RESIDENTIAL TENANCIES

Ninth Edition

Richard A. Feldman, B.A., LL.B., B.ED.

CARSWELL®

A cataloguing record for this publication is available from Library and Archives Canada.

ISBN 978-0-7798-2264-5

Composition: Computer Composition of Canada Inc.

Printed in Canada by Thomson Reuters

CARSWELL, A DIVISION OF THOMSON REUTERS CANADA LIMITED

One Corporate Plaza
2075 Kennedy Road
Toronto, Ontario
M1T 3V4

Customer Relations
Toronto 1-416-609-3800
Elsewhere in Canada/U.S. 1-800-387-5164
Fax: 1-416-298-5082
www.carswell.com
E-mail www.carswell.com/email

Acknowledgement and Dedication

My thanks go to the editorial staff at Carswell for ensuring the quality and accuracy of this new edition, to my family, friends and colleagues for their continued support and encouragement and, finally, to my wife, Irene, for her enduring patience, love and understanding.

Preface

The *Residential Tenancies Act, 2006* has been in place now for almost three years and the Landlord and Tenant Board has finally started releasing more of its decisions. As a result, there is now sufficient experience with the new legislation to comment upon it with greater certainty than was possible when the eighth edition of this text was released (shortly after the new legislation came into effect).

There have also been significant changes in other areas of the law since the release of the eighth edition. In particular, there have been significant changes in the area of human rights in Ontario. Consequently, Chapter 15 (Human Rights Issues) has been greatly expanded in this edition.

There have been more convictions under the penal provisions of both the T.P.A. and the R.T.A. and Chapter 19 (Penal Sanctions) has been updated accordingly.

In addition, this ninth edition includes reference to hundreds of new court and Board decisions that were not available when the previous edition was released. Finally, for the first time, all of the Landlord and Tenant Board's forms have been included with this text (on CD).

As a former Member of the Ontario Rental Housing Tribunal (as the Landlord and Tenant Board was known under the *Tenant Protection Act*), I have tried to bring my experience to bear in making this edition as practical and accessible as possible. Where appropriate, I have offered some opinions or suggestions that I hope the reader will find to be informative and helpful.

The Quick Reference Guide found at Appendix 1 is based upon a document I originally designed for my own use while sitting as a Member of the Tribunal. That document was used by me and other Members of the Tribunal as a handy reference tool. Each common type of application is represented by a brief summary that identifies the sections of the Act that are applicable, the forms that are required, the time limits involved, the facts that must be proven by the applicant, possible defences to consider and the type of order that can be granted if the application is successful.

All relevant statutes, regulations, Rules and Interpretation Guidelines have been included at the back of the text for ease of reference. Also, in this edition, all of the Board's forms have been provided on a compact disc to make it easier for you to both refer to the forms and to complete them (i.e., fill in the blanks) on your own computer. Since amendments may be made after the date this book is published, it is always recommended that you check with the Landlord and Tenant Board to ensure that you are referring to the most up-to-date version of the law and that you are using the current version of a form. The Board's filing and administrative fees may also change from time to time.

As always, it is my hope that landlords, tenants, property managers, legal representatives, adjudicators, legislators, educators and students will find this text to be of use.

October 2009 Richard A. Feldman, B.A., LL.B., B.ED.

About the Author

Richard Feldman possesses undergraduate degrees in Geography and Education from York University and the University of Toronto, respectively. He graduated from Osgoode Hall Law School in 1988 and was called to the Ontario Bar in 1990. He is the recipient of numerous academic honours, including the James A. Priestley Admission Scholarship, York University In-course Scholarship, the Hans Carol Prize, the Robert Laidlaw Cup for Academic Excellence and the Arnolds Balins Award.

As a lawyer in a Toronto firm for approximately seven years, Mr. Feldman's practice focused primarily on civil litigation, administrative law, family law and real estate transactions.

In 1998, Mr. Feldman joined the newly-formed Ontario Rental Housing Tribunal (as the Landlord and Tenant Board was then known) as one of its founding members. He served as a full-time Member of the Tribunal until the end of his second term in 2004. In his capacity as a Member of the Rental Housing Tribunal, Mr. Feldman trained and mentored new adjudicators, participated in various committees and issued over 9,000 orders.

Mr. Feldman is a member of the Law Society of Upper Canada, the Ontario College of Teachers and the Society of Ontario Adjudicators and Regulators. He has taught numerous courses on litigation and administrative law and has lectured on advocacy skills and administrative procedure.

Since 2004, Mr. Feldman has served with distinction as an Arbitrator with the Financial Services Commission of Ontario, where he adjudicates disputes that arise under the *Statutory Accident Benefits Schedule* of the *Insurance Act*. He continues to teach, write and lecture on landlord and tenant law as well as other areas of administrative law.

Contents

Table of Cases

1

Residential Tenancy Law in Ontario — A Historical Perspective and Recent Developments

1. BRIEF HISTORICAL OVERVIEW

For many years, a distinction has been made in the law between residential and commercial tenancies. The prevailing belief has been that a person's right to security and enjoyment of his home is deserving of special protection, even if that home is a rented one. Some provincial governments have also believed that rent and rent increases for residential tenancies need to be regulated, perhaps because of a perceived imbalance in the respective bargaining power of residential tenants and professional landlords. Rent controls were introduced in Ontario in 1975 with the enactment of the *Residential Premises Rent Review Act, 1975*[1] and have existed, in one form or another, since then.[2]

Until the late 1990's, both commercial and residential tenancies were governed by the *Landlord and Tenant Act*, R.S.O. 1990, c. L.7. Part IV of the *Landlord and Tenant Act* dealt specifically with residential tenancies. Issues arising between residential landlords and tenants (that fell within the purview of the *Landlord and Tenant Act*) were resolved by application to the superior court; this typically involved applications by landlords to evict tenants for failure to pay rent or other breaches of the *Landlord and Tenant Act* or applications by tenants seeking remedies for breaches of the Act by landlords. Most issues related to the lawfulness of the rent charged for a residential unit or to the ability of a landlord to raise the rent were, however, governed

---

[1] S.O. 1975 (2nd Sess.), c. 12.

[2] A more detailed discussion of the history of rent control legislation is found in Chapter 9.

by the *Rent Control Act*, S.O. 1992, c. 11. Disputes under the *Rent Control Act* were dealt with as administrative proceedings. The Ministry of Housing would appoint a "rent control officer" who had the authority to conduct a hearing and render a decision that was binding upon the parties.

A number of criticisms were levelled at the legislative regime as it existed in Ontario throughout most of the 1980's and 1990's.

First, numerous statutes, instead of one unified statute, were governing residential tenancies at any one time. Some felt this represented an unnecessarily complex and confusing legislative framework.

Second, disputes between the same parties concerning the same rental unit (and possibly concerning related issues) might have to be resolved through very different procedures before different decision-making bodies (i.e., either by application to court or to a branch of the Ministry of Housing). Many felt that "one stop shopping" would be preferable.

Third, it was argued that court was not the best place to resolve disputes between residential landlords and tenants. Courts tend to be very formal and intimidating places, and the parties involved in tenancy disputes, especially parties who lack legal representation, might be at a considerable disadvantage. Also, many of the judges only occasionally had to hear these types of cases (because of the way in which their schedules rotated); notwithstanding their excellent credentials, many judges lacked expertise in residential tenancy law. Courts tend to engender an adversarial atmosphere and (until recently) put little effort into assisting parties in resolving their disputes through alternative means such as mediation. The application process itself was criticized (especially by landlords) for taking too long. Finally, there was pressure upon the judicial system to clear out its considerable backlog of cases (including commercial, family and criminal matters) and many people felt that the court's scarce resources could better be directed towards resolving those other types of cases.

The solution to many of these problems appeared to be the creation of one, overarching statute that would govern all aspects of residential tenancies in Ontario and that would create a new tribunal with the resources and expertise to fairly and efficiently resolve disputes arising between residential landlords and tenants. The problem with implementing such a solution was that it was not clear whether constitutional jurisdiction existed to allow anyone other than federally appointed judges to adjudicate such matters. In 1996, the Supreme Court of Canada resolved this issue. In *Reference re: Act to Amend the Residential Tenancies Act (NS)*[3], the Court held that since residential tenancy disputes were not exclusively within the jurisdiction of federally appointed judges at the time of Confederation, it was not necessary

---

[3] (1996), (sub nom. *Reference re Act to Amend Chapter 401 of the Revised Statutes, 1989, the Residential Tenancies Act (N.S.), ss.7, 8(2)*), 131 D.L.R. (4th) 609, 1996 CarswellNS 166 (S.C.C.).

to have judges at that level make decisions in these matters. This opened the door for the Ontario government to create a whole new legislative scheme to deal with residential tenancies.

2. THE TENANT PROTECTION ACT, 1997

On June 17, 1998, the *Tenant Protection Act, 1997*[4] (T.P.A.) came into effect, replacing Part IV of the *Landlord and Tenant Act*, the *Rent Control Act, 1992* and the *Rental Housing Protection Act*.[5] The T.P.A. governed all aspects of residential tenancies, including the creation of a tenancy, the form and content of tenancy agreements, the rights and responsibilities of landlords and tenants, and the termination of tenancies. It also established the Ontario Rental Housing Tribunal, the independent, quasi-judicial tribunal charged with resolving disputes between residential landlords and tenants and with giving effect to the provisions of the T.P.A.

Although the T.P.A. was designed to address many of the criticisms of the previous system,[6] it did not mark a complete departure from that regime. For instance, Part IV of the *Landlord and Tenant Act* was transported (with a few changes) almost in its entirety into the new T.P.A. Court cases decided under Part IV of the *Landlord and Tenant Act*, therefore, continued to be relevant.

The repeal of the *Rental Housing Protection Act* permitted landlords to convert to condominiums or to demolish, with some compensation to existing tenants, residential complexes of more than five units. Local municipalities, however, retained the power to pass by-laws limiting the granting of building or demolition permits for such purposes.

The fear, expressed by some, that the T.P.A. would completely eliminate rent controls turned out to be unfounded. The amount by which a landlord could increase the rent for a "sitting" tenant continued to be strictly controlled. Under the T.P.A., however, when a unit became vacant, the landlord could negotiate any rent with the prospective new tenant, without regard to the rent that had been charged to the previous tenant of that unit. This is sometimes referred to as "vacancy decontrol".

Under the *Rent Control Act*, a guideline figure was published annually by the Ministry of Housing. In general terms, this guideline represented the maximum percentage by which a landlord in Ontario could increase a tenant's rent. In special circumstances, a landlord could seek permission to increase the rent by more than the guideline amount. Under the T.P.A., the concept of an annual rent guideline continued, but there was an expansion of the conditions under which a landlord would be permitted to increase the rent of

---

[4] S.O. 1997, c. 24.

[5] R.S.O. 1990, c. R.24.

[6] Described earlier in this Chapter.

sitting tenants above the guideline. When the T.P.A. came into force, landlords were also given a limited opportunity to attempt to recoup capital expenditures they had incurred years earlier. Not surprisingly a very large number of these above-guideline increase (AGI) applications were filed and the provisions of the T.P.A relating to rent increases became some of the more controversial changes introduced by this legislation. To some extent, however, market factors mitigated the effect of those provisions. Just because a landlord had the legal right to raise the rent for a unit did not mean that doing so was always advisable. As vacancy rates in large urban centres continued to rise,[7] landlords found that they could not charge a higher rent than the market would bear, or they would find themselves with many empty units.

Although the T.P.A. arguably achieved many of the objectives of its drafters (i.e., quicker resolution of disputes with less cost to the parties and the government, in a forum more accessible to the public), both landlord and tenant groups took issue with specific provisions of the T.P.A., with the most scathing comments often coming from tenant advocates. Some of the more common criticisms of the T.P.A. were as follows:

1. Vacancy decontrol, it was alleged, permitted rents across Ontario to skyrocket. The suggested solution was the introduction of more stringent rent controls, including the reinstatement of a Rent Registry;
2. The default process was unfair to tenants and resulted in many tenants being evicted without even having an opportunity to plead their case in person before an adjudicator;
3. Tenants ought to be able to raise concerns about the condition of the building when the landlord is seeking to increase the rent; and
4. Rent increases above the guideline that are based on capital expenditures ought to be structured in such a way that the rents would eventually be reduced once the landlord recouped the expenditure. Similarly, if rents increased because the landlord's operating costs increased, tenants should be able to seek a reduction of the rent when those costs decrease so that the landlord does not obtain a windfall.

When the Liberals defeated the Conservatives in Ontario in 2003, they did so, in part, based upon a promise to replace the T.P.A. with new legislation. In the spring of 2004, the Ministry of Municipal Affairs and Housing

---

[7] According to the Canada Mortgage and Housing Corporation (CMHC), the average Canadian rental apartment vacancy rate rose dramatically between 2001 and 2004 and then generally remained stable or declined slightly between 2004 and 2006. During this period, vacancy rates in many major urban centres in Ontario were at the highest levels reported since the 1970's. The average vacancy rates in Ontario have decreased slightly since 2006. For more detailed information, please visit the CMHC website at *www.cmhc.ca*.

began a public consultation process (the Residential Tenancy Reform Consultation). The government held several public meetings and invited the public to make written submissions on a number of areas of possible reform. On May 3, 2006, the government of Ontario introduced new legislation — the *Residential Tenancies Act, 2006* (Bill 109) — to replace the T.P.A.

3. THE RESIDENTIAL TENANCIES ACT, 2006

The *Residential Tenancies Act, 2006*[8] (R.T.A.) received Royal Assent on June 22, 2006, but did not come into force until **January 31, 2007,** in order to allow the Rental Housing Tribunal (now called the "Landlord and Tenant Board") and stakeholders time to prepare for the new legislation.

The bulk of the provisions under the T.P.A. have been carried forward, unchanged, into the *Residential Tenancies Act*. The R.T.A. attempts, however, to organize topics in a more rational manner — keeping related provisions grouped together.

As a practical matter, the two most significant changes under the R.T.A. are:

1. the elimination of the default process; and
2. the right of a tenant to raise any issue the tenant wishes at an application brought by the landlord to deal with arrears of rent.

Approximately one-half of all applications filed with the Tribunal under the T.P.A. were resolved without a hearing (i.e., they were resolved through the "default" process). Where the respondent (usually the tenant) failed to file a Dispute within five days of receiving the application and notice of hearing, the Tribunal would usually cancel the hearing and issue an order in favour of the applicant based upon the documents filed. Since the vast majority of applications were filed by landlords to evict tenants for failing to pay rent, this meant that, in most cases, landlords obtained eviction orders without a hearing about one week after filing an application. A respondent could seek to have such a default order set aside (by demonstrating that he or she was not reasonably able to participate in the process) but such motions were not always successful.

It should be noted that this default process was not a creation of the T.P.A. It was, in fact, a modification of a similar process that permitted Deputy Registrars of the Court to sign eviction orders where a tenant failed to attend a preliminary meeting and failed to indicate in writing that the tenant wished the matter to proceed to a hearing before a judge. Although the Rental Housing Tribunal was created, at least in part, to provide for the efficient processing of applications, it was this very efficiency that was most often

[8] S.O. 2006, c. 17.

criticized in the press and led some to label the Tribunal (unfairly in my view) as an "eviction factory".

During the Residential Tenancy Reform Consultation, the government studied a number of issues, but gave special attention to the default process. Ultimately, rather than extend the deadlines or otherwise modify the existing default process, the government chose to eliminate the default process altogether. Eliminating the default process, however, would likely effectively double the number of cases that would proceed to a hearing and there was a concern that this could result in a backlog of cases and considerable delay. In anticipation of this substantial increase in workload, the government appointed many new Members to the Landlord and Tenant Board. As it turns out, roughly the same proportion of tenants who failed to file disputes under the T.P.A. now fail to attend hearings under the R.T.A. Therefore, despite an increase in the number of cases proceeding to hearing, the Board has been able to deal efficiently with the many simple and uncontested arrears applications that come before it.

The other major procedural change introduced by the R.T.A. is the right of a tenant to raise, at an application commenced by the landlord with respect to arrears of rent,[9] any issue the tenant wishes (s. 82) and to be granted the same relief as if the tenant had commenced his or her own application. This is a relatively surprising addition for the following reasons: (1) it seems contrary to the principles of natural justice; (2) it is not necessary in order to protect tenants from eviction applications brought by landlords who are in serious breach of their obligations; and (3) it is open to abuse.

It is contrary to the principles of natural justice because (subject to the Board creating rules to the contrary), at a hearing held at the request of the landlord, a tenant will be able to surprise a landlord with accusations and allegations of which the landlord had no previous warning. The landlord will not know in advance what evidence or witnesses to bring to the hearing because the landlord will not know what issues a tenant might raise. In the past, tenants who had issues that they wished to be heard were told to file their own application which then could be heard at a later date on its own or at the same time as the landlord's application. At least in that way, the landlord and the Tribunal had some warning of the issues being raised and the relief being sought by the tenant.

A tenant who wished to avoid eviction always had the right (under s. 84(1) of the T.P.A.) to raise any issues that could be relevant to the Tribunal's decision about whether or not it would be fair to deny or to delay the eviction. Furthermore, under s. 84(2) of the T.P.A., the Tribunal had to refuse to grant an eviction where a tenant could prove that a landlord was in serious breach

---

[9] Either an eviction application (Form L1) brought under ss. 59 and 69 of the R.T.A. (subsection 82(1)) or an application for arrears of rent without an eviction (Form L9) brought under s. 87 of the R.T.A. (subsection 87(2)).

of the landlord's obligations or was bringing the eviction application in retaliation for the tenant trying to assert his or her legal rights. These protections are continued under s. 83 of the R.T.A.

Finally, s. 82 of the R.T.A. is open to abuse because unscrupulous tenants may make spurious accusations against their landlord when faced with possible eviction for arrears of rent. They will realize that the landlord will be faced with the difficult choice of either proceeding with the hearing although unprepared to respond to these new allegations, or requesting an adjournment in order to prepare a defence.

Section 82 of the R.T.A. may also have the effect of encouraging "rent strikes". A tenant who feels that he or she has a legitimate complaint but does not want to bother commencing an application may decide to simply withhold the rent. The landlord will then either have to capitulate to the tenant's demands or commence an eviction application based upon non-payment of rent. At the hearing of the landlord's application, pursuant to s. 82, the tenant will have the opportunity to raise his or her own issues without having incurred any expense and without having gone to the trouble of commencing his or her own application.

Fortunately, my review of the available cases from the Landlord and Tenant Board suggests that s. 82 has not, as a practical matter, created any significant problems at the Board. The most common issue raised by tenants under s. 82 appears to be in relation to maintenance concerns. Often, the problems about which the tenants are complaining appear to be relatively minor in nature. Also, tenants who make such allegations rarely come to the hearings properly prepared with cogent, corroborative evidence (such as inspection reports, photographs, copies of documents to prove that the landlord was aware of the problem(s), etc.). Consequently, the rent abatements that have been awarded are typically quite modest (usually less than $500) and any abatement awarded is simply deducted by the Board from the arrears of rent the tenant owes the landlord.[10] The Board may also order that repairs

[10] See Landlord and Tenant Board File No. SOL-00505 (March 22, 2007); Landlord and Tenant Board File No. SOL-00304 (March 19, 2007); Landlord and Tenant Board File No. SOL-00750 (March 30, 2007); Landlord and Tenant Board File No. SOL-00434 (March 14, 2007); Landlord and Tenant Board File No. SOL-00219 (March 5, 2007); Landlord and Tenant Board File No. SOL-00396 (March 16, 2007); Landlord and Tenant Board File No. SOL-00178 (March 16, 2007); Landlord and Tenant Board File No. NOL-00178 (March 15, 2007); Landlord and Tenant Board File No. EAL-00743 (March 30, 2007); Landlord and Tenant Board File No. CEL-00480 (March 9, 2007); Landlord and Tenant Board File No. CEL-00060 (Feb. 22, 2007); Landlord and Tenant Board File No. EAL-13121 (Jan. 13, 2009); Landlord and Tenant Board File No. SOL-18140 (Jan. 13, 2009); Landlord and Tenant Board File No. NOL-05876 (Jan. 14, 2009); Landlord and Tenant Board File No. EAL-00358 (March 12, 2007); Landlord and Tenant Board File No. NOL-00039 (Feb. 22, 2007); and Landlord and Tenant Board File No. TSL-19733 (Jan. 12, 2009).

be done, but that will be of little comfort to a tenant who has been evicted from the unit prior to the date by which the work must be done.[11]

Where the issues raised by the tenant under s. 82 appear to be more complex, some Members have issued interim orders adjourning the hearing and, in the intervening period, requiring disclosure by the tenant(s) of details of the issues being raised and copies of any evidence to be relied upon (so that the landlord has a reasonable opportunity to know the case the landlord has to meet) and/or requiring the tenant to pay at least some rent into the Board. Should the tenant fail to comply with the interim order, the Member may then refuse to deal with the s. 82 issues when the hearing reconvenes and proceed to hear the landlord's application to terminate the tenancy for non-payment of rent.[12]

Thus, for the most part, the introduction into the R.T.A. of the new provisions contained in s. 82 have not resulted in undue delays or other abuses of process.

Some of the other significant changes made under the R.T.A. are as follows:

Part I (Introduction)

Definition of vital service (s. 1)

Under the T.P.A., "vital service" was defined as fuel, hydro, gas or hot or cold water. Under the R.T.A., the definition also includes heat (during the part of each year prescribed by regulations). This should make it easier for the Landlord and Tenant Board and for the Investigation and Enforcement Unit of the Ministry of Municipal Affairs and Housing to penalize a landlord who fails to ensure that a rental unit is continuously provided with adequate heat during the prescribed times of the year (September 1 through June 15).[13]

Part II (Tenancy Agreements)

Landlords to provide information to new tenants (s. 11)

For tenancies that are entered into after the R.T.A. is proclaimed, landlords must provide their new tenants (on or before the tenancy

---

[11] See, for example, Landlord and Tenant Board File No. SWL-21938 (Jan. 9, 2009) and Landlord and Tenant Board File No. SWL-21702 (Jan. 29, 2009).

[12] This power comes from ss. 195 and 201 of the R.T.A. and s. 23 of the *Statutory Powers Procedure Act* (see Appendix 9). For examples of cases where this approach has been used, please see: Landlord and Tenant Board File No. NOL-00177 (March 28, 2007); Landlord and Tenant Board File No. SWL-00176 (March 6, 2007); Landlord and Tenant Board File No. SOL-17433 (Jan. 13, 2009); Landlord and Tenant Board File No. SOL-17643 (Jan. 16, 2009); and Landlord and Tenant Board File No. TSL-18941 (Jan. 26, 2009).

[13] Section 4 of O. Reg. 516/06.

begins) with information in writing (and in the approved form) about the rights and responsibilities of landlords and tenants, the role of the Landlord and Tenant Board and how to contact the Board. Note, however, that there appears to be no penalty for landlords who fail to comply with this requirement.

Part III (Responsibilities of Landlords)

Right of entry on 24 hours notice (s. 27)

1. Under s. 21 of the T.P.A., a landlord could enter the unit (after first providing proper advance notice in writing) to "carry out a repair or do work in the rental unit". Under the R.T.A., this has been clarified by amending the phrase as follows: "to carry out a repair *or replacement* or do work in the rental unit."

2. The T.P.A. stated that a landlord could enter the rental unit to show it to a potential purchaser. Landlords would often leave it up to their real estate agent to show the premises to potential buyers but some tenants objected on the basis that the T.P.A. only authorized entry by a landlord, not by an agent of the landlord. Subsection 27(2) of the R.T.A. seeks to resolve this problem by specifying that a licenced broker or real estate agent may enter the unit (without the landlord) to show it to a potential purchaser as long as the agent/broker has the written authorization of the landlord.

3. Under the T.P.A., a landlord had no general right to enter a rental unit to inspect it unless the landlord specifically reserved such a right in the tenancy agreement. Under the R.T.A., a landlord can now enter the rental unit (on notice) to inspect its condition so that the landlord can fulfill the landlord's maintenance obligations. This right, however, must be exercised in a reasonable fashion.

Orders prohibiting rent increases (s. 30)

In addition to the remedies that were previously available (under the T.P.A.) to tenants who brought applications concerning maintenance, under the R.T.A. another "weapon" has been added to the arsenal: an order prohibiting a rent increase (or "OPRI").

Where a landlord is found to be in serious breach of the landlord's maintenance obligations, in addition to other relief that may be granted, the Landlord and Tenant Board may: (1) prohibit the landlord from charging a new tenant[14] under a new tenancy agreement

[14] Other than tenants in rent-geared-to-income housing.

more than the last lawful rent charged to the former tenant; (2) prohibit the landlord from giving a notice of rent increase; or (3) prohibit the landlord from taking a rent increase for which a notice has been given but which has not yet taken effect.

Once an OPRI is issued, it remains in effect until the landlord completes the ordered repairs; the Board is not required to issue an order "lifting" the OPRI.

Evicting a tenant on a tenant's application (s. 32)

Under the T.P.A., when a tenant brought an application against his or her landlord, one of the things the tenant could request from the Tribunal was an order terminating the tenancy. If the Tribunal granted such an order, however, and the tenant changed his or her mind about moving out, the landlord had no way to enforce the order. This has now been remedied by s. 32 of the R.T.A., which provides that the Board may now also order the tenant's eviction (but, again, only where it is the tenant who is requesting that the tenancy be terminated).

Part IV (Responsibilities of Tenants)

No substantial changes.

Part V (Security of Tenure and Termination of Tenancies)

Additional time to remove property after eviction (s. 41)

Under the R.T.A., the amount of time a landlord must wait before disposing of a tenant's property after the enforcement of an eviction order by a sheriff has been increased to 72 hours (up from 48 hours under the T.P.A.).

Also, under the T.P.A., a former tenant had no way to enforce his or her rights with respect to property left behind in the rental unit except through court action. This problem has been rectified by the inclusion in s. 41 of the R.T.A. of remedies for a landlord's breach of this provision. Amongst other relief, the Board can order the landlord to pay the former tenant for their reasonable costs to repair or replace the property that was damaged, destroyed or disposed of as well as the former tenant's out-of-pocket expenses and the Board can impose an administrative fine not exceeding the greater of $10,000 and the monetary jurisdiction of the Small Claims Court.[15]

---

[15] The monetary jurisdiction of the Small Claims Court is scheduled to be increased to $25,000, effective January 2010.

Landlord/Purchaser requires possession of the unit for occupation by a caregiver (ss. 48 and 49)

In addition to being able to terminate a tenancy on the basis that the landlord or purchaser requires the unit for their own occupation or for occupation by certain select family members, the rights of the landlord/purchaser have now been expanded to include situations where they (or prescribed members of their families) require occupation of the unit for a person who will be providing care services to a prescribed class of persons who reside or shall reside elsewhere within the same residential complex.

Former tenant's application where notice given in bad faith (s. 57)

Under the T.P.A., in certain circumstances, a former tenant had the right to bring an application against a former landlord who had given the tenant a notice of termination in bad faith and where the tenant vacated the rental unit as a result of receiving the notice of termination. It was not clear, however, whether the tenant had the right to bring such an application where the tenant refused to comply with the notice of termination, forced the landlord to bring an application and then, ultimately, was forced to vacate the rental unit as a result of an eviction order from the Tribunal following a determination by the Tribunal that the landlord was, in fact, acting in good faith. Under the R.T.A., it is now clear that a tenant does retain the right to commence such an application, even if there was an earlier finding by the Tribunal that the landlord was acting in good faith. Presumably, this is on the basis that the landlord's actions subsequent to the original hearing provide new evidence upon which the Board can arrive at a different conclusion.

Shorter notice for wilful damage or misuse of premises that could result in serious damage (s. 63)

Under the R.T.A., in most circumstances, the notice period to terminate the tenancy for undue damage remains the same as under the T.P.A.: 20 days for a "first" notice (s. 62) and 14 days for a "second" notice (s. 68). However, if the tenant (or another occupant or a person the tenant permits in the residential complex) is wilfully causing damage, using the rental unit or complex in a manner that is inconsistent with use as a residential premises or has caused or is likely to cause significant damage to the premises, the landlord may choose to rely upon s. 63 and provide only 10 days' notice.

Shorter notice for interference with reasonable enjoyment of landlord in small building (s. 65)

Under the R.T.A., in most circumstances, the notice period to terminate the tenancy for interference with reasonable enjoyment of other tenants or the landlord remains the same as under the T.P.A.: 20 days for a "first" notice (s. 64) and 14 days for a "second" notice (s. 68). However, if the tenant (or another occupant or a person the tenant permits in the residential complex) is substantially interfering with the reasonable enjoyment of a landlord who also resides in the residential complex and the complex has three or fewer residential units, the landlord may choose to rely upon s. 65 and provide only 10 days' notice.

Pay and stay provisions (s. 74)

Under the T.P.A., a tenant who was being evicted for non-payment of rent had the opportunity to pay the full amount owing (plus any costs ordered by the Tribunal) up to (but not including) the date the eviction order could be filed with the sheriff's office. That right continues to exist under the R.T.A. but it has been expanded so that, **once per tenancy,** the tenant can even save the tenancy by paying all amounts owing plus the sheriff's fees after the order has been filed with the sheriff but prior to the actual enforcement of the eviction order.

Lower threshold on motions to set aside *ex parte* applications (ss. 77 and 78)

Where a tenant has given a landlord a notice of termination, where the tenant has agreed to terminate the tenancy or where there has been a breach by a tenant of certain terms of a mediated agreement or order of the Board, the landlord can apply for an order terminating the tenancy and evicting the tenant without notice to the tenant (*ex parte*). When the tenant receives the *ex parte* order, the tenant may then bring a motion to have it set aside. This is not a change from the relevant provisions as they existed under the T.P.A. What is new, is that the R.T.A. makes it clear that a hearing must be held on the motion and that the *ex parte* order can be set aside if the Board is satisfied that it would not be unfair to do so (even if the landlord has proven that the landlord was legally entitled to an eviction order).

Effective date of eviction order can pre-date the termination date in some cases (s. 80)

An eviction order is normally effective not earlier than the date of termination set out in the notice of termination. The R.T.A., however, now provides that the ordered date (the date the order can be filed with the sheriff for enforcement of the eviction) can be earlier than the termination date in the notice if the notice is given under s. 63 (short notice due to risk of significant damage) or s. 66 (serious impairment of safety).

Expedited enforcement of some evictions (s. 84)

Under the T.P.A., the Tribunal would generally indicate in each eviction order that was based upon impaired safety that the order was to be enforced by the sheriff in priority to others. Now, under s. 84 of the R.T.A., orders from the Board will include a similar direction not just in cases of impaired safety but also in cases of illegal drug activity, serious damage and interference with a landlord's reasonable enjoyment (in a building with three or fewer residential units).

Limitation on arrears where tenancy not properly terminated (s. 88)

Under the T.P.A. and the caselaw developed thereunder, a tenancy could not be terminated by a tenant simply vacating the unit or by giving a short or otherwise defective notice of termination. This left tenants potentially liable for the rent on the unit for an indefinite period (i.e., until the landlord was able to re-rent the unit for a comparable rent).

Under the R.T.A., a "cap" has now been placed upon a tenant's maximum liability for arrears of rent in circumstances where the tenancy was not properly terminated by the tenant.

If a tenant gave an improper notice of termination, arrears are owed for the period starting from the date the tenant gave the defective notice up to the termination date that would have been specified in the notice if the tenant had given proper notice of termination.

If the tenant gave no notice of termination at all, arrears are owed from the date the landlord knew or ought to have known that the tenant had vacated the unit up to the termination date that would have been specified in the notice of termination if proper notice had been given.

If a landlord gives a notice of termination for landlord's or purchaser's own use, or for demolition/conversion/renovation and the tenant moves without giving the required 10 days notice of early termination, the tenant will owe rent for up to 10 days from the earlier of the following dates: (1) the date the tenant gave the improper notice; (2) where no notice was given, the date the landlord knew or ought to have known the tenant had vacated the unit; and (3) the termination date in the landlord's notice of termination.

Despite these rules, however, a landlord is still obliged to make reasonable efforts to mitigate its losses by finding a new tenant for the unit. If a landlord rents the unit to a new tenant, the former tenant's liability ends on the day before the day the new tenant is entitled to occupy the unit.

Part VI (Assignment, Subletting and Unauthorized Occupancy)

Tenancy terminated when unauthorized occupant evicted (s. 100)

Under the T.P.A., where a tenant transferred occupancy of the rental unit to an unauthorized occupant, the Tribunal had the power to evict the unauthorized occupant but had no statutory authority to terminate the original tenancy. Section 100 of the R.T.A. allows the landlord in such circumstances to now file an application to terminate the tenancy and evict both the tenant and the unauthorized occupant.

Part VII (Rules Relating to Rent)

Interest on rent deposit (s. 106)

Interest on the rent deposit will be the same as the annual guideline (i.e., the percentage change from year-to-year in the *Consumer Price Index* (CPI) for Ontario, instead of the fixed rate of six per cent).

Automatic rent payments cannot be required (s. 108)

The T.P.A. stated that a landlord cannot require a tenant to pay rent by way of post-dated cheques or other negotiable instruments. The R.T.A. *also* prohibits a landlord from insisting on payment by automatic debit or automatic credit card charges.

Rent receipts (s. 109)

The R.T.A. extends the requirement for a landlord to provide a receipt to a tenant to include former tenants, as long as the request for a receipt is made within 12 months of the end of the tenancy.

Discounts (s. 111)

The R.T.A. will allow landlords more flexibility in offering discounts to tenants, without affecting the lawful rent (as long as they follow the prescribed rules).

Notice of OPRI (ss. 114 and 115)

If an order prohibiting a rent increase is in effect for a unit, the landlord must provide written notice of the details (in the approved form) to a prospective new tenant of that unit, and where the OPRI is issued after the tenancy agreement is made, written notice must be provided to the tenant. If the landlord breaches these provisions, the tenant has up to one year to commence an application for relief (the return of excess rent collected illegally) and the landlord can be fined an amount not exceeding the greater of $10,000 and the monetary jurisdiction of the Small Claims Court.[16]

Circumstances where notice of rent increase not required (s. 117)

Where a new tenancy is entered into after an OPRI has been issued and the landlord subsequently does the required work, the landlord does not have to serve the tenant with a notice of rent increase (NORI) in order to raise the rent to the amount that the landlord would have been entitled to charge if the OPRI had not been issued. Presumably, that amount will be whatever the landlord and tenant agreed would be the lawful rent at the time the tenancy agreement was entered into.

Where an OPRI (that prohibits the landlord from collecting a rent increase) is issued after the landlord has given a NORI, and the landlord subsequently does the required work, the landlord may take the rent increase without giving a new NORI.

The effective date of the rent increase in both cases would be the first day of the first rental period following the date on which the landlord completes the work. For the purpose of the *next* lawful increase, the rent increase is deemed to have been taken at the time the landlord would have been entitled to take it, had the OPRI not been issued.

Rent increase guideline (s. 120)

The rent increase guideline will be the percentage change from year-to-year in the *Consumer Price Index* (CPI) for Ontario. This figure will be published in the Ontario Gazette by August 31 of the year preceding that in which it will take effect.

Agreements to increase rent (s. 121)

The R.T.A. states that the maximum increase that a landlord and tenant can agree to will be capped at three per cent above the guideline (rather than the four per cent cap under the T.P.A.).

[16] The monetary jurisdiction of the Small Claims Court is scheduled to be increased to $25,000, effective January 2010.

Above guideline increases (s. 126)

This is one of the areas with the most significant changes to the legislation. The changes will be discussed in detail in Chapter 9. Some of the more significant changes can be summarized as follows:

1. A landlord can apply for an above-guideline increase (AGI) if there has been an extraordinary increase in the cost for municipal taxes and charges or utilities or both for the residential complex *or any building in which the rental unit is located.* This suggests that a landlord can apply if there has been an extraordinary increase in operating costs related to only one building within the complex regardless of whether there has been such an increase for the complex as a whole.

2. The determination of whether an increase in operating costs is "extraordinary" is no longer tied to a table of cost categories but is to be determined in accordance with the regulations.

3. Only "eligible" capital expenditures can be used as the basis for an AGI application. What is eligible has been restricted somewhat. In particular, a capital expenditure to replace a system or thing will generally not be eligible if the system or thing did not require major repair or replacement. Also, a capital expenditure will not be eligible if it relates to work done before a tenancy commenced (i.e., a new tenant cannot be required to pay for work done before the tenancy began).

4. A new "cap" has been placed on the size of the increase that can be obtained in relation to capital expenditures. Under the T.P.A., the "cap" was four per cent per year with no limit on the total aggregate increase or the number of years over which the increase could be taken. This meant that if the landlord justified a 20 per cent increase in rent based on capital expenditures, the rent increase would have to be phased in over a five year period (four per cent per year for five years). Under the R.T.A., the Board cannot grant an increase based upon capital expenditures of more than three per cent per year with a maximum limit of three years (thus, a maximum aggregate increase of nine per cent).[17]

5. If the landlord is in serious breach of the landlord's maintenance obligations, the Board may dismiss the AGI application or delay the effect of the rent increase order until the landlord has complied with its obligations. This means that tenants can now raise maintenance

---

[17] Actually, because of the effect of compounding, the total increase is somewhat more than 9%.

concerns at AGI hearings and attempt to prove that the landlord has not complied with an existing work order or order of the Board related to a *serious* breach of its maintenance obligations or otherwise prove that the landlord is in *serious* breach of its maintenance obligations. This provision applies to applications made under the R.T.A. as well as those commenced under the T.P.A. for which a final order was not issued prior to January 31, 2007.[18]

Rent reductions and costs no longer borne (ss. 128 and 129)

Where the Board issues an AGI order based upon an extraordinary increase in utility costs, the order will set out the percentage increase that is attributed to the increased utility costs as well as the landlord's obligation to keep tenants informed about the total costs of utilities for the complex. Where the utility costs subsequently decline by more than the prescribed percentage in the prescribed period, the landlord will be required to reduce the rent accordingly.

Where the Board issues an AGI order based upon capital expenditures, the order will set out the percentage increase that is attributed to the capital expenditures, a date by which the rent must be reduced (according to prescribed rules) and information about the landlord's obligation to reduce the rent as of that date. Note that many capital expenditures are amortized over at least a 15-year period. A tenant will, therefore, likely only see a benefit from this provision if he or she remains in the same unit for at least 15 years, the relevant provisions of the R.T.A. do not change during the intervening period, the tenant keeps a copy of the Board's order and he or she remembers to insist on the rent reduction at the appropriate time.

These provisions apply to AGI applications commenced under the R.T.A. as well as to those commenced under the T.P.A., but which were not yet resolved at the time these provisions came into effect.[19]

Part VIII (Smart Meters and Apportionment of Utility Costs)

Smart Meters (s. 137)

Where a landlord pays for the supply of electricity to a rental unit (i.e., where the tenant does not pay extra for electricity because that cost is included in the rent), the R.T.A. allows the landlord to install a separate electricity meter (a "smart" meter), without the tenant's consent, if the landlord complies with certain strict criteria. Once the smart meter is installed and a minimum of 12 months have passed

[18] Subsection 242(7) of the R.T.A.

[19] Section 258(2) of the R.T.A.

from the date of installation, the landlord can require the tenant to pay for the electricity actually consumed within the unit. In exchange, the landlord will have to reduce the tenant's rent based upon the average monthly cost of electricity for that unit during the preceding 12-month period. Unfortunately, this may encourage some tenants to use more electricity, not less, immediately following installation of a smart meter since the higher the hydro bill during that period, the greater will be the subsequent rent reduction. A landlord who installs a smart meter is also obliged to install new, energy-efficient appliances in the unit. Accordingly, it is unclear how many landlords will find it attractive to voluntarily install smart meters in their buildings. The government is still working out some of the details concerning implementation of this program so these provisions have not yet gone into effect.

Apportionment of Utility Costs (s. 138)

For a building containing no more than six units, where the landlord supplies a utility to each of the units, the R.T.A. allows the landlord to unilaterally change the tenancy agreements and charge each tenant a portion of the utility costs, provided that the landlord gives adequate notice, reduces the rent and ensures that any appliances in the unit and other aspects of the unit and building meet the prescribed requirements relating to energy conservation. It should be noted that the separate charge for the utility is still not considered to be "rent". The regulations necessary for implementation of this section of the Act have not yet been passed. Thus, implementation of s. 138 will not occur until some time in the future.

<u>Part IX (Care Homes)</u>

Abatement of rent if tenancy agreement not written (s. 139)

In a care home, the tenancy agreement must be written. If the landlord does not comply, the tenant can apply for an abatement of rent.

Limit on liability for care services and meals (s. 145)

A tenant who terminates the tenancy in a care home can also require the landlord to stop providing care services and meals prior to the termination date by giving 10 days notice and has no obligation to pay for such services thereafter. If the tenant dies, the estate has no obligation to pay for care services and meals that would otherwise have been provided under the tenancy agreement more than 10 days after the death of the tenant.

External care providers (s. 147)

The R.T.A. states that the landlord must not do anything to prevent a tenant from obtaining additional care services from an external care provider or interfere with the provision of additional care services by an external care provider of the tenant's choice.

Part X (Mobile Home Parks and Land Lease Communities)

Park rules (s. 154)

Where a landlord establishes rules for a mobile home park or land lease community, the R.T.A. requires that the landlord provide a written copy of the rules to each tenant and must inform the tenants in writing of any changes to the rules. Where a landlord fails to comply with this provision, the tenant's obligation to pay rent is suspended (until the landlord does comply, at which time all of the past rent becomes due).

Property tax notice to be provided to tenant (s. 155)

Where a tenant is obliged to reimburse the landlord for property taxes with respect to a mobile home owned by the tenant, and the Municipal Property Assessment Corporation gives the landlord written notice of the value of the mobile home for tax purposes, the landlord must promptly provide the tenant with a copy of that information. Where a landlord fails to comply with this provision, the tenant's obligation to reimburse the landlord for the property taxes is suspended (until the landlord does provide the information, at which time the landlord may require the tenant to pay any property taxes that the tenant withheld).

Assignment to potential assignee/purchaser (s. 159)

Under s. 108 of the T.P.A., the landlord had no right to refuse the assignment of a mobile home site if the potential assignee had purchased or had entered into an agreement to purchase the mobile home on that site. Under the R.T.A., if the landlord wishes to prevent such an assignment, the landlord has 15 days in which to apply to the Board for a determination of whether the landlord's reasons for refusing consent to the requested assignment are reasonable.

Greater compensation where notice given for demolition/conversion/ repairs (s. 164)

Under the T.P.A., where a tenant had to vacate a rental unit located in a mobile home park or land lease community because the landlord intended to demolish the site, do work that was so extensive that the tenant could not safely remain in the unit or convert the site to non-residential use, the tenant would be entitled to the same compensation as any other tenant (i.e., three months rent) but was also entitled to much more advance notice (at least one year) than tenants in other types of rental accommodations. Under the R.T.A., the notice period remains the same but the amount of compensation has been increased to the lesser of the following amounts:

1. One year's rent; and
2. $3,000 or the amount prescribed in the regulations, whichever is greater.

Part XI (The Landlord and Tenant Board)

The name of the adjudicative body has been changed from the Rental Housing Tribunal to the Landlord and Tenant Board, but otherwise, no substantial changes to the structure or jurisdiction of this body have been made.

Part XII (Board Proceedings)

Notice by Board (s. 189)

Under the T.P.A., it was the applicant's responsibility to serve the respondent with a copy of the application and notice of hearing and to provide proof of service. Many respondents (especially tenants) complained, however, that they did not actually receive such notice. Although not required by law to do so, the Rental Housing Tribunal began in or about 2005 to also mail notices to respondents in an effort to ensure that respondents were aware that proceedings had been commenced against them at the Tribunal. Under the R.T.A., the onus remains upon the applicant to serve the respondent with a copy of the application and notice of hearing but there is now also a statutory obligation upon the Landlord and Tenant Board to notify the respondent in writing that an application has been made and to provide the Board's file number for the application, the date of the hearing (where it has been scheduled), and contact information for the Board.[20]

Payment into Board pending resolution of maintenance application (s. 195)

Where a tenant has commenced a maintenance application, pending hearing of the application and the issuance of a final order, the Board may order or permit the tenant to pay his or her rent directly into the

[20] Subsection 54(1) of O. Reg. 516/06.

Board. This power is not new, but the fact that it is specifically tied in the statute to maintenance applications seems to be another signal that, under the R.T.A., rent strikes are not only condoned, but encouraged.

"Hands off" policy towards the calculation of rent and subsidies in social housing (s. 203)

Under the T.P.A., Members struggled with the issue of whether they could or should look behind the rent charged by landlords in rent-geared-to-income housing, the subsidies provided to tenants in social housing and determinations by landlords as to tenants' eligibility for, or the amount of, any prescribed form of housing assistance. Section 203 of the R.T.A. makes it clear that the Board is *not* to make any determinations or review decisions of the landlord or other bodies concerning these issues. In essence, the Board must simply accept the information provided by the landlord with respect to the lawful rent payable by such tenants. In *Peel Housing Corp. v. Ellis*,[21] the Divisional Court has confirmed that this section means exactly what it says and this is one provision of the R.T.A. with which Board Members seem quite content to comply.[22]

Agreement to settle (s. 206)

On a landlord's application to terminate the tenancy for non-payment of rent and/or for the payment of rent arrears, the parties can sign a written settlement (typically, a repayment schedule) and file it with the Board before the hearing has commenced. The Board can then incorporate the terms of this settlement into a consent order. Such an order, however, cannot include any provision for termination of the tenancy or even termination in the event of a breach of any terms of the agreement. The most that can happen is that, upon a breach of the agreement by the tenant, the landlord may request that the application be re-opened and a new hearing date set. Either party can also seek to have the consent order set aside on the basis that the agreement was only obtained through misrepresentation or coercion.

In my view, landlords are not likely to take advantage of this provision for the following reasons: (1) the consent order is, for all intents and purposes, unenforceable; (2) upon a breach by the tenant, there could be considerable delay before a new hearing can be scheduled; (3) the new hearing will be more complex (i.e., there will be

---

[21] (2009), 2009 CarswellOnt 693 (Ont. Div. Ct.).

[22] See, for example, Landlord and Tenant Board File No. NOL-05875 (Jan. 22, 2009); Landlord and Tenant Board File No. SWL-22456 (Jan. 22, 2009); and Landlord and Tenant Board File No. TNL-19695 (Jan. 29, 2009).

more issues to resolve) and the onus upon the landlord will be twofold as the landlord will have to prove a breach of the agreement before there can even be a hearing of the merits of the landlord's original application. Therefore, there is little, if any, advantage to the landlord making a deal with the tenant in advance of the originally scheduled hearing date. A landlord who wishes to negotiate with the tenant would likely be better off waiting until the day of the hearing and then entering into a mediated agreement or a consent order *at* the hearing.

Power to review clarified (s. 209)

Under the T.P.A., the Tribunal had the power to review its hearing orders where there was a serious error in law or in fact. A serious error in law included a denial of natural justice. Therefore, if a person was unable to attend a hearing, the Tribunal could and usually would order a new hearing. For the sake of clarity, s. 209(2) of the R.T.A. makes it explicit that the Board's power to review its decisions includes the power to do so where a party was not reasonably able to participate in the proceeding.

Part XIII (Municipal Vital Services By-Laws)

No substantive changes.

Part XIV (Maintenance Standards)

No substantive changes.

Part XV (Administration and Enforcement)

No substantive changes.

Part XVI (Offences)

New offences (s. 234)

The following new offences are added:

1. failure to provide a tenant *or former tenant* with a receipt in accordance with s. 109;[23]
2. failure to give a new tenant the required notice that sets out the lawful rent to be charged or giving false information in the notice where there is an OPRI;[24]

---

[23] Clause 234(h) of the R.T.A.

[24] Clause 234(i) of the R.T.A.

3. failure to provide information on the total cost of utilities in accordance with subsection 128(2);[25]

4. doing anything to prevent a tenant of a care home from obtaining care services from a person of the tenant's choice contrary to clause 147(a);[26] and

5. interfering with the provision of care services to a tenant of a care home contrary to clause 147(b).[27]

Increased fines (s. 238)

The maximum fine that can be imposed on an individual has been increased from $10,000 under the T.P.A. to $25,000 under the R.T.A. The maximum fine that can be imposed on a corporation has been increased from $50,000 under the T.P.A. to $100,000 under the R.T.A.

Part XVII (Regulations)

There are no substantive changes to the types of regulations that can be made under the R.T.A. The actual regulations, however, have been changed significantly.

Part XVIII (Transition)

For applications that were commenced under the T.P.A. but that were not resolved by January 30, 2007, the application shall be resolved in accordance with the T.P.A. That is, the *substantive* law that will apply on such applications will be the provisions of the T.P.A., with the following two exceptions:

1. the matter must proceed to a hearing (the default process ceases to exist on January 31, 2007);[28] and

2. if it is an eviction application, the tenant will have the rights and protections afforded by sections 82 and 83 of the R.T.A.[29]

The *procedural* Rules that will apply will be those in existence at the time the step is taken.

If an eviction order based upon arrears of rent has not yet been enforced and the tenant retains rights under subsection 72(4) to (10)

---

[25] Clause 234(k) of the R.T.A.

[26] Clause 234(n) of the R.T.A.

[27] Clause 234(o) of the R.T.A.

[28] Subsection 242(2) of the R.T.A.

[29] Subsections 242(1), (3) and (5) of the R.T.A.

of the T.P.A., upon proclamation of the R.T.A. that tenant will also be afforded the additional rights set out in subsections 74(11) to (18) of the R.T.A.[30]

For above-guideline rent increase (AGI) applications commenced under the T.P.A., the following transitional rules apply:

1. If the hearing does not take place until after January 30, 2007, tenants can raise maintenance concerns at the hearing as if the application had been made under the R.T.A.;[31]
2. If the application was made (i.e., filed) on or after May 3, 2006, and it is based in whole or in part on capital expenditures, the order shall specify the percentage increase that is attributable to the capital expenditures and the date and amount by which the rent must eventually be decreased by the landlord (if the same tenant still resides in the unit on that date).[32]

Under the T.P.A., the Tribunal had access to information from the Rent Registry (maintained under the *Rent Control Act, 1992*) and was obliged to provide that information to members of the public on request. Under s. 245 of the R.T.A., that obligation will end on January 31, 2008 (i.e., one year after the R.T.A. is proclaimed).

The old notice of rent increase and notice of termination forms used under the T.P.A. can continue to be used for two months after the R.T.A. is proclaimed (i.e., up to the end of March 2007).[33]

Part XIX (Other Matters)

Unless, prior to May 3, 2006, a landlord gave a notice of rent increase to raise the rent to the "maximum rent" set as of the date the T.P.A. came into effect, the landlord can no longer do so. The concept of "maximum rent" has been abolished.[34]

4. REMEDIAL LEGISLATION

The objectives of Part IV of the *Landlord and Tenant Act* were to redress the imbalance between landlords and tenants.

---

[30] Subsection 242(4) of the R.T.A.

[31] Subsection 242(7) of the R.T.A.

[32] Subsection 258(2) of the R.T.A.

[33] Section 246 of the R.T.A.

[34] Subsection 258(1) of the R.T.A.

A general statement of remedial interpretation is found in *Thompson v. Lord Clanmorri.*[35]

> In construing any . . . enactment, regard must be had not only to the words used, but to the history of the Act, and the reasons which led to its being passed. You must look at the mischief which had to be cured as well as at the cure provided.

This approach was certainly followed by the Supreme Court of Canada in *Herbold v. Pajelle Investments Ltd.*[36] The court quoted with approval the statement from the Court of Appeal judgment in the case:[37]

> The legislation reflects the effort on the part of the legislators to govern and control the standard of social behaviour of inhabitants of large modern multiple housing units not only towards their lessors but also towards each other with a view to promoting peace and tranquility from a social as well as from an environmental standpoint.

In another case, *Gagnon v. Centre-Town Developments Ltd.*,[38] the court in considering the remedial objective of the legislation applied s. 10 of the *Interpretation Act*,[39] which states in effect that remedial legislation should receive such liberal interpretation as will ensure the attainment of the statute according to its true intent and spirit.

Another statement of the remedial objective of Part IV is found in *Anglo-Keno Developments Inc. v. Langan*:[40]

> [T]he object of the Act is to provide for an increase of security to the tenant. . . . the true intent and spirit can be best arrived at by that interpretation which enables its remedial aspect to be effective at the earliest possible date.

It was stated in *Lounsbury Realty Ltd. v. Shekter*[41] that Part IV provided the complete code for obtaining possession of residential premises: "the process is intended to be speedy, informal and inexpensive; to engraph discovery proceedings on to the structure would defeat this intention".

Expressions from the above few cases indicate that the courts interpreted the residential sections of Part IV of the *Landlord and Tenant Act* with a liberal attitude consistent with the continued expressed intent of the Legislature. The intent was stated in the explanatory notes to the Bill when Part

---

35 [1900] 1 Ch. 718 at 725 (Eng. C.A.).

36 (1975), [1976] 2 S.C.R. 520 (S.C.C.).

37 (1974), 4 O.R. (2d) 133 at 138 (Ont. C.A.), varied (1975), [1976] 2 S.C.R. 520 (S.C.C.).

38 (1975), 10 O.R. (2d) 245 (Ont. Co. Ct.), reversed on other grounds (1976), 14 O.R. (2d) 550 (Ont. Div. Ct.).

39 *Interpretation Act*, R.S.O. 1970, c. 225 [now R.S.O. 1990, c. I.11].

40 (February 29, 1976) (Ont. Co. Ct.).

41 (1978), 23 O.R. (2d) 309 at 313 (Ont. Co. Ct.).

IV was first introduced in the Ontario Legislature, and that was to implement the recommendations of the Ontario Law Reform Commission, which were aimed at achieving a fair balance of rights and obligations between landlords and tenants. The reports of the Commission were guidelines for the courts for interpreting the objects of Part IV for tenants.

Another remedial aspect of the *Landlord and Tenant Act* is found in s. 121 which specifies that a judge may refuse a landlord's application for possession if it would be unfair, and thus interposes a statutory equity.

Part IV of the *Landlord and Tenant Act* was clearly intended to have remedial effect and, accordingly, it was given liberal interpretation by the courts.

The same remedial spirit was implicit in the wording of the T.P.A. and was found by the Members of the Rental Housing Tribunal and the courts to be a guiding principle in interpreting and applying that legislation.

Although tenant advocates sometimes scoffed at the title of the former legislation, many of those same advocates are now concerned that the change of the title from the "Tenant Protection Act" to the "Residential Tenancies Act" will send the wrong signal that somehow protection of tenants is no longer at the heart of the legislation. Likely in response to this concern, a new section was added to the R.T.A., to explicitly state the purposes of the Act. Section 1 of the R.T.A. reads as follows:

> The purposes of this Act are to provide protection for residential tenants from unlawful rent increases and unlawful evictions, to establish a framework for the regulation of residential rents, to balance the rights and responsibilities of residential landlords and tenants and to provide for the adjudication of disputes and for other processes to informally resolve disputes.

The R.T.A. does not represent a marked departure from the T.P.A. About 90 per cent of the R.T.A. was taken word-for-word from the T.P.A., which in turn was taken in large part from Part IV of the *Landlord and Tenant Act*. The wording and, arguably, the intention behind most of the legislative provisions governing residential tenancies in Ontario have not really changed in over 20 years. Thus, in light of both its history and its objectives (as expressed in s. 1 of the *Act*), the *Residential Tenancies Act*, 2006 ought properly to be viewed as remedial legislation.

5. LEGISLATIVE FRAMEWORK

The R.T.A. is the single most important part of the legislative framework governing Ontario residential tenancies. It is the foundation upon which this "framework" rests. The R.T.A. does not, however, constitute the entire scheme. Furthermore, although s. 3 of the R.T.A. states that the R.T.A. takes priority over other statutes, there are a couple of exceptions. First, subsection

3(4) of the R.T.A. specifically provides that the provisions of the Ontario *Human Rights Code* are paramount. Second, provisions of the R.T.A. can be struck down if they are found to be unconstitutional. Subject to these caveats, the R.T.A. is paramount in the field of residential tenancies in Ontario. As previously indicated, however, the R.T.A. is only one part of a larger legislative framework.

As the governing statute, the R.T.A. creates the basic rights and obligations of landlords and tenants and provides remedies for breaches of its provisions. It created the Landlord and Tenant Board to assist in the resolution of disputes arising between residential landlords and tenants. As with many statutes, however, it is relatively long and cumbersome and leaves some details (concerning procedures in particular) to be worked out at a later date. Such details are contained in the regulations.[42] The key regulation under the R.T.A. is Ontario Regulation 516/06, which (amongst other things): defines key terms; sets rules for care homes and mobile home parks; establishes rules for calculating lawful rent, rent discounts, rent increases above the guideline and rent reductions resulting from a reduction in municipal taxes; establishes which additional charges are legal; and establishes the useful life of capital expenditures.

Another noteworthy regulation is Ontario Regulation 517/06 which establishes maintenance standards in places without municipal standards.[43] Regulations are subordinate to the statutes under which they were created. These regulations, therefore, are subordinate to the R.T.A.; in the event of a conflict, the provisions of the R.T.A. prevail.

Although the Landlord and Tenant Board was created by the R.T.A., the Board was left to create its own procedures.[44] In order to fulfill its mandate, the Board has established and published Rules of Practice (found at Appendix 7). Anyone appearing before the Board should be familiar with these Rules.

In addition, the Board is bound by the provisions of the *Statutory Powers Procedure Act*, R.S.O. 1990, c. S.22.[45]

The Board has also published Interpretation Guidelines[46] to assist its Members and the public in understanding how certain provisions of the R.T.A. are generally interpreted and applied; while not binding upon the Members of the Board, it is expected that a Member will follow the interpre-

---

[42] It is usually easier for a government to amend an existing regulation or pass a new regulation rather than attempt to modify the empowering statute. In this way, regulations offer governments greater flexibility.

[43] See s. 224(1) of the R.T.A. Where a municipality has its own maintenance standards, O. Reg. 517/06 does not apply.

[44] Section 176 of the R.T.A.

[45] Pursuant to s. 184(1) of the R.T.A. (see, however, the exceptions listed in ss. 184(2) and 184(3)).

[46] See Appendix 8.

tations contained in the Guidelines unless the Member provides a clear rationale for departing from the suggested approach.[47]

Finally, there is the issue of the common law. To what extent are Members bound by the decisions of their colleagues and the courts? Members of the Board are *not* bound by decisions of other Members of the Board or of Vice-chairs. While it is hoped that the Board will achieve a consistent interpretation of provisions of the R.T.A. and the regulations and that Members will adopt similar approaches to dealing with similar issues, one Member is not legally obligated to follow the decision of another. The Board is bound by decisions of the Divisional Court, the Ontario Court of Appeal and the Supreme Court of Canada. Decisions from courts other than the ones listed above[48] may be persuasive, but they are not strictly binding upon Members of the Board. Similarly, decisions made under predecessor statutes (such as the *Tenant Protection Act*, *Landlord and Tenant Act* or the *Rent Control Act*) may be persuasive, but only to the extent that the legislative provisions under consideration are similar to those contained in the R.T.A.

---

[47] See Rule 26.3 of the Board's Rules of Procedure.

[48] Such as the Superior Court of Justice, Small Claims Court or courts outside of Ontario.

2

The Landlord and Tenant Board

1. INTRODUCTION

This chapter is meant to provide an overview of the nature, jurisdiction and powers of the Landlord and Tenant Board. Additional information about the Board and the *Residential Tenancies Act, 2006*[1] (R.T.A.) can be obtained by visiting the Board's website (www.ltb.gov.on.ca) or by calling the Board's Telephone Information Centre at 416-645-8080 (from within the Toronto calling area) or 1-888-332-3234 (from outside Toronto). While every effort has been made to ensure that this text is accurate at the time of printing, the law is constantly changing and it is always recommended that you consult the Board's official website to obtain the most up-to-date information.

2. NATURE OF THE BOARD

The Landlord and Tenant Board (formerly known as the Ontario Rental Housing Tribunal)[2] is a "quasi-judicial" tribunal, meaning that it is similar, but not identical, to a court of law. The head of the Board is known as the Chair. There are seven Vice-chairs and, at any given time, between about thirty and forty full-time Members (also known as adjudicators) and approximately five to ten part-time Members. The Chair, Vice-chairs and Members are appointed[3] to their positions by the provincial government (i.e., by Order-in-Council) and serve for limited terms[4]. The background, education and training of Members vary widely. Some are lawyers. Some have experience in politics or in other forms of public service. Members of the Landlord and Tenant Board are expected to comply with the Board's published "Principles

---

[1] S.O. 2006, c. 17.

[2] Section 168 of the R.T.A.

[3] Sections 169 and 170 of the R.T.A. (formerly ss. 158 and 159 of the T.P.A.).

[4] Usually for no more than three terms and usually not exceeding an aggregate of ten years of service. Prior to 2007, appointments were usually for no more than two three-year terms (six years in total).

of Conduct for Members" (see Appendix 5). Biographies of the Chair, Vice-chairs and Members can be found on the Board's website. The appointment process is described in more detail on the website of the Public Appointment Secretariat (www.pas.gov.on.ca).

The Board also relies heavily upon its staff, including, mediators, managers, analysts, financial officers and client service representatives. In total, the Board employs about 300 people across the province.

Pursuant to s. 232 of the R.T.A.,[5] Members of the Board and all other employees of the Board acting in good faith in the performance of their duties are exempt from civil actions (i.e., they cannot be "sued" for damages for alleged negligence or default in the performance of their duties).[6]

The Board operates from eight regional offices, located in: London (Southwest Region), Hamilton (Southern Region), Mississauga (Central Region), Ottawa (Eastern Region), Sudbury (Northern Region) and Toronto (Toronto East, Toronto North and Toronto South). In addition to holding hearings at its regional offices, the Board also regularly holds hearings in other locations (such as Newmarket and Whitby), and less frequently, in more remote locations.

In some (but not all) locations where the Board holds hearings, Duty Counsel is available to provide legal assistance to tenants. The Duty Counsel is a lawyer or other legal professional who assists tenants who lack legal representation. This is a service provided by the Advocacy Centre for Tenants Ontario (ACTO) and is funded by Legal Aid Ontario. Duty Counsel are not part of the Board.

The Board attempts to assist parties in resolving their disputes through mediation. Participation in mediation is voluntary.[7] Board mediators are available for most types of applications and are on duty at most locations where the Board holds hearings. Most mediators are former Rent Officers (and, in some instances, former Members of the Rental Housing Tribunal) who have considerable experience in this field and have been specifically trained in assisting parties to negotiate a settlement of disputes arising from residential tenancies. Mediators must conform to a Code of Ethics and Professional Conduct (see Appendix 6). Mediators provide a means of dispute resolution which is neutral, fair to all participants, confidential, collaborative and which promotes empowerment of the participants.

If the parties are unable or unwilling to resolve their disputes through negotiation, then the matter will proceed to a hearing. Hearings are conducted by individual Members sitting alone, not by a panel.[8]

---

[5] Formerly, s. 205 of the T.P.A.

[6] See, for example, *Taylor v. Levitt* (2008), [2008] O.J. No. 4088, 170 A.C.W.S. (3d) 414 (Ont. S.C.J.).

[7] Except in the case of a landlord's application to have a tenant of a care home moved to another facility, in which case mediation is mandatory (see Chapter 21).

[8] Section 171 of the R.T.A. (formerly s. 160 of the T.P.A.).

Documents can be filed by parties or their representatives at the regional offices in person, by fax or electronically.

Under the *Tenant Protection Act, 1997*[9] (T.P.A.), the Rental Housing Tribunal typically resolved about 70,000-75,000 applications (i.e., disputes) annually. Approximately 90% of applications were filed by landlords, while only 10% of applications were initiated by tenants. Under the T.P.A., approximately three-quarters of all applications were L1 applications filed by landlords seeking termination of the tenancy and payment of rent arrears. In its first year of operation,[10] the Landlord and Tenant Board resolved almost 75,000 applications and in its second year[11] it resolved approximately 88,000 applications. In both years, approximately 90% of applications were filed by landlords and L1 applications made up about 70% of all applications resolved by the Board. In short, the number and nature of the applications being heard by the Board under the R.T.A. are roughly the same as were heard by the Tribunal under the T.P.A.

As discussed in Chapter 1, the two main differences under the R.T.A. are that: (1) *virtually all* applications proceed to a hearing (since the default process has been eliminated);[12] and (2) on landlord applications concerning rent, tenants can raise their own concerns and seek relief for the landlord's breaches of the *Act* without first having to file their own applications.[13]

3. JURISDICTION OF THE BOARD

(a) General

According to s. 168(2) of the R.T.A. (formerly s. 157(2) of the T.P.A.), the Board has "exclusive jurisdiction to determine all applications under this Act and with respect to all matters in which jurisdiction is conferred on it by this Act". Pursuant to s. 174 of the R.T.A. (formerly s.162 of the T.P.A.), the Board "has authority to hear and determine all questions of law and fact with respect to all matters within its jurisdiction under this Act."

What is within the jurisdiction of the Board? At the risk of oversimplifying matters, I would say that the Board has exclusive jurisdiction over all matters falling within the jurisdiction of the R.T.A. and which do not exceed the monetary jurisdiction of the Board.

---

9 S.O. 1997, c. 24.

10 January 31, 2007 to January 30, 2008.

11 January 31, 2008 to January 30, 2009.

12 There are some exceptions to this, such as: (1) L4 applications (to terminate the tenancy under s. 78 for breach of a mediated agreement or order of the Board) that generally are meant to be resolved, *ex parte* (i.e., without notice to the tenant and without a hearing); and (2) motions to void an eviction order where all arrears of rent (and other amounts ordered) have been paid.

13 Pursuant to s. 82 of the R.T.A.

The exclusive nature of the Rental Housing Tribunal's jurisdiction was reaffirmed by the Ontario Court of Appeal in *Beach v. Mofatt*.[14] The appellants were the residential tenants of an illegal rooming house in Ottawa. The respondents were neighbours who had brought an action against the landlords seeking damages for nuisance and for an interim and final injunction restraining them from operating the rooming house. The defendants (who did not participate in the appeal) were the landlords of the rooming house. The Superior Court of Justice had granted what amounted to an eviction order against the tenants of this rooming house (even though the action had been commenced by the owners of a neighbouring property and not by the tenants' landlords). The single legal issue in the appeal was whether the Superior Court of Justice had jurisdiction to order the eviction of the tenants or whether the Tribunal had exclusive jurisdiction to do so. The Court of Appeal found that the Tribunal had exclusive jurisdiction to terminate these tenancies on a properly constituted application by the landlords. Therefore, the appeal was allowed and the Superior Court's "eviction order" was overturned.

Similarly, in *Barrett v. 731229 Ontario Ltd.*,[15] a landlord was charging tenants an administrative charge over and above the charge for electricity that they were consuming. A number of tenants objected and commenced an application with the Rental Housing Tribunal for a ruling on whether this constituted an illegal charge. The Tribunal ruled in favour of the tenants. The landlord appealed this decision on the basis that the Tribunal lacked the jurisdiction to deal with this matter and that the billing issue ought to have been brought before the Ontario Energy Board. The Divisional Court held that while the Ontario Energy Board asserts paramountcy through a regulation, the paramountcy provision contained in the T.P.A. trumps it. Thus, the Tribunal did have jurisdiction to deal with the issues raised. The Divisional Court also found that the Tribunal's decision was reasonable in the circumstances.

In *Progressive Investments v. Harris*,[16] the landlord brought an action for arrears of rent against a tenant who was still in possession of the rental unit. The Kitchener Small Claims Court held that this issue was exclusively within the jurisdiction of the Landlord and Tenant Board and dismissed the claim for want of jurisdiction.

In *Theriault v. O'Shanter Development Co.*,[17] a former tenant sought to bring an action for general and punitive damages against her former landlord arising from her loss of enjoyment of the unit during balcony repairs. Justice P.A. Thomson stated that the courts have generally been taking the approach that the Ontario Rental Housing Tribunal (now the Landlord and Tenant

---

[14] (2005), [2005] O.J. No. 1722, 2005 CarswellOnt 1693 (Ont. C.A.).

[15] (2006), [2006] O.J. No. 1499 (Ont. Div. Ct.).

[16] (2008), [2008] O.J. No. 5163 (Ont. S.C.J.).

[17] (2007), 2007 CarswellOnt 5277 (Ont. S.C.J.).

Board) has exclusive jurisdiction over matters within its expertise and where the amount in issue is within the statutory limits ($10,000 at the time this decision was rendered). Justice Thomson went on to conclude that a former tenant cannot oust the jurisdiction of the Board by calling a demand for what is essentially an abatement of rent "damages" or by adding a claim for punitive damages (where it is clear that such claim is simply a further attempt to evade the jurisdiction of the Board). Justice Thomson noted that the one-year limitation under s. 32(2) of the T.P.A. (now s. 29(2) of the R.T.A.) had elapsed before the former tenant had even commenced the court proceedings. I suspect that that is why the former tenant attempted to bring her complaint before the Superior Court of Justice (i.e., because she waited too long and lost her right to commence an application under the T.P.A.). In any event, the Court dismissed her claim on the basis that the matter was within the exclusive jurisdiction of the Landlord and Tenant Board.

On the other hand, where the one-year limitation period under s. 29(2) of the R.T.A. has expired and the former tenant's claim would be statute-barred from proceeding before the Board, it appears that the court may be prepared to adopt a more "flexible" interpretation in order to find that the claim of a former tenant was *not* exclusively within the jurisdiction of the Board.[18]

In *Rhee v. Zilberman*,[19] upon default of a second mortgage, the second mortgagee obtained a judgment against the owner of the property in power of sale proceedings. The second mortgagee found that the property was occupied and that the occupants were obstructing her efforts to sell the property. It appears that she may have locked the occupants out of the property. Those occupants commenced a proceeding at the Ontario Rental Housing Tribunal for a declaration that they were tenants of the property in question and that the mortgagee had illegally entered their unit and illegally evicted them. The second mortgagee received notice of those proceedings before the Tribunal but chose not to participate. Based upon the evidence available, the Tribunal found the occupants to be tenants of the property and issued an interim order to allow them to regain possession. The second mortgagee then brought a motion before the Court to add the occupants as parties to the original proceeding and for a Writ of Possession against those occupants. In these circumstances, the Court declined to intervene, holding that the second mortgagee ought to seek redress at the Tribunal and/or seek remedies under s. 52 of the *Mortgages Act* (which permits the Court to set aside a fraudulent tenancy agreement created to frustrate a mortgagee's attempts to enforce the terms of the mortgage).

---

[18] See, for example, *Batey v. Transglobe Property Management Services*, [2008] O.J. No. 4135 (Ont. S.C.J., London Small Claims Court).

[19] (2006), 2006 CarswellOnt 6868 (Ont. S.C.J.).

In *Dewar v. Athwal*,[20] Ms. Dewar brought what was essentially a motion for an order restraining the defendants (who were her landlords) from dealing with their assets and an order that the defendants be ordered to surrender their passports (and remain in the country). Ms. Dewar had a number of complaints related to her tenancy, including an allegation that damage was caused to her personal property as a result of a fire at the residential complex. Ms. Dewar had not yet commenced any action in the court but she was scheduled to appear at a hearing before the Landlord and Tenant Board (apparently concerning an eviction application brought be the landlords). Justice Sproat suggested that the Landlord and Tenant Board was the proper place for Ms. Dewar to raise any issues arising from this tenancy and, in the absence of any properly constituted court action, declined to make any further orders.

(b) Residential Tenancies

Section 3 of the R.T.A. (formerly s. 2 of the T.P.A.) states that, "This Act applies with respect to rental units in residential complexes, despite any other Act and despite any agreement or waiver to the contrary." Sections 5, 6 and 7 of the R.T.A., however, list types of tenancies that are partially or completely exempt from the Act; there are, therefore, exceptions. The definition of "residential" tenancies and these exceptional cases are discussed in more detail in Chapter 4.

First, for the R.T.A. to apply (and for the Board to have jurisdiction over the matter), there must be a "tenancy" as defined by the *Act*. There must be a landlord and tenant relationship (see Chapter 3). Thus, where the Board finds that there is no landlord and tenant relationship, it will decline jurisdiction.[21]

Non-residential tenancies in Ontario are generally governed by the *Commercial Tenancies Act*, R.S.O. 1990, c. L.7. The Landlord and Tenant Board has no jurisdiction over commercial tenancies.[22]

The Board has jurisdiction only over residential tenancies. The Board may, therefore, refuse to intervene where the relationship between the parties is other than a normal "landlord and tenant" relationship. For instance, the Board may find that it lacks jurisdiction to adjudicate a dispute between a vendor and purchaser of real property, even where the purchaser has been allowed to occupy the premises pending the completion of the sale.[23] The Board may also refuse to accept jurisdiction where a tenant has been locked out of the rental unit as a result of the enforcement of an order of the Superior

---

20 (2007), 2007 CarswellOnt 5505 (Ont. S.C.J.).

21 See, for example, Landlord and Tenant Board File NO. EAT-01664 (Feb. 24, 2009).

22 Landlord and Tenant Board File No. CET-01671 (Jan. 8, 2009).

23 *308237 Ontario Ltd. v. Lask* (Feb. 19, 2001), SWL-23039 (Ont. Rental Housing Trib.).

Court obtained in power of sale proceedings brought by the condominium corporation against the owner of the unit (i.e., the tenant's landlord).[24]

The Board may refuse to assume jurisdiction where there is a related pending Superior Court application or where the matter is more properly within the jurisdiction of the court. For instance, the Tribunal declined jurisdiction where there was a dispute over a person's ownership of or interest in the property.[25] The Tribunal also adjourned a set aside motion where the landlord was a mortgagee in possession and there was a pending court challenge to the validity of the mortgage in question.[26]

The Board may also be reluctant to intervene in matters which are essentially family disputes.[27]

In *Breton v. Milks*[28], the two owners of the property were estranged spouses. The tenant living in the unit only dealt with the husband. The wife attempted to evict the tenant in furtherance of her claims to the matrimonial property and her dispute over the fairness of the separation agreement. The Tribunal declined to intervene until a court decided the issue of which spouse had control over the property. In *Brickson v. Pennock*[29], a court granted one spouse the right to occupy the premises on payment of occupation rent to the other. It was unclear whether the court had created a tenancy. When there was an alleged failure to pay the occupancy rent, the Tribunal declined to intervene and referred the parties back to the court that made the original order.

In Landlord and Tenant Board File No. TEL-09610 (February 27, 2008), the parties were former common law spouses. Title to the subject property was in the name of only one of the spouses (the Applicant). After the property was purchased in the name of the Applicant, the parties entered into a written trust agreement that provided for co-ownership and detailed how mortgage

2 — THE L.T.B.

---

[24] *Whitt v. McDowall* (Oct. 4, 2001), TNT-02206, [2001] O.R.H.T.D. No. 128, 2001 CarswellOnt 6307 (Ont. Rental Housing Trib.).

[25] *Tannous v. Tannous* (Aug. 31, 1999), SWL-09268 (Ont. Rental Housing Trib.); *Mercer v. Mercer* (July 6, 2006), SWL-81450, [2006] O.R.H.T.D. No. 96 (Ont. Rental Housing Trib.); Landlord and Tenant Board File No. TEL-18936 (Dec. 10, 2008).

[26] *Toronto-Dominion Bank v. Couto* (April 21, 2006), SWL-78675-SA, [2006] O.R.H.T.D. No. 35 (Ont. Rental Housing Trib.).

[27] See, for example, Landlord and Tenant Board File No. SOL-14704-RV, in which it was held that no tenancy ever existed between the Applicant and the Respondent. Rather it was determined that the dispute between the parties arose as a result of a breakdown in the relationship between family members (i.e., when the Applicant's marriage failed, it affected the relationship between him and his stepson, who lived in the basement of the matrimonial home and who the Applicant wished to now treat as a regular tenant and evict from the home). See also Landlord and Tenant Board File No. TEL-19566 (Feb. 18, 2009), which involved a dispute between brothers.

[28] (Sept. 18, 2001), EAL-23478, [2001] O.R.H.T.D. No. 131, 2001 CarswellOnt 6323 (Ont. Rental Housing Trib.).

[29] (July 11, 2001), EAL-20706-RV, [2001] O.R.H.T.D. No. 101, 2001 CarswellOnt 6342 (Ont. Rental Housing Trib.).

and utility payments were to be made and how the property would devolve in the future. The parties also purported to execute a "temporary" tenancy agreement. A dispute arose between the parties and the Applicant filed an application before the Landlord and Tenant Board for arrears of rent and to evict the Respondent for persistent late payment of rent. Pursuant to the definition of "tenant" found in s. 2 of the R.T.A., it was held that the Respondent could not be a tenant if the Respondent's right to occupy the unit is by virtue of being a co-owner. Looking at the real substance of the matter (*per* s. 202 of the R.T.A.), it was found that this was not a landlord and tenant relationship. Furthermore, given that the Respondent might also have an interest in the property by virtue of a constructive or resulting trust (having contributed to its acquisition and/or upkeep), the Member ruled that the dispute between the parties was better determined before the courts than the Board.

Even where there clearly exists a residential tenancy subject to the R.T.A., the Board's jurisdiction is still limited to a particular period of time. In general, the Board has little power to grant relief for events that occur prior to the commencement of the tenancy.[30] In *Fortin v. Reiter-Nemetz*,[31] the tenant was upset about the noise of construction on the road outside her rental unit. She stated that the landlord promised her it would be quiet. The application was dismissed both on the grounds that it was out of time (the tenant had waited more than one year from the commencement of the construction before bringing this application) and on the grounds that the Tribunal is not the proper forum to seek damages flowing from an alleged misrepresentation that occurred prior to the commencement of the tenancy.

Furthermore, under the T.P.A., the Rental Housing Tribunal had no jurisdiction to grant relief to a former tenant for conduct of the landlord that occurred during or after the enforcement of an eviction order (i.e., after termination of the tenancy). In *Lorini v. Lombard*,[32] for example, the Divisional Court held that the Tribunal cannot grant relief to a former tenant for conduct of the landlord during or after the enforcement of an eviction order. This was held to be true even though the landlord had a statutory obligation under the T.P.A. to hold the tenant's property available for retrieval by the tenant for at least 48 hours following an eviction.[33] Under the T.P.A., the landlord may have been liable to the tenant as a bailee of the personal property that the tenant leaves behind in a rental unit (see *Cruickshank v. Mobal Khan Enterprises*[34]), but the former landlord's liability had to be determined by a

---

[30] With the possible exception of ordering the return of the deposit where the tenancy never commences.

[31] (Dec. 13, 2002), TNT-02907, 2002 CarswellOnt 5014 (Ont. Rental Housing Trib.).

[32] (2001), 2001 CarswellOnt 5380 (Ont. Div. Ct.).

[33] Subsection 42(2) of the T.P.A.

[34] (2002), 2002 CarswellOnt 2811 (Ont. S.C.J.).

court and not by the Tribunal. The approach taken by the Divisional Court in *Lorini v. Lombard* was followed in a number of Tribunal decisions.[35]

Unlike the Tribunal, however, the Board does have some power under the R.T.A. to grant relief for events that occur after termination of the tenancy but those powers are limited to specific situations and prescribed time periods. For instance, new provisions in the R.T.A. (s. 41) allow the Board to order the return of the tenant's property or compensation for loss or damage to the tenant's property that occurs after the tenancy ends.

(c) Monetary Jurisdiction

The monetary jurisdiction of the Board is set out in s. 207 of the R.T.A. (formerly s. 193 of the T.P.A.), which reads as follows:

> 207. (1) The Board may, where it otherwise has jurisdiction, order the payment to any given person of an amount of money up to the greater of $10,000 and the monetary jurisdiction of the Small Claims Court.
>
> (2) A person entitled to apply under this Act but whose claim exceeds the Board's monetary jurisdiction may commence a proceeding in any court of competent jurisdiction for an order requiring the payment of that sum and, if such a proceeding is commenced, the court may exercise any powers that the Board could have exercised if the proceeding had been before the Board and within its monetary jurisdiction.
>
> (3) If a party makes a claim in an application for payment of a sum equal to or less than the Board's monetary jurisdiction, all rights of the party in excess of the Board's monetary jurisdiction are extinguished once the Board issues its order . . .

Thus, the monetary jurisdiction of the Board is tied to that of the Small Claims Court. The monetary jurisdiction of the Small Claims Court is currently $10,000 per claim throughout the province.[36] Pursuant to para. 23(1)(a) of the *Courts of Justice Act*, R.S.O. 1990, c. C.43, the Small Claims Court has jurisdiction in any action for the payment of money where the amount claimed does not exceed this amount (i.e., $10,000), exclusive of interest and costs. I would therefore conclude that the Landlord and Tenant Board currently has jurisdiction over any application for the payment of money where the amount claimed does not exceed $10,000, exclusive of interest and costs.[37]

Now $25,000

[35] See *Ilunga v. Wright* (March 13, 2002), CET-02551, [2002] O.R.H.T.D. No. 32 (Ont. Rental Housing Trib.).

[36] O. Reg. 626/00.

[37] See *Bazos v. Norrena* (Sept. 27, 2002), TNL-38188-RV, 2002 CarswellOnt 3782 (Ont. Rental Housing Trib.); Landlord and Tenant Board File No. TNL-20541 (Jan. 9, 2009); Landlord and Tenant Board File Nos. TNL-18268 / TNL-20272 / TNT-01306 (Jan. 20, 2009); and Landlord and Tenant Board File No. TNL-20879 (Jan. 23, 2009).

Recently, the Attorney General announced that, effective January 1, 2010, the monetary jurisdiction of the Small Claims Court will be increased to $25,000.[38] If and when that occurs, the monetary jurisdiction of the Landlord and Tenant Board will also automatically increase to $25,000 (exclusive of interest and costs).

One issue that arose rather frequently under the T.P.A. was whether the Tribunal could indicate in an order for arrears of rent that, in order to avoid the eviction, the tenant(s) must pay an amount in excess of the monetary jurisdiction of the Tribunal. Pursuant to s. 72(3) of the T.P.A. (now s. 74(3) of the R.T.A.), whenever the Tribunal issued an order terminating the tenancy for non-payment of rent, the Tribunal had to include in the order a paragraph informing the tenant and the landlord that the order would become void if, before the order becomes enforceable (i.e., before the date it can be filed with the Sheriff's Office), the tenant paid to the landlord or to the Tribunal the amount required under s. 72(4) and specifying the amount. Assuming that a tenant owes the landlord $20,000, it was clear that the Tribunal could only order that the tenant pay to the Landlord $10,000 plus costs (when that was the limit of the Tribunal's monetary jurisdiction). What amount should the order specify needs to be paid in order to void the order pursuant to ss. 72(3) and 72(4) of the T.P.A. (now ss. 74(3) and 74(4) of the R.T.A.)? Members of the Tribunal were not entirely consistent on this issue.

One view was that the amount specified in an arrears order pursuant to s. 72(3) of the T.P.A. was not being *ordered* and, therefore, the monetary jurisdiction of the Tribunal was irrelevant. The Members who adopted this approach took the position that the Tribunal was not ordering the tenant to pay this amount; rather, the Tribunal was merely informing the tenant how much money must be paid in order to avoid eviction. The benefit of this approach was that it prevented a tenant who owed more than $10,000 to a landlord from gaining a windfall by waiting until the landlord commenced an application in the Tribunal and then wiping out the entire debt by merely paying $10,000. The problem with this approach is that it tends to gloss over the provisions of both ss. 193(1) and (3) of the T.P.A. (now ss. 207(1) and (3) of the R.T.A.) and the ruling of the Divisional Court in *Ip v. King*.[39]

The alternative approach (and the one apparently endorsed by the Divisional Court in *Ip v. King*[40]) is to strictly apply the monetary limit, both to the amounts ordered and to the amount referred to in s. 72(3) of the T.P.A. (now s. 74(3) of the R.T.A.). After all, the landlord has the option of pursuing in court a claim that exceeds the Board's monetary jurisdiction; by choosing

---

[38] O. Reg. 439/08, ss. 1 and 2.

[39] (December 23, 1998), Doc. V1124/98 (Ont. Div. Ct.) (unreported), in which the Divisional Court held that the amount specified in an eviction order as necessary to void the order also cannot exceed $10,000 (which was the limit of the Tribunal's monetary jurisdiction at that time).

[40] *Ibid.*

to commence the application at the Board, a landlord is deemed to waive any claim to any amount in excess of the maximum amount that can be awarded by the Board. Subsection 207(3) of the R.T.A. (formerly subsection 193(3) of the T.P.A.) clearly states that all rights of the landlord in excess of the Board's monetary jurisdiction are extinguished once the Board issues its order. This approach may be somewhat narrower, but its adoption would lead to greater certainty and I am now convinced that it is the preferable approach.

Another issue that can arise in the context of the monetary jurisdiction of the Board is how to calculate set-offs.[41] In *Ryshpan v. Bayview Summit Development Ltd.*,[42] the landlord brought an application based upon non-payment of rent. The tenants brought their own application for an abatement of rent. The tenants owed almost $17,000 in arrears of rent but the Member found that the tenants were entitled to a rent abatement of $4,500. The question was whether to deduct the $4,500 from the $17,000 owed to the landlord or from the $10,000 which was the most that the Tribunal could grant to the landlord at that time. The Member deducted (or "set off") the $4,500 from the total amount owing. After giving the tenants credit for the last months' rent deposit (and interest thereon) and the $4,500 rent abatement, the Member found that the tenants still owed the landlord about $11,000 and ordered the payment of this amount. On appeal, the Divisional Court agreed with this approach (i.e., the manner in which the rent abatement was set off against the total rent arrears) but reduced the amount ordered to $10,000 to accord with the monetary jurisdiction of the Tribunal.

The monetary limitation would appear to be per application. A party with several different potential grounds might therefore consider commencing a number of separate applications in order to "get around" the monetary jurisdiction of the Board. Such a strategy is, however, unlikely to succeed. It will likely be viewed as an abuse of the Board's process (since a party with a claim or claims in excess of the Board's jurisdiction always has the option of pursuing such claims in court). The Board has the discretionary power to combine applications[43] and it can use that power to effectively limit the total amount of a party's claim.[44] Bringing a series of applications (one after the other) will also likely prove an ineffective way of "getting around" the

2 — THE L.T.B.

---

[41] This applies to legal set-offs only (i.e., where the Board deducts a debt owed by the landlord to the tenant from a debt owed by the tenant to the landlord, or *vice versa*, provided that both obligations arise from the tenancy). The Board cannot grant equitable set-offs as it lacks the jurisdiction to grant equitable relief (except as specifically provided in the provisions of the R.T.A.).

[42] (April 12, 2000), Doc. 53312/99 (Ont. Div. Ct.) (re CEL-04319 and CET-00429).

[43] Pursuant to s. 186 of the R.T.A. (formerly s. 173 of the T.P.A.).

[44] This is the approach the Tribunal took in *Campbell and Lee v. Toronto Housing Co. Inc.* (on the review of the original orders TNL-08147 and TNL-08149) in order to restrict the award to $10,000; on appeal, this review decision was upheld by the Divisional Court (September 21, 2001), Doc. 747/99 (Ont. Div. Ct.).

Board's monetary jurisdiction as the Board may dismiss applications that seek to raise issues that could have been raised in an earlier application.[45]

Pursuant to s. 207(2) of the R.T.A. (formerly s. 193(2) of the T.P.A.), a person entitled to apply under the R.T.A. but whose claim exceeds the Board's monetary jurisdiction may commence a proceeding in any court of competent jurisdiction.

Where a large number of persons, each of whom has a potential claim under the R.T.A. that exceeds the maximum amount that may be granted by the Board, and where those persons wish to pursue their respective claims, they can now apparently band together and commence a class action under the *Class Proceedings Act, 1992*, S.O. 1992, c. 6.[46]

Note that the Board will not make an order for the payment of an amount of money if the amount is less than five dollars (s. 207(4) of the R.T.A. and s. 58 of O. Reg. 516/06).

(d) Constitutional Questions

Constitutional issues are rarely raised in the context of hearings before the Landlord and Tenant Board. The Board's jurisdiction to deal with such issues is also poorly understood.

The Supreme Court of Canada has confirmed that where an empowering statute clearly confers upon a tribunal explicit jurisdiction to decide questions of law arising under provisions of that statute, there is a presumption that the tribunal's jurisdiction includes the authority to consider the constitutional validity of the challenged provisions.[47] Since the Landlord and Tenant Board explicitly has the authority to "hear and determine all questions of law and fact with respect to all matters within its jurisdiction",[48] it appears that the Board does have the power and the responsibility to deal with any constitutional issues that arise in applications brought before it. Constitutional questions may involve challenges to the constitutionality of specific provisions of the R.T.A. or regulations made thereunder (including, but not limited to, challenges raised under the *Canadian Charter of Rights and Freedoms*) or

---

[45] Based on the doctrine of abuse of process by re-litigation, discussed later in this Chapter.

[46] *Politzer v. 170498 Canada Inc.* (2005), 2005 CarswellOnt 7035 (Ont. S.C.J.). Note, however, that Cullity J. defined the class based in part on the assumption that the Tribunal has the power to award punitive damages (see paras. 31 to 33) and was apparently unaware of the Divisional Court's decision to the contrary in *Campbell v. Maytown Inc.* (2005), 2005 CarswellOnt 8300 (Ont. Div. Ct.).

[47] *Martin v. Nova Scotia (Workers' Compensation Board)*, [2003] 2 S.C.R. 504, 4 Admin. L.R. (4th) 1, 231 D.L.R. (4th) 385, 2003 CarswellNS 360 (S.C.C.).

[48] Section 174 of the R.T.A. (formerly s. 162 of the T.P.A.).

issues with respect to the types of tenancies that are properly within the powers of the Province to regulate.[49]

Where a party wishes to raise a constitutional question, the party must comply with the provisions of s. 109 of the *Courts of Justice Act*, R.S.O. 1990, c. C.43.[50] This typically involves serving notice (in a prescribed form) upon the Attorney General of Canada and the Attorney General of Ontario at least 15 days prior to the day on which the question is to be argued. The Attorneys General then have the option of participating in the proceedings.

(e) Human Rights

Subsection 3(4) of the R.T.A. (formerly s. 2(4) of the T.P.A.) provides that, "If a provision of this Act conflicts with a provision of another Act, other than the *Human Rights Code*, the provision of this Act applies." It is clear that, in the field of residential tenancies, the *Residential Tenancies Act* takes priority over all other provincial statutes, except the *Human Rights Code*. Not only must Members be alert to possible contraventions of the Ontario *Human Rights Code*, they may also be expected to enforce some of the provisions of the *Human Rights Code*. As will be discussed in detail in Chapter 15, courts in Ontario have made it clear that tribunals have the jurisdiction and obligation to consider human rights issues that arise in the context of their hearings and cannot refuse to consider such issues on the assumption that all such matter sare more properly argued before the Human Rights Tribunal.

(f) In Possession

Most landlord applications can only be brought while the tenant remains "in possession" of the rental unit (see Chapter 3). If a landlord wishes to pursue a claim for arrears of rent or damages against a *former* tenant, the landlord must do so in court.

(g) Small Claims Court

During a tenancy, the Landlord and Tenant Board has exclusive jurisdiction over most[51] disputes that might arise between the landlord and tenant.

---

[49] Such as tenancies located on Crown land or "lands reserved for Indians" which may be exclusively within federal jurisdiction (this topic is discussed further in Chapter 4).

[50] Subsection 109(6) of the *Courts of Justice Act* specifically states that the provisions of s. 109 apply to proceedings before boards and tribunals as well as to court proceedings.

[51] The Board would generally not have jurisdiction over criminal matters, family law disputes or matters involving allegations of negligence or intentional torts resulting in serious personal injuries or damages that exceed its monetary jurisdiction.

Once the landlord and tenant relationship ends, however, landlords have no right to commence proceedings under the R.T.A. and tenants have only limited rights, for certain types of claims, to commence an application before the Board within one year. Thus, a former landlord or tenant, who wishes to commence proceedings after the tenancy is over, may have to do so in court rather than before the Landlord and Tenant Board. Since, effective January 1, 2010, the monetary jurisdiction of the Small Claims Court will be increased to $25,000, such disputes will likely be resolved in that court.

Pursuant to s. 4 of the *Limitations Act*, 2002, S.O. 2002, c. 24, Sched. B, in general, a proceeding must be commenced in respect of a claim within two years of the day on which the claim was discovered.[52] The Rules of the Small Claims Court are found in O. Reg. 258/98 under the *Courts of Justice Act*, R.S.O. 1990, C. 43. For more information on the Small Claims Court, including a link to its forms, rules and information pamphlets, visit the nearest court office or the attorney general's website at *www.ontariocourtforms.on.ca/english/scc*.

4. POWERS OF THE BOARD

Earlier in this chapter, I indicated that the Landlord and Tenant Board is a quasi-judicial tribunal, which means that it is similar to a court. It is not, however, identical to a court nor was that the intention when the Board (formerly known as the "Ontario Rental Housing Tribunal") was created. The Board handles a very large number of applications and its procedures are designed to be as simple and expeditious as possible. In general terms, this means: simplified forms, short time-frames, no formal discovery process, relatively informal hearings, simplified evidentiary rules and a more active and inquisitorial role played by adjudicators who have been granted broad discretionary powers. Pursuant to Rule 2.1 of the Board's Rules of Practice, Members may exercise any of their powers under the Rules or under the R.T.A. on their own initiative or at the request of a party. It is these powers that I will explore further in this section. Some of the topics discussed in this chapter will be analyzed in further detail in later chapters.

(a) Jurisdictional Powers

The Board has authority to hear and determine all questions of law and fact with respect to all matters within its jurisdiction under the R.T.A.[53] It is

[52] There are exceptions specified in the *Limitations Act* for minors, persons under a disability and for certain types of claims.

[53] Section 174 of the R.T.A. (formerly s. 162 of the T.P.A.).

the Board that decides the limits of its jurisdiction, subject only to an appeal or application for judicial review made to the higher courts.

(b) Procedural Powers

(i) General

The Board is required to adopt the most expeditious method of determining the questions arising in a proceeding that affords to all persons directly affected by the proceeding an adequate opportunity to know the issues and be heard on the matter.[54] Pursuant to Rule 2.2 of the Board's Rules of Practice, the Member may decide the procedure to be followed for an application and may make specific procedural directions or orders at any time and may impose such conditions as are appropriate and fair.

Although the Board's procedures are governed by the *Statutory Powers Procedure Act* and the Board's Rules of Practice, situations may arise for which there are no clearly defined procedures. The Member presiding over a hearing may have to "invent" a procedure.[55] As long as it affords all parties a fair opportunity to present their case, novel procedural rulings will likely be upheld by the appellate courts. For example, in ***Metropolitan Toronto Housing Authority v. Godwin***,[56] the Member was faced with the prospect of hearing evidence from 312 tenants in this multi-tenant application. In an interim order, she indicated her intention to hear "representative" evidence from 11 of the tenants rather than hearing from each and every tenant named as a party to the application. The landlord brought a judicial review application to challenge this procedural order and was successful; the Divisional Court quashed the Tribunal's order. That decision was then appealed to the Court of Appeal, which overturned the order of the Divisional Court and restored the decision of the Tribunal. The Court of Appeal noted that the purpose of the *Tenant Protection Act* is to encourage speedy, fair and efficient access to justice in residential tenancy matters, that the Act is tenant-centred and that a liberal approach should govern the interpretation of the T.P.A. It held that the Tribunal did have the jurisdiction to control its process and to make the challenged order.

Pursuant to Rule 1.5 of the Board's Rules of Practice, a Member may also waive or vary a Rule where appropriate. This rule is authorized by s. 4(2) of the *Statutory Powers Procedure Act*. A party is entitled to present reasons why any Rule should be waived in the particular circumstances of

---

[54] Section 183 of the R.T.A. (formery s. 171 of the T.P.A.) and Rule 1.1 of the Board's Rules of Practice.

[55] See Rule 1.3 of the Board's Rules of Practice.

[56] (2002), 2002 CarswellOnt 2051, 161 O.A.C. 57 (Ont. C.A.), overturning (2000), 2000 CarswellOnt 3223 (Ont. Div. Ct.) (re interim order TST-01206 issued March 10, 2000).

that case. In most cases, a Rule will not be waived by a Member without inviting and considering submissions from all parties. The following Rules, however, cannot be waived: the Rules concerning computation of time, the Rules protecting the confidentiality of mediations and the requirement that reasons be provided where a Member decides to depart from the interpretation suggested in an Interpretation Guideline (see Rules 4.5, 13.22, 26.6).

(ii) Adding and Removing Parties

The parties to an application are the landlord and any tenants or other persons directly affected by the application.[57] The Board has the power to add or remove parties as it considers appropriate.[58] A sub-tenant, for instance, ought to be included in any application brought by the landlord to terminate the head tenancy as the sub-tenant will clearly be affected by the outcome of that application. The failure to include the sub-tenant as a party to the proceeding may invalidate the proceedings.[59]

(iii) Joining and Severing Applications

Pursuant to s. 198 of the R.T.A. (formerly s. 185 of the T.P.A.), the Board may direct that two or more applications be joined or heard together if the Board believes it would be fair to determine the issues raised by them together. The Board may also order that applications that have been joined be severed or that applications that had been ordered to be heard together be heard separately.

In *Orchard v. Barrick*,[60] a Member decided to hear together three related tenant applications (involving different tenants from the same residential complex who had similar complaints). The landlord requested a review on the basis that proceeding in this manner prevented a fair and independent hearing of each case and the landlord questioned the authority of the Member to have proceeded in this manner. The request for review was denied. It was held that s. 185(1) of the T.P.A. specifically gave the Tribunal the power to hear applications together and that the landlord failed to demonstrate any unfairness in this case in having the three cases heard together.

Pursuant to s. 199 of the R.T.A. (formerly s. 185.1 of the T.P.A.), the Board may also sever one application into parts and deal with each part as though it were a separate application. This is especially useful where one tenant has combined several applications but a Member determines that each

---

[57] Subsection 187(1) of the R.T.A. (formerly subsection 174(1) of the T.P.A.).

[58] Subsection 187(2) of the R.T.A. (formerly subsection 174(2) of the T.P.A.).

[59] *Baker v. Hayward* (1977), 78 D.L.R. (3d) 762 (Ont. C.A.).

[60] (May 27, 1999), CET-00224-RV (Ont. Rental Housing Trib.).

application ought to be heard separately or where several tenants of different units join together to file one application against the same landlord but the Board determines that each tenant's application should continue as a separate proceeding.

(iv) Amending Applications

An application can be amended by the applicant at any time in a proceeding (on notice to the respondent). An amendment generally requires the consent of a Member of the Board.[61] Where, however, the parties resolve the application through mediation conducted by the Board and the parties agree to the requested amendment, the application will be considered amended and permission by a Board Member is not required.[62] The Board may also amend an application on its own initiative.[63]

The Member will consider the following factors when a request to amend an application is made:[64]

(a) whether the amendment was requested as soon as the need for it was known;
(b) any prejudice a party may experience as a result of the amendment;
(c) whether the amendment is significant enough to warrant any delay that may be caused by the amendment;
(d) whether the amendment is necessary and was requested in good faith; and
(e) any other relevant factors.

(v) Permitting Withdrawal of Applications

Prior to the commencement of the hearing, an applicant may withdraw an application without the consent of the Board.[65] The exception to this is a tenant's application alleging harassment; in such cases, the application cannot be withdrawn without the consent of the Board.[66] Once a hearing begins, an application may only be withdrawn with the consent of the Board.[67]

---

[61] Subsection 200(1) of the R.T.A. (formerly subsection 186(1) of the T.P.A.) and Rule 16.2 of the Board's Rules of Practice.

[62] Rule 16.5 of the Board's Rules of Practice.

[63] Paragraph 200(1)(f) of the R.T.A. (formerly para. 187(1)(f) of the T.P.A.).

[64] Rule 16.4 of the Board's Rules of Practice.

[65] Subsection 200(2) of the R.T.A. (formerly subsection 186(2) of the T.P.A.).

[66] Subsection 200(3) of the R.T.A. (formerly subsection186(3) of the T.P.A.). Presumably, the concern is that the landlord who has been threatening or harassing the tenant has coerced or intimidated the tenant into withdrawing the application. It is implicit that before granting such consent the Board will investigate the circumstances surrounding the tenant's request.

[67] Subsection 200(4) of the R.T.A. (formerly subsection 186(4) of the T.P.A.).

An oral or electronic hearing has begun when the parties first appear before a Member, even if the appearance is only to deal with a preliminary matter.[68] A written hearing has begun when the respondent's deadline to file responses has passed.[69]

There is a significant distinction between an application that is withdrawn and one that is dismissed. Where an application is withdrawn, it is open to the applicant to later file an identical application (assuming that no relevant limitation period has elapsed). Where an application is dismissed, subject to the discretion of the Board, the matter is considered closed and cannot be re-litigated at a later date (unless the order dismissing the previous application specifically states that the dismissal is being made "without prejudice").

(vi) Extending and Shortening Time

The Board may extend or shorten *most* time requirements with respect to any matter in its proceedings.[70] Rule 15 sets out the procedure to follow for a party seeking an order extending or abridging the usual time requirements. Pursuant to Rule 15.6, a Member shall consider the following factors in deciding whether to extend or shorten any time requirement under the Act or these Rules:

(a) the length of the delay, and the reason for it;
(b) any prejudice a party may experience;
(c) whether any potential prejudice may be remedied;
(d) whether the request is made in good faith; and
(e) any other relevant factors.

However, a Member does not have the power to extend or shorten a number of prescribed time requirements. These are set out in s. 56 of O. Reg. 516/06 (formerly s. 36 of O. Reg. 194/98). The more significant of these time periods that cannot be altered include: the minimum notice periods required for notices of termination; all deadlines for filing applications (except for above-guideline increase applications, applications concerning a landlord's refusal to consent to an assignment of a mobile home site or land lease site and applications to review a work order[71]); and the 24-hour (written) notice required when a landlord intends to enter a rental unit pursuant to s. 27(1) of the R.T.A. Before any time period set out in the R.T.A., the regulations or the Rules is extended or shortened by a Member, the complete list contained

---

[68] Rule 17.1 of the Board's Rules of Practice.

[69] Rule 17.2 of the Board's Rules of Practice.

[70] Subsection 190(2) of the R.T.A. (formerly subsection 176(2) of the T.P.A.).

[71] Subsection 190(1) of the R.T.A. (formerly subsection 176(1) of the T.P.A.).

in s. 56 of O. Reg. 516/06 should be consulted to ensure that the time period under consideration is one that a Member is permitted to alter.

(vii) Controlling the Proceedings

Pursuant to s. 25.1 of the *Statutory Powers Procedure Act*, a tribunal may make rules governing the practice and procedure before it. The Landlord and Tenant Board has done so.

Pursuant to s. 25.0.1 of the *Statutory Powers Procedure Act*, a tribunal also has the power to determine its own procedures and practices and may for that purpose make orders with respect to the procedures and practices that apply in any *particular* proceeding.

Inherent in the power of any quasi-judicial tribunal is the power to control its own process. The fair and efficient administration of justice is dependent upon this. The *Statutory Powers Procedure Act* and the Board's Rules have provided Members with some tools to assist in maintaining control over hearings.

Although hearings are generally open to the public,[72] the Board does have the power to hold a hearing in the absence of the public where matters that involve public security may be disclosed or intimate financial or personal matters may be disclosed that are of such a nature that the desirability of avoiding disclosure thereof in the interests of any person affected or in the public interest outweighs the desirability of adhering to the principle that hearings be open to the public.[73]

Subsection 9(2) of the *Statutory Powers Procedure Act* provides that a tribunal may make such orders or give such directions as it considers necessary for the maintenance of order at a hearing and, if any person disobeys or fails to comply with any such order or direction, the tribunal or member thereof may call for the assistance of any peace officer to enforce the order or direction and every peace officer so called upon shall take such action as is necessary to enforce the order or direction and may use such force as is reasonably required for that purpose.

Subsection 23(3) of the *Statutory Powers Procedure Act* permits a tribunal to exclude from a hearing anyone, other than a person licensed under the *Law Society Act* appearing on behalf of a party or as an advisor to a witness, if it finds that such person is not competent to properly represent or to advise the party or witness or does not understand and comply at the hearing with the duties and responsibilities of an advocate or adviser.[74]

---

72 Subsection 9(1) of the *Statutory Powers Procedure Act*.

73 Subsection 9(1) of the *Statutory Powers Procedure Act* and Rule 24 of the Board's Rules of Practice.

74 This section of the *Statutory Powers Procedure Act* used to allow a tribunal to exclude as a representative anyone who was not a barrister or solicitor. With the passage of the *Access to*

(viii) Disclosure

Under s. 5.4 of the *Statutory Powers Procedure Act*, a tribunal may, at any stage of its proceedings up to the end of the hearing, make orders for the exchange of documents, the exchange of reports of expert witnesses, the provision of particulars and any other form of disclosure. The tribunal must adopt rules of practice in order to use this authority. The tribunal cannot use these powers to require the production of privileged information. The power of a tribunal to order such disclosure was affirmed by the Court of Appeal in *Ontario (Human Rights Commission) v. Dofasco Inc.*[75]

Formal disclosure was rarely ordered in proceedings before the Rental Housing Tribunal as it was seen as a step that could result in unnecessary delay and add to the cost of the proceedings (see Rule 17 of the Tribunal's Rules).

Rule 19 of the Rules of the Landlord and Tenant Board grants Members of the Board the authority to order disclosure. The preamble to Rule 19 suggests a somewhat more flexible attitude on this issue. It reads as follows:

> Disclosure may be useful to facilitate a better hearing, especially if proper consideration is given to the type of proceedings, the knowledge of the parties about procedures, and the desire for an expeditious and fair procedure.

From this statement, it would seem to be a reasonable inference that orders for production may now become more common.

In *Cooke v. Mathur*,[76] the tenant refused to disclose her documents to the landlord (even at the hearing). The Member dismissed the application and ordered costs to the landlord. The Member also ordered that the tenant could file no further applications until those costs were paid. This decision was upheld on review and on appeal to the Divisional Court.[77]

For most types of cases that come before the Board, disclosure is not mandatory. As usual, there is an exception and it is in relation to a landlord's application to increase rents above the guideline. Pursuant to Rule 19.2, a landlord who applies for an above-guideline rent increase related to an extraordinary increase in operating costs or an increase in the operating costs related to security services must be prepared to disclose at the hearing the rent for each rental unit in the residential complex and the date that rent was established (for a new tenant) or was last increased (for an existing tenant).

Justice Act, 2006 and the governance of paralegals by the Law Society of Upper Canada, the power of tribunals to exclude a representative is now restricted to the exclusion of persons who are not licensed by the Law Society.

[75] (2001), 57 O.R. (3d) 693 (Ont. C.A.).

[76] (Nov. 22, 2000), EAT-02249 (Ont. Rental Housing Trib.).

[77] (2003), 2003 CarswellOnt 5868 (Ont. Div. Ct.), leave to appeal refused (2004), 2004 CarswellOnt 3042 (Ont. C.A.).

Other detailed disclosure requirements relating to above-guideline rent increase applications are contained in ss. 22 and 23 of O. Reg. 516/06. If a landlord fails to comply with these provisions, the Board can dismiss the application, refuse to consider the part of the expenditure for which supporting documentation was not properly disclosed or make such other order as the Board considers appropriate in the circumstances.

(ix) *Compelling and Admitting Evidence*

Pursuant to s. 12 of the *Statutory Powers Procedure Act* and Rule 23 of the Board's Rules of Practice, any Member may, by signing a summons, require a witness to attend a hearing and give sworn or unsworn testimony and to produce documents, records and things that are relevant and admissible. The party requesting that a summons be issued shall provide a written request stating the necessity and relevance of the summons.[78] While the requested summons will usually be issued, it is not automatic. Based upon the information provided in the request for summons, it is within the discretion of the Member considering the request to decide whether or not to sign the summons. This decision to issue or refuse to issue the summons may later be reviewed by the Member presiding at the hearing.[79] If a witness who has been properly served with a summons fails to appear before the Board, the party who seeks their attendance may apply to a judge of the superior court for a bench warrant for their arrest.[80] Furthermore, if a witness who has been properly served with a summons fails to appear before the Board, fails to remain in attendance, fails to produce required documents or fails to answer proper questions, the Board may bring a motion to the Divisional Court to have that person punished as if he or she had been guilty of contempt of that court.[81]

The Board may admit as evidence at a hearing, whether or not given or proven under oath or affirmation or admissible as evidence in a court,

(a) any oral testimony; and
(b) any document or other thing,

relevant to the subject-matter of the proceeding as long as it is not inadmissible

---

[78] Rules 23.2 and 23.3.

[79] Rule 23.4.

[80] Subsection 12(4) of the *Statutory Powers Procedure Act*.

[81] Section 13 of the *Statutory Powers Procedure Act*. Given the time and effort that would be involved in bringing such a motion, I would think that the Board would only use this power in the most exceptional circumstances.

by reason of any privilege[82] under the law of evidence or specifically declared inadmissible under the R.T.A.[83]

People who testify at hearings have the option of *swearing* that they shall tell the truth (while holding the religious text of their choice) or solemnly *affirming* that they shall tell the truth. Both are equally binding. In order to avoid offending the person about to testify (by asking questions about the person's religious beliefs), many adjudicators simply ask all witnesses to take an affirmation and will not ask a witness to swear an oath unless the witness specifically requests it. The power to administer oaths and affirmations comes from s. 22 of the *Statutory Powers Procedure Act*. The Board also has the option of hearing testimony without having the witness take an affirmation or oath. In my experience, people who are going to tell the truth will do so whether or not they are first made to promise to tell the truth and those who intend to lie are not likely to be deterred by the formality of an affirmation or oath. Nevertheless, the courts seem to place some weight on whether or not there was "sworn testimony" so it is probably best for Members to retain this formality. It is also very important for the Board to be consistent; having only some witnesses affirmed or sworn in but not others, even if by accident, could give the impression that the presiding adjudicator prejudged that some parties or witnesses were inherently more trustworthy than others or could raise concern that the adjudicator will give more weight to the "sworn" testimony than the "unsworn" testimony.

As a result of s. 15 of the *Statutory Powers Procedure Act*, the Board can accept as evidence virtually anything that is relevant, as long as it is not privileged. This provision is meant to avoid embroiling tribunals in complex and lengthy arguments over the admissibility of evidence. Lawyers, law students and people who watch too many courtroom dramas on television often come before the Board eager to make objections over the smallest of procedural and evidentiary issues. These objections not only unnecessarily lengthen the proceedings, they also, more often than not, have no valid basis in law. For instance, there is little point in objecting to hearsay evidence — such evidence is admissible in proceedings before the Board.[84] The only real issue is the weight that ought to be given to such evidence since it is second- or third-hand information, which may not be very reliable.[85] As long as

[82] Such as a privileged communication between a solicitor and his or her client.

[83] Subsections 15(1) and (2) of the *Statutory Powers Procedure Act*.

[84] Nevertheless, a Member *can* refuse to accept hearsay evidence if it is so unreliable that its prejudicial nature far outweighs its probative value. See *Cappuccitti v. Lawson* (Feb. 14, 2003), TEL-32960, 2003 CarswellOnt 1591 (Ont. Rental Housing Trib.).

[85] In *Doherty v. Minto Developments Inc.* (November 19, 2003), Doc. 02-DV-000820 (Ont. Div. Ct.) (re EAL-31684), for instance, the Divisional Court criticized the Tribunal for apparently failing to recognize that less weight should be given to hearsay evidence. From the Tribunal's order, it appears that as much weight was given by the Member to the testimony of a police officer who could only offer hearsay evidence (because he had arrived at the

evidence is relevant, it is likely to be admitted.[86] Therefore, instead of objecting to the admission of that evidence, a party is usually better off arguing that it be given little or no weight (if the evidence can be shown to be unreliable).[87]

(x) *Granting Adjournments*

Pursuant to s. 21 of the *Statutory Powers Procedure Act* and rule 12.3 of the Board's Rule of Practice, the Board has the power to adjourn a hearing on its own motion or, where it is shown to the satisfaction of the Board that the adjournment is required, to permit an adequate hearing to be held. For more information about rescheduling hearings, see the Board's Interpretation Guideline #1, Rule 12 and Chapter 16 of this text.

(xi) *Ordering and Permitting Payment Into the Board*

The Board may require a *respondent* to pay a specified sum into the Board within a specified time.[88] The Board cannot order money to be paid into the Board after it has issued its final order in an application.[89] The procedures for paying money into and out of the Board are set out in Rule 31 of the Board's Rules of Practice.[90] If the respondent fails to make the required payment, the Board may refuse to consider the evidence and submissions of the respondent.[91] Note that this provision only applies to respondents.

This provision provides Members with a useful tool for preventing an abuse of the Board's process. Where, for instance, a respondent requests an adjournment of the hearing but admits owing money to the applicant, it may be appropriate when granting the requested adjournment to order payment by the respondent into the Board of some of the money currently owing. If the respondent is the tenant, it may make sense to order payment into the Board of the rent that will fall due in the intervening period. This will ensure

---

complex after the incident was over and had not actually witnessed the incident himself) as was given to the testimony of witnesses who had actually observed the incident first-hand.

[86] In Landlord and Tenant Board File Number TEL-12667 (May 15, 2008), the case against a tenant alleging an illegal act (assault on another tenant) and serious impairment of safety was entirely based on hearsay evidence. The Member accepted this evidence and found it sufficient to grant the landlord's application to terminate the tenancy and evict the tenant.

[87] For example, a letter will usually be given less weight than a sworn affidavit and a sworn affidavit will usually be given less weight than a witness who testifies at the hearing because, unlike the witness, the affidavit cannot be subjected to cross-examination in order to test its accuracy.

[88] Paragraph 195(1)(a) of the R.T.A. (formerly subsection182(1) of the T.P.A.).

[89] Subsection 195(3) of the R.T.A.

[90] The creation of such procedures is authorized by subsection 195(2) of the R.T.A.

[91] Subsection 195(4) of the R.T.A. (formerly subsection 182(3) of the T.P.A.).

that the landlord is in no worse financial position when the matter returns and will permit the tenant to demonstrate some good faith. Making such an interim order is appropriate where the tenant indicates that he or she has the money available but has been withholding rental payments from the landlord until, for example, the landlord deals with a maintenance problem (sometimes referred to as a "rent strike"). The power to order a respondent to pay money into the Board must be used sparingly, however, because it is not meant to deprive people with limited financial means from having an opportunity to get a fair hearing of their case upon its merits.

A new provision under the R.T.A. enables the Board to permit a tenant who is making an application concerning alleged maintenance problems (i.e., where the tenant is the applicant) to pay all or part of the rent for the tenant's rental unit into the Board.[92] This provision also applies to maintenance applications commenced under the T.P.A. but that were not finally disposed of prior to the R.T.A. coming into effect (on January 31, 2007).[93] The tenant's request for permission can be in writing (if made before the hearing) or in person at the hearing.[94] The detailed procedures are set out in Rule 31 of the Board's Rules of Practice. Where the Board grants permission and the tenant pays the money into the Board, the tenant is given credit for such payments and will not be considered to be in default of payment of that rent.[95] The idea is that, at the end of the hearing, the Board can decide if some or all of the rent that has been paid in trust into the Board ought to be given back to the tenant as an abatement of rent or for damages (etc.) that the Board has found to be owing to the tenant by the landlord as a result of breaches by the landlord of the landlord's maintenance obligations. The Act does not indicate what consequence should follow a failure by the tenant to pay money into the Board after requesting permission to do so. After all, the Board is not ordering the applicant to pay his or her rent into the Board but is *permitting* the applicant to do so (albeit this permission comes in the form of an interim order[96]). At the very least, the tenant will be considered to be in arrears of rent if that money has not been paid to the landlord and, thus, the tenant risks termination of the tenancy (on an application commenced by the landlord).

---

[92] Paragraph 195(1)(b) of the R.T.A.

[93] Subsection 242(6) of the R.T.A.

[94] Rules 31.11 to 31.13 of the Board's Rules of Practice.

[95] Subsection 195(5) of the R.T.A.

[96] Rule 31.14 of the Board's Rules of Practice.

(xii) Interim Orders

Board Members have the express authority to make interim orders and may impose conditions therein.[97] An interim decision or order need not be accompanied by reasons.[98]

(xiii) Pre-hearing Conferences

Although rarely used, the Board has the power to conduct pre-hearing conferences.[99] The purpose of such a conference is to discuss the preparations for the hearing and the hearing itself, including attempts to define and narrow the issues in dispute, disclose potential evidence and witness lists, and discuss the possibility of settlement. Generally speaking, the Board will only direct a conference to be held where a lengthy hearing lasting one or more days is anticipated, and the hearing could be shortened or made more effective. A Member of the Board or an employee of the Board can conduct the pre-hearing conference but it can only be held at the direction of a Member and only a Member can issue an interim order (with respect to such things as production of documents). Thus, it is preferable for a pre-hearing conference to be conducted by a Member. If settlement discussions take place during the pre-hearing conference then, unless the parties agree otherwise, the Member who was involved in the pre-hearing discussion should not preside over the hearing of the application.[100]

(xiv) Stay of Proceedings

At one point in time, the Rental Housing Tribunal was having problems with parties and representatives who owed money to the Tribunal but who would continue filing new applications. They were able to ignore Tribunal cost orders and administrative fines with impunity and/or continue filing applications when the fee for earlier applications had not been paid in full. Consequently, s. 182.1 of the T.P.A. was enacted. This section has been carried forward into the R.T.A. as s. 196. It permits the Board to refuse to accept new applications, discontinue applications that have already been filed or refuse to issue an order (for an application that has been heard) until the fine, fee or costs have been paid. "Fine, fee or costs" does not include money that has been ordered to be paid into the Board pursuant to s. 195 of the

---

[97] Subsections 16.1(1) and (2) of the *Statutory Powers Procedure Act*.

[98] Subsection 16.1(3) of the *Statutory Powers Procedure Act*.

[99] Under s. 5.3 of the *Statutory Powers Procedure Act* and Rule 20 of the Board's Rules of Practice.

[100] Subsection 5.3(4) of the *Statutory Powers Procedure Act*.

R.T.A.[101] The actual procedure for dealing with these situations is contained in Rule 9 of the Board's Rules of Practice.

In Landlord and Tenant Board File No. TSL-20188 (Feb. 23, 2009), the landlord's application was discontinued by the Board (and the landlord was ordered to pay the tenant's costs) because the landlord had not yet paid an administrative fine imposed on the landlord in an earlier (interim) order of the Board in the same proceeding.

(xv) Pre-screening of Applications

The Board has added a new Rule (Rule 8) which permits its staff to reject certain types of defective applications. In other cases of apparent errors or deficiencies (for instance, in the Notice of Termination), staff will be able to point out the apparent problem to the applicant but will still permit the applicant to file the material if the applicant insists.

This is meant to save the parties and the Board from an unnecessary waste of time and money. If a flawed application is permitted to proceed to a hearing and is then dismissed, the applicant will not be better off than if the problem was pointed out and if the applicant was given an opportunity to fix the problem or start over again at an earlier stage in the process. The problem with staff rejecting applications is that no one other than a duly appointed Member of the Board has the jurisdiction to make determinations or orders.

The jurisdiction for staff to reject defective applications comes from two sources: subsection 185(1) of the R.T.A. and s. 4.5 of the *Statutory Powers Procedure Act*.

Subsection 185(1) of the R.T.A. provides that an application *shall* be filed in the form approved by the Board, *shall* be accompanied by the prescribed information and *shall* be signed by the applicant.

Pursuant to s. 4.5 of the *Statutory Powers Procedure Act*, if a tribunal adopts the necessary rules, a tribunal or its administrative staff may decide not to process the documents relating to the commencement of a proceeding if:

1. the documents are incomplete;
2. the documents are received after the time required for commencing the proceeding has elapsed;
3. the fee required for commencing the proceeding is not paid; or
4. there is some other technical defect in the commencement of the proceeding.

[101] Subsection 196(2) of the R.T.A.

In such circumstances, the tribunal or its administrative staff must give the applicant notice of its decision with its reasons and the requirements for resuming the processing of the documents.[102]

Thus, an application will be rejected by the Board's staff if it is not accompanied by the prescribed information (Rule 8.1), if the tenant is not in possession of the unit (for certain types of landlord applications — Rule 8.2), if the application is being filed earlier than permitted under the R.T.A. (Rules 8.3 and 8.4) or is being filed too late (Rule 8.5). Special rules apply to above-guideline increase applications (Rules 8.5.1 and 8.5.2)[103] and a hearing for this type of application will not be scheduled until all of the required material has been filed with the Board. Staff may also (pursuant to Rules 8.6 through 8.10) point out potential errors or omissions in the documents filed by the applicant but it will always be the applicant's decision whether or not to make any changes to the application or file it as is (Rule 8.11). Ultimately, the responsibility remains on the applicant, not the Board, to ensure that the application is complete, accurate and in compliance with the R.T.A. (Rule 8.12).

One final note of caution. While many situations will be unambiguous, there is the potential for a dispute to arise between an applicant and Board staff as to how to interpret provisions of the R.T.A. For instance, a landlord might want to argue that even though a tenant is no longer living in the rental unit, the tenant is still "in possession" of the unit. There may be a difference of opinion as to how to calculate time (especially where the last day of a limitation period falls on a weekend or holiday). Where such disputes arise, staff should probably allow the applicant to proceed if he or she insists so that a Member of the Board can hear the arguments and make a ruling. The refusal by administrative staff to permit a party to present a case to the Board may end up being challenged by way of judicial review.

(c) Investigative Powers

As mentioned earlier, the Board is not meant to be exactly like a court. Traditionally, courts employ an adversarial model in which it is believed that the truth can best be obtained by allowing the adverse parties to adduce evidence and make arguments, while the judge sits back and observes the proceedings. Judges have been discouraged from "entering the fray" (i.e., taking too active a part in the hearing), for fear of losing the appearance of impartiality.[104] Intervention by Board Members, however, is often necessary

---

[102] Subsection 4.5(2) of the *Statutory Powers Procedure Act*.

[103] Introduced on December 8, 2008.

[104] See *Ross v. Hern* (2004), 2004 CarswellOnt 1104, [2004] O.J. 1186 (Ont. C.A.) in which the Court of Appeal overturned the judgment of the Superior Court of Justice in a civil action because the sheer number of questions and interruptions by the trial judge and the

to expedite the proceedings and to fulfill the Board's mandate of public education. Appellate courts sometimes criticize Board Members for becoming too involved; for instance, in the questioning of witnesses. It appears to me, though, that some judges are missing the point. The question that ought to be asked is whether or not the parties received a fair hearing before an adjudicator who treated the parties in an even-handed manner; it should not be whether the Board Member conducted the hearing in exactly the way it would have been conducted in a court.

Hearings before the Board are meant to be somewhat inquisitorial (i.e., the Members are *expected* to ask questions of the parties and witnesses); this is a reflection of the fact that many parties who appear before the Board are relatively unsophisticated or inexperienced in legal proceedings and are often unrepresented and require guidance from the adjudicator as to what issues and evidence are relevant and admissible. As long as the Board Member does not go too far or make statements that create a reasonable apprehension of bias, adopting an inquisitorial model is not contrary to the principles of natural justice — it represents the exercise of powers specifically granted to the Member by the provisions of the *Residential Tenancies Act*. Many of these powers are found in s. 201 of the R.T.A. (formerly s. 187 of the T.P.A.), which reads as follows:

> 201. (1) The Board may, before, during or after a hearing,
>
> (a) conduct any inquiry it considers necessary or authorize an employee of the Board to do so;
>
> (b) request a provincial inspector or an employee of the Board to conduct any inspection it considers necessary;
>
> (c) question any person, by telephone or otherwise, concerning the dispute or authorize an employee of the Board to do so;
>
> (d) permit or direct a party to file additional evidence with the Board which the Board considers necessary to make its decision;
>
> (e) view premises that are the subject of the hearing; or
>
> (f) on its own motion and on notice to the parties, amend an application if the Board considers it appropriate to do so and if amending the application would not be unfair to any party.
>
> (2) In making its determination, the Board may consider any relevant information obtained by the Board in addition to the evidence given at the hearing, provided that it first informs the parties of the additional information and gives them an opportunity to explain or refute it.

---

types of questions he asked made the judge an "active participant in the case" instead of an impartial arbiter.

(3) If a party fails to comply with a direction under clause (1)(d), the Board may,

(a) refuse to consider the party's submissions and evidence respecting the matter regarding which there was a failure to comply; or

(b) if the party who has failed to comply is the applicant, dismiss all or part of the application.

(4) If the Board intends to view premises under clause (1)(e), the Board shall give the parties an opportunity to view the premises with the Board.

Unfortunately, these powers are not widely known or understood and present practical difficulties with actually trying to use them. For instance, the Board does not have staff readily available to conduct inquiries and then testify at a proceeding. The Ministry of Housing does have staff who are competent to inspect a residential unit or complex but such staff are usually reluctant to become involved where the municipality in which the complex is located has its own inspectors.

Although Members can question people by telephone, if it is done outside of the hearing room the parties will not be able to observe the conversation and there will be no official record of it. Also, although a Member is permitted to gather additional evidence, it is crucial that all parties be advised of the evidence being considered by the adjudicator so that they have a chance to test that evidence or at least make submissions with respect to that evidence. Not only is this required by the principles of natural justice, it is specifically required by the provisions of s. 201(2) of the R.T.A. In ***Marks v. Charlton***,[105] the Divisional Court held that it was a serious error for the Member to contact witnesses after the hearing had concluded without affording the party against whom the Member ruled an opportunity to be aware of and to challenge this evidence.

The power to require a party to file additional documentary evidence can be a very powerful one as it permits the Board to gather additional evidence without the necessity of adjourning and then reconvening the hearing. Furthermore, failing to comply with the Board's direction, can result in very significant consequences pursuant to s. 201(3): the Board may refuse to consider the party's submissions and evidence with respect to the matter regarding which there was a failure to comply, and if the party is the applicant, the application can be dismissed in whole or in part.

The power to inspect the premises is another extremely useful, but regrettably, seldom utilized tool. Board Members may be reluctant to use this power for a number of reasons including lack of time and the fear of putting

---

[105] Doc. 778/2000, (Ont. Div. Ct.), overturning TET-01379.

themselves at risk.[106] In my six years on the Rental Housing Tribunal, I only used this power once. The landlord alleged that the tenants had damaged the windows in such a way that they could not be repaired. The tenants denied damaging the windows and testified they were still functional. It was late in the day and difficult to tell who was telling the truth. I advised both parties I would meet them at the rental unit early the next morning to inspect the windows. My inspection revealed that the windows were still functional. The landlord's credibility had been destroyed and the landlord's application was dismissed.

Similarly, in *Peel Non-Profit Housing Corp. v. Pickles*,[107] the tenants brought a motion to set aside an eviction order on the basis that they did not have a reasonable opportunity to participate in the proceedings. The tenants challenged the accuracy of the landlord's certificate of service and alleged that it was impossible for documents to be slid under their door. The Member attended the unit to put this assertion to the test. The landlord was able to demonstrate for the Member that it was possible to slip the documents under the door. The tenants' testimony was found not to be credible and their motion was denied.

In Landlord and Tenant Board File No. TET-01535 (Jan. 13, 2009), an application was brought against a former landlord, alleging that the landlord had given the tenant a notice of termination in bad faith. In reliance upon a notice of termination from the landlord (that claimed the landlord required the rental unit for occupation by the landlord's son), the tenant vacated the rental unit. The tenant later received information that suggested that the landlord's son did not take possession of the unit and that the unit was listed for rent. The landlord denied this and stated that his son had moved into the unit and had been living there for months. The landlord also claimed that his son had gone to Japan for a couple of months but would be returning to the unit in a matter of days. The Member arranged to meet the landlord and tenant at the rental unit. The Member found that the unit was, for all intents and purposes, empty. Based upon all of the evidence, including his observations at the rental unit, the Member found in favour of the former tenant.

This power (to inspect the premises) was also used by the reviewing Member in Landlord and Tenant Board File No. TEL-05179-Remand / TEL-07243-Remand (Feb. 20, 2009). One of the central issues in this case is whether the tenant had caused undue damage to the common areas of the complex (especially to the carpeting in the hallway). Given the long and complex history of this dispute (having been sent by the Divisional Court back to the Board for a new hearing after a successful appeal by the tenant),

---

[106] Some disputes can be extremely volatile and may raise legitimate concerns with respect to safety and security.

[107] (June 24, 2002), CEL-24614-SA, [2002] O.R.H.T.D. No. 73 (Ont. Rental Housing Trib.).

the Vice-chair conducting the new hearing decided that it would be best if he personally inspected the condition of the complex.

(d) Fact-Finding Powers

More often than not, cases that appear before the Board turn upon their facts rather than upon any disagreement over the interpretation of the law. A Board Member's primary function is making findings of fact, especially since a party only has a right to appeal on questions of law (not fact).[108] Unless quashed by another Member through the Board's internal review process, a Member's findings of fact are, for all intents and purposes, final. It is therefore crucial that Board Members have broad powers to search for the truth and, in appropriate cases, look beyond outward appearances. This is the purpose behind s. 202 of the R.T.A. (formerly s. 188 of the T.P.A.), which reads as follows:

> 202. In making findings on an application, the Board shall ascertain the real substance of all transactions and activities relating to a residential complex or a rental unit and the good faith of the participants and in doing so,
>
> (a) may disregard the outward form of a transaction or the separate corporate existence of participants; and
>
> (b) may have regard to the pattern of activities relating to the residential complex or the rental unit.

There are few cases yet under s. 202 of the R.T.A. but since the wording has not changed, it is useful to consider decisions made under s. 188 of the T.P.A. The following cases provide examples where s. 188 of the T.P.A. played an important role in the decision reached by the Tribunal. Note that this provision does not grant Members any substantive powers and it does not permit Members to disregard other provisions of the Act.[109] It is merely meant to assist Members in making findings of fact.

In *Lee v. Hepburn*,[110] the landlord tried to create the appearance of operating a hotel so that the rental unit would be exempt from the T.P.A.[111] The Member relied upon s. 188 to look beyond this outward appearance and found that, based upon the real substance of the relationship between the parties, the rental unit was not a hotel room and was not exempt from the Act.

---

108 Section 210 of the R.T.A. (formerly s. 196 of the T.P.A.).

109 *Burton v. Leadway Apartments Ltd.* (2002), 2002 CarswellOnt 2771 (Ont. Div. Ct.).

110 (Feb. 7, 2000), TEL-09512, 2000 CarswellOnt 6340, (sub nom. *Lee v. Lee*) [2000] O.R.H.T.D. No. 25 (Ont. Rental Housing Trib.).

111 Pursuant to s. 3(a) of the T.P.A., discussed in more detail in Chapter 4.

Generally, the Tribunal's position was that a corporate landlord cannot apply to terminate a tenancy based upon the desire of the landlord (or a specified member of the landlord's family) to reside in the rental unit because a corporation cannot require a unit for "residential occupation" as that term is used in s. 51 of the T.P.A. (now s. 48 of the R.T.A.) and a corporation is incapable of having any of the relatives listed in that section of the Act.[112] In *DeMercado v. Brumm*,[113] however, the Member pierced the corporate veil and found that, although title to the property was held in the name of a corporation, in reality, the landlord was a natural person (not a corporation). Looking at the real substance of this case, the landlord was found to be an individual who required possession of the unit for residential occupation by his daughter. Consequently, the landlord's application was granted.

In *Tiago v. Tinimint Housing Non-Profit Inc.*,[114] it was alleged that the tenants misrepresented their income in a rent-geared-to-income situation and that, consequently, they owed substantial arrears of rent. The Tribunal permitted the landlord to produce evidence concerning the financial records of the tenants and their closely held corporations. Based upon this evidence, the Member ruled in favour of the landlord. The tenants appealed. The Divisional Court held that, under s. 188 of the T.P.A., the Tribunal had every right to consider the financial circumstances of the tenants' corporations as well as their personal financial records.

Another interesting case that turned upon a determination of the real substance of the matters in issue is found in *Tenants of 28 & 32 Corinth Gdns v. Forum Homes (Corinth) Inc*.[115] The properties known municipally as numbers 28 and 32 Corinth Gardens were two separate, adjacent triplexes. The corporate landlord purchased one of the properties; another related corporation bought the other. Each of the two corporate owners served upon each of the tenants of their respective buildings a notice of termination for demolition. Since each building had less than five units, no compensation was offered to the tenants.[116] The tenants moved out but then joined together to bring this application. After the tenants vacated the buildings, Forum Homes (Corinth) Inc. acquired title to the second of the two properties. Looking at the real substance of this matter (relying upon s. 188 of the T.P.A.), the Tribunal found that the management of both of these properties and the identities of the two corporate owners were so intermingled, that the two properties be-

---

112 See *Rodgers v. Thompson* (Oct. 1, 1998), EAL-01315-RV (Ont. Rental Housing Trib.).

113 (June 1, 2001), EAL-21140, [2001] O.R.H.T.D. No. 80, 2001 CarswellOnt 6060 (Ont. Rental Housing Trib.).

114 Doc. 02-BN-12223 and 02-BN-8911 (Ont. Div. Ct.) (CEL-28530 issued Dec. 20, 2002 and CEL-24823 issued Sept. 20, 2002).

115 (May 2, 2003), TNT-03257, 2003 CarswellOnt 2640 (Ont. Rental Housing Trib.).

116 Pursuant to s. 55 of the T.P.A.(now s. 52 of the R.T.A.), compensation in an amount equal to three months rent is only required if the residential complex contains at least five residential units.

came one *residential complex* containing six units. The landlord was therefore ordered to pay the tenants the compensation required by s. 55 of the T.P.A. (now s. 52 of the R.T.A.).

In *Twin Elms Estates Ltd. v. Parsons*,[117] the Landlord set up a scheme to take this trailer park out of the jurisdiction of the *Rent Control Act* and the T.P.A. The occupants became "shareholders" and thereby purportedly obtained the right to occupy the site. The Member who originally heard this case looked only at the outward appearances and found that the occupants of the units did not fall squarely within the definition of "tenant". On review, the Tribunal reversed this decision, finding that the "real substance of the relationship is clearly one of landlord and tenant". On appeal, the Divisional Court agreed with reviewing the Member's application of s. 188 of the T.P.A., stating that: "In our view, s. 188 is a direction to the Tribunal to ascertain the real substance of all transactions relating to the rental unit. It is a direction to find the true facts about the relationship, regardless of the form in which they may be clothed." The Court of Appeal refused to grant the Landlord leave to appeal the matter further.[118]

Finally, the Divisional Court has held that, s. 202 of the R.T.A. permits a Member of the Board to determine (on a case-by-case basis) whether a sole shareholder of a corporate landlord is also a "landlord" within the meaning of the Act, capable of delivering a notice of termination for "own use".[119]

(e) Substantive Powers

(i) Declaratory Relief

The Board has the power to make declarations under the law. For instance, pursuant to s. 9 of the R.T.A. (formerly s. 7 of the T.P.A.), the Board can declare whether or not the R.T.A. (or a specific provision of the R.T.A.) applies to a particular rental unit or residential complex. Furthermore, before the Board can grant relief to a tenant under either s. 30 or 31 of the R.T.A. (formerly ss. 34 and 35 of the T.P.A.), the Board must first make a determination[120] that the landlord, superintendent or agent of the landlord has breached specified provisions of the Act. Similarly, the Board must make a determination under subsection 35(2) of the Act (i.e., that the tenant altered the locking system on the door without the consent of the landlord) before it

---

[117] Doc. London 1125 (Ont. Div. Ct.) (re SWT-00300).

[118] Doc. M27519 (Ont. C.A.).

[119] *Edward Slapsys c/o 1406393 Ontario Inc. v. Abrams*, Court File No. 80/08, June 22, 2009 (unreported), upholding Landlord and Tenant Board review order TSL-01748-RV (Feb. 1, 2008). Note that the unsuccessful tenant in this case may be seeking leave to appeal the decision of the Divisional Court to the Court of Appeal.

[120] Under section 29, 57 or 98 of the R.T.A.

can grant relief under subsection 35(3). Another example of declaratory relief is found in s. 74 of the R.T.A. (formerly s. 72 of the T.P.A.). Pursuant to s. 74(4), an eviction order based upon arrears of rent becomes void if, before the date it can be filed with the sheriff, the tenant pays all amounts set out in the order. Where a tenant believes that the correct amount has been paid, the tenant can file an affidavit with the Board and request that an order be issued declaring the eviction order void. The tenant can then file the "voiding" order with the sheriff in order to stop the enforcement of the eviction order.[121] Other examples of declaratory relief include declarations by the Board as to the legal rent for a particular unit and the amount by which the rent for a unit or units can be increased or decreased.

(ii) Monetary Compensation

The Board routinely orders one party to pay monetary compensation[122] to another based upon a number of different grounds, including (but not limited to) the following:

1. Ordering an abatement of rent to a tenant where the landlord has breached the landlord's obligations;[123]
2. Ordering a landlord to pay compensation to a tenant for the cost the tenant incurred or will incur to repair or replace property that was damaged or destroyed as a result of the landlord's misconduct;[124]
3. Ordering a landlord to pay compensation to a tenant for reasonable out-of-pocket expenses the tenant incurred or will incur as a result of the landlord's breach(es) of the Act;[125]
4. Ordering payment to the tenant of all or any portion of any increased rent which the tenant has incurred or will incur for a one-year period after the tenant has left the rental unit (if the tenant was induced to vacate the rental unit as a result of the landlord's misconduct);[126]
5. Ordering payment to the tenant of reasonable out of pocket moving, storage and other like expenses which the tenant has incurred or will incur (if the tenant was induced to vacate the rental unit as a result of the landlord's misconduct);[127]
6. Ordering payment to the landlord of the reasonable out of pocket

---

[121] This process will be discussed in more detail in Chapter 14.
[122] Up to the monetary limit described earlier in this Chapter.
[123] Paragraphs 30(1)2, 31(1)c and 57(3)2 of the R.T.A.
[124] Clauses 30(1)5.i. and 31(1)(b)(i) of the R.T.A.
[125] Clauses 30(1)5.ii. and 31(1)(b)(ii) of the R.T.A.
[126] Paragraph 31(2)(a) and clause 57(3)1.i. of the R.T.A.
[127] Paragraph 31(2)(b) and clause 57(3)1.ii. of the R.T.A.

expenses necessary to change the locking system (where the tenant changed the system without the consent of the landlord);[128]

7. Ordering payment to the landlord of arrears of rent, compensation for use and occupation of the rental unit and NSF cheque charges;[129]
8. Ordering payment to the landlord of compensation for damage to the unit or the complex;[130]
9. Ordering the difference between what a tenant did pay and what they should have paid in rent-geared-to-income housing (where the tenant has misrepresented his or her income);[131]
10. Ordering the repayment of any amount illegally collected or retained by the landlord;[132] and
11. Ordering payment of any amount owing as a result of an order increasing rents above the guideline.[133]

Pursuant to paras. 30(1)9, 31(1)(f) and 57(3)4 of the R.T.A., in addition to any other relief the Board may award, the Board may make "any other order that it considers appropriate". The limits of these provisions are not entirely clear and some Members have used these paragraphs to award to successful tenants some of the remedies that the courts awarded under Part IV of the *Landlord and Tenant Act*. Given the comments of the Divisional Court and the Court of Appeal about the remedial nature of the *Act* and its precursors and the broad and liberal interpretation that should be given to its provisions, it may well be open to Members to interpret these provisions in a more expansive fashion. This is discussed further in Chapters 11 and 12.

(iii) Administrative Fines

Where a landlord has breached certain provisions of the R.T.A.,[134] in addition to any other order the Board may make, the Board may order that the landlord pay to the Board an administrative fine (of up to $10,000, given the Board's current monetary jurisdiction).[135] An administrative fine should

---

[128] Subsection 35(3) of the R.T.A.

[129] Section 87 of the R.T.A.

[130] Section 89 of the R.T.A.

[131] Section 90 of the R.T.A.

[132] Section 135 of the R.T.A.

[133] Section 126 of the R.T.A. Subsections 205(2), (3) and (4) of the R.T.A. also permit the amounts ordered to be paid in installments over a period of up to one year in such circumstances.

[134] Paragraphs 2 to 6 of subsection 29(1), subsections 41(2) and (3), subsection 57(1) and s. 114 of the R.T.A. (see Interpretation Guideline 16 for further details).

[135] Clauses 31(1)(d) and 57(3)3 of the R.T.A. Effective January 2010, this may increase to $25,000.

not be confused with costs (see Interpretation Guideline 16). According to the Board's Interpretation Guideline 6:

> An administrative fine is a remedy to be used by the Board to encourage compliance with the RTA and to deter landlords, superintendents and agents from engaging in similar actions in the future. This remedy is appropriate in serious cases where the landlord has shown a blatant disregard for the RTA and other remedies will not provide adequate deterrence and compliance.

According to the Board's Interpretation Guideline 16:

> An administrative fine should not be confused with costs. Administrative fines are payable to the Minister of Finance and not to a party. Costs may be ordered where a party's conduct in the proceeding before the Board was unreasonable and may be ordered payable to a party or to the Board. See Guideline 3, Costs, for details.

A Member may impose a conditional fine in an interim order to encourage compliance with the R.T.A. For example, a Member may order a fine for each day that the landlord fails to comply with a term or condition in the interim order. The interim order should state precisely what the landlord is required to do and the consequences of failing to comply. The total amount of the fine, if any, should be set out in the final order.

In setting the amount of the fine, the Member may consider: (1) the nature and severity of the breach; (2) the effect of the breach on the tenant; and (3) any other relevant factors.[136] The amount of the fine should be commensurate with the breach. Prior to 2007, Interpretation Guideline 16 suggested the following amounts:

(a) $250 to $1,500 for a first fine;
(b) $1,000 to $3,000 for a second fine; and
(c) up to the maximum amount for any subsequent fine.

These recommendations have now been removed from Interpretation Guideline 16, suggesting that the appropriate amount of the fine is entirely within the discretion of the presiding Member. Therefore, if the conduct of the landlord is particularly egregious, a large fine may be appropriate even if this landlord has never before been ordered to pay an administrative fine.

Examples of situations where the Rental Housing Tribunal imposed administrative fines include cases where:

[136] See Interpretation Guideline 16.

- the landlord threatened to report to the police allegedly criminal conduct of the tenant if the tenant did not agree to vacate the unit;[137]
- the landlord, having lost an application to terminate the tenancy, proceeded to cut off the gas and electricity to this unit and threatened to lock out the tenant, who was nine months pregnant at the time;[138]
- the landlord engaged in conduct designed to harass the tenant into vacating the unit (which the tenant did do);[139]
- the landlord verbally abused the tenants, repeatedly making racist comments to them and, ultimately, coerced the tenants into moving out;[140]
- the landlord attempted to threaten and intimidate the tenant into moving out;[141]
- the landlord refused to drill a new well for the tenants when the old one went dry on the basis that it would cost too much and the tenants had no running water in their unit for several months;[142]
- the landlord illegally entered the rental unit, changed the locks and seized, damaged or disposed of the tenant's personal property;[143]
- the landlord threatened the tenant, illegally entered the rental unit, took the tenant's dog and then assaulted the tenant;[144] and
- the landlord gave the tenant a notice of termination in bad faith.[145]

(iv) Termination of the Tenancy

One of the most important powers of the Board is the ability to terminate a tenancy. Pursuant to s. 37 of the R.T.A. (formerly s. 39 of the T.P.A.), a tenancy may be terminated only in accordance with the Act. If a landlord and

---

[137] *Osibayo v. James* (Sept. 12, 2001), EAT-02975, [2002] O.R.H.T.D. No. 84 (Ont. Rental Housing Trib.).

[138] *McClement v. Kisiel* (March 3, 1999), SWT-00388 (Ont. Rental Housing Trib.).

[139] *Gervais v. Yoon* (July 2, 1999), SOT-00442 (Ont. Rental Housing Trib.).

[140] *Wu v. Singh* (Oct. 14, 1998), SOT-00109 (Ont. Rental Housing Trib.).

[141] *Dean v. Fitchett* (May 20, 1999), TET-00233 (Ont. Rental Housing Trib.).

[142] *Loughlean v. Perri* (Dec. 18, 1998), SWT-00236 (Ont. Rental Housing Trib.).

[143] *Keller v. Blair* (Aug. 20, 1999), EAT-00776 (Ont. Rental Housing Trib.); *Ellison v. Thornton* (Aug. 4, 2006), TST-08160, 2006 CarswellOnt 9171, [2006] O.R.H.T.D. No. 111 (Ont. Rental Housing Trib.); *436235 Ontario Ltd. and Volpi v. Mountfort* (Sept. 20, 2002), Div. Ct. File Nos. 405/00 and 499/00, re Ontario Rental Housing Tribunal File Nos. TST-02063, TST-02095 (Ont. Div. Ct.); *Leitao v. Ruffolo* (March 13, 2001), CET-00244-RV, 2001 CarswellOnt 6340 (Ont. Rental Housing Trib.); *Essex v. Lee* (June 2, 1999), TNT-00486, 1999 CarswellOnt 5804 (Ont. Rental Housing Trib.); *Idrissou v. Hoseine* (Oct. 13, 1998), TST-00190, 1998 CarswellOnt 6413 (Ont. Rental Housing Trib.); and Landlord and Tenant Board File No. SOT-00269-AM (issued July 24, 2007 and amended Sept. 18, 2007).

[144] *Seguin v. Fontaine* (July 27, 2006), SWT-07419, [2006] O.R.H.T.D. No. 84 (Ont. Rental Housing Trib.).

[145] *Duguag v. Venittelli* (Feb. 2, 2006), SOT-05261 (Ont. Rental Housing Trib.).

tenant cannot agree to terminate the tenancy, an application will have to be made to the Board.[146]

Typically, an application will be filed by a landlord under s. 69 for an order terminating a tenancy. This can be due to misconduct on the part of the tenant, another occupant of the rental unit or a guest of the tenant. Such "fault" grounds for termination include: persistent late payment of rent;[147] non-payment of rent;[148] commission of an illegal act within the residential complex;[149] misrepresentation of income in rent-geared-to-income housing;[150] serious impairment of the safety of other persons in the complex;[151] causing undue damage to the unit or the complex;[152] substantially interfering with the reasonable enjoyment of other tenants or the lawful rights of the landlord;[153] and, having more people living in the unit than permitted by health, safety and housing standards.[154]

A landlord can also apply to terminate a tenancy even when the tenant has done nothing wrong. Such "no-fault" grounds for termination include situations where the landlord or a prescribed member of the landlord's family (or a person providing care services to one of them) wants to live in the rental unit;[155] the purchaser of the complex or a prescribed member of their family (or a person providing care services to one of them) wants to live in the rental unit;[156] the landlord plans to demolish or renovate the unit to the extent that it must be vacant during the work or plans to convert the unit to a non-residential use;[157] the tenant no longer qualifies to continue living in public housing;[158] the tenancy was contingent upon the tenant's employment by the landlord and that employment has terminated;[159] and, the tenancy arose by virtue of or collateral to an agreement of purchase and sale of a proposed condominium unit and the agreement of purchase and sale has been terminated.[160]

Occasionally, a tenant will seek an order terminating a tenancy. In addition to the other relief a tenant might seek, a tenant may request of the

---

[146] Even when the parties can agree, the parties may wish to obtain an order just to be on the safe side (by bringing an application under s. 77 of the R.T.A., formerly s. 76 of the T.P.A.).

[147] Paragraph 58(1)1 of the R.T.A. (formerly para. 60(1)1 of the T.P.A.).

[148] Section 59 of the R.T.A. (formerly s. 61 of the T.P.A.).

[149] Subsection 61(1) of the R.T.A. (formerly subsection 62(1) of the T.P.A.).

[150] Subsection 60(1) of the R.T.A. (formerly subsection 62(2) of the T.P.A.).

[151] Section 66 of the R.T.A. (formerly s. 65 of the T.P.A.).

[152] Sections 62 and 63 of the R.T.A. (formerly s. 63 of the T.P.A.).

[153] Sections 64 and 65 of the R.T.A. (formerly s. 64 of the T.P.A.).

[154] Section 67 of the R.T.A. (formerly s. 66 of the T.P.A.).

[155] Section 48 of the R.T.A. (formerly s. 51 of the T.P.A.).

[156] Section 49 of the R.T.A. (formerly s. 52 of the T.P.A.).

[157] Section 50 of the R.T.A. (formerly s. 53 of the T.P.A.).

[158] Paragraph 58(1)2 of the R.T.A. (formerly para. 60(1)2 of the T.P.A.).

[159] Paragraph 58(1)3 of the R.T.A. (formerly para. 60(1)3 of the T.P.A.).

[160] Paragraph 58(1)4 of the R.T.A. (formerly para. 60(1)4 of the T.P.A.).

Board that he or she be released from the tenancy agreement where the landlord has unlawfully withheld consent to an assignment or sublet,[161] has failed to properly repair and maintain the unit or the complex,[162] or has done one or more of the activities set out in paras. 2 to 6 of subsection 29(1) of the R.T.A.[163]

For more information about termination of tenancies, please refer to Chapter 6.

(v) Eviction

Sometimes people use the terms "eviction" and "termination" interchangeably. This is incorrect. Termination of a tenancy signifies the lawful ending of a contract (the tenancy agreement) — by notice, by death,[164] by agreement or by order of the Board. The term "eviction" refers to the act of physically removing a person from the rental unit. Where the Board has granted an order to a landlord terminating a tenancy, the order will also *usually* contain provisions for the eviction of the tenant. At the appropriate time, the landlord will have to file the order with the Court Enforcement Office (sheriff) and make arrangements to have the eviction order enforced.

It is possible, however, to obtain an order terminating a tenancy without an order for an eviction.

Where the landlord believes that a tenant has abandoned a rental unit, the landlord may apply to the Board under s. 79 of the R.T.A. (formerly s. 78 of the T.P.A.) for an order terminating the tenancy; no eviction will be ordered because the termination is being granted on the basis that no one is occupying the unit (therefore, there is no one to evict).

Under the T.P.A., where a tenant applied for and obtained an order terminating the tenancy, no eviction was ordered because the termination was being granted at the request of the tenant and the Tribunal assumed the tenant would vacate the rental unit. If the tenant changed his or her mind and remained in the unit, the landlord had no recourse. This has now been rectified by the addition into the R.T.A. of s. 32, which provides that the Board may now also order the tenant's eviction on a tenant's application (but, again, only where it is the tenant who is requesting that the tenancy be terminated). If the tenant does not vacate by the date specified in the order, the landlord may have the eviction order enforced by the sheriff.

Under the T.P.A., where a landlord applied for an order to remove an unauthorized occupant from a rental unit (pursuant to s. 81 of the T.P.A.), the Tribunal could order the eviction of the unauthorized occupant but could

---

[161] Paragraph 98(3)3 of the R.T.A. (formerly para. 33(1)3 of the T.P.A.).

[162] Paragraph 30(1)1 of the R.T.A. (formerly para. 34(1)1 of the T.P.A.).

[163] Paragraph 31(1)(e) of the R.T.A. (formerly para. 35(1)(d) of the T.P.A.).

[164] Section 91 of the R.T.A. (formerly s. 49 of the T.P.A.).

not terminate the tenancy of the original tenant who had transferred possession of the rental unit without the consent of the landlord.[165] Under s. 100 of the R.T.A., this has been changed so that the Landlord and Tenant Board now has the power to both evict the unauthorized occupant *and* terminate the tenancy of the tenant who transferred possession of the unit to the unauthorized occupant.

Thus, under the R.T.A., while most orders that terminate a tenancy will also contain specific provisions for the eviction of the tenant and any other occupants of the rental unit, the concepts of "termination of the tenancy" and "eviction" remain distinct.

(vi) *Injunctive Relief*

Injunctions tend to be of two varieties: mandatory orders ("You shall do . . .") and prohibitive orders ("You shall not do . . ."). Although the Board has no general power to grant injunctive relief, it does have the statutory power, in specific cases, to make orders that have the character of either mandatory or prohibitive injunctions.

One example is found in para. 31(1)(a) of the R.T.A. (formerly para. 35(1)(a) of the T.P.A.) which grants the Board the power (where it has determined that the landlord, superintendent or agent has engaged in wrongful conduct) to order that the landlord, superintendent or agent "not engage in any further activities listed in [paragraphs 2 to 6 of subsection 29(1)] against any of the tenants in the residential complex."

Another example is found in subsection 31(3) of the R.T.A. (formerly s. 35(3) of the T.P.A.). In the situation of an illegal "lockout", in addition to any other relief that may be ordered, the Board can order that the landlord "allow the tenant to recover possession of the rental unit and that the landlord refrain from renting the unit to anyone else".

Yet another example I shall offer is found in subsection 35(3) of the R.T.A. (formerly s. 37 of the T.P.A.). If the Board finds that the tenant has altered the locking system to the door to the unit (or complex), the Board may order that the tenant provide the landlord with keys to the new lock.[166]

Finally, a new power given to the Board under the R.T.A. is the power to issue an order prohibiting rent increases (OPRI) where the landlord is found to be in serious breach of the landlord's maintenance obligations.[167]

---

[165] In *Jasper Homes v. Brennan* (2004), 2004 CarswellOnt 947 (Ont. Div. Ct.) (re TSL-44487), the Divisional Court confirmed that the Tribunal did not have jurisdiction to terminate the tenancy on an application to evict an unauthorized occupant pursuant to s. 81 of the T.P.A. This interpretation is supported by comments made by the Court of Appeal in *Samuel Property Management Ltd. v. Nicholson* (2002), 2002 CarswellOnt 3004 (Ont. C.A.).

[166] Or pay the landlord the reasonable out of pocket expenses necessary to change the locking system.

[167] Paragraphs 6, 7 and 8 of subsection 30(1) of the R.T.A.

(vii) Equitable Remedies

The Board is not a court and therefore does not inherently possess any power to grant relief in equity. This does not mean that the Board cannot try to affect just results — only that it must do so by using the powers specifically granted to it by statute.

(viii) Costs

The statutory authority for the Board to order costs is found in subsections 204 (2), (3) and (4) of the R.T.A., which read as follows:

> (2) The Board may order a party to an application to pay the costs of another party.
> (3) The Board may order that its costs of a proceeding be paid by a party or a paid agent or counsel to a party.
> (4) The amount of an order for costs shall be determined in accordance with the Rules.[168]

The Board's Rules and Interpretation Guidelines set out the usual approach of the Board to ordering costs against a party or representative of a party.

In general, a successful applicant will be granted an order for recovery of the application filing fee they have paid.[169] In addition, the Board may award a party's representation fees of up to $75 per hour for the services of a lawyer or paid agent (in the preparation and presentation of a case).[170] As with (almost) any Rule, a Member can waive the usual Rule and impose such terms as he or she deems just (i.e., a Member could, in the appropriate circumstances, award to a party costs for legal representation at a rate higher than $75 per hour).[171] Interpretation Guideline 3 suggests that costs over and above the application fee will generally only be ordered against a party who has been responsible for unreasonable conduct and also suggests situations in which a party is not entitled to costs even if there has been unreasonable conduct by another party.

The Board may also order a party (or their representative) to pay the *Board's* costs; this relatively rare remedy may be used by the Board where

---

[168] Rule 27 of the Board's Rules of Practice.

[169] Rule 27.1 of the Board's Rules of Practice.

[170] Rules 27.2 and 27.3 of the Board's Rules of Practice.

[171] See *Cardillicchio v. Urmodia* (Oct. 16, 2002), TNL-39579-RV and TNT-03017, 2002 CarswellOnt 3813 (Ont. Rental Housing Trib.). Also see *Quam Agencies Ltd. v. Poulter*, (April 19, 1999), EAL-03347 (Ont. Rental Housing Trib.), in which costs of $1,900.00 were awarded to the successful party.

the unreasonable conduct of a party or their representative has squandered valuable Board resources. An example of where such an order might be appropriate would be where an applicant requests a "special" hearing in which a room and adjudicator have been reserved specifically for this case and then the applicant chooses on the day set for the hearing to abandon the application without any prior warning to the opposing party or the Board. It will be too late to schedule any other hearings and the room will sit empty. In such circumstances, a Member might consider ordering Board costs against the applicant. Other situations where Board costs may be ordered include cases in which: (1) a party knowingly misled the Board; (2) a party was reckless or indifferent about the truthfulness of their evidence; (3) a party failed to comply with directions from the Member about the orderly conduct of the hearing; and (4) a party attempted to harass the opposing party in order to prevent that person from commencing or continuing with the proceeding or from defending the proceeding (see Interpretation Guideline 3).

Pursuant to Rule 27.4, expenses of the Board, which a party or representative may be ordered to pay shall not exceed $75 per hour for the hearing or $500 in total in respect of the proceedings as a whole. Again, a Member could choose to exercise his or her power under Rule 1.5 to waive these usual limits and order a larger amount.

In *Luskey v. Thomas*,[172] for instance, the applicant's conduct during the hearing was rude and contemptuous towards the Member. At the conclusion of the hearing, the application was dismissed and the applicant was ordered to pay $500 to the Tribunal.[173]

Costs, other than the application fee, are considered to be discretionary. As long as the Member exercises that discretion in a reasonable fashion, their decision is unlikely to be overturned upon review or appeal.

(ix) Other Terms and Conditions

Subsection 204(1) of the R.T.A. (formerly subsection 190(1) of the T.P.A.) states that, "The Board may include in an order whatever conditions it considers fair in the circumstances." This grants Members of the Board considerable freedom to add to their orders conditions that will ensure a just result. The only limit (other than that the conditions must not exceed the Member's jurisdiction or be contrary to public policy) is the imagination of the adjudicator. This is particularly useful in conjunction with ss. 83 and 78 of the Act; where appropriate, a Member can exercise their discretion under s. 83(1) by refusing to grant an eviction but issue an order that imposes upon

---

[172] (July 12, 2006), CET-05862, [2006] O.R.H.T.D. No. 91 (Ont. Rental Housing Trib.).

[173] Unfortunately, the Member referred to this as an "administrative fine" (which the Tribunal had no jurisdiction to award against a tenant on a tenant's application) rather than as Tribunal costs (which the Tribunal had every right to impose in the circumstances).

the tenant strict terms (such as a repayment schedule or requiring or prohibiting certain types of conduct[174]) and stating in the order that if those terms are breached then the landlord may apply to the Board, without further notice to the tenant, for an order terminating the tenancy pursuant to s. 78 of the R.T.A.[175]

The only *caveat* (or words of caution) concerning a Member's power in this regard is that the terms and conditions need to be clear, enforceable and within the jurisdiction of the Member. For more information, please refer to "Orders and Reasons" in Chapter 16.

(x) *Transferring a Tenancy*

Pursuant to s. 148 of the R.T.A. (formerly s. 99 of the T.P.A.), a landlord may apply to the Board for an order transferring a tenant out of a care home and evicting the tenant if,

(a) the tenant no longer requires the level of care provided by the landlord; or
(b) the tenant requires a level of care that the landlord is not able to provide.

The Board may only issue such an order, however, if:

1. the landlord has first participated in mediation provided by the Board; and
2. the Board is satisfied that appropriate alternate accommodations are available for the tenant and that the level of care that the landlord is able to provide when combined with the community based services provided to the tenant in the care home cannot meet the tenant's care needs.[176]

(xi) *Preventing Abuse of Process*

Pursuant to s. 197(1) of the R.T.A. (formerly s. 183(1) of the T.P.A.), the Board may dismiss an application without holding a hearing or refuse to allow an application to be filed if, in the opinion of the Board, the matter is frivolous or vexatious, has not been initiated in good faith or discloses no reasonable cause of action. This section has been used very rarely.

---

[174] See, for example, Landlord and Tenant Board File Nos. TSL-19140 / TSL-19176 (Jan. 26, 2009) and Landlord and Tenant Board File No. EAL-14114 (Jan. 23, 2009).

[175] The provisions of s. 78 can only be invoked where the terms that have been breached are of the same nature that gave rise to the original application. See Chapter 13.

[176] See Chapter 21 for more information about Care Homes.

In *Martin v. Lavallee*,[177] a tenant filed an application but failed to attend the hearing; the application was dismissed. The tenant then filed a second, identical application and again failed to attend the hearing; that application was also dismissed. The tenant then filed a third, identical application and failed to attend that hearing; that application was dismissed as being frivolous and vexatious. In *MacNeil v. Rourke*,[178] the Tribunal used its power to dismiss the tenant's applications as being frivolous and vexatious and an abuse of process and also ordered the tenant be prohibited from filing any further applications with respect to this tenancy.

Pursuant to s. 197(2) of the R.T.A. (formerly s. 183(2) of the T.P.A.), the Board may dismiss a proceeding without holding a hearing if the Board finds that the applicant filed documents that the applicant knew or ought to have known contained false or misleading information. Very few cases have been adjudicated under this subsection.

In *8 Godstone Road v. Tenants of 8 Godstone Road*,[179] the landlord applied to the Tribunal to increase rents above the guideline. Most of the expenditures had already been claimed (and allowed) in an earlier application. The landlord was alerted to the problem but did nothing until confronted at the hearing and then asked to withdraw the duplicated claims. The Member found that the application was misleading and abusive and dismissed the entire application without a hearing. This decision was upheld upon review. On appeal, however, the Divisional Court sent the matter back to the Tribunal for rehearing because the original Member based his decision on submissions[180] rather than upon evidence. The Divisional Court did not explain why it was necessary to hear testimony when s. 183(2) of the Act stated that the Tribunal may dismiss the application *without holding a hearing*. One can only infer that the Divisional Court's interpretation of s. 183(2) of th T.P.A. was as follows: first, the Tribunal/Board must hold a hearing in order to determine whether false or misleading documents have been filed by the applicant and whether the applicant knew or ought to have known they were false or misleading; second, if the Tribunal/Board is satisfied that this has been proven, the Tribunal/Board must then consider whether or not to dismiss the application without holding a hearing on the merits of that application.

Pursuant to s. 23(1) of the *Statutory Powers Procedure Act*, the Board may also make such orders or give such directions as it considers proper to

---

[177] (March 29, 1999), SWT-00417 (Ont. Rental Housing Trib.).

[178] (Nov. 1, 2000), EAT-02070 and EAT-02071, [2000] O.R.H.T.D. No. 147, 2000 CarswellOnt 4435 (Ont. Rental Housing Trib.).

[179] (February 4, 2004), Doc. 633/02 (Ont. Div. Ct.) (unreported), overturning (Sept. 27, 2002), TNL-34383, [2002] O.R.H.T.D. No. 103, 2002 CarswellOnt 3780 (Ont. Rental Housing Trib.).

[180] No testimony was required by the Tribunal since duplication of the claims was apparent from the face of the record and s. 183(2) of the T.P.A. authorized dismissal of the application, in such circumstances, *without* holding a hearing.

prevent abuse of its processes. Numerous court cases deal with the concept of "abuse of process" in the context of civil litigation — it is a rather fluid concept which can encompass any conduct on the part of a litigant that would tend to bring the administration of justice into disrepute or that would lead to the issuance of an order that would be contrary to public policy.

Some situations in which the Rental Housing Tribunal exercised its discretion to prevent an abuse of process include:

- preventing a landlord from enforcing an old eviction order where the landlord had subsequently entered into a new tenancy agreement with the tenant;[181]
- finding that an eviction order had been effectively voided (through payment of the arrears) even though the tenant's payment to the landlord was technically 18 cents less than the amount required by the terms of the eviction order;[182]
- refusing to evict the tenant (on an application under s. 77 of the T.P.A.) where the tenant's inability to fulfill the terms of a mediated agreement with the landlord resulted from the landlord's own conduct (the landlord refused to provide the tenant with evidence of the tenancy so the tenant was unable to obtain financial assistance);[183]
- dismissing an application brought by a tenant where the issue raised by the tenant was known to the tenant at the time that a similar earlier application that had been brought by the same tenant was settled with the landlord and which issue could have been included in that earlier application;[184]
- putting a tenant back into possession of the rental unit where the

[181] *Morguard Residential Inc. v. Belair* (July 25, 2003), CEL-31220-RV, 2003 CarswellOnt 4191 (Ont. Rental Housing Trib.).

[182] *41-51 Brookwell Drive Ltd. v. Daniel* (July 30, 2003), TNL-47186-SV, [2003] O.R.H.T.D. No. 106, 2003 CarswellOnt 4258 (Ont. Rental Housing Trib.).

[183] *Coronado Court Apartments v. Rosier* (July 11, 2003), TNL-47543-SA, 2003 CarswellOnt 4259 (Ont. Rental Housing Trib.).

[184] *Shiffman v. Bathurst Sheppard Apartments* (June 8, 2004), TNT-03769-RV, 2004 CarswellOnt 3627 (Ont. Rental Housing Trib.). This decision considers the concept known as abuse of process by relitigation and stands for the proposition that parties ought to bring forward in one proceeding all issues arising from the same cause of action and not hold back a part of the claim they know or ought to know exists at the time of the commencement of the application; failure to do so may preclude the party from later commencing a second application based upon the same type of application whether or not the specific issue was raised in the first application. A similar approach was taken in *Mandel v. Morguard Residential Inc.* (Nov. 6, 2003), TST-05662-RV, 2003 CarswellOnt 5675 (Ont. Rental Housing Trib.), where the Member dismissed the tenant's application because the issues raised could have been advanced in a previous application by the tenant.

eviction order was obtained or enforced in such a manner as to constitute an abuse of process;[185] and,

- refusing to grant an eviction based upon an agreement to terminate the tenancy where the tenant was "tricked" into signing the agreement in reliance upon misrepresentations made by the landlord's agent and as a result of the tenant's ignorance of the law.[186]

(xii) Granting Relief from Forfeiture

Some of the most important provisions in the R.T.A. are found in s. 83 of the Act (formerly s. 84 of the T.P.A.). These provisions permit the Board to grant "relief from forfeiture".

Subsection 83(3) outlines situations in which the Board must, for reasons of public policy, refuse to grant an eviction order even if the landlord has proven all elements normally required in order to obtain such an order. The Board must refuse to grant an eviction order where, for instance, the landlord is in serious breach of the landlord's obligations or is attempting to retaliate because the tenant has organized a tenants' association, has complained to a government official about the landlord or has otherwise attempted to enforce his or her rights as a tenant (by, for instance, filing an application against the landlord).

Subsection 83(1) grants a Member the discretion to refuse to grant an eviction or to delay an eviction where such relief is warranted. Under the T.P.A., the Divisional Court held that it was crucial for the Tribunal to consider granting such relief in every case where the facts may warrant it, even if the tenant did not specifically refer to the section or ask for such relief, and that an order should make it clear that the Member turned his or her mind

---

[185] *Metropolitan Toronto Housing Authority v. Ahmed* (2001), 2001 CarswellOnt 1347 (Ont. Div. Ct.), confirming (July 29, 1999), TNL-06552-SA (Ont. Rental Housing Trib.). This decision was followed in *Commvesco Levinson Viner Group v. Pershaw* (Oct. 11, 2001), EAL-23388-RV and EAT-03169, [2001] O.R.H.T.D. No. 134 (Ont. Rental Housing Trib.), in which the landlord was ordered to allow the tenant back into possession because the landlord should not have allowed the eviction order to be enforced by the sheriff when the landlord knew that the eviction order had been stayed (as a result of the tenant filing a motion to set aside the eviction order). Since these decisions, the T.P.A. was amended to specifically grant to the Tribunal the power to put tenants back into possession on an "illegal lockout". These cases demonstrate that the court will often support the Tribunal's efforts to find creative ways to fulfill the purpose of the *Tenant Protection Act* and to prevent abuses of the Tribunal's process. See also *Kwak v. Marinecorp Mgt. Inc.*, (2007) 2007 CarswellOnt 4335 (discussed in more detail in Chapter 14).

[186] *Hawkins v. Foster* (Sept. 16, 1998), CEL-00749 (Ont. Rental Housing Trib.). The Member does not explicitly state the grounds for dismissing this application but it could have been on the basis that it would have amounted to an abuse of process to have ordered otherwise or on the basis of the exercise of discretion under s. 84(1) of the T.P.A.

to this issue.[187] It is now mandated by statute that the Board must review the circumstances and consider whether or not it should exercise its powers under subsection 83(1) in every case where a landlord is seeking to evict a tenant.[188]

See Chapter 14 for a more thorough discussion of the Board's power to grant relief from forfeiture.

(xiii) Correcting Errors

Pursuant to s. 21.1 of the *Statutory Powers Procedure Act* and Rule 28 of the Board's Rules of Practice, even after an order has been issued, the Member who issued it may amend the order to correct a typographical error, error of calculation or similar error contained in the decision or order. Any request for such an amendment should be made within 30 days of the date the order is issued.

It should be noted that this power is meant to correct clerical or arithmetic errors made by the Board or a party. In the past, many Members refused to correct orders containing errors in the name of a party or the address of the rental unit where the error was made by the applicant and not by the Tribunal. In such circumstances, the applicant's only other alternative was to seek to have the original order reviewed on the basis that for the Tribunal to refuse to correct the order (even though it was not the Tribunal's fault) would result in a denial of natural justice. By amendments made on April 24, 2006 to Rule 26 (now Rule 28) and to Interpretation Guideline 15, the Tribunal attempted to address this problem by permitting Members to correct clerical errors that were made by a party and inadvertently carried through into the Tribunal's order (as well as clerical errors made by the Tribunal itself). These changes have been carried forward into the Board's Rules and Interpretation Guidelines.

When an order is amended to correct a clerical error, care should be taken by the Member to ensure that it is still possible for the respondent to comply with the order. Consider the following hypothetical example. On an application to terminate a tenancy based on arrears of rent, it is determined that the tenant owes $300 in rent. The Board issues an order on October 15, which mistakenly states that the tenant must pay $3,000 plus the landlord's costs by October 26 if the tenant wishes to void the order and avoid termination of the tenancy and eviction. The tenant is confused about what should be paid and requests that the order be amended to correct the apparent clerical error. On October 27, an amended order is issued but the only change to the order is that "$3,000" has now been changed to "$300". No other part of the order is changed. The deadline for paying the money ordered remains October 26

[187] *Luray Investments Ltd. v. Recine-Pynn* (1999), 1999 CarswellOnt 3055 (Ont. Div. Ct.) (re TNT-00213, TNT-00124, TNT-01992).

[188] Subsection 83(2) of the R.T.A.

and that date has already passed. There is no way for the tenant to comply with the order. This could be highly prejudicial to the tenant. In such circumstances, it is very important that Members consider amending not only the amounts in question but also the deadlines contained within the order.[189] For an actual example of just such a situation, please see *3414493 Canada Inc. v. Leyser*.[190]

(xiv) Power to Review Decisions

Pursuant to s. 209 of the R.T.A. (formerly s. 195 of the T.P.A.), except where the Act provides otherwise, an order of the Board is final, binding and not subject to review except under s. 21.2 of the *Statutory Powers Procedure Act*. This section permits a tribunal to create procedures for reviewing its own decisions. The Landlord and Tenant Board has created just such a review process and the details are set out in Rule 29 of the Board's Rules of Practice. In essence, a person who is affected by an order that finally disposes of an issue (as opposed to most interim orders) and who feels that it contains a serious legal or factual error, may (within 30 days) file a written request for a review of that order. If, upon reading the request for review, a Member finds that there may be some merit to the request, a review hearing will be scheduled. Any Member may review the decision of any other Member of the Board. The Board may also, on its own initiative, arrange for an order to be reviewed where it appears to the Chair or a Vice-chair that the order may contain a serious error. At the conclusion of a review hearing, the original order may be affirmed, quashed (in which case a new hearing will usually take place) or amended. A more thorough discussion of the review process is contained in Chapter 16.

(xv) Order Prohibiting a Rent Increase (OPRI)

In addition to the remedies previously available to tenants who brought applications concerning maintenance, under the R.T.A. another "weapon" has been added to the arsenal — an order prohibiting a rent increase (or "OPRI").[191] Where a landlord is found to be in serious breach of the landlord's maintenance obligations, in addition to other relief that may be granted, the Landlord and Tenant Board may:

(1) prohibit the landlord from charging a new tenant[192] under a new

---

[189] For further discussion of this issue, see Interpretation Guideline No. 15.

[190] (Nov. 18, 2003), TSL-56202-SA, [2003] O.R.H.T.D. No. 138, 2003 CarswellOnt 5709 (Ont. Rental Housing Trib.).

[191] Paragraphs 6, 7 and 8 of subsection 30(1) of the R.T.A.

[192] Other than tenants in rent-geared-to-income housing.

tenancy agreement more than the last lawful rent charged to the former tenant;
(2) prohibit the landlord from giving a notice of rent increase; or
(3) prohibit the landlord from taking a rent increase for which a notice has been given but which has not yet taken effect.

Once an OPRI is issued, it remains in effect until the landlord completes the ordered repairs; the Board is not required to issue an order "lifting" the OPRI.

5. PRINCIPLES OF NATURAL JUSTICE

(a) Introduction

Administrative tribunals have a duty to act fairly. In November 2000, the Government of Ontario, through the Management Board Secretariat and the Public Appointments Secretariat, published a Model Code of Conduct for Appointees to Regulatory & Adjudicative Agencies. This is what the Model Code (at p. 5) has to say about this duty of fairness:

> Fairness is a broad concept that eludes simple definition but is recognizable in the conduct of adjudicative proceedings and, specifically, in the actions of tribunal members. Fairness is a matter of how the proceedings as a whole are conducted; the concept of procedural fairness embodies the method by which we achieve substantive fairness. It embraces a complex set of elements, including matters of law and matters of attitude and demeanour.
>
> At a minimum, fairness refers to a person's right to hear the case against him or her, the right to respond and the right to an unbiased hearing. To act fairly, members must follow the law, including all relevant statute and common law, and the proceedings must be conducted in accordance with the principles of fundamental justice.
>
> The obligation to act fairly also requires that members conduct themselves in accordance with the principles and standards set out in this Code. For example, fairness requires that the process be transparent and accessible, and that the persons be accorded their rights without discrimination or favouritism. Fairness requires that members conduct proceedings in an effective, expert and timely fashion. Proceedings must be conducted efficiently — with minimal delays and cost to the parties and the tribunal — without sacrificing fairness and a just resolution.
>
> Beyond these requirements, the varied nature of administrative tribunals dictates that procedural fairness will vary from case to case and situation to situation.

As for the conduct of its Members, the Board has published on its website the following basic principles to which its Members are expected to adhere:

1. A Member will approach every hearing with an open mind with respect to every issue.
2. A Member will listen carefully to the submissions of the parties and their representatives.
3. A Member will at all times show respect for the parties and their representatives and witnesses, and for the hearing process itself, through his or her demeanour, timeliness, dress, and conduct.
4. A Member will demonstrate a high degree of sensitivity to issues of gender, ability, race, language, culture and religion which may affect the conduct of a hearing and assessment of credibility.
5. A Member will endeavour to conduct all hearings expeditiously, commencing at the appointed time and preventing unnecessary delay, while ensuring that all parties have a fair opportunity to present their evidence and argument.
6. A Member will conduct a hearing in a firm but courteous manner and should likewise require courteous behaviour from hearing participants. The Member will promote mutual respect among hearing participants, and will not allow unprofessional, sexist, racist, ethnocentric or inappropriate religious comment or contemptuous conduct.
7. A Member will permit parties and agents to present their evidence and arguments without undue interruption from other participants or the Member him/herself.
8. A Member will attempt to ensure that parties who are unrepresented are not unduly disadvantaged at the hearing, although he or she cannot advise or take the side of an unrepresented party.
9. A Member will not communicate directly or indirectly with any party, witness or representative in respect of a proceeding outside of a hearing or pre-hearing conference, except in the presence of all parties and their representatives. He or she will behave in a manner that ensures parties view the Member as impartial towards all participants and representatives.
10. A Member will decide each case in good faith to the best of his or her ability. The prospect of disapproval from any person, institution, media representative or community will not deter the Member from making the decision which he or she believes is correct based on the law and the evidence.
11. A Member accepts responsibility for the accuracy and correctness of his or her Orders and Reasons.
12. A Member is responsible for ensuring that all decisions are rendered promptly. Written reasons for decisions will be prepared without undue delay.
13. A Member will consider any Interpretation Guidelines and relevant Board decisions on a question at issue before him or her, although

neither are binding. A Member is not required by law to follow a Guideline or its reasoning, but must be prepared to explain clearly in the reasons why he or she does not find a Guideline or previous decision relevant or why he or she has adopted different reasoning. The Member will give due weight to the need for a degree of consistency in the interpretation of the law.

(b) Bias

To be fair, a hearing must be presided over by an adjudicator who deals with the parties in a courteous and even-handed manner and comes to the hearing with an open mind. In everyday parlance, "bias" is often synonymous with bigotry. In an administrative law context, the word "bias" has broader implications; it implies lack of neutrality or impartiality. When someone alleges that an adjudicator is biased, they are alleging that the adjudicator is favouring, or is likely to favour, the other party. The person who feels that he or she is not being treated equally might assume that it is because of any number of reasons, including: the class to which they belong (be it landlord or tenant), their socio-economic status; their racial, ethnic, religious or cultural background; their educational level; the attitudes of the adjudicator towards relevant issues (as expressed in this or earlier cases); or, the existence of a relationship between the adjudicator and the opposing party (or that party's representative).

An allegation that an adjudicator is biased is very serious. It is an assertion that a particular adjudicator will not conduct the hearing in a fair manner, listening attentively to the evidence and submissions of both sides, carefully weighing the evidence and coming to a just decision based solely upon the merits of the case. In other words, it is an allegation that the adjudicator cannot or will not do his or her job properly. It is very difficult for a party to establish actual bias.

The existence of a "reasonable apprehension" of bias is more commonly alleged and somewhat easier to establish. Typically, such an allegation is made by a party who feels that the presiding Member's questions or comments during the hearing demonstrate that the adjudicator is favouring one side over the other before all of the evidence and submissions have been received (that the Member has made up his or her mind before the end of the hearing). Alternatively, a party may raise such an allegation before the hearing has even begun based on a fear of bias that comes from knowledge of prior dealings or relationships between the adjudicator and any of the parties involved in the current dispute or their witness(es).

The test to be applied when there is an allegation of a reasonable apprehension of bias is: What would an informed person, viewing the matter realistically and practically — and having thought the matter through —

conclude? Would he think that it is more likely than not that the decision-maker, whether consciously or unconsciously, would not decide fairly?[193]

In *R. v. S. (R.D.)*,[194] the Supreme Court of Canada summarized the principles that apply to a claim of judicial bias. These principles were then repeated by the Ontario Court of Appeal in *Marchand (Litigation Guardian of) v. Public General Hospital Society of Chatham* as follows:[195]

1. All adjudicative tribunals owe a duty of fairness to the parties who appear before them. The scope of the duty and the rigour with which the duty is applied vary with the nature of the tribunal. Courts, however, should be held to the highest standards of impartiality.
2. Impartiality reflects a state of mind in which the judge is disinterested in the outcome and is open to persuasion by the evidence and submissions. In contrast, bias reflects a state of mind that is closed or predisposed to a particular result on material issues.
3. "Fairness and impartiality must be both subjectively present and objectively demonstrated to the informed and reasonable observer. If the words or actions of the presiding judge give rise to a reasonable apprehension of bias to the informed and reasonable observer, this will render the trial unfair." (at p. 524 S.C.R.)
4. The test for bias contains a twofold objective standard: the person considering the alleged bias must be reasonable and informed; and the apprehension of bias must itself be reasonable.
5. The party alleging bias has the onus of proving it on the balance of probabilities.
6. Prejudgment of the merits, prejudgment of credibility, excessive and one-sided interventions with counsel or in the examination of witnesses and the reasons themselves may show bias. The court must decide whether the relevant considerations taken together give rise to a reasonable apprehension of bias.
7. The threshold for a finding of actual or apprehended bias is high. Courts presume that judges will carry out their oath of office. Thus, to make out an allegation of judicial bias requires cogent evidence. Suspicion is not enough. The threshold is high because a finding of bias calls into question not just the personal integrity of the judge but the integrity of the entire administration of justice.

---

193 See *Barrett v. Layton* (2003), [2003] O.J. No. 5572, 2003 CarswellOnt 5602 (Ont. S.C.J.); *Osterbauer v. Ash Temple Ltd.* (2003), [2003] O.J. No. 948, 2003 CarswellOnt 866 (Ont. C.A.); *R. v. S. (R.D.)*, [1997] 3 S.C.R. 484, 118 C.C.C. (3d) 353 (S.C.C.); and *Committee for Justice & Liberty v. Canada (National Energy Board)* (1976), [1978] 1 S.C.R. 369 (S.C.C.).

194 [1997] 3 S.C.R. 484, 118 C.C.C. (3d) 353 (S.C.C.).

195 (2000), 51 O.R. (3d) 97 (at pp. 130-1).

8. Nonetheless, if the judge's words or conduct give rise to a reasonable apprehension of bias, it colours the entire trial and cannot be cured by the correctness of the subsequent decision. Therefore, on appeal, a finding of actual or apprehended bias will ordinarily result in a new trial.

Therefore, it is vital that a Member not only approach every case with an open mind but also be seen to be dealing with parties and witnesses in a courteous, sensitive and even-handed manner. An unfortunate comment or poorly phrased question could create a reasonable apprehension of bias (even where no actual bias exists).

In *60 Montclair Ltd. v. Kizemchuk*,[196] the landlord alleged that the appearance of a swastika on a Thanksgiving Day card and the defacing of a Chanukah card (both posted in the building) were interpreted by some of the residents (who were elderly and Jewish) as incidents of discrimination that gave rise to fears for their safety. Although the Member did not agree that it was a swastika on the Thanksgiving Day card, he went on to make comments about it that were, according to the Divisional Court, "insensitive and highly inappropriate". The Court went on to state that, "Although he later explained why he made the comments, his initial remarks created a reasonable apprehension of bias." The Divisional Court ruled that "the comments of the member about the swastika could lead an informed person, viewing the matter realistically and practically and having thought the matter through, to conclude that this element of the landlord's application would not be dealt with impartially". The decision of the Tribunal was quashed and the matter was remitted back to the Tribunal for hearing before a different adjudicator.

This does not mean that an adjudicator does not have the right to intervene in the proceedings. The Ontario Court of Appeal has stated that, "A trial judge has the *right, indeed the duty*, to intervene to clarify and understand the evidence or *to control the trial, provided* that in intervening, the trial judge does *not prejudge* the issue in dispute or the credibility of the witnesses."[197]

In *Kwak v. Marinecorp Mgt. Inc.*,[198] a Member of the Tribunal had to deal with a hotly contested and lengthy proceeding in which it was alleged that the landlord enforced an eviction order in circumstances that made it an abuse of process. At several points during the hearing, the Member indicated that he was considering adjourning the hearing and issuing an interim order reinstating the tenancy. When the landlord's representative strenuously objected, the Member held off making such an interim decision and allowed the hearing to proceed. On appeal, amongst other alleged errors, the landlord argued that the comments made by the Member during the hearing gave rise

---

[196] (June 6, 2002), Doc. 524/01 (Ont. Div. Ct.) (re TSL-23799).

[197] *Marchand (Litigation Guardian of) v. Public General Hospital Society of Chatham* (2000), 51 O.R. (3d) 97 (at p. 139) (Ont. C.A.), leave to appeal refused [2001] 2 S.C.R. x (S.C.C.).

[198] (2007), 2007 CarswellOnt 4335 (Ont. Div. Ct.).

to a reasonable apprehension of bias. The Divisional Court disagreed. It held that, when the statements were taken in the context of the hearing as a whole, they did not give rise to a reasonable apprehension of bias by the Member against the landlord: "In our view, a person fully informed of all that had transpired would not reach the conclusion that the Member was not likely to decide fairly on the basis of his [the Member's] proposal for an adjournment and an interim order."

On the other hand, in *Jung v. Toronto Community Housing Corp.*,[199] the Divisional Court overturned two related decisions of the Tribunal because the Tribunal appeared biased. In this case, Jang-Soon Jung was a tenant living in rent-geared-to-income housing. The tenant's granddaughter, Lauren Jung, moved in with the tenant in 1989 to assist the tenant with daily living. In April 2006, the tenant was hospitalized and it was expected that she would be moving into a nursing home. Lauren Jung went to the landlord's office to request that her name be added to the lease so that she might stay in the rental unit. Jang-Soon Jung returned briefly to the apartment before she died on May 3, 2006. The landlord has a long list of people waiting for units to become vacant; it apparently considered this to be an attempt by Lauren Jung to "jump the queue". The landlord told her that it deemed the tenancy terminated as of June 3, 2006 (30 days after the death of the tenant), and that she should move out by then as the locks to the unit would be changed at that time. Lauren Jung commenced an application seeking, among other things, a declaration from the Tribunal that she was a tenant of the rental unit. The landlord responded by bringing its own application for an order evicting Lauren Jung as an unauthorized occupant. The two applications were heard together by the same Member. The Member allowed the landlord's representative to dominate the proceedings. The Member did not allow Ms. Jung to present evidence but, instead, based his decision upon the submissions of the representatives. From the outset and repeatedly throughout the proceedings, the Member made comments that indicated he had already made up his mind that Ms. Jung was not a tenant - the very issue that had to be decided. The Member granted the landlord's application and dismissed Ms. Jung's application on the grounds that, since she was not a tenant, she had no right to file an application against the landlord.

On appeal, the Divisional Court found that Ms. Jung was entitled to have an oral hearing in which evidence would be led and legal submissions would be heard and considered as to her status. Procedural fairness required that she be given notice of the facts, arguments and considerations upon which the decision was to be based and an opportunity to make submissions. Simply because the landlord raised jurisdiction as a "preliminary matter" did not mean that the Tribunal could dispense with procedural fairness. The Court found that the Member demonstrated bias both from his comments and from

[199] (2007), 2007 CarswellOnt 7295 (Ont. Div. Ct.).

the manner in which the hearing was conducted. Both decisions were quashed and both applications were sent back to the Tribunal for hearing by a different adjudicator.

Where an allegation of bias is made in the course of a hearing, the Member is required to invite and consider the submissions of all parties and make a ruling on the issue of whether or not he or she can continue to preside over the hearing of this case. The Member's decision is, of course, subject to review and appeal. Regardless of the decision reached by the Member, the Member should inform the Chair of the allegation of bias and whether or not the Member removed himself or herself from the case.

Note that an allegation of bias (or reasonable apprehension of bias) should be made directly to the presiding Member (not to a Regional Manager, Vice-chair or the Chair) as soon as practicable after the facts upon which the allegation is based become known and before a decision is rendered. A party who delays in raising an allegation of bias until after the proceeding has concluded (i.e., waits to see the result) may be barred later from raising the issue or, at the very least, as a result of undue delay, that party's motives may be considered suspect.[200]

Finally, where a party raises an allegation of bias at a Board proceeding but the presiding adjudicator refuses to recuse himself or herself, the party who made the objection should not storm out of the hearing room or refuse to participate further in the proceeding. They should note their objection on the record and then proceed with the case. Abandoning the proceeding is not required by the law and is very risky as it will jeopardize the success of not only the Board proceeding but also any subsequent review or appeal.[201]

2 — THE L.T.B.

---

[200] See, for example: *Authorson (Litigation Guardian of) v. Canada (Attorney General)*, [2002] O.J. No. 2050, 161 O.A.C. 1, 32 C.P.C. (5th) 357, 2002 CarswellOnt 1724 (Ont. Div. Ct.), additional reasons at (2002), 2002 CarswellOnt 2939 (Ont. Div. Ct.); *Stabile v. Milani Estate* (2002), [2002] O.J. No. 3833 (Ont. S.C.J.), additional reasons at (2002), 2002 CarswellOnt 3293 (Ont. S.C.J.), affirmed (2004), 2004 CarswellOnt 831 (Ont. C.A.); *Suguitan (Re)* (2006), [2006] O.J. No. 360 (Ont. S.C.J.); *Metrin Mechanical Contractors Ltd. v. Big H Construction Inc.* (2001), [2001] O.J. No. 3387 (Ont. S.C.J.); *Southridge Apartments v. Hastings* (2007), 2007 CarswellOnt 777 (Ont. Div. Ct.); *Canada (Human Rights Commission) v. Taylor*, [1990] S.C.J. No. 129 (S.C.C.); and *UFCW Canada v. Rol-Land Farms Ltd* (2008), (sub nom. *United Food and Commercial Workers International Union v. Rol-Land Farms Ltd.*) 235 O.A.C. 172 (Ont. Div. Ct.), additional reasons at (2008), 2008 CarswellOnt 3707 (Ont. Div. Ct.).

[201] *Rando Drugs v. Scott* (2007), 86 O.R. (3d) 653 (Ont. C.A.), leave to appeal refused (2008), 2008 CarswellOnt 353 (S.C.C.). Failure to participate in the entire proceeding deprives the party from an opportunity to present evidence, to cross-examine the other party's witnesses, to make submissions on other issues that arise (or that could have been raised had the party not absented themselves). If, on review or appeal, the party is unable to convince the reviewing body that the allegation of bias has sufficient merit to justify ordering a new hearing, no other grounds of appeal will likely be entertained where the party refused to continue to participate in the original hearing.

(c) Language

Language can pose a barrier to accessibility and transparency, both of which are important to a fair process. A significant number of people who appear before the Landlord and Tenant Board are unable to effectively participate in a hearing conducted in English. Nevertheless, the Board does not provide or pay for interpreters. A party who requires such assistance must arrange for their own professional interpreter or ask for permission from the presiding Member to permit a friend or family member to act as an interpreter. Having such persons act as interpreters is clearly fraught with difficulties: they are usually untrained, they are not neutral, they may have an interest in the outcome of the proceeding, they may not be familiar with the Board's proceedings, may not be familiar with legal terminology and they may not be interpreting what is said accurately. One can only imagine that the decision of the Board not to provide such services was based on cost considerations rather than on considerations of procedural fairness. It is difficult to fathom the logic in a legal system that provides interpreters to individuals facing conviction for a provincial offence (such as a "speeding ticket") but not to individuals facing eviction from their home. The Divisional Court, however, has found in at least one case[202] that the failure of the Board to provide an interpreter did not constitute a denial of natural justice.

There is one exception to the general rule that the Board does not provide interpreters. Pursuant to the *French Language Services Act,* R.S.O. 1990, c. F.32, the Board is obliged to provide a French interpreter or conduct the hearing in French if requested by a party but only in cases where the rental unit is located or the party making the request resides in a "designated area" of Ontario. This is now explicitly recognized by the Board in Rule 7 of the Board's Rules of Practice. Even where the Board fails to comply with this requirement, however, it does not automatically mean that the resulting order will be quashed. In *Sebastiao v. Toronto Community Housing Corporation,*[203] the tenant requested a French-language interpreter but was not provided with one by the Tribunal (probably as the result of an oversight). On appeal, the Divisional Court did not overturn the Tribunal's decision because no denial of natural justice occurred; the transcript and the documents filed showed clearly that the tenant was able to fully participate in English.

---

[202] *Karrum v. Yolanda Enterprises Ltd.* (July 7, 2000), TSL-12922, [2000] O.R.H.T.D. No. 184, 2000 CarswellOnt 3850 (Ont. Div. Ct.).

[203] (November 20, 2003), Doc. 706-02 (Ont. Div. Ct.) (re TSL-44947-RV).

(d) Right to be Represented

Pursuant to s. 10 of the *Statutory Powers Procedure Act*,[204] a party to a proceeding has the right to be represented by a representative. Generally, this means that a party must be given a reasonable opportunity to retain a legal representative, which may necessitate an adjournment. While there is an obligation upon a party to exercise this right with reasonable diligence, a refusal by the Board to grant an adjournment to enable a party to retain counsel may be a reversible error.[205] In fact, where a fundamental and complex legal issue is raised by the applicant for the first time at the hearing and the respondents are unrepresented, it may be incumbent upon the Board to *offer* the respondents an opportunity to obtain counsel and the failure to do so may constitute a denial of natural justice.[206]

(e) Procedural Fairness

Each party is entitled to a fair opportunity to present his or her case. It was, therefore, found to be a serious error for a Member to invite one side to call evidence but not the other.[207] Similarly, in *Eickmeier v. 395321 Ontario Ltd.*,[208] it was found to be a serious error for the original Member not to hear from both parties and for the Member to use the mantle of the Member's authority to coerce the parties into "settling" their dispute.

Although the Board can proceed with a hearing in the absence of one of the parties, it is advisable to give the missing party some "grace" period in case that party was unavoidably detained. Where the Board only waited five minutes before proceeding in the tenant's absence, on appeal, the Divisional Court held that this amounted to a denial of natural justice and a reversible error.[209]

In *Manpel v. Greenwin Property Management*,[210] the Divisional Court found that, due to a very large number of interruptions and objections by counsel for the landlord, and the Member's failure to control this disruptive conduct, the tenant was denied a fair hearing. The tenant was not permitted by the Member to have a verbatim reporter present (for at least part of the hearing), was not allowed to read an opening statement, was not allowed to

---

204 As amended by the *Access to Justice Act*, 2006, S.O. 2006, c. 21.

205 *Doherty v. Minto Developments Inc.* (November 19, 2003), Doc. 02-DV-000820 (Ont. Div. Ct.) (re EAL-31684).

206 *Kizemchuk v. Kizemchuk* (2000), 2000 CarswellOnt 2547 (Ont. Div. Ct.) (re TSL-11717).

207 *Klein v. Cohen* (2000), 2000 CarswellOnt 5138 (Ont. Div. Ct.).

208 (Aug. 23, 2001), CET-01857-RV, [2001] O.R.H.T.D. No. 113, 2001 CarswellOnt 6313 (Ont. Rental Housing Trib.).

209 *Sutherland v. Lamontagne* (March 3, 2008) Court File No. DV-756-07 (unreported).

210 (2005), 34 R.P.R. (4th) 82 (Ont. Div. Ct.), additional reasons at (2005), 2005 CarswellOnt 6862 (Ont. Div. Ct.) (re TST-06638).

adduce all of his evidence and was not granted an adequate opportunity to respond to the submissions made by the landlord's representative, especially concerning the landlord's motion for a non-suit.

Although the Board does have the jurisdiction to dismiss an application upon a nonsuit motion brought by the respondent,[211] this power should only be exercised in the clearest of cases. The Board is required to apply the principles of procedural fairness and natural justice. The parties are entitled to be heard and are entitled to a fair hearing. Failure to adhere to these requirements will result in the Board's decision being quashed.[212]

Parties are entitled to know the evidence that is being considered by the adjudicator. If a Member considers evidence that was not presented at the hearing, it is incumbent upon the Member to advise the parties and either reconvene the hearing or, at the very least, take written submissions from the parties before reaching a final decision.

In *Marks v. Charlton*,[213] the Divisional Court found that it was a serious error for the Member to contact witnesses after the hearing without affording the parties the right to confront or attempt to contradict the evidence.

In *Barker v. Park Willow Developments*,[214] the tenants applied for a reduction in rent based upon the loss of use of a balcony during restoration work.[215] The Member rejected the landlord's evidence with respect to the cost of providing this service. This was the only evidence presented at the hearing concerning the value of this "facility". The Member came up with his own calculation for the value of the balcony, based on the proportional floor space of the balcony compared to the area of the entire rental unit. The Divisional Court held that, in these circumstances (where the Member intended to adopt an approach other than one suggested at the hearing), it was an error for the Member not to have reconvened the hearing to accept evidence and submissions from the parties. The matter was sent back to the Board for reconsideration.

All parties to a proceeding must be given an adequate opportunity to fully present their case. The failure to do so will be a reversible error.[216]

In *Lesseeleur v. Homes First Society*,[217] it was held upon the review that the tenant, who due to mental impairment was not able to effectively represent himself at the original hearing, did not have a meaningful opportunity to

---

211 See *Burton-Lesbury Holdings Ltd. v. Daley* (June 20, 2003), Doc. 556/02, [2003] O.J. No. 3643 (Ont. Div. Ct.) (re TNL-38573).

212 *Baker v. Canada (Minister of Citizenship & Immigration)*, [1999] 2 S.C.R. 817 (S.C.C.).

213 Doc. 778/2000 (Ont. Div. Ct.) (re TET-01379).

214 (2004), 2004 CarswellOnt 2848 (Ont. Div. Ct.).

215 In this case, the landlord conceded that balconies were "facilities" for the purposes of s. 142.

216 *Sheppard v. Suraski* (April 21, 2006), TST-08126-RV-RV, 2006 CarswellOnt 4424, [2006] O.R.H.T.D. No. 42 (Ont. Rental Housing Trib.).

217 (August 31, 2006), TSL-83969-IN (Ont. Rental Housing Trib.).

participate in the hearing and was therefore denied natural justice. A new hearing was ordered.

Finally, where a party, through an error on the part of the Board, has been prevented from participating in a hearing,[218] on review, the order should be quashed and a new hearing ordered automatically.[219]

6. RES JUDICATA

The best description I have found of the concept of *res judicata*, comes from an article by Paul M. Perell, entitled "Res Judicata and Abuse of Process":[220]

> The complex idea of *res judicata* is that a final judgement on the merits by a tribunal of competent jurisdiction, including an administrative tribunal, is binding and determinative of the rights of the parties or their privies in all subsequent legal proceedings with respect to claims, defences and fundamental issues decided in the former legal proceedings and, in some instances, with respect to claims, defences and fundamental issues that ought to have been decided in the former legal proceedings. There are two types of *res judicata*: cause of action estoppel and issue estoppel. Cause of action estoppel precludes a person or his privies from bringing a proceeding or raising a defence against another or his privies when the cause of action or the defence was decided or ought to have been decided in an earlier proceeding. Issue estoppel precludes a person or his privies from relitigating a fundamental issue after that issue was finally decided in an earlier proceeding between the same parties or their privies, even if the causes of action or defences in the proceedings are different. The underlying policies for both kinds of *res judicata* are that there should be an end to litigation and a party should not be harassed with a duplicative proceeding. These policies encourage consistency, conclusiveness, finality and judicial economy in the administration of justice in situations where a party has had his day in court.

Res judicata is solely a judicial doctrine (i.e., it is not found in any statute). A tribunal can apply this doctrine as part of its jurisdiction to control its own process and prevent abuses of that process.

(a) Cause of Action Estoppel

Cause of action *estoppel* is the legal "rule" that a claim that has been heard and resolved by a court or tribunal cannot be heard again. For this doctrine to apply, three conditions must be satisfied:

---

[218] If, for instance, the notice of hearing contained an incorrect date, time or place for the hearing.

[219] *Seifennasr v. Ottawa (City) Non-Profit Housing Corp.* (2003), 2003 CarswellOnt 5182 (Ont. Div. Ct.) (re EAL-25821-RV).

[220] Advocates Quarterly, Vol. 24, 2001 at pp. 189-191.

(i) the same claim currently being advanced has already been decided in an earlier proceeding;
(ii) that decision was final; and
(iii) the parties (or their privies) are the same now as in that earlier proceeding.

As stated in the paper by Mr. Perell, the doctrine is grounded in principles of fairness and public policy. It is not fair to force the litigant to face the same litigation twice. The community has an interest in having disputes resolved once and for all. This promotes confidence and predictability in the process.[221]

As indicated above, one of the elements that must be present is that the parties (or their privies) in both proceedings must be the same. This is not always as obvious as one might imagine. In *Clarke v. Bielak*,[222] an individual landlord brought an application to terminate the tenancy for use of the unit by her daughter. Just two months previously, however, the landlord had brought an identical application but had named her corporation as landlord; that earlier application had been dismissed.[223] The second application was granted. On appeal by the tenant, the Divisional Court overturned the eviction order arising from the second application on the basis that the Rental Housing Tribunal had erred in failing to consider whether the corporate landlord and the individual controlling it were really one and the same for the purposes of the doctrine of *res judicata*.

In *Parker v. Wendler*,[224] the Landlord's original application (EAL-00825) to evict the Tenant based upon intended use of the unit by the Landlord's son was dismissed. The Landlord immediately filed another (identical) application hoping to adduce new evidence and be more successful on this new application. The application was dismissed as it was *res judicata*. Similarly, in *Ehmke v. Johnson*,[225] the tenants brought an earlier application for the same relief that was dismissed. This application was, therefore, dismissed. The Tribunal suggested that if the tenants were unhappy with the earlier decision, they must seek to have it overturned. They cannot simply ignore it and commence a new application. In *MacLean v. Benaissa*,[226] the tenant brought an application alleging harassment by her landlord. As evidence of harassment, she relied upon the fact that the landlord had previously brought a series of (unsuccessful) applications seeking to evict her. The Tribunal dismissed her application on the basis that she could not re-litigate those

---

221 *Brown v. Marwieh* (1995), 36 C.P.C. (3d) 1 (N.S. S.C.), affirmed (1995), 39 C.P.C. (3d) 372 (N.S. C.A.), at 7.

222 (2003) 2003 CarswellOnt 4351, [2003] O.J. No. 4479, 178 O.A.C. 233 (Ont. Div. Ct.).

223 On the basis that a corporation cannot bring this type of application because a corporation, not being a natural person, is incapable of having any relatives who can occupy the unit.

224 (Nov. 23, 1998), EAL-02476 (Ont. Rental Housing Trib.).

225 (July 24, 2002), TET-02565, 2002 CarswellOnt 3818 (Ont. Rental Housing Trib.).

226 Doc. 123/03 (Ont. Div. Ct.) (re TST-04923 and TST-04924).

applications. On appeal, the Divisional Court found that there was nothing wrong with the Tenant raising, as evidence of harassment, a series of previous attempts by the Landlord to evict her. While the previous applications cannot be re-litigated, the history of the Landlord's repeated efforts to end this tenancy could conceivably constitute evidence of harassment.

For the most part, courts have strictly applied *res judicata* to prevent a multiplicity of proceedings. Since, however, the doctrine of *res judicata* is designed primarily to prevent an abuse of process, there are times where its strict application may not be appropriate. Examples of cases where a court has decided not to apply *res judicata* include situations where the law (or its interpretation) has changed since the prior proceeding or where the application of this doctrine would cause unfairness or work an injustice.[227] An example of such a situation arose in *Nesha v. Bezrukova ("Nesha")*.[228]

In the *Nesha* case, the tenant originally brought an application for, amongst other things, damages for the value of property that had gone missing from a storage space. The member held that the Tribunal lacked jurisdiction to award damages under s. 35 of the T.P.A. At that time, the Tribunal's decisions were not entirely consistent on this point. Some members felt that the power of the Tribunal to make "any other order it considers appropriate" (as that term was used in paras. 34(1)5 and 35(1)(c) of the T.P.A.) included the power to award damages; other Members did not agree with this interpretation and could find no statutory authority to award damages. Subsequently, s. 35 of the T.P.A. was amended to specifically allow for claims for the cost of repairing or replacing property. The tenant filed a new application (TNT-02274) based upon the same facts and claiming the relief that was previously denied (i.e., damages). The member hearing this application ruled that the matter was *res judicata* and that the amendment of the T.P.A. did not allow the tenant to re-litigate the matter. This decision was upheld on review.[229] Both decisions were, however, overturned on appeal to the Divisional Court on the basis that either the Tribunal erred in its interpretation of the doctrine of *res judicata* or that it was unfair to strictly apply that doctrine in this case.

For a straightforward example, see Landlord and Tenant Board File No. TSL-21516 (Feb. 6, 2009), in which the landlord's application was dismissed because it was based upon the same facts and documents that were the subject of an earlier application that was dismissed with prejudice.

---

[227] See *Hocklin v. Bank of British Columbia* (1995), 3 B.C.L.R. (3d) 193 (B.C. C.A.), leave to appeal refused (1995), 195 N.R. 238 (note) (S.C.C.); *Lexogest Inc. v. Manitoba* (1994), 91 Man. R. (2d) 260 (Man. Q.B.); and *Minott v. O'Shanter* (1999), 42 O.R. (3d) 321 (Ont. C.A.).

[228] (2003), 2003 CarswellOnt 3674 (Ont. Div. Ct.).

[229] (July 15, 2002), TNT-02274-RV, 2002 CarswellOnt 5727 (Ont. Rental Housing Trib.), reversed (2003), 2003 CarswellOnt 3674 (Ont. Div. Ct.).

(b) Issue Estoppel

Issue *estoppel* is the legal "rule" meant to prevent a party from raising an issue that has already been decided in an earlier proceeding. For this doctrine to apply, three conditions must be satisfied:[230]

(i) the same question (issue) currently being advanced has already been decided in an earlier proceeding;
(ii) that earlier decision was final; and
(iii) the parties (or their privies) are the same now as in that earlier proceeding.

The philosophy behind issue *estoppel* is basically the same as for cause of action *estoppel*. Therefore, even if all three preconditions are present, the court (or tribunal) must still decide whether, as a matter of discretion, issue *estoppel* ought to be applied.[231]

In *Glimjem Holdings v. Weidenfeld*,[232] the tenant had brought an application for an abatement of rent and damages based upon alleged breaches by the landlord of its maintenance obligations. After that case had been heard, but before the order was issued, the landlord commenced an application to evict the tenant for non-payment of rent. The tenant sought to have the landlord's application stayed until the issuance of the order on his application. The tenant argued that if the Tribunal found as a fact in his application that the landlord was in breach of the maintenance obligations, the landlord would be *estopped* from denying that fact (by issue *estoppel*) in the current application and, pursuant to s. 84(2) of the T.P.A., no eviction order could be made against him. It was held that issue *estoppel* did not apply in this case because no decision had yet been made on the tenant's application. Furthermore, the test under s. 24 of the T.P.A. (i.e., whether there was a *breach* of the landlord's maintenance obligations) is different than the test under s. 84(2) of the T.P.A. (which only prevents an eviction if the landlord is found to be in *serious breach* of its obligations). Also, the test under s. 84(2) refers to whether the landlord is (currently) in serious breach (i.e., at the time the eviction application is heard); even if the landlord was found in the tenant's application to have been in breach of its maintenance obligations at some point in the past, it would not be determinative of whether the landlord was still in breach of those obligations or how serious those breaches are as of the date of the hearing of the landlord's application. The tenant was requesting adjournments

---

230 *Danyluk v. Ainsworth Technologies Inc.*, [2001] 2 S.C.R. 460 (S.C.C.).

231 See *Danyluk v. Ainsworth Technologies Inc.*, [2001] 2 S.C.R. 460 (S.C.C.) in which the Supreme Court of Canada found that it would be wrong to apply the principle of issue estoppel in a situation where the original decision was achieved through an unfair process.

232 (Dec. 16, 2002), TNL-41312-SA, 2002 CarswellOnt 5012 (Ont. Rental Housing Trib.).

but demonstrated an unwillingness to comply with the terms the Tribunal set as conditions for those adjournments. The Tribunal therefore ordered that the hearing of the landlord's application would proceed and not wait for the outcome of the tenant's application.

In Landlord and Tenant Board File No. NOT-00940 (Jan. 22, 2009), the tenant brought an application against the landlord. The Member pointed out that the same parties had previously appeared before the Board on an earlier application (NOT-00883), in which it was determined that the unit had not been intended for residential occupation and, in fact, had never been used for residential occupation and, as a result, the R.T.A. did not apply and the Board had no jurisdiction over the relationship between these parties. It was held that the doctrine of *res judicata* (issue estoppel) applied and the application was dismissed.

One case where I think the Member misapplied this principle of issue *estoppel* is *Rocheleau v. Gonsalves*.[233] The landlord brought an application against the tenant. As part of the tenant's defence, the tenant raised the issue of whether the landlord was in serious breach of the landlord's maintenance obligations due to the alleged failure of the landlord to repair or replace a faulty refrigerator and stove and to address other maintenance concerns. Somewhat surprisingly (since it was the landlord's application) the Tribunal ordered the landlord to effect some repairs (in order TEL-56852-SA). An inspector from the City of Toronto Property Standards Dept. attended at the unit in mid-January 2006 and issued a Work Order. The tenant vacated the unit at the end of January 2006 and then commenced an application (TET-05552) for an abatement of rent based upon alleged breaches by the landlord of its maintenance obligations. The Member awarded some relief for the failure of the landlord to comply with the City's Work Order but indicated that the Tribunal had "no jurisdiction" to "again" address the issue of the fridge and stove as that issue was dealt with in order TEL-56852-SA issued on December 19, 2005.

Respectfully, I believe this pronouncement (that the Tribunal lacked jurisdiction to consider the claims with respect to the fridge and stove) was incorrect for the following reasons. First, whether or not to apply the principle of issue *estoppel* is a matter of discretion, not a question of jurisdiction. Second, the issue under s. 84(2) of the T.P.A.[234] (i.e., whether the landlord *is in serious breach* of its obligations at the time of the hearing) is different from the issue of whether the tenant can prove that the landlord was (at some point within one year prior to filing the application) in breach of its obligations under s. 24(1) of the T.P.A.[235] Third, although the Tribunal heard evidence

[233] (March 27, 2006), TET-05552, [2006] O.R.H.T.D. No. 23, 2006 CarswellOnt 2152 (Ont. Rental Housing Trib.).

[234] Now s. 83(3) of the R.T.A.

[235] Now s. 20(1) of the R.T.A.

concerning the fridge and stove as part of the tenant's defence to the landlord's eviction application, on that application the Tribunal lacked jurisdiction to grant relief under s. 34 of the T.P.A. (now s. 30 of the R.T.A.). Therefore, although the parties may be bound in the tenant's application by testimony they gave during the previous proceeding (assuming that a transcript was available) and may be bound by findings of fact set out in that earlier order, the issues that can properly be raised and the remedies available in the two applications are not identical and the principle of issue *estoppel* does not apply.

Another case where the Member misdirected himself was *Wamboldt v. Wellman*.[236] In an earlier case between the parties, the Ontario Rental Housing Tribunal granted relief to the tenant because of the landlord's failure to properly maintain the unit. The landlord was, among other things, ordered to effect repairs. On a subsequent application by the tenant, the Member refused to hear evidence about ongoing, similar maintenance problems on the basis that those issues had already been dealt with in the earlier application. On appeal by the tenant, the Divisional Court held that the principles of *res judicata* and *issue estoppel* did not apply in this case, as the tenant was perfectly entitled to seek relief for breaches of the Act that occurred subsequent to the issuance of the Tribunal's previous order, even if those breaches by the landlord represented a continuation of pre-existing maintenance problems (i.e., "ongoing breaches"). As a consequence, a new hearing was ordered.

In Landlord and Tenant Board File No. SOL-18469 (Feb. 2, 2009), the landlord brought an application to terminate the tenancy based upon arrears of rent. In both the notice of termination (Form N4) and the application (Form L1), the landlord showed the monthly rent as being greater than the lawful rent determined in a previous order concerning the same tenancy. It was held that the landlord was estopped from claiming a rent different than that already determined by the Board in a previous application and the current application was dismissed. Essentially, this constituted a collateral attack by the landlord on the earlier order; if the landlord wished to challenge the findings in that earlier order, the landlord was required to do so by way of request for review or appeal of that order.

(c) Abuse of Process by Re-litigation

The principles against permitting duplicative claims are: finality (there should be an end to litigation), avoidance of inconsistent results, prevention of harassment, and judicial economy.

---

236 (2007) 2007 CarswellOnt 8328 (Ont. Div. Ct.).

In *Shiffman v. Bathurst Sheppard Apartments*,[237] the tenant commenced an application for maintenance concerns and settled with the landlord through mediation. The tenant knew of an additional maintenance concern (alleged inadequate heat) not specifically raised in that application but was advised by his lawyer at that time not to mention that issue. The mediated agreement was not entirely clear on whether it was meant to cover ALL possible maintenance issues to that date but that was certainly the landlord's intention. Subsequently, the tenant filed a new maintenance application about lack of heat. The landlord objected to this type of litigation by installments (or by ambush) and argued that the tenant was *estopped* from filing a new maintenance application based upon the same time period covered in the agreement. The member who originally heard this case ruled that since there had not been a hearing on the original application (since that case had settled), the principles of cause of action *estoppel* and issue *estoppel* did not apply. On review, it was held that it was an error for the member not to also consider the doctrine of abuse of process by re-litigation.

Parties must have confidence that mediated agreements shall represent full and final settlements of all issues (unless clearly worded to the contrary). This doctrine applies equally to both landlords and tenants. Thus, parties ought to bring forward in one proceeding all issues arising from the same cause of action and not hold back a part of the claim they know or ought to know exists at the time of the commencement of the application. Failure to do so may preclude the party (as in this case) from later commencing a second application based upon the same type of application whether or not the specific issue was raised in the first application. The review was granted and the tenant's application was dismissed. A similar ruling was made by the reviewing Member in *Mandel v. Morguard Residential Inc.*,[238] in which the tenant's application was dismissed because the issues raised in it could have been included in an earlier application that had been brought by the tenant against the landlord.

In Landlord and Tenant Board File No. TNT-00020 (March 16, 2007), the tenant was once again raising issues that had been raised, or *that ought to have been raised*, in the numerous Tribunal and court proceedings that the tenant had previously initiated against the landlord. The Member dismissed the tenant's current application as an abuse of process.

Courts are equally concerned with avoiding a multiplicity of proceedings and in preventing an unsuccessful party from trying to relitigate issues that have already been decided. In *Muir v. Disher*,[239] there was a history of antagonism and harassment by the tenant of his landlords. This tenancy was the subject of extensive proceedings under the R.T.A. On several occasions,

2 — THE L.T.B.

---

[237] (June 8, 2004), TNT-03769-RV, 2004 CarswellOnt 3627 (Ont. Rental Housing Trib.).

[238] (Nov. 6, 2003), TST-05662-RV, 2003 CarswellOnt 5675 (Ont. Rental Housing Trib.).

[239] (2009), 2009 CarswellOnt 254 (Ont. S.C.J.).

the landlord believed that the matter had been resolved through negotiation only to find that a new application had been commenced or that the tenant sought to re-open the former proceeding for the flimsiest of reasons. In a decision from the Board, the presiding Member noted that the landlords were highly prejudiced by having to face numerous applications, that they deserved some finality and that the practice of the tenant continually filing applications regarding the same issues and same time period amounted to an abuse of process and would not be permitted. The tenant's application before the Board was dismissed. The tenant then filed two actions in Small Claims Court to deal with essentially the same issues. The presiding deputy judge found that the issues before the Court were either previously raised in the Board proceedings or could have been raised therein and that these actions constituted an abuse of process. The actions were stayed and costs were awarded to the defendant landlords.

7. CHOICE OF FORUM

While most disputes arising between residential landlords and tenants are resolved at the Landlord and Tenant Board, the choice of where to have the dispute adjudicated is not always so obvious. For instance, not every dispute that arises between a landlord and tenant necessarily arises out of (or in connection with) the tenancy. If a landlord terminates the employment of a superintendent who lives in the residential complex, the landlord may wish to evict the former superintendent from the complex and the former employee may wish to pursue a claim against the landlord for wrongful dismissal. The landlord can commence eviction proceedings before the Landlord and Tenant Board; the former superintendent must pursue his or her claim in court. Similarly, a landlord can generally only commence an application against a tenant. If there is a guarantor (or co-signer) for the tenant's obligations under the tenancy agreement and the landlord wishes to pursue a claim against such a person, it will have to be in court and not before the Board.[240]

Some parties who are owed more than the monetary limit that may be awarded by the Board assume they can obtain an order at the Board for the maximum amount the Board is permitted to grant and then pursue a claim for the balance of the debt in court. According to s. 207(3) of the R.T.A. (formerly s. 193(3) of the T.P.A.), this clearly is not permitted. When a party chooses to have the dispute adjudicated by the Board, "all rights of the party in excess of the Board's monetary jurisdiction are extinguished." It may make sense, however, for the applicant to waive the excess and choose to proceed before the Board. For example, it is possible that a landlord who is owed

[240] The topics of superintendents and guarantors will be analyzed in more detail in subsequent chapters.

more than the monetary limit of the Board might nevertheless choose to commence an application in the Board in order to obtain an order faster and with less legal expense than would likely be involved in a proceeding before the Superior Court of Justice. A landlord will also sometimes come to the conclusion that it is unlikely the landlord will ever actually collect the monies owing to it; in such circumstances, the goal may be to obtain an eviction order as quickly as possible and the amount of money ordered is of little practical significance (since the landlord never expects to actually collect on the debt). There may, therefore, be perfectly rational reasons to commence proceedings in the Board and waive any part of the claim that exceeds the monetary limit of the Board. It is important, however, for the applicant to realize that he or she is forever giving up the right to pursue any amount in excess of the Board's monetary jurisdiction.

Another tactic tried by a landlord more recently was to seek an order terminating the tenancy based on arrears that exceeded $33,000 but not seek an order for payment of that amount; in this way, the landlord hoped to be able to get a quick eviction order at the Board and then try to obtain a judgment for the full amount of the debt in court. The Board is required in such eviction orders, however, to state the amount that the tenant is required to pay to void the order and the amount in this case exceeded the monetary jurisdiction of the Board. The presiding Member would not permit this and put the landlord to the election of either continuing with the application before the Board and waiving any claim to the amount in excess of the Board's monetary jurisdiction or withdrawing the application and pursuing the entire claim by way of application before the Superior Court of Justice. The landlord elected the latter option and the application was dismissed on a "without prejudice" basis. The Member's approach in this case is consistent with that adopted by the Divisional Court in its unreported decision in *Ip v. King*.[241]

A person also takes the risk that, if they choose the wrong forum, by the time they discover their error, it will be too late. In *Assor v. Cando Property Management Ltd.*,[242] the tenant chose to commence an action against her landlord in Small Claims Court. Eventually, a judge of the Small Claims Court ruled that the action could not proceed as the Tribunal has exclusive jurisdiction over disputes arising out of residential tenancies.[243] By that time, however, it was too late for her to commence an application in the Tribunal as the relevant limitation period had expired.[244] The Small Claims Court

2 — THE L.T.B.

[241] (December 23, 1998), Doc. V1124/98, discussed earlier in this Chapter under Section 3 (Jurisdiction of the Board) under the heading, "Monetary Jurisdiction".

[242] (Feb. 28, 2003), TNT-03233, [2003] O.R.H.T.D. No. 31, 2003 CarswellOnt 1509 (Ont. Rental Housing Trib.).

[243] See s. 168(2) of the R.T.A. (formerly s. 157(2) of the T.P.A.).

[244] A one-year limitation period exists for most tenant applications pursuant to subsections 29(2), 57(2) and 98(2) of the R.T.A. (formerly subsection 32(2) of the T.P.A.) and the Board has no jurisdiction to extend or waive this limitation period.

attempted to assist the tenant by "transferring" the matter to the Tribunal[245] but the Tribunal held, correctly in my view, that the Small Claims Court had no jurisdiction to "transfer" the matter to the Tribunal as it had purported to do. Since the relevant limitation period had expired and the tenant had not commenced an application in the correct forum (i.e., the Tribunal), she was now statute-barred from doing so. In other words, by the time the tenant found out she was in the wrong place, it was too late to start over in the right place and she lost any right to pursue her claim against the landlord.

In *Bailey v. Viscount Properties — Division of Aaron Construction Ltd.*,[246] the drain in the basement of this townhouse backed up and sewage entered the basement once in 2001 and twice in 2002. In 2004, the tenant commenced an application at the Rental Housing Tribunal concerning these problems but then, after speaking to duty counsel and realizing that there was a one-year limitation period, she chose to abandon her application and, instead, commenced a claim in Small Claims Court in November 2004. The Court found that, pursuant to s. 157(2) of the T.P.A. (now s. 168(2) of the R.T.A.), it did not have jurisdiction to decide this case as the relief sought by the plaintiff was within the exclusive jurisdiction of the Ontario Rental Housing Tribunal.

Finally, a party who chooses to commence an application before the Superior Court of Justice under the R.T.A. should recognize that the Court will have no greater powers than the Board, except that the Court can grant an order payment of an amount that exceeds the maximum amount that could be granted by the Board. An application that is heard by the Court, however, is still a proceeding under the R.T.A. and the Court is bound by the provisions of the R.T.A.[247]

8. APPLICATIONS TO DETERMINE WHETHER THE ACT APPLIES (s. 9)

Usually, it will be obvious whether or not the R.T.A. applies to a particular tenancy, unit or complex. This is not always the case, however. There are situations where the parties cannot agree on whether the R.T.A. applies. Such issues can arise during the course of a hearing and it often comes as a surprise to the Member since the issue of jurisdiction is rarely identified in the documents filed by parties. Where jurisdiction becomes an issue, the Member must explicitly deal with that issue in his or her decision.

Where, however, a party knows in advance that jurisdiction is going to be an issue, it may be preferable to obtain a ruling on that issue before proceeding with any other application. A party who wishes to obtain a ruling

[245] As if the Tribunal were another court, pursuant to s. 110 of the *Courts of Justice Act*.

[246] (2006), [2006] O.J. No. 3309 (Ont. S.C.J.).

[247] Subsection 207(2) of the R.T.A. (formerly subsection 193(2) of the T.P.A.).

on the applicability of the R.T.A. before commencing other proceedings, may do so by filing with the Board an application (Form A1) pursuant to s. 9 of the R.T.A. (formerly s. 7 of the T.P.A.).[248] After hearing evidence and submissions from the parties, the Board will then issue an order determining whether the R.T.A. (or any provision of it) applies to the particular rental unit or residential complex.

9. ACCESS TO BOARD DECISIONS

From 1998 through 2006, the Rental Housing Tribunal likely issued more than 600,000 decisions. Less than 1,000 have been made public by the Tribunal.[249] The failure of the Rental Housing Tribunal to release more of its decisions made it difficult for scholars and practitioners and even for Members themselves to determine how the law in this field was developing and it made it difficult for parties appearing before the Tribunal (and now the Landlord and Tenant Board) to make cogent arguments about how the law has been or ought to be interpreted.

There were also problems with the manner in which the Tribunal chose which decisions would be released to the public. Historically, the Tribunal permitted Members to decide for themselves whether or not to "flag" their decisions as "significant". Then a committee (composed primarily of administrative staff) would choose from amongst those decisions that were "flagged" by the Members to decide which ones should actually be released to the public. This process was problematic for a number of reasons.

First, some Members identified many of their decisions as significant while other Members rarely (if ever) did so. As a result, the decisions that were released by the Tribunal tended to come from only a handful of Members and did not represent a good cross-section of decisions from all Members of the Tribunal.

Second, the system I have described above raises questions about who gets to decide which decisions are significant enough to be released and upon what criteria those decisions are made. It raises concerns that staff at the Tribunal may inadvertently affect the development of the law by failing to release decisions that really are significant. This system may also create a fear (in the conspiracy-minded) that management could deliberately attempt to affect the development of the law by disseminating decisions with which management agrees and withholding from the public novel or controversial decisions.

Third, by releasing such a small number of decisions and releasing them through reporting services that are generally only available to lawyers (for a

---

[248] See Chapter 13 for more information about this type of application.

[249] By way of comparison, between 2000 and 2006, the Ontario Labour Relations Board made available to the public over 44,000 of its decisions.

fee), the Tribunal made it difficult for the public to gain access to even those few decisions that it did choose to release. This is especially troubling for an adjudicative process that was intended to be more accessible and accommodating to parties who were expected to represent themselves.

By way of comparison, the Environmental Review Tribunal, the Financial Services Commission of Ontario, the Ontario Human Rights Tribunal, the Licence Appeal Tribunal, the Ontario Labour Relations Board, the Ontario Municipal Board and the Workplace Safety and Insurance Appeals Tribunal are quasi-judicial tribunals in Ontario that make *all* their decisions available online through their respective websites. Many of these websites facilitate legal research by allowing the public to search for cases by keywords, the names of the parties and/or the name of the decision-maker, the date of the decision and so forth and this is done free of charge.[250]

Some individuals at the Rental Housing Tribunal expressed concern about releasing decisions that contain identifying information about the parties (such as the names and addresses of the parties). This concern was occasionally used by the Tribunal as an explanation for its reluctance to release its decisions. Between 2003 and 2006, the Information and Privacy Commission ("I.P.C.") released a number of decisions that supported this growing trend towards secrecy at the Rental Housing Tribunal.[251] On October 6, 2006, the I.P.C. upheld the Tribunal's decision to withhold from its orders the names of tenants and their unit numbers as this constituted confidential personal information.[252] Anticipating that the Tribunal might use this order as an excuse to further restrict access to its decisions, the Senior Adjudicator at the I.P.C., who issued this decision, went on to write the following post-script:

> I urge the Tribunal to consider adopting the practice of many administrative tribunals, including this office, of drafting its Orders in a manner which removes personal information and identifiers to better facilitate the public's access to its body of case law.

The decisions of many administrative tribunals in Ontario continue to contain the names of parties. The same is true of the decisions of the courts. The Landlord and Tenant Board, however, is now prohibited from releasing identifying information about tenants. I have some reservations about this trend towards secrecy in administrative justice and I am concerned about the inconsistencies that decisions such as this one by the I.P.C. have created

---

[250] For example, see the official websites of the Consent and Capacity Board, the Ontario Labour Relations Board, the Ontario Municipal Board, and the Workplace Safety and Insurance Appeals Tribunal.

[251] See, for example, Information and Privacy Commission Orders PO-2109 (Feb. 7, 2003); PO-2418 (Sept. 27, 2005); PO-2265 (April 28, 2004); and PO-2510 (Oct. 6, 2006).

[252] Information and Privacy Commission Order PO-2511 by Senior Adjudicator John Higgins.

between different administrative tribunals and between tribunals and the courts. Amongst other problems created by these inconsistencies, it is now virtually impossible to cross-reference appeal decisions of the Divisional Court (which are reported by the names of the parties) with the original Board decisions under consideration (which are identified solely by file number and not by the names of the parties). It is, however, beyond the scope of this Chapter for me to analyze the development and the current state of privacy law in Ontario.

In any event, until the law is changed or this issue is reconsidered by the I.P.C., the Landlord and Tenant Board is bound by I.P.C. Order PO-2511. In my view, however, the Board has overreacted to the decision of the I.P.C. Instead of just withholding identifying information about tenants (i.e., the tenant's name and unit number), the Board is now removing from many (but, interestingly, not all) of its decisions the entire address of the residential complex, the names of *all* parties (despite the fact that the I.P.C. has issued at least three decisions in which it has been held that the names of landlords need not be removed),[253] and even the names of the parties' respective representatives and witnesses.

In its first two years of operation as the Landlord and Tenant Board, the Board only made public about 60 of its decisions (out of the more than 150,000 decisions issued during that period). This completely unsatisfactory state of affairs was roundly criticized by both practitioners in this field and by academics.[254] Under mounting pressure to rectify this problem, the Board finally (as of March 2009) began to release (in redacted form) decisions resulting from contested hearings.[255] This is a very significant move on the part of the Board and the Board deserves credit for addressing this long-standing issue. Hopefully, in the future, the Board will be able to add even more value to its database by making the cases contained therein searchable by key word(s) and/or section number(s).

---

[253] Orders PO-2268 (April 24, 2004), PO-2269 (April 28, 2004), and PO-2225 (January 12, 2004).

[254] See my comments in Chapter 2 of the 7th and 8th editions of this text for a sample of some of the criticisms that have been levelled at the Board with respect to this issue.

[255] The Board considers an application to have been contested if someone from each side attends the hearing to present their case.

3

Landlords and Tenants

1. INTRODUCTION

The *Residential Tenancies Act, 2006* (R.T.A.)[1] applies only to residentialtenancies.[2] In very basic terms, a residential tenancy is created when a personwith control over premises agrees to allow another person to reside in thosepremises for a period of time, usually in exchange for payment of rent. Theperson allowing the occupancy is the "landlord" and the person renting thepremises from the landlord is the "tenant". The relationship between a landlord and tenant is governed primarily by the terms of their contract (the"tenancy agreement") and by the provisions of the R.T.A.

Not all situations, however, where one person provides living space toanother involve a landlord and tenant relationship. For instance, an employerwith a live-in helper may not fall within the jurisdiction of the R.T.A.; it maybe seen simply as a master and servant relationship and not that of a landlordand tenant. The court so held in ***Kruciak v. Antoniuk***,[3] where the owner hadsomeone living in his home in order to prepare his meals, do laundry, andotherwise look after him, and for these services, "rent-free" accommodationin one room was provided as well as the use of the house except the owner'sbedroom. The servant was not found to be a tenant.

This chapter is devoted to examining the types of persons and relationships covered by the R.T.A.

2. LANDLORD

The term "landlord,"as defined in s. 2 of the R.T.A., includes:

(a) the owner or other person permitting occupancy of a rental unit,

---

[1] S.O. 2006, c. 17.

[2] This was also true of the precursor legislation, the *Tenant Protection Act, 1997* (T.P.A.).

[3] [1946] 3 W.W.R. 252 (Man. C.A.).

(b) their heirs, assigns, personal representatives and successors in title,and
(c) a person entitled to possession of the residential complex who attempts to enforce any of the rights of a landlord.

As will be discussed in more detail later, a tenant can become the "landlord" of a sub-tenant, but not if the tenant continues to occupy the rental unit.If the tenant continues to occupy the rental unit and allows others to moveinto the unit as well, the additional occupants will be considered to be hisroommates and not his tenants.

It is sometimes assumed that any given residential complex can onlyhave one landlord. This, I think, would be too narrow an interpretation of thelaw. Take, for instance, the case of an apartment building that is owned by acorporation (let's call it "ABC Ltd.") but run, on a day-to-day basis, by aproperty management company hired by the owner. By the definition contained in the R.T.A., *both* ABC Ltd. (as the owner) *and* the property management company (as the person[4] permitting occupancy of the rental unitswithin the complex and the person entitled to possession of the complex andwho is attempting to enforce the rights of a landlord) would be considered tobe landlords of this complex. This is, in fact, quite a common scenario in myexperience. To most tenants, it is irrelevant who actually owns the complex; of their dealings will be with the property management company. Propertymanagement companies show units to prospective tenants, negotiate tenancyagreements, maintain and repair the complex, collect rent and commenceproceedings before the Landlord and Tenant Board (the "Board").

Since the term "landlord" includes successors in title, questions sometimes arise as to a new landlord's rights and responsibilities regarding eventsthat occurred prior to that landlord taking over. The Divisional Court heldthat a landlord can apply to raise the rents in a residential complex basedupon capital expenditures incurred by the previous landlord.[5] Although thisdecision was merely an endorsement of the record without any reasons, itwas a well-known decision of the Divisional Court and the Rental HousingTribunal felt constrained to follow this precedent.[6] The Landlord and TenantBoard will likely take the same position.

If a landlord can derive a benefit from the conduct of the previouslandlord, can a successor landlord also be liable for the conduct of the previouslandlord? The answer to that question is less certain. The prevailing view

[4] A corporation is, for most legal purposes, considered to be a person.

[5] *Rossvan Holdings Limited et al. v. C. McCarthy and all other tenants*, Doc. 442/94 (Ont. Div. Ct.) (unreported).

[6] *Fane v. Sawden* (Feb. 24, 2003), TNL-36220-RV, 2003 CarswellOnt 1502 (Ont. Rental Housing Trib.) refers to other Tribunal decisions in which *Rossvan* has been followed: TNL-03984 (Nov. 24, 1999) and TNL-27000 (Oct. 10, 2001).

under the *Landlord and Tenant Act* was that a successor landlord is only liable to a tenant for an abatement of rent from the date the successor landlord acquires the property.[7] In *Tenants of 10 Shallmar Blvd. v. Shallmar Court Apartments Inc.*,[8] the Rental Housing Tribunal held that a current landlord is not responsible for breaches of the Act by the former landlord. In the same decision, the Member also concluded that tenants have no right under the T.P.A. to commence an application against a person who is not a landlord at the time the application is filed. Similarly, once a landlord ceases to be a landlord of a residential complex, that former landlord loses the right to commence any applications under the T.P.A. (now the R.T.A.).[9]

One might then wonder about rent or a rent deposit that was collected by the previous landlord. Is a new landlord responsible for money that was collected illegally by the previous landlord or for money that ought to have been held in trust by the former landlord and, presumably, was accounted for in the transfer of the property? In *Blizzard v. Hanford Holdings Ltd. Partnership*,[10] a new landlord was ordered to repay excess (i.e., illegal) rent collected by the previous landlord. In *Spencer Properties Ltd. v. Zrebeic*,[11] a new landlord purchased the building and brought an application to force the tenants to provide one month's rent deposit. The tenants argued that they had already provided such a deposit to the previous landlord. In finding in favour of the tenants, the Court held that the mandatory requirement to apply such deposits to the last month's rent creates an implied covenant which, pursuant to s. 88 of the *Landlord and Tenant Act* (now s. 18 of the R.T.A.), runs with the land and binds an assignee of the landlord. Applying the doctrine of *caveat emptor* ("let the buyer beware") in light of the implied covenant that the Court had found to exist, the Court concluded that the landlord should have satisfied itself, at the time of purchasing the apartment building, as to the existence of security deposits, and it failed to do so.

Different considerations may apply when the new landlord is a mortgagee who takes control of the residential complex; this will be discussed below under the heading "Mortgagee in Possession".

3 — LANDLORDS AND TENANTS

---

[7] *Prenor Trust Co. of Canada v. Forrest* (1993), [1993] O.J. No. 1058, 1993 CarswellOnt 3653 (Ont. Gen. Div.); *981673 Ontario Ltd. v. Jessome* (1994), [1994] O.J. No. 3039, 1994 CarswellOnt 1812 (Ont. Gen. Div.); *Graff v. Dama* (1995), [1995] O.J. No. 452, 1995 CarswellOnt 2428 (Ont. Gen. Div.); *CIBC Trust Corp. v. Mullings* (1996), [1996] O.J. No. 197, 1996 CarswellOnt 175 (Ont. Gen. Div.); and *Alta Place Property Inc. v. MacMillan* (1997), [1997] O.J. No. 911, 1997 CarswellOnt 644 (Ont. Gen. Div.).

[8] (Aug. 25, 2000), TNT-00632 and TNT-00677, 2000 CarswellOnt 4422 (Ont. Rental Housing Trib.).

[9] *Metro Capital v. Douglas* (Mar. 9, 2001), SWL-23877 (Ont. Rental Housing Trib.).

[10] (May 1, 2003), TST-05739, 2003 CarswellOnt 2656 (Ont. Rental Housing Trib.).

[11] (1992), [1992] O.J. No. 2944, 1992 CarswellOnt 1760 (Ont. Gen. Div.).

3. TENANT

The term "tenant" as defined in s. 2(1) of the R.T.A., includes a person who pays rent in return for the right to occupy a rental unit and includes the tenant's heirs, assigns and personal representatives, but "tenant" does not include a person who has the right to occupy a rental unit by virtue of being,

(a) a co-owner of the residential complex in which the rental unit is located, or
(b) a shareholder of a corporation that owns the residential complex.

Because the definition of tenant uses the term "includes", it is meant to be illustrative rather than exhaustive.

The absence of an agreement to pay rent, for instance, will not always determine whether or not a landlord and tenant relationship exists.[12] The fact that a person has lived in a rental unit, even for a long time, does not necessarily make him a tenant;[13] he may have simply been living with the tenant. Also, a tenant is defined as a person who has the *right* to occupy the rental unit. By s. 13 of the R.T.A., a tenancy commences on the day the tenant is entitled to occupy the rental unit, whether or not the tenant actually occupies it. Therefore, it is possible to be a tenant of a rental unit but to have never lived in the unit.

The fact that a person has paid rent to a landlord does not necessarily mean that he is a tenant; although rent is usually paid to a landlord *by* a tenant, it can also be paid *on behalf* of a tenant. Some landlords are reluctant to accept money from a person who is not the tenant listed on the tenancy agreement for fear that it will later be determined by the Board that the landlord accepted this person as a tenant. This concern, and the proper method of dealing with such situations, was discussed in *Parkway Realty Ltd. v. Jani.*[14] In *Jani*, the landlord refused to accept rent payments from the wife of the tenant for fear of making her a tenant. It was held that this was a failure to mitigate on the part of the landlord and that the proper course would have been to accept the money as paid on behalf of the tenant and put the wife and tenant on written notice that the landlord was not creating or acknowledging the existence of any tenancy agreement with the wife. Other typical cases where rent is paid on behalf of the tenant involve payments made by welfare or other government agencies. The fact that the rent is paid for a tenant by

---

[12] *Kizemchuk v. Kizemchuk* (2000), 2000 CarswellOnt 2547 (Ont. Div. Ct.) (re TSL-11717).

[13] *Belleau v. Victoria Park Community Homes* (Jan. 11, 1999), SOT-00229 (Ont. Rental Housing Trib.).

[14] (March 23, 2000), TNL-13873, [2000] O.R.H.T.D. No. 46, 2000 CarswellOnt 6357 (Ont. Rental Housing Trib.).

such an agency does not make the welfare agency the tenant (unless the agency itself enters into the tenancy agreement with the landlord).[15]

Although the definition of "tenant" includes the tenant's heirs and personal representatives, a tenancy cannot be passed on to such persons upon the death of the tenant. The provisions of s. 91 of the R.T.A. (formerly s. 49 of the T.P.A.) take priority and stipulate that the tenancy "shall be deemed to be terminated" 30 days after the death of the tenant.[16] During that 30-day period, however, the heirs or personal representatives of the deceased tenant become "tenants" of the rental unit and, thus, during that period have the same rights and obligations as other tenants in the complex. There may be an exception for the tenant's surviving spouse (please see "Protection for the Spouse of a Tenant" below).

Trespassers on residential premises were not entitled to the protection of Part IV of the *Landlord and Tenant Act*[17] and are not protected by the R.T.A.

In *Hamilton et al. v. 611283 Ontario Ltd.*,[18] K.H. took on the identity of her sister (who had a better credit history) and kept up this pretence for almost a year. At some point, K.H. moved out and allowed her boyfriend to remain in the unit. When he left the country (temporarily), the landlord discovered the truth about these people and, treating the tenancy as a nullity, simply changed the locks and took back possession. In the unique circumstances of this case, it was held that there was no valid tenancy and that K.H. and her boyfriend were not entitled to any relief under the T.P.A.

4. TENANT "IN POSSESSION"

As discussed in Chapter 2, a landlord with a potential claim against a tenant must decide where to pursue that claim (i.e., in which forum). In broad terms, a landlord will generally be seeking one or both of the following remedies:

(1) an order that will enable the landlord to regain possession of the rental unit; and
(2) an order for the payment of money.

A "money order" will usually represent an order for payment of arrears of rent owing to the landlord or for payment of compensation for damage to the rental unit or residential complex . Under the T.P.A. (ss. 86, 87 and 88), a landlord's right to commence an application for monetary compensation was

[15] *Park Realty Ltd. v. Mentuck* (1981), 10 Man. R. (2d) 380 (Man. Co. Ct.).

[16] *1500 Tansley C/O Lakeshore Management v. Smith* (Aug. 22, 2002), SOL-33570, 2002 CarswellOnt 3788 (Ont. Rental Housing Trib.).

[17] *Phillips v. Kranjcec* (1977), 4 C.P.C. 91 (Ont. H.C.).

[18] (Nov. 26, 2001), TNT-02353 (Ont. Rental Housing Trib.).

contingent upon the tenant being *in possession* of the rental unit at the time the application was commenced. If the tenant was not in possession, the landlord would have to pursue a claim in court for damages. This principle (that the tenant must be in possession of the rental unit at the time such applications are commenced) has been carried forward into the R.T.A. (ss. 87, 89 and 90).

In *George V. Apartments Ltd. v. Cobb* (*"George V"*),[19] the landlord served a notice of termination upon the tenant but the tenant did not vacate the unit by the termination date and the landlord did not commence an application based upon the notice. Therefore, the notice of termination became void. The tenant then announced she would be vacating the unit in mid-November (giving approximately three weeks notice). The tenant did not pay any rent for November, expecting her last month's deposit to cover that month (which she considered to be the last month of the tenancy). Before the tenant moved out of the rental unit (i.e., while she was still in possession of the rental unit), the landlord filed an application for an order for arrears of rent (i.e., but not seeking to terminate the tenancy). The Member held that November was the last month of the tenancy and that the rent deposit covered that rent. On appeal by the landlord, the Divisional Court held that, absent a valid notice of termination, the tenancy was not terminated and the landlord need *not* apply the rent deposit to cover November's rent (since November was *not* the last month of the tenancy). This decision has since been followed in numerous decisions of the Tribunal.[20]

George V had far-reaching implications. It confirmed that a tenant cannot end a tenancy either through a defective notice of termination or by simply moving out. As a result of *George V*, rather than having to commence proceedings in court for damages where a tenant "skipped out", landlords were able to go to the Tribunal and obtain an order for any rent owing to the landlord up to the date that the landlord was able to find a new tenant for the vacated rental unit.[21] For the Tribunal to grant relief to the landlord, however,the landlord still had to prove that the tenant was in possession of the rental unit at the time the application was commenced. What concerned some tenant advocates about the *George V* decision, was that it left tenants who failed to terminate their tenancies in accordance with the strict provisions of the *Tenant Protection Act* potentially liable for the rent on the unit for an indefinite period (i.e., until the landlord was able to re-rent the unit for a comparable rent).

---

[19] (2002), 2002 CarswellOnt 5553 (Ont. Div. Ct.).

[20] See for example *Mitt, Re* (March 10, 2006), TET-05493, 2006 CarswellOnt 2141, [2006] O.RH.T.D. No. 22 (Ont. Rental Housing Trib.) and *Stlascht & Deutschmann Ltd. v. Quesnel* (June 22, 2006), SWL-81278, [2006] O.R.H.T.D. No. 67, 2006 CarswellOnt 4429 (Ont. Rental Housing Trib.).

[21] Subject to the landlord's obligation to mitigate its losses (s. 13 of the T.P.A.).

The Legislature has attempted to address this latter concern by the introduction into the *Residential Tenancies Act* of a limit on a tenant's liability for rent arrears where the tenant has provided a defective notice of termination or no notice of termination to the landlord. Section 88 of the R.T.A. now places a "cap" upon a tenant's maximum liability for arrears of rent in circumstances where the tenancy was not properly terminated by the tenant (see Chapter 13 for a more detailed analysis of the provisions of s. 88).

Section 88 of the R.T.A. sets a limit on a tenant's liability for arrears of rent where the tenancy has not been properly terminated and it also establishes a method of calculating arrears of rent in such cases. It does not expand the jurisdiction of the Board. Therefore, for the Board to have the jurisdiction to grant *any* relief to a landlord for arrears of rent, the tenant must still be "in possession" of the unit at the time the application is commenced (s. 87(1)(b)of the R.T.A.).

Similarly, for the Board to have jurisdiction to grant relief to a landlord for damage to the premises (s. 89 of the R.T.A.) or for misrepresentation of income in rent-geared-to-income housing (s. 90 of the R.T.A.), the tenant must be "in possession" of the rental unit at the time the application is commenced.

Thus, cases under the *Landlord and Tenant Act* and the T.P.A. that discuss the issue of when a tenant can be considered to be "in possession" ofthe rental unit remain relevant and important under the R.T.A. One of the more difficult issues facing landlords is whether or not an application for relief under what are now ss. 87, 89 and 90 of the R.T.A. can be commenced after the tenant has vacated the unit. Can such a tenant still be considered to be "in possession" of the unit even if the tenant is no longer residing at the unit?

One of the hallmarks of possession is control over the unit. If the tenant has moved out of the rental unit but has not returned to the landlord the key(s) to the unit (and if the landlord has done nothing inconsistent with its position that the tenancy continues), the Board could find that the tenant is still in possession of the rental unit. This issue was considered by the Divisional Court in the case of *Tenser v. Norquay Developments Limited*.[22] On August26, 2003, the tenant provided written notice to the landlord that he intended to terminate his tenancy on September 1, 2003. He vacated the unit on August 30, 2003. He did not return the rental unit keys to the landlord. The tenant was aware that the locks to all units in the complex were being changed on September 2, 2003, and that keys to the altered locks would be provided by the landlord to all tenants on that date. On September 9, 2003, the landlord applied for arrears of rent for the months of August and September 2003.

The crucial issue, both at first instance and on appeal to Divisional Court, was whether the tenant was "in possession" of the rental unit on the date that

[22] (November 9, 2004), Doc. London 1426 (Ont. Div. Ct.) (re SWL-52858).

3 — LANDLORDS AND TENANTS

the application was commenced by the landlord (since the landlord would have no right to commence such an application if the tenant were not in possession of the unit). On this issue, the Divisional Court agreed with the Tribunal's finding that the tenant was still in possession of the rental unit. The retention by the tenant of the keys to the unit and mailbox, his right to obtain a key to the new lock and his continuing right to occupy the unit were indicia of his ability to gain access to and control over the unit. This decision confirmed that a tenant can be deemed to be "in possession" of a rental unit without actually occupying or having immediate physical control of the unit.

This reasoning has generally been accepted by the Landlord and Tenant Board, as it was by the Rental Housing Tribunal. Where a tenant has clearly vacated the rental unit and returned the keys to the landlord, barring unusual circumstances, the Board will find that the tenant ceased to be "in possession" of the unit on the day the unit was vacated and any application commenced by the landlord after that date (pursuant to s. 87, 89 or 90 of the R.T.A.) will be dismissed.[23]

Of course, if the landlord changes the locks, prevents the tenant from re-entering the unit or begins major renovations to the unit without the knowledge or consent of the tenant, this is inconsistent with the landlord's argument that the tenant has retained control over the unit.

In *Yaganeh v. Sabra Properties*[24] the tenants vacated the unit in late-September 2000 without giving the landlord a proper written notice of termination. When the tenants were advised that they would be responsible for October's rent (i.e., that the rent deposit would be applied to the rent owing for October as the landlord considered October to be the last month of the tenancy), the tenants asked to be allowed back into the unit to use it for the month of October. The landlord refused to allow the tenants back into the unit. The Tribunal found the landlord's conduct to be inconsistent with its argument that the tenancy continued past September and ordered the refund of the tenant's rent deposit.

The situation may become even more complex where several tenants are under one tenancy agreement. What if one tenant has moved out of the rental unit but the other tenants have remained in the unit? Can the landlord commence an application against all the tenants named in the lease and can the landlord obtain an order for the payment of money against all of them? The Ontario Court of Appeal answered these questions in *1162994 Ontario Inc.*

---

[23] See, for example: Landlord and Tenant Board File No. SOL-00170 (March 6, 2007); Landlord and Tenant Board File No. EAL-00303 (March 15, 2007); Landlord and Tenant Board File No. EAL-00294 (March 15, 2007); Landlord and Tenant Board File No. CEL-00418 (March 28, 2007); Landlord and Tenant Board File No. SWL-00542 (March 16, 2007); Landlord and Tenant Board File No. TNL-15859 (Feb. 20, 2009); Landlord and Tenant Board File No. SOL-18374 (March 3, 2009); and Landlord and Tenant Board File No. TNL-20521 (Feb. 13, 2009).

[24] (Feb. 6, 2001), TNT-01459, 2001 CarswellOnt 6283 (Ont. Rental Housing Trib.).

v. Bakker.[25] In the *Bakker* case, four tenants originally signed the lease. At the time the landlord filed an application for arrears of rent, unbeknownst to the landlord, three of the original tenants had moved out and been "replaced" by other people. On appeal, the Divisional Court held that as long as one of the original tenants was still in possession of the unit, they were all deemed to be in possession and, therefore, all four (original) tenants remained jointly liable for the debt. On further appeal, the Tribunal's original order was restored. The Court of Appeal upheld the original decision of the Tribunal that removed from the application three of the tenants on the basis that they were not in possession of the rental unit at the time the application was commenced. The Court of Appeal ruled that whether the tenants are jointly and severally liable under the tenancy agreement (i.e., whether they owe rent) is a different issue than whether the landlord has the right to commence an application under the T.P.A. against tenants who are no longer in possession of the rental unit. The Court wrote as follows:

> I think the requirement that the tenant be "in possession of the rental unit" at the time of the application reflects a determination that rent arrears disputes can be resolved efficiently and fairly through the Tribunal where the tenant at the time of the application continues to have some connection with the rental unit and, therefore, some relationship with the landlord. Situations where the connection has been severed and the relationship is gone are best resolved through the more formal court processes.

The *Bakker* decision has been followed by the Tribunal in *Delisle Holdings v. Ferry*,[26] *Carter v. Patterson*[27] and *Miller v. Carlyle II Rental Pool*[28] and by the Landlord and Tenant Board in File Number SWL-14748 (June 5, 2008).

In *Boardwalk General Partnership, Re*,[29] the Member purports to distinguish the facts of this case from *Bakker* on the basis that the tenant vacated the unit in the middle of the initial term of the tenancy. It was held that, in such a case, the landlord could commence an application for arrears of rent at the Tribunal even though the tenant had moved out because the tenant was

---

25 (2004), [2004] O.J. No. 2565, 2004 CarswellOnt 869 (Ont. C.A.) (re SWL-40290).

26 (July 22, 2004), TSL-58363, 2004 CarswellOnt 3620, [2004] O.R.H.T.D. No. 23 (Ont. Rental Housing Trib.).

27 (Sept. 27, 2004), TEL-42067-RV, 2004 CarswellOnt 5463 (Ont. Rental Housing Trib.). The tenants moved out prior to the landlord filing his application. The tenants had not returned the keys to the unit but they were no longer using or occupying the unit. Following the *Bakker* decision, the Member ruled that the tenants were not in possession of the rental unit at the time the application was commenced. The application was, therefore, dismissed.

28 (Aug. 6, 2004), CET-039997 and CEL-36003-SA-RV, 2004 CarswellOnt 3643 (Ont. Rental Housing Trib.).

29 (July 26, 2006), SWL-82124, [2006] O.R.H.T.D. No. 86, 2006 CarswellOnt 9163 (Ont. Rental Housing Trib.).

constructively "in possession" of the unit "by virtue of the lease" that was "still in force". The Member held that this was distinguishable from the facts in *Bakker* where the lease "had already expired" by the time the landlord commenced proceedings.

The Member fails to consider that at the end of the initial term of a tenancy agreement, unless the parties agree otherwise, it is deemed to renew as a periodic tenancy (month-by-month) on the same terms and conditions. I am not sure in what sense the tenancy agreement in *Bakker* can be considered to have "expired". I fail to see a meaningful distinction between a tenant who vacates the unit without giving proper notice during the initial term of the tenancy and a tenant who does so after the initial term. In my view, the reasoning in this decision is not persuasive and Members of the Board are still obliged to follow the decision of the Ontario Court of Appeal in *Bakker*.

The *Bakker* decision has been criticized by some landlords for making a complex situation even more complex. The most common criticisms of this decision are summarized below.

First, *Bakker* does not allow for "one-stop shopping"; that is, a landlord-could not come to the Tribunal (now the Board) for *all* claims arising from a residential tenancy. Although many claims could be brought to the Tribunal, others would have to be pursued (if at all) by way of court proceedings. In reality, this was not new. The requirement that a tenant be in possession of the rental unit in order for a landlord to commence an application under ss. 86, 87 and 88 of the T.P.A. existed since the enactment of the T.P.A. All that*Bakker* really did was address situations where some of the tenants listed on the tenancy agreement had permanently moved out of the unit prior to the commencement of the application. In such a case, the Divisional Court ruled that the landlord could commence an application in the Tribunal against the tenants who were still in possession of the rental unit but not against the tenants who were no longer in possession. If, according to the tenancy agreement, the liability of the tenants is joint and several, the landlord would be able to obtain an order for the *entire* debt against the tenants who remained in possession. It would then be up to those tenants to decide whether they wished to try to collect some money from the co-tenants who vacated the rental unit prior to the commencement of the landlord's application.

Second, although the *Bakker* decision reinforced that a landlord did not have the right to commence an application under the T.P.A. against a tenant who was no longer in possession of the rental unit, *the Court did not define "possession"*. This term was not defined in the T.P.A. (nor is it defined in the R.T.A.). Few cases are directly on point, but as described earlier in this Chapter, the case law suggests that it is possible for a tenant to be considered in possession of a rental unit although not actually residing in the unit at the time the application is commenced.

Third, the *Bakker* decision does not seem to "mesh" well with the approach mandated by the Divisional Court in *George V.*[30] *George V* stood for the proposition that a tenant continues to be liable under the terms of a tenancy if the tenancy has not been properly terminated (such as where the tenant abandons the unit) but *Bakker* suggested that a landlord could not commence an application in the Rental Housing Tribunal for arrears of rent against tenants who had already vacated the rental unit.

In one case,[31] a Member of the Tribunal attempted to distinguish the facts of the case before him from those of *Bakker*. He held that since *Bakker* was a case in which the tenancy was month-to-month but the case before him was still during the initial term of the tenancy, he was not obliged to follow *Bakker*and could make an order against both tenants even though one of the two tenants was no longer in possession of the rental unit. The Member does not explain why, in law, it makes a difference whether the tenancy in question is periodic or for a fixed term in deciding whether or not the tenant was in possession of the rental unit at the time the application was commenced. Personally, I do not find this Member's reasoning to be persuasive and I prefer the approach taken in *Delisle Holdings v. Ferry*[32] (in which, in similar circumstances, the Tribunal found that it was bound by the *Bakker* decision).

In a more recent decision,[33] a Member of the Board again tried to distinguish the case before him on its facts from those in the *Bakker* decision. The Member found that since the two tenants were jointly and severally liable, even though one of the tenants claimed that he had vacated the rental unit, he still ought to be considered a tenant. Of course, in *Bakker*, the tenants may also have been jointly and severally liable and I fail to see how a person's potential liability in contract establishes that that person in fact continues to be "in possession" of the rental unit. The Member also states that both tenants remained "involved" with the rental unit but fails to elaborate on the nature of that involvement. Ultimately, it seems to me that the Member was placing the onus upon the tenant who was alleging that he was no longer in possession of the unit to prove that fact (in part, by providing evidence that he had established a residence elsewhere) and the Member found that the tenant had failed to meet that evidentiary burden.

Ultimately, what does all this mean? I would draw the following conclusions from the interplay of the Court decisions as well as the new provisions contained in s. 88 of the R.T.A.:

1. (a) Where a tenant has given a defective notice of termination or

---

[30] *George V. Apartments Ltd. v. Cobb* (2002), 2002 CarswellOnt 5553 (Ont. Div. Ct.).

[31] *Boardwalk General Partnership v. Dye* (July 26, 2006), SWL-82125, [2006] O.R.H.T.D. No. 87, 2006 CarswellOnt 9163 (Ont. Rental Housing Trib.).

[32] 2004 CarswellOnt 3620 (Ont. Rental Housing Trib.).

[33] Landlord and Tenant Board File No. TNL-20986 (Jan. 29, 2009).

3 — LANDLORDS AND TENANTS

where the tenant has verbally advised the landlord of the tenant's intention to vacate the unit but delivers no written notice of termination, a prudent landlord will ensure that it commences its application with the Board (under ss. 87, 89 or 90 of the R.T.A.) while the tenant is still residing in the rental unit. In that way, there will be no doubt that the tenant was "in possession" of the unit at the time the application was commenced.

(b) If the application is under s. 87 of the R.T.A., there must actually be arrears of rent when the application is commenced. There is no provision for commencing an application based upon the landlord's expectation that there will be rent owing at some point in the future, based on events that have not yet occurred. Since most tenants incorrectly assume that the rent deposit will cover the month that he or she is moving out, there usually will be at least one month's rent owing in these cases.[34] Section 88 determines how the arrears are to be calculated and sets a limit on the maximum amount that can be ordered in such cases.

2. Where the tenant has given no warning and has simply vacated the unit or where the landlord has otherwise failed to commence an application under s. 87, 89 or 90 of the R.T.A. prior to the tenant-vacating the unit, the landlord may still commence an application at the Board *if and only if* the landlord can demonstrate that the tenant somehow remained "in possession" of the unit at the time the application is commenced (usually by proving that the tenant retained some control over the rental unit). Otherwise, the landlord should pursue the claim by way of court action and not in an application to the Landlord and Tenant Board.

3. If there are several tenants listed on the tenancy agreement and some of them have moved away, an application filed by the landlord with the Board should probably only seek an order for the payment of money against the tenant(s) who actually remain in possession of the unit (*Bakker*). Tenants who the landlord knows vacated the rental unit prior to the commencement of the application and who have not retained any control over the unit should not be named as respondents to the application.

Finally, where the issue arises at a hearing before the Landlord and Tenant Board as to whether a tenant was in possession of the rental unit at the time

[34] A rent deposit must be applied to the last rental period (s. 106(10) of the R.T.A.). If the tenant has failed to properly terminate the tenancy by delivering a valid notice of termination, the period in which they vacate the unit will not actually be the *last* period of the tenancy; the tenancy continues (*George V*). Therefore, the landlord need not apply the deposit in payment of the rent for that period and the tenant will be in arrears of rent.

the application was commenced, the presiding Board Member must make a finding on this issue. The failure to specifically make a finding of fact as to whether the tenant was in possession of the rental unit at the time the application was commenced has been considered by the Divisional Court to be a reversible error.[35]

5. PROTECTION FOR THE SPOUSE OF A TENANT (NEW)

It is not uncommon, especially in older tenancies, for only one spouse to be listed on the tenancy agreement as the "tenant". If that person then dies, can the landlord treat that person's surviving spouse as a mere occupant of the rental unit who has no right to remain in the unit? This problem has arisen from time to time and, until recently, there was no guidance provided by the governing legislation. Subsection 3(1) of the O. Reg. 516/06 now provides that:

> If a tenant of a rental unit dies and the rental unit is the principal residence ofthe spouse of that tenant, the spouse is included in the definition of "tenant" insubsection 2(1) of the Act unless the spouse vacates the unit within the 30-day period described in subsection 91(1) of the Act.

This permits the surviving spouse (who is not listed on the tenancy agreement as a tenant) the option of either vacating the unit within 30 days of the death of the tenant or remaining in the unit as a "tenant", with all of the rights and obligations that entails. However, pursuant to subsection 3(4) of O. Reg. 516/06, surviving spouses have no such protection in cases of social housing,[36] care homes[37] and certain types of government housing.[38]

In cases where only one person is listed as the tenant on a tenancy agreement, it is also not uncommon (usually in cases where there is a breakdown in the relationship) for that person to simply vacate the rental unit and leave their spouse behind without providing any notice of termination to the landlord and without agreeing with the landlord that the tenancy will be terminated. In such cases, if the rental unit is the principal residence of the tenant's spouse, the spouse shall now be deemed to be a "tenant"[39] (with allof the rights and obligations of a tenant that entails) *unless*:

1. the rental unit is in a building that contains three or fewer residential units and the landlord resides in the building;[40]

[35] *Kissell v. Milosevic* (2008), 2008 CarswellOnt 3300 (Ont. Div. Ct.).

[36] I.e., a rental unit described in s. 7 of the R.T.A.

[37] I.e., a rental unit that is in a care home to which Part IX of the R.T.A. applies.

[38] I.e., a rental unit to which s. 6 of O. Reg. 516/06 applies.

[39] Subsection 3(2) of O. Reg. 516/06.

[40] Paragraph 3(3)1 of O. Reg. 516/06.

2. the spouse vacates the rental unit no later than 60 days after the tenant vacated the rental unit;[41]
3. the tenant who vacated the rental unit was not in arrears of rent, the landlord commences an application under s. 100 of the R.T.A. to terminate the tenancy because the tenant has transferred occupancy of the rental unit without the consent of the landlord, the spouse who remains in the unit does not oppose that application or otherwise indicate that he or she intends to remain in the rental unit and the Board issues an order terminating the tenancy under s. 100;[42]
4. the tenant who vacated the rental unit was in arrears of rent, the landlord gives the spouse a notice (in a form approved by the Board) within 45 days after the date the tenant vacated the unit and the spouse fails, within 15 days after receiving the notice:

   i. to advise the landlord that he or she intends to remain in the rental unit; or
   ii. to agree in writing with the landlord to pay the arrears of rent;[43]

5. the tenant who vacated the rental unit was in arrears of rent, the landlord does not give the spouse a notice but brings an application to terminate the tenancy under s. 100 of the R.T.A. (for an unauthorized transfer of occupancy) and the spouse fails, before the order under s. 100 is issued:

   i. to advise the landlord that he or she intends to remain in the rental unit; or
   ii. to agree in writing with the landlord to pay the arrears of rent;[44]

6. the tenancy falls within one of the following: social housing, a care home or certain types of government housing.[45]

For further analysis, please refer to "Joint and Several Liability and the Evolution of a Tenancy" in Chapter 5.

6. ROOMMATES

The R.T.A. is meant to govern the relationship between landlords and tenants and sets out the rights and responsibilities of each. The Landlord and Tenant Board is given exclusive jurisdiction over all residential tenancies that are not specifically excluded from the Act.

---

[41] Paragraph 3(3)2 of O. Reg. 516/06.
[42] Paragraph 3(3)3 of O. Reg. 516/06.
[43] Paragraph 3(3)4 of O. Reg. 516/06.
[44] Paragraph 3(3)5 of O. Reg. 516/06.
[45] Subsection 3(4) of O. Reg. 516/06.

The definition of "landlord" specifically excludes a "tenant occupying a rental unit". Although a tenant can become the landlord of a subtenant, if the head tenant continues to occupy the rental unit, it will not be considered as ublet[46] and, therefore, a new landlord and tenant relationship will not have been created. It will be viewed as a tenant sharing his or her unit with a roommate. If a dispute arises between the roommates, neither has the right to file an application with the Board because the R.T.A. does not apply to their relationship.[47]

Even with these definitions, cases can still arise where it is difficult to properly characterize the relationship between the parties. What if the tenant rents out part of his or her space to another person or turns one unit into more than one unit? Leaving aside the issue of remedies the landlord may have against the tenant for altering the rental unit without the landlord's consent, the question remains as to the nature of the relationship between the original tenant and the person who rents space from that tenant. Does the original tenant become the landlord of the new occupant? Is it wrong to characterize the head tenant as a "landlord" because he still occupies part of the original rental unit? Should the new occupant be denied the protection of the R.T.A. because his "landlord" created a distinct rental accommodation without the permission of the owner of the house? Should the two tenants be treated as roommates?[48] Is it possible to sublet a portion of the original rental unit? None of these issues is specifically addressed in the R.T.A. or its regulations. Since these questions go to the very jurisdiction of the Board, when there is a dispute between such parties, Members will have to carefully define the boundaries of the rental unit in question and make a determination as to whether or not there exists a landlord and tenant relationship between the original tenant and additional person(s) that the original tenant later brought into the premises. Each case will turn upon its own facts.

7. SUBLETS AND ASSIGNMENTS

(a) General

The terms "sublet" and "assignment" are often confused. They are related, but very different, concepts.

When a tenant *sublets* his rental unit, he is renting his unit to someone else for a period no longer than the term of the head lease. The head tenant

[46] See s. 2(2) of the R.T.A.

[47] *Chung v. Mondville* (Aug. 24, 1998), TSL-00415 (Ont. Rental Housing Trib.); *Thompson v. Carpenter* (Oct. 2, 1998), TSL-02200 (Ont. Rental Housing Trib.); Landlord and Tenant Board File No. TNT-01407 (Jan. 16, 2008).

[48] This was the conclusion reached in *Greig v. Matthews* (Oct. 11, 2000), TNL-19827 and TNT-01368, 2000 CarswellOnt 5591, [2000] O.R.H.T.D. No. 140 (Ont. Rental Housing Trib.).

vacates the rental unit but has the express intention of returning and taking back the unit before the expiration of the head lease. There is no contract between the subtenant and the head landlord. The head tenant becomes the landlord of the subtenant but the head tenant is still responsible to the head landlord for all obligations under their tenancy agreement, including the payment of rent (s. 97(4) of the R.T.A.). The subtenant has no greater rights than the head tenant. The subtenancy is subordinate to the main tenancy. Thus, if the main tenancy is terminated, the subtenancy will also end.

When a tenant *assigns* her rental unit, she is having someone else permanently take over the tenancy agreement. The original tenant retains no right to later return and reassert control over the rental unit. The new tenant is bound by the terms of the original tenancy agreement. Although there is a new tenant, a new tenancy agreement does not exist; therefore, the landlord cannot raise the rent as a result of the assignment (s. 113 of the R.T.A.).

If a tenant wishes to be released early from a tenancy agreement, then what he or she really wants to do (short of reaching an agreement with the landlord to terminate the tenancy) is to assign the tenancy to someone else. This will take the original tenant completely out of the picture. By way of contrast, a sublet will still leave the original tenant legally responsible to the landlord for the balance of the term of the tenancy.[49]

To clarify matters, the term "sublet" is defined in s. 2(2) of the R.T.A."Sublet" refers to a situation in which:

i. the tenant vacates the rental unit;
ii. the tenant gives one or more other persons the right to occupy the rental unit for a term ending on a specified date before the end of the tenant's term or period; and
iii. the tenant has the right to resume occupancy of the rental unit on that specified date.

A few important points from the above definition are worth noting.

First, the tenant must vacate the rental unit; the R.T.A. does not apply to disputes between the tenant and other persons with whom the tenant shares the rental unit (i.e., disputes between roommates).[50]

Second, the subtenancy must have a specified end date and that date must be *before* the end of the head tenancy. This detail is often overlooked by tenants who wish to sublet their unit.

---

[49] See *Fisher Kay Ltd. v. Haggert et al.* (Nov. 20, 2000), TNL-20362 (Ont. Rental Housing Trib.), in which the tenant was held responsible for damage caused to the rental unit by the subtenant and guests of the subtenant.

[50] The Legislature also amended the definition of "landlord" under the T.P.A. (and now the R.T.A.) to exclude a tenant occupying a rental unit.

A tenant does not have an absolute right to sublet or assign a rental unit. Consent must be obtained from the landlord. The landlord must act reasonably in dealing with a request from a tenant to assign or sublet the rental unit.

The question of whether or not the landlord is unreasonably withholding consent depends on the circumstances of each case and includes the personal relationship as between the lessor and lessee, and the nature of the user of the property: *Cowitz v. Siegel*.[51] The landlord cannot refuse consent on grounds entirely personal to the landlord and wholly extraneous to the lessee. Another way of putting it is that the landlord should be able to withhold consent to an assignment or subletting which might result in the premises being used or occupied in an undesirable way or by an undesirable tenant. However, the landlord is not limited to these grounds, as all the circumstances of his refusal will be considered: *Shields v. Dickler*.[52]

It is up to the tenant to prove that the landlord has unreasonably withheld consent. The burden is on the tenant, not on the landlord.[53]

An acceptable reason for a landlord refusing consent to an assignment was found when the landlord had a waiting list for apartments and a policy of allotting vacant apartments to persons at the top of the waiting list: *Burns v. Belmont Construction Co.*[54]

In *Colasanti v. Katz*,[55] the court indicated there is a broader approach to the surrounding circumstances within the reasonable person standard.

In *Bowley v. McMenemy*,[56] the tenant's right to sublet was refused. The tenant applied to the Tribunal. The property was a large house and all tenants were female. The tenant wished to sublet to a male. The Tribunal found that the Landlord's refusal in these circumstances was not unreasonable.

If a landlord discovers that a tenant has transferred occupancy of the rental unit to someone else without the landlord's consent, the landlord has three choices. First, the landlord can accept the person as a tenant and (within 60 days of discovering the presence of the unauthorized occupant) negotiate a new tenancy agreement.[57] Second, the landlord can commence proceedings (within 60 days of discovering the presence of the unauthorized occupant) to evict the occupant of the rental unit.[58] Third, the landlord can do nothing. If, within 60 days, the landlord has not negotiated a new tenancy or filed an application to remove the unauthorized occupant, the landlord will be deemed to have consented to the assignment or sublet, as the case may be.[59] Similarly,

[51] [1954] O.W.N. 833 (Ont. C.A.).

[52] [1948] O.W.N. 145 (Ont. C.A.).

[53] *Moore v. New Progress Construction Ltd.* (1980), 9 Man. R. (2d) 434 (Man. Co. Ct.).

[54] (1987), 4 T.L.L.R. 15 (Ont. Dist. Ct.).

[55] (1996), 1 R.P.R. (3d) 200 (Ont. Gen. Div.).

[56] (May 3, 1999), SWT-00495 (Ont. Rental Housing Trib.).

[57] Subsections 104(1) and (2) of the R.T.A. (formerly ss. 125(1) and (2) of the T.P.A.).

[58] Section 100 of the R.T.A. (formerly s. 81 of the T.P.A.).

[59] Subsection 104(4) of the R.T.A. (formerly subsection 125(4) of the T.P.A.).

if a landlord accepts rent after knowing of a subletting this will amount to a waiver of the right to forfeiture or refusal of consent: *Capitalex Holding Inc. v. Gartamk Investments Ltd.*[60]

The statutory right that a tenant may assign or sublet does not apply to any rental units described in s. 7 of the R.T.A., presumably because such-housing is set aside for persons with special needs and/or low incomes and there are long waiting lists for such housing.

(b) Sublets

Subletting is dealt with in s. 97 of the R.T.A. (formerly s. 18 of the T.P.A.). Subtenants whose subtenancy has been consented to by the landlord are included in the R.T.A. in s. 2 (under the definition of subtenant) and s. 97.

Subsection 97(1) states that, "A tenant may sublet a rental unit to another person with the consent of the landlord." A landlord cannot arbitrarily or unreasonably withhold consent to the sublet of a rental unit to a potential subtenant (s. 97(2)). The landlord may only charge reasonable out of pocket expenses when giving consent (s. 97(3)).

If a landlord does arbitrarily or unreasonably refuse to consent to a sublet of a rental unit to a potential subtenant, then the tenant may commence an application to the Board for an order declaring that the landlord has violated the provisions of s. 98(1) of the Act and, pursuant to s. 98(3):

1. authorizing the proposed sublet;
2. authorizing an alternative sublet proposed by the tenant;
3. terminating the tenancy; and/or
4. granting an abatement of the tenant's or former tenants' rent.

Also, by s. 98(4) of the R.T.A., the Board may establish terms and conditions of the assignment.

If the Board authorizes it, the sublet will have the same legal effect as if the landlord had consented to it (s. 98(5)).

There were a couple of interesting Tribunal decisions dealing with the question of whether a landlord's refusal to consent to a sublet had been unreasonable or arbitrary. In *Dover v. Shkimba*,[61] the landlord refused the tenants' request to sublet the unit without making any inquiries with respect to the proposed subtenant. The landlord's mind was closed from the beginning. This was held to be unreasonable and the Tribunal authorized the proposed sublet. In *Bowley v. McMenemy*,[62] the rental unit had been rented to seven female tenants who shared one bathroom. One of the tenants re-

---

[60] (1975), 11 O.R. (2d) 578 (Ont. H.C.).

[61] (March 1, 2005), TST-07738, 2005 CarswellOnt 1290 (Ont. Rental Housing Trib.).

[62] (May 3, 1999), SWT-00495 (Ont. Rental Housing Trib.).

quested the landlord's consent to sublet to a male. In all of the circumstances, the Tribunal did not find to be unreasonable the landlord's decision to refuse consent to a sublet to a male person.

A landlord is entitled to charge the tenant for the landlord's reasonable out of pocket expenses incurred in giving consent to a subletting (s. 97(3)). Presumably, this is meant to cover the cost of such things as a credit or reference check on the potential subtenant. A set administrative or processing fee would not normally be considered to be an out of pocket expense "incurred" by the landlord. There are no permitted allowances for a standard charge or internal administrative procedures: *Geeves v. Keewatin Management*[63] and *Kelly v. Carslake*.[64] The reasonable expenses of a landlord might include the costs of the landlord's solicitor in drafting or approving of a subletting.

When the landlord is applying for termination of the head lease, the landlord should add the subtenant as a party in the notice of termination. The subtenant is a proper party to the application because he or she will be affected by the order being sought. Also, pursuant to s. 83(1) of the R.T.A. (formerly s. 84(1) of the T.P.A.), the Board may refuse to grant the application if it would be unfair having regard to all the circumstances.

In *Baker v. Hayward*,[65] the landlord obtained an order for possession against the head tenant because of non-payment of rent, and the subtenant applied for relief from forfeiture. The court stated that a subtenant could apply for relief from forfeiture either under s. 113(1)(*g*) of Part IV of the *Landlord and Tenant Act*, on his own application or in the landlord's application for possession, and if the landlord is applying for possession, notice of the application for possession must be served on the subtenant.

When applying to terminate the lease of a subtenant of a tenant member of a non-profit co-operative apartment, the R.T.A. does apply. It has been held in a British Columbia case that the member must comply with the *Residential Tenancy Act*,[66] even though a non-profit co-operative is excluded from the Act, as it is in Ontario by s. 5(c) of the R.T.A.: *R.K. Investment Ltd.v. McElney*.[67]

In *Daye v. Feder*,[68] the county court judge found that an unauthorized subtenant was a trespasser and was not protected under Part IV of the *Landlord and Tenant Act*. Today, the person to whom occupation of the rental unit had been transferred (without the consent of the landlord) would be treated as an unauthorized occupant who could be evicted by the landlord pursuant to s. 100 of the R.T.A.

---

[63] (1987), 61 O.R. (2d) 125 (Ont. Dist. Ct.), affirmed (1989), 4 T.L.L.R. 190 (Ont. Div. Ct.).

[64] (1989), 1989 CarswellOnt 2569 (Ont. Prov. Ct.).

[65] (1977), 16 O.R. (2d) 695, 78 D.L.R. (3d) 762 (Ont. C.A.).

[66] S.B.C. 1977, c. 61.

[67] (1981), 21 R.P.R. 173 (B.C. C.A.).

[68] (April 13, 1979), Doc. 45416/77 (Ont. Co. Ct.).

(c) Assignments

The applicable provisions are found in s. 95 of the R.T.A. (formerly s. 17 of the T.P.A.). The tenant must first obtain the landlord's consent. The request can be either general[69] or specific (s. 95(3)).[70] In a decision of the Court of Appeal,[71] the Court referred to this as the difference between a request for consent to "Assignment in Principle" versus consent to a "Specific Assignment".

If the request is general, the landlord has the option of consenting to the assignment or refusing the assignment;[72] this is tant amount to the landlord giving blanket approval or a blanket refusal without regard to whom the assignee may be. If the request is specific, the landlord has three options:

1. consent to the assignment to the named potential assignee;
2. refuse consent to the assignment of the rental unit to that potential assignee; or
3. refuse consent to the assignment of the rental unit (to anyone).[73]

Upon the landlord's consent to the assignment, the assignee takes on the obligations of the tenant and the benefits of the landlord's obligations (s. 95(8)(*a*)). The assignee will not, however, be responsible to the landlord for any breaches of the Act or of the tenancy agreement by the original tenant (s. 95(8)(*b*)).[74]

A landlord shall not arbitrarily or unreasonably refuse to consent to an assignment of a rental unit to a potential assignee (s. 95(5)). If a landlord does arbitrarily or unreasonably refuse to consent to an assignment of a rental unit to a potential assignee, the tenant may then commence an application to the Board for an order declaring that the landlord has violated the provisions of s. 98(1) of the Act and, pursuant to s. 98(3):

1. authorizing the proposed assignment;
2. authorizing an alternative assignment proposed by the tenant;
3. terminating the tenancy; and/or
4. granting an abatement of the tenant's or former tenant's rent.

---

69 That is, asking for consent to assign the unit without specifying the intended assignee. In other words, asking the landlord, as a general proposition, whether the landlord will permit any assignment of the rental unit.

70 That is, asking for consent to assign the unit to a particular, specified assignee.

71 *North York General Hospital Foundation v. Armstrong* (2005), 34 R.P.R. (4th) 173 (Ont. C.A.).

72 Section 95(2) of the R.T.A. (formerly s. 17(2) of the T.P.A.).

73 Section 95(3) of the R.T.A. (formerly s. 17(3) of the T.P.A.).

74 For instance, the assignee will not be liable for any arrears of rent that accumulated prior to the assignment: Landlord and Tenant Board File No. CEL-00351 (March 2, 2007).

Also, by s. 98(4), the Board may establish terms and conditions of the assignment. If this happens, the assignment will have the same legal effect as if the landlord had consented to it (s. 98(5)).

If a landlord refuses to consent to assignment as a general proposition (under s. 95(2)(*b*) or 95(3)(*c*)), or fails to respond within seven days of the date the landlord receives the request for consent, the tenant may give the landlord a notice of termination under s. 96 within 30 days after the date the request is made.[75]

The landlord's refusal can be constructive or implied, as well as actual. In *Prutkin v. Heath Residences*,[76] the landlord consented to the idea of assigning the rental unit but then began asking potential assignees to pay rent higher than the current amount. This frustrated the tenant's efforts to find a potential assignee (and was illegal pursuant to s. 124 of the T.P.A., now s. 113 of the R.T.A.). The Tribunal held that such conduct was improper and amounted to an unreasonable refusal to permit an assignment.

A landlord is entitled to charge the tenant for the landlord's reasonable out of pocket expenses incurred in giving consent to an assignment to a potential assignee (s. 95(7) of the R.T.A.). Presumably, this is meant to cover the cost of such things as a credit or reference check on the potential assignee. A set administrative or processing fee would not normally be considered to be an out of pocket expense "incurred" by the landlord. There is no permitted allowance for a standard charge or for internal administrative procedures: *Geeves v. Keewatin Management*[77] and *Kelly v. Carslake*.[78] The reasonable expenses of a landlord might include the costs of the landlord's solicitor in drafting or approving of an assignment.

In *Dale v. Country Club Towers*,[79] the tenant requested the landlord's consent to *assign* the unit (without naming a potential assignee). The landlord responded (within seven days) in writing that it would consent, in theory, to a *sublet*. The Tribunal found that since the response was silent with respect to the requested assignment, it amounted to either a refusal or a failure to respond within the permitted time limit. However, since the request for consent did not name a potential assignee, the tenant had no right to seek relief under s. 33 of the T.P.A. (now s. 98 of the R.T.A.) and the application was dismissed.[80] In such a situation, what the tenant ought to have done was

3 — LANDLORDS AND TENANTS

[75] Section 95(4) of the R.T.A. (formerly s. 17(4) of the T.P.A.).

[76] (Dec. 14, 1998), TNT-00214 (Ont. Rental Housing Trib.).

[77] (1987), 61 O.R. (2d) 125 (Ont. Dist. Ct.), affirmed (1989), 4 T.L.L.R. 190 (Ont. Div. Ct.).

[78] (1989), 1989 CarswellOnt 2569 (Ont. Prov. Ct.).

[79] (July 9, 2001), TNT-01979, 2001 CarswellOnt 6373, [2001] O.R.H.T.D. No. 95 (Ont. Rental Housing Trib.).

[80] The tenant's remedies would have been found in s. 48 of the T.P.A. (now s. 96 of the R.T.A.) but, since the tenant did not exercise her rights in a timely fashion (i.e., within 30 days of her request), she likely lost her right to terminate the tenancy based upon the landlord's refusal or failure to respond.

give 30 days notice, vacate the rental unit and then claim a refund of any money illegally retained by the landlord.[81]

The estate of a deceased tenant did not have the right to assign under s. 89 of Part IV: *O'Brien Estate v. Frastell Property Management*;[82] and *Valleyview Apartments Ltd. v. Rothbart Estate*.[83] This is now so by reason of s. 91(1) of the R.T.A. (unless there are other tenants of the rental unit). If the deceased tenant was not the sole tenant, the surviving tenant(s) would retain the right to request permission to assign the tenancy.

8. SUPERINTENDENTS AND OTHER EMPLOYEES OF THE LANDLORD

A landlord often needs to hire employees to manage and maintain a residential complex. Sometimes, such employees are provided with a rental unit (for no rent or at a reduced rent) as part of their compensation. The provision of such a rental unit is typically conditional upon the continuation of the employment. This is because the landlord will need to quickly replace the employee on the termination of their employment and the landlord must be in a position to offer the new employee a place to live. The rental unit that is provided to such employees is termed "superintendent's premises"; this term is somewhat misleading since it refers to a rental unit occupied, not only by a superintendent of the building, but "by a person employed as a janitor, manager, security guard or superintendent and located in the residential complex with respect to which the person is employed".[84] Special provisions are contained in the R.T.A. to deal with such premises.

Section 93 of the Act reads as follows:

> 93.(1) If a landlord has entered into a tenancy agreement with respect to a superintendent's premises, unless otherwise agreed, the tenancy terminates on the day on which the employment of the tenant is terminated.
>
> (2) A tenant shall vacate a superintendent's premises within one week after his or her tenancy is terminated.
>
> (3) A landlord shall not charge a tenant rent or compensation or receive rent or compensation from a tenant with respect to the one week period mentioned in subsection (2).

In view of the phrase "unless otherwise agreed", the terms of the employment contract and/or tenancy agreement must be examined. In *Medeiros v.*

[81] As was successfully done by the tenant in *Morgan v. Wright* (Nov. 2, 1998), EAT-00273 (Ont. Rental Housing Trib.).

[82] (1989), 8 R.P.R. (2d) 179 (Ont. Dist. Ct.).

[83] (1988), 65 O.R. (2d) 209 (Ont. Div. Ct.).

[84] Section 2 of the R.T.A.

ForestLane Properties,[85] the contract required two months notice of termination. The superintendent was entitled to two months pay — an amount for apartment accommodation in lieu of two months notice.

If the tenant has not vacated within one week of the termination of his or her employment, pursuant to s. 94 of the R.T.A. (formerly s. 80 of the T.P.A.), the landlord may apply to the Board for an order terminating the tenancy and for an eviction.

The class of employees identified in the definition of "superintendent's premises" have a unique position within a residential complex. They are agents of the landlord and, thus, the landlord is responsible for their actions and statements made in their professional capacity and, especially, with respect to their dealings with the tenants within the complex. They are employees of the landlord and have all the rights and responsibilities that accompany such a role. They are also tenants of the residential complex, with all of the rights and responsibilities that entails.

For instance, in *Bellrose v. Almeida*,[86] the landlord attempted (by way of an employment contract) to obtain a security deposit that exceeded one month's rent. The Tribunal ruled that although the superintendent was an employee of the landlord, he was also a tenant entitled to the protection of ss. 118 and 144 of the T.P.A. (now ss. 106 and 135 of the R.T.A.). The Tribunal ordered the landlord to refund the tenant (with interest) the amount by which the rent deposit exceeded one month's rent.

In some ways, such employees have fewer rights than other tenants. First,they have no right to assign or sublet their rental unit;[87] this protects the landlord's right to control the superintendent's premises and make it available only to specified employees. Second, unlike other tenants, such employees lack security of tenure (as a result of s. 93); their right to occupy their unit is dependent upon the continuation of their employment (unless they are able to make an agreement with the landlord to the contrary).

On the surface, the law seems pretty straightforward. When the employment of a superintendent (or janitor, manager, or security guard) is terminated, they are required to vacate their rental units within one week and, if they do not do so, the landlord can commence an eviction application. However, these cases can become complicated in a number of ways. For instance, it is not always clear whether a person falls within one of the specified categories of employees listed above. Alternatively, they may admit that they work for the landlord, but claim that they perform their duties in a building other than the one in which they live. The former employee may assert that there was an express agreement with the landlord that occupation of the rental unit is not contingent upon the continuation of their employment. The former em-

[85] (October 29, 1986), Doc. 207664/83 (Ont. Dist. Ct.).

[86] (June 30, 1999), NOT-00166 and NOT-00169 (Ont. Rental Housing Trib.).

[87] See subsections 95(9) and 97(6) of the R.T.A.

ployee may have been a tenant in the unit before becoming an employee of the landlord and may assert that the unit is not a "superintendent's premises" or that there is an implied (if not express) agreement that occupation of the rental unit is not contingent upon the continuation of employment. The former employee may allege that the landlord agreed to allow him or her more than one week to remain in the unit while looking for new accommodations. The employee may be challenging the termination of their employment (by, for-instance, commencing a court action for wrongful dismissal or filing a complaint with the Employment Standards Branch of the Ministry of Labour and/or with the Human Rights Commission) and may argue he or she has the right to remain in the rental unit pending the outcome of that other proceeding. I have included, below, some cases dealing with these types of issues.

In *Stewart-Kerr Properties Ltd. v. Fitzgerald*,[88] the defendant started off as a tenant, later agreed with the landlord to be responsible for cleaning and maintenance, and moved from the first apartment to another and the rent was to be deducted from his salary; the judge held that the latter apartment was "caretaker's premises" (as it was referred to under the *Landlord and Tenant Act*).

Somewhat contrary to that case is *Rondinelli v. Cain*,[89] in which the tenant was asked to do caretaking duties part-time. The judge did not refer to *Stewart-Kerr*. The decision depended on the facts of there being no caretaker's unit and that there was no specific and primary purpose of a tenancy agreement for caretaker's services.

In *J. Kugler Partnership v. Love*,[90] the tenant did about 15 hours of custodial work per month for the landlord. The Tribunal ruled that s. 68 of the T.P.A. and related provisions were intended to deal with a person hired on a full-time basis, that this tenant was not a "caretaker, janitor, manager, watchman, security guard, or superintendent" and that the tenancy was not conditional on her continued performance of any services for the landlord.

In Landlord and Tenant Board File No. TEL-06892 (October 25, 2007), the tenancy agreement referred to the tenant as a superintendent but the Member found that, in reality, this was not the case. The residential complex consisted of only one rental unit, meaning that the tenant could only possibly be responsible for the tenant's own unit. No remuneration or responsibilities (beyond maintaining the lawn in good condition) were outlined in the agreement. Looking at the real substance of the matter (per s. 202 of the R.T.A.), the Member found that the landlord chose to call the tenant a "superintendent" in the agreement merely in an attempt to circumvent the R.T.A.

---

[88] (1979), 25 O.R. (2d) 374 (Ont. Co. Ct.).

[89] (1989), 67 O.R. (2d) 382 (Ont. Dist. Ct.).

[90] (Aug. 19, 1998), EAL-00833, 1998 CarswellOnt 6029 (Ont. Rental Housing Trib.).

In Landlord and Tenant Board File No. SOL-15389 (September 19, 2008), the tenant argued that he is more of a janitor than a caretaker, that he was paid for only a few hours per day and that he did not occupy "superintendent's premises". The Member found that a janitor is one of the classes of employees covered by this section of the Act, that the rental unit in this case was located in the residential complex where the tenant's duties were carried out, that the rental unit was provided to the tenant when his employment commenced and that his employement had been terminated. As a result, it was determined that ss. 93 and 94 of the *Act* applied and the tenancy was terminated.

Caretaker's premises were considered in *Rio Algom Ltd. v. Mostaway.*[91] The contract between the parties stated that the tenant was not an employee, presumably to avoid various employee benefits, and was a "janitorial contractor". The tenant therefore contended that the tenancy agreement was not for caretaker's premises and that s. 115 of Part IV did not apply. The court held that the effect of the employment agreement was that the tenant was employed as a caretaker and so s. 115 applied and, therefore, the landlord could apply for a writ of possession on termination of the caretaker's agreement and the one week's grace permitted by s. 115(1), without having to also give notice of termination of the tenancy.

A number of judges and Tribunal Members once held a view that in order to be a "superintendent's premises" the rental unit had to be specifically designated as such by the landlord.[92] This approach is no longer valid. In *Eng v. Z2K Properties*,[93] the Divisional Court dispenses with the old argument that premises need to be specially designed or designated in order to qualify as superintendent's premises. Any unit occupied by a superintendent (or other specified employee) can qualify as superintendent's premises. If, however, a person was a tenant before becoming an employee of the landlord, then it may be found that they are not occupying superintendent's premises.[94]

In *Parkette Place Apartments c/o Investors Property Services Ltd. v. MacIntosh*,[95] the tenant had lived in this unit for 30 years. For the last 20 of those years, she had been employed as a superintendent in the building. Although she alleged that the former landlord had promised her that she could remain in the unit even if she were no longer the superintendent, she had no corroborative evidence to support this assertion. The new landlord (who had terminated her employment as superintendent) adduced a written agreement, signed by the tenant, stating that she could remain in this unit only as long

---

[91] (April 19, 1982), Kurisko D.C.J. (Ont. Dist. Ct.).

[92] See, for instance, *Osgoode Properties Ltd. v. Taylor* (July 31, 2003), EAL-36489, 2003 CarswellOnt 4195 (Ont. Rental Housing Trib.).

[93] Doc. 103/2000 (Ont. Div. Ct.) (re TSL-14647), unreported.

[94] On this point, see also *J. Kugler Partnership v. Love* (Aug. 19, 1998), EAL-00833, 1998 CarswellOnt 6029 (Ont. Rental Housing Trib.).

[95] (May 25, 2006), TEL-61007, 2006 CarswellOnt 4417 (Ont. Rental Housing Trib.).

as she was the superintendent. Based upon this evidence, the Tribunal found in favour of the landlord and granted an eviction order.

In *Frastell Property Management v. Landsiedel*,[96] it was reiterated that upon termination of a caretaker's employment, the landlord is not required to give notice of termination of the tenancy.

In a Manitoba case, *Globe General Agencies Ltd. v. Antiuk*,[97] the judge stated the obvious reason for a section in the Manitoba statute similar to that of the Ontario Statute:

> If an employee occupying the caretaker's suite turned out to be unsatisfactory. . . and the employer, namely the landlord, did not have an expeditious method of removing him and replacing him with a suitable person, the tenancy relationship with all of the other tenants would be placed in jeopardy.

The effect of s. 115 of Part IV of the *Landlord and Tenant Act* for regaining early possession of caretaker's premises on termination of the employment was questioned by the janitor or superintendent as being discriminatory and offending s. 15 of the *Canadian Charter of Rights and Freedoms* and thus unconstitutional: *Garfella Investments Ltd. v. Carniero.*[98] This argument was rejected on the basis that the interests of the landlord and the tenants for efficient operation of an apartment building were paramount to that of giving a caretaker or superintendent the same period of notice as other tenants after termination of employment.

The next issue to consider is whether s. 83 of the R.T.A. (which gives the Board power to refuse to grant an eviction on grounds that "it would be unfair") applies to termination of a superintendent (etc.).

In *Reid v. Canada Tungsten Mining Corp.*,[99] the supervisor of bunkhouses who lived in one of them, served meals and did general clean-up chores, was not entitled to stay in possession after her employment had beenterminated. The owner landlord obtained an order for possession under the *Landlord and Tenant Ordinance*,[100] similar to superintendent's premises in the R.T.A. The other interesting point in the case is that the tenant employee contended that the notice to quit was retaliatory and relief from forfeiture ought to be granted to the tenant. In refusing the tenant relief, the court stated that the relief section only applied to the normal landlord and tenant relationship and was not applicable when the parties were also employer and employee.

Section 83 of the R.T.A. applies to all applications to evict a tenant. Where, however, the tenant is an employee of the landlord who must be

[96] (1987), 1987 CarswellOnt 2742 (Ont. Dist. Ct.).
[97] (1983), 21 Man. R. (2d) 259 (Man. Co. Ct.).
[98] (1986), 1986 CarswellOnt 2897 (Ont. Dist. Ct.).
[99] [1974] 3 W.W.R. 469 (N.W.T. S.C.).
[100] R.O.N.W.T. 1956, c. 56.

replaced quickly for the sake of all tenants in the complex, I would think that it would be extremely rare for the Board to refuse to grant an eviction. Similarly, given the fact that the tenant knew or ought to have known when taking the position that he or she would only have seven days to vacate the rental unit and given the potential harm to the complex and its residents of a lengthy delay in replacing the employee, I would think that the Board would also be reluctant to delay the eviction. Nevertheless, Members retain the power to grant such relief and each case will have to be decided upon its own unique circumstances.

A grievance procedure will not delay a landlord in obtaining possession. In *Onucki v. Fudge*,[101] in which the notice of dismissal was questioned, the Ontario Divisional Court stated quite definitely:

> Whether or not sufficient notice of termination of employment was given to the erstwhile superintendent is a matter for another forum. It is also clear that the employment of the appellant was terminated, and that is all that is required under s. 115. The approach adopted in *Rio Algom Ltd. v. Turcotte* (1978), 20 O.R. (2d) 769 (Ont. Div. Ct.), should be followed.

In *North-Wright Air Ltd. v. Petak*,[102] the summary stated that even if dismissal was wrongful, it had legal effect and the tenancy was terminated.

In a later case, *Westdale Construction Co. v. Rapea*,[103] the judge com mented on that point that, "managerial chaos would result if access to the caretaker's apartment had to await the resolution of the claim by the caretaker that he had been wrongly terminated." The judge refused a request for delay until the grievance procedure before the Ontario Labour Relations Board could be ruled on and granted a writ of possession. Rather oddly, the judge went on to say that if the Ontario Labour Relations Board restored the caretaker to his employment his replacement would have to vacate to permit there occupation by the caretaker. That would, no doubt, result in more chaos.

This approach (i.e., that an allegation of wrongful dismissal is not defence to, and will not delay, an application under to evict the tenant) was followed by the Tribunal in *Stanmore Developments v. Fourmie*,[104] *Channel Properties Ltd. v. Groff*[105] and *Northwestern Property Management Limited v. Woodbeck*.[106]

When such a tenant's employment is terminated, the landlord cannot charge rent or compensation for one week (s. 93(3) of the R.T.A.). It is less clear whether the landlord is entitled to occupation rent there after until the

---

[101] (1990), 1990 CarswellOnt 2344 (Ont. Dist. Ct.).

[102] [1990] 2 W.W.R. 565 (N.W.T. S.C.).

[103] (1990), 74 O.R. (2d) 29 (Ont. Dist. Ct.).

[104] (Aug. 9, 1999), TNL-08766 (Ont. Rental Housing Trib.).

[105] (Oct. 29, 1998), SOL-01850 (Ont. Rental Housing Trib.).

[106] (January 26, 2005), NOL-13066-RV (Ont. Rental Housing Trib.).

premises are vacated. The court has found that such compensation is due to the landlord.[107] In at least one decision, however, the Tribunal has ruledo therwise;[108] this may be because s. 86(2) of the T.P.A. (now s. 87(3) of the R.T.A.), which gives the landlord the right to apply to the Tribunal for compensation for use and occupation of a rental unit after a tenancy has been terminated, only applies where a "notice of termination or an agreement to terminate the tenancy has taken effect". Since no notice of termination or agreement to terminate was required by ss. 68 and 80 of the T.P.A. (now ss. 93 and 94 of the R.T.A.), s. 86(2) of the T.P.A. (now s. 87(3) of the R.T.A.) could not be relied upon by a landlord. Section 86 of the R.T.A. states that a landlord is entitled to compensation for the use and occupation of a rental unit by a person who is a tenant who does not vacate the unit after his or her tenancy is terminated by *order*, notice or agreement. This seems to cover the situation where the Board orders the termination of the tenancy of a superintendent (or other specified employee) living in superintendent's premises. Pursuant to s. 86, daily compensation is clearly owing to the landlord for every day the tenant remains in the unit after the expiration of the one-week grace period. The problem is that no section of the R.T.A. specifically provides that a landlord can apply to the Board for an order for payment of this compensation.[109] I am not aware of any decision that adequately addresses this apparent gap in the legislation and it may be that most parties and Members have simply assumed that landlords are entitled to such compensation because of the way in which the application form has been drafted.

Another issue arises where the landlord permits the former superintendent to stay in the unit for a while in exchange for the payment of compensation. In one such case,[110] the former superintendent then took the position that, by accepting such payments, the landlord is deemed to have created a new tenancy. Section 45 of the T.P.A. (now s. 45 and 86 of the R.T.A.) usually protects landlords who accept money from tenants whose tenancies have been or are about to be terminated. Section 45, however, only applies where the tenant does not vacate the unit after the tenancy is terminated by an order, a notice of termination of the tenancy or an agreement. In the case of a superintendent, there is no separate notice of termination of the tenancy. Thus, it has been held that s. 45 of the T.P.A. did not apply in these cases and whether or not the acceptance of money from the former superintendent should be taken to create a new tenancy will depend upon whether or not

---

[107] *York (Region) Housing Corp. v. Sipos* (1994), 1994 CarswellOnt 2874 (Ont. Gen. Div.).

[108] *35 Brock Street Ltd. v. Smith* (Feb. 17, 1999), SOL-03767 (Ont. Rental Housing Trib.).

[109] If the tenant was not paying any rent for the unit, there may also be the practical problem of calculating a *per diem* rate for use and occupation of the unit.

[110] *Bell-Am Apartments Ltd., Re* (Sept. 8, 2006), TEL-64464, 2006 CarswellOnt 9159 (Ont. Rental Housing Trib.).

there was an express or implied agreement to create a new tenancy or continue the existing tenancy.[111]

9. BOARDERS/LODGERS

In the R.T.A. the definition of "rental unit" in s. 2(1) includes a room in a boarding house, rooming house or lodging house. These terms, however, are not defined in the R.T.A. Presumably, they refer to relatively transient (daily, weekly or monthly) accommodations (other than a hotel or motel) where a room is provided in which to sleep but other facilities (such as a kitchen, bathroom, etc.), if provided at all, are shared with other tenants. In a boarding house, the name implies that meals are also provided as part of the service. Despite the fact that such tenancies tend to be short-lived, the government has extended to tenants living in such accommodations the security of tenure and other protections afforded by the R.T.A. Landlords ofsuch facilities must abide by the provisions of the R.T.A.

10. CONDOMINIUM PURCHASERS

In condominium projects, delays usually occur in getting the declaration registered. As a result, the condominium has not been constituted at the time the premises are ready for occupation and purchasers wish to move in. Developers have therefore permitted the purchasers to occupy under what are called occupancy agreements, pending final closing and the transfer of ownership; and for developers it is also important to require purchasers to move in as interim occupants, and so be an early source of revenue. These agreements provide for rent or occupancy licence fees and include various contractual provisions common to the landlord and tenant relationship.

The question arises when there is default by a purchaser whether re-entry should be in accordance with the R.T.A. If the interim occupancy arrangement is considered to be a tenancy agreement, the procedure for repossession will be under the R.T.A.

As default under the occupancy agreement will also constitute default under the agreement of purchase and sale, separate action will have to be taken by the developer, which may include cancellation, forfeiting the deposit, damages, as well as possession. All claims can be in the one action.

Although procedure under the R.T.A. might be more expeditious for repossession, that still leaves for determination the rights of the parties under the agreement of purchase and sale.

---

[111] *Ibid.*

Two early cases decided that the interim occupancy arrangement was that of landlord and tenant. Termination of the outstanding agreement of purchase and sale was apparently not an issue.

The first case in which it was decided that this was a landlord and tenant matter was *Bransfield Construction Co. v. Cox.*[112] The parties were the developer of a condominium project and an agreement purchaser of a proposed condominium unit who had gone into possession under the terms of an interim occupancy agreement. Payments by the interim occupant were in arrears. The County Court judge held that the occupancy was a landlord and tenant arrangement and made an order terminating the lease and for possession under Part IV of the *Landlord and Tenant Act*. This order was appealed to the Divisional Court. The Court confirmed the County Court judge's jurisdiction to make the order under the applicable section of Part IV, although varying the order. The Court simply stated: "This is a residential matter under PartIV".

In *W.B. Sullivan Construction Ltd. v. Barker*,[113] the respondents were-purchasers in occupation of proposed condominium units. They had been tenants in the apartment building that was being converted into a condominium. The respondents objected to the carrying charges, which were called "rent" under the interim occupancy agreement, and which were higher than the rents that they had been paying. They applied for rent review under the *Residential Premises Rent Review Act, 1975*[114] (then in force) and succeeded in having the rent reduced. The Divisional Court upheld the decision of the rent review officer on the basis that although there were "Two relationships that exist between the parties to the contract — that of vendor and purchaser, and also that of landlord and tenant . . . the dominant relationship can only be that of landlord and tenant".[115]

However, it does seem that rent control would not apply. Section 80(4) of the *Condominium Act, 1998*[116] limits the monthly charges to interest onthe unpaid balance of the purchase price at the prescribed rate, an estimate damount for taxes and projected monthly common expenses for the unit. These amounts may increase during a period of interim occupancy, without having to comply with rent control.

Section 3 of the R.T.A. (formerly s. 2 of the T.P.A.) makes the R.T.A. applicable to tenancies notwithstanding any other Act, which would include the *Condominium Act*.

The R.T.A. applies to an interim occupancy agreement, but apparently not exclusively when the rights under the agreement of purchase and sale have also to be litigated.

---

112 [1973] 3 O.R. 989 (Ont. Div. Ct.).

113 (1976), 14 O.R. (2d) 529 (Ont. Div. Ct.), leave to appeal refused (1976), 14 O.R. (2d) 529n (S.C.C.).

114 S.O. 1975 (2nd Sess.), c. 12.

115 (1976), 14 O.R. (2d) 529 (Ont. Div. Ct.) at 548.

116 S.O. 1998, c. 19.

It is also to be noted that the *Condominium Act, 1998* limits or modifies for interim occupancy some of the provisions of the R.T.A.

Section 80(6) of the *Condominium Act, 1998* lists the rights and duties of a proposed declarant:

> [T]he declarant,
>
> (a) shall provide those services that the corporation will have a duty to provide to owners after the registration of the declaration and description that creates the unit;
>
> (b) shall repair and maintain the proposed property and the proposed unit in the same manner as the corporation will have a duty to repair after damage and maintain after the registration of the declaration and description that creates the unit;
>
> (c) has the same right of entry that the corporation will have after the registration of the declaration and description that creates the unit;
>
> (d) may withhold consent to an assignment of the right to occupy the proposed unit;
>
> (e) may charge a reasonable fee for consenting to an assignment of the right to occupy the proposed unit; and
>
> (f) shall, within 30 days of the registration of the declaration and description that creates the unit, notify the purchaser in writing of the date and instrument numbers of the registration, unless within that time the purchaser receives a deed to the unit that is in registerable form.

But this does not refer to re-entry. Termination of interim occupancy and re-entry would have to be either under the R.T.A., or in an action based upon default under the agreement of purchase and sale.

Any other matters between occupant and declarant may be dealt with in the interim occupancy agreement subject to the rights and obligations of the landlord and tenant in the R.T.A. To mention only one, by s. 33 of the R.T.A. a tenant is responsible for ordinary cleanliness and for repair of damage by wilful or negligent conduct. This obligation of the interim occupant may be spelled out in the interim occupancy agreement. Its implementation by the declarant would likely be under the *Condominium Act, 1998*, but could be under the R.T.A.

Few cases for re-entry in the case of interim occupancy of a condominium unit were ever brought before the Tribunal. This could indicate there has not been a problem with interim occupancy agreements or that the parties involved in such disputes have proceeded to court.

Failure to pay the monthly rent or occupancy charge could lead to early termination of the occupancy for the arrears with short notice under s. 59 of the R.T.A. (formerly s. 61 of the T.P.A.).

In *Donnol Enterprises Ltd. v. Norley*,[117] the developer declarant was seeking an order for possession against a defaulting purchaser and interim occupant. The application was brought pursuant to s. 106(1) of Part IV of the*Landlord and Tenant Act* and relied on s. 51(7) of the *Condominium Act* [now s. 80(6) of the *Condominium Act, 1998*]. It was argued that the interim occupant was a tenant and that Part IV of the *Landlord and Tenant Act* applied. The judge held otherwise, and stated that "the key to the status of [the person in occupation under the occupancy agreement] must be found in the agreement of purchase and sale itself and not in the *Condominium Act*,"[118] and went on to state that it is "not to say that every occupancy provision in every agreement automatically becomes a lease so as to bring into play the provisions of Pt. IV".[119] The judge concluded that he had no jurisdiction to deal with the application for termination and possession under the *Landlord and Tenant Act*. This case continues to be of interest in that the judge considered the effect and the intention expressed in the agreement of purchase and sale as paramount, thus a landlord and tenant relationship was avoided.

In *Symphony Place Corp. v. Angelini*,[120] a vendor who terminated theoffer to purchase for failure to close applied for and was granted possession against a tenant of the purchaser. The tenant was in possession without the consent of the owner and so was considered a trespasser. The court referred to s. 110(3)(*e*) of Part IV for jurisdiction, that is, that the tenancy arose by virtue of or collateral to a bona fide agreement of purchase and sale of a proposed unit within the meaning of the *Condominium Act*, as is now in s. 58(1)4 of the R.T.A. Another ground for the decision was that the occupant or the purchaser who let the occupant into possession was, in the words of s. 107(1)(*c*) of Part IV "conduct of the tenant or a person permitted in the residential premises . . . such that it substantially interfered with the reasonable enjoyment of the premises for all usual purposes by the landlord" (now the words of s. 64(1) of the R.T.A.), which was to resell the unit and not to rent.

Pursuant to s. 58(1), para. 4 of the R.T.A., a landlord may give a tenant notice of termination of their tenancy where the tenancy arose by virtue of or collateral to an agreement of purchase and sale of a proposed unit within the meaning of the *Condominium Act, 1998* in good faith and the agreement of purchase and sale has been terminated. In *Whitby Harbour Development Corp. v. Cater*,[121] a case concerning a condominium unit, the court went ahead with the application under s. 110(3)(*e*) of Part IV (the predecessor to s. 58(1) para. 4 of the R.T.A.) although noting that similar relief was also

[117] (1980), 14 R.P.R. 214 (Ont. Co. Ct.).
[118] (1980), 14 R.P.R. 214 (Ont. Co. Ct.) at 218.
[119] (1980), 14 R.P.R. 214 (Ont. Co. Ct.) at 220.
[120] (1992), 7 O.R. (3d) 151 (Ont. Gen. Div.).
[121] (1992), 23 R.P.R. (2d) 25 (Ont. Gen. Div.).

being sought in an action in the Ontario Court, General Division. A similar decision was released more recently in Landlord and Tenant Board File No. TEL-00235-A (released March 7, 2007 and amended on March 15, 2007).

To sum up on this point, the R.T.A. does apply for an application for possession against a defaulting purchaser as interim occupant. However, similar relief can be applied for in a separate action, along with the declarant vendor's remedies for default. Most developers would prefer to avoid the strictures and obligations of the residential landlord and tenant relationship, except for the summary application for possession under s. 59(1) of the R.T.A. (for arrears of rent), against a defaulting purchaser as interim occupant.

11. MORTGAGEE IN POSSESSION

In certain circumstances, a mortgagee has the right to take control of a property in order to protect the mortgagee's interests. Usually, this occurs where the mortgagor (the owner of the property) defaults on mortgage payments. The rights of a mortgagee emanate from both the contract between the parties (i.e., the terms of the mortgage itself[122]) and from statute.[123] A mortgagee may take control of a residential complex to protect its interests in the short term, until it can sell the property and recover the money it lent to the owner and any expenses it incurs in collecting on the debt. In order to be deemed a landlord, a mortgagee must be *in possession* of the mortgaged residential complex.[124] This term is not defined. It is generally held that, to be "in possession", the mortgagee must exercise control over the property (directly or through an agent) or must assert the rights of a landlord.[125] Collecting rent from the mortgagor's tenant(s) (by attornment of rents) *may* be found to be sufficient exercise of control so as to put the mortgagee "in possession".

Falconbridge on Mortgages[126] states that a mortgagee becomes a mortgagee in possession where the mortgagee, "deprives the mortgagor of the control and management of the mortgaged property".

A finding by the Landlord and Tenant Board as to whether a mortgagee is a mortgagee in possession is a question of fact (not a question of law) and, therefore, cannot be appealed.[127]

When a mortgagor defaults on a mortgage, the mortgagee may wish to make some inquiries concerning the existence of any tenancy agreements.

---

[122] Including the standard terms incorporated by reference into the mortgage.

[123] The *Mortgages Act*, R.S.O. 1990, c. M.40, as amended by S.O. 1991, c. 6, and further amended by s. 106 of the R.T.A.

[124] Section 47(1) of the *Mortgages Act*.

[125] For instance, seeking to terminate a tenancy: s. 48(2) of the *Mortgages Act*.

[126] (5th ed., May 2007), at pp. 31-32.

[127] *Bank of Montreal v. Weidenfeld* (2008), 2008 CarswellOnt 3016 (Ont. Div. Ct.).

The mortgagee may question the mortgagor and may require the mortgagor to provide a list of tenants, if any.[128] The mortgagee may also enter the common areas of the complex to conduct an inspection, demand production from the mortgagor or the mortgagor's tenant of a copy of any written tenancy agreement and demand from the mortgagor or the mortgagor's tenant any particulars of any tenancy agreement.[129] The mortgagor and tenant(s) have an obligation to co-operate with these inquiries[130] and the mortgagee can attempt to enforce its rights in this regard by court order.[131] Taking any (orall) of these steps, however, does not constitute taking possession and, therefore, does not automatically turn the mortgagee into a landlord.[132]

If there is a long-term lease that is not registered on title, whether or not the mortgagee is bound by it may depend on a number of factors. Once the mortgagee takes possession of the property, the mortgagee steps into the shoes of the landlord and is bound by all existing tenancy agreements, subject to the right of the mortgagee under s. 52 of the *Mortgages Act* to seek to have set aside any bogus tenancy agreements the mortgagor may have purported to enter into after default on the mortgage. Thus, if there is a *bona fide* tenancy agreement for a term of ten years that pre-dates the mortgage, once the mortgagee takes possession, the mortgagee may well be bound by that tenancy agreement, even if it was unaware of its existence at the time the mortgage was created. On the other hand, if the mortgagee has not yet taken possession, the mortgagee may be able to argue that it is not bound by the tenancy agreement since it is for a term greater than three years and it is not registered on title (and, pursuant to s. 72 of the *Land Titles Act*, the mortgagee would not deemed to have notice of it).[133]

Once a mortgagee is in possession of a residential complex, the mortgagee is deemed to be the landlord of the complex and the original landlord under the tenancy agreement ceases to be the landlord.[134] The mortgagee in possession is subject to all existing tenancy agreements[135] and is bound by the provisions of the R.T.A. (i.e., has all of the rights and responsibilities of a landlord).[136] Although the *Mortgages Act* purports (in s. 46(1)) to take priority (in the case of conflict) over any other statute, the Court of Appeal made it clear that the procedures for terminating a tenancy set out in the

---

[128] Section 50(1) of the *Mortgages Act.*

[129] Section 50(2) of the *Mortgages Act.*

[130] Sections 50(4) and (5) of the *Mortgages Act.*

[131] Section 50(6) of the *Mortgages Act.*

[132] Section 50(3) of the *Mortgages Act.*

[133] For a case on point, see *Bank of Montreal v. Smith*, (2008) 2008 CarswellOnt 3473 (Ont. S.C.J.).

[134] Section 47(2) of the *Mortgages Act.*

[135] Section 47(3) of the *Mortgages Act.*

[136] Section 48(1) of the *Mortgages Act.* See Landlord and Tenant Board File No. SOL-00562 (March 30, 2007) and Landlord and Tenant Board File No. TSL-20501 (Jan. 23, 2009).

T.P.A. (including the prescribed forms and notice periods) prevail over any conflicting provisions contained in the *Mortgages Act*.[137] This ruling would also apply to the R.T.A., which is the successor to the T.P.A.

The person deemed the landlord by the above must serve notice on all tenants of the change in landlord.[138] The notice must be in writing and must contain the name and address of the person deemed to be the landlord.[139] The notice may be in the form prescribed in the regulations made under the *Mortgages Act*.[140] Service of all documents should be in accordance with s. 191 of the R.T.A. (formerly s. 178 of the T.P.A.)[141] and the proof of service should be kept for future reference. Rent must be paid to the person deemed to be the landlord from the date of service of this notice (unless the mortgagee instructs or a court orders otherwise).[142]

Failure to comply with the requirements as to the form and service of the notice may prevent the mortgagee from successfully pursuing its rights as a mortgagee in possession. In *CIBC v. Unrau*,[143] the mortgagee's application-was dismissed as the notice of change of landlord and notice of attornment of rents were found to be invalid for lack of a signature. Similarly, in *TD Bank v. Miral*,[144] the Tribunal found that the applicant mortgagee was not "in possession" because the notice given by the bank failed to comply with the relevant provisions of the *Mortgages Act*.

If the mortgagee decides to actually take possession of the residential-complex, it faces numerous practical problems. What if the mortgagor refuses to answer any questions about the premises and its occupants or if the mortgagor has disappeared altogether? What if the tenants also refuse to co-operate and will not even give their names? What if they claim that the tenancy agreements have not been reduced to writing? Can the mortgagee confirm that the alleged terms of the oral tenancy agreements are being accurately reported by the tenants? What if the mortgagee suspects that the mortgagor is colluding with others in an attempt to discourage the mortgagee from taking possession or is otherwise trying to adversely affect the value of the mortgagee's interest in the complex?

Where the identity of the tenant(s) is known and the terms of the tenancy are clear, the mortgagee in possession can enforce its rights under the R.T.A. as would any other landlord. It can seek to terminate the tenancy for occupation of the rental unit by a purchaser or specified members of the pur-

---

[137] *Canada Trustco Mortgage Co. v. Park* (2004), [2004] O.J. No. 3215, 2004 CarswellOnt 3184 (Ont. C.A.).

[138] Section 47(6) of the *Mortgages Act*.

[139] Section 47(7) of the *Mortgages Act*.

[140] Section 47(8) of the *Mortgages Act*.

[141] Section 57 of the *Mortgages Act*.

[142] Section 49 of the *Mortgages Act*.

[143] (Nov. 16, 1998), NOL-00408-SA (Ont. Rental Housing Trib.).

[144] (March 8, 1999), EAL-03070-RV (Ont. Rental Housing Trib.).

chaser's family under s. 49 of the R.T.A. If the mortgagee is a natural person wishing to reside in the unit, he or she can also apply for possession under s. 48 of the R.T.A. If the tenant has not been paying rent, the mortgagee in possession may bring an application for payment of the arrears of rent and/or for termination of the tenancy. The only difference between a mortgagee and any other landlord is that the mortgagee may need to adduce evidence to prove that it is, in fact, a mortgagee in possession of the residential complex and that it has served proper notice of this fact upon the tenant(s) in question.

Where, however, the identity of the tenant(s) is unknown or the terms of the tenancy are unclear, the mortgagee in possession should probably proceed in court rather than bring an application before the Landlord and Tenant Board. The court can attempt to force the mortgagor and the tenants to disclose the information and documents the mortgagee requires (under s. 50 of the *Mortgages Act*) or can, pursuant to s. 52 of the *Mortgages Act*, vary or set aside a tenancy agreement, or any of its provisions if the object of that agreement was to discourage the mortgagee from taking possession or to adversely affect the value of the mortgagee's interest in the complex.[145] The court will also have available to it powers in equity that the Board lacks. Although the Board may seem attractive because its proceedings are generally faster and less expensive than in court, it is very risky for a mortgagee to commence an application without having all of the necessary information.

In Landlord and Tenant Board File No. CEL-02248 (Oct. 2, 2007), the mortgagee in possession was facing a tenant who purportedly had a fixed-term tenancy of five years. The mortgagee in possession, as landlord, served a sixty-day notice of termination for use of the unit by a purchaser. This notice could only be sufficient if the tenancy were month-to-month and the Board somehow ignored that the end of the term of the tenancy was still almost five years away. The applicant suggested that, given the alleged below-market rent being charged and the unusual length of the term of the tenancy, the Board ought to find that it was a fraudulent transaction and declare the tenancy agreement void. The Board stated that the mortgagee in possession could have pursued such a declaration from the court under the *Mortgages*

---

[145] See *Rhee v. Zilberman* (2006), 2006 CarswellOnt 6868 (Ont. S.C.J.), in which the judge dismisses a motion by the plaintiff on the basis that the plaintiff (a mortgagee) ought to proceed under s. 52 of the *Mortgages Act* if the plaintiff wishes to have an allegedly fraudulent tenancy agreement set aside. The judge also noted that this motion was a collateral attack on an order of the Rental Housing Tribunal and that the plaintiff could have, but chose not to, participate in the proceeding before the Tribunal and cannot now complain of the repercussions of that decision. Also see *Canada Mortgage & Housing Corp. v. Seetarram* (2008), 2008 CarswellOnt 1372 (Ont. S.C.) in which the court declared that a purported five-year lease was invalid either because it exceeded three years and had not been registered on title (and was therefore not valid against the mortgagee under the *Land Titles Act*) or because it was a sham lease and was invalid under s. 52 of the *Mortgages Act*. The court found that there was a tenancy, but that it was month-to-month and not for the term (five years) set out in the document.

Act. The Board declined to look behind the tenancy agreement and found that the notice of termination was void.

In *CIBC Mortgages Inc. v. "All male and female tenants"*,[146] the Tribunal dismissed the application of this mortgagee in possession because it had failed to properly identify the tenants. A similar approach was taken in *RoyalBank v. Occupants*.[147] The Member indicated that the onus rests upon the applicant to prove the existence of a tenancy, the identity of the tenant(s) and to prove that they were in possession of the rental unit at the time the application was commenced. Royal Bank failed to adduce such evidence and the application was dismissed. The Member also indicated that, in an application for arrears of rent, the applicant must establish the amount of rent lawfully owing. In *Montreal Trust Co. v. Khaper*,[148] the notice of termination for non-payment of rent was found to be void because it did not set out the amount of rent that was due; the fact that the applicant was a mortgagee in possession and may not have known the amount of lawful rent owing was found not to be a valid excuse.

In Landlord and Tenant Board File No. TEL-16435 (September 18, 2008), the mortgagee in possession could not readily ascertain the actual rent the landlord had been charging and so claimed arrears of rent, arbitrarily setting the rent at what it considered to be a fair market value. The Board dismissed the application, stating that the mortgagee in possession needed to prove the rent actually owing (if any) and pointed out that the mortgagee had available to it under s. 50 of the *Mortgages Act* a method of attempting to obtain any information it might require.

A somewhat different approach, however, was taken in Landlord and Tenant Board File No. TSL-7876 (November 7, 2008). In this case, the tenants refused to cooperate and refused to provide information about their tenancy to a mortgage in possession. The mortgagee in possession brought an application to terminate the tenancy for substantial interference with its lawful rights. The Member agreed that, in such circumstances, a mortgagee in possession should not have to pursue a separate legal proceeding in court in order to obtain basic information about a tenancy and ordered the tenants to provide to the mortgagee in possession particulars of the tenancy by a specified date, failing which the mortgagee in possession was free to obtain an *ex parte* order terminating the tenancy pursuant to s. 78 of the R.T.A. for breach of the Board's order.

Once a mortgagee becomes the landlord by becoming a mortgagee in possession, the tenants are obliged to pay their rent to the mortgagee. Tenants who continue to pay the original landlord after receiving proper notice from

---

[146] (Jan. 14, 2002), SWL-34539, [2002] O.R.H.T.D. No. 4 (Ont. Rental Housing Trib.).

[147] (Nov. 21, 2000), TSL-24149, [2000] O.R.H.T.D. No. 148, 2000 CarswellOnt 6416 (Ont. Rental Housing Trib.).

[148] (Feb. 1, 2002), CEL-22701 (Ont. Rental Housing Trib.).

the mortgagee in possession, will not be given credit for those payments and risk eviction for non-payment of rent.[149] Conversely, if the tenants pay their rent to the mortgagee in possession, the original landlord (the mortgagor) cannot successfully claim that there are arrears of rent (simply because the mortgagor was not the one to receive the rent).[150]

The mortgagee in possession may wish to obtain possession for occupation on behalf of himself or herself or his or her family[151] (where the mortgagee is a person) or, more commonly, on behalf of a purchaser[152] (where the mortgagee is exercising its right to sell the property on default of the mortgage).

Subsection 53(4) of the *Mortgages Act* says that in such cases, regardless of the term of the tenancy, 60 days notice of termination is sufficient. According to the Court of Appeal, however, s. 53(4) of the *Mortgages Act* is superseded by the relevant provisions of the T.P.A. (now the R.T.A.).[153] Note that, for a fixed term tenancy, the termination date in the notice of termination cannot be earlier than the last day of the term of the tenancy (which could be many months, or even years, away).

As some protection for the tenant being evicted, s. 54 of the *Mortgages Act* states that if the purchaser or his or her family does not occupy the premiseswithin 180 days the tenant can obtain a court order to re-occupy on the same terms as before, providing the tenant applies within 210 days of the termination date. That serves more as a warning that the sale must be *bona fide* than as a useful right for a tenant who has re-located.

The offer to purchase when a mortgagee is selling a single family home under power of sale or after foreclosure should modify the usual vacant possession term so that the mortgagee vendor or the prospective purchaser will make the necessary application for termination of the tenancy and possession, or that if by a certain date the application is refused the purchaser may withdraw or waive vacant possession, or the vendor may withdraw if unable to provide vacant possession. A further comment is that some flexibility should be allowed for the closing date to accord with the finality of the order for possession.

---

[149] *Royal Bank v. Faith* (June 23, 2006), TEL-62563, 2006 CarswellOnt 4388, [2006] O.R.H.T.D. No. 81 (Ont. Rental Housing Trib.).

[150] Landlord and Tenant Board File No. TEL-19530 (Jan. 9, 2009).

[151] In accordance with s. 48 of the R.T.A.

[152] In accordance with s. 49 of the R.T.A.

[153] *Canada Trustco Mortgage Co. v. Park* (2004), [2004] O.J. No. 3215, 2004 CarswellOnt 3184 (Ont. C.A.). See also the decisions in Landlord and Tenant Board File Numbers CEL-02248 (Oct. 2, 2007) and TEL-03366-RV (July 18, 2007), both available on the Board's website, in which the Board has held that the relevant provisions of the R.T.A. (which state that the R.T.A. takes priority over all statutes except the *Human Rights Code*) are essentially identical to those of the T.P.A. and, thus, the Board remains bound by the Court of Appeal's decision in *Canada Trustco Mortgage Co. v. Park*.(cited above).

In *Royal Bank v. Boutis*,[154] the plaintiff bank as first mortgagee in possession had complied with the applicable sections of the *Mortgages Act* to obtain possession for a purchaser. The tenants' defence that the two-storey detached house was not a single family home was not accepted by the court. The two illegal apartments did not negate finding that it was a single family home. Possession for the purchaser was ordered.

In *Regional Trust Co. v. Briggs*,[155] a purchaser from the mortgagee in power of sale proceedings wished possession for himself and family. The premises were zoned for single family. The court held that it was a single family home. As proper notices had been served, a writ of possession was ordered.

What are the rights of a mortgagee in possession when the mortgagor, without the consent of the mortgagee, made extensive renovations to a house in turning it into five subdivided units? This was considered in *Royal TrustCorp. v. James.*[156] The judge held that the substantial renovations and change of use were in contravention of the mortgage. He granted an order for possession against all "tenants".

In *Premier Trust Co. v. Heckhausen*,[157] the mortgagee was selling a single family home under power of sale to a purchaser with vacant possession. The applicable sections of the *Mortgages Act* were followed. Judgment for possession was reserved until past the original date for closing the sale and vacant possession. The sale contract provided for an extension of the closing date. However, the tenant appealed and was automatically granted a stay of the order for possession. Fortunately, the stay was lifted and the appeal was settled just in time for the extended closing date. This case illustrates the importance of providing in such a contract an adequate extension date for closing.

When a mortgagor has given a lease after the mortgagee has gone into possession, the court on an application of the mortgagee will set aside the tenancy, *Mortgages Act*, s. 52(1)(*a*), and order possession for arrears of rent: *Sun Life Trust Co. v. Thomas.*[158]

Somewhat similar is *Royal Trust Corp. v. Mahoney.*[159] The plaintiff trust company as mortgagee in possession sold under power of sale the single family home to a purchaser who wished personal possession. The tenant claimed that a term of the lease gave an option to purchase and right of first refusal, notices of which were registered. The trust company included in the application to court for possession for the purchaser that the option to purchase and first right of refusal are not properly integral to or normally incidental to

[154] (1994), 1994 CarswellOnt 2638 (Ont. Gen. Div.).
[155] (1993), 30 R.P.R. (2d) 69 (Ont. Gen. Div.).
[156] (July 20, 1992), Doc. L4455/82 (Ont. Gen. Div.).
[157] (1993), 37 R.P.R. (2d) 165 (Ont. Gen. Div.).
[158] (1995), 1995 CarswellOnt 2726 (Ont. Gen. Div.).
[159] (1993), 34 R.P.R. (2d) 65 (Ont. Gen. Div.).

a tenancy agreement. The court agreed first that the trust company is not bound by the option and first right of refusal, and secondly, ordered the registration expunged from the title, and granted an order for possession.

A mortgagee in possession is not liable for breaches of the R.T.A. (or T.P.A.) committed by the former landlord.[160] For instance, a mortgagee who goes into possession will not be responsible for illegal rents charged by a former landlord or for abatements for non-repair but will be liable to the tenant from the date of going into possession and becoming the landlord untildisrepair and work orders are satisfied: s. 47(1) of the *Mortgages Act*.[161]

The mortgagee in possession may, however, be liable to account for rent deposits collected by the former landlord. Subsection 106(4) of the R.T.A. (formerly s. 118(4) of the T.P.A.) provides that a new landlord of a rental unit or a person who is deemed to be a landlord under s. 47(1) of the *Mortgages Act* shall not require a tenant to pay a rent deposit if the tenant has already paid a rent deposit to the prior landlord of the rental unit. The onus is,therefore, upon the mortgagee in possession to satisfy itself as to what rent deposits the mortgagor ought to have been holding in trust as the mortgagee will have to account for these monies.[162] If, however, the rent deposit exceeds one month's rent or the tenant has made "advance payments" of rent to the mortgagor, the mortgagee in possession may not have to account for these amounts (to the extent that they exceed one month's rent).[163]

A mortgagee ceases to be deemed to be a landlord once it is no longer "in possession" (i.e., control) of the rental unit.[164] Nevertheless, the mortgagee remains liable to the tenant(s) for events that occurred while the mortgagee was deemed to be the landlord.[165]

---

[160] *Irving v. AGC Inc.* (December 20, 2001), NOT-00582, [2001] O.R.H.T.D. No. 151 (Ont. Rental Housing Trib.).

[161] *981673 Ontario Ltd. v. Jessome* (1994), 21 O.R. (3d) 343 (Ont. Gen. Div.).

[162] This is so by reason of s. 47(1) of the *Mortgages Act* which deems the mortgagee in possession to be the landlord under the tenancy agreement: *Royal Trust Corp. of Canada (Trustee of) v. Parmentier* (1996), 1996 CarswellOnt 140 (Ont. Gen. Div.). This was again revisited in *Gardner v. Industrial Alliance Insurance Co.* (1997), 22 O.T.C. 252 (Ont. Div. Ct.) in which *Chiappino v. Bishop* (1988), 49 R.P.R. 218 (Ont. Dist. Ct.) was questioned and *Spencer Properties Ltd. v. Zrebiec* (1992), 1992 CarswellOnt 1760 (Ont. Gen. Div.) was followed. See also *Top Link Investments Ltd. v. Hutchinson* (1997), 15 R.P.R. (3d) 67 (Ont. Gen. Div.) in which *Gardner, supra*, and *Spencer, supra*, were applied and *Chiappino, supra*, and *Dollar Land Corp. v. Solomon*, [1963] 2 O.R. 269 (Ont. H.C.) were not followed. *Royal Trust Corp. of Canada v. Roche* (1994), 20 O.R. (3d) 551 (Ont. Gen. Div.): It is up to the purchaser to check and find out about any security deposits.

[163] *Royal Bank v. Boutis* (1994), 1994 CarswellOnt 2638 (Ont. Gen. Div.).

[164] Section 47(4) of the *Mortgages Act*.

[165] Section 47(5) of the *Mortgages Act*.

12. DEATH OF A TENANT

Under the R.T.A., s. 91(1), if a tenant of a rental unit dies and no other tenants of the rental unit remain, the tenancy shall be deemed to be terminated 30 days after the death of the tenant.

By s. 91(2) of the R.T.A., the landlord shall give the executor or members of the family access to the premises for the purpose of removing the tenant's property. The mechanism for enforcing this right is less certain. In *Nugent v. Simzer*,[166] the daughter of a deceased tenant brought a motion in the name of her father and herself before the Tribunal, on an expedited basis, prior to even commencing an application. She was seeking access to her father's unit in order to retrieve personal belongings. By way of an interim order, the Member ordered the landlord to provide the daughter with keys to the unit and to permit her access to the unit. The Member indicated that failure to comply with this interim order could result in monetary sanctions against the landlord.

If the tenant's property has not been removed within the 30 days, the landlord may sell or retain it (s. 92 of the R.T.A.), subject to request within six months by the executor or a family member for the return of property retained or, if sold, the proceeds, less the landlord's costs for moving, storing and any arrears of rent.

By s. 92(5) a landlord and the tenant's executor or administrator may agree to other terms about termination. In the absence of such an agreement, the tenancy is terminated 30 days after the death of the tenant; the ignorance of the landlord or the representatives of the estate about these provisions does not affect its application.[167]

The above two sections *do not* apply when a tenant of a mobile homesite dies if the tenant owns the mobile home: s. 163 of the R.T.A. Sections 91 and 92 of the R.T.A. *do* apply if the tenant of the mobile home site who dies did not own the mobile home that is located on that site. Please see Chapter 20.

In *Birk v. Hadcock*,[168] the Member held that during the 30-day period following the death of the tenant, although the estate has the right to access the unit, it is not a "tenant" and therefore cannot assert the rights of a tenant. This appears to me to be a very narrow reading of the definition of tenant, which in s. 1 of the T.P.A. (now s. 2 of the R.T.A.) is said to include a tenant's heirs, assigns and personal representatives. Also, this leaves the estate with no recourse (at least not under the R.T.A.) against a landlord who contravenes the Act during that 30-day period following the death of the tenant.

---

[166] (April 12, 2002), no file number (Ont. Rental Housing Trib.).

[167] *Hershorn Estate v. Silverberg* (Oct. 30, 2000), TNT-01401, 2000 CarswellOnt 6426 (Ont. Rental Housing Trib.).

[168] (Jan. 27, 2003), TET-02951, 2003 CarswellOnt 1532 (Ont. Rental Housing Trib.).

A deceased tenant's heir, however, does not have any right to take over the tenancy. In *Portree Properties Ltd. v. Morris*,[169] the tenant lived with her son. She then died. The son wished to remain in the unit and considered himself to be a tenant. The landlord considered the son to be an unauthorized occupant. The Tribunal found that the only tenant was the deceased and that by operation of s. 49 of the T.P.A. (now s. 91 of the R.T.A.), the tenancy was terminated 30 days after her death.

It has also been held that a child of a deceased tenant needs to prove tha the or she is an "heir" in order to have standing to commence any proceeding on behalf of their deceased parent against the landlord.[170] Presumably, a personal representative (an executor or administrator of the estate of thedeceased) would also have the right to commence such proceedings if they can provide evidence that they have the authority to act on behalf of the estate. This is because the definition of "tenant" in s. 2 of the Act includes a tenant's "heirs, assigns and personal representatives."

Since the tenancy is deemed terminated 30 days after the death of the sole tenant (subject to the new provisions concerning spouses), in the absence of evidence that this deadline was extended by agreement or that a new tenancy was created, the Board may refuse to hear any application raising disputes between a landlord and the family of the deceased tenant that arises more than 30 days after the date the tenancy was terminated pursuant to s.91 of the R.T.A.[171]

Under the R.T.A., there is new protection for a surviving spouse who is not actually listed as a tenant on the tenancy agreement. Please refer to the section entitled, "Protection for the Spouse of a Tenant", above.

13. BANKRUPTCY AND INSOLVENCY

The bankruptcy[172] of a tenant can have an impact on the landlord's ability to collect on any debt that exists as of the date of the assignment and on the landlord's ability to commence or continue proceedings against that tenant. As a general rule, all property of the bankrupt vests in the trustee in bankruptcy and the bankrupt person ceases to have any capacity to dispose of or otherwise deal with his property. Among this property is the bankrupt's interest in rental property.[173] Upon a bankruptcy, therefore, all dealings must involve the trustee in bankruptcy.

---

[169] (March 28, 1999), TSL-07281 (Ont. Rental Housing Trib.).

[170] *Sarault, Re* (April 4, 2006), EAT-07297, 2006 CarswellOnt 9165 (Ont. Rental Housing Trib.).

[171] Landlord and Tenant Board File No. TNL-19746 (Jan. 20, 2009).

[172] Usually through an assignment in bankruptcy or by a receiving order under the *Bankruptcy and Insolvency Act*, R.S.C. 1985, c. B-3 (as amended).

[173] *Wyssling Esate v. Latrielle Estate* (1990), 71 O.R. (2d) 577 (Ont. H.C.) at 586 and *Minto*

The *Bankruptcy and Insolvency Act* also governs insolvency. Insolvency occurs where a person either files a proposal or a notice of intention to file a proposal under Part III of the Act. In the case of insolvency, unlike bankruptcy, the insolvent person's property does not pass to the trustee or other officer but remains the property of the insolvent.

Immediately upon an insolvency or a bankruptcy, there is a stay of any proceeding against the bankrupt or insolvent person where the proceeding is for a claim "provable in bankruptcy". The purpose of the stay is to avoid a multiplicity of proceedings and to prevent any unsecured creditor from obtaining priority over any other unsecured creditors. It gives the bankrupt or insolvent persons some "breathing room" and allows for arrangements to be made to deal with all of the outstanding claims or potential claims against the person.

What are claims provable in bankruptcy? According to s. 121(1) of the *Bankruptcy and Insolvency Act*, they are:

> All debts and liabilities, present and future, to which the bankrupt is subject on the day on which the bankrupt becomes bankrupt or to which the bankrupt may become subject before the bankrupt's discharge by reason of any obligation incurred before the day on which the bankrupt becomes bankrupt . . .

A debt for past rent would clearly be a claim provable in bankruptcy. A claim against the tenant for compensation for damage to the rental unit or complex would also qualify as a claim provable in bankruptcy.

If a tenant owes money to his or her landlord and then becomes bankrupt, what are the implications? If the landlord has not yet commenced a proceeding against the tenant *and the claim is one that is provable in bankruptcy*, the landlord will not be able to commence an application once notified of the bankruptcy (or insolvency); the landlord can only file a claim with the trustee and hope that, along with other unsecured creditors, the landlord may eventually collect some of the money owing to it. If a proceeding for a claim *provable in bankruptcy* has already been commenced, it will automatically be stayed (i.e., it cannot proceed).[174]

This does not mean that landlords have no recourse. Although, as a practical matter, a landlord will not be able to proceed to obtain an order for arrears of rent or an eviction based upon those arrears once a tenant has become bankrupt or insolvent, that does not preclude the landlord from commencing proceedings for any *new* arrears that accrue after the date the

---

Yorkville Inc. v. Trattoria Fieramosca Inc. (September 29, 1997), Sharpe J. (Ont. Gen. Div.) (unreported).

[174] Sections 69, 69.1, 69.2 and 69.3 of the *Bankruptcy and Insolvency Act*. See *Metropolitan Toronto Housing Authority v. Mohamed* (May 20, 1999), TSL-04858-RV (Ont. Rental Housing Trib.) and *Badenhurst Properties Ltd. in Trust v. Grandez* (June 15, 2006), TSL-82470 (Ont. Rental Housing Trib.)

tenant becomes bankrupt or insolvent.[175] Also, it is arguable that the landlord can commence eviction proceedings that are not based upon a claim provable in bankruptcy. In *Portree Properties Ltd. v. Vanoostrum*,[176] for instance, sincethe application was based upon persistent late payment of rent and no claim was made for payment of any rent, the Tribunal ruled that the proceeding was not stayed by the tenant's assignment in bankruptcy.[177]

Similarly, an application to terminate a tenancy based upon a breach of a mediated agreement (so long as no arrears of rent are being sought as part of the application) has been held by the Divisional Court not to be a claim provable in bankruptcy and, therefore, this type of application is not precluded by the tenant's assignment in bankruptcy, even if the terms of the mediated agreement that have been breached relate to payment by the tenant of arrears of rent that arose prior to the assignment in bankruptcy.[178]

In Landlord and Tenant Board File No. SWL-16920 (August 12, 2008), the Board Member distinguished the facts of the case before her from those in *Peel Housing Corp. v. Siewnarine*[179] and chose instead to follow the Divisional Court's earlier decision in *Forestwood Co-operative Homes Inc. v. Pritz*.[180] The Member held that since the landlord was seeking arrears of rent in addition to termination of the tenancy (based upon the breach of the tenant of a mediated agreement that had been entered into by the parties one day after the tenant made an assignment in bankruptcy), the landlord's application was stayed. The tenant's motion to set aside the *ex parte* eviction order was granted and the landlord's application was dismissed.

Where a tenant has filed a Consumer Proposal under the *Bankruptcy and Insolvency Act*, this will stay proceedings against the tenant. If, however, there is a Deemed Annulment of the tenant's Proposal, the landlord's right to claim rent arrears will be revived.[181]

Although less common, the same principles apply when a landlord becomes bankrupt or insolvent. Any proceeding for a claim provable in bankruptcy is stayed.[182]

---

175 *Freure Management v. Lederman* (July 24, 2000), SWL-17937 (Ont. Rental Housing Trib.) and *Badenhurst Properties Ltd. — In Trust v. Grandez* (July 6, 2006), TSL-78159-RV (Ont. Rental Housing Trib.).

176 (Nov. 25, 2003), TSL-56260, [2003] O.R.H.T.D. No. 143, 2003 CarswellOnt 5710 (Ont. Rental Housing Trib.).

177 The Member did, however, exercise his discretion and refused to grant an eviction in the circumstances of this case.

178 *Peel Housing Corp. v. Siewnarine* (2008), 2008 CarswellOnt 3807 (Ont. Div. Ct.).

179 (2008), 2008 CarswellOnt 3807 (Ont. Div. Ct.).

180 (2002), [2002] O.J. No. 550 (Ont. Div. Ct.).

181 See ss. 66.31 and 66.32 of the *Bankruptcy and Insolvency Act* and Landlord and Tenant Board File No. CEL-07769-RV (March 5, 2008).

182 *Pataky v. Lagace* (April 7, 2003), EAT-04386, 2003 CarswellOnt 1589 (Ont. Rental Housing Trib.).

14. GUARANTORS

A guarantor (sometimes referred to in a tenancy agreement as a co-signor) is, in simple terms, a person who promises to be financially responsible for another person. In some cases, a landlord will only agree to accept a new tenant if someone else will guarantee that the rent will be paid. For example, students living out-of-town sometimes need such a guarantee. In the early days of the Tribunal, there was a lively debate amongst Members as to whether an order for the payment of money could be made by the Tribunal against a tenant's guarantor.

On the one hand, efficiency was one of the goals of establishing the Rental Housing Tribunal and landlords were hoping for "one-stop shopping". This goal would not be fully realized if a landlord could only obtain an order against a tenant at the Tribunal and then had to pursue a separate court action against the guarantor. Also, the parties to an application are supposed to be the landlord and the tenant and "any other persons directly affected by the application".[183] Guarantors might want to have an opportunity to participate in the proceedings in order to protect their interests in the matter. These were arguments in favour of including guarantors in applications before the Tribunal and making one order against both the tenant(s) and the guarantor.

On the other hand, the T.P.A. only permitted the Tribunal to order the payment of rent (for example) against *a tenant*. In the context of arrears of rent, the guarantor may have been legally obliged to take responsibility for the debt of the tenant to the landlord, but that did not mean that the amounts owed by the guarantor constituted "rent". Rent is, by definition, paid for the right to occupy a unit and a guarantor has no such right.[184] Ultimately, the Tribunal adopted this approach, as was reflected in the Tribunal's Interpretation Guideline 11:

> In most cases, the guarantor has no express right of possession and, even if they do, no one expects them to ever occupy the rental unit. The Tribunal will not usually make an order against guarantors because they are not tenants. The claim against them is for damages, not rent. The Act does not authorize the Tribunal to deal with such claims, even if they are related to the issue of rent arrears. Landlords should seek enforcement of such obligations through the Courts.

The Board has also accepted this interpretation.[185] Nevertheless, the Board's Interpretation Guidelines are not binding upon its Members and it is still open to an individual Member to take a different approach, if the Member can provide cogent reasons for adopting a different interpretation.

3 — LANDLORDS AND TENANTS

---

[183] Subsection 174(1) of the T.P.A. (now s. 187(1) of the R.T.A.).

[184] See TSL-00469 (Aug. 28, 1998), overturned on review, and TNL-04119 (Jan. 27, 1999).

[185] See the Board's Interpretation Guideline No. 11 (p. 4).

15. LICENSEES

Licensees of residential premises were included in Part IV of the *Landlord and Tenant Act* by the amendment to the definition of "tenancy agreement" in s. 79 to include "a licence to occupy residential premises". Thedefinition of "tenancy agreement" in s. 2 of the R.T.A. specifically includesa licence to occupy a rental unit.

It may be academic to consider the distinction between a licence and a tenancy. The distinction is expressed in 27 Hals., 4 ed., 588. A licence is normally created where a person is granted the right to use premises without becoming entitled to exclusive possession of them, or the circumstances show that all that was intended was that the grantee should be granted a personal privilege ". . . while the property remains in the owner's possession and control . . .".

An obvious example, but not exempted from the R.T.A., would be nurses in a hospital residence who pay weekly or monthly for their accommodation. They merely enjoy a licence to live there while employed.[186] However, nurses as employees do not have security of tenure if their employment is terminated: s. 58(1)3 of the R.T.A.

For a licensee to be under the R.T.A., he or she must be a licensee of the landlord. Merely being an occupant does not make that person a licensee. In *S.R.G. Construction v. Zara*,[187] an occupant shared the accommodation with the tenant without the landlord's consent and was held to be a squatter and so a trespasser.[188]

16. LIFE TENANCY

A lease for the term of a tenant's life cannot be terminated under Part IV: *Oliver v. Harvey*.[189] The same holds true under the R.T.A. The very fact that the lease is for life precludes notice of termination being given under the R.T.A., unless there are termination provisions in the lease which might make the Act applicable.

The right of a tenant to be permitted to occupy for life usually arise sunder the terms of a will, and the obligations of landlords and tenants in the R.T.A. are not applicable to the life tenancy. Often a will may stipulate that the life tenant will be responsible for taxes, fire insurance, repairs and maintenance. If so, it is up to the tenant to look after repairs and expenses and not the estate which is the owner.

---

[186] (1971), [1972] 1 O.R. 244 (Ont. H.C.).

[187] (September 18, 1986), Davidson D.C.J. (Ont. Dist. Ct.).

[188] (1977), 4 C.P.C. 91 (Ont. H.C.).

[189] (1974), [1975] 2 W.W.R. 39 (Sask. Dist. Ct.).

In *Waters, Re*,[190] the question asked of the court was whether the life tenant or the executors of the estate must do the repairs required by a City of Toronto work order. The will stated that the life tenant should be responsible for repairs. The judge so held. There was no thought, apparently, of considering the effect of Part IV of the *Landlord and Tenant Act* and the obligation of the estate to repair.

Sometimes a life tenancy gives the life tenant the right to income from the property. If so, and the life tenant rents the property to a third party, the R.T.A. would apply to that tenancy. Nevertheless, the life tenancy terminate son death of the life tenant, and a lease by a life tenant terminates even if the expiry date happened to extend beyond the death of the life tenant: *CamstonLtd. v. Volkswagen Yonge Ltd.*[191]

17. CO-OWNERSHIP

Several years ago, before the current boom in condominium living, people devised various schemes in which they could collectively own the building in which they lived.

One method of accomplishing this was for the existing owner of the apartment building to sell percentage interests in the building to purchasers who then held their respective interests as tenants in common. Each tenant in common had a right to occupy a specific unit within the residential complex. If the purchaser already lived within the complex, by purchasing a percentage interest in the building, they also acquired the right to remain in the unit they currently occupied. If the purchaser was not already living in the building, he or she acquired the right to live in a particular unit and, if that unit was currently occupied by a tenant, to evict that tenant.

Another scheme involved the transfer of ownership of an apartment building to a corporation. Various individuals would own shares of the corporation and enter into a shareholders agreement with each other whereby each shareholder would have the right to occupy a specific unit in the building. If that unit was already occupied by a tenant, the shareholder would have the right to evict the tenant.

These co-ownership arrangements posed some difficulties under the existing law of residential tenancies. For instance, a particular co-owner may have had the right to occupy a specific unit in the complex that was currently occupied by a tenant. Did that make the co-owner the landlord of the tenant in that specific unit?

In *Blok-Glowczynski v. Stanga*,[192] the court held that there was no relationship of landlord and tenant between one tenant in common, that is, one

[190] (1978), 21 O.R. (2d) 124 (Ont. H.C.).

[191] [1968] 2 O.R. 65 (Ont. Co. Ct.), affirmed [1968] 2 O.R. 65 at 68n (Ont. C.A.).

[192] (1978), 22 O.R. (2d) 376 (Ont. Co. Ct.).

of the purchasers from the owner of the building, and the tenant of an apartment allotted by a right of occupancy agreement to that tenant in common. The landlord and tenant relationship is between all tenants in common, that is, all the owners and each apartment tenant. In other words, each tenant in common has an undivided small percentage interest in the entire building and in each apartment in the building.

Similarly, in *Kirsic v. Cyr*,[193] the judge discussed the interest of a tenant in common who had a right of occupancy agreement with all the other tenants in common for a specific apartment and held that the tenant in common was not the landlord with respect to that apartment. The landlord was all the tenants in common, that is, all the owners of the apartment building. The co-ownership agreement signed by the tenants in common regulated only the relationship between each tenant in common with respect to possession and occupancy of the various apartments, and was binding on them alone, and could not affect the relationship between a tenant in common and an existing tenant.

Subsequently, in *Mohammad v. Campbell*,[194] there was an easier fact situation to consider. The applicant for possession for himself under Part IV, s. 110(3)(*a*) was again a tenant in common with the right of occupancy, but who had rented his apartment to the tenant for a few years and then wished to obtain possession. An order was given terminating the lease and ordering possession. The above two cases were distinguished.

In *Medeiros v. Fraleigh*,[195] the facts were that the applicant for possession had purchased from a tenant in common who had the right of occupancy of the specific apartment and the predecessor had previously rented the apartment to the tenant who was still in possession. There was thus clearly established a landlord and tenant relationship. An order for possession was granted. The importance of the case is that the Ontario Divisional Court virtually overruled the *Blok-Glowcynski* and *Kirsic* cases. Accordingly, a tenant in common, whether a first purchaser or a subsequent purchaser, could obtain possession and evict an existing tenant.

The concern following the *Medeiros v. Fraleigh* decision was that more owners of apartment buildings might sell to purchasers who, as tenants in common, could evict existing tenants and so further deplete the stock of rental housing within the Province. By an amendment to the *Landlord and Tenant Act*, s. 110(4), Part IV, a person with a right of occupancy could no longer obtain possession for himself or his family, except in a building with six units or less or in the case where the person or his family had previously occupied the apartment.

---

[193] (1979), 25 O.R. (2d) 464 (Ont. Co. Ct.).

[194] (December 10, 1981), Doc. M58267/81 (Ont. Co. Ct.).

[195] (1983), 40 O.R. (2d) 793 (Ont. Div. Ct.).

The amendment effectively protected tenants' tenure[196] in apartment buildings which had been sold to tenants in common or to a corporation whose shareholders each had a right of occupancy of a specific apartment, with only the following two exceptions: (1) small buildings[197] and (2) situations where the landlord or a member of his or her family had previously occupied the unit.

Medeiros v. Fraleigh was followed in a case where one of two tenants in common satisfied the court that he required possession for occupation by himself and his family: *Wong v. Mercer*.[198] Although the notice of termination in this case was after the above amendment which added Part IV, s. 110(4), the prohibition did not apply as the building contained fewer than six units.

Wong v. Mercer was referred to but not followed in *Ciampini v. Dedman*,[199] because the court applied the amendment, s. 110(4), as there was an implied occupancy agreement and the unit in question was in a building containing 100 units, and so refused the application. The six-units exclusion did not apply.

Again in *Jan v. Quenneville*,[200] the application of a landlord for possession for her son was refused because neither exceptions in s. 110(4) applied, although the court did approve of *Medeiros v. Fraleigh* and there was anoccupancy agreement and the landlady had purchased the apartment unit.

Medeiros v. Fraleigh was applied in *Megan Investments Ltd. v. Funston*.[201] The single family house on a farm was owned as tenants in common 9/10, and a sole corporation of which Mr. Zahoruk was the sole shareholder and 1/10 by Mrs. Zahoruk, and when she received the transfer, there was included an endorsement that she was given the right to occupy. She desired to have possession for her daughter. The appropriate application for possession under s. 103, *bona fide* or as it is now called, good faith, was accepted and an order for possession followed.

Provisions similar to those under s. 110(4) of the *Landlord and Tenant Act* were carried forward first into the T.P.A. (s. 70(2)) and, now, into the R.T.A. (s. 72(2)).

Pursuant to s. 72(2) of the R.T.A., the Board cannot terminate a tenancy based upon ss. 48 or 49 ("own use" or "purchaser's use" applications) where the landlord's claim is based on a tenancy agreement or occupancy agreement that purports to entitle the landlord to reside in the rental unit unless:

3 — LANDLORDS AND TENANTS

---

[196] See *Cohen v. Klein* (May 11, 2001), TNL-17189(2), [2001] O.R.H.T.D. No. 66, 2001 CarswellOnt 6410 (Ont. Rental Housing Trib.).

[197] I.e., six or fewer residential units (under the *Landlord and Tenant Act*).

[198] (1985), 11 O.A.C. 158 (Ont. Div. Ct.).

[199] (September 23, 1986), Doc. York M1358541/86 (Ont. Dist. Ct.).

[200] (1988), 1 R.P.R. (2d) 191 (Ont. Dist. Ct.).

[201] (1992), 25 R.P.R. (2d) 63 (Ont. Gen. Div.).

1. the building contains four or fewer residential units; or
2. if the landlord, the landlord's spouse, a child or parent of the landlord or the landlord's spouse or a person who provided care services to one of them previously lived in the unit (was "a genuine occupant of the premises").

Special provisions apply if a part or all of a residential complex is converted to a condominium (s. 51 of the R.T.A.). In such circumstances, a tenant in possession at the time the declaration is registered cannot be given notice of termination for personal occupation (under s. 48 or 49 of the R.T.A.). Such a tenant has, as it were, lifetime protection.

4

Rental Premises Governed by the Residential Tenancies Act

1. INTRODUCTION

Non-residential tenancies in Ontario are generally governed by the *Commercial Tenancies Act*, R.S.O. 1990, c. L.7. The Landlord and Tenant Board has no jurisdiction over commercial tenancies.[1]

Only *residential* rental accommodations are governed by the *Residential Tenancies Act, 2006* (R.T.A.)[2] and its regulations. Section 3 of the R.T.A. states that the Act applies with respect to rental units in residential complexes, despite any other Act and despite any agreement or waiver to the contrary. Parties cannot opt out of this legislative scheme. Even if a residential landlord and tenant sign an agreement that states that the R.T.A. will not apply to the tenancy, that agreement has no legal effect. Furthermore, any provision in a tenancy agreement that is inconsistent with the R.T.A. or the regulations is void.[3]

According to s. 2 of the Act,[4] "rental unit" and "residential unit" both mean any living accommodation used or intended for use as rented residential premises and include: a site for a mobile home or site on which there is a land lease home; a room in a boarding house, rooming house or lodging house; and a unit in a care home.

"Residential complex" means:

(a) a building or related group of buildings in which one or more rental units are located;
(b) a mobile home park or land lease community;
(c) a site that is a rental unit;

---

[1] Landlord and Tenant Board File No. CET-01671 (Jan. 8, 2009).
[2] S.O. 2006, c. 17.
[3] Section 4 of the R.T.A. (subject only to s. 194).
[4] Most definitions are found in s. 2 of the R.T.A.

(d) a care home; and
(e) includes all common areas and services and facilities available for the use of its residents.

The definition of "residential premises" has been interpreted as including "all of those common facilities which are available to the tenants of a building": *Gagnon v. Centre-Town Developments Ltd.*[5] In this case the common facilities included the recreational areas such as the sun-deck, sauna room, squash court and swimming pool. It was also stated that the *Landlord and Tenant Act* shall be deemed to be remedial[6] and shall accordingly receive such liberal construction as will best ensure the attainment of the object of the Act according to its true intent, meaning and spirit: s. 10 of the *Interpretation Act.* The Supreme Court of Canada likewise held in *Herbold v. Pajelle Investments Ltd.*,[7] that the words "rented premises" have a broader connotation than mere physical space of the apartment suite, and include the swimming pool and sauna and whatever a tenant is entitled to under the terms of a written lease or the implied tenancy agreement. Although these decisions were made under previous legislation, they would apply equally to a rental unit and residential complex as defined in s. 2 of the R.T.A.

The provision of recreational facilities and other extras can be at a separate charge for use, but this should be clearly stated in the original tenancy agreement. Although a fairly long specific list of services and facilities may be stated in a lease, that would not limit the number of services and facilities which might be made available by a landlord, and so various other non-listed services and facilities might well be the obligation of a landlord if they had been promised to a prospective tenant.

The fact that two buildings are owned or operated by the same landlord does not necessarily mean that they form one residential complex. Where the buildings are on different streets and are not adjacent to each other (i.e., are separated by property owned by others), they will likely not be considered to form one residential complex.[8]

The general rule is that the R.T.A. applies to all residential rental accommodations in Ontario unless the tenancy is of a type specifically excluded from the Act. Some rental units are *partially* exempt from the Act (i.e., they are exempt from specified provisions of the R.T.A. but not from the entire

---

[5] (1975), 10 O.R. (2d) 245 (Ont. Co. Ct.), reversed on other grounds (1976), 14 O.R. (2d) 550 (Ont. Div. Ct.).

[6] (1975), 10 O.R. (2d) 245 at 247 (Ont. Co. Ct.), reversed on other grounds (1976), 14 O.R. (2d) 550 (Ont. Div. Ct.).

[7] (1975), [1976] 2 S.C.R. 520 (S.C.C.).

[8] See Landlord and Tenant Board File No. TEL-13012 (Aug. 13, 2008) in which an application to terminate a tenancy was dismissed as the alleged illegal act occurred in another building owned by the same landlord but which building was not part of the residential complex in which the tenant resided.

Act) and other rental units are *completely* exempt from the Act. The partial exemptions are listed in ss. 6, 7 and 8 of the R.T.A. and ss. 5, 6 and 7 of O. Reg. 516/06.

Complete exemption from the R.T.A. is determined either by the character of the parties involved[9] or by the fact that the tenancy falls within one of the categories listed in s. 5 of the R.T.A. Tenancies that are completely exempt from the R.T.A. generally fall into one of the following categories:

1. Non-residential tenancies.
2. Tenancies on property owned by the provincial Crown, where the Crown has an interest (s. 5(m) of the R.T.A.) or that is exclusively under federal jurisdiction.
3. Vacation and seasonal accommodations (s. 5(*a*)).
4. Business/agricultural use with accommodation attached (s. 5(*j*)).
5. Rentals to employees (ss. 5(*b*) and (*h*)).
6. Accommodations in institutions (ss. 5(*d*), (*e*), (*f*), (*k*) and (*l*)).
7. Living accommodation provided by a non-profit housing co-operative (s. 5(*c*)).
8. Accommodations at certain educational institutions (s. 5(*g*)).
9. Accommodations in which the tenant and owner share a kitchen or bathroom (s. 5(*i*)).

The remainder of this chapter will be devoted to explaining what types of rental units are governed by the R.T.A. and which ones are partially or completely exempt from this legislation.

2. RENTING AND RE-RENTING UNITS AS A BUSINESS

The point for consideration here is not whether a lease comes within the exclusion of s. 5(*j*) for "business or agricultural purposes with living accommodation attached", but whether a commercial lease of residential units comes within the R.T.A.

When there is a commercial lease of an apartment building to a head tenant who then rents the apartment suites for residential premises, one would have thought that the head lease would not be under the R.T.A. Although the "head tenant" is renting a number of residential units from the landlord, that tenant has no intention of actually residing in any of the units in the building. The head tenant rents several units in the complex (or the entire complex) with the express intention of subletting the units to other persons. The relationship between the head tenant and the various subtenants who actually

[9] See the definitions of "landlord" and "tenant" under s. 2 of the R.T.A. and the analysis of this issue found in Chapter 3.

rent and live in the rental units is clearly governed by the R.T.A. but it is less certain whether this is also true of the contract between the owner of the building and the head tenant (which is strictly a commercial transaction[10]).

The term "residential premises" was considered in *Matlavik Holdings Ltd. v. Grimson*,[11] in which the owner of 31 apartments leased all of them, that is, the whole building, to a tenant for a term of five years with a right of renewal so that the tenant in the course of his business could lease each of the apartments on short terms of daily, weekly or monthly tenancies. Again one would have thought that the basic lease was a commercial transaction but the Divisional Court in a majority judgment simply held it was a lease of residential premises and that the *Residential Premises Rent Review Act*,[12] then in force, applied. The dissenting judge felt that, as essentially a business contract, the relationship between the owner and the head tenant ought not to be governed by law applicable to residential tenancies.

The *Matlavik* case, *supra*, was distinguished in *Deerhurst Investment Ltd. v. FPI Management Systems Ltd.*[13] The head landlord had leased a number of apartments to a tenant company for the carrying on of the tenant's business of renting furnished apartments on a daily, weekly or monthly basis. This was quite similar to the commercial arrangement in *Matlavik*. The question was whether the head lease was of commercial or residential premises. The trial judge held that it was a commercial lease. It was held that the tenant company had no intention of occupying the apartments but rented them from the landlord for business purposes; renting the suites out at per diem rates. The trial judge went on to say that he would have preferred to follow the dissenting judgment in *Matlavik*. However, he got around the majority judgment in *Matlavik* and distinguished that case on the basis that the business of the head tenant was the operating of a hotel that was excluded from "residential premises" by s. 1(*g*) and so was not under Part IV of the *Landlord and Tenant Act* (now s. 5(*a*) of the R.T.A.). In *552838 Ontario Ltd. v. London Executive Suites Inc.*,[14] the court followed the *Deerhurst* case, *supra*, and held that the units were for hotel type use and were excluded by s. 1(*g*) of Part IV of the *Landlord and Tenant Act* and therefore the head lease of all the units to a tenant to operate the units was a commercial lease.

Whether or not the Act applies apparently does not depend upon what the head landlord and head tenant intended, albeit a business matter; rather, it depends on the nature and use of the premises. The last statement follows

---

[10] One might wonder how such an arrangement can be profitable, since a head tenant cannot legally charge more rent to a subtenant than the head tenant pays for the unit to the landlord (s. 134(1)(*c*) of the R.T.A.).

[11] (1979), 24 O.R. (2d) 92 (Ont. Div. Ct.).

[12] S.O. 1975 (2nd Sess.), c. 12.

[13] (1984), 50 O.R. (2d) 687 (Ont. Co. Ct.), affirmed (1985), 50 O.R. (2d) 687n (Ont. Div. Ct.).

[14] (1992), 1992 CarswellOnt 4017 (Ont. Gen. Div.).

from *Queen Elizabeth Hospital v. Campbell.*[15] The head tenancy was to a tenant operating a rooming house, which at the time of the lease was excluded from Part IV. Rooming houses are now covered under the R.T.A. As rooming houses were then excluded, the court could have followed *Deerhurst*. However, the head lease included a covenant by the tenant to use the premises for residential purposes, and rent increases had been under the *Residential Premises Rent Review Act.*[16]

A different, and perhaps preferable, approach was taken by the District Court in *European Style Bldgs. Ltd. v. 191 St. George Street Ltd.*[17] The head lease was of a 100 suite apartment building. All units, except the superintendent's unit, were then rented by the head tenant. The judge held that the head lease was commercial and Part IV did not apply. The judge referred to an obiter statement in *Mount Citadel Ltd. v. Ibar Developments Ltd.*:[18] "assuming, as [the judge did], that the head lease is not a residential lease but a commercial tenancy as between the plantiff [lessor] and defendent [lessee]." The judge expressed approval of the dissent in *Matlavik, supra*. The judge also mentioned *Prucyk v. Bay-Gerrard Foods Ltd.*,[19] which concerned a head lease of a mobile home park. It was noted by the judge in that case that the head landlord proceeded under Part IV against the head tenant and the subtenants, and the court held that Part IV applied. Next, the judge considered the *Queen Elizabeth Hospital* case, *supra*, and distinguished that case as it was of a lease of a house, even though the tenant was operating a rooming house. In finishing the reasons, the judge stated that the head landlord was not seeking to evict any of the residential sub-tenants, but only to take over the operation of what was presumably a profitable enterprise. This judgment makes sense, as did the dissent in *Matlavik*.

The *Matlavik* dissent was accepted and followed in *Northwest Territories Housing Corp. v. Yellowknife Syndicate.*[20] The court held that the basic lease of a residential building to a corporation, which was in the business of renting the units, was a commercial lease, but it must be noted that the wording of the legislation considered in this case[21] differed from the Ontario statute (Part IV of the *Landlord and Tenant Act*).

In a more recent case, *Port Sarnia Property Professionals v. Gateway Property Management Corp.*,[22] the Rental Housing Tribunal adopted an approach similar to that of the District Court in *European Style Bldgs. Ltd. v.*

---

[15] (1985), 53 O.R. (2d) 14 (Ont. Div. Ct.).

[16] S.O. 1975 (2nd Sess.), c. 12.

[17] (1987), 1987 CarswellOnt 2937 (Ont. Dist. Ct.).

[18] (1976), 14 O.R. (2d) 318 (Ont. H.C.) at 327.

[19] (October 21, 1983), Carnwath Co. Ct. J. (Ont. Co. Ct.).

[20] [1990] N.W.T.R. 269 (N.W.T. S.C.).

[21] *Residential Tenancies Act*, R.S.N.W.T. 1988, c. R-5.

[22] (April 12, 2006), SWT-07262, 2006 CarswellOnt 4422, [2006] O.R.H.T.D. No. 47 (Ont. Rental Housing Trib.).

191 St. George Street Ltd.[23] Port Sarnia Property Professionals leased 12 residential units of the 155 located within this residential complex managed by Gateway Property Management Corp. Port Sarnia Property Professionals then furnished the units and re-rented the units to various individuals. It was acknowledged that the tenancy agreements between the persons living within the units and Port Sarnia Property Professionals were governed by the provisions of the T.P.A. What was in question was whether the Act applied to the relationship between Port Sarnia Property Professionals and Gateway Property Management Corp. After considering the definitions set out in the Act for "rent", "tenant", "rental unit" and "landlord", the Member concludes there is no residential "landlord" and "tenant" relationship between the parties. There is no analysis of the larger policy issues and no reference is made in this decision to any case law on this point (i.e., it appears that the Member was unaware of the Divisional Court decisions on this issue).

In *Optimal Space Inc. v. Margana Holdings Inc.*,[24] a judge of the Superior Court was asked to decide the nature of the contract between the landlord of five properties and the tenant who rented those properties. It was essentially a commercial contract between two sophisticated corporations. The corporate tenant, however, rented these properties to individuals as care homes. The tenant sought a declaration that the fact that it rented the properties out as care homes, governed by the *Tenant Protection Act*, rendered the premises "residential" and, therefore, the agreement between itself and the head landlord was also governed by the T.P.A. The tenant relied upon the Divisional Court decisions in the *Matlavik* and *Queen Elizabeth Hospital* cases.[25] The Superior Court judge, who clearly did not want to follow *Matlavik*, distinguished it on the basis that under the *Residential Premises Rent Review Act, 1975*, the definition of "tenancy agreement" referred to an agreement for *possession* of residential premises whereas the definition under the *Tenant Protection Act* referred to a tenancy agreement as an agreement for *occupancy* of a rental unit. The judge distinguished the *Queen Elizabeth Hospital* case on the basis that in that case, the Divisional Court had to be concerned with the predominate nature of the premises since the properties were multi-use or multi-purpose whereas care homes remain care homes even where receiving care services is not the primary purpose of their occupation. The judge therefore felt free not to follow these Divisional Court decisions and found that the fact that the subtenancies were governed by the T.P.A. did not change the commercial nature of the tenancy between the head landlord and the head tenant, both of whom were sophisticated parties whose original intention was to enter into a commercial transaction not governed by the T.P.A.

---

23 (1987), 1987 CarswellOnt 2937 (Ont. Dist. Ct.).

24 (2005), [2005] O.J. No. 1708 (Ont. S.C.J.).

25 *Matlavik Holdings Ltd. v. Grimson* (1979), 24 O.R. (2d) 92 (Ont. Div. Ct.) and *Queen Elizabeth Hospital v. Campbell* (1985), 53 O.R. (2d) 14 (Ont. Div. Ct.).

The leading cases on this point from the Ontario Divisional Court suggest that, unless the unit is exempted by what is now s. 5 of the R.T.A., if the re-renting, subletting or making available is for "residential premises," then the head lease will be treated as a lease of residential accommodation governed by the R.T.A. and will not fall under the *Commercial Tenancies Act*.[26] Nevertheless, there has recently been some movement by the courts away from the principles laid down in *Matlavik* and *Queen Elizabeth Hospital* cases.[27] Until the Divisional Court has an opportunity to revisit this issue, some uncertainty will remain in this area.

3. RESIDENTIAL RENTAL PREMISES ON INDIAN LANDS

The question of whether a residential tenancy on an Indian Reserve should be dealt with under the *Indian Act*[28] or the R.T.A. is not entirely clear. The question really is whether the Province has jurisdiction to regulate an interest in property over which the federal government may have exclusive legislative authority.

Anderson v. Triple Creek Estates[29] held that the *Indian Act* applied to an application for possession, and the judgment refers to a number of cases on the subject.

Subsequently, in *Matsqui Indian Band v. Bird*,[30] the court stated that legislative jurisdiction was exclusively federal. The British Columbia *Residential Tenancy Act*[31] did not apply. The common law did. One month's notice to terminate monthly tenancy was sufficient.

In an earlier case, *Millbrook Indian Band v. Nova Scotia (Northern Counties Residential Tenancies Board)*,[32] the Nova Scotia Court of Appeal confirmed the trial judge's decision that the *Residential Tenancies Act* has no application to Indian Reserve lands, which are in the exclusive jurisdiction of the federal government.

An apparent opposite view was taken in *Fort William First Nation v. Pervais*,[33] that is, the court dealt with the plaintiff First Nation's claim for possession for arrears of rent under Part IV (of the *Landlord and Tenant Act*) and for the tenant the lack of repair under s. 94(1) of Part IV and for the arrears of rent. There was the tenant's request for relief under s. 121 of Part IV, for which the judge granted relief for the tenant. Oddly, no mention was

[26] R.S.O. 1990, c. L.7, which is applicable to non-residential tenancies in Ontario.

[27] *Matlavik Holdings Ltd. v. Grimson* (1979), 24 O.R. (2d) 92 (Ont. Div. Ct.) and *Queen Elizabeth Hospital v. Campbell* (1985), 53 O.R. (2d) 14 (Ont. Div. Ct.).

[28] R.S.C. 1985, c. I-5.

[29] (1990), 1990 CarswellBC 1048 (B.C. S.C.).

[30] (1992), [1993] 3 C.N.L.R. 80 (B.C. S.C.).

[31] S.B.C. 1984, c. 15.

[32] (1978), 28 N.S.R. (2d) 268 (N.S. C.A.).

[33] (1996), 19 O.T.C. 253 (Ont. Gen. Div.).

made of the *Indian Act* and lack of jurisdiction to deal with Part IV matters. The decision was appealed by the landlord on the basis of the *Indian Act*, even though the action and the trial had gone ahead without reference to the *Indian Act*. Counsel for the First Nations was of the opinion that the *Indian Act* applied. However, the case was settled before the appeal was heard.

The Rental Housing Tribunal has had to wrestle with this issue on a couple of occasions under the T.P.A. In *Lightfoot v. Big Canoe*,[34] it was held that it is possible for some provisions of the *Tenant Protection Act* to apply to a tenancy located on lands reserved for Indians (such as the sections that permit the Tribunal to protect the rights of tenants) but for the Tribunal to lack jurisdiction to enforce other provisions of the Act (such as those concerning termination of the tenancy).

Similarly, in *Nolan v. Charlie*,[35] the Tribunal held that the question of its jurisdiction over tenancies on Indian land must be decided on the facts of each case. In *Nolan*, because the tenants were not "Indians or band members", it was held that a valid tenancy agreement did not exist and that the T.P.A. did not apply.

In Landlord and Tenant Board File No. SWT-01763 (Jan. 21, 2009), it was held that "lands reserved for Indians" under paragraph 91.24 of the *Constitution Act, 1867* need not necessarily be located on lands that have the official status of "Reserve lands". In this case, the residential complex was constructed by the Band for occupation by Band Members and the Band Council acted as the landlord. The complex, however, was located outside of the Reserve (on land that the Band hoped, through court action, to have added to the Reserve at some point in the future). The Board Member was satisfied on the facts of this case that, although the land upon which the residential complex was located was not currently part of the Reserve, it was nevertheless "lands reserved for Indians" and, as such, fell within the exclusive jurisdiction of the federal government.

Therefore, whether or not the R.T.A. applies to a residential rental accommodation located on an Indian Reserve depends on the exact nature of the tenancy, the parties involved (i.e., whether they are covered by the *Indian Act*) and the nature of the relief being sought. Such cases tend to be rare. By their nature, though, they also tend to be very complex, involving legal arguments about constitutional issues.

4. CROWN LANDS

A recent decision of the Divisional Court seems to conclude that the T.P.A. has no application to land owned by the Province. In *Wheeler v.*

---

[34] (Sept. 12, 2001), TNT-01748, 2001 CarswellOnt 6305, [2001] O.R.H.T.D. No. 119 (Ont. Rental Housing Trib.).

[35] (June 19, 2002), NOT-00316, [2002] O.R.H.T.D. No. 71 (Ont. Rental Housing Trib.).

Ontario (Minister of Natural Resources),[36] a number of individuals leased summer resort lots within a provincial park. The rental agreements provided that the premises were for recreational purposes and not as year-round permanent residences and specifically excluded the premises from the predecessor legislation to the T.P.A. The Ontario Rental Housing Tribunal ruled that the T.P.A. did not apply to the leases. Three individuals appealed this decision. The Divisional Court, in dismissing the appeal, ruled that the T.P.A. does not apply to property owned by the provincial Crown because the *Interpretation Act*, R.S.O. 1990, c. I.11 provides in s. 11 that "No Act affects the rights of Her Majesty, Her heirs or successors, unless it is expressly stated therein that Her Majesty is bound thereby." In the alternative, the Court held that it would have found that such recreational properties could not be characterized as "residential units" within a "residential complex" or as a "land lease community" as contemplated by the T.P.A. The Divisional Court distinguished the facts in this case from *Moss v. Jackson*[37] on the basis that the structures being considered in *Moss* were permanent and intended as such, were not located in a provincial park and were not subject to rental agreements that restricted their use to summer recreation. Presumably, the Divisional Court's decision in *Wheeler* would apply equally to the R.T.A.

While this decision may make sense when it comes to provincial parks, its potential broader implications are of real concern. At one time, the provincial government (through various agencies) was one of the biggest landlords (if not the biggest) in Ontario. It owned and operated numerous residential complexes containing thousands of rental units, primarily subsidized housing for the most vulnerable segment of the population. Disputes concerning such properties have always been adjudicated under the provincial law relating to residential tenancies (i.e., the R.T.A. and the predecessor legislation). Although the responsibility for such complexes was "downloaded" a few years ago from the Province onto various municipal governments across Ontario, the Province still owns a considerable amount of real estate and if *Wheeler* is applied broadly, residential tenancies owned or operated by the Province may be found to be completely outside of the scope of the R.T.A.

I suggest that a distinction must be made between land owned by the Province itself and residential premises owned or operated by a corporation or other agency of the Crown. A distinction between the Crown and Crown agencies and corporations already exists in law.[38] Making such a distinction would enable Members to follow the *Wheeler* decision but restrict it to cases with similar facts. Such an approach would avoid undoing years of practice,

[36] (2005), 75 O.R. (3d) 113 (Ont. Div. Ct.).

[37] (February 18, 2002), Doc. 00-DV-000512 (Ont. Div. Ct.) (re EAL-07687), discussed below in the section on vacation and seasonal accommodations.

[38] *Proceedings Against the Crown Act*, R.S.O. 1990, c. P.27.

and respect the intention of the legislators that the R.T.A. apply to *all* residential rental premises except for those specifically excluded by the provisions of the Act.

5. COMPLETE EXEMPTIONS

Assuming that it has been established that a landlord and tenant relationship exists between the parties,[39] there are still situations where the tenancy will be exempt from the provisions of the R.T.A. Some of those situations are discussed below. It should be noted that once it has been established that the unit is a rental unit in a residential complex, it will be presumed that the R.T.A. applies; if a party alleges that the R.T.A. does not apply to such a unit, the burden of proof will rest upon that party who is claiming the exemption.[40]

(a) Non-Residential Use and Mixed Use

Since the R.T.A. only regulates rental units in residential complexes, non-residential tenancies are exempt from the Act. Disputes that arise between commercial (i.e., non-residential) landlords and tenants must generally be resolved in the courts as the Landlord and Tenant Board has no jurisdiction over such relationships. For instance, in *Bogoros v. Grossi*,[41] the plaintiff was renting a garage from the defendant in which he stored a vehicle and some other goods. The plaintiff lived elsewhere and did not rent any other premises from the defendant – only the garage. The plaintiff alleged that the garage had been broken into and that there had been damage done to his property and he sought damages against the defendant in Small Claims Court. The Court agreed that the *Tenant Protection Act* did not apply to the garage as it was not a "living accommodation" within a "residential complex".

In *Lake v. Kalpakis*,[42] the tenant commenced an application against the landlord for an order determining whether the landlord harassed, obstructed, coerced, threatened or interfered with her, and determining whether the landlord failed to meet his maintenance obligations. As a preliminary matter, the landlord raised the issue of whether or not the T.P.A. applied to this rental unit; the landlord argued that the T.P.A. did not apply to the unit because it

---

[39] See Chapter 3.

[40] *Ramsay v. Heselmann* (1983), 42 O.R. (2d) 255 (Ont. Div. Ct.); *Koressis v. Turner* (1986), 54 O.R. (2d) 571 (Ont. Div. Ct.); *Foster v. Lewkowicz* (1993), 34 R.P.R. (2d) 74 (Ont. Gen. Div.); *Marshall v. Cao* (June 9, 2003), EAT-04545, [2003] O.R.H.T.D. No. 79, 2003 CarswellOnt 2664 (Ont. Rental Housing Trib.); *Lanthier v. 963324 Ontario Ltd.* (1992), 1992 CarswellOnt 2469 (Ont. Gen. Div.).

[41] (2007) 2007 CarswellOnt 8635 (Ont. S.C.J.).

[42] (Dec. 10, 1999), TNT-00793 (Ont. Rental Housing Trib.).

was zoned for commercial use. The Tribunal ruled that whether or not the T.P.A. applied to this tenancy was determined by how the unit was being used, not by how the property was zoned.

A similar conclusion was reached by the Divisional Court in *436235 Ontario Ltd. and Volpi v. Mountfort.*[43] In 1991, a court order was issued declaring that a portion of this complex could not be used for residential purposes because such a use violated municipal zoning by-laws. In 1998, a tenancy that was the subject matter of the applications before the Tribunal began in another part of the complex. Although the lease purported to be for commercial use, both parties were aware that the tenant intended to live in the unit and did live in the unit. When the tenant later refused to pay an illegal rent increase, the landlord threatened to remove him by any means necessary. The landlord locked the tenant out of the unit. The tenant applied to the Tribunal, which issued an order requiring the landlord to provide keys to the tenant and requiring the landlord pay to the tenant $500 per day until the landlord allowed the tenant back into the rental unit. The landlord refused to comply with this order and the Tribunal then issued a second order against the landlord for $10,000. This latter order was upheld upon appeal. The Divisional Court ruled that the landlord could not hide behind either the 1991 court order or the municipal by-laws.

In the *Mountfort* case,[44] the landlord relied upon the case of *Curnew et al. v. 463235 Ontario Ltd.*[45] The landlord argued that *Curnew* stands for the proposition that if a tenancy violates the municipal by-laws, it should be treated as a nullity. If this is actually what *Curnew* means, then I suggest that it is not good law and ought not to be followed. While such an interpretation might relieve a tenant of his or her obligations under the tenancy agreement, it would also have the effect of stripping such a tenant of all rights and protections afforded by the R.T.A. In my view, such an interpretation is contrary to public policy and flies in the face of s. 3 of the R.T.A., which provides that the R.T.A. applies with respect to rental units in residential complexes, despite any other Act (which I would think includes zoning by-laws) and despite any agreement or waiver to the contrary.

In *Scarlett v. Mpampas*,[46] a Member of the Rental Housing Tribunal held that, in determining whether or not the tenancy was residential or commercial, his decision turned not on whether the tenant was actually living in the unit but upon the intention of the parties at the time they made their contract (as reflected in the terms of the tenancy agreement). The Member held that the rental unit in question was exempt from the Act by the provisions of s. 3(*j*) of the T.P.A. (now s. 5(j) of the R.T.A.).

---

[43] (September 20, 2002), Doc. 450/00, 499/00 (Ont. Div. Ct.) (re TST-02063 and TST-02095).

[44] (September 20, 2002), Doc. 450/00, 499/00 (Ont. Div. Ct.) (re TST-02063 and TST-02095).

[45] (April 6, 1998), Doc. Toronto 97-LT-145330 (Ont. Gen. Div.).

[46] (Jan. 21, 2003), TST-05448, 2003 CarswellOnt 1595 (Ont. Rental Housing Trib.).

Where the use to which a rental unit is put changes over time or where a rental unit is used for a combination of residential and non-residential purposes, characterizing the premises is not always a simple task. Since only *residential* premises are subject to the R.T.A., if the issue is raised, the Board must make a determination.[47]

How the premises are treated will depend, in large part, upon the intention of the parties. If the rental unit was intended to be used as a residence, then the fact that the tenant also does some business in the unit may not change its character.[48] If the tenancy agreement was for exclusively non-residential purposes (say, for example, the renting of industrial space to be used as an auto repair shop), then the tenant should not be able to avail himself of the protections of the R.T.A. by later taking up residence in the shop without the knowledge or consent of the landlord. In such circumstances, it might be appropriate to take the approach suggested in *Scarlet v. Mpampas, supra*, and determine the nature of the tenancy by the terms of the original agreement (thereby preventing one party from unilaterally altering the fundamental nature of their contract). This approach would arguably not be appropriate, however, where the change in the nature of the tenancy was based upon an express or implied agreement of the parties. Imagine a case where a person rents commercial space and then, after the tenancy has already commenced, asks the landlord for permission to also live in the space. If the landlord agrees (and perhaps even assists by adding some amenities to the unit to make the space more habitable), should the landlord later (when the relationship between the parties sours) be able to treat the rental unit as commercial space that is exempt from the R.T.A.? What if the space was rented from the beginning with the understanding that it would be used for both residential and non-residential purposes?

Combined business and residential uses were dealt with in *Hahn v. Kramer*.[49] The tenant was running a music publishing business in the residential premises. He did not have any other business premises. The trial judge held that the premises were not residential. Nevertheless, on appeal to the Divisional Court, the majority held that the premises were residential premises and that Part IV of the *Landlord and Tenant Act* applied. One judge stated that the wording of the exclusion from the Act, "business purposes with living accommodation attached", indicated that the business purposes

---

[47] Whether or not a rental premises is residential is a different question than whether the property is exempt from the R.T.A. pursuant to s. 5(*j*) of the Act; that topic will be dealt with later in this Chapter.

[48] If the business is illegal or is substantially interfering in the lawful rights of the landlord or in the reasonable enjoyment of other tenants in the complex, then this may be grounds for the landlord to seek to terminate the tenancy. The business activities, however, will generally not be deemed to change the character of the residential unit or the tenancy, which remain subject to the provisions of the R.T.A.

[49] (1979), 23 O.R. (2d) 689 (Ont. Div. Ct.).

should *predominate* in order for the premises not to be considered residential. Another member of the court agreed but preferred the reasoning that the word "attached" implied separation of the business and residential uses or areas of the premises. The dissenting judge's opinion was that when there is an acknowledged *combined* use and one of the uses is for business purposes, the premises do not come within the definition of residential premises.

This "predominant use" test suggested by the Divisional Court is useful in situations where the rental unit is used for both residential and non-residential purposes. In such circumstances, the predominant use to which the unit is put will determine whether or not the unit will be considered to be a residential premises (and, therefore, subject to the provisions of the R.T.A.).

In *Interpark Developments Ltd. v. McLaughlin*,[50] the rented property consisted of a house, barn and shed. The tenant lived in the house and operated a dog kennel in and around the rented buildings. It was held to be a combined use and therefore not residential premises (applying the "combined use" test referred to in the dissenting opinion in *Hahn v. Kramer*[51]). Note that, in situations of combined use, if the business use is discontinued, the exemption no longer applies.[52]

Interpark Developments, supra, was followed in *Petrolo v. Winstone*.[53] This case related to a lease of a farmhouse and 62 acres. The tenant was operating a horse boarding and training business. The applicant landlord's position was that the lease was non-residential and was exempt from Part IV of the *Landlord and Tenant Act*. The court agreed and was satisfied that the residential premises were functionally (although not physically) "attached" to the barn, paddocks and the land. In deciding that the lease was non-residential the judge relied on either the predominating factor of the business as per *Hahn v. Kramer, supra*, or the combined use as in *Interpark Developments, supra*. The court also considered that the lease was for agricultural purposes with living accommodation attached. The relevant zoning was for agricultural uses, which included riding and/or boarding stables or for pasturing horses. The court therefore relied on the "predominant use" test, the "combined use" test and the precursor to s. 5(*j*) of the R.T.A. to find that the property was not subject to Part IV of the *Landlord and Tenant Act*.

In *Bindex Engineering Corp. v. Elliott*,[54] the landlord rented space in an old building as an artist's studio. The tenant made some renovations and took up residence in the unit. The judge distinguished *Hahn v. Kramer*, *supra*, and did not rely on the predominant use test of the majority judgment in that case, but held that as it was a combined use, that the premises were not residential

---

[50] (December 14, 1979), Quinlan J. (Ont. Co. Ct.).

[51] (1979), 23 O.R. (2d) 689 (Ont. Div. Ct.).

[52] *Carere v. Power* (1989), 1989 CarswellOnt 1557 (Ont. Div. Ct.).

[53] (1997), 12 R.P.R. (3d) 46 (Ont. Gen. Div.).

[54] (1987), 59 O.R. (2d) 245 (Ont. Dist. Ct.).

and were, therefore, exempt from Part IV. The judge stated that it was unrealistic to try and determine what was predominant since living and doing artistic work in an artist's studio was simply a combined use.

The *Bindex* case was then distinguished in *Dicks v. Maxbel Upholstery Ltd.*[55] A tenant was doing dressmaking in one room. The court followed *Hahn v. Kramer*, *supra*, and decided that doing dressmaking was not the predominant use and, accordingly, that the accommodations were residential premises.

The predominant purpose test of *Hahn* was followed in *Degasper v. Bateman.*[56] Although the lease was for a "general office and studio facility" the tenant intended to use the premises as her residence. The tenant was a writer and provided bookkeeping and financial consulting services. She saw no clients at her residence, had no employees, and except for her telephone used for business and a computer, there were few if any visible manifestations of her business on the premises. The court held that the predominant purpose was residential.

In *Petrakos, Re*[57] the tenant rented the main floor of this house, where she lived with her husband and their three children. She also operated an in-home day care in her unit. The landlord, who lived in this house, on the second floor, commenced an application to regain possession of the main floor so that she could occupy the entire house. The tenant argued that her unit was exempt from the T.P.A. on the basis that either: (1) her unit was used primarily for commercial, not residential purposes; or (2) it was occupied for business purposes with living accommodation attached (s. 3(j) of the T.P.A.). The Member ruled against the tenant on both points, finding that the predominant use of the unit was residential and that there was no separation of the business and residential premises so that it could not be said that the living accommodation was "attached" to business premises.

In conclusion, where one rental unit is being used for both residential and non-residential purposes and it becomes necessary for the Board to ascertain whether or not the rental unit is truly residential in nature, applying the "predominant use" test rather than the "combined use" test makes more sense to me. Many residential tenants work, at least part of the time, from their apartments or operate home-based businesses. For instance, in *Waterloo Apts. v. Lind*,[58] the tenant did his business by telephone from the apartment; it was held that this was not sufficient to exclude the lease from Part IV of the *Landlord and Tenant Act* as being for business purposes. Had the "combined use" test been applied, the result could have been quite different. The "combined use" test, if adopted by the Board, has the potential of depriving

---

[55] (March 31, 1988), Doc. 325492/88 (Ont. Dist. Ct.).

[56] (1990), 10 R.P.R. (2d) 56 (Ont. Dist. Ct.).

[57] (July 21, 2006), TSL-84285, 2006 CarswellOnt 9168 (Ont. Rental Housing Trib.).

[58] (1986), 1986 CarswellOnt 3118 (Ont. Dist. Ct.).

such tenants of the protection of the R.T.A. Since the "predominant use" test is the one that is more consistent with the purpose of the R.T.A. and seems to be the preferred approach of the Divisional Court, I would suggest that it is the better tool for analysing mixed use tenancies.

(b) Vacation and Seasonal Accommodations

Pursuant to s. 5(*a*) of the R.T.A. (formerly s. 3(a) of the T.P.A.), the Act does not apply with respect to living accommodation intended to be provided to the travelling or vacationing public or occupied for a seasonal or temporary period in a hotel, motel or motor hotel, resort, lodge, tourist camp cottage or cabin establishment, inn, campground, trailer park, tourist home, bed and breakfast vacation establishment or vacation home.

In *Rogers v. Fisherman's Cove Tenant & Trailer Park Ltd.*,[59] the Divisional Court has interpreted this provision to mean that the *Act* does not apply with respect to living accommodation that is:

(1) intended to be provided to the travelling or vacationing public; **or**

(2) occupied for a seasonal or temporary period in a hotel, motel or motor hotel, resort, lodge, tourist camp cottage or cabin establishment, inn, campground, trailer park, tourist home, bed and breakfast vacation establishment or vacation home.

Only one of the above criteria needs to be met in order to exempt the premises from the Act. With respect to the *second* of these two criteria, it is not the *intent* of the parties that determines whether the *Act* applies; rather, it is how the premises are actually being used that will decide the issue (i.e., whether the premises are occupied for a seasonal or temporary period).

It is sometimes assumed that *every* rental unit within a hotel, motel, inn or similar establishment is automatically completely exempt from the R.T.A. This is incorrect. In cases involving establishments that normally cater to the travelling or vacationing public, whether or not the R.T.A. applies to a rental unit within the complex is *not* determined by the nature of the establishment. Rather, it is determined by how that particular unit is being used (or is intended to be used).

In *Gohlisch and Rosetown Inn*,[60] exemption from the T.P.A. was claimed by the landlord as the operation was an inn for the travelling or vacationing public and was under the *Innkeepers Act*.[61] The Tribunal held that the unit occupied by the tenants was not exempted (i.e., the T.P.A. *did* apply to this unit) even if the rest of the complex was an inn. Similar rulings have

4 — RENTAL PREMISES GOVERNED

[59] Court File No. 1265, London, October 10, 2002 (unreported).

[60] (Feb. 18, 1999), CET-00245 (Ont. Rental Housing Trib.).

[61] R.S.O. 1990, c. I.7.

been made by the Tribunal in *Lee v. Hepburn*,[62] *Harret v. Park*,[63] and *Caissie v. Inn on the Creek*.[64] Calling the complex an "inn" or "hotel" does not make it so; the Board will consider the real substance of the transactions between the parties.[65] In any event, it is the character of the tenancy in question that is of paramount importance, not the character of the complex as a whole.

In situations such as these, the Board must ascertain whether occupation of the rented unit is transient or of a more enduring nature. In deciding the nature of the relationship between the parties, the Rental Housing Tribunal and the courts have considered such things as: the intention of the parties (in particular, whether the person renting the unit intends to make the unit his or her sole residence);[66] whether the unit comes furnished;[67] whether typical hotel services are provided;[68] the arrangements the parties have made for payment for occupation of the unit;[69] the degree of control the landlord retains over the unit and whether the landlord can enter at will;[70] and the intended and actual duration of the occupation.[71] Generally, the longer the stay, the less transient the relationship appears and the stronger the argument that the occupant has made the rental unit his or her home and is, therefore, entitled to the protections (and is burdened with the responsibilities) set out in the R.T.A.

In a couple of older cases,[72] however, the courts found certain rental units located within hotels to be exempt from Part IV of the *Landlord and Tenant Act*, notwithstanding that the units in question had been occupied continuously by the same person(s) for over a decade. It is difficult to understand how the courts could find such occupation to be of a transient nature. Given

---

[62] (Feb. 7, 2000), TEL-09512, 2000 CarswellOnt 6340 (Ont. Rental Housing Trib.).

[63] (Nov. 30, 2001), TNT-02185, 2001 CarswellOnt 6306 (Ont. Rental Housing Trib.).

[64] (March 10, 2003), TET-03037, 2003 CarswellOnt 1555 (Ont. Rental Housing Trib.).

[65] *Hooey v. Rahbari* (March 10, 2003), TET-03002 (Ont. Rental Housing Trib.) and *Millwared v. Park* (July 19, 2001), TST-03314 (Ont. Rental Housing Trib.).

[66] *Caissie v. Inn on the Creek* (March 10, 2003), TET-03037, 2003 CarswellOnt 1555 (Ont. Rental Housing Trib.); *Harrett v. Park* (Nov. 30, 2001), TNT-02185, 2001 CarswellOnt 6306 (Ont. Rental Housing Trib.).

[67] *Sohlisch and Rosetown Inn* (Feb. 18, 1999), CET-00245 (Ont. Rental Housing Trib.).

[68] *Ibid.*; *Curtis Property Management v. Rezai*, (March 28, 1989), Doc. York M17705/89 (Ont. Dist. Ct.).

[69] *Foster v. Lewkowicz* (1993), 34 R.P.R. (2d) 74, 14 O.R. (3d)339 (O.C. G.D.).

[70] *Curtis Property Management v. Rezai* (1989), 1989 CarswellOnt 2731 (Ont. Dist. Ct.).

[71] *Harrett v. Park* (Nov. 30, 2001), TNT-02185, 2001 CarswellOnt 6306 (Ont. Rental Housing Trib.); *Curtis Property Management v. Rezai* (1989), 1989 CarswellOnt 2731 (Ont. Dist. Ct.); *Alexander v. City View Motel* (May 12, 1999), SOT-00338 (Ont. Rental Housing Trib.).

[72] *Canadian Pacific Hotels Ltd. v. Hodges* (1978), 23 O.R. (2d) 577 (Ont. Co. Ct.) and *Deerhurst Investment Ltd. v. FPI Management Systems Ltd.* (1984), 50 O.R. (2d) 687 (Ont. Co. Ct.), affirmed (1985), 50 O.R. (2d) 687n (Ont. Div. Ct.).

the broader definition of the terms "tenant", "tenancy agreement"[73] and "rental unit" found in the R.T.A. (and, previously, in the T.P.A.), the supremacy of the R.T.A. over other provincial statutes[74] and the current emphasis upon security of tenure, these cases are unlikely to be followed by the Board.

Another issue that the Board will be called upon to adjudicate under s. 5(*a*) is whether or not the rental unit in question is "occupied for a seasonal or temporary period". Neither "seasonal" nor "temporary" are defined in the R.T.A.

This issue sometimes arises in the context of trailer parks. Where a trailer is found to be used only seasonally, it will be exempt from the R.T.A.[75] Where a trailer is accessible, useable and used throughout the year, the rental unit is not exempt (i.e., the R.T.A. does apply).[76]

The issue of seasonal or temporary use also arises in connection with cottages and cabins. In *Ross v. Minister of Natural Resources*,[77] the tenant had a 30-year lease to use this cottage, but only on a seasonal basis. The Tribunal held that the cottage was exempt from the T.P.A. pursuant to s. 3(*a*) (now s. 5(a) of the R.T.A.). This decision was upheld on appeal to the Divisional Court.

In *Putnam v. Grand River Conservation Authority*,[78] the landlord owned thousands of acres of land designated as conservation areas. Some lakes were located within these lands. The landlord permitted some use of the land around the lakes for summer cottagers. Although there was no question that the use was seasonal, the Tribunal held that the exemption in s. 3(*a*) of the T.P.A. (now s. 5(a) of the R.T.A.) did not apply because, in order to be exempt, the living accommodation had to be occupied for a seasonal or temporary period in a "cottage [establishment] or cabin establishment". These individual cottages were not located in a cottage establishment that was analogous to a hotel, motel, resort, lodge, tourist camp, inn, campground, trailer park and so forth. By this interpretation, it is not only the seasonal nature of the dwelling that is important but whether it is located within an establishment set up to

[73] By including in the definition of "tenancy agreement" a "licence to occupy a rental unit" and thereby eliminating the distinction between a tenant and a licensee which distinction may have been at the heart of this line of decision.

[74] Except for the *Ontario Human Rights Code*.

[75] *Paul Bunyan Trailer Camp Ltd. v. McCormick* (Sept. 25, 1998), SWL-00680 (Ont. Rental Housing Trib.), upheld on appeal (1999), 1999 CarswellOnt 5466 (Ont. Div. Ct.); *Currie v. Highland Pines Campground Ltd.* (1996), 15 O.T.C. 339 (Ont. Gen. Div.); and *Cousineau v. McCreary's Beach Vacation Resort Inc.* (Nov. 13, 1998), EAT-001917 (Ont. Rental Housing Trib.).

[76] *Coveny v. Teti* (Nov. 17, 2001), EAT-03179, 2001 CarswellOnt 6330 (Ont. Rental Housing Trib.) and *Becker v. Sedlezky* (May 27, 2005), SWT-06127-IN (Ont. Rental Housing Trib.).

[77] (June 10, 2002), Doc. 010016/2001 (Ont. Div. Ct.) (re NOT-00151).

[78] (2006), [2006] O.J. No. 2217, 2006 CarswellOnt 3365, 210 O.A.C. 191 (Ont. Div. Ct.), reversing (April 1, 2005), SWT-05672, SWT-05673, SWT-04384, SWT-04385, 2005 CarswellOnt 1287 (Ont. Rental Housing Trib.).

run a business catering to tourists and vacationers. The Divisional Court agreed with this interpretation of s. 3(a) of the T.P.A.[79]

In *Moss v. Jackson*,[80] the landlord granted to individuals long-term leases of lots of land around a lake and permitted those individuals to erect cottages on these lots. It was clearly a land lease community. Following the reasoning in the *Paul Bunyan* case (which related to a trailer park),[81] the Tribunal concluded that the properties were intended as summer vacation properties and that s. 3(*a*) of the T.P.A. (now s. 5(a) of the R.T.A.) applied, exempting the properties from the T.P.A. On appeal, the Divisional Court overturned the decision of the Tribunal and held that the property was subject to the T.P.A. Unlike the *Putnam* decision, the Court in this case did not analyze whether or not this cottage was located within a "cottage or cabin establishment". Instead, in a tersely written decision, the Court merely stated that whether the use of the cottages was seasonal or temporary was irrelevant because land lease communities are not specifically listed in s. 3(*a*) of the T.P.A. as one of the exempt establishments.

In Landlord and Tenant Board File No. CET-00058 (April 30, 2007), the tenant rented a cottage from the landlord. Typically, this landlord rents out cottages for short periods to the vacationing public during the summer months. In this case, the tenant rented the cottage in the off-season and anticipated staying from October 2006 until some time in June 2007. There was no written tenancy agreement. The tenant initially paid rent for October 2006 and June 2007 (first and last month's rent) and was required by the landlord to put the gas account into her name. The landlord charged a separate amount for electricity. Problems arose between the parties and the landlord locked the tenant out of the premises. The tenant commenced an application before the Board and the landlord alleged that the Board had no jurisdiction to intervene as this relationship was not governed by the R.T.A. as it was "living accommodation intended to be provided to the traveling or vacationing public, or occupied for a seasonal or temporary period . . . in a cottage establishment." On the facts of this case, the Member held that the exemption set out in s. 5(a) of the R.T.A. did not apply and that the tenancy was subject to the *Act* (i.e., that the tenant did have the right to bring an application before the Board). The Member held that it was the nature of the particular agreement between these parties that determined the nature of the tenancy rather than the character of the establishment as a whole or the landlord's usual business

[79] The Divisional Court, however, sent the matter back to the Tribunal for reconsideration because the Tribunal in its original decision failed to address the fact that the parties had previously entered into a mediated agreement in which they purported, pursuant to s. 181 of the T.P.A., to contract out of the provisions of the Act.

[80] (February 18, 2002), Doc. 00-DV-000512 (Ont. Div. Ct.) (re EAL-07687).

[81] *Paul Bunyan Trailer Camp Ltd. v. McCormick* (Sept. 25, 1998), SWL-00680 (Ont. Rental Housing Trib.), upheld on appeal (1999), 1999 CarswellOnt 5466 (Ont. Div. Ct.); *Currie v. Highland Pines Campground Ltd.* (1996), 15 O.T.C. 339 (Ont. Gen. Div.).

practices. In the absence of a written tenancy agreement, the agreement between the parties had to be implied from the documents that did exist and the conduct of the parties, including the amounts that were paid and accepted as the monthly rent. Having found that it had the jurisdiction, the Board proceeded to hear the application, found in favour of the tenant, terminated the tenancy and ordered the landlord to pay to the tenant the following: (1) damages for the value of the tenant's goods that were lost or destroyed as a result of the landlord's conduct; (2) the amount illegally collected by the landlord as a damage deposit; (3) an abatement of rent for the time during which the tenant was locked out of the unit; (4) moving and other related expenses ($1,500.00); and (5) costs.

For more information about mobile homes and land lease homes, please see Chapter 20.

(c) Business/Agricultural Use with Accommodation Attached

Section 5(j) of the R.T.A. (formerly s. 3(*j*) of the T.P.A.) exempts premises occupied for business or agricultural purposes with living accommodation attached if the occupancy for both purposes is under a single lease and the same person occupies the premises and the living accommodation.

In other words, a lease of a store (or factory, warehouse, garage, barn, etc.) with living accommodations attached is exempt from the R.T.A. if all of the conditions set out in s. 5(*j*) are present. For instance, s. 5(*j*) also states that there must be a single lease and that it must be the same person who occupies both the non-residential premises and the living accommodation. Accordingly, the exemption would not apply if there were separate tenancy agreements for the residential and non-residential portions of the rented space.

The issue of combined business and residential uses was discussed earlier under the heading, "Non-residential Use and Mixed Use". The "predominant use" test suggested by the Divisional Court is applicable where there is one rental unit that is being used for a combination of residential and non-residential purposes. In my view, s. 5(*j*) of the Act is meant to deal not with situations of multiple uses within a single unit but with situations where the premises are occupied for business or agricultural purposes and there is a "living accommodation attached" (i.e., where there is some physical separation of the living space from the non-residential activities). By the wording of s. 5(*j*), it is implicit that, for this exemption to apply, the business or agricultural purpose must be the focus of the tenancy; the attached residence is like a "bonus" feature of the tenancy. That is why cases decided under s. 5(*j*) (and its precursors) also enter into discussions about which purpose is predominant. This has lead to some blurring of the distinction between mixed use situations and those falling under s. 5(*j*). The similarity is that, in both types of cases, the tenancy will be exempt from the R.T.A. if it is determined that the true (or predominant) nature of the tenancy is other than residential (notwithstanding that the tenant might also live in the rented premises or in accommodations attached thereto).

When a farm property is rented together with the house, the predominant use is agricultural and so would be excluded from s. 5(*j*) of the R.T.A., as being "premises occupied for business or agricultural purposes with living accommodation attached under a single lease".

In *Petrolo v. Winstone*,[82] for instance, the tenant rented a farmhouse and 62 acres. The tenant was operating a horse boarding and training business. The relevant zoning was for agricultural uses, which included riding and/or boarding stables or for pasturing horses. The applicant landlord's position was that the lease was exempted from Part IV of the *Landlord and Tenant Act*. The court agreed and was satisfied that the lease was for agricultural purposes with living accommodation attached (*functionally*, not physically, attached).[83] A similar result was achieved in *Conley v. Walker*.[84] In *Conley*, the tenants rented part of a farm, which included the farmhouse. The tenants operated the following businesses on the premises: trail riding, a children's camp and a petting zoo. It was held that the premises were exempt pursuant to s. 3(*j*) of the T.P.A.

In *Silver v. Goldberry Inc.*,[85] the ground floor of the building was rented by the corporate tenant to be used as a store and the second and third floors were for the residence of the company's officer and director. The court decided that the building (including the residential part) were for business purposes. Whether a similar case decided under the R.T.A. would have been found to be exempt pursuant s. 5(*j*) would depend on whether both the residential and business uses were covered by a single lease and on whether the corporation occupying the business space was found to be the "same person" as the officer and director who occupied the residential portion of the building.[86] These were the issues with which the Tribunal had to wrestle in the case of *Karrum Properties Inc. v. Yolanda Enterprises Ltd.*[87]

In *Karrum Properties Inc. v. Yolanda Enterprises Ltd.*, *supra*, the landlord owned a three-storey property on a major downtown street where most buildings were used solely for commercial purposes. The area was zoned commercial-residential. The corporate tenant's skin and beauty care business

---

[82] (1997), 12 R.P.R. (3d) 46 (Ont. Gen. Div.).

[83] The judge also found this was not a residential tenancy, applying either the "predominant use" or "combined use" tests discussed earlier in this chapter.

[84] (2001), 2001 CarswellOnt 1356 (Ont. S.C.J.).

[85] (1985), Doc. York M116911/85 (Ont. Co. Ct.).

[86] Which would likely necessitate an analysis under s. 202 of the Act and a decision by the Board of whether or not to "pierce the corporate veil".

[87] (July 13, 2000), TSL-12922, 2000 CarswellOnt 3850, [2000] O.R.H.T.D. No. 184 (Ont. Rental Housing Trib.), affirmed (2001), 2001 CarswellOnt 1839 (Ont. Div. Ct.), affirmed (2002), 2002 CarswellOnt 3483 (Ont. C.A.).

occupied most of the second and third floors of the building. The original written lease was a commercial one. The principal of the corporate tenant and her close relatives and friends resided in units carved off from the business areas. The landlord applied for an order determining that the T.P.A. did not apply to the premises. Applying the test set out in *Hahn v. Kramer, supra*, the Member found that the predominant purpose here was commercial, not residential. Looking at the real substance of the matter (s. 188 of the T.P.A., now s. 202 of the R.T.A.), he also found that the business and residential portions of the unit were occupied by the same persons (members of the same family) and that both the business premises and the living accommodation were covered by a single lease with the landlord. Therefore, it was held that, pursuant to s. 3(*j*) of the T.P.A. (now s. 5(*j*) of the R.T.A.), the T.P.A. did not apply to these premises.

In *Petrakos, Re*[88] the tenant rented the main floor of this house, where she lived with her husband and their three children. She also operated an in-home day care in her unit. The landlord, who lived in this house, on the second floor, commenced an application to regain possession of the main floor so that she could occupy the entire house. The tenant argued that her unit was exempt from the T.P.A. on the basis that either: (1) her unit was used primarily for commercial, not residential purposes; or (2) it was occupied for business purposes with living accommodation attached (s. 3(j) of the T.P.A.). The Member ruled against the tenant on both points, finding that the predominant use of the unit was residential and that there was no separation of the business and residential premises so that it could not be said that the living accommodation was "attached" to business premises.

In a more recent case heard by the Landlord and Tenant Board, where the tenancy agreement provided for both residential occupation by the tenant as well as permission for the tenant to operate a small engine repair shop and to raise cattle, the Board held that, pursuant to s. 5(j) of the R.T.A., the Act did not apply.[89]

(d) Employees

An employee who is provided with a rental unit as part of his or her job is not automatically exempt from the R.T.A. In fact, as discussed in greater detail in Chapter 3, para. 58(1)3 and s. 93 of the R.T.A. contain specific provisions dealing with such tenancies.

There are, however, a couple of exceptions (i.e., tenancies involving employees to which the Act does not apply). These exemptions are found in ss. 5(*b*) and 5(*h*) of the Act.

[88] (July 21, 2006), TSL-84285, 2006 CarswellOnt 9168 (Ont. Rental Housing Trib.).

[89] Landlord and Tenant Board File No. TET-01314-RO (Jan. 13, 2009).

Section 5(*b*) exempts residential accommodations situated on or off a farm when occupancy is conditional upon the employee continuing to be employed on the farm. The tenancy of a farm manager who lives on the farm conditional on continuing to be employed would come within this exclusion.

Section 5(*h*) exempts an employee who lives in a building or project used in whole or in part for non-residential purposes when the occupation is conditional on the employee continuing to be employed.

During such tenancies, neither the landlord nor the tenant will have any recourse to the provisions of the R.T.A. and when the employment (and, therefore, the tenancy) ends, the landlord will have no right to commence proceedings under the R.T.A. If the tenant will not leave voluntarily, possession of the rental unit would have to be regained through court action.

The fact that a tenant of residential premises happens to be an employee of the landlord who is the owner of a business where the tenant was employed, does not give the owner as landlord the right to terminate the tenancy when the employment in the business is terminated: *Huron Dairy Equipment Ltd. v. Leppington.*[90]

Section 110(3)(*d*) of Part IV (*Landlord and Tenant Act*), which provides for the termination of a tenancy where the tenant is an employee whose services have been terminated, was given a broad interpretation in *Rio Algom Ltd. v. Roberts.*[91] In this case the tenant was not employed by the landlord, but was employed by a construction company, which had a contract with the landlord. By the terms of the contract the employee of the construction firm was provided with residential premises by the landlord while he continued to be employed by the construction firm. The employment was terminated. The court held that the subsection applied, and as the employment was terminated, the lease could also be terminated even though the tenant was not an employee of the landlord. The court noted that the subsection refers to accommodation "provided" by the employer, but does not specifically say that the employee must be an employee of the actual landlord.

This broad interpretation was not accepted in *Pan Properties Ltd. v. Vance*,[92] for two reasons. One was rather obvious: the tenancy agreement was for a reduced rent during employment and was to be increased after termination of employment and therefore was to continue after termination. The other reason was the judge's interpretation that the intent of the subsection was only for landlords who "offer accommodation [to their employees] as an incident of the employment or as an inducement to the employee" and so the landlord employer should be able to have the accommodation available if the tenant employee's employment was terminated. Here the tenant was an em-

---

[90] (1989), 1989 CarswellOnt 2695 (Ont. Dist. Ct.).

[91] (1979), 27 O.R. (2d) 288 (Ont. Dist. Ct.).

[92] (1980), 31 O.R. (2d) 234 (Ont. Co. Ct.).

ployee of a company whose major shareholder was also a shareholder of the landlord company, but the tenant was not in fact an employee of the landlord.

In *Harbour View (Sault Ste. Marie) Ltd. v. Greene*,[93] the tenant was an on-site salesperson, employed by the condominium corporation. As part of her compensation, she was allowed to live rent-free in one of the condominium units. It was held that this tenancy was not exempt from the *Landlord and Tenant Act*. A similar conclusion would likely have been reached under the R.T.A. (since the entire building is residential and, therefore, s. 5(*h*) would not apply).[94]

(e) Institutional Accommodations

(i) Accommodation for Rehabilitative or Therapeutic Purposes

Two types of accommodations fall within this category of exemptions. The first type is described in s. 5(k) of the R.T.A. It excludes living accommodation occupied by a person for the purpose of receiving rehabilitative or therapeutic services agreed upon by the person and the provider of the living accommodation, where:

(i) the parties have agreed that,

(A) the period of occupancy will be of a specified duration, or

(B) the occupancy will terminate when the objectives of the services have been met or will not be met, and

(ii) the living accommodation is intended to be provided for no more than a one year period.

"Rehabilitative" was defined in *Keith Whitney Homes Society v. Payne*[95] as "restoration of the individual to his or her greatest potential whether physically, mentally, socially or vocationally"; and "therapeutic" is defined by the Shorter Oxford English Dictionary as "to treat medically, pertaining to the healing of disease".

The other exemption is found in s. 5(l). It excludes living accommodation in a care home occupied by a person for the purpose of receiving short-term respite care.

Note that both exemptions are meant to deal only with a short-term stay in a facility for the purpose of receiving rehabilitative or therapeutic services. They do not represent a general exemption of long-term care facilities (i.e.,

[93] (March 19, 1982), Doc. 6729/82 (Ont. Dist. Ct.).

[94] (March 19, 1982), Doc. 6729/82 (Ont. Dist. Ct.).

[95] (1992), 9 O.R. (3d) 186 (Ont. Gen. Div.).

care homes[96]). In fact, the R.T.A. has specific provisions dealing with care homes (Part IX of the R.T.A.).

In *Barrie v. St. Michael's Halfway Houses, Matt Talbot House Division*,[97] numerous tenants commenced applications for a determination of whether or not the *Tenant Protection Act* applied to this residential complex. The landlord opposed the applications on several grounds, including the assertion that the complex was completely exempt from the T.P.A. under subsections 3(k) and 3(l) of the T.P.A. (now subsections 5(k) and 5(l) of the R.T.A.).

The Member found that s. 3(k) of the T.P.A. did not apply to many of the tenancies since they were not for fixed terms and even for the tenancies that were for fixed terms, the landlord was not providing rehabilitative or therapeutic services. Assistance with daily living or arranging for treatment to be provided elsewhere did not constitute the provision by the landlord of "rehabilitative or therapeutic services". The Member also found that the tenancies were *not* short-term so that, even if the landlord was providing respite care, the exemption provided by s. 3(l) of the T.P.A. would not apply. Thus, the landlord had failed to prove that these tenancies were completely exempt from the T.P.A. The landlord went on to argue, successfully, that one of the two buildings was partially exempt under para. 2 of subsection 5(1) of the T.P.A. (now para. 3 of subsection 7(1) of the R.T.A.).

(ii) Emergency Shelter

Section 5(f) of the R.T.A. (formerly s. 3(f) of the T.P.A.) excludes short-term living accommodation provided as emergency shelter. The Act does not define "short term" or "emergency shelter".

In *Gill v. A. Paladino Holdings Ltd.*,[98] the landlord had obtained an eviction order and the tenant was evicted by the sheriff. The "former" tenant persuaded the landlord to agree to let him back in temporarily and not to pay rent until he could find other accommodation. The "former" tenant would not move out. The landlord called the police. But before getting him out, the "former" tenant applied to the Tribunal that the landlord was harassing him. The Tribunal refused the application about harassment. It was determined that the temporary and invalid agreement was not a tenancy agreement. The unit was "short term living accommodation provided as emergency shelter", which is exempt from the T.P.A. by s. 3(*f*).[99] See also *Gallan v. Maggiolo*,[100]

---

[96] As defined in s. 2(1) of the R.T.A. (and extended by O. Reg. 516/06). For a more detailed analysis of care homes, please refer to Chapter 21.

[97] (January 29, 2004), TST-06105, TST-06106, [2004] O.R.H.T.D. No. 8 (Ont. Rental Housing Trib.).

[98] (February 2, 2000), SOT-00811, 2000 CarswellOnt 6337 (Ont. Rental Housing Trib.).

[99] (February 2, 2000), SOT-00811, 2000 CarswellOnt 6337 (Ont. Rental Housing Trib.).

[100] (Nov. 16, 1998), SWT-00111 (Ont. Rental Housing Trib.).

in which the Tribunal found that the Act did not apply to a situation where the landlord provided emergency shelter to the tenants.

(iii) Penal or Correctional Accommodation

Pursuant to s. 5(*d*) of the Act, living accommodation occupied by a person for penal or correctional purposes is exempt from the R.T.A.

(iv) Other Specified Institutions

Accommodations specifically listed in s. 5(*e*), such as those provided in public or private hospitals, psychiatric facilities, nursing homes and certain charitable institutions, are excluded from the R.T.A. Please refer to s. 5(*e*) for the complete list of exempt institutions. As usual, the onus will be upon the party claiming that the rental unit is exempt from the R.T.A. to specify the section of the Act upon which that party is relying and to prove to the Board that the unit meets the requirements for exemption. In Landlord and Tenant Board File No. CET-00022 (Feb. 28, 2007), the landlord (Simcoe County Christian Senior Home Tollendale Village) raised this issue at the outset of the hearing and was able to prove that, pursuant to s. 5(*e*) of the R.T.A., the Act did not apply to this complex.

(f) Non-Profit Co-Operative Housing Corporation

Pursuant to s. 5(*c*) of the R.T.A., the Act does not apply to living accommodation provided by a non-profit housing co-operative to tenants in member units. It is the *Co-operative Corporations Act*[101] which applies. By s. 171.7(1) of the *Co-operative Corporations Act*, the R.T.A. does not apply to member units. Housing charges are set by the members: s. 171.6(1) of the *Co-operative Corporations Act*. As members set the rents there is no need for rent control and so it is not applicable.

Section 171.8 of the *Co-operative Corporations Act* provides the procedure for terminating membership and occupancy. This procedure is by the board of directors of the co-operative and can be appealed to the members at a duly constituted meeting, as it has been for some years.

If the member refuses to vacate, repossession can only be by a writ of possession on application to a judge of the Ontario Superior Court of Justice. This procedure is set out in s. 171.13 of the *Co-operative Corporations Act* and is very similar to the procedure provided in the R.T.A. The judge may order termination and possession and arrears of housing charges, and "may

[101] R.S.O. 1990, c. C.35, as amended by S.O. 1992, c. 19.

impose such terms and conditions as the judge considers appropriate" (s. 171.13(12)). Where the *Co-operative Corporations Act* is silent as to procedures to be followed, the court can determine the methodology to be adopted, having reference to the *Rules of Civil Procedure.*[102]

In addition, the judge is given similar powers as in s. 83 of the R.T.A. These powers are in s. 171.21 of the *Co-operative Corporations Act.* The judge hearing an appeal is directed to refuse the application for possession if satisfied that:

1. the co-operative has contravened the Act or its by-laws and the contravention is material,
2. the reason for the application is that the applicant has complained to any governmental authority about housing standards,
3. the applicant has sought to enforce his or her legal rights, or
4. the member unit is occupied by children, provided there is not overcrowding.

Notwithstanding these considerations for the judge, the fact is that the application for possession against a member of a co-operative has already been dealt with by the board of the co-operative and affirmed by the members.

Accordingly, when an application comes before a judge under the procedure of the amended *Co-operative Corporations Act*, one would think that the important considerations apply, namely were there fair hearings at the board meeting and the members meeting and was there no bias, and that the decision was a reasonable one.

Amendments to the *Co-operative Corporations Act* require the judge hearing an appeal from a board's decision to determine not only whether the applicable by-laws for termination were not unreasonable or arbitrary but to be satisfied as to the evidence supporting the board's decision to terminate.

In the case of *Tamil Co-operative Homes Inc. v. Arulappah,*[103] by the time the appeal was heard the matter had been settled. As a result, the appeal was moot. Nevertheless, counsel for both parties requested the Divisional Court to consider and rule on the standard of review, by reason of the amendments, when the board applies to the court for an order for possession. Prior to the amendments, the order for possession would be by a judge, if satisfied that there was procedural fairness, no bias and that the board's decision for termination was reasonable. The question asked was whether the standard of review was not only as just stated but whether the judge should consider and be satisfied with the evidence supporting the board's decision for termination; that is a trial *de novo*.

---

[102] *Woodsworth Housing Co-operative Inc. v. Tarling* (2006), [2006] O.J. No. 624, 2006 CarswellOnt 906 (Ont. S.C.J.).

[103] (1999), 25 R.P.R. (3d) 85 (Ont. Div. Ct.), affirmed (2000), 36 R.P.R. (3d) 58 (Ont. C.A.).

The Divisional Court by a majority decided that the standard of review by the amendments did require a trial *de novo*. So that is the law. But the dissenting judgment is well reasoned. Basically, it gives deference to the board's decision pointing out that the resident member was given the reasons for termination, an opportunity to be heard, decision by a majority of the board who were elected by the members, an appeal to the members at a duly constituted meeting where the resident member and their majority decision would be heard. And when it comes before a judge for an order for possession there will be the consideration of procedural fairness, natural justice and reasonableness, with the overriding jurisdiction by s. 171.21(1) to refuse the application for possession if it would be unfair.

When a future application for possession comes before a judge, the dissenting judgment will at least have some persuasive effect to give deference to the proceedings that led to the board's decision. It can be said that the amendments were to preserve the distinctive democratic character of co-operatives and member control.

Assuming that may be so, the following cases are mentioned as guidelines of how an appeal from the decision of the co-op may be considered.

In *Hugh Garner Housing Co-op. Inc. v. Hamid*,[104] the judge reviewed the proceedings before the Board and the members meeting and said that there was a fair hearing:

> The Board was in a position to know the participants . . . . A Co-operative is a unique living arrangement which calls for co-operative living . . . . To allow the tenants to stay on would be asking this court to do little more than second-guess the board.

In *Chautauqua Co-op. Homes Inc. v. Wilson*,[105] a writ of possession was ordered after the court considered the procedural fairness leading up to the notice of termination.

The rules of the co-operative should apply. The courts should not interfere with a *bona fide* decision to expel and obtain possession. There can be relief from forfeiture by s. 171.21 of the *Co-operative Corporations Act* or by the court's equitable jurisdiction in s. 98 of the *Courts of Justice Act*.[106]

Before the amendments, the hearing by a court of an application for possession following a decision of the co-operative was not considered a hearing *de novo* but was limited to the court being satisfied that the proper procedures had been followed and that the principles of fundamental justice had been observed. In *Beech Hall Housing Co-op. Inc. v. Titova*,[107] the co-operative's application for possession was dismissed for at least the reason

[104] (1987), 1987 CarswellOnt 2617 (Ont. Dist. Ct.).

[105] (October 5, 1986), Doc. DCOM1119/86 (Ont. Dist. Ct.).

[106] R.S.O. 1990, c. C.43. See on this point *McBride v. Comfort Living Housing Co-op. Inc.* (1992), 7 O.R. (3d) 394 (Ont. C.A.).

[107] (1986), 1986 CarswellOnt 2793 (Ont. Dist. Ct.).

that the complainant, who was another member, sat on the board which heard the complaint and determined that the other tenant member should be evicted. Bias and lack of fairness were the factors.

Nevertheless, in addition to procedural fairness considerations there is, as stated above, the discretion of the judge in s. 117.13(12) of the *Co-operative Corporations Act* to "impose such terms and conditions as the judge considers appropriate", and the above directions to the judge in s. 117.21.

In *Quigley v. Charles Darrow Housing Co-operative Inc.*,[108] the court considered and decided that the notice to the member and occupant by the Board of Directors failed to give any real or substantive indication of the complaints to the member in order to respond, and so there was failure to provide procedural fairness. The co-operative's application for termination and possession was dismissed.

Unreasonably disturbing other members, noise complaints and refusal to allow a fire safety check were allegations accepted by the board of directors for termination of membership and possession in *Forestwood Co-operative Homes Inc. v. Gellert.*[109] The member did not appeal to the other members, which would be the next procedure, but applied to the court on basis of procedural unfairness. There was not sufficent disclosure to the member before the hearing by the board. The court was not satisfied that there was "a reasonable basis for its [the board's] decision", and also that there was not advance disclosure of the material being considered, and so there was procedural unfairness. The application to terminate was refused.

In certain co-ops, some members may receive subsidy support for the rent. They are normally required by by-law to update income and the number of persons in the household. In *Rouge Valley Co-operative Homes Inc. v. Kerr*,[110] the member refused the inquiry requests of the manager. The subsidy was revoked and the member continued to pay only the subsided housing charge. The court confirmed the termination and ordered for possession.

In another case, complaints were made of late parties and noise caused by the daughter and her friends. The board ordered termination and eviction. By the time of the appeal the situation had improved as there was only one new complaint. The court noted that the member had been in her unit for a number of years. As the judge said, "the court should proceed very carefully in authorizing an eviction, particularly where there appears to be a positive change in circumstances." The judge refused the eviction decision, relying on the discretion in s. 171.21 of the *Co-operative Corporatons Act*: *Ellen McGrail Housing Co-operative Inc. v. Hall.*[111]

---

[108] (1993), 30 R.P.R. (2d) 310 (Ont. Gen. Div.).

[109] (1998), 1998 CarswellOnt 4497 (Ont. Gen. Div.).

[110] (1998), 1998 CarswellOnt 1579 (Ont. Gen. Div.).

[111] (November 5, 1997) (Ont. Gen. Div.).

In a case in which the member was a psychiatric out-patient, his conduct was a nuisance to other members; also, he did not keep his unit clean and, in fact, on one visit by the fire department the report was that the condition was a fire hazard. However, by the time this got to court the member was complying. The judge noted that this type of accommodation is to foster a spirit of collegiality and co-operation among members. To make an order terminating the membership and for possession would have a serious impact on the member. The unfairness was such that an order for possession was refused, leaving it to the board of directors to watch over the member and if there was more trouble to proceed again for termination and possession: *Changemakers Co-operative Homes (Kitchener) Inc. v. Audrassy.*[112]

A sublease by a tenant member of a non-profit co-operative may not come within the co-operative exclusion: *R.K. Investment Ltd. v. McElney.*[113] Therefore, a tenant member who wishes to regain possession from his or her sub-tenant likely will be able to rely upon the provisions of the R.T.A.

(g) Accommodations at Certain Educational Institutions

Pursuant to s. 5(g) of the R.T.A., living accommodation provided by an educational institution to its students or staff is exempt from the Act where,

(i) the living accommodation is provided primarily to persons under the age of majority, or all major questions related to the living accommodation are decided after consultation with a council or association representing the residents, and

(ii) the living accommodation does not have its own self-contained bathroom and kitchen, or is not intended for year-round occupation by full-time students or staff and members of their households.

The exclusion of students makes sense as it would be impractical to consider them as tenants with security of tenure. Such accommodation is for an academic term and has to be available for other students in the next academic term. Note, however, that this exemption would not apply to university or college residences, dormitories or apartments (since the students would generally be at or above the age of majority and many of the units will have a self-contained bathroom or kitchen, or both).

If the above exclusion by s. 5(g) of the R.T.A. does not apply there may be partial exemption for students or staff by s. 7(1)5. There can be no assigning or subletting or rent control. There are other subsections of s. 7(1) that also apply to this partial exemption.

4 — RENTAL PREMISES GOVERNED

---

[112] (1999), 1999 CarswellOnt 771 (Ont. Gen. Div.).

[113] (1981), 21 R.P.R. 173 (B.C. C.A.).

In *Durski v. Tyndale College & Seminary*,[114] the tenant had been a student and volunteer at the College. At the time she applied for this apartment, however, she was no longer enrolled as a student. Although the College apparently intended its rental units to be used only by staff and students, its standard form of written tenancy agreement did not make the creation or the continuation of the tenancy contingent upon a tenant being a student or providing services to the College. When, several years later, the College discovered that the tenant was no longer enrolled as a student, it asked her to vacate the unit. She resisted this suggestion and brought an application to determine whether the T.P.A. applied to her tenancy. It was held that the landlord had failed to demonstrate that the rental unit fell within any of the exceptions enumerated in the T.P.A. (with particular reference to paras. 3(g) and (h), now paras. 5(g) and (h) of the R.T.A.) and that the Act did apply to this rental unit. There was no determination of whether the unit might be partially exempt from the T.P.A. under s. 5 of the Act (now s. 7 of the R.T.A.) since neither party had raised that issue.

Apparently concerned by the precedent that may have been created by the *Durski* decision, Tyndale College commenced its own application[115] seeking a determination as to whether (all) the rental units on its campus were completely or partially exempt from the T.P.A. The Tribunal found that for some tenants, it was an implied term of the tenancy agreement that occupancy was conditional upon continued employment at the College; those tenancies were found to be completely exempt from the Act under s. 3(*h*) of the T.P.A. For the rest of the tenancies, the Tribunal found that although not completely exempt, the tenancies were exempt from *some* provisions of the Act (i.e., they were partially exempt) either on the basis that they were rental units provided by an educational institution to a student or staff member (s. 5(1)4 of the T.P.A., now s. 7(1)5 of the R.T.A.) or on the basis that they were rental units located in a residential complex owned, operated or administered by a religious institution for a charitable use on a non-profit basis (s. 5(1)5 of the T.P.A., now s. 7(1)6 of the R.T.A.).

(h) Accommodations in Which the Tenant and Owner Share a Kitchen or Bathroom

This type of accommodation is excluded from the R.T.A. by the provisions of s. 5(i) of the Act. The section, however, is more complex than it may first appear.

One commonly misunderstood condition is that the exemption only applies where the bathroom or kitchen is shared with the *owner* of the property

[114] (April 22, 2002), TNT-02581 (Ont. Rental Housing Trib.).

[115] *Tyndale College & Seminary v. Aavasalmi* (Jan. 14, 2003), TNL-40238, 2003 CarswellOnt 1512 (Ont. Rental Housing Trib.).

or specified members of the owner's family. It is not enough that the tenant share a bathroom or kitchen with the "landlord". Not every landlord is an owner. Therefore, if the landlord is relying upon this section, he or she must come to the Tribunal prepared to prove that the person with whom the tenant must share a kitchen or bathroom is "the owner, the owner's spouse, child or parent or the spouse's child or parent". Furthermore, that person must be living in the same building as the tenant for this exemption to apply.

Also, it must be proven that the tenant is "required" (by the terms of the tenancy agreement) to share a kitchen or bathroom with this person; that the tenant occasionally permits the person in question to use the kitchen or bathroom is not enough.[116] The parties must have agreed from the outset that this sharing of the kitchen or bathroom with the owner (or specified family member) was part of the deal. This requirement, however, can be implied (for instance, from the lack of separate kitchen and/or bathroom facilities).[117]

Finally, the landlord must be acting in good faith. Pursuant to s. 202 of the Act, the Board must ascertain the real substance of the situation, whether the parties are acting in good faith and may disregard the outward form of a transaction or may have regard to the pattern of activities relating to the residential complex or the rental unit in making findings of fact. The Board, therefore, has the power and obligation to ascertain whether, by the terms of the tenancy agreement, the tenant is required to share a kitchen or bathroom with an owner (or other designated person) who lives in the building or whether it is really a sham — an effort on the part of the landlord to make the unit appear to be exempt from the R.T.A. when this is not really the case.

The exemption of "shared" accommodations was considered in *Kutzak v. Gauthier*.[118] The landlord had a separate bathroom and kitchen. The tenant had rooms in the basement including a kitchen and a bathroom which were also shared with the landlord. The judge held that the tenant's lease was exempt from Part IV of the *Landlord and Tenant Act*. There was a sharing of facilities, even though the landlord had her own bathroom and kitchen.

A more limited sharing was not within the exclusion in *Crawford v. Drake*.[119] The tenant had private rooms, but shared the recreation room with the landlord and a washroom with another tenant.

The shared accommodation exclusion continued to apply upon the death of the landlady when the executor applied under Part III of the *Landlord and*

---

[116] See *Pepevnak v. Milne* (October 26, 1999), TST-01391 (Ont. Rental Housing Trib.) in which it was found that the landlord failed to prove that, by the terms of the tenancy agreement, the tenant was *required* to share his bathroom.

[117] See *Gawtrey v. Landrigan* (Jan. 23, 2006), TET-05270, 2006 CarswellOnt 2140 (Ont. Rental Housing Trib.); *Clamp v. Ramsay* (February 19, 2002), CEL-22484 and CET-02477 (Ont. Rental Housing Trib.); and Landlord and Tenant Board File No. NOL-00299 (March 28, 2007).

[118] (1988), 4 T.L.L.R. 201 (Ont. Dist. Ct.).

[119] (February 3, 1989), Gotlib D.C.J. (Ont. Dist. Ct.).

Tenant Act for possession having given one month's notice to vacate: *Hooey v. Bomze.*[120]

The shared kitchen exception, s. 3(i) of the T.P.A. (now s. 5(i) of the R.T.A.), was considered in *Hamel v. Farzam.*[121] The Tribunal held that a head tenant was an owner and landlord, as described in that section, who shared the kitchen and a bathroom with her subtenant.

In *Mason v. Wilson,*[122] the Member found that this unit was exempt from the Act under s. 3(i) of the T.P.A. as the tenant was required to share the kitchen and bathroom with the owner's spouse and child.

In *Campbell v. Wu,*[123] the Tribunal found that it is not sufficient for the landlord to show that the owner (etc.) used the same bathroom or kitchen as the tenant. It must be proven that, by the terms of the tenancy agreement, the tenant is *required* to share the bathroom or kitchen. Since that was not proven in this case, the Member ruled that the rental unit was governed by the T.P.A. and that the Tribunal had jurisdiction to adjudicate the dispute. A similar ruling was made by the Board in Landlord and Tenant Board File No. TEL-02602 (May 31, 2007).

If the unit was exempt under this provision, that exempt status does not change when a mortgagee becomes the landlord by virtue of being a mortgagee in possession.[124]

In other cases, the issue has been whether the owner actually lives in the complex. In *Marshal v. Cao,*[125] it was held that the landlord had not presented sufficient evidence to prove he lived in the building. In *Elgasuani v. Niazof,*[126] the landlord/owner of this house took the position that he slept in a room in the house two or three nights per week and that the tenants who rented rooms in the house were required to share a bathroom and kitchen with him. He admitted having an apartment elsewhere in Toronto, but stated that he lived in both his own apartment and in the house in question. His "bedroom" in the house consisted of a mattress on the floor of a room not much larger than the mattress itself. Although it was found that the owner attended at the house almost daily in order to keep the various tenants under surveillance, the Tribunal found that he did not really live in the house and, therefore, that the rental units were not exempt from the T.P.A. The tenant was, therefore,

---

120 (1993), 1993 CarswellOnt 2047 (Ont. Gen. Div.).

121 (Oct. 8, 1999), EAL-08557 and EAT-01012 (Ont. Rental Housing Trib.).

122 (Sept. 1, 1998), SOL-00742 (Ont. Rental Housing Trib.).

123 (Jan. 19, 1999), TNT-00233 (Ont. Rental Housing Trib.), followed in *Fasulo v. Finn* (November 30, 2005), CET-05089, 2005 CarswellOnt 7928 (Ont. Rental Housing Trib.).

124 *Choi v. Gowling Lafleur Henderson LLP* (April 26, 2006), TET-05694, [2006] O.R.H.T.D. No. 43, 2006 CarswellOnt 4390 (Ont. Rental Housing Trib.).

125 (June 9, 2003), EAT-04545, [2003] O.R.H.T.D. No. 79, 2003 CarswellOnt 2664 (Ont. Rental Housing Trib.).

126 (Jan. 25, 2000), TNT-00852, 2000 CarswellOnt 6452, [2000] O.R.H.T.D. No. 188 (Ont. Rental Housing Trib.).

permitted to proceed with his application against the landlord for, amongst other things, harassment and interference with reasonable enjoyment.

In *Fedewicz v. Neelin*,[127] the landlord relied on this exemption. The rental unit was within a house in Ottawa. At the time of the commencement of the tenancy and throughout the tenancy, the landlord (owner) was living and working in Toronto. The Tribunal found, however, that the landlord maintained her primary residence in Ottawa and intended to return to her house in Ottawa before the end of the term of the tenancy, at which time the tenants would be required to share the kitchen and bathroom with the landlord. Based on these facts, the Tribunal found that the premises were exempt from the T.P.A. On appeal by the tenant, the Divisional Court upheld the Tribunal's interpretation and application of s. 3(i) of the T.P.A. (now s. 5(i) of the R.T.A.).

(i) Purchasers

Commonly in the purchase of new condominium units, and less frequently in other types of real estate transactions, purchasers are permitted to occupy the premises prior to the completion ("closing") of the transaction.

In condominium projects, delays often occur in getting the declaration registered. As a result, the condominium has often not been constituted at the time that the premises are ready for occupation and purchasers wish to move in. Developers have therefore permitted the purchasers to occupy under what are called occupancy agreements, pending final closing and the transfer of ownership; and for developers it is also important to require purchasers to move in as interim occupants, and so be an early source of revenue. These agreements provide for rent or occupancy licence fees and include various contractual provisions common to the landlord and tenant relationship.

Typically, during this period of occupancy, the purchasers will have to pay some compensation to the vender for the use of the unit. Has a tenancy been created between the vendor and purchase that is subject to the provisions of the R.T.A.? If a dispute arises between the parties concerning this occupancy, where should that dispute be resolved?

A somewhat unusual fact situation (involving property *other* than a condominium) was dealt with in *Hassani v. Marchewka*.[128] In this case, there was an accepted offer to purchase with an extended closing date of over one year. The parties also entered into a lease of the premises for that period. The purchaser did not close on the scheduled date and would not give up possession. The vendors brought a summary application for possession under Rule

[127] (2007), 2007 CarswellOnt 4908 (Ont. Div. Ct.).

[128] (July 22, 1992), Doc. 1064/92 (Ont. Gen. Div.).

14.05(3) of the *Rules of Civil Procedure*,[129] and for forfeiture of the deposit and damages.

One would have thought that the predominant factor was the default of the purchaser tenant failing to close and that all remedies of the vendor including regaining possession could have and should have been dealt with in one action. However, the court could not avoid the fact that possession was under the lease. Applying the definition in s. 1 of the *Landlord and Tenant Act*, the vendors were also the landlords "giving or permitting the occupation". Accordingly, Part IV of the *Landlord and Tenant Act* applied and had possession to be obtained for non-payment of rent by the owners as landlords serving a notice of termination under s. 106(1)(*b*). The judge did order the forfeiture of the deposit and a reference to determine damages which presumably would include further damages while the purchaser as tenant stayed in possession.

Unlike the courts, however, the Board may be reluctant to assume jurisdiction over a dispute that arises from an agreement of purchase and sale.[130] This will be especially true if court proceedings have already been commenced with respect to the failed real estate transaction. Each case will have to be carefully considered. The Board will have to determine the following points:

1) whether the parties meet the definition of "landlord" and "tenant" (as those terms are used in the R.T.A.);
2) whether the Board has the jurisdiction to adjudicate the dispute; and (if it does have jurisdiction)
3) whether that jurisdiction is exclusive.

Where it is determined that the Board has exclusive jurisdiction over the matter, the Board will have to hear the dispute arising from the purchaser's tenancy but the Board will not be able to make orders with respect to the underlying agreement of purchase and sale. If the Board's jurisdiction is not exclusive (i.e., its jurisdiction is concurrent with that of the superior court), the parties might be better off having their dispute adjudicated by the court (which can consider not only the alleged breach of the interim occupancy agreement and the claim for possession of the property but also the broader rights, obligations and remedies that may arise from the agreement of purchase and sale).

If the R.T.A. is found to apply to premises occupied by purchasers pursuant to an occupation agreement, then the landlord/vendor will have to comply with all notice provisions and procedures set out in the R.T.A. in

---

[129] R.R.O. 1990, Reg. 194.

[130] *308237 v. Lask* (Feb. 19, 2001), SWL-23039 (Ont. Rental Housing Trib.) and Landlord and Tenant Board File No. TEL-00274 (March 7, 2007). For a contrary view, see Landlord and Tenant Board File No. TEL-00047 (March 8, 2007).

order to obtain an eviction order against the tenant/purchaser. To the extent that any provision of the *Condominium Act* or any other statute (except the *Human Rights Code*) is inconsistent with the provisions of the R.T.A., the provisions of the R.T.A. prevail.[131]

In *Symphony Place Corp. v. Angelini*,[132] a vendor who terminated the offer to purchase for failure to close applied for and was granted possession against a tenant of the purchaser. The tenant was in possession without the consent of the owner and so was considered a trespasser. The court referred to s. 110(3)(*e*) of Part IV for jurisdiction, that is, that the tenancy arose by virtue of or collateral to a *bona fide* agreement of purchase and sale of a proposed unit within the meaning of the *Condominium Act*, as is now in s. 58(1)4 of the R.T.A. Another ground for the decision was that the occupant or the purchaser who let the occupant into possession was, in the words of s. 107(1)(*c*) of Part IV "conduct of the tenant or a person permitted in the residential premises ... such that it substantially interfered with the reasonable enjoyment of the premises for all usual purposes by the landlord" (now the words of s. 64(1) of the R.T.A.), which was to resell the unit and not to rent.

Note that para. 58(1)4 of the R.T.A. now specifically grants the Board the power to terminate a tenancy that arose by virtue of or collateral to an agreement of purchase and sale of a proposed condominium unit where that agreement has been terminated.

To sum up this point, most developers prefer to avoid the strictures and obligations of the R.T.A. and, therefore, do not commence applications before the Board. The exception is that the vendor/landlord may wish to take advantage of the Board's streamlined eviction procedures (and then seek any other relief in a later court action).

(j) Residential Complex in which the Crown has an Interest (NEW)

By virtue of s. 5(m) of the R.T.A., a residential complex is exempt from the R.T.A. if the provincial Crown has an interest in the complex and if: (1) the property was forfeited to the Crown under federal or provincial legislation relating to unlawful activities;[133] or (2) if possession of the complex has been or may be taken in the name of the Crown under the *Escheats Act*.

4 — RENTAL PREMISES GOVERNED

---

[131] Subsection 3(4) of the R.T.A.

[132] (1992), 7 O.R. (3d) 151 (Ont. Gen. Div.).

[133] I.e., the complex was forfeited under the *Remedies for Organized Crime and Other Unlawful Activities Act, 2001*, the *Prohibiting Profiting from Recounting Crimes Act, 2002* or the *Criminal Code* (Canada).

6. PARTIAL EXEMPTIONS

Partial exemptions from the R.T.A. are listed in ss. 6, 7 and 8 of the R.T.A. and ss. 5, 6 and 7 of O. Reg. 516/06. Some of the more common examples are discussed further below.

(a) Homes for Special Care

Pursuant to s. 6(1)(a) of the R.T.A., many sections of the Act (concerning such things as conversion or demolition of rental units and rules related to rent) do not apply with respect to accommodation that is subject to the *Homes for Special Care Act*.[134]

(b) Accommodation Subject to the Developmental Services Act

Pursuant to s. 6(1)(b) of the R.T.A., many sections of the Act (concerning such things as conversion or demolition of rental units and rules related to rent) do not apply with respect to accommodation that is subject to the *Developmental Services Act*[135] and that is not otherwise exempt under s. 5(*e*) of the R.T.A.

(c) New Units

As an incentive for the construction or creation of new rental accommodation, s. 6(2) of the R.T.A. (formerly s. 4(2) of the T.P.A.) provides for an exemption from most of the rent control provisions for "new" rental units. Under this section, a rental unit is "new" if it has never been "occupied" for any purpose prior to June 17, 1998, or, alternatively, it has not been "rented" since July 29, 1975. In addition, a rental unit will be considered new if it is in a building no part of which was occupied prior to November 1, 1991.

The real incentive for the creation of "new" units is that landlords of "new" units may increase the rent by any amount, even for existing tenants. The landlord must still provide the tenant with 90 days' written notice, and the rent may only be increased once every 12 months.

Other rent rules that apply, even to "new units", are found in ss. 105 through 109 of the R.T.A. They are the provisions dealing with rent deposits, the prohibition against requiring post-dated cheques (etc.) and the rule requiring the landlord to provide rent receipts.

---

134 R.S.O. 1990, c. H.12.

135 R.S.O. 1990, c. D.11.

(d) Subsidized and Non-profit Public Housing

Pursuant to s. 7 of the R.T.A., many sections of the Act (concerning such things as the right to assign or sublet a rental unit, conversion or demolition of rental units and rules related to rent) do not apply to subsidized and non-profit public housing. Such housing is developed or acquired under a prescribed[136] federal, provincial or municipal program, typically (but not always) operated under the *Social Housing Reform Act, 2000*.[137]

Such housing is provided for low or modest income persons at reduced rents and, generally, takes one of two forms. In one model, the unit itself is located in a residential complex in which some of the rental units are set aside for tenants who have qualified for rental subsidies. The total rent being charged for the subsidized units remains at, or close to, market levels. The tenant pays a portion of that rent (based upon the tenant's household income) and the rest of the rent is paid to the landlord by the government. The rent subsidy is the difference between the total rent being charged for the unit by the landlord and the amount the tenant is expected to contribute towards that rent. The other typical model is a large housing project that is run by a corporation set up by the local municipality in which the rent that is charged for each unit is based upon the income of the tenant living in that unit ("rent-geared-to-income" or "RGI" housing).

In such housing, the rent being charged to the tenant varies with the income of the tenant (and members of the tenant's household). This explains why such rental units must be exempt from most of the usual provisions of the R.T.A. dealing with rent and rent increases. For instance, pursuant to s. 119 of the R.T.A., the monthly rent for a non-subsidized rental unit can usually only be raised once every 12 months and only if a written notice is provided to the tenant at least 90 days in advance (s. 116). Obviously, if a tenant's rent can be different for each rental period (as the tenant's income rises and falls), the usual rules about the timing and amount of rent increases and decreases cannot apply.

Also, in order to get into subsidized housing the tenant must meet strict criteria. If, at some point, the landlord discovers that the tenant no longer qualifies for subsidized housing or has misrepresented his or her income, the landlord must have a means to remove the tenant and to recover any amount the tenant should have been paying. Paragraph 58(1)2 provides the means for terminating the tenancy of a tenant who no longer qualifies for this type of housing. Subsection (1) permits a landlord to seek to terminate the tenancy of any tenant in subsidized housing who has knowingly and materially misrepresented his or her income, s. 90 of the R.T.A. grants the Tribunal the power, in such circumstances, to order the tenant to pay to the landlord the

[136] Prescribed in ss. 5 and 6 of O. Reg. 516/06.

[137] S.O. 2000, c. 27.

rent that the tenant would have been required to pay if the tenant had not misrepresented his or her income. In order for the landlord to be aware of the tenant's financial circumstances, the tenant is obliged to provide the landlord with information about his or her income and household composition on at least an annual basis; in addition, the tenant has an ongoing responsibility to promptly advise the landlord of any material change in the income of his or her household.

Low-rental housing buildings constructed pursuant to the *National Housing Act*,[138] sometimes referred to as "limited dividend rental projects", were assisted by low interest loans from Canada Mortgage and Housing Corporation (CMHC). Pursuant to s. 15 of the *National Housing Act*, the rents were set by contract between the owner and CMHC and had to be fair and reasonable having regard to the family income. Tenants did not have the right to dispute rental rates set in this manner: *Mountbriar Building Corp. (Toronto) Ltd. v. McMurray*.[139] A more recent decision dealing with limited dividend rental projects was *Luray v. Tenants of 1307 Wilson Ave.*[140] in which it was held that the tenants in the complex had no right to enforce the agreement made under the *National Housing Act* between the CMHC and the previous landlord.[141]

One of the more difficult issues that plagued the Tribunal was the extent to which the Tribunal would and should look behind the rents being claimed by landlords in subsidized public housing cases. Such cases posed both practical and jurisdictional problems.

The practical problems were related primarily to the caseload of the Tribunal and the amount of time allotted to rental arrears applications. These types of cases were allotted very little time by the Tribunal, on the assumption that they would be relatively simple. In typical arrears applications, the parties will usually agree on the lawful monthly rent for the unit. Often, they will even agree on the amount of the arrears. More often than not, in such cases, the tenant merely wishes to explain his or her circumstances (i.e., to explain why he or she fell into arrears) and ask for additional time in which to pay the arrears (in order to "save" the tenancy) or to find alternative accommodations. Obviously, such hearings tend to be fairly expeditious. If the lawfulness of the rent charged or the amount of the arrears becomes an issue, the hearing will take considerably longer. In the case of subsidized and rent-

---

[138] R.S.C. 1985, c. N-11.

[139] (1978), 19 O.R. (2d) 30 (Ont. Div. Ct.).

[140] (March 12, 2001), TNL-03937 (Ont. Rental Housing Trib.), affirmed (March 11, 2002), Doc. 257/0199 (Ont. Div. Ct.).

[141] This was because the tenants were not parties to that contract. It was also because the only remedy provided in the agreement for the landlord raising rents without the consent of CMHC was the immediate recall of a loan; in this case, the mortgage had already been discharged (so there was no loan to recall) and CMHC had released the landlord from any obligations under the agreement.

geared-to-income housing, the complexity was compounded by the fact that few Members had any training in, or understanding of, how the rent (or rent subsidy) ought to be calculated. Even the landlords' representatives who attended the hearings were seldom able or willing to justify the amounts being claimed by the landlord. These landlords grew accustomed to having Members accept their figures without question. Because such units were exempt from many of the provisions of the T.P.A. that deal with rent, it was generally assumed that the Tribunal had no jurisdiction to look behind the amount of rent charged by such landlords. This approach certainly helped to keep hearings brief by avoiding entangling the Tribunal in complex rent calculations[142] and issues of the landlord's internal polices and procedures.

Even if a Member might be willing to explore these issues further (i.e., look into the rent being charged or the amount of subsidy being granted to a tenant), the Tribunal as a whole never reached a consensus on whether or not the Tribunal even had the jurisdiction to do so. There were essentially two schools of thought within the Tribunal.

One school of thought was that the Tribunal had no jurisdiction to review how these landlords calculated the monthly rent or the amount of a subsidy.[143] Members who subscribed to this view felt that tenants who wish to challenge either the amount of rent that had been charged by the landlord or the amount of the subsidy provided may have other avenues to seek redress, including an internal review process under the *Social Housing Reform Act, 2000*, S.O. 2000, c. 27 (s. 82) and, possibly, judicial review. These Members, however, were generally willing to concede that the conduct of the landlord, including the reasonableness of the landlord's actions and whether or not the landlord had complied with its own policies and procedures may be relevant to the Tribunal's decision about whether to use its discretionary power under s. 84(1) of the T.P.A. (now s. 83(1) and (2) of the R.T.A.) to delay or deny an eviction.

The other school of thought focused upon the fact that the landlord was bringing an application before the Tribunal based upon the alleged failure of the tenant to pay rent "lawfully owing" under a tenancy agreement (s. 61 of the T.P.A., now s. 59 of the R.T.A.).[144] These Members took the position that the Tribunal had the power and the duty in arrears cases to ensure that the

[142] Complex because the amount that can lawfully be charged may change for each rental period (as the tenant's income rises and falls) and because the formula used to calculate the rent may itself be complicated.

[143] See the following examples: *Supportive Housing Coalition v. Mark* (April 6, 2000), TSL-16387, [2000] O.R.H.T.D. No. 54, 2000 CarswellOnt 6375 (Ont. Rental Housing Trib.) and *Toronto Community Housing Corp. v. Thompson* (Dec. 22, 2003), TSL-56721, [2003] O.R.H.T.D. No. 145, 2003 CarswellOnt 5711 (Ont. Rental Housing Trib.).

[144] Or, pursuant to s. 88 of the T.P.A. (now s. 90 of the R.T.A.), to ascertain the rent that would have been lawfully owing if the tenant had not misrepresented his or her income.

rent being claimed by the landlord was in fact, lawfully owing.[145] The onus of proving all necessary elements rests upon the applicant (in these cases, the landlord). In non-subsidized rent cases, the Tribunal does not simply take the word of the landlord that the monthly rent is lawful; if a tenant challenges the legality of the rent being charged, evidence and submissions are received from all parties and a determination of that issue is made by the Tribunal. Why should landlords of public housing not have to meet the same onus of proof? If the landlord cannot prove that the rent being claimed is correct and lawful, then the landlord has failed to meet its onus of proof and the application ought to be dismissed.

By the inclusion of s. 203 into the R.T.A., the Legislature has now made it clear that the Board has no jurisdiction to look behind the rent charged or the subsidies granted in such housing. Section 203 reads as follows:

> The Board shall not make determinations or review decisions concerning,
>
> (a) eligibility for rent-geared-to-income assistance as defined in the *Social Housing Reform Act, 2000* or the amount of geared-to-income rent payable under that Act; or
>
> (b) eligibility for, or the amount of, any prescribed form of housing assistance.

In *Peel Housing Corp. v. Ellis*,[146] the Divisional Court has confirmed that this section means exactly what it says.

While this is clearly an attempt to restrict the Board's enquiries into how the landlord in such housing has calculated the rental arrears, it will be interesting to see how the Board reconciles the direction under s. 203 with its mandatory obligation under s. 83 to examine *all* relevant facts in deciding whether and how to exercise its discretion and to ascertain what other terms or conditions (if any) it may need to make in order to prevent an abuse of its process.

(e) Non-Member Unit Provided by a Non-Profit Housing Co-operative

Pursuant to para. 7(1)4 of the R.T.A., many sections of the Act (concerning such things as the right to assign or sublet a rental unit, conversion or demolition of rental units and rules related to rent) do not apply to a rental unit provided by a non-profit housing co-operative to tenants in *non-member* units. This is distinct from the total exemption of *member* units provided under s. 5(c) of the Act.

---

[145] See *Metropolitan Toronto Housing Authority v. Atufa* (Dec. 17, 1998), TSL-02803, 1998 CarswellOnt 6414 (Ont. Rental Housing Trib.) and *York Presbytery v. Plourde* (May 14, 2001), TNL-22694 and TNL-24908 (Ont. Rental Housing Trib.).

[146] (2009), 2009 CarswellOnt 693.

(f) Educational and Religious Institutions

Pursuant to para. 7(1)5 of the R.T.A., many sections of the Act (concerning such things as the right to assign or sublet a rental unit, conversion or demolition of rental units and rules related to rent) do not apply to a rental unit provided by an educational institution to a student or member of its staff and that is not exempt from the Act under s. 5(g).

Pursuant to para. 7(1)6 of the R.T.A., the same is true of a rental unit located in a residential complex owned, operated or administered by a religious institution for a charitable use on a non-profit basis.

The Tyndale College case[147] provides a good example of a partial exemption based upon both of the grounds listed above. Tyndale College commenced an application seeking a determination as to whether the rental units on its campus were completely or partially exempt from the T.P.A. The Tribunal found that for some tenants, it was an implied term of the tenancy agreement that occupancy was conditional upon continued employment at the College; those tenancies were found to be completely exempt from the Act under s. 3(*h*) of the T.P.A. (now s. 5(h) of the R.T.A.). For the rest of the tenancies, the Tribunal found that although not completely exempt, the tenancies were exempt from *some* provisions of the Act (i.e., partially exempt) either on the basis that they were rental units provided by an educational institution to a student or staff member (s. 5(1)4 of the T.P.A., now s. 7(1)5 of the R.T.A.) or on the basis that they were rental units located in a residential complex owned, operated or administered by a religious institution for a charitable use on a non-profit basis (s. 5(1)5 of the T.P.A., now s. 7(1)6 of the R.T.A.).

Pursuant to s. 37(6) of the R.T.A., post-secondary educational institutions are also exempt from ss. 37(4) and (5) of the R.T.A. The usual rule is that an agreement or notice to terminate a tenancy signed by the tenant at the commencement of the tenancy is void. These provisions are meant to prevent a landlord from coercing a tenant into signing such an agreement or notice at the outset of the tenancy and then holding that document (and the implied threat of a swift termination of the tenancy) "over the head" of the tenant for the rest of the tenancy. An exception has been made, however, in the case of post-secondary educational institutions that provide housing for their students. Security of tenure is considered to be of less importance in such housing than the institution's ability to control its housing stock and quickly remove students (through an abbreviated procedure that permits the institution to obtain an eviction order without any prior notice to the student it is seeking to evict[148]).

---

[147] *Tyndale College & Seminary v. Aavasalmi* (Jan. 14, 2003), TNL-40238, 2003 CarswellOnt 1512 (Ont. Rental Housing Trib.).

[148] Pursuant to s. 77 of the R.T.A.

In *Queen's University (Apartment & Housing Services) v. Clandfield*,[149] it was confirmed that, as a university, Queen's is permitted to have a student execute a notice of termination (or agreement to terminate) at the time the original tenancy agreement is created (which is an exception to the usual rule). In this case, however, the University relied upon that agreement to indirectly enforce a "no pets" policy where it could not legally do so directly.[150] The Tribunal found this to be inappropriate and held that the agreement to terminate was void. The Divisional Court overturned the Tribunal's decision. On further appeal, the Court of Appeal was not prepared to find that the agreement was void but it did rule that the landlord could not use a valid agreement to terminate a tenancy for the improper purpose of enforcing a "no pets" policy. The Court of Appeal was not prepared to permit the University to do indirectly what it could not legally do directly. It was a question of abuse of process rather than of the validity of the notice of termination signed by the tenant.

7. TENANCY AT WILL

Tenancies at will are extremely rare and there are few cases on point.

In *Hubbard v. Hamburgh*,[151] the plaintiff was a tenant at will of Metropolitan Toronto. She had been a tenant and her tenancy was terminated and a writ of possession was ordered. Due to political negotiations about houses on the Toronto Islands, the writ of possession was not enforced. She continued to pay rent and taxes to Metropolitan Toronto. Hence, the court declared that she was a tenant at will. She had sublet to the defendant. The court held that, as a tenant at will, the head tenant could sublet and that the sub-tenant was also a tenant at will. Arrears of rent owed by the sub-tenant were ordered to be paid. In order for the plaintiff, the head tenant, to obtain possession from the subtenant, she would have had to proceed under Part IV of the *Landlord and Tenant Act* for whatever statutory reason for termination might be available. If Metropolitan Toronto had decided to go ahead with the writ and possession then both the tenant and sub-tenant would have had to give up possession.

8. MOBILE HOMES AND LAND LEASE HOMES

Mobile homes within a mobile home park and land lease homes within a land lease community are defined in s. 2, of the R.T.A. and are covered by

---

[149] (2001), 200 D.L.R. (4th) 661, 54 O.R. (3d) 475, 146 O.A.C. 299, [2001] O.J. No. 2095, 2001 CarswellOnt 1893 (Ont. C.A.).

[150] Since "no pets" provisions are void pursuant to s. 15 of the T.P.A. (now s. 14 of the R.T.A.).

[151] (1993), 16 O.R. (3d) 368 (Ont. Gen. Div.).

the provisons of Part X (ss. 152-167) of the Act. The Landlord and Tenant Board has exclusive jurisdiction over disputes arising with respect to such rental premises.[152]

For a full discussion of this topic, please refer to Chapter 20.

9. DIPLOMATIC IMMUNITY

Diplomatic immunity of a tenant was submitted by the tenant in a landlord's application for termination and eviction in *Juneau and Rouder*.[153] The Tribunal refused the tenant's motion, quoting from Article 31 of the *Vienna Convention on Diplomatic Relations* that this matter was of private immoveable property which was not held for the purposes of the diplomatic mission, being an exception to diplomatic immunity.

[152] See *Swire v. Walleye Trailer Park Ltd.* (2001), 2001 CarswellOnt 2832, (Ont. Div. Ct.) in which the Divisional Court held that the Tribunal was the proper forum to adjudicate a dispute over whether the landlord (a trailer park) could pass along as an additional charge to tenants of the park a share of the property taxes.

[153] (September 16, 1999), EAL-08713-SA (Ont. Rental Housing Trib.).

5

Tenancy Agreements

1. INTRODUCTION

The purpose of a tenancy agreement is to establish and define the relationship between a landlord and a tenant. In s. 2 of the *Residential Tenancies Act, 2006* (R.T.A.)[1] "tenancy agreement" is defined as a "written, oral or implied agreement between a tenant and a landlord for occupancy of a rental unit and includes a licence to occupy a rental unit". The basic topics that ought to be covered in any tenancy agreement include: (1) the identity of the landlord(s) and tenant(s); (2) the premises being rented; (3) the use to which the premises may be put; (4) the rent being charged and details about how and when the rent is to be paid; and (5) the term of the tenancy (the start date and end date, if any). Historically, a lease was different from a licence: a lease provided the tenant with the right to exclusive use and occupation of the rented premises whereas a licence merely provided the licensee with permission to use the premises with no promise of exclusivity and no security of tenure. Since the definition of tenancy agreement now includes a licence to occupy a rental unit, there is no longer any meaningful distinction, at least in the residential context, between a lease and a licence. However, the term "lease" is still often used in common parlance to refer to a written tenancy agreement.

This chapter will also focus on how a tenancy is created, terms that may be included in a tenancy agreement, how tenancies can change over time and how they are renewed. The various methods of terminating a tenancy are described in Chapter 6.

[1] S.O. 2006, c. 17.

2. WRITTEN AGREEMENTS

Like most contracts, written tenancy agreements have advantages over less formal agreements. The expectations, rights and responsibilities of the parties can be clearly set out in a written agreement, making it much easier later, when a dispute arises, to refer back to the written agreement and know with certainty the terms to which the parties agreed. With a written tenancy agreement, a judge or Board Member adjudicating the dispute does not have to rely on the memory of the parties or their subjective interpretation of what was agreed upon when the tenancy was created. Even if the individuals who executed the agreement are not available to testify, the intention of the parties will be manifest from the written agreement. For these reasons, professional landlords almost always rely on written tenancy agreements. In fact, they often utilize a two-step process.

The landlord first has the prospective tenant(s) complete an application form. Typically, this form indicates the unit for which the prospective tenant is applying, the rent the landlord is demanding and the term of the tenancy. The prospective tenant is asked to complete the parts of the form that provide the landlord with the names of references and information about the prospective tenant's employment and financial circumstances, credit history and rental history. The prospective tenant may also be asked to submit a deposit with the application form. The application form usually states that, upon acceptance of the application, the tenant(s) will be required to execute a tenancy agreement.

If the application is accepted by the landlord, the tenant(s) will then typically be granted a limited period of time in which to execute a longer, more detailed written tenancy agreement and provide a further payment of one month's rent. Such tenancy agreements can be several pages long and often have attached to them a schedule that sets out Rules and Regulations describing what the landlord considers to be acceptable (and unacceptable) conduct within the residential complex. Occasionally, the parties never actually get around to signing a lease. In such circumstances, the application form may be found to constitute a written tenancy agreement. Alternatively, the terms of the tenancy may be inferred from the application form and/or from the conduct of the parties.

By signing the tenancy agreement, the tenant is deemed to agree to all of the terms contained therein. Evidence concerning oral promises that occur around the time of the execution of a written contract (and that are inconsistent with the terms of the contract) is generally not admissible; in other words, if it is not in the contract, it does not count. Therefore, both parties must be careful that the terms of the written tenancy agreement actually reflect what the parties have agreed to orally.[2]

Written tenancy agreements often contain rules prohibiting (for example) the installation of dishwashers, washing machines and/or dryers inside the rental unit and of satellite dishes outside the unit. These are issues that can become a source of conflict later. Before signing the agreement, a prospective tenant should discuss any objections to such provisions with the landlord.

Such agreements tend to be standardized so that every tenancy agreement within a complex looks pretty much the same. Since they are usually drafted by landlords, they tend to favour landlords. Until recently, there wasn't much room for negotiation and landlords would be reluctant to alter the standard terms contained in their tenancy agreements. Given the recent increase in vacancy rates, however, prospective tenants are in a much stronger bargaining position than they have been for many years and tenants may now be able to negotiate more favourable terms.

3. ORAL AGREEMENTS

Where a landlord and tenant do not execute a written tenancy agreement, a tenancy can still exist. It can be created by oral agreement. In order for a tenancy created by oral agreement to be legally binding, there must have been a "meeting of the minds" with respect to the essential elements of the tenancy (i.e., the premises, the rent and the term). Oral agreements are uncommon for large apartment buildings; professional landlords prefer the certainty of a written contract. Oral agreements are more common in less formal settings, such as where a homeowner rents out the basement of their house. Unfortunately this leaves much room for misunderstanding and people tend to make assumptions and leave important details unspoken. Problems can arise when the parties later disagree about the terms of their agreement. Even honest people tend to remember the details of conversations differently when a dispute arises several months or years later. The lack of a written record creates uncertainty for the parties and evidentiary problems should a dispute lead to legal proceedings.

In *Carere et al. v. Blagrove*,[3] the landlords purchased a property through a sale by the sheriff. They found the house occupied by a tenant and, initially, took his word with respect to the terms of the alleged existing tenancy agreement. They later became suspicious that the tenant had not been honest with them about the terms of that agreement. They indicated that they were prepared to allow the tenant to remain in possession of the house if he negotiated with them a new tenancy agreement. The tenant agreed. The tenant

[2] For instance, the agreement should reflect what services and facilities are included in the rent and what additional fees, if any, will be charged.

[3] (Nov. 24, 2000), TNL-18384, 2000 CarswellOnt 6443 (Ont. Rental Housing Trib.).

then defaulted on payments under the new agreement. The landlords commenced an application to terminate the tenancy and evict the tenant. The tenant alleged that the new tenancy agreement was not binding upon him and that he was entitled to rely upon the terms of the former agreement. It was held that the evidence of the tenant with respect to the (extremely favourable) terms of the alleged former tenancy agreement was not credible and that the tenant was bound by the terms of the oral agreement he made with the new landlords.

4. IMPLIED AGREEMENTS

In rare cases, there will be neither a written agreement nor an oral agreement between the parties. In such cases, the terms of the tenancy agreement must be inferred from the conduct of the parties.

A good example of a case in which the Tribunal found an implied tenancy agreement is *Kizemchuk v. Kizemchuk*.[4] The parties to the application were a brother and his wife, who occupied a rental unit in a residential complex operated by his sister (the landlord). The parties could not agree on whether a tenancy existed here or on the terms of that tenancy. The building was previously run by the parents of the brother and sister. The brother had, from time to time, paid rent or provided services for the right to occupy this unit in the building. At some point during his occupancy of this unit, his parents transferred ownership of the residential complex to their daughter (his sister), who then became the landlord. There was no specific written or oral tenancy agreement. The Tribunal was, however, able to ascertain the essential terms of an implied tenancy agreement by examining the history of the conduct of the parties, the amounts that had been paid by the brother and the value of the services he performed. The Tribunal was thus able to determine the amount of rent owing to the landlord and issued an order in accordance with its findings. That decision was upheld on appeal to the Divisional Court and the tenants' motion for leave to appeal to the Court of Appeal was denied.

In a somewhat similar case, however, the Court of Appeal was not prepared to find that there was an implied tenancy agreement. In *Bluestone v. Dagarsho Holdings Ltd.*,[5] a mother was the president and sole shareholder of the defendant holding company that owned the property in question. The plaintiff son, who was the property manager, and his wife occupied the property for about 20 years without paying any rent. In 1995, the son had a falling out with his mother, who then took various steps to reclaim possession of the property. The son and his wife argued, amongst other things, that they were tenants of the premises who were entitled to protection under the pro-

---

[4] (2000), 2000 CarswellOnt 2547, [2002] O.J. No. 2284 (Ont. Div. Ct.) (re TSL-11717).

[5] (2005), 37 R.P.R. (4th) 53, 2005 CarswellOnt 5193 (Ont. C.A.).

visions of the T.P.A. The trial judge found that they were not tenants and that the T.P.A. did not apply in this situation; rather, their rent-free occupation of the lands arose by reason of their familial relationship. This finding was upheld on appeal by the Court of Appeal.

Where there is neither a written nor an oral tenancy agreement and the essential terms of a tenancy cannot be inferred from the conduct of the parties, the Board may determine that no tenancy exists and decline to assume jurisdiction over the matter.[6]

Even if the relationship outwardly appears to be that of a landlord and tenant, if the true nature of the relationship between the parties is something else, the Board may find that it lacks the jurisdiction to adjudicate on the matter. In Landlord and Tenant Board File No. TSL-00031 (Feb. 27, 2007), the Member found that the "tenant" was really the beneficial owner of the property (despite title being taken in someone else's name) and that this was not really a tenancy. The Member found that the Board lacked jurisdiction over the matter and dismissed the application.

Even where a written agreement exists, additional terms will sometimes be implied from the conduct of the parties. In *Pinedale Properties Ltd. v. Dimitrijevski*,[7] the tenants parked two cars in the outdoor lot, free of charge, for 18 years. A new landlord took over and assigned specific spaces to the tenants of the complex and sought to charge these tenants for one of the two parking spaces. When these tenants refused to pay, the landlord brought an application to terminate their tenancy for non-payment of rent. Although the written tenancy agreement and previous rent orders did not indicate that two spaces were included in the rent, the Member inferred from the conduct of the tenants and the previous landlord over 18 years that two spaces were included in the basic rent of these tenants. The landlord's application was dismissed.

5. WAIVER AND FORBIDDEN TERMS

The R.T.A. applies to residential tenancies notwithstanding any other statute or any agreement or waiver to the contrary.[8] This statutory protection for tenants is to ensure that they cannot be required to contract out of their rights given by the R.T.A. Any future or even present waiver clauses in leases affecting these rights are of no effect. In *Fleischmann v. Grossman Holdings Ltd.*,[9] it was held that the common exclusionary clause in residential leases

[6] Landlord and Tenant Board File No. TNT-01078 (Jan. 12, 2009).

[7] (June 7, 1999), TNL-07253 (Ont. Rental Housing Trib.). For a similar case, see also *Heinemann v. Haverlock* (Oct. 30, 1998), CEL-01594 (Ont. Rental Housing Trib.), discussed later in this chapter.

[8] Section 3 of the R.T.A. (formerly s. 2 of the T.P.A.).

[9] (1976), 16 O.R. (2d) 746 (Ont. C.A.).

could no longer be relied on by a landlord who was sued by a tenant because the landlord had failed to fulfil the statutory duty to repair and a tenant had suffered damages as a result of the lack of repair.

There is a *general* prohibition against including in a tenancy agreement any provision that is inconsistent with the R.T.A. or the regulations; any provision in a tenancy agreement that is inconsistent with the Act or regulations is void.[10]

In *Ferguson v. Stirpe*,[11] the landlady rented out her basement to a student. The landlady tried to exert control over all aspects of the tenant's conduct, including trying to limit or prevent the tenant from having guests visit her. It was held that if a landlord chooses to rent out part of her home, she must respect the right of her tenant to privacy and to quiet and reasonable enjoyment of the rental unit. It was further confirmed that any provision of a tenancy agreement that is inconsistent with these fundamental rights is void. At the request of the tenant, the tenancy was terminated and an abatement of rent was awarded.

Landlords will sometimes try to control who resides within a rental unit. Obviously, landlords have a statutory right to screen potential tenants and potential assignees or subtenants. What about cases where the tenant remains in possession of the unit but wants to bring someone else into the unit? It seems absurd that a tenant should need permission from the landlord to share the unit with another person (a relative, friend, spouse, significant other or simply a roommate) or should have to obtain permission from the landlord to have a child. Nevertheless, some landlords try to exert this type of control over their units.

In Landlord and Tenant Board File No. SOT-00022 (March 26, 2007), the landlord inserted into its standard tenancy agreements a provision that required a tenant to obtain prior written approval before allowing another person to stay (i.e., sleep) in the unit for more than three weeks in aggregate in any three-month period, failing which the landlord could treat the guest as a trespasser and/or terminate the tenancy and evict the tenant. The tenant in this case became engaged to be married. In an attempt to comply with the tenancy agreement, his fiancée completed an "application for permission to reside" with the tenant in the rental unit. She was not seeking permission to be added to the tenancy agreement as a tenant. Her application was denied because she had a poor credit history and the tenant was advised that if his fiancée moved in with him the landlord would evict them both.

The tenant filed an application with the Board, alleging that the landlord was substantially interfering with his reasonable enjoyment of the rental unit. The landlord argued that, upon the death of the tenant or upon a breakdown in their marriage, the fiancée (who would then be a spouse) might have the

---

[10] Section 4 of the R.T.A. (formerly s. 16 of the T.P.A.).

[11] (Sept. 2, 1999), TNT-00627, 1999 CarswellOnt 5825 (Ont. Rental Housing Trib.).

right to become a tenant under the new provisions of the R.T.A. and s. 3 of O. Reg. 516/06. The landlord therefore argued that the tenant's fiancée was a prospective tenant and that, pursuant to s. 10 of the R.T.A., the landlord could screen out (deny permission to) a prospective tenant who had a bad credit history. The Board rejected this argument finding that a "prospective tenant" is a person who is currently applying to become a tenant not someone who could conceivably, under certain circumstances, at some point in the future, have the right to become a tenant. The landlord was ordered to cease its attempts to block the tenant's fiancée from moving into the unit or threatening to evict the tenant for this reason. This decision upholds the underlying principle that a tenant's home is their castle and, subject to the limitations specifically set out in the R.T.A.,[12] the landlord cannot dictate to a tenant with whom the tenant may share his or her home.

While the prohibition against contracting out of the provisions of the Act usually serves to protect tenants, it can have the opposite effect. In *1086891 Ontario Inc. v. Barber*,[13] the tenant entered into an agreement with the property manager that the rent would be "frozen" as of May 2003, and the rent would not be increased as long as the tenant remained in the unit. The consideration for this agreement was that the tenant agreed to pay a rent increase in 2002 and agreed not to vacate the rental unit when he had the opportunity to do so. Notwithstanding this agreement, the landlord subsequently purported to increase the rent, and when the tenant refused to pay the higher rent, brought an application to evict the tenant for non-payment of rent. The Rental Housing Tribunal ruled in favour of the landlord on the basis that the agreement between the parties was inconsistent with the T.P.A. and, pursuant to s. 2 of that Act (now s. 3 of the R.T.A.), that agreement was void. On appeal, the majority of the Divisional Court agreed with this analysis and upheld the Tribunal's decision. In a strongly worded but well-reasoned dissent, however, Justice Cumming concluded that it is not contrary to the Act for a landlord to agree to take less rent than it might be otherwise entitled to charge:

> I do not find any provision of the *TPA* which mandates that the landlord has a statutory "right" to *increase* the rent in contradiction of a freely-negotiated tenancy agreement which fixes indefinitely a frozen rent. . .[14]
>
> . . .It would not seem uncommon in a period when the vacancy rate for residential rental housing is significant (given increased supply) for landlords and tenants in the competitive marketplace to negotiate and agree upon increases of rent on lease renewals that are less than the maximum rent allowed under the *TPA*. In my view, it would be contrary to the *TPA*, its underlying policy, and the reality

[12] For instance, prohibiting tenants from having so many people residing in the unit that it violates health and safety regulations.

[13] 2007 CarswellOnt 3267 (Ont. Div. Ct.).

[14] *1086891 Ontario Inc. v. Barber*, 2007 CarswellOnt 3267 (Ont. Div. Ct.) at para 30.

in practice, to conclude that a landlord would have the statutory "right" (because of s. 2(1)) to later renege upon this agreed-upon rent (if the market later changed such that a higher rent – up to the maximum rent allowed under the *TPA* – could now be obtained from a prospective new tenant) within the still continuing renewal term at the agreed-upon fixed rent.[15]

The decision in *1086891 Ontario Inc. v. Barber*[16] has been followed recently by Landlord and Tenant Board File No. SWL-13073 (April 17, 2008). Despite a letter from the property management purporting to verify with the tenant that the rental payments "will remain at $699.00 as long as you occupy the above said property", the Board held that the parties could not contract out of the Act and that this agreement was not binding upon the landlord. Since the building was relatively new, pursuant to s. 6(2) of the Act, the landlord was also permitted to increase the rent by more than the guideline (see discussion of this in Chapters 4 and 9).

In addition to the general prohibition against attempting to contract out of the Act, there are also specific terms that cannot be included in tenancy agreements. Two examples are "acceleration" clauses[17] and "no pet" clauses.[18] If a landlord attempts to include such clauses in a tenancy agreement, those provisions (not the entire agreement) are void.[19]

Although the prohibition against "no pets" clauses has been around for a number of years, cases still occasionally arise in which landlords try to find creative ways to exclude pets from their buildings. In *Queen's University v. Clandfield*,[20] the university relied upon a notice of termination that it had the tenant execute at the time the tenancy commenced[21] in an effort to enforce the University's "no pets" policy. The Court of Appeal agreed with the Tribunal that the University could not do indirectly what it would not be entitled to do directly. The landlord's application to terminate this tenancy, although founded upon a notice of termination, was ultimately motivated by the landlord's desire to enforce an illegal, blanket "no pets" policy. The landlord's application was dismissed.

In *215 Glenridge Ave. Ltd. Partnership v. Waddington,*[22] the owner of a condominium unit rented the unit to a tenant. The tenancy agreement con-

---

[15] *1086891 Ontario Inc. v. Barber*, 2007 CarswellOnt 3267 (Ont. Div. Ct.) at para 33.

[16] (2007), 2007 CarswellOnt 3267 (Ont. Div. Ct.).

[17] Section 15 of the R.T.A. (formerly s. 14 of the T.P.A.).

[18] Section 14 of the R.T.A. (formerly s. 15 of the T.P.A.).

[19] "Void" means that the provision in question has no legal affect because it is as if it never existed.

[20] (2001), 200 D.L.R. (4th) 661, 54 O.R. (3d) 475, 146 O.A.C. 299, [2001] O.J. No. 2095, 2001 CarswellOnt 1893 (Ont. C.A.).

[21] Forcing a tenant to sign an agreement or notice to terminate the tenancy as a condition to entering into a tenancy agreement is normally illegal (s. 37(4) and (5) of the R.T.A.) but it is permitted in the case of certain educational institutions (s. 37(6) and (7) of the R.T.A.).

[22] (2005), 2005 CarswellOnt 688 (Ont. S.C.J.).

tained a blanket "no pets" clause. This was consistent with the Declaration and Rules of the condominium corporation. The tenant had two cats in the unit. The landlord was aware that s. 15 of the T.P.A. made the "no pets" provision void. The landlord therefore chose to bring an application under s. 134(1) of the *Condominium Act, 1998* for an order declaring that the tenant was in breach of the condominium corporation's Declaration and Rules and ordering the removal of the cats. The application was dismissed. The condominium corporation's blanket "no pets" rule contravened s. 58(1) of the *Condominium Act* which allows prohibition of pets *only* if they compromise safety, security or the welfare of unit owners or if they unreasonably interfere with the use and enjoyment of common elements.

Note, however, that a unit in a housing co-operative may be exempt from the R.T.A. and, in such a case, the co-operative may be able to enforce a by-law that prohibits pets (or certain types of pets).[23]

Section 108(a) of the R.T.A. (formerly s. 119 of the T.P.A.) states that neither a landlord nor a tenancy agreement shall require a tenant to provide post-dated cheques or other negotiable instruments for payment of rent. In *Stanbar Properties Limited v. Rooke*,[24] the tenant signed a tenancy agreement, which required the tenant to make arrangements with his own bank for the payment of his monthly rent by "pre-authorized direct debit as required by the Landlord." As well, the agreement included a provision that required the tenant to maintain insurance coverage with respect to certain perils and to provide proof of the insurance coverage to the landlord upon request. The tenant refused to honour these provisions. The landlord applied to terminate the tenancy under s. 64(1) of the T.P.A. (now s. 64(1) of the R.T.A.), on the basis that the tenant's failure to comply with these terms of the tenancy agreement substantially interfered with a lawful right, privilege or interest of the landlord. At first instance, the Tribunal found that the landlord had no right to insist on pre-authorized direct debit and that the Tribunal lacked the jurisdiction to deal with "breaches of contractual obligations". On appeal, the Divisional Court overturned the Tribunal's decision on both points. The Court held that the Tribunal does have jurisdiction under s. 64(1) to decide whether a breach of the tenancy agreement substantially interferes with a lawful right, privilege or interest of the landlord. The Court also held that the Tribunal erred in regarding pre-authorized direct debit as "a form of negotiable instrument" as it is neither negotiable nor an instrument and its use is not prohibited by s. 119 of the T.P.A.

In response to this decision, the Legislature has now introduced s. 108(b) to the R.T.A., which prohibits a landlord from requiring a tenant to pay rent by the automatic debiting of the tenant's account at a financial institution or

[23] *Scarborough Bluffs Co-operative Inc. v. Loomes* (2003), 2003 CarswellOnt 328 (Ont. S.C.J.), additional reasons at (2003), 2003 CarswellOnt 428 (Ont. S.C.J.).

[24] (November 9, 2005), Doc. Hamilton 04-212DV (Ont. Div. Ct.).

by an automatic charge to the tenant's credit card or by any other form of automatic payment.

Finally, the common law concerning contracts also applies to tenancy agreements (which are simply a particular type of contract). For instance, an agreement (or part of an agreement) obtained as a result of misrepresentation, duress or undue influence may be struck down.[25]

6. FRUSTRATION OF CONTRACT

The legal doctrine of "frustration" is simply that contractual obligations are discharged when an unexpected event takes place, which neither party contemplated and which materially affects the basis of the contract, or the contractual obligations of one party become impossible to perform. Frustration can be pleaded when the subject matter of the contract has been destroyed or there has been an interruption of performance under the contract that is so critical and protracted as to bring an end in a full and fair sense to the contract as a whole (and no resumption is reasonably possible).

The weight of judicial authority has been that the doctrine of frustration does not apply to leases, although it has been applied to other types of contracts. It had long been the law of landlord and tenant relationships that a tenant must continue to pay rent even though the demised property can no longer be used for the intended purpose, or if the property is destroyed by fire.

This was clearly stated in *Merkur v. H. Shoom & Co.*,[26] where the lessee was unable to use his commercial premises for the purpose contemplated, and the court stated that although the object of the lease was thereby defeated, the doctrine of frustration did not apply. A number of leases do have clauses permitting abatement of rent under such circumstances, but very few leases permit the tenant to terminate the lease.

The unfairness of this state of law was made manifest in the case of *Macartney v. Queen-Yonge Investment Ltd.*[27] Fire had partially destroyed a downtown office building in Toronto, not damaging the tenant's premises, but putting the heating system out of action. The tenant sought to get out of the lease because of the landlord's breach of covenant to heat. When these matters were dealt with by the court, the judgment stated that the tenant only had a right to damages, and that only if the lease terms did not exclude the tenant's right to damages. Quoting from *Johnston v. Givens*,[28] the court stated:[29]

---

[25] See, for example, Landlord and Tenant Board File No. TSL-07526 (March 3, 2008).

[26] (1953), [1954] O.W.N. 55 (Ont. C.A.).

[27] (1960), [1961] O.R. 41 (Ont. H.C.).

[28] [1941] O.R. 281 (Ont. C.A.).

[29] (1960), [1961] O.R. 41 (Ont. H.C.) at 49.

> The rule is of general application that in default of any express provision [in the lease] to that effect the landlord's breaches of covenant do not entitle the tenant to declare the lease at an end.

The judge held that he was bound by the law on this point, but went on to say:[30]

> It seems to me, with respect, to be surprising to find that ... [a] breach of a covenant to supply heat in a country where premises are uninhabitable in winter without heat [does not give the tenant the right to treat the lease as being at an end] .... One would reasonably expect such a covenant to be a condition.

The judgment concludes that "a right to damages . . . is cold comfort to a shivering tenant".

This formerly unfair result for a tenant of residential premises was changed by s. 86 of the *Landlord and Tenant Act*, now s. 19 of the R.T.A., which provides that the doctrine of frustration of contract is now made applicable to residential tenancy agreements. In addition, the section makes the *Frustrated Contracts Act*[31] applicable. This statute provides the blueprint for a court to determine and adjust, on an equitable basis, the respective rights and obligations of the parties in the event of an unanticipated occurrence which frustrates the lease.

Section 86 of Part IV was applied in *Caithness Caledonia Ltd. v. Goss.*[32] The tenant's apartment was directly over the laundromat which gave off substantial heat. The landlord installed an air conditioner to offset the problem, but the air conditioner was not working for a number of months. The judge decided that the apartment was not fit for habitation, and by virtue of ss. 86 and 87 of Part IV, there was at least partial frustration and so he allowed the tenant an abatement of the rent.

The *Caithness* case was considered in *Binder v. Key Property Management Corp.*[33] The tenant moved in and shortly after found that she was allergic to the fresh paint and new carpeting and had to move out. She was diagnosed with chronic fatigue syndrome. The medical evidence indicated that she could not live there. She gave notice to vacate and applied to court for an order terminating the lease relying on s. 86 of Part IV that the *Frustrated Contracts Act*[34] applied. The judge accepted the law of the *Caithness* case, but stated that the law did not apply to physical incapacity. The apartment was habitable. As the judge stated a lease would not be terminated if a tenant was hospitalized, so on that analogy, the application for termination was refused.

---

[30] (1960), [1961] O.R. 41 (Ont. H.C.) at 49-50.

[31] R.S.O. 1990, c. F.34.

[32] [1973] 2 O.R. 592 (Ont. Co. Ct.).

[33] (1992), 26 R.P.R. (2d) 80 (Ont. Gen. Div.).

[34] R.S.O. 1990, c. F.34.

In another case, *Shippam v. Johnson*,[35] the landlord was unable to supply potable water as specified in the lease. This was due to a deteriorating supply and the extreme expense to replace the entire system. The court held that the landlord was frustrated in an attempt to comply and granted the application for termination of the lease.

In *Giroux v. Doran*,[36] the premises burned down. It was not the fault of either party. The contract was found to be frustrated and the tenancy was terminated as of the date of the fire.

In *Guest v. Groleau*,[37] a flood made the unit temporarily uninhabitable. The landlord was required to pay the tenants' reasonable living expenses while they awaited the repair of the unit. The tenants, however, could not "walk away" from the tenancy. The doctrine of frustration was held not to apply in these circumstances.

7. INFORMATION THAT MUST BE PROVIDED TO THE TENANT ON THE COMMENCEMENT OF A TENANCY

(a) Requirements of Section 11

For tenancies that are entered into after the R.T.A. is proclaimed, landlords must provide their new tenants (on or before the tenancy begins) with information in writing (and in the approved form) about the rights and responsibilities of landlords and tenants, the role of the Landlord and Tenant Board and how to contact the Board. Note, however, that there appears to be no penalty for landlords who fail to comply with this requirement.

(b) Requirements of Section 12

Section 12 of the R.T.A. (formerly s. 8 of the T.P.A.) requires landlords to do one or more of the following (for tenancy agreements made on or after June 17, 1998):

(1) if the tenancy agreement is written, include in the tenancy agreement the legal name and address of the landlord to be used for the purpose of giving notices or other documents under the R.T.A. (s. 12(1));
(2) provide a copy of the written tenancy agreement (signed by the landlord and tenant) to the tenant within 21 days after the landlord receives it signed by the tenant (s. 12(2)); and
(3) if the tenancy agreement is not in writing, give the tenant written

[35] (1984), 45 O.R. (2d) 307 (Ont. Co. Ct.).

[36] (Nov. 1, 2000), EAT-02070 and EAT-02071, [2001] O.R.H.T.D. No. 147 (Ont. Rental Housing Trib.).

[37] (Aug. 28, 2002), EAT-03581, 2002 CarswellOnt 3747 (Ont. Rental Housing Trib.).

notice of the landlord's legal name and address for service within 21 days after the tenancy begins (s. 12(3)).

A tenant requires this information so that the tenant will have written evidence as to the identity of the landlord and will have an address at which the landlord can be served with notices or other documents required under the R.T.A.

If a landlord fails to comply with these provisions, there are very serious consequences: the tenant's obligation to pay rent is suspended and the landlord cannot require the tenant to pay rent (s. 12(4)). Note that the obligation to pay rent is suspended, not eliminated. When the landlord finally complies with the requirements of s. 12, the tenant will then owe any rent that the tenant withheld (s. 12(5)).

Until a landlord complies with the provisions of s. 12, the landlord cannot serve upon a tenant a valid notice of termination for non-payment of rent.[38] This is because, at the time the notice of termination is given to the tenant, the tenant's obligation to pay rent is suspended and the landlord has no right to demand payment of rent (pursuant to s. 12(4)). The landlord also cannot use a "bootstrap" argument; the notice of termination cannot be the notice contemplated by s. 12(3) and, at the same time, be considered to be a valid notice of termination. If the notice of termination is considered to be sufficient to comply with the requirements of s. 12(3), the landlord can proceed with an application for arrears of rent but will not be able to seek termination of the tenancy (for non-payment of rent) unless a second, valid notice of termination is served upon the tenant.[39]

In *Carvhalho v. Haman*,[40] the landlord did not set out his address in the tenancy agreement and did not provide the tenant with written notice of that information. The reviewing Member found that the fact that a cheque delivered to the tenant from the landlord may have shown an address for the landlord did not constitute compliance with the requirements of s. 8 of the T.P.A. (now s. 12 of the R.T.A.). It was therefore held that the landlord had no right to commence an application for arrears of rent as the tenant's obligation to pay rent had been suspended. The application form itself, however, contained the landlord's address for service and was sufficient to comply with the requirements under s. 8 of the T.P.A. The Member ruled that from

---

[38] *Doren v. Ryshpan et al.* (Dec. 5, 2001), TNL-31595 (Ont. Rental Housing Trib.) and *Firm Capital Properties Inc. v. Cabenero* (Dec. 18, 1998), SOL-02546 (Ont. Rental Housing Trib.) and Landlord and Tenant Board File No. SWL-22606 (Jan. 26, 2009). See also *Huang & Danczkay Property Management Inc. v. Lin* (1992), 1992 CarswellOnt 2842 (Ont. Gen. Div.) in which the court held that it was premature for the landlord to serve a notice of termination for non-payment of rent when the landlord had not yet provided a copy of the tenancy agreement to the tenant.

[39] *Abraham v. Paquette* (Nov. 30, 2000), TEL-15971, [2000] O.R.H.T.D. No. 166 (Ont. Rental Housing Trib.).

[40] Aug. 24, 2006 (amended Aug. 31, 2006), TSL-79719-RV, [2006] O.R.H.T.D. No. 110 (Ont. Rental Housing Trib.).

the time the tenant received the application form, the arrears became due and the landlord could pursue those arrears of rent should the landlord wish to commence a *fresh* application.

A rather unique and somewhat restrictive interpretation was given to these provisions in *Belgrave Avenue (London) Inc. v. Franze*.[41] The evidence suggests that the landlord never provided the tenant with a copy of the tenancy agreement at any time prior to serving upon her the notice of termination and application. In fact, a copy of the tenancy agreement was not delivered until during the hearing of this application. At the time the notice of termination was served and at the time the application was commenced, there were no arrears of rent because the tenant's obligation to pay rent was suspended. Nevertheless, the Member glosses over this point and finds that, since the tenancy agreement was delivered to the tenant at the hearing, the obligation to pay rent was no longer suspended and the landlord was entitled to proceed with this application based upon those arrears of rent.

8. INITIAL TERM AND RENEWAL

Pursuant to s. 13 of the R.T.A. (formerly s. 9 of the T.P.A.), the term or period of a tenancy begins on the day the tenant is entitled to occupy the rental unit under the tenancy agreement, whether or not the tenant actually occupies it.[42]

Once a tenancy has been created, it can only be terminated in accordance with the R.T.A. (s. 37(1) of the R.T.A.); this generally means termination by agreement, by notice or by order of the Board.[43]

Most tenancies start out with a fixed term (usually one year). What happens at the end of that year? Are any steps required to renew the tenancy? The parties can expressly renew such a tenancy or terminate it. If the parties take no action, however, the tenancy does not automatically end at the conclusion of the initial term; it is deemed to be automatically renewed as a consequence of s. 38(1) of the R.T.A. Subsection 38(1) states that, "If a tenancy agreement for a fixed term ends and has not been renewed or terminated, the landlord and tenant shall be deemed to have renewed it as a monthly tenancy agreement containing the same terms and conditions that are in the expired tenancy agreement and subject to any increases in rent charged in accordance with this Act."

Not all tenancies are for a fixed term, however. They may be day-to-day, week-to-week or month-to-month, etc., without any specified term. Do periodic tenancies need to be renewed at the end of each period? According to

[41] (April 18, 2006), SWL-79013, [2006] O.R.H.T.D. No. 31 (Ont. Rental Housing Trib.).

[42] See Landlord and Tenant Board File No. SOT-00474 (Aug. 3, 2007), discussed further in Chapter 8 (under the heading "Applying or Refunding the Rent Deposit").

[43] Termination of a tenancy is discussed in detail in Chapter 6.

s. 38(2) of the R.T.A. (formerly s. 40(2) of the T.P.A.), such tenancies are also automatically renewed.

Subsection 38(2) states that, "If the period of a daily, weekly or monthly tenancy ends and the tenancy has not been renewed or terminated, the landlord and tenant shall be deemed to have renewed it for another day, week or month, as the case may be, with the same terms and conditions that are in the expired tenancy agreement and subject to any increases in rent charged in accordance with this Act."

Subsection 38(3) states that, "If the period of a periodic tenancy ends, the tenancy has not been renewed or terminated and subsection (2) does not apply, the landlord and tenant shall be deemed to have renewed it as a monthly tenancy, with the same terms and conditions that are in the expired tenancy agreement and subject to any increases in rent charged in accordance with this Act."

Landlords typically send out notices of rent increase each year at least 90 days before the date the rent increase is to take effect; in practical terms, this means that such notices are sent out about four months before the anniversary of the commencement of the tenancy. Although the form of such notices is mandated by regulation, some landlords have taken it upon themselves to add at the bottom of the forms a place for the tenant to request (by checking a box and signing the form) that the tenancy be renewed for another year. The benefit to the landlord is that it can "lock in" a tenant for another year and help ensure a more stable flow of income. There is also some potential benefit to the tenant. Certain types of applications for termination by a landlord may only take effect at the end of the term; if the tenancy is renewed for a one-year term, the tenant's security of tenure is enhanced somewhat during that year. The "downside" for tenants is that it commits them to remain in the rental unit for at least another year.

The way in which the added portion is drafted by landlords suggests to tenants that they have only two options: renew for a one-year term (or longer) or indicate their intention to terminate the tenancy. This is, at the very least, misleading. Tenants have the third option of taking no action, in which case the tenancy will be automatically renewed as a month-to-month tenancy on the same terms as before.[44] Many tenants, though, are ignorant of this third option.

In my view, this practice of trying to fool or scare tenants into renewing their tenancies for a fixed term is unethical. Furthermore, by altering the notice of rent increase in this way, the landlord takes the risk that it will be considered to be neither a valid renewal of the tenancy agreement (for a fixed

[44] Except that the rent may be higher (but this would be true whether the tenancy is specifically renewed by the parties or if it is deemed to be renewed by operation of s. 38).

term)[45] nor a valid notice of rent increase.[46] It is recommended that landlords who wish to offer tenants the opportunity to renew their tenancies for a fixed term should: (1) send separate correspondence to the tenants (not alter a prescribed form); and (2) explain that this is, indeed, optional.

9. UNILATERAL CHANGE OF TERMS

As in any contractual situation, one party to the contract generally cannot unilaterally change the terms of that contract.[47]

In *Garrick v. Chakarvarty*,[48] the landlord's habit was to come in person to retrieve the rent. The rent was due on the first day of each month and the landlord used to come to collect the rent at the beginning of each month. The landlord then began coming around the middle of the month. In such circumstances, the Tribunal held that the landlord could not complain then that the rent was being paid late.

In *Heinemann v. Haverlock*,[49] the tenant had used three parking spaces for years. The new landlord took the position that the tenant was only entitled to one space and that, by using three, this tenant was interfering in the lawful rights of the landlord and the reasonable enjoyment of the other tenants. The Tribunal found that the parking arrangement (i.e., the use of three spaces) was long-standing and that the landlord could not unilaterally alter the terms of the tenancy agreement. The landlord's application was dismissed.

There are two situations, however, where the R.T.A. permits a landlord to change the terms of an existing tenancy agreement, even if the tenant objects.

First, under s. 137 of the R.T.A., where a landlord supplies electricity to a rental unit, the R.T.A. allows the landlord to withdraw the supply of electricity and install a separate electricity meter (a "smart" meter), without the tenant's consent, if the landlord complies with certain strict criteria. Once the smart meter is installed and a minimum of 12 months have passed from the date of installation, the landlord can charge separately for the electricity actually consumed in the rental unit. In exchange, the landlord will have to reduce the tenant's rent based upon the average monthly cost of electricity for that unit during the preceding 12-month period.

---

45 *Realstar Management Partnership v. Rostovsky*, (June 18, 2004), TNL-52825-RV (Ont. Rental Housing Trib.) and *Digiglio and Turret Realties Inc., Re*, Divisional Court, June 28, 1995 (unreported).

46 See Landlord and Tenant Board File No. TSL-03635 (Sept. 24, 2007). There is a further discussion of this issue in Chapter 9 under the heading "Notice of Rent Increase".

47 Unless expressly permitted by the terms of the contract itself or specifically authorized by statute.

48 (Nov. 12, 1998), TSL-02726 (Ont. Rental Housing Trib.).

49 (Oct. 30, 1998), CEL-01594 (Ont. Rental Housing Trib.).

Second, under s. 138 of the R.T.A., for a building containing no more than six units, where the landlord supplies a utility to each of the units, the R.T.A. allows the landlord to unilaterally change the tenancy agreements and charge each tenant a portion of the utility costs, provided that the landlord gives adequate notice, reduces the rent and ensures that any appliances in the unit and other aspects of the unit and building meet the prescribed requirements relating to energy conservation. It should be noted that the separate charge for the utility is still not considered to be "rent".

Due to a delay in the passage of the required regulations, neither s. 137 nor s. 138 is yet in effect.

10. FUNDAMENTAL BREACH AND MISREPRESENTATION (COVENANTS INTERDEPENDENT)

Traditionally, the common law provided that the tenant's obligations under a lease continued in full force notwithstanding that the landlord was not fulfilling the landlord's covenants. According to the common law of landlord and tenant relations, the respective obligations of landlords and tenants were deemed to be independent.

In *Macartney v. Queen-Yonge Investment Ltd.*,[50] the commercial tenant was not relieved of his obligation to pay rent when the landlord did not or could not provide heat. The tenant's only remedy for the breach of a landlord's covenant was to sue for damages, only if the lease terms did not include a waiver of damages by the tenant.

On the other hand, a landlord had been able to treat a breach of covenant by a tenant as a condition of the lease, and the landlord then had the right to re-enter and terminate the lease, or as will be discussed later, the right to apply to court for an order terminating the lease.

The usual rules of contract law make the respective covenants or obligations of the parties mutually dependent and, therefore, a breach of a material obligation of one party will excuse the other from further performance.

The recommendation of the Ontario Law Reform Commission was that the respective obligations of landlords and tenants should be *interdependent*, similar to the common law rules applicable to contracts. The response to this recommendation was the addition of s. 11 to the T.P.A.

Section 11 of the T.P.A. originally provided that, subject to the other rights and remedies contained in Part II of the Act, "the common law rules respecting the effect of *the breach* of a material covenant by one party to a contract on the obligation to perform by the other party apply with respect to tenancy agreements" (emphasis added). This created some confusion as to whether even minor breaches by one party would relieve the other party of

[50] (1960), [1961] O.R. 41 (Ont. H.C.).

the obligation to honour the contract. To clarify matters, s. 11 was amended in 2000 to read as follows:

> Subject to this Part, the common law rules respecting the effect of *serious, substantial or fundamental breach* of a material covenant by one party to a contract on the obligation to perform of the other party apply with respect to tenancy agreements. (emphasis added)

This provision has been imported, virtually unchanged, into s. 17 of the R.T.A.

Section 17 of the R.T.A., at least in theory, applies equally to landlords and tenants. Practically speaking, however, s. 17 will be of greater benefit to tenants able to take advantage of its provisions in two ways.

First, a tenant may be able to raise s. 17 as a defence to a landlord's eviction application. Take, for example, the case where a landlord is seeking to terminate the tenancy and evict the tenant for non-payment of rent. In addition to other defences that may be available to the tenant (including ss. 83(1) and (3)), where it can be proven that the landlord was in serious, substantial or fundamental breach of a material covenant under the tenancy agreement, the tenant can argue that the landlord's breach or breaches relieved the tenant of his obligations under the agreement, including the obligation to pay rent. If this argument is accepted, it will be a complete defence to the landlord's application.

Second, where the landlord's breach goes to the root of the contract, it may be considered so fundamental as to permit the tenant to consider the tenancy agreement to be at an end.

In *Temlas Apartments Inc. v. Desloges*,[51] the tenants vacated the unit because the hot water was unusable and the landlord failed to deal with the problem. The landlord sued in Small Claims Court for lost rental income for the balance of the term of the tenancy. The trial judge found that a fundamental breach of the tenancy agreement had occurred and dismissed the landlord's action. On appeal, the Divisional Court found that the contamination of the hot water did not constitute a breach fundamental enough to discharge the contract. The Court discusses what constitutes a "fundamental breach" and concludes that, to be fundamental, the breach must frustrate the real purpose of the contract.

Cases of fundamental breach of a tenancy agreement will be very rare. Since Part III of the R.T.A. already provides numerous remedies for most potential breaches by a landlord of the Act (or of a tenancy agreement), the Board will rarely have to resort to the provisions of s. 17 in order to grant relief to a tenant.[52] Nevertheless, the seriousness of the breach by the landlord will be relevant to the Board's decision as to the appropriate remedy.

---

[51] (1980), 29 O.R. (2d) 30 (Ont. Div. Ct.).

[52] Including, in appropriate circumstances and at the request of the tenant, an order terminating the tenancy early.

In *Petsinis v. Santos*,[53] the landlord had promised to paint this luxurious home as one of the key terms negotiated at the commencement of the tenancy. The tenant even agreed to pay higher rent based upon that promise. The landlord breached this term by failing to paint the house. The tenants brought an application based upon an alleged failure of the landlord to repair and maintain the rental unit. The Member ruled that since the painting of the house was a fundamental part of the tenancy agreement, the appropriate remedy here was to allow the tenant out of the tenancy agreement (i.e., order termination of the tenancy). This decision was upheld upon appeal to the Divisional Court.

A tenant induced into entering a tenancy agreement through negligent or fraudulent misrepresentations may be able to seek damages in a court of competent jurisdiction but, generally, conduct that occurs before a tenancy commences falls outside the jurisdiction of the Board.[54]

In *Boulay. v. Chizmar*,[55] the Tribunal found that a lack of any electricity to the unit constituted a fundamental breach of contract that relieved the tenants of their obligations under the tenancy agreement, including their obligation to pay rent (until electric service was restored to the property).

In Landlord and Tenant Board File No. SOT-01771 (Jan. 14, 2009), the tenants were renting a basement apartment. It turned out that the apartment violated local by-laws and the landlords were required to remove the kitchen from the basement. It was determined that this was so significant an alteration to the terms of the agreement that it constituted a fundamental breach that justified termination of the tenancy.

It is not just tenants, however, who can rely upon the concept of fundamental breach.

Where a tenant intentionally defrauds a landlord by lying about her identity and then transfers the unit to someone else, the landlord may be able to treat the entire contract as a nullity and to treat any stranger living in the unit as a trespasser.[56]

In *Annett v. Robert Breadner Children's Trust (Trustees of)*,[57] the landlord rented the premises to the tenant with an option to purchase the property. Although the option to purchase was independent of the tenancy agreement, its operation was tied inextricably to the fulfillment of the terms of the tenancy agreement. The tenant was persistently late in paying rent and fell into arrears. The tenant then purported to exercise the option to purchase. Justice Stong

---

[53] (September 10, 2001), Doc. 726/00 (Ont. Div. Ct.) (re TNT-01335).

[54] *Fortin v. Reiter-Nemetz* (Dec. 13, 2002), TNT-02907, 2002 CarswellOnt 5014 (Ont. Rental Housing Trib.).

[55] (May 23, 2002), SWT-03249 (Ont. Rental Housing Trib.).

[56] *Hamilton et al. v. 611283 Ontario Ltd.* (Nov. 26, 2001), TNT-02353 (Ont. Rental Housing Trib.).

[57] (2007), [2008] O.J. No. 84 (Ont. S.C.J.), affirmed (2008), 2008 CarswellOnt 6892 (Ont. C.A.).

of the Ontario Superior Court of Justice held that persistently late and non-payment of rent were material breaches going to the root of the lease and the option to purchase agreement. Such fundamental breaches relieved the landlord from its obligations under the option agreement, but the landlord was ordered to return advances the tenant had made towards the purchase of the property.

11. COVENANTS RUNNING WITH THE LAND

By s. 18 of the R.T.A. (formerly s. 12 of the T.P.A.), covenants other than personal service covenants, run with the land and bind assignees whether the covenantor has covenanted on behalf of his assigns or not. This overcomes the distinction in the ancient rule of landlord and tenant law that only covenants which refer to something in existence (*in esse*) run with the land, and that covenants relating to something not in existence (*in posse*) do not run with the land. As to the latter, neither the assignee of the reversion nor the assignee of the tenant is bound, that is, unless by the original lease the lessor or lessee, as the case may be, had covenanted for himself and his assigns.

Covenants of the first type (*in esse*) are covenants to pay rent, to pay taxes, to repair, and to use the premises only for certain purposes.

Covenants of the second type (*in posse*) are covenants to rebuild in case of destruction by fire or to erect improvements.[58]

Section 18 of the R.T.A. states:

> Covenants concerning things related to a rental unit or the residential complex in which it is located run with the land, whether or not the things are in existence at the time the covenants are made.

When the subjects of covenants running with the land or the reversion are discussed in landlord and tenant textbooks, a distinction is also made between covenants which directly concern or benefit the land demised, and covenants which are collateral and therefore personal between the original parties which do not touch or concern the land demised, and do not run with the land or the reversion, even if assignees are named.

Examples of the latter type are an option to purchase and a provision for forfeiture if execution should issue against the tenant's goods. Some doubt may be held as to whether an option to purchase is purely personal. In the case of *Re Avard; Nook v. Parker*,[59] it was held that an option to purchase was not personal to the tenant and was transmissible to his personal representatives. But in *Devine v. Ferguson*,[60] an option to purchase was said to be

---

[58] For a further explanatory reference see Williams & Rhodes, *Canadian Law of Landlord and Tenant*, 6th ed. (Toronto: Carswell, 1988) at 15:7:7.

[59] [1948] Ch. 43 (Eng. Ch. Div.).

[60] [1946] O.R. 736 (Ont. H.C.).

wholly outside the relationship of landlord and tenant and therefore did not run with the land. However, in *Maynard v. Regent Refining (Can.) Ltd.*,[61] an assignee of the tenant was able to enforce an option to purchase, by reason of the terms of the assignment consented to by the lessor.

The covenant to repay an existing security deposit for damages did not bind the assignee of the landlord who did not receive the security deposit from the assignor in *Dollar Land Corp. v. Solomon*,[62] and so did not bind the assignee of the reversion to repay. But see the further judicial analysis of this point in the subsequent paragraphs.

It should be noted that in this case although there was the usual clause that "lessor" included "assigns", the particular clause referring to the deposit specifically referred only to the lessor. Whether this should have made any difference, it was nevertheless a stated ground in the judge's reasons for holding that the purchaser from the landlord was not responsible for the security deposit, the refund or its application. In any event, by s. 18 of the R.T.A. the purchaser is liable for the return of the deposit or its proper application. Therefore a purchaser from a landlord should obtain an accounting from the landlord of security deposits held and interest thereon and the payment of them to the purchaser or a suitable adjustment.

As by s. 18 of the R.T.A. that covenants run with the land, it is submitted that an option to purchase should be available to the assignee of a tenant or to a tenant against an assignee of the reversion. Certainly the tenor of the amendments to ameliorate the position of tenants would dictate that this be so.

One would think that an option to purchase given to a tenant can be considered as a "thing related to the rented premises": s. 88 of Part IV, now s. 18 of the R.T.A.

In an earlier edition of this book, it was stated that an assignee of the reversion is not obliged to repay or account for a security deposit paid by a tenant to the former owner landlord and for that statement relied on *Dollar Land Corp. v. Solomon*.[63] It was, however, also mentioned in the text of that edition that s. 88 of Part IV, which provides that covenants run with the land, may and probably should fix a purchaser with the liability for the return of the security deposit or its proper application. Subsequent to that edition, the *Dollar Land* case was confirmed in *Chiappino v. Bishop*[64] and the successor landlord did not have to repay or account for security deposit which was not received by the successor landlord.

[61] [1956] O.W.N. 251 (Ont. H.C.).
[62] [1963] 2 O.R. 269 (Ont. H.C.).
[63] *Ibid.*
[64] (1988), 49 R.P.R. 218 (Ont. Dist. Ct.).

By another round of judicial consideration, however, it has now been decided in favour of the tenant: *Spencer Properties Ltd. v. Zrebiec.*[65] The judge held that the obligation to repay a security deposit in s. 82(1) of Part IV, now s. 105(2) of the R.T.A., amounts to an implied covenant by the landlord which runs with the land by s. 88 of Part IV, now s. 18 of the R.T.A. So it is up to the successor landlord to make due inquiry about outstanding security deposits. If there were any security deposits the successor landlord is required to repay or account for them to the tenants who paid them.

The suggestion that s. 88 of Part IV, now s. 18 of the R.T.A., does include all but purely personal covenants can be a suggestion until there is judicial interpretation of the words "things related to the rented premises", but the word "things" seems to be as general a word as there is in our language.

If there is some substance to this suggestion, and if the original parties do not wish particular covenants to affect or benefit assignees, such a covenant should clearly state that it is for the benefit of and the burden is only upon the parties to the lease and has no effect so far as assignees of the tenant or reversion are concerned.

This is more or less what was stated by the Ontario Law Reform Commission in its report:[66]

> [A]ll covenants are to be enforceable by or against an assignee, unless ... the parties to the tenancy agreement have argued otherwise, or unless it is intended that performance of a service under the covenant is to be by the covenantor, and by him alone.

12. DUTY TO MITIGATE

Pursuant to s. 16 of the R.T.A. (formerly s. 13 of the T.P.A.), when a landlord or tenant becomes liable to pay any amount as a result of a breach of a tenancy agreement, the person entitled to claim the amount has a duty to take reasonable steps to minimize the person's losses. This is known as mitigation of damages. It applies equally to landlords and tenants.

For landlords, this means that if a tenant vacates a rental unit, without giving proper notice of termination, the landlord must make reasonable efforts to re-rent the unit as quickly as possible. Landlords who have a number of vacant units may seek to rent first those units that have been vacant the longest[67] but this may not be considered acceptable mitigation,[68] especially

[65] (1992), 1992 CarswellOnt 1760 (Ont. Gen. Div.).

[66] Report of the Ontario Law Reform Commission (15 March 1976) at 29.

[67] *Parkway Realty Ltd. v. Jani* (March 23, 2000), TNL-13873, [2000] O.R.H.T.D. No. 46, 2000 CarswellOnt 6357 (Ont. Rental Housing Trib.).

[68] *Bonshaw Estates v. Murphy* (1993), 1993 CarswellOnt 3356 (Ont. Gen. Div.).

where the units are different in character.[69] It also means accepting any payment offered by or on behalf of the tenant that will reduce the debt; a landlord should not reject a payment simply because it is less than the full amount owing or is tendered by someone other than the tenant (if it is clear that the payment is being made *on behalf of* the tenant). Similarly, a landlord should not be reluctant to accept arrears of rent or compensation for use or occupation of a rental unit. Unless the landlord and tenant agree otherwise, accepting money from the tenant in such circumstances is not deemed to waive the notice of termination, reinstate the tenancy or create a new tenancy.[70]

For tenants, mitigation may mean that where a landlord fails (after repeated requests) to effect relatively minor repairs, the tenant ought to take steps to have the repairs done and seek reimbursement for the expense of those repairs, rather than allowing the problem to continue indefinitely and then seek an abatement of rent over a period of months or years.

13. INTERESSE TERMINI

The archaic principle of *interesse termini* was abolished by s. 85(1) of Part IV of the *Landlord and Tenant Act*. The application of the principle was to deprive a tenant, who had not been able to obtain possession, of the right to sue the landlord for specific performance. The tenant might have signed a lease or agreement to lease, and before going into possession, the landlord may have decided to refuse possession. The tenant had no legal right arising from *interesse termini* (interest in a term) to require the landlord to honour the lease and let the tenant into possession.

Although a tenant was not able to sue for specific performance, a tenant could sue the landlord for damages flowing from not being permitted into possession.

Damages were awarded when accommodation was not ready for two months after the date specified in the offer to lease. Damages included motel accommodation less what would have been paid as rent, plus extra moving costs and storage: *Tolgyesi v. Freure Homes Ltd.*[71]

---

[69] For instance, it might be easier to re-rent a one-bedroom apartment than a three-bedroom unit or to rent out a newly renovated unit over one that is in poor condition. A blanket "last in, last out" policy may not be acceptable. A landlord must be prepared to prove what efforts it has made to minimize its losses and to explain the reasonableness of its actions.

[70] Section 45 and 103(2) of the R.T.A. Of course, if an order terminating a tenancy is based solely upon arrears of rent (and other sums specified in s. 87 of the Act) and the tenant pays the full amount the order specifies as necessary to void the order, the landlord really has no choice but to accept the money and the tenancy will be reinstated by operation of s. 74(4) of the R.T.A.

[71] (1987), 1987 CarswellOnt 2825 (Ont. Dist. Ct.).

Seldom has a prospective residential tenant been adversely affected by being unable to sue for specific performance. Accordingly, giving tenants the right to sue for specific performance is not likely to change landlord and tenant relations materially. Not many tenants will wish to resort to legal action.

Nevertheless, it was a further step in effecting a better balance between the respective and vital interests of landlords and tenants.

The above s. 85(1) of Part IV was not carried forward into the T.P.A. or the R.T.A. Therefore, it is an open question as to whether or not the principle of *interesse termini* has been reintroduced into the realm of residential tenancies.

14. DISTRESS

In non-residential tenancies, landlords are often permitted to seize a tenant's property for default in payment of rent or for other breaches of the tenant's obligations. It was felt by the government that such a remedy was generally not appropriate for residential tenancies and, therefore, distress was abolished as a remedy in Part IV of the *Landlord and Tenant Act*. That prohibition has been continued in s. 40 of the R.T.A. (formerly s. 31 of the T.P.A.).

However, in a few situations, a landlord may deal with personal property left in a rental unit or residential complex. Where a tenancy has been terminated and the tenant does not retrieve his or her property within 72 hours after the enforcement of an eviction order, the landlord may, pursuant to s. 41of the R.T.A. sell, retain or otherwise dispose of the tenant's property. Similarly, a landlord may dispose of property in a rental unit that a tenant has abandoned (pursuant to s. 42 of the R.T.A.) if the landlord first obtains an order from the Board or provides proper notification to the tenant and to the Board. Finally, where the sole tenant of a rental unit has died, the landlord may immediately remove any property that is unsafe or not hygienic, and after 30 days, may sell, retain for the landlord's own use or otherwise dispose of any other property still remaining in the rental unit (s. 92 of the R.T.A.). These topics are discussed more fully in Chapter 18.

15. JOINT AND SEVERAL LIABILITY AND THE EVOLUTION OF A TENANCY

Most written tenancy agreements provide that, if there is more than one tenant, each tenant is jointly and severally responsible for any liability arising out of the agreement. This means that each tenant is 100% responsible. Take the example of two friends who decide to rent an apartment together. The monthly rent is $1,400. If the tenancy agreement provides that they are jointly and severally liable, they are each responsible for 100% of the debt to the landlord. The friends may have agreed between themselves that they would each pay $700 towards the rent but the landlord need not be concerned with their arrangement. Legally, the landlord can attempt to collect any rent owing from either tenant or from both of them. The same is true for liability for damage to the unit or any other liability arising form the tenancy agreement. Each tenant is fully responsible for the actions of the other tenant(s) and what occurs during the tenancy. A tenant can even be responsible for what occurs after they vacate the unit. Although the landlord may not be able to pursue a claim in an application before the Landlord and Tenant Board against a tenant who is no longer in possession of a rental unit,[72] the landlord may nevertheless pursue such a claim in court. In *George V Apartments Ltd. v. Cobb*,[73] the Divisional Court confirmed that merely vacating a rental unit does not end a tenancy or a tenant's liability under the tenancy agreement. This, then, brings me to the next topic: How tenancies evolve.

Consider the following hypothetical situations:

Scenario 1.

Two friends, Sharon and Sandra, share an apartment. Both are listed on the tenancy agreement as tenants but the landlord has always exclusively dealt with Sharon. Sharon advises the landlord that she and Sandra wish to terminate their tenancy and hands the landlord a notice of termination, signed only by Sharon. Is the notice of termination valid?

Most decisions from the Tribunal have answered this question in the negative; unless the person signing has clear authority to do so on behalf of all other tenants, a notice of termination or agreement to terminate a tenancy should be signed by *all* of the tenants.[74]

Scenario 2.

Spouses rent an apartment in both of their names. There is a breakdown of the relationship and one spouse vacates the unit. Can she be released from her obligations under the tenancy agreement?

Situations where one (or more) of several tenants named in the tenancy agreement vacate the rental unit is actually fairly common. What seems to be poorly understood is that, until the tenancy is properly terminated, all of the tenants may remain liable to the landlord and to each other under the

[72] As a result of the Court of Appeal's decision in *1162994 Ontario Inc. v. Bakker* (2004), 2004 CarswellOnt 869 (Ont. C.A.) (re SWL-40290).

[73] (2002), 2002 CarswellOnt 5553 (Ont. Div. Ct.).

[74] *Jenkins v. Hammond* (Aug. 27, 2003), EAL-36153, EAT-04770 and EAL-36615-RV, [2003] O.R.H.T.D. No. 112, 2003 CarswellOnt 4202 (Ont. Rental Housing Trib.); *Wilson v. Gilboa Management* (Jan. 20, 1999), EAT-00378 (Ont. Rental Housing Trib.); and *Victoria Park Community Homes v. Carson et al.* (June 16, 2003), SOL-40820 (Ont. Rental Housing Trib.).

tenancy agreement. That sometimes comes as quite a surprise to individuals who may have had nothing to do with the rental unit for years.

The problem is that the R.T.A. does not expressly provide a mechanism whereby one tenant can end his or her liability by having themselves removed from the tenancy or by unilaterally terminating the entire tenancy.[75] This problem (but not a solution) was discussed at some length in *Ladowsky v. Bell*,[76] in which a tenant who had moved out of the unit a long time before the landlord obtained an order for arrears of rent (amongst other things) requested a review of that order. She felt that it was unfair that she should be responsible to pay rent for a unit in which she had not lived for quite some time. In the absence of her having given the landlord any notice and in the absence of any statutory provision relieving her of liability, the Member felt he had no choice but to deny this request for review. Even if she had given written notice to the landlord, it is unlikely that such notice would be found to be effective to terminate the tenancy since it would not have been signed by all of the tenants. Presumably, if all parties consented, one tenant could be released from a tenancy. Short of that, however, there is no clear mechanism for severing a tenancy.

The R.T.A. fails to deal with conflicts that might arise between tenants to a single tenancy agreement and fails to provide any mechanism whereby one of several tenants can either end their liability under the tenancy agreement or force an end to the entire tenancy. In the absence of any express statutory provisions or clear guidance from the courts on this issue, people should be wary of co-tenancies since it is much easier to get into such a relationship than it is to get out. In my view, the R.T.A. needs to be amended to specifically deal with such situations.

One possible solution is through amendment to the assignment provisions (s. 95). A co-tenant who wishes to be released from liability under the tenancy agreement could provide a written request to assign his or her interest in the tenancy to the remainder of the original tenants. If the landlord consents to the assignment, everyone is happy.[77] If the landlord refuses to consent to the assignment or fails to respond within the specified time period, that could trigger a right for the person who is requesting consent to commence an application to seek an order from the Board authorizing the assignment, authorizing an alternate assignment, terminating this tenant's interest in (and liability under) the tenancy or terminating the entire tenancy. All parties to

---

[75] Note that subsection 3(2) of O. Reg. 516/06 does not apply in situations where both spouses are listed as tenants on the tenancy agreement.

[76] (Feb. 13, 2003), TSL-35330-RV, [2003] O.R.H.T.D. No. 23, 2003 CarswellOnt 1533 (Ont. Rental Housing Trib.).

[77] The tenants who remain in the unit can always bring in a roommate to help defray their expenses but the R.T.A. will not apply to the relationship between the roommates and the landlord will not need to be apprised of the new occupant (unless the new occupant wants to be added as a tenant on the tenancy agreement).

the tenancy will then have the right to attend before the Board and argue their respective positions.

Alternatively, the R.T.A. could be amended to allow any tenant (even where there is more than one) to deliver a notice terminating either the entire tenancy or their interest in the tenancy.

Neither of the above proposals is perfect and each would come with its own set of problems. A process is needed, however, to resolve these issues amongst co-tenants because, currently, short of consent by all parties or termination of the tenancy, a tenant has no clear way to end his joint and several liability under a tenancy agreement and can, at least theoretically, be responsible for that tenancy for the rest of his life, even if he no longer lives in or has any connection to the rental unit.

Scenario 3.

A husband and wife rented an apartment. Only his name was listed on the tenancy agreement as the tenant. The couple lived in the unit together for 40 years until his death last month. During the tenancy, all rent was paid by cheques drawn from a joint bank account. Informally, the landlord treated both the husband and wife equally as tenants but all official correspondence from the landlord (such as notices of rent increase) was addressed solely to the male tenant. Now that the husband has died, the landlord has given notice to the female occupant of the unit that the tenancy will terminate 30 days after the death of her husband. The landlord is taking the position that she is not a tenant of this unit, merely an occupant (but the landlord has indicated that it would be willing to discuss the possibility of negotiating a new tenancy agreement with her, at a substantially higher monthly rent). Is she a tenant or is the landlord right to treat her as a mere occupant?

This problem has arisen from time to time and, until recently, there was no guidance provided by the governing legislation. Subsection 3(1) of the O. Reg. 516/06 now provides that:

> If a tenant of a rental unit dies and the rental unit is the principal residence of the spouse of that tenant, the spouse is included in the definition of "tenant" in subsection 2(1) of the Act unless the spouse vacates the unit within the 30-day period described in subsection 91(1) of the Act.

This permits the surviving spouse (who is not listed on the tenancy agreement as a tenant) the option of either vacating the unit within 30 days of the death of the tenant or remaining in the unit as a "tenant", with all of the rights and obligations that entails. However, pursuant to subsection 3(4) of O. Reg. 516/

06, surviving spouses have no such protection in cases of social housing,[78] care homes[79] and certain types of government housing.[80]

Tenancies are not static. They change over time. They evolve. Tenants get married, have children, separate, divorce and die. Tenants often forget to keep the landlord informed of changes in their household composition or assume that such changes are immaterial. Tenancy agreements that may have been accurate when executed begin to reflect with less and less accuracy what is actually occurring within the rental unit. A tenancy agreement, however, is a legally binding contract that creates both rights and responsibilities and the failure to keep that agreement up-to-date can create serious problems for both landlords and tenants.

[78] I.e., a rental unit described in s. 7 of the R.T.A.

[79] I.e., a rental unit that is in a care home to which Part IX of the R.T.A. applies.

[80] I.e., a rental unit to which s. 6 of O. Reg. 516/06 applies.

6

Termination of a Tenancy

1. INTRODUCTION

A tenancy agreement may be terminated *only* in accordance with the *Residential Tenancies Act, 2006* (R.T.A.).[1] A tenancy can be lawfully terminated: (1) upon the death of the sole tenant; (2) by agreement; (3) by notice of termination; and (4) by order of the Landlord and Tenant Board. Assignment of the tenancy is sometimes also thought of as a method of terminating the tenancy. From the point of view of the original tenant, the tenancy is at an end because he or she has been released from the contract. Technically, however, the tenancy continues and the rights and obligations of the original tenancy have simply been transferred to the new tenant (the assignee).

If a tenancy is not terminated in accordance with the provisions of the R.T.A., the tenancy continues and all parties may be liable to fulfill their obligations under the tenancy agreement. More often than not, this means that a tenant who fails to properly terminate his tenancy will be liable to pay rent even after he has vacated the rental unit.[2] Tenants also get themselves into trouble by assuming that they can simply walk away from a tenancy at the end of the term of a fixed-term tenancy. They may be unaware that, pursuant to s. 38 of the R.T.A., the tenancy *automatically* renews unless proper notice has been given to the landlord of the tenant's intention to terminate the tenancy. Some provisions have been added to the R.T.A., however, which limit a tenant's liability where the tenant has failed to properly terminate the tenancy.[3]

Pursuant to s. 88 of the R.T.A., a tenant who vacates a rental unit without providing proper notice now has *some* protection as a "cap" has been placed

---

[1] Subsection 37(1) of the R.T.A.

[2] *George V Apartments Ltd. v. Cobb* (2002), 2002 CarswellOnt 5553 (Ont. Div. Ct.).

[3] Section 88 of the R.T.A.

on such a tenant's liability for rent. It should be noted, however, that s. 88 does *not* explicitly terminate the tenancy.[4]

2. DEATH OF THE TENANT

Pursuant to s. 91(1) of the R.T.A. (formerly s. 49(1) of the T.P.A.), if a tenant of a rental unit dies and there are no other tenants of the rental unit, the tenancy shall be deemed to be terminated 30 days after the death of the tenant. The landlord and the tenant's executor are, however, permitted to negotiate other arrangements (s. 92(5)). Please refer to Chapters 3 and 18 for a more complete analysis of this topic. Also, note that the tenancy of a site in a mobile home park or land lease community is not automatically terminated upon the death of the owner of the home (see Chapter 20).[5]

3. TERMINATION BY AGREEMENT

A landlord and tenant can agree to terminate a tenancy at any time during the tenancy. Such an agreement is void, however, if entered into at the beginning of the tenancy or as a condition of entering into the tenancy agreement.[6] This is meant to prevent a landlord from coercing a tenant into signing an agreement to terminate the tenancy at the beginning of the tenancy and then holding that agreement "over the head" of the tenant. With such an agreement in hand, the landlord could terminate the tenancy at any time and for any reason; this would put the tenant in a very vulnerable position. Thus, the usual rule is that an agreement to terminate a tenancy made at the beginning of the tenancy or as a condition of entering into the tenancy agreement is void. In certain circumstances, however, rental units occupied by students of post-secondary educational institutions are exempt from this rule.[7]

The termination agreed to between the landlord and tenant can take effect on any date (i.e., it need not be the last day of a term or period). The agreement can be oral or written. Obviously, a written agreement will have greater certainty and be easier to enforce. There must, however, be an agreement — a meeting of the minds.[8]

---

[4] It should also be noted that the provisions of s. 88 likely do not relieve the tenant of liability should the landlord choose to commence a court action for other damages flowing from the tenant's breach of contract.

[5] Section 163 of the R.T.A.

[6] Subsection 37(5) of the R.T.A. (formerly subsection 39(3) of the T.P.A.).

[7] See subsections 37(6) and (7) of the R.T.A.

[8] See *Canadian Apt. Properties Real Estate v. Moser* (Feb. 26, 2001), SWL-25346-SA (Ont. Rental Housing Trib.) and *Behar v. Lalonde* (April 5, 2006), SWL-80002, [2006] O.R.H.T.D. No. 36 (Ont. Rental Housing Trib.).

In *Aoun v. Haider*,[9] the tenant advised the landlord that she would try to find another place to live and that, if she did find a new place, she would move. It was held that such an imprecise commitment is insufficient to establish an agreement to terminate the tenancy.

In *Menendez Holdings Ltd. v. Chu*,[10] the landlord gave the tenants written notice that the failure of the tenants to advise the landlord of their intention to renew the tenancy would be taken as an agreement to terminate the tenancy; the Tribunal found that such a self-serving letter did not actually prove the existence of an agreement between the parties. Similarly, it has been held that an oral announcement by the tenant of his intention to terminate the tenancy followed by silence on the part of the landlord will usually not be sufficient to prove that the parties actually agreed to terminate the tenancy.[11]

In *425343 Ontario Ltd. v. Gohari* [12] the tenants notified the landlord of their intention to terminate the tenancy. The landlord, through its representative, said, "OK" and accepted the keys from the tenants on the day they were moving out. On these facts, the Divisional Court inferred from the conduct of the parties that there existed an oral agreement to terminate the tenancy.

There may be circumstances, however, where even a duly signed agreement to terminate that is in the correct form may nevertheless be found to be invalid. Fraud, duress or a complete lack of understanding by one party as to the nature of the document may invalidate the agreement.

In *Metropolitan Toronto Housing Authority v. Bowler*,[13] an agreement to terminate was held to be invalid as the tenant's signature was obtained under threats from the landlord of eviction and criminal proceedings.

In *Windsor-Essex County Housing Corp. v. Graham*,[14] the landlord misled the tenant into believing that he could be evicted within 24 hours and that by signing an agreement to terminate the tenancy, he would be gaining 30 days in which to find alternate accommodations. The tenant was under considerable emotional stress, had limited formal education and did not have the opportunity to obtain legal advice before signing the agreement. In these circumstances, it was held that the agreement was invalid.

In *Wajchendler v. Kaufmann*[15] the tenant delivered a written notice of termination to terminate the tenancy effective October 31, 2000. The tenant then discovered that the house being built for him would not be completed

---

9 (August 13, 1998), SWL-00672-SA (Ont. Rental Housing Trib.).

10 (Aug. 25, 2000), SWL-19253 (Ont. Rental Housing Trib.).

11 *Dadiala v. Griffin* (June 13, 2001), EAL-20894-RV, [2001] O.R.H.T.D. No. 84, 2001 CarswellOnt 6343 (Ont. Rental Housing Trib.). See also *Fort Erie Municipal Non Profit Housing Corp. v. Putman* (June 17, 1999), SOL-05896-SA (Ont. Rental Housing Trib.).

12 (2003), 2003 CarswellOnt 4534 (Ont. Div. Ct.).

13 (April 3, 2002), Doc. 814/00 (Ont. Div. Ct.).

14 (June 12, 2006), SWL-80983-SA (Ont. Rental Housing Trib.).

15 (Nov. 2, 2000), TNL-20934-SA (Ont. Rental Housing Trib.).

on time. The tenant alleged that he made an oral agreement with an agent of the landlord to extend the tenancy by one month and he filed a motion to set aside the *ex parte* order obtained by the landlord. The motion was granted so that the matter could be heard on its merits. The Tribunal found that the person with whom the tenant allegedly made the agreement did not have apparent authority to bind the landlord and that the tenant's testimony concerning the alleged oral agreement was unreliable. As a result, the Tribunal granted the landlord's application for termination of the tenancy and for an eviction order.

If reduced to writing, the agreement should be in Form N11 and should be signed by the landlord(s) and tenant(s). If there is more than one landlord or tenant, each party should sign on their own behalf. If, for instance, one of the tenants fails to sign the agreement, this may render it invalid.[16] If a person is signing on behalf of someone else, there should be clear evidence that they have the authority to do so (such as written authorization or a duly executed power of attorney) or the agreement may be open to attack later.

If a tenant has agreed to terminate the tenancy and vacates the rental unit by the date upon which the parties agreed, no further steps need be taken by either side. If, however, the landlord is concerned that the tenant may not keep her end of the bargain, pursuant to s. 77 of the R.T.A. (formerly s. 76 of the T.P.A.), the landlord may apply to the Board in advance of the termination date for an order terminating the tenancy and evicting the tenant (not to be enforced until after the termination date agreed upon by the parties). The application is in Form L3 and it is an *ex parte* application (i.e., the tenant is not notified of the proceedings). The cost of filing this application is $150. If the agreement is in writing, a copy of that agreement must be filed with the application. The landlord must also file a sworn affidavit verifying the details of the agreement (s. 77(2)). Assuming that everything is in order, the landlord will obtain an eviction order that can be filed with the sheriff if the tenant does not vacate the unit on the date upon which the parties agreed.

Alternatively, the landlord can wait until the termination date upon which the parties agreed to see whether or not the tenant actually moves out. If the tenant does not move out, the landlord can then file an application under s. 77. Such an application must be filed within 30 days of the termination date;[17] if the landlord waits too long, the landlord will forever have lost the right to enforce the agreement.

When an *ex parte* order is issued by the Board under s. 77, a copy is forwarded to the tenant at the rental unit. If the tenant wishes to challenge the *ex parte* order, the tenant has 10 days (unless an extension is granted) in

---

[16] *Jenkins v. Hammond* (2003), [2003] O.R.H.T.D. No. 112, 2003 CarswellOnt 4202, EAL-36153, EAT-04770, EAL-36615-RV (Ont. Rental Housing Trib.). See also *Shabudin v. Lee* (Sept. 21, 1999), TNL-09817 (Ont. Rental Housing Trib.).

[17] Subsection 77(3) of the R.T.A.

which to bring a motion (in Form S2) to have the order set aside.[18] Pending the hearing of that motion, the eviction order is stayed.[19] Although the Board *may* advise the sheriff of this fact, pursuant to Rule 30.1 of the Board's Rules of Practice, it is the responsibility of the party who files a set aside motion to immediately take a copy of the motion and notice of hearing to the Court Enforcement Office. This will ensure that the eviction is not enforced prior to the determination of the motion. The motion and notice of hearing must be served upon the landlord at least 48 hours prior to the time set for the hearing (Rule 10.7).

No criteria are listed in the R.T.A. for determining whether or not an *ex parte* order ought to be set aside. The wording of subsection 77(8), however, suggests that the Board ought to hear all of the relevant evidence and decide whether the landlord has failed to prove that there was an agreement to terminate the tenancy. However, even where the landlord has proven that there was a valid agreement to terminate the tenancy, the Board may nevertheless exercise its discretion under para. 77(8)(b) and set aside the *ex parte* eviction order if the Board is satisfied, having regard to all the circumstances, that it would not be unfair to do so.

Also, on such motions, even when finding in favour of the landlord (i.e., denying the set-aside motion) and allowing enforcement of the *ex parte* eviction order, the Board has the discretionary power to delay the lifting of the stay on that order and, thereby, delay the eviction. This power comes from paragraph 77(8)(c) of the R.T.A. which provides that the Board can order that the stay be lifted immediately or "on a future date specified in the order". See Landlord and Tenant Board File No. SOL-00961-SA (April 12, 2007) for an example of a case where the Board granted such relief.

Although applications under s. 77 are meant to be resolved primarily as written hearings based solely upon the documents filed by the landlord, the R.T.A. recognizes that Members of the Board have discretion whether or not to grant such applications.[20] Where a Member determines that an oral hearing is required, a hearing date will be set and, pursuant to Rule 10.2 of the Board's Rules of Practice, the applicant will be asked to give the application and the notice of hearing to the tenant(s) as soon as possible but not later than ten days before the time set for the hearing, unless otherwise directed by the Board. Under similar provisions of the T.P.A., some landlords argued that there was no specific authority in *Act* for a Member to convert an *ex parte* procedure into an oral hearing on notice to the tenant. My response to this was (and, under the R.T.A., continues to be) as follows:

1. The Board always retains the power to control its processes and to

---

[18] Subsection 77(6) of the R.T.A.

[19] Subsection 77(7) of the R.T.A.

[20] Subsection 77(4) of the R.T.A. states that the Board *may* make an order terminating the tenancy and evicting the tenant.

make such orders as it deems necessary to fully and fairly adjudicate disputes that come before it; so long as the Board does not violate any express provision of the Act, there is no prohibition against the methodology that has been adopted by the Board.

2. Subsection 188(2) of the R.T.A. (formerly subsection 175(2) of the T.P.A.) requires the applicant to serve on the other parties a copy of *any* notice of hearing issued by the Board in respect of an application.
3. Where the written material filed by the landlord appears to a Member to be inadequate, the alternative to holding a *viva voce* hearing could be to simply dismiss the landlord's application at the initial stage (without providing any further opportunity to the landlord to prove its case); I doubt that landlords would find such an approach to be preferable to the one currently employed by the Board.

4. TERMINATION BY NOTICE OF TERMINATION

(a) Form and Content

Timely delivery of a proper notice of termination is usually required to effectively terminate a tenancy. Section 43 of the R.T.A. (formerly s. 43 of the T.P.A.) specifies the formal requirements for a notice of termination. The notice must be in a form approved by the Board and must: (a) identify the rental unit for which the notice is given; (b) state the date on which the tenancy is to terminate; and (c) be signed by the person giving the notice, or the person's agent.

Apparently, the actual signing by the landlord may not be strictly required. Typing of the landlord's name was accepted in *Darragh Construction & Investments Ltd. v. Cain.*[21] The court stated this was sufficient compliance and was preferable to an illegible signature. Notices to terminate signed by the landlord by stencil and then duplicated were held to be properly signed: *Atkinson v. Metropolitan Toronto (Municipality)*.[22] This point was not argued when the appeal was allowed by the Supreme Court of Canada.[23] If the person signing the notice of termination is doing so not as the landlord, but as agent for the landlord, this should be made clear.[24] If there is more than one landlord, the notice should probably be signed by all of the landlords.[25]

---

[21] (1988), 30 O.A.C. 1 (Ont. Div. Ct.).

[22] (1976), 12 O.R. (2d) 401 (Ont. C.A.), reversed (1977), [1978] 1 S.C.R. 918 (S.C.C.).

[23] (1977), [1978] 1 S.C.R. 918 (S.C.C.), reversing (1976), 12 O.R. (2d) 401 (Ont. C.A.).

[24] *Chassid v. Kadosh* (Nov. 28, 2000), TNL-20799, 2000 CarswellOnt 6446 (Ont. Rental Housing Trib.).

[25] *Atkinson v. Calloo et al.* (Aug. 19, 1999), TNL-09094 (Ont. Rental Housing Trib.). In this case, two people, an estranged husband and wife, owned this house, and at the time of the hearing were involved in a family law dispute over this property (which had been the

If the notice is given by a landlord, it must also set out the reasons and details respecting the termination and inform the tenant that:

(a) if the tenant vacates the rental unit in accordance with the notice, the tenancy terminates on the date set out in the notice;
(b) if the tenant does not vacate the rental unit, the landlord may apply to the Board for an order terminating the tenancy and evicting the tenant; and
(c) if the landlord applies for an order, the tenant is entitled to dispute the application.[26]

If the notice omits this advice to the tenant, the notice will be invalid.[27]

In May 2007, the Board discovered that a number of the notices of termination it had made available to the public did not contain the information required by s. 43(2)(a). Effective May 22, 2007, the Board replaced the defective notices with revised forms. Landlords should be sure to use forms that comply with the statutory requirements. Any tenant who has received a defective notice of termination may have grounds to challenge any subsequent application or order based upon that notice.[28]

Although there is no statutory requirement that a tenant's name must appear on a notice of termination served by a landlord, it has been held in at least one case that the failure of the landlord to name one of two tenants rendered the notice void. The Board concluded that the tenant, whose name did not appear on the notice, may have been misled into believing that his tenancy was not in jeopardy and, thus, he would then have been deprived of an opportunity to pay the arrears of rent in time to void the notice.[29] It is therefore recommended that, in every notice of termination, the name of all landlords and tenants subject to the tenancy agreement be named on the notice and that each and every respondent be served with the notice.

These are the minimum requirements for a notice of termination. Although, pursuant to s. 212 of the R.T.A. (formerly s. 198 of the T.P.A.), substantial compliance with the *Act* respecting the contents of notices is

---

matrimonial home). One spouse wanted to regain possession of the unit for her own use and the other spouse did not agree. The wife unilaterally served a notice of termination upon the tenants. It was held that, on this type of application, one landlord cannot act without the knowledge and consent of the other landlord and the application was dismissed.

[26] Subsection 43(2) of the R.T.A.

[27] *Dumi Construction Ltd. v. Greenspan* (1977), 15 O.R. (2d) 808 (Ont. Co. Ct.) and *Forrest Estates Home Sales Inc. v. Gwyn* (1987), 1987 CarswellOnt 3072 (Ont. Dist. Ct.).

[28] In Landlord and Tenant Board File No. CEL-02248 (Oct. 2, 2007), however, it was found by the presiding Member that the earlier Form N12 (i.e., the one issued by the Board prior to May 22, 2007) used by the landlord substantially complied in form and content with the requirements of the R.T.A. and, therefore, was saved by s. 212 of the *Act*.

[29] Landlord and Tenant Board File No. SWL-05726 (Sept. 13, 2007).

sufficient,[30] the Tribunal took a rather strict view when it came to the form and contents of a notice of termination and the Board is likely to adopt a similar approach. Failing to use the correct form, failing to properly complete the form or altering the form can render the notice void. In the past, this was often not discovered until a Member made a ruling on the issue and, by that point, many weeks, perhaps months, may have been wasted. That is one of the reasons why the Board is now pre-screeing applications (Rule 8).

For most notices of termination from tenants (Form N9) and for certain types of notices from landlords (Forms N8, N12 and N13), the termination date must be the last day of the rental period or, if the tenancy is for a fixed term, the last day of the fixed term. In such a case, naming May 30 as the termination date was found to invalidate the notice since the last day of May is the 31st, not the 30th.[31]

Similarly, landlords and tenants sometimes think that the termination date should be the first day of the next period to allow the tenant until that date to move out. If the relevant provision of the *Act* requires that the termination date be the last day of a rental period, choosing the first day of the following month as the termination date (for a monthly tenancy) will invalidate the notice.[32] Also, the termination date must be a date that actually exists (and has not yet passed). For instance, there is no such date as November 31. Although the Divisional Court was, on at least once occasion, willing to overlook just such a clerical error,[33] the Tribunal generally took a narrower view.[34]

A notice of termination from a landlord will have to withstand even closer scrutiny because of the additional requirements imposed by s. 43(2). Notices of termination take many different forms, corresponding to the different grounds upon which a landlord may seek to terminate a tenancy and the different notice periods required for such grounds. A landlord must ensure that the correct form is being used and that an adequate amount of notice is

---

[30] For instance, it was found that using an older version of the Form N4 was sufficient in *McCormick v. Chatterson* (March 17, 2006), SWL-79296, [2006] O.R.H.T.D. No. 7 (Ont. Rental Housing Trib.).

[31] *Falls Masonry Limited v. Collee et al.* (July 29, 1999), SOL-06497 (Ont. Rental Housing Trib.).

[32] *Kam v. Bodnar* (Oct. 12, 1999), TNL-10325 (Ont. Rental Housing Trib.). The termination date specified in the notice of termination for persistent late payment of rent was September 1 and not August 31. Although the landlord had given more than 60 days notice, the Tribunal held that the notice of termination was void.

[33] *Mallia v. Wolch* (1991), 16 R.P.R. (2d) 317 (Ont. Div. Ct.).

[34] See *Golden Hauer Investments Ltd. v. Makipaa* (Nov. 2, 2000), TEL-15244, [2000] O.R.H.T.D. No. 148, 2000 CarswellOnt 4451 (Ont. Rental Housing Trib.), *Falls Masonry Limited v. Collee et al.* (July 29, 1999), SOL-06497 (Ont. Rental Housing Trib.) and *Young v. Nicholson* (February 20, 2006), CEL-50892, 2006 CarswellOnt 2138, [2006] O.R.H.T.D. No. 11 (Ont. Rental Housing Trib.).

being provided (taking into account any additional time required for service of the notice upon the tenant(s)).

A notice of termination must be clear and unequivocal. In *Simpson v. Young & Biggin Ltd.*,[35] the notice given by the landlord permitted the tenant to stay on in possession for an additional period beyond the date by which the landlord was entitled to give notice to terminate, and for that reason the notice was held to be invalid.

(b) Service of the Notice

Permitted methods of service of a notice are set out in s. 191 of the R.T.A. (formerly s. 178 of the T.P.A.) and in Rule 5 of the Board's Rules of Practice. Pursuant to s. 191(1) of the R.T.A., a notice or document is sufficiently given to a person (other than the Board):

(a) by handing it to the person;
(b) if the person to be served is a landlord, by handing it to an employee of the landlord (who is exercising authority in respect of the residential complex to which the notice or document relates);
(c) if the person to be served is a tenant (or subtenant or occupant), by handing it to an apparently adult person in the rental unit;
(d) by leaving it in the mail box where mail is ordinarily delivered to the person;
(e) if there is no mail box, by leaving it at the place where mail is ordinarily delivered to the person;
(f) by sending it by mail to the last known address where the person resides or carries on business; or
(g) by any other means allowed in the Rules.

Rule 5.1 also permits a notice to be given to another person by any of the following methods:

(a) by courier to that person;
(b) if there is a fax machine where the person carries on business or in the residence of the person, by fax;
(c) for service on a person who *occupies* the rental unit, by placing it under the door of the unit or through a mail slot in the door;
(d) for service on a tenant of a notice under section 27 of the R.T.A. (i.e., notice to enter the rental unit), by any permitted method of service or posting it on the door of the rental unit.

Note that, except for a notice to enter the unit under s. 27 of the R.T.A., no other document can be served by posting the document on the door to the rental unit. This was a common method of service under the *Landlord and*

[35] (1971), [1972] 1 O.R. 103 (Ont. C.A.).

Tenant Act but, with only the one stated exception, this type of service has been prohibited since the enactment of the T.P.A. in June 1998. A landlord that posts a notice of termination on a tenant's door may not only find that it is an invalid method of service but that he may have exposed himself to allegations of harassment by the tenant and potential liability should the tenant choose to commence an application against the landlord or should the Investigation & Enforcement Unit choose to prosecute the landlord for a provincial offence under s. 233 of the R.T.A.

Rule 5.2 also gives a Member the power to give written directions to a party, either on his or her own initiative or on that party's request, regarding one or both of the following: (1) who shall be served with the application or any other document; or (2) how an application or document shall be served. Finally, if a document is given to a person by a method other than an approved method, if it is proven that the contents of the document actually came to the attention of the person for whom it was intended within the required time period, service will be considered valid.[36] For example, improper service was accepted when the Tribunal was satisfied that the notice did come to the attention of the tenant in *H. & R. Property Management v. Kutusa*.[37]

For most methods of service, a document is deemed to be served on the same date it is delivered. This is not true, however, for service by mail or by courier. A notice or document given by mail shall be deemed to have been given on the fifth day after mailing;[38] a notice or document given by Xpresspost is deemed to be given by mail (not by courier).[39] If a notice or document is delivered to another person by courier, it is deemed to be given on the day following the day it was given to the courier but, if that is a non-business day, it is deemed to be given on the next business day.[40] Notwithstanding these presumptive rules, if a party can prove that the document was actually received earlier than the date of deemed service, the Board will find that it was served on that earlier date.[41]

(c) Timing

Pursuant to s. 193 of the R.T.A. (formerly s. 180 of the T.P.A.), time shall be computed in accordance with the Rules. In general, the time between two events is computed by excluding the day on which the first event occurs and including the day on which the second event occurs (Rule 4.1). For example, if a landlord is counting 14 days required between the date a notice of termination is given to a tenant and the date of termination to be set out in

---

[36] Subsection 191(2) of the R.T.A. (formerly subsection 178(2) of the T.P.A.).
[37] (June 4, 1999), TNL-07551 (Ont. Rental Housing Trib.).
[38] Subsection 191(3) of the R.T.A. (formerly subsection 178(3) of the T.P.A.).
[39] Rule 5.4 of the Board's Rules of Practice.
[40] Rule 5.3 of the Board's Rules of Practice.
[41] Rule 5.6 of the Board's Rules of Practice.

the notice, they would not count the date the notice will be given (the "first event") but will include the proposed date of termination (the "second event"). All weekend days and other holidays are counted. Thus, a notice given on the 10th of the month could be effective as early as the 24th. These Rules may not be waived by a Member of the Board (Rule 4.5).

If the notice is sent by mail or courier, the termination date in the notice will have to be adjusted to take into account the time that type of service is deemed to take. For the example set out above, if the notice of termination were mailed to the tenant on the 10th of the month, the earliest that the notice can be effective is the 29th. The document will be deemed to be served on the fifth day after mailing (i.e., on the 15th) and the landlord must then allow 14 days (in this example) before the termination date. The 14th day after the 15th (not counting the 15th) is the 29th.

If a landlord or tenant fails to provide sufficient notice, the Board will not be able to "save" the subsequent application by abridging the statutory time requirements. The Board has the power to shorten or extend many time requirements set out in the R.T.A., the regulations and the Rules but the Board is specifically prohibited from extending or shortening time requirements related to notice requirements for terminating tenancies (pursuant to s. 56, O. Reg. 516/06). An error within the notice of termination or in the timing of its service is, therefore, often fatal to both the notice itself and any application founded upon the flawed notice.

(d) Notice of Termination from the Tenant

When a tenant wishes to terminate a tenancy in the normal course (i.e., at the end of a period of the tenancy or at the end of the term of a tenancy for a fixed term), in the absence of an agreement with the landlord (under s. 37), the tenant must serve upon the landlord a notice of termination.[42] In order to be valid, the written notice served by the tenant must either be in Form N9 or must substantially comply in form and content with that form (s. 212 of the R.T.A., formerly s. 198 of the T.P.A.).[43]

Normally, the notice of termination must take effect on the last day of the term or period.[44] In addition to terminating a tenancy at the end of the term or period of a tenancy, under some special circumstances, a tenant may terminate a tenancy early (and on a day other than the last day of a rental period) by delivering a notice of termination. Such circumstances include the following: where the tenant asks the landlord to consent to an assignment

---

[42] Section 47 of the R.T.A. (formerly s. 46 of the T.P.A.).

[43] See *Fort Erie Municipal Non Profit Housing Corp. v. Putman* (June 17, 1999), SOL-05896-SA (Ont. Rental Housing Trib.) and *Stanmore Developments v. Badal* (Feb. 5, 1999), TNL-04206-SA (Ont. Rental Housing Trib.).

[44] Subsection 44(1) of the R.T.A. (formerly subsection 47(1) of the T.P.A.).

and the landlord refuses consent or fails to respond within seven days;[45] and, where the tenant has received notice of termination from the landlord under ss. 48, 49 or 50 of the R.T.A. (formerly ss. 51, 52 and 53 of the T.P.A.) and the tenant wants to terminate the tenancy earlier than the date set out in the landlord's notice.[46]

Like an agreement to terminate the tenancy, a notice of termination from the tenant is void if given at the beginning of the tenancy or as a condition of entering into the tenancy agreement.[47] Unlike an agreement to terminate a tenancy, a *notice* of termination must be in writing.

The notice cannot be equivocal or uncertain. It is not sufficient, for instance, for a tenant to write to the landlord that "I will try to be out by the end of June."[48]

The amount of advance notice required depends on the nature of the tenancy; the required notice periods are set out in s. 44 of the R.T.A. (formerly s. 47 of the T.P.A.). For a daily or weekly tenancy, the notice of termination must be given to the landlord at least 28 days before the end of a period. For a monthly tenancy, the notice must be given to the landlord at least 60 days before the end of the month. For a yearly tenancy, the notice must be given at least 60 days before the end of the year. For a fixed-term tenancy, the notice must be given at least 60 days before the end of the term.

Since February is a short month, in the past, tenants have run into problems by only providing 58 or 59 days' notice. To avoid this problem, where a tenant delivers a notice of termination that is to be effective on the last day of February, s. 44(5) of the R.T.A. provides that the tenant shall be deemed to have given at least 60 days notice if the notice of termination is given to the landlord no later than January 1 of that year. Where the notice is to take effect on March 31, s. 44(5) provides that the tenant shall be deemed to have given at least 60 days notice if the notice of termination is given to the landlord no later than February 1 of that year. Note that no similar provisions exist for notices given by landlords to tenants in and around February.

If there is more than one tenant, the notice should be signed by all of the tenants.[49] The failure to provide proper notice can mean that the tenancy shall be deemed to continue even after the tenant has vacated the rental unit; this

---

[45] Section 96 of the R.T.A. (formerly s. 48 of the T.P.A.).

[46] Subsections 48(3), 49(4) and 51(4) of the R.T.A.

[47] Subsection 37(4) of the R.T.A. (formerly subsection 39(4) of the T.P.A.). Certain post-secondary educational institutions are exempt from s. 37(4) subsections 37(6) and (7) of the R.T.A.

[48] *Jordan & Geisel Management Ltd. v. Gallant* (July 21, 1998), SOL-00216 (Ont. Rental Housing Trib.). See also *Fort Erie Municipal Non-profit Housing Corp. v. Putnam* (June 17, 1999), SOL-05896-SA (Ont. Rental Housing Trib.).

[49] See *Wilson v. Gilboa Management* (Jan. 20, 1999), EAT-00378 (Ont. Rental Housing Trib.) and *Victoria Park Community Homes v. Carson et al.* (June 16, 2003), SOL-40820 (Ont. Rental Housing Trib.); and *Greater Sudbury Housing Corporation v. Mahdavi et al.* (April 28, 2004), NOL-11017 and NOL-10838 (Ont. Rental Housing Trib).

can leave the tenant liable to the landlord for rent, amongst other things.[50] Of course, such liability is subject to the landlord's duty to mitigate its losses[51] and the new provisions of s. 88 of the R.T.A.[52]

The prevailing view at the Tribunal was that, once a tenant has given a landlord a valid notice of termination, no provision in the T.P.A. permitted the tenant to change his or her mind and rescind the notice.[53] The landlord may agree to ignore the notice but it will likely depend on whether the landlord believes that a new tenant will pay substantially higher rent for the unit in question, how many vacant units there are in the complex, whether the existing tenant has been a good tenant who the landlord would like to keep in the complex and whether or not the landlord has already contracted to rent the unit to someone else.

If the notice of termination was obtained from the tenant through misrepresentation or duress, however, this may invalidate the document. In *Goldlist Property Management v. Rizq*,[54] the landlord's notice of rent increase informed the tenants that their only options were to either renew the tenancy for a one-year period or to sign that they wished to terminate their tenancy. In fact, by law, the tenants had the option of taking no action and their tenancy would be renewed on a month-to-month basis. Since the signature of the tenants on the notice of termination was obtained through misrepresentation, it was held that the tenants could rescind their notice.

If a tenant has served upon the landlord a valid notice of termination and vacates the rental unit by the date set out in the notice, no further steps need be taken by either side; the notice will have effectively terminated the tenancy. If, however, the landlord is concerned that the tenant may not actually vacate the unit, pursuant to s. 77 of the R.T.A. (formerly s. 76 of the T.P.A.), the landlord my apply to the Board in advance of the termination date for an order terminating the tenancy and evicting the tenant (not to be enforced until after the termination date agreed upon by the parties). The application is in

---

[50] *Malahide Developments Ltd. v. Gruszecki* (January 9, 1978) (Ont. Div. Ct.) and *George V Apartments Ltd. v. Cobb* (Dec. 6, 2002), 2002 CarswellOnt 5553, Doc. Newmarket 61791/02 (Ont. Div. Ct.).

[51] In *Dudley v. Mackay* (2000), 131 O.A.C. 75 (Ont. Div. Ct.), the judge found that the landlord, who had been given short notice of termination by the tenant, failed to mitigate by failing to show the premises promptly or advertise. See also c*Hunters Lodge Apartments v. Varontsov et al.*, (July 12, 2001), TNL-27754 (Ont. Rental Housing Trib.).

[52] This places a "cap" on a tenant's potential liability for arrears of rent where the tenant vacates the unit without properly terminating the tenancy.

[53] See *Causyn v. Marrello* (July 17, 2000), EAT-01897, EAL-14808, 2000 CarswellOnt 4433 (Ont. Rental Housing Trib.) and *Red Pine Apartments Ltd. v. Speller* (Sept. 26, 2001), TNL-301460-SA (Ont. Rental Housing Trib.). The opposite view was expressed, however, in *Ibrans Inv. Ltd. v. Pereira* (Oct. 27, 2000), TEL-15359-SA (Ont. Rental Housing Trib.) and in *Goldlist Property Management v. Rizq* (Dec. 7, 1998), CEL-02115 (Ont. Rental Housing Trib.).

[54] (Dec. 7, 1998), CEL-02115 (Ont. Rental Housing Trib.).

Form L3 and it is an *ex parte* application (i.e., the tenant is not notified of the proceedings). The cost of filing this application is $150. A copy of the notice of termination must be filed with the application. The landlord must also file a sworn affidavit verifying the details of the notice of termination (s. 77(2)). Assuming that everything is in order, the landlord will obtain an eviction order that can be filed with the sheriff if the tenant does not vacate the unit on the date set out in the notice.

Alternatively, the landlord can wait until the termination date set out in the notice of termination to see whether or not the tenant vacates the unit. If the tenant does not move out, the landlord can then file an application under s. 77. Such an application must be filed within 30 days of the termination date;[55] if the landlord waits too long, the landlord will forever have lost the right to enforce the notice that had been served by the tenant.

Once the landlord has filed the application under s. 77, the procedures are the same regardless of whether the application is based upon an *agreement* to terminate or a *notice* of termination from the tenant. I therefore refer the reader to the discussion in the section entitled "Termination by Agreement" (above) for a review of procedural issues that often arise on applications brought under s. 77 of the R.T.A.

(e) Notice of Termination from the Landlord

One of the basic principles underlying the R.T.A. is the notion of security of tenure. A landlord cannot end a tenancy on a whim or merely because of the passage of a certain amount of time. Absent an agreement with the tenant, a landlord cannot terminate a tenancy unless the tenant has contravened the provisions of the R.T.A. or of the tenancy agreement or the landlord legitimately requires the rental unit for certain approved purposes that are given priority in the legislation. A landlord cannot terminate a tenancy without first having served upon the tenant proper notification (the notice of termination) specifying the grounds for termination and the date upon which the termination is to take effect. The notice will effectively terminate the tenancy if the tenant vacates the rental unit by the termination date specified in the notice of termination (s. 46(1) of the R.T.A.). If the tenant does not vacate the rental unit by that date, the landlord must commence an application[56] to seek an order terminating the tenancy.

The four most common errors made by landlords seeking to terminate tenancies are: (i) choosing an invalid termination date; (ii) giving insufficient notice; (iii) altering the approved forms; and (iv) failing to include sufficient reasons and details. I shall discuss each of these topics in turn.

---

[55] Subsection 77(3) of the R.T.A.

[56] Usually within 30 days, except for applications based upon arrears of rent (see ss. 46(1) and 46(2) of the R.T.A.).

(i) Choosing a Termination Date and Giving Adequate Notice

For certain types of notices from landlords (Forms N8, N12 and N13), the termination date must be the last day of the rental period or, if the tenancy is for a fixed term, the last day of the fixed term. This includes notices based upon the following situations:

- persistent late payment of rent;
- ceasing to qualify to live in public or subsidized housing;
- termination of employment by the landlord where the tenancy is conditional upon the continuation of that employment;
- termination of an Agreement of Purchase and Sale for a proposed condominium unit where the tenancy was created in contemplation of the completion of that Agreement;
- the ending of the period of rehabilitative or therapeutic services where that was the sole purpose for the tenancy;
- the landlord or a purchaser or specified members of their families want to live in the unit;
- the landlord is converting the unit or complex to a use other than residential;
- the landlord intends to demolish the unit or the complex; and,
- the landlord requires the unit to be vacant in order to do repairs or renovations that are so extensive they require vacant possession and a building permit.

In such cases, not only must the landlord provide the minimum amount of notice, but the termination date must be the last day of a rental period or of the term, as the case may be. If it is a fixed-term tenancy (such as a one-year lease), the termination date cannot be earlier than the last day of that term, even if that is many months (or even years) later.[57] Also, although most tenancies end on the last day of a month, this is not true for all tenancies. If, for instance, the rent is always due on the 15th of the month, it is likely that the last day of each rental period falls on the 14th of each month; for a notice of termination Form N8, N12 or N13, the termination date in such a case would have to be the 14th of a month sufficiently distant to provide the minimum number of days notice.

For other notices (Forms N4, N5, N6 and N7), the only requirement is that the minimum amount of notice be given; the termination date does not have to be the last day of a period or term of the tenancy. This includes notices based upon the following situations:

- non-payment of rent;
- damage to the unit or complex;

---

[57] *Lypny v. Rocca* (1986), 55 O.R. (2d) 46 (Ont. Dist. Ct.), affirmed (1988), 63 O.R. (2d) 595 (Ont. Div. Ct.).

- substantial interference with the reasonable enjoyment of other tenants or with the reasonable enjoyment or legal rights of the landlord;
- having more people living in the unit than is permitted by health, safety or housing standards;
- committing an illegal act or carrying on an illegal business in the complex (including drug-related offences);
- misrepresentation of income in rent-geared-to-income housing;
- and serious impairment of the safety of other persons in the complex.

These matters are considered more urgent and cannot necessarily wait until the end of the term or a period of the tenancy.

The relevant notice periods (for notices of termination served by a landlord) are summarized in the following table.

Grounds	Sec. No.	Notice Period	Form
Possession for landlord's use	48(2)	• at least 60 days notice before end of period or term*	N12
Possession for purchaser's use	49(2)	• at least 60 days notice before end of period or term*	N12
Demolition, conversion, extensive repairs or renovation	50(2) 164(1)	• at least 120 days notice before end of period or term* • at least one years notice before end of period or term* in the case of a mobile home or land lease home owned by the tenant	N13
Persistent late payment of rent <u>and</u> other grounds listed under para. 58(1)1	58(2) 44	• at least 28 days before end of period or term for daily/weekly tenancy* • at least 60 days before end of period or term for other tenancies*	N8
Non-payment of rent	59(1)	• at least 7 days for daily/weekly tenancy • at least 14 days for other tenancies	N4
Illegal act or business	61(2) 68(2)	• at least 10 days notice if related to the production, trafficking or possession for trafficking of an illegal drug • for other matters, at least 20 days notice if first notice or at least 14 days if this notice is given within 6 months of the tenant voiding an earlier notice of termination given under s. 62, 64 or 67	N6
Misrepresentation of Income	60(2) 68(2)	• at least 20 days notice if first notice • at least 14 days if this notice is given within 6 months of the tenant voiding an earlier notice of termination given under s. 62, 64 or 67	N6
Undue damage (typical)	62(2) 68(2)	• at least 20 days notice if first notice • at least 14 days if this notice is given within 6 months of the tenant voiding an earlier notice of termination given under s. 62, 64 or 67	N5
Undue damage (fast-track)	63(1)	• at least 10 days notice	N7
Interference with reasonable enjoyment (typical)	64(2) 68(2)	• at least 20 days notice if first notice • at least 14 days if this notice is given within 6 months of the tenant voiding an earlier notice of termination given under s. 62, 64 or 67	N5
Interference with reasonable enjoyment (fast-track)	65(1)	• at least 10 days notice	N7
Impairment of safety	66(2)	• at least 10 days notice	N7
Overcrowding	67(2) 68(2)	• at least 20 days notice if first notice • at least 14 days if this notice is given within 6 months of the tenant voiding an earlier notice of termination given under s. 62, 64 or 67	N5

* Where indicated, the termination date must be the last day of a rental period or of the term (for a fixed-term tenancy).

Whether a new landlord can commence an application based upon a notice of termination served upon a tenant by a former landlord remains an open question. The courts have not been entirely consistent on this issue. One view is that a notice of termination given by a landlord who shortly thereafter sells the property is no longer valid and the new owner landlord must serve a new notice; it is only the landlord who served a notice of termination who may apply for termination and possession: *Dumi Construction Ltd. v. Greenspan.*[58] This was confirmed in *Wise v. Fawcet*[59] in which notice of termination for extensive repairs was served by the former landlord prior to selling the property. The present landlord then commenced the application, which was held to be no longer valid. The result has been a different, however, when the notice to terminate is for non-payment of rent served on the tenant by a landlord owner who sells the property. The purchaser, the successor landlord, was permitted to proceed to obtain possession based on the notice to terminate served by the predecessor landlord: *P.J. Construction Ltd. v. Dunn.*[60]

(ii) Altering the Approved Forms

The Board's forms contain important information for tenants about their rights under the R.T.A. The entire notice can be invalidated if a landlord deletes any of that information from the notice of termination or attempts to add to the form additional information that may not be consistent with the legislation. In once case decided under the T.P.A., a landlord added to the Form N4 (notice of termination for non-payment of rent) the following: "This notice of termination is being served upon you pursuant to a statutory requirement and not as an election on the part of the Landlord to terminate your tenancy. If you abandon the rented premises without remedying your default, you will continue to be liable for all past and prospective rent losses and any other damages suffered by the Landlord, including . . . solicitor and client costs". [61] Another landlord added a slightly different clause to the Form N4 (no doubt with the same intended effect): "Notwithstanding this notice of termination, you are being held responsible for the rent for the remainder of the tenancy".[62] In both cases, the Tribunal held that the insertion of these additional clauses invalidated the notices of termination.

In cases where a tenant has allegedly damaged the rental unit or the residential complex (but not so much to justify a fast-track notice under s. 63),

---

[58] (1977), 15 O.R. (2d) 808 (Ont. Co. Ct.).

[59] (1987), 4 T.L.L.R. 404 (Ont. Dist. Ct.).

[60] (November 25, 1987), Doc. M152960/87 (Ont. Dist. Ct.).

[61] *Minto Management v. McCormick* (June 1, 2000), SWL-17516 (Ont. Rental Housing Trib.).

[62] *Sheppard Manor v. Petsinis* (Sept. 14, 2000), TEL-14389, [2000] O.R.H.T.D. No. 122, 2000 CarswellOnt 4444 (Ont. Rental Housing Trib.).

para. 62(2)(c) of the R.T.A. provides the tenant with a number of options. These are reflected in Part C of Form N5 as follows:

> If this notice is for Reason #1 [damage], you can correct the problem by:
>
> - repairing the damaged property,
> - paying me $____________, which is the reasonable cost of repairing the damaged property,
> - replacing the damaged property if it is not reasonable to repair it,
> - paying me $____________, which is the reasonable cost or replacing the damaged property, if it is not reasonable to repair it, or
> - making arrangements satisfactory to me to either,
>   - repair or replace the damaged property, or
>   - pay me the reasonable cost of repairing or replacing the damaged property.

If the landlord strikes out or omits any of these options, it has been found to invalidate the notice of termination.[63]

As explained in the section below entitled, "Second Notices", a "first" notice of termination under s. 62, 64 or 67 is significantly different than a "second" notice under s. 60, 61, 62, 64 or 67. A "second" notice has a shorter notice period and cannot be cured by stopping or correcting the conduct about which the notice complains. Therefore, if a "first" notice is marked as if it were a "second" notice, the tenant will have been misled into believing that he or she has no opportunity to void the notice. The defective notice will be void and any application that is based upon that notice will be dismissed.[64]

(iii) Reasons and Details

Subsection 43(2) of the R.T.A. requires that the notice set out the "reasons and details respecting the termination". In essence, the landlord must provide the tenant with sufficient information so that the tenant knows the reason the landlord is seeking to end the tenancy and sufficient details so that the tenant knows the allegations being made and can prepare a defence. For instance, if the ground for termination of the tenancy is persistent late payment of rent, that is the *reason*. Writing in the notice of termination that "the tenant is always late in paying rent" does not provide any *details*. Lack of such details

---

[63] *Fisher Kay Ltd. v. Bowen* (Sept. 17, 1999), TNL-09813, 1999 CarswellOnt 5803 (Ont. Rental Housing Trib.) and *Clarke et al. v. Roach et al.* (Oct. 26, 1998), TEL-01660 (Ont. Rental Housing Trib.).

[64] *Booth v. Snider* (March 23, 2000), TNL-13842, 2000 CarswellOnt 6436 (Ont. Rental Housing Trib.).

may invalidate a notice[65] and an invalid notice cannot be saved by providing further details at the hearing. An inaccurate, vague or confusing notice may be void.[66]

The reasons and details must be "precise and informative": *Krakus Apartments Ltd. v. Stanga*;[67] *Lypny v. Rocca*;[68] and *King v. Toms*.[69] Furthermore, on the hearing of the application only evidence in support of the particulars stated in the notice of termination will be permitted.[70]

The test for sufficiency of a notice of termination is that particulars be given so that the tenant is not misled: *Bhagwandin v. Wright*.[71] In that case a letter with sufficient particulars accompanied the notice to terminate, and this was accepted. The court went on to say that validity of a notice should not rest on a narrow technicality and that subtleties are to be disregarded in the interpretation of the validity of a notice.

A notice that lacks details *may* be "saved", however, if the landlord provides to the tenant (before or along with the notice of termination) the requisite details in other documents. Under the *Landlord and Tenant Act*, the Ontario Court of Appeal ruled that an otherwise invalid notice of termination can be "saved" if the requisite information that ought to have been included in the notice of termination is contained in a separate document that is served together with the notice of termination.[72] More recently, the Divisional Court ruled that a notice of termination that does not contain sufficient details may be found to substantially comply with the requirements of s. 43(2) if the landlord advised the tenant of these details in some other way.[73] Similarly, in

---

[65] *698077 Ontario Ltd. v. Garcia* (Aug. 3, 2000), TEL-13582, [2000] O.R.H.T.D. No. 105, 2000 CarswellOnt 4377 (Ont. Rental Housing Trib.); *Tavernier v. Morell* (June 28, 2001), EAL-21801, [2001] O.R.H.T.D. No. 91, 2001 CarswellOnt 6341 (Ont. Rental Housing Trib.); *Kam. v. Bodnar*, (Oct. 12, 1999) TNL-10325 (Ont. Rental Housing Trib.); and *Pinecrest Heights v. Futi* (Sept. 6, 2000), EAL-15062, [2000] O.R.H.T.D. No. 116, 2000 CarswellOnt 4347 (Ont. Rental Housing Trib.).

[66] *1255074 Ontario Inc. v. Mak* (June 10, 1999), TNL-05155-RV (Ont. Rental Housing Trib.); *Green Ash Dvpt. v. McDonald* (April 14, 1999), TNL-05851 (Ont. Rental Housing Trib.); *Cerase Holdings Ltd. v. Veres-Bafford* (March 8, 2000), TNL-13127, 2000 CarswellOnt 6435 (Ont. Rental Housing Trib.).

[67] (1978), 20 O.R. (2d) 642 (Ont. Co. Ct.).

[68] (1986), 55 O.R. (2d) 46 (Ont. Dist. Ct.), affirmed (1988), 63 O.R. (2d) 595 (Ont. Div. Ct.).

[69] District Court File No. 5060/90, Peterborough (July 31, 1990), unreported.

[70] *Dean v. Grohal* (1980), 27 O.R. (2d) 643 (Ont. Div. Ct.), *Atchison v. Rogers* (May 15, 2006), SWL-80511, [2006] O.R.H.T.D. No. 37 (Ont. Rental Housing Trib.), and *Morguard Residential Inc. v. Begum* (Nov. 29, 2005), TSL-76882 (Ont. Rental Housing Trib.).

[71] (1988), 65 O.R. (2d) 204 (Ont. C.A.).

[72] *Bhagwandin v. Wright* (1988), 65 O.R. (2d) 204 (C.A.), reversing (1987), [1988] O.J. No. 3, 1987 CarswellOnt 1066 (Ont. Div. Ct.).

[73] For example, in letters given to the tenant before or along with the notice of termination: *Kuzyk v. SK Properties* (2001), 2001 CarswellOnt 6074, [2001] O.J. No. 5260 (Ont. S.C.J.). Since the tenant's appeal in this case was granted on other grounds, this statement may constitute *obiter dictum* and may, therefore, not be binding upon the Board.

Rowenaville Holdings Ltd. v. Nahhas[74] a notice of termination for persistent late payment of rent that lacked details was found to nevertheless be valid because of the information provided to the tenants by the landlord in the numerous notices of termination (for non-payment of rent) previously served by the landlord upon the tenants.

Since 2002, however, the Divisional Court seems to have moved away from the position it adopted in *Rowenaville* and to have taken a harder line on notices of termination. In *Ball v. Metro Capital et al.*,[75] the Divisional Court ruled that a notice of termination was void for lack of details. It stated that a tenant needs sufficient information to know the case that must be met, to decide whether to dispute the allegations and to consider whether (and how) to cease the conduct or correct the omission within the permitted time period. Particulars should include dates and times of alleged offensive conduct together with a detailed description of the alleged conduct engaged in by the tenant.

Lack of details in the notice of termination has been found to invalidate the notice in numerous cases, including those involving allegations of: persistent late payment of rent; causing undue damage; substantially interfering with the reasonable enjoyment of other tenants or with the lawful rights of the landlord; committing illegal acts; serious impairment of safety; and failing to pay rent.[76] The Landlord and Tenant Board appears to be applying the principles set out in the *Ball v. Metro Capital* case more often and more broadly than was the case under the T.P.A. Landlords will need to be particularly careful when completing notices of termination to ensure that sufficient *reasons and details* are provided therein.

While the landlord is required to provide details of the alleged offensive conduct, the landlord need not go so far as to name every potential witness.[77]

In *Bragg v. Blackman*,[78] the Tribunal found a notice of termination for non-payment of rent (Form N4) to be invalid as the amounts claimed therein were inconsistent and confusing.

---

[74] (2000), [2000] O.J. No. 466, 2000 CarswellOnt 350 (Ont. Div. Ct.)

[75] (Dec. 19, 2002), Div. Ct. File No. 48/02, (Dec. 10, 2001), (Ont. Div. Ct.) on appeal from Tribunal decision TNL-31297.

[76] *Franbern Investments Inc. v. White* (May 26, 1999), TSL-05918-RV, 1999 CarswellOnt 5794 (Ont. Rental Housing Trib.); *G&G Leasing v. Lessard* (Oct. 6, 2001), EAL-24301, 2001 CarswellOnt 6325 (Ont. Rental Housing Trib.); *Andreacchi v. Rossi* (June 30, 1999), TNL-08007 (Ont. Rental Housing Trib.); *Drouin v. Peabody* (Sept. 10, 2003), EAL-37548, 2003 CarswellOnt 4196 (Ont. Rental Housing Trib.); *Peel Living v. Lannon* (Feb. 16, 2005), CEL-41229, 2005 CarswellOnt 1286 (Ont. Rental Housing Trib.); *Montreal Trust Co. of Canada v. Khaper* (Feb. 1, 2002), CEL-22701 (Ont. Rental Housing Trib.); and *Grota v. Kirk* (May 30, 2006), SWL-80726, [2006] O.R.H.T.D. No. 51 (Ont. Rental Housing Trib.).

[77] *Merkur Properties v. Singh* (2004), 2004 CarswellOnt 1076 (Ont. Div. Ct.), (Sept. 5, 2003), re TEL-37786 (Ont. Rental Housing Trib.).

[78] (May 25, 2006), SWL-79901, [2006] O.R.H.T.D. No. 41 (Ont. Rental Housing Trib.).

In *Shah v. Kolarova*,[79] it was held that a notice of termination for use by the landlord (Form N12) was invalid as it did not identify both landlords and did not specify the identity of the specific person(s) who intended to occupy the rental unit.

(iv) When Notice of Termination Becomes Void

As previously stated, all Board-approved notices of termination contain important information for tenants about their rights under the R.T.A. One of the most important pieces of information for a tenant is that the tenant need not vacate the unit but can instead choose to remain in possession and wait to see if the landlord commences an application. Pursuant to s. 46(1) of the R.T.A., a notice of termination becomes void 30 days after the termination date specified in the notice unless: (a) the tenant vacates the rental unit before that time; or (b) the landlord applies for an order terminating the tenancy and evicting the tenant before that time. The only exception to this is a notice of termination for non-payment of rent (Form N4), which has no "expiry" date (s. 46(2)). This is important information and, if it is omitted or struck from the notice, it will invalidate the notice.

Thus, with the exception of the Form N4, all notices of termination become void at the end of 30 days after the termination date named in the notice if the landlord has not commenced an application to terminate the tenancy and evict the tenant by then. Certain types of notices can also become void if the tenant resolves the problem identified in the notice. Such notices can be thought of as being "curable".[80] These include notices of termination based upon non-payment of rent (Form N4), undue damage under s. 62 (Form N5), interfering with reasonable enjoyment under s. 64 (Form N5) and having too many people living in the unit (Form N5).

Pursuant to s. 59(3) of the R.T.A., the notice of termination for non-payment of rent is void if, before the day the landlord applies to the Board for an order terminating the tenancy and evicting the tenant based upon the notice, the tenant pays the rent that is in arrears under the tenancy agreement and the additional rent that would have been due under the tenancy agreement as at the date of payment by the tenant had notice of termination not been given.[81] The Form N4 must inform the tenant of this right (to pay and void

---

[79] (June 21, 2006), TEL-62456, 2006 CarswellOnt 4423 (Ont. Rental Housing Trib.).

[80] At least on the first notice. See the next section for a discussion of the effect of receiving a second notice of termination within six months.

[81] The notice becomes void if, before the landlord commences an application, the tenant pays all rent owing to the landlord (both the rent listed in the notice of termination and any rent that has come due since service of that notice).

the notice).[82] The omission of that advice or warning will result in the notice of termination being held invalid.[83]

Pursuant to s. 62(3) of the R.T.A., the notice of termination (given under s. 62, not under s. 63) based upon damage to the rental unit or residential complex is void if the tenant, within seven days after receiving the notice repairs or replaces the damaged property or pays the landlord the reasonable cost to repair or replace the damaged property. The notice of termination must advise the tenant of this right.[84] The Form N5 does contain this information and, as previously indicated, if the landlord deletes or omits any of the tenant's options in this regard it will invalidate the notice.

Pursuant to s. 64(3) of the R.T.A., the notice of termination based upon substantial interference with the reasonable enjoyment of other tenants or the lawful rights of the landlord (given under s. 64, not s. 65) is void if the tenant, within seven days after receiving the notice, stops the conduct or activity or corrects the omission. Again, the notice of termination must advise the tenant (if it is the first such notice given in the last six months) that the tenant has seven days in which to comply.[85] Failure to advise the tenant of this right will invalidate the notice.[86]

Pursuant to s. 67(3) of the R.T.A., the notice of termination based upon overcrowding[87] is void if the tenant, within seven days after receiving the notice, sufficiently reduces the number of persons occupying the rental unit. Again, the notice of termination must advise the tenant that the tenant has seven days in which to comply.[88] Failure to advise the tenant of this right will invalidate the notice.

In the past, a landlord who served a notice of termination upon a tenant might be concerned about accepting money from the tenant or serving subsequent documents (such as a notice of rent increase) that might be taken as an indication that the landlord was waiving the notice of termination or creating a new tenancy.[89] To alleviate this concern, s. 45 of the R.T.A. attempts to make clear that a landlord can give a tenant a notice of rent increase or accept arrears of rent or compensation for use or occupation of

---

[82] Subsection 59(2) of the R.T.A.

[83] *Cory v. Carmo* (1978), 19 O.R. (2d) 340 (Ont. Dist. Ct.).

[84] Subsection 62(2) of the R.T.A.

[85] Subsection 64(2) of the R.T.A.

[86] *Lugano View Ltd. v. Grannum* (1988), 64 O.R. (2d) 468 (Ont. Div. Ct.).

[87] I.e., if the number of persons occupying the rental unit on a continuing basis results in a contravention of health, safety or housing standards required by law.

[88] Subsection 67(2) of the R.T.A.

[89] See *Aaron Construction Ltd. v. Kelley* (1982), 35 O.R. (2d) 244 (Ont. Co. Ct.) in which it was held that a valid notice of termination is nullified if the landlord subsequently serves notice of a rent increase; and *Nicholson v. Michalas* (1988), 64 O.R. (2d) 238 (Ont. Div. Ct.) in which the Divisional Court overruled the *Aaron* decision and held that the landlord had a right to give a notice of rent increase without that having the effect of waiving the earlier notice to terminate the tenancy.

the rental unit after service of a notice of termination without waiving that notice of termination, reinstating the tenancy or creating a new tenancy (unless the landlord and tenant specifically agree otherwise).[90]

(v) *Second Notices*

As previously indicated, a tenant has an opportunity to void a Form N5. If, within six months after the first notice becomes void, the tenant contravenes the provisions of s. 60, 61, 62, 64 or 67 of the R.T.A., the landlord may serve another notice of termination (either Form N5 or N6). This "second" notice of termination generally has a shorter notice period and indicates that the tenant does not have any right to void the notice by compliance.[91] Note that a "second" notice can only be given if the first notice became void "as a result of the tenant's compliance with the terms of that notice" (para. 68(1)(a)). If the first notice was not voided as a result of compliance, the landlord should commence an application based upon that first notice. If it is too late (i.e., if the notice has become void because the landlord did not commence an application within 30 days of the termination date set out in the first notice), the landlord will have to start again with another first ("curable") notice.[92]

Similarly, if the landlord fails to commence an application within 30 days of the termination date set out in a valid "second" notice, that notice becomes void (s. 46 of the R.T.A.). If there is then a further problem with the tenant, the landlord may have to start over with a new "first" (i.e., voidable) notice of termination (even if it occurs within six months of the first notice) as there is no provision in the R.T.A. for delivering a second "second" notice.[93]

Finally, there cannot be a "second" notice without a valid "first" notice. In *Quann Agencies Ltd. v. Poulter*,[94] it was held that since the first notice of termination given by the landlord was invalid, the landlord had no right to serve a "second" notice and the landlord's application was dismissed. Similarly, where the first N5 notice of termination was invalid as the termination date did not comply with the Act, the second notice also had to be declared void (since the landlord had no right to serve a second notice).[95]

---

[90] Similarly, pursuant to subsection 103(2), unless the parties agree otherwise, a landlord can accept compensation from an unauthorized occupant without fear of creating a tenancy.

[91] Subsection 68(1) of the R.T.A.

[92] *Bosmworth v. Shirley* (March 31, 2006), SOL-63194-RV, [2006] O.R.H.T.D. No. 15 (Ont. Rental Housing Trib.); *Concord Pacific Property Inc. v. Hope* (April 12, 2006), TEL-60237, 2006 CarswellOnt 4414, [2006] O.R.H.T.D. No. 45 (Ont. Rental Housing Trib.); and *Chaplin v. Drake* (August 4, 2004), EAL-43000 (Ont. Rental Housing Trib.).

[93] Landlord and Tenant Board File No. NOL-05483 (Feb. 3, 2009).

[94] (May 17, 1999), EAL-03347-RV (Ont. Rental Housing Trib.).

[95] Landlord and Tenant Board File No. NOL-05863 (Jan. 19, 2009).

5. TERMINATION BY ORDER

When either the landlord or the tenant wishes to end a tenancy early and the other party will not agree, it may become necessary to commence an application.

Typically, an application will be filed by a landlord under s. 69 for an order terminating a tenancy. This can be due to misconduct on the part of the tenant, another occupant of the rental unit or a guest of the tenant. Such "fault" grounds for termination include: persistent late payment of rent;[96] non-payment of rent;[97] commission of an illegal act within the residential complex;[98] misrepresentation of income in rent-geared-to-income housing;[99] serious impairment of the safety of other persons in the complex;[100] causing undue damage to the unit or the complex;[101] substantially interfering with the reasonable enjoyment of other tenants or the lawful rights of the landlord;[102] and, having more people living in the unit than permitted by health, safety and housing standards.[103]

A landlord can also apply to terminate a tenancy even when the tenant has done nothing wrong. Such "no-fault" grounds for termination include situations where: the landlord or a prescribed member of the landlord's family (or a caregiver for such a person) wants to live in the rental unit;[104] the purchaser of the complex or a prescribed member of their family (or a caregiver for such a person) wants to live in the rental unit;[105] the landlord plans to demolish or renovate the unit to the extent that it must be vacant during the work or plans to convert the unit to a non-residential use;[106] the tenant no longer qualifies to continue living in public housing;[107] the tenancy was contingent upon the tenant's employment for the landlord and that employment has terminated;[108] and, the tenancy arose by virtue of or collateral to an agreement of purchase and sale of a proposed condominium unit and the agreement of purchase and sale has been terminated.[109]

---

[96] Paragraph 58(1)1 of the R.T.A. (formerly para. 60(1)1 of the T.P.A.).

[97] Section 59 of the R.T.A. (formerly s. 61 of the T.P.A.).

[98] Subsection 61(1) of the R.T.A. (formerly subsection 62(1) of the T.P.A.).

[99] Subsection 60(1) of the R.T.A. (formerly subsection 62(2) of the T.P.A.).

[100] Section 66 of the R.T.A. (formerly s. 65 of the T.P.A.).

[101] Section 62 of the R.T.A. (formerly s. 63 of the T.P.A.) and s. 63 of the R.T.A. (new).

[102] Section 64 of the R.T.A. (formerly also s. 64 of the T.P.A.) and s. 65 of the R.T.A. (new).

[103] Section 67 of the R.T.A. (formerly s. 66 of the T.P.A.).

[104] Section 48 of the R.T.A. (formerly s. 51 of the T.P.A.).

[105] Section 49 of the R.T.A. (formerly s. 52 of the T.P.A.).

[106] Section 50 of the R.T.A. (formerly s. 53 of the T.P.A.).

[107] Paragraph 58(1)2 of the R.T.A. (formerly para. 60(1)2 of the T.P.A.).

[108] Paragraph 58(1)3 of the R.T.A. (formerly para. 60(1)3 of the T.P.A.).

[109] Paragraph 58(1)4 of the R.T.A. (formerly para. 60(1)4 of the T.P.A.).

A landlord can also seek an order terminating the tenancy on an *ex parte* basis where the tenant has served upon the landlord a notice of termination;[110] the landlord and tenant have agreed to terminate the tenancy;[111] or, the tenant has breached a specified provision of a mediated agreement or order of the Board.[112]

Occasionally, a tenant will seek an order terminating a tenancy. In addition to the other relief a tenant might seek, a tenant may request of the Board that he or she be released from the tenancy agreement where the landlord has taken the following actions: unreasonably withheld consent to an assignment or sublet;[113] failed to properly repair and maintain the unit or the complex;[114] done one or more of the activities set out in paras. 2 to 6 of subsection 29(1);[115] or charged the tenant for a portion of utility costs under s. 138 without first bringing the unit and the appliances within the unit into compliance with the prescribed requirements.[116]

---

[110] Section 77 of the R.T.A. (formerly s. 76 of the T.P.A.).
[111] Section 77 of the R.T.A. (formerly s. 76 of the T.P.A.).
[112] Section 78 of the R.T.A. (formerly s. 77 of the T.P.A.).
[113] Paragraph 98(3)3 of the R.T.A. (formerly para. 33(1)3 of the T.P.A.).
[114] Paragraph 30(1)1 of the R.T.A. (formerly para. 34(1)1 of the T.P.A.).
[115] Paragraph 31(1)(e) of the R.T.A. (formerly para. 35(1)(d) of the T.P.A.).
[116] Paragraph 138(7)1 of the R.T.A. (new). Note that this provision is not yet in effect.

7

Rent and Other Charges

1. DEFINITION OF RENT

Rent, simply stated, is the consideration payable by the tenant for the accommodation provided according to the terms of the lease. Rent is defined in s. 2 of the *Residential Tenancies Act, 2006* (R.T.A.) as the amount of any consideration for the right to occupy and for any services and facilities and any privilege, accommodation or thing that the landlord provides for the tenant whether or not a separate charge is made.

Although rent is usually paid in money, the use of the term "consideration" means that anything of value given to the landlord for the right to occupy the unit can be considered to be payment of rent. For instance, if the landlord and tenant agree, "rent" could include services provided by the tenant. In *Authier v. Tamai*,[1] the rental unit was in a terrible state at the time the tenancy commenced. The parties agreed that the tenant, who was an experienced contractor, would effect repairs to the unit and the cost of labour and materials would be deducted from the rent that would otherwise have been owed to the landlord. The Tribunal therefore found that there was no rent owing for the second and third months of the tenancy (the first month's rent had been paid at the commencement of the tenancy). Although the tenant did not actually pay any amount to the landlord for those two months, the *consideration* given to the landlord was the value of the labour and materials provided by the tenant (with the consent of the landlord) in restoring the rental unit from its formerly dilapidated state. Similarly, in Landlord and Tenant Board File No. SOL-02104 (June 11, 2007), the Board held that, based upon the agreement between the parties, the value of work done by the tenant was valuable consideration accepted by the landlord to permit the tenant to remain in the unit and, therefore, constituted "rent".

---

[1] (June 19, 2006), SWL-81126, 2006 CarswellOnt 4409, [2006] O.R.H.T.D. No. 65 (Ont. Rental Housing Trib.).

In a court decision from Nova Scotia (under similar legislation),[2] it was held that "an agreement . . . to pay the power bill constitutes an agreement to pay rent since it would constitute an amount paid in consideration of the right to occupy the premises."

Rent also includes any consideration paid for the following "services and facilities and any privilege, accommodation or thing that the landlord provides":

(a) furniture, appliances and furnishings
(b) parking and related facilities
(c) laundry facilities
(d) elevator facilities
(e) common recreational facilities
(f) garbage facilities and related services
(g) cleaning and maintenance services
(h) storage facilities
(i) intercom systems
(j) cable television facilities
(k) heating facilities and services
(l) air-conditioning facilities
(m) utilities and related services
(n) security services and facilities

The above listing does not mean that all of these items are automatically included for a tenant. Each rental unit comes with its own set of services and facilities that are included in the rent. Such services and facilities may be included as part of the tenancy agreement, either explicitly or by implication. Vital or essential services such as water, heat, light and garbage disposal would be implied in the tenancy agreement if not so stated.

Amenities and services not covered by the lease terms or implied as such may be made available by separate contract and apart from the statutory rights and obligations of the R.T.A. For example, recreational facilities such as a swimming pool, tennis courts and so on can be used by tenants, if desired, at charges that are not rent, and on terms apart from the residential tenancy rights and obligations.

By the definition contained in s. 2 of the R.T.A., rent does not include an amount paid by a tenant to a landlord to reimburse the landlord for property taxes paid by the landlord with respect to a mobile home or a land lease home owned by a tenant[3] or an amount that a landlord charges a tenant of a rent

---

[2] *Vallée v. Balsom* (2007), 2007 CarswellNS 405 (N.S. Small Cl. Ct.).

[3] See s. 2 of the R.T.A. See also Landlord and Tenant Board File No. CEL-14835 (Feb. 10, 2009).

unit in a care home for care services[4] or meals.

Rent control is dealt with in Chapters 9 and 10.

2. OTHER CHARGES

Pursuant to s. 134 of the R.T.A. (formerly s. 140 of the *Tenant Protection Act* (T.P.A.)), a landlord may not, directly or indirectly, attempt to collect any other charge unless specifically prescribed by regulation. A landlord may not charge a fee, premium, commission, bonus, penalty or other consideration except as may be prescribed. Section 17 of O. Reg. 516/06 (formerly s. 29 of O. Reg. 194/98) sets out charges that are permissible:

1. Payment for additional keys, remote entry devices or cards requested by the tenant, not greater than the direct costs;
2. Payment for replacement keys, remote entry devices or cards, not greater than the direct replacement costs, unless the replacement keys, remote entry devices or cards are required because the landlord, on the landlord's initiative, changed the locks;
3. Payment of a refundable key, remote entry device or card deposit, not greater than the expected direct replacement costs;
4. Payment of NSF fees charged by a financial institution to the landlord;
5. Payment of an administration charge, not greater than $20, for an NSF cheque;
6. Payment by a tenant or subtenant in settlement of a court action or potential court action or an application or potential application to the Board;
7. Payment to a landlord or tenant of a mobile home park or land lease community at the commencement of the tenancy as consideration for the rental of a particular site;
8. Payment of a charge not exceeding $250 for transferring, at the request of the tenant,
   i. between rental units to which subsections 6(1) or (3) of this Regulation applies, if the rental units are located in the same residential complex, or
   ii. between rental units in a residential complex that is described in paragraph 1, 2, 3 or 4 of subsection 7(1) of the Act;
9. Payment of an amount to reimburse the landlord for property taxes paid by the landlord with respect to a mobile home or a land lease home owned by the tenant.

[4] See s. 2 of the R.T.A. and s. 2 of O. Reg. 516/06 for the definition of "care services". Please refer to Chapter 21 for a more in-depth analysis of the provisions relating to care homes.

A landlord of a mobile home park may also charge for the landlord's reasonable out of pocket expenses incurred with regard to entry of a mobile home into the park, the exit of the mobile home from the park, the installation of the mobile home, the removal of the mobile home, and the testing of water or sewage in the park.[5]

An important fact is that such charges, even when permitted, are considered to be in addition to rent — they are not themselves part of the rent. Therefore, a landlord cannot enforce payment of these amounts in the same manner as rent.

In *Swire v. Walleye Trailer Park Ltd.*,[6] for example, the Divisional Court considered the question of whether the landlord of this trailer park could pass on to the tenants the property taxes paid by landlord with respect to the mobile homes in question. Justice Maloney wrote:

> In my view, section 29 of Ontario Regulation 194/98 provides a complete answer to the question in the case at bar. While reimbursement for property taxes in respect of mobile homes is not considered rent under the *TPA*, it is also not considered an illegal charge. As a result, it is my opinion that the governing law allows landlords to charge tenants of mobile home parks for this expense.[7]

Similarly, in *Hearst Trailer Park v. Guilbault*,[8] the Tribunal held that property taxes the landlord had to pay on the tenant's mobile home could not be included in an application for arrears of rent (because taxes are not rent).

In *Black Creek Retirement Homes Ltd. v. Hurford et al.*,[9] the landlord operated a 272-unit mobile home park and charged rent at a monthly rate. The landlord also charged each tenant an annual administrative fee of $100 plus $7 GST. The tenants claimed that this was an illegal charge (as it was not one of the charges permitted by s. 29 of O. Reg. 194/98). The landlord claimed that it was really just part of the rent. The Tribunal found (in two separate orders) in favour of the tenants. These decisions were upheld upon appeal to the Divisional Court.

---

[5] Section 166 of the R.T.A. (formerly s. 115 of the T.P.A.). See Chapter 20.

[6] (2001), 2001 CarswellOnt 2832 (Ont. Div. Ct.).

[7] At para. 26. This may be *obiter* since ultimately the tenant's appeal was granted on the basis that the Small Claims Court that originally found in favour of the landlord had no jurisdiction to deal with a dispute that arose between a residential landlord and tenant and that was clearly within the exclusive jurisdiction of the Ontario Rental Housing Tribunal.

[8] (Feb. 25, 2002), NOL-06722, [2002] O.R.H.T.D. No. 26 (Ont. Rental Housing Trib.).

[9] (May 29, 2001), Div. Ct. File Nos. 00-2320-DV and 00-2321-DV, re SOT-00780 and SOT-00759.

3. CHARGES FOR UTILITIES

(a) General

Section 17 of O. Reg. 516/06 does not refer to payment for utilities (heat, electricity, water). It is widely assumed that a tenant can be made to pay for the cost of vital services[10] although there is no provision of the R.T.A. that expressly permits this.

Landlords have employed different schemes for collecting amounts from tenants for fuel, electricity, gas or hot or cold water.

The parties can agree that the rent "includes utilities"; this means that there will be no separate charge to the tenant for the cost of any of the utilities as the landlord deems the rent to be sufficient to cover this expense. This is the simplest approach and clearly is permitted by the legislation.

Alternatively, the parties can also agree that the rent is, for example, $x per month *plus* utilities (or certain selected utilities). The parties will then have to agree if the tenant will pay the service providers directly or will reimburse the landlord periodically when the landlord receives a bill from the various utility companies.

If there is a separate charge for utilities, it should be understood that such a charge does not constitute "rent" under the R.T.A. By law, rent must generally remain constant throughout a 12-month period,[11] whereas utility charges typically fluctuate from month to month, changing with both consumption and unit price. Unlike rent that is usually paid in advance, utilities will generally have to be paid in arrears. Therefore, such charges cannot be considered rent and non-payment of such charges cannot be enforced in the same manner as for arrears of rent. This was the accepted interpretation of the Rental Housing Tribunal and will, in all likelihood, continue to be the interpretation adopted by the Landlord and Tenant Board.[12] In practice, this means that if a landlord charges separately for utilities and the tenant falls into arrears of both rent and payments for utilities (and if the tenant is still in possession of the rental unit), the landlord will have to pursue the claim for arrears of rent (and/or eviction based upon the arrears of rent) before the Landlord and Tenant Board and the claim for money owing for utilities in court (usually, the Small Claims Court). Unfortunately, not all judges are familiar with the law in this area and, as a result, have on occasion dismissed

---

[10] Defined in s. 2 of the R.T.A. as "hot or cold water, fuel, electricity, gas, or during the part of each year prescribed by the regulations, heat".

[11] Pursuant to s. 119 of the R.T.A., subject to exceptions: (1) where certain rent discounts are provided; (2) where the parties agree to add or withdraw services or facilities; and (3) for tenancies that are exempt from the usual "12-month rule" (for instance, rent-geared-to-income housing).

[12] As reflected in Interpretation Guideline 11. Also see subsection 138(2) of the R.T.A., which clearly indicates that the charge for a utility does not fall within the definition of "rent".

7 — RENT AND OTHER CHARGES

a landlord's claim (for money owing for utilities) based upon the misapprehension that such a claim merely constitutes a claim for arrears of rent and that such a claim is solely within the jurisdiction of the Landlord and Tenant Board.[13] This is another reason why it may be better to simply include the cost of utilities in the rent and not charge separately for them.

(b) Increasing the Rent Based on Utilities

Pursuant to s. 123 of the R.T.A., the landlord can increase the rent to cover the cost of providing a prescribed "service, facility, privilege, accommodation or thing". The list of permitted services (etc.) found in subsection 16(1) of O. Reg. 516/06 includes, an air conditioner, extra electricity for an air conditioner, extra electricity for a washer or dryer in the rental unit, blockheater plug-ins, heat, electricity, and water or sewage services (excluding capital work). Therefore, where it was not part of the original agreement and the landlord agrees with the tenant to add one of these services or things, the landlord can raise the rent by a set (not fluctuating) amount to be determined in accordance with the Act and subsections 16(2), (3) and (4) of O. Reg. 516/06.

If such an additional service (etc.) is later discontinued, the rent must be reduced by the same amount it was increased.[14]

One result of these provisions is that it appears to permit a landlord, for example, to temporarily raise the rent during the summer months if the tenant uses an air conditioner in the unit and if the landlord follows the procedures set out in ss. 123 and 125 of the Act.[15] This was the opinion of the Tribunal in *Burnhamdale Investments Ltd. v. Metlin*.[16]

In *Burnhamdale Investments Ltd. v. Metlin*, the parties had agreed that the tenants would pay an additional charge each summer for use of an air conditioner. The tenants failed to pay this amount and the landlord brought an application to terminate the tenancy and evict the tenants for non-payment of rent. The real issue here was whether this seasonal charge was "rent" within the meaning of the T.P.A. The Vice-chair held that, during the months this additional service was provided to the tenants, it was legal for the landlord to increase the rent in this way. Therefore, it was found that the tenants had failed to pay the full rent owing for the months in question and the Vice-chair granted the landlord's application.

---

[13] See, for example, *389160 Ontario Ltd. v. MacIntyre* (2008),[2008] O.J. No. 5166 (Ont. S.C.J.).

[14] See s. 125 of the R.T.A. and subsection 16(5) of O. Reg. 516/06.

[15] The landlord could raise the rent even more if it is the landlord who supplies the air conditioner (para. 3 of subsection 16(1)).

[16] (Sept. 22, 2000), CEL-14134, [2000] O.R.H.T.D. No. 126, 2000 CarswellOnt 4579 (Ont. Rental Housing Trib.).

A landlord can therefore agree with a tenant to raise the rent in an existing tenancy in exchange for *adding* new services, facilities, privileges, accommodations or things (if they are listed in s. 16 of O. Reg. 516/06) and this additional service or thing can be provided for a limited period of time. If the rent is increased because of the addition of a service or thing, the amount by which the rent is increased must be a set (i.e., "flat") amount and not one that fluctuates.

See Chapter 9 for a more thorough discussion of rent increases based upon the provision of additional services and Chapter 10 for a discussion of rent decreases based upon the discontinuance of prescribed services.

(c) Allocation of Utility Cost

If a complex contains more than one rental unit, but only one meter (and, therefore, one charge for the entire complex), apportioning the utility costs between the units is sometimes difficult. This can be a source of friction amongst the tenants in the complex and between the tenants and the landlord. One tenant may argue that she uses less electricity (for example) because she lives alone. Another tenant may argue that he should pay a smaller proportion of the gas bill because his unit is the smallest in the complex. This continues to be a source of contention in many smaller buildings.

Some landlords have avoided this problem by paying for the utilities directly and ensuring that the rent charged to the tenants is sufficient to cover the cost of the utilities. The current government, however, wants to encourage conservation and believes that tenants are more likely to consume less (gas, electricity, water, etc.) if they have to pay for those services based upon their actual use.

Section 138 was added to the R.T.A. in order to permit a landlord of a smaller building (up to six units) to charge tenants a portion of the utility costs for the building even if, previously, utilities had been included in their rent.

The concept is that the landlord would provide adequate notice to the tenant, ensure that any appliances in the unit and other aspects of the unit and building meet the prescribed requirements relating to energy conservation, reduce the tenant's rent by an appropriate amount, and then charge them separately for an allocated proportion of the actual utility charges for the entire complex. The allocation of the utility costs amongst the tenants in the building must be done in accordance with the "prescribed rules". Such rules have not yet been established. Thus, implementation of s. 138 has been delayed.

Note that, pursuant to subsection 138(3), the amounts charged for utilities will still not be considered "rent" and failure to pay for utilities cannot be enforced in the same manner as arrears of rent.

(d) Smart Meters

As indicated in the previous section, the current provincial government wants to encourage conservation and believes that tenants are more likely to consume less electricity if they have to pay for it based upon their actual use. The government is, therefore, encouraging landlords (especially in larger apartment buildings) to install meters that will monitor the electricity consumption within each rental unit.

Where a landlord pays for the supply of electricity to a rental unit (i.e., where the tenant does not pay extra for electricity because that cost is included in the rent), s. 137 of the R.T.A. allows the landlord to install a separate electricity meter (a "smart" meter), without the tenant's consent, if the landlord complies with the prescribed rules. Once the smart meter is installed and a minimum of 12 months have passed from the date of installation, the landlord can require the tenant to pay for the electricity actually consumed within the unit. In exchange, the landlord will have to reduce the tenant's rent based upon the average monthly cost of electricity for that unit during the preceding 12-month period. Unfortunately, this may encourage some tenants to use more electricity, not less, immediately following installation of a smart meter since the higher the hydro bill during that period, the greater will be the subsequent rent reduction. A landlord who installs a smart meter is also obliged to install new, energy-efficient appliances in the unit. Accordingly, it is unclear how many landlords will find it attractive to voluntarily install smart meters in their buildings.

The "prescribed rules" necessary for implementation of this section have not yet been published. Thus, implementation of s. 137 has been delayed.

For more information about smart sub-meters and time-of-use rates, visit the Smart Meters Ontario website at *www.smartmetersontario.ca.*

(e) Hydro Sub-Metering

Because several years have passed since the enactment of the R.T.A. but the provisions concerning smart meters have still not been implemented, some landlords have decided to take it upon themselves to try to come up with ways to encourage tenants to conserve energy and, at the same time, reduce their operating costs.

One method that is being explored is to get tenants to agree to pay separately for electricity (based on usage), even though, by the terms of the tenancy agreement, the cost of electricity is supposed to be included in their rent. Typically, the landlord will propose to reduce the tenant's monthly rent by a specified amount, monitor the usage of electricity and then bill the tenant for the electricity actually consumed. If the cost of the electricity consumed is less than the rent reduction, there is a net gain for the tenant. Although this may sound attractive, there are some points to consider.

First, while a tenant may be able to agree to such an arrangement, it is far from clear that, in the absence of any clear statutory authority, a landlord can force such a unilateral change in the terms of the tenancy agreement over the objection of an unwilling tenant.

Second, without careful monitoring over at least 12 months of an individual tenant's usage of electricity (which is not possible in most buildings where there is no sub-metering of individual units), it is impossible to know whether the rent reduction proposed by the landlord is a reasonable one.

Third, even if the landlord installs a sub-meter for an individual rental unit so that actual electricity usage can be monitored for that unit, in the absence of any statutory authority, it appears to me that the landlord has no right to force a tenant to pay separately for electricity if the original agreement between the parties was for the rent to include all utilities.

Fourth, if a tenant agrees *now* to such an arrangement, that tenant may not later (if and when the smart meter provisions of the R.T.A. are implemented) have the benefit of the provisions of the R.T.A. that are designed to protect tenants (such as requiring the landlord to install new, energy-efficient appliances in the unit and to monitor electricity use for a year before forcing the tenant to pay directly for electricity in order to determine a fair rent reduction).

Fifth, there may be "administration" fees charged by the company monitoring the sub-meters, over and above the actual cost of the electricity. This may mean that the tenant will actually end up paying more in total than if they, the tenant, had not agreed to pay separately for electricity.

Sixth, some tenancy agreements provide that, although electricity is included in rent currently, at some point in the future the landlord may, at the landlord's sole discretion, decrease the rent and force the tenant to pay separately for electricity. Whether such terms are actually enforceable may depend upon the exact wording of the contract. Tenants should be careful about signing tenancy agreements that contain such a provision and those who have already signed an agreement containing such a clause should consider seeking legal advice.

There are two recent decisions that have clarified the situation, one from the Landlord and Tenant Board and the other from the Ontario Energy Board.

In Landlord and Tenant Board File No. TST-01693-AM,[17] the landlord had installed sub-meters and attempted to force tenants whose rent included electricity to pay separately for electricity based upon their actual consumption. The landlord purported to reduce each tenant's rent to compensate for this change. A "third party service provider" monitored the system and billed tenants for the electricity and tenants were instructed by the landlord to pay

[17] Issued on July 2, 2009 and amended on July 20, 2009.

the amounts billed directly to the third party service provider. Approximately 70 tenants got together and brought an application before the Landlord and Tenant Board to challenge the landlord's conduct. The presiding Member found that,

> [B]y transferring the hydro (electricity) payment obligation from the Landlord to the Tenant[s] without the consent agreement that is contemplated by section 125 of the *Residential Tenancies Act, 2006* (the "*Act*"), the Landlord has harassed, coerced and threatened the Tenants and substantially interfered with the reasonable enjoyment of the rental unit or residential complex by the Tenants or by a member of their household.

The Member ordered the landlord to cease this activity.

Some of the tenants had executed tenancy agreements that stated that, even though rent would initially include electricity, at some later point in time the landlord could unilaterally require tenants to pay separately for electricity. The Landlord and Tenant Board found that such an agreement was unenforceable because it did not comply with s. 125 of the R.T.A. and this part of the tenancy agreement lacked sufficient particulars (for example, how the rent reduction would be determined) to form a binding contract. For the tenants with older tenancy agreements (in which no such change in billing was contemplated), the landlord's conduct was determined to represent an attempt to unilaterally change the terms of the contract without any consent on the part of the tenants; such a unilateral change was also found to be contrary to the R.T.A. One party simply cannot change the terms of the contract without express authority to do so under the R.T.A.

In 2009, the Ontario Energy Board initiated a proceeding respecting discretionary metering activities in residential buildings, including the installation of smart sub-meters, and released its decision on August 13, 2009.[18] The Ontario Energy Board was receiving numerous complaints from tenants with respect to the implementation of smart sub-metering in their apartment buildings. The volume of complaints, their nature and the scope of the sub-metering activity being undertaken in the province led the Energy Board's Chief Compliance Officer to issue a Compliance Bulletin which "unequivocally characterized the discretionary metering activity being undertaken as unauthorized, and inconsistent with the requirements of the *Electricity Act, 1998*". In the absence of any regulation governing this type of activity, the Energy Board decided to intervene and create some ground rules (at least, that is, until the government comes up with a legislative solution). The Energy Board's decision has the following implications:

1. Any smart sub-metering installation in bulk metered residential com-

[18] EB-2009-0111 (August 13, 2009), available on the Ontario Energy Board website: *www.oeb.gov.on.ca*.

plexes on or after November 3, 2005, is unauthorized and any resulting changes to financial arrangements respecting the payment of electricity charges by tenants is unenforceable;[19]

2. Landlords who have engaged in such activities during this period must restore tenants to the position they were in prior to the installation of the sub-meters;

3. If section 137 of the R.T.A. is ever proclaimed and the necessary regulations passed, it will apply only to the smart metering activities of "licensed distributors" and not to landlords and their agents who are considered to be "exempt distributors";

4. Landlords who are exempt distributors may, from the date of this decision onwards, install smart sub-metering systems in residential complexes, provided they obtain the express, voluntary and informed written consent of the tenants to be affected, which requires the landlord:

    a. to have a third party perform an energy audit and to share the methodology and results with tenants;

    b. to disclose the amount of any administrative charge that will be included on the electricity bills;

    c. to specify the amount of the rent reduction being offered and to provide tenants with a detailed description of the methodology used to arrive at the rent reduction;

    d. to disclose the methodology used to apportion the delivery charges amongst the customers;

    e. to obtain the consent at the time that the change in billing is being proposed.[20]

Note, however, that although this order purports to permit this type of activity if a landlord complies with the conditions listed therein, this is only from the point of view of the Ontario Energy Board. The Landlord and Tenant Board retains exclusive jurisdiction over residential tenancies in the province and it is conceivable that the Landlord and Tenant Board may find that such a change in billing, even with the "informed" consent of tenants, may be inconsistent with the provisions of the R.T.A. The issue of hydro sub-metering is likely to remain a "hot topic" for the next few years and it will be interesting to see how the law in this area develops.

---

[19] I.e., any consent obtained by a distributor prior to August 13, 2009, is ineffective and cannot be relied upon.

[20] I.e., not in advance, such as when the tenancy agreement is being executed.

For more information on this topic, please refer to Chapter 10 ("Reduction or Discontinuance of a Service or Facility (s. 130) and Sub-metering of Electricity").

4. LAWFUL RENT: HOW MUCH CAN THE LANDLORD CHARGE?

No landlord shall charge rent for a rental unit in an amount that is greater than the lawful rent permitted under Part VII of the R.T.A. (s. 111(1)).

(a) How is "Lawful Rent" Determined?

The rent for a rental unit is lawful if the landlord has abided by the rules set out in Part VII of the R.T.A. (ss. 105 through 136).

Prior to enactment of the T.P.A. on June 17, 1998, the rent was "linked" to the unit not to the tenant. Under the T.P.A., if the tenancy began prior to June 17, 1998, the landlord retained the right to increase the rent to any amount not exceeding the maximum rent set for the unit under the previous legislation (ss. 123 and 135 of the T.P.A.). The concept of maximum rent was created under the *Residential Rent Regulation Act, 1986*, S.O. 1996, c. 63 and continued under the *Rent Control Act, 1992*, S.O. 1992, c. 11. Although not continued under the T.P.A., the concept of "maximum rent" was still relevant for the purpose of determining the lawful rent for tenants who occupied the same rental unit both before and after the T.P.A. took effect (June 17, 1998).

Maximum rent was the most rent a landlord could collect for a rental unit if all allowable increases had been taken. It was a notional amount, which increased every year regardless of whether the landlord actually increased the rent charged to the tenant. This led to some instances in which the "maximum rent" for a rental far exceeded what the market could reasonably bear for the unit. Since the landlord could increase the rent to the maximum rent on proper notice, the tenants of such units were vulnerable to economic eviction. In cases where the maximum rent as of June 17, 1998, was considerably higher than the market rent, those long-time tenants remained vulnerable.

Because the T.P.A. did not contain provisions for increasing the maximum rent for a rental unit, the "maximum rent" was effectively frozen as of June 17, 1998.

If the landlord was charging an amount equal to the "maximum rent" on June 17, 1998, then the "maximum rent" designated for that unit became irrelevant. However, if the landlord was collecting less than the "maximum rent" for the unit on June 17, 1998, the landlord had the right under s. 135 of the T.P.A. to increase the rent to the maximum.[21] Each year, the landlord could increase the rent by the guideline amount or up to the maximum, whichever was greater. A landlord, however, was not permitted to increase the rent up to the "maximum rent" and then apply the guideline increase at the same time (or even in the same 12-month period).

Due to the passage of time, most tenants who had been in the same unit since before June 17, 1998, were already paying rent that exceeded the "maximum rent" that was fixed on June 17, 1998. Thus the concept of "maximum rent" no longer had any relevance. Consequently, the government abolished this concept, effective May 3, 2006. Unless, prior to May 3, 2006, a landlord gave a notice of rent increase to raise the rent to the "maximum rent", the landlord can no longer do so.[22]

Under the T.P.A., the Tribunal had access to information from the Rent Registry (maintained under the *Rent Control Act, 1992*) and was obliged to provide that information to members of the public on request. Pursuant to s. 245 of the R.T.A., that obligation will end on January 31, 2008 (i.e., one year after the R.T.A. is proclaimed).[23]

Under the T.P.A., for any new tenancy that began on or after June 17, 1998, the initial rent charged by the landlord became the new lawful rent for the unit (s. 124 of the T.P.A.). In such cases, the landlord could charge whatever initial rent the market would bear. This was referred to as "vacancy de-control". Each time a unit became vacant, the rent would be de-controlled, and the landlord could charge whatever amount the market would bear. Once a new rent had been established, that new rent would then be controlled by the provisions in the T.P.A. governing the permitted timing and amounts of rent increases and decreases.

The concept of vacancy de-control has been continued under the R.T.A., with one notable exception. Where the Board finds that a landlord is in serious breach of the landlord's maintenance obligations, the Board may (amongst other things) prohibit the landlord from charging a new tenant[24] under a new tenancy agreement more than the last lawful rent charged to the former tenant (until the ordered work has been completed).[25] Orders preventing rent increases (OPRI's) are discussed in more detail in Chapters 9 and 11. Once the lawful rent for a rental unit has been established, provisions under the R.T.A. strictly govern the permitted timing and amounts of rent increases and decreases. These provisions are discussed in detail in Chapters 9 and 10.

---

[21] Subject to proper written notice and provided no increase had been taken in the previous 12 months.

[22] Subsection 258(1) of the R.T.A.

[23] Although the government may choose to preserve the information that was contained in the Rent Registry.

[24] Other than tenants in rent-geared-to-income housing.

[25] Paragraph 30(1)6 of the R.T.A.

(b) Deemed Lawful Rent

Under the R.T.A. (as was the case under T.P.A.), the tenant has only one year to challenge the legality of the rent.[26] This has been confirmed recently by the Court of Appeal in *Turnbull's Grove Inc. v. Price*[27] In that same case, however, the Court made a distinction between an unlawful rent charge or rent increase (to which the one-year limitation applies) and a rent increase that is void.

According to the Court of Appeal, if a landlord collects an illegal charge from a tenant, the tenant will have one year in which to commence an application.[28] Similarly, if the landlord serves upon the tenant a notice of rent increase that purports to increase the rent by an amount that exceeds prescribed limits but otherwise substantially complies with the requirements of the Act, the rent will be deemed to be lawful if not challenged by the tenant within one year of the date the rent was first charged. The challenge must take the form of an application to the Board in which "the lawfulness of the rent charged is in issue in application."[29] Although s. 136 indicates that rent that has not been challenged within one year shall be deemed to be lawful, the use of the word "deemed" does not create a rebuttable presumption. It does not mean that the rent will be assumed to be lawful unless the tenant can prove otherwise. Section 136 creates a one-year limitation period.[30] For instance, in *Coe v. Philp et al.*,[31] the tenant moved into the premises (before enactment of the T.P.A.) and commenced paying $300 per month for rent. The tenant then obtained a historical rent report for the unit that indicated that she should only have paid $231.88 per month. Because she waited more than one year to commence her application, it was held that the relevant limitation period had expired and she could no longer challenge the lawfulness of the $300 per month rent. Even if a tenant has been misled as to the lawfulness of the rent charged, it does not alter the one-year limitation for bringing an application.[32]

What is new about the Court of Appeal's decision in *Turnbull's Grove Inc. v. Price*,[33] however, is that the Court states that if the landlord purports to increase a tenant's rent without providing the notice of rent increase required by s. 127 of the T.P.A. (now s. 116 of the R.T.A.), the increase is

---

[26] Section 135(4) of the R.T.A. (formerly s. 144 of the T.P.A.).

[27] (2007), 2007 CarswellOnt 3494, 85 O.R. (3d) 641 (Ont. C.A.).

[28] Section 141(1) of the T.P.A. (now s. 136(1) of the R.T.A.).

[29] Section 141(2) of the T.P.A. (now s. 136(2) of the R.T.A.).

[30] *Kizemchuk et al. v Kizemchuk* (June 7, 2002), File No. 134/2001, TSL-11717 (Ont. Rental Housing Trib.).

[31] (Aug. 24, 2001), SWL-01417 (Ont. Rental Housing Trib.).

[32] *Crich v. Goodwood Apartments Limited* (June 11, 1999), TST-00930 (Ont. Rental Housing Trib.).

[33] (2007), 2007 CarswellOnt 3494, 85 O.R. (3d) 641 (Ont. C.A.).

void. It is as if it never existed and, according to the Court of Appeal, a void rent increase cannot be saved by the passage of time. In this case, the landlord gave only an oral notice of rent increase and the tenant paid the increased amount for about ten months. Eventually she brought an application to recover the "excess" rent collected by the landlord but the Tribunal dismissed her application as it was not commenced within one year of the date the landlord first collected or retained money in contravention of the Act.[34] The tenant then began paying only the rent she considered to be lawful and the landlord commenced an application to evict her for arrears of rent. The Tribunal ruled in favour of the landlord on the basis that the higher rent was deemed lawful as it had been more than one year since the increase was first charged.[35] This decision was upheld by the Divisional Court. On further appeal, the Court of Appeal overturned both earlier decisions on the basis that the challenged rent increase was of no force and effect from the date of its imposition since it had not been based on a proper notice of rent increase and a notice that is void pursuant to s. 127 of the T.P.A. (now s. 116 of the R.T.A.) cannot be saved by the provisions of s. 141 of the T.P.A. (now s. 136 of the R.T.A.). This decision is binding upon the Landlord and Tenant Board.

Thus, the law as interpreted by Ontario's highest court is that a rent increase that is not based upon a notice of rent increase[36] is a nullity and is not deemed lawful because of the passage of one year. Although the tenant will be barred from commencing an application more than one year after the illegal rent was first charged,[37] if the landlord brings an application concerning rent, the tenant may be able to challenge the lawfulness of the rent (as a defence to the landlord's application) even if it is more than one year after it was first charged. The one-year deeming provisions do not apply to a rent increase that is void.

(c) Determining the Amount of Rent Being Charged

Usually, the landlord and tenant agree on the amount that the landlord is charging for rent. In most cases, the amount being charged is set out clearly in the original written tenancy agreement and/or in a written Notice of Rent Increase. There may, however, be situations where there is no written agreement and/or where the landlord and tenant agree to a lower rent than the landlord could legally charge the tenant for the rental unit (based upon the original agreement). If the arrangement is made informally and is not reduced

[34] Section 144(4) of the T.P.A. (now s. 135(4) of the R.T.A.).

[35] Section 141 of the T.P.A. (now s. 136 of the R.T.A.).

[36] Or, perhaps, a rent increase that is based upon a notice that does not substantially comply in form and content with the approved form.

[37] See s. 135(4) of the R.T.A. and Landlord and Tenant Board File No. SWT-00924 (February 1, 2008).

to writing, a dispute may arise later between the parties as to how much rent the tenant was really supposed to be paying. This is most likely to arise where it is the landlord's agent who makes the informal arrangement with the tenant and the landlord does not discover this fact until some time later. In such circumstances, the Board will have to consider whether there is sufficient evidence that an explicit agreement was made or whether such an agreement can be inferred from the conduct of the parties over time and whether the person purporting to act on behalf of the landlord had the apparent authority to make such a deal.

In Landlord and Tenant Board File No. SOL-12512 (June 23, 2008), the landlord brought an application to terminate the tenancy on the basis that the tenant had not paid all the rent lawfully owing to the landlord. It was undisputed that for the first year of the tenancy, the monthly rent was $805.00. The tenant received a Notice of Rent Increase toward the end of the first year advising that the monthly rent would be increasing to $846.00. Throughout that second year of the tenancy, however, the tenant only paid $825.00 per month. The following year, the tenant received a notice that the monthly rent would be increased to $867.00. The tenant responded by paying $846.00. The Board found that the monthly rent for the second year of this tenancy was in fact $825.00 based upon an informal agreement between the tenant and the superintendent of the building. The Board accepted that there was such an agreement based upon the testimony of the tenant and the failure of the landlord during the year in question to take any steps to advise the tenant that it objected to the tenant paying only $825.00 per month. Since the lawful monthly rent for that period was only $825.00, the Notice of Rent Increase for the following year contained incorrect calculations and was, therefore, found to be void. As a result, there were found to be no arrears of rent owing and the landlord's application was dismissed.

5. DISCOUNTS

(a) Introduction

Landlords sometimes offer incentives to tenants to attract them to the unit or to encourage (through economic incentives) prompt payment of rent. Rent discounts fell out of favour during the late 1990s and early part of this decade but, given the current vacancy rates,[38] landlords may consider offering financial incentives to attract new tenants. Rent discounts can make determining the lawful rent for a rental unit more complicated (since the rent charged for every period during the term or during a 12-month period may not be identical). Subsections 111(3) and (4) of the R.T.A. provide that,

[38] See the discussion of current trends in vacancy rates in Chapter 1.

subject to subsection 111(2), where discounts are offered, the lawful rent shall be calculated in accordance with the prescribed rules. These "rules" are found in ss. 10, 11, 12, 13 and 14 of O. Reg. 516/06.

The discount rules under the R.T.A. represent a marked departure from the rules under the T.P.A. and are described below.

(b) Discounts That Do Not Affect the Lawful Rent

It is important to understand that many discounts will not in any way affect the calculation of the lawful rent for a rental unit if the landlord follows the rules set out in subsection 111(2) of the R.T.A. and ss. 10 and 11 of O. Reg. 516/06.

The lawful rent will *not* be affected where the following types of discounts are offered:

RENT-FREE PERIODS (not exceeding three months rent)

1. A discount in rent at the beginning of, or during, a tenancy, that consists of up to three months rent in any 12-month period, if the discount is provided in the form of rent-free periods and meets the following prescribed conditions:[39]
   a. the discount must be provided for in a written agreement;
   b. if the rent is paid monthly and the discount is equal to the rent for one month or less, the entire discount must be taken during one rental period;
   c. if the rent is paid monthly and the discount is equal to the rent for a period greater than one month but not more than two months, the discount equal to the rent for one month must be taken during one rental period and the balance within one other rental period;
   d. if the rent is paid monthly and the discount is equal to the rent for a period greater than two months but not more than three months, the discount equal to the rent for two months must be taken for two rental periods and the balance within one rental period.
   e. If the rent is paid daily or weekly, the discount must be taken in periods that are at least one week in duration.

[39] See para. 111(2)(a) of the R.T.A. and subsection 10(1) of O. Reg. 516/06.

Under the T.P.A., to be an "eligible discount" (i.e., one that would not affect the calculation of the lawful rent) a rent-free period could not exceed *one* month's rent and had to be offered within the first eight months of the 12-month period.[40]

PROMPT PAYMENT DISCOUNT (not exceeding 2%)

2. A discount in rent at the beginning of, or during, a tenancy, of up to 2% of the rent that could otherwise be lawfully charged for a rental period, if the discount is provided for paying rent on or before the date it is due and the discount is provided for in a written or oral agreement.[41]

OTHER PRESCRIBED DISCOUNTS[42]

3. A discount provided for in a written agreement, if the total amount of the discount that is provided during the first eight months of the 12-month period does not exceed the rent for one month.
4. A discount provided for in a written agreement, if:
   a. the total amount of the discount that is provided in the 12-month period does not exceed the rent for two months;
   b. the total amount of the discount that is provided in the first seven months of the 12-month period does not exceed the rent for one month; and
   c. any discount that is provided in the last five months of the 12-month period is provided in only one of those months and does not exceed the rent for one month.
5. A discount provided for under a tenancy agreement that operates under the Strong Communities Housing Allowance Program – Toronto Pilot and that complies with the other requirements of para. 11(1)3 of O. Reg. 516/06.

Where any of these provisions apply, the landlord can offer a tenant a discount without actually altering the lawful rent.

(c) Discounts that Affect the Calculation of the Lawful Rent

Where a landlord offers the tenant a discount that does not comply with the provisions set out above, it will affect the calculation of the lawful rent.

---

[40] Paragraph 1 of subsection 12(1) of O. Reg. 194/98. Also see *Phoenix Property Services Corp., Re* (Sept. 5, 2006), EAL-58401, 2006 CarswellOnt 9161 (Ont. Rental Housing Trib.) in which the rent-free period was not considered to be an "eligible discount" because it was offered in the 11th month of the 12-month period.

[41] See para. 111(2)(b) of the R.T.A. and subsection 10(2) of O. Reg. 516/06.

[42] See para. 111(2)(c) of the R.T.A. and subsection 11(1) of O. Reg. 516/06.

In such cases, the lawful rent is to be calculated in accordance with s. 12 of O. Reg. 516/06.[43] The calculation of the lawful rent in such cases under the R.T.A. is similar to that required under the T.P.A.

When calculating the lawful rent, generally one adds the sum of the rents that are actually charged or to be charged in each of the rental periods in the 12-month period, add the **largest eligible discount**, divide that sum by the number of rental periods in the 12-month period and then add any rent increase (under s. 123) or subtract any rent decrease (under s. 125).[44]

The definition of "largest eligible discount" is very complex and is much more restrictive if the discount is not provided for in a *written* agreement.[45] Landlords should, therefore, be sure to include in the written tenancy agreement any details concerning rent discounts to be provided to the tenant.

Special rules are given for calculating the lawful rent in the following cases:

i. A prompt payment discount exceeding 2%[46]
ii. Multiple types of discounts provided to the same tenant[47]
iii. The landlord provides a discount to a tenant under the Strong Communities Housing Allowance Program but does not comply with para. 3 of subsection 11(1) of O. Reg. 516/06
iv. The rent charged for the first rental period is greater than the rent charged for subsequent periods[48]

For the purpose of calculating lawful rent under ss. 12 and 13, the "12-month period" has the same meaning as in s. 11 of O. Reg. 516/06[49] and the "rent actually charged or to be charged" does not include amounts that cannot be lawfully charged, rent increases under s. 123 or rent decreases under s. 125.[50]

I shall now describe these four situations in greater detail.

Prompt payment discount exceeding 2%

Subsection 11(3) of O. Reg. 516/06 provides that in such cases, the lawful rent is calculated by dividing the discounted rent by 0.98. Consider the following example.

EXAMPLE 1: The base monthly rent is $1,000 but a 5% discount is given for prompt payment. What is the lawful monthly rent for the unit?

---

[43] Subsection 111(3) of the R.T.A.
[44] Subsection 12(2) of O. Reg. 516/06.
[45] See the definition contained in subsection 11(6) of O. Reg. 516/06.
[46] Subsection 11(3) of O. Reg. 516/06.
[47] Subsections 11(4) and (5) of O. Reg. 516/06.
[48] Section 13 of O. Reg. 516/06.
[49] Subsection 12(8) of O. Reg. 516/06.
[50] Section 14 of O. Reg. 516/06.

O. REG. 516/06	DESCRIPTION	CALCULATION OF LAWFUL RENT
s. 11(3)	The lawful rent is calculated by dividing the discounted rent by 0.98.	= (Discounted rent) ÷ 0.98 = ($1,000 - 5%) ÷ 0.98 = ($950) ÷ 0.98 = $969.39

Answer: The lawful monthly rent is $969.39.

Note that the calculation of the lawful rent where prompt payment discounts are offered by a landlord does not appear to be contingent upon whether or not the tenant actually "earned" or received the discount in any particular month. Where the discount is 2% or less, it is immaterial whether or not the discount was ever received by the tenant since the lawful rent is equal to the undiscounted rent. Where, however, the prompt payment discount exceeds 2% and the tenant has been consistently late in paying his or her rent, a landlord could argue that the lawful rent should be based upon the undiscounted rent (not the formula set out in s. 11(3) of O. Reg. 516/06) as the tenant did not earn the prompt payment discounts. There appears to be no provision for this in the Regulation itself and the calculation of the lawful rent seems to be determined without regard to whether or not the tenant actually receives the prompt payment discount offered by the landlord.

Multiple discounts

If the landlord provides a discount of up to 2% for prompt payment (under clause 111(2)(b) of the R.T.A.) and also provides another discount (other than a discount described in clause 111(2)(a) or (c) of the Act), then the lawful rent for any rental period in the 12-month period shall be calculated in accordance with subsection 11(4) of O. Reg. 516/06.

If the landlord provides a prompt payment discount greater than 2% and also provides another discount in rent (other than a discount described in clause 111(2)(a) or (c) of the Act), then the lawful rent for any rental period in the 12-month period shall be calculated in accordance with subsection 11(5) of O. Reg. 516/06.

Strong Communities Housing Allowance Program

If a tenancy agreement operates under the Strong Communities Housing Allowance Program – Toronto Pilot, and the landlord does not comply with para. 3 of subsection 11(1), the lawful rent shall be the undiscounted rent that was permitted under the Act at the time the tenancy agreement began to operate under the Program.

Higher rent charged in first rental period

What if the landlord charges more for the first rental period than for the subsequent rental periods? Section 13 of O. Reg. 516/06 deals with this situation. The calculation is the same as it was under the T.P.A.

EXAMPLE 2: The rent for the first month is $1,200 and the monthly rent for the next 11 months is $1,000. What is the lawful monthly rent for the unit?

O. REG. 516/06	DESCRIPTION	CALCULATION OF LAWFUL RENT
s. 13	Add all the rents actually charged or to be charged by the landlord during the 12-month period.	= $1,200 + ($1,000 × 11) = $1,200 + $11,000 = $12,200
	Subtract from that sum the rent for the first rental period.	$12,200 - $1,200 = $11,000
	Divide that amount by a number equal to the number of rental periods in the 12-month period minus 1.	= $11,000 ÷ (12 – 1) = $11,000 ÷ 11 = $1,000

Answer: The lawful monthly rent is $1,000 (even though the rent for the first month is higher).

6. PAYMENT OF RENT

(a) Timing of Payment

The timing of rental payments is a matter of contract between the landlord and tenant. Rent can be paid at whatever times and periods the parties agree upon. Most landlords insist on payment of rent in advance (i.e., on the first day of a rental period) but nothing in the R.T.A. makes this arrangement mandatory.

The parties can change their agreement about when the rent is due either by express agreement or implicitly by their conduct. The landlord may thus lose the right to insist on payment of the rent on the date set out in the tenancy agreement if the landlord has consistently permitted payment on other dates without complaint. In *Cottam v. Smith*,[51] for instance, the Ontario Court of Appeal found that "by a course of conduct ... it had been recognized that the

[51] [1947] O.W.N. 880 (Ont. C.A.).

rent would be properly paid if paid at any time during the first fifteen days of the month".[52]

Even if rent is payable monthly by the terms of the lease, a landlord and tenant may agree to different payment dates due to the tenant's circumstances, provided of course that any such arrangement can be proven. In *Lecours v. Cyr*,[53] the tenant satisfied the Tribunal that the landlord and tenant had agreed that the tenant could pay lump sum payments of rent on July 31 and October 31. The Member wrote, "there is no reason in public policy or clear authority in the T.P.A. that a landlord and tenant should not be able to make arrangements for payment of rent including intermittent and lump sum payments."

Similarly, where the landlord previously allowed the tenant until the end of the month to pay the rent for that month, then it is an implied term of the tenancy that the tenant has until the last day of each month to pay the rent and the landlord cannot unilaterally change that term of the agreement.[54]

A tenant has the whole of the due date to pay the rent, and is not in arrears until after midnight on that day.[55]

Failure to pay rent is a cause for termination of the tenancy (s. 59 of the R.T.A.). Persistent late payment of rent is also a cause for termination (s. 58(1) of the R.T.A.).

Prepayment of rent is risky for both the tenant and the landlord.

First, if the property changes hands, the tenant may not get credit for the amount paid in advance (to the former landlord) and will risk having to pay those amounts a second time to the new landlord. Prepayment of rent before it is due has been held not to be in fulfillment of the covenant to pay rent, that is, until the due date for that rent, but it is treated as an advance to the landlord.[56] Rent so paid to the landlord before it is due has been said to be paid at the tenant's risk in case of a change of ownership[57] or where a mortgagee takes over control of the property.[58] That may be so for ordinary prepayment, but for prepayment as a security deposit, a decision has held that a new landlord must account to the tenant for the security deposit whether received by the new landlord or not.[59] The judge referred to s. 82(1) of Part IV (of the *Landlord and Tenant Act*) which states that a security deposit "shall be applied in payment of the rent for the last rent period immediately preceding the termination of the tenancy", and that mandatory requirement creates

---

52 [1947] O.W.N. 880 (Ont. C.A.) at 881 [O.W.N.].

53 (February 4, 1999), Eastern District #NOL-00844 (Ont. Rental Housing Trib.).

54 Landlord and Tenant Board File No. SWL-22520 (Jan. 30, 2009).

55 *Urbach v. McClarty* (1952), [1953] O.W.N. 58 (Ont. C.A.); Landlord and Tenant Board File No. SOL-00776 (April 12, 2007); and Landlord and Tenant Board File No. TSL-00411 (March 15, 2007).

56 For a further discussion of this issue, see the section on "Prepayment of Rent" in Chapter 8.

57 *Cavell v. Canada Dry Ginger Ale Ltd.*, [1945] O.W.N. 799 (Ont. Co. Ct.).

58 Landlord and Tenant Board File No. CEL-11712 (August 25, 2008)..

59 *Spencer Properties Ltd. v. Zrebiec* (1992), 1992 CarswellOnt 1760 (Ont. Gen. Div.).

an implied covenant which, pursuant to Part IV, s. 88, now s. 18 of the R.T.A., runs with the land and binds an assignee of the original landlord. The judge distinguished the *Cavell* case, *supra*, as not applying to residential tenancies. The judge went on to say that a new landlord should inquire about any security deposits.

Second, a landlord who accepts rent in advance may be found to be holding an illegal rent deposit and may be forced to re-pay to the tenant the amounts that were paid in advance,[60] with interest on all money paid in advance. The landlord may also be prosecuted for violating para. 234(d) of the R.T.A.[61]

Some confusion arises between the prepayment of rent and the collection by the landlord of an illegal rent deposit. This confusion may have been created by a blurring of the distinction between the *term* of a tenancy and the rental *periods* within that term. Let us take the example of a tenancy that is, at least initially, to run for one year; the term of the tenancy is one year. That does not tell us how often rent is to be paid. Usually, tenancy agreements provide for payment of rent monthly. There is no reason in law, however, why rent payments cannot be specified to be weekly or bi-weekly or some other period to which the parties have agreed. If no rental period is specified within that fixed term, there is also no reason in law why the landlord could not insist on payment of the full year's rent at the commencement of the tenancy. If, by the terms of the tenancy agreement, rent is supposed to be paid monthly, demanding payment for all 12 rental periods at the beginning of the year would amount to prepayment of the rent. If only one rental period (one-year in length) exists, then requesting payment of rent for this one period at the beginning of that period is not prohibited. This was the approach taken by a British Columbia court in *Metropolitan Trust Company of Canada v. Beverly Hills Holdings Ltd.*[62] Four residential leases were being considered. Each was for a specific period; two were three months each for a fixed rent paid at the outset, one for six months and the other for eight months. Each of these were for fixed amounts of rent paid upon going into possession. The court held that the leases were for fully paid terms and not monthly rental paid in advance.

Sometimes, apartments rented to university students are rented at an annual rental payable monthly for eight months or during the academic year. Rent so pro-rated has the effect of prepaying the rent. This was approved of at trial in *Gallant v. Veltrusy Enterprises Ltd.*,[63] but overturned on appeal on

---

[60] *Li v. Sympthony Square Ltd.* (2007), 2007 CarswellOnt 1059 (Ont. Div. Ct.). In this case, the Divisional Court also approved of the trial judge having awarded punitive damages for the landlord's conduct.

[61] See an example of such a prosecution in Chapter 19 (case heard in Newmarket on October 10, 2008, before Justice of the Peace Douglas W. Clark).

[62] (September 28, 1988), Doc. Vancouver H900171 (B.C. S.C.).

[63] (1980), 28 O.R. (2d) 349 (Ont. Co. Ct.), reversed (1981), 32 O.R. (2d) 716 (Ont. C.A.).

the basis that the County Court judge did not have jurisdiction for his decision.[64] In *Boyd v. Earl & Jennie Lohn Ltd.*,[65] a similar arrangement was not accepted by the court and the lease was declared void. It was held that the pro-rated rent, or that is, a part of each month's rent, was in effect a security deposit which in total was for more than one month's rent and so was in conflict with s. 82 of Part IV (*Landlord and Tenant Act*). If, however, the parties had agreed to an eight-month tenancy (without reference to pro-rating a year's rental over the eight months) and if the security deposit did not exceed one month's rent, that would not appear to contravene the R.T.A.

(b) Method of Payment

The acceptable method of paying rent is also a matter of contract between the parties, with a couple of exceptions. A landlord *cannot* require a tenant to:

1. provide post-dated cheques or other negotiable instruments for payment of rent;[66] or
2. permit automatic debiting of the tenant's account at a financial institution, automatic charging of a credit card or any other form of automatic payment for the payment of rent.[67]

Although the landlord cannot *demand* rent payments be made in the forms prohibited by s. 108 of the R.T.A., the Act does not prohibit a tenant from doing so voluntarily.

Delivering the rent money to the landlord is the tenant's responsibility. Although the landlord may develop the habit of collecting the rent from the tenant, ultimately, the onus is on the tenant to ensure the rent is paid. The method of delivering the rent ought to be specified in the tenancy agreement. For instance, the landlord should specify if the rent can be delivered by mail. If the landlord does not agree to payment through the mail, a tenant would be in default if a rent payment was mailed and not received: *Lastaff v. Lorenson.*[68]

Once the landlord establishes a method of payment, however, the tenant cannot be faulted for making delivery in accordance with the landlord's instructions. In Landlord and Tenant Board File No. SWL-22318 (Jan. 22, 2009), the landlord permitted tenants to put their rent through the slot into the locked utility (hydro) room. The tenant put cash in an envelope and delivered the envelope as usual into the locked utility room. There was a

---

64 (1981), 32 O.R. (2d) 716 (Ont. C.A.).

65 (1984), 47 O.R. (2d) 111 (Ont. H.C.).

66 Paragraph 108(a) of the R.T.A. (formerly s. 119 of the T.P.A.).

67 Paragraph 108(b) of the R.T.A. (new).

68 (1930), 38 O.W.N. 119 (Ont. C.A.).

breach in the landlord's security and someone obtained the key to the utility room and stole the cash. The landlord brought an application to evict the tenant for non-payment of rent. The Member did not accept the landlord's assertion that tenants were aware that only cheques were to be dropped off in the hydro room and cash was to be given to the superintendent and found that the rent had in fact been paid (in other words, it was delivered in the usual way and if it was then stolen from the landlord's possession, that was not the tenant's problem).

Similarly, unless the landlord has clearly specified otherwise, payment of the rent will be considered valid if the rent is delivered to an employee of the landlord who has apparent authority to accept rent payments.[69] If that employee absconds with the money, that ought not to be the concern of the tenants.[70]

A tenant cannot unilaterally change the method of paying the rent. In *373041 Ontario Ltd. v. Nettlefield*,[71] the tenant had paid the rent by delivery for a number of years, then, without the landlord's approval, changed to providing it by registered mail. For some reason, the rent for each of three months was not received by the landlord. The tenant was liable to make up the outstanding amount, with whatever recourse she might have against Canada Post. An agreement to deliver the rent by mail, even if not expressed, could however be implied from the conduct of the parties.[72]

Also, although payment by cheque is commonplace these days, some landlords still insist on payments in cash or by money order or certified cheque.[73] If the tenant has agreed, as a term of the tenancy agreement, to make payments in a specific form, the tenant may be bound by that agreement. If, however, the agreement is silent with respect to how payment is to be made, the landlord may have to accept the rent in whatever form it is tendered.

In *Cornwall Non-Profit Corporation v. Gaffney*,[74] the tenancy agreement provided for payment by money order or certified cheque. It was held by the Tribunal that this did not offend s. 119 of the T.P.A. (now para. 108(a) of the R.T.A.). This decision was upheld on appeal to the Divisional Court.[75]

In *Stanbar Properties Limited v. Rooke*,[76] the tenant signed a tenancy agreement, which required the tenant to make arrangements with his own

---

69 Issuing rent receipts would be a good indication that the employee was authorized by the landlord to accept rent payments.

70 See Landlord and Tenant Board File No. EAL-00095 (Feb. 26, 2007).

71 (August 17, 1992) (Ont. Gen. Div.).

72 *Cottam v. Smith*, [1947] O.W.N. 880 (Ont. C.A.).

73 In *Kamin v. Kirby* (1949), [1950] O.W.N. 68 (Ont. H.C.) the High Court held that rent ought to be paid in cash unless the landlord has agreed otherwise, but given the realities of modern finance, this decision may no longer represent the law in Ontario.

74 (March 26, 1999), EAL-03940 (Ont. Rental Housing Trib.).

75 Div. Ct. File No. 99-DV-328.

76 (Nov. 9, 2005), Div. Ct. File No. 04-212DV Hamilton.

bank for the payment of his monthly rent by "pre-authorized direct debit as required by the Landlord." As well, the agreement included a provision that required the tenant to maintain insurance coverage with respect to certain perils and to provide proof of the insurance coverage to the landlord upon request. The tenant refused to honour these provisions. The landlord applied to terminate the tenancy on the basis that the tenant's failure to comply with these terms of the tenancy agreement substantially interfered with a lawful right, privilege or interest of the landlord. At first instance, the Tribunal found that the landlord had no right to insist on pre-authorized direct debit and that the Tribunal lacked the jurisdiction to deal with "breaches of contractual obligations". On appeal, the Divisional Court overturned the Tribunal's decision on both points. The Court found that the Tribunal did have jurisdiction under s. 64(1) of the T.P.A. to decide whether a breach of the tenancy agreement substantially interfered with a lawful right, privilege or interest of the landlord. The Court also held that the Tribunal erred in regarding pre-authorized direct debit as "a form of negotiable instrument" as it is neither negotiable nor an instrument and its use is not prohibited by s. 119 of the T.P.A. At least in part because of this decision, some landlords began to insist on payment of rent by pre-authorized direct debit. By the addition of para. 108(b) to the R.T.A., the government has now made it clear that landlords are no longer entitled to insist upon payments in this manner.

As always, a tenant should carefully review a tenancy agreement before signing and should remove or modify any terms the tenant finds objectionable, or refuse to sign an agreement that contains terms with which the tenant is uncomfortable. Once the agreement is signed, unless the terms of the agreement are contrary to the provisions of the R.T.A. or the *Human Rights Code*, the terms of the contract will be binding.

Where a rent cheque received from a tenant is returned NSF (i.e., the cheque is not honoured by the bank because there are "Not Sufficient Funds" in the tenant's account to cover the amount of the cheque), the landlord is entitled to pass on to the tenant the fee (if any) that the landlord is actually charged by its bank when the cheque fails to clear and up to $20 to cover the landlord's administrative costs of processing the NSF cheque.[77] Landlords can include a claim for such amounts in an application to collect arrears of rent (under s. 87). Note, however, that the R.T.A. *only* provides these remedies where a cheque is returned NSF. If the cheque is dishonoured by the bank for some *other* reason or the tenant orders his or her financial institution to "stop payment" on the cheque, the landlord does not have a statutory right to recover administrative or out-of-pocket expenses related to that cheque.

[77] Sections 74, 87 and 134 of the R.T.A. and s. 17 of O. Reg. 516/06.

(c) Proof of Payment

The onus of proof always rests upon the person who commences a legal proceeding. If a tenant commences an application alleging that the landlord has collected or retained money illegally, the onus will rest upon the tenant to prove the amounts that have been paid to the landlord and the circumstances surrounding those payments. If a landlord seeks to evict a tenant for non-payment of rent or for persistent late payment of rent, the onus will rest upon the landlord to prove that rent was not paid or that it was not paid on time. Proving a negative, however, can be very difficult. How does a landlord prove that the rent was not received? The best way is through meticulous record-keeping.

A landlord is required to provide upon the tenant's request, free of charge to the tenant, a receipt for the payment of any rent, rent deposit, arrears of rent or any other amount paid to the landlord.[78] This also applies to a request by a former tenant (if the request is made within 12 months after the tenancy terminated).[79] In fact, it is an offence to fail to do so.[80] Aside from all that, it is in the *landlord's* best interests to provide receipts. A landlord who has maintained meticulous records and issued receipts for all amounts received, will be able to put forth a much more convincing case. If the tenant insists that the landlord's records are not accurate, a bald assertion to this effect will likely be insufficient to persuade the adjudicator. The tenant will likely have to produce some documentary evidence to contradict the records produced by the landlord. Proof of payment could consist of additional receipts, cancelled cheques and so forth. Since the tenant is the one asserting that a payment was made, the tenant is in the best position to offer proof of that fact.

Pursuant to s. 9 of O. Reg. 516/06, a document constitutes a receipt for the purposes of s. 109 of the Act if it includes, at a minimum:

a. the address of the rental unit to which the receipt applies;
b. the name of the tenants to whom the receipt applies;
c. the amount and date for each payment received for any rent, rent deposit, arrears of rent, or any other amount paid to the landlord and shall specify what the payment was for;
d. the name of the landlord of the rental unit; and
e. the signature of the landlord or the landlord's authorized agent.

Proving payment of rent often becomes difficult (at least for the Board Member) where the payments were allegedly made in cash and neither party has any documentary evidence to support their position. A Member might well decide such a case on the basis of the credibility of the parties. The

[78] Subsection 109(1) of the R.T.A. (formerly s. 120 of the T.P.A.).
[79] Subsection 109(2) of the R.T.A. (new).
[80] Paragraph 234(h) of the R.T.A. (formerly s. 206(2)13 of the T.P.A.).

Member may also consider upon whom rests the burden of proof. If the burden rests upon the landlord, the lack of accurate and reliable financial records may weigh heavily against the landlord. After all, this is supposed to be the landlord's business. A landlord who insists upon cash payments, refuses to issue receipts, fails to deposit the rent into a separate bank account and fails to keep proper books of accounting will not appear to the Board to be the most reliable of witnesses. Poor record-keeping on the part of the landlord often represents either sloppiness or an effort to evade having to report the rental income to Revenue Canada. In either case, the reliability of the landlord's testimony will be suspect. If, on the other hand, the onus of proving payment of rent lies on the tenant, lack of corroborating documents may prove detrimental to the tenant.[81]

7. EFFECT OF NON-DELIVERY OF TENANCY AGREEMENT

A landlord's obligations to provide a copy of the tenancy agreement (or, in certain circumstances, written notice of the landlord's address for service) is found in s. 12 of the R.T.A. (formerly s. 8 of the T.P.A.). Failing to comply with these provisions results in very serious consequences for the landlord — the tenant's obligation to pay rent is suspended and the landlord cannot require the tenant to pay rent (s. 12(4)). Note that the obligation to pay rent is suspended, not eliminated. When the landlord finally complies with the requirements of s. 12, the tenant will then owe any rent that the tenant withheld (s. 12(5)). For a more detailed analysis, please refer to "Requirements of Section 12" in Chapter 5.

8. SUBSIDIZED RENT

For a discussion of how such rents are calculated and the Board's jurisdiction to "look behind" the landlord's calculations, please see "Subsidized and Non-profit Public Housing" in Chapter 4.

Subsidized public housing is a scarce commodity. The federal government has not played an active role in this field for years. The Ontario government "downloaded" social housing onto the municipalities in the early part of this decade. Large metropolitan centres do not have nearly enough units and municipalities apparently lack the will or the resources to build new units. Public housing operators typically complain that deserving low-income individuals and families can wait five to seven years before a unit becomes available. Therefore, considerable pressure is placed upon landlords of such housing to remove any tenants who are not fulfilling their obligations or who

---

[81] See, for example, Landlord and Tenant Board File No. SWL-00436 (March 16, 2007).

are trying to "cheat" the system. In addition to the usual reasons for terminating a tenancy, in subsidized housing a landlord can also seek to terminate the tenancy of a tenant based upon misrepresentation of income (s. 60(1) of the R.T.A.) or because the tenant no longer qualifies for this type of housing (s. 58(1)2 of the R.T.A.).

9. IS THE DEPOSIT RENT?

The more prevalent view amongst Members (and the one supported by Interpretation Guideline 11) is that the deposit is not "rent" *per se*. Rather, it is security for payment of rent for the final rental period. It does not actually become rent until the last period of the tenancy. Similarly, the amount a tenant is required to pay to "top up" the rent deposit is also generally not considered rent (although there are some decisions to the contrary). For further analysis of this issue, please refer to Chapter 8 ("Topping Up" the Rent Deposit).

Pursuant to s. 106(1) of the R.T.A. (formerly s. 118(1) of the T.P.A.), a landlord can only demand a rent deposit prior to, or upon, entering into a tenancy agreement. If a landlord fails to collect a rent deposit at the beginning of the tenancy or allows the tenant to use up the deposit prior to the last rental period, the landlord will likely be unsuccessful in trying to treat the unpaid deposit as arrears of rent. This problem is discussed in detail under the heading "Collection of the Rent Deposit" in Chapter 8.

10. COMPENSATION WHEN PREMISES ARE NOT VACATED

Pursuant to s. 103 of the R.T.A. (formerly s. 45 of the T.P.A.), a landlord is entitled to compensation for the use and occupation of a rental unit by a person who is an unauthorized occupant of the unit or a tenant who does not vacate the unit after his or her tenancy is terminated by order, notice or agreement. This would include a tenant who occupies a superintendent's premises and who does not vacate the unit within seven days of notice of termination.[82]

Subsection 87(3) of the R.T.A. (formerly s. 86(2) of the T.P.A.) states that a landlord shall be entitled to compensation for the use and occupation of premises after the tenancy has been terminated. Subsection 100(3) of the R.T.A. (formerly s. 86(2.1) of the T.P.A.) provides similar relief against unauthorized occupants. Section 102 of the R.T.A. (formerly s. 89 of the T.P.A.) permits a tenant to seek compensation against an overholding subtenant.

---

[82] Pursuant to s. 98(3) of the R.T.A. (formerly s. 68(3) of the T.P.A.), but the landlord is not entitled to any rent or compensation for the first seven days after the notice is given.

Compensation is not the same as rent. Rent is the consideration given to the landlord for the right to occupy the rental unit *during* the tenancy. The amount an occupant must pay for continuing to use a rental unit after the tenancy has been terminated (but before the occupant actually vacates the unit voluntarily or by enforcement of an eviction order) is meant to compensate the landlord financially for not yet being able to rent the unit to a new tenant. The compensation is a *per diem* (i.e., daily) rate calculated based upon the lawful rent that was charged immediately prior to the termination of the tenancy.

The formulae used by the Board to calculate this rate are very simple. If the rental period is monthly, the monthly rent payable immediately prior to the termination of the tenancy is multiplied by 12 and then the resulting figure is divided by 365 to arrive at a daily rate. If the rental period is weekly, the weekly rent payable immediately prior to the termination of the tenancy is multiplied by 52 and then the resulting figure is divided by 365 to arrive at a daily rate.

11. EFFECT OF OVERHOLDING TENANT PAYING RENT

Section 45 and subsection 103(2) of the R.T.A (formerly para. 45(2)(*a*) of the T.P.A.) ensure that receipt by a landlord of rent or compensation for use or occupation from an overholding tenant does *not* waive any notice of termination or reinstate the tenancy or create a new tenancy (unless the parties agree otherwise).[83]

These provisions lessen or make no longer applicable the statement in *R.M. Ballantyne Co. v. Olympic Knit & Sportwear Ltd.*,[84] that the payment of money is an important element in presuming a new tenancy.

In view of these provisions, more than the payment of rent by an overholding tenant whose tenancy has been terminated will be required to reinstate the lease, and the tenant who wishes to assert a waiver by the landlord will have to adduce some definite evidence of the landlord's agreement to waive the notice of termination.

Such evidence was accepted in *Couotoulakis and Lines.*[85] The court decided that the landlord had given verbal assurance that if the tenants paid the arrears and costs they could remain in the premises, which they did. On accepting that evidence, the court held that a new tenancy on a monthly basis was thereby created.

---

[83] These provisions codify the principles enunciated by the Divisional Court in *Nicholson v. Michalas* (1988), 64 O.R. (2d) 238, 48 R.P.R. 280, 50 D.L.R. (4th) 170, 28 O.A.C. 142 (Ont. Div. Ct.).

[84] [1965] 2 O.R. 356 (Ont. C.A.).

[85] (October 27, 1982) (Ont. Co. Ct.).

In *Prucyk and Chaisson*,[86] the landlord had accepted post-dated cheques from the tenant to a date beyond the date of termination in a notice to terminate for own use: Part IV, s. 103. The court found that "by the landlord's conduct ... he sanctioned a tenure extending beyond the date of termination".

In Landlord and Tenant Board File No. TSL-06975-RV (December 11, 2007), after an order was issued to evict a tenant, the tenant provided a series of payments to the landlord, which the landlord accepted in partial payment of arrears of rent owing to the landlord. One of the cheques, however, indicated that it was in payment of "rent" for a month that was subsequent to the termination of the tenancy. The tenant argued before the Board that accepting payment of rent for a period after the tenancy had been terminated was evidence that the landlord had agreed to create a new tenancy. The Member ruled otherwise:

> [I]t is illogical to believe that . . .a tenant [can] purposely defeat the intention of the Act and orders of the Board by creating a new tenancy simply by adding a notation to payment made to direct a payment to a liability not yet incurred. The addition of a notation does not create any agreement and is not an acknowledgement of terms if the other party accepted the payment.

So although it seems clear from ss. 45 and 103 of the R.T.A. that a landlord can accept arrears of rent after notice of termination, it might be wise to explicitly advise the tenant (in writing) that any amount received after notice of termination is accepted in payment of past debts or for compensation for use and occupation of the rental unit (as opposed to "rent") and that acceptance of money from the tenant does not constitute a waiver by the landlord, reinstatement of the tenancy or the creation of a new tenancy. Simply advising the tenant that the money is being accepted on a "without prejudice" basis may not be sufficiently clear to protect the landlord.[87]

12. SOLICITORS' DUTIES CONCERNING VERIFICATION OF RENT

It is beyond the scope of this text to provide a comprehensive guide to solicitors acting on the purchase or sale of residential rental properties or with respect to the financing of such transactions. Nevertheless, it may be helpful for solicitors to keep the following points in mind when retained to act in such matters.

From the vendor's point of view, ideally, the property should be sold on an "as is" basis, with no representations or warranties. Such terms, however, are unlikely to be attractive to a purchaser and it is advisable that the vendor

[86] (March 24, 1982) (Ont. Co. Ct.).

[87] *Chernec v. Smith*, [1946] O.W.N. 513 (Ont. C.A.).

retain a solicitor to assist in the drafting of the agreement of purchase and sale in an effort to limit the vendor's obligations. However, given some of the new provisions of the R.T.A. (discussed below), the vendor should not be surprised that the purchaser will demand disclosure of virtually all of the vendor's business records (including all financial records) going back many years and will expect those records to have been kept meticulously.

If the purchaser is *not* buying the property as an investment (for example where a person buys a house that contains a basement apartment and intends to reside in the entire house or to allow a prescribed family member or a care giver to live in the basement apartment), the purchaser will not really care what rent is being charged for the rental unit. The purchaser's main interest will be in obtaining vacant possession of the property and the agreement of purchase and sale should require that the rental unit be vacated by a particular date as a precondition to closing the deal.[88] The purchaser can wait until he owns the property and then seek to evict the tenant but this places the burden on the purchaser and the outcome of an eviction application is never certain; if unsuccessful, the purchaser will end up with a (now hostile) tenant when he never wanted to be a landlord in the first place and had intended to use the space for other purposes.

If the purchaser is interested in the property as an investment, the stream of rental income it produces will be crucial (to both determining the price that is paid and to the attractiveness of the property as an investment). Unless the solicitor acting for the purchaser/mortgagee is very clear about limiting the scope of his or her retainer, the solicitor will have the unenviable task of confirming the rents being charged, the lawfulness of those rents, the deposits being held and discovering if there is *anything* that might now or in the foreseeable future affect the income stream.

I will now discuss some of the things that can affect the rental income generated by a residential building.

On the positive side, the purchaser will want to know not just how much rent is currently being charged, but how much rent can potentially legally be charged for each unit in the building. For most units, the rent currently being charged *is* the most that can be charged until the next guideline increase takes effect. The purchaser will want a complete file for each tenant. To confirm the lawfulness of the current rent, for each rental unit the purchaser will need

---

[88] The purchaser may need to cooperate with the vendor by having the person who will be living in the unit sign an affidavit to this effect and that person should be ready to testify at a hearing before the Landlord and Tenant Board if the current tenant refuses to leave voluntarily. The purchaser should also be made aware that should the person named in the notice of termination not actually move into the unit within a reasonable time after completion of the sale, the former tenant has up to one year to commence an application for compensation. Normally, this application would be against the former landlord (the vendor). However, the vendor could, in turn, commence legal proceedings against the purchaser for any damages that resulted from any misrepresentations made by the purchaser.

written confirmation as to the amount of rent that is actually being paid, the previous rent for this tenant, the anniversary date of the increase, a copy of the last notice of rent increase and proof of service, and a copy of any current notice of rent increase that has been served but has not yet taken effect (together with proof of service). If the landlord has offered a "prompt payment" or other discount, the purchaser will need even more detailed information about the amount and timing of all rent payments over *at least* the last one-year period.

The purchaser must be aware of any existing above-guideline rent increase (AGI) orders that have not yet been fully applied as an existing AGI will permit the purchaser (as assignee of the former landlord) to increase the rents for the affected tenants by more than the guideline amount as specified in the order.

Finally, a new landlord can apply for an above-guideline rent increase based upon work done and paid for by the previous landlord. Therefore, if the previous landlord has done some major work and has not yet commenced (or completed) an above-guideline rent increase (AGI) application, the purchaser may do so if the purchaser can obtain all of the documents and other evidence needed to support such an application. Since this has the potential of increasing the rent stream, it is worth exploring.

On the other side, many things can negatively impact on the rental revenue generated by a residential complex and the R.T.A. has made this list even longer.

First, there is the power of the Board to "freeze" rents either through an order prohibiting a rent increase (OPRI) under s. 30 of the R.T.A. or, during an AGI application, through an order that effectively stays the application pursuant to s. 126(13) of the R.T.A. Such orders can only be made where the landlord is in serious breach of the landlord's maintenance obligations. This can have a significant financial impact upon the landlord, preventing (or limiting) rent increases until the ordered work has been completed. That work could potentially be very costly. A purchaser does not want to "inherit" the previous landlord's problems. To protect itself, amongst other investigations, the purchaser should consider:

1. retaining experts to examine the building (including all rental units) and confirm that it is in good condition and that it complies with all relevant health, safety, housing and maintenance standards;
2. making enquiries with the Fire Department, Health Department, the municipal or regional property standards department and so forth to determine if any work has been ordered that remains outstanding;
3. obtaining from the vendor all records (over a reasonable period of time) relating to the maintenance of the building including any inspection reports and any written maintenance requests from tenants;
4. conducting a search (with written authorization from the current

landlord) at the Landlord and Tenant Board to obtain copies of *all* orders and pending applications affecting the property, especially any OPRI's, AGI orders, pending maintenance applications or pending AGI applications;[89] and

5. obtaining from the vendor, copies of all Tribunal/Board and court orders, information about any pending Board or court cases and appropriate warranties (to survive closing) concerning the lawfulness of the rents charged and that the vendor has disclosed all information about orders or proceedings that could affect the rent.

Second, there are new rent "roll back" provisions in AGI orders made in applications filed on or after May 3, 2006 for "costs no longer borne" (see Chapter 9). With respect to AGI orders based on capital expenditures, each order will indicate for each unit the dates by which the expenditures will have been fully recovered — the date upon which the rent must be reduced by a specified amount (if the same tenant remains in that unit on that date). Since these dates can be as much as 25 years after the date the order is issued, purchasers will need copies of all AGI orders related for the complex for the last 25 years (or at least as far back as May 2006). With respect to AGI orders based on an extraordinary increase in operating costs, new provisions require a landlord who obtains such an order to disclose its operating costs to tenants for the following five years (s. 35 of O. Reg. 516/06). If a reduction in operating costs occurs during that period, the tenants who were affected by the order may apply for a corresponding rent decrease. Thus, a purchaser should require a copy of any such order made in the last five years (under the R.T.A.) as well as the names and unit numbers of the tenants affected and proof of compliance with the disclosure requirements up to the date of closing. The purchaser should also be made aware that if such an order has been made and operating costs decrease, the Board (on application by the tenants) may order a rent reduction.

Third, there are numerous other reasons why rents can be reduced (see Chapter 10). For instance, rent reductions are automatic where property taxes have decreased by 2.5% or more.[90] Therefore, a purchaser will need to obtain property tax records for at least one or two years. Tenants can also apply for a decrease in rent where services or facilities have been reduced or discontinued. A purchaser will need to know if any orders exist requiring a temporary

---

[89] *Travers v. Reilley,* [1996] O.J. 273 (Ont. Gen. Div.). Unfortunately, it is currently unclear whether the Landlord and Tenant Board will cooperate in allowing a purchaser access to its decisions. It *may* help if the purchaser has a signed authorization from the current landlord. In any event, if the Board continues its current practice of removing all identifying information (such as the tenants' names and unit numbers) and specific financial information from its orders, access to such redacted orders will be of little, if any, value to a purchaser (see Information and Privacy Commission Order PO-2347 (Nov. 25, 2004)).

[90] See s. 131 of the R.T.A. and s. 41 of O. Reg. 516/06.

or permanent rent reduction and whether any services (etc.) have been reduced or discontinued in the previous one-year period.

Fourth, successor landlords have been held accountable for rent deposits and unpaid interest on such deposits. Thus, a purchaser will need detailed information about the deposits on hand as well as information about interest that has been paid on those deposits. These amounts will have to be adjusted for on closing.

Thus, the purchaser will need to obtain all business records from the vendor going back at least two years. For many properties this will include such things as: copies of all tenancy agreements; information about the tenants, their spouses and other occupants of the rental units; copies of any notices of rent increases together with proof of service; copies of notices/orders from government authorities concerning taxes or concerning maintenance, health or safety concerns; copies of invoices, receipts and bank records; financial statements and income tax returns; information about the deposits on hand and details about interest earned thereon and interest paid to the tenants; municipal tax records; information about any pending applications or court cases; copies of any OPRI's as well as evidence that new tenants were provided with the required information concerning any outstanding OPRI's. A purchaser will want to obtain copies of *all* AGI orders relating to the property (dating back to at least 1998) and copies of any other court and/or Tribunal/Board orders that could affect the rent that can be charged. This is just a sampling of the type of information that a purchaser will require. The purchaser should probably consider retaining an accountant with experience in property management to review all of the relevant financial records.

In drafting the agreement of purchase and sale, the purchaser's solicitor should consider including a right in favour of the purchaser to terminate the agreement if the purchaser is not satisfied that all rents currently being charged are legal, that required notices have been given and that all necessary rebates have been paid. Included would be extensive representations and warranties that will live on relating to compliance with the legislation and a statutory declaration confirming the same to be delivered on closing. Security such as vendor take-back mortgage with a right of set-off to protect the purchaser in the event that any representations are inaccurate should be considered. Documents such as those listed above should be requisitioned and delivered to the purchaser. Solicitors are warned to beware of any broad statements found in the commitment or mortgage document itself to the effect that the property complies in all ways with the statute unless the purchaser is in a position to satisfy itself as to these matters.

When acting for the vendor, the vendor should be made aware that the true value of the property will be directly related to the legality of the rents and as such the vendor should be prepared to prove the legality of the rents to the purchaser. All representations and warranties should be explained to the vendor. Ensure that the vendor has the necessary advice to determine the compliance of the property with the statutes even if that involves seeking outside assistance.

When acting for the mortgagee, the commitment should require the borrower to deliver all documentation needed to establish the legality of the rents such as registration forms, old orders, current applications and a current rent roll. It should contain representations and warranties regarding compliance with the statutes and in particular a warranty that all rents are legal and that any rebates have been repaid. Searches similar to those of the purchaser's solicitor should be conducted. The loan should become due and payable in full at the option of the lender in the event that illegal rents are discovered. Beware of broad statements in the instructions to the solicitor and in the reports on title. It is impossible for a solicitor to give an unqualified opinion on the legality of rents and compliance with the statutes. The lender's solicitor should seek instructions that the statutory declaration of the borrower will be sufficient.

Solicitors should be aware that failure to conduct the appropriate searches or obtain undertakings or to take appropriate steps limiting a retainer, may be subject to negligence proceedings.

8

Security Deposits

8 — SECURITY DEPOSITS

1. INTRODUCTION

"Security deposit" is defined in s. 105(2) of the *Residential Tenancies Act* (R.T.A.)[1] as, "money, property or a right paid or given by, or on behalf of, a tenant of a rental unit to a landlord or to anyone on the landlord's behalf to be held by or for the account of the landlord as security for the performance of an obligation or the payment of a liability of the tenant or to be returned to the tenant upon the happening of a condition." Essentially, this means that a security deposit can be anything of value[2] given to a landlord as security for a tenant's obligations under the Act or the terms of the tenancy agreement.

In general, the only security deposit that a landlord may collect is a rent deposit (s. 105(1) of the R.T.A., formerly s. 117(1) of the T.P.A.) and only if it is collected in accordance with s. 106 of the R.T.A. (formerly s. 118 of the T.P.A.). As usual however, there are exceptions to the rule.

Pursuant to para. 3 of s. 17 of O. Reg. 516/06 (formerly para. 3 of s. 29 of O.Reg. 194/98), a landlord may charge a refundable key or card deposit, not greater than the expected direct replacement costs.[3] Also, s. 2 of O. Reg 290/98 to the *Human Rights Code* entitles a landlord to require a prospective tenant to obtain a guarantee for the rent. This appears to be in addition to the landlord's right to require the tenant to pay a rent deposit. What the word "guarantee" means in this context is not entirely clear. It could simply mean that the landlord can, without violating Ontario's *Human Rights Code*, insist that a prospective tenant have someone with substantial income or assets or a better credit history guarantee the tenant's financial obligations to the landlord. If this is all it means, there is no real impact upon the provisions of ss. 105 and 106 of the R.T.A. (formerly ss. 117 and 118 of the T.P.A.). In

---

[1] Formerly, s. 117(2) of the *Tenant Protection Act* (T.P.A.).

[2] Including services performed by the tenant for the landlord: *Marignani v. Randall* (1995), 1995 CarswellOnt 587 (Ont. Gen. Div.).

[3] An automatic garage door opener is akin to a key or access card: *West v. Rockcliffe* (Dec. 15, 1998), SOT-00166 (Ont. Rental Housing Trib.).

2960 Don Mills Rd. Apts. v. Hitchcock,[4] however, the landlord attempted to rely upon this regulation made under the *Human Rights Code* as a legal justification for forcing the tenant to provide an irrevocable bank letter of credit in favour of the landlord as *additional* security and in an amount that far exceeded one month's rent; the Tribunal disapproved of this attempt to circumvent the provisions of s. 118 of the T.P.A. and found, on the facts of this case, that the irrevocable letter of credit did not constitute a "guarantee" for rent.

Since the only permitted type of deposit (other than a refundable key deposit) is a *rent* deposit, any other security requested by a landlord is illegal. These include security deposits for damage[5] and for administrative charges.[6]

Failing to comply with s. 105 or with many of the provisions of s. 106 of the R.T.A. not only leaves the landlord potentially liable to the tenant in question, it also leaves the landlord vulnerable to prosecution for committing offences under s. 234 of the R.T.A. (punishable, upon conviction, by a fine of up to $25,000 for an individual and up to $100,000 for a corporation).

2. PRE-PAYMENT OF RENT

Avoidance of the restrictions on security deposits was achieved in a British Columbia case: *R. v. Benetos*.[7] The British Columbia statute has a more detailed definition of a security deposit than the Ontario statute and includes "an advance payment of more than one-half of one month's rent". The rent was $450 per month. The landlord requested and received at the outset $675, i.e., the first month's rent of $450 and $225, "as a rent payment to be applied on account of the rent for the final month of the above term". The majority judgment of the British Columbia Court of Appeal held that the $225 was merely an advance payment on account of rent, being not more than one-half, and a bit inexplicably stated that it was not given as a security, and went on to say that once it was paid "it became [the landlord's] to do with as he wished". While this interpretation is hardly in accord with the intent of the British Columbia or Ontario statutes, it is authority that an advance payment even referable to the last month of the tenancy is not simply a security deposit.

---

4 (October 3, 2001), TNL-27583-RV, 2001 CarswellOnt 6310 (Ont. Rental Housing Trib.), overturning (July 12, 2001), TNL-27583 and referring to TNT-01688.

5 *Zaker v. Harripersad* (September 28, 1981), McNeely J. (Ont. Co. Ct.). And Landlord and Tenant Board File No. TST-02054 (Jan. 7, 2009)

6 *Kelly v. Carslake* (1989), 1989 CarswellOnt 2569 (Ont. Prov. Ct.) and *690981 Ontario Ltd. v. Park* (January 5, 1993), Doc. No. 92-LT-42153, 92-LT-44157 (Ont. Gen. Div.).

7 (1978), 5 R.P.R. 44 (B.C. C.A.).

Even though the above case has become authority for an advance payment not being a security deposit, landlords should not put too much reliance on that way of avoiding the restrictions on security deposits.

A later Ontario case, *Gallant v. Veltrusy Enterprises Ltd.*,[8] questioned and distinguished *R. v. Benetos*.[9] The lease in question is fairly typical when a landlord rents to university students with the rent for a one-year term pro-rated over eight months to coincide with the academic year. Thus the rent for each of the eight months was more than what the monthly rental would be if it was spread over twelve months. The tenant's argument was that, accordingly, each month's rent included an amount which was, in effect, a security deposit and the amount required to be deposited for the last month of the eight months term was a security deposit for a larger amount "than the rent for a rent period not exceeding one month": s. 82 of Part IV.[10] The trial judge held that the additional amount each month resulting from the pro-rating was prepayment of rent and not a series of security deposits, but that the amount required as a deposit was a security deposit for more than one month's rent and the difference must be refunded. Also, in that case a deposit of $10 was required for extra keys. This was held to be a security deposit and had to be refunded.

The *Veltrusy* case was appealed.[11] The court decided, without dealing with the merits, that the County Court judge did not have jurisdiction to determine the rights of the landlord and tenant. It would have been a help to have commented on the merits.

Prepayment of rent in lieu of or in addition to a security deposit of rent was not permitted in *Boyd v. Earl & Jennie Lohn Ltd.*[12] The court stated that s. 82 of Part IV was enacted to prevent undue hardship to those tenants who required housing accommodation but could not afford to come forward with large amounts of money in advance. At the same time it provides landlords with a specific sum as security against rent. A requirement in a lease for the advance payment of pro-rated rent is contrary to this section and is thus not binding on a tenant.

The consensus of the Rental Housing Tribunal was that collecting pre-paid rent constituted an unlawful attempt to collect greater security than was permitted under ss. 117 and 118 of the T.P.A. A number of landlords who collected pre-paid rent were also convicted under s. 206(2)10 of the T.P.A. and, as a result, had to pay substantial fines (see Chapter 19).

More recently, the Ontario Divisional Court has disapproved of a landlord of residential premises collecting prepaid rent in *Li v. Sympthony Square*

8 — SECURITY DEPOSITS

---

[8] (1980), 28 O.R. (2d) 349 (Ont. Co. Ct.), reversed (1981), 32 O.R. (2d) 716 (Ont. C.A.).

[9] (1978), 5 R.P.R. 44 (B.C. C.A.).

[10] In this instance and hereinafter, the phrase "Part IV" refers to Part IV of the *Landlord and Tenant Act*, R.S.O. 1990, c. L.7.

[11] (1980), 28 O.R. (2d) 349 (Ont. Co. Ct.), reversed (1981), 32 O.R. (2d) 716 (Ont. C.A.).

[12] (1984), 47 O.R. (2d) 111 (Ont. H.C.).

Ltd.[13] and upheld the order that the landlord pay to the former tenants general damages (including interest on the prepaid rent), punitive damages and costs.

Also, a landlord and the landlord's agent have recently been successfully prosecuted for collecting a year's rent in advance. This case was heard in the Provincial Offences Court in Newmarket on October 10, 2008, before Justice of the Peace Douglas W. Clark. The owner of a single-family dwelling hired an agent to find a suitable tenant. The agent found a prospective tenant but then discovered that this prospective tenant was unemployed. The owner advised the agent that, if the prospective tenant paid one year's rent in advance, he could rent the property and he would get a reduction in the monthly rent (down from $2,400 to $2,000). The agent instructed the tenant to make the funds payable to his corporation. The tenant paid first and last month's rent and a further, separate payment of $20,000 to the corporation in question. The tenant took possession of the property. Within about six weeks, the tenant was advised that the owner had not been making the mortgage payments and the mortgagee was looking to the tenant to pay monthly rent directly to the bank. Since the tenant had already paid the rent for a year, he refused to pay the bank. The bank made an application to the Landlord and Tenant Board seeking to have the tenant evicted for non-payment of rent. The Board found in the tenant's favour and dismissed the bank's application.

Charges were then laid against the owner, her agent and the corporation in question pursuant to clause 234(d) of the R.T.A. The owner failed to appear at the trial. The agent appeared on behalf of himself and the corporation. He argued that the $20,000 was "pre-paid rent" and did not fall within the definition of "security deposit". He also argued that the corporation was not involved with this tenancy – it was merely a "banking convenience". The Court found that pre-paid rent is a form of security deposit and that the corporation was involved in the unlawful transaction. All three defendants were convicted. The corporation was fined $10,000 and both individuals were fined $2,500 (for a total penalty of $15,000).

I would, therefore, recommend caution to any landlord considering demanding or accepting pre-paid rent.

There is also risk to a tenant in pre-paying rent. Where the tenancy agreement does not provide for it, pre-paying the rent will not be considered to be a covenant that runs with the land (see "Responsibilities of Assignee of Landlord" at end of this Chapter) and, therefore, will not bind a subsequent landlord or a mortgagee who takes over possession of the rental complex. A tenant who pre-pays the rent in such circumstances runs the risk of being ordered to pay the rent again to the assignee of the original landlord.[14]

---

[13] (2007), 2007 CarswellOnt 1059 (Ont. Div. Ct.).

[14] Landlord and Tenant Board File No. CEL-11712 (Aug. 25, 2008).

3. RENT DEPOSITS

Sections 106 and 107 of the R.T.A. (formerly ss. 118 and 118.1 of the T.P.A.) contain the following provisions relating to rent deposits:

1. a landlord can only demand a rent deposit prior to or upon entering into a tenancy agreement (s. 106(1));
2. the rent deposit cannot exceed the lesser of the amount of rent for one rent period and the amount of rent for one month (s. 106(2));
3. if the rent increases, the landlord may require the tenant to "top up" the rent deposit (s. 106(3));
4. a mortgagee in possession cannot ask for a new rent deposit if one was already paid to the mortgagor (s. 106(4));
5. the landlord shall pay interest to the tenant annually on the rent deposit (s. 106(6));
6. the landlord may use this interest to "top up" the rent deposit (s. 106(7));
7. if the landlord fails to pay this interest when it is due, the tenant may deduct the appropriate amount from a subsequent rent payment (s. 106(9));
8. the landlord shall apply a rent deposit for (and only for) rent owing to the landlord for the last rent period before the tenancy terminates (s. 106(10)); and
9. if a landlord collects a rent deposit from a prospective tenant and then does not give vacant possession of the unit to the prospective tenant, the landlord must return the rent deposit (unless the tenant agrees to take a different rental unit) (s. 107).

(a) Collection of the Rent Deposit

Pursuant to s. 106(1) of the R.T.A. (formerly s. 118(1) of the T.P.A.), a landlord can only demand a rent deposit prior to, or upon, entering into a tenancy agreement. This seems straightforward. Also, a new landlord cannot insist on a security deposit from an existing tenant: *673078 Ont. Ltd. v. Mandowsky*.[15]

In my experience, there are two situations where landlords fail to properly protect their interests in this regard. In both situations, the landlord may suffer as a result of an act of kindness.

In the first typical scenario, the tenant does not have quite enough money to pay first and last month's rent prior to the date the tenancy is to commence or the tenant asks to be allowed to move into the unit early (and before first and last month's rent have been paid in full). The tenant promises to pay the

[15] (1987), 1987 CarswellOnt 3047 (Ont. Dist. Ct.).

balance of the deposit at a later date (or over a period of time). The landlord agrees and gives possession of the unit to the tenant. The tenant then fails to pay the deposit as agreed. Once the tenancy has commenced, the landlord can no longer demand payment of the rent deposit. If a landlord wishes to protect himself, the landlord should insist on receiving two months' rent before handing over the keys to the unit. At the very least, if a landlord is inclined to give the tenant a "break", the landlord should obtain the full rent deposit and allow the tenant some additional time to pay the rent owing for the first month of the tenancy (and ensure that it is explicit how the money is being applied). At least in this way, if the tenant defaults in the payment of the first month's rent, the landlord has the potential remedy of evicting the tenant for non-payment of rent. That remedy does not exist for non-payment of a rent deposit.

In the second typical scenario, at some point after the tenancy has commenced, the tenant fails to pay the usual monthly rental payment. Either through ignorance or a desire to assist the tenant, the landlord uses the rent deposit to cover the rent payment that the tenant has just missed. If the tenant later replaces the deposit, the landlord has not really suffered any prejudice. If, however, the tenant is unable or unwilling to do so, the landlord has no right to commence an application for this money. By the terms of s. 106(1), a landlord may "require a tenant to pay a rent deposit . . . if the landlord does so *on or before entering into the tenancy agreement*". Furthermore, pursuant to s. 106(10), a landlord *shall* apply a rent deposit in payment of the rent for the last rent period before the tenancy is terminated. A landlord has no right to use the rent deposit for any period other than the last rental period. A landlord who uses a rent deposit to cover rent owing for any period other than the last one, may have lost that deposit forever.

(b) Amount of the Rent Deposit

Pursuant to s. 106(2) of the R.T.A. (formerly s. 118(2) of the T.P.A.), the amount of a rent deposit shall not be more than the lesser of the amount of rent for one rent period and the amount of rent for one month. Therefore, it is not strictly true that the rent deposit will always be one month's rent. In the case of a daily tenancy, the maximum rent deposit would be equivalent to the rent for one day. In a weekly tenancy, it would be one week's rent. The usual amount for a rent deposit (and the absolute maximum amount that a landlord may require) is one month's rent. In *Trozzo v. Cerullo et al.*,[16] the landlord charged first and last month's rent plus an extra deposit of $300; the Tribunal ordered the return of this illegal extra deposit.

---

[16] (Feb. 25, 1999), TNT-00305 (Ont. Rental Housing Trib.).

Similarly, in Landlord and Tenant Board File Nol TST-02228 (Feb. 25, 2009), where a landlord collected first and last months' rent plus an additional amount equal to one month's rent, the landlord was ordered to return this illegal additional security.

(c) "Topping Up" the Rent Deposit

Pursuant to s. 106(3) of the R.T.A. (formerly s. 118(3) of the T.P.A.), if the lawful rent increases after a tenant has paid a rent deposit, the landlord may require the tenant to pay an additional amount to increase the rent deposit up to the amount permitted by s. 106(2). In other words, as the rent goes up each year, the rent deposit should also be increased so that it continues to represent the rent for one rental period.[17]

Under the T.P.A. there was a problem, however, because the T.P.A. provided no clear method for landlords to enforce this right. Some landlords used the interest they owed to the tenant to "top up" the deposit. Others simply allowed the deposit to remain the same, even though the rent increased over time and, thus, the deposit no longer represented the rent for one rental period. Still other landlords commenced applications against tenants for payment of the shortfall in the deposit, on the premise that the shortfall represented arrears of rent. The difficult issue in those cases is whether failing to pay a portion of a rent deposit constitutes a failure to pay "rent".

Two schools of thought surround this issue. One view is that a tenant is legally obliged to "top up" the rent deposit and that this is part of the consideration the tenant is required to give for the right to occupy the unit. By the definition of "rent" contained in the T.P.A., the "top up" can be considered rent and failing to pay this amount does create arrears of rent for which the landlord may bring an application under s. 86 (and, potentially, s. 69 for termination of the tenancy).[18] The more prevalent view amongst Tribunal members (and the one supported by the Tribunal's Interpretation Guideline 11), however, was to the contrary. According to this interpretation, since the deposit is intended to represent security for payment of rent that is not yet due (i.e., rent for the last period of the tenancy), no part of it can be said to be in arrears; the deposit is security for rent and does not actually become rent until the last period of the tenancy. The amount necessary to "top up" the deposit may be a debt owed to the landlord but that does not make it rent.[19]

---

[17] *Cando Property Management v. Wilson* (1983), 44 O.R. (2d) 123 (Ont. Div. Ct.).

[18] See *549 North Service Road v. Sills et al.* (Oct. 27, 1998), CEL-01763 (Ont. Rental Housing Trib.). See also decisions TSL-20860, *Dunelm Holdings v. Beals* (Nov. 22, 2000), TEL-15854, 2000 CarswellOnt 6398 (Ont. Rental Housing Trib.) and TSL-23227.

[19] See *Medallion Properties Inc. v. Otteanu* (Nov. 19, 1998), TSL-03727 (Ont. Rental Housing Trib.); *Medallion Properties Inc. v. Dempster* (May 29, 2001), TNL-26550, 2001

The Legislature has attempted to resolve this issue by adding subsection 106(7) to the R.T.A. This permits a landlord to use the interest payable on the deposit (see "Interest on the Rent Deposit" below) to "top up" the rent deposit. Since, under the R.T.A. provisions, the annual guideline increase will always be the same as the interest rate applicable to deposits, the interest that would otherwise be payable to the tenant will usually be sufficient to cover the amount needed to "top up" the deposit.

(d) Interest on the Rent Deposit

Under the *Landlord and Tenant Act* and the *Tenant Protection Act*, landlords were required to pay interest on rent deposits at the rate of 6% per year.[20] The rate of interest had been fixed at this rate for decades. Under the R.T.A., the rate of interest shall now fluctuate with the change in the Consumer Price Index for Ontario.[21] Pursuant to s. 106(6) of the R.T.A., a landlord of a rental unit shall pay interest to the tenant annually on the amount of the rent deposit "at a rate equal to the guideline determined under s. 120 that is in effect at the time payment becomes due".

In the one-year period following the date of proclamation of the R.T.A. (January 31, 2007), the interest payable to a tenant on his or her deposit will be a hybrid amount based upon the following:

1. interest payable in respect of the period ending before January 31, 2007 shall be based on 6% per year;
2. interest payable in respect of the period commencing on or after January 31, 2007 shall be based on the published guideline amount.

This transitional provision (s. 106(8) of the R.T.A.) is poorly drafted because for most tenancies (which are monthly), the period ending before January 31, 2007 is December 2006 and the period commencing on or after January 31, 2007 is February 2007, which begs the question, "What interest rate is applicable to January 2007?"

In Landlord and Tenant Board File No. TST-01025 (January 30, 2008), the Member resolved this issue by awarding interest on the rent deposit at 6% up to and including January 30, 2007, and at 2.6% from January 31, 2007, onwards.

The guideline amount for 2007 (and, therefore, the rate for calculating interest on rent deposits for the period after January 30, 2007) was 2.6%. The

---

CarswellOnt 6368 (Ont. Rental Housing Trib.); *6161/6171 Bathurst Street Prt. v. Levy* (Mar. 27, 2000), TNL-13960, [2000] O.R.H.T.D. No. 47, 2000 CarswellOnt 6358 (Ont. Rental Housing Trib.).

[20] At times, this interest rate (6%) was well below the average return that could be earned on a typical bank savings account and at other times (especially in recent years) it was above the going bank rate.

[21] See s. 120 of the R.T.A.

guideline amount for 2008 was 1.4%. The guideline amount for 2009 is 1.8%. The guideline amount for 2010 is 2.1%. For a complete listing of all guideline amounts back to 1975, please refer to Appendix 14.

(e) Applying or Refunding the Rent Deposit

Pursuant to s. 106(10) of the R.T.A. (formerly s. 118(8) of the T.P.A.), a landlord shall apply a rent deposit that a tenant has paid to the landlord or to a former landlord in payment of the rent for the last rent period before the tenancy terminates.

There is no specified procedure for retention or repayment. Using the deposit for the last month's rent is not a problem. If the lease is terminated prior to the last month by the landlord or the tenant, the landlord must apply the security deposit for the rent for the last rent period immediately preceding the termination of the tenancy. If the rent has already been paid for that month, the security deposit should be repaid to the tenant, with interest and, if it is not repaid, it is an offence (s. 234(f) of the R.T.A., formerly s. 206(2)12 of the T.P.A.). The tenant can also commence an application under s. 135 of the R.T.A. (formerly s. 144 of the T.P.A.) for an order for the payment of money illegally retained by the landlord.

The landlord cannot hold the security deposit as a set-off for damages: *Zaker v. Harripersad.*[22] The rent deposit can only be used for one thing — payment of rent for the final rental period. If the rent for the final rental period has already been paid or if the tenancy never commenced (in which case there can be no rent owing), the rent deposit must be returned to the tenant.

Pursuant to s. 107 of the R.T.A. (formerly s. 118.1 of the T.P.A.), a landlord shall repay the amount received as a rent deposit in respect of a rental unit if vacant possession of the rental unit is not given to the prospective tenant.[23] Where the landlord cannot or will not deliver possession of the unit to a prospective tenant, clearly that tenant is entitled to the return of his or her deposit. In fact, in such circumstances, it is an offence for the landlord to retain the deposit.[24] The landlord may also be held responsible in an action for damages for the financial losses suffered by the prospective tenant in finding alternative accommodations[25] and, possibly, for the stress and mental suffering of the prospective tenant.[26]

8 — SECURITY DEPOSITS

---

[22] (Sept. 28, 1981), McNeely J. (Ont. Co. Ct.). See also *Saunders v. Webster*, (January 30, 2003), TST-05105-RV (Ont. Rental Housing Trib.) and Landlord and Tenant Board File No. TST-02222 (Feb. 11, 2009).

[23] Unless the tenant decides to take a different unit in the complex (s. 107(2)).

[24] Pursuant to s. 234(g) of the R.T.A. (formerly para. 206(2)12.1 of the T.P.A.). Please refer to Chapter 19 for a more detailed discussion of the various offences related to deposits.

[25] *Tolgyesi v. Freure Homes Ltd.* (1987), 1987 CarswellOnt 2825 (Ont. Dist. Ct.).

[26] *Hazlewood v. Hazen* (1985), 30 A.C.W.S. (2d) 179 (Ont. Dist. Ct.).

The tenancy commences on the day that the tenant is entitled to take possession of the rental unit, whether or not the tenant actually does take possession (s. 13 of the R.T.A., formerly s. 9 of the T.P.A.). Once the tenancy has commenced, the tenant is responsible for rent and may only terminate the tenancy in accordance with the Act.[27]

In Landlord and Tenant Board File No. SOT-00474 (Aug. 3, 2007), the tenancy was to commence on July 1, 2007. The tenant paid a deposit when he signed the application. The tenant never moved in. On July 3, 2007, the tenant informed the landlord that he no longer required the rental unit and requested the return of his rent deposit. The landlord refused, taking the position that the tenancy had commenced on July 1 and that it was too late to find a tenant for July. The landlord did find a new tenant for the unit as of August 1 and applied the rent deposit to cover the rent owing for July. The tenant commenced an application for the refund of his rent deposit. The Member held that the tenant could not rely on s. 107 of the R.T.A. since the landlord had not prevented him from taking possession of the unit. Pursuant to s. 13 of the R.T.A., the tenancy commenced on July 1, whether or not the tenant actually occupied the unit on that date. Therefore, the landlord was entitled to apply the deposit to the rent owing for July and the tenant's application was dismissed. A similar decision was reached in Landlord and Tenant Board File No. TNT-01319 (Jan. 9, 2009).

Of course, a tenant may be released from the obligations of a tenancy agreement and may therefore be entitled to a refund of the rent deposit if the tenant can establish (on application to the Board) that there has been a fundamental breach of the tenancy agreement.[28]

Where the unit is habitable but a few things require repair, the tenant will be expected to take possession and give the landlord an opportunity to rectify the problems.[29] A tenant who simply walks away from the tenancy because she does not think the unit is in good condition risks being held responsible for the rent for that unit until the landlord is able to find a new tenant or until the date that the tenancy could have been terminated had the tenant delivered a valid notice of termination, whichever comes first.

What if the tenant advises the landlord of a change of heart *prior* to the commencement of the tenancy? Section 107 of the R.T.A. is silent on the consequences of an anticipatory breach by the tenant. Since s. 107 only refers

---

[27] I.e., with the agreement of the landlord, with proper notice to the landlord or with an order from the Board. See Chapter 6.

[28] See *Au et al. v. Gracile Productions Inc.* (Oct. 18, 2001), TNT-02189 (Ont. Rental Housing Trib.).

[29] In *Rojas et al. v. Roman Group Properties* (Feb. 27, 2004), TNT-03946 (Ont. Rental Housing Trib.) the tenants paid a deposit and were given possession of the unit. Shortly after receiving the keys, the tenants changed their minds and advised the landlord they would not be taking the unit. They sought the return of their deposit. Since the tenancy had commenced and there was no fundamental breach by the landlord, the tenants' application was dismissed.

to repayment of the rent deposit where possession of the unit is not *given* to the tenant, where it is the tenant's decision not to take possession, it could be inferred that the tenant is not entitled to the return of the deposit. This is the approach taken by a Member in Landlord and Tenant Board File No. TST-00935-RV (April 28, 2008), in which it was held that s. 107(1) was intended to address the situation where a landlord refused or was unable to deliver vacant possession to a tenant on the date set for commencement of the tenancy and was not applicable where a tenant attempted to repudiate the agreement prior to its commencement.

Cases from the Rental Housing Tribunal, however, suggest that the Members generally did not adopt such an interpretation under similar provisions of the *Tenant Protection Act*. Instead, the Tribunal Members focused upon the response of the landlord to the anticipatory breach of contract by the prospective tenant to decide whether or not the landlord was entitled to retain the monies.

In most cases, the landlord accepts the prospective tenant's repudiation of the contract. The contract is then considered to be at an end and the landlord is free to sue (in court) for any damages that flow from the tenant's breach of contract. Since, however, the repudiation of the contract is accepted prior to the commencement of the tenancy, the tenancy never actually starts and no "rent" is owing to the landlord. In such cases, the landlord must refund any rent deposit collected from the prospective tenant and cannot retain the deposit to offset other financial losses the landlord may have suffered as a result of the breach (such as the cost of advertising for a new tenant, etc.).[30]

Similarly, where the landlord imposes a condition precedent in the contract that the prospective tenant is not able to satisfy and the landlord is not prepared to waive, the tenancy never commences and the landlord will have to refund the deposit and pursue a claim for damages in court. In *Benedetto v. Clenland*,[31] the landlord obtained a deposit from these prospective tenants (and advised the tenants that it was "non-refundable") and insisted that they obtain a guarantor. They could not obtain a guarantor so no lease was signed and the tenants asked for their deposit back. The landlord refused. The Tribunal concluded that since vacant possession of the unit was not given to the tenants, the rent deposit had to be refunded. On appeal by the landlord, the Divisional Court upheld the decision of the Tribunal.

It is not entirely clear how the Landlord and Tenant Board will deal with cases in which the prospective tenant repudiates the agreement prior to the commencement of the tenancy.

---

[30] *Abdulkarimov v. Melnyk* (Jan. 13, 2003), TNT-03161 (Ont. Rental Housing Trib.); *Wang v. Lee* (April 7, 1999), TNT-00383, 1999 CarswellOnt 5799 (Ont. Rental Housing Trib.); *Bousserghine v. Thornton* (Sept. 7, 2001), TET-02007, [2001] O.R.H.T.D. No. 115, 2001 CarswellOnt 6300 (Ont. Rental Housing Trib.); *Liao v. Cheng*, (October 4, 2005), TST-08392 (Ont. Rental Housing Trib.).

[31] (September 8, 2005), No. 325/05 (Ont. Div. Ct.), unreported, re TST-08299.

In one case,[32] the Board held that the tenants were entitled to the return of the rent deposit where the tenants revoked their offer to lease the rental unit before their offer had been accepted by the landlord (and, hence, no tenancy agreement existed).

Based on my review of the decisions that have been released by the Board, it appears that the Board Members have not yet reached a consensus on this issue.

Some Members are taking the position that if the tenancy never commences, there can be no rent owing and, since the deposit can only be used to pay rent, it must be returned (leaving the landlord free to sue for any damages that the landlord suffered as a result of the tenant's anticipatory breach of contract).[33]

Other Members are taking different approaches.

One position is that, since s. 107 of the R.T.A. only requires the landlord to return the deposit where vacant possession of the rental unit is not *given* to the tenant, if the unit is available and the tenant chooses not to take it, the landlord has no legal obligation (at least, not pursuant to s. 107) to repay the deposit.[34]

Another position is that the landlord is not obliged to accept the repudiation, can deem the tenancy to commence on the date the tenant could have taken possession of the unit and can then treat the unit as if the tenant abandoned the unit without giving proper notice of termination (although it is not entirely clear to me how a tenant can abandon a unit that they never occupied). In this way, the landlord can apply the deposit to the rent owing.[35]

Finally, there are Members who see nothing wrong in the landlord using the deposit monies to offset against the damages the landlord has suffered (in lost rent and expenses related to finding a new tenant) as a result of the prospective tenant's unilateral breach of contract.[36]

(f) Responsibility of Assignee of Landlord

Prepayment of rent to a landlord does entail some risk for a tenant. In *Cavell v. Canada Dry Ginger Ale Ltd.*,[37] it was stated:

---

[32] Landlord and Tenant Board File Number SOT-01293 (July 18, 2008).

[33] Landord and Tenant Board File No. NOT-00031 (March 19, 2007) and Landlord and Tenant Board File No. SWT-00004 (March 19, 2007).

[34] Landlord and Tenant Board File Number TST-00935-RV (April 28, 2008).

[35] Landlord and Tenant Board File No. TNT-01319 (Jan. 9, 2009). Presumably, the maximum amount of rent arrears to which the deposit could be applied in such situations would be the lesser of the maximum amount permitted under s. 88 of the R.T.A. and the rent actually owing for the period up to the date the landlord is able to re-rent the unit.

[36] Landlord and Tenant Board File No. NOT-00006 (March 2, 2007) and Landlord and Tenant Board File No. TST-00028 (March 21, 2007).

[37] [1945] O.W.N. 799 (Ont. Co. Ct.).

> Payment of rent before it is due is not fulfilment of the obligation imposed by the covenant to pay rent, but is ... an advance to the landlord ... Rent paid to the landlord before it is due is paid at the tenant's risk in case of a change of ownership.

The *Cavell* decision was followed in a residential tenancy case, *Chiappino v. Bishop*,[38] which also followed *Dollar Land Corp. v. Solomon*.[39] A new owner who was unaware that the tenant had paid a security deposit to a previous owner was not liable to the tenant for the security deposit. These decisions, however, fail to make a distinction between prepayment of rent and providing security for the future payment of rent.

In an earlier edition of this book it was suggested that s. 88 of Part IV of the *Landlord and Tenant Act*, now s. 18 of the R.T.A., probably applied to "covenants concerning things related to the rented premises run with the land". Also, "landlord" includes assigns: s. 1(*b*) of Part IV, now s. 2(1) of the R.T.A.; and by s. 82 of Part IV, now s. 106(10) of the R.T.A., there is the statutory obligation that the security deposit "shall be applied in payment of the rent for the last rent period", and the assignee of the reversion must comply with that obligation, and the new landlord, an assignee of the reversion, would be liable for the security deposit to the tenant.

This was confirmed in *Spencer Properties Ltd. v. Zrebiec*.[40] The judge stated that by s. 82 of Part IV, "the security deposit shall be applied in payment of the rent for the last rent period immediately preceding the termination of the tenancy" and this amounts to an implied covenant by the landlord, and by s. 88 of Part IV, runs with the land, binding the new landlord, the assignee. This is a fairer result, obviously, for the tenant. The judge pointed out that the assignee was obliged to inquire about security deposits.

The *Spencer* case, *supra*, was followed in *Top Link Investments Ltd. v. Hutchinson*,[41] holding that a mortgagee in possession or a purchaser from a mortgagee in possession is obligated to apply any security deposits paid to the original landlord pursuant to s. 82 of Part IV toward the payment of the last month's rent prior to the termination of the tenancy. Apart from the judicial interpretation of the applicable sections in Part IV, the equities were also stated. "The purchaser is in the best position to include the security deposits in the negotiations of the purchase price. If the purchaser does not, it is his or her own fault and so should suffer the consequences of absorbing the loss of the security deposits." Otherwise it would not be equitable for tenants.

Subsection 106(4) of the R.T.A. (formerly s. 118(4) of the T.P.A.) provides that a new landlord of a rental unit or a person who is deemed to be a

---

[38] (1988), 49 R.P.R. 218 (Ont. Dist. Ct.).

[39] [1963] 2 O.R. 269 (Ont. H.C.).

[40] (1992), 1992 CarswellOnt 1760 (Ont. Gen. Div.).

[41] (1997), 37 O.R. (3d) 107 (Ont. Gen. Div.).

landlord under s. 47(1) of the *Mortgages Act* (i.e., a mortgagee in possession) shall not require a tenant to pay a deposit if the tenant has already paid a rent deposit to the prior landlord of the rental unit.

Subsection 106(5) of the R.T.A. (formerly subsection 118(5) of the T.P.A.) provides an exception to the usual rule that the new landlord cannot require a deposit where one was paid to the previous landlord; where the tenant has received some or all of the rent deposit from the proceeds of the sale of the property, the new landlord may require the tenant to turn over such proceeds in order to bring the deposit back up to the correct amount. Situations where tenants receive proceeds from the sale of a rental property are likely to be extremely rare.

This illustrates the importance to both the landlord and tenant of keeping accurate written records and the importance to a purchaser of a rental complex to use due diligence in obtaining all relevant information about the vendor's accounting, including information about all rent deposits collected by the vendor. The vendor will have to give credit to the purchaser in the statement of adjustments for the amount of the outstanding security deposits together with accrued interest thereon. The important thing is that the purchaser, assignee of the reversion, should be aware that security deposits will have to be applied against the rents or may have to be repaid to the tenants. As a tenant can claim to have the security deposit applied to the rent by an assignee of the reversion, a purchaser from the original landlord, i.e., assignee, should at the time of the purchase satisfy by due inquiry as to what security deposits are outstanding. A purchaser of an apartment building or other multiple rental accommodation should obtain from the landlord a statement of security deposits held by the landlord and the accrued interest thereon and reimburse the landlord for the same in the statement of adjustments. It should be further noted that in the *Spencer Properties* case, *supra*, the new landlord purchased from a second mortgagee selling under power of sale. Nevertheless the implied covenant ran with the land and as stated, the assignee, the purchaser, became liable to the tenants for the security deposits which had been paid to the previous owner as mortgagor.

Obviously, a mortgagee in possession is at somewhat of a disadvantage because the mortgagor is unlikely to cooperate by providing information and documentation and the information provided by the tenants themselves (if they are willing to provide any information at all to the mortgagee) may not be reliable. The best evidence that a tenant can produce to verify that a deposit was paid to the landlord will usually consist of a written acknowledgement of this fact contained in the application form or the tenancy agreement, a receipt signed and dated by the landlord who received the deposit or a cancelled cheque.

9

Rent Increases

1. INTRODUCTION

When rent controls were first introduced in Ontario in 1975, they weren't expected to last longer than 18 months. Now, over 30 years and six statutes later, it appears that rent regulation, in one form or another, is here to stay. This chapter will address some of the more significant rules relating to rent increases. I will explore the rules relating to rent decreases in Chapter 10.

(a) History of Rent Control

Rent regulation was originally introduced in Ontario by the *Residential Premises Rent Review Act, 1975*.[1] The purpose of the Act was to limit the amount by which landlords would be permitted to increase the rent for a residential rental unit and restrict increases to once in each 12-month period.

At the same time, security of tenure was introduced in 1975 by an amendment to the *Landlord and Tenant Act*.[2] Although rent regulation and security of tenure were dealt with in separate statutes and have their own distinctive purposes they were also interrelated. Without rent regulation, security of tenure would be ineffective. Through excessive rent increases, a landlord could obtain possession from tenants unable to pay. By the same token, without security of tenure it is unlikely that tenants would feel comfortable policing their landlord's compliance with rent regulation guidelines.

When first enacted, the *Residential Premises Rent Review Act, 1975* provided for its repeal on August 1, 1977. This date was extended by a series of amendments until November 30, 1979, when it was replaced by the *Residential Tenancies Act, 1979*.[3]

---

[1] S.O. 1975 (2nd Sess.), c. 12.

[2] S.O. 1975 (2nd Sess.), c. 13. Security of tenure was continued under the *Tenant Protection Act, 1997*, and currently, under the *Residential Tenancies Act, 2006*.

[3] S.O. 1979, c. 78, then R.S.O. 1990, c. R.29.

The *Residential Tenancies Act, 1979* was intended to be a detailed legislative code covering all aspects of the law relating to residential landlords and tenants. A Residential Tenancy Commission was to replace the County and District Courts as the sole tribunal for resolution of all manner of disputes.

In response to a massive sale of the residential rental holdings of the Cadillac Fairview Corporation and the potential of significant rent increases to be passed through to tenants, further limits on rent increases were introduced with the *Residential Complexes Financing Costs Restraint Act, 1982*[4] amending the *Residential Tenancies Act*. The *Residential Tenancies Act* was further amended in 1985 limiting annual guideline rent increases to 4%, a reduction from 6%.

In 1986, the *Residential Tenancies Act* and its amendments were replaced by the *Residential Rent Regulation Act, 1986*.[5] This Act broadened the scope of rent regulation to include virtually all privately owned residential rental units. Under the previous legislation, only rental units situated in a building, no part of which was occupied before January 1, 1976, were covered by rent regulation. Now "post-1975" rental units, that is, those first occupied since December 31, 1975, were subject to rent regulation beginning August 1, 1985. Further limitations on rent increases that could be approved on landlord applications were imposed by the *Residential Rent Regulation Amendment Act, 1991*.[6]

On August 10, 1992, the *Rent Control Act, 1992*[7] replaced the *Residential Rent Regulation Act, 1986*. The *Rent Control Act, 1992* established an absolute upper limit by which maximum rents could be increased when a landlord applies for a rent increase above the annual percentage guideline, that is, no more than 3% above the annual guideline. Also, extensive regulations were under the *Rent Control Act, 1992*.

As of June 17, 1998, the *Tenant Protection Act, 1997*[8] replaced the *Rent Control Act, 1992*. The rent control provisions under the T.P.A. were described in great detail in the seventh edition of this text.

The *Residential Tenancies Act, 2006* replaced, the T.P.A. on January 31, 2007.[9] Most of the rent control provisions contained in the T.P.A., including "vacancy decontrol", have been carried forward into the R.T.A. with only minor changes. There are, however, some new provisions in the R.T.A. that are designed to address specific concerns raised by tenant advocates during the public consultation process that began in 2004 (see Chapter 1).

---

[4] S.O. 1982, c. 59, as amended by S.O. 1983, c. 69, s. 1; S.O. 1984, c. 65, s. 1; S.O. 1986, c. 63, s. 128.

[5] S.O. 1986, c. 63, then R.S.O. 1990, c. R.29.

[6] S.O. 1991, c. 4.

[7] S.O. 1992, c. 11.

[8] S.O. 1997, c. 24 (hereinafter referred to as the T.P.A.).

[9] S.O. 2006, c. 17 (hereinafter referred to as the R.T.A.).

This Chapter will focus on the rent control provisions of the current legislation.

(b) Challenges to the Constitutionality of Rent Regulation

Over the years, several attempts have been made to challenge the authority of the provincial government to regulate the rents collected by private landlords. In *Haddock v. Ontario (Attorney General)*,[10] a landlord challenged the constitutionality of the *Residential Rent Regulation Act, 1986* on the grounds that the Act severely impaired landlords' abilities to carry on business and earn a livelihood from their property contrary to s. 7 of the *Canadian Charter of Rights and Freedoms*[11] and that the Act violated s. 15 of the *Charter* by discriminating against certain landlords of older buildings. Mr. Justice Henry of the High Court of Justice dismissed the application finding that ss. 7 and 15 of the *Charter* did not guarantee a "right" to a better economic return on investment in property and that there was no justification on the evidence for finding that landlords are a disadvantaged group for whom s. 15 affords protection.

In *A & L Investments Ltd. v. Ontario (Minister of Housing)*,[12] a number of landlords claimed they were entitled to compensation from the Provincial Court for their losses resulting from the expropriation, taking, destruction or extinguishment of their property and property rights, by reason of the *Residential Rent Regulation Amendment Act, 1991*. They also claimed that their *Charter* rights were violated by the Act. The Court of Appeal disagreed, and struck the landlords' claim completely.[13]

2. OVERVIEW: WHEN CAN THE RENT BE INCREASED AND BY HOW MUCH?

No landlord shall charge rent for a rental unit in an amount that is greater than the lawful rent permitted under Part VII of the R.T.A. (s. 111(1)). For a full discussion of how the lawful rent for a unit is determined, please refer to Chapter 7.

---

[10] (1990), 73 O.R. (2d) 545 (Ont. H.C.).

[11] Part I of the *Constitution Act, 1982*, being Schedule B to the *Canada Act 1982* (U.K.), 1982, c. 11.

[12] (1993), (sub nom. *A & L Investments Ltd. v. Ontario*) 13 O.R. (3d) 799 (Ont. Gen. Div.), leave to appeal allowed (sub nom. *A & L Investments Ltd. v. Ontario*) 15 O.R. (3d) 643 (Ont. Gen. Div.), affirmed (1994), 1994 CarswellOnt 1938 (Ont. Div. Ct.).

[13] (1997), 36 O.R. (3d) 127 (Ont. C.A.), leave to appeal refused (1998), 227 N.R. 281 (note) (S.C.C.), leave to appeal refused (1998), 227 N.R. 282 (note) (S.C.C.).

Section 110 of the R.T.A. provides that, "No landlord shall increase the rent charged to a tenant for a rental unit, except in accordance with [Part VII]."

Generally, when a unit becomes vacant, a landlord can charge a new tenant any rent upon which the parties can agree (s. 113). For tenancies that existed prior to the R.T.A. coming into force (on January 31, 2007), unless otherwise prescribed, the lawful rent is either the rent that was being charged as of the day before the R.T.A. came into force or, if the rent being charged was not lawful, then the lawful rent will be the amount that it was lawful to charge on that day pursuant to the *Tenant Protection Act* (s. 112 of the R.T.A.).

Even if the rent being charged is not lawful, if it is not challenged within one year from the date it is first charged, it will become lawful (s. 136(1)).[14]

Once the rent has been established, a landlord can only raise the rent in accordance with certain strict rules (which will be discussed in detail later in this Chapter). For most tenancies, the rent can only be raised once every 12 months (s. 119)[15] and only upon giving the tenant written notice, in the approved form, at least 90 days prior to the date the rent increase is to take effect (s. 116).

Usually, an annual rent increase will be restricted to a "guideline" increase (i.e., an increase by up to a maximum percentage set each year by the government) for which the landlord does not require any special permission (s. 120). As long as the landlord serves proper notice, the tenant has no legal right to object to a guideline increase.[16] A tenant who receives a notice of rent increase and thinks that the increase is unlawful can commence an application for a determination of the issue by the Landlord and Tenant Board. If the tenant acknowledges that it is lawful but simply finds it to be unfair in the circumstances, the tenant can always try negotiating with the landlord; depending on the relationship between the parties and market conditions, the landlord may be willing to accommodate a tenant's request for a smaller rent increase, no rent increase or, in special circumstances, possibly even a rent reduction. If a tenant is unable to reach a satisfactory arrangement with the landlord (which, of course, should always be reduced to writing), the tenant always has the option of delivering a notice of termination and ending the tenancy pursuant to s. 47 of the R.T.A.

---

[14] Unless the unlawful rent resulted from a rent increase that was void for lack of a proper notice of rent increase. See the discussion in Chapter 7 on the significance of the Ontario Court of Appeal's decision in *Turnbull's Grove Inc. v. Price* (2007), 2007 CarswellOnt 3494, 85 O.R. (3d) 641 (Ont. C.A.).

[15] A purported rent increase that took place less than 12 months after the previous increase was deemed to be void for failing to comply with s. 119 of the R.T.A.: Landlord and Tenant Board File No. EAL-00186 (March 8, 2007).

[16] Unless an order from the Board prohibiting rent increases is in place. This is discussed later in this chapter.

Under the T.P.A., if the tenancy began prior to June 17, 1998, the landlord retained the right to increase the rent to any amount not exceeding the maximum rent set for the unit under the previous legislation (ss. 123 and 135 of the T.P.A.). For such tenancies, the "maximum rent" was "frozen" as of June 16, 1998.[17] Under the T.P.A., landlords had the option of raising the rent (once every 12 months and upon proper written notice) by any amount up to the "maximum rent", even if that resulted in an increase that exceeded the guideline (s. 135 of the T.P.A.).[18] A landlord could not, however, try to raise the rent to the maximum rent *and* further increase that amount by the guideline, all in one year.[19]

Since more than eight years have passed since enactment of the T.P.A., most tenants who have been in the same unit since before June 17, 1998 are already paying rent that exceeds the "maximum rent" that was fixed on June 17, 1998. For the vast majority of tenants, therefore, the concept of "maximum rent" no longer has any relevance. Consequently, the government decided to abolish this concept, effective May 3, 2006. Unless, prior to May 3, 2006, a landlord gave a notice of rent increase to raise the rent to the "maximum rent", the landlord can no longer do so.[20]

In addition to the usual guideline increase, rent can be increased *at any time*, pursuant to s. 123, if the landlord and tenant agree that the landlord will add a parking space or a prescribed (by s. 16 of O. Reg. 516/06) service, facility, privilege, accommodation or thing. Section 16 of O. Reg. 516/06 also sets out the amount by which the rent can be increased.

Rent can be increased above the guideline if the landlord and tenant agree that the rent will be increased in exchange for the landlord carrying out a specified capital expenditure or in exchange for the landlord providing a new or additional service (s. 121). Rent can also be increased above the guideline, without the consent of a tenant, if the landlord has incurred operating costs related to security services, has incurred an extraordinary increase in the cost of municipal taxes and charges or utilities (or both) or has incurred eligible capital expenditures related to the residential complex *and* has applied for and obtained an order from the Board permitting a rent increase above the guideline (s. 126).

It has also been held that discontinuance by the landlord of a gratuitous rent discount that has the effect of increasing the amount paid by the tenant by more than the guideline amount did not offend the Act.[21]

---

[17] Some landlords mistakenly believe that the maximum rent notionally increases each year by the guideline amount. This is incorrect. The maximum rent was "frozen" as of June 16, 1998 and could not be increased thereafter.

[18] *Theman Holdings v. Lewis* (Dec. 3, 1998), TSL-02231 (Ont. Rental Housing Trib.). And Landlord and Tenant Board File No. EAL-00186 (March 8, 2007).

[19] *Dixon v. Some Property Co.* (Dec. 9, 1999), TNT-01963-RV (Ont. Rental Housing Trib.).

[20] Subsection 258(1) of the R.T.A.

[21] *Ilijevski v. Nubury Properties Ltd.* (Nov. 3, 1999), TNT-00739, 1999 CarswellOnt 5827

3. EXEMPTION FROM RENT CONTROL

(a) General

The general rule is that the R.T.A. applies to all residential rental accommodations in Ontario unless the tenancy is of a type specifically excluded from the Act. Some rental units are *partially* exempt from the Act (i.e., they are exempt from specified provisions of the R.T.A. but not from the entire Act) and other rental units are *completely* exempt from the Act. The partial exemptions are listed in ss. 6, 7 and 8 of the R.T.A. and ss. 5, 6 and 7 of O. Reg. 516/06. Complete exemption from the R.T.A. is determined either by the character of the parties involved[22] or by the fact that the tenancy falls within one of the categories listed in s. 5 of the R.T.A. These exemptions are examined in detail in Chapter 4.

Remember that the onus of proving that a rental unit is exempt from the R.T.A. (or from a specific provision of the R.T.A.) rests upon the person making that claim.[23]

Obviously if a tenancy is completely exempt from the R.T.A., then it would not be subject to the rent control provisions contained within the R.T.A. For tenancies partially exempt from the R.T.A., specific rent control provisions in the Act may or may not apply; it will depend on the nature of the tenancy and whether the section of the R.T.A. under consideration is listed as one of the sections that does not apply to this particular type of tenancy. Tenancies that are typically at least partially exempt from the rent control provisions of the R.T.A. include social housing units, institutional units and "new" units. I shall discuss these types of units below. Please also refer to the section entitled "Partial Exemptions" in Chapter 4.

(b) Social Housing Units

Rental units in social housing projects owned, operated or administered by or on behalf of the Ontario Housing Corporation, the Government of Canada or agencies thereof, municipalities, and non-profit housing projects funded under various programs are partially exempt from the provisions concerning the amount of rent which may be collected (s. 7). The usual rent

---

(Ont. Rental Housing Tribunal). In this case, it was also found that the tenant had not been misled as the lawful rent for the unit (before the discount was applied) was always clearly shown on the notices of rent increase forms.

22 See the definitions of "landlord" and "tenant" under s. 2 of the R.T.A. and the analysis of this issue found in Chapter 3.

23 See the discussion contained in Chapter 4 and see also *Koressis v. Turner* (1986), 54 O.R. (2d) 571 (Ont. Div. Ct.).

control provisions may apply, however, if the tenant in these premises pays rent to a landlord other than the type of landlord listed in s. 7.[24]

(c) Institutional Units

If the rental accommodation is governed by specific legislation that regulates the operation of the units, including the regulation of rents charged to tenants, the units will be exempt from most of the rules regulating rent. Those provisions that will apply include the provisions limiting the landlord to one increase every 12 months, the requirement to provide 90-day written notices of rent increases, the limitations on the collection and use of security deposits, the prohibition concerning the requirement to provide payments be post-dated cheque or automatic debit (etc.) and the requirement that the landlord provide rent receipts.

A partial exemption also applies to educational institutions, religious institutions operating for a charitable use on a non-profit basis, and where the tenant pays rent in an amount geared to income due to public funding.[25] Ninety-day written notices of rent increases are required but, unlike the units referred to above, increases are not limited to once in a 12-month period. There is a limitation to the exemption for student accommodation: the exemption will apply only if an existing student council or staff association has been consulted about the increase.[26] Thus all rent control provisions apply where there is no consultation. No definition or case law sets a standard for the type of consultation and it is assumed that most educational institutions conduct at least a minimum amount of consultation.

(d) New Units

As an incentive for the construction or creation of new rental accommodation, s. 6(2) of the R.T.A. (formerly s. 4(2) of the T.P.A.) provides for an exemption from most of the rent control provisions for "new" rental units. Under this section, a rental unit is "new" if it has never been "occupied" for any purpose prior to June 17, 1998, or, alternatively, it has not been "rented" since July 29, 1975. In addition, a rental unit will be considered new if it is in a building no part of which was occupied prior to November 1, 1991.

The real incentive for the creation of "new" units is that the landlord of "new" units may increase the rent by any amount, even for existing tenants. The landlord must still provide the tenant with 90 days' written notice, and the rent may only be increased once every 12 months.

---

24 See ss. 7(4) and 7(5) of the R.T.A.

25 See subsections 7(1) and 8(1) of the R.T.A.

26 Subsection 7(6) of the R.T.A.

Other rent rules that still apply to "new units" are found in ss. 105 through 109 of the R.T.A. They are the provisions dealing with rent deposits, the prohibition against requiring post-dated cheques (etc.) and the rule requiring the landlord to provide rent receipts.

In Landlord and Tenant Board File Number SWL-13073 (April 17, 2008), the landlord purported to raise the rent by more than the guideline amount. The Board held that this was permissible in this case as the residential complex had been constructed in 1994. Thus, no part of the building had been occupied prior to November 1, 1991, and, pursuant to s. 6(2) of the R.T.A., this complex was exempt from many of the provisions of the *Act* relating to rent and rent increases.

(e) Mobile Homes

As a result of "vacancy de-control", when a unit becomes vacant the landlord can normally charge the new tenant whatever rent the market will bear. An exception to this rule is where the new tenant has purchased from the former tenant a mobile home on a rented site (see s. 165 of the R.T.A.). In such circumstances, the landlord may not charge the new tenant more than the last lawful rent charged for the site plus an amount prescribed by regulation. This "prescribed amount" is set out in s. 50 of O. Reg. 516/06. For more details about the provisions related to mobile homes, please see Chapter 20.

4. GUIDELINE INCREASE

Section 120(1) of the R.T.A. states:

> No landlord may increase the rent charged to a tenant or to an assignee under section 95 during the term of their tenancy by more than the guideline, except in accordance with section 126 or 127 or an agreement under section 121 or 123.

The landlord may, by right, increase the rent charged to a sitting tenant by up to the annual "guideline" each year. The guideline is the annual percentage rent increase determined by the Ministry of Municipal Affairs and Housing. Each year, the Minister is required to announce the guideline increase for the upcoming year by August 31 of the prior year, thus giving landlords at least four months notice of the guideline before it takes effect.[27]

Under the T.P.A., the Ministry determined the annual guideline amount using a complicated formula based on three-year moving averages of prescribed operating costs[28] plus 2% for capital expenditures. The government

---

[27] Subsection 120(3) of the R.T.A.

[28] Insurance, heating, hydro, water, municipal taxes, administration, maintenance and miscellaneous costs.

has now decided to simplify the calculation of the guideline and to have parity between the guideline amount and the amount of interest the landlord must pay on rent deposits.

Pursuant to subsection 120(2) of the R.T.A., the guideline for a calendar year is the percentage change from year to year in the Consumer Price Index for Ontario for prices of goods and services reported monthly by Statistics Canada, averaged over the 12-month period that ends at the end of May of the previous calendar year, rounded to the first decimal point. In short, the annual guideline will reflect the annual change in the Consumer Price Index (CPI).

The guideline fluctuates each year. The guideline was at its highest in the mid-1970's (8%). Recently, the guideline has been at an all-time low. The guideline for 2009 is 1.8% and for 2010 is 2.1%. For a complete list of the annual rent increase guidelines from 1975 through 2010, please see Appendix 14. Additional information can be obtained from the Landlord and Tenant Board or through the Ministry of Municipal Affairs and Housing.

5. ORDERS PROHIBITING RENT INCREASES

In addition to the remedies that were previously available to tenants who brought applications concerning maintenance, under the R.T.A. another "weapon" has been added to the arsenal: an order prohibiting a rent increase (or "OPRI"). This idea is not new. A similar provision existed under the *Rent Control Act, 1992*.[29] The goal is to give the landlord a financial incentive to keep the building in a good state of repair and to comply with any work orders that may be issued against the building or any orders of the Board that require the landlord to rectify *serious* maintenance problems. In essence, once an OPRI is issued by the Board, the landlord cannot raise the rent for the affected units until the required repairs have been completed. This prohibition on any rent increase applies not only to the original tenant (i.e., the tenant who obtained the OPRI) but also applies to any new tenant whose tenancy commences while the OPRI remains in effect. The R.T.A. also requires landlords to inform prospective tenants about the existence of an outstanding OPRI. Obviously it will be difficult for a landlord to find a tenant willing to move into a rental unit when the landlord has to inform the prospective tenant that there are serious outstanding maintenance problems with the unit or the building.

Pursuant to paras. 6, 7 and 8 of s. 30(1) of the R.T.A., where a landlord is found to be in serious breach of the landlord's maintenance obligations, in addition to other relief that may be granted, the Landlord and Tenant Board may: (1) prohibit the landlord from charging a new tenant[30] under a new

---

[29] S.O. 1992, c. 11, s. 38.

[30] Other than tenants in rent-geared-to-income housing.

tenancy agreement more than the last lawful rent charged to the former tenant; (2) prohibit the landlord from giving a notice of rent increase; or (3) prohibit the landlord from taking a rent increase for which a notice has been given but which has not yet taken effect.

Once an OPRI is issued, it remains in effect until the landlord completes the ordered repairs; the Board is not required to issue an order "lifting" the OPRI. Where the OPRI was based on an outstanding municipal or provincial work order, there may be a problem if the responsible governmental authority does not have in place a system for issuing written confirmation when the work order has been satisfied. This may lead to disagreements between the tenants and the landlord as to whether or not the necessary work has been completed and it may result in further proceedings before the Landlord and Tenant Board, at which point the inspector will likely have to be called as a witness. Hopefully, inspectors will soon be empowered to issue notices indicating when a work order has been satisfied or they may end up spending most of their time testifying at hearings instead of performing their intended functions.

Pursuant to s. 114 of the R.T.A., if an order prohibiting a rent increase is in effect for a unit, the landlord must provide written notice of the details (in the approved form) to a prospective new tenant of that unit and, where the OPRI is issued after the tenancy agreement is made (but before the tenancy actually commences), written notice must also be provided to the tenant.[31] The notice must contain information[32] about:

- the order that is in effect
- the amount of rent that the landlord may lawfully charge the new tenant until the prohibition ends
- the amount of rent that the landlord may lawfully charge the new tenant after the prohibition ends
- the last lawful rent charged to the former tenant
- such other information as is prescribed

If an OPRI takes effect in respect of a rental unit after a new tenancy agreement relating to the rental unit takes effect, the landlord must promptly give to the new tenant written notice (in the approved form) about the lawful rent for the rental unit, the order that has been issued and such other information as is prescribed.[33]

If the landlord breaches these provisions (i.e., s. 114), the tenant has up to one year to commence an application for relief (the return of excess rent collected illegally) and the landlord can be fined an amount not exceeding the greater of $10,000 and the monetary jurisdiction of the Small Claims

---

[31] Subsections 114(1) and (2) of the R.T.A.
[32] Subsection 114(3) of the R.T.A.
[33] Subsections 114(4) and (5) of the R.T.A.

Court.[34] Furthermore, failing to give a new tenant the required notice that sets out the lawful rent to be charged or giving false information in the notice where there is an OPRI is an offence under clause 234(i) of the R.T.A. (see Chapter 19).

6. NOTICE OF RENT INCREASE

In most circumstances, the landlord may increase the rent for a rental unit only once every 12 months (s. 119) provided the tenant is given at least 90 days written notice,[35] in the prescribed form (Form N1), setting out the landlord's intention to increase the rent, the date the new rent will take effect and the amount of the new rent (s. 116).[36] Even for tenancies partially exempt from the R.T.A., a written notice of a rent increase is usually required (unless the rent is geared to the tenant's income);[37] where such notice is required, the prescribed form is Form N2.

The importance of the notice of rent increase cannot be underestimated. The legislation clearly states "An increase in rent is void if the landlord has not given the notice required by this section, and the landlord must give a new notice before the landlord can take the increase" (s. 116(4)). The wording of the previous three statutes, the *Tenant Protection Act*, *Residential Rent Regulation Act* and the *Rent Control Act*, was similarly strict with respect to the need to adhere to the rules set out in the statute. For instance, in *Moscatiello v. Fiume*,[38] the tenant agreed to a rent increase on the renewal of her tenancy. Since, however, the landlord had failed to provide her with proper written notice of a rent increase, the increase was more than the guideline amount and it was not a case where the landlord was going to be providing additional services, the Tribunal found the rent increase to be illegal and found that the rent continued to remain at its former level.

Similarly, in *Shah, Re*,[39] the landlord purported to serve a notice increasing the rent by 2.5% although the applicable guideline amount at the time was only 1.5%. The tenant refused to pay the higher amount and the landlord commenced an application based upon, amongst other things, arrears of rent. The Tribunal found that, since the notice of rent increase was invalid, there were no arrears of rent and dismissed this part of the landlord's application.

---

[34] Section 115 of the R.T.A. The monetary jurisdiction of the Small Claims Court is scheduled to be increased to $25,000, effective January 2010.

[35] Oral notice is insufficient: *Lopez v. Lupo* (Aug. 25, 1998), TST-00093 (Ont. Rental Housing Trib.).

[36] For discussion of the exceptions, see Agreements to Increase Rent, later in this chapter.

[37] Sections 6, 7 and 8 of the R.T.A. do not exempt the subject properties from the requirements of s. 116, except in the case of rent-geared-to-income housing (subsection 7(3) of the R.T.A.).

[38] (July 20, 1999), TNT-00593 (Ont. Rental Housing Trib.).

[39] (June 21, 2006), TEL-62456, 2006 CarswellOnt 4423 (Ont. Rental Housing Trib.).

Notwithstanding the strict wording of these provisions, however, the courts have on occasion found it necessary to interpret the rules regarding a notice of rent increase more liberally. In the following cases, rent increases were recognized despite less than complete compliance with the statutory provisions.

Service of the notice in less than 90 days had been permitted in *Cando Property Management v. Wilson,*[40] which found that the validity of a notice should not rest on narrow technicalities. In *Macey Avenue Apartments Inc. v. McKenzie,*[41] the court followed *Cando* and found that less than 90 days notice (89 days) was not fatal as the tenant had sufficient time to decide whether to continue or terminate her tenancy.

This line of cases has, arguably, been overturned by the Court of Appeal in the case *Wolkow v. Dunnell.*[42] In that case, decided under the *Rent Control Act, 1992* a Rent Officer had determined that several notices, given 60 days prior to the effective date of the rent increase, were invalid and of no effect. In addition to failing to comply with the requirement to give 90 days notice, the notices given by the landlord also failed to properly inform the tenants of the new rent to be charged. As a result, the tenants were awarded a rent rebate in the amount of $4,632.

On appeal to the Divisional Court, it was ruled that the notices were valid, effective 90 days after they were served. Essentially, the court allowed the rent to be increased 30 days after the rent increase was actually collected by the landlord. As a result, the rebate was reduced to a mere $68.

However, the ruling of the Divisional Court was overturned on appeal to the Court of Appeal. The Court of Appeal considered the precise wording used in s. 7 of the *Rent Control Act* and s. 5 of the *Residential Rent Regulation Act,* both of which contain wording similar to the wording found in s. 127(4) of the T.P.A. On the issue of the requirement to give notice, the court stated:

> In my view, a fundamental objective of both Acts is to clearly define the amount and the circumstances in which rents may be increased by a landlord. Consistent with this objective, the legislation provides that a tenant shall be given at least 90 days' notice, in the prescribed form, of a landlord's intention to increase the rent. As the Divisional Court held in *Devitt v. Sarochyn* (sic), *supra,*[43] the purpose of the 90-day period is to allow a tenant sufficient time to accept the increase, or to serve the required 60-day notice to terminate the tenancy.[44]

---

[40] (1983), 44 O.R. (2d) 123 (Ont. Div. Ct.).

[41] (1992), 1992 CarswellOnt 3184 (Ont. Gen. Div.), additional reasons at (1992), 1992 CarswellOnt 2064 (Ont. Gen. Div.).

[42] (1998), 40 O.R. (3d) 783 (Ont. C.A.).

[43] See *Devitt v. Sawchyn* (1976), 12 O.R. (2d) 652 (Ont. Div. Ct.), affirmed (1977), 14 O.R. (2d) 135n (Ont. C.A.).

[44] (1983), 44 O.R. (2d) 123 (Ont. Div. Ct.) at 787 per Austin J.A.

The Court of Appeal further ruled that the failure to provide notice in the prescribed form prejudiced the tenants by failing to give sufficient information, such as the exact amount of the new rent, required by the tenants to make an informed decision on whether to continue the tenancy.

The Court of Appeal specifically cited *Kasprzycki v. Abel*[45] and *Dipetta v. Mardarowicz*[46] as representing the correct approach on the issue of the validity of the notices of rent increase. Interestingly, the court did not specifically overrule *Cando Property Management v. Wilson, supra.* This leaves open the possibility that *Wolkow v. Dunnell* could be narrowly interpreted to mean that the notice will be void only where the tenant is not given "sufficient time to accept the increase, or to serve the required 60-day notice to terminate the tenancy." One could argue that in *Cando* the notice was only one day late (89 days before the effective date), leaving the tenant sufficient time (29 days) to make the decision to stay or leave. It is, however, doubtful that such an argument would be successful[47] and it is far more prudent for landlords to provide the minimum notice required by the Act.

A notice given by the landlord that is defective or "short" is completely void and cannot be relied upon at all. The landlord must start from scratch and serve a new notice of rent increase.[48]

Although the notice of rent increase form is mandated by regulation, in Chapter 5 (under the heading "Initial Term and Renewal") I discussed the questionable practice of some landlords of altering the form by adding at the bottom of the form a section that makes it appear that tenants only have the option of either renewing the tenancy for another year or ending the tenancy. Some Members have held that altering the notice of rent increase in this way renders it void.[49] It is also recommended that prescribed forms not be altered by parties.

Not every error in a notice of rent increase is fatal. In Landlord and Tenant Board File No. TNL-18527 (Feb. 3, 2009), it was held that the notice delivered by the landlord was in substantial compliance with the requirements of the *Act* and that any errors contained in the notice did not mislead or confuse the essential information in the notice.

Finally, if a landlord is making an application for an above guideline rent increase, the landlord will often have to serve notices of rent increase to tenants in the complex before the hearing has been held and before the Board has rendered its decision as to the amount (above the guideline) by which the

---

[45] (1986), 55 O.R. (2d) 536 (Ont. Dist. Ct.).

[46] (1989), 69 O.R. (2d) 143 (Ont. Dist. Ct.).

[47] See, for example, *Noguera v. Cerase Holdings Ltd.* (Feb. 10, 1999), TNT-00280 (Ont. Rental Housing Trib.).

[48] Section 116(4) of the R.T.A. (formerly s. 127(4) of the T.P.A.).

[49] *3414493 Canada Inc. v. Rozsavolgyi* (Sept. 1, 2003), TSL-52280 (Ont. Rental Housing Tribunal), amended Sept. 18, 2003. For a more recent decision, see Landlord and Tenant Board File No. TSL-03635 (Sept. 24, 2007).

landlord may increase the rent for specified tenants within the complex. It is therefore difficult for the landlord to know what percentage increase to use for the notices of rent increase. Most landlords use their best estimate of the largest possible percentage (i.e., the guideline amount plus the largest percentage increase that could be ordered if the landlord were completely successful on the pending above-guideline increase application). Although this practice has been challenged, the Tribunal has held that it does not invalidate the notice of rent increase for the landlord to include in a notice of rent increase an increase that is greater than the amount ultimately permitted by the Board.[50] The way the notices are drafted, it will be obvious to tenants that for at least part of the rent increase identified in the notice, the landlord requires the permission of the Landlord and Tenant Board.

Pursuant to s. 126(5) of the R.T.A., until an order from the Board authorizing the rent increase takes effect, the landlord cannot "require" the tenant to pay the full amount it is seeking. Tenants can, however, choose to pay the full amount if they wish (s. 126(6)). Therefore, pending the outcome of the landlord's application, tenants who have received a notice of rent increase seeking more than the guideline amount have the option of paying the full amount set out in the notice or paying only the guideline increase. If a tenant chooses to pay only the guideline increase and the landlord is successful in obtaining an order for an amount above the guideline, the tenant will have a specified time in which to make up the difference. If a tenant pays the full amount set out in the notice of rent increase but then the landlord does not obtain an order for the amount originally anticipated by the landlord, the landlord will have a specified time in which to repay to the tenant the excess rent that had been paid by the tenant.

7. AGREEMENT TO INCREASE RENT

(a) In Exchange for Capital Expenditure or New/Additional Service (s. 121)

A tenant may agree to accept a rent increase of up to 3% above the guideline amount in exchange for a specific capital expenditure or new service or facility.[51] Agreements to increase rent pursuant to s. 121 of the R.T.A. must be in form N10. The agreement must set out the new rent, the effective date of the rent increase and the tenant's right to cancel the agreement within

[50] *Ahmad v. TZS Holdings Inc.* (Feb. 25, 2004), TET-03832, 2004 CarswellOnt 1015 (Ont. Rental Housing Trib.).

[51] Under the T.P.A., the limit was 4%. Most agreements to increase rent pursuant to s. 121 will concern capital expenditures. A new service or facility will not be the subject of an agreement under s. 121 unless the service or facility is not prescribed (see discussion of s. 123, later in this chapter).

five days. The agreement must also set out the specific capital expenditure or new service offered by the landlord. Failure to set out the terms of the agreement in sufficient detail could render the agreement unenforceable by either party.

A tenant may cancel the agreement within five days of the date the agreement was signed.[52] To cancel the agreement, the tenant must provide the landlord with written notice of their intent to cancel the agreement.[53] There is no prescribed form for cancelling an agreement.

The signed agreement takes the place of the notice of rent increase, and can take effect in as little as six days after the agreement is signed (to allow for the five-day cooling off period).[54]

Unlike applications under s. 126, under s. 121 there is no definition of "capital expenditure" and there are no restrictions as to what constitutes a capital expenditure or new service for the purpose of the agreement, or how much each expenditure or service must be worth. Those issues are decided between the parties to the agreement. The only limitation is that the rent increase may not exceed the guideline plus 3%. Finally, the 12-month rule applies to rent increases under s. 121 (i.e., it must have been at least 12 months since the last rent increase).

Given the new complexities inherent in above-guideline rent increase applications under s. 126 of the R.T.A. (discussed later in this Chapter), landlords who are contemplating doing major work (especially work *within* a rental unit as opposed to work on common areas of the complex) may now find s. 121 to be an attractive alternative method of increasing rents above the guideline.

Once a binding agreement under s. 121 is in place, if the landlord fails to comply with the terms of the agreement (for instance, by failing to incur the specific capital expenditure set out in the agreement), the tenant may apply to the Board pursuant to s. 122 to determine whether the portion of the increase above the guideline was valid.[55] The tenant has two years from the effective date of the increase to file the challenge (s. 122(2)). Once the tenant files the application with the Board, the Board will give the tenant a notice of hearing. The tenant must give the landlord a copy of the application and the notice of hearing at least 10 days before the hearing (Rule 10.1). The tenant should then file a certificate of service with the Board within five days after effecting service upon the landlord (Rule 11.2).

---

[52] Subsection 121(4) of the R.T.A.

[53] Section 191 of the R.T.A. lists the methods by which a notice may be given to a person (handing it to the person, mailing it to the person, etc.).

[54] Subsections 121(5), (6) and (7) of the R.T.A.

[55] Form T4. All forms prescribed under the R.T.A. may be obtained directly from the Board, or through the Board's official website, www.ltb.gov.on.ca.

(b) In Exchange for Parking Space or Addition of a Prescribed Service, Facility, Privilege, Accommodation or Thing (s. 123)

As in previous legislation,[56] a landlord and tenant may agree to increase or decrease the rent for a unit to reflect the addition or removal of a prescribed service or facility. The T.P.A. differed from the *Rent Control Act* with respect to the number of services or facilities that could be the subject of such an agreement. The list of prescribed services and facilities remains unchanged under the R.T.A.

In addition to a parking space, the landlord and tenant may agree to add or subtract any of the following services or facilities: cable television, satellite television, an air conditioner, extra electricity for an air conditioner, extra electricity for a washer or dryer in the rental unit, blockheater plug-ins, lockers or other storage space, heat, electricity, water or sewage services excluding capital work, floor space, and property taxes with respect to a site for a mobile home or a land lease home.[57]

There is no upper limit to the amount of the increase achieved through an agreement under s. 123, but the method of calculating the increase is prescribed by the regulation.[58] The increase in rent (or decrease, if the service is being withdrawn) will be equal to the actual cost to the landlord of providing the service or facility, except in the case of agreements concerning floor space.[59] However, if establishing a cost is not possible, or no direct cost is attributable to the landlord, the rent will be increased or decreased by "a reasonable amount based on the value of the service, facility or thing".[60]

Unlike agreements under s. 121, no form is prescribed for this agreement, although caution dictates that the agreement be in writing. Finally, there is no cooling off period for agreements under s. 123, and neither the 12-month rule nor the notice of rent increase provisions apply.

(c) Coerced Agreements (s. 124)

Any agreement to increase the rent above the guideline, whether pursuant to s. 121 or s. 123, is void and thereby unenforceable "if it was entered into as a result of coercion or as a result of a false, incomplete or misleading representation by the landlord or an agent of the landlord" (s. 124). A tenant who wishes to challenge an agreement may do so by filing an application

---

[56] Section 46 of the *Rent Control Act*, 1992 and s. 132 of the T.P.A.

[57] Subsection 16(1) of O. Reg. 516/06.

[58] Subsections 16(2) through (5) of O. Reg. 516/06.

[59] See subsections 16(2), (3) and (4) of O. Reg. 516/06 for the rules for calculating increases or decreases due to the addition or removal of floor space from the rental unit. For rent decreases based on a reduction of services or facilities, also see Chapter 10.

[60] Subsection 16(2) of O. Reg. 516/06.

under s. 135 of the R.T.A., claiming that the agreement is void, and therefore resulted in an unlawful rent increase. A tenant who wishes to challenge an agreement to increase rent should do so within one year of the date of the rent increase.[61]

8. LANDLORD'S APPLICATION FOR ABOVE-GUIDELINE INCREASE (s. 126)[62]

(a) General

(i) Grounds

If the landlord wishes to increase the rent for a rental unit by more than the guideline, and an agreement under s. 121 is either impossible or impractical, a landlord may make an application to the Board for an order increasing the rent by more than the guideline.

The landlord may base such an application on any of the three grounds listed in s. 126(1) of the R.T.A. (formerly s. 138(1) of the T.P.A.): eligible capital expenditures, extraordinary increases in municipal taxes or utilities, and operating cost increases related to the provision of security services (by persons not employed by the landlord).

Increases in other categories of operating costs, such as maintenance costs, insurance or superintendent's salary, may not be used to justify an increase above the guideline. In addition, increases in the cost of financing a residential complex may not be used to justify an increase above the guideline.

The portion of the justified rent increase based on eligible capital expenditures or operating costs related to security services is capped at 3% above the guideline (s. 126(11)). However, any portion of the justified increase beyond 3% may be passed through in up to two subsequent 12-month periods, again limited to 3% above the guideline each year (s. 126(11)).[63] The order of the Board will set out the increase permitted above the guideline in the initial year, and subsequent years, until the entire justified increase or the maximum permissible increase (whichever is lesser) has been passed through to the tenants.

The portion of the justified increase based on an extraordinary increase in operating costs is not capped, and may be passed through to the tenants in one year.

---

[61] However, applying the same reasoning as in *Turnbull's Grove Inc. v. Price* (2007), 2007 CarswellOnt 3494, 85 O.R. (3d) 641 (Ont. C.A.), where a rent increase is *void*, the unlawful rent may *not* be deemed to be lawful after one year, despite s. 136(2) of the R.T.A.

[62] Please refer to the Board's Interpretation Guideline #14 (released July 5, 2007).

[63] Thus the total aggregate rent increase above the guideline that is permissible based on eligible capital expenditures or operating costs related to security services is just over 9% (taken over a three-year period).

The general rules for making findings on this type of application are found in ss. 24 and 25 of O. Reg. 516/06. Subsection 24(1) of the Regulation provides that, in determining the amount of any capital expenditure or the amount of operating costs, the Board shall:

1. include any G.S.T. and provincial sales tax paid by the landlord;
2. exclude any penalties, interest or other similar charges for late payment;
3. exclude any amount that has already been included in calculating the amount of a capital expenditure or operating costs in the same application or for which the landlord has obtained relief in a previous order under the R.T.A. or T.P.A.; and
4. subtract the amount of all grants, other forms of financial assistance, rebates and refunds received by the landlord that effectively reduce the operating costs.

Subsection 24(2) of O. Reg. 516/06 deals with allocating costs where the residential complex forms part of a larger project. Section 25 of O. Reg. 516/06 deals with determining a landlord's costs arising out of a transaction that is not an arm's length transaction. Each of these sections will be discussed further below.

As in all applications under the R.T.A., the Board may include any conditions in the order which it considers fair in the circumstances.[64] This includes the power, in certain circumstances, to permit a tenant who must pay an above-guideline increase and who owes money to the landlord as a result of the Board's order to pay the amount owing in up to 12 monthly installments.[65]

Unlike applications concerning security of tenure, however, applications about rent increases are governed by extensive regulations and the Board's discretion is much more limited.

(ii) Changes Under the R.T.A.

The provisions under the R.T.A. and regulations made thereunder relating to above-guideline rent increase applications reflect some dramatic differences from the provisions that were in effect immediately prior to the enactment of this legislation. Some of the more significant changes can be summarized as follows:

1. A landlord can apply for an above-guideline increase (AGI) if there has been an extraordinary increase in the cost for municipal taxes and charges or utilities or both for the residential complex *or any*

---

[64] Section 204(1) of the R.T.A.

[65] Subsections 205(2), (3) and (4) of the R.T.A.

building in which the rental unit is located. This suggests that a landlord can apply if there has been an extraordinary increase in operating costs related to only one building within the complex regardless of whether there has been such an increase for the complex as a whole.

2. The determination of whether an increase in operating costs is "extraordinary" is no longer tied to a table of cost categories but will be determined in accordance with the regulations.
3. Only "eligible" capital expenditures can be used as the basis for an AGI application. What is eligible has been restricted somewhat. In particular, a capital expenditure to replace a system or thing will generally not be eligible if the system or thing did not require major repair or replacement. Also, a capital expenditure will not be eligible if it relates to work done before a tenancy commenced (i.e., a new tenant cannot be required to pay for work done before the tenancy began).
4. There is a new "cap" on the size of the increase that can be obtained in relation to capital expenditures. Under the T.P.A., the "cap" was 4% per year with no limit on the total aggregate increase or the number of years over which the increase could be taken. This meant that if the landlord justified a 20% increase in rent based on capital expenditures, the rent increase would have to be phased in over a five year period (4% per year for five years). Under the R.T.A., the Board cannot grant an increase based upon capital expenditures of more than 3% per year with a maximum limit of three years (thus, a maximum aggregate increase of 9%).[66]
5. If the landlord is in serious breach of the landlord's maintenance obligations, the Board may dismiss the AGI application or delay the effect of the rent increase order until the landlord has complied with its obligations. This means that tenants can now raise maintenance concerns at AGI hearings and attempt to prove that the landlord has not complied with an existing work order or order of the Board related to a *serious* breach of its maintenance obligations or otherwise prove that the landlord is in *serious* breach of its maintenance obligations. This provision applies to applications made under the R.T.A. as well as those commenced under the T.P.A. for which a final order was not issued prior to January 31, 2007.[67]
6. There are new provisions concerning what information must be disclosed by the landlord to the tenants, both before the application is heard and after the order is issued.

---

[66] Actually, because of the effect of compounding, the total increase is somewhat more than 9%.

[67] Subsection 242(7) of the R.T.A.

7. Pursuant to s. 128, where the Board issues an AGI order based upon an extraordinary increase in utility costs, the order will set out the percentage increase that is attributed to the increased utility costs as well as the landlord's obligation to keep tenants informed about the total costs of utilities for the complex. Where the utility costs subsequently decline (by more than the prescribed percentage in the prescribed period), the landlord will be required to reduce the rent accordingly. Similarly, pursuant to s. 129, where the Board issues an AGI order based upon capital expenditures, the order will set out the percentage increase that is attributed to the capital expenditures, a date by which the rent must be reduced (according to prescribed rules) and information about the landlord's obligation to reduce the rent as of that date. These provisions are discussed in detail in Chapter 10.

(iii) Procedural Rules

The application, Form L5, must be filed with the Board at least 90 days before the effective date of the first increase proposed in the application (s. 126(3)). There is a filing fee of $200 for the first 1-10 units, plus $10 for every additional unit to a maximum of $1,000. The landlord must give a copy of the application and the notice of hearing to the tenants named in the application as soon as possible, but not later than 30 days before the hearing date.[68]

While both of these time periods[69] are important, failure to strictly comply with them is not necessarily fatal to an application. Section 190(1) of the R.T.A. permits the Board to extend or shorten the time for filing an application under s. 126; Rule 15 of the Board's Rules of Practice sets out the procedure for requesting the Board to exercise this power and the criteria to be considered upon such a request.[70]

Pursuant to s. 22 of O. Reg. 516/06, an application under s. 126 must be accompanied by the following documentary evidence to support the application:

---

[68] Rule 10.4 of the Board's Rules of Practice. Originally, only 10 days' notice was required under the Tribunal's Rules but the Tribunal increased this to 30 days in order to give tenants more time in which to organize and prepare for the hearing and avoid unnecessary adjournments. This practice has been continued by the Board.

[69] For filing the Application and serving it with the notice of hearing.

[70] For examples of cases where the Rental Housing Tribunal abridged the usual time requirements for AGI applications under the T.P.A., see: *Re 2260 Weston Rd., Toronto* (Feb. 26, 2001), TNL-13575 (Ont. Rental Housing Trib.); *Re 2816 Keele St., Toronto* (Oct. 5, 2000), TNL-09077 (Ont. Rental Housing Trib.); and *Re 1533 and 1537 Wilson Ave., Toronto* (March 12, 2001), TNL-14556 (Ont. Rental Housing Trib.).

If the application is based on:	The landlord must file (with the application):
1. an extraordinary increase in the cost for municipal taxes and charges or utilities or both	i. evidence of the costs for the base year and the reference year and evidence of payment of those costs, and ii. evidence of all grants, other forms of financial assistance, rebates and refunds received by the landlord that effectively reduce those costs for the base year or the reference year.*
2. capital expenditures incurred	i. evidence of all costs and payments for the amounts claimed for capital work, including any information regarding grants and assistance from any level of government and insurance, resale, salvage and trade-in proceeds;* ii. details about each invoice and payment for each capital expenditure item, in the form approved by the Board; iii. details about the rents for all rental units in the residential complex that are affected by any of the capital expenditures, in the form approved by the Board.
3. operating costs related to security services	i. evidence of the costs claimed in the application for the base year and the reference year and evidence of payment of those costs

* Some of this information can be provided to the Board later if it is not available when the application is commenced (subsection 22(2) of O. Reg. 516/06).

An application under s. 126 based in whole or in part on capital expenditures must be accompanied by two additional photocopies of the application, by two additional photocopies of the material that accompanies the application under subsection 22(1) of O. Reg. 516/06, and by a compact disc containing the material that accompanied the application in portable document format.[71] Similarly, where supporting documents are filed late (under subsection 22(2) of O. Reg. 516/06), two additional copies and a compact disc must be provided.[72] However, if the residential complex contains six or fewer residential units *and* is located in a rural or remote area *and* the landlord cannot reasonably provide a compact disc, the landlord can simply file the photocopies of the supporting documents and need not also provide a compact disc.[73]

The best evidence available should be filed by the landlord. For proof of payment, the best evidence will often be copies of *cancelled* cheques (not merely copies of cheques or cheque stubs) or signed and dated receipts.

[71] Subsections 22(3) and (6) of O. Reg. 516/06.

[72] Subsections 22(4) and (6) of O. Reg. 516/06.

[73] Subsection 22(5) of O. Reg. 516/06.

Page two of Form L5 (under the heading "Important Information"), states as follows:

> If the landlord does not file the required supporting documents at the time the application is made, a Member may refuse to allow the landlord to file these documents at a later date. This may result in the landlord being unable to prove their claim.

A landlord is required to serve upon the tenants named in the application a copy of the L5 application and notice of hearing at least 30 days prior to the date set for the hearing.

A landlord is not required to serve the supporting documents on the tenants. Tenants who are interested in seeing the supporting documentation, however, have a right to obtain them from the landlord.[74] If the landlord was required to file a compact disc with the Board, upon the request of a tenant subject to the application, the landlord must also provide a copy of that CD to the tenant for a charge of not more than $5. Alternatively, if the tenant agrees, the landlord can provide the material to the tenant in paper form (at a reasonable charge) or by e-mail (free of charge).[75] However, if the landlord was supposed to file a CD with the Board but fails to do so, upon the request of a tenant subject to the application, such a landlord must provide a photocopy of all supporting documents for a charge of not more than $5.[76] If the landlord has an office in or close to the residential complex, the landlord must also make a photocopy of all supporting material available for viewing by the tenants subject to the application.[77] The Form L5 advises tenants of their right to view and/or obtain copies of this material from the landlord.

With respect to the requirement to file certain supporting documents with the application, a Member has no discretion to waive these requirements.[78] If a landlord fails to file the documentary evidence required by the regulations at the same time the application is filed, what is the result? It depends upon how much of the application is affected. If the required documents were filed for all of the amounts claimed in the application except for one or two capital expenditures (for example), in all likelihood the landlord will be able to proceed on all issues except the two items for which supporting documentation was not filed on time. If the landlord filed the documentation that was required by s. 22 of O. Reg. 516/06 but wishes to add supplementary material at the hearing, this would likely be a matter for the discretion of the Member. Remember that there is a specific provision (subsection 22(2) of O. Reg. 516/

---

[74] Section 23 of O. Reg. 516/06.

[75] Subsection 23(3) of O. Reg. 516/06.

[76] Subsection 23(4) of O. Reg. 516/06.

[77] Subsection 23(5) of O. Reg. 516/06.

[78] *Overbank Towers v. Tenants of 2360 Eglinton Ave E.* (April 29, 2003), TEL-32148, 2003 CarswellOnt 2669 (Ont. Rental Housing Trib.). See also *Dunelm Holdings v. Abugalal* (April 19, 2002), TEL-22592-RV (Ont. Rental Housing Trib.).

06) that permits certain information to be filed late if it was not available at the time the application was commenced. If none of the supporting material was filed with the application, however, the application will probably be dismissed in its entirety.[79]

In *Gramercy Apartments Ltd. v. Anthony*,[80] the landlord applied to increase the rents above the guideline based upon, amongst other things, over $200,000 in capital expenditures related to lobby and corridor renovations. Although the total cost of this work was shown on the application, the landlord or its agent accidentally forgot to attach to the application the sheets with the detailed breakdown of this cost. The landlord offered several times at the hearing to provide the missing detailed information. The Member did not respond to these offers, did not invite submissions from the parties on this issue and never specifically ruled on whether the landlord was or was not going to be permitted to do so. Ultimately, the expenditure question was disallowed for lack of detailed information. On appeal by the landlord, the Divisional Court found it to be a reversible error that the adjudicator did not at least give the landlord an opportunity to make submissions with respect to the admissibility of the additional information the landlord sought to file (late) and that the adjudicator failed to give reasons for refusing to accept that information from the landlord.

In calculating the permissible rent increase, it is crucial to know the total rent charged for the rental units covered by the application.[81] In applications based in whole or part upon capital expenditures, the landlord is required to file, in the prescribed form, details about the rents for all rental units in the residential complex that are affected by any of the capital expenditures. In applications where the claim is not based upon capital expenditures, such information need not be filed with the application. Nevertheless, the landlord must be prepared to disclose at the hearing the rent for each rental unit in the residential complex, and the date that rent was established for a new tenant under s. 113 of the R.T.A. or last increased for an existing tenant (Rule 19.2).

Finally, in any application, upon the request of a Member, a party may be required to clarify the contents of an application or other document filed with the Board or to provide further details according to the method and within the time set out in the request (i.e., direction), failing which the Board may refuse to consider the evidence and submissions of that party (Rule 19.1).

---

[79] The issue of how to deal with the failure to comply with s. 18 of O. Reg. 194/98 (now s. 22 of O. Reg. 516/06) is discussed in the following cases: *Finch Main Gardens Ltd. v. Tenants of 2431 Finch Ave. W.* (Nov. 4, 2002), TNL-30175, [2002] O.R.H.T.D. No. 116, 2002 CarswellOnt 3779 (Ont. Rental Housing Trib.) and *Minto Developments Inc. v. Tenants of Northview Rd. and Eleanor Dr., Nepean* (Feb. 25, 2003), EAL-23847 (Ont. Rental Housing Trib.).

[80] (2008), 2008 CarswellOnt 906 (Ont. Div. Ct.).

[81] See para. 1 of s. 31 of O. Reg. 516/06.

Despite the fact the landlord must file various documents in support of this type of application, when the hearing proceeds, the landlord will be required to introduce its evidence through the testimony of one or more witnesses. The witness(es) should have first-hand information about the various expenses and costs that form the foundation of the application and be very familiar with the residential complex. This is particularly important where capital expenditures are claimed. The witness should know when the work was done, why it was done, where it was done, how much it cost, the details concerning all payments and any holdbacks, and so on. The witness must be able to answer any relevant questions asked by the tenants or by the adjudicator. It is extremely risky for a landlord to come to a hearing believing that it can rely solely upon the documents filed.[82] If, as is sometimes the case, the witness is a property manager who was not employed at the complex at the time the work in question was done, then the property manager must familiarize him- or herself with all of the documentation related to the work, inspect the work that was done (on site) and thoroughly prepare for the hearing.

Similarly, tenants must prepare for the hearing. Since only experts are entitled to give opinion evidence, the tenants may need to retain an expert to review the documentation and the work that was done. They may need to retain a legal representative to argue their case or to negotiate with the landlord. Landlords have been willing to negotiate in recent years. In fact, in my experience, in 2003 and 2004, most above-guideline increase applications were resolved by way of consent orders (orders issued based upon the joint submissions of the parties, after they had reached a settlement). Given the current vacancy rates,[83] and the time, expense and risk of pursuing an application under s. 126 to its conclusion, landlords will likely continue to be willing to negotiate with their tenants and just because a landlord can legally increase a tenant's rent does not mean the landlord will attempt to do so. Finally, tenants who do not participate in the hearing will nevertheless be bound by any order issued by the Board.

---

[82] See *Re, 420 Eglinton Ave. E., Toronto* (Aug. 13, 1999), TNL-03859 (Ont. Rental Housing Trib.) in which the application was granted, with some hesitation, despite the inability of the witness to answer questions; *Re 391 Major Mackenzie Dr. E., Richmond Hill* (Nov. 27, 2001), TNL-29193 (Ont. Rental Housing Trib.) in which the ignorance of the witness proved fatal to the case; and *Re 101 Marlee Ave., Toronto* (June 29, 2001), TNL-23115 (Ont. Rental Housing Trib.) in which approximately $30,000 in alleged balcony repairs was disallowed, at least in part, because the property manager was unable to describe the scope of the work done by a related corporation.

[83] See the discussion of current trends in vacancy rates in Chapter 1.

(iv) Tenants Who Are Not Affected

Depending on when a new tenancy commences, the tenant may be exempt from an above-guideline rent increase order. A tenant will not be subject to a rent increase based upon any capital expenditures completed before his or her tenancy agreement took effect.[84] Also, a tenancy that commences during the 90-day period before the first effective date (FED) of a rent increase in such an order (or a tenancy that commences after the FED), is not affected by that order.[85] Finally, the order only affects the tenants named in the order. If a tenant who was subject to an above-guideline rent increase application ends his tenancy and a new tenant moves into the unit (under a new tenancy agreement), that new tenant is not affected by the order.

(v) Non-Arm's Length Transactions

Section 25 of O. Reg. 516/06 sets out complex rules for identifying and dealing with non-arm's length transactions. In essence, while such transactions are not forbidden, precautions must be taken to ensure that the amounts paid by the landlord are not greater than would be reasonable for the landlord to have paid in an arm's length transaction. There is no place on the L5 application form for disclosure of the existence of a non-arm's length transaction and the tenants are unlikely to discover such a relationship. As a result, this rarely becomes an issue at the hearing of these applications. If the tenants allege that a transaction that is the subject of an application was not arm's length, the tenants will have to prove it. Once such a transaction has been established, the Board may then place the onus upon the landlord to provide evidence to demonstrate that the amounts paid to the related person were less than or equal to the costs that would arise from a similar market transaction. If the landlord fails to adduce such evidence, then the landlord's claim based upon the cost of that transaction may be disallowed.[86]

When such an allegation is raised, it is important for the Board Member to obtain sufficient information to permit the Member to make a finding as to whether there was a non-arm's length transaction and, if so, whether the amount paid was reasonable in the circumstances. The Board Member must be wary of presuming a non-arm's length relationship without having sufficient evidence to actually establish that fact. In *Gramercy Apartments Ltd. v. Anthony*,[87] the adjudicator disallowed over $200,000 in capital expenditures

---

[84] Subsection 126(9) of the R.T.A.

[85] Subsection 126(14) of the R.T.A.

[86] *Marks v. Barcewicz* (February 7, 2001), TEL-15662, 2001 CarswellOnt 6251 (Ont. Rental Housing Trib.) and *Re 101 Marlee Ave., Toronto* (June 29, 2001), TNL-23115 (Ont. Rental Housing Trib.).

[87] (2008) 2008 CarswellOnt 906 (Ont. Div. Ct.).

related to lobby and corridor renovations. Based upon comments of the adjudicator, it appears that this may have been, at least in part, because of the adjudicator's concerns about the landlord's good faith as a result of the presumed non-arm's-length relationship between the property management company retained by the landlord and the contractor retained to do the work. The evidence presented at the hearing did not support such a finding and, on appeal, it was held that this was a reversible error.

(vi) Allocation

Pursuant to s. 24(2) of O. Reg. 516/06, where a residential complex forms part of a larger project, the operating costs for the project and the amount of capital expenditures that benefit both the residential complex and the other parts of the project shall be allocated between the residential complex and the other parts of the project in accordance with one or more of the following factors:

1. The area of each part of the project.
2. The market value of each part of the project.
3. The revenue generated by each part of the project.

If the allocation described above will be unreasonable considering how much of the costs and expenditures are attributable to each part of the project, the operating costs and capital expenditures shall be allocated among the parts of the project in reasonable proportions according to how much of the costs and expenditures are attributable to each part of the project (s. 24(3) of O. Reg. 516/06).

Part C to Schedule 1 of the L5 application form provides a place for the landlord to report if any of the operating cost categories relate to non-residential portions of the complex or other residential complexes. Part D to Schedule 2 of the L5 application form provides a place for the landlord to report if any of the capital expenditure items relate to non-residential portions of the complex or other residential complexes. If part of the costs or expenditures relate to non-residential portions of the complex or to other residential complexes, the Board must allocate only the appropriate portion of those costs and/or expenditures to the residential portion of the subject complex (using one of the methods outlined above).

In *Re 125 Neptune Dr., Toronto,*[88] the landlord acknowledged that it received a small revenue from Bell Mobility Cellular Inc. for allowing this company to erect an antenna on the roof of the building. This was considered a non-residential use and the municipal taxes and charges and operating costs were adjusted based upon the respective revenue generated from the residential and non-residential parts of the complex.

---

[88] (June 22, 2001), TNL-19802 (Ont. Rental Housing Trib.).

In *Re 3400 Weston Rd., Toronto*,[89] the application was based, in part, upon capital expenditures that affected both this complex and a neighbouring property that was also owned by this landlord. For expenditures that benefited both complexes, the landlord attributed 50% of the cost to 3400 Weston Road. The tenants challenged this allocation. After hearing the testimony of the property manager, examining a site plan showing the layout of the two complexes and considering the relative benefit derived by the tenants of each complex, the Tribunal approved of the manner in which the landlord allocated the expenditures in question.

The landlord must come prepared with information concerning the respective areas for each part of the project (or the areas of the various residential complexes affected), the market value of each part, the revenue generated by each part and the breakdown of the costs/expenditures (if known) for each part. Although the landlord may be tempted to provide only that information which yields the best allocation (at least from the landlord's point of view), the landlord should come with the information necessary to calculate the allocation by all of the different methods as the tenants or the Member may wish to compare the results that are produced using the various factors listed above. If that data is not made available at the hearing, the Member may adjourn the hearing to another date and insist that the landlord produce that information at the next hearing (and the landlord could be made to pay the costs of the reconvened hearing) or insist that the necessary information be provided by way of post-hearing written submissions.

(vii) Rebates, Refunds, etc.

Paragraph 1, item ii of subsection 22(1) of O. Reg. 516/06 states that an application based upon an extraordinary increase in the cost of municipal taxes and charges or utilities or both must be accompanied by, "evidence of all grants, other forms of financial assistance, rebates and refunds received by the landlord that effectively reduce those costs for the base year or the reference year."

Paragraph 2, item i of subsection 22(1) of O. Reg. 516/06 states that the application must be accompanied by, "evidence of all costs and payments for the amounts claimed for capital work, including any information regarding grants and assistance from any level of government and insurance, resale, salvage and trade-in proceeds." One of the more common examples is where a municipality provides a financial incentive (by way of a rebate) to landlords to install devices (such as low-flow toilets, aerators for taps and water-conserving shower-heads) in order to reduce water consumption.

[89] (Oct. 28, 2002), TNL-29451 (Ont. Rental Housing Trib.).

If the information referred to above is not available at the time the application is filed but becomes available before the end of the hearing, the landlord must disclose this information before or during the hearing (subsection 22(2) of O. Reg. 516/06).

It is important that such information be disclosed because rebates and refunds (etc.) must be deducted from the landlord's costs in order to determine the true *net* cost to the landlord of the capital expenditure(s) incurred or of the tax or charge levied by the municipality or of the utility charges. The L5 application contains a section for the landlord to indicate for both operating costs and capital expenditures whether any refunds, rebates, etc. have been received by the landlord. There is also a place for the landlord to indicate whether the landlord received any money from an insurer, government grants or forgivable loans or other assistance, or proceeds from trade-in, salvage or resale for any capital expenditure items. Failing to provide this information when the landlord knew or ought to have known of the grant, rebate (etc.), can invalidate the entire application as it may be found that the documents filed by the landlord were false or misleading (s. 197(2) of the R.T.A.). Filing false or misleading information with the Board is also an offence (see Chapter 19).

(viii) Multiple Applications/Orders

Since a rent increase above the guideline based upon security costs and/or capital expenditures cannot exceed the 3% "cap" in any one year, it is not uncommon for a single order to provide for several years of above-guideline increases. For instance, if the landlord justifies an 8% rent increase above the guideline (based upon security costs and/or capital expenditures), the order will provide that the landlord can increase rents by 3% above the guideline in the first 12-month period, by 3% in the next 12-month period and by the remaining 2% in the subsequent 12-month period.

What happens if, during this three-year period, the landlord applies for another rent increase above the guideline? If the application is based upon an extraordinary increase in operating costs, the rent increase permitted by the Board as a result of this new application can be taken *in addition* to the increase already permitted by the previous order. If the new application is based upon security costs and/or capital expenditures, any permitted rent increase will have to wait until the year where the maximum (3%) increase has not already been ordered. In the example given above, that would mean that 1% of the new rent increase above the guideline could be taken in the third year (so that the aggregate rent increase from the first and second order does not exceed 3% in that year) and any remaining permitted rent increase would have to be taken in subsequent years. This is sometimes referred to as a "stacking" of orders. The rules governing this interplay of orders are set out in s. 127 of the R.T.A. and s. 33 of O. Reg. 516/06. Note that, pursuant to s. 33 of O. Reg. 516/06, if a landlord increases a tenant's rent by less than the maximum amount permitted by an order of the Board or fails to raise the rent above the guideline at all, the difference between the actual rent charged and the amount by which the landlord could have legally increased the rent is lost forever and cannot be taken in a subsequent period (ss. 33(2) and (3) of O. Reg. 516/06).

A landlord can generally only increase a tenant's rent once every 12 months. The question is occasionally asked whether this means that a landlord is forbidden from filing more than one above-guideline rent application in the same 12-month period. It appears that there is no prohibition against this. In *Flemingdon Apartments v. Tenants of 55 Wynford Heights Cres.*,[90] the tenants argued that since there was already an order for an increase in rent above the guideline (TNL-03497) with a first-effective-date of March 1, 1999, this second application with a first-effective-date of September 1, 1999, should not be allowed as it would constitute more than one increase in rent in a 12-month period. The Tribunal did not agree and provided the following reasons:

> Depending on when the Landlord serves the Notices of [Rent] Increase and the amount of increase claimed therein, individual tenants may face only one increase in rent but that increase may include a combined increase above the guideline based upon application TNL-03497 and upon this application. Whether or not the increase claimed of a particular tenant is lawful and the amount of that increase will depend upon the particular facts of each case and cannot be decided on this application. There is nothing in the Tenant Protection Act or the regulations thereto which prohibits the Landlord from proceeding as it has done in bringing first an application based upon capital expenditures and then bringing an application (within twelve months of the first application) based upon an extraordinary increase in its operating costs.

(ix) Serious Maintenance Problems

Under the *Rent Control Act, 1992*,[91] on an application by a landlord to increase rent above the guideline, the presiding rent officer could consider the condition of the building as a factor in deciding whether the previous maximum rent should be reduced. For instance, an application for a rent increase above the guideline could be refused because of an inadequate standard of maintenance or repair of the residential complex or of a rental unit in it. This tended to make such hearings long, complicated and hotly contested affairs in which numerous tenants would insist on testifying, each

---

[90] (May 9, 2000), TNL-07922, 2000 CarswellOnt 4455 (Ont. Rental Housing Trib.).

[91] S.O. 1992, c. 11, subsection 13(8).

with his or her own concern(s) about the condition of his or her rental unit or the complex as a whole.

When the *Tenant Protection Act* came into effect in the summer of 1998, tenants were no longer permitted to raise maintenance concerns at AGI hearings. Instead, they were told that they had the right to commence separate proceedings but that neglect of the complex was not a defence to an above-guideline rent increase application. While this had the desired effect of reducing the length and complexity of such hearings, it left many tenants frustrated and angry.

The R.T.A. has re-introduced the right of tenants to defend against a landlord's application to increase rents above the guideline on the basis that the landlord has neglected the landlord's obligations with respect to the condition of the residential complex.

Pursuant to subsections 126(12) and (13) of the R.T.A., the Board can dismiss the landlord's AGI application with respect to a rental unit or delay the rent increase otherwise justified by the landlord if the Board finds that the rental unit of a tenant who is subject to the application is affected by:

1. the failure of the landlord to complete items in a work order (by the deadline set out in the work order) that represent a serious breach of a health, safety, housing or maintenance standard;
2. the failure of the landlord to complete specified repairs or replacements or other work ordered by the Board under paragraph 4 of subsection 30(1) and that is related to a serious breach of the landlord's obligations under subsection 20(1) or s. 161 of the Act; or
3. a serious breach of the landlord's obligations under subsection 20(1) or section 161 of the Act.

Note that in each case, the breach must be a *serious* one and can only be raised as a defence by tenants who are actually affected by the breach.

The phrase "serious breach" is also used in para. 83(3)(a) of the R.T.A. (formerly para. 84(2)(a) of the T.P.A.). Some guidance may be derived from the case law developed under those provisions (see Chapter 14). An early case from the Landlord and Tenant Board, however, suggests that the Board may be setting a surprisingly low threshold.

In *Murjay Construction Ltd. c/o Oxford Properties Group, Re*,[92] the landlord filed an application for an above-guideline rent increase one day before enactment of the R.T.A. Nevertheless, as a result of transitional provisions in the R.T.A. (s. 242(7)), ss. 126(12) and 126(13) of the R.T.A. applied. Without any forewarning, the tenants who appeared at the application brought forward allegations that the landlord was in serious breach of its maintenance obligations because: there were dryers and washing machines in the laundry room that needed repair; the treadmill in the exercise room

[92] (July 26, 2007), TNL-84211 (L.T.B.).

required repair; the sandbox in the playground required maintenance; there were a few spots in common areas of the building where wallpaper was torn or missing; and the hallway carpets were badly in need of cleaning. After hearing the evidence presented by the tenants on this issue, the landlord was put in the unenviable position of choosing between requesting an adjournment (in order to either effect some repairs or to bring witnesses or other evidence to the hearing to respond to the tenants' allegations) or trust that, even if uncontested, the tenants' allegations were insufficient to prove that the landlord was in "serious breach" of the landlord's maintenance obligations within the meaning of s. 126(12) of the R.T.A. The landlord chose not to request an adjournment and, as it turns out, this was a tactical error.

The presiding Vice-chair identified the following criteria to be considered in determining whether there was a **breach** of the landlord's maintenance obligations:

1. whether the problem is current (unresolved/ongoing);
2. whether the landlord knew or ought to have known of the problem.

The Vice-chair then indicated that whether the breach would be considered **serious** would depend upon:

1. the nature of the problem;
2. the duration of the time since the landlord became aware (or ought to have been aware) of the need for repair or maintenance; and
3. the significance of the impact upon the tenant(s) as a result of the breach.[93]

The Vice-chair found the failure of the landlord to deal with the problems listed above to be a serious breach of the landlord's maintenance obligations (separately and collectively) and ordered that the rent charged for any rental unit affected by the AGI application could not be increased until he was satisfied, on motion made by the landlord within 30 days, that all of the breaches had been remedied.

The Divisional Court, on the other hand, seems to be going in the other direction, setting the threshold considerably higher (albeit in a somewhat different context) and making an important distinction between very poor conditions (i.e., a serious *problem*) and a serious *breach* by the landlord of its maintenance obligations.[94]

---

[93] It appears from the reasons that accompany this order that the Vice-Chair was prepared to conclude from the nature of certain breaches that they were likely to have an adverse and substantial impact on the tenants of the complex, without necessarily hearing testimony to this effect.

[94] See *Puterbough v. Canada (Public Works & Government Services)* (2007), [2007] O.J. No. 748, 55 R.P.R. (4th) 189, 2007 CarswellOnt 2222 (Ont. Div. Ct.), additional reasons at (2007), 2007 CarswellOnt 7645 (Ont. Div. Ct.) discussed in detail in Chapter 14.

Assuming that the courts treat identical words found in different sections of the Act in the same manner, one thing is clear: whether or not a breach is "serious" will be viewed as a question of fact, not law, from which there will be no right to appeal to the Divisional Court.[95]

If the Board finds that there has been a serious breach that affects one or more tenants named in the landlord's AGI application and the Board chooses not to simply dismiss the application as against those tenants, the Board can delay the effect of the order until such time as the landlord has rectified the problem. In such a case, the Board will issue the AGI order, but in addition to the usual provisions, it will specify the period of time in which the landlord will have the opportunity to resolve the problem and will provide that the rent charged for the rental unit(s) affected shall not be increased pursuant to the order until the Board is satisfied that the problem has in fact been rectified within the time limit specified. The landlord will have to bring a motion (within the time period specified by the Board), on notice to the tenants of the rental units in order to prove that the necessary work has been done or the problem has otherwise been rectified so that the landlord is no longer in serious breach of the landlord's obligations under subsection 20(1) or s. 161 of the Act.[96] Presumably, if successful, such a motion will result in an order being issued by the Board that finds that the landlord is no longer in serious breach and that the landlord may now increase the rent above the guideline in accordance with the terms of the AGI order.

While it is difficult to predict the long-term effect of these provisions, in the short-term it is reasonable to assume that AGI hearings will once again become long, complicated and contentious.

(x) Other Considerations

In deciding whether it makes sense to commence such an application, a landlord must perform a cost-benefit analysis. This involves more than merely weighing the likelihood of success against the legal and other costs associated with the application. It also involves a consideration of market forces. If, for instance, most tenants are already paying rent that is at or above market levels, any attempt to increase the rent may simply drive tenants out of the complex and leave the landlord with empty units. Landlords now also face the possibility of having to respond to complaints about maintenance at these hearings. Even if successful, there is a potential cap on the amount of increase that can be awarded. There is an administrative cost associated with having to track certain types of rent increases so that they can be rolled back at a later date. Thus, just because a landlord *can* bring such an application does not mean that it is always advisable.

---

[95] See the discussion in Chapter 14 concerning para. 83(3)(a) of the R.T.A.

[96] Paragraph 126(13)(b) of the R.T.A.

Between 1998 and 2001, when market and other conditions were favourable, landlords rushed to file above-guideline increase ("AGI") applications. The zenith for these applications was reached in 2001, in which year over 1,600 AGI applications were filed. Beginning in 2002, however, there was a dramatic drop in the number of AGI applications filed by landlords, primarily as a result of a marked decrease in heating costs combined with a marked increase in vacancy rates. More complicated procedural rules and legislative changes have also made these applications less attractive to landlords in recent years. From 2003 to the present, the number of such applications has remained in the range of only about 200 to 300 applications per year.

(b) Increase in Cost of Security Services

Paragraph 3 of s. 126(1) of the R.T.A. allows landlords to apply for an above-guideline increase based upon operating costs related to security services provided in respect of the residential complex or any building in which the rental units are located by persons who are not employed by the landlord. The allowance will be determined according to the rules set out in s. 30 of O. Reg. 516/06.

For the application to be allowed, the landlord must prove an increase from the Reference Year to the Base Year (but need not prove an *extraordinary* increase as is required for other operating costs). The Board shall exclude from the calculation of the increased cost of security services any such costs that are no longer being provided to the tenant at the time the application is heard.[97]

Any rent increase justified as a result of an increase in the cost of providing security services will be subject, together with any increase justified based upon eligible capital expenditures, to an annual cap of 3% above the guideline (s. 126(11)).

(c) Extraordinary Increase in Operating Costs

An increase above the guideline may be justified by an extraordinary increase in the landlord's operating costs. For the purposes of the R.T.A., operating costs are limited to utilities, municipal taxes and charges. Utilities are defined as heat, electricity and water (s. 2 of the R.T.A.). Municipal taxes and charges are defined under s. 2 of the R.T.A.

Municipal taxes and charges mean taxes charged to a landlord by the municipality and charges levied on a landlord by a municipality (and include

[97] Subsection 30(3) of O. Reg. 516/06.

education taxes levied under Div. B of Part IX of the *Education Act* and taxes levied on a landlord's property in unorganized territory).

Municipal taxes and charges *do not* include the following:

- charges for inspections done by a municipality related to an alleged breach of a health, safety, housing or maintenance standard
- charges for emergency repairs carried out by a municipality
- charges for work in the nature of a capital expenditure carried out by a municipality
- charges for services, work or non-emergency repairs performed by a municipality related to the landlord's non-compliance with a by-law
- penalties, interest, late payment fees and fines
- any amount spent by a municipality under subsection 219(1) or any administrative fee applied to that amount under subsection 219(2) (i.e., charges by the municipality in the form of a lien or administrative fees related to vital services provided to the residential complex by the municipality)
- any other prescribed charges

The rules for making findings related to an extraordinary increase in operating costs are set out in s. 29 of O. Reg. 516/06.

Under the T.P.A., whether or not an increase in operating costs was considered "extraordinary" was based on whether this particular landlord's costs increased by more than the average (as set out in a Table of Operating Cost Categories (TOCC)).

Things have been simplified considerably under the R.T.A. The annual guideline amount each year is now based on the percentage change in the Consumer Price Index for Ontario. Pursuant to s. 28 of O. Reg. 516/06, an increase in the cost of municipal taxes and charges or utilities is "extraordinary" if it is at least 1.5 times the guideline amount that is in effect for the calendar year in which falls the effective date of the first intended rent increase referred to in the application. For example, if the guideline amount for the calendar year in which the landlord hopes to increase the rent is 2%, an increase in operating costs will only be considered to be "extraordinary" if it represents an increase of at least 3% (1.5 multiplied by 2%). If the annual guideline amount is ever less than zero, *any* increase in operating costs will be deemed to be extraordinary.[98]

To make a claim for extraordinary operating costs, the landlord must provide evidence of the operating costs (municipal taxes and charges and/or utilities if applicable) over a two-year period. These two years are called the "base year" and the "reference year".[99] For claims based on utilities, the base

---

[98] Subsection 28(3) of O. Reg. 516/06.

[99] Section 19 of O. Reg. 516/06.

year is the 12-month accounting period, chosen by the landlord,[100] most recently completed 90 days before the first effective date of the application. For claims based on municipal taxes, the base year is the calendar year most recently completed 90 days prior to the effective date of the application. In each case, the reference year is simply the 12-month period immediately preceding the base year.

The amount of the increase justified by the extraordinary operating cost increase is calculated by comparing the actual increase in the cost (reference year to base year) with the annual guideline.[101] The formula for calculating the allowance for an extraordinary increase in the cost for municipal taxes and charges is set out in subsection 29(2) of O. Reg. 516/06. The formula for calculating the allowance for an extraordinary increase in the cost for utilities is set out in subsection 29(3) of O. Reg. 516/06.

Since utility costs must be claimed on an all or nothing basis (i.e., a landlord *must* include heat, water and electricity costs even if there were not extraordinary increases in all three categories), an increase in one category may be offset by a decrease in another.[102] For example, if the landlord's water costs increased, but the heating costs decreased, the decreased heating costs will offset some or all of the increased water costs.

Unlike rent increases based upon increased security costs or capital expenditures, there is no limit to the amount of rent increase that can be granted based upon an extraordinary increase in operating costs and there is no provision in the R.T.A. for consideration by the Board of the reasonableness of operating costs.[103]

However, unlike the former legislation, the R.T.A. does contain provisions that require the rent increase to be rolled back if, subsequently, the landlord's operating costs decrease (see Chapter 10).

---

[100] A landlord is free to choose its 12-month accounting period under the R.T.A., even if that landlord used a different accounting period under former legislation: *Re 505 Cummer Ave., Toronto* (April 25, 2002), TNL-29733 (Ont. Rental Housing Trib.). Once the landlord has chosen an accounting period under the R.T.A. and an order has been issued for a rent increase based upon an extraordinary increase in costs for utilities or for operating costs related to security services, however, the landlord must be consistent in future years and use the same accounting period (s. 19(2) of O. Reg. 516/06).

[101] Since the guideline (based on the percentage change in the Consumer Price Index) generally reflects the average change in the cost of goods and services since the preceding year.

[102] By looking at the cost of water *only*, it appears to me that the Board got it wrong (i.e., failed to follow the methodology mandated by s. 29(3) of O. Reg. 516/06) in Landlord and Tenant Board File No. EAL-11885 (Jan. 26, 2009). It is also curious in this case how the Member resolved an issue of credibility (i.e., whether the tenants were properly served with a copy of the Application and Notice of Hearing as alleged by the landlord but denied by the tenants) when the hearing was conducted only by way of written submissions.

[103] *Re 1061 Don Mils Rd., Toronto* (Nov. 26, 2001), TNL-25712-RV (Ont. Rental Housing Trib.).

(d) Capital Expenditures

(i) General

Under the regulations to the T.P.A., a capital expenditure was defined as "an expenditure on a major renovation, repair, replacement or new addition, the expected benefit of which extends for at least one year". Under the R.T.A., this term has been re-defined. In addition, under the R.T.A. not all capital expenditures are "eligible" to be considered.

The landlord may claim any eligible capital expenditure related to work that was completed during the 18-month period ending 90 days before the first intended rent increase proposed in the application.[104]

The increase with respect to a capital expenditure is calculated by amortizing the total cost of the expenditure over the anticipated useful life of the item, at a prescribed rate of interest.

Under the T.P.A., the total cost of the expenditure would automatically be increased by 5% for most items, representing a management and administration allowance.[105] Under the R.T.A., such management and administration charges have been eliminated. The total cost of the item, however, may include any reasonable amount to reflect the landlord's labour used in the completion of the work.[106]

A list of the anticipated useful lives of various capital expenditures is found in the Schedule attached to Ont. Reg. 516/06. If the specific expenditure is not found in the Schedule, the Board may determine a reasonable useful life, with reference to similar items found in the Schedule.

The issues that typically must be resolved on this type of application are as follows:

1. Did the landlord follow the correct procedures in serving and filing the application and supporting documentation and in providing notice of the hearing?
2. Does each expenditure claimed meet the definition of a "capital expenditure"?
3. Is it an "eligible" capital expenditure?
4. Has the landlord proven that the expenditure has been "incurred"?
5. Has the landlord proven that the work (for which the expenditure was incurred) was completed within the prescribed time period?
6. Should the cost be spread over the entire complex or be borne by the tenant(s) of one or more specific units?

---

[104] Subsection 26(2) of O. Reg. 516/06.

[105] Management and administration allowances did not apply to capital expenditures for furniture or appliances and did not apply to a landlord's own labour. See O. Reg. 194/98, s. 22, para. 6 (repealed).

[106] Subsection 26(3) of O. Reg. 516/06.

7. For each capital expenditure, what is the "useful life" of the work done or thing purchased?
8. Is there any non-residential part to the complex that will require an allocation of costs?
9. Were any transactions non-arm's length and, if so, what amount should be attributed to that expenditure?
10. Are there any existing above-guideline increase applications that need to be taken into account in phasing in any rent increase justified by the current application?
11. Ultimately, based upon the answers to the questions above, what is the amount of the rent increase above the guideline justified by the landlord, over what period of time can the landlord apply the permitted increase and when and by how much will the landlord have to reduce the rent (in accordance with s. 129 of the Act)?[107]

(ii) Definition of "Capital Expenditure"

The term "capital expenditure", as used in the context of an above-guideline increase application, does not have the same meaning as it may have under income tax legislation or under generally accepted accounting principles.

Under the regulations to the T.P.A., a capital expenditure was defined as "an expenditure on a major renovation, repair, replacement or new addition, the expected benefit of which extends for at least one year". It could include an expenditure with respect to a leased asset or an expenditure that the landlord was required to pay on work undertaken by a municipality, local board or public utility (other than work undertaken because of the landlord's failure to do it).

As stated above, a capital expenditure was defined under the T.P.A. as an expenditure on a *major* renovation, repair, replacement or new addition. Therefore, the Rental Housing Tribunal would not include an expenditure where it determined that the expenditure was not made in respect of a "major" renovation, etc. The adjective "major" attempted to distinguish capital expenditures from ongoing maintenance costs, with somewhat inconsistent results.

At least one landlord tried to argue that the adjective "major" only qualified the word "renovation" and did not apply to repairs, replacements or new additions. This interpretation was expressly rejected by the Tribunal

[107] Section 129 of the R.T.A. requires the above-guideline rent increase to be rolled back once the rent increase has been fully paid for and it requires the AGI order to advise the tenants the date upon which the landlord is required to reduce the rent and the amount by which the rent ought to be reduced at that time (see Chapter 10).

in *Treegreen Apartments Inc. v. Tenants of Trethewey Dr.*[108] and in the Tribunal's Interpretation Guideline (No. 14). In *Treegreen*, it was held that the word "major" modified the entire phrase and that: "in order to be considered as a capital expenditure, the Landlord must have incurred an expenditure on a major renovation, major repair, major replacement or major new addition, the expected benefit of which extends for at least one year."[109] In the same case, the Tribunal rejected the landlord's argument that if a landlord incurs an expenditure on work or an item that is listed in the Schedule entitled, "Useful Life of Work Done or Thing Purchased," then that expenditure *must* be deemed to be capital in nature. In rejecting this argument, the Tribunal provided the following reasoning:

> ... caulking is listed in the Schedule. It is absurd to argue that a superintendent who caulks the corner of one window in a large residential complex could apply for the cost of the caulking as being a capital expenditure. Similarly painting is listed in the Schedule. Painting a spot on a door where paint has chipped off is significantly different than painting all common areas of a building ... (para. 16)
>
> By the Legislature including the word 'major' in the definition of a capital expenditure and failing to define the term or set out a mathematical formula for determining which expenditures are 'major' (such as stating a minimum threshold level based upon a proportion of revenue), it must be assumed that members are meant to analyze the facts of each case and make a determination as to which expenditures qualify as capital expenditures. The natural consequence of this will be some uncertainty amongst parties as each case will turn upon its own particular facts and upon the interpretation of the law given by each member of the Tribunal. . . (para. 22)

The Tribunal adopted the reasoning contained in the *Treegreen* decision in its Interpretation Guideline (No. 14).

Under the *Residential Rent Regulation Act*, certain minor capital expenditures were not allowed unless the expenditure affected 25% of the rental units in the complex or the amount of the rent increase resulting from the expenditure exceeded 1% of the total annual rent for the complex.[110] Although a similar provision was not included under the regulations to the T.P.A., some Members nevertheless attempted to define "major" in a similar manner, creating arbitrary rules of thumb; these Members held that, in order to be considered "major", an expenditure must be more than a certain minimum dollar amount or must represent more than a certain proportion of rent revenue for the residential complex (or the rent revenue for the rental units affected).

---

[108] (June 19, 2001), TNL-14364-RV, [2001] O.R.H.T.D. No. 89, 2001 CarswellOnt 6411 (Ont. Rental Housing Trib.).

[109] *Treegreen Apartments Inc. v. Tenants of Trethewey Dr.*, (June 19, 2001), TNL-14364-RV, [2001] O.R.H.T.D. No. 89, 2001 CarswellOnt 6411 (Ont. Rental Housing Trib.) at para. 15.

[110] See the definition of "capital expenditure" in O. Reg. 440/87, s. 1.

For instance, in one case a Member defined the term "major" to mean "any expenditure over $1,000".[111]

Setting arbitrary thresholds was supported neither by the T.P.A. nor by the Tribunal's Guidelines. In determining whether a renovation, repair, replacement or new addition qualifies as a capital expenditure or whether it is more in the nature of routine maintenance, the approach approved of by the Tribunal and the approach adopted by most Members was to consider all of the relevant factors, including: how often this type of work was likely to be done by the landlord, the total cost involved (both in absolute terms and in comparison to the total rent received from all tenants in the complex or from the tenants in the subject units), the nature and scope of the work done and the impact of the item on the residential complex.[112]

Pursuant to s. 18 of O. Reg. 516/06, "capital expenditure" is now defined as "an expenditure for an *extraordinary or significant* renovation, repair, replacement or new addition, the expected benefit of which extends for at least *five* years". The definition still includes an expenditure with respect to a leased asset or an expenditure which the landlord was required to pay on work undertaken by a municipality, local board or public utility (other than work undertaken because of the landlord's failure to do it). By lengthening the requisite period of expected benefit and changing "major" to "extraordinary or significant", presumably the legislators were intending to raise the threshold. However, since the terms "extraordinary" and "significant" are not defined, the current definition is likely to be as problematic as its predecessor.

On the other hand, the current definition is somewhat more helpful in that it goes on to say that it does not include:

1. routine or ordinary work undertaken on a regular basis or undertaken to maintain a capital asset in its operating state, such as cleaning and janitorial services, elevator servicing, general building maintenance, grounds-keeping and appliance repairs; and
2. work that is substantially cosmetic in nature or is designed to enhance the level of prestige or luxury offered by a unit or residential complex.[113]

To further limit such applications, not all capital expenditures can be considered on an AGI application. The capital expenditure must be "eligible". A capital expenditure is NOT eligible:

---

[111] See *Re 358 McArthur Avenue, Vanier* (May 21, 1999), EAL-03242 (Ont. Rental Housing Trib.), where the Tribunal disallowed a claim of $963 for a chimney liner on the ground that it fell short of the $1000 threshold for a "major" expenditure.

[112] *Treegreen Apartments Inc. v. Tenants of Trethewey Dr.*, (June 19, 2001), TNL-14364-RV, [2001] O.R.H.T.D. No. 89, 2001 CarswellOnt 6411 (Ont. Rental Housing Trib.) and *Re 358 McArthur Ave.*, Vanier (May 21, 1999), EAL-03242 (Ont. Rental Housing Trib.).

[113] Subsection 18(1) of O. Reg. 516/06.

1. if it was incurred before the tenancy in question existed;[114]
2. if it was incurred to replace a system or thing (unless it needed major repair or replacement or it promoted access for persons with disabilities, energy or water conservation or the security of the complex).[115]

In order to be eligible, a capital expenditure must:

1. be necessary to protect or restore the physical integrity of the residential complex;[116]
2. be necessary for the landlord to comply with the landlord's repair and maintenance obligations;[117]
3. be necessary to maintain the provision of a plumbing, heating, mechanical, electrical, ventilation or air conditioning system;[118]
4. provide access for persons with disabilities;[119]
5. promote energy or water conservation; or[120]
6. maintain or improve the security of the residential complex or part of it.[121]

The expenditure must also relate to a renovation, repair, replacement or new addition. An interesting type of work that remains problematic is the removal of old oil storage tanks. A number of properties still have such tanks buried under the ground, adjacent to the apartment building. They pose an environmental hazard and must be removed. The cost of removing such tanks, removing any affected soil, re-filling the hole and replacing the sod can be substantial. Under the T.P.A., some landlords successfully claimed the cost as a capital expenditure.[122] There is no question that such work is both reasonable and significant. Not all Members agreed, however, that the cost meets the definition of "capital expenditure" because removal of an oil tank from the ground cannot easily be regarded as a "repair, replacement, renovation or new addition".[123] Similarly, removal of a hot water tank has been held not to qualify as a capital expenditure.[124]

---

[114] Subsection 126(9) of the R.T.A.

[115] Subsection 126(8) of the R.T.A.

[116] Paragraph 126(7)(a) of the R.T.A. and subsection 18(1) of O. Reg. 516/06 (definition of "physical integrity").

[117] Paragraph 126(7)(b) of the R.T.A.

[118] Paragraph 126(7)(c) of the R.T.A.

[119] Paragraph 126(7)(d) of the R.T.A.

[120] Paragraph 126(7)(e) of the R.T.A.

[121] Paragraph 126(7)(f) of the R.T.A.

[122] *Re 20 Esterbrooke Ave., Toronto* (Dec. 1, 1999), TNL-03907 (Ont. Rental Housing Trib.).

[123] *Re 18, 14, 25 and 27 Seeley Dr., Toronto* (April 30, 2002), TNL-20607 (Ont. Rental Housing Trib.).

[124] *Re 1533 to 1537 Wilson Ave., Toronto* (March 31, 1999), TNL-03600 (Ont. Rental Housing Trib.).

(iii) Capital Work

Section 126 of the R.T.A. permits a landlord to apply to the Board for an order allowing the rent charged to be increased by more than the guideline for any or all of the rental units in a residential complex where capital expenditures have been incurred respecting the residential complex or one or more of the rental units. In determining these applications, s. 126(10) requires the Board to follow the "prescribed rules" (i.e., the relevant provisions of O. Reg. 516/06).

One of those provisions sets time limits beyond which landlords may not apply to increase rents based upon capital expenditures. For the first six months after the T.P.A. was enacted, landlords were permitted to file applications based upon expenditures related to *work* "completed on or after June 25, 1996" (para. 2 of s. 22, O. Reg. 194/98). After that six-month transitional period, applications based upon capital expenditures could only include expenditures for *work* "completed prior to the 18-month period ending 90 days before the effective date of the first intended rent increase referred to in the application".[125]

Many landlords were quite pleased[126] that, at least during the early days of the T.P.A., they could seek a rent increase based upon work they had done as much as two and one-half years earlier. Some landlords sought a way to recover even older expenditures. The main reason for this was that many landlords incurred substantial expenditures in the mid-1990s in an effort to comply with amendments to the Fire Code. As a result of these amendments, landlords were required to install or upgrade emergency lighting, exit signs, sprinkler and other fire-suppression systems, smoke alarms, automatic door closers and so on. In many cases, at least some of the work related to such "Fire Code retrofits" was completed before June 25, 1996. Landlords wanted to claim a rent increase based upon their *entire* expenditure and not just the expenditures incurred with respect to work completed after June 25, 1996.

Such landlords focused on the word "work" as that term was used in s. 22 of O. Reg. 194/98, arguing that all of the expenditures related to the Fire Code retrofit were part of one project. It was argued that according to the Regulation it doesn't matter when the work commenced — it only matters when the work was completed. If "work" is interpreted as all work related to this "fire retrofit project", then it didn't matter that some of the work was done prior to June 25, 1996. As long as the Tribunal was willing to consider that different contracts for different types of work could all be considered part of one large project and that "work" can mean a project involving

---

[125] Paragraph 1 of s. 22, O. Reg. 194/98 and subsection 26(2) of O. Reg. 516/06. For practical purposes, this meant work completed no more than about 21 months prior to the first effective date and no less than three months before the first effective date.

[126] Judging by the large number of above-guideline increase applications received by the Tribunal in the initial six-month period.

disparate types of capital improvements, then this argument would succeed.[127] If the Tribunal insisted on examining each individual contract as a separate capital expenditure, then this argument would fail. Since the term "work" was not defined in either the T.P.A. or in Regulation 194/98, Tribunal Members generally found this argument reasonable and persuasive.[128]

In a somewhat similar vein, it is not unusual for landlords to include in their claims the cost of any experts retained for the project, such as architects or engineers. Landlords often use engineers and other specialists to determine what work needs to be done, to draw up specifications, to oversee a tendering process, to hire the needed contractor(s), to oversee the work and to advise the landlord when certain phases of a project are complete so that the landlord can make interim payments to the contractor(s). Obviously, such an expert will charge a fee for his or her services. Although the cost of those services may not appear to be capital in nature, the repair, replacement, renovation or new addition would often not be possible without the assistance of such an expert and the Tribunal generally permitted such expenses to be included with the cost of the actual work.[129] If, however, the capital work for which the expert's report was prepared is never actually done, the cost of the report itself will not be permitted as a capital expenditure on its own.[130]

Grouping together different but related types of work (and calling it a "project") may sometimes be legitimate, but it is also open to abuse. Increasingly, it has represented an effort on the part of landlords either to make "work" appear major (where individual contracts might not meet that definition) or to capture older expenditures that might otherwise be outside of the permissible time-period. Perhaps because of this potential for abuse, around the year 2000, Members began to take a more critical look at the

---

[127] Of course, this would often require the Tribunal to calculate an average useful life (i.e., amortization period) for the "project" as various types of work within the project would often be assigned different "useful lives" in the Schedule.

[128] See, for example, *Re 5 & 15 Tangreen Crt., Toronto* (May 18, 1999), TNL-03791 (Ont. Rental Housing Trib.) and *Re 2928 – 2932 Yonge St., Toronto* (April 15, 1999), TNL-03493 (Ont. Rental Housing Trib.).

[129] As long as it was not a duplication of the management duties of the landlord (for which 5% was added to almost all capital expenditures under the T.P.A.). See *2250 Kennedy Rd. Apartments v. Tenants of 2250 Kennedy Rd.* (Sept. 3, 1999), TNL-03952, 1999 CarswellOnt 5820 (Ont. Rental Housing Trib.).

[130] The cost of an engineer's report was not allowed where the report recommended against doing the capital work in question, and as a result, the work was not done: *Re 4109 and 4111 Bathurst St, Toronto* (Oct. 13, 2000), TNL-09078 (Ont. Rental Housing Trib.). See also *Re 65 Forest Manor Rd., Toronto* (May 8, 2001), TNL-16323 (Ont. Rental Housing Trib.). In *Re 130 George Henry Blvd., Toronto* (May 18, 2000), TNL-04059 (Ont. Rental Housing Trib.), the expert hired by the landlord came to the conclusion that the emergency lighting system complied with the Fire Code and that no capital work was required; while obtaining this report was reasonable, since it did not relate to any capital work, the cost of the report was not considered to be a capital expenditure.

nature and cost of the various types of work that were being presented as a single project.[131]

(iv) When Is the Work Complete?

As indicated above, an expenditure can only be included in an application by a landlord if it relates to work that was completed within the time period specified in s. 26(2) of O. Reg. 516/06. This begs the question, "When is work complete?" No guidance can be found within the R.T.A. or the Regulation itself.

The onus is upon the landlord to prove when the work was completed. If the landlord fails to do so, the expenditure may not be allowed.[132] A Member may allow the landlord to provide additional information either at a reconvened hearing or by way of written post-hearing submissions, but this is solely within the discretion of the Member. If a Member does provide such an opportunity, the parties must comply with the directions of the Member as documents that are filed late may not be considered by the Member and, absent some very good explanation for the default, it is unlikely that the landlord will be able to successfully challenge the Member's decision.[133]

Imagine an extraordinary or significant renovation contract costing one million dollars. The work commences in 2003 and 99% of the work is completed and paid for in 2004. In 2006, the last 1% of the work is done and paid for. In 2007 the landlord files an application to increase rents above the guideline based upon this capital expenditure. If the work were considered to have been completed in 2006, the entire capital expenditure of one million dollars can be claimed in 2007. The landlord can argue that the work called for in the contract was not completed until 2006 and that there is no reason why the capital expenditure incurred by the landlord cannot form the basis of an above-guideline increase application in 2007. The landlord could further submit that had the landlord filed the application earlier (back in 2003 or 2004), the tenants could have objected on the basis that the work was not yet complete.[134] On the other hand, the tenants can argue that the work was

---

[131] *Princess Gardens v. Ablog* (Feb. 29, 2000), TSL-05143, [2000] O.R.H.T.D. No. 37, 2000 CarswellOnt 6343 (Ont. Rental Housing Trib.); *Re 60 Callowhill Drive and 695 Martingrove Rd., Toronto* (Jan. 11, 2000), TNL-03983 (Ont. Rental Housing Trib.); *Re 15 Shallmar Blvd., Toronto* (Nov. 14, 2001), TNL-26420 (Ont. Rental Housing Trib.).

[132] *Metro Capital Management Inc. v. Tenants of 120 George Henry Blvd.* (March 27, 2000), TNL-04049 (Ont. Rental Housing Trib.) and *Re 391 Major Mackenzie Dr. E., Richmond Hill* (Nov. 27, 2001), TNL-29193 (Ont. Rental Housing Trib.).

[133] *Re 12 Castelgrove Blvd., Toronto* (Dec. 2, 1999), TNL-03816-RV (Ont. Rental Housing Trib.).

[134] See *Re 15 Shallmar Blvd., Toronto* (Nov. 14, 2001), TNL-26420 RV (Ont. Rental Housing Trib.). In an earlier application by the same landlord (TNL-04072 (Ont. Rental Housing Trib.)), an expenditure was disallowed because the project had not yet been completed. Once the project was complete, the landlord again claimed for the cost of the entire project

substantially completed in 2004 and that it makes a mockery of the limitation period set out in subsection 26(2) of O. Reg. 516/06 to allow this type of "bootstrapping". Both sides would have made good points and the decision could be difficult for the Board.

In an effort to avoid these types of situations, where projects are quite lengthy, there has been some approval for the idea of claiming the cost of the project in phases, with each phase representing a distinct capital expenditure.[135] This allows the landlord to claim the individual phases of the expenditure as they are completed, rather than waiting until the entire project is complete. For large projects or smaller buildings, this may also make sense since there is a 3% per year cap on rent increases attributable to capital expenditures (for a maximum of three years) and, by breaking the project into phases, the landlord may be able to pass along to the tenants a greater proportion of the total cost of the project. Note, however, that the "planning phase" of a capital expenditure may not be passed on to the tenants as a separate expenditure, because "the tenants should not be subjected to the cost of increased rent before they are enjoying the benefit of the work".[136]

Now imagine a scenario in which the work is completed but problems with the work require repairs. The repairs will be done by the original contractor at no cost to the landlord. The landlord commences an application to raise the rents above the guideline based upon the cost of the original contract. The tenants object on the basis that the work is still ongoing and has not, therefore, been completed. In this scenario, the landlord may invite the Board to interpret the word "completed" as meaning "substantially completed" as was done by the Rental Housing Tribunal in *Re 2601 to 2621 Meadow Brook Lane, Windsor.*[137]

In one case, the tenants argued the work was not completed because it had not been inspected and approved by a government official.[138] This argument was rejected by the Tribunal (at least on the facts of the case).

Ultimately, each case will turn upon its own facts and the Board may need to resort to its powers under s. 202 of the R.T.A. to ascertain the real

---

(including the earlier invoice that had previously been rejected as premature) and the tenants argued work related to that first invoice had been completed outside of the permissible time period (i.e., it was too old). The Tribunal found that this would be completely unfair to the landlord and ruled that the landlord could claim for the cost of the entire project (including the original invoice rejected in the earlier application) as the project was completed within the relevant time-frame.

[135] *Re Warrender Avenue, Toronto* (Feb. 29, 2000), TSL-05143 (Ont. Rental Housing Trib.).

[136] *Re Stein Resorts Inc.* (May 10, 1999), SOL-02169-RV (Ont. Rental Housing Trib.), affirming (Oct. 19, 1998), SOL-02169 (Ont. Rental Housing Trib.).

[137] (May 10, 1999), SWL-01549-RV (Ont. Rental Housing Trib.). The reviewing Member wrote, "To take the position that the work was not complete until there were not any problems may mean a project of this size would never be complete."

[138] *Re 20 Esterbrooke Ave., Toronto* (Dec. 1, 1999), TNL-03907 (Ont. Rental Housing Trib.).

substance of all transactions and activities relating to the residential complex and the good faith of the parties.

(v) When Is the Expenditure "Incurred" By the Landlord?

The term "incurred" is defined in subsection 18(1) of O. Reg. 516/06 to mean (in relation to a capital expenditure):

- (a) the payment in full of the amount of the capital expenditure, other than a holdback withheld under the *Construction Lien Act*,
- (b) if the expenditure relates to a lease, the assumption, when the lease commences, of the obligations under it, or
- (c) if the expenditure relates to work undertaken by a municipality, local board or public utility, when the work is completed.

Virtually all cases that come before the Board rely on the first of these three definitions.

Note that s. 126 only requires that the capital expenditures be incurred respecting the residential complex or one or more of the rental units in it. It does not require that the expenditure be incurred by the landlord who files the application seeking to raise rents above the guideline. It has been held that the expenditure can be incurred by a third party on behalf of the landlord[139] or even by a previous landlord of the complex.[140] The onus remains upon the applicant, however, to prove the expense was incurred (i.e., paid for in full) and that the work was completed within the permitted time period. In *Re 211 Wilson Ave., Toronto*,[141] the landlord's application with respect to an expenditure allegedly incurred by the previous landlord was dismissed because the applicant (the current landlord) failed to prove these things.

An interesting case to consider is *Nistico v. Hill*.[142] The rental unit was located within an "equity co-op". The landlord was the owner of approximately 1.6% of the complex, with exclusive rights over the unit in question. The tenant had lived in this unit for approximately 28 years at the time of the application; Ms. Nistico had been the landlord of this unit for the last 16 of those 28 years. In or about May 2000, the Board of Directors for the complex decided that major exterior brick repairs were necessary. The work was scheduled to commence around June 2000. The Board approved a special

---

[139] *Re 2603 Bathurst St., Toronto*, TNL-14662 (March 21, 2001) (Ont. Rental Housing Trib.).

[140] *Shallmar Court Apartments Inc. v. Abonyi* (Nov. 24, 1999), TNL-03984 (Ont. Rental Housing Trib.) and *Fane v. Sawden* (Feb. 24, 2003), TNL-36220-RV, [2003] O.R.H.T.D. No. 27, 2003 CarswellOnt 1502 (Ont. Rental Housing Trib.), both following the Divisional Court's decision in *Rossvan Holdings Ltd. v. McCarthy*, Doc. 442/94 (Ont. Div. Ct.) (unreported).

[141] (Oct. 10, 2001), TNL-27000 (Ont. Rental Housing Trib.).

[142] (July 16, 2001), TNL-19919, 2001 CarswellOnt 6302 (Ont. Rental Housing Trib.).

assessment of $60,000 to finance the repair program and levied a monthly charge against co-owners. Ms. Nistico's share was $78.98 per month for 12 months commencing June 1, 2000. On September 8, 2000, she filed an application seeking an order to increase the tenant's rent above the guideline based upon this "capital expenditure". At the time she commenced the application, the landlord had paid only a fraction of the charge levied against her. At the hearing, she failed to adduce any evidence as to whether or not the brick repairs had been completed and whether the cost of the work had been paid for in full. Without deciding whether a landlord in such a situation even has the right to commence this type of application, the Tribunal dismissed the application because the expense upon which this application was based had not yet been "incurred" within the meaning of s. 15 of O. Reg. 194/98.

(vi) Reasonableness

Subsection 138(7) of the T.P.A. gave the Tribunal the authority to disallow "unreasonable" capital expenditures. That power has been removed under the R.T.A., and instead, has been replaced with the concept of "eligible" capital expenditures.[143]

(vii) Apportionment of the Expenditure Amongst Tenants

When people think of capital expenditures, they tend to think of large, expensive projects that affect the entire residential complex — things like balcony restoration projects or major repairs to the roof of the building, replacing all windows in the complex or replacing all carpeting throughout the common areas of an apartment building. Landlords will invariably seek to spread such costs over the entire complex. The rationale is that where the work affects the common areas or the physical integrity or safety of the building, all tenants benefit and all should bear a small part of the expense. Apportioning the expense amongst a large number of tenants also reduces each tenant's share of the expense. The landlord may choose to exclude some tenants from the application (such as the superintendent or tenants who are already paying market rent) but this will not prejudice the tenants who are named in the application; the way a rent increase is calculated, no tenant will pay more than his or her proportionate share of an expense regardless of how many tenants are included or excluded from the application.

Some tenants will argue, however, that they should not have to pay (through a rent increase) for some of the capital expenditures claimed in these types of applications. A tenant on the ground floor may argue, for instance, that they should not have to pay for balcony repairs because their unit does

---

[143] Discussed above under the heading: Definition of "Capital Expenditure".

not have a balcony. Invariably, the landlord's response to such statements is that it is in everyone's interests that chunks of cement not fall from balconies and that all tenants have an interest in ensuring the building is kept safe and structurally sound. The Rental Housing Tribunal typically agreed with this philosophy that most expenditures should be borne by all the tenants named in the application. However, this rule has some exceptions.

Where work is done to improve a specific rental unit within a larger complex, having the tenants who most directly benefit bear the cost of those improvements may be more appropriate. Where, within a specific unit, the floors are refinished or new floor covering is installed, the kitchen and/or bathroom is renovated, new appliances are installed (such as a stove and/or refrigerator) or the entire apartment is painted, the landlord may seek to have the associated cost attributed only to the tenant(s) of that unit. Such expenditures are a good example of work that was not terribly expensive but was typically accepted by the Tribunal as meeting the definition of a capital expenditure (as it was under the T.P.A.). Most appliances, for instance, cost around $500 each but were typically allowed by the Tribunal as capital expenditures, probably because such expenditures are relatively infrequent and are not part of the routine maintenance of the building. It is unclear whether such expenditures will be seen as "extraordinary" or "significant" under the current definition of a capital expenditure.

The fact that a tenant may have to pay for work done prior to the commencement of their tenancy often came as an unpleasant surprise to new tenants under the T.P.A. Under the R.T.A., this should no longer be a concern.[144]

Landlords frequently include claims based upon "in-suite" work in above-guideline rent increase applications. The Board will take submissions from all parties present at the hearing as to how the cost of such work should be apportioned (i.e., whether the expenditure should be treated as a "whole building" expense or as "unit-specific"). One of the factors the Board is likely to consider is how such expenditures have been treated by the landlord on previous applications. Once the landlord has created a precedent for certain types of expenditures within the residential complex, it will usually be followed in subsequent applications.

A tenant whose unit has not been upgraded in many years might question why she should have to pay for the renovation of another tenant's unit. On the other hand, if and when she gets new appliances, she might prefer not having to bear the cost of those appliances on her own. Good arguments can be advanced for either position. Ultimately, the Board will decide how the expenditures should be apportioned amongst the tenants and this will form part of the Board's order. Expenditures treated as unit-specific will be reflected in the fact that the rent increase permitted by the Board will not be

---

[144] See subsection 126(9) of the R.T.A.

the same for each tenant in the complex. A schedule will be attached to the Board's order setting out the rent increase permitted for each rental unit. Note, however, that unlike the scheme under the *Rent Control Act*, under the R.T.A. the rent and permitted rent increases do not attach to the rental unit; they apply only to the specific tenant named in the order. Once that tenancy ends, the order no longer has any effect (s. 126(14)) because the landlord is free to negotiate with the new tenant of that unit any rent the landlord deems appropriate (s. 113).

(viii) Useful Life

An eligible capital expenditure accepted by the Board must still be amortized over the "useful life" of the work done or the thing that was purchased.[145] From the tenants' point of view, the longer the amortization period, the smaller the rent increase will be.

The rules for determining an expenditure's useful life are set out in s. 27 of O. Reg. 516/06. In general terms, the useful life of work done or a thing purchased is determined by reference to the Schedule to O. Reg. 516/06 or, if it is not specifically listed in the Schedule, by analogy to something similar that is in the Schedule or failing that, by what is generally accepted as the useful life of such work or thing. If the thing purchased is not brand new (i.e., it is a "used" item), then the useful life must be reduced to take into account the length of time of that previous use. In no event, however, shall the useful life be deemed to be less than ten years.

Effective January 2009, the L5 Application form required by the Board was amended to ensure that landlords indicate on the form the useful life of any capital expenditure being claimed.

If work is grouped together and claimed as one capital expenditure, it is possible that each type of work will have a different useful life. The Board can deal with this in several ways. The various components can be separated and the Board can insist that each one, on its own, must meet the definition of a capital expenditure and, if it does, the appropriate useful life will be assigned to that work. The Board can accept the expenditure in the form in which it is presented and calculate an average useful life based upon the useful lives of the component parts of the project; this is the approach that was most often adopted by the Tribunal under the T.P.A. Finally, the Board could determine which single type of work best characterizes the project and assign to the entire expenditure the useful life designated in the Schedule for that type of work.

Because the useful life attributed to a capital expenditure can have a significant impact on the potential rent increase, Members should always invite submissions from the parties with respect to this issue.

---

[145] Subsections 26(6) and (7) of O. Reg. 516/06.

10

Rent Decreases and the Return of Amounts Collected or Retained Illegally

1. INTRODUCTION

Rent can be reduced in essentially five ways:

1. On the agreement of the landlord and tenant to reflect the removal of a prescribed service or facility (or for any other reason);
2. Automatically, where property taxes on the residential complex have decreased by 2.5% or more;
3. By order of the Board (on application by the tenant under s. 133) where property taxes on the residential complex have decreased by 2.49% or less and the landlord and tenant cannot agree on the amount of the appropriate rent reduction;
4. By order of the Board (on application by the tenant under s. 130) where the landlord is found to have unilaterally reduced or discontinued a service or facility; and
5. By order of the Board (on application by the tenant under s. 135) where the landlord is found to have charged an unlawful amount of rent (or illegal additional charges).

Where a service or facility is discontinued by a landlord, the rules for calculating the appropriate rent reduction are determined by whether the service/facility is a "prescribed" one (i.e., parking or a service/facility listed in s. 16 of O. Reg. 516/06), whether the tenant agreed to the removal of the service/facility and whether the removal was "reasonable" (see Chart below).

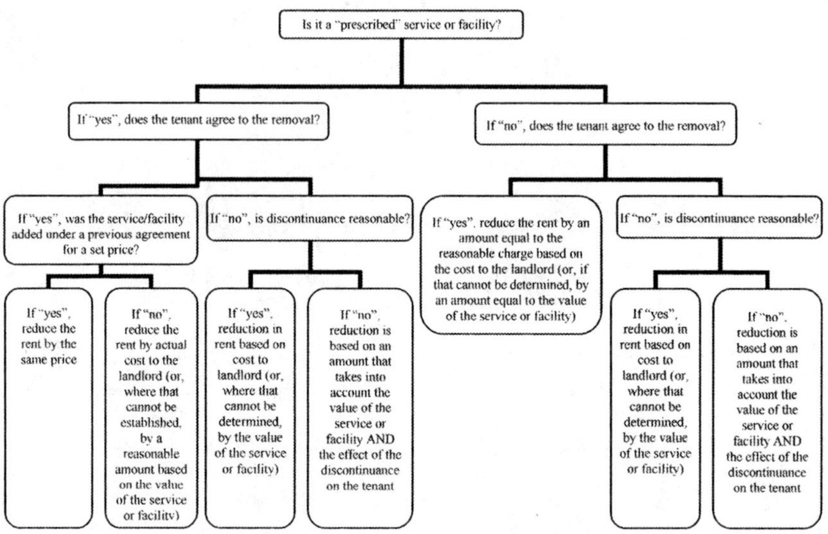

An application for a *rent reduction* should not be confused with an application under s. 29 or 57 of the *Residential Tenancies Act, 2006* (R.T.A.) in which the tenant seeks an *abatement of rent.* When the rent is *reduced,* this indicates that the lawful rent for the unit has been lowered, usually permanently, subject only to the next lawful increase that the landlord can take upon proper notice to the tenant. A rent decrease will be based upon the legality of the rent, as determined by the rules relating to rent set out in Part VII of the R.T.A. (i.e., ss. 105 through 135). When rent is *abated,* the lawful rent does not change; the Board is merely ordering a refund of some or all of rent paid for a period during which the landlord failed to comply with the landlord's obligations under the tenancy agreement and the R.T.A. or failed to comply with an order of the Board. While abatements are usually granted for past rental periods, abatements can also be ordered to continue into the future until specified events occur (such as the landlord performing repairs ordered by the Board). Although an abatement alters the amount a tenant must pay to the landlord for a specified period of time, it does not affect the lawful rent. Therefore, when the rent abatement ends, the rent that the tenant must pay returns to its former level.

A tenant can bring both an abatement application and a rent reduction application at the same time, if the situation warrants. In such a case, the Board should deal with both applications at the same time, but each ground for the application should be addressed distinctly. For a further discussion of the differences between rent abatements and rent reductions, see *Green v. 35 Walmer Road Construction Co.*[1]

[1] (1998), 42 O.R. (3d) 301 (Ont. Gen. Div.).

2. AGREEMENT TO DECREASE RENT (s. 125)

As in previous legislation,[2] a landlord and tenant may agree to decrease the rent for a unit to reflect the removal of a prescribed service or facility (s. 125). In addition to parking and cable service, the landlord and tenant may agree to subtract any of the following services or facilities: satellite television, an air conditioner, extra electricity for an air conditioner, extra electricity for a washer or dryer in the rental unit, blockheater plug-ins, lockers or other storage space, heat, electricity, water or sewage services (excluding capital work), floor space, and property taxes with respect to a site for a mobile home or a land lease home.[3]

The minimum decrease in rent will be equal to the landlord's actual cost of providing the service or facility, except in the case of agreements concerning floor space.[4] However, where it is not possible to establish a cost, or where there is no direct cost to the landlord, the rent will be decreased by "a reasonable amount based on the value of the service, facility or thing".[5]

While rent increases are strictly controlled, this is not the case with rent decreases. Nothing prohibits a landlord and tenant from agreeing to reduce the rent for any reason. For instance, a landlord may wish to accommodate a good, long-standing tenant who is experiencing difficulty in paying the rent. There is no prescribed form for an agreement to reduce the rent. Regardless of the reason for the agreement, however, caution dictates that it be reduced in writing.

3. RENT REDUCTION AS A RESULT OF A PROPERTY TAX DECREASE

(a) Automatic Rent Reduction (s. 131)

Pursuant to s. 131 of the R.T.A. and the relevant regulations,[6] rents for residential complexes are automatically reduced if the municipal property taxes paid by the landlord for the complex have decreased by at least 2.5% from the previous year's taxes.[7] The rent reductions are "automatic" because tenants do not have to apply to the Board to have the rent reduction approved in a Board order and they do not have to get permission from the landlord to

[2] Section 46 of the *Rent Control Act, 1992* and s. 134 of the *Tenant Protection Act, 1997*.

[3] O. Reg. 516/06, s. 16(1).

[4] See O. Reg. 516/06, ss. 16(3) and (4) for the rules for calculating increases or decreases due to the addition or removal of floor space from the rental unit.

[5] O. Reg. 516/06, s. 16(2).

[6] Sections 41 through 45 of O. Reg. 516/06.

[7] Subsection 41(1) O. Reg. 516/06. Of course, tenants who live in complexes exempt from ss. 131 and 132 of the R.T.A have no right to such a rent reduction.

reduce the rent. The automatic rent reductions take effect on December 31 of the year the taxes for the complex decrease.[8] A tenant is not entitled to any rent reduction that took effect before his or her tenancy began.

(b) Notice of Automatic Rent Reduction

How will the tenants know that the property taxes for the complex have decreased by at least 2.5%? If the complex has seven or more rental units, the municipality must calculate the percentage rent reduction that applies to the rental units in the complex and send out notices of rent reduction to landlords and tenants.[9] The notice sets out the percentage rent reduction that applies to the units in the complex and the date the rent reduction is effective.[10] Pursuant to subsection 41(6) of O. Reg. 516/06, the notice is supposed to be sent to landlords between June 1 and September 15[11] and to tenants between October 1 and December 15.[12]

If the complex has fewer than seven units, the municipality is not obligated to notify the tenants of the complex. Such tenants may never become aware of the decrease in property taxes or their right to an automatic rent reduction. Tenants who live in smaller buildings and are interested in preserving their rights in this regard may be well-advised to contact the municipality directly around November each year. If they cannot agree with their landlord as to the correct amount of the rent reduction, they then may have no alternative (if they wish to pursue the matter further) but to commence an application under s. 133 for an order determining the amount of the rent decrease. The onus will be on the tenant to prove the amount by which the

---

[8] Subsection 41(4) of O. Reg. 516/06.

[9] Subsections 131(3) of the R.T.A. and 41(5) of O. Reg. 516/06. The relevant question is not whether the building contains seven or more rental units, but whether there are seven or more rental units within the *complex*. Under the definition of "residential complex" found in s. 2 of the R.T.A., a residential complex can consist of a group of small buildings. As long as at least seven rental units are in the *complex* and the rent reduction is at least 2.5%, the tenants are entitled to notice of the rent reduction. While simple in theory, in practice this can become complicated where the municipality assigns a separate tax roll number and issues a separate tax bill for each building within the residential complex. In such cases, the municipality may fail to recognize that the buildings form one residential complex containing seven or more units and, as a result, may fail to issue the necessary notices of rent reduction. Tenants living in such complexes would likely never learn of this error.

[10] Subsections 131(3) and (4) of the R.T.A.

[11] The notice is sent out to landlords first so that they can calculate each tenant's new, reduced rent and incorporate that information into any notices of rent increase the landlord intends to issue. It also provides the landlord with an opportunity to challenge the municipality's calculations or assumptions.

[12] Under the T.P.A., some municipalities sent the notices out late, which created great confusion and necessitated a complex amendment to the regulations (creating even greater uncertainty). Hopefully, this will not occur again.

property taxes have decreased for the complex so there is no point in commencing such an application without that information.

(c) When Rent Reduction Is Not Automatic (s. 133)

When the property taxes for a complex have decreased, tenants are entitled to a rent reduction, regardless of the amount by which the property taxes have decreased. It is just that the reduction is not *automatic* if the decrease in taxes for the complex is 2.49% or less. Taxes can also be decreased as a result of a review or appeal, but because of the passage of time, the municipality may not issue a notice of rent reduction to the affected tenant(s). In such circumstances, a tenant can still apply to the Board under s. 133 of the R.T.A. for a rent reduction due to decreased taxes. The application will be in Form T3. The Board will generally only consider the taxes for the complex for the two calendar years prior to the date the application is filed. If, however, the taxes for an earlier year were decreased by an appeal decision, the Board will consider the taxes for the calendar year that changed as a result of the appeal decision and the calendar year before that but only if the T3 application is filed within 12 months of the date the appeal decision was issued.[13]

Where the tax decrease is 2.49% or less, the resulting rent reduction may be so small that the tenant may not consider it worthwhile to file such an application, considering the time and effort involved and the fact that it costs $45 to file such an application.

(d) Calculating Rent Reduction

The first step in calculating rent reduction is to calculate the percentage decrease in property taxes. This must be calculated using only the actual property taxes for the complex and not any other charges the municipality may have levied on the landlord.

The formula for calculating the percentage decrease in property taxes is as follows:

$$\frac{\text{Taxes for year prior to reduction} - \text{Taxes for year in which taxes were reduced}}{\text{Taxes for year prior to reduction}} \times 100\%$$

The resulting figure (i.e., the percentage decrease in property taxes) is then multiplied by 20% for properties that fall under the multi-residential property class as defined in s. 4 of O. Reg. 282/98 (General) made under the *Assessment Act*[14] to arrive at the percentage rent reduction, or by 15%

[13] O. Reg. 516/06, s. 45(2), para. 3, item ii.

[14] See Appendix 11.

10 — RENT DECREASES

otherwise.[15] This is based upon the assumption that landlords of multi-residential properties typically pay approximately 20% of their total annual revenue from rent in municipal property taxes and landlords of other residential rental properties pay approximately 15% of their total annual revenue from rent in municipal property taxes. The calculation is the same whether or not the rent reduction is automatic.

Example

A landlord of a residential complex that falls under the multi-residential property class as defined in s. 4 of O. Reg. 282/98 (General) made under the *Assessment Act* paid $20,000 in municipal property taxes in 2006 but only $15,000 in 2007. To calculate the percentage decrease in property taxes, refer to the formula above.

Rent Reduction = Percentage Tax Decrease × 20%

Step 1: Calculation of Percentage Tax Decrease

$$= \frac{\text{Taxes for year prior to reduction} - \text{Taxes for year in which taxes were reduced}}{\text{Taxes for year prior to reduction}} \times 100\%$$

$$= \frac{\text{2006 Property Taxes} - \text{2007 Property Taxes}}{\text{2006 Property Taxes}} \times 100\%$$

$$= \frac{\$20{,}000 - \$15{,}000}{\$20{,}000} \times 100\%$$

$$= \frac{\$\,5{,}000}{\$20{,}000} \times 100\%$$

$$= 0.25 \times 100\%$$

$$= 25\%$$

Step 2: Calculation of Rent Reduction

Rent Reduction = Percentage Tax Decrease × 20%

= 25% (calculated in Step 1) × 20%

= 5%

Therefore, in the example given above, where property taxes for the complex have decreased by 25%, the tenants are entitled to a rent reduction equal to 20% (one-fifth) of that figure, or 5%. Since the municipal property tax decreased by more than 2.49%, the rent reduction would be automatic and the municipality should notify the tenants of the complex (if the complex has at least seven units). Effective December 31 of the year in which the taxes were decreased (in this example, December 31, 2007), each tenant's rent will automatically be reduced by 5%. So, for example, if the monthly rent for a

---

[15] Subsection 41(3) of O. Reg. 516/06.

tenant used to be $1,000, the reduced rent as of December 31, 2007, would be $950 ($1,000 minus 5%) and the next time the landlord is permitted to increase the tenant's rent (which date is not affected by this rent decrease), the increase will be based upon the reduced rent of $950.

Since a distinction is now made between properties that do or do not fall under the multi-residential property class as defined in s. 4 of O. Reg. 282/98 (General) made under the *Assessment Act*, it is worth further considering this distinction.

The multi-residential property class as defined in s. 4 of O. Reg. 282/98 (General) made under the *Assessment Act* includes vacant land principally zoned for multi-residential development and land used for residential purposes that has **seven or more self-contained units**. The multi-residential property class does not include the following (set out in para. 1 of subsection 3(1) of O. Reg. 282/98):

1. land that does not have seven or more self-contained residential units;
2. a condominium unit;
3. land owned by a co-operative;
4. co-ownership arrangements (where the right to occupy a rental unit is based on owning shares of the corporate owner or being one of several co-owners of the complex);
5. a timeshare;
6. a group home;
7. a care home;
8. land used for seasonal occupation;
9. a life lease project; and
10. a municipally-licensed rooming house.

For properties that do not fall under the multi-residential property class as defined in s. 4 of O. Reg. 282/98 (General) made under the *Assessment Act*, it will be presumed that municipal property taxes represent 15% of rent revenue, not the usual 20%.[16]

(e) Application to Vary the Amount of the Rent Reduction (s. 132)

(i) Introduction

If a landlord believes that the amount of the rent reduction set out in a notice from the municipality is too high, the landlord may apply to the Board to vary the amount of the rent reduction.[17] Similarly, if a tenant believes that the amount of the rent reduction set out in the notice is too low, the tenant

[16] Thus, for such properties, the rent reduction is calculated by multiplying the percentage tax decrease by 15%.

[17] Section 132 of the R.T.A. and ss. 42 to 44 of O. Reg. 516/06.

may apply to the Board to vary the amount of the rent reduction.[18] Since tenants generally do not have access to the landlord's property tax and other financial records, in reality, tenants rarely apply to the Board to vary the amount of the rent reduction; historically, this type of application is one that is almost exclusively used by landlords.

Pursuant to s. 42(1) of O. Reg. 516/06, a person may apply to the Board for an order varying the rent reduction determined under s. 131 of the Act if:

(a) other charges that are in addition to the municipal property tax and that are not set out in clauses (a), (b), (c), (d), (e) and (f) of the definition of "municipal property tax" in subsection 41(2) were levied upon the landlord by the municipality in the base year;[19]
(b) the percentage of the rent charged in the residential complex that the municipal property tax comprises is not 20% for properties that fall under the multi-residential property class as defined in s. 4 of O. Reg. 282/98 (General) made under the *Assessment Act*, and 15% otherwise;[20]
(c) there is an error in the notice of rent reduction with respect to the amount by which the municipal property tax is reduced or the amount by which the rent is to be reduced; or
(d) the municipal property tax is increased or decreased during the period from the day the notice of rent reduction was issued to March 31 of the year following the date the rent reduction takes effect.

The latter two reasons are premised upon the issuance of a notice of rent reduction. They would obviously not apply to a residential complex with less than seven rental units as no notices are issued for such complexes. Each of the above-noted grounds for application shall now be discussed in greater detail.

For clauses 42(1)(a), (c) and (d), if the landlord files sufficient evidence to establish the annual rents for the complex, that total will be used in calculating the rent decrease. If the landlord fails to prove the annual rents, the calculation will be based upon 20% of the actual decrease, if any, in the municipal taxes and charges from the reference year to the base year for properties that fall under the multi-residential property class as defined in s. 4 of O. Reg. 282/98 (General) made under the *Assessment Act*, and 15% of

---

[18] Also under s. 132 of the R.T.A.

[19] For the purposes of calculating the rent reduction to which the tenants are entitled as a result of a decrease in municipal taxes, the regulations utilize the concept of a "base year" and "reference year". These terms are defined in s. 43 of O. Reg. 194/98 and have meanings similar, but not identical, to the meanings ascribed to the same terms when used in the context of an above-guideline rent increase application. In the context of calculating a rent reduction, the "base year" means the calendar year in which the rent reduction takes effect and the "reference year" means the calendar year immediately preceding the base year.

[20] See Appendix 11.

the actual decrease, if any, in the municipal taxes and charges from the reference year to the base year otherwise.[21]

(ii) Other Charges

If a landlord has paid charges to the municipality and thinks those amounts should be taken into account when determining the percentage of the automatic rent reduction for property taxes (and they were not taken into account), the landlord can apply to vary the amount of the rent reduction.

"Municipal taxes and charges" are defined in s. 2 of the R.T.A. A rent reduction under s. 131 of the R.T.A., however, is *not* based upon a reduction of municipal taxes and charges. It is based upon a reduction in the "municipal property tax" for a residential complex. "Municipal property tax" is given a specific definition for the purpose of s. 131 applications (in s. 41(1) of O. Reg. 516/06):

"Municipal property tax" means taxes charged to a landlord by a municipality and includes taxes levied on a landlord's property in unorganized territory and taxes levied under Division B of Part IX of the *Education Act*, but does not include,

(a) charges for inspections done by the municipality on a residential complex if those charges are related to an alleged breach of a health, safety, housing or maintenance standard,
(b) charges for emergency repairs carried out by the municipality on a residential complex,
(c) charges for work in the nature of a capital expenditure carried out by the municipality,
(d) charges for work, services or non-emergency repairs performed by a municipality in relation to a landlord's non-compliance with a by-law;
(e) penalties, interest, late payment fees or fines;
(f) any amount spent by a municipality under subsection 219(1) of the Act or any administrative fee applied to that amount under subsection 219(2) of the Act, or
(g) any other charges levied by the municipality.

The Board can consider charges such as user fees (for example, tipping fees for dumping garbage) or special levies. The Board has in at least one case also considered water/sewer charges part of the municipal property taxes (and, therefore, properly included in the calculation of the rent decrease), although the reasoning in this case is difficult to follow and it did not ade-

[21] Subsection 43(2) of O. Reg. 516/06.

quately explain how such charges were not excluded by para. 28.1(2)(e) of O. Reg. 194/98 under the T.P.A. (now para. 41(1)(g) of O. Reg. 516/06).[22]

(iii) 20% Factor

If the property falls under the multi-residential property class in s. 4 of O. Reg. 282/98 (General) made under the *Assessment Act* and if a tenant believes the municipal property taxes represent more than 20% of the landlord's rental revenue for the residential complex, the tenant can apply to the Board for an order to vary the amount of the rent reduction. The greater the taxes are as a proportion of rent revenue, the greater will be the rent reduction. Remember that 20% was based upon an assumption by the government as to the typical ratio between property taxes and rent revenue. Where it can be demonstrated that the ratio is different than 20%, the actual ratio will be applied by the Board.

As previously discussed, however, tenants rarely have access to the information necessary to bring forward such an application and, typically, such applications are filed by landlords who wish to demonstrate that taxes represent less than 20% of rent revenue (which will result in a smaller rent reduction for tenants). This is probably the most common basis for A4 applications.

The formula for calculating the rent decrease is:

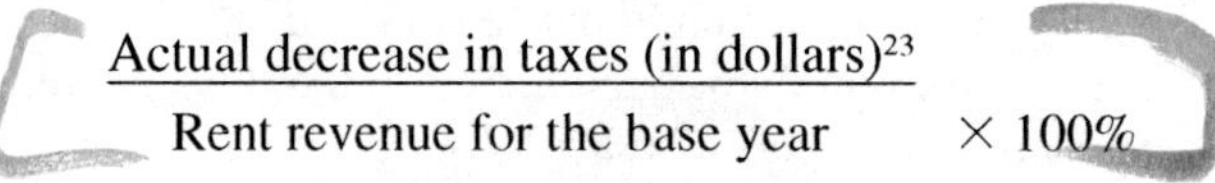

$$\frac{\text{Actual decrease in taxes (in dollars)}^{23}}{\text{Rent revenue for the base year}} \times 100\%$$

The landlord will have to file documentary evidence of the property taxes for the base year and reference year and of the rent revenue for the complex for the base year.[24]

The lower the taxes are in comparison to the rent revenue, the lower the rent reduction will be. Unless the accuracy of the property taxes for the base year and reference year are questioned, the landlord's best bet in attempting to demonstrate that the rent reduction should be lower than that shown on the notice issued by the municipality is to show that the rent revenues are substantially more than five times the property taxes in the base year. Some landlords have been rather creative in attempting to find ways to inflate the rent revenue for a residential complex.

---

[22] *1277897 Ontario Ltd. v. Audette* (Apr. 23, 2003), NOL-06654-RV, [2003] O.R.H.T.D. No. 55, 2003 CarswellOnt 2666 (Ont. Rental Housing Trib.).

[23] Actual decrease in taxes = (reference year taxes – base year taxes).

[24] Section 44 of O. Reg. 516/06.

In *Briarlane Property Management Inc. v. Ali*,[25] the landlord submitted that it ought to include in total annual rents for the base year not only the rent actually received but also the potential rental income that could have been received for the rental units if none of the units had been vacant at any time during the year. The landlord argued that this would be fair since property taxes are based, at least in part, upon the potential income that can be generated from the complex. The Tribunal rejected this argument. Clause 28.5(2)2, item ii. of O. Reg. 194/98 (now item ii. of clause 43(2)2 of O. Reg. 516/06) required the Tribunal to determine the percentage rent decrease for a rental unit by dividing the actual tax decrease by the "total of the annual rents for all of the rental units in the residential complex" and multiplying that quotient by 100. The Tribunal interpreted "total of the annual rents for all of the rental units in the residential complex" to mean the rents actually received for the rental units during the base year, not the potential rental income that the complex might have generated.

In *Briarlane Property Management Inc. v. Ali*, the landlord also argued that part of the rent revenue should be allowed to include income received from "sundries, the fee charged to some tenants for use of air conditioning units, interest on deposits and income derived from the laundry facilities of the complex." The Tribunal pointed out that not all revenue a landlord receives from a residential complex is necessarily exclusively derived from the rent from rental units. It was held that sublet charges, sundry income, air conditioner revenue or interest on deposits were not "rent for rental units in the complex". Similarly, while the laundry room formed part of the complex, it was not a rental unit as defined in s. 1 of the T.P.A. and any rent derived therefrom was not considered to have been rent "for a rental unit".

Finally, the figure provided by the landlord to the Tribunal in the *Briarlane* case as the total of the annual rents for all of the rental units in the residential complex turned out to be misleading. The figure provided by the landlord was actually obtained by taking the rent revenue for December of the base year and multiplying that figure by 12. By using this method of calculating the rent revenue, the landlord overstated the total rent revenue by $140,000! The Tribunal found this to be inappropriate.[26] Since the base year was completed at the time the application was filed, there was no need for the landlord to estimate or extrapolate from the data for December of the base year. The landlord ought to have had available to it actual rent revenue figures for that year. At the direction of the Tribunal, the landlord filed the actual rent revenue figures and the rent reduction was calculated using the actual total of the annual rents for the rental units in the complex.

[25] (Aug. 8, 2003), TNL-45816, [2003] O.R.H.T.D. No. 109, 2003 CarswellOnt 4257 (Ont. Rental Housing Trib.).

[26] A similar ruling was made in *Lifestyle Retirement Communities Ltd. v. Tenants of 8 The Donway E.* (Jan. 28, 2004), TNL-49319 (Ont. Rental Housing Trib.).

(iv) 15% Factor

If the property does not fall under the multi-residential property class in s. 4 of O. Reg. 282/98 (General) made under the *Assessment Act*, a tenant can apply to the Board to vary the amount of the rent reduction if they believe that municipal taxes represent more than 15% of the landlord's rental revenue for the residential complex. The greater the taxes are as a proportion of rent revenue, the greater will be the rent reduction. Remember that 15% was based upon an assumption by the government as to the typical ratio between property taxes and rent revenue for these types of properties. Where it can be demonstrated that the ratio is different than 15%, it will be the actual ratio that is applied by the Board.

As previously discussed, however, tenants rarely have access to the information necessary to bring forward such an application and, such applications are more likely to be filed by landlords who wish to demonstrate that taxes represent less than 15% of rent revenue (which will result in a smaller rent reduction for tenants).

The formula for calculating the rent decrease is:

$$\frac{\text{Actual decrease in taxes (in dollars)}^{27}}{\text{Rent revenue for the base year}} \times 100\%$$

The landlord will have to file documentary evidence of the property taxes for the base year and reference year and of the rent revenue for the complex for the base year.[28]

The lower the taxes are in comparison to the rent revenue, the lower the rent reduction will be. Unless the accuracy of the property taxes for the base year and reference year are questioned, the landlord's best bet in attempting to demonstrate that the rent reduction should be lower than that shown on the notice issued by the municipality is to show that the rent revenues are substantially more than 6.66 times the property taxes in the base year. Some landlords have been rather creative in attempting to find ways to inflate the rent revenue for a residential complex (see the discussion of *Briarlane Property Management Inc. v. Ali*[29] in the previous section).

In *Lifestyle Retirement Communities Ltd. v. Tenants of 8 The Donway E.*,[30] the residential complex was a care home. As such, it was taxed somewhat differently from other residential complexes. The municipal taxes for this complex were based upon its total potential income. The landlord's income was derived from both rent and from charges for care services. Rent only

---

27 Actual decrease in taxes = (reference year taxes – base year taxes).

28 Section 44 of O. Reg. 516/06.

29 (Aug. 8, 2003), TNL-45816, [2003] O.R.H.T.D. No. 109, 2003 CarswellOnt 4257 (Ont. Rental Housing Trib.).

30 (Jan. 28, 2004), TNL-49319 (Ont. Rental Housing Trib.).

accounted for approximately 51% of the total revenue generated from this complex. The landlord argued that it was unfair to base the rent reduction calculation on a comparison of 100% of the tax reduction to only 49% of the revenue upon which the taxes were based. The landlord suggested that the Tribunal ought to either only utilize 51% of the tax decrease or, if using the entire tax decrease, include *all* revenue generated by the complex (and not just the annual revenue from rent). The landlord could provide no statutory authority for departing from the calculations required by the relevant regulations and, as a result, its submissions failed.

(v) Mistake in the Notice

Landlords and tenants can apply to vary the amount of the rent reduction if they believe there is an error in the notice of rent reduction issued by the municipality. The error may be in the amount of the tax reduction or the amount of the rent reduction.

(vi) Change in Taxes after Notice Issued

The property taxes for the year could change after the notices are sent out because of reconsiderations or appeals to the property tax assessment for the complex. If the property taxes were either increased or decreased after the notices of rent reduction were sent out by the municipality but before March 31 of the year following the effective date of the rent reduction, either the landlord or the tenant can apply under s. 132 of the R.T.A. to vary the amount of the rent reduction set out in the notice.

(vii) Procedure

The application is filed using form A4 and the filing fee is $45. If a tenant is applying, the tenancy must be in existence; former tenants cannot apply under this section. The deadline for filing this type of application is the later of:

1. 90 days following the day on which the person who will be the applicant is given the notice of rent reduction (or 90 days following the day on which the tax notice is issued if a notice of rent reduction is not required); and
2. March 31 of the year following the effective date of the rent reduction.[31]

[31] Subsection 42(2) of O. Reg. 516/068.

The Board cannot extend this deadline.[32]

Pursuant to s. 44 of O. Reg. 516/06, the following must be filed with the application:

1. Evidence of the amount of municipal taxes in the reference year and in the base year.
2. If the application is made under clause 42(1)(*a*), evidence of the other charges levied by the municipality in the reference year and in the base year.
3. If the application is made under clause 42(1)(*b*), evidence of the rents charged for the residential complex.
4. If notice of a reduction of rent has been given under subsection 131(3) of the Act, a copy of that notice.

The applicant must complete the application form (A4) and, if a notice of rent reduction was issued by the municipality, attach a copy of that notice to the application. The applicant must then file the application, together with any documents required by s. 44 of O. Reg. 516/06 (listed above) and the filing fee. Once the Board has received the necessary documents and the filing fee, normally a written hearing is scheduled.[33] The applicant must then serve a copy of the application and the notice of written hearing on each respondent no later than 20 days after the notice of written hearing is issued.[34] Parties are not required to serve copies of any of the supporting documentation (other than the copy of the notice of rent reduction attached to the application) on the other parties to the application.[35] The applicant must file with the Board a certificate of service according to Rule 11.1 no later than 25 days after the notice of written hearing is issued,[36] failing which the Board may dismiss the application.[37] In a written hearing, landlords and tenants file their evidence and written submissions with the Board[38] and a Member makes a decision based upon the documents filed, without holding a face-to-face hearing.

Upon the objection of a party or upon its own initiative, the Board may[39] consider whether it is inappropriate for the matter to proceed by way of a written hearing. If the Board finds it is not appropriate for the matter to be

---

[32] Paragraph 2 of s. 56, O. Reg. 516/06.

[33] Rule 22 of the Board's Rules of Practice.

[34] Rule 22.4 of the Board's Rules of Practice.

[35] Section 184(3) of the R.T.A. and Rule 22.5 of the Board's Rules of Practice.

[36] Rule 22.6 of the Board's Rules of Practice.

[37] Rule 22.7 of the Board's Rules of Practice.

[38] The dates they are required to submit and reply to documents are set out in the notice of written hearing.

[39] By s. 184(2) of the R.T.A., s. 5.1(2) of the *Statutory Powers Procedure Act* does not apply to this type of application and, therefore, the Board can decide to conduct the hearing as a written hearing whether or not a party to the proceeding objects.

decided by way of a written hearing, it can order that the matter continue as an oral hearing.[40]

The effective date of the rent decrease is always December 31 of the year in which the taxes decreased.

4. REDUCTION OR DISCONTINUANCE OF A SERVICE OR FACILITY (s. 130) AND SUB-METERING OF ELECTRICTY

A tenant can apply for an order reducing the rent for the rental unit due to a reduction or discontinuance of a service or facility provided to the tenant.[41] The application, on Form T3, must be filed by the tenant within 12 months of the date of the reduction or discontinuance.[42] A former tenant may also apply under s. 130 if they were affected by the discontinuance or reduction of the services or facilities while they were a tenant of the rental unit.[43] The fee for making the application is $45.[44]

Unlike the similar application under s. 23 of the *Rent Control Act*, the Board does not have the authority to add as parties all other tenants of the residential complex affected by the reduction. Under s. 130 of the R.T.A., each tenant affected by the reduction must generally file his or her own application. However, under s. 186(2) of the R.T.A., two or more tenants (from different rental units) of a residential complex may together file an application (if each tenant signs it) and, pursuant to s. 198(1) of the R.T.A., the Board has the authority to join similar applications and hear them together in a single hearing, if it would be fair to do so.

The provisions for calculating the appropriate rent reduction, if any, to which a tenant is entitled as a result of a reduction or discontinuance of a service or facility, are found in s. 39 of O. Reg. 516/06. These provisions can be summarized as follows:

1. *If the discontinuance or reduction is temporary* and its duration is reasonable, taking into account the effect on the tenant, there shall be no reduction of rent;[45]

2. Where a service or facility was previously provided under an agreement under s. 123 of the R.T.A. (or similar provisions of predecessor legislation), the reduction in rent on *discontinuing* the service or

---

[40] Rules 22.1, 22.2 and 22.3 of the Board's Rules of Practice.

[41] Section 130 of the R.T.A.

[42] Section 130(5) of the R.T.A.

[43] Section 130(2) of the R.T.A.

[44] If tenants of more than one unit within the same complex choose to bring one application to deal with a common complaint, the fee is $45 for the tenant(s) of the first unit plus $5 for the tenant(s) of every additional unit up to a maximum of $450.

[45] Subsection 39(7), O. Reg. 516/06.

facility shall be equal to either the most recent amount of the separate charge for the service or facility or, where there is no separate charge, the increase in rent which the landlord took when the service or facility was first provided, adjusted upwards to take into account rent increases since that time;[46]

3. Otherwise, where a service or facility is *discontinued* (permanently or for an unreasonably long duration) and
   - (a) *the discontinuance was reasonable* in the circumstances, the rent shall be reduced by an amount that is equal to what would be a reasonable charge for the service or facility based on the cost of the service or facility to the landlord or, if the cost cannot be determined or if there is no cost, on the value of the service or facility, including the cost to the tenant or former tenant of replacing the discontinued service or facility;[47]
   - (b) *the discontinuance was not reasonable* in the circumstances, the rent shall be reduced by an amount that takes into account the following:
     - (i) the value of the service or facility, including the cost to the tenant or former tenant of replacing the discontinued service or facility;
     - (ii) the effect of the discontinuance on the tenant or former tenant; and
     - (iii) the fact that the amount of rent reduction granted under this provision cannot be less than would be given had the discontinuance been reasonable.[48]
4. If a service or facility is *reduced* (permanently or for an unreasonably long duration), the amount of the reduction of rent shall be a reasonable proportion, based on the degree of the reduction of the service or facility, of the amount by which the rent would have been reduced if the service had been discontinued.[49]

Although the "reasonable charge" for a discontinued service or facility is based upon the cost to the landlord, the rent reduction will not necessarily be identical to the landlord's actual cost of providing the service or facility. In *Re 198 Springbank Drive, London,*[50] the Rental Housing Tribunal ordered a rent reduction of $5 per unit per month, notwithstanding the fact that the landlord's actual cost of providing the service was $0.36 per unit per month.

---

46 Subsection 39(5), O. Reg. 516/06.

47 Subsection 39(2), O. Reg. 516/06.

48 Subsections 39(3) and (4), O. Reg. 516/06.

49 Subsection 39(6), O. Reg. 516/06.

50 SWT-00764 (September 30, 1999).

In making this order, the Tribunal ruled that the actual cost to the landlord is only one factor to be considered in determining the reasonable charge for the facility.

During major balcony repairs, it is common for tenants to lose access to their balconies. This has sometimes formed the basis for rent reduction applications. Tenants who feel they are not receiving full value for the rent they are paying (since they cannot enjoy the use of their balconies) may commence applications seeking a temporary reduction of their rent (during the period of the balcony repairs). In the past, such applications were frequently combined with applications seeking other relief (including abatements of rent) for interference with their reasonable enjoyment of their rental units as a result of the noise, dust and vibrations caused by the balcony work. However, given the limited relief available to tenants on applications based upon interference in their enjoyment caused by necessary repairs to the complex,[51] tenants in such circumstances may now choose to restrict their applications to a demand for a temporary reduction in rent as a result of a reduction in services or facilities.

Two main difficulties arise with the cases in which a tenant or tenants have based a rent reduction application (under s. 130) upon the temporary "loss" of a balcony.

The first is in determining the value of the balcony. In *Barker v. Park Willow Developments*,[52] the landlord adduced evidence at the hearing as to the value of the balcony that was based upon spreading its annual costs for the complex over the total floor space of the complex (resulting in a nominal value of pennies per day for each balcony). The Member rejected this evidence and calculated the value of the balcony based on the proportional floor space of the balcony in comparison to the area of the entire rental unit and then using the ratio by which the floor space had been reduced to calculate a proportional reduction in monthly rent. The Divisional Court held that it was an error in law for the Member not to have reconvened the hearing to hear evidence and take submissions if he intended to adopt an approach other than the only one that had been suggested at the hearing.[53] The matter was remitted back to the Tribunal. The decision from the second hearing is reported as *Totzek v. Park Willow Developments*.[54]

This brings us to the second difficulty. It is not entirely clear whether a balcony is a "facility" as that term is defined in s. 2 of the Act. Balconies are not specifically identified as a service or facility in the definition (s. 2); the list provided in the definition is illustrative rather than exhaustive and it

---

[51] Discussed in greater detail in Chapters 11 and 12.

[52] (March 13, 2004), TNT-02909 and TNT-02911 (Ont. Rental Housing Trib.).

[53] *Barker v. Park Willow Developments* (2004), 2004 CarswellOnt 2848, 188 O.A.C. 276 (Ont. Div. Ct.).

[54] (Oct. 18, 2004), TNL-02909, TNT-02911, 2004 CarswellOnt 5468 (Ont. Rental Housing Trib.).

leaves this question open. Despite the fact that the landlord apparently conceded that the balcony was a "facility" and that the tenant was entitled to at least some rent reduction under s. 142 of the T.P.A.,[55] when the *Totzek* matter returned to the Tribunal for a new hearing, the tenants' application for a rent reduction was dismissed on the basis that a balcony is not a "service or facility" but is part of the rental unit itself.[56] A similar interpretation under the R.T.A. has been adopted by a Member of the Landlord and Tenant Board more recently in *Cap Reit or Canadian Apartment Properties Real Estate Investment Trust, Re.*[57]

The rather fluid nature of the definition of "services and facilities" is illustrated in the case of *Boudreau et al. v. Shelter Canadian Properties Limited.*[58] In this case, the residential complex was comprised of row houses in which each rental unit had an outside area enclosed by fencing. The outside area included patios for each rental unit and a common play area. The landlord removed the fencing, which the tenants claimed resulted in a loss of privacy and created an increased risk of harm to their children and pets. The landlord apparently planned to replace the fencing but stated this could take one to three years. The Tribunal found that the enclosed patio space and common play area was a recreational facility and concluded that there had been a discontinuance of this facility because of the loss of the fence. A 10% rent reduction was ordered (until the fencing was replaced). On appeal by the landlord, the Divisional Court upheld the Tribunal's ruling that the fence was a part of the service and facility to which the tenants were entitled under the tenancy but directed the Tribunal to re-examine the issue of how the rent reduction should be calculated, as the Member failed in the first instance to make specific reference to ss. 30(2) and (5) of O. Reg. 194/98 and failed to make explicit findings of fact to support the amount of rent reduction awarded.

Other examples of cases in which tenants have been granted a rent reduction include: a 10% reduction for two months (June and July) as a result of the temporary discontinuance of air conditioning;[59] a reduction in rent based upon the loss of use of a community hall;[60] a rent reduction for the

---

[55] See *Barker v. Park Willow Developments* (2004), 2004 CarswellOnt 2848, 188 O.A.C. 276 (Ont. Div. Ct.), at para. 6.

[56] *Totzek v. Park Willow Developments* (Oct. 18, 2004), TNL-02909, TNT-02911, 2004 CarswellOnt 5468 (Ont. Rental Housing Trib.). See also *Papas v. Montcrest Apartment* (Aug. 20, 1999), TST-00361 (Ont. Rental Housing Trib.) in which it was held that quiet enjoyment is not a service or facility as contemplated by s. 130 of the *Act.*

[57] Landlord and Tenant Board File No. CET-00506 (Oct. 29, 2007).

[58] (January 13, 2003), Div. Ct. File 01-BN-10854, re (Nov. 15, 2001), SOT-01968 (Ont. Rental Housing Trib.).

[59] *Fatemi v. Residential II GP Ltd.* (August 20, 1998), TST-00075, 1998 CarswellOnt 6419 (Ont. Rental Housing Trib.). The landlord commenced an appeal of this decision but the outcome is unknown.

[60] *Tenants v. Cove Mobile Home Park* (Sept. 30, 1999), SWT-00764 (Ont. Rental Housing Trib.).

discontinuance of storage lockers;[61] a rent reduction of $25 per month for loss of the use of a parking space at the residential complex;[62] a rent reduction of $97.50 per month for loss of the use of washer and dryer facilities at no charge (previously included in the rent);[63] and a temporary rent reduction of $400 per month for the 5.5 month period that the landlord moved into the basement of the house, which effectively deprived the tenants of the use of that space during that period of time.[64]

In *Dixon et al. v. LT Greenwin Property Management Inc.*,[65] the existing hot water boiler in the building was no longer able to provide an adequate supply of hot water to the units in question. As a result, the supply of hot water was temporarily reduced from September 28, 1999, through January 31, 2000, (at which time the landlord replaced the old boiler with a new one that was able to provide an adequate supply of hot water). Although the Member found that the landlord was not in breach of its maintenance obligations, considering the duration of the problem and the impact upon the tenants, the Member deemed it appropriate to order a 20% reduction in the rent of the effected tenants for four months (October 1999 through January 2000).

As discussed in Chapter 1, in an effort to encourage tenants to conserve electricity, the R.T.A. included a new provision (s. 137) permitting landlords to install smart meters and, ultimately, have tenants pay for the amount of electricity they use, even if electricity was originally included in the rent. There are some strict conditions, however, with which the landlord must comply, including monitoring electricity usage for the unit for 12 months and installing new, energy-efficient appliances. The government decided to delay having this part of the R.T.A. take effect and it has not yet been proclaimed.

Some landlords have decided to take matters into their own hands.[66] Either they are tired of waiting for s. 137 to be proclaimed or they would

---

[61] *Taber et al. v. Doublesweet Investments* (Nov. 26, 2001), TNT-02215, TNT-02216 (Ont. Rental Housing Trib.). On appeal, the landlord introduced evidence that it had restored the lockers to the tenants as of January 2002. At the hearing before the Tribunal, the landlord had given no indication that the discontinuance of this service or facility was intended to be temporary. Given this new information, the Court decided to alter the Tribunal's order by ending the rent reduction as of December 2001. On the issue of the lockers' value, the Court agreed that since the landlord had adduced no evidence at the hearing as to the cost of providing the lockers or as to the value of such service/facility, the Tribunal was correct in accepting the tenants' evidence (which was the only evidence) as to the value of the lockers: *Taber v. Doublesweet Investments* (April 30, 2003), 172 O.A.C. 130 (Ont. Div. Ct.). In Landlord and Tenant Board File No. NOT-00001 (Feb. 23, 2007), the Board awarded a 5% rent reduction ($32.50 per month) for loss of the use of a storage locker.

[62] Landlord and Tenant Board File No. SOT-00005 (March 8, 2007).

[63] Landlord and Tenant Board File No. TST-02071 (Jan. 12, 2009).

[64] Landlord and Tenant Board File No. TNT-00014 and TNT-00052 (March 14, 2007). The total rent reduction awarded was $2,200.

[65] (Apr. 11, 2000), TNT-00964 (Ont. Rental Housing Trib.).

[66] See Chapter 7, "Hydro Sub-Metering".

rather try to install a sub-metering system before they are forced to comply with the conditions of s. 137. Such landlords are attempting to install meters (sub-meters) that can monitor the electricity usage in individual rental units and then they are purporting to reduce the rent by some amount they deem to be reasonable and to have the tenant billed for the amount of electricity actually being consumed in the unit.

Although this may sound attractive, there are some points to consider.

First, while a tenant may be able to agree to such an arrangement, it is far from clear that, in the absence of any clear statutory authority, a landlord can force such a unilateral change in the terms of the tenancy agreement over the objection of an unwilling tenant.[67]

Second, without careful monitoring over at least 12 months of an individual tenant's usage of electricity (which is not possible in most buildings where there is no sub-metering of individual units), it is impossible to know whether the rent reduction proposed by the landlord is a reasonable one.

Third, even if the landlord installs a sub-meter for an individual rental unit so that actual electricity usage can be monitored for that unit, in the absence of any statutory authority, it appears to me that the landlord has no right to force a tenant to pay separately for electricity if the original agreement between the parties was for the rent to include all utilities.

Fourth, if a tenant agrees *now* to such an arrangement, that tenant may not later (if and when the smart meter provisions of the R.T.A. are implemented) have the benefit of the provisions of the R.T.A. that are designed to protect tenants (such as requiring the landlord to install new, energy-efficient appliances in the unit and to monitor electricity use for a year before forcing the tenant to pay directly for electricity in order to determine a fair rent reduction).

Fifth, there may be "administration" fees charged by the company monitoring the sub-meters, over and above the actual cost of the electricity. This may mean that the tenant will actually end up paying more in total than if they, the tenant, had not agreed to pay separately for electricity.

Sixth, some tenancy agreements provide that, although electricity is included in rent currently, at some point in the future, the landlord may, at the landlord's sole discretion, decrease the rent and force the tenant to pay

---

[67] It is unclear whether a landlord may unilaterally change the terms of the tenancy agreement and begin to charge separately for electricity even though, previously, it was included as part of the rent. In *Flemingdon Apartments*, (July 30, 1999) TNL-03497 (Ont. Rental Housing Trib.), I expressed my doubts about the legality of one party to the contract unilaterally changing the terms of that contract. The landlord in that case argued that a landlord has the absolute right to discontinue a service (in this case, electricity) whether or not a tenant consents, as long as an appropriate rent reduction is provided. I found, however, that simply billing differently for the same service did not amount to a discontinuance of the service and that a landlord had no right to unilaterally change the terms of the tenancy agreement, absent clear statutory authority.

separately for electricity. Whether such terms are actually enforceable may depend upon the exact wording of the contract. Tenants should be careful about signing tenancy agreements that contain such a provision and those who have already signed an agreement containing such a clause should consider seeking legal advice.

There are two recent decisions that have clarified the situation, one from the Landlord and Tenant Board and the other from the Ontario Energy Board.

In Landlord and Tenant Board File No. TST-01693-AM,[68] the landlord had installed sub-meters and attempted to force tenants, whose rent included electricity, to pay separately for electricity based upon their actual consumption. The landlord purported to reduce each tenant's rent to compensate for this change. A "third party service provider" monitored the system and billed tenants for the electricity and tenants were instructed by the landlord to pay the amounts billed directly to the third party service provider. Approximately 70 tenants got together and brought an application before the Landlord and Tenant Board to challenge the landlord's conduct. The presiding Member found that,

> [B]y transferring the hydro (electricity) payment obligation from the Landlord to the Tenant[s] without the consent agreement that is contemplated by section 125 of the *Residential Tenancies Act, 2006* (the "*Act*"), the Landlord has harassed, coerced and threatened the Tenants and substantially interfered with the reasonable enjoyment of the rental unit or residential complex by the Tenants or by a member of their household.

The Member ordered the landlord to cease this activity.

Some of the tenants had executed tenancy agreements that stated that, even though rent would initially include electricity, at some later point in time the landlord could unilaterally require tenants to pay separately for electricity. The Landlord and Tenant Board found that such an agreement was unenforceable because it did not comply with s. 125 of the R.T.A. and this part of the tenancy agreement lacked sufficient particulars (for example, how the rent reduction would be determined) to form a binding contract. For the tenants with older tenancy agreements (in which no such change in billing was contemplated), the landlord's conduct was determined to represent an attempt to unilaterally change the terms of the contract without any consent on the part of the tenants; such a unilateral change was also found to be contrary to the R.T.A. One party simply cannot change the terms of the contract without express authority to do so under the R.T.A.

In 2009, the Ontario Energy Board initiated a proceeding respecting discretionary metering activities in residential buildings, including the in-

[68] Issued on July 2, 2009 and amended on July 20, 2009.

stallation of smart sub-meters, and released its decision on August 13, 2009.[69] The Ontario Energy Board was receiving numerous complaints from tenants with respect to the implementation of smart sub-metering in their apartment buildings. The volume of complaints, their nature and the scope of the sub-metering activity being undertaken in the province led the Energy Board's Chief Compliance Officer to issue a Compliance Bulletin (Bulletin 200901, March 24, 2009) which "unequivocally characterized the discretionary metering activity being undertaken as unauthorized, and inconsistent with the requirements of the *Electricity Act, 1998*". In the absence of any regulation governing this type of activity, the Energy Board decided to intervene and create some ground rules (at least, that is, until the government comes up with a legislative solution). The Energy Board's decision has the following implications:

1. Any smart sub-metering installation in bulk metered residential complexes on or after November 3, 2005, is unauthorized and any resulting changes to financial arrangements respecting the payment of electricity charges by tenants is unenforceable;[70]
2. Landlords who have engaged in such activities during this period must restore tenants to the position they were in prior to the installation of the sub-meters;
3. If section 137 of the R.T.A. is ever proclaimed and the necessary regulations passed, it will apply only to the smart metering activities of "licensed distributors" and not to landlords and their agents who are considered to be "exempt distributors";
4. Landlords who are exempt distributors may, from the date of this decision onwards, install smart sub-metering systems in residential complexes, provided they obtain the express, voluntary and informed written consent of the tenants to be affected, which requires the landlord:

    a. to have a third party perform an energy audit and to share the methodology and results with tenants;
    b. to disclose the amount of any administrative charge that will be included on the electricity bills;
    c. to specify the amount of the rent reduction being offered and to provide tenants with a detailed description of the methodology used to arrive at the rent reduction;
    d. to disclose the methodology used to apportion the delivery charges amongst the customers;

---

[69] EB-2009-0111 (August 13, 2009), available on the Ontario Energy Board website: *www.oeb.gov.on.ca*.

[70] I.e., any consent obtained by a distributor prior to August 13, 2009 is ineffective and cannot be relied upon.

e. to obtain the consent at the time that the change in billing is being proposed.[71]

Note, however, that although this order purports to permit this type of activity if a landlord complies with the conditions listed therein, this is only from the point of view of the Ontario Energy Board. The Landlord and Tenant Board retains exclusive jurisdiction over residential tenancies in the province and it is conceivable that the Landlord and Tenant Board may find that such a change in billing, even with the "informed" consent of tenants, may be inconsistent with the provisions of the R.T.A.

Thus, until the Ontario Energy Board changes its position or s. 137 of the R.T.A. (or some similar provision) is actually proclaimed to be in force, tenants should be wary of any attempt by a landlord to install or use hydro sub-meters in residential complexes (other than condominiums). Tenants should be very cautious about agreeing to pay separately for something that used to be included as part of their rent. A tenant faced with such a situation should obtain legal advice before making any agreement with the landlord.

5. RENT REDUCTION RELATED TO AN AGI ORDER ("COSTS NO LONGER BORNE")

(a) Introduction

One of the biggest complaints from tenants under the *Tenant Protection Act*, revolved around the fact that there were a number of mechanisms by which a landlord could seek to increase the rent charged, but no reciprocal method for tenants to have the rent reduced. Tenants would ask, "If my rent goes up to pay for improvements to the building, once the capital costs have been fully paid for, why doesn't my rent come back down?" They would also ask, "If my rent is increased to cover a spike in utility costs, why isn't my rent reduced when the cost of utilities falls?"

Even the Divisional Court was troubled that there appeared to be no good answers to these questions and urged the government (in *Burton v. Leadway Apartments Ltd.*[72]) to take another look at the relevant provisions. After public consultation, the government has incorporated into the R.T.A. provisions that allow a rent increase (above the guideline) to be "rolled back" once the capital expenditures that justified the rent increase have been paid for or once the cost of utilities has decreased substantially.

[71] I.e., not in advance, such as when the tenancy agreement is being executed.

[72] (2002), 165 O.A.C. 114, 2002 CarswellOnt 2771, [2002] O.J. No. 3252 (Ont. Div. Ct.) File No. 86/02 (Aug. 26, 2002) re (Sept. 17, 2001), TNL-29284 (Ont. Rental Housing Trib.).

(b) Utilities (s. 128)

Where the Board issues an above-guideline increase order (under s. 126 of the R.T.A.) based in whole or in part upon an extraordinary increase in utility costs, the order will set out the percentage increase attributed to the increased utility costs as well as the landlord's obligation to keep tenants informed about the total costs of utilities for the complex.[73] Where the utility costs subsequently decline (by more than the prescribed percentage in the prescribed period), the landlord will be required to reduce the rent accordingly.[74] This does not apply to a tenant of a rental unit in respect of a utility if the landlord ceases to provide the utility to the rental unit in accordance with the R.T.A. or in accordance with an agreement between the landlord and tenant.[75]

The "prescribed" rules are set out in ss. 35 to 37 of O. Reg. 516/06. Each year for the five years immediately following the first effective date of the rent increase,[76] if the landlord's utility costs decrease, the tenant affected by an AGI order (based on an extraordinary increase in utility costs) may be entitled to a rent decrease if the reduction in utility costs is sufficient to result in a rent reduction of at least 0.5% of the tenant's rent.[77] If, after calculating the rent reduction under subsections 36(1) and (2) of O. Reg. 516/06, the decrease turns out to be less than 0.5% of the current rent, the landlord need not reduce the tenant's rent.

Each year for five years, on the anniversary of the first effective date of the rent increase, the landlord must provide information[78] in an approved form to a tenant affected by such an order and who remains in the rental unit.[79] A tenant can insist upon the landlord providing a compact disc containing all utility bills used to justify current utility costs (if the tenant's demand is made within two years of being given information by the landlord about those costs).[80] The landlord can charge up to $5 for the compact disc.[81] Alternatively, the landlord and tenant can agree that the supporting documentation will be provided by e-mail or in paper form[82] or the landlord can unilaterally decide to provide the information in paper form if: (1) the resi-

---

73 Subsections 128(1) and (2) of the R.T.A.

74 Subsection 128(3) of the R.T.A.

75 Subsection 128(4) of the R.T.A.

76 I.e., for five 12-month periods that begin and end on the same days of the year as the base year used in the Board's order permitting the rent increase based on an extraordinary increase in utility costs (s. 37(2) of O. Reg. 516/06).

77 Subsection 37(1) of O. Reg. 516/06.

78 Listed in subsection 35(3) of O. Reg. 516/06.

79 Subsections 35(1) and (2) of O. Reg. 516/06.

80 Subsections 35(5) and (6) of O. Reg. 516/06.

81 Subsection 35(7) of O. Reg. 516/06.

82 Subsection 35(8) of O. Reg. 516/06.

dential complex contains six or fewer units and is located in a rural or remote area; (2) the landlord cannot reasonably provide a compact disc; and (3) the landlord provides the tenant with a photocopy of the information required under subsection 35(5) for a charge of not more than $5.[83]

Over the five-year period following the first effective date of the rent increase, the tenant can receive one or more reductions as long as the total of all rent reductions during that period does not exceed the amount by which the rent was increased as a result of the AGI order. If a rent decrease is to take effect on the same day as a rent increase, the rent decrease shall be deemed to take effect one day earlier, so that the rent increase will be calculated on the lower rent (i.e., the rent after the decrease has been applied).[84]

In theory, it should be simple to calculate the amount of the rent reduction. According to an example given on the website of the Ministry of Municipal Affairs and Housing, if a $10,000 extraordinary increase in utility costs resulted in a 2% above guideline rent increase for the tenant and if the utility costs later decrease by $10,000, the tenant will get a 2% rent reduction. The usual formula for calculating the rent decrease (if any) is set out in subsection 36(1) of O. Reg. 516/06. A more complicated calculation must be performed if, during the relevant five-year period, the landlord stopped providing one of the utilities that originally justified the above-guideline rent increase. In such a case, the method of calculating the rent reduction (if any) is found in subsection 36(2) of O. Reg. 516/06. It may be beyond the ability of most tenants (and many landlords) to calculate the rent reduction required under these provisions and, unless the Board distributes software to assist parties in this regard, parties may wish to consider retaining the services of an expert advisor.

The onus is upon the landlord to keep track of these matters and to automatically reduce the rent for tenants who are affected by such orders and who continue to occupy their units when the cost of utilities decreases by more than the prescribed amount. No specific provision permits a tenant to commence an application against a landlord who does not comply with s. 128 of the R.T.A. It is not clear at this time how a tenant will be able to enforce his or her rights under s. 128. Hopefully, this will be resolved in the near future.

(c) Capital Expenditures (s. 129)

If an application by a landlord for an above-guideline rent increase (AGI) under s. 126 of the R.T.A. (or s. 138 of the T.P.A.) was filed on or after May 3, 2006 and is based in whole or in part on capital expenditures, and if that

[83] Subsection 35(9) of O. Reg. 516/06.

[84] Subsection 36(6) of O. Reg. 516/06.

application is granted, the order issued by the Board (or Tribunal, prior to January 31, 2007) shall specify the percentage increase that is attributable to the capital expenditures and the date and amount by which the rent must eventually be decreased by the landlord (if the same tenant still resides in the unit on that date).[85] That date is determined in accordance with the rules prescribed in subsection 38(1) of O. Reg. 516/06.

If the rent charged to the tenant for a rental unit is increased pursuant to the order by the maximum percentage permitted by the order and the tenant continues to occupy the rental unit on the date specified (for rolling back the rent), the landlord must, on that date, reduce the rent charged to the tenant by the percentage specified in the order.[86]

If the rent charged to the tenant for a rental unit is increased pursuant to the order by less than the maximum percentage permitted by the order and the tenant continues to occupy the rental unit on the date specified, the landlord must, on that date, reduce the rent charged to the tenant by the percentage determined by the regulations.[87]

If the increase in rent (above the guideline) was due in whole to eligible capital expenditures, the percentage reduction shall be equal to the percentage increase taken by the landlord.[88]

If the increase in rent (above the guideline) was due only in part to eligible capital expenditures, the percentage reduction shall be the percentage for eligible capital expenditures as determined under s. 34 of O. Reg. 516/06.[89]

In any event, every AGI order will contain a schedule that seeks to explain to tenants how to determine when and by how much the rent should be reduced. The landlord is required to keep track of these matters and to automatically reduce the rent for tenants who are affected by such orders and who continue to occupy their units on the date specified in the order. No specific provision permits a tenant to commence an application against a landlord who does not comply with s. 129 of the R.T.A. If the landlord does not reduce the rent on the specified date, a tenant should communicate with the landlord and remind the landlord about the obligation to roll-back the rent as of the specified date. If the landlord refuses to co-operate and the tenant has paid more rent that the landlord could legally charge, the tenant could conceivably commence an application under s. 135, claiming that the landlord has collected or retained money illegally (discussed later in this chapter). Alternatively, the tenant would be justified in calculating the new, lower rent and then beginning to pay that reduced rent; if the landlord wishes to then

---

[85] Section 129 and subsection 258(2) of the R.T.A.

[86] Clause 129(c)(i) of the R.T.A.

[87] Clause 129(c)(ii) of the R.T.A.

[88] Paragraph 1 of subsection 38(2), O. Reg. 516/06.

[89] Paragraph 2 of subsection 38(2), O. Reg. 516/06.

challenge the tenant's calculation, it will be the landlord who has to bring an application before the Board (based upon alleged arrears of rent).

Of course, the usefulness of this provision is yet to be seen. It will depend on whether the same tenant remains in the same unit long enough for the "roll-back" provisions to take effect and whether the landlord or tenant remembers to keep track of the relevant date. It will also depend on whether the relevant provisions of the legislation remain in effect years from now, when the rent reduction is supposed to occur.

6. TENANT'S APPLICATION TO RECOVER MONEY COLLECTED OR RETAINED ILLEGALLY

A tenant, former tenant or prospective tenant may apply to the Board to recover any money collected or retained illegally by the landlord, superintendent or agent of the landlord.[90] This application is made on Form T1 and must be filed within one year of the date the unlawful rent was first collected.[91] In some circumstances, if the landlord is still retaining the money, it may be possible to rely on that fact and commence an application more than one year after it was collected.[92] The fee for making this type of application is $45.[93] The application and notice of hearing must be served at least 10 days before the hearing (Rule 10.1) and the applicant must file the certificate of service with the Board within five days of service being effected (Rule 11.2). As discussed in Chapter 2, the monetary jurisdiction of the Landlord and Tenant Board is currently $10,000.[94]

This type of application is typically commenced where a tenant (or former tenant or prospective tenant) alleges that the landlord has:

1. collected or retained an illegal charge;[95]
2. collected or retained an excessively large rent deposit;
3. failed to refund the rent deposit;

---

[90] Subsections 135(1) and (2) of the R.T.A. (formerly subsections 144(1) and (2) of the T.P.A.).

[91] Pursuant to subsection 135(4) and s. 136 of the R.T.A. See, for example, *Smith v. Jansen* (June 22, 2006), TET-05762, [2006] O.R.H.T.D. No. 82, 2006 CarswellOnt 4418 (Ont. Rental Housing Trib.) and Landlord and Tenant Board File No. SWT-00924 (February 1, 2008). The only exception to this is an application under s. 122 of the R.T.A., for which there is a two year limitation period (ss. 136(3) and 122(2) of the R.T.A).

[92] Please refer to the discussion of this topic in Chapter 8.

[93] If tenants of more than one unit within the same complex choose to bring one application to deal with a common complaint, the fee is $45 for the tenant(s) of the first unit plus $5 for the tenant(s) of every additional unit up to a maximum of $450.

[94] The monetary jurisdiction of the Small Claims Court is scheduled to be increased to $25,000, effective January 2010. Since the monetary jurisdiction of the Board is tied to that of the Small Claims Court, the monetary jurisdiction of the Board will also be increased to $25,000 at that time.

[95] See s. 17 of O. Reg. 516/06 for a list of permitted charges.

4. failed to pay interest on the rent deposit; or
5. charged a higher rent than is legally permissible.[96]

Although an application under s. 135 of the R.T.A. may have the effect of reducing the amount of rent a tenant must *pay* to a landlord, such an application does *not* actually result in a reduction of the lawful rent. If the allegation by the tenant or former tenant is that the landlord has charged illegally high rent and if the application is granted, the Board shall make a finding as to the lawful rent for the unit and will order that the landlord repay any amounts collected in excess of the lawful rent. The Board is making a declaration as to the rent that the landlord can lawfully charge to the tenant; the Board is not by such an order reducing the lawful rent. If the tenancy is a continuing one, the Board may permit the tenant to collect the amounts owed to the tenant by deducting those amounts from future rent payments. If the tenancy no longer exists, the former tenant will have to collect the amount ordered in the same manner as any other court order.

If the allegation by the tenant (or former tenant or prospective tenant) is that the landlord has collected an illegal charge (i.e., a charge in addition to the rent) and if the application is granted, the Board will order the landlord to repay to the applicant any charges that were collected in contravention of the R.T.A. and O. Reg. 516/06. Such an order does not affect the rent at all (although the Board may again permit the debt to be deducted from future rent payments if the tenancy is a continuing one).

Applications under s. 135 of the R.T.A. can also be brought where a tenant (or former tenant or prospective tenant) believes that the landlord has illegally retained money (such as a rent deposit) that should have been returned to the applicant. Although a successful applicant will be granted an order that the landlord must repay a specified sum, the lawful rent will not be changed as a result.

Recent examples of amounts that were found to have been collected or retained illegally include:

- a key deposit that was not refunded when the key was returned;[97]
- interest owing on the rent deposit;[98]
- an extra charge of $50 per month for the four months that the tenant's brother stayed with the tenant in the unit;[99]

---

[96] This can result from such things as: increasing the rent without providing a proper and timely written notice of rent increase; increasing the rent more than once in a 12-month period (except were specifically permitted by the Act); and increasing the rent by an amount that is greater than permitted by law.

[97] Landlord and Tenant Board File No. SOT-01787 (Jan. 21, 2009) and Landlord and Tenant Board File No. NOT-00012 (March 1, 2007).

[98] Landlord and Tenant Board File No. TNT-01345 (Jan. 12, 2009).

[99] Landlord and Tenant Board File No. NOT-00012 (March 1, 2007).

- $200 charged by the landlord as an "early termination fee";[100]
- amounts the landlord withheld from the deposit as a set-off against damages;[101]
- an extra charge of $50 per month to permit the tenant to keep a dog in the rental unit.[102]

Where the Board has made an order prohibiting the landlord from increasing the rent for a unit and a new tenant moves into that unit (i.e., a new tenancy agreement is entered into with respect to that unit), the new tenant is entitled to receive a notice advising the new tenant of the existence of the order prohibiting rent increases (OPRI), the last lawful rent that was charged to the former tenant, the amount the landlord may lawfully charge the new tenant until the prohibition ends and the amount that may be charged once the prohibition ends (s. 114 of the R.T.A.). If the landlord does not provide such a notice and/or has charged the new tenant more than legally permitted, pursuant to s. 115 of the R.T.A., the new tenant has one year[103] in which to commence an application for an order:

1. determining the amount of rent that the new tenant may lawfully be charged until the prohibition ends;
2. determining the amount of rent that the new tenant may lawfully be charged after the prohibition ends;
3. requiring the landlord to rebate to the new tenant any rent paid by the new tenant in excess of the rent that the tenant may lawfully be charged; and
4. if the landlord failed to provide the required notice, imposing an administrative fine not exceeding the greater of $10,000 and the monetary jurisdiction of the Small Claims Court.[104]

Pursuant to subsection 115(5), s. 135 does not apply in such situations. Nevertheless, the application under s. 115 will also be in Form T1. In addition to the usual material that must be filed, on an application under s. 115 of the R.T.A., the *landlord* must file with the Board, at or before the hearing, an affidavit sworn by the landlord setting out the last lawful rent charged to the former tenant and any available evidence in support of the affidavit.[105]

---

[100] Landlord and Tenant Board File No. TET-01745 (Jan. 20, 2009). Note, however, that it is not clear that the Board had jurisdiction to deal with this matter if the payment in question was made after the tenancy had been terminated.

[101] Landlord and Tenant Board File No. SOT-01775 (Jan. 13, 2009).

[102] Landlord and Tenant Board File No. EAT-01640 (Jan. 30, 2009).

[103] Subsection 115(2) of the R.T.A.).

[104] Subsection 115(3) of the R.T.A. The monetary jurisdiction of the Small Claims Court is scheduled to be increased to $25,000, effective January 2010.

[105] Subsection 115(4) of the R.T.A. and s. 15 of O. Reg. 516/06.

See Chapters 7, 8 and 9 for detailed discussions about lawful rent, rent deposits, additional charges that are permitted under the R.T.A. and when rent and rent increases are deemed to be lawful as a result of the passage of time.

11

Maintenance Obligations of Landlords

1. INTRODUCTION

For years, the common law rule had been that a landlord could rent a tumble-down house. Also, there had been no liability on the part of the landlord to put demised premises in repair, or to maintain them in repair, unless such obligation had been a term of the lease, which was seldom, if ever, the case. In fact, the usual clause in written leases referring to repairs was a covenant by the tenant to repair, with reasonable wear and tear excepted.

With reference to written leases and the common repair clause just mentioned, the tenant's obligation to repair was considered unfair. Many tenants were not aware that the clause was in their leases. If they were aware of it, they thought mistakenly that they were only required to repair reasonable wear and tear, although careful reading of the clause, or noting the punctuation, made it obvious that reasonable wear and tear was excepted. Very few tenants seek legal advice before signing leases, and so the implication of the repair clause was not brought home to them. The fact that the clause required a tenant to repair structural damage in the demised premises would surely have surprised 90% of tenants. Similarly, if the plumbing or refrigerator did not work for causes other than wear and tear, it was the tenant's responsibility to repair.

Although the reasonable wear and tear exception meant that a tenant did not have to repair ordinary wear and tear, the landlord was also not obligated to do so. Good landlords may have made these repairs to protect their property. Other landlords left their tenants to effect repairs or suffer the inconvenience of not having them made.

In short term leases, which most residential tenancies are, the burden of the former repair clause was even more onerous on tenants.

When there was no written lease, there again was no obligation on the landlord to repair.

It was also a general principle of landlord and tenant law that no covenant or warranty on the part of a landlord will be implied as to the suitability of the premises for the purpose for which they are intended to be used. The one exception was in the case of furnished premises for which there was an implied warranty by the landlord that the premises were fit for habitation. That implied covenant is now carried forward as an obligation by the landlord to keep the premises (furnished or unfurnished) fit for habitation during the term of the lease: ss. 20(1) and (2) of the *Residential Tenancies Act, 2006* (R.T.A.).

As the Ontario Law Reform Commission recommended, it was a matter of public interest that tenants' interests should be brought into balance with the landlords' interests in this troubled area of repair of premises. Landlord and tenant laws afforded tenants little help when premises were unsafe and unhealthy.

Now, by the terms of s. 20 of the R.T.A. (formerly s. 24 of the T.P.A.), a landlord must not only provide from the beginning, but must also maintain, the rented premises in a good state of repair and fit for habitation during the tenancy and must comply with health, safety and housing standards. This obligation on the landlord exists even if the tenant is aware that the rental unit is in poor condition before agreeing to rent the premises (s. 20(2)). These statutory requirements for landlords and tenants apply notwithstanding the common law or the lease terms.[1]

Some leases now incorporate the landlord's statutory obligation to repair as a covenant to repair, in which case the effect of covenants being interdependent would apply to the landlord's covenant to repair, as well as the statutory duty to repair in s. 20 of the R.T.A., and the tenant can be relieved of the tenant's obligations (in particular, the obligation to pay rent).

Even if the statutory obligation to repair is not stated in the lease as a covenant by the landlord it has been held that the landlord's obligation to repair by s. 94 of Part IV of the *Landlord and Tenant Act* is an implied covenant by the landlord, and the effect of s. 87 of Part IV (now s. 17 of the R.T.A.) is that the tenant may withhold rent: *Quann v. Pajelle Investments Ltd.*[2]

The landlord's obligation is not merely to keep the tenant's unit in a good state of repair. This duty extends to the entire *residential complex*, which includes common areas and facilities such as hallways, lobbies, elevators, stairwells, parking areas, swimming pools and athletic facilities and the grounds around the building(s).[3]

---

[1] Remember that, pursuant to s. 4 of the R.T.A., a landlord and tenant cannot contract out of the Act.

[2] (1975), 7 O.R. (2d) 769 (Ont. Co. Ct.).

[3] See the definition of "residential complex" in s. 2(1) of the R.T.A. A landlord's maintenance responsibilities have long been held to apply to the common areas and facilities of a residential

Section 2 of the R.T.A. contains a long list of "services and facilities" which might be included if they were presumed to be provided by a landlord or reasonably anticipated by a tenant. It would of course be better for a tenant to request that services be specifically listed in the lease. Even if not specified in the lease terms, the Board might well deem them included, depending on the circumstances.

For fixtures put in by the tenant, the obligation to repair would be that of the tenant. Fixtures that are the landlord's are the responsibility of the landlord to repair.

The landlord's obligation to repair does not apply when the tenant is overholding, in possession of the unit after an order terminating the tenancy agreement, or when the tenant is no longer in possession: *Bruns v. Fancher*.[4]

Subsection 20(1) states that a landlord is responsible:

- for providing and maintaining a residential complex, including the rental units in it, in a good state of repair and fit for habitation, and
- for complying with health, safety, housing and maintenance standards.

Both of these obligations will now be discussed in greater detail below.

2. GOOD STATE OF REPAIR AND FIT FOR HABITATION

A landlord must *provide* the residential complex in a good state of repair and fit for habitation. It was held in *Smith v. 736923 Ontario Ltd.*,[5] that it was irrelevant that the tenant was aware of the (poor) condition of the unit at the time of entering into the tenancy. That principle is now enshrined in s. 20(2) of the R.T.A., which states that a landlord's obligations under s. 20(1) of the R.T.A. applies "even if the tenant was aware of a state of non-repair or a contravention of a standard before entering into the tenancy agreement."[6]

In view of the landlord's obligation to provide premises in good repair one may expect landlords to obtain from prospective tenants acknowledgements that the premises are satisfactory and in a good state of repair, or a list of items needing the landlord's attention. There is no provision prohibiting such an acceptance of the premises by a tenant, although if treated as a clear

complex and not just to the individual rental units: *Herbold v. Pajelle Investments Ltd.* (1975), [1976] 2 S.C.R. 520 (S.C.C.). See also *Lewis v. Westa Holdings Ltd.* (1975), 8 O.R. (2d) 181 (Ont. Co. Ct.) in which the landlord was ordered to repair an indoor parking area and locker storage space and *Tate v. Deehurst Investments Ltd.* (1987), 62 O.R. (2d) 221 (Ont. Div. Ct.) in which relief was granted on the basis of the landlord's failure to properly maintain common areas (such as hallways, elevators, the lobby and pool facilities) and failure to repair the broken intercom system.

4 (1977), 16 O.R. (2d) 781 (Ont. Div. Ct.).

5 (1996), 1996 CarswellOnt 1396 (Ont. Gen. Div.).

6 Also see Landlord and Tenant Board File No. NOL-18614 / NOT-00017 (March 8, 2007).

contracting out of his rights, it will not be binding. If a tenant later complains about the condition of the premises, the tenant's acknowledgement would afford some evidence that the accommodation was and still is satisfactory, but it would not be conclusive. In fact in *Claydon v. Quann Agencies Ltd.*,[7] the substandard conditions had existed for 12 years for one tenant, 14 months for another and four months for another, and so there was obviously knowledge on the part of the tenants of existing non-repair. Nevertheless the judge held that the statutory obligation under s. 94(1) of Part IV of the *Landlord and Tenant Act* to make the premises fit for habitation must be complied with by the landlord. So the obligation of the landlord is one which the courts will interpret favourably for the tenant.

A landlord must also *maintain* the complex in a state of good repair. In general, maintaining the complex in a good state of repair requires a landlord to: (1) have a regular maintenance regime in place; (2) perform major repairs when necessary; (3) respond promptly to requests from tenants for routine maintenance concerns; and (4) respond even faster in emergency situations. Landlords may also now be expected to conduct regular inspections of rental units.[8]

The duty to inspect and maintain an urban apartment building is a high standard: *Phillips v. Dis-Management*[9] (citing *Quann v. Pajelle, supra).* In *Quann v. Pajelle Investments Ltd.*,[10] the court held that s. 94(1) of Part IV of the *Landlord and Tenant Act* casts a duty on the landlord to inspect to ensure that the ongoing obligation to repair is fulfilled.

It has been stated that incidental to the landlord's obligation to repair, is the obligation to inspect, particularly so in the case of an older building: *MacLennan v. 587125 Ontario Ltd.*[11] In this case, the judge also stated that it is not a sufficient answer for a landlord to say that the anticipated resistance from tenants made routine inspections impracticable.

Landlords who wished to perform routine inspections of rental units may have been deterred from doing so in the past because of the privacy provisions set out in the *Tenant Protection Act, 1998* (T.P.A.). Under s. 21 of the T.P.A., a landlord had no right to enter a rental unit to conduct a routine inspection unless the landlord specifically reserved such a right in the tenancy agreement. Absent such an express provision in the contract, a landlord could be punished for illegally entering the rental unit. Paragraph 4 of subsection 27(1) of the R.T.A. now specifically grants landlords the right to conduct such inspections (on at least 24 hours written notice) and I suggest that landlords ought to take advantage of this provision for two reasons. First, regular (perhaps annual)

---

[7] [1972] 2 O.R. 405 (Ont. Co. Ct.).

[8] See Landlord and Tenant Board File No. SOT-00484 (January 17, 2008).

[9] (1995), 24 O.R. (3d) 435 (Ont. Gen. Div.).

[10] (1975), 7 O.R. (2d) 769 (Ont. Co. Ct.).

[11] (1990), 11 R.P.R. (2d) 28 (Ont. Dist. Ct.).

inspection of the rental units will permit the landlord to determine if there are any unreported maintenance problems that need to be addressed. Second, the information gathered during such inspections may assist the landlord in defending against any allegations that may later be made by a tenant that the rental unit was not in good condition.

Consideration will now be given to what is meant by a "good state of repair". It is to be noted that there is no exception for reasonable wear and tear, nor indeed are there any exceptions, and so the obligation can be said to be absolute and not qualified.

Nevertheless, the landlord's obligation to repair and to decorate has a reasonable expense limitation: Klippert, *Residential Tenancies in British Columbia* (Toronto: Carswell, 1976) at 100. In *Buswell v. Goodwin*,[12] the landlord was not liable to the tenant for a closing order by the local municipal authority when a house was not fit for habitation. A landlord does not have to repair a house at whatever the cost.

The words "in a good state of repair" are considered similar to "good tenantable repair". The latter words were defined in the still leading case of *Proudfoot v. Hart*, as follows:

> Good tenantable repair ... [is] such repair as, having regard to the age, character, and locality of the house, would make it reasonably fit for the occupation of a reasonably-minded tenant of the class who would be likely to take it.[13]

These words were used in *Waters, Re*,[14] concerning the extent of the obligation to "repair" imposed on a life tenant by the terms of a will. A further statement is in *Gordon v. Goodwin*:[15]

> The house must be so reasonably fit for habitation at the time of the beginning of the term .... Of course, there is no need for the tenement to answer every whim of a finical tenant; but common sense should be applied in determining whether it does fulfil the required conditions.

Another case concerning a commercial tenancy, in referring to such a state of repair, held that the premises should be such that they might be used not only with safety, but with reasonable comfort by the class of persons by whom and for the sort of purposes for which the premises were to be occupied: *United Cigar Stores Ltd. v. Buller*.[16]

In *Vicro Investments Ltd. v. Adams Brands Ltd.*,[17] also a commercial tenancy, many of the reported decisions on the repair covenant were discussed. In this case it was held that the tenant cannot insist on repairs that

[12] [1971] 1 W.L.R. 92.

[13] (1890), 25 Q.B.D. 42 (Eng. C.A.) at 55.

[14] (1978), 21 O.R. (2d) 124 (Ont. H.C.).

[15] (1910), 20 O.L.R. 327 (Ont. C.A.).

[16] (1931), 66 O.L.R. 593 (Ont. C.A.).

[17] [1963] 2 O.R. 583 (Ont. H.C.).

will make the building new or that will give him a building substantially different from that which he rented, nor can he require mere signs of age to be eliminated.

Some guidance as to the standard of repair required of a landlord will be found in *McPhail v. Islington London Borough Council.*[18] The case dealt with whether hot water must be provided by a landlord to satisfy a statutory requirement of personal washing facilities. Lord Justice Russell, putting the matter somewhat quaintly said,

> ...a household of one person may rub along well enough on the occasional boiled kettle for that one's personal washing ... [but for a household of six] a piped supply of hot water ... may be far more necessary.[19]

Another member of the Court of Appeal put it more usefully for our purposes of interpretation of what is a good state of repair. It is: "a matter of fact and degree in which regard must be had to ... the general conditions prevailing in the locality".[20] This may vary with the area in question and the type of housing available, and also in that one must look at the whole tenor of the obvious intentions of the legislature.

This was stated in a more recent Ontario case, *611406 Ontario Inc. v. Cunningham*[21] — that in considering the state of repair, the age and character of the building are relevant factors.

A full discussion and guidance as to the responsibilities of landlords to repair will be found in *Quann v. Pajelle Investments Ltd.*,[22] one statement being:

> [T]he landlord [is] responsible for supplying and maintaining housing in a state of repair that would give effect to the desire to eliminate the substandard conditions which may have severe physical, emotional and psychological impacts on the tenants.

In *Quann v. Pajelle*, the judge ordered the landlord to provide security guards to prevent unwanted intruders and vandalism.

In a later case, over 200 tenants applied under s. 94(4) of Part IV of the *Landlord and Tenant Act* for an injunction to prevent the removal of security guards and for an order directing the landlord to continue providing security guards for the underground garage. The judge held that s. 94 was for non-repair and was not available as a remedy to order the provision of "an essential service" whether contracted for or not or for injunction proceedings to prevent the withdrawal of security guards: *Hart v. Consolidated Building Ltd.*[23]

---

[18] [1970] 1 All E.R. 1004 (C.A.).

[19] [1970] 1 All E.R. 1004 (C.A.) at 1006.

[20] [1970] 1 All E.R. 1004 (C.A.) at 1007.

[21] (1997), 1997 CarswellOnt 590 (Ont. Gen. Div.).

[22] (1975), 7 O.R. (2d) 769 (Ont. Co. Ct.).

[23] (November 29, 1978) (Ont. Co. Ct.).

The distinction may be that the *Quann v. Pajelle* case, which was cited to the judge, concerned an apartment building which was in a serious state of disrepair and subject to vandalism.

The judge in the *Hart* case referred to the security guards as an essential service if contracted for by the tenants. It will remain for some other court to determine which case to follow, and whether security guard service can be considered an essential service that shall not be withheld. Under the R.T.A., it is unlikely that withdrawal of security services would be considered to be either a maintenance issue or an issue of interference with the supply of "vital services" (as currently defined). Lack of needed security would more likely be characterized as interference with the tenants' reasonable enjoyment of the residential complex.

In a later case concerning lack of proper security for the buildings, *Quann v. Pajelle Investments Ltd.* was followed and one month's rent was allowed as an abatement: *Taten Holdings Ltd. v. Lyons*.[24]

In *Offredi v. 751768 Ontario Ltd.*,[25] a number of tenants brought an application against the landlord based upon an alleged failure by the landlord to comply with its maintenance obligations. The complaints included a power outage that lasted five days and a general poor level of maintenance throughout the complex. The landlord took the position that it had taken reasonable steps to maintain the building and that the deplorable state of the maintenance was due to the misconduct of the tenants themselves. The judge at first instance rejected these arguments and ordered the landlord to repay to the tenants about 20% of their rents over the period in question. On appeal, this decision was upheld by the Divisional Court who wrote as follows:

> In our judgement, this is not a case that turns on whether the landlord can be said to have acted reasonably. What the tenants claim is a breach of contract. The tenants were paying full rent for premises which the landlord was under an obligation, under the *Landlord and Tenant Act*, to keep in a good state of repair and fit for habitation. The landlord failed to do that. That is the basis of the claim for an abatement.

As previously stated, at all times the complex must be "fit for habitation". The term "fit for habitation" hardly needs any explanation. It was referred to in *Hahn v. Kramer*,[26] where the judge said "the heating of the premises was inadequate to non-existent; that cooking was impossible, there was a lack of hot water ... and a failure to comply with an outstanding work order", and so rather obviously he found the premises to be "totally lacking in fitness for habitation".

---

[24] (February 18, 1983), Doc. York 74667/82 (Ont. Co. Ct.).

[25] (1994), 72 O.A.C. 235, 116 D.L.R. (4th) 757 (Ont. Div. Ct.).

[26] (1979), 26 O.R. (2d) 558 (Ont. Co. Ct.).

A leading case on the meaning of "fit for habitation" is *Summers v. Salford (Borough)*.[27] If the state of disrepair is such that by ordinary use damage may naturally be caused to the occupier, either in respect of personal injury to life or limb or injury to health, the house is not reasonably fit for habitation. The Board will also consider whether the defects affect the tenant's reasonable enjoyment of the premises (s. 29(1) para. 3 of the R.T.A.). Finally, as the R.T.A. is remedial legislation, its provisions will be given a liberal and broad interpretation.

In one case of premises not in a good state of repair and not fit for habitation the tenant moved in for one night then left. The landlord sued the tenant for the rent because of no notice to terminate. The court reviewed the evidence and found that the house was not fit for habitation. The furnace was not working, the house was infested with mice, and general substandard conditions existed inside and outside. An order terminating the tenancy was granted under s. 94 of Part IV (*Landlord and Tenant Act*) and the landlord's claim for rent was dismissed: *Kucora v. Bodula*.[28]

The state of non-repair in a new apartment building still under construction when the tenant moved in was considered in *Gagnon v. Centre-Town Developments Ltd.*[29] The trial judge had ordered an abatement of rent. The Divisional Court allowed the appeal on the basis that the apartment was fit for habitation and that the landlord's obligation to repair by s. 94 of Part IV was not applicable to items of non-completion, leaving open the question of whether the tenant could sue for damages in an ordinary action.

In *Stephos Management Services v. McGregor*,[30] the tenants sought an abatement of rent on the basis that the presence of cockroaches constituted a breach of the obligation to provide premises fit for habitation. The Court rejected this argument, declaring instead that a landlord will only be in breach of its maintenance obligations if it fails to take all reasonable measures to rid the premises of pests once the landlord becomes aware of the problem.

3. HEALTH, SAFETY, HOUSING AND MAINTENANCE STANDARDS

Subsection 20(1) provides that a landlord is responsible for complying with health, safety, housing and maintenance standards. These standards come from many sources, including provincial legislation such as the *Health Protection and Promotion Act*,[31] the *Building Code Act, 1992*,[32] the *Fire*

---

[27] [1943] 1 All E.R. 68 (U.K. H.L).

[28] (May 18, 1984), Doc. 400/83 (Ont. Small Claims Ct.).

[29] (1975), 10 O.R. (2d) 245 (Ont. Co. Ct.), reversed (1976), 14 O.R. (2d) 550 (Ont. Div. Ct.).

[30] (1993), 1993 CarswellOnt 3655, [1993] O.J. No. 1179 (Ont. Gen. Div.).

[31] R.S.O. 1990, c. H.7.

[32] S.O. 1992, c. 23.

Protection and Prevention Act, 1997,[33] the *Electricity Act, 1998*,[34] and the *Technical Standards and Safety Act, 2000*.[35]

Housing and maintenance standards are also contained in municipal by-laws and, where such by-laws do not exist, in O. Reg. 517/06 of the R.T.A. Municipalities have power under the *Municipal Act*,[36] to pass various health by-laws, for example garbage collection, minimum heat standards and rodent control. Section 15.2 of the *Building Code Act, 1992* provides that a landlord shall comply with these municipal standards.

These statutes, regulations and by-laws create a complex mosaic of health, safety, housing and maintenance standards. Landlords are expected to be familiar, and to comply, with all applicable standards.

There had been some concern before the enactment of Part IV of the *Landlord and Tenant Act* that a tenant would be intimidated into not complaining about the premises because of possible retaliatory action by the landlord. To protect against this, paras. 121(3)(b) and (c) of Part IV provided that a tenant who complained to a governmental or municipal authority about non-compliance would be protected from retaliatory eviction. The section stated that a judge hearing a landlord's application for possession must refuse the order for possession if it appeared the landlord was so proceeding because of the tenant's complaint. The wording under s. 83(3) of the current R.T.A. (formerly s. 84(2) of the T.P.A.) is virtually identical. It provides that the Board shall refuse to grant an eviction if the landlord's application is brought in retaliation for the tenant complaining to a government authority of the landlord's violation of a law dealing with health, safety, housing or maintenance standards or because the tenant attempted to secure or enforce his or her legal rights. It is also contrary to the R.T.A. and is an offence for the landlord to harass, coerce or threaten a tenant (see s. 23 and para. 233(i) of the R.T.A.).

Health standards generally originate from the *Health Protection and Promotion Act*, which sets out certain minimum requirements for residential premises (such as potable water and sanitation facilities) and provides for the creation of local boards of health. Safety and housing standards are contained in the Building Code, the Fire Code, the Electrical Safety Code and the *Technical Standards and Safety Act, 2000* (viz. elevator safety).

Complaints about alleged violations of health standards are generally investigated by local health inspectors. Alleged violations of the Fire Code are dealt with by the Fire Marshall or representatives of the local fire department. Concerns about the safety of elevators may be investigated by the

[33] S.O. 1997, C. 4.

[34] S.O. 1998, c. 15, Sched. A.

[35] S.O. 2000, c. 16.

[36] R.S.O. 1990, c. M.45.

Technical Standards and Safety Association (T.S.S.A). Concerns about electrical safety may be investigated by the Electrical Safety Association.

Maintenance standards are generally found in municipal by-laws. For instance, the City of Toronto has a Property Standards By-law which specifies minimum standards with respect to such topics as: pest control; yard maintenance; landscaping and drainage; retaining walls; signs; walls, columns and beams; stairs, guards and handrails; roofs; garbage/debris storage and disposal; steps, walks, driveways, parking and loading areas; the condition of floors, stairs, landings, walls, ceilings, doors, passageways, exits, etc.; elevators; mail; kitchen facilities; electrical service; lighting; plumbing; heating and air conditioning; ventilation; parking and storage garages; and garage doors and exit doors.

Alleged violations of housing and maintenance standards are generally investigated by municipal property standards officers. These inspectors have expertise in the Building Code and the relevant municipal property standards by-laws. There may be an overlap between local property standards and health, fire, electrical and technical safety standards; a local property standards officer may deal with all of the various complaints or may refer to the appropriate authorities concerns that are outside his or her area of expertise.

After an inspection of the site, the property standards officer will advise the landlord of any property standards violations. The notification can be informal or through a written notice of violation. No specific time limit is given in the by-law. Therefore, an inspector can use his discretion in setting a reasonable time for the problem to be corrected. If the landlord fails to correct the problem within the time specified in the notice of violation, the inspector may choose to allow the landlord some additional time, may close the file (if, for instance, the inspector is convinced that the tenant is obstructing the landlord from completing the necessary work) or may issue a Work Order. A Work Order will specify the work that must be done and the date by which it must be completed. Failure to comply with a Work Order can result in prosecution.[37] The *City of Toronto Act, 2006*[38] (in particular, s. 386) permits the City to proceed with repairs if the owner fails to do so, and the cost becomes a lien against the property enforced in the same manner as for arrears of taxes.

The type of testing that may be performed by local authorities is limited. For instance, for reasons of expense and potential liability, the local health department may decline to perform a lab analysis of mould found within a residential complex or test air quality, choosing to rely primarily or exclu-

---

[37] See *R. v. Mintz*, [1973] 2 O.R. 257 (Ont. C.A.) and *R. v. Merrick* (September 23, 1983), (Ont. C.A.).

[38] S.O. 2006, c. 11.

sively upon a visual inspection.[39] This leaves it to the landlord and tenant to decide whether they wish to bear the cost of retaining a consultant to perform additional tests.

It is to be noted that if a housing standards by-law is passed by a municipality under the *Planning Act* section, enforcement proceedings cannot be taken until an owner is given at least six months to effect repairs. Some doubt arose as to whether the City of Toronto housing standards by-laws were passed pursuant to the *City of Toronto Act* or the *Planning Act*, and in particular whether the period of six months for an owner to do repairs under the latter statute prevailed. This question was resolved in *R. v. Hall*.[40] The Court of Appeal held that the Toronto housing standards by-law was validly passed by virtue of the *City of Toronto Act* and was not enacted under the powers given to municipalities by then s. 36(2) of the *Planning Act*. Therefore the six months' moratorium does not apply.

If a residential complex is located in an unorganized territory or if no municipal property standards by-law applies to the residential complex, then the standards contained in O. Reg. 517/06 (made under the R.T.A.) apply to the complex (see Appendix 3).[41] In such cases, complaints are made to the Minister (through the Investigations and Enforcement Unit of the Ministry of Municipal Affairs and Housing)[42] who will have an inspection done and a work order may be issued with a time limit for compliance: ss. 221 to 226 of the R.T.A. (formerly ss. 151 to 156 of the T.P.A.). Failure to comply with the work order is an offence under para. 234(t) of the R.T.A. (formerly para. 206(2)17 of the T.P.A.).

In addition to any fines or other sanctions that may be imposed upon the landlord for failing to comply with an order from the agency responsible for enforcing health, safety, housing and maintenance standards, a tenant may seek redress by application to the Landlord and Tenant Board under ss. 20, 29(1)1, 30 and 161 of the R.T.A. (discussed below).

Although a Notice of Violation or Work Order issued by a public authority is not necessary for a finding of a breach of s. 20 of the R.T.A. (see Interpretation Guideline 5), the existence of a Notice of Violation or a Work Order and the testimony at the hearing of a qualified inspector or property standards officer can be crucial to the success of such an application.[43]

---

[39] This was the gist of the evidence of the local health inspector in the case of *Orton v. La Haye* (Aug. 12, 2003), TNT-03028, [2003] O.R.H.T.D. No. 110, 2003 CarswellOnt 4238 (Ont. Rental Housing Trib.). The additional testing paid for by the tenant failed to prove, however, the existence of a mould problem within the house.

[40] [1970] 2 O.R. 576 (Ont. C.A.).

[41] Section 224 of the R.T.A. (formerly s. 154 of the T.P.A.).

[42] 12th Floor, 777 Bay Street, Toronto ON M5G 2E5. Tel. 1-888-772-9277 or 416-585-7214.

[43] For example, evidence from the local fire prevention department and the Public Health Inspector were instrumental in the tenants obtaining a substantial abatement of rent (25% for one year and a lesser abatement thereafter) in the case of *Brine v. Glaser* (1985), 34 A.C.W.S. (2d) 204 (Ont. Dist. Ct.).

Attempts to prove that a landlord has violated health, safety, housing and maintenance standards without such evidence are rarely successful. There are two main reasons for this. First, since the government inspector is an impartial and expert witness, his or her testimony will generally be given greater weight than that of the tenant alone. Second, most tenants do not understand how to gather and present the type of evidence necessary to prove their case.

For example, a common complaint from tenants is that their apartment is too cold. Such a statement is subjective and of little, if any, evidentiary value.[44] A room temperature that feels "too cold" to one person may feel too warm to another. The property standards for the City of Toronto require that every dwelling and unit shall be provided with a heating system capable of maintaining a room temperature of 21 degrees Celsius (from September 15 to June 1). Other municipalities and regions may have by-laws that set slightly different minimum temperature standards. For residential complexes for which there are no municipal (i.e., local) property standards, O. Reg. 517/06 requires that the temperature of all rooms must be at least 20 degrees Celsius (s. 15).[45] Property standards usually also specify the manner in which temperature readings must be taken. In Toronto, the room temperature must be measured at 1.5 metres above the floor level. In places where O. Reg. 517/06 applies, the room temperature must be measured at 1.5 metres above floor level *and* 1 metre from exterior walls. It will also have to be shown that the thermometer used for taking the measurements is accurate. Tenants rarely come to a hearing with reliable data taken using the prescribed methodology and, as a result, are often disappointed with the result of their applications.

At the same time, good landlords ought not fear an inspection. If there exists only minor problems (or none at all), the official report will reflect that fact and the landlord will then have evidence from an objective and expert third party that there were no serious deficiencies.[46]

What follows are brief descriptions of some cases in which tenants have been successful in proving a breach of health, safety, housing and maintenance standards.

---

[44] See Landlord and Tenant Board File No. SWT-00003 (Feb. 22, 2007), in which the Member lamented the fact that the tenants provided him with "nothing more than a vague allegation that the unit is cold" and that such evidence was "far from satisfactory" and Landlord and Tenant Board File No. TSL-20145 (Jan. 13, 2009), in which the Member stated that "the Tenant has led insufficient evidence to establish that the temperature within her rental unit failed to comply with municipal standards."

[45] See Appendix 3.

[46] See, for example, Landlord and Tenant Board File No. CEL-15502 / CET-01662 (Jan. 19, 2009), in which the tenants' application was dismissed, in large part, because the evidence demonstrated that the City Inspector found only a few minor violations that were remedied by the landlord within a few days.

In *Claydon v. Quann Agencies Ltd.*,[47] the landlord was ordered to comply with municipal work orders issued by the municipality under a housing standards by-law.

Many repairs were ordered in *Quann v. Pajelle Investments Ltd.*,[48] to comply with the Toronto housing standards by-law and with the *Public Health Act*.[49] Rent withholding and abatements of rent were approved although it is not apparent from the judgment that abatements of rent were granted.

The liability of a landlord for breach of the duty to comply with safety standards, s. 24(1) of the T.P.A. and the Fire Code, to have installed an operable smoke alarm was determined in *Pacifico v. Ryan*.[50]

In *Beyer v. Absamco Developments Ltd.*,[51] full abatement of rent was ordered until the landlord completed the work required by many work orders issued against the landlord pursuant to the City of Toronto housing standards by-law and to do the necessary repairs "so as not to interfere with the reasonable enjoyment of the premises for all usual purposes by the tenants".

A lengthy list of deficiencies was considered by the judge in *Endcliffe Construction Co. Ltd. v. MacLeod*.[52] There was a report by an electrical inspector as to the danger of the poor wiring, a public health inspector as to the unsanitary condition of the septic tank system, and a property standards enforcement officer as to items of disrepair. The judge ordered all work to be done to comply with health and safety standards within 60 days and an abatement of rent until compliance. The landlord's application for termination was dismissed.

Exemplary damages were granted, rent abatement and an order to comply with the property standards violations: *Desjardins v. Castlecap Holdings Corp.*[53] The judge stated that the landlord refused to heed the complaints of the tenant and the notice of violation by the property standards department.

In *Hahn v. Kramer*,[54] an order for termination was made because the premises were unfit for habitation. There was an outstanding work order under the City of Toronto housing standards by-law, heating was inadequate to non-existent, cooking was impossible and there was a lack of hot water. Reference back to *Temlas Apartments Inc. v. Desloges*,[55] would indicate that when the premises are totally unfit for habitation there may be frustration of the lease contract as in s. 86 of Part IV, now s. 19 of the R.T.A., in addition

---

[47] [1972] 2 O.R. 405 (Ont. Co. Ct.).

[48] (1975), 7 O.R. (2d) 769 (Ont. Co. Ct.).

[49] R.S.O. 1970, c. 377.

[50] (1994), 1994 CarswellOnt 2560 (Ont. Gen. Div.).

[51] (1976), 12 O.R. (2d) 768 (Ont. Co. Ct.).

[52] (December 3, 1981), Doc. 5913/80 (Ont. Co. Ct.).

[53] (June 14, 1991), Doc. 1109-013 (Ont. Gen. Div.).

[54] (1979), 23 O.R. (2d) 689 (Ont. Div. Ct.).

[55] (1980), 29 O.R. (2d) 30 (Ont. Div. Ct.).

to the right of applying to the court for termination of the tenancy under s. 30 of the R.T.A.

In *Satchithananthan v. Cacciola*,[56] the tenant was able to prove that the landlord failed to clear the walkways and parking area of snow and ice within twenty-four hours of a snowfall, contrary to the City of Toronto Property Standards.

There may be a limit on what will be expected of a landlord if the cost of repairs, particularly to comply with municipal by-laws, is beyond the landlord's financial ability. In *Shippam v. Johnson*,[57] the landlord was granted an order terminating the tenancy and for possession when he was unable to supply potable water and there was the extreme expense of replacing the water system. The court applied the *Frustrated Contracts Act*.[58] In another case, *Lypny v. Rocca*,[59] the landlord who could not afford the major repairs was granted possession in order to convert the unit to non-residential use.

In a mobile home park case the water supply and sewage system were badly in need of repair or replacement. The landlord satisfied the court of his *bona fide* efforts to rectify the problem but could not obtain the necessary mortgage financing unless rents were increased to which the tenants objected. The court faced with this "merry-go-round" refused an abatement, ordered withheld rent to be paid to the landlord and refused the landlord's application for possession. The judge noted that if repairs are not possible to the two systems there is no statutory requirement by s. 94 (of the *Landlord and Tenant Act*) to replace the equipment which is beyond repair. The only comment which might be made is that the judge accepted that the landlord *bona fide* would replace the system if mortgage financing could be obtained, and that the tenants would have to accept rent increases or move out: *Bellevue Homeowners' Assn. v. Bellevue Mobile & Motor Homes Ltd.*[60]

In *Bissonnette v. Wynn Family Properties*,[61] the tenants complained of inadequate heat in the rental unit. According to the tenants, after unsuccessful attempts to have the landlord deal with this problem, they had a city inspector attend at the unit to take temperature readings. Contrary to the municipal property standards (which required a minimum room temperature of 21 degrees Celcius), the readings on January 17, 2000 showed that the temperatures in the bedrooms were 15 degrees Celcius and in the dining and living rooms were 16 degrees Celcius. The landlord had baseboard heaters installed within a day or two and, by January 19, 2000, the rental unit had adequate heat. Based upon this breach of the relevant housing standards, the tenants requested an order for an abatement of rent and termination of the tenancy. The

---

[56] (Dec. 30, 2002), TST-04047, 2002 CarswellOnt 5023 (Ont. Rental Housing Trib.).
[57] (1984), 45 O.R. (2d) 307 (Ont. Co. Ct.).
[58] R.S.O. 1980, c. 179, now R.S.O. 1990, c. F.34.
[59] (1986), 55 O.R. (2d) 46 (Ont. Dist. Ct.), affirmed (1988), 63 O.R. (2d) 595 (Ont. Div. Ct.).
[60] (1982), 1982 CarswellOnt 1906 (Ont. Co. Ct.).
[61] (March 3, 2000), TNT-00946, 2000 CarswellOnt 6413 (Ont. Rental Housing Trib.).

landlord consented to an order terminating the tenancy but submitted that no abatement was warranted in these circumstances. The Tribunal agreed with the landlord's submissions and granted only an order terminating the tenancy.

In *Wamboldt v. Pillon*,[62] the Tribunal found that: (1) the electrical system in the house did not comply with the Ontario Electrical Safety Code, (2) the wood-burning stove did not comply with the Fire Code, and (3) there was a problem with mould growing under the house and within the house. The Tribunal therefore found that the landlord had failed to comply with the relevant health, safety, housing and maintenance standards. By the time of the hearing, the problem with the wood-burning stove and mould had been rectified. The Tribunal ordered that the landlord rectify the remaining problem (i.e., the electrical problem) within about three weeks.

In Landlord and Tenant Board File No. SOL-18346, the Board heard that the local fire department had inspected the rental unit and found that it did not comply with the requirements of the Fire Code. For this and other breaches of the landlord's maintenance obligations, the Member awarded the tenant a 30% rent abatement for six months (equal to $1,305.00).

4. MAINTENANCE RESPONSIBILITIES IN MOBILE HOME PARKS AND LAND LEASE COMMUNITIES

Pursuant to s. 161 of the R.T.A., in addition to fulfilling its obligations under s. 20 of the R.T.A., the landlord of a mobile home park or land lease community has these *additional* responsibilities:

(a) removing or disposing of garbage or ensuring the availability of a means of removing or disposing of garbage in the park/community at reasonable intervals;
(b) maintaining the park/community in a good state of repair;
(c) removing snow from park/community roads;
(d) maintaining the water supply, sewage disposal, fuel, drainage and electrical systems in the park/community in a good state of repair;
(e) maintaining the park/community grounds and all buildings, structures, enclosures and equipment intended for the common use of tenants in a good state of repair; and
(f) repairing damage to a tenant's property, if the damage is caused by the wilful or negligent conduct of the landlord.

The landlord will still be expected to comply with any health, safety, housing or maintenance standards applicable to the site. If there are no municipal property standards, the provincial standards (set out in O. Reg. 517/06) will apply. These standards, amongst other things, require a landlord

[62] (Feb. 5, 2001), TNT-01432, 2001 CarswellOnt 6258 (Ont. Rental Housing Trib.).

to: maintain a supply of potable water and water pressure sufficient for normal household use; maintain adequate water and pressure for fire fighting; maintain roads free of potholes, snow and other obstructions, and control dust on them; and, empty sewage holding tanks.

Maintenance of roads in a good state of repair in mobile home parks was enforced by court order in *Guillemette v. Kingsway Villa Ltd.*[63]

A tenant or former tenant may apply (under para. 29(1)1 of the R.T.A.) to the Board for relief as a result of a breach of the landlord's obligations under s. 161. The tenant only has one year to commence the application from the date of the breach by the landlord (s. 29(2)) and, in determining the appropriate remedy (if any) to grant, the Board must consider whether the tenant or former tenant advised the landlord of the alleged breaches (s. 39(2)). The list of possible remedies is contained in s. 30(1) of the R.T.A.

For complete lack of repair, *Lacey v. Shaughnessy Brothers Investments Ltd.*[64] tells a full story. Adequate disposal of garbage was not available, the roads were in poor shape and the grounds and structures for common use were in poor repair. Court orders to comply were disregarded. The judge said there was total failure by the landlord and there would be 100% abatement gradually reduced as the landlord complied. Punitive damages of $200 were awarded and solicitor and client costs.

A somewhat similar lack of repair and proper services in a mobile home park is found in *Plachta v. Minnie.*[65] The landlord of a mobile home park wanted to close it down and convert the property to vacant land. His application was according to s. 105(1)(*b*) of Part IV, now s. 53(1)(*b*) of the T.P.A. The court accepted the genuineness of the landlord's intention, noting that the reasonableness, economically or otherwise, was not to be considered. However, the application was refused based on the counter-claim of the tenants that the judge should not grant termination and possession as it would be unfair: Part IV, s. 121, now s. 83 of the R.T.A. The landlord had allowed the park to deteriorate: roads were not properly maintained, garbage was not disposed of, plumbing and electrical were left in disrepair, water was not potable. As in *Lacey, supra*, abatement was ordered of 20%; the estimate of the trial judge was the difference between the fair value of the premises if they had been repaired and the fair value in the present state. The judge ordered repairs and ordered the landlord to have the water supply properly working as to quantity, quality and pressure, to repair the roads, remove snow soon after a snowfall, then sand the roads, to replace outdoor lights, and to promptly and regularly remove garbage. The judge refused the landlord's application for termination of the tenancy. Costs were awarded to the successful tenant.

---

[63] (1991), 1991 CarswellOnt 2079 (Ont. Gen. Div.).

[64] (1993), 1993 CarswellOnt 1968 (Ont. Gen. Div.).

[65] (1994), 1994 CarswellOnt 3277 (Ont. Gen. Div.).

Note that these extra responsibilities (under s. 161 of the R.T.A.) relate to the condition of the park or community. The landlord of a mobile home park and land lease community is responsible for the condition of the site that is rented, the surrounding grounds and the common services and facilities. Such a landlord is generally not responsible for the condition of the mobile home or land lease home.

If the owner of a mobile home or land lease home rents that home (and sublets the site) to someone else, that owner becomes the landlord of the new occupant and has all of the maintenance obligations of a landlord. There will be no contractual relationship between the occupant of the home and the landlord of the park/community.

A tenant or former tenant may apply (under s. 30) to the Board for relief as a result of a breach of the landlord's maintenance obligations. There is a one-year limitation period. This process is described later in this chapter.

For more information about mobile homes and land lease homes, please refer to Chapter 20.

5. LIMITS ON A LANDLORD'S LIABILITY

While the R.T.A. clearly makes it the landlord's responsibility to ensure that the residential complex, and all units within the complex, are properly maintained in a good state of repair and fit for habitation, the liability of the landlord is not absolute. A landlord has limited liability when it comes to the condition of the complex. The principles underlying these limits can be described as follows:

1. A new landlord is generally not liable for the failure of the former landlord to properly maintain the complex;
2. A tenant has some responsibility to keep the rental unit clean and to repair any damage caused by the tenant, other occupants of the unit or persons the tenant has allowed into the complex;
3. A landlord will usually not be penalized for failing to fix a problem that was never brought to the attention of the landlord;
4. The landlord's obligation to maintain the unit in a good state of repair does not mean that the landlord must cater to the unreasonably high expectations of a hypersensitive tenant;
5. The landlord is not the insurer of the tenant's property;
6. A tenant must take reasonable steps to minimize his or her losses; and
7. A landlord may be able to contract with a tenant to have the tenant perform some routine maintenance.

(a) Liability of a New Landlord

A new landlord is generally not liable for the failure of the former landlord to properly maintain the residential complex or the units therein.[66] This does not mean, however, that the new landlord can ignore an ongoing problem; the landlord (including a mortgagee in possession) has the responsibility to fulfill its obligations under s. 20 and promptly make any necessary repairs to the complex. It simply means that a new landlord will not be liable to pay any amounts to tenants for breaches of the R.T.A. (or predecessor legislation) that occurred prior to this landlord becoming the landlord.[67]

When a mortgagee goes into possession and is deemed to be the landlord[68] and where there is a lack of repair of the premises, an abatement of rent can be ordered but will be limited to the period during which the mortgagee has been the landlord.[69] Nevertheless, it is up to the mortgagee in possession to do repairs even though the disrepair was the fault of the predecessor landlord.[70]

In another case of a mortgagee in possession, *981673 Ontario Ltd. v. Jessome*,[71] the apartment building had 720 apartments. Extensive repairs were needed, affecting heat, hot water, fire protection, lack of security, garage use, balconies, and others. The owner landlord, faced with 600 work orders, abandoned the property and disappeared. The second mortgagee went into possession, and became the landlord. The court awarded the tenants a 30% abatement from the time the mortgagee went into possession, to be reduced from time to time by stages of one-third, as each stage as set by the court for repairs were done and work orders were satisfied. The judge noted that the second mortgagee was making great strides in getting the repairs done and must maintain the work with speed and to the satisfaction of the City and other regulatory authorities.

---

[66] *Irving et al. v. AGC Inc.* (Dec. 20, 2001), NOT-00582, [2001] O.R.H.T.D. No. 151 (Ont. Rental Housing Trib.), and *Tenants of 10 Shallmar Blvd. v. Shallmar Court Apartments Inc.* (Aug. 25, 2000), TNT-00632, TNT-00677, 2000 CarswellOnt 4422 (Ont. Rental Housing Trib.). See also *Kottabi et al. v. DiGiovanni* (Feb. 1, 2002), CET-02319-RV (Ont. Rental Housing Trib.) in which it was held that it is not proper to allow tenants to deduct from the rent owing to a new landlord an abatement of rent related to events that occurred prior to the new landlord acquiring title to the property.

[67] Landlord and Tenant Board File No. TEL-19200 / TET-01680 (Jan. 5, 2009).

[68] By virtue of the *Mortgages Act*, R.S.O. 1990, c. M.40.

[69] *Prenor Trust Co. of Canada v. Forrest* (1993), 1993 CarswellOnt 3653 (Ont. Gen. Div.). Also see Landlord and Tenant Board File No. SOT-01658 / SOT-01751 (Feb. 2, 2009).

[70] *Hayward v. Shaughnessy Brothers Investments Ltd.* (1996), 1996 CarswellOnt 3783 (Ont. C.A.).

[71] (1994), 21 O.R. (3d) 343 (Ont. Gen. Div.).

(b) Tenant's Responsibility for Cleanliness and Damage

Pursuant to s. 33 of the R.T.A. (formerly s. 29 of the T.P.A.), the tenant is responsible for ordinary cleanliness of the rental unit, except to the extent that the tenancy agreement requires the landlord to clean it. Pursuant to s. 34 of the R.T.A. (formerly s. 30 of the T.P.A.), the tenant is responsible for repairing damage to the rental unit or residential complex caused by the wilful or negligent conduct of the tenant, other occupants of the rental unit or persons who are permitted in the residential complex by the tenant.

If the tenant is responsible for the damage to the rental unit or to the residential complex, it is highly unlikely that the tenant will receive a very sympathetic hearing if that tenant chooses to commence an application against the landlord for any relief as a result of that damage.

Similarly, if the tenant's conduct contributed to the problem or if the tenant failed to take reasonable steps to mitigate, that may affect both the type of relief granted by the Board and the amount of any abatement (or other monetary relief) awarded. For instance, in *Fisher v. Murovec*,[72] the Tribunal awarded an abatement of rent for a serious, on-going mould problem but reduced the amount of the award because of the tenant's role in contributing to this problem.

What if a tenant (or another occupant of the tenant's unit or a guest of the tenant) has caused damage to the complex and the tenant refuses to take responsibility and repair the damage or pay for such repairs? Can the landlord leave the damage until the issue has been resolved by the Board (or by a court)? If the damage is to the common areas of the complex, then the answer to this question would clearly be "no". The landlord has an obligation to all tenants within the complex to make necessary repairs within a reasonable period of time. The landlord may also be held responsible by the municipal or provincial government for breaches of zoning or waste control by-laws or environmental protection legislation should the landlord fail to step in and rectify problems created by a tenant.[73] If the tenant responsible for the damage does not agree to repair the damage or pay for the repairs, the landlord must proceed to have the repairs effected and then seek an order for reimbursement of the cost (and any other relief permitted by the R.T.A.) by commencing an application against the responsible tenant.

If the damage is within the unit of the tenant who caused the damage and it will not affect the tenants of any other units within the complex or other persons outside of the rental unit, the answer is less clear. Although the landlord has an ongoing obligation to keep the rental unit in a good state of repair, the landlord might be reluctant to effect repairs if the landlord believes

---

[72] (Oct. 16, 1998), TST-00193 (Ont. Rental Housing Trib.).

[73] *Springwater (Township) v. 829664 Ontario Ltd.* (2008), 2008 CarswellOnt 1124 (Ont. S.C.J.).

that the tenant is wilfully damaging the rental unit and will continue to do so; it would be a waste of time, money and effort. The landlord may also be reluctant to enter the unit if the tenant is potentially dangerous or has refused to allow the landlord access to the unit. In such circumstances, the landlord may be justified in seeking to terminate the tenancy and then wait until after the tenant has been evicted before repairing the damage to the rental unit.

(c) Notification of the Landlord

Although the R.T.A. does not make the landlord's obligation to repair and maintain the residential complex contingent upon being advised of problems by the tenants, pursuant to s. 30(2) of the Act, the Board *must* consider whether or not a tenant notified the landlord of the problem when determining the appropriate remedy to grant to that tenant.[74] In some circumstances, the landlord's responsibility can only be expected to be fulfilled after notice has been given by a tenant to a landlord.

In *Racz v. Szoboszloi*,[75] the landlord applied to court for possession for non-payment of rent and the tenant countered by alleging that there were cockroaches in the flat which came from the landlord's adjoining premises. The judge held that there should have been notice of the complaint to the landlord, and cited in support *O'Brien v. Robinson*,[76] which held that the landlord's obligation to repair only arose after notice of the alleged defect, or, of course, if the landlord became aware of defects on inspection. In *O'Brien v. Robinson* it was a latent defect in a ceiling which fell down and injured the tenant. As neither the tenant nor the landlord was aware of the defect, there was no obligation on the landlord to repair, and thus no liability.

In *Mackay v. Sanghera*,[77] the Divisional Court held that the landlord was not liable to the tenant for lack of maintenance because the tenant never notified the landlord of the problem. This case follows the Court of Appeal decision in *McQuestion v. Schneider*,[78] in which it was held that liability for injuries or damages could not be imposed on a landlord who had no knowledge or could not reasonably be expected to have knowledge of a maintenance problem.

Some cases, however, suggest that a landlord cannot rely solely upon tenants' complaints to identify repairs that are necessary and that, subject to a tenant's right to privacy, a landlord has a positive, ongoing obligation to periodically inspect rental units and to maintain them in a good state of

---

[74] See s. 30(2) and Interpretation Guideline 5.

[75] (1974), 4 O.R. (2d) 306 (Ont. Co. Ct.).

[76] [1973] 1 All E.R. 583 (C.A.).

[77] (June 20, 2001), 2001 CarswellOnt 2349 (Ont. Div. Ct.).

[78] (1975), 8 O.R. (2d) 249 (Ont. C.A.).

repair.[79] Now that the R.T.A. permits landlords to enter rental units periodically (on notice) for the purpose of conducting maintenance inspections, a heavier onus may be placed upon landlords to be aware of the state of their buildings, whether or not they have received complaints from the tenants.

Once a maintenance problem has been identified, the landlord has an obligation to take reasonable steps to fix that problem. This obligation (to do the necessary work) is not eliminated by the failure of the tenant to bring it to the landlord's attention at an earlier date. The delay of the tenant in informing the landlord, however, may well influence the Board's decision about whether or not to grant any monetary relief to the tenant and the amount of any such relief. Once aware of the problem, the landlord must act promptly.

In *Antoniou v. Feder*,[80] the tenant did not immediately advise the landlord of the serious problems with this house. The Tribunal ultimately granted a substantial abatement in rent but only commencing from the date the landlord was advised of the problems.

In *Egesi v. Yorkville North Developments*,[81] the tenants suffered three serious leaks between January and April 1999. They sought a substantial abatement of rent. Although the leaks were serious, an abatement was not deemed the appropriate remedy because the tenants failed to promptly advise the landlord of the problem and then interfered in the landlord's attempts to gain access to the unit in order to effect the necessary repairs. The landlord was ordered to complete the necessary work but no abatement of rent was granted.

In *Catana v. Centennial Manor Apt. Inc.*,[82] it was ruled that tenants cannot wait for months, then complain about the lack of repairs in order to obtain a larger abatement of rent; the tenants ought to have immediately brought these problems to the attention of the landlord.

In *Kapelos v. Heine*,[83] the tenant provided no evidence that he advised the landlords of maintenance problems in a timely fashion. Once the landlords were made aware of the leak in the roof, they responded immediately and repaired the problem. The Tribunal therefore found that the landlords did not fail to meet their maintenance obligations and the tenants' application was dismissed.

In Landlord and Tenant Board File No. SWT-00529 (Sept. 28, 2007), the tenants informed the landlord in 2005 about some mould around some of the windows in the unit and the landlord recommended that the tenants try cleaning the affected areas with bleach. The problem apparently got worse over time but the tenants said nothing further about this problem to the

---

[79] See *Roy v. Frisz* (June 23, 1999), SOT-00397 (Ont. Rental Housing Trib.).

[80] (Oct. 2, 2000), TNT-01154, 2000 CarswellOnt 6429 (Ont. Rental Housing Trib.).

[81] (1999), TNT-00466, 1999 CarswellOnt 5798 (Ont. Rental Housing Trib.).

[82] (Jan. 28, 2000), SWT-01030 (Ont. Rental Housing Trib.).

[83] (Aug. 17, 2006), TEL-63573, TET-05940, [2006] O.R.H.T.D. No. 108 (Ont. Rental Housing Trib.).

landlord until some time in 2007 and then refused the landlord's offer of assistance at that time. The tenants brought an application for an order terminating the tenancy and for an abatement of rent. In these circumstances, the Board declined to grant any relief to the tenants.

In Landlord and Tenant Board File No. SWT-01955 (Jan. 20, 2009), the Member dismissed the tenant's application for the following reasons:

> The Tenant did not inform the Landlord that the down-spout required attention and the Landlord would not have reasonably been aware of this strange issue. The Landlord, therefore, cannot be seen to be in breach of her maintenance obligations. The remedy sought by the Tenant is, therefore, not appropriately considered.

Similarly, in Landlord and Tenant Board File No. TEL-00054 (March 5, 2007), the Member refused to grant an abatement with respect to an allegedly defective seal on the refrigerator because the Member was not satisfied that the tenant advised the landlord prior to raising that issue at the hearing.

(d) Objective vs. Subjective Standard

The determination of the condition of the premises, the required state of repair and compliance with health, housing and safety standards is by application of an objective rather than a subjective test. The issue is not whether the condition of the unit or complex meets with the approval of a particular tenant; rather, the issue is whether the condition of the premises complies with the relevant minimum health, safety and housing standards and whether, in all of the circumstances, a *reasonable* tenant would find the premises to be in a good state of repair and fit for habitation.

An overly sensitive tenant complained that a new soundproof ceiling should be installed by the landlord and failure to do so was a breach of the landlord's obligation to repair and maintain the apartment fit for habitation: *Lockwood v. Edwards*.[84] The court stated that the apartment was in an old building and that noise from the rooms above was normal, tolerable and acceptable, and further held that it did not constitute a nuisance. In a somewhat similar case, the Tribunal found that although sound was transmitted readily through the floor of the bedroom of this unit (located in an older building above a barber shop), since the unit complied with all relevant health, safety and housing standards and was otherwise in a good state of repair, the landlord had not violated his obligations under s. 24 of the T.P.A (now s. 20 of the R.T.A.).[85]

---

[84] (1982), 16 A.C.W.S. (2d) 492 (Ont. Co. Ct.).

[85] *Satchithananthan v. Cacciola* (Dec. 30, 2002), TST-04047, 2002 CarswellOnt 5023 (Ont. Rental Housing Trib.). The Tribunal found, however, that the amount of noise coming into the unit was substantially interfering with the tenant's reasonable enjoyment of the unit and ordered the landlord to take steps to soundproof the affected room.

(e) Forseeability

A landlord is not absolutely liable for everything that goes wrong within a residential complex or for all losses incurred by tenants as a result of maintenance problems. In general, a landlord will only be held financially responsible to a tenant where the landlord was negligent in fulfilling the obligations under s. 20 (i.e., where the landlord knew or ought to have known of a maintenance problem or potential problem and failed to take reasonable and timely steps to address that problem).

In *McQuestion v. Schneider*,[86] the Court of Appeal held that liability for injuries or damages could not be imposed on a landlord who had no knowledge or could not reasonably be expected to have knowledge of a maintenance problem. This decision was followed by the Divisional Court in *Mackay v. Sanghera*.[87]

In *O'Brien v. Robinson*,[88] as a result of a latent defect, a ceiling fell down and injured the tenant. Neither the tenant nor the landlord was aware of the defect so the court found that there was no liability on the landlord.

The landlord was found not to be in breach of s. 24(1) of the T.P.A. when a refrigerator stopped working. This was not foreseeable. The landlord did not know nor should the landlord have known that the refrigerator was about to break down. The landlord responded promptly. The tenant's application for an order determining that the landlord had failed to properly maintain the unit and for damages for spoiled food was dismissed.[89]

Similarly, a landlord was not found liable for damages arising from leaks where no negligence was found on the part of the landlord.[90] A similar approach has been adopted more recently in Landlord and Tenant Board File No. TST-02101 (Jan. 19, 2009)[91] and Landlord and Tenant Board File No. TNT-01332 (Jan. 13, 2009).[92]

In *Martin v. Sterling Karamar Property Management*,[93] a radiator burst in a unit, resulting in the flooding of the unit below. The flooded rental unit was uninhabitable for two weeks. The flood was in no way the result of any negligence on the part of the landlord and the landlord's response was exemplary. The tenant rejected the landlord's offer to temporarily move the tenant into another unit. The tenant claimed an abatement of rent and com-

---

[86] (1975), 8 O.R. (2d) 249 (Ont. C.A.).

[87] (June 20, 2001), 2001 CarswellOnt 2349 (Ont. Div. Ct.).

[88] [1973] 1 All E.R. 583 (C.A.).

[89] *Nixon v. Pelentsky* (Oct. 29, 1999), TST-01247 (Ont. Rental Housing Trib.).

[90] *Cripps v. Peterborough Housing Authority* (1990), 20 A.C.W.S. (3d) 276 (Ont. Dist. Ct.).

[91] In which it was held that there was no forewarning that there was a problem with the municipal pipes outside the rental property.

[92] In which it was found that this flood "was in the nature of an unforeseeable act of God for which the Landlord ought not to be held accountable."

[93] (July 4, 2003), TNT-03453, 2003 CarswellOnt 4239 (Ont. Rental Housing Trib.).

pensation for damage to her property. In these circumstances, no monetary relief was awarded.

In *Bramar Holdings Inc. v. Deseron*,[94] heavy rain caused a sewer backup in the tenant's basement on two occasions. The landlord's response was exemplary but, for approximately five weeks, the tenant could not reside in the house while repair work was being done. The landlord was found not to be in breach of its obligations to maintain the rental unit but, because the tenant had been deprived of the physical use and enjoyment of the premises for approximately five weeks, the rent was abated for that period of time. No other relief was granted.

In *Exeter v. Osgoode Properties Ltd.*,[95] a toilet failed and the unit was flooded. There was no prior indication of any problem with this toilet. The landlord was not held responsible since there was no negligence on the part of the landlord.

The landlord was not held responsible for damages when part of the ceiling fell and damaged the tenant's stereo and desk. There was no evidence that the landlord failed to inspect or should have known this might happen. The landlord was not a guarantor: *Jensen v. Debly*.[96]

In Landlord and Tenant Board File No. SOT-00042 (April 20, 2007), a pipe burst in the residential complex, causing a flood and major damage to 64 units and the common areas of the complex. The pipe in question underwent routine inspection and had just passed its annual inspection about four months prior to its failure. The Board found that there was no evidence to suggest that the landlord could have predicted or prevented this incident. In addition, the Board found the landlord's response to have been exemplary. Consequently, the tenant's application based upon the damage and inconvenience caused by the flood was dismissed.

It is a different matter, however, if the landlord knew or ought to have known of the existence of a potential problem. In *MacLennan v. 587125 Ontario Ltd.*,[97] the tenant brought an action for damages caused by a burst water pipe. In view of the age of the building and evidence of similar pipe corrosion in other units, the landlord was found to have breached its maintenance obligations by failing to carry out general routine inspections that would have detected the problem.

Even though the landlord, in the absence of any negligence, may not be held responsible for the initial problem, the landlord can nevertheless be held liable if appropriate and prompt action is not taken once the damage has

[94] (1996), 1996 CarswellOnt 1185 (Ont. Gen. Div.).

[95] (Sept. 11, 2000), EAT-01578-RV, [2000] O.R.H.T.D. No. 119, 2000 CarswellOnt 4519 (Ont. Rental Housing Trib.), varied (2000), 2000 CarswellOnt 4507 (Ont. Rental Housing Trib.).

[96] (1995), 167 N.B.R. (2d) 230 (N.B. Q.B.).

[97] (1990), 11 R.P.R. (2d) 28, 1990 CarswellOnt 527 (Ont. Dist. Ct.).

occurred. The landlord has an obligation to minimize the damage and to ensure it does not worsen.

In *200 Keele St. Tenants and Kasmani*,[98] tenants complained to the landlord because of water damage to their units and furniture, which affected their reasonable enjoyment and that the landlord was in breach of s. 24(1) of the T.P.A. They asked for reductions in rent. The evidence was that an exceptionally heavy snowfall occurred in January 1999. The sudden accumulation of the snow and the freeze/thaw cycle were outside of the usual. The Tribunal said that the landlord acted "as fast and as attentive as reasonably possible". The tenants' applications were dismissed by the Tribunal.

Similarly, the Board dismissed a tenant's application where it found that the landlord responded promptly and in a reasonable manner to routine maintenance concerns and responded in an exemplary fashion when there was a major flood caused when a pipe burst.[99]

On the other hand, the landlord was held responsible where, although the flood was not the landlord's fault, the repairs took too long, in the Member's opinion. In Landlord and Tenant Board File No. TET-01712 (Jan. 26, 2009), the Board awarded the tenant $1,200 as compensation for damaged personal property, a 25% abatement of rent (totaling $422.50) and $450 for the out-of-pocket expenses related to living in a motel and having to eat in restaurants.

Similarly, in Landlord and Tenant Board File No. CET-00006 (March 19, 2007), although the tenant failed to prove that a sewer backup into the rental unit resulted from any failure on the landlord's part to properly maintain the unit, because of the landlord's delay in repairing the unit, the tenant was awarded a rent abatement of $1,500 (equal to the tenant's out-of-pocket expenses in temporarily renting alternate accommodations).

In *Makhiter v. Toronto Community Housing Corp.*,[100] a garage door caused damage to the tenant's vehicle. The tenant was unable to prove that the incident resulted from any failure of the landlord to properly maintain the complex so the application was dismissed.

In *Sheppard v. Suraski*,[101] the tenant experienced inconvenience (and damage to his property) due to repeated water leakage into the rental unit. The Tribunal found that, at least for the period of time that could be considered in this application, the landlord had an adequate preventative maintenance program in place and had responded in a reasonably timely fashion to the tenant's complaints. The Tribunal pointed out that the Act does not impose absolute liability upon a landlord with respect to maintenance/repair issues

[98] (April 14, 1999), TST-00612 (Ont. Rental Housing Trib.).

[99] Landlord and Tenant Board File No. SOT-00042, (April 20, 2007).

[100] (Jan. 18, 2002), TET-02239 (Ont. Rental Housing Trib.).

[101] (April 21, 2006), TST-08126-RV-RV, 2006 CarswellOnt 4424, [2006] O.R.H.T.D. No. 42 (Ont. Rental Housing Trib.).

and that, in this case, the landlord had not breached his maintenance obligations during the relevant time period. As a result, the tenant's application was dismissed.

Sometimes, it will be difficult to ascertain whether the landlord actually foresaw the risk but it can be inferred from the circumstances that the landlord ought to have foreseen it. In Landlord and Tenant Board File No. SOT-01762 (Jan. 14, 2009), a large old tree on the grounds of a residential complex fell over onto a number of cars of the complex's tenants. Three tenants joined together to bring an application to the Board against the landlord for compensation for damage to their respective vehicles (on the basis that the landlord had failed to comply with its maintenance obligations). In granting the tenants' application (at least for those who had documented proof of the cost of repairs), the Member applied the legal principle of *res ipsa loquitur* (i.e., the thing speaks for itself) and found that "a healthy tree does not just fall down". The Member held that, in circumstances such as this, negligence is assumed unless the landlord can prove otherwise. The landlord adduced no credible evidence that the tree fell because of unusual weather conditions. The landlord also failed to provide any other reasonable explanation and failed to produce any evidence concerning the health of the tree from the company that the landlord stated provided it with "tree services". The Member stated that, "When a tree falls on cars it is up to the owner of the tree to demonstrate that this occurrence is not as a result of failing to take proper care of the tree." Since no such evidence was adduced, the application was granted.

In conclusion, a landlord is not the insurer of the tenant's property and will not be held financially responsible for maintenance problems that the landlord could not reasonably have prevented through the exercise of reasonable diligence. Tenants who are concerned about their possessions should consider obtaining insurance. The lack of such insurance, however, cannot be used as a defence by a landlord who has failed to comply with the landlord's obligations under s. 20 of the R.T.A.[102] This is sometimes raised as an issue by landlords but is, in reality, a "red herring". Even if a tenant has contents insurance, if the contents are damaged as a result of the landlord's negligence, although the tenant will likely be compensated by his or her insurance company, that company will then have a legal right to commence proceedings against the landlord in the name of the tenant (a "subrogated" claim) to collect any amounts to which the tenant is entitled. The existence of insurance does not, therefore, relieve the landlord of liability. Whether the tenant has insurance or not, the landlord will still be held responsible for the landlord's failure to comply with its maintenance obligations.[103]

---

[102] Landlord and Tenant Board File No. TET-01712 (Jan. 26, 2009).

[103] Nevertheless, if the tenancy agreement requires the tenant to have insurance and provide proof to the landlord of such insurance, the failure of the tenant to do so may be grounds to

(f) Mitigation

When a problem arises, the tenant must take reasonable steps to minimize the impact. This may involve informing the landlord of the problem as quickly as possible, co-operating with the landlord's efforts to address the problem or temporarily vacating the unit. If the landlord is unresponsive, it may sometimes also mean taking steps to address the problem on one's own. For instance, after failing to receive an appropriate response from the landlord to repeated requests for maintenance, the tenant may be justified (and required by his/her duty to mitigate) in having the repairs done at his/her own expense and then seeking reimbursement by the landlord for that expense.

In one case that came before the Tribunal, a tenant complained that the smoke detector in the unit was not working because the battery needed to be replaced. Admittedly, it was the landlord's responsibility to ensure that all smoke detectors were functioning. The tenant was asked why, if he felt that it was a matter of life and death, he did not replace the battery himself. His response was that it was not his job. Although the tenant was technically correct, the Tribunal will take such matters into account in deciding what relief, if any, to grant a tenant who is complaining about lack of maintenance.

For instance, in *Cino v. Standard Land Investments*,[104] the Tribunal reduced the rent abatement ordered from 10% to 5% because the tenants could easily have mitigated the situation by purchasing and installing their own smoke detectors when the landlord neglected to do so.

In *Burr et al. v. The Azuria Group*,[105] the farmhouse rented to the tenants was in very poor condition. Mr. Burr agreed to do the necessary work and to deduct the cost of his labour and materials from rent payments. The landlord assumed that the problems had been rectified. They had not. Eventually, the tenants complained about the condition of the house. The Tribunal held that the tenants ought to have mitigated the situation: by doing the work (or having the work done) and then submitting bills to the landlord, by advising the landlord of the work that was necessary and demanding that the landlord do the work, or by promptly commencing an application to force the landlord to do the work. Since the tenants utterly failed to mitigate the situation, no abatement of rent was granted.

A tenant is not, however, required to terminate the tenancy and move out of the unit in order to mitigate the landlord's failure to fulfill the landlord's maintenance obligations.[106]

---

terminate the tenancy under s. 64(1) of the Act: *Stanbar Properties Limited v. Rooke* (Nov. 9, 2005), Doc. Hamilton 04-212DV (Ont. Div. Ct.).

104 (April 18, 2006), SWT-07421, [2006] O.R.H.T.D. No. 62 (Ont. Rental Housing Trib.).

105 (Aug. 20, 2002), TNT-02653 (Ont. Rental Housing Trib.).

106 *Goodman v. Menyhart* (2009), 2009 CarswellOnt 2205 (Ont. Div. Ct.)

(g) Where Tenant Agrees to Perform Routine Maintenance

Generally, the view of the Landlord and Tenant Board has been that a landlord cannot contract out of the landlord's obligations to maintain and repair the residential complex. Thus, landlords who purported to enter into agreements with tenants to have the tenants perform lawn maintenance or snow removal ran the risk that such agreements would be found to be of no force or effect. A recent decision from the Ontario Superior Court of Justice, however, suggests that such agreements may be upheld.

In *Montgomery v. Van*,[107] a tenant slipped and fell on some ice on the property and suffered injuries as a result. The tenant commenced a civil action against the landlord for damages alleging that the landlord was negligent in failing to remove the snow and ice from the walkway. It was, however, a term of the tenancy agreement that "Tenants are responsible for keeping their walkway and stairway clean (including snow removal)".

The landlord brought a motion for determination of a question of law; in particular, whether the provision that required the tenant to remove ice and snow from the common walkways was void. The landlord submitted that the T.P.A. (and the regulations thereto) do not specifically require a landlord to personally complete snow removal tasks from common areas. A landlord is simply required to "ensure" that such tasks are completed. On that basis, it was submitted that landlords may fulfil their statutory obligations by delegating snow removal tasks to others. It was argued that the T.P.A. and associated regulations do not state that snow removal tasks may never be assumed by a tenant and, as such, the Conditions of Lease executed by the tenant were not inconsistent with the *Act* and should not be considered to be void. The Court agreed and found that the provision in question did not violate the *Act*.

6. PROCEDURE

When a maintenance problem occurs within a rental unit or elsewhere in the residential complex, a tenant's first move should be to notify the landlord. Most multi-unit buildings have a set procedure for requesting repairs. In many cases, a telephone call to the superintendent will be all that is needed. It is recommended, however, that all requests be made in writing. The request should be specific about the problem, should identify the rental unit or affected area of the building and should be dated and signed by the tenant. If possible, the tenant should retain a copy and have the landlord stamp it or sign it as proof that the landlord has received the work request. Such documents will be very important later if the landlord alleges that the tenant never advised the landlord of the problem.

---

[107] (2009), 2009 CarswellOnt 182 (Ont. S.C.J.).

Unless it is an emergency situation, the landlord is required to provide written notice, at least 24 hours in advance, before entering a rental unit (ss. 26 and 27). The notice must specify the reason for entry, the day of entry and a time of entry between the hours of 8 a.m. and 8 p.m. (s. 27(3)). The tenant need not be at home when the landlord enters the unit.

Notwithstanding the usual rules about entry, a landlord may enter a rental unit at any time without written notice if the tenant consents to the entry at the time of entry (para. 26(1)(b)). Some landlords try to obtain such consent by having the tenant sign a request for maintenance form which states that the tenant is consenting to the landlord entering the unit to effect the repairs. While it is not illegal to request such confirmation, such an acknowledgement may not actually protect the landlord since the consent is not being given "at the time of entry" as required by para. 26(1)(b).

Both landlords and tenants are expected to act reasonably. A superintendent who shows up at the apartment door to fix a routine problem at 1:00 a.m. should not be surprised if he is not greeted warmly and welcomed into the rental unit. Since the landlord has not complied with the usual notice provisions for entry to the unit and has come at a time outside the usually permitted time for entry, the tenant is within his or her rights to refuse the superintendent into the unit. A tenant who wishes repairs to be done, however, should not set so many conditions on the time and manner of entry that the landlord is effectively prevented from doing the necessary work. Landlords rely upon professionals such as plumbers and electricians; such workers often have to give an estimate of the time of entry (e.g., between noon and 4:00 p.m.) rather than a precise time. It is not always possible to pick a time or date that is convenient to the tenant. Both sides should attempt to work together to resolve the problem. Unfortunately, people do not always act as they should and those people often end up appearing before the Tribunal/ Board.

Before commencing an application at the Board, a tenant may wish to consider contacting the appropriate government authority (Fire Marshall, local health department, municipal property standards department, Investigations Branch of the Ministry of Municipal Affairs and Housing, etc.) in order to lodge a complaint and arrange for an inspection of the premises. The intervention of a government agency may be sufficient to convince the landlord to do the necessary work. If not, the intervention will at least provide additional independent evidence that the landlord has failed to meet its maintenance obligations.

The tenant may also apply to the Board for various types of relief (listed in s. 30 of the R.T.A. and described in detail in the next section of this chapter). The application is Form T6. The fee is $45. If tenants of several units join together to file one application, the fee is $45 for the first unit plus $5 for each additional unit to a maximum of $450.

The application is made pursuant to para. 29(1)1 of the R.T.A. for an order determining that the landlord breached the obligations under s. 20(1). The application may be filed by a tenant or a former tenant.[108] There is, however, a deadline for filing such an application. Pursuant to s. 29(2), the application cannot be brought more than one year after the day "the alleged conduct giving rise to the application occurred". It is up to the tenant to apply promptly.[109]

This does not necessarily mean that a tenant must live with a problem that has existed for more than one year. The Board has ruled that landlords' maintenance obligations are ongoing.[110] It would be contrary to the intention of the legislation to rule that if a building is bad enough for long enough, the landlord does not have to address the poor condition of the building because the tenant(s) did not commence an application within one year of the first appearance of the problems. Since a landlord's maintenance obligations are ongoing, the "alleged conduct giving rise to the application" (i.e., failure to effect repairs) continues until the necessary work has been done and a tenant's application is not barred by the expiration of a limitation period.

While it is clear that the Board can consider evidence as to the condition of the unit or the complex going back more than one year prior to the filing of the application, it remains an open question whether tenants can be granted *relief* for any period more than one year prior to the filing of the application. Members of the Rental Housing Tribunal generally refused to grant relief for any period earlier than one year prior to the filing of the tenant's application as it was believed that that would be contrary to the intent of s. 32(2) of the T.P.A. (what is now s. 29(2) of the R.T.A.). There are indications, however, that some Members of the Board may be adopting a different interpretation when it comes to "ongoing" maintenance problems (i.e., problems that have persisted for more than one year).[111]

The Divisional Court has recently considered this issue. In *Goodman et al. v. Menyhart*,[112] the landlords were neglecting the maintenance of the residential complex. Beginning in February 2005, a series of orders were issued by the City of Toronto's property standards and health departments.

---

108 Even after the tenancy has ended, a former tenant can apply for relief (usually an abatement of rent previously paid to the landlord) for breaches of the landlord's obligations under s. 20 that occurred during the tenancy.

109 See, for example, Landlord and Tenant Board File No. CET-00084 (March 27, 2007), in which a number of claims were dismissed as being out of time. For a similar interpretation, also see Landlord and Tenant Board File No. SWL-21951 (Jan. 9, 2009).

110 See the Board's Interpretation Guideline 5.

111 See, for example, Landlord and Tenant Board File No. TNT-01298 (Jan. 12, 2009), Landlord and Tenant Board File No. NOT-00927 (Feb. 4, 2009) and Landlord and Tenant Board File No. TSL-87099-RV / TST-01120-RV (October 27, 2008). Note that this last decision is currently under appeal to the Divisional Court.

112 An unreported decision of the Divisional Court (Court File No. DC-07-00000321-0000, April 9, 2009).

In February 2006, the tenants of two units in the complex brought an application under the T.P.A. against their landlords for, among other things, breach of the landlords' maintenance obligations. The hearing took nine days to hear over a period of almost a year. The hearing concluded in January 2007 and the Board's order was issued in May 2007. The Member awarded the tenants a 25% abatement of rent from May 2006 onwards. The Member found that he could not grant relief for any period earlier than one year immediately preceding the date upon which the order was issued. On appeal by the tenants, the Divisional Court considered the interpretation of s. 32(2) of the T.P.A. (which is now s. 29(2) of the R.T.A.) and found that this provision imposes a limitation period for the *bringing* of an application but "does not limit the duration of an abatement of rent to 12 months before the date of the Order".

Some may interpret this decision as standing for the proposition that there is no limitation on the period for which a tenant may seek an abatement of rent (for long-standing maintenance problems). Unfortunately, the wording used by the Divisional Court is not clear. It merely states that a tenant's claim for relief is not restricted to the 12-month period prior to the *issuance of the order*. The Divisional Court is silent on the issue of whether a claim that is made in time (within one year of the conduct giving rise to the application) has any restrictions as to the period for which relief can be granted. For instance, it is possible that the effect of s. 32(2) of the T.P.A. (now s. 29(2) of the R.T.A.) is to prohibit the Board from granting relief for any period earlier than one year prior to the *date the application is made*.

In this case, the Divisional Court granted the tenants' appeal and awarded to the tenants an additional abatement of rent going back to February 2006, which just happens to be one year prior to the date the tenants commenced their application. Members of the Rental Housing Tribunal routinely granted abatements of rent for up to one year prior to the commencement of the application. In this respect, there is nothing revolutionary about this decision from the Divisional Court. Since the Divisional Court did not award an abatement of rent for any period earlier than one year prior to the commencement of the application, its position on this issue remains unclear. Until the Board amends its Interpretation Guideline No. 5 (see Appendix 8) to specifically address this issue or the Divisional Court clarifies its position, this will remain an open question.

It is crucial for a tenant to present at the hearing good supporting documentation in order to be successful on this type of application. The testimony of the tenant may not be enough on its own. Successful tenants often present photographs (or video) to support their case. Such evidence can be very persuasive. The tenant should file copies of all written requests for repairs, etc., given to the landlord. The tenant may also wish to file a copy of any notice of violation, Work Order or similar document issued against the landlord for violation of health, safety, housing and maintenance standards; if the tenant experiences difficulty in obtaining such documents, the tenant can obtain and serve a summons upon the inspector to compel the inspector to attend the hearing (to testify) and bring to the hearing all relevant notes and records pertaining to the unit or complex in question.

It may also be necessary to call an expert witness. In Landlord and Tenant Board File No. NOT-00013 (March 1, 2007), the tenant was complaining that there was mould in her unit and that it was adversely affecting her health. A note from her doctor to this effect was given no weight by the Board as the doctor had never attended at the rental unit. Digital images were presented at the hearing but the Member stated that the images were too small to determine if the dark spots were mould, mildew, dirt or something else altogether. The Member noted that the tenant did not call expert witnesses or submit any compelling documentary evidence in support of the claim of mould. As a result, it was found that the tenant had failed to meet her burden of proof and the application was dismissed.

Finally, under the T.P.A., a tenant would sometimes file a T6 application in response to a landlord's application (more often than not, an application to evict the tenant for non-payment of rent). The tenant's application was often scheduled for a later date than the landlord's application. Typically, on the date scheduled for the hearing of the landlord's application, the tenant would request that the hearing be adjourned so that both applications could be heard together on the date scheduled for the tenant's application. While such requests were often granted, it was not automatic and there were some risks involved.

Hearing the two applications together made sense because if the landlord was found to be in serious breach of the maintenance obligations, no eviction could be granted. Furthermore, because covenants are interdependent, a fundamental breach by the landlord would relieve the tenant of the obligation to pay rent (so there would not actually be any arrears). Sometimes, however, the landlord or the Tribunal suspected that the request for an adjournment was simply a stalling tactic. After all, if there were legitimate or serious maintenance problems, why would the tenant wait until the landlord commenced an application to do something about it?

Under the R.T.A., tenants may not need to seek such adjournments since, pursuant to s. 82, they can raise maintenance issues (or any other issues they want) at the hearing of the landlord's application concerning arrears of rent without actually filing their own application and without providing any prior notification to the landlord. My review of the available cases from the Board suggests that tenants are raising (under s. 82) maintenance concerns at an eviction hearing initiated by the landlord (based upon arrears of rent) more often than they are commencing their own maintenance applications (T6). Unfortunately, many tenants are not coming to such hearings properly prepared with cogent, corroborative evidence (such as inspection reports, photographs, copies of documents to prove that the landlord was aware of the problem(s), etc.) and, as a result, they get little, if any, relief.[113] Typically, on a s. 82 maintenance complaint, a tenant will receive an abatement of up to $500.00 (occasionally more), which will then be deducted by the Board from the arrears of rent the tenant owes the landlord.[114] The Board may also order that repairs be done, but that will be of little comfort to a tenant who has been evicted from the unit prior to the date by which the work must be done.[115]

7. REMEDIES FOR BREACH

(a) General

Pursuant to s. 30(1) of the R.T.A., once the Board has determined (under para. 29(1)1) that a landlord has breached the obligations under s. 20(1), the Board may do one or more of the following:

1. Terminate the tenancy;
2. Order an abatement of rent;
3. Authorize a repair that has been or is to be made and order its costs to be paid by the landlord to the tenant;
4. Order the landlord to do specified repairs or other work within a specified time;
5. Order the landlord to pay a specified sum to the tenant as compensation for:
   (i) costs the tenant has incurred or will incur in repairing or replacing property of the tenant that was damaged, destroyed or disposed of as a result of the landlord's breach or breaches of the obligations under s. 20(1); and
   (ii) other reasonable out-of-pocket expenses that the tenant has in-

---

[113] See, for example, Landlord and Tenant Board File No. TEL-00572 (March 28, 2007); Landlord and Tenant Board File No. TSL-00509 (March 28, 2007); and Landlord and Tenant Board File No. TSL-20145 (Jan. 13, 2009).

[114] See Landlord and Tenant Board File No. SOL-00505 (March 22, 2007); Landlord and Tenant Board File No. SOL-00304 (March 19, 2007); Landlord and Tenant Board File No. SOL-00750 (March 30, 2007); Landlord and Tenant Board File No. SOL-00434 (March 14, 2007); Landlord and Tenant Board File No. SOL-00219 (March 5, 2007); Landlord and Tenant Board File No. SOL-00396 (March 16, 2007); Landlord and Tenant Board File No. SOL-00178 (March 16, 2007); Landlord and Tenant Board File No. NOL-00178 (March 15, 2007); Landlord and Tenant Board File No. EAL-00743 (March 30, 2007); Landlord and Tenant Board File No. CEL-00480 (March 9, 2007) ; Landlord and Tenant Board File No. CEL-00060 (Feb. 22, 2007); Landlord and Tenant Board File No. EAL-13121 (Jan. 13, 2009); Landlord and Tenant Board File No. SOL-18140 (Jan. 13, 2009); Landlord and Tenant Board File No. NOL-05876 (Jan. 14, 2009); Landlord and Tenant Board File No. TSL-19733 (Jan. 12, 2009).

[115] See, for example, Landlord and Tenant Board File No. SWL-21938 (Jan. 9, 2009); and Landlord and Tenant Board File No. SWL-21702 (Jan. 29, 2009).

curred or will incur as a result of the landlord's breach or breaches of the obligations under s. 20(1);

6. Issue an order prohibiting a rent increase; and
7. Make any other order that it considers appropriate.

Each of these remedies is discussed further below.

(b) Terminate the Tenancy

This remedy can only be granted at the request of the tenant. It is suggested that the Board should only grant an order terminating a lease for lack of repairs when the non-repair is of a substantial nature or has rendered the premises unfit for habitation or where the parties consent to such an order being made. This was the view expressed by the presiding Member in *Tetrault v. 1203279 Ontario Ltd.*,[116] in which the Member declined to grant the tenant's request for an order terminating the tenancy on the basis that such an order "should only be made where the landlord is in serious breach of the duties imposed by the *Tenant Protection Act* and it is not reasonable to expect that the breach will be remedied."

The Board's Interpretation Guideline 5 indicates that termination of the tenancy and eviction of the tenant should only "be used in serious cases and only where the tenant requests them or a public authority has required the unit to be vacated . . . if the unit is not fit for human habitation . . . [or] if the condition of the unit is so poor as to threaten the safety of the inhabitants or threaten their well-being." For examples of how this Interpretation Guideline has been applied, see Landlord and Tenant Board File No. SWL-21683 / SWT-01988 (Feb. 9, 2009), Landlord and Tenant Board File No. EAT-01531/ EAT-01575 (Feb. 9, 2009) and Landlord and Tenant Board File No. CET-01725 (Feb. 4, 2009).

Termination of the tenancy is also appropriate where the landlord cannot or will not provide a habitable unit or a unit that meets the basic requirements upon which the parties have agreed. The breach of the statutory obligation of the landlord to repair is treated in a similar manner to a breach of a landlord's convenant. It has already been noted that, under s. 17 of the R.T.A., convenants by the landlord and tenant are interdependent and a breach by one relieves the other of performance of obligations. By s. 19 of the R.T.A., the doctrine of frustration of contract also applies to tenancy agreements.

In *Leach v. White Knight Investments Ltd.*,[117] the tenant's application for an order under s. 94 of Part IV (*Landlord and Tenant Act*) for termination of the tenancy, return of the security deposit and an abatement of rent, could be

---

[116] (Jan. 7, 2000), TST-01642, [2000] O.R.H.T.D. No. 3, 2000 CarswellOnt 6326 (Ont. Rental Housing Trib.).

[117] (1978), 19 O.R. (2d) 142 (Ont. Co. Ct.).

made even after the tenant had moved out because of the landlord's failure to repair under s. 94. This was restated in *Blatt Holdings Ltd. v. Stumpf.*[118] Namely, that the tenant could bring an application under s. 94 of Part IV for alleged non-repair and presumably an abatement of rent even after the tenant had gone out of possession.

In *Babineau and Kaswood Apartments, Re.*,[119] the landlord knew of the presence of cockroaches and did not act promptly to have them eradicated. The tenant was successful in obtaining an order terminating the tenancy and for an abatement of rent.

These considerations were dealt with in *Temlas Apartments Inc. v. Desloges.*[120] The lease contained a covenant by the lessor (landlord) to maintain the premises in a good state of repair and fit for habitation. The tenant complained that the hot water system was contaminated by rust and impossible to use for bathing. The tenant moved out, not having first applied under s. 94(4)(*a*) of Part IV for an order terminating the tenancy. The court held that the water condition was not a fundamental breach of the landlord's covenant amounting to frustration of the lease contract, s. 86 of Part IV, now s. 19 of the R.T.A., that is, it was not "an accumulation of defects which taken en masse, constitute such a ... breach going to the root of the contract"; nor was the condition so fundamental that s. 87 of Part IV, now s. 17 of the R.T.A., covenants interdependent, applied to the extent that the tenant could terminate the lease. The court did find that the tenant suffered inconvenience and discomfort for which damages were allowed by way of an abatement of the rent.

In *Petsinis v. Santos*,[121] the landlord had promised, as part of the negotiation of a tenancy agreement for a three-year term, to paint the interior of this luxurious home. To the tenants, this was a crucial term of the agreement and they had agreed to pay a higher rent based upon this condition. After the commencement of the tenancy, when it became clear the landlord was not going to fulfill this promise and paint the house, the tenants brought an application to end the tenancy early. The Member ruled that since the painting of the house was a fundamental part of the tenancy agreement, terminating the tenancy was an appropriate remedy. This decision was upheld on appeal to the Divisional Court.

Mention should be made of damage to premises caused by fire, other than as the result of a tenant's negligence. Many leases provide for rent to be abated while fire damage is repaired, or for termination of the lease if the fire damage is very extensive. The statutory obligation of the landlord to repair in s. 94(1) of Part IV, now s. 20(1) of the R.T.A., would not be considered

---

[118] (1982), 16 A.C.W.S. (2d) 200 (Ont. Div. Ct.).

[119] (1982), 13 A.C.W.S. (2d) 390 (Ont. Co. Ct.).

[120] (1980), 29 O.R. (2d) 30 (Ont. Div. Ct.).

[121] (Sept. 10, 2001), Div. Ct. File No. 726/00, TNT-01335 (Ont. Rental Housing Trib.).

mandatory in the face of the usual fire clauses. However, the termination of the lease or the temporary reduction in rent would have to be worked out with the tenant, either on the tenant's consent in accordance with the terms of the lease applicable to fire damage, or by resort to adjudication before the Board.

Finally, it is important for landlords and Members of the Board to remember that this remedy can only be granted at the tenant's request or with the tenant's consent. It is the tenant's application and the tenancy cannot be terminated unless that is something the tenant desires. In essence, the Board cannot evict the tenant when it is the tenant who came to the Board looking for help! Once the order is issued, however, the tenant cannot change his or her mind about vacating the unit. Pursuant to s. 32 of the R.T.A., a termination order requested by a tenant shall also contain provisions that will permit the landlord to file the order with the Court Enforcement Office and have the tenant evicted if the tenant does not vacate the unit voluntarily by the date set out in the order.

(c) Withholding Rent

Prior to the enactment of the *Tenant Protection Act* in 1998, courts occasionally approved of tenants withholding rent when there were serious maintenance problems with which the landlord refused to deal.[122]

For instance, rent was withheld and an abatement of rent was granted when the landlord cut off the electricity and hot water and the tenant had paid the rent to the tenant's lawyer: *Hill v. Ebony Realty Corp.*[123]

In general, courts approved the withholding of rent in cases where the landlord's breach of its maintenance obligations was so serious that the tenant could rely upon the common law principle of interdependent covenants (i.e., the serious breach of a material covenant by one party to a contract has the effect of relieving the other party of the obligations under that contract). In other words, if the landlord is in serious, substantial or fundamental breach of its obligations to repair and maintain the rental unit or residential complex, the tenants affected are relieved of their obligations under the tenancy agree-

---

[122] See *Tagwerker v. Zaidan Realty Corp.* (1991), 19 R.P.R. (2d) 137 (Ont. Gen. Div.) in which the judge stated that the standard of maintenance was so poor that it bordered on abandonment by the landlord. He ordered an abatement of 25% for the common areas and 10% for the apartment units effective until proof of satisfactory compliance with 900 outstanding work orders. The rent strike was approved. Over $200,000 had been paid into a strike fund and then into court. Abatements were ordered to be paid out first, the balance to be made available for repairs and any amount left over to be paid to the landlord.

[123] (May 25, 1976), Doc. M11583 (Ont. Co. Ct.).

ment(s), including the obligation to pay rent.[124] This common law principle has been incorporated in the *Residential Tenancies Act* (s. 17).[125]

For this principle to apply, however, the breach must be very serious indeed. In *Temlas Apartments Inc. v. Desloges*,[126] the court said that the tenants suffered inconvenience and discomfort but since they had shelter — the basic or fundamental purpose of the contract (heat, light, privacy, water for drinking, and every other amenity, except hot water) it could not be said that the breach discharged the contract.

Withholding rent has never been a recommended strategy, however, because it puts the tenancy in jeopardy (the tenancy could be terminated and the tenant evicted for non-payment of rent or for persistent late payment of rent). There is also the concern that permitting tenants to resort to such self-help measures will lead to chaos. As the Divisional Court stated in *Blatt Holdings Ltd. v. Stumpf*:[127]

> It is hardly necessary to state that if every tenant withheld rent on grounds either real or fancied ... there would be complete anarchy in this important aspect of community relationships.

Similarly, in *Elieff Investments Ltd. v. Kovacich*,[128] the Ontario District Court wrote that:

> ... the tenants had their remedies under [Part IV of the *Landlord and Tenant Act*] which they chose to ignore. They arbitrarily and unilaterally stopped paying their rent. Deliberate flouting of our laws can only lead to anarchy.

For a tenant whose complaints are being ignored, it can be very tempting to withhold the rent. This will certainly get the landlord's attention. However, there are a number of problems with this strategy.

First, as previously stated, it puts the tenancy at risk. The landlord can commence eviction proceedings based upon the unpaid rent. Even if the tenant eventually pays the rent, the landlord can later seek to evict the tenant based upon the fact that the rent has persistently been paid late.

Second, it can put the tenant's credibility into issue. Unless the landlord capitulates and does the work demanded by the tenant, the parties will likely end up before the Landlord and Tenant Board. If the landlord has commenced an application for arrears of rent, the Board may order that all or a portion of the unpaid rent be paid into the Board to be held in trust pending the outcome of the application(s). Although many tenants claim that they have been with-

---

124 See, for example: *Pajelle Investments Ltd. v. Chisholm* (1974), 4 O.R. (2d) 652 (Ont. H.C.); *Quann v. Pajelle Investments Ltd.* (1975), 7 O.R. (2d) 769 (Ont. Co. Ct.); and *Hill v. Ebony Realty Corp.* (May 25, 1976), Doc. M11583 (Ont. Co. Ct.).

125 Formerly s. 11 of the T.P.A.

126 (1980), 29 O.R. (2d) 30 (Ont. Div. Ct.).

127 (1982), 16 A.C.W.S. (2d) 200 (Ont. Div. Ct.).

128 (1987), 1987 CarswellOnt 2428 (Ont. Dist. Ct.).

holding rent because of maintenance concerns, the truth is that many tenants use the alleged lack of maintenance as a an excuse when they are unable to pay their rent for other, unrelated reasons. In such cases, the tenants have not actually been withholding and saving the rent money and they will not be able to comply with the Board's order. The failure of a tenant to comply with the Board's order can have a devastating effect upon the tenant's application (see s. 195) and will likely negatively impact upon the Board Member's assessment of the credibility of that tenant.

Third, if a group of tenants from the same building get together and withhold their rent (a "rent strke"), this can financially ruin the landlord and end up hurting the tenants as well. Without the stream of rental income coming from the tenants, a landlord may not be able to meet ongoing expenses. If mortgage payments are missed, the mortgagee may end up taking over the building. If taxes are not paid, the municipality may take over. No creditor of the landlord, however, will be interested in doing major work on the building and they will find it difficult to sell the property since few purchasers will want to buy a dilapidated building filled with militant tenants who are not paying their rent. In the meantime, the landlord may declare bankruptcy or may simply disappear. In the end, instead of getting the building fixed, the effect of the "rent strike" may be to get the building condemned or purchased by a developer looking to demolish the building or convert the apartments into condominiums.

Rather than withholding rent, tenants are recommended to commence their own applications when the landlord refuses to address legitimate maintenance concerns. The Board will then decide what remedies are appropriate. The Board has a number of ways to rectify the problems and compensate a tenant that will not put the tenancy in jeopardy.

Nevertheless, new provisions in the R.T.A. seem to encourage tenants to withhold their rent. Pursuant to s. 82 of the R.T.A., a tenant can raise any issue they want at the hearing of an application commenced by the landlord concerning arrears of rent. Therefore, a tenant with a maintenance problem could simply withhold his rent, wait for the landlord to commence an application for arrears of rent and then raise the maintenance issue at that hearing. Also, even if the tenant chooses to commence his own application about maintenance, he can withhold his rent and then, pursuant to s. 195(1)(b) request permission to pay into the Board all of the rent that has been withheld plus any future rent as it comes due (pending the outcome of the tenant's application). It therefore appears to me that the current legislation encourages tenants to use their rent as leverage in getting landlords to effect repairs. There is still some risk to such a strategy and tenants who decide to pursue this avenue had better have all of the rent money available to pay into the Board or they may find themselves evicted.

(d) Abatement of Rent

An abatement of rent is a monetary award expressed in terms of past or future rent. It may be a lump sum payment the landlord is ordered to pay the tenant (which effectively orders the landlord to refund a part of the rent paid) or it may be an order to allow the tenant to pay less rent by a certain amount or percentage (or even to pay no rent) for a specified period, or a combination of these. For instance, in Landlord and Tenant Board File No. NOL-18614/NOT-00017 (March 8, 2007), in addition to ordering the landlord to perform a long list of repairs, the Board also awarded the tenants a 25% abatement of rent for the seven months prior to the hearing and ordered that abatement to continue indefinitely into the future "until all repairs are properly completed by the Landlord". A similar order was also issued in Landlord and Tenant Board File No. EAT-01610 (Feb. 6, 2009).

An abatement of rent is generally not appropriate where the landlord was not aware of the problem until the application was filed or where the landlord quickly rectified the problem once notified.[129] In determining the amount to be ordered, the Member will consider the period of time that the problem existed and the severity of the problem (in terms of the impact this problem would have on a reasonable tenant in the same circumstances). According to the Board's Interpretation Guideline (No. 5), an abatement of rent should not be seen as punishment for landlord conduct or inaction; it is "compensation to the tenant for the inadequate state of repair and any inconvenience or actual loss of use of the rental unit or common facilities".

Sometimes, major repairs are required to a residential complex. Such repairs can be quite disruptive. A tenant who is disturbed by such repairs should not file a T6 application. The landlord's failure to repair and maintain the complex is not in question. Rather, it is the disturbance created by the repair work that is at the heart of the tenant's complaints. Such an application would usually be based upon an allegation that the landlord was substantially interfering with the tenant's reasonable enjoyment of the residential complex. Section 8 of O. Reg. 516/06 places strict limits on the amount of a rent abatement that can be granted in such circumstances. This issue is discussed in greater depth in Chapter 12.

Abatements of rent were commonplace under s. 94(3) of Part IV[130] for lack of repairs extending beyond a reasonable time. Often the tenant's application for an abatement under that section was coupled with reliance on s. 87 of Part IV, now s. 17 of the R.T.A., on the basis that as the landlord is not fulfilling the landlord's obligations to keep the premises in good repair, the tenant's obligation to pay rent should be reduced accordingly.

---

[129] See Interpretation Guideline 5.

[130] In this instance and hereinafter, the phrase "Part IV" refers to Part IV of the *Landlord and Tenant Act*, R.S.O. 1990, c. L.7.

A magic formula for determining what an appropriate abatement ought to be does not exist. Ultimately, the abatement has to depend on the good sense of the Board Member balancing all the equities given the circumstances of each case. The cases mentioned in this chapter should be of some help.

As was stated in *Biltmore Terrace Apartments v. Nazareth*:[131]

> What is appropriate in each case will depend on the circumstances, including the amount of rent, the age and general condition of the premises, the nature and degree of the non-repair and its duration, the efforts of the landlord to inspect, the co-operation or otherwise of the tenant and the efforts made by the landlord to rectify the defect.

That is about as clear a guideline as there can be. The judge, having said that, dealt with inadequate heating, exposed wiring, ceiling leaks in the living room and dining room that were not attended to by the landlord for some period of time. The tenant had placed tins and other containers to collect the leaking water. They overflowed a number of times. There was considerable damage to the tenants' furniture and other articles. The rent was $570 per month, which had been withheld. The abatement was $150 per month for seven months, and $300 per month for ten months until the tenants moved out. Damages of $2,000 were allowed for water damage.

When a tenant applies for an abatement of rent, sufficient evidence should be put forward to assist the Board to determine the amount of the abatement. In *Quann v. Pajelle Investments Ltd.*,[132] it was stated:

> The true abatement would be the difference between the fair value of the premises if in good condition they had been as rented and the fair value of the premises as they were during the occupancy by the tenant while the landlord was in breach.

In that case the judge went on to comment about the difficulty of assessing the abatement when there was so little evidence.

In *Victoria Park Community Homes Inc. v. Buzza*,[133] the premises were shockingly filthy. The judge said that right justice, equity and good conscience would be served if no rent were paid for the months until the premises were put in habitable condition.

In *Manhattan House v. Ziegler*,[134] the tenants were frustrated with the landlord's delays in repairs and moved out. There was very poor maintenance, the landlord made no effort to stop tenants' parties, harassment by other tenants, non-repair, poor ventilation and smells from the garbage chute. The landlord's inaction was, as the judge said, "reprehensible". The judge held

---

131 (1997), 1997 CarswellOnt 1667 (Ont. Gen. Div.), additional reasons at (1997), 1997 CarswellOnt 2380 (Ont. Gen. Div.).

132 (1975), 7 O.R. (2d) 769 (Ont. Co. Ct.).

133 (1975), 10 O.R. (2d) 251 (Ont. Co. Ct.).

134 (1997), 28 O.T.C. 294 (Ont. Gen. Div.).

that the tenants were entitled to abatement over a three year period at $200 per month for a total of $7,200, and ordered solicitor and client costs.

In *Croteau v. Collins*,[135] substantial repairs were required but were not completed before the tenants moved in. There was no water, the premises were totally unfit for habitation and there were outstanding work orders. The tenants moved out within the first week. The court held that they were entitled to move out. The court ordered an abatement of $172.75, being rent proportioned for the period in occupation, return of rent of $422.25 for balance of month, return of security deposit, and damages of about $1,000 for costs of moving in and out. The latter was within s. 94(1)(*c*) of Part IV, now s. 30(1)9 of the R.T.A., the making of "an order which the judge [Board]considers appropriate".

In *373041 Ontario Ltd. v. Amiri*,[136] the dishwasher did not work, there were fractures in the ceiling and balcony, there were cockroaches and the metal railing of the balcony was rusty. The landlord did not do repairs for six weeks. The judge said that the lives of the tenants were materially affected. An abatement of $1,500 was granted for the lack of repair.

For the failure of the landlord to repair for three months an overflowing toilet and sink in the apartment above the tenant's, causing water damage, the Tribunal ordered under s. 34(1) para. 2 a rent abatement of $200 for each of the three months and payment of $513 for compensation for cleaning the water damage: *Foreman and 11 Eby Street South Ltd.*[137]

In *Alta Place Property Inc. v. Evans*,[138] the court determined that the landlord was in breach of its obligations to repair and comply with health safety and housing standards for the premises and the building. Also there was cockroach infestation. The landlord's position was that the age of the building required major capital construction repairs and that the tenants voluntarily accepted the risks of the poor conditions. The tenants had signed the lease with the acknowledgement terms that the tenants accepted occupancy on an "as is" basis. The court did not accept that as an excuse for the landlord, referring to s. 94(1) of Part IV that the landlord is responsible for repair "despite the fact that any state of non-repair existed to the knowledge of the tenant". An abatement of $100 per month was ordered for the duration of the tenancy as long as the landlord continued to be in breach of the relevant health, safety and housing standards.

In *Herbold v. Pajelle Investments Ltd.*,[139] the Supreme Court of Canada approved the principle of granting abatements of rent for the failure of the landlord to supply air-conditioning and for lack of repair of the swimming

---

[135] (1996), 12 R.P.R. (3d) 181 (Ont. Gen. Div.).

[136] (1995), 12 O.T.C. 3 (Ont. Gen. Div.).

[137] (August 31, 1999), Review Office, #SWT-00373-RV (Ont. Rental Housing Trib.).

[138] (1997), 1997 CarswellOnt 601 (Ont. Gen. Div.).

[139] (1975), [1976] 2 S.C.R. 520 (S.C.C.).

pool and sauna. The proper calculation of the abatements was referred back to the County Court for the hearing of more evidence. It is noted that the Court stated:[140]

> [I]t would be only in the most exceptional circumstances that a Court should grant an abatement for rent because of failure to provide the repairs and services during a short period.

In *Endcliffe Construction Ltd. v. MacLeod*,[141] the landlord was in breach of s. 96[142] [later s. 94 of Part IV], now s. 20 of the R.T.A., as to repairs and the local municipal by-law as to housing standards, lack of hot water heater and malfunction of toilet facilities. Rent was abated until all work was done to the satisfaction of municipal authorities. The landlord was cited for contempt of court for failure to comply with this order.

A full abatement of rent was ordered in *Dumi Construction Ltd. v. Greenspan*.[143] The landlord went ahead with reconstruction while tenants were still in possession. Notices to vacate because of extensive repairs were invalid. Apart from the abatement of rent, the landlord was ordered to repair the occupied premises and to clear all corridors and exit areas.

Also, in *Beyer v. Absamco Developments Ltd.*,[144] the landlord started to gut the building while tenants were still in occupation. Full abatement of rent was ordered until City of Toronto work orders were complied with and the premises were put back in a good state of repair.

Kitchen appliances and a washer and dryer were part of the rented premises in *Nitsotolis v. Marois*.[145] These appliances were not working properly. The judge allowed an abatement, ordered the landlord to repair or replace them within 60 days and adjourned the hearings until that time to consider the landlord's compliance and to set some further abatement.

An abatement of 30% of the rent was granted to tenants in an apartment building for the period in which, because of lack of security, some apartments were being used at all hours by drug traffickers, drug users and prostitutes: *Guiliani v. Eelkins*.[146]

A lengthy list of tenants' complaints resulted in a 20% abatement over two years in *Offredi v. 751768 Ontario Ltd.*[147] The deficiencies included an underground garage out of use for one year for repairs, elevators frequently

---

[140] (1975), [1976] 2 S.C.R. 520 (S.C.C.) at 528 [S.C.R.].

[141] (December 3, 1981), Doc. 5913/80 (Ont. Co. Ct.).

[142] *Landlord and Tenant Act*, R.S.O. 1980, c. 232.

[143] (1977), 15 O.R. (2d) 808 (Ont. Co. Ct.).

[144] (1976), 12 O.R. (2d) 768 (Ont. Co. Ct.).

[145] (June 25, 1985), Doc. York M114504/85 (Ont. Dist. Ct.).

[146] Lawyer's Weekly #946-004 (Ont. Dist. Ct.).

[147] (July 10, 1991), Doc. Toronto L9023/90 (Ont. Gen. Div.), affirmed (1994), 72 O.A.C. 235 (Ont. Div. Ct.).

out of service in a 20-storey building, dirty corridors, infrequent garbage collection and deficient security.

In *Smith v. 736923 Ontario Ltd.*,[148] there were many complaints about fire safety, the intercom system not working and poor or no lighting in the corridors. As the judge said, "[T]his building is a disaster waiting to happen." Windows and doors were in a deplorable condition. These complaints were from day one of the tenants going into possession. Counsel for the landlord submitted that the tenants knew what they were getting into. But s. 94(1) of Part IV, that the landlord must repair and maintain in good repair, includes that "despite the fact that any state of non-repair existed to the knowledge of the tenant before the tenancy agreement was entered into." The judge ordered that repairs be done forthwith, and granted an abatement of $200 per month from the commencement of tenancy, then reduced to 10%, and continuing until the fire department was satisfied the building was in a safe condition, and the building inspector was satisfied that all his and the tenants' complaints had been corrected.

Combining a claim for damages and abatement because of the landlord's lack of proper repair was approved in *Phillips v. Dis-Management.*[149] A pipe broke in the common area and the tenant's apartment was flooded. The judge referred to s. 94(4)(*c*) of Part IV, which gave the jurisdiction to make such further order as may be considered appropriate — as the Tribunal can do by s. 30(1) para. 9 of the R.T.A. — and so for damages. The judge also said that a multiplicity of proceedings should be avoided by the judge dealing with damages and abatement in the same proceeding. By failing to inspect and promptly repair, the landlord was in breach. Abatement of $300 per month was granted for the disruption of the tenant's quiet enjoyment, and damages of $1,400 for replacing carpets and some chattels.

This case was followed in *Alta Place Property Inc. v. MacMillan.*[150] Abatement of $100 per month for 13 months was granted for the landlord's continuing and inexcusable neglect to repair and failure to deal with a vermin infestation, which affected the tenant's right to her use and enjoyment of the premises.

Another case of damages and abatement caused by lack of inspection and repair by the landlord is *Pillon v. 933886 Ontario Ltd.*[151] A leaky roof caused considerable water damage. The tenant had to move out for two days. A number of her chattels had to be cleaned and repaired. Some clothes had to be thrown out. For the disruption affecting her reasonable quiet enjoyment of her premises the judge granted abatement of 50% for three months and $3,500 in damages.

---

[148] (1996), 1996 CarswellOnt 1396 (Ont. Gen. Div.).

[149] (1995), 24 O.R. (3d) 435 (Ont. Gen. Div.).

[150] (1997), 24 O.T.C. 311 (Ont. Gen. Div.).

[151] (1996), 8 O.T.C. 397 (Ont. Gen. Div.).

Abatement of $20 per month was granted for poor garbage service, $15 per month for failure to repair an apartment unit, and $15 per month for the tenant's inconvenience, annoyance and discomfort. The landlord was ordered to make repairs: *Aprioi Investments v. Moreno.*[152]

In *Bellanda Holdings Ltd. v. Barnaby*,[153] the tenant withheld the rent because of lack of repairs. By the time of the hearing most of the repairs had been attended to, but for earlier problems of lack of heat and cockroaches the judge allowed an abatement of $500, and gave the tenant time to pay the remainder of the arrears in rent.

In *Murovec v. Fisher*,[154] the Tribunal awarded a 20% abatement of rent over a 10-month period because of a severe moisture and mould problem in the unit.

In *Antoniou v. Feder*,[155] the landlord failed to deal with serious maintenance problems and totally disregarded work orders from the municipality and an interim order from the Tribunal. A 100% rent abatement was ordered from the time the landlord was aware of the problem until such time as the work ordered by the Tribunal was completed.

In *Hatton v. Del Management Solutions Inc.*,[156] the main issue concerned the water supply. The well-water had become contaminated; although no E. coli was found, the water tests indicated the water was "unsafe". The landlord provided bottled water for drinking but the tenants were told by the landlord to continue using the well water for bathing and other domestic uses (washing clothes, doing dishes, etc.). After consulting with the local health officials, the tenants remained concerned about the health and safety of themselves and their young children and arranged for a holding tank to supply clean water until the landlord dug a new well. The tenants requested an abatement of rent equal to the cost of renting the holding tank and having it filled periodically with clean water. The tenants' application was granted. The landlord filed an appeal but apparently the parties settled the underlying issues before the appeal could be heard.

In *Martin v. Sterling Karamar Property Management*,[157] a radiator burst in a unit, flooding the unit below. As a result, the unit below was uninhabitable for two weeks. The flood was in no way the result of any negligence on the part of the landlord and the landlord's response was exemplary. The tenant rejected the landlord's offer to temporarily move the tenant into another unit. She claimed an abatement of rent and compensation for damage to her property. In these circumstances, no monetary relief was awarded.

---

[152] (November 7, 1991), 1991 CarswellOnt 2323 (Ont. Gen. Div.).

[153] (1982), 17 A.C.W.S. (2d) 363 (Ont. Co. Ct.).

[154] (Oct. 16, 1998), TST-00193 (Ont. Rental Housing Trib.).

[155] (Oct. 2, 2000), TNT-01154, 2000 CarswellOnt 6429 (Ont. Rental Housing Trib.).

[156] (Dec. 19, 2000), TNT-01396, 2000 CarswellOnt 6425 (Ont. Rental Housing Trib.).

[157] (July 4, 2003), TNT-03453, 2003 CarswellOnt 4239 (Ont. Rental Housing Trib.).

In *Griffin et al. v. Paolini et al.*,[158] the tenants alleged numerous breaches by the landlords of their maintenance obligations. The tenants were able to prove that a Work Order had been issued against the landlord by the municipality. Nevertheless, only a relatively modest abatement ($200) was awarded because: (1) the tenants had not advised the landlord of many of the problems; (2) the landlord generally acted responsibly once aware of a maintenance problem; and (3) when the landlord did attempt to address the tenants' concerns, they obstructed the landlord's efforts to gain access to the unit. In a somewhat similar application brought by neighbouring tenants in the same complex,[159] an abatement of $1,000 was awarded because the tenants were able to prove that the landlords failed to investigate and remedy in a timely manner a number of problems, including: windows that were ill-fitting, cracked and not weather-tight; insufficient lighting in common areas of the complex; and, the collapse of a portion of the bathroom ceiling.

In *MacDonald et al. v. Congi*,[160] water penetration into the basement of this rented house was a recurring problem. Although the landlord made some efforts to deal with the problem, the landlord's response was slow and ineffective. It was determined that the tenants were entitled to an abatement of $3,225 for the period from June through October 2003.

In *Simone v. Lai*,[161] it was determined that the landlords failed to repair within a reasonable period of time the air conditioner, the windows and the loose bricks on the front steps. Also, the unit was not ready for occupation on the date agreed upon. The monthly rent was $2,100. The tenants were awarded a lump-sum abatement in the amount of $1,450.

In *Glawe v. Skeoch*,[162] the tenant entered into a 19-month agreement to rent a house for $1,800 per month. The house included an outdoor pool. In addition to a number of relatively minor complaints, the tenant's main concern was that the heater for the swimming pool did not work (rendering the pool unusable). The tenant was aware at the time the tenancy was created that the pool heater was not working and had not worked for years. Nevertheless, the landlord specifically warranted that all pool related equipment would be in good working order on the date of occupancy. That provision, together with s. 24(2) of the T.P.A., meant that the tenant was entitled to expect that the landlord would rectify the problem prior to the commencement of the tenancy (or promptly thereafter). The repairs were never done. The Tribunal awarded a total rent abatement of $650 for the four months during which the tenant could reasonably have been expected to have used the swimming pool.

---

[158] (Feb. 26, 2003), TNT-03091 (Ont. Rental Housing Trib.).

[159] *Hedley et al. v. Paolini et al.* (Feb. 26, 2003), TNT-03092 (Ont. Rental Housing Trib.).

[160] (Jan. 19, 2004), TNT-03720 (Ont. Rental Housing Trib.).

[161] (Dec. 7, 1999), CET-00693, 1999 CarswellOnt 5812 (Ont. Rental Housing Trib.).

[162] (Dec. 17, 1999), TNT-00752, 1999 CarswellOnt 5828 (Ont. Rental Housing Trib.).

In *Gallinger v. Franklin*,[163] the landlord failed to respond to the tenants' complaints about a faulty refrigerator. Eventually, the refrigerator ceased functioning altogether. The tenants purchased a new refrigerator. The Tribunal awarded a 5% abatement during the period that the old refrigerator was not operating reliably and ordered the landlord to reimburse the tenants for the cost ($650) of the new refrigerator (at which point, the refrigerator would become the landlord's property).

In *Clark et al. v. Morris et al.*,[164] the roof had been leaking for three years. This caused severe mildew problems in the unit and damaged the tenants' property. A work order was issued against the property by the municipality but the landlords chose to ignore it. The Member ordered the landlord to perform the necessary repairs (and authorized the tenants to do the work if the landlord did not complete it by a specified date) and awarded to the tenants an abatement of $6,000.00 (almost a complete abatement from one year prior to filing their application to the date of hearing) plus $715.00 for the cost of repairing or replacing their damaged property.

For numerous breaches of the municipal property standards by-law by the landlord, a tenant was awarded a 50% abatement for 12 months plus an additional 50% abatement for 3.5 months (November 1 through February 16) during which the furnace was not functioning (for a total abatement of $4,082.00).[165] The landlord was also ordered to effect the necessary repairs to the complex.

In *McDonald v. Chang Shinn-Der in Trust et al.*,[166] the landlords had been neglecting the property for some time and had ignored previous orders from the municipality and from the Rental Housing Tribunal. The tenants were awarded an abatement of rent (15% for one year) and the landlords were ordered to effect all necessary repairs.

In *Strange et al. v. Tuz*,[167] the landlord failed to comply with fire department work orders and failed to address numerous maintenance problems within the complex. The Member ordered the landlord to do certain work, including the work identified in a Fire Safety Inspection Report. The Member also granted to the tenants a 100% abatement in rent from six months prior to the hearing until such time as all of the work had been completed. Since the landlord has threatened the tenants with eviction when they complained about the condition of the complex, the landlord was also fined $3,000.00.

In *Christopher v. Philip*,[168] of the four burners on the tenant's stove, only the two smaller burners were operating. It took the landlord 36 days to deal

---

[163] (July 28, 2006), CET-05864, [2006] O.R.H.T.D. No. 92 (Ont. Rental Housing Trib.).

[164] (September 9, 2004), EAT-05652 (Ont. Rental Housing Trib.).

[165] *Fleming v. Lyons*, (July 29, 2004), EAT-05672 (Ont. Rental Housing Trib.).

[166] (June 16, 2003), SWT-04418 (Ont. Rental Housing Trib.).

[167] (December 7, 2001), SWT-02452 and SWT-02779 (Ont. Rental Housing Trib.).

[168] (July 25, 2006), TET-05880, [2006] O.R.H.T.D. No. 103 (Ont. Rental Housing Trib.).

with this problem. The Tribunal awarded an abatement of $20 per day for each of these 36 days (a total of $720).

In *Rahim v. Bennett*,[169] the Tribunal granted a 5% abatement for the four months that the tenant could not use the hot tub located in the house that she rented.

For a five-month infestation of insects and rodents, a tenant in a rooming house received a 25% abatement of rent over that entire period, for a total rent abatement of $375.00.[170]

In Landlord and Tenant Board File No. SOT-01737 (Jan. 15, 2009), the landlord had new toilets installed in the units of this complex. One toilet was not properly installed and the water from the toilet bowl continually leaked into the unit below. The landlord was very slow in responding to the complaints of the tenants from the lower unit. As a result, those tenants were awarded an abatement of approximately 20-25% from the time the landlord was first informed of the problem until it was rectified (which represented a total abatement of about $1,800.00).

In another case involving water penetration, water was entering the unit through cracks in the foundation.[171] The landlord took over eight months to deal with the problem. This resulted in damage throughout the unit, including mould. The landlord brought an application to terminate the tenancy for non-payment of rent and alleged damage caused to the unit by the tenants. Pursuant to s. 82 of the R.T.A., the tenants raised their maintenance issues. From the amounts awarded to the landlord (over $5,000 in total), the Board deducted over $4,000 in rent abatements, representing a 25% abatement in rent over ten months.

(e) Authorize Repairs by Tenant

Sometimes, a tenant cannot wait for a landlord to do the work. For instance, if it is an emergency and the tenant cannot reach the landlord, the tenant may have to take immediate action. A tenant may get tired of having repeated requests for maintenance ignored by a landlord and may opt to do the work himself or hire a contractor to do the necessary work. A tenant may be frustrated by a landlord whose attempts to effect repairs are unprofessional and/or unsafe and may choose to have the work done properly by an independent contractor. By taking matters into his or her own hands, the tenant will likely incur some expense and potentially risks penalties (including eviction) for any damage (which can include unauthorized "improvements") caused to the unit or the complex.

---

169 (April 28, 2006), TEL-59923, TET-05581, 2006 CarswellOnt 4413 (Ont. Rental Housing Trib.).

170 Landlord and Tenant Board File No. EAL-61660/EAT-00016 (March 16, 2007).

171 Landlord and Tenant Board File No. TNL-18402 (Jan. 9, 2009).

In order to protect himself, such a tenant needs to bring an application before the Board to obtain an order authorizing the work that the tenant had done. In the same application, the tenant can seek reimbursement for the expense of such work. It will have to be proven that both the work and the expense involved were reasonable. If the tenant is unsuccessful on such an application, the tenant will have improved the landlord's property at the tenant's expense[172]— that is another risk of doing the work without first obtaining authorization from the landlord or the Board.

The tenant can also seek authorization *before* doing any necessry work. The Board's preference is probably to order that any necessary work be done by the landlord. Where, however, there is good reason to believe that the landlord may not perform the work even if ordered to do so, the Board may authorize the tenant to have the work done if the landlord fails to do the work by a specified deadline; this at least gives the landlord one last opportunity to do the necessary work.[173] If there is good reason to believe that the landlord is unwilling or unable to have the work done properly, the Board may simply authorize the tenant to do the work without any further opportunity for the landlord to effect the necessary repairs. The Board's order can also specify that the cost of such work can be deducted by the tenant from future rent payments. Where such orders are issued, the Board may wish to order that the tenant provide copies of receipts to the landlord as evidence of the expenditures incurred by the tenant, and may wish to consider placing a "cap" on such expenses so that the tenant does not take advantage of the situation and run up excessive repair bills. Such conditions can be included in the Board's order by virtue of paras. 30(1)3 and 30(1)9 and ss. 204 and 205 of the R.T.A.

There is no automatic right to deduct or withhold from rent ("set off") amounts incurred by the tenant to repair the unit. This was re-stated by the Ontario Court of Appeal in *Milley v. Hudson*.[174] This can only be authorized by the Board, on application by the tenant.

In *Armstrong and O'Halloran*,[175] the Tribunal dealt with this a little differently. The tenant went ahead with painting that was needed when the tenant moved in. The landlord had agreed to pay $350 for the cost of the paint, but the tenant did not have the authorization for the painters at a total cost of $2,000. The Tribunal's order was for an abatement of rent for the

---

[172] See *Kashyap v. Moore* (April 20, 1982), Doc. 7451/82 (Ont. Co. Ct.). The cost of cleaning and decorating done by the tenant for her own benefit, installation of a new fence and landscaping done by the tenant in anticipation of purchasing the property were disallowed. The court said that when the premises were rented they were in good repair and fit for habitation.

[173] See the Board's Interpretation Guideline 5 under the heading "Any Other Order that is Appropriate".

[174] (September 27, 1971) (Ont. C.A.).

[175] (March 30, 2000), TET-00882, 2000 CarswellOnt 6356 (Ont. Rental Housing Trib.).

difference of $1,650 rather than simply ordering the landlord to pay the cost to the tenant right away. Although this may be a sensible solution, it may not have strictly complied with the wording of s. 34(1) para. 3 of the T.P.A. (which stated that the Tribunal may "order [the cost of the work] to be paid by the landlord").

In another case, the tenant sought to set off the cost of work which had not been authorized by the landlord against arrears of rent. Some of the items not allowed were additional outdoor lighting, cleaning of eavestroughing and erection of new fences. These were not the responsibility of the landlord and could not be deducted from the rent: *Higgins v. Mathot.*[176]

In both these cases the items disallowed were obviously not the responsibility of the landlords, but the cases do point to the advisability of obtaining the landlord's authorization in advance. Before a tenant proceeds to make repairs relying on s. 30 of the R.T.A., the tenant should notify the landlord of the necessity for the repairs and give the landlord a reasonable time to make them. In the case of a tenant who conducts repairs without notifying the landlord and then applies to the Board, one would expect the Board to be more sympathetic to the position of the landlord.

In *Glawe v. Skeoch*,[177] the tenants requested an order authorizing the work they had done and reimbursement for the cost ($244.47) of replacing the vegetable "crisper" drawer in the refrigerator and the pool skimmer basket and of patching the pool and repairing the air conditioning unit. The tenants had the work done because they were "frustrated trying to deal with a landlord with whom it was difficult to communicate, who seemed not to be responding promptly to requests for small repairs and who, at the time, may not have had a property manager." The repairs were authorized by the Tribunal and the landlord was ordered to pay $244.47 to the tenants.

In *Grimard v. Knight*,[178] the landlord was notified by the tenants on November 4, 2005 about a hole in the roof but failed to take any steps to address the problem because, according to the landlord, the tenants agreed in the contract to accept the property in an "as is" condition. After waiting several months, the tenants finally made their own arrangements to have the roof repaired. The Tribunal authorized the repairs, ordered the landlord to reimburse the tenants for the cost of this repair ($2,825.95) and ordered a 10% abatement of rent commencing from November 4, 2005.

In *Rahim v. Bennett*,[179] the tenant had various repairs done to the house she rented. The Tribunal authorized the work she had done in repairing the pool, hot tub and security system and ordered the landlord to reimburse the

---

[176] (1983), 45 O.R. (2d) 377 (Ont. Co. Ct.).

[177] (Dec. 17, 1999), TNT-00752, 1999 CarswellOnt 5828 (Ont. Rental Housing Trib.).

[178] (March 2, 2006), SWT-07217, [2006] O.R.H.T.D. No. 5 (Ont. Rental Housing Trib.).

[179] (April 28, 2006), TEL-59923, TET-05581, 2006 CarswellOnt 4413 (Ont. Rental Housing Trib.).

tenant for the cost of those repairs. The Tribunal did not hold the landlord responsible for the tenant's cost of painting the house as the Tribunal found that the tenant had this done for aesthetic reasons not because the existing paint was in poor condition.

(f) Order Landlord to Do Repairs

If a tenant has raised legitimate maintenance concerns and those problems have not been resolved by the time the matter comes before the Board, the Board's first priority is usually to ensure that any necessary repairs are effected as quickly as possible. Since it is the landlord's responsibility, the landlord would typically be ordered to have the work done. To be enforceable, such an order must be specific as to the exact nature of the work and the deadline for completing the work (see Chapter 19).

If such a term is contained in a *final* order, the Board has no way to monitor whether or not the landlord actually complies with the order (i.e., whether the landlord actually effects the repairs). Depending upon the other terms of the order, the landlord's failure to do the work ordered by the Board can result in the continuation of a rent abatement or the continuation of a prohibition on rent increases. If, however, the tenant's primary goal in bringing the application is to force the landlord to effect the necessary repairs, an abatement of rent (or moratorium on rent increases) may not satisfy the tenant. Also, depending on the size of the abatement, it may amount to little more than a licence for the landlord to neglect the complex. It is contrary to public policy for the Board to issue orders that parties can ignore with virtual impunity. Although it is true that a breach of such an order can theoretically lead to prosecution under s. 234(y) of the R.T.A., such prosecutions are relatively rare and involve a lengthy process which will not ultimately benefit the tenant. To the extent possible, the goal of the Board should be to ensure parties comply with the provisions of the R.T.A. and to issue orders that will actually achieve the desired results. Sometimes, that takes a bit of creativity on the part of the presiding Member.

In my view, a better alternative to issuing a final order at the conclusion of the initial hearing is to issue an *interim* order requiring the landlord to complete the necessary repairs by a specified deadline. The hearing can then be reconvened on a later date before the same Member to ascertain whether the landlord complied with the interim order. At that time, the Member can decide whether any further relief is warranted (such as an abatement of rent and the amount of that abatement). Obviously, the Member will be much more favourably disposed towards a landlord who complies with the interim order than with a landlord who has made no effort to comply with the order and who has shown contempt for both the tenant and the Board. By issuing an interim order first, the Member is able to retain some control over the process and provide a meaningful incentive for the landlord to do the work that has been ordered. This is also an approach suggested in the Board's Interpretation Guideline (No. 5).[180]

Another alternative for the Board is to order the landlord to do the work, but provide that if the landlord fails to complete the work by a specified date, the tenant may arrange to have the work done and may deduct the cost from future rent payments. This approach has been adopted in a number of cases.[181]

In *McDonald v. Chang Shinn-Der in Trust et al.*,[182] the landlords had been neglecting the property for some time and had ignored previous orders from the municipality and from the Rental Housing Tribunal. In addition to awarding the tenants an abatement of rent (15% for one year), the Member ordered the landlords to effect all necessary repairs. Expecting that the landlords would not move quickly on this order, the Member authorized the tenants to get two written estimates and then present them to the landlords. If the landlords did not retain one of the two contractors within five days of receipt of the estimates, the tenants were instructed to refer the matter to the Investigations and Enforcement Branch (presumably for prosecution of the landlords).

(g) Damages

Compensation had long been awarded by courts to tenants for damage to a tenant's property as a result of the deliberate or negligent conduct of the landlord and for reasonable out-of-pocket expenses incurred by a tenant as a result of a landlord's failure to fulfill the landlord's statutory, contractual or common law obligations. When the T.P.A. was first enacted and these disputes were moved from the courts to the Rental Housing Tribunal, it was not entirely clear whether the Tribunal had the same power to award damages. This debate ended in 2000 when s. 34 of the T.P.A. was amended by the addition of para. 4.1, which gave the Tribunal the explicit power to award such damages. That provision now appears in the R.T.A. as para. 30(1)5, which permits the Board to order the landlord to pay a specified sum to the tenant as compensation for:

i. the reasonable costs that the tenant has incurred or will incur in repairing or, where repairing is not reasonable, replacing property of the tenant that was damaged, destroyed or disposed of as a result of the landlord's breach, and

---

[180] Under the heading "Any Other Order that is Appropriate".

[181] Including *Clark et al. v. Morris et al.* (September 9, 2004), EAT-05652 (Ont. Rental Housing Trib.); Landlord and Tenant Board File No. SOT-00012 (Feb. 28, 2007); Landlord and Tenant Board File No. SOT-00003 (Feb. 21, 2007).

[182] (June 16, 2003), SWT-04418 (Ont. Rental Housing Trib.).

ii. other reasonable out-of-pocket expenses that the tenant has incurred or will incur as a result of the landlord's breach.

In general, relatively simple claims for damage to property and out-of-pocket expenses that are within the monetary jurisdiction of the Board can be included as part of a T6 application. A claim arising from particularly complex circumstances or that is for a type or amount of relief beyond the jurisdiction of the Board ought to be pursued as a separate court action. As the Divisional Court said about similar proceedings under the *Landlord and Tenant Act*, this summary process "was never intended for an assessment of damages . . . to do that might frustrate the very intent and purpose of the summary procedure provided by the Act."[183]

Similarly, damages for personal injuries suffered by a tenant, his family or a visitor to the complex for lack of repair of the rented premises and the common areas should be pursued by way of civil action.[184] For instance, in *Bakhtiari v. Axes Investments Inc.*,[185] the landlord, the City of Toronto and a tenant were all held liable in damages for injuries suffered by the plaintiffs as a result of a fire in an apartment building. The defendant tenant's cigarette started a fire in his unit. He fled the unit leaving the door open. The door remained open as it was not equipped with a self-closing device and the fire spread into the hallway and stairwell. The plaintiffs, mother and son, were trapped by smoke in the stairwell and ultimately suffered brain damage. The plaintiffs brought action against the building for damages for negligence in failing to have installed self-closing devices on the doors (as required by the Fire Code). The trial judge allowed the action, awarded substantial damages and apportioned liability as follows: 10% to the tenant who started the fire; 20% to the City for failing to enforce its by-law and failing to take the opportunity to rectify the situation when the landlord applied for an extension of time to retrofit the building (in order to comply with the Fire Code); and, 70% to the landlord for failing to have self-closing devices on the doors in the complex. The landlord appealed. The Court of Appeal allowed the appeal to the extent that it apportioned 20% of the liability to the tenant who started the fire, 35% to the City and only 45% to the landlord.

What follow are other examples of court and Tribunal decisions where damages were either awarded or were at least considered as a remedy.

---

[183] *Hahn v. Kramer* (1979), 23 O.R. (2d) 689 (Ont. Div. Ct.) at 692-693.

[184] For negligence, breach of contract, breach of a statutory obligation under the *Occupiers' Liability Act*, R.S.O. 1990, c. O.2, etc.

[185] 2004 CarswellOnt 456, 182 O.A.C. 185, 46 M.P.L.R. (3d) 33, 22 C.C.L.T. (3d) 200, 69 O.R. (3d) 671 (Ont. C.A.), additional reasons at (2004), 2004 CarswellOnt 1031 (Ont. C.A.), leave to appeal refused (2004), 2004 CarswellOnt 3779 (S.C.C.).

Modest damages were allowed for moving expenses and the cost of meals while out of possession while the premises were unfit for habitation: *Hahn v. Kramer.*[186]

The general principle against awarding damages under the broad discretion given a judge by s. 94(4)(*c*) of Part IV was stated in *Beyer v. Absamco Developments Ltd.*,[187] where the court ordered the landlord to repair and comply with municipal work orders and granted an abatement of rent, but refused to consider the tenants' claims for damages to their personal property and for exemplary damages for the landlord's lack of repair, stating that such claims should be dealt with in a civil action with pleadings and examinations for discovery. It has been between landlords and tenants as to payment of arrears of rent, possession, repairs and maintenance and is not available for complicated cases of damages: *Carney and Kovod Investments Ltd.*[188]

In a later case under s. 94 of Part IV concerning a landlord's lack of repair, *Pena v. Grossman*,[189] the judge allowed a claim of damages to proceed, stating that there was the jurisdiction by s. 94(4)(*c*) to "make such further order as the judge considers appropriate". The specific amounts claimed by the tenant were for replacement of furniture and a carpet damaged by the alleged lack of repair of the premises. The judge stated that while the claim was in theory for general damages, it was rather specifically for the expense which the tenant would incur for replacement, if the evidence supported the claim. The judge somewhat distinguished the *Beyer v. Absamco Developments Ltd.* case,[190] probably because in that case the damages would have been substantial due to the landlord going ahead with renovations of the building when some tenants were still in possession.

Damages should be awarded only if the landlord already had, or should have had, notice of the defective condition, or the tenant had notified the landlord of the defect and the latter had failed to remedy it properly: *Adams Furniture Co. v. Johar Investments Ltd.*[191] However, in *Quann v. Pajelle Investments Ltd.*,[192] the court stated that notice by the tenant is not necessary to bring into being the landlord's obligation to repair, particularly where the landlord should have known of the lack of repair.

Damages can be awarded for lack of heat: *Head v. Community Estates & Building Co.*[193]

---

[186] (1979), 26 O.R. (2d) 558 (Ont. Co. Ct.).

[187] (1976), 12 O.R. (2d) 768 (Ont. Co. Ct.).

[188] (May 23, 1979) (Ont. Co. Ct.).

[189] (December 16, 1982), Doc. M71731/82 (Ont. Co. Ct.).

[190] (1976), 12 O.R. (2d) 768 (Ont. Co. Ct.).

[191] [1961] O.R. 133 (Ont. H.C.).

[192] (1975), 7 O.R. (2d) 769 (Ont. Co. Ct.).

[193] [1944] O.R. 353 (Ont. H.C.).

In *Roy v. Aubin*,[194] damages were awarded against the landlord for smoke damage from the furnace. The landlord was aware of the defective furnace and was held to have been negligent in failing to have it repaired.

A landlord was responsible for damage caused by mice which got into a tenant's apartment in a newly-constructed building, through openings where service pipes were installed and which had not been properly sealed off. Notice to the landlord or knowledge of the non-repair or non-completion of this minor item of construction was apparently not argued on behalf of the landlord: *Levin v. Active Builders Ltd.*[195]

Damages were given in *Cockburn v. Smith*,[196] for injury to a tenant's health by reason of lack of repair.

Combining a claim for damages and abatement because of the landlord's lack of proper repair was approved in *Phillips v. Dis-Management.*[197] A pipe broke in the common area and the tenant's apartment was flooded. The judge referred to s. 94(4)(*c*) of Part IV, which gave the jurisdiction to make such further order as may be considered appropriate — as the Tribunal could do by s. 34(1) para. 5 of the T.P.A. (now s. 30(1) para. 9 of the R.T.A.) — and so for damages. The judge also said that a multiplicity of proceedings should be avoided by the judge dealing with damages and abatement in the same proceeding. By failing to inspect and promptly repair, the landlord was in breach. Abatement of $300 per month was granted for the disruption of the tenant's quiet enjoyment, and damages of $1,400 for replacing carpets and some chattels.

Another case of damages and abatement caused by lack of inspection and repair by the landlord is *Pillon v. 933886 Ontario Ltd.*[198] A leaky roof caused considerable water damage. The tenant had to move out for two days. A number of her chattels had to be cleaned and repaired. Some clothes had to be thrown out. For the disruption affecting her reasonable quiet enjoyment of her premises the judge granted abatement of 50% for three months and $3,500 damages.

Damages can be awarded for damage to the tenant's chattels caused by the landlord's breach of the obligation to repair: *Amell v. Maloney*[199] and *Pembery v. Lamdin.*[200]

In *Cunningham v. Moore*,[201] it was stated that s. 94 of Part IV (of the *Landlord and Tenant Act*) created a civil liability and that the remedy available to the tenant was not confined to the procedure in s. 94. However, in the

---

[194] (1930), 39 O.W.N. 183.

[195] [1973] 6 W.W.R. 279 (Man. C.A.).

[196] [1924] 2 K.B. 119 (Eng. C.A.).

[197] (1995), 24 O.R. (3d) 435 (Ont. Gen. Div.).

[198] (1996), 8 O.T.C. 397 (Ont. Gen. Div.).

[199] (1929), 64 O.L.R. 285 (Ont. C.A.).

[200] [1940] 2 All E.R. 434 (C.A.).

[201] (1972), [1973] 1 O.R. 357 (Ont. H.C.).

more recent case of *Gentles v. Toronto (City) Non-Profit Housing Corp.*,[202] Lane J. seems to be of the opinion that breach of provisions of the T.P.A. (and now, presumably, the R.T.A.) give rise to remedies under that Act and do *not* give rise to a separate cause of action.

In *Gallinger v. Franklin*,[203] the landlord failed to respond to the tenants' complaints about a faulty refrigerator. Eventually, the refrigerator ceased functioning altogether. The tenants claimed damages equal to 25% of every purchase they made at a grocery store for 4.5 months because they say they lost that much in perishable food items over the course of the intermittent failure of the refrigerator. This part of the claim was denied because the tenants provided insufficient documentary evidence to satisfy the Tribunal as to the value of the groceries lost as a result of the malfunctioning refrigerator.

Similarly, in *Hunt v. Laughlin*,[204] the Member was satisfied that the landlord failed to take adequate steps to prevent snow from falling off the roof of the complex but granted no compensation to the tenants as they had failed to adduce sufficient evidence to prove that any damage was caused to their vehicle by snow falling from the roof.

In Landlord and Tenant Board File No. TNT-01116 (Jan. 2, 2009), the tenants' personal property was damaged by water that entered the rental unit. Based upon the uncontested evidence presented by the tenants (no one appeared for the landlord at the hearing), the Board determined that the landlord was responsible for this problem. The tenants requested (among other types of relief) compensation for the cost of repairing the damaged personal property and, in the absence of written estimates, the Board was only prepared to award the tenant the modest amount of $300 for this part of the claim.

Although the Divisional Court generally took the view that the Rental Housing Tribunal lacked the jurisdiction to award damages in tort (i.e., damages beyond out-of-pocket expenses), a recent decision from the Divisional Court states that the Tribunal (now the Board) did have the jurisdiction to grant damages flowing from the landlord's breach of the tenancy agreement. In *Mejia v. Cargini*,[205] the landlord had three friends assault the tenant in order to pressure the tenant and his family to vacate the rental unit. The Tribunal terminated the tenancy at the tenant's request and awarded an abatement of rent and moving expenses and fined the landlord for this conduct but declined to award general damages on the basis that the Tribunal lacked the jurisdiction to grant such relief even though the T.P.A. permitted the Tribunal to "make any other order that it considers appropriate". On appeal by the

[202] (2006), 2006 CarswellOnt 1538 (Ont. S.C.J.), additional reasons at (2009), 2009 CarswellOnt 659 (Ont. S.C.J.).

[203] (July 28, 2006), CET-05864, [2006] O.R.H.T.D. No. 92 (Ont. Rental Housing Trib.).

[204] (Feb. 28, 2006), CET-05580, 2006 CarswellOnt 2143, [2006] O.R.H.T.D. No. 12 (Ont. Rental Housing Trib.).

[205] (2007), 2007 CarswellOnt 666 (Ont. Div. Ct.).

tenant, the Divisional Court found that the Tribunal did have the jurisdiction to award general damages flowing from the landlord's breach of the covenant of quiet enjoyment (i.e., interference with reasonable enjoyment) and amended the order of the Tribunal in order to grant the tenant damages in the amount of $4,000. Although this was not a case involving any alleged breach of the landlord's maintenance obligations, it may signal that the Landlord and Tenant Board does have the jurisdiction, in appropriate cases, to award general damages that flow directly from a breach of the landlord's contractual and statutory obligations.

(h) Order Prohibiting a Rent Increase (OPRI)

In addition to the remedies that were previously available to tenants who brought applications concerning maintenance, under the R.T.A. another "weapon" has been added to the arsenal — an order prohibiting a rent increase (or "OPRI"). This idea is not new. A similar provision existed under the *Rent Control Act, 1992*.[206] The goal is to give the landlord a financial incentive to keep the building in a good state of repair and to comply with any work orders that may be issued against the building or any orders of the Board that require the landlord to rectify *serious* maintenance problems. In essence, once an OPRI is issued by the Board, the landlord cannot raise the rent for the affected units until the required repairs have been completed. This prohibition on any rent increase applies not only to the original tenant (i.e., the tenant who obtained the OPRI) but also applies to any new tenant whose tenancy commences while the OPRI remains in effect. The R.T.A. also requires landlords to inform prospective tenants about the existence of an outstanding OPRI. Obviously, it will be difficult for a landlord to find a tenant willing to move into a rental unit when the landlord has to inform the prospective tenant that there are serious outstanding maintenance problems with the unit or the building.

Pursuant to paras. 6, 7 and 8 of s. 30(1) of the R.T.A., where a landlord is found to be in serious breach of the landlord's maintenance obligations, in addition to other relief that may be granted, the Landlord and Tenant Board may make the following orders: (1) prohibit the landlord from charging a new tenant[207] under a new tenancy agreement more than the last lawful rent charged to the former tenant; (2) prohibit the landlord from giving a notice of rent increase; or (3) prohibit the landlord from taking a rent increase for which a notice has been given but which has not yet taken effect.

Once an OPRI is issued, it remains in effect until the landlord completes the ordered repairs; the Board is not required to issue an order "lifting" the

---

[206] S.O. 1992, c. 11, s. 38.

[207] Other than tenants in rent-geared-to-income housing.

OPRI. Where the OPRI was based on an outstanding municipal or provincial work order, there may be a problem if the responsible governmental authority does not have in place a system for issuing written confirmation when the work order has been satisfied. This may lead to disagreements between the tenants and the landlord as to whether or not the necessary work has been completed and it may result in further proceedings before the Landlord and Tenant Board, at which the inspector will likely have to be called as a witness. Hopefully, inspectors will soon be empowered to issue notices indicating when a work order has been satisfied or they may end up spending most of their time testifying at hearings instead of performing their intended functions.

In Landlord and Tenant Board File No. EAT-01383 / EAT-01609 / EAL-14091 (Feb. 9, 2009), the landlord had neglected his maintenance obligations for years. Finally, workers were sent by the landlord to the rental property, but they hooked a pick-up truck to the rear addition and proceeded to rip it off of the building, causing serious structural damage and making the situation even worse. Despite intervention by property standards, the landlord continued to ignore his responsibilities. In addition to awarding a substantial abatement of rent, the Board also imposed an OPRI until the landlord completed all repairs ordered by the Board and complied with any outstanding Work Orders from the City of Ottawa.

Pursuant to s. 114 of the R.T.A., if an order prohibiting a rent increase is in effect for a unit, the landlord must provide written notice of the details (in the approved form) to a prospective new tenant of that unit and, where the OPRI is issued after the tenancy agreement is made (but before the tenancy actually commences), written notice must also be provided to the tenant.[208] The notice must contain the following information:[209]

- the order that is in effect
- the amount of rent that the landlord may lawfully charge the new tenant until the prohibition ends
- the amount of rent that the landlord may lawfully charge the new tenant after the prohibition ends
- the last lawful rent charged to the former tenant
- such other information as is prescribed

If an OPRI takes effect in respect of a rental unit after a new tenancy agreement relating to the rental unit takes effect, the landlord must promptly give to the new tenant written notice (in the approved form) about the lawful rent for the rental unit, the order that has been issued and such other information as is prescribed.[210]

---

208 Subsections 114(1) and (2) of the R.T.A.

209 Subsection 114(3) of the R.T.A.

210 Subsections 114(4) and (5) of the R.T.A.

If the landlord breaches these provisions (i.e., s. 114), the tenant has up to one year to commence an application for relief (the return of excess rent collected illegally) and the landlord can be ordered to pay to the Board an administrative fine not exceeding the greater of $10,000 and the monetary jurisdiction of the Small Claims Court.[211] Furthermore, failing to give a new tenant the required notice that sets out the lawful rent to be charged or giving false information in the notice where there is an OPRI is an offence under clause 234(i) of the R.T.A. (see Chapter 19).

(i) Any Other Order the Board Considers Appropriate

The Board, hearing an application under s. 30, has the power "to make such further order as it considers appropriate": s. 30(1) para. 9 of the R.T.A.

Some adjudicators relied upon an identical provision of the T.P.A. to order damages prior to the addition of para. 4.1 to s. 34 of the T.P.A., which explicitly granted to the Tribunal the power to award certain types of damages.

When the Board orders that the landlord do specified work within the rental unit, if the landlord alleges that it has had difficulty gaining access to the unit or the parties are having difficulty agreeing on the dates and times for entry, the Board can include terms in the order specifying the dates and times of entry or that the tenant shall allow the landlord to enter the unit upon proper written notice given at least 24 hours in advance, in accordance with s. 27 of the R.T.A.

In *M.F. Arnsby Property Management Ltd., Re*,[212] the tenants were experiencing recurring problems with mould. The landlord responded promptly to calls from the tenants and, eventually, came to believe that the presence of large fish tanks in the unit may have been contributing to the problem. The landlord sent notices to the tenants demanding the removal of these fish tanks. The tenants then spent thousands of dollars to retain experts to conduct tests and write reports as to the cause of the mould problems. The tenants, however, did not share these reports with the landlord. The tenants then commenced an application against the landlord seeking an order declaring that the landlord had failed to properly maintain the unit and for an order that the landlord reimburse the tenants for the cost (over $3,800) of the experts they had retained and for complete indemnification for all of their legal costs associated with this application (almost $2,400). Although the Tribunal ultimately agreed with the tenants that the aquaria did not contribute to the mould problem, it felt that the landlord's conclusion was a reasonable one given the information it had available to it at the time. In any event, the tenants failed

---

[211] Section 115 of the R.T.A. The monetary jurisdiction of the Small Claims Court is scheduled to be increased to $25,000, effective January 2010.

[212] (June 5, 2006), SWT-07337, 2006 CarswellOnt 4412, [2006] O.R.H.T.D. No. 60 (Ont. Rental Housing Trib.).

to prove that the landlord had breached its maintenance obligations under the Act and the Tribunal dismissed the application on this basis. The Tribunal went on to state that even if it had found in favour of the tenants, the amounts claimed by the tenants as "costs" were excessive.

The Divisional Court has recently confirmed that this provision gives the Tribunal (now the Board) the power to grant general damages for a breach by the landlord of the tenancy agreement. In *Mejia v. Cargini*,[213] the landlord had three friends assault the tenant in order to pressure the tenant and his family to vacate the rental unit. The Tribunal terminated the tenancy at the tenant's request and awarded an abatement of rent and moving expenses and fined the landlord for this conduct but declined to award general damages on the basis that the Tribunal lacked the jurisdiction to grant such relief even though the T.P.A. permitted the Tribunal to "make any other order that it considers appropriate". On appeal by the tenant, the Divisional Court found that the Tribunal did have the jurisdiction to award general damages flowing from the landlord's breach of the covenant of quiet enjoyment (i.e., interference with reasonable enjoyment) and amended the Tribunal's order to grant the tenant damages in the amount of $4,000. Although this was not a case involving any alleged breach of the landlord's maintenance obligations, it may signal that the Landlord and Tenant Board does have the jurisdiction, in appropriate cases, to award general damages that flow directly from a breach of the landlord's contractual and statutory obligations.

Finally, under the *Landlord and Tenant Act*, courts relied upon a provision similar to s. 30(1) para. 9 to award exemplary (punitive) damages in appropriate circumstances.[214] Exemplary damages are meant to be punishment for particularly egregious conduct. Unlike an administrative fine (available under s. 31 for other types of breaches by landlords but *not* available under s. 30 for a breach of a landlord's maintenance obligations), exemplary damages are ordered to be paid to the applicant (not the government); thus, an award of exemplary damages not only serves as punishment and deterrent but also benefits the aggrieved party. The following are examples of cases in which exemplary damages were awarded under the *Landlord and Tenant Act* for a landlord's failure to properly repair and maintain the rental unit or the residential complex.

A guideline about exemplary damages, if such is necessary, is found in *Nantel v. Parisien*,[215] a commercial lease case. The judge said that the landlord acted in a high-handed and shockingly contemptuous manner, and went on to put it feelingly:[216]

---

213 (2007), 2007 CarswellOnt 666 (Ont. Div. Ct.).

214 See *Shaw v. Pajelle Investments Ltd.* (1985), 11 O.A.C. 70 (Ont. Div. Ct.) in which an abatement was ordered for poor maintenance and infestation by mice and cockroaches. The Court also awarded special and exemplary damages.

215 (1981), 22 R.P.R. 1 (Ont. H.C.).

216 (1981), 22 R.P.R. 1 (Ont. H.C.) at 11 [R.P.R.].

> [T]he law must do what it can to ensure, by whatever means are at its disposal to ensure that the legal rights of a citizen are protected from the tyranny of another.

In another case, lack of repair and continued failure by the landlord to comply with demands from the municipal property standards department resulted in a 50% abatement of rent for the lack of repairs under s. 94 of Part IV, and an award of $1,000 in punitive damages: *Desjardins v. Castlecap Holdings Corp.*[217]

In *Musiol v. Malamas*,[218] the judge awarded exemplary damages of $500 for each of the three tenants for: "[T]he very high-handed manner in which the landlord dealt with [tenants'] complaints, his callous disregard for their concerns over an extensive period of time, and his blatant refusal to remedy the situation despite outstanding work orders."

Exemplary damages of $1,000 were ordered in *Menyhart v. Pearlman*,[219] for considerable lack of repair, and the landlord's "deliberate, protracted and unrelenting conduct to a degree that has unreasonably interfered with the tenant's quiet enjoyment". On appeal the exemplary damages of $1,000 were set aside. However the judge on appeal stated that,

> ...the landlords were in complete disregard of the tenant's rights and convenience ... and undoubtedly caused great anguish and stress for the tenant ... and the landlords have substantially interfered with the tenant's reasonable enjoyment ... with the intent to cause her to give up possession.

Under the T.P.A., awards of exemplary damages were rare and it was not clear whether there was a concensus amongst Tribunal Members as to whether or not the Tribunal even had the jurisdiction to grant such relief. There are a few cases where the Tribunal has granted such relief, although not in the context of a maintenance application.[220]

In 2005, the Divisional Court ruled that the Tribunal "has no jurisdiction to award exemplary or punitive damages".[221] This is the first decision on this point as far as I am aware and, subject to a statutory amendment or reconsideration of this issue by the Divisional Court or a higher authority, this is the last word on this issue.

---

[217] (June 14, 1991), Doc. 1109-013 (Ont. Gen. Div.).

[218] (1988), 1988 CarswellOnt 2849 (Ont. Dist. Ct.), additional reasons at (November 15, 1989), Doc. M159801-7/88, M160565/88 (Ont. Dist. Ct.).

[219] (1988), 4 T.L.L.R. 235 (Ont. Dist. Ct.), reversed (April 28, 1994), Doc. 92-LT-40758 (Ont. Gen. Div.).

[220] *Van Schyndel v. Johnson* (Jan. 19, 2002), EAT-03360, [2002] O.R.H.T.D. No. 8 (Ont. Rental Housing Trib.), and *Simpson v. Milligan* (Oct. 7, 1999), SOT-00544 (Ont. Rental Housing Trib.).

[221] *Campbell v. Maytown Inc.* (2005), 204 O.A.C. 136 (Ont. Div. Ct.), at para. 23.

Since the Rental Housing Tribunal did not have the authority to award exemplary or punitive damages under para. 34(1)5 of the T.P.A. and since para. 30(1)9 of the R.T.A. is identical to para. 34(1)5 of the T.P.A., the Landlord and Tenant Board also appears to lack the authority to grant such relief.

12

Other Obligations of Landlords

1. INTRODUCTION

In addition to the obligation to properly maintain the residential complex in a good state of repair, landlords have many other obligations towards the tenants and occupants of a residential complex. Put another way, tenants, members of their households and their guests have rights that must be respected by landlords. Some of the obligations of a landlord already discussed in this text include the following:

1. To maintain the rented premises in a good state of repair and fit for habitation during the tenancy and to comply with health, safety and housing standards;[1]
2. To provide a tenant with the landlord's legal name and address for service;[2]
3. To provide a copy of a written tenancy agreement;[3]
4. To provide new tenants with information about the rights and responsibilities of landlords and tenants (in the approved form);[4]
5. Not to require a tenant to pay illegal rent or prohibited additional charges;[5]
6. Not to increase the rent too frequently or by more than is legally permitted;[6]
7. To decrease the rent when required to do so by law;[7]

---

[1] See Chapter 11.

[2] See Chapter 5 — Information That Must be Provided to a Tenant on the Commencement of the Tenancy.

[3] See Chapter 5 — Information That Must be Provided to a Tenant on the Commencement of the Tenancy.

[4] See Chapter 5 — Information That Must be Provided to a Tenant on the Commencement of the Tenancy.

[5] See Chapter 7.

[6] See Chapter 9.

[7] See Chapter 10.

8. Not to collect any security deposit other than a rent deposit, not to collect a rent deposit that exceeds the rent for one rental period and to pay interest on that deposit;[8]
9. Not to arbitrarily or unreasonably withhold consent to an assignment or sublet;[9] and
10. Not to charge a tenant more than the appropriate portion of the cost of utilities.[10]

Additional obligations of a landlord under the *Residential Tenancies Act, 2006* (R.T.A.) include:

11. To permit candidates for election reasonable access to a residential complex (s. 28);
12. Not to enter the rental unit except in accordance with the R.T.A. (ss. 25-27);
13. Not to alter the locking system to the unit or the complex without giving keys to the tenant (s. 24);
14. Not to withhold or interfere with the supply of vital services (s. 21);
15. Not to interfere with (or allow others to interfere with) the tenant's reasonable enjoyment of the rental unit or residential complex (s. 22);
16. Not to harass, obstruct, coerce, threaten or interfere with a tenant (s. 23);
17. To make an evicted tenant's property available for retrieval for 72 hours (s. 41); and
18. Not to give a notice of termination under s. 48, 49 or 50 in bad faith (s. 57).

It should be noted that while a landlord is responsible for the landlord's own conduct, the landlord is also responsible for and is bound by the conduct[11] of the superintendent and other agents acting on behalf of the landlord. For instance, where the Member found that a tenant had paid rent to the superintendent who then disappeared with the money, the landlord's application to terminate the tenancy for alleged arrears of rent was dismissed.[12]

Also, recall that any term of a tenancy agreement inconsistent with the provisions of the R.T.A. is void (s. 4);[13] thus, a landlord cannot contract out of these obligations and a tenant cannot legally waive his or her rights under the R.T.A.

---

[8] See Chapter 8.

[9] See Chapter 3.

[10] See Chapter 10.

[11] Actions, statements and omissions.

[12] Landlord and Tenant Board File No. EAL-00095 (Feb. 26, 2007) and Landlord and Tenant Board File No. SWL-00379 (March 29, 2007).

[13] See Chapter 5.

A tenant generally has one year in which to pursue relief for a breach by the landlord of the tenant's rights under the R.T.A.[14] Usually, the tenant must commence his or her own application in order to get the issue before the Landlord and Tenant Board. If, however, the landlord brings the tenant before the Board to collect alleged arrears of rent, pursuant to s. 82 of the R.T.A. (and subsection 87(2)),[15] the tenant can raise any issue(s) the tenant wants at that hearing and have the issue(s) heard by the Board as if the tenant had filed his or her own application.

For most breaches related to tenant rights, the possible remedies are listed in s. 31 of the R.T.A. For breaches related to the handling of an evicted tenant's property, the rights and remedies are set out in s. 41. Finally, if a landlord is found to have given a notice of termination (under s. 48, 49 or 50) in bad faith, the former tenant may seek relief under s. 57 of the R.T.A. A breach of these rights can also constitute an offence under ss. 233-239 of the R.T.A., punishable on conviction by fines of up to $25,000 for an individual and up to $100,000 for a corporation (see Chapter 19).

2. TENANT'S RIGHT TO PRIVACY vs. LANDLORD'S RIGHT TO ENTER THE UNIT

One of the most fundamental rights of a tenant is the right to privacy. A person's home is still their castle, even if the accommodations are rented. From time to time, however, a landlord will have legitimate need to enter a rental unit. The R.T.A. therefore permits a landlord to enter a rental unit during the tenancy,[16] but only in limited circumstances and only where the landlord follows the correct procedures. A landlord who illegally enters a rental unit may be subject to an order by the Board and/or to prosecution under the *Provincial Offences Act* or even the *Criminal Code*.

A landlord may enter a rental unit only in accordance with ss. 26 and 27 of the R.T.A. (formerly ss. 20 and 21 of the *Tenant Protection Act, 1997* (T.P.A.)).[17] Section 26 describes situations in which a landlord may enter a rental unit without notice. Section 27 describes situations in which a landlord may enter a rental unit after first providing at least 24 hours' written notice to the tenant.

Pursuant to s. 26, a landlord may enter a rental unit *without* written notice:

---

[14] Subsections 29(2) and 57(2) of the R.T.A. Note that since a time limit does not appear to be set out in the R.T.A. for applications commenced under s. 41, presumably a two-year limitation period will apply as per the *Limitations Act*.

[15] I.e., the landlord has filed an L1 or L9 application.

[16] Obviously different considerations apply where a rental unit has been abandoned or an eviction order has been enforced by the landlord; the restrictions on a landlord's right to enter a rental unit in ss. 26 and 27 of the R.T.A. do not apply in such circumstances.

[17] Section 25 of the R.T.A. (formerly s. 19 of the T.P.A.).

1. At any time, in cases of emergency;[18]
2. At any time, if the tenant consents to the entry at the time of entry;[19]
3. At the time agreed to by the parties (or, if no time was specified, between 8 a.m. and 8 p.m.) where the tenancy agreement requires the landlord to enter the unit in order to clean it;[20] and
4. Between 8 a.m. and 8 p.m. to show the unit to prospective tenants if the landlord and tenant have agreed that the tenancy will be terminated or one of them has given notice of termination to the other and if, before entering, the landlord informs or makes a reasonable effort to inform the tenant of the intention to do so.[21]

Although s. 26 only refers to a "landlord" having a right to enter the rental unit, this has generally been interpreted to mean "the landlord, superintendent or other agent of the landlord".

The potential need for a landlord to gain immediate access to a rental unit in cases of emergency is obvious. Some things cannot wait 24 hours. If there has been a flood or fire or some other emergency that endangers the lives of tenants in the complex or the physical structure of the complex or that is likely to result in substantial loss of or damage to property if not acted upon immediately, this must take priority over a tenant's privacy interests.[22] There must be a genuine emergency however and not some excuse manufactured by the landlord to gain quick access to the unit. Also, even in an emergency, the landlord should still make reasonable efforts to respect the tenant's right to privacy; such efforts may include knocking on the door to the unit and allowing the tenant a minute or two to answer the door rather than simply barging in unannounced.

Where the relationship between the landlord and tenant is a good one, the parties may simply agree on a time for the landlord to enter the unit. This may be as a result of a request by the tenant for repairs or maintenance. Some landlords include on their standard maintenance request forms a statement (above the signature of the tenant) that indicates that the tenant consents to the landlord entering the unit without further notification. Such consents, whether oral or written, do not technically comply with the requirements of para. 26(1)(b) of the R.T.A. which only permits entry without notice where the tenant consents to the entry "*at the time of entry*". This implies a landlord

[18] Paragraph 26(1)(a) of the R.T.A.

[19] Paragraph 26(1)(b) of the R.T.A.

[20] Subsection 26(2) of the R.T.A.

[21] Subsection 26(3) of the R.T.A.

[22] Where the superintendent had to enter the unit on three occasions to turn off the water supply in the kitchen in order to respond to a backup and overflow in the unit below, this was considered to be a *bona fide* emergency situation and none of the entries were found to be illegal: Landlord and Tenant Board File No. SOT-01743 (Jan. 22, 2009).

or superintendent coming to the tenant's door and asking if they may enter and the tenant granting permission and allowing them to enter.

The consent must come at the time of entry. Such consent must be voluntary, not coerced. Also, if the landlord continually seeks (without giving any written notice) to enter the unit late at night or at other times that the tenant has indicated are inconvenient, even if the tenant permits the entry it does not mean that the tenant may not later claim that the landlord's conduct substantially interfered with the tenant's reasonable enjoyment of the unit or that it amounted to harassment. A tenant could also consent to the entry but then later deny they had done so. Acting in such an informal manner may work well when the relationship between the landlord and tenant is good, but it exposes the landlord to potential risk later on should that relationship sour.

Consent by the tenant at the time of entry will not, however, save a defective written notice! The Divisional Court has ruled that where the landlord has provided written notice to the tenant that fails to comply with the requirements of the *Act*, even if the tenant grants permission at the time of entry, the entry may still be considered to be illegal.[23]

Obviously, if it is a term of the tenancy agreement that the landlord will clean the rental unit at regular intervals, the tenant should have no objection to the landlord entering the unit for this purpose. In such circumstances, the R.T.A. does not require the landlord to provide a notice before each entry since the parties have already worked out the details as part of their agreement. If the tenancy agreement does not provide any specific times, however, the Act states that the entry must occur between 8 a.m. and 8 p.m.

Finally, where the tenancy is coming to an end, the landlord may need to show the unit to prospective new tenants, often on very short notice. Subsection 26(3) permits this, as long as the landlord makes reasonable efforts to advise the tenant of the intention to enter the unit (which can be by way of a telephone call) and as long as the entry occurs between 8 a.m. and 8 p.m. The landlord is responsible for what occurs during such viewings and, therefore, should not allow prospective tenants to enter the unit unattended.

In *McGarvey v. Purton*,[24] a landlord entered the rental unit to show it to prospective tenants. Upon entering the unit, the landlord discovered what appeared to be a marijuana-growing operation. The landlord then called the police and allowed the police to enter the unit without a search warrant. The Tribunal found that the landlord had no authority under s. 20 or 21 of the T.P.A. to allow the police into the rental unit.[25] The Tribunal also found that

12 — LL OBLIGATIONS: OTHER

---

[23] *Wrona v. Toronto Community Housing Corp.* (2007), 2007 CarswellOnt 693 (Ont. Div. Ct.). In this case, the landlord was ordered to pay the tenant a rent abatement of $1,000 and costs.

[24] (May 9, 2003), EAL-31352, EAT-03878, [2003] O.R.H.T.D. No. 64, 2003 CarswellOnt 2665 (Ont. Rental Housing Trib.).

[25] The Member in this case appears to have been concerned with the landlord inviting the police into the rental unit. Even if the police had obtained a warrant, there would still have been no *express* authority in s. 20 or 21 of the T.P.A. for the landlord granting the police access to

the landlord should not have taken matters into his own hands by changing the locks to the rental unit and removing the tenant's property from the complex. The Tribunal awarded to the tenant a 50% abatement of rent for a two-month period.

Pursuant to s. 27(1), a landlord may enter a rental unit in accordance with *written notice* given to the tenant at least 24 hours before the time of entry under the following circumstances:

1. To carry out a repair or replacement or do work in the rental unit;[26]
2. To allow a potential mortgagee or insurer of the residential complex to view the rental unit;
3. To allow a person who holds a certificate of authorization within the meaning of the *Professional Engineers Act* or a certificate of practice within the meaning of the *Architects Act* or another qualified person to make a physical inspection of the rental unit to satisfy a requirement imposed under subsection 9(4) of the *Condominium Act, 1998*;
4. To carry out an inspection of the rental unit if the inspection is for the purpose of determining whether or not the rental unit is in good condition and fit for habitation and complies with health, safety and maintenance standards and if it is reasonable to carry out the inspection;[27]
5. For any other reasonable reason for entry specified in the tenancy agreement.

The T.P.A. stated that a landlord could enter the rental unit to show it to a potential purchaser. Landlords would often leave it up to their real estate agent to show the premises to potential buyers but some tenants objected on the basis that the T.P.A. only authorized entry by a landlord, not by an agent of the landlord. Subsection 27(2) of the R.T.A. seeks to resolve this problem by specifying that a licenced broker or real estate agent may enter the unit (without the landlord) to show it to a potential purchaser as long as the tenant has been provided with at least 24 hours written notice before the time of entry, and the agent/broker has the written authorization of the landlord.

---

the rental unit because of suspected illegal activity within the unit. Does this mean that the landlord should have insisted that the police break down the door? From an economical and practical point of view, this makes little sense. Nevertheless, from a strict interpretation of the T.P.A., this seems to be what the law required unless the landlord could demonstrate that the presence of the marijuana plants, grow lights and watering devices created such a hazard that it constituted an emergency that justified immediate entry into the rental unit.

[26] Under s. 21 of the T.P.A., a landlord could enter the unit (after first providing proper advance notice in writing) to "carry out a repair or do work in the rental unit". Under the R.T.A., this has been clarified by amending the phrase as follows: "to carry out a repair *or replacement* or do work in the rental unit."

[27] This is new. A similar right did not exist under the T.P.A.

The written notice required by s. 27 must specify: (1) the reason for entry; (2) a day of entry; and (3) a time of entry between 8 a.m. and 8 p.m.[28] If the reason for entry is omitted or the time given is not specific, the notice does not comply with the requirements of s. 27(3) and any entry into the unit relying upon such a notice would be illegal.[29]

The reason for entry must be one permitted under subsection 27(1) or (2) and it must be *bona fide*. There is no *general* right of a landlord to enter a rental unit. It is also not enough that the reason be reasonable. If a landlord desires a right to enter a rental unit for a reason other than those listed in clauses 1 to 4 of subsection 27(1) or in subsection 27(2), a specific term to this effect must be included in the tenancy agreement. For instance, a landlord could reserve the right to enter the rental unit on 24 hours notice where it appears that the unit may have been abandoned or where it appears to the landlord that the rental unit is being used for illegal activities. By specifying in the tenancy agreement additional situations in which the landlord may want to gain access to the rental unit, the landlord can then rely upon clause 5 of subsection 27(1) of the R.T.A. (i.e., entry for "any other reasonable reason . . . specified in the tenancy agreement").

In *Johansen v. Carlton Apartments Ltd.*,[30] the tenant had commenced an application against the landlord. The landlord wanted to gather photographic evidence and gave a notice to the tenant that the landlord's agent would be entering the unit to "view the state of repair". The tenant then commenced this application on the basis that such entry was not legally justified and amounted to harassment. The member agreed. There was no provision in the T.P.A. that permitted a landlord to enter a rental unit to gather evidence for a hearing or gave the landlord the general right to inspect the unit. The Member awarded an abatement of rent equal to one month's rent. Presumably, with the addition of clause 4 to subsection 27(1), a similar case might now be decided differently under the R.T.A.

The notice should indicate the date the landlord intends to enter the unit. Whether one notice can be given for several dates is questionable and it may be safer for a landlord to give a separate notice for each entry. Finally, the time of entry must be specified. This is often difficult for landlords who rely on workers (plumbers, electricians, etc.) who may not be able to tell the landlord the exact time they will be arriving at the complex or who may be working on several units in the complex and may not be sure when they will get to any specific unit in the building. Nevertheless, s. 27(3) requires that a notice of entry specify a time of entry.[31] A landlord cannot indicate a six- or

---

[28] Subsection 27(3) of the R.T.A.

[29] *Muir v. Heinemann et al.* (Nov. 6, 2001), TNT-02202 (Ont. Rental Housing Trib.) and *Park v. Realstar Management* (May 19, 1999), TNT-00426, 1999 CarswellOnt 5800 (Ont. Rental Housing Trib.).

[30] (Feb. 10, 1999), SOT-00254 (Ont. Rental Housing Trib.).

[31] *Muir v. Heinemann et al.* (Nov. 6, 2001), TNT-02202 (Ont. Rental Housing Trib.).

nine-hour period during which an entry will occur; the notice must specify a time within the 12-hour window permitted by the R.T.A.[32]

In addition to other permitted methods of serving such a notice upon the tenant(s),[33] a notice of entry is the only document that can be served upon a tenant by posting it on the door of the rental unit.[34]

In *Muir v. 1045838 Ontario Inc. et al.*,[35] the tenant was awarded an abatement equal to roughly one month's rent because the landlord (amongst other things): (1) attempted to gain entry to the unit on more occasions than reasonably necessary; (2) relied upon notices that failed to specify the reason and/or time or entry; and (3) entered the unit when there was no emergency and no valid written notice had been given to the tenant.

Although entry for repairs after notice may be permissible, the repairs must be necessary. In *Mayrand v. 768565 Ontario Ltd.*,[36] the landlord entered to do repairs and renovations to upgrade the unit and planned to then apply for rent increases. The Ontario Court of Appeal considered and decided that the repairs were not "necessary".

In *Robson v. Shabudin*,[37] the landlord entered the unit illegally on a number of occasions without prior notification and without there being any emergency or other lawful excuse. This conduct continued even after the tenant posted a notice requesting that it cease. The Tribunal found that these illegal entries were alone sufficient grounds to justify granting the tenant's request for a termination of the tenancy.

In *Elgasuani v. Niazof*,[38] the landlord entered the house (shared by a few tenants) on an almost daily basis without any notice to the tenant(s). He kept this tenant awake at night by making noise and turning on lights in the house. He deprived the tenant of access to his mail. He engaged in a course of conduct designed to drive the tenant out of the complex. The landlord was ordered to cease such activities. A few months later, another tenant of this house complained about this landlord's conduct. The Tribunal found that the landlord had continued to enter the house without any notice or other legal justification. This time, the landlord was ordered to pay an administrative fine.[39]

---

[32] *Wrona v. Toronto Community Housing Corp.* (2007), 2007 CarswellOnt 693(Ont. Div. Ct.). See also Landlord and Tenant Board File No. SOT-01677 (Feb. 2, 2009).

[33] See s. 191 of the R.T.A. and Rule 5 of the Board's Rules of Practice.

[34] Rule 5.1(d) of the Board's Rules of Practice.

[35] (Nov. 6, 2001), TNT-02202 (Ont. Rental Housing Trib.).

[36] (1990), 75 O.R. (2d) 167 (Ont. C.A.).

[37] (Sept. 22, 1999), TNT-00678 (Ont. Rental Housing Trib.).

[38] (Jan. 25, 2000), TNT-00852, [2000] O.R.H.T.D. No. 188, 2000 CarswellOnt 6452 (Ont. Rental Housing Trib.).

[39] *Mijango v. Niazof*(April 3, 2000), TNT-01000, 2000 CarswellOnt 6420 (Ont. Rental Housing Trib.).

In *Simpson v. Milligan*,[40] the landlord harassed the tenant, illegally entered, and cut off water supplies to get the tenant to vacate. The Tribunal awarded an abatement of rent of 50%, and 100% for the month when the water was cut off. As for illegal entry, the Tribunal said that the landlord wrongly did so without lawful justification, which constituted a trespass, and ordered damages of $2,500 be paid to the tenant. The Tribunal then considered punitive damages, stating that the landlord's conduct was reprehensible and was deserving of condemnation and punishment and ordered the landlord to pay the tenant exemplary damages of $1,000.[41]

One further decision of the Tribunal to mention is *Gervais v. Yoon*.[42] There was harassment, illegal entry on six occasions and withholding of water service. The landlord substantially interfered with the tenant's reasonable enjoyment. The Tribunal ordered a rent abatement of 50% and an administrative fine of $2,000, saying that the landlord deliberately and completely disregarded the rights of the tenant.

Sections 26 and 27 refer to entry by the "landlord". The question therefore sometimes arises whether the landlord has the right to bring others along into the unit or whether others (agents of the landlord) can attend without the landlord being present. The *Act* itself is silent on this point. I think that it is clear that the landlord can bring along other persons if it is reasonable to do so. For instance, the landlord may need to bring into the unit an engineer or insurance inspector or workers needed to effect repairs to the unit. In Landlord and Tenant Board File No. SOL-01458 (June 19, 2007), the Board held that it was reasonable for the landlord to bring along his wife to inspect the unit as she had previously done work in the unit and occasionally acted as property manager. I also think that it is unrealistic to expect that the landlord will remain in the rental unit for the duration of a lengthy repair. Of course, the landlord is liable for the conduct of the landlord's agents and ought to take care to carefully select and supervise those who are permitted to enter rental units on the landlord's behalf.

3. OBLIGATION NOT TO ALTER THE LOCKING SYSTEM WITHOUT GIVING KEYS TO THE TENANT (ILLEGAL LOCKOUTS)

It is not illegal for a landlord to alter the locking system on a door giving entry to a rental unit or residential complex during the tenant's occupancy of the rental unit. A landlord can change the locking system as often as the

---

[40] (Oct. 7, 1999), SOT-00544 (Ont. Rental Housing Trib.).

[41] An administrative fine would have been permissible but, as will be discussed later, the Divisional Court has ruled that the Tribunal (Board) has no jurisdiction to grant punitive or exemplary damages.

[42] (July 2, 1999), SOT-00442 (Ont. Rental Housing Trib.).

landlord wishes (within reason) as long as the landlord gives the tenant keys to the new lock(s).[43] If the landlord does not provide the tenant with keys to the new lock(s), then the landlord has effectively locked the tenant out of the unit, or the complex, as the case may be.

Where a landlord locks the tenant out of the unit without going through a formal eviction, it is sometimes referred to as an "illegal lockout" or "wrongful eviction". Pursuant to s. 39 of the R.T.A., a landlord shall not recover possession of a rental unit subject to a tenancy unless the tenant has vacated or abandoned the unit or an order of the Board evicting the tenant has authorized the possession.

Locking a tenant out of their home without due process is one of the worst things that a landlord can do. Landlords who are found[44] to have engaged in such conduct, therefore, ought to expect the response of the Board to be quite severe.

Wrongful eviction was very seriously dealt with by the Tribunal in *Keller v. Blair*.[45] The landlord illegally entered the rental unit and changed the locks. There was harassment and the landlord seized the tenant's property (contrary to s. 31 of the T.P.A.). The Tribunal ordered abatement of rent of 50%, $10,000 damages for property not returned and an administrative fine of $2,500. The Tribunal said that the landlord's conduct was extreme, vicious, absolutely reprehensible and unacceptable.

In another wrongful eviction case, *Leitao v. Ruffolo*,[46] the tenant's family of five spent the night of the eviction in their van. Their goods were put in storage. The Tribunal ordered the return of the tenant's goods, full abatement of rent, $3,042 for accommodation costs for five weeks, moving costs, and an administrative fine of $2,000.

In *Bartok v. Rose*,[47] there was harassment by the landlord and illegal entry. Also, the landlord changed the locking system, withheld water service on two occasions, and cut cable service. The Tribunal ordered a 50% abatement of rent and moving expenses.

In *436235 Ontario Ltd. and Volpi v. Mountfort*,[48] the landlord locked out a tenant who refused to pay an illegal rent increase. The Tribunal made an interim order that the landlord provide keys to the tenant and that the landlord pay an administrative fine of $500 per day until compliance. The landlord continued to refuse to comply and the Tribunal ordered a $10,000 fine for this flagrant disregard of the rights of the tenant and of the interim order of the Tribunal. This was upheld on appeal by the Divisional Court.

---

[43] Subsecton 24(1) of the R.T.A.

[44] Under para. 29(1)5 of the R.T.A.

[45] (Aug. 20, 1999), EAT-00776 (Ont. Rental Housing Trib.).

[46] (Oct. 1, 1999), CET-00244-RV (Ont. Rental Housing Trib.).

[47] (Aug. 10, 1999), TST-01108 (Ont. Rental Housing Trib.).

[48] (Sept. 20, 2002), Div. Ct. File Nos. 405/00 and 499/00, re Ontario Rental Housing Tribunal File Nos. TST-02063, TST-02095 (Ont. Div. Ct.).

In *Ellison v. Thornton*,[49] the landlord entered the unit illegally, assaulted the tenant, damaged the tenant's personal possessions and locked the tenant out of the unit for one and a half days. The Member ordered the landlord to pay an administrative fine of $1,000, a rent abatement of approximately $350, $300 for the cost of repairing or replacing the tenant's damaged property and aggravated damages in the amount of $1,000.

In *Kahlon v. AGF Trust Co.*,[50] the applicants claimed that AGF illegally locked them out of this unit. The Member found that AGF was acting upon a writ of possession it obtained from the Ontario Superior Court. In fact, the Tribunal concluded that there never existed a tenancy in this case. Rather, the application was part of an effort by relatives of the mortgagors (who were in default), in collusion with the mortgagors, to deceive the Tribunal and maintain some control over the property. The Member dismissed the application, ordered that the applicants pay Tribunal costs of $500 and referred the matter to the Investigations and Enforcement Branch for possible prosecution of the persons who attempted to mislead the Tribunal.

In Landlord and Tenant Board File No. SOT-00269-AM,[51] the tenant was having a number of problems with the condition of the rental unit. Despite repeated requests from the tenant and even from the Enforcement Branch of the Ministry of Municipal Affairs and Housing, the landlord refused to do anything about the poor condition of the unit. In desperation, the tenant withheld her rent for January 2007 in order to get the landlord's attention. The landlord then proceeded to cut off the electricity to the unit and, while the tenant was away, the landlord changed the locks to the unit and threw the tenant's possessions out into the snow. On application by the tenant, the Board ordered the landlord to pay to the tenant $250.00 for moving expenses, $4,029.00 in damages for the cost of replacing the property lost as a result of the landlord's conduct and to pay to the Board an administrative fine of $2,500.00.

In Landlord and Tenant Board File No. NOT-00932 (Feb. 11, 2009), the landlord illegally locked the tenants out of the rental unit and improperly disposed of their property. The Board awarded to the former tenants $5,500.00 for the value of the damaged, lost or stolen items and $250.00 as a reasonable estimate of their out-of-pocket and moving expenses and ordered the landlord to return to the tenant the personal property the landlord admitted still having in storage.

In Landlord and Tenant Board File No. NOT-00793 (Feb. 5, 2009), the landlord illegally locked the tenants out of the rental unit and improperly disposed of their property. The Board awarded to the former tenants $6,218.00

[49] (Aug. 4, 2006), TST-08160, [2006] O.R.H.T.D. No. 111 (Ont. Rental Housing Trib.).

[50] (Feb. 28, 2006), CET-05665, 2006 CarswellOnt 2144, [2006] O.R.H.T.D. No. 13 (Ont. Rental Housing Trib.).

[51] Issued July 24, 2007 and amended September 18, 2007.

for the value of the damaged, lost or stolen items, $2,035.00 as a reasonable estimate of their out-of-pocket and moving expenses, $1,747.00 for "emotional distress and extreme inconvenience" (for a total of $10,000.00) and fined the landlord an additional $2,000.00.

4. OBLIGATION NOT TO WITHHOLD OR INTERFERE WITH THE SUPPLY OF VITAL SERVICES

Some landlords have, in the past, relied on self-help to regain possession from a defaulting tenant, either by physical re-entry or by cutting off the electricty, heat and/or water.

By s. 121(1) of the *Landlord and Tenant Act*, physical re-entry was prohibited and a landlord only had recourse to court proceedings to obtain a writ of possession to be enforced by the sheriff. This prohibition continued under the T.P.A. (s. 41) and, now, under the R.T.A. (s. 39).

In view of s. 17 of the R.T.A., that covenants are interdependent, it might seem that when a tenant is in breach of the covenant to pay rent, the landlord would be relieved from the covenant to heat and supply other vital services. To avoid this recourse of landlords, s. 21 of the R.T.A. provides that a landlord shall not at any time during a tenant's occupancy of a rental unit and before the day on which an order evicting the tenant is executed, "withhold reasonable supply of any vital service, care service or food that it is the landlord's obligation to supply under the tenancy agreement or deliberately interfere with the reasonable supply of any vital service, care service or food." Note that it is contrary to the Act for the landlord to deliberately interfere with the reasonable supply of any vital service, care service or food whether or not the landlord is obliged by the terms of the tenancy agreement to provide such services or goods.

"Vital service" is defined in s. 2 of the R.T.A. as hot or cold water, fuel, electricity, gas, or during the part of each year prescribed by the regulations (i.e., September 1 through June 15),[52] heat.

"Care services" are defined in s. 2 of the R.T.A. as:

- health care services;
- rehabilitative or therapeutic services; or
- services that provide assistance with the activities of daily living.

The term "rehabilitative" was defined in *Keith Whitney Homes Society v. Payne*[53] as "restoration of the individual to his or her greatest potential whether physically, mentally, socially or vocationally"; and "therapeutic" is defined by the Shorter Oxford English Dictionary as "to treat medically, pertaining to the healing of disease".

---

[52] Section 4 or O. Reg. 516/06.

[53] (1992), 9 O.R. (3d) 186 (Ont. Gen. Div.).

Pursuant to s. 2(1) of O. Reg. 516/06, care services include:

- Nursing care
- Administration and supervision of medication prescribed by a medical doctor
- Assistance with feeding
- Bathing assistance
- Incontinence care
- Dressing assistance
- Assistance with personal hygiene
- Ambulatory assistance
- Personal emergency response service

If provided along with one or more of the services list above, care services can also include:[54]

- Recreational or social activities
- Housekeeping
- Laundry services
- Assistance with transportation

Where it is the landlord's obligation to provide these services, they cannot be withheld as a means of getting rid of a tenant who is in arrears of rent, or a tenant who is just objectionable in the eyes of the landlord. The landlord must continue the supply of these services until an eviction order has been obtained and enforced by the sheriff.

Withholding of care services or food could potentially result in a tenant's illness or death. Thankfully, there are no reported decisions of a landlord withholding care services or food. There are, however, numerous cases of landlords who have withheld or interfered with the reasonable supply of vital services.

Of course, not every interruption in the supply of vital services is the result of an illegal attempt to force the tenant to vacate the rental unit. It also frequently results from the inability of the landlord to pay the utility bills as they come due. In circumstances where the interruption results from the inability (as opposed to unwillingness) of the landlord to pay for the utility, it is probably more properly characterized as an interference with the tenant's reasonable enjoyment of the unit rather than as a withholding of, or interference with, the reasonable supply of a vital service (as contemplated by s. 21 and para. 29(1)2). In any event, while lack of malice on the part of the landlord may be relevant to the Board's decision as to the appropriate relief to grant under s. 31, it is not a complete defence. The landlord may also face prosecution under s. 233 (see Chapter 19).

[54] Subsection 2(2) of O. Reg. 516/06.

In *Hill v. Ebony Realty Inc.*,[55] a landlord cut off the electricity. An abatement of rent was ordered and the landlord had to pay damages for spoilt food caused by the electric refrigerator being out of service.

In an ordinary action by a tenant for damages against the landlord for cutting off the water supply, the landlord was held liable in tort and for breach of contract. Damages were awarded including refund of rent paid, general damages of $200 and $500 for punitive damages: *Tefft v. Kooiman.*[56]

In *Speiran v. Verrilli*,[57] it was held that, where a landlord is obliged by the terms of the tenancy agreement to pay for hydro, the failure of the landlord to do so (which results in the cutting off of hydro to the rental unit) constitutes withholding or interfering in the supply of a vital service.

Occasional interruption of the supply of services will not be compensable if the interruptions were not the result of any deliberate conduct on the part of the landlord.[58]

In *Balausiak et al. v. Talaluddin*,[59] the tenants brought an application alleging that the landlord had withheld the reasonable supply of potable water. The Member found that the landlord did provide a reasonable supply of potable water for normal household consumption and that the landlord was not required to meet the increased demand for water created by the presence of the tenants' thirty pets. In *Laporte v. Ladouceur*,[60] however, it was held on the facts of this case that failing to take immediate steps to ensure the uninterrupted supply of potable water constituted the withholding of that vital service.

In *McClement v. Kisiel*,[61] the same day that the landlord's application to evict the tenant was dismissed by the Tribunal, the landlord cut off the gas and hydro to the unit (presumably in an effort to force the tenant to vacate the unit). The hydro remained off for ten days and the gas for thirteen days. The landlord also threatened to change the locks to the unit. At the time, the tenant was nine months pregnant. The Tribunal awarded a rent abatement and fined the landlord $1,000.

In *2030859 Ontario Inc., Re*,[62] a group of approximately 50 tenants brought an application against their landlord because the gas had been shut off to the apartment building from July 28, 2004 to August 4, 2004 and from

---

[55] (May 25, 1976), Doc. M11583 (Ont. Co. Ct.).

[56] [1978] 5 W.W.R. 175 (Man. Q.B.).

[57] (Oct. 21, 1999), TNT-00773, 1999 CarswellOnt 5830 (Ont. Rental Housing Trib.).

[58] *Terriah et al. v. Mishra* (Feb. 16, 1999), EAT-00398 (Ont. Rental Housing Trib.). Relief in this case was granted based upon harassment by the landlord.

[59] (Jan. 18, 2002), EAT-03301 (Ont. Rental Housing Trib.).

[60] (Sept. 12, 2001), EAT-02975, [2001] O.R.H.T.D. No. 120, 2001 CarswellOnt 6329 (Ont. Rental Housing Trib.).

[61] (March 3, 1999), SWT-00388 (Ont. Rental Housing Trib.).

[62] (Feb. 27, 2006), SOT-04875, 2006 CarswellOnt 2148, [2006] O.R.H.T.D. No. 28 (Ont. Rental Housing Trib.).

April 6, 2005 to April 14, 2005. The gas had been shut off due to non-payment of the utility bill by the landlord. The landlord did not participate in the hearing. Each tenant was awarded a rent abatement of $610 and the landlord was fined $500.

In *Brooks v. Banelopolous*,[63] the electricity to the rental unit was disconnected as a result of the landlord's failure to pay the bill. The tenants were awarded a small abatement of rent to compensate them for their out-of-pocket expenses. Since the landlord had previously been fined $1,000 by the Tribunal for similar conduct (see order TET-05072 issued on August 25, 2005), the Tribunal imposed a fine of $1,250 for this most recent incident.

Where it is the tenant's responsibility to pay for the utilities, however, and they are cut off when the tenant fails to pay the utility bills, the landlord cannot be held responsible.[64] Furthermore, where the interruption in the service was temporary and due to an error on the part of the municipality or utility company, it cannot be said that the landlord interfered with the supply of a vital service.[65]

The Landlord and Tenant Board has demonstrated a willingness to deal swiftly with emergency situations caused by the cutting off of vital services. In File No. SOT-00248, the Board issued an interim order on May 22, 2007, that the landlord give the utility authorities access to the building to restore electricity and ordered the landlord to have electricity service restored that same day or, in the alternative, provide a power generator sufficient to meet specified needs of the tenant. The landlord did not comply with this interim order and about a week later, the Board issued a second interim order[66] that further clarified the original order, granted a 100% abatement of rent until electricity was restored to the unit, fined the landlord $500 *per day* from May 31, 2007, until the power was restored or the tenants chose to terminate the tenancy, which the Member ordered they could do (for a limited time) on 48 hours' written notice to the landlord.

[63] (May 15, 2006), TET-05494, TET-05667, 2006 CarswellOnt 4389, [2006] O.R.H.T.D. No. 59 (Ont. Rental Housing Trib.).

[64] But see Landlord and Tenant Board File No. SOT-00163 (April 27, 2007), in which the Board found that it constituted interference with the tenant's reasonable enjoyment of the rental unit for the landlord to force one tenant to put the gas account for a house containing two units into her name and then try to put the burden on her to collect half of each bill from the tenant of the other unit.

[65] *Quadera Ltd., Re* (Sept. 29, 2006), NOT-02386, 2006 CarswellOnt 9162 (Ont. Rental Housing Trib.).

[66] File SOT-00248-IN(2), (June 1, 2007).

5. OBLIGATION NOT TO INTERFERE WITH THE REASONABLE ENJOYMENT OF THE UNIT/COMPLEX

(a) General

The covenant for quiet enjoyment is said to protect a tenant from acts of the lessor or those lawfully claiming under him substantially interfering with the tenant's ordinary and lawful enjoyment of the premises. The concept of interference with "quiet enjoyment" does not necessarily relate only to disturbances caused by excessive noise. The term can relate to *any* substantial interference with the tenant's enjoyment of the premises.

The covenant for quiet enjoyment is implied by the common law and by s. 23 of the *Conveyancing and Law of Property Act*,[67] although in most written leases it is expressed.

It is, as stated, either an express or implied covenant of every residential tenancy agreement. It was made a statutory obligation of landlords under Part IV of the *Landlord and Tenant Act*. The covenant for quiet enjoyment is now, under s. 22 of the R.T.A., expressed in terms of reasonable enjoyment rather than quiet enjoyment but the underlying principles remain the same:

> A landlord shall not at any time during a tenant's occupancy of a rental unit and before the day on which an order evicting the tenant is executed substantially interfere with the reasonable enjoyment of the rental unit or the residential complex in which it is located for all usual purposes by a tenant or members of his or her household.

Originally, courts interpreted this covenant rather narrowly. A landlord would only be found to have breached this obligation if the acts of the landlord physically interfered with the tenant's ability to use the premises; mere inconvenience or discomfort was not enough.[68]

In the "Report on Landlord and Tenant Law" by the Ontario Law Reform Commission of March 15, 1976, there was a discussion of the problems inherent in the prevailing, narrow view of the covenant for quiet enjoyment. The following recommendations were made as a result (these recommendations may still be useful when considering whether a breach of the covenant for quiet enjoyment has occurred and the appropriate remedy):

1. In every tenancy agreement the landlord shall be deemed to have covenanted that the tenant shall have the right to quiet enjoyment, including the right to peaceably possess and have the full benefit of the rented premises, together with the right to use and enjoy them in reasonable peace, comfort and privacy, without interference, interruption or disturbance from the landlord or any other person or persons lawfully claiming by, from or under him.

---

[67] R.S.O. 1990, c. C.34.

[68] *Greenbranch Investments Ltd. v. Goulborn* (1972) (Ont. C.A.).

2. A landlord should be deemed to have committed a breach of the covenant for quiet enjoyment if he knew or ought to have known that the act complained of would interfere with the peaceable possession of the tenant or with the reasonable peace, comfort or privacy of the tenant or members of the household.
3. The nature of the acts constituting a breach of the covenant should not necessarily be limited to those which at present comprise a breach of the implied or usual express covenant for quiet enjoyment. Without limiting the generality of the foregoing, a breach of the covenant should arise from any acts which result in the tenant's reasonable peace, comfort or privacy being interfered with, whether due to liquids, gases, vapours, solids, odours, vibration, noise, abusive language, threats, fire, the total or partial withholding of heat, electricity, water, gas or other essential services, or the removal of windows, doors, walls or other parts of the rented premises. The Commission recommends, however, that the proposed legislation should not expressly delimit the types of acts which might constitute a breach of the covenant; rather, it should be left to the court to determine whether, in all the circumstances of the case, the covenant has been breached.
4. In the appropriate circumstances, the court should be empowered to make a finding that the covenant has been breached, notwithstanding that the acts complained of have not taken place nor originated on the rented premises.
5. In order for the court to find that the covenant has been breached, it should not be necessary for the tenant to have quit the rented premises, nor should it be necessary that the tenant be expected to do so.
6. The imposition of liability for breach of the covenant should not automatically turn on any arbitrary distinction between acts committed on or off the rented premises, between rightful or wrongful acts of persons claiming by, from or under the landlord, between acts performed in pursuance of a statutory duty or otherwise, or, with respect to acts committed by tenants of adjacent premises, between situations where the consent of the common landlord has been given or not given.
7. A breach of the covenant should entitle the tenant to damages, injunctive relief, or an order declaring the tenancy agreement terminated. The latter remedy, however, ought to be available only where, having regard to the nature and seriousness of the breach, the court is of the view that damages or injunctive relief, or both, are in all the circumstances inadequate remedies.
8. Contracting out of the covenant for quiet enjoyment should not be permitted in the case of residential tenancies.

In *Ryan v. Parkinson*,[69] for profane and abusive language by the landlord amounting to harassment, the judge was satisfied there was a breach of the covenant (for quiet enjoyment) and granted an abatement.

Some of the matters which obviously interfere with a tenant's enjoyment of his premises were dealt with in *Parkes v. Howard Johnson Restaurants Ltd.*[70] The landlord embarked on a course of conduct designed to force the tenant out, including the removal of a padlock by smashing it, the removal of the doors to part of the premises occupied by the tenant, deliberate interruption of the elevator service and interference with the electrical supply so that the tenant had insufficient light, and cutting off the heating, all of which were obviously breaches of the covenant for quiet enjoyment. Some of these acts are now prohibited under sections of the R.T.A. In the case just mentioned, punitive damages were directed to be paid by the landlord because of his high-handed actions.

Another pretty obvious breach of the covenant for quiet enjoyment was the removing of doors and windows by a landlord: *Lavender v. Betts.*[71] Punitive damages were awarded to the understandably outraged tenant.

One other case concerned pipes bursting and damage to the tenant's premises resulting from water leaking into his premises, and it was held to be a breach of the covenant for quiet enjoyment: *Broben Investment Ltd. v. Cadillac Contractors & Developments Ltd.*[72]

Complaint by a tenant about the noise and construction work on a neighbouring property that substantially interfered with her reasonable enjoyment of the rental unit was heard by the Tribunal in *Teachout v. Sifton Properties Ltd.*[73] The tenant was attracted to renting here, having been told by a representative of the landlord that the adjoining wooded property owned by a company associated with the landlord was not for development. Soon after moving in, construction work started for a new building. The Tribunal was sympathetic but held that ss. 26 and 32(1) para. 6 of the T.P.A. for her right to reasonable enjoyment only applied to her rental unit and the residential complex, and not to whatever was going on at an adjoining property. The Tribunal did say that the misrepresentation by the landlord's agent may give her an action in tort in another forum. The contrary conclusion was reached by a different Member on somewhat similar facts in *Weeks v. Paquette*[74] in which the Member found in favour of the tenant as a result of the landlord creating unreasonable levels of noise by its construction activities on land near the residential complex.

---

[69] (1994), 19 O.R. (3d) 475 (Ont. Gen. Div.).

[70] (1970), 74 W.W.R. 255 (B.C. S.C.).

[71] [1942] 2 All E.R. 72 (Eng. K.B.).

[72] (1961), [1962] O.R. 207 (Ont. H.C.).

[73] (February 28, 2000), SWT-01067, 2000 CarswellOnt 6353 (Ont. Rental Housing Trib.).

[74] (April 14, 2003), EAT-03150, EAT-03215, EAT-03312, [2003] O.R.H.T.D. No. 50, 2003 CarswellOnt 1585 (Ont. Rental Housing Trib.).

Noise bothering a tenant was dealt with in *Fox v. Atlantis Real Estate Corp.*[75] The court ordered the landlord under s. 94(4)(*c*) of Part IV (*Landlord and Tenant Act*) to have adjustments made to machinery in part of the buildings under the tenant's apartment to relieve the noise, and adjourned the application for an abatement for a period so as to effect the necessary work.

Over the years, the Legislature, the courts, the Rental Housing Tribunal and now the Landlord and Tenant Board have gradually adopted a broader view. Substantial interference with the reasonable enjoyment of a tenant or a member of their household now includes both acts and omissions by the landlord, including the failure of the landlord to take reasonable steps to protect one tenant from disturbance or harassment by another.[76]

This does not mean that every complaint received by a landlord from one tenant about another should immediately result in the landlord seeking to evict the tenant about whom the complaint is made. Care must be taken to independently verify that there is a problem and, except in the most serious cases, the landlord ought to give the "offending" tenant a warning and an opportunity to ameliorate the situation.[77]

In *Hu v. Metropolitan Toronto Housing Authority*,[78] the tenant (who was a Ph.D. student) was disturbed by an 11-year-old in the unit above practicing on the piano. The landlord did not take action against the noisy tenant as should have been done. An abatement of 25% was granted and was ordered to continue until the disturbance ceased. The judge referred to the wide authority under s. 113(1)(*g*) of Part IV, now s. 31(1)(f) of the R.T.A., to make such further order that the judge (now the Board Member) considers appropriate, and included in her order that the tenant has the right to move if the piano noise continued, with moving expenses of $500 to be paid by the landlord.

In *Hassan v. Niagara Housing Authority*,[79] another tenant was unreasonably disturbing or harassing the applicant tenant. On appeal, the Divisional Court held that, in such circumstances, the landlord must step in and take prompt and effective action against the offending tenant. Writing stern letters and meeting with the offending tenant is not enough if the harassment continues. The landlord must then commence an application to terminate the

---

[75] (December 3, 1985), Doc. York M120648/85 (Ont. Dist. Ct.).

[76] See *Chartrand v. Zouzoulas* (Feb. 27, 2004), EAT-05347, [2004] O.R.H.T.D. No. 15, 2004 CarswellOnt 1014 (Ont. Rental Housing Trib.); *Deschênes v. Commvesco Levinson Viner Group Inc.* (April 27, 2004), EAT-05480, 2004 CarswellOnt 2195, 2004 CarswellOnt 2196 (Ont. Rental Housing Trib.); Landlord and Tennat Board File No. SWT-01921 (Jan. 19, 2009); and Landlord and Tenant Board File No. CET-01732 (Feb. 19, 2009).

[77] *Stott v. Sterling Silver Development Corp.* (Dec. 12, 2000), TNT-00744 (Ont. Rental Housing Trib.).

[78] (1994), 1994 CarswellOnt 2565 (Ont. Gen. Div.).

[79] (Feb. 5, 2001), 2001 CarswellOnt 4890, 48 R.P.R. (3d) 297, [2000] O.J. No. 5650 (Ont. Div. Ct.).

tenancy of the offending tenant. The landlord must act quickly (within weeks, not months) to effectively correct the problem. In this case, the landlord failed to take such action. The Divisional Court awarded the applicant tenant an abatement of rent equal to one-half the rent paid during the relevant time period.

Disputes between neighbours living in close proximity are inevitable. As stated in *1068434 Ontario Inc. v. 500 Windsor Ave. (Tenants of)*:[80]

> Life in any apartment comlex involves an unavoidable clash of individual interest, and the risk of interference with other people's enjoyment of the complex. These interferences range from trifling annoyances to serious disruptions in the lives of others. Each individual in an apartment community must put up with a certain amount of annoyance, inconvenience and interference. The very principle of apartment living depends on the principle of "give and take, live and let live".

For instance, in *Stansbury v. Chatterjee*,[81] other tenants were complaining about the cooking odours emanating from this rental unit. The Tribunal held that the tenants residing in this unit had done nothing wrong and that unfamiliar cooking smells were simply something one had to live with when living in an apartment building.

When confronted with a dispute between tenants, there is therefore a heavy onus upon the landlord to decide on an appropriate course of action and to deal with the matter promptly. It may be difficult for the landlord to ascertain which tenant is at fault. As tempting as it may be, a landlord cannot simply throw up his or her hands and say, "This is a matter between the tenants and I refuse to get in the middle." The landlord must investigate the allegations being made and take appropriate steps to deal with the problem.[82] In conducting the investigation and in dealing with complaints from or about a tenant, the landlord must act in a fair and even-handed manner.[83] The failure to take such steps can result in the landlord being held legally and financially responsible to the tenant who has been deprived of his or her right to reasonable enjoyment of the rental unit or the residential complex.

Similarly, a landlord may be held responsible for failing to properly "screen" prospective tenants. In *Donahue v. Clace*,[84] the applicant tenant was "driven out" of this residential complex by the disruptive conduct of a relatively new tenant. The Tribunal held that a landlord has a duty to take

---

[80] (June 8, 2001), SWL-15779 (Ont. Rental Housing Trib.) at para. 88.

[81] (Nov. 8, 1999), SOL-08895 (Ont. Rental Housing Trib.).

[82] *Norton v. Lenuzza* (Oct. 14, 1999), TNT-00706 (Ont. Rental Housing Trib.); *Ellis v. New Country Investors* (March 8, 2001), SOT-01401-RV, 2001 CarswellOnt 6352 (Ont. Rental Housing Trib.); *Laporte v. Ladouceur* (Sept. 12, 2001), EAT-02975, [2001] O.R.H.T.D. No. 120, 2001 CarswellOnt 6329 (Ont. Rental Housing Trib.); and *Farrel v. Kohens* (March 26, 2004), TNT-03924, 2004 CarswellOnt 2187 (Ont. Rental Housing Trib.); Landlord and Tenant Board File No. CET-01732 (Feb. 19, 2009).

[83] *Kirk v. McGrath* (March 1, 2001), TNT-01705 (Ont. Rental Housing Trib.).

[84] (Dec. 4, 2000), NOT-00511, [2000] O.R.H.T.D. No. 168 (Ont. Rental Housing Trib.).

reasonable steps to protect tenants from interference with their enjoyment of the complex and that this duty includes the duty to carefully screen prospective tenants. In this case, the landlord had not done background checks and the Tribunal found that this represented a failure of the landlord to fulfill his obligation under s. 26 of the T.P.A. (now s. 22 of the R.T.A.).

It can constitute interference with reasonable enjoyment if the landlord attempts to prevent a tenant from having guests in the rental unit or otherwise attempts to exert an undue level of control over how the tenant lives.[85]

It can also be a breach of s. 22 of the R.T.A. where a landlord is aware of a tenant's fears and those fears are reasonable but the landlord fails to take reasonable steps to address the cause of that fear. In *Barrett et al. v. Norquay Developments Ltd.*,[86] the tenants suffered a break-in through the apartment window. They asked the landlord to inspect the window and make it more secure. The landlord ignored this request. The Tenants were afraid of further break-ins and decided to move out. They brought an application against the landlord asking for termination of the tenancy and an abatement of rent on the basis that the landlord's failure to address their legitimate security concerns substantially interfered in their ability to enjoy their unit. The Tribunal agreed, terminated the tenancy and awarded a 100% abatement of rent for the last two months of the tenancy. On appeal by the Landlord, the Tribunal's decision was upheld.

It is not enough that a landlord avoid doing things that disturb a tenant. A landlord has a positive obligation to safeguard and/or restore a tenant's reasonable enjoyment of his or her rental unit. In *Satchithananthan v. Cacciola*,[87] tobacco smoke and unreasonable amounts of noise entered this rental unit from the residential and commercial units below, thereby interfering with the tenant's reasonable enjoyment of her unit. Although the building complied with all relevant building and housing standards, because of its age and unusual construction, sound and odours travelled easily though the unit's rather "porous" floor. An abatement of rent was awarded and the landlord was ordered to renovate the tenant's bedroom floor in order to reduce noise transmission from below. Subsequently, the tenant brought another application alleging (amongst other things) that, although the renovation had helped reduce the noise, it was still too noisy in her unit. This application was dismissed. It was found that the landlord had complied with the earlier order and had taken reasonable and sufficient steps to protect the tenant's reasonable enjoyment of the unit.[88]

---

[85] *Ferguson v. Stirpe* (Sept. 2, 1999), TNT-00627, 1999 CarswellOnt 5825 (Ont. Rental Housing Trib.) and *Radokovic v. Stoney Creek Non Profit Housing Corp.* (Aug. 8, 2001), SOT-00994l, [2001] O.R.H.T.D. No. 107 (Ont. Rental Housing Trib.).

[86] (Oct. 27, 2003), Div. Ct. File No. 1372/02 re SWT-03890 (Ont. Rental Housing Trib.).

[87] (Dec. 30, 2002), TST-04047, 2002 CarswellOnt 5023 (Ont. Rental Housing Trib.).

[88] *Satchithananthan v. Cacciola* (June 25, 2003), TNT-03370, 2003 CarswellOnt 2641 (Ont. Rental Housing Trib.).

In a case[89] involving a complaint about second-hand cigarette smoke, a Member had this to say:

> In the situation of a building where smoking is not prohibited, complaints from a non-smoker about smoking in the building present a difficulty for landlords because telling a tenant who smokes that he or she cannot smoke in their own home might very well be a breach of the smoking tenant's right to reasonable enjoyment of their rental unit. Rather a reasonable response in a building where smoking is permitted might be to attempt to ameliorate the problem for the non-smoker by investigating how the ventilation system might be improved, by installing an air filter system, or by providing the complaining tenant with an air purifier.

Since the landlord in this case took no steps to investigate or ameliorate the problem, the tenant was awarded a rent abatement of 10% over five months.

In *Akinlade v. Sunday*,[90] the landlord was to complete the construction of this unit prior to the tenants taking possession (on September 1, 2001). When the tenancy commenced, much of the work on this unit had not been completed. The tenants took possession anyway and hoped that the work would soon be finished. It was not. Although promised, the unit did not have a separate entrance, a functioning bathroom or kitchen or any separation from the furnace. The tenants also had to deal with a rodent infestation. The landlord failed to complete the work and ignored the complaints of the tenants. It was found that this constituted not only a breach of the landlord's maintenance obligations but also resulted in substantial interference in the tenants' reasonable enjoyment of the rental unit for all usual purposes. At the request of the tenants, the tenancy was terminated and they were awarded an abatement equivalent to two months' rent.

In a more recent case,[91] a tenant rented the basement of a house and agreed to pay the utility charges in connection with the rental unit. The tenant set up the gas account (for the house) in her name. At the time, the upper unit in the house was vacant. About one week later, a tenant moved into the upper unit. As the units were not separately metered, the gas bills the basement tenant would be receiving would reflect the gas consumption related to both rental units. The landlord told the basement tenant that it was her responsibility to collect one-half of the cost of each monthly gas bill from the upstairs tenant. The basement tenant tried to comply but had difficulties collecting the money from the other tenant. The basement tenant could not afford to pay the now substantially higher gas bill by herself and the gas account went into arrears. It was held by the Board that, failing to set up a separate gas account for each unit and trying to shift the responsibility onto the basement

---

[89] Landlord and Tenant Board File No. TST-01913 / TSL-20119 (Feb. 19, 2009).

[90] (Jan. 18, 2002), TNT-02372 (Ont. Rental Housing Trib.).

[91] Landlord and Tenant Board File No. SOT-00163 (April 27, 2007).

tenant to collect money from the other tenant constituted substantial interference with the basement tenant's reasonable enjoyment of her unit. The Board ordered the landlord to pay to the basement tenant one-half of all gas bills, including the amount in arrears (failing which the basement tenant could deduct the appropriate sum from the rent she would otherwise have to pay the landlord). While, traditionally, interference with reasonable enjoyment was taken to mean interference with the tenant's ability to actually use and enjoy the rental unit, it appears that at least one of the Members of the Landlord and Tenant Board is prepared to expand the concept of interference with reasonable enjoyment to include interference with the tenant's economic interests.

A landlord is not absolutely liable for every disturbance or event that may affect a tenant's enjoyment of the residential complex. For one thing, a landlord need only protect a tenant's *reasonable* enjoyment; a landlord is not required to satisfy the expectations of a hypersensitive or excessively demanding individual.[92] Furthermore, a landlord need only safeguard a tenant's enjoyment of a residential unit for all *usual purposes*.

A landlord will not generally be held responsible for the conduct of others over whom the landlord has no control. For instance, in *Peters v. Landstake Investments Ltd.*,[93] the landlord was not held responsible for vandalism to the tenant's vehicle. Similarly, in *Furlong v. Century Park Apartments*,[94] the landlord was not held responsible for the theft of the tenant's motorcycle from the underground parking garage; the tenant failed to prove that the theft of the motorcycle was the direct result of anything the landlord had done or had failed to do with regard to the security of the garage or that this loss substantially interfered with the tenant's reasonable enjoyment of the residential complex for all usual purposes. Following the *Furlong* decision, in Landlord and Tenant Board File No. TNL-18086 / TNT-01463 (Jan. 19, 2009), the landlord was absolved of responsibility for the theft of the tenant's vehicle from a residential complex as the tenant did not establish a

---

[92] See *Raniere v. Iana Development Ltd.* (March 29, 1999), TNT-00376 (Ont. Rental Housing Trib.), *Bassier v. Tedford Gardens Apts.* (Nov. 14, 2001), TNT-02145 (Ont. Rental Housing Trib.) and *Reid v. Manulife Financial*, [2007] Landlord and Tenant Board File No. TST-09871 in which the tenants were found to be unusually sensitive to noise. See also: *Thomas v. W.A. Construction Benleigh Apts.* (Jan. 14, 1999), TET-00207 (Ont. Rental Housing Trib.) in which it was held that the fact that the tenant was forced to park his vehicle in a new location did not constitute substantial interference with the tenant's reasonable enjoyment of the rental unit for all usual purposes; and Landlord and Tenant Board File No. TNT-00937 (Jan. 9, 2009), in which a tenant who chose to live in a unit adjacent to the common room for the complex and overlooking the squash courts, pool lounge and outdoor patio was found to have no right to complain about a normal amount of noise coming from other tenants and their guests using these facilities during normal operating hours (especially where the landlord offered to move the tenant to other vacant units but the tenant refused all such offers).

[93] (March 3, 2003), TNT-03081, 2003 CarswellOnt 1507 (Ont. Rental Housing Trib.).

[94] (Nov. 7, 2002), CET-02977, 2002 CarswellOnt 5025 (Ont. Rental Housing Trib.).

clear connection between something the landlord did or failed to do and the tenant's loss.

In *Gates v. Noble*,[95] the landlord was not held responsible for the conduct of the police towards a tenant. An employee of the landlord called the police and alleged that the tenant had threatened him. The police attended at the complex and told the tenant that if he did not want to be charged with an offence, he should pack up and leave. He did. The tenant later brought an application against the landlord based on (amongst other things) harassment and interference with reasonable enjoyment. The Tribunal found that, although the police attended at the unit because of a call from the landlord, when the police officers threatened to lay charges against the tenant if he did not vacate the complex they were acting on their own and not as agents for the landlord. Therefore, this part of the tenant's application was dismissed.

Contrast the previous case with *Cromwell v. Modest*,[96] in which the landlord had the police remove the tenant from the rental unit. Apparently, the police were convinced that the *Tenant Protection Act* did not apply to this rental unit and refused to look at a previous order from the Tribunal that indicated to the contrary. The police instructed the tenant to vacate the unit immediately and that if he returned to the property he would be charged with trespassing. Subsequently the unit was re-rented so that it was not possible for the Tribunal to put the tenant back into possession. In this case, the Member found that the police were acting as agents for the landlord and that the landlord was ultimately responsible for this interference with the tenant's reasonable enjoyment of the rental unit. The landlord was ordered to pay to the tenant compensation for the expenses the tenant incurred as a result of this illegal eviction and the Tribunal fined the landlord $1,500.

In *Panoramic Properties Inc., Re*,[97] the tenant alleged that the landlord was substantially interfering with her reasonable enjoyment of the rental unit by the way in which the landlord set her parking charge. The tenant alleged that the landlord was discriminating against her because her rent was subsidized. As it turns out, this tenant has been paying a lower parking rate than almost all other tenants in the complex and parking charges in the complex were not determined based upon whether or not the rent was subsidized. Consequently, the tenant's application was dismissed.

Imposing unreasonable restrictions on visitor parking can constitute interference with the reasonable enjoyment of the complex.[98]

---

[95] (Oct. 29, 1999), TNT-00768, 1999 CarswellOnt 5831 (Ont. Rental Housing Trib.).

[96] (March 23, 2006), TET-05615, 2006 CarswellOnt 2153, [2006] O.R.H.T.D. No. 24 (Ont. Rental Housing Trib.).

[97] (Aug. 8, 2006), SOT-05733, 2006 CarswellOnt 9156 (Ont. Rental Housing Trib.).

[98] *Marshall v. Bayview Summit Development Ltd.* (2001), 2001 CarswellOnt 6371 (Ont. Rental Housing Trib.).

In *Kraft v. Colavita*,[99] it was held to constitute substantial interference with the reasonable enjoyment of the tenants (as well as harassment) where the landlord deliberately withheld oil (for heating) and hot water, refused to allow an inspection of the oil tank, transferred utility accounts into the names of the tenants, unilaterally changed the parking arrangements, seized the tenants' property and attempted to charge the tenants for work that it was the landlord's responsibility to perform. The landlord was ordered to return the tenants' property and the tenants were awarded an abatement in rent of $8,125.00.

In Landlord and Tenant Board File No. TET-01640 (Jan. 30, 2009), the landlord failed to pay the gas bill and, as a result, the tenants were without gas service for approximately two weeks in October 2008. It was found that this substantially interfered with the tenants' reasonable enjoyment of the unit and the tenants were awarded an abatement equal to just over 50% of the rent for that month.

In Landlord and Tenant Board File No. EAT-01617 (Jan. 12, 2009), the landlords and their son were found to have substantially interfered with the tenant's reasonable enjoyment of the rental unit by: showing up unannounced and using the tenant's yard, shooting the tenant's cat with a B.B.-Gun, threatening to burn down the house and serving several written and oral notices of termination, all improperly served and without any real justification. The fact that they had paid for the tenant's vet bills was considered by the Member to be a mitigating factor but the amused attitude of the landlords at the hearing was considered to be an aggravating factor. Nevertheless, only a modest abatement of rent ($250) was awarded.

Failing to maintain and repair the unit, in addition to giving rise to rights and remedies under s. 30 of the R.T.A., may also constitute substantial interference with the reasonable enjoyment of the rental unit (giving rise to additional possible remedies under s. 31 of the *Act*).[100]

In Landlord and Tenant Board File No. SOT-01867 (Feb. 23, 2009), the superintendent illegally entered the tenants' unit on two occasions. On the second occasion, the tenants called the police. The superintendent discovered confidential and embarrassing information about the female tenant (possibly while illegally in the rental unit). In retaliation for calling the police, the superintendent circulated a letter to other tenants of the complex, disclosing what he had discovered about the female tenant. The Board found that this conduct substantially interfered with the tenants' reasonable enjoyment of the rental unit and awarded them $1,500 as compensation for the effects of the superintendent's conduct.

---

[99] (March 5, 2001, amended May 2, 2001) CET-01644 (Ont. Rental Housing Trib.).

[100] Landlord and Tenant Board File No. EAT-01620 (Feb. 10, 2009) and Landlord and Tenant Board File No. SOT-01778 / SOT-01779 (Feb. 3, 2009).

Finally, the timing of the alleged interference is important. Section 22 of the R.T.A. only protects tenants for events that occur during the tenant's occupancy of the rental unit. If the conduct of which the tenant complains occurred prior to the commencement of the tenancy, there will be no remedy available under this section.[101] For example, if the landlord prevents the tenant from taking possession of the rental unit, this may constitute obstruction or be actionable in court but it will not likely be covered under s. 22 since the interference did not occur during the tenant's "occupancy" of the rental unit. Similarly, the protection of s. 22 does not extend to events that occur on the day an eviction order is enforced or any time thereafter.

(b) Interference with Enjoyment Caused by Repairs/Maintenance

Every building requires maintenance and, from time to time, will require repairs. Occasionally, the work will be extensive. Rental accommodations are no exception. Tenants must expect that, from time to time, a landlord will have to perform maintenance and repairs; in fact, it is the landlord's legal obligation to do so. Unfortunately, such work may disturb the tenants who live in the building. When the disturbance is minor or lasts only for a short duration, most tenants accept the inconvenience without complaint. When the disturbance is significant (in nature or duration), tenants may seek redress; they may argue that the landlord has breached its covenant to ensure the tenants' quiet or reasonable enjoyment of the premises.

Therefore, two competing interests are in tension. On one hand is a tenant's right to have quiet and reasonable enjoyment of the rental unit and of the residential complex as a whole. On the other hand is the landlord's obligation to perform all necessary repairs (as well as the public interest in encouraging landlords to act responsibly and not allow their buildings to deteriorate). When the landlord is required to undertake a major repair project (such as balcony restoration or underground parking garage restoration), the conflict between these two interests becomes obvious. The solution to this problem is less obvious.

In the past, tenants have commenced proceedings against their landlords in such circumstances on the basis that: (1) the noise, dust, vibrations, etc., caused by the repair work substantially interfered with their reasonable (or quiet) enjoyment of their rental unit/complex; and/or (2) they were deprived of the use of part of the facilities normally provided by the landlord and for which they were paying. Such proceedings have met with mixed results, probably because courts have been loathe to penalize a landlord financially (by granting an abatement to tenants) where the landlord has done nothing

---

[101] See *Fortin v. Reiter-Nemetz* (Dec. 13, 2002), TNT-02907 (Ont. Rental Housing Trib.) in which the tenant complained about misrepresentations allegedly made to her by the landlord at the time the tenancy agreement was negotiated.

wrong and is merely attempting to fulfill the landlord's obligations to repair and maintain the building. Nevertheless, tenants have been granted relief in some cases.

In *Herbold v. Pajelle Investments Ltd.*,[102] the Supreme Court of Canada considered the question of whether an abatement is warranted for a temporary loss of use of facilities during necessary repairs and renovations. The action was initiated under s. 96 of the *Landlord and Tenant Act*, which provided that the landlord is responsible for providing and maintaining the rented premises in a good state of repair and fit for habitation. The trial judge ordered an abatement of rent to the tenants for the loss of use of the air conditioning unit for the month of July 1971 and the sauna and swimming pool from November 1971 to March 1972. The landlord appealed the decision. Ultimately, the case made its way up to the Supreme Court of Canada where the trial judge's decision was upheld. At page 528 of the decision, the Court wrote the following:

> I am ready to agree that it would only be in the most exceptional circumstances that a court should grant an abatement for rent because of failure to provide the repairs and services during a short period required for necessary repairs and renovations . . . the evidence is that the air-conditioning was not supplied at all during the mid-summer month of July in the year 1971 and that no use of the sauna bath or swimming pool was provided from November 1971 to March 1972. Those are important and long continuing delays in providing the facilities which it was the responsibility of the landlord to provide and the learned County Court Judge was perfectly justified in considering they would have to be compensated for by an abatement in rental.

In *Reid v. Roar Enterprises Ltd.*,[103] the landlord had undertaken a substantial program of renovation involving plumbing, wiring, bathroom fixtures, kitchen fixtures and cupboards. These renovations disrupted the lives of the tenants and they sought compensation by way of an abatement of rent. In granting an abatement to the tenants, the Ontario District Court commented that the fact that it was difficult to do the work without disruption and the reasonableness of the landlord's actions were both irrelevant in determining this issue. In essence, the court found that tenants should pay less when they get less.[104]

In *Flewelling v. Minto Developments Inc.*,[105] the Ontario Court (General Division) considered whether an abatement was warranted under s. 96(3) of the *Landlord and Tenant Act* in circumstances where the landlord undertook extensive repairs to the balconies of a high rise apartment building. The tenants lost all access to the balconies for approximately one year. The tenants

---

[102] (1975), [1976] 2 S.C.R. 520 (S.C.C.).

[103] (1988), 1 R.P.R. (2d) 97 (Ont. Dist. Ct.).

[104] (1988), 1 R.P.R. (2d) 97 (Ont. Dist. Ct.) at 104 [R.P.R.].

[105] (1991), [1991] O.J. No. 3496, 1991 CarswellOnt 608, 21 R.P.R. (2d) 138 (Ont. Gen. Div.).

testified that they were severely disturbed by excessive heat during the summer months and by noise and dust throughout the period of the repairs. In granting to the tenants a 10% abatement of rent for one year, the Court wrote the following (at paras. 29 and 32):

> Notwithstanding Minto's efforts, all of these applicants were denied reasonable enjoyment of the rented premises by being denied access to the balcony which was fundamental to the enjoyment of their apartments . . . To each of these four tenants the use of the balconies, I accept, was central to the enjoyment of their apartment. The denial of use of the balconies in these cases for the period of 1 year constitutes a long, continuing delay in providing the facilities, which was the responsibility of the landlord.

In *Offredi v. 751768 Ontario Limited*,[106] the Divisional Court upheld the decision of Hoilett, J. of the General Division, which granted an abatement in rent to tenants for, amongst other things, disruption during necessary repairs to the garage in their building. The tenants alleged that the landlord had breached its covenant of quiet enjoyment. The garage repairs had lasted for approximately one year, during which time the tenants had to park their cars elsewhere at considerable inconvenience. At the Divisional Court, the landlord advanced the argument that it should not bear the burden for making repairs to the garage because those repairs were necessary for the structural safety of the building. In dismissing the landlord's argument in this regard, the Court stated (at para. 7):

> In our view, there is no merit whatsoever in that submission. It goes without saying that there was an obligation, and a very serious one, on the landlord to maintain the building in a sound structural condition. If the carrying out of essential repairs resulted in a failure to give to the other tenants the quiet possession of their apartments to which they were entitled, it is the landlord that must bear the burden and not the tenants.

In *Zand v. Highmark Properties*,[107] the Ontario Court of Justice (General Division) again considered the question of the tenants' entitlement to an abatement during necessary repairs. In this case, the landlord undertook extensive exterior repairs to the building, resulting in noise, dust and loss of use of the exterior grounds, including the parking lot, for a period of eight months. The Court found that a rent abatement in the amount of 10% was warranted. The Court's conclusion in this case, however, was premised on a finding that these extensive repairs were only necessary because of the previous neglect of the building by the landlord.

In *Thompson et al. v. Metropolitan Toronto Housing Authority*,[108] the landlord was doing necessary major repairs to the building (especially to the

---

[106] (1994), [1994] O.J. No. 1204, 72 O.A.C. 235, 1994 CarswellOnt 2204 (Ont. Div. Ct.).

[107] (1995), 49 R.P.R. (2d) 69 (Ont. Gen. Div.).

[108] (November 26, 1996), Court File no. 96-LT-119698 (Ont. Gen. Div.) (unreported).

balconies) that caused considerable inconvenience to the tenants. They complained that they paid full rent for their apartments but did not receive that for which they had bargained. The noise, dust and vibrations made it impossible for the tenants to fully enjoy their units. The court awarded a 40% abatement of rent and found it was irrelevant that these tenants lived in subsidized housing or rent-geared-to-income housing. On this issue, Madam Justice Molloy wrote (at p. 21) that tenants in such housing, "have the same right to an abatement of rent as a tenant in any other building" and that they "have the same right to quiet enjoyment of their premises as a tenant in any other building."

In *Caldwell v. Valiant Property Management*,[109] considerable necessary repair work was being done over a period of eight months. As the judge stated, for the breach of covenant of quiet enjoyment implied by s. 23(1) of the *Conveyancing and Law of Property Act*, an abatement of rent is justified when a tenant does not receive, for a significant period of time, a substantial benefit of the leased premises. Actual physical interference is not necessary. There is substantial inconvenience and discomfort — and this is so even where the landlord is fulfilling the duty to keep the premises in good repair. Following the reasoning of the *Reid* decision, the judge ruled that the reasonableness of doing the repairs and the reasonableness of the manner of performing them are irrelevant factors.

Shortly after the *Caldwell* decision, the T.P.A. was enacted. Thus, the Rental Housing Tribunal was created at a time of considerable uncertainty when it came to the issue of what relief, if any, was available to tenants who suffered through major building repairs and renovations. In the earliest version of the Tribunal's Interpretation Guideline (No. 5) on landlords' maintenance obligations, it was suggested that a landlord should only be held liable for an abatement of rent as a result of disruptions caused by repairs in exceptional circumstances (i.e., where the disruption is substantial and lasts a long time and where there was some fault on the part of the landlord such as the repairs being necessitated by earlier neglect of the building by the landlord). The concern was that routinely awarding an abatement of rent for disruptions caused by repairs would deprive landlords of funds needed to do the work and would discourage landlords from making necessary improvements.

Although Members were bound to consider this Guideline, they were free to choose not to follow it. Many Tribunal Members chose, instead, to follow the more tenant-centred approach adopted in many of the more recent court decisions (such as the *Offredi* and *Caldwell* decisions, cited above).[110]

---

[109] (1997), 33 O.R. (3d) 187 (Ont. Gen. Div.).

[110] See *Flogell v. Greenwin Property Management* (May 11, 1999), TST-00745 (Ont. Rental Housing Trib.); *Papas v. Montcrest Apartment* (Aug. 20, 1999), TST-00361 (Ont. Rental Housing Trib.); *Krivdyuk v. Westwood Management International* (Aug. 16, 1999), TNT-

That, however, does not mean that all such applications by tenants were successful before the Tribunal. No relief was awarded, for instance, in cases where the interference was for a relatively short duration, where the landlord acted reasonably, where the interference was not *substantial* because most of the work occurred while the tenant was at work (i.e., absent from the complex) or where the tenant failed to mitigate (by failing to take advantage of other temporary accommodations offered by the landlord).[111]

Apparently, the government was not entirely satisfied with the direction being taken by the Tribunal. As part of the *Government Efficiency Act, 2001*, s. 30.1 was added to O. Reg. 194/98.[112] This new and relatively complicated section dictated how the Tribunal was to determine whether a landlord, in carrying out work in a rental unit or a residential complex, substantially interfered with the reasonable enjoyment of the unit or complex for all usual purposes by the tenant of the unit. Although it did not actually say so, presumably it was also meant to apply to interference with the enjoyment of members of the tenant's household as well. Section 30.1 also strictly limited the amount of abatement that could be awarded even where the Tribunal found a tenant's reasonable enjoyment had been substantially interfered with as a result of work on the unit or the complex. The approach mandated by the new regulations were then reflected in the Tribunal's revised Interpretation Guidelines 5 and 6.

In broad terms, s. 30.1 of O. Reg. 194/98 precluded the Tribunal from finding that there was a breach of s. 26 of the T.P.A. as a result of a landlord doing work in a residential complex unless the *effect* on the tenant was substantial and the interference with the tenant's use and enjoyment of the unit or complex was both substantial and *unreasonable* in the circumstances. Even where it was found that the effect on the tenant was substantial and the interference was substantial and unreasonable, no abatement could be awarded as long as the following conditions were met:

(1) the landlord gave advance notice to the tenant;
(2) the notice was accurate and timely;
(3) the work was "eligible work" as defined in s. 30.1(2) of the regulation;
(4) the landlord obtained any permit(s) required by the *Building Code*;

00569 (Ont. Rental Housing Trib.); *Gavriline v. Westwood Management International* (Nov. 23, 1999), TNT-0573 (Ont. Rental Housing Trib.); and *Hui v. Greenwin Property Management Inc.* (June 24, 1999), TST-00964 (Ont. Rental Housing Trib.).

[111] *Noorani v. Cando Property Management Ltd.* (Jan. 27, 2000), TNT-00748 (Ont. Rental Housing Trib.); *Kawar v. LT Greenwin Property Management Inc.* (May 19, 2000), TNT-01097, 2000 CarswellOnt 4420 (Ont. Rental Housing Trib.); *Muir v. Wise Management Inc.*, (July 31, 2000), CET-01060 (Ont. Rental Housing Trib.); and *Mill v. Gallery Towers 2001* (Nov. 5, 2002), TST-05098, 2002 CarswellOnt 3776 (Ont. Rental Housing Trib.) upheld on review (March 17, 2003), TST-05098-RV (Ont. Rental Housing Trib.).

[112] This amendment came into effect as of October 7, 2002 (O. Reg. 268/02).

(5) the work was done at reasonable times;
(6) the duration of the work was reasonable; and
(7) the landlord took reasonable steps to minimize the impact from noise associated with the work.

Where it was found that the effect on the tenant was substantial *and* the interference was substantial and unreasonable *and* it was determined that the landlord failed to comply with one or more of the seven requirements listed above, an abatement of rent *could* be granted. Unless the interference greatly exceeded the level that would normally be expected in all of the relevant circumstances, however, the abatement could not exceed 10% of the monthly rent.

In practical terms, this test was so convoluted and restrictive that a tenant would rarely be successful on an application for an abatement of rent based upon interference caused by major work on the building.[113] Even if a tenant did manage to somehow navigate his or her way through this complex regulatory scheme and prove entitlement to an abatement of rent, the abatement granted would almost certainly be no greater than 10%. Given the likely outcome, rarely was it worth the time and effort (and, possibly, expense) involved in bringing such an application. This point is perfectly illustrated by the case of *Haidar v. York University*.[114]

In *Haidar v. York University*,[115] a student living in residence brought an application against the university for the disturbance being created by nearby construction on the campus. After attempting to weave his way through the relevant statutory and regulatory provisions, the Member determined that it was unreasonable for the university to have carried on this construction work during the exam period when it ought to have known that resident students would need a quiet environment in which to study. The Member awarded the tenant a 100% abatement for a 19-day period. This represented an award of $450.39. One has to wonder if, at the end of the day, the tenant felt that it was worthwhile attending before the Tribunal on eight separate occasions over a nine-month period in order to obtain an order for $450.00.

Despite criticism of these provisions, they have been carried forward into the current regime with only slight modifications. Section 8 of O. Reg. 516/06 now replaces s. 30.1 of O. Reg. 194/98. It is very similar to (and just as complicated as) the predecessor regulation but has a few differences. For instance, landlords must now provide advance notice about major work that is planned not only to "sitting" tenants but also to prospective tenants (who may, therefore, choose to look elsewhere for accommodations). Section 8 of

---

[113] See, for example, *Paramount Property Management, Re* (Aug. 15, 2005), EAT-06454 (Ont. Rental Housing Trib.) and *Bibber et al. v. Paramount Property Management*, [2005] EAT-06464 (Ont. Rental Housing Tribunal).

[114] (June 6, 2006), TNT-04721, [2006] O.R.H.T.D. No. 113 (Ont. Rental Housing Trib.).

[115] (June 6, 2006), TNT-04721, [2006] O.R.H.T.D. No. 113 (Ont. Rental Housing Trib.).

O. Reg. 516/06 is also organized in a slightly different fashion than its predecessor. The most significant change is that, unless the interference greatly exceeds the level that would normally be expected in all of the relevant circumstances and the work was not of the prescribed type or was not carried out in the prescribed fashion, the abatement cannot exceed 25% of the monthly rent; this is an increase from the amount (10%) permitted under the T.P.A.

In any event, landlords who are planning to do major work should carefully review the requirements of s. 8 of O. Reg. 516/06 and attempt to comply with its provisions so as to minimize the interference with the reasonable enjoyment of the tenants in the complex and reduce the risk of having to later provide to the tenants an abatement of rent.

I have only found a few decisions by the Landlord and Tenant Board dealing with this issue. In every case, the tenant's application was dismissed.

In Landlord and Tenant Board File No. TST-00227 (Aug. 15, 2007), the tenant, who worked primarily from the rental unit, was disturbed while the residential complex underwent a noisy phase of renovation of the balconies. The Member found that the work was necessary, that it was carried out at reasonable hours and within a reasonable duration, that the landlord made reasonable efforts to notify the tenants and to minimize the interference due to the noise. Thus, pursuant to s. 8(3)(b) of O.Reg. 516/06, the Member was unable to find that the interference was unreasonable (and substantial) and the tenant's application was dismissed.

In Landlord and Tenant Board File No. CET-00506 (Oct. 29, 2007) , the tenant demonstrated that the balcony repairs caused a considerable amount of interference but failed to prove that the interference was *unreasonable*, as defined in s. 8 of O. Reg. 516/06. The tenant's application was, therefore, dismissed.

In another application[116] concerning disruption caused to a different tenant by the same balcony repairs (as in CET-00506), the presiding Member found that the noise and dust created by the balcony repairs did cause substantial disruption to this tenant. Pursuant to s. 8 of O. Reg. 516/06, however, the onus was upon the tenant to establish that the interference was also "unreasonable in the circumstances" which, according to the Member, involves a combined two-part test which is both objective and subjective. Paragraph 8(3)(a) specifically instructs the Board to consider the effect of the work on the individual tenant involved; one must ask whether the effect on this tenant was disproportionate or particularly severe. The Member held that this part of the analysis was subjective. The evidence in this case indicated that the effect on this tenant was severe, ultimately requiring the tenant to seek medical attention. The other part of the analysis is objective: "Was the disruption reasonable given the nature and extent of the work that needed to

---

[116] Landlord and Tenant Board File No. TST-00183 (Sept. 26, 2007).

be done?" In this case, the Member found that since there was no evidence before her that the work could have been done in a less disruptive manner, the interference was not "unreasonable" and, pursuant to s. 8(3) of O. Reg. 516/06, it cannot be said to be substantial. Although not necessary, the Member went on to find that the landlord had complied with the requirements of s. 8(4) of O. Reg. 516/06 and, therefore, she would not have granted a rent abatement in any event. If this analysis is correct, one might well wonder how any tenant, short of retaining and calling an engineer to give expert testimony (which is likely to be cost-prohibitive), is going to be able to prove to the Board that the repairs that caused substantial disruption could have been done in a less disruptive manner.

In another case about repairs to balconies and railings,[117] the Board determined that the landlord carried out the work in a manner and over a period of time that was reasonable in the circumstances. Accordingly, the tenant's application was dismissed.

In Landlord and Tenant Board File No. SOT-01796 (Jan. 12, 2000), the landlord engaged in a major project to convert 148 units from electric heat to gas. Each unit had substantial work done to facilitate this conversion, to install a new gas furnace, a new water heater and a new air conditioner. The work included running air ducts throughout each unit, which involved making holes in walls and ceilings and then repairing the drywall. This tenant lost patience and vacated the unit after three days of construction. The tenant stated that the work being done substantially interfered with her reasonable enjoyment and requested that the Board terminate her tenancy as of the date she moved out of the unit (December 31, 2008). Pursuant to s. 8 of O. Reg. 516/06, in such circumstances, the interference cannot be found to be substantial unless it was unreasonable. The Member found that, on the facts of this case, the interference with the tenant's enjoyment of the unit was not unreasonable. As a result, the tenant's application was dismissed.[118]

6. OBLIGATION NOT TO HARASS, OBSTRUCT, COERCE, THREATEN OR INTERFERE WITH A TENANT

Pursuant to s. 23 of the R.T.A. (formerly s. 27 of the T.P.A.), a landlord "shall not harass, obstruct, coerce, threaten or interfere with a tenant." In order to violate s. 23 of the R.T.A., a landlord need only do one of the prohibited acts listed therein. Each word used in this section ("harass", "obstruct", "coerce", "threaten" and "interfere") is deemed to have a unique meaning.

[117] Landlord and Tenant Board File No. TST-00353 (July 7, 2008).

[118] The Member also found that, contrary to the assertions of the tenant, a valid notice of termination had not been received by the landlord early enough for it to have been effective on December 31, 2008.

12 — LL OBLIGATIONS: OTHER

In *Walker v. Lawson*,[119] it is said that these words must be given their usual meaning, which is not particularly helpful, but the Tribunal then quoted dictionary definitions as follows:

> Harass: to worry, vex, weary by prolonged or often repeated molestation or importunity; to annoy, fatigue by incessant attacks, surprises, skirmishes, or raids.
>
> Obstruct: to block, bar, render impassable; to prevent, hinder from passing; to hinder, prevent, intercept passage of light or sound; to oppose, hinder, impede the progress of.
>
> Threaten: to utter a threat to, state intention of injuring, punishing; to express intention of hurting, punishing in a specified way; to state intention to inflict; to present appearance, manifest a probability of immanent occurrence, approach; to menace.
>
> Interfere: to intervene, especially in matters which do not concern one; to meddle; to interpose, mediate; to hinder, prevent, act as an obstacle; to annoy, pester, molest; to thwart, prevent, interrupt, be an obstacle to; to affect prejudicially, injure; to intermeddle with.

In *Cino v. Standard Land Investments*,[120] the Tribunal suggested that harassment can be defined as "conduct which one knows or should know to be unwelcome by the other person and which one pursues for no legitimate purpose."

Harassment usually connotes a pattern of objectionable statements or other conduct by a person that causes distress to the person subjected thereto and that the person engaging in the conduct knows or ought to know is unwelcome.[121] In particularly egregious cases, however, a single act may constitute harassment. Harassment by a landlord of a tenant has been found to include such things as:

- a series of attempts to evict the tenant when no legitimate grounds existed for early termination of the tenancy;[122]
- continually confronting and threatening the tenant;[123]
- verbally abusing the tenants, repeatedly making racist comments;[124]
- threatening the tenant and having others make harassing telephone calls to the tenant;[125]
- continuing to send the tenant notices of termination and other threatening notices purportedly based on arrears of rent even after the

---

119 (July 19, 1999), SOT-00476 (Ont. Rental Housing Trib.).

120 (April 18, 2006), SWT-07421, [2006] O.R.H.T.D. No. 62 (Ont. Rental Housing Trib.), at para. 5.

121 See Landlord and Tenant Board File No. NOT-00967 (Feb. 6, 2009).

122 *MacLean v. Benaisssa*, Div. Ct. 123/03 re TST-04923 and TST-04924 (Ont. Div. Ct.).

123 *Terriah et al. v. Mishra* (Feb. 16, 1999), EAT-00398 (Ont. Rental Housing Trib.).

124 *Wu v. Singh* (Oct. 14, 1998), SOT-00109 (Ont. Rental Housing Trib.).

125 *Young v. Benoit* (March 15, 1999), SWT-00363 (Ont. Rental Housing Trib.).

tenant had met with the landlord several times in order to correct the errors in the landlord's records and to provide evidence that, in fact, there was no rent owing;[126]

- showing up at the rental unit almost daily, entering the unit without notice or permission, interfering with the tenant's access to his mail, etc.;[127]
- the superintendent screaming at tenants, members of their households and their guests, making obscene and racist comments and generally treating tenants in an abusive and demeaning manner;[128]
- demanding post-dated cheques and yelling at the tenant on several occasions for refusing to provide post-dated cheques;[129]
- making unwanted sexual advances and remarks and threatening to raise the rent if the tenant did not yield to these advances;[130]
- serving a notice of termination for use of the unit by the Landlords' daughter when the Landlords had no actual intention of having their daughter move in and were actually seeking to avoid dealing with various maintenance issues;[131]
- taking petty and punitive actions against the tenants and withdrawing services because the tenants brought pets into the rental unit.[132]

In *Cino v. Standard Land Investments*,[133] the property manager made a practice of calling all of his tenants before the end of each month to remind them that the rent was about to come due. He testified that, if he waited for tenants to fall into arrears, it would cost the landlord much more than placing a few friendly reminder calls beforehand. These tenants had no record of

---

[126] *Abdi v. Toronto Community Housing Corp.* (Dec. 20, 2002), TNT-02263, TNT-02699, 2002 CarswellOnt 5022 (Ont. Rental Housing Trib.). In this case, the absence of malice was found not to be an excuse. It was, however, a factor considered in determining the appropriate remedy. The landlord was directed by the Tribunal to improve its administrative system in order to avoid these types of problems in the future. See also *Fu v. Sherbourne Estates Management Inc.* (March 24, 2004), TSL-57159, TST-06602, 2004 CarswellOnt 2198 (Ont. Rental Housing Trib.) and *Khan v. Riverside Residences* (March 21, 2001), TNT-01689, 2001 CarswellOnt 6372 (Ont. Rental Housing Trib.) where it was held that it constitutes harassment for a landlord to serve notices of termination for money that is not owing or to which the landlord is not legally entitled.

[127] *Elgasuani v. Niazof* (Jan. 25, 2000), TNT-00852, [2000] O.R.H.T.D. No. 188, 2000 CarswellOnt 6452 (Ont. Rental Housing Trib.).

[128] *Blyth et al. v. Feudale* (Oct. 30, 2001), TNT-02197 (Ont. Rental Housing Trib.). The landlord was held responsible for the conduct of the superintendent and was ordered to pay abatements of rent to the applicant tenants.

[129] Landlord and Tenant Board File No. SOT-01685 (Jan. 26, 2009).

[130] Landlord and Tenant Board File No. TNT-01176 / TNL-16360 (Jan. 8, 2009).

[131] Landlord and Tenant Board File No. EAT-01460 / EAT-01572 (Feb. 3, 2009).

[132] Landlord and Tenant Board File No. TET-01511 (Feb. 20, 2009).

[133] (April 18, 2006), SWT-07421, [2006] O.R.H.T.D. No. 62 (Ont. Rental Housing Trib.), at para. 5.

missing rental payments and they were annoyed by these unwarranted and, frankly, patronizing telephone reminders to pay their rent. The Member concluded that this conduct constituted harassment and awarded the tenants a 2% abatement of rent (up to the point in time when they actually did fall into arrears of rent).

In *Grimard v. Knight*,[134] the tenant ceased paying rent because of the landlord's refusal to repair the roof. Instead of dealing with the problem or commencing proceedings to terminate this tenancy (for non-payment of rent), the landlord simply treated the tenancy as if it did not exist and had his agent place a "for rent" sign on the tenants' front lawn. Although this represented only a single incident, the Tribunal found that it constituted harassment and awarded the tenants a 35% rent abatement because "the Landlord's actions represent such intentional disregard for the rights of the Tenants and disrespect for the processes established under the TPA that, in our view, an abatement of rent at the higher end of the spectrum is called for."[135]

In *Campbell v. Workman*,[136] the landlord wrote at least one letter to social assistance alleging that the tenant was not trustworthy and had lied to the landlord and then threatened to call the social assistance hotline and inform on the tenant. On appeal, the Divisional Court upheld the finding of the Member that this conduct constituted harassment and awarded to the tenant an abatement of $6,500.[137]

Obstruction in the context of s. 23 of the R.T.A. may mean preventing a tenant from engaging in lawful activities related to the rental unit or the residential complex, including efforts by the landlord to prevent the tenant from securing or enforcing his or her legal rights as a tenant. In *Hoang v. Marmorato*,[138] the tenant was arrested and charged with drug trafficking. He had allegedly turned this rented house into a marijuana growing operation. When the landlord discovered this, he took back possession of the house (without first obtaining an order from the Tribunal) and refused to return to the tenant any of the personal property that had been left behind when the tenant had been arrested. It was found that the tenancy had not been terminated and that, therefore, the landlord had no legal right to prevent the tenant from re-entering the unit or from retrieving his property. This was found to be obstruction.

---

[134] (March 2, 2006), SWT-07217, [2006] O.R.H.T.D. No. 5 (Ont. Rental Housing Trib.).

[135] *Grimard v. Knight*, (March 2, 2006), SWT-07217, [2006] O.R.H.T.D. No. 5 (Ont. Rental Housing Trib.), para. 22.

[136] (2007), 2007 CarswellOnt 7084 (Ont. Div. Ct.).

[137] The appeal was allowed in part, however, because the Divisional Court held that there was no evidence to support the Member's finding that the landlord had interfered with the tenant's parking space. As a result, the $10,000 abatement that had originally been ordered by the Tribunal for both harassment and substantial interference with reasonable enjoyment was reduced by $3,500.

[138] (Aug. 19, 2002), TNT-02594 (Ont. Rental Housing Trib.).

Coercion typically refers to persuading a person to do something that they do not wish to do (or to refrain from doing something they wish to do) through the use of force or the threat of force.

The concept of *threats* is generally well understood. To offend s. 23 of the R.T.A., the threat need not be one of violence. A landlord is not permitted to threaten a tenant in any way.

In *1109223 Ontario Ltd. v. Plummer*,[139] there was lack of repairs for a long time, and the tenant had to put plastic over her furniture. There were outstanding work orders. The landlord complained about cheques that were N.S.F. (they were not). The tenant felt that she was harassed by management. An abatement of $100 per month was ordered and for harassment, $800.

In *Terriah et al. v. Mishra*,[140] the landlord's continual confrontations and threats of eviction were found to constitute harassment. The Tribunal allowed a 100% abatement of rent for two months and granted the tenants' request to terminate the tenancy.

In *Dean v. Fitchett*,[141] the tenant brought two dogs into the unit, even though the tenant had promised that there would be no pets in the unit. The landlord was very upset. He attempted to threaten and intimidate the tenant into vacating the unit. The tenant brought an application before the Tribunal. The Tribunal awarded an abatement of rent and ordered an administrative fine of $1,000.

In *Young v. Benoit*,[142] the landlord left threatening messages on the tenant's answering machine, broke into the tenant's apartment and threatened the tenant with a knife, sent threatening notes to the tenant, damaged the tenant's vehicle and had others make harassing telephone calls to the tenant's unlisted telephone number. The tenant vacated the rental unit because of this conduct. The Tribunal awarded the tenant a 50% abatement of rent for the period of September 1998 through February 1999 plus a 100% abatement for an additional two months. Since criminal charges were pending against the landlord, the Tribunal declined to impose an administrative fine.

In *McClement v. Kisiel*,[143] in addition to other heinous conduct (including cutting off the heat and electricity to this unit), the landlord threatened to change the locks to the unit (i.e., lock the tenant out). The Tribunal awarded a rent abatement of $1,000 and ordered a fine of $1,000.

Threatening to report alleged criminal conduct (unless the tenant agrees to move out) is a crime and was contrary to the T.P.A.[144] Similarly, it was considered to be a violation of the T.P.A. for a landlord to tell a tenant that

---

[139] (1997), 32 O.T.C. 285 (Ont. Gen. Div.).

[140] (Feb. 16, 1999), EAT-00398 (Ont. Rental Housing Trib.).

[141] (May 20, 1999), TET-00233 (Ont. Rental Housing Trib.).

[142] (March 15, 1999), SWT-00363 (Ont. Rental Housing Trib.).

[143] (March 3, 1999), SWT-00388 (Ont. Rental Housing Trib.).

[144] *Osibayo v. James* (Aug. 6, 2002), TET-02577, [2002] O.R.H.T.D. No. 84, 2002 CarswellOnt 3777 (Ont. Rental Housing Trib.). The landlord in this case was fined $500.

if she did not pay a greater portion of the utility bills, the landlord would report her to the Workplace Safety and Insurance Board.[145]

In *Malik v. Pezzente*,[146] the tenants had caused substantial damage to the unit (see TNL-19048). The landlord's agents threatened to physically remove the tenants and their property if they did not vacate the unit. An abatement equal to one month's rent was awarded to the tenants.[147]

In *Seguin v. Fontaine*,[148] the tenant fell behind in his rent. Instead of following the steps necessary to commence a proceeding before the Rental Housing Tribunal, the landlord sent the tenant notes threatening to lock him out of the rental unit. The landlord then illegally entered the unit while the tenant was absent and either took the tenant's dog or allowed it to follow him home. When the tenant went to see the landlord to confront him about this illegal entry, the landlord assaulted the tenant. The landlord also placed a call to Ontario Works to report that, while he was (illegally) in the rental unit, he saw documents that might indicate that the tenant was not accurately reporting to the government his current address and the rent that he was being charged. The Member described the landlord's conduct as "utterly atrocious" and found that it constituted harassment and a threat as well as an illegal entry into the rental unit. In addition to terminating the tenancy and awarding to the tenant his moving expenses and the difference in rent, the Tribunal also imposed an administrative fine of $500.

Interference is not defined. It *may* mean substantial interference with a lawful right, privilege or interest of the tenant. This would give to tenants rights equivalent to those given to landlords in ss. 64 and 65 of the R.T.A. (including the right to seek remedies before the Board for breach by the landlord of an important term of the tenancy agreement). This was the interpretation adopted in *Tenants of 10 Humberline Dr. v. Toronto Community Housing Corp.*[149]

In *Tenants of 10 Humberline Dr. v. Toronto Community Housing Corp.*,[150] the landlord began to insist that tenants who wished to continue using the parking facilities must provide the landlord with a copy of the vehicle ownership and proof of insurance on the vehicle. Many tenants objected on the basis that this had not been required in the past, that it was an invasion of their privacy and that it was not required by the terms of the tenancy agreement. The Tribunal held that, as the tenancy agreements were currently drafted, the landlord had no legal right to insist on proof of insur-

---

[145] *Oliver v. Satar* (May 28, 2001), TET-01758, [2001] O.R.H.T.D. No. 73, 2001 CarswellOnt 6356 (Ont. Rental Housing Trib.).

[146] (Sept. 14, 2000), TNT-01321, 2000 CarswellOnt 6424 (Ont. Rental Housing Trib.).

[147] Which was then deducted from the amount the tenants were ordered to pay the landlord for the damage they had caused to the unit.

[148] (July 27, 2006), SWT-07419, [2006] O.R.H.T.D. No. 84 (Ont. Rental Housing Trib.).

[149] (June 10, 2004), TNT-03761 (Ont. Rental Housing Trib.).

[150] (June 10, 2004), TNT-03761 (Ont. Rental Housing Trib.).

ance. Therefore, to the extent that the landlord had insisted on proof of insurance, the landlord had interfered with the tenants. The landlord was ordered to refrain from this conduct in the future.[151]

In a similar case,[152] a new landlord took over the building and requested that tenants provide information regarding the make, model and other identifying information regarding their vehicles that they wished to park in the parking lot of the complex. A tenant objected to providing this information and brought an application seeking a declaration that this constituted harassment. She also sought to raise other issues that had been dealt with in a previous application (SOT-01453). The presiding Member found the claim of harassment to be frivolous and found that attempting to re-litigate matters that had already been adjudicated was vexatious. Accordingly, the tenant's application was dismissed, with costs awarded to the landlord.

7. OBLIGATION NOT TO GIVE A NOTICE OF TERMINATION IN BAD FAITH

Landlords are always expected to act in good faith towards their tenants. This is especially true where a landlord gives a notice of termination under s. 48, 49 or 50 of the R.T.A. (formerly ss. 51, 52 and 53 of the T.P.A.). Notices of termination given under s. 48, 49 or 50 are based upon the landlord's statement that the rental unit will be renovated or demolished or converted to a non-residential use or that the rental unit is required for occupation by the landlord or a purchaser or by a specified member of the family of the landlord or a purchaser (or for a caregiver for one of the prescribed persons). The notices of termination, therefore, are grounded upon what the landlord says will be done in the future and not upon events that have already transpired. Because eviction applications under these sections are very difficult to defend against, there is a real potential for abuse by unscrupulous landlords.

The Legislature recognized that a tenant might receive a notice of termination from a landlord given under s. 48, 49 or 50 of the R.T.A. and comply with that notice (i.e., vacate the rental unit by the date set out in the notice of termination), only to later discover that the proposed occupant never moved in or the proposed work was never done. It was therefore felt that a tenant who was duped in this way ought to have some recourse against the landlord who had acted in bad faith. That relief is provided in s. 57 of the R.T.A. The purpose of this section is to discourage landlords from using s. 48, 49 or 50 to obtain vacant possession of a rental unit on false pretences.

Under the T.P.A., an application could only be brought by a tenant who vacated the unit "as a result of the notice". If the tenant vacated the unit for

---

[151] Subject, of course, to the right of the landlord to modify the standard terms of its tenancy agreements (for new tenancies).

[152] Landlord and Tenant Board File No. SOT-01795 (Jan. 12, 2009).

other reasons, no relief was available to the tenant. Decisions concerning whether the Tribunal had the jurisdiction to grant relief where the tenant was forced to vacate the unit as a result of an order (i.e., where the tenant opposed the landlord's eviction application but lost) were inconsistent. One view was that, if the Tribunal made a finding on the landlord's application that the landlord gave the notice in good faith, the tenant was *estopped* from returning to the Tribunal later (on a T5 application) to allege that new evidence shows that the landlord did not, in fact, give the notice of termination in good faith.[153] Not all Members of the Tribunal, however, agreed with this interpretation.[154]

This dilemma has now been resolved by subsection 57(4) of the R.T.A., which provides that in an application under subsection 57(1), the Board may find that the landlord gave a notice of termination in bad faith "despite a previous finding by the Board to the contrary."

Subsection 57(1) of the R.T.A. provides that if a tenant receives a notice of termination under s. 48, 49 or 50 of the R.T.A. and the former tenant vacates the rental unit as a result of the notice or as a result of an application to or order made by the Board based on that notice and then the event described in the notice does not occur within a reasonable period of time (i.e., the person named in the notice has not moved into the rental unit or the work described in the notice has not been done), the tenant may apply to the Board (in Form T5) for a determination that the landlord's notice was given in bad faith. The application must be made within one year after the former tenant vacated the rental unit.[155] If the Board determines that the landlord gave such a notice in bad faith, then the Board may grant such relief as it deems appropriate under subsection 57(3).[156]

In order to be successful on this type of application, a tenant must prove that:

(1) the notice of termination had been given in bad faith; and
(2) the rental unit was not occupied by the person specified in the notice within a reasonable period of time (in the case of a notice under s. 48 or 49) or the unit was not demolished, converted, repaired or renovated as specified in the notice within a reasonable period of time (in the case of a notice under s. 50).

---

[153] *Narine v. Lewis* (Nov. 10, 2003), TEL-28366-RV, 2003 CarswellOnt 5715 (Ont. Rental Housing Trib.).

[154] See *O'Brien v. Williamson* (June 9, 2004), CET-04155, 2004 CarswellOnt 3644 (Ont. Rental Housing Trib.).

[155] Subsection 57(2) of the R.T.A.

[156] See, for example, *McMahon v. Gordon* (June 6, 2003), TST-05710, 2003 CarswellOnt 2655 (Ont. Rental Housing Trib.) in which the Tribunal awarded the tenant $8,400 for the difference in rent as a result of having vacated the rental unit in reliance upon a notice of termination that had been given by the landlord in bad faith.

In *Crawford v. Vos*,[157] the landlord gave a notice to the tenant to vacate the unit so that the landlord's father could reside in the unit. After the tenant vacated the unit, she discovered that the landlord's father was only occasionally staying in the unit and that it was not his principal residence. The Member found this to have been a bad faith misrepresentation:

> To displace this Tenant . . .from her full-time home, to make room for a part-time occupier, whose main use of the unit occurs while engaging in social activities, is not what was contemplated by the legislature. As a result, the Tenant is entitled to compensation for the inconvenience of having to leave.

A lengthy delay between the tenant vacating the unit and the landlord taking possession may raise questions about whether or not the landlord gave the notice in good faith. It will also look very suspicious if a landlord gave a notice indicating that he wanted to move in and then, instead, the unit is rented to a new tenant. In both cases, however, there may be a perfectly innocent explanation. It is possible that, at the time the notice was given, the landlord was acting in good faith but that later events forced the landlord to change his plans.

In *Barnes v. Speers*,[158] the landlords gave a notice of termination for "own use" (under s. 51 of the T.P.A.) but then failed to occupy the rental unit. The tenants commenced a T5 application. The evidence from the landlords was that they had intended to move in but then one of the landlords was diagnosed with cancer and was very ill and could not move. The Member held that although the landlords had not occupied the unit within a reasonable period of time, the Member was not convinced that the notice of termination had been given in bad faith. Since the tenants had failed to prove one of the two essential elements, their application was dismissed.

In *Beatson and Agostino*,[159] the Tribunal held that the landlord acted in bad faith when giving notice of termination for personal possession and not moving in but selling the house. The Tribunal imposed a fine of $1,000 and also awarded the tenant her moving costs and the difference in rent. The Tribunal declined to grant compensatory damages as this would not come within s. 35(1)(*e*) of the T.P.A. (now clause 57(3)4 of the R.T.A.).

In *Morritt v. Sedore*,[160] the landlord gave a notice that he required the house for his own use. The tenants complied with the notice and vacated the house. The tenants noticed that, almost one year later, the landlord had still not moved into the house. They filed a T5 application. Around the same time, the landlord finally moved into the house. The landlord was able to explain his delay in occupying the unit (due largely to unforeseen serious health

---

[157] (May 29, 2003), EAT-04416 (Ont. Rental Housing Trib.).

[158] (Oct. 8, 1999), SWT-00291 (Ont. Rental Housing Trib.).

[159] (May 27, 1999), SOT-00382 (Ont. Rental Housing Trib.).

[160] (Feb. 4, 2003), TNT-03196, [2003] O.R.H.T.D. No. 18, 2003 CarswellOnt 1508 (Ont. Rental Housing Trib.).

problems). The application was dismissed both on the basis that the landlord was found to have given the notice in good faith and on the basis that, on the facts of this particular case, a year was a reasonable period of time.

In *Diamand v. Sheep Island Investment Corp.*,[161] the reviewing Member found that, at the time the notice of termination was given to the tenant, the landlord did genuinely intend to move into the rental unit but that the landlord's plans changed due to events that occurred subsequent to the tenant vacating the unit. As a result, the former tenant's application alleging that the landlord had acted in bad faith was dismissed.

In Landlord and Tenant Board File No. NOT-00964 (Feb. 24, 2009), due to economic and personal difficulties, the landlords planned to sell their large home and move into the smaller one they were renting out. After receiving a notice of termination the tenants vacated the unit (although they had probably planned to leave in any event). The landlords renovated the small house in anticipation of moving in and listed their home for sale but found that they could not sell it. They then became aware of a single mother who was looking for a home and decided to allow her to rent the small house. The former tenants brought an application under s. 57 of the R.T.A. The presiding Member held that, at the time the notice of termination was given, the landlords genuinely intended to move into the rental unit and that they had not given the notice in bad faith.

Another case where circumstances changed can be found in Landlord and Tenant Board File No. TET-00001 (Feb. 19, 2007). The landlord and his wife and child lived on the main floor of the house. There was a rental unit in the basement. The landlord's wife, as a result of mental illness, was abusing their child and, because she refused to get treatment, Children's Aid intervened and required her to live apart from the rest of the family. The landlord and his wife executed a separation agreement. Apparently, it was acceptable to Children's Aid if the landlord's wife moved into the self-contained basement unit. Thus, the landlord gave notice to the tenant occupying that unit that he required the unit for occupation by his wife. Because the tenant was pregnant, the landlord gave her some additional time before having to move out and she did agree to vacate the premises. Subsequently, she discovered that the landlord had rented the unit to someone else. The evidence disclosed that, after the tenant vacated the unit, the landlord's wife agreed to get treatment, was allowed to continue living with her family and, consequently, did not require the basement apartment. Based on the foregoing, the Member found that when the landlord gave the tenant the notice of termination, the landlord had been acting in good faith and the tenant's application was dismissed.

---

[161] (July 25, 2002), TST-03634-RV (Ont. Rental Housing Trib.).

In *Venittelli, Re*,[162] the tenants filed an application concerning an illegal rent increase. Four days later, the landlord served upon the tenants a notice requiring them to vacate the unit so that the landlord's son could move in. The tenants complied with the notice of termination and vacated the rental unit. The landlord's son moved into the unit but within two or three days the unit was advertised as "for rent" and the son moved out of the unit shortly thereafter. The Member found that the landlord had "enacted this elaborate scheme in order to remove the Tenants from the first floor apartment so that she might achieve the desired rent increases". The Member found that the landlord gave the tenants the notice in bad faith and ordered the landlord to pay the tenants $900 (representing the difference in rent at their new unit) and $224.46 for moving and other out-of-pocket expenses. The Member also imposed an administrative fine of $250.

In *Cottrell v. Howell*,[163] a Member gave a rather unique interpretation to para. 32(1)10 of the T.P.A. The landlord in this case gave the tenants 90 days notice to vacate based upon the landlord's stated intention of doing extensive renovations (s. 53 of the T.P.A.). The landlord did not inform the tenants of their right to first refusal (s. 56 of the T.P.A.). The tenants moved out and then commenced a T5 application. The parties in this case agreed that the renovations were completed within a reasonable period of time. Nevertheless, for failing to inform the tenants of their right of first refusal, the Member found that the notice had been given in bad faith and awarded to the tenants one year's difference in rent. The main problem with this decision, as I see it, is that it ignores that para. 32(1)10 of the T.P.A. made relief conditional on a finding that the notice of termination was given in bad faith AND that the landlord did not renovate the rental unit within a reasonable time after the tenant vacated the unit. It also blurs the distinction between giving a notice that is deficient and giving a notice in bad faith; the fact that a notice may be void because it does not contain all of the required information does not necessarily mean that it was given by the landlord in bad faith. Given the unusual facts of this case and the unique interpretation adopted by the Member, I would suggest caution in relying upon this decision as a precedent.

An interesting issue arises where a landlord gives a notice of termination on behalf of a purchaser. If the purchaser does not actually move into the unit within a reasonable period of time, against whom should the former tenant seek relief? It is not clear that the Board has any power to make an order against a former landlord. Since "landlord" includes a successor in title and since the former landlord was acting on behalf of the purchaser, it would seem to make sense to hold that purchaser and only that purchaser accountable. This was the reasoning in *Quan, Re*[164] in which the Vice-chair overturned

---

[162] (February 2, 2006), SOT-05261, 2006 CarswellOnt 9155 (Ont. Rental Housing Trib.).

[163] (July 8, 2004), CET-04190, 2004 CarswellOnt 3638 (Ont. Rental Housing Trib.).

[164] (April 18, 2006), TST-08544-RV, 2006 CarswellOnt 9172 (Ont. Rental Housing Trib.).

an earlier decision of the Tribunal and ruled that the innocent landlord who had served the notice of termination on behalf of a purchaser should not have to bear responsibility for the subsequent conduct of that purchaser. One wonders whether the Tribunal might have come to a different conclusion had there been evidence that the vendor and purchaser had knowingly colluded to deceive the tenant.

8. OBLIGATIONS WITH RESPECT TO EVICTED TENANT'S PROPERTY

Section 41 of the R.T.A. (formerly s. 42 of the T.P.A.) applies if the premises are vacated as a result of:

(a) a notice of termination,
(b) an agreement between the parties to terminate the tenancy,
(c) the tenant of superintendent's premises voluntarily leaving the unit when his or her employment ends (s. 93(2)), or
(d) an order of the Board terminating the tenancy or evicting the tenant.

With respect to a rental unit that has been vacated as a result of (1) a notice of termination, (2) the landlord and tenant agreeing to terminate the tenancy, or (3) the tenant vacating the superintendent's premises within one week of the termination of the tenancy, the landlord is free to sell, retain for the landlord's own use or otherwise dispose of property in the rental unit or in the residential complex. In other words, the landlord is free to do as the landlord wishes with goods left behind by a tenant who vacates the rental unit without enforcement of an eviction order.[165]

Where the landlord actually has to enforce an eviction order in order to regain possession of the rental unit, the landlord may not sell, retain or otherwise dispose of the tenant's property before 72 hours have elapsed after the enforcement of the eviction order.[166] This is an increase from the 48-hour period formerly required under the T.P.A. During that 72-hour period, the landlord must make the evicted tenant's property available between the hours of 8 a.m. and 8 p.m.[167] If the tenant has not collected his or her property within the stated 72-hour period, the landlord is then free to sell, retain for the landlord's own use or to otherwise dispose of the property left behind by the evicted tenant.

A landlord and a tenant may agree to terms other than those set out in s. 41 with regard to the disposal of the tenant's property.[168] To avoid misunderstandings, any such agreement should be in writing.

---

[165] Subsection 41(1) of the R.T.A.
[166] Subsection 41(2) of the R.T.A.
[167] Subsection 41(3) of the R.T.A. and s. 46 of O. Reg. 516/06.
[168] Subsection 41(5) of the R.T.A.

Where a former tenant believes that the landlord has not complied with the requirements of s. 41 of the R.T.A., the former tenant may commence an application under subsection 41(6). Unlike other tenant applications, no time limit is imposed by the R.T.A. for commencing this type of application. Presumably, that means that the time limit imposed by the *Limitations Act* applies (i.e., two years). It is advisable, however, to commence this type of application immediately, as any delay will make it more difficult to retrieve the property in question or to prove the nature or value of this property.

For more information about disposal of property, please refer to Chapter 18.

9. PROCEDURE

A tenant generally has one year in which to pursue relief for a breach by the landlord of the tenant's rights under the R.T.A.[169] Usually, the tenant must commence his or her own application in order to get the issue before the Landlord and Tenant Board. If, however, the landlord brings the tenant before the Board to collect alleged arrears of rent, pursuant to s. 82 of the R.T.A. (and subsection 87(2)), the tenant can raise any issue(s) the tenant wants at that hearing and have the issue(s) heard by the Board as if the tenant had filed his or her own application.[170]

In this part of the chapter, I will describe the typical steps that must be taken by a tenant who wishes to commence his or her own application against the landlord.

If a tenant or former tenant[171] believes that the landlord has violated the tenant's rights described in ss. 21 through 27 of the R.T.A., the tenant may apply to the Board under s. 29 for various types of relief (listed in s. 31 of the R.T.A. and described in detail in the next section of this chapter). If a landlord does not comply with the provisions of subsections 41(2) and (3) of the R.T.A. (i.e., the landlord does not make an evicted tenant's property available for retrieval during the relevant period), the former tenant may apply to the Board for relief under subsection 41(6) of the R.T.A. An application under s. 29 or 41 is made in Form T2. There is no filing fee.

Pursuant to s. 29(2), the application (based upon a breach of ss. 21 through 27) cannot be brought more than one year after the day "the alleged conduct giving rise to the application occurred". It is up to the tenant to apply promptly.

---

[169] Subsections 29(2) and 57(2) of the R.T.A. Note that since a time limit does not appear to be set out in the R.T.A. for applications commenced under s. 41, presumably a two-year limitation period will apply as per the *Limitations Act.*

[170] See Chapters 1 and 16 for further analysis of the impact of s. 82.

[171] Even after the tenancy has ended, a former tenant can apply for relief (usually an abatement of rent previously paid to the landlord) for breaches of the landlord's obligations that occurred during the tenancy.

There is a concept in some areas of tort law that a limitation period does not begin to run until the injured party knows or ought to know of the harm (the "discoverability doctrine"). The Tribunal held that this doctrine does not apply to cases before the Tribunal and that the limitation period created by s. 29(2) is a strict one.[172] The Board has adopted the same approach and has held that "there will be no extension of the limitations imposed by the statute."[173]

There is no deadline set out in the R.T.A. for filing a T2 application concerning an alleged breach of s. 41 (regarding the property of an evicted tenant). Obviously, the quicker such an application is brought, the more likely the tenant will be able to recover his or her property or at least prove the nature and value of the property in question.

A tenant should not choose to file a T2 application simply because it is free. If the complaint is really about maintenance, a T6 application should be filed. If the complaint is really about the reduction or discontinuance of services, a T3 application should be filed. If the complaint is really about money collected or retained illegally, a T1 application should be filed. If the complaint is really about the failure of the landlord to consent to an assignment or sublet, a Form A2 should be filed. If a tenant commences the wrong type of application, the Board may dismiss the application and make the tenant start over again.[174] If a limitation period has expired in the meantime, this could prove fatal to the tenant's claims.

Of course, some issues may involve breaches of more than one provision of the R.T.A. For instance, a serious maintenance problem can also affect a tenant's reasonable enjoyment of the unit. Combining several types of applications and having them heard together can also be appropriate for a tenant. This will be discussed further in Chapter 16.

Under the T.P.A., tenants sometimes filed a T2 application in response to a landlord's application. The tenant's application was often scheduled for a date later than the landlord's application. Typically, on the date scheduled for the hearing of the landlord's application, the tenant would request that the hearing be adjourned so that both applications could be heard together on the date scheduled for the tenant's application. While such requests were often granted, that was not always the case.

Hearing the two applications together made sense because if the landlord was found to be in serious breach of the landlord's obligations, no eviction could be granted (para. 84(2)(a) of the T.P.A. — now para. 83(3)(a) of the R.T.A.). Sometimes, however, the landlord or the Tribunal would suspect

---

[172] *Mota v. 1138639 Ontario Inc.* (Jan. 26, 2005), TST-07152, 2005 CarswellOnt 1282 (Ont. Rental Housing Trib.).

[173] Landlord and Tenant Board File No. SOL-17144 (Feb. 18, 2009).

[174] *Vega v. 1413211 Ontario Ltd.* (Dec. 12, 2001), TET-02219, [2001] O.R.H.T.D. No. 147, (Ont. Rental Housing Trib.).

that the request for an adjournment was simply a stalling tactic. After all, if there were legitimate or serious problems, why did the tenant wait to do something about it until the landlord commenced an application?

Given the new ability of tenants (under s. 82) to raise issues at the hearing of the landlord's arrears application, the Board may be more reluctant to grant a tenant's request for an adjournment. Since it is the tenant who is raising the issue at the hearing, the tenant should be ready to present evidence to support his or her allegations. It is the landlord who will likely request an adjournment if the landlord is taken by surprise by the tenant's allegations.

Finally, the events about which the tenant is complaining must have occurred during the tenancy. The Board generally has no jurisdiction to deal with events that occur before the commencement of the tenancy or after the termination of the tenancy (with the exception of the landlord's obligations under s. 41).

If a former tenant believes that the landlord has given a notice of termination under s. 48, 49 or 50 in bad faith, the former tenant may apply to the Board under subsection 57(1) for relief under subsection 57(3) of the R.T.A. The application is in Form T5. There is no filing fee. The application must be filed within one year after the former tenant vacated the rental unit.[175]

Regardless of the type of application, unless the tenant is relying upon s. 82, the tenant must file a completed application with the Board, obtain a notice of hearing and then serve the application and notice of hearing upon the landlord.[176]

For most tenant applications, the application form and the notice of hearing must be served on the landlord at least 10 days before the hearing (Rule 10.1) and the certificate of service should be filed with the Board within five days after service has been completed. For illegal lockout cases and cases where the landlord is preventing an evicted tenant from retrieving the property left behind at the residential complex, the tenant need only provide five days notice of the hearing (Rule 10.5(a) and Rule 10.5(b) of the Board's Rules of Practice).

10. REMEDIES

(a) General

(i) Remedies for Breach of Sections 21-27

Most tenant applications concern an allegation that one or more of ss. 21 through 27 of the R.T.A. have been violated. Such applications are com-

---

[175] Subsection 57(2) of the R.T.A.

[176] See Chapter 16 for a discussion about proper methods for service.

menced under s. 29. Before any relief can be granted in such cases, the Board must make a determination that such a breach has occurred. This determination must appear in the order.[177] Once there has been such a determination, the Board can then consider what relief is appropriate to grant from the list of possible remedies set out in subsection 31(1) of the R.T.A.

Pursuant to s. 31(1) of the R.T.A. (formerly s. 35(1) of the T.P.A.), once the Board has determined that a landlord, superintendent or agent of the landlord has done one or more of the activities set out in paras. 2 to 6 of subsection 29(1), the Board may do one or more of the following:

i. Terminate the tenancy;
ii. Prohibit similar conduct in the future;
iii. Order an abatement of rent;
iv. Award compensation for lost or damaged property and other reasonable out-of-pocket expenses;
v. Impose an administrative fine not exceeding the greater of $10,000 and the monetary jurisdiction of the Small Claims Court;[178]
vi. Make any other order that it considers appropriate.

Where the tenant was induced by the conduct of the landlord, the superintendent or an agent of the landlord to vacate the rental unit, the Board may, in addition to the remedies set out above, order that the landlord pay compensation for the tenant's moving expenses and all or any portion of any increased rent (for up to one year) that the tenant will have to pay as a result of the move (s. 31(2)).

(ii) Special Provisions Relating to Illegal Lockouts

When a tenant has been illegally locked out of his or her rental unit, usually the first thing that the tenant wants is to regain access to the unit. The tenant's personal possessions are in the unit, the tenant may have a pet inside the unit and the tenant may have nowhere else to live. Time is of the essence. Occasionally, the police are willing to intervene; usually, however, the police take the position that it is a landlord and tenant matter and that the parties should take their dispute before the Landlord and Tenant Board.

When the T.P.A. was first enacted, it was not clear whether the Tribunal had the jurisdiction to put a tenant back into possession in such circumstances.[179] Some Tribunal Members found that the Tribunal did have the power to grant such a remedy under s. 23 of the *Statutory Powers Procedure Act* (which permits a tribunal to make such orders as are necessary to prevent

---

[177] Subsection 29(1) of the R.T.A.

[178] The monetary jurisdiction of the Small Claims Court is scheduled to be increased to $25,000, effective January 2010.

[179] Subsections 35(3), (4) and (5) of the T.P.A. did not exist at that time.

an abuse of process). There was, however, no standard procedure for dealing with illegal lockout cases and no practical means of forcing the landlord to comply with an order of the Tribunal ordering that the tenant be put back into possession. There was also the issue of what to do about an innocent new tenant who may have just moved into the unit and who would be dispossessed if the former tenant were allowed to take back the rental unit. Consequently, subsections (3), (4) and (5) were added to s. 35 of the T.P.A. to provide a uniform and practical approach to these situations. These provisions are now found in subsections 31(3), (4) and (5) of the R.T.A.

The most important step for the tenant to take is to get the matter before the Board as quickly as possible. The tenant can commence a T2 application and can request an order, on an emergency basis, abridging the normal time for service upon the landlord of the application and notice of hearing. The tenant should request that the hearing be within 24 to 48 hours. The tenant must then serve the landlord with the application, notice of hearing and interim order (if any) in accordance with the Rules (and any direction from the Board) to ensure that the landlord is aware of and participates in the hearing. If the tenant cannot obtain an order abridging the time for service, then Rule 10.5(a) provides that the tenant must serve a copy of the application and notice of hearing upon the landlord at least five days before the hearing date.

In addition, or in the alternative, the tenant can contact the Investigations and Enforcement Unit of the Ministry of Municipal Affairs and Housing. They are often willing to intervene to assist tenants by educating landlords about the R.T.A. and the possible consequences to the landlord (including prosecution) for breaches of the Act. Sometimes a telephone call from this Unit is all that is needed to solve the problem.

Once the parties actually appear at a hearing before a Member, if the Member determines that the landlord, superintendent or agent of the landlord has altered the locking system on a door giving entry to the rental unit or the residential complex, or caused the locking system to be altered, during the tenant's occupancy of the rental unit and without giving the tenant replacement keys and *if the Board is satisfied that the rental unit is vacant*, the Member may, in addition to the other remedies set out in ss. 31(1) and 31(2), order that the landlord allow the tenant to recover possession of the rental unit and that the landlord refrain from renting the unit to anyone else (s. 31(3) of the R.T.A.). Since this type of order cannot be granted unless the Board is satisfied that the rental unit is vacant, the tenant will need to adduce evidence to this effect. This is why it is so important to have the landlord or a representative of the landlord present at these hearings.

Such an order will typically be an interim order as the Member will likely wish to retain jurisdiction over the matter and decide what other remedies are appropriate once the Member knows whether or not the landlord cooperated in allowing the tenant back into the unit. Pursuant to s. 31(4), such an order has the same effect and can be enforced in the same manner as a writ of possession. This means that the tenant can file the order with the Sheriff's Office and enlist the services of the sheriff in helping the tenant physically take back control of the rental unit. This type of order has a limited lifespan, however. Such an order automatically expires at the end of the 15th day after it is issued if it has not been filed with the appropriate Sheriff's Office (para. 31(5)(a)). Alternatively, if it has been filed with the correct Sheriff's Office, it will automatically expire at the end of the 45th day after it was issued (para. 31(5)(b)). In other words, such an order must be filed with the sheriff within 15 days and be enforced by the sheriff within 45 days of the date it was issued.

(iii) Remedies for Bad Faith Notice (s. 57)

Pursuant to s. 57 (3) of the R.T.A., once the Board has determined that a landlord gave a notice of termination in bad faith contrary to subsection 57(1), the Board may do one or more of the following:

i. order that the landlord pay a specified sum to the former tenant for all or any portion of any increased rent that the former tenant has incurred or will incur for a one-year period after vacating the rental unit;
ii. order that the landlord pay a specified sum to the former tenant for reasonable out-of-pocket moving, storage and other like expenses that the former tenant has incurred or will incur;
iii. order an abatement of rent;
iv. impose an administrative fine not exceeding the greater of $10,000 and the monetary jurisdiction of the Small Claims Court;[180]
v. make any other order that it considers appropriate.

(iv) Remedies Where Evicted Tenant Is Denied Access to Property (s. 41)

If the Landlord and Tenant Board determines that a landlord has breached an obligation under subsection 41(2) or (3), the Board may, pursuant to s. 41(6) of the R.T.A., do one or more of the following:

1. order that the landlord not breach the obligation again;
2. order that the landlord return to the former tenant property of the former tenant that is in the possession or control of the landlord;
3. order that the landlord pay a specified sum to the former tenant for,

---

[180] The monetary jurisdiction of the Small Claims Court is scheduled to be increased to $25,000, effective January 2010.

i. the reasonable costs that the former tenant has incurred or will incur in repairing or, where repairing is not reasonable, replacing property of the former tenant that was damaged, destroyed or disposed of as a result of the landlord's breach, and
ii. other reasonable out-of-pocket expenses that the former tenant has incurred or will incur as a result of the landlord's breach;

4. order that the landlord pay to the Board an administrative fine not exceeding the greater of $10,000 and the monetary jurisdiction of the Small Claims Court;[181]

5. make any other order that it considers appropriate.

For more information about disposal of property, please refer to Chapter 18.

(b) Terminate the Tenancy

Paragraph 31(1)(e) of the R.T.A. provides the Board with the power to terminate a tenancy at the request of a tenant where the Board finds that a landlord, superintendent or agent of the landlord has done one or more of the activities set out in paras. 2 to 6 of s. 29(1). The Board's Interpretation Guideline 6 suggests the types of situations where termination of the tenancy may be appropriate:

(1) Where the conduct of the landlord, superintendent or agent of the landlord has induced the tenant to vacate the unit and the Board wishes to relieve the tenant of any potential liability to the landlord under the tenancy agreement;
(2) Where the landlord and tenant agree that the tenancy should be terminated;
(3) Where the health or safety of the tenant is put in jeopardy by the continuation of the tenancy; and
(4) Where the relationship between the landlord and tenant has deteriorated to such a degree that it is unreasonable for the tenancy to continue.

It is important for landlords and Members of the Board to remember that this remedy can only be granted at the tenant's request or with the tenant's consent. It is the tenant's application and the tenancy cannot be terminated unless that is something the tenant desires. In essence, the Board cannot evict the tenant when it is the tenant who came to the Board looking for help! Once the tenant has requested and been granted such an order, however, there is

[181] The monetary jurisdiction of the Small Claims Court is scheduled to be increased to $25,000, effective January 2010.

no going back.[182] A new provision under the R.T.A. (s. 32) now permits landlords to enforce such orders by way of eviction. Thus, if the Board terminates the tenancy at the tenant's request, the tenant must leave by the termination date set out in the order or the landlord can file the order with the Sheriff's Office and have the tenant evicted.

In Landlord and Tenant Board File No. SOT-00078 (March 27, 2007), the superintendent received a package for the tenants, opened the tenants' door a crack and placed the package inside the unit, then relocked the door to the unit. Unbeknownst to the superintendent, he had triggered a silent alarm that the tenants had installed in their unit. Although, in most circumstances, this would be considered a relatively minor breach of the *Act*, the male tenant in this case was a protected refugee who had endured unpleasant events in his past. For this tenant, his past experiences put this breach of privacy in a whole different context. He testified that, since the incident, he had flashes of past events that he had been trying to forget, that he could not sleep at night and that he simply no longer felt secure within this complex. This was, admittedly, an isolated incident where the superintendent did not physically enter the unit and had meant to be helpful. The landlord had apologized to the tenants. Nevertheless, the effect was disproportionate because of the particular sensitivity of one of the tenants. In these circumstances, the Member granted the tenants' request to terminate the tenancy but declined to grant any other relief against the landlord. A similar approach was taken in Landlord and Tenant Board File No. SWT-02002 (Feb. 13, 2009).

(c) Prohibit Conduct

Where the Board determines that a landlord, superintendent or agent of the landlord has done one or more of the activities set out in paras. 2 to 6 of s. 29(1), according to para. 31(1)(a) of the R.T.A., the Board may "order that the landlord, superintendent or agent may not engage in any further activities listed in those paragraphs against any of the tenants in the residential complex."

Such a prohibition may be used in conjunction with other remedies or on its own. For instance, where there has been an isolated and relatively minor breach of the R.T.A. (such as entry into the unit for a legitimate reason but without strict compliance with the notice requirements), the Board may simply order that, in the future, the landlord not enter any rental unit except in compliance with the provisions of the *Act*.[183]

---

[182] Unless, of course, the tenant is able to negotiate with the landlord an extension of time, a continuation of the old tenancy or the creation of a new tenancy.

[183] See, for example, Landlord and Tenant Board File No. SOT-01847 (Feb. 10, 2009) and Landlord and Tenant Board File No. SOT-01850 (Feb. 10, 2009).

The Board's Interpretation Guideline 6 suggests that the main factor for the Board in deciding whether or not to make such an order is whether it is in the public interest to deter the respondent from any further occurrence of actions against tenants. In practical terms, there is no way to enforce such an order. Its real value is in helping another Member or judge decide an appropriate penalty on a subsequent application or prosecution should an allegation be made that, notwithstanding the earlier order of the Board (or Tribunal), the landlord, superintendent or agent continued to engage in the prohibited conduct against a tenant or tenants of the residential complex. Obviously, if the landlord has ignored an earlier order, the penalty the second time around is likely to be much more severe.

(d) Abatement of Rent

An abatement of rent is a monetary award expressed in terms of past or future rent. It may be a lump sum payment the landlord is ordered to pay the tenant (which effectively orders the landlord to refund a part of the rent paid) or it may be an order to allow the tenant to pay less rent by a certain amount or percentage (or even to pay no rent) for a specified period, or a combination of these.

The Rental Housing Tribunal generally took the view that an abatement of rent was the "starting point for deciding among the possible remedies" and was the "principal remedy which compensates the tenant for the respondent's actions".[184] Since rent is paid to the landlord, an abatement of rent can only be ordered against the landlord.[185] If the offensive conduct represents an isolated but very serious event (such as an illegal lockout) then it may be appropriate to award an abatement equal to one to two months' rent. If the conduct is less serious but occurs over a period of time, it is usually more appropriate to calculate the abatement as a proportion of the rent over the months during which the tenant had to endure that conduct. The size of the abatement should reflect the seriousness of the conduct in question. For relatively minor breaches of the R.T.A., an abatement of rent, if granted, will typically be in the range of 5% to 10%. More serious breaches typically result in abatements of up to 50%. If the degree of disruption changes over time, the abatement awarded should reflect this as well. Ultimately, there are no hard and fast rules and the matter is within the discretion of the adjudicator.

An abatement of 30% of the rent was granted to tenants in an apartment building for the period in which, because of lack of security, some apartments

---

[184] Ontario Rental Housing Tribunal Interpretation Guideline No. 6. Although these quotes can no longer be found in the Board's Interpretation Guideline (No. 6), it is expected that the Board will adopt a similar approach.

[185] I.e., the superintendent or other agent of the landlord cannot be ordered to pay an abatement of rent.

were being used at all hours by drug traffickers, drug users and prostitutes: *Guiliani v. Eelkins.*[186]

In the past, where work within the residential complex has substantially interfered with a tenant's reasonable enjoyment of the complex, abatements have been awarded in the range of 5% to 25%. Section 8 of O. Reg. 516/06 (discussed previously in this Chapter) will make it more difficult for tenants to succeed on such applications. Given the restrictions of s. 8 of O. Reg. 516/06, even where the Board finds that it can grant an abatement, the amount of the abatement will rarely exceed 25% of the rent charged during the period of the disturbance.

Harassment and illegal entry by the landlord were considered by the Tribunal in *Simpson and Mulligan.*[187] The landlord took some unexplained objection to the tenant having a lady friend visit from time to time and demanded by threatening letters that this must not happen again, followed up by notice of termination. The landlord also alleged that she had caused damage to the apartment. The landlord entered illegally and forcibly removed the lady friend. Also, in an effort to drive out the tenant, the landlord told a plumber not to finish repairs to the kitchen and bathroom sinks, which could not be used for six weeks. For harassment, s. 32(1)3 of the T.P.A., the Tribunal ordered a partial abatement of rent for four months and 100% for one month. Next, under s. 35(1)(*e*) of the T.P.A. (make any other order the Tribunal considers appropriate), for the illegal entry and trespass the Tribunal ordered general damages of $2,500 and exemplary damages of $1,000.[188]

In another lack of repair and damages case, over a period of two years, the tenants complained about mice and a leaking ceiling. The court referred to the loss of use and enjoyment of the premises and awarded damages of $3,000 to be paid forthwith: *Scott v. Toronto (City) Non-Profit Housing Corp.*[189]

A somewhat unusual application by a tenant for an abatement of rent occurred because the landlord had cut down a number of trees which the judge said "virtually denuded the land surrounding the residence". He reduced the rent by $100 per month retroactive to the date the trees were cut down and ongoing until there was a replanting of trees: *Dovey v. Glynn.*[190]

An abatement of $20 per month was granted for poor garbage service, $15 per month for failure to repair an apartment unit, and $15 per month for

---

[186] Lawyer's Weekly #946-004 (Ont. Dist. Ct.).

[187] (October 7, 1999), SOT-00544 (Ont. Rental Housing Trib.).

[188] Note that this decision came before amendments to s. 35 of the T.P.A. that specifically allowed for the award of certain types of damages and before the Divisional Court decision determining that the Tribunal did not have the jurisdiction to award punitive or exemplary damages: *Campbell et al. v. Maytown Inc. et al.* (Nov. 7, 2005), Div. Ct. File No. 71732/04.

[189] (October 14, 1988), Doc. M135788/86 (Ont. Dist. Ct.).

[190] (1991), 1991 CarswellOnt 2461 (Ont. Gen. Div.).

the tenant's inconvenience, annoyance and discomfort. The landlord was ordered to make repairs: *Aprioi Investments v. Moreno.*[191]

Harassment of a tenant by the landlord or the landlord's superintendent can lead to an abatement of rent, as it did in *Ryan v. Parkinson.*[192] The landlord deliberately and unjustifiably used verbally abusive and profane language and demanded that the tenant vacate, which caused her personal upset and discomfort of a substantial nature, and breached the tenant's right to enjoy the covenant of quiet enjoyment. An abatement of $475 was ordered. The landlord was told by the court to desist.

For allowing the police into a tenant's unit without a warrant, which then resulted in the tenant being arrested and charged for growing marijuana plants, the Tribunal awarded an abatement of rent equal to one month's rent (a 50% abatement over a two-month period).[193]

The Tribunal ordered a rent abatement of $500 where the landlord had threatened to report the tenant to the WSIB.[194]

For illegal entry by the landlord into the rental unit, threatening to evict the tenant and failing to properly maintain the unit, the Tribunal awarded a lump sum abatement roughly equal to one month's rent.[195]

For an illegal lockout by the landlord, the Tribunal awarded an abatement of one month's rent (as well as moving expenses and imposing an administrative fine).[196]

In a case where the landlord harassed the tenants with continual confrontations and threats of eviction, the Tribunal allowed a 100% abatement of rent for two months and granted the tenants' request to terminate the tenancy.[197]

In *Wu v. Singh,*[198] the landlords verbally abused the tenants, repeatedly made racist comments to them and coerced them into moving out. The Tribunal awarded an abatement equal to two months' rent and imposed an administrative fine equal to four months' rent.

For the landlord's failure to deal with the tenant's legitimate complaints about interference with her enjoyment of the rental unit caused by intermittent noise and cigarette smoke coming through the "porous" floor of this rental

---

[191] (1991), 1991 CarswellOnt 2323 (Ont. Gen. Div.).

[192] (1994), 19 O.R. (3d) 475 (Ont. Gen. Div.).

[193] *McGarvey v. Purton* (May 9, 2003), EAL-31352, EAT-03878, [2003] O.R.H.T.D. No. 64, 2003 CarswellOnt 2665 (Ont. Rental Housing Trib.).

[194] *Oliver v. Satar* (May 28, 2001), TET-01758, [2001] O.R.H.T.D. No. 73, 2001 CarswellOnt 6356 (Ont. Rental Housing Trib.).

[195] *Muir v. 1045838 Ontario Inc. et al.* (Nov. 6, 2001), TNT-02202 (Ont. Rental Housing Trib.).

[196] *Essex v. Lee* (June 2, 1999), TNT-00486, 1999 CarswellOnt 5804 (Ont. Rental Housing Trib.).

[197] *Terriah et al. v. Mishra* (Feb. 16, 1999), EAT-00398 (Ont. Rental Housing Trib.).

[198] (Oct. 14, 1998), SOT-00109 (Ont. Rental Housing Trib.).

unit, the tenant was awarded an abatement roughly equal to 10% of the rent over the period she was affected.[199]

In *Speiran v. Verrilli*,[200] the landlord refused to pay the hydro bills for the rental unit. As a result, the hydro service was cut off and was only reconnected (at a cost of $128 to the tenants) when the tenants transferred the hydro account into their name. The landlord was ordered to have the hydro account transferred back into his name and to pay the tenants $128 as an abatement of rent. It was further ordered that, if the landlord failed to comply with these terms, the tenants could deduct from future rent the rent abatement ordered plus any further amounts they were forced to pay to ensure uninterrupted hydro service to the rental unit.

In *Chadwick v. MacDonald*,[201] the tenant claimed (amongst other things) that the landlord failed to take adequate steps to address her complaints about the conduct of the basement tenant and the guests of that tenant that substantially interfered with Ms. Chadwick's reasonable enjoyment of the complex. The tenant also complained about the $491.25 she had to pay for a hydro bill that ought to have been paid by the basement tenant or the landlord. The tenant was awarded a lump-sum abatement of $600 for the landlord's failure to take appropriate steps to deal with the conduct of the basement tenant (and his guests) and a further abatement of $491.25 to compensate the tenant for the hydro payment she was wrongly forced to incur.

In *Laporte v. Ladouceur*,[202] the basement tenant was disturbing the tenant in the unit above. The landlord failed to take effective action to deal with the problem. The tenant was awarded an abatement equal to one month's rent.

The Divisional Court awarded a 50% rent abatement for the period during which the tenant and members of his family were being harassed by other tenants of the complex and the landlord failed to take reasonable steps within a reasonable period of time to restore to the tenant the quiet enjoyment to which he was entitled.[203]

Where the landlord was held responsible for failing to adequately screen a tenant who was permitted to move into the unit and then disturbed his neighbours, the neighbouring tenant was awarded a 10% abatement of rent over the relevant time period (as well as moving expenses and the difference in rent for twelve months).[204]

---

[199] *Satchithananthan v. Cacciola* (Dec. 30, 2002), TST-04047, 2002 CarswellOnt 5023 (Ont. Rental Housing Trib.). The landlord was also ordered to renovate the floor of the unit to help reduce sound transmission from below.

[200] (Oct. 21, 1999), TNT-00733, 1999 CarswellOnt 5830 (Ont. Rental Housing Trib.).

[201] (Feb. 29, 2000), TNT-00903 (Ont. Rental Housing Trib.).

[202] (Sept. 12, 2001), EAT-02975, [2001] O.R.H.T.D. No. 120, 2001 CarswellOnt 6329 (Ont. Rental Housing Trib.).

[203] *Hassan v. Niagara Housing Authority* (2000), 48 R.P.R. (3d) 297, 2001 CarswellOnt 4890, [2000] O.J. 5650 (Ont. Div. Ct.).

[204] *Donahue v. Clace* (Dec. 4, 2000), NOT-00511, [2000] O.R.H.T.D. No. 168, 2000 CarswellOnt 6407 (Ont. Rental Housing Trib.).

In *Blyth et al. v. Feudale*,[205] an application was brought by tenants of two different units to complain about harassment and verbal abuse by the superintendent. The landlord was aware of the allegations but did nothing to control the conduct of the superintendent. The tenant of one unit was awarded a lump-sum abatement equal to one month's rent. The other tenant, who was more the focus of the superintendent's harassment, was awarded an abatement equal to two months' rent.

In *Malik and Pezzente*,[206] agents of the landlord threatened that if the tenant and his family did not vacate the rental unit by a specified date, they would be forcibly removed (without an eviction order) and that their possessions would be thrown into the street. The tenant's wife was threatened with physical violence. The tenant was awarded a rent abatement equal to one month's rent.[207]

For the failure of the landlord to complete the renovations to the rental unit prior to the date of the commencement of the tenancy and for the landlord's failure to provide all of the promised amenities, which resulted in substantial interference with the tenants' reasonable enjoyment of the unit, the tenants were granted (amongst other relief) an abatement equal to two months' rent.[208]

For illegal entries into the rental unit by the landlord, for going through the tenants' mail and for continual efforts by the landlord over a period of about six months to harass the tenants into vacating the rental unit, the Tribunal awarded a lump-sum abatement equal to two months' rent.[209]

In *Kraft v. Colavita*,[210] it was held to constitute substantial interference with the reasonable enjoyment of the tenants (as well as harassment) where the landlord deliberately withheld oil (for heating) and hot water, refused to allow an inspection of the oil tank, transferred utility accounts into the names of the tenants, unilaterally changed the parking arrangements, seized the tenants' property and attempted to charge the tenants for work that it was the landlord's responsibility to perform. The landlord was ordered to return the tenants' property and the tenants were awarded an abatement in rent of $8,125.00. Although the Member does specify how this abatement was calculated, to put it into context, it may be helpful to note that the monthly rent in this case was $1,250.00.

12 — LL OBLIGATIONS: OTHER

---

205 (Oct. 30, 2001), TNT-02197 (Ont. Rental Housing Trib.).

206 (Sept. 14, 2000), TNT-01321 (Ont. Rental Housing Trib.).

207 This sum was then deducted from the amount awarded to the landlord in order TNL-19048, issued September 14, 2000, for the estimated cost of repairing the damage caused to the rental unit by the tenant or members of his household.

208 *Akinlade et al. v. Sunday* (Jan. 18, 2002), TNT-02372 (Ont. Rental Housing Trib.).

209 *Lauzon et al. v. Leo et al.* (Jan. 30, 2001), TNT-01570 (Ont. Rental Housing Trib.).

210 (March 5, 2001, amended May 2, 2001) CET-01644 (Ont. Rental Housing Trib.).

In *Young v. Benoit*,[211] one of the worst cases to come before the Tribunal, the landlord left threatening messages on the tenant's answering machine, broke into the tenant's apartment and threatened the tenant with a knife, sent threatening notes to the tenant, damaged the tenant's vehicle and had others make harassing telephone calls to the tenant's (unlisted) telephone number. The tenant vacated the rental unit because of this conduct. The Tribunal awarded the tenant a 50% abatement of rent for the period from September 1998 through February 1999 plus a 100% abatement for an additional two months thereafter.

Where the landlord had the hydro and gas cut off and threatened to lock this tenant (who was nine months pregnant at the time) out of the unit, the Tribunal awarded a rent abatement of $1,000 and ordered a fine of $1,000.[212]

In *Gervais v. Yoon*,[213] the landlord engaged in conduct designed to harass the tenant into vacating the rental unit. The tenant did ultimately vacate the unit as a result of this conduct. The Tribunal ordered a 50% abatement of rent for the period of the harassment (January through April 1999) and fined the landlord $2,000.

In Landlord and Tenant Board File Number CET-01181 (June 30, 2008), for illegally taking back possession of a rental unit, the landlord was ordered to pay the former tenants $2,000.00 as an abatement of rent.

(e) Damages

(i) Introduction

Speaking generally, damage claims for substantial amounts are better litigated in a separate ordinary action: *Beyer v. Absamco Developments Ltd.*[214] The rationale is that since applications under Part IV of the *Landlord and Tenant Act* (now under the R.T.A.) were meant to be summary, without pleadings and the procedures of an ordinary action, they were not suitable for adjudicating the complex issues of damages.

The Ontario Divisional Court said much the same quite succinctly in *Hahn v. Kramer*:[215]

> The summary process of the *Landlord and Tenant Act* was never intended to be used for an assessment of damages ... to do that might frustrate the very intent and purpose of the summary procedure provided by the Act.

Similarly, in a case concerning a tenant of a mobile home and s. 128 of Part IV (*Landlord and Tenant Act*), the tenant was claiming damages for

---

[211] (March 15, 1999), SWT-00363 (Ont. Rental Housing Trib.).

[212] *McClement v. Kisiel* (March 3, 1999), SWT-00388 (Ont. Rental Housing Trib.).

[213] (July 2, 1999), SOT-00442 (Ont. Rental Housing Trib.).

[214] (1976), 12 O.R. (2d) 768 (Ont. Co. Ct.).

[215] (1979), 23 O.R. (2d) 689 (Ont. Div. Ct.).

damage to personal property, threats by the landlord and emotional upset caused by the threats. The judge held that the section did not give jurisdiction to deal with *tortious* liability of the landlord: *Solomon v. Valley View Mobile Village.*[216]

Damages claimed by a tenant of $6,000 for personal items including computer equipment when there was flooding due to the landlord's failure to repair should be in a civil action according to *Latimer v. Wassaf.*[217]

Nevertheless, in rare cases under the *Landlord and Tenant Act,* modest damages were awarded where the damages directly flowed from a breach of that Act and were easily quantifiable.

In *Phillips v. Dis-Management,*[218] the judge said "[T]o require ... one proceeding for abatement and a subsequent proceeding for damages would violate the principles enshrined in the Courts of Justice Act." It can be noted that the damages were readily quantifiable.

In *Croteau v. Collins,*[219] substantial repairs required before moving in were not completed. There was no water and the premises were totally unfit for habitation and there were outstanding work orders. The tenants moved out within the first week. The court held that they were entitled to move out. Abatement, return of deposit for the last month's rent, and damages of $1,000 for costs of moving in and out were ordered.

When the T.P.A. was first enacted, it was unclear whether the Tribunal had the jurisdiction to grant any type of damage award beyond the compensation specifically referred to in s. 35(2). A paragraph in s. 35(1) of the T.P.A. permitted the Tribunal to make any other order it considered appropriate. Nevertheless, a Member of the Tribunal could not grant an order that he or she considered appropriate but was beyond the legislated powers of the Tribunal. Some Members concluded that, because the courts sometimes awarded damages under similar provisions of the *Landlord and Tenant Act,* the Tribunal could also grant such relief.[220] The majority of Members, however, adopted a more conservative approach and declined to award damages as it was a type of relief not specifically enumerated in s. 35 of the T.P.A.[221]

Effective December 2000, s. 35(1) of the T.P.A. was amended by the addition of para. (a.1). This paragraph specifically empowered the Tribunal to award certain types of compensation for monetary losses suffered by a

---

216 (September 24, 1981), Smith J. (Ont. Dist. Ct.).

217 (June 22, 1995), Doc. Ottawa 98254/95 (Ont. Gen. Div.).

218 (1995), 24 O.R. (3d) 435 (Ont. Gen. Div.).

219 (1996), 12 R.P.R. (3d) 181 (Ont. Gen. Div.).

220 *Harper and Panier* (October 12, 1999), EAT-01082 (Ont. Rental Housing Trib.); *Lochead and Bascelli* (August 17, 1999), EAT-00800 (Ont. Rental Housing Trib.); and *Yang v. Hird* (Sept. 25, 1999), EAL-06337, EAT-00801 (Ont. Rental Housing Trib.).

221 See *Bilindo Marcocchio Ltd. and Thorndyke* (June 15, 1999), TST-00680, TSL-06874 (Ont. Rental Housing Trib.) and *Blackbaum and Singh* (March 30, 1999), TST-00700 (Ont. Rental Housing Trib.).

tenant as a result of the conduct of the landlord. The types of damages (or compensation) that the Tribunal could award were clearly set out in para. 35(1)(a.1) and in s. 35(2) of the T.P.A. Nevertheless, some uncertainty remained as to whether the Tribunal had the jurisdiction (under para. 35(1)(e)) to award punitive or exemplary damages. Ultimately, the Divisional Court considered this question and concluded that the Tribunal did not have the power to grant such relief.[222] Presumably, that is equally true of the Landlord and Tenant Board.

Although the Board has exclusive jurisdiction to determine all applications under the R.T.A. and with respect to all matters in which jurisdiction is conferred on it by the R.T.A.,[223] the Board does not have exclusive jurisdiction to determine *all* possible disputes that may arise between a landlord and a tenant. Where a claim for damages by a tenant against a landlord falls outside the scope of the *Residential Tenancies Act, 2006*, the tenant still has the right to pursue that claim in a court of competent jurisdiction. If for instance, as a result of the negligence of the landlord, the tenant suffers some serious personal injury within the residential complex that results in pain and suffering, hospital and other medical expenses, loss of current and future income and other damages, these are issues over which the Board lacks jurisdiction. Such issues ought to be determined by way of a court action.

Although the Divisional Court generally took the view that the Rental Housing Tribunal lacked the jurisdiction to award damages in tort, a recent decision from the Divisional Court states that the Tribunal did have the jurisdiction to grant damages flowing from the landlord's breach of the tenancy agreement. In *Mejia v. Cargini*,[224] the landlord had three friends assault the tenant in order to pressure the tenant and his family to vacate the rental unit. The Tribunal terminated the tenancy at the tenant's request and awarded an abatement of rent and moving expenses and fined the landlord for this conduct but declined to award general damages on the basis that the Tribunal lacked the jurisdiction to grant such relief even though the T.P.A. permitted the Tribunal to "make any other order that it considers appropriate". On appeal by the tenant, the Divisional Court found that the Tribunal did have the jurisdiction to award general damages flowing from the landlord's breach of the covenant of quiet enjoyment (i.e., interference with reasonable enjoyment) and amended the order of the Tribunal in order to grant the tenant damages in the amount of $4,000.

It should be noted that many tenancy agreements contain exculpatory clauses which rule out any claim by the tenant for damages in such circumstances, unless a landlord has specifically excluded the implied covenant for quiet enjoyment. Even so, in view of ss. 3(1) and 4 of the R.T.A., that tenants

---

[222] *Campbell v. Maytown Inc.* (2005), 204 O.A.C. 136 (Ont. Div. Ct.), at para. 23.

[223] Subsection 168(2) of the R.T.A.

[224] (2007), 2007 CarswellOnt 666 (Ont. Div. Ct.).

cannot be required to waive their rights under the R.T.A. and s. 17, that covenants are interdependent, the common exculpatory or exclusion of damages clauses no longer have full protective effect for landlords. For example, in *Fleischmann v. Grossman Holdings Ltd.*,[225] the exculpatory clause could not be relied on by a landlord who had failed to fulfil the statutory duty to repair and a tenant had suffered damages as a result of the lack of repair.

In another case concerning the exculpatory clause, a tenant suffered chronic carbon monoxide poisoning, but did not die, from fumes in her apartment which escaped from the landlord's garage located underneath the apartment. It was held to be a breach of the covenant for quiet enjoyment. It is also noted that the usual exculpatory clause was pleaded by the landlord, but not argued, and the judge commented that such a clause will be strictly construed against the landlord: *Federic v. Perpetual Investments Ltd.*[226]

(ii) *Compensation for Lost or Damaged Property and Out-of-Pocket Expenses*

Clause (i) of para. 31(1)(b) states that the Board may order that the landlord, superintendent or agent pay a specified sum to the tenant as compensation for, "the reasonable costs that the tenant has incurred or will incur in repairing or, where repairing is not reasonable, replacing property of the tenant that was damaged, destroyed or disposed of as a result of the landlord, superintendent or agent having engaged in one or more of the activities listed in those paragraphs [2 to 6 of subsection 29(1)]."

The onus rests upon the tenant to establish not only that property was damaged, destroyed or disposed of as a result of the respondent's conduct, but also the value of the subject property and the reasonable cost of repairing or replacing the item. Photographs and receipts are some of the best evidence a tenant can offer as to the nature and value of the lost or damaged property and written estimates, advertisements or receipts may be the best evidence that a tenant can offer as to the expected or actual cost of repairing or replacing the items in question. Where, however, the tenant's list of lost or damaged items is highly detailed and the estimated values are unchallenged by the landlord and appear reasonable to the Member, the Member may accept such estimates without requiring much in the way of substantiating documentation.[227]

---

[225] (1976), 16 O.R. (2d) 746 (Ont. C.A.).

[226] (1968), [1969] 1 O.R. 186 (Ont. H.C.).

[227] See Landlord and Tenant Board File No. SOT-00269-AM (issued July 24, 2007) and amended on Sept. 18, 2007), in which the Board ordered the landlord to pay the tenant, among other things, $4,029.00 for the reasonable expense the tenant had incurred or would incur in replacing property that was lost as a result of an illegal lock-out by the landlord.

Note that the tenant is entitled to be put back into the same position he or she was in before the misconduct by or on behalf of the landlord; the tenant is not entitled to be put into a better position. For instance, if a 20-year-old 14-inch television set is destroyed, the tenant is not entitled to the cost of a new, 42-inch flat-screen high definition plasma television.

Whether or not the tenant has contents insurance (i.e., apartment insurance) is irrelevant. Even if the tenant did have such coverage, the tenant's insurer would be entitled to pursue a subrogated action against the landlord, superintendent or agent. The presence or absence of insurance does not in any way affect the liability of the landlord, superintendent or agent for engaging in conduct that contravenes the R.T.A. and that has resulted in the loss of, or damage to, the tenant's property.

Clause (ii) of para. 31(1)(b) states that the Board may also order that the landlord, superintendent or agent pay a specified sum to the tenant as compensation for, "other reasonable out-of-pocket expenses that the tenant has incurred or will incur as a result of the landlord, superintendent or agent having engaged in one or more of the activities listed in those paragraphs [2 to 6 of s. 29(1)]".

Note that, unlike an abatement of rent (that can only be ordered to be paid by the landlord), an order for payment of compensation under paragraph 31(1)(b) can be made against one or more of the superintendent, agent of the landlord and the landlord. Of course, before an order is made against the superintendent or other agent of the landlord, they should be named as parties to the application, served with notice of the proceedings and given an opportunity to participate in the proceedings.

(iii) Moving Expenses and the Difference in Rent

Pursuant to s. 31(2) of the R.T.A., if in an application under any of the paras. 2 to 6 of s. 29(1), it is determined that the tenant was induced by the conduct of the landlord, the superintendent or an agent of the landlord to vacate the rental unit, the Board may, in addition to the remedies set out in subsection (1), order that the *landlord* pay a specified sum to the tenant as compensation for,

(a) all or any portion of any increased rent which the tenant has incurred or will incur for a one-year period after the tenant has left the rental unit; and
(b) reasonable out of pocket moving, storage and other like expenses which the tenant has incurred or will incur.

Two types of relief are available under s. 31(2): out of pocket moving and storage expenses, and the difference in rent. Note that both types of relief are only available where the tenant was *induced* to vacate the rental unit by the conduct of the landlord, superintendent or agent of the landlord. Where the evidence demonstrates that the tenants were planning to vacate the unit anyway (i.e., for reasons unrelated to any conduct on the part of the landlord or the landlord's agents), no relief is available under s. 31(2).[228] The Board's Interpretation Guideline No. 6 suggests that the tenant's intentions are immaterial and that the real question is whether a reasonable tenant would have been induced to vacate the rental unit. This statement may be somewhat misleading. The R.T.A. specifically requires the tenant to prove that he or she was *induced* to vacate the unit as a result of the conduct in question. If the evidence demonstrates that the tenant had already made concrete plans to move out before the landlord (or agent) did anything wrong, the tenant will not be able to claim that the landlord's conduct induced the tenant to vacate the unit.

With respect to the moving and storage expenses, tenants should bring invoices and receipts to prove the actual expenses they have incurred (if they have already moved out) or will have to incur (if they have not yet vacated the rental unit). Reimbursement of expenses such as truck and equipment rentals, gasoline for the truck, the cost of temporary storage facilities, the purchase of boxes and packing material, the cost of redirecting mail, obtaining new telephone service and so forth is likely to be allowed by the Board if the tenant can produce documentation to substantiate the claim. Examples of cases in which this type of relief has been granted include: *Essex v. Lee*;[229] *Norton v. Lenuzza*;[230] *Ferguson v. Stirpe*;[231] Landlord and Tenant Board File No. SOT-00269-AM;[232] and Landlord and Tenant Board File No. TET-01535 (Jan. 13, 2009).

With respect to claiming the difference in rent, the Board will generally only grant this relief if the rental units are comparable. The tenant should not take advantage of the situation to rent a much larger or nicer unit and then expect the former landlord to pay the difference in rent. If, however, the situation was urgent (such as where the tenant's health or safety was at risk) and the tenant can demonstrate that he or she made reasonable efforts to find alternative accommodations but the only reasonably suitable unit available was a more expensive one, the former landlord may be ordered to pay the difference in rent (for up to 12 months) even if that unit does represent an upgrade. Examples of cases in which this type of relief has been granted include: *Donahue v. Clace*;[233] *McMahon v. Gordon*;[234] Landlord and Tenant

12 — LL OBLIGATIONS: OTHER

---

228 *Klians et al. v. Lipszyc et al.* (April 12, 2000), TNT-00929 (Ont. Rental Housing Trib.).

229 (June 2, 1999), TNT-00486, 1999 CarswellOnt 5804 (Ont. Rental Housing Trib.).

230 (Oct. 14, 1999), TNT-00706 (Ont. Rental Housing Trib.).

231 (Sept. 2, 1999), TNT-00627, 1999 CarswellOnt 5825 (Ont. Rental Housing Trib.).

232 Issued July 24, 2007 and amended September 18, 2007.

233 (Dec. 4, 2000), NOT-00511, [2000] O.R.H.T.D. No. 168, 2000 CarswellOnt 6407 (Ont. Rental Housing Trib.).

234 (June 6, 2003), TST-05710, 2003 CarswellOnt 2655 (Ont. Rental Housing Trib.) in which

Board File No. TET-01535 (Jan. 13, 2009); and Landlord and Tenant Board File No. SOT-01771 (Jan. 14, 2009).

For two recent cases in which the former tenants were awarded both moving expenses and the difference in rent, see Landlord and Tenant Board File No. SOL-01866 (Feb. 24, 2009) and Landlord and Tenant Board File No. EAT-01620 (Feb. 10, 2009).

(iv) Exemplary and Punitive Damages

Under the *Landlord and Tenant Act*, courts relied upon a provision similar to para. 31(1)(f) to award exemplary (punitive) damages in appropriate circumstances.[235] For instance, in *Leach v. Stubbe*,[236] punitive damages of $1,000 were ordered for illegally locking out the tenant.

Exemplary damages are meant to be a punishment for particularly egregious conduct. Unlike an administrative fine, exemplary damages are ordered to be paid to the applicant (not the government); thus, an award of exemplary damages not only serves as punishment and deterrent but also benefits the aggrieved party.

Although exemplary and punitive damages may still be remedies available to tenants who proceed by way of court action against their landlords, it now appears settled that the Board cannot use para. 31(1)(f) to grant such relief. In 2005, considering an identical provision of the T.P.A., the Divisional Court ruled that the Tribunal "has no jurisdiction to award exemplary or punitive damages".[237] This is the first decision on this point as far as I am aware and, subject to a statutory amendment or reconsideration of this issue by the Divisional Court or a higher authority, this is the last word on this issue. The Board does *not* have the authority to award exemplary or punitive damages.

(v) Aggravated Damages

Although the Divisional Court held that the Tribunal (now the Board) does not have the jurisdiction to award *exemplary* or *punitive* damages,[238] that does not necessarily mean that the Board cannot award *aggravated*

$8,400 was awarded as the difference in rent where the landlord was found to have given a notice of termination under s. 51 in bad faith.

235 See *Shaw v. Pajelle Investments Ltd.* (1985), 11 O.A.C. 70 (Ont. Div. Ct.) in which an abatement was ordered for poor maintenance and infestation by mice and cockroaches. The Court also awarded special and exemplary damages.

236 (1988), 4 T.L.L.R. 206 (Ont. Prov. Ct.).

237 *Campbell v. Maytown Inc.* (2005), 204 O.A.C. 136 (Ont. Div. Ct.), at para. 23.

238 *Campbell v. Maytown Inc.* (2005), 204 O.A.C. 136 (Ont. Div. Ct.), at para. 23.

damages in the appropriate circumstances. According to a couple of decisions, the Board does have the jurisdiction to grant aggravated damages.

In one case that came before the Rental Housing Tribunal,[239] the Member gave the following analysis of this issue:

> It is noted that punitive damages are not compensatory in nature. Aggravated damages are compensatory in nature taking into consideration not just the tangible injuries, but also the intangible injuries such as distress and humiliation caused by the actions of the offending party. The Supreme Court of Canada in *Vorvis v. Insurance Corp. of British Columbia*, [1989] 1 S.C.R. 1085, confirmed that aggravated damages are compensatory in nature.
>
> I find and confirm that the Tribunal has jurisdiction to award compensatory damages including aggravated damages.
>
> The Ontario Rental Housing Tribunal is better equipped to deal with matters relating to damages arising out of landlord and tenant relationships as it specializes and is experienced in landlord and tenant matters. It is good law and public policy for the Tribunal to adjudicate fully and completely upon every remedial aspect of a landlord and tenant dispute with out (sic) the dispute resolution process being duplicated and undermined . . .
>
> Pursuant to *Vorvis*, supra, there is a three part test to be applied in assessing aggravated damages:
>
> 1. that (sic) must be damage;
> 2. the damage should be such that it is capable of being reasonably anticipated; and
> 3. there is a connection between the damage and the breach.

In this case, the landlord entered the unit illegally, assaulted the tenant, damaged the tenant's personal possessions and locked the tenant out of the unit for one and a half days. The Member concluded that the physical and psychological harm suffered by the tenant was foreseeable by the landlord and was connected to the landlord's breaches of the *Tenant Protection Act*. As a result, the Member ordered the landlord to pay an administrative fine of $1,000, a rent abatement of approximately $350, $300 for the cost of repairing or replacing the tenant's damaged property and aggravated damages in the amount of $1,000.

In a more recent case,[240] the tenant brought an application against the landlord for harassment. The landlord was ordered to provide rent receipts and to unseal the tenant's mail slot. The tenant was awarded $2,500 as a rent abatement and a further $2,500 in aggravated damages. Finally, an administrative fine of $1,000 was also levied against the landlord.

---

[239] *Thornton, Re* (Aug. 4, 2006), TST-08160, [2006] O.R.H.T.D. No. 111, 2006 CarswellOnt 9171 (Ont. Rental Housing Trib.).

[240] Landlord and Tenant Board File No. TST-09833 (April 11, 2007).

Since there are very few cases directly on point, it remains an open question whether other Members of the Landlord and Tenant Board will also conclude that they have the power to award aggravated damages in the appropriate circumstances under para. 31(1)(f) of the R.T.A.

(f) Administrative Fine

Pursuant to para. 31(1)(d) of the R.T.A., if the Board determines that a landlord, a superintendent or an agent of a landlord has done one or more of the activities set out in paras. 2 to 6 of s. 29(1), the Board may order that the landlord pay to the Board an administrative fine not exceeding the greater of $10,000 and the monetary jurisdiction of the Small Claims Court. The monetary jurisdiction of the Small Claims Court is scheduled to be increased to $25,000, effective January 2010.

According to the Board's Interpretation Guideline No. 6, an administrative fine is a remedy designed to deter landlords, superintendents and agents from engaging in similar actions in the future and should be used "in serious cases where the landlord has shown a blatant disregard for the RTA and other remedies will not provide adequate deterrence and compliance." Unlike the former Rental Housing Tribunal, the Landlord and Tenant Board has not attempted to set ranges for first fines, second fines and so forth. Instead, the Board is leaving the matter within the discretion of the Member who hears the case but suggests (in Interpretation Guideline No. 16) that, in setting the amount of the fine, the Member may consider:

1. the nature and severity of the breach;
2. the effect of the breach on the tenant; and
3. any other relevant factors.

Whenever the Board is considering making such an order against a landlord, the landlord should be invited to make submissions as to the appropriateness and the amount of any such fine.[241]

If a party fails to pay a fine imposed by the Board, in addition to other steps the Board may take to collect the debt, Rule 9 of the Board's Rules of Practice prevents that party from filing any new applications.[242] Rule 9 also prevents a party from proceeding with an existing application if that party has failed to pay to the Board any fee, *fine* or costs (until the amount owing to the Board has been paid).

Examples of cases in which fines have been imposed upon landlords include the following: $500 for an illegal lockout;[243] $500 per day for an

---

241 See Interpretation Guideline No. 16.

242 Except in urgent cases (Rule 9.1). Pursuant to Rule 9.2, applications for or based upon arrears of rent are not considered urgent.

243 *Idrissou v. Hoseine* (Oct. 13, 1998), TST-00190, 1998 CarswellOnt 6413 (Ont. Rental Housing Trib.).

illegal lockout and then $10,000 for ignoring the interim order of the Tribunal;[244] $500 for threatening to report the tenant's alleged criminal conduct;[245] $2,300 (equal to four months' rent) for harassing the tenants until they vacated the rental unit;[246] $500 for an illegal lockout;[247] $750 for an illegal lockout;[248] $1,000 for cutting off utilities and threatening to lock the tenant out of the unit;[249] $2,000 for harassing the tenant into vacating the unit;[250] $1,000 for threatening and attempting to intimidate the tenant into moving out of the unit because of the presence of pets;[251] $1,000 to deter the landlord from collecting non-refundable key deposits from socially vulnerable people and for an illegal eviction;[252] and $2,500 for cutting off the electricity to the unit, locking the tenant out of the unit and throwing the tenant's possessions out into the snow while she was absent from the unit.[253]

(g) Any Other Order the Board Considers Appropriate

Under para. 31(1)(f) of the R.T.A., the Board hearing an application also has the discretionary power "to make such further order as it considers appropriate." Given the breadth of the other relief set out in s. 31(1), it is difficult to think of many situations where the Board will need to resort to this provision.

One example in which this provision was used can be found in *Satchithananthan v. Cacciola*.[254] The Tribunal relied upon para. 35(1)(e) of the T.P.A. (now para. 31(1)(f) of the R.T.A.) to order the landlord to renovate the unit in an effort to reduce the amount of noise entering the unit and interfering with the tenant's reasonable enjoyment of the unit.

Thus, unlike para. 31(1)(a) of the R.T.A., which only permits the Board to prohibit the landlord from certain conduct in the future, para. 31(1)(f) may permit the Board to order a landlord to take positive steps to rectify a situation or take action that will help prevent similar problems from recurring.

---

244 *436235 Ontario Ltd. v. Mountfort* (2002), 2002 CarswellOnt 8561(Ont. Div. Ct.) re Ontario Rental Housing Tribunal File Nos. TST-02063, TST-02095 (Ont. Div. Ct.).

245 *Osibayo v. James* (Aug. 6, 2002), TET-02577, [2002] O.R.H.T.D. No. 84(Ont. Rental Housing Trib.).

246 *Wu v. Singh* (Oct. 14, 1998), SOT-00109 (Ont. Rental Housing Trib.).

247 *Essex v. Lee* (June 2, 1999), TNT-00486, 1999 CarswellOnt 5804 (Ont. Rental Housing Trib.).

248 Landlord and Tenant Board File Number CET-01181 (June 30, 2008).

249 *McClement v. Kisiel* (March 3, 1999), SWT-00388 (Ont. Rental Housing Trib.).

250 *Gervais v. Yoon* (July 2, 1999), SOT-00422 (Ont. Rental Housing Trib.).

251 *Dean v. Fitchett* (May 20, 1999), TET-00233 (Ont. Rental Housing Trib.).

252 Landlord and Tenant Board File No. SOT-01787 (Jan. 21, 2009).

253 Landlord and Tenant Board File No. SOT-00269-AM (issued July 24, 2007 and amended Sept. 18, 2007).

254 (Dec. 30, 2002), TST-04047, 2002 CarswellOnt 5023 (Ont. Rental Housing Trib.).

Another example is ordering that a landlord allow an evicted tenant to take back possession of the rental unit. Subsections 31(3), (4) and (5) deal with remedies that may be granted where there has been an illegal lockout. What I am referring to here is a situation in which a landlord has obtained possession of a rental unit through the enforcement of an eviction order issued by the Board but in circumstances where the Board subsequently finds that it was an abuse of its process for the landlord to have obtained the order in the manner it did or for the landlord to have enforced the eviction order. Examples might include cases where a landlord obtains an eviction order through misrepresentation or where a landlord enforces an order that the landlord knows has been stayed by a subsequent order of the Board or by operation of law. Although, thankfully, such cases are rare, the Tribunal found jurisdiction under s. 23 of the *Statutory Powers Procedure Act* to put a tenant back into possession. The Divisional Court confirmed that the Tribunal did possess the power to put a tenant back into possession even after the sheriff has enforced an eviction order.[255]

Finally, the Divisional Court recently confirmed that this provision gives the Tribunal (now the Board) the power to grant general damages for a breach by the landlord of the tenancy agreement. In *Mejia v. Cargini*,[256] the landlord had three friends assault the tenant in order to pressure the tenant and his family to vacate the rental unit. The Tribunal terminated the tenancy at the tenant's request and awarded an abatement of rent and moving expenses and fined the landlord for this conduct but declined to award general damages on the basis that the Tribunal lacked the jurisdiction to grant such relief even though the T.P.A. permitted the Tribunal to "make any other order that it considers appropriate". On appeal by the tenant, the Divisional Court found that the Tribunal did have the jurisdiction to award general damages flowing from the landlord's breach of the covenant of quiet enjoyment (i.e., interference with reasonable enjoyment) and amended the Tribunal's order to grant the tenant damages in the amount of $4,000.

---

[255] *Metropolitan Toronto Housing Authority v. Ahmed* (2001), 2001 CarswellOnt 1347 (Ont. Rental Housing Trib.), re TNL-06552 (Ont. Rental Housing Trib.); followed in *Commvesco Levinson Viner Group v. Pershaw* (Oct. 11, 2001), EAL-2388-RV, EAT-03169, [2001] O.R.H.T.D. No. 134, 2001 CarswellOnt 6322 (Ont. Rental Housing Trib.).

[256] (2007), 2007 CarswellOnt 666 (Ont. Div. Ct.).

13

Obligations of Tenants and Common Applications by Landlords

1. OBLIGATIONS OF TENANTS

In the previous two chapters, I have described the obligations of landlords under the *Residential Tenancies Act, 2006* (R.T.A.). Seen from another perspective, I have described the rights of tenants. But tenants also have obligations and the failure of tenants to fulfill their obligations often permits the landlord to seek termination of the tenancy. In this chapter, I shall describe the obligations of tenants under the R.T.A. and the rights of landlords when tenants fail to fulfill these obligations.

It should be noted that, just as a landlord is responsible for the conduct of the superintendent, property manager and other employees and agents, a tenant can be responsible for the conduct of other members of the tenant's household, guests, subtenants and other persons permitted into the complex by the tenant. Some of the obligations of a tenant under the R.T.A. include:

1. Not to change the locks without the landlord's consent (s. 35(1));
2. Not to harass, etc., the landlord (s. 36);
3. To be responsible for the cleanliness of the unit (s. 33);
4. Not to damage the unit or complex and to pay for any such damage (ss. 34, 62, 63 and 89);
5. To pay the rent (s. 59);
6. To pay the rent on time (para. 58(1)1);
7. Not to commit an illegal act or carry on an illegal business or permit others to do so in the complex (s. 61(1));
8. Not to misrepresent income in rent-geared-to-income housing and to pay the back-rent that should have been paid (ss. 60(1) and 90);

9. Not to substantially interfere with the reasonable enjoyment of other tenants or with the lawful rights of the landlord (ss. 64 and 65);
10. Not to seriously impair the safety of others in the complex (s. 66);
11. Not to overcrowd the unit (s. 67);
12. To comply with an order of the Board or the terms of a mediated agreement (s. 78);
13. If the tenant is the superintendent of the complex, to move out within one week of his or her employment being terminated (s. 94).

If a tenant breaches any of these obligations, the landlord may simply warn the tenant or may begin a more formal process that can, ultimately, lead to the issuance of an order by the Board. The landlord may merely seek an order for monetary compensation or other relief (see "Non-eviction Applications" below). Usually, however, the landlord will seek an eviction order (with or without an order for monetary compensation).

There is no provision for notice of termination by a landlord when a tenant is in breach of a covenant in a lease, other than when a breach of covenant can be brought within the causes for termination specified in the R.T.A.[1]

If the landlord is considering seeking an order to terminate the tenancy, the first step will be to serve the appropriate notice of termination upon the tenant. The necessary steps to terminate a tenancy are described in Chapter 6 and the basic steps for commencing an application are described in Chapter 16.

2. NON-EVICTION APPLICATIONS

(a) General

Some applications, by their nature, will not result in an eviction order even where the landlord is completely successful. These are described below. It should be noted, however, that even in applications where a landlord was originally seeking an eviction order, the landlord and tenant can agree to some compromise solution short of termination of the tenancy.[2]

(b) To Determine if the R.T.A. Applies

Usually, whether or not the R.T.A. applies to a particular tenancy, unit or complex will be obvious. However, this is not always the case, such as in situations where the parties cannot agree on whether the R.T.A. applies. Such

---

[1] The topic of a landlord's rights on a tenant's breach of a covenant is discussed further in this chapter under the heading, "Interference with Reasonable Enjoyment, etc."

[2] See "Negotiation and Mediation" in Chapter 16.

issues can arise during the course of a hearing and often come as a surprise to the Member since the issue of jurisdiction is rarely identified in the documents filed by parties. Where jurisdiction becomes an issue, the Member must explicitly deal with that issue in his or her decision.

Where, however, a party knows in advance that jurisdiction is going to be an issue, obtaining a ruling on that issue before proceeding with any other application may be preferable. A party who wishes to obtain a ruling on the applicability of the R.T.A. before commencing other proceedings may do so by filing with the Board an application (Form A1) pursuant to s. 9 of the R.T.A. (formerly s. 7 of the T.P.A.). The filing fee is $45. The applicant must serve the application and notice of hearing upon the other party or parties at least ten days prior to the date of the hearing (Rule 10.1 of the Board's Rules of Practice) and file a certificate of service with the Board within five days of effecting service (Rule 11.2).

After hearing evidence and submissions from the parties, the Board will then issue an order determining whether the R.T.A. (or whether a specified provision of the R.T.A.) applies to the particular rental unit or residential complex.

The *Tyndale College* cases are a good example of two related applications brought under s. 7 of the T.P.A. They arose from questions about whether the T.P.A., or certain provisions of the T.P.A., applied to rental units located within this Christian college. These cases are described in detail in Chapter 4 (under the heading, "Accommodations at Certain Educational Institutions").

Once it is established that the rental premises in question are used for residential purposes, the onus is upon the party alleging that the rental unit is exempt from the R.T.A. to prove this.[3]

In Landlord and Tenant Board File No. TSL-05535 (January 21, 2008), an alumni association (the landlord) owned a frat house located near the University of Toronto. Members of a specific fraternity were permitted to reside in the premises, in exchange for paying rent (as well as annual dues). The landlord brought an application to the Landlord and Tenant Board (under s. 9 of the *Act*) for a determination as to whether the premises were governed by the R.T.A. The Board found that the landlord had failed to demonstrate that the premises fell within any of the exemptions specified in s. 5 of the *Act* and, therefore, that the *Act* applies to this residential complex.[4]

---

[3] *Ramsay v. Heselmann* (1983), 42 O.R. (2d) 255 (Ont. Div. Ct.); *Koressis v. Turner* (1986), 54 O.R. (2d) 571 (Ont. Div. Ct.); *Foster v. Lewkowicz* (1993), 34 R.P.R. (2d) 74 (Ont. Gen. Div.); *Marshall v. Cao* (2003), [2003] O.R.H.T.D. No. 79, 2003 CarswellOnt 2664 (Ont. Rental Housing Trib.); *Lanthier v. 963324 Ontario Ltd.* (1992), 1992 CarswellOnt 2469 (Ont. Gen. Div.); and Landlord and Tenant Board File No. TSL-05535 (January 21, 2008).

[4] Note, however, that the Board did not go on to analyze whether the premises may be *partially* exempt (i.e., exempt from some of the provisions of the R.T.A.) pursuant to para. 5 of s. 7 of

(c) Tenant has Changed Locks

A tenant may not alter the locking system on a door giving entry to a rental unit or residential complex (or cause the locks to be altered) without the consent of the landlord. It is prohibited under s. 35(1) of the R.T.A. (formerly s. 23(2) of the T.P.A.) and is an offence under para. 233(b) of the R.T.A.

If a tenant alters a locking system, contrary to s. 35(1), the landlord may apply to the Board for an order determining that the tenant has altered the locking system on a door giving entry to the rental unit or the residential complex or caused the locking system to be altered during the tenant's occupancy of the rental unit without the consent of the landlord (s. 35(2)). The application is in Form L8 and must be served on the tenant, along with the notice of hearing, at least 10 days before the date set for the hearing (Rule 10.1). The filing fee is $150.00. The landlord must then file a certificate of service with the Board within five days of effecting service (Rule 11.2).

The only relief the Board can grant on such an application (other than costs) is to order the tenant to provide the landlord with keys or to pay the landlord the reasonable out of pocket expenses necessary to change the locking system (s. 35(3)). The Board cannot terminate the tenancy on an application under s. 35. If, however, changing the locks has resulted in a breach of other provisions of the R.T.A., a landlord may seek termination of the tenancy through other types of applications. For instance, the change of locks by the tenant may be grounds to terminate the tenancy if it was part of a scheme to wrongly deprive the landlord of access to the unit and this has substantially interfered with the lawful rights of the landlord. Also, since it is an offence under s. 233, it could be argued that changing the locks without the consent of the landlord is an "illegal act" that justifies terminating the tenancy under s. 61(1).[5]

The question of who owns the locks is irrelevant; the focus of these applications should be on whether or not the landlord consented to the change of locks.[6] Once given, the landlord's consent binds the landlord for the duration of the occupancy of that tenant.[7]

In *837 Roselawn Avenue v. Johnson*,[8] the tenant placed an additional deadbolt lock on the door to the rental unit. The landlord was not provided

---

the R.T.A. (i.e., a rental unit provided by an educational institution to a student that is not otherwise exempt from the *Act*).

5 *Swansea Village Co-op v. Balcerzak* (1988), 63 O.R. (2d) 741 (Ont. Div. Ct.).

6 *Briarlane Property Management Inc. v. Bradt* (2004), 2004 CarswellOnt 1393, 185 O.A.C. 198 (Ont. Div. Ct.).

7 *Briarlane Property Management Inc. v. Bradt* (2004), 2004 CarswellOnt 1393, 185 O.A.C. 198 (Ont. Div. Ct.). See also *Wm. Squibb & Daughters Ltd. v. Hamlin* (November 14, 2005), SWL-74621, 2005 CarswellOnt 7831 (Ont. Rental Housing Trib.).

8 (March 31, 2000), TNL-14224, 2000 CarswellOnt 6438 (Ont. Rental Housing Trib.).

with a key to this lock. The evidence showed that after two break-ins, the tenant requested and was granted permission by the property manager at the time (around 1983) to install the lock in question. The new property manager purportedly brought this application in 2000 because he was concerned that the landlord would not be able to quickly gain access to the unit in an emergency situation. While the Tribunal expressed some understanding of the landlord's desire to have quick access to all rental units in an emergency, since the landlord had given the tenant permission to change (i.e., add) the lock in question, no relief was available under ss. 36 and 37 of the T.P. A.

(d) For Arrears of Rent

For a general review of issues about rent and rent deposits, please see Chapters 7 and 8.

A landlord may apply to the Board if the tenant has not paid rent lawfully required under the tenancy agreement and if the tenant is still in possession of the rental unit (s. 87). If the tenant has vacated the unit, the landlord will have to seek compensation by way of a court action as the Board will have no jurisdiction to grant relief under s. 87.

This type of application is almost always combined with an application to terminate the tenancy (for non-payment of rent). Nevertheless, it is possible for a landlord to seek arrears of rent *without* seeking to terminate the tenancy.

Under the T.P.A., the same application form (Form L1) was used for arrears of rent, whether or not the landlord was seeking an eviction order. Under the R.T.A., a *new* form is to be used where the landlord is seeking an order for arrears of rent without an order terminating the tenancy. The application is in Form L9 and the filing fee is $170.[9] The application and notice of hearing must be served upon the tenant at least 10 days prior to the hearing (Rule 10.1). No time limit is set out in the R.T.A. for this type of application.[10] The certificate of service for the application and notice of hearing should be filed within five days after service has been effected (Rule 11.2).

Whenever a landlord brings an application for arrears of rent, the landlord may also include a claim for NSF cheque charges actually incurred by the landlord[11] and the landlord's administrative charges in respect of NSF

13 — LL APPLICATIONS

---

9 Effective April 2009. From 2002 through March 2009, the fee was $150.

10 See *McAughey v. Drosos* (June 28, 1999), TNL-07871 (Ont. Rental Housing Trib.). Although the general limitation period for claims is now two years from the date of discovery of the claim (s. 4 of the *Limitations Act*, 2002, S.O. 2002, c. 24), there is a specific six-year limitation period on claims for recovery of arrears of rent pursuant to s. 17 of the *Real Property Limitations Act*, R.S.O. 1990, c. L. 15.

11 I.e., the amount the landlord was charged by the financial institution because of insufficient funds in the payor's account to cover the amount of the cheque (see para. 87(5)1 and para. 4 of s. 17 of O. Reg. 516/06).

cheques (not to exceed $20 per cheque).[12] Other than this, a landlord is not entitled to claim anything on this type of application other than *rent*.[13] Pursuant to s. 1 of the R.T.A.:

> **"rent"** includes the amount of any consideration paid or given or required to be paid or given by or on behalf of a tenant to a landlord or the landlord's agent for the right to occupy a rental unit and for any services and facilities and any privilege, accommodation or thing that the landlord provides for the tenant in respect of the occupancy of the rental unit, whether or not a separate charge is made for services and facilities or for the privilege, accommodation or thing, but **"rent"** does not include,
>
> (a) an amount paid by a tenant to a landlord to reimburse the landlord for property taxes paid by the landlord with respect to a mobile home or a land lease home owned by a tenant, or
>
> (b) an amount that a landlord charges a tenant of a rental unit in a care home for care services or meals.

If the landlord is *not* seeking to terminate the tenancy (i.e., the landlord has *not* combined the L9 application with an eviction application), the tenant is not entitled to credit for the rent deposit. A rent deposit can only be applied to rent owing for the *last* rental period just before a tenancy ends. If the tenancy is not ending, the tenant is not entitled to have the deposit deducted from the total arrears ordered on an L9 application.

How the Form L9 is completed is very important. Section 1 of Part 4 of the application form has only three rows in which to show how the arrears of rent are calculated. If rent is owed for more than three rental periods, what do you do? My suggestion is to group several rental periods together. The Board's Form L9 instruction booklet also recommends this but makes it clear that the third row should always contain the most recent rent information and should relate to only one rental period. In a complicated situation, it is acceptable to attach a ledger or account summary to the Form L9 but the information must still be summarized by completing the table in Section 1 of Part 4 (within the three rows provided). Let's take a concrete example to illustrate these points.

Let's say that the rent is $1,000 per month, due on the first day of each month, and that in 2007 the tenant paid $500 in January, $800 in February, $1000 in March, $950 in April, $850 in May and the landlord is filing an L9 application with the Board in May 2007. Section 1 of Part 4 of the Form L9 should be completed as follows:

---

[12] Paragraph 87(5)2 of the R.T.A. (formerly subsection 86(4) of the T.P.A.) and para. 5 of s. 17 of O. Reg. 516/06.

[13] See Chapter 7 for a full description of what is, and is not, included in the definition of the word "rent".

Rent Period From: (dd/mm/yyyy)	To: (dd/mm/yyyy)	Rent Charged $	Rent Paid $	Rent Owing $
01/01/2007	31/01/2007	1,000.00	500.00	500.00
01/02/2007	30/04/2007	3,000.00	2,750.00	250.00
01/05/2007	31/05/2007	1,000.00	850.00	150.00
		Total Rent Owing $		900.00

The Board's software is designed to allow only three lines of input so to make things easier for the Board staff, organize the information to fit into three lines. You may also wish to attach a month-by-month breakdown to show the details for the months that have been "lumped together". This will be especially important if the rent has changed during the period in question. If the application is also for an order terminating the tenancy, it is absolutely critical that the rental period in which the termination date falls be left on its own (i.e., that rental period should have its own row) and that it not be combined on the form with any other rental period. Finally, please note that you can claim the rent for the entire rental period even if filing the application in the middle of the period or if the notice of termination (when seeking termination) falls in the middle of the rental period. If the application is just for arrears of rent (without termination), a landlord is entitled to claim for the entire rental period as the rent was due at the beginning of the period. If the application also seeks an order terminating the tenancy, the Board's software will make the necessary adjustments and calculate the arrears of rent up to the date of termination.

Under the T.P.A. and the caselaw developed thereunder, a tenancy could not be terminated by a tenant simply vacating the unit or by giving a short or otherwise defective notice of termination. This left tenants potentially liable for the rent on the unit for an indefinite period (i.e., until the landlord was able to re-rent the unit for a comparable rent). Pursuant to s. 88 the R.T.A., a "cap" has now been placed upon a tenant's maximum liability for arrears of rent in circumstances where the tenancy was not properly terminated by the tenant.

If a tenant gave an improper notice of termination, arrears are owed for the period starting from the date the tenant gave the defective notice up to the termination date that would have been specified in the notice if the tenant had given proper notice of termination.[14] If the tenant gave no notice of termination at all, arrears are owed from the date the landlord knew or ought to have known that the tenant had vacated the unit up to the termination date that would have been specified in the notice of termination if proper notice had been given. If a landlord gives a notice of termination for landlord's or purchaser's own use, or for demolition/conversion/renovation and the tenant

[14] See, for example, Landlord and Tenant Board File No. TNL-00388 (April 17, 2007) and Landlord and Tenant Board File No. TSL-13807-RV (Jan. 8, 2009).

moves without giving the required ten days' notice of early termination, the tenant will owe rent for up to ten days from the earlier of the following dates: (1) the date the tenant gave the improper notice; (2) where they gave no notice, the date the landlord knew or ought to have known that they had vacated the unit; and (3) the termination date in the landlord's notice of termination.

Despite these rules, however, a landlord is still obliged to make reasonable efforts to mitigate its losses by finding a new tenant for the unit. If a landlord rents the unit to a new tenant, the former tenant's liability ends on the day before the day the new tenant is entitled to occupy the unit (s. 88(3)).

Note that when bringing an application before the Board on the basis of arrears of rent, in addition to preparing to prove its own case, the landlord should also try to anticipate and prepare for the issue(s) that the tenant may raise at the hearing, either under s. 82 or s. 83 of the R.T.A. This topic is discussed further in Chapter 16.

(e) Compensation for Damage to the Unit/Complex

A landlord may apply to the Board for an order for compensation if the tenant, another occupant of the rental unit or a person whom the tenant permits in the residential complex wilfully or negligently causes undue damage to the rental unit or the residential complex and the tenant is in possession of the rental unit at the time the appreciation is commenced (s. 89). If the tenant has vacated the unit, the landlord will have to seek compensation by way of a court action as the Board will have no jurisdiction to grant relief under s. 89.

Although there was one case in which it was suggested that the term "undue damage" could include purely economic loss by the landlord,[15] a more natural reading of the words "damage to the rental unit or the residential complex" implies physical damage to the building or its contents.

This type of relief is almost always combined with an application to terminate the tenancy (because of the damage done to the unit or the complex). Nevertheless, it is possible for a landlord to seek compensation for the damage *without* seeking to terminate the tenancy.

The application will be in Form L2 and the filing fee is \$170.[16] The application and notice of hearing must be served upon the tenant at least 10 days prior to the hearing (Rule 10.1). The certificate of service for the application and notice of hearing should be filed within five days after service has been effected (Rule 11.2).

The landlord must prove who caused the damage.

---

[15] *Saikaly and Swanson* (April 27, 1999), EAL-05232 (Ont. Rental Housing Trib.).

[16] Effective April 2009. From 2002 through March 2009, the fee was \$150.

If it is alleged that someone other than the tenant caused the damage, the landlord will need to prove that the tenant permitted that other person into the complex. Where damage was done to the door of the rental unit during a police raid, the tenant was not held responsible because the tenant did not cause the damage or permit the police into the complex.[17] In *Fisher Kay Ltd. v. Haggart et al.*,[18] the tenant sublet the unit to a friend who then turned the unit into a "flop-house". The tenant was held responsible for the damage caused to the unit by persons he permitted in the unit.

In *Charolais Developments Inc. v. Griffin*,[19] a tow truck driver attempted to drive his vehicle into the garage of this complex in order to remove the tenant's vehicle. In doing so, he damaged the premises. The evidence showed that the tenant did not permit the tow truck driver to enter the residential complex, but in fact, warned him not to attempt to enter the premises. Consequently, the landlord's application against the tenant was dismissed.

A minor child of the tenant will usually not be considered to be a tenant of the rental unit since the child was not a party to the tenancy agreement and has no legal obligation to pay rent. Nevertheless, the Rental Housing Tribunal and the Landlord and Tenant Board have generally held parents responsible for the acts of their children. Typically, the child will either be an occupant of the unit or will have been permitted into the complex by the tenant. On this basis, a tenant will usually be ordered to compensate a landlord for undue damage caused to the unit or the complex by the tenant's child.[20] Alternatively, pursuant to the *Parental Responsibility Act, 2000*, S.O. 2000, c. 4 (Appendix 15), a person whose property has been damaged, destroyed or stolen by a minor (a person under 18 years of age) may bring a claim against the minor's parents for damages in the Small Claims Court.

If it is the tenant who is alleged to have caused the damage, this must be proven. It is not enough to say, "The damage must have been caused by the tenant." In *Singh v. Giannone*,[21] the tenant of this basement unit suffered from a "bi-polar" mental disorder. She took herself off of her medication and her behaviour became erratic and potentially dangerous. The police were called and, as a result, the tenant was taken to a local hospital where she was

[17] *Grenoble Properties v. Nura* (Feb. 13, 2003), TEL-32753-SA, 2003 CarswellOnt 1554 (Ont. Rental Housing Trib.).

[18] (Nov. 20, 2000), TNL-20362 (Ont. Rental Housing Trib.).

[19] (June 26, 2003), CEL-31287, [2003] O.R.H.T.D. No. 89, 2003 CarswellOnt 2659 (Ont. Rental Housing Trib.).

[20] In *Pezzente v. Malik* (Sept. 14, 2000), TNL-19048, 2000 CarswellOnt 6445 (Ont. Rental Housing Trib.), the tenants were held responsible for allowing their children to write and draw on the walls of the rental unit. In *Tellier v. Boddy*, (May 26, 2006), SWL-79869, [2006] O.R.H.T.D. No. 48 (Ont. Rental Housing Trib.), the tenants were held liable (and evicted) for damage done to the exterior of the property when the tenants allowed their children to play soccer and hockey near the building despite the repeated requests of the landlord that this not be permitted.

[21] (Jan. 13, 2003), TNL-38679-RV (Ont. Rental Housing Trib.).

forced to remain for observation for approximately one month. Through the hospital staff, the tenant made arrangements to return to the unit to pick up a few personal possessions. The landlord, who had changed the locks, allowed her into the unit to retrieve some of her property. She arranged to return two days later to collect more of her things. On that occasion, the landlord and tenant found that the basement was flooded. The landlord jumped to the conclusion that the tenant must have done something two days earlier to cause the flood (which, by the way, caused substantial damage to the tenant's property). The landlord believed that the tenant had caused the flood but was unable to offer any evidence to substantiate this allegation. This part of the application was, therefore, dismissed.

In all cases, the landlord will need to prove that the damage was caused wilfully or negligently[22] and that the damage is "undue" — that is, more than the usual deterioration or "wear and tear" expected to occur over time from normal use of the premises.[23]

There is an interesting discussion of what constitutes usual wear and tear in the case of *Kamoo v. Brampton Caledon Housing Corp.*[24] In this civil action for damages, the plaintiff was a landlord who had rented a unit to the defendant non-profit organization. The defendant assisted persons with developmental disabilities in gaining independence in the community by providing, amongst other things, housing. The defendant had rented this unit for about eight years and permitted various persons to occupy the unit from time-to-time. At the end of the tenancy, the landlord claimed that he incurred well over $10,000 in expenses to repair the unit and to replace appliances, window coverings, sinks and carpeting. The defendant alleged that the unit simply reflected eight years of occupancy and exhibited the signs of usual wear and tear, especially since the landlord never visited the unit and never effected any repairs at all during the tenancy. Reasonable wear and tear is generally defined as "unavoidable deterioration in the dwelling and its fixtures resulting from normal use".[25] The court found that the length of occupancy can be relevant to the question of what is normal wear and tear (the longer the occupancy, the more wear and tear can be expected). In the end, the Court found that the former tenant was responsible for the cost of some of the repairs but not for the cost of replacing the stove and refrigerator and not for the cost of repairing the effects of normal wear and tear.

---

[22] See *1050 Castlefield Ave. Ltd. v. Dos Santos* (June 10, 1999), TNL-06842, 1999 CarswellOnt 5815 (Ont. Rental Housing Trib.) in which the landlord failed to prove that the damage was caused by the wilful or negligent conduct of the tenants.

[23] *Rosati v. Naalband* (July 6, 1999), TNL-07926, 1999 CarswellOnt 5797 (Ont. Rental Housing Trib.). For a more recent case, see Landlord and Tenant Board File No. SWL-025683 (Feb. 27, 2009).

[24] (2005), 2005 CarswellOnt 4405 (Ont. S.C.J.).

[25] *Kamoo v. Brampton Caledon Housing Corp.* (2005), 2005 CarswellOnt 4405 (Ont. S.C.J.) at para. 16.

Undue damage must be more than mere knicks, scrapes and dents associated with normal occupation of a rental unit.[26] The fact that the landlord has to clean up garbage left behind by a tenant does not mean that the presence of the debris has *damaged* the residential complex.[27] The fact that something in the rental unit has ceased to function normally is not sufficient, in the absence of any other evidence, to prove that the tenant has caused the problem. For instance, the fact that a refrigerator breaks down or a toilet becomes clogged does not prove that the tenant caused undue damage to the rental unit.[28]

In *Taylor v. Hickson*,[29] the landlords brought an action in small claims court against their former tenants for arrears of rent and damage to the rental unit. Amongst other defences, the defendants argued that the "damage" was little more than normal wear and tear. The judge considered the analysis in the *Kamoo* decision and found that extensive damage to carpeting caused by pet urine (requiring replacement of the carpeting at a cost of over $5,000) and holes of various sizes in the walls (necessitating over $7,000 in repairs) did not constitute normal wear and tear.

The landlord must prove the exact nature of the damage. Potential damage or the risk of damage is not enough. In *Rosati v. Naalband*,[30] the tenant went onto the roof to remove Christmas lights about which the landlord had complained. The landlord alleged that walking on the roof on a warm day could damage the shingles but offered no evidence that any damage had, in fact, occurred. This part of the application was dismissed.

The landlord must also establish the reasonable cost of repairing the damage or, where repairing is not reasonable, the cost of replacing the damaged property.[31] The landlord is entitled to the reasonable cost of restoring the unit or complex to the condition it was in prior to the undue damage but is not entitled to be put into a better position. The landlord should come with actual receipts or written estimates of the cost of repairing the damage or, where that is not possible, the cost of replacing the item in question with one of similar quality to the original item.

Significantly altering the interior structure of a rental unit without the consent of the landlord has been held to constitute both undue damage and

---

26 *Khanna v. Masterman et al.* (Nov. 25, 1999), SOL-06827, SOT-00588, SOT-00637 (Ont. Rental Housing Trib.).

27 *Khanna v. Masterman et al.* (Nov. 25, 1999), SOL-06827, SOT-00588, SOT-00637 (Ont. Rental Housing Trib.) and *Sankar v. Tomlinson et al.* (March 26, 1999), TNL-05582 (Ont. Rental Housing Trib.).

28 *Sankar v. Tomlinson et al.* (March 26, 1999), TNL-05582 (Ont. Rental Housing Trib.).

29 (2006), 2006 CarswellOnt 256 (Ont. S.C.J.).

30 (July 6, 1999), TNL-07926, 1999 CarswellOnt 5797 (Ont. Rental Housing Trib.).

31 *Rosati v. Naalband* (July 6, 1999), TNL-07926, 1999 CarswellOnt 5797 (Ont. Rental Housing Trib.). Also see Landlord and Tenant Board File No. EAL-14380 / EAT-01663 (Feb. 12, 2009).

substantial interference with a lawful, right, privilege and interest of the landlord.[32] In *Srivastava v. Campbell et al.*,[33] the tenants rented a house. Without the knowledge or consent of the landlord, they erected a partition in the basement, removed a bar and removed carpeting on the main floor and in the basement, damaged flooring, knocked down a fence on the property and damaged the lawn by parking vehicles on the lawn. This was all held to be undue damage (and grounds for termination of the tenancy). Tenants have also been held responsible where the manner in which they have installed a satellite dish has caused undue damage to the rental unit.[34]

If the tenants have already vacated the rental unit, if the landlord wants to claim relief as against a guarantor or if the extent of the damage is beyond the monetary jurisdiction of the Landlord and Tenant Board, then the landlord may choose to pursue an action against the former tenants (and/or guarantor) in the Ontario Superior Court of Justice. In *Eskritt v. MacKay*,[35] the landlord commenced an action against former tenants and their guarantor for, amongst other things, damage to the premises. The Court found that, pursuant to s. 30 of the T.P.A. (now s. 34 of the R.T.A.), the tenants were responsible for undue damage they or their guests caused to the rental unit and, in this case, awarded almost $30,000 for the property damage claim.

(f) Abandonment[36]

Pursuant to s. 39 of the R.T.A. (formerly s. 41 of the T.P.A.), a landlord may recover possession of a rental unit, without an order of the Board, where a tenant has vacated or abandoned the unit.[37] Where a landlord believes that a tenant has abandoned a rental unit, the landlord may also apply to the Board for an order terminating the tenancy (s. 79). It is not necessary (or possible) to obtain an eviction order in such circumstances since the landlord is alleging that no one lives in the unit (i.e., there is no one to evict).

Dictionary meanings for "vacated" include: "having no tenant and devoid of furniture"; "uninhabited and unoccupied". Dictionary definitions of "aban-

---

[32] *Toronto Community Housing Corp. v. Borys* (July 4, 2002), TEL-28626, [2002] O.R.H.T.D. No. 79 (Ont. Rental Housing Trib.).

[33] (May 26, 1999), TNL-07066 (Ont. Rental Housing Trib.).

[34] See *Parkview Management v. Dehas* (Sept. 27, 2001), EAL-22575, [2001] O.R.H.T.D. No. 126, 2001 CarswellOnt 6317 (Ont. Rental Housing Trib.). There is no liability under s. 87, however, where the installation of the satellite dish has not caused any damage to the rental unit: *Kitchener Alliance Community Homes Inc. v. Brine* (Dec. 16, 2002), SWL-43674, 2002 CarswellOnt 5027 (Ont. Rental Housing Trib.) and *Turret Management Inc. v. Joanisse* (December 3, 2002), NOL-07535-RV (Ont. Rental Housing Trib.).

[35] (2006), 2006 CarswellOnt 6910 (Ont. S.C.J.), reversed (2008), 2008 CarswellOnt 5165 (Ont. C.A.)

[36] See Board's Interpretation Guideline No. 4.

[37] See, for example, *Michaud v. Wright*, (August 10, 1999), NOT-00209 (Ont. Rental Housing Trib.).

doned" include "deserted" and "forsaken". The word "vacant" was considered in a fire insurance case, *Golob v. Dumfries Mutual Fire Insurance Co.*[38] where it was stated: "the term vacant implies entire abandonment, non-occupancy for any purpose". Any of these additional meanings should emphasize, if it is necessary, that a landlord cannot physically re-enter unless it is perfectly obvious that the tenant has left the premises and it is clearly apparent to the landlord that the tenant has no intention of returning.

Obviously this would not include a situation where a tenant is away on holidays, even extended holidays, while the rent is being paid. In fact, as long as the rent is being paid, the unit cannot be considered "abandoned".[39]

If the landlord is absolutely certain that the unit has been abandoned, the landlord can take possession of the unit without an order from the Board (s. 39). If the landlord is in any doubt of the tenant's abandonment of the unit (or if the landlord simply wants some additional assurance before taking back possession of the unit), the landlord should apply to the Board for an order terminating the tenancy. The application is in Form L2 and it can be commenced at any time. The filing fee is $170.[40] Notwithstanding the landlord's belief that the unit is vacant, the application and notice of hearing must still be served on the tenant(s) at least ten days prior to the date set for the hearing (Rule 10.1). In such circumstances, the most practical way to effect service would likely be by mail or by slipping the documents under the door (or through the mail slot) to the unit.[41] The certificate of service for the application and notice of hearing should be filed within five days after service has been effected (Rule 11.2).

On such an application, the Board will need to be satisfied that all the tenants have moved away and have no intention of returning. Indications of this may include evidence that the tenants have disconnected their telephone service, have had their mail forwarded, have removed all of their belongings from the unit and so forth. Photographs of the interior of the unit may assist in demonstrating that all the furniture and other possessions have been removed. The problem for the landlord is obtaining such photographs without violating the law. It would be difficult to argue that such a situation constitutes an emergency justifying entry into the unit without notice (under s. 26). Section 27 of the R.T.A., however, allows for entry on 24 hours written notice to inspect the unit to determine if it is in a good state of repair and fit for habitation (para. 27(1)4) or for "any other reasonable reason for entry specified in the tenancy agreement" (para. 27(1)5). If a landlord includes in the tenancy agreement a provision that allows for entry (on notice) where it

[38] (1979), 25 O.R. (2d) 65 (Ont. C.A.).

[39] Subsection 2(3) of the R.T.A.

[40] Effective April 2009. From 2002 through March 2009, the fee was $150.

[41] If the documents are mailed, the landlord must remember to place the documents in the mail at least 15 days prior to the hearing to allow five days for mail delivery.

appears that the unit has been abandoned, the landlord would be able to lawfully enter the unit in such circumstances (after giving the required written notice at least 24 hours in advance).

In order to form an intention to abandon a rental unit, the tenant must have been acting of his or her own free will. If, for instance, the tenant has been arrested and taken into custody, the landlord cannot treat the unit as being abandoned.[42]

In a bizarre recent case,[43] the landlord brought an application to terminate the tenancy on the basis that the tenant had abandoned the rental unit. Both the landlord and tenant attended the hearing. In the resulting order, the Member makes no finding with respect to the issue of abandonment of the unit but goes on to terminate the tenancy and evict the tenant (notwithstanding that there is no indication that the tenant consented to this) because, in the opinion of the Member, it was a bad relationship and it would be better for the parties if the tenancy were ended!

In Landlord and Tenant Board File No. TNL-00769 (March 23, 2007), there were two tenants, a husband and wife. There was a marital breakdown and the wife left her husband, who remained for a time in the rental unit. The husband then advised the landlord that he would be moving out and he returned his key to the unit. The landlord never heard from the wife. In these circumstances, the Board found that the rental unit could be considered abandoned and granted the landlord's application to terminate the tenancy.

Given that applications for abandonment are relatively rare, I suspect that many landlords simply take possession of abandoned rental units without seeking an order.

Some landlords, however, may have chosen to pursue an application based upon arrears of rent rather than based upon abandonment of the rental unit. In such circumstances, there is a potential problem with such a tactic. An application to terminate a tenancy based upon arrears of rent may only be commenced while the tenant remains in possession of the rental unit.[44] If the unit has been abandoned, it is questionable whether the tenant could be said to be in possession of the unit. The Court of Appeal, in *1162994 Ontario Inc. v. Bakker*, [45] has now raised serious doubts about whether a tenant who no longer lives in a rental unit can be said to be in possession of the unit.[46] A

---

[42] *Clatney v. Genova* (2005), [2005] O.J. No. 1285, 2005 CarswellOnt 1552 (Ont. Div. Ct.) and *Sophmeric Investments A.J. Hofstader v. Misasi* (Feb. 14, 2000), TEL-09996, [2000] O.R.H.T.D. No. 30, 2000 CarswellOnt 6341 (Ont. Rental Housing Trib.).

[43] Landlord and Tenant Board File No. TNL-21516 (Jan. 22, 2009).

[44] Paragraph 87(1)(b) of the R.T.A. (formerly para. 86(1)(b) of the T.P.A.).

[45] [2004] O.J. No. 2565, 2004 CarswellOnt 869 (Ont. C.A.) (SWL-40290).

[46] Notwithstanding that the Divisional Court held that a tenancy continues (i.e., is not terminated) where a tenant vacates a rental unit without first giving proper notice of termination (*George V Apartments Ltd. v. Cobb* (2002), 2002 CarswellOnt 5553 (Ont. Div. Ct.)) and that a tenant who vacates a rental unit without giving proper notice to the landlord and who

landlord should also consider that it is a serious offence to file false or misleading documents with the Board, and declaring on the Form L1 that the tenant remains in possession of the rental unit when the landlord knows that the tenant has abandoned the unit may well expose the landlord and those acting for the landlord to the risk of prosecution and, upon conviction, the very real possibility of having to pay substantial fines.

Special provisions apply where a mobile home or land lease home has been abandoned. Please refer to Chapters 18 and 20 for more information on this topic.

3. SELECTED EVICTION APPLICATIONS

(a) General

Pursuant to s. 39 of the R.T.A. (formerly s. 41 of the T.P.A.), a landlord may not recover possession of a rental unit subject to a tenancy unless the tenant has vacated or abandoned the unit or the landlord has obtained an order of the Board authorizing the landlord to have the tenant evicted and to regain possession of the unit. If a landlord attempts to re-enter a unit without following the correct procedures, the landlord may be penalized by the Board (on application by the tenant) and may be subject to prosecution for an offence under one or more of ss. 233 through 237 of the R.T.A.

Where a tenant breaches his or her obligations under the R.T.A., this can often constitute grounds for eviction. Termination of the tenancy and eviction is the ultimate consequence as it represents an end to the landlord-tenant relationship; it results in the forcible removal of a tenant from his or her home.

Every eviction application is commenced in reliance by a landlord upon the specific provisions of the R.T.A. that have been breached by the tenant and upon s. 69 which states: "A landlord may apply to the Board for an order terminating the tenancy and evicting the tenant if the landlord has given notice to terminate under this Act or the *Tenant Protection Act,* 1997."

The earliest date upon which an application may be commenced depends upon the nature of the application. For certain types of breaches, the application cannot be commenced until after the notice period set out in the notice of termination has expired. For example, if a landlord gives a notice of termination for non-payment of rent (a Form N4) which provides the tenant with 14 days notice, the application cannot be commenced until the 15th day after the notice was given (the day after the termination date specified in the notice of termination).[47] For notices that provide the tenant with seven days

---

retains a key (and therefore some control) can be said to be in possession of the unit (*Tenser v. Norquay Developments Limited*, Div. Ct. File No. 1426, re SWL-52858).

[47] Subsection 74(1) of the R.T.A. (formerly subsection 72(1) of the T.P.A.).

to rectify the problem identified in the notice, an application to terminate the tenancy cannot be commenced until after the full seven-day period has expired.[48] If the specific section relied upon by the landlord is silent on this issue, then the application may be commenced immediately after serving the notice of termination upon the tenant (s. 71).

There is also a time limit (i.e., deadline) for commencing most applications. Except for applications based upon arrears of rent, all other applications must be commenced no later than 30 days after the termination date specified in the notice of termination.[49] There is no deadline for applications based upon arrears of rent.[50] The filing fee for most landlord applications is $170.[51]

Usually, the landlord applies under s. 69 for an order that both terminates the tenancy and evicts the tenant. In at least one circumstance, however, a landlord will apply for one but not the other.[52] As discussed earlier in this chapter, where the landlord believes that the tenant has abandoned the rental unit, the landlord may apply to the Board under s. 79 for an order terminating the tenancy, but since the unit is supposedly vacant, the Board has no power to order an eviction on such an application.

Under the T.P.A. (s. 81), where the Tribunal found that there had been an unauthorized transfer of the unit, the Tribunal had the power to evict the unauthorized occupant but not to terminate the tenancy. This has changed under the R.T.A. Now, the Board has the power under s. 100 of the R.T.A. to both evict the occupant(s) of the unit and terminate the tenancy.

In every case where *eviction* is being sought, the Board must weigh the facts and decide whether it would be appropriate to delay the eviction or to deny the landlord's request for an eviction (subsections 83(1) and (2)). In certain circumstances, where the landlord is acting improperly, the Board is required to deny a request for an eviction order (subsection 83(3)). Relief from forfeiture and the effect of s. 83 are discussed at length in Chapter 14.

---

[48] Section 70 of the R.T.A.

[49] Subsection 69(2) of the R.T.A.

[50] See subsection 69(3) of the R.T.A. Note that although there is no deadline specified in the R.T.A. for commencing an application based upon arrears of rent, a landlord attempting to rely upon an old notice of termination may encounter some difficulties (discussed later in this chapter, in the section on evictions based upon non-payment of rent). Although there is no time limit in the R.T.A. for such applications, there is a six-year limitation set out in the *Real Property Limitations Act*, R.S.O. 1990, c. L. 15.

[51] There is no charge for an application under s. 78 and there is a fee schedule for applications under s. 126. Always consult with the Board to ascertain the current fee schedules.

[52] See Chapter 2 for a discussion of the power of the Board to terminate a tenancy and order evictions, and the difference between the two.

(b) Unauthorized Occupant

Under s. 100(1) of the R.T.A. (formerly s. 81(1) of the T.P.A.), if a tenant transfers the occupancy of a rental unit to a person in a manner other than by an assignment authorized under s. 95 or a subletting authorized under s. 97, the landlord may apply to the Board for an order terminating the tenancy and evicting the tenant and the person to whom the occupancy of the rental unit was transferred. Although rarely requested, the landlord is also entitled to request on this type of application an order for the payment of compensation by the unauthorized occupant for the use and occupation of the rental unit[53] as well as an order for the payment to the landlord of an amount necessary to reimburse the landlord for bank charges and the landlord's administration charges related to NSF cheques the landlord has received.[54]

The application is commenced by the landlord having a Form A2 application issued and then serving the application and notice of hearing upon the tenant and the occupant(s) at least ten days prior to the date of the hearing (Rule 10.1).[55] The filing fee is $170.[56] The application must be made no later than 60 days after the landlord discovers the unauthorized transfer of occupancy (s. 100(2)). If the landlord does not commence an application under s. 100 within 60 days of discovering the transfer of occupancy and does not negotiate a new tenancy agreement with the occupant, an assignment of the rental unit is deemed to have occurred (i.e., the occupant is permitted to "take over" the existing tenancy and becomes a tenant).[57] The clock starts to run from the time the landlord discovers the *transfer* of occupancy, not from the time the landlord discovers the person in question is occupying the unit.[58] This is a distinction that may have been overlooked by the Board in Landlord and Tenant Board File No. TEL-19428 (Jan. 16, 2009) as there is no determination that there was actually ever a transfer of occupancy but the Member was nevertheless prepared to find that the landlord's application was out of time.

The Board may also examine whether the landlord has expressly or implicitly[59] accepted the occupant as a tenant.

---

[53] Subsection 100(3) of the R.T.A. (formerly subsection 86(2.1) of the T.P.A.). The amount of daily compensation is based on the rent. For monthly rent, multiply the rent by 12 and then divide that product by 365 to calculate a daily rate of compensation. For weekly rent, multiply the rent by 52 and then divide the product by 365.

[54] Subsection 100(4) of the R.T.A.

[55] The proper parties to an application are the landlord and tenant(s) and any person who may be directly affected by the application (s. 187(1)).

[56] Effective April 2009. From 2002 through March 2009, the fee was $150.

[57] Subsection 104(4) of the R.T.A. (formerly subsection 125(4) of the T.P.A.).

[58] *Valela v. Hinds et al.* (Dec. 24, 2001), TNL-31825-RV (Ont. Rental Housing Trib.). Also see Landlord and Tenant Board File No. CEL-00427 (March 8, 2007) and Landlord and Tenant Board File Nos. TSL-19736 / TSL-20767 (Feb. 18, 2009).

[59] See *Pezza et al. v. Altberg et al.* (March 6, 2003), TNL-44119 (Ont. Rental Housing Trib.).

In *Lee v. Duarte*,[60] M. and J. Duarte were the original tenants. Their adult son, A. Duarte, also lived in the unit. In November 1998, the landlord discovered that J. Duarte had died and that M. Duarte had moved out of the unit. The landlord commenced an application against A. Duarte and his wife as unauthorized occupants. The application was dismissed. For approximately four years the landlord had been dealing with A. Duarte as if he were a tenant of the unit. In fact, the landlord dealt exclusively with A. Duarte and A. Duarte paid all of the rent during that period. Although A. Duarte may not have originally been named as a tenant, a tenancy was implied by the conduct of the parties.

In a somewhat similar case,[61] a written tenancy agreement showed only one tenant. Subsequently, and with the knowledge and consent of the landlord, another adult person moved into the unit with the original tenant. That person began paying one-half of the rent directly to the landlord. The landlord communicated directly with that person with respect to maintenance and other aspects of the tenancy. Eventually, the original tenant named in the tenancy agreement gave notice that she was vacating the unit. When she left, the landlord brought an application to evict the other person who remained in the rental unit on the basis that she was an unauthorized occupant. She responded that, given the conduct of the parties over time, it was implicit that she was a tenant (even if not listed on the written tenancy agreement) and not merely an occupant. The Member agreed and dismissed the landlord's application.

It is not uncommon for family members of the tenant (who may have been living with the tenant) to remain in the unit when the tenant dies. Under s. 91 of the R.T.A. (formerly s. 49 of the T.P.A.), the tenancy is automatically terminated 30 days after the death of the tenant. As long as the landlord does not accept as a tenant the person who continues to occupy the unit after the death of the tenant and commences an application under s. 100 in time, the Board will likely grant the landlord's application and evict the family members as unauthorized occupants.[62]

As discussed in detail in Chapter 3, however, the surviving spouse of a tenant may be entitled now to remain in the unit as a tenant pursuant to the provisions of subsection 3(1) of O. Reg. 516/06, which reads as follows:

> If a tenant of a rental unit dies and the rental unit is the principal residence of the spouse of that tenant, the spouse is included in the definition of "tenant" in

---

[60] (Feb. 22, 1999), TSL-05399, 1999 CarswellOnt 5808 (Ont. Rental Housing Trib.).

[61] Landlord and Tenant Board File No. EAL-00576 (April 27, 2007).

[62] *1500 Tansely c/o Lakeshore Management v. Smith* (Aug. 22, 2002), SOL-33570, 2002 CarswellOnt 3788 (Ont. Rental Housing Trib.); *Portree Properties Limited v. Morris* (March 28, 1999), TSL-07281 (Ont. Rental Housing Trib.); and *Toronto Community Housing Corp., Re* (June 19, 2006), TEL-62490, 2006 CarswellOnt 9154 (Ont. Rental Housing Trib.).

subsection 2(1) of the Act unless the spouse vacates the unit within the 30-day period described in subsection 91(1) of the Act.

This permits a surviving spouse (who is not listed on the tenancy agreement as a tenant) the option of either vacating the unit within 30 days of the death of the tenant or remaining in the unit as a "tenant", with all of the rights and obligations that entails. However, pursuant to subsection 3(4) of O. Reg. 516/06, surviving spouses have no such protection in cases of social housing,[63] care homes[64] and certain types of government housing.[65]

In cases where only one person is listed as the tenant on a tenancy agreement, it is also not uncommon (usually in cases where there is a breakdown in the relationship) for that person to simply vacate the rental unit and leave their spouse behind without providing any notice of termination to the landlord, without agreeing with the landlord that the tenancy will be terminated and without seeking the landlord's permission to assign or sublet the unit to the spouse. In such cases, if the rental unit is the principal residence of the tenant's spouse, the spouse shall now be deemed to be a "tenant"[66] (with all of the rights and obligations that entails) *unless*:

1. the rental unit is in a building that contains three or fewer residential units and the landlord resides in the building;[67]
2. the spouse vacates the rental unit no later than 60 days after the tenant vacated the rental unit;[68]
3. the tenant who vacated the rental unit was not in arrears of rent, the landlord commences an application under s. 100 of the R.T.A. to terminate the tenancy because the tenant has transferred occupancy of the rental unit without the consent of the landlord, the tenant does not oppose that application or otherwise indicate that he or she intends to remain in the rental unit and the Board issues an order terminating the tenancy under s. 100;[69]
4. the tenant who vacated the rental unit was in arrears of rent, the landlord gives the spouse a notice (in a form approved by the Board) within 45 days after the date the tenant vacated the unit and the spouse fails, within 15 days after receiving the notice:
   i. to advise the landlord that he or she intends to remain in the rental unit; or
   ii. to agree in writing with the landlord to pay the arrears of rent;[70]

---

[63] I.e., a rental unit described in s. 7 of the R.T.A.

[64] I.e., a rental unit that is in a care home to which Part IX of the R.T.A. applies.

[65] I.e., a rental unit to which s. 6 of O. Reg. 516/06 applies.

[66] Subsection 3(2) of O. Reg. 196/06.

[67] Paragraph 3(3)1 of O. Reg. 196/06.

[68] Paragraph 3(3)2 of O. Reg. 196/06.

[69] Paragraph 3(3)3 of O. Reg. 196/06.

[70] Paragraph 3(3)4 of O. Reg. 196/06.

5. the tenant who vacated the rental unit was in arrears of rent, the landlord does not give the spouse a notice but brings an application to terminate the tenancy under s. 100 of the R.T.A. (for an unauthorized transfer of occupancy) and the spouse fails, before the order under s. 100 is issued:
   i. to advise the landlord that he or she intends to remain in the rental unit; or
   ii. to agree in writing with the landlord to pay the arrears of rent;[71]
6. the tenancy falls within one of the following: social housing, a care home or certain types of government housing.[72]

Thus, if the sole tenant listed on the tenancy agreement vacates the rental unit without providing a notice of termination or dies, leaving behind a spouse who continues to use the rental unit as his or her principal residence, the landlord will have to carefully consider the provisions of s. 3 of O. Reg. 516/06 before deciding whether or not the spouse is a "tenant" or an "unauthorized occupant". In order to protect its interests, a landlord may have to either give the appropriate notice to the spouse requesting that the spouse elect whether or not to remain in the unit as a tenant or the landlord may have to commence an application under s. 100 to see whether or not the spouse will oppose it. Where it appears to the landlord that the sole tenant has vacated the unit, leaving a spouse remaining in the unit, the landlord should consider delivering to the remaining spouse a notice in Form N14.

Section 100 of the R.T.A. does not apply to situations in which the tenant has invited a person to share the rental unit and where the landlord does not approve of an additional person living in the unit or does not approve of the particular person in question. As long as the original tenant continues to occupy the rental unit, a *transfer* of occupancy has not occurred.[73]

The new provisions of the R.T.A., however, only serve to protect a "spouse" and only in certain specified situations. What if the person left behind in the unit does not meet the definition of "spouse"? In certain circumstances, it may be inferred that such a person was in fact a tenant, even if their name did not appear on the tenancy agreement.[74] If that is the finding of the Board, that person cannot be considered to be an unauthorized occupant. Each case will turn on its own facts, including details of all interactions between the landlord and that person.

---

[71] Paragraph 3(3)5 of O. Reg. 196/06.

[72] Subsection 3(4) of O. Reg. 196/06.

[73] *Gallery Towers v. Schpactenko* (Dec. 13, 1999), TNL-07692-SA (Ont. Rental Housing Trib.); *Sheldon Stein Construction Co. Ltd. v. Geist* (Feb. 12, 1999), TNL-03910 (Ont. Rental Housing Trib.).

[74] See Landlord and Tenant Board File No. TNL-18268 / TNL-20272 / TNT-01306 (Jan. 20, 2009) and Landlord and Tenant Board File No. SWL-21996 (Jan. 13, 2009).

In *Belaga v. Hastilow*,[75] the tenant invited another person to share his unit. The situation changed and the tenant requested that person to leave. They refused. With the co-operation of the landlord, an application was commenced to evict that person from the unit as an "unauthorized occupant". Since, however, there had not been a *transfer* of the unit from the tenant to that person (i.e., since the tenant also continued to occupy the unit), the application had to be dismissed.

Whether the original tenant retains sufficient connection with the rental unit to allow the Board to find that the tenant continues to "occupy" it is a question of fact.

In *Jane-Oak Apartments Inc. v. Bosco*,[76] the tenants moved to another city but allowed their adult children to remain in the unit. The father continued to reside in the unit, on average, two or three days per week and he continued to pay the rent for the unit. It was held that there had not been a transfer of occupancy and that, therefore, the children were not unauthorized occupants. In the alternative, the landlord had known about this situation for almost a year so if there had been a transfer of occupancy, there would be deemed to be an assignment of the tenancy to the children (who would now be considered tenants).

In *Murphy v. Despres*,[77] the tenant had originally rented an entire house. He then allowed others to move into the house and he spent most of his time at his girlfriend's house and moved most of his personal belongings there. The rental unit was no longer his home. He had turned the garage at the house into an auto body shop, however, and attended at the house almost daily to carry on his business. It was held that he no longer occupied the rental unit for residential purposes and that there had been a transfer of occupancy without the consent of the landlord. The unauthorized occupants were evicted.

In *Toots v. Chacko*,[78] the tenant allowed her brother and his family to move into the rental unit. She had moved in with her boyfriend and had removed most of her possessions from the rental unit. She failed to demonstrate that she maintained a substantial connection with the rental unit and it was held that she had transferred occupancy of the rental unit to her brother (and his family). The landlord's application was granted.

In Landlord and Tenant Board File No. SWL-22625 (Feb. 12, 2009), the Board found that there had not been a transfer of occupancy because the tenants were only temporarily out of the province dealing with family problems and they expected to return soon to the rental unit.

[75] (October 29, 1999) TSL-14006 (Ont. Rental Housing Trib.).

[76] (Feb. 22, 1999), TSL-05399 (Ont. Rental Housing Trib.).

[77] (Oct. 31, 2002), TNL-40892, 2002 CarswellOnt 3816 (Ont. Rental Housing Trib.).

[78] (Jan. 20, 2003), TNL-43192, 2003 CarswellOnt 1503 (Ont. Rental Housing Trib.).

The seminal case in this area is now *Nicholson v. Samuel Property Management Ltd.*[79] The tenant ceased to reside full-time at the unit. He slept at the unit once or twice a week. He continued to pay the rent to the landlord and to pay for the utilities. He allowed others to live in the unit. The landlord sought to evict them as unauthorized occupants. The Member who heard this case held that the tenant's continuing connection to the unit was not substantial enough to support a finding that he maintained a residence there. It was held that there had been a transfer of occupancy and the application was granted.

On appeal, the Divisional Court held that the Member was wrong in law to base his decision upon a "substantial connection" test which is not enunciated in the *Act*. On further appeal, the Court of Appeal overturned the decision of the Divisional Court and restored that of the Tribunal:

> Nicholson's limited use of the rental unit makes it impossible to conclude that he had not transferred the occupancy of it to his two friends. The unit is, in truth, not the home of Nicholson, who occasionally stays there and keeps his clothes there, but of his two friends, who carry on all usual living activities there. (para. 24)

The Court of Appeal held that occupation is a question of fact and degree. If that is so, one might wonder what jurisdiction the Divisional Court has to hear an appeal of such an issue since the Divisional Court is restricted to considering only alleged errors in law (and not findings of fact). Unfortunately, the Court of Appeal did not specifically deal with this issue in its decision.

(c) "No-Fault" Grounds for Termination of the Tenancy

(i) Landlord Requires Unit[80]

By s. 48(1) of the R.T.A. (formerly s. 51(1) of the T.P.A.), a landlord may give notice of termination if, in good faith, the landlord, their spouse or a child or parent of one of them or a person who will provide care services to one of them (and who will live in the residential complex) requires possession of the rental unit for the purpose of residential occupation. Notice of termination (Form N12) may be given to take effect at the end of the period of tenancy, whether weekly, monthly, or yearly, or at the end of a tenancy of a fixed term, for example two years. The notice period cannot be less than 60 days.

---

[79] (2002), 2002 CarswellOnt 3004, 3 R.P.R. (4th) 66 (Ont. C.A.), reversing (2001), 2001 CarswellOnt 3570 (Ont. Div. Ct.) and restoring the Tribunal's decisions in TSL-22331 and TSL-24516.

[80] Please refer to the Board's Interpretation Guideline No. 12.

"Child" does not include a grandchild of the landlord,[81] although it may include a foster child.[82] "Child" also does not include an adult niece whom the landlord has demonstrated a settled intention to treat as a dependent or for whom the landlord has the obligations of a father because of his religion.[83]

"Spouse" includes an estranged spouse.[84]

A landlord cannot give this type of notice for a grandchild as this is not one of the classes of relatives listed under s. 48(1) of the R.T.A. (formerly s. 51(1) of the T.P.A.).[85]

New under the R.T.A. is the right of a landlord to give this notice for use of the rental unit by a person who will provide care services to the landlord (or specified members of the landlord's family). In Landlord and Tenant Board File No. TSL-04977 (Aug. 21, 2007), the landlord, an 89-year-old woman, resided on the main floor of the residential complex. She required assistance with daily tasks. Although she had outside assistance for two to three hours every day, she had no one to assist her in the evenings. She sought to evict the tenant of the basement unit so that the unit could be occupied by a person who would provide her with additional care services. The landlord and prospective care provider testified at the hearing and were found to be credible. Despite the fact that another unit was available in the complex, the Member found that the landlord was acting in good faith and was entitled to choose to have the care provider live in the basement unit if that was her desire. Given the fact that the basement tenant had lived there for over 18 years, however, the Board delayed the eviction for approximately two months to allow him additional time in which to find alternate accommodations.

In *Shah, Re*,[86] it was held that a notice of termination for use by the landlord (Form N12) was invalid as it did not identify both landlords and did not specify the identity of the specific person(s) who intended to occupy the rental unit. The date of termination specified in the notice of termination must be at least 60 days after the notice is given <u>and</u> shall be the day a period of the tenancy ends, or where the tenancy is for a fixed term, the end of the term

13 — LL APPLICATIONS

---

[81] *Pasek v. Thompson* (1989), 1989 CarswellOnt 3103 (Ont. Dist. Ct.); *Kohot and Mullen* (May 7, 1999), TEL-04995 (Ont. Rental Housing Trib.); *Lazar v. Bouzane* (Aug. 16, 2002), TNL-36315, 2002 CarswellOnt 3781 (Ont. Rental Housing Trib.); and *Lackner v. Smith* (May 16, 2001), TNL-26384, [2001] O.R.H.T.D. No. 69, 2001 CarswellOnt 6366 (Ont. Rental Housing Trib.).

[82] *McLean v. Mosher* (1992), 9 O.R. (3d) 156 (Ont. Gen. Div.) and *Ouellette v. Lecuyer* (Feb. 1, 1999), EAL-03494 (Ont. Rental Housing Trib.).

[83] *Anwar v. Martins* (March 4, 1999), TSL-06296 (Ont. Rental Housing Trib.).

[84] *Bobotsis v. Brown* (June 7, 2006), SWL-81221, 2006 CarswellOnt 4425, [2006] O.R.H.T.D. No. 61 (Ont. Rental Housing Trib.).

[85] *Fox v. Brown* (Sept. 16, 2002), TSL-43167-SA (Ont. Rental Housing Trib.).

[86] (June 21, 2006), TEL-62456, 2006 CarswellOnt 4423 (Ont. Rental Housing Trib.).

(s. 48(2)).[87] See Chapter 6 for a more detailed discussion of the statutory requirements for a valid notice of termination.

Having given notice of termination, the landlord may immediately commence an application for possession (s. 71). The application is in Form L2. The filing fee is $170.[88] The application cannot be commenced more than 30 days after the termination date specified in the notice of termination (s. 69(2)). The application and notice of hearing should be served on the tenant(s) at least 10 days before the hearing (Rule 10.1) and the certificate of service for the application and notice of hearing should be filed within five days of service (Rule 11.2).

The Board cannot make an order terminating a tenancy and evicting the tenant in an application based on notice under s. 48 (or 49) unless the person who requires the rental unit files with the Board an affidavit certifying that the person in good faith requires the rental unit for his or her own personal use (s. 72(1)).[89] The affidavit should be as specific as possible. Simply stating "I require the unit" may not be sufficient. The affidavit should indicate the identity of the person and their relationship to the landlord and that they require the unit for their residence (i.e., that they intend to live in the unit). Finally, the affidavit must be signed by the person who actually intends to live in the rental unit.[90]

Special provisions apply to a tenant living in a residential unit that is being, or has been, converted to a condominium. The possible rights and limitations of a landlord are spelled out in s. 51(1) to (7) of the R.T.A.

"Requires" should not be interpreted to the point that a landlord seeking possession of his or her own premises must prove that this accommodation and no other will suffice. "Requires" is answered by the landlord having a *bona fide* intention to regain possession for the landlord's own or family's occupancy. In *Kennealy v. Dunne*[91] the applicant had a residence elsewhere and also the use of his daughter's flat. The Court of Appeal rejected an objective inquiry into the landlord's needs as being irrelevant, and stated that the landlord's genuine desire was sufficient.

---

[87] The application will be dismissed if the termination date identified in the notice of termination does not comply with the requirements of the R.T.A. For instance, an application was dismissed where the landlord chose a termination date of December 31, 2008, but the tenancy was for a fixed term that did not end until September 2009: Landlord and Tenant Board File No. CEL-15584 (Jan. 14, 2009).

[88] Effective April 2009. From 2002 through March 2009, the fee was $150.

[89] If the affidavit is not signed by the person who will be living in the rental unit or is not sworn, the application will be dismissed: *Akhtar v. Adamson* (April 26, 2006), TEL-60864, [2006] O.R.H.T.D. No. 44, 2006 CarswellOnt 4415 (Ont. Rental Housing Trib.) and Landlord and Tenant Board File No. EAL-14064 (Feb. 4, 2009).

[90] *1461313 Ontario Limited v. Clarke* (January 17, 2002), TSL-36355 (Ont. Rental Housing Trib.).

[91] (1976), [1977] 2 All E.R. 16 (Eng. C.A.).

Both "bona fide" and "requires" were considered in *Robertson v. Heinrich.*[92] The judge stated that "bona fide" has the ordinary meaning of "in good faith, or real, actually genuine". As for "requires" this does not mean that the landlord must prove a justifiable need. The point was more fully dealt with in *Ireland v. Taylor*[93] where Tucker L.J. said:

> If the landlord in fact desires possession of this [the additional rooms of his] house [for a studio] and genuinely intends to use it for this purpose, I can see no ground for saying that he does not "require" it.

"Requires" and "bona fide" were also analyzed in *Winchur v. Louwe,*[94] in which the judge questioned whether the landlady honestly required the premises for her son. There was no clear evidence that she would move in if vacant possession was obtained and there had been previous court proceedings between the landlady and the tenant about lack of repairs.

Another way of stating "requires" is that it is the genuine want and intent of the landlord which is fundamental and not the reasonableness of the landlord: *Cove Mobilehome Park & Sales Ltd. v. Welch.*[95]

This was re-stated in *McLean v. Mosher*[96] — a landlord need not establish that his requirement is reasonable, only that he *bona fide* wanted and genuinely had the immediate intention to occupy. The landlord applied for possession under s. 51 of the T.P.A. to provide living accommodation for a foster child.

The meaning of the expression "in good faith" is said to have the literal meaning of "bona fide", and has been defined in legal dictionaries as "honestly, without fraud, collusion or participation in wrong doing", or that the landlord must truly intend to do what it says and that the landlord must not be guilty of dishonesty, deception or pretence: *Semeniuk v. White Oak Stables Ltd.*[97] The concept of "good faith" was examined by the Tribunal in *Slater v. Beljinac*[98] and *Stockla v. Wolff.*[99]

Usually, the size of the residential complex is irrelevant on this type of application. If, however, the application is based on a tenancy or occupancy agreement purporting to entitle the landlord to reside in the unit, the Board shall not make an order terminating a tenancy and evicting the tenant(s) unless the building contains not more than four units *or* the landlord, spouse,

13 — LL APPLICATIONS

---

92 (May 12, 1978) (Ont. Co. Ct.).

93 (1948), [1949] 1 K.B. 300 (Eng. K.B.).

94 (September 2, 1981), Doc. L&T98/81 (Ont. Co. Ct.).

95 (1979), 27 O.R. (2d) 65 (Ont. Div. Ct.).

96 (1992), 9 O.R. (3d) 156 (Ont. Gen. Div.).

97 (1991), 56 B.C.L.R. (2d) 371 (B.C. C.A.).

98 (Oct. 4, 2000), TSL-21378 (Ont. Rental Housing Trib.).

99 (May 19, 2000), NOL-02972 (Ont. Rental Housing Trib.) with reference to *Feeney v. Noble* (1994), 19 O.R. (3d) 762 (Ont. Div. Ct.).

child or parent had previously been a genuine occupant of the premises (s. 72(2)).[100]

In *Cosentino v. Lowden*,[101] the judge accepted the landlord's *bona fides* but questioned whether the landlord required the tenant's apartment. It was to be for the landlord's son *if* he separated from his wife. Therefore, the application was refused as no present need or requirement existed. The judge apparently took into account the competing equities of the son possibly moving in as against "the substantial upset and hardship" for the tenants having to find similar accommodation. It is suggested this should not be a factor in determining whether the landlord "requires" possession. It would, however, be relevant to the Board's consideration as to whether or not to grant relief from forfeiture under s. 83(1).

There must be a genuine desire to occupy the rental unit as a residence immediately or within a reasonable period of time.[102] What is a reasonable period of time depends upon the circumstances of each case.

In *Chenard v. Foster*,[103] four siblings inherited a 350-acre, lakefront property that had been in their family for 175 years. A land lease community (consisting mostly of seasonal cottages) was located on the property and, thus, the siblings became landlords. The landlords wished to sever the property and to each build a retirement home on his/her own portion of the land. They intended to make those new homes their respective residences. They obtained permission from the local Land Division Committee to sever their land on the condition that the existing land lease homes be removed first. The tenants objected so the landlord commenced 17 separate applications before the Ontario Rental Housing Tribunal to terminate these tenancies under what was s. 51 of the T.P.A. The landlord was successful on all applications. The tenants then appealed those decisions to the Divisional Court, which heard all of these matters together. The Court recognized that there would be a delay between the removal of the land lease homes and the erection by each landlord of his or her new home but that this delay was reasonable in the circumstances. In any event, the Court held that once the land lease homes were removed, the process to erect the new homes would be underway and the landlord could be said to be "occupying" the lots for the purposes of their residential occupation (even if they were not yet actually residing there). The appeals were dismissed with costs to the respondents in the amount of $7,500 (inclusive of GST and disbursements).

---

[100] See *Cohen v. Klein* (May 11, 2001), TNL-17189(2), [2001] O.R.H.T.D. No. 66, 2001 CarswellOnt 6410 (Ont. Rental Housing Trib.), and *Capelas v. Osmond et al.* (July 9, 2001), TNL-27003-RV (Ont. Rental Housing Trib.).

[101] (March 16, 1982), Doc. M60558/82 (Ont. Co. Ct.).

[102] *Salter v. Beljinac* (2001), 201 D.L.R. (4th) 744 (Ont. Div. Ct.) and *Chenard v. Foster* (2007), 2007 CarswellOnt 7709 (Ont. Div. Ct.).

[103] (2007), 2007 CarswellOnt 7709 (Ont. Div. Ct.).

The landlord must require possession of the rental unit for the purpose of *residential occupation*. It has been held that leaving the unit empty does not constitute *residential occupation*. In Landlord and Tenant Board File No. TEL-01943 (May 22, 2007), the landlords rented out their basement. They served a notice of termination and then commenced an application to terminate the basement apartment tenancy so that they could regain possession of the basement for their own use. At the hearing, however, it became apparent that, if the application were granted, the landlords "would not use this space for any purpose". Aside from the doubts that the Member may have had about the true motives for the landlord's application (given the troubled history between the parties), the Vice-chair based his decision on his determination that leaving a unit vacant does not constitute "residential occupation". He went on to state,

> If leaving a rental unit empty was considered to be "residential occupation", then the remedy contained [in] Subsection 57(1)(a) would be rendered meaningless and unavailable, as it would be impossible for a tenant to establish that the landlord or other specified person did not occupy the rental unit with[in] a reasonable time.

While the reasoning of the Vice-chair may be logical in many settings, it seems too narrow an approach to take with respect to situations such as this where a landlord trying to reclaim a part of his or her own home. The R.T.A. contains a number of new provisions (for example, providing for expedited evictions) that recognize that tenancies within a landlord's home may require special treatment. In this case, the Vice-chair found as a fact that the landlords genuinely intended not to re-rent the basement apartment. Given their experiences with this tenant, they decided that they no longer wished to be landlords at all and they wanted to reclaim their entire house for their family. Their mistake was in stating that the unit would be left empty. Had they simply stated that they would be using the basement as a part of their home for storage or for other normal residential purposes then their application may well have been granted.

Where units are vacant in a multi-unit building but the landlord insists that he or she genuinely desires to move into a particular unit that is currently occupied, the Board may wish to enquire further. Although, in order to be acting in good faith, a landlord's desire for a unit need only be genuine and not necessarily reasonable,[104] the reasonableness of the landlord's conduct will be relevant in two ways. First, capriciousness on the part of the landlord may lead the Board to the conclusion that the landlord is really acting out of ulterior motives;[105] this is especially true where there is a history of animosity

[104] *DaVinci Towers Apartments v. Harris* (October 7, 1985), Zalev D.C.J. (Ont. Dist. Ct.) and *Decristofano v. Darr* (September 17, 1986), Salhany J. (Ont. Dist. Ct.).

[105] See Landlord and Tenant Board File No. TEL-00222 (March 5, 2007).

or conflict between the parties. Second, the Board retains the discretionary power under s. 83(1) to refuse to grant an eviction. If the disruption to the life of the tenant would be substantial and the landlord cannot give a good explanation as to why it is critical that the landlord live in the particular rental unit in question, especially where there are other units available in the building, the Board may refuse to grant the landlord's application (notwithstanding that the landlord's intention to move into the rental unit was found to be genuine).[106]

In any case, where the parties have a history of conflict or where it appears the landlord may be retaliating against the tenant, the Board may decline the landlord's application either on the basis that the landlord is not acting in good faith or in reliance upon either s. 83(1) or (3) of the R.T.A. The Board's assessment of the credibility of the parties will often be determinative of the result.[107]

The person who intends to reside in the unit is not required to testify at the hearing. The Board may rely upon the affidavit of that person and the other evidence presented at the hearing.[108] While the affidavit may not be the best possible evidence, in some cases it may be sufficient.[109] There is a risk, however, that by not calling a key witness, the case may be weakened and may not succeed; the Board may draw an adverse inference from the absence of a crucial witness or may simply find that the applicant has failed to meet the onus of proof.[110]

In *Dremin v. Beckner*,[111] the landlord applied to terminate the tenancy on the basis that the landlord's son required possession of the unit. The Tribunal found that the landlord was not acting in good faith and was, in fact, bringing the application in retaliation for what the landlord perceived to be the tenant's role in preventing the landlord from using the rear of the property as a commercial parking lot.

In *DeAcetis v. Rogers*,[112] shortly after the tenants were successful in obtaining an order for an abatement of rent and requiring the landlords to effect repairs, the landlords served the tenants with a notice that they required the unit for use by their daughter. The Member hearing this case inferred

---

[106] *Horst v. Beingessner* (Nov. 14, 2002), SWL-43648, 2002 CarswellOnt 5019 (Ont. Rental Housing Trib.).

[107] See, for example: *Groe v. Motchuk* (November 18, 2002), TSL-41387 (Ont. Rental Housing Trib.) and Landlord and Tenant Board File No. SOL-18674 (Feb. 20, 2009).

[108] *Walsh v. 580472 Ontario Ltd. et al.* (Nov. 6, 2002), Div. Ct. File No.: Toronto 578/02 re CEL-25335 (Ont. Rental Housing Trib.).

[109] *Lombardi v. Brenke-Leach* (Dec. 14, 2000), TNL-21991-SA, 2000 CarswellOnt 6409 (Ont. Rental Housing Trib.) and Landlord and Tenant Board File No. SWL-20646 (Jan. 20, 2009).

[110] *Afzalzada v. Murray* (May 18, 2001), TNL-25657 (Ont. Rental Housing Trib.) and Landlord and Tenant Board File No. TNL-20842 (Jan. 14, 2009).

[111] (Aug. 24, 1998), TSL-00419, 1998 CarswellOnt 6409 (Ont. Rental Housing Trib.).

[112] (Aug. 1, 2000), TEL-12408, [2000] O.R.H.T.D. No. 103, 2000 CarswellOnt 4370 (Ont. Rental Housing Trib.).

from the timing of these events and from comments of the landlords that they were not acting in good faith. In the alternative, the Member would have refused to grant an eviction in reliance on para. 84(2)(c) of the T.P.A. (now para. 83(3)(c) of the R.T.A.).

In *Capuccinello v. MacDonald*,[113] there was a long history of problems between the parties. The landlord served a notice of rent increase upon the tenant and the tenant indicated that he would be challenging that rent increase. The landlord responded that, "If you are going to try to give me problems, I have ways to get you out." The landlord then served the tenant with notice that the landlord's son wished to move into the unit. The Tribunal found that the landlord was not acting in good faith and dismissed the landlord's application.

In *Ferreira v. Greco*,[114] after several failed attempts to evict the tenant on other grounds, the landlord served the tenant with notice that he and his wife wanted to move from Portugal and take up residence in the unit. Based upon the evidence presented, the Member found that it was more likely that the landlord intended to sell the property and wished to evict the tenants because the landlord believed that he would get a higher price for the property and find it easier to sell if it were vacant. The landlord's application was dismissed as he had failed to prove that he was acting in good faith.

In *Smiley v. Klempan*,[115] the landlord stated that she required the tenant's unit because she was no longer able to walk up and down the stairs to her own unit. This was found to be incredible as she was still able to do many vigorous activities. Even if her mobility was restricted, the landlord offered no explanation for why she had not moved into another ground floor unit when it became vacant. The application was also commenced shortly after the tenant contacted the City concerning lack of maintenance of the complex. In these circumstances, the Member found that the landlord was acting in bad faith.

In *Cacciola v. Satchithananthan*,[116] the delivery of the notice of termination (for use of the unit by the landlord's daughter) came only ten days after the tenant demanded a rent reduction and commenced an application against the landlords. This raised serious questions about whether the landlords were acting in good faith (even though the daughter probably would have moved into the rental unit, given the opportunity). The landlords' application was dismissed.

[113] (July 20, 1999), SOL-06120 (Ont. Rental Housing Trib.).

[114] (November 6, 2001), TNL-29969 (Ont. Rental Housing Trib.).

[115] (June 13, 2001), EAL-20738, EAT-02682, [2001] O.R.H.T.D. No. 88, 2001 CarswellOnt 6406 (Ont. Rental Housing Trib.).

[116] (Dec. 30, 2002), TSL-40340, 2002 CarswellOnt 5015 (Ont. Rental Housing Trib.).

In *Bobotsis v. Brown*,[117] the landlord delivered the notice of termination shortly after the tenant was successful in obtaining an order against the landlord. During the hearing, the landlord kept repeating that "I have had enough" of the tenant and that "I just want him out". In these circumstances, the Member was not satisfied that the landlord had proven that she was acting in good faith and the application was dismissed.

In *Welker v Marcotte*,[118] the notice of termination was delivered by the landlord shortly after a dispute erupted between the parties over whether or not the tenant was responsible for a problem that developed with respect to the sewage pump. In these circumstances, the Member was not satisfied that the landlord was acting in good faith. The Member also found that the application was retaliatory contrary to the provisions of para. 84(2)(a) of the T.P.A. (now s. 83(3)(a) of the R.T.A.). For both reasons, the application was dismissed.

In *Persaud v. Lear*,[119] the landlord's agent and the tenant got into a heated discussion about the tenant's use of the utilities. A few days later, the landlord served a notice of termination for the landlord's own use. At the hearing, the landlord, who continued to live with his family in Toronto, offered no explanation why he wished to move into this unit in Brantford. The Vice-chair found the timing to be very suspicious and did not find the landlord to be credible. As a result, the Vice-chair found that the landlord had failed to prove that he in good faith required the rental unit for his own residential occupation and she dismissed his application.

Other cases where applications have been denied for lack of good faith include: *Korenowsky v. Kremko*[120] and *Alter v. Baron*.[121] It should also be noted that if, at the time the landlord serves the notice of termination, the landlord was acting in bad faith, this cannot be "cured" by the landlord subsequently developing a genuine intention to reside in the rental unit.[122]

A history of animosity does not, however, automatically mean that the Board will be convinced that the landlord is acting in bad faith. In Landlord

---

117 (June 7, 2006), SWL-81221, 2006 CarswellOnt 4425, [2006] O.R.H.T.D. No. 61 (Ont. Rental Housing Trib.).

118 (June 12, 2006), TEL-62031, TET-05780, 2006 CarswellOnt 4386, [2006] O.R.H.T.D. No. 79 (Ont. Rental Housing Trib.).

119 (July 14, 2006), SOL-68467-SA, [2006] O.R.H.T.D. No. 95 (Ont. Rental Housing Trib.).

120 (Sept. 24, 1998), TSL-00634, 1998 CarswellOnt 6405 (Ont. Rental Housing Trib.).

121 (Oct. 30, 2000), TNL-20728 (Ont. Rental Housing Trib.).

122 *Lacombe v. Duval* (June 28, 2002), EAL-26736, EAL-28533, EAT-03340, [2002] O.R.H.T.D. No. 74, (Ont. Rental Housing Trib.). Also see Landlord and Tenant Board File No. TNL-20808 (Jan. 29, 2009) in which the Member concluded that, at the time the notice of termination was given, the landlords were not acting in good faith. Subsequently, the landlords' circumstances changed and, by the time of the hearing, it was possible that they genuinely intended to occupy the rental unit. The Member dismissed the application but, in the circumstances, did so without prejudice to their right to serve a new notice of termination and commence a fresh application upon the same grounds.

and Tenant Board File No. EAL-00662 (April 4, 2007), despite the fact that the notice of termination followed shortly after two previous failed attempts by the landlord to evict the tenant for non-payment of rent, heated arguments and threatening notes between the parties and a restraining order obtained by the landlord against the tenant, the Member was satisfied that the landlord's daughter genuinely wanted to live in the rental unit for three or four months so that she could be close to her summer job. Aside from the Member's conclusion that the landlord was acting in good faith, which obviously turned upon the Member's assessment of the credibility of the landlord and his daughter, one might wonder why, given the fact that the landlord admitted to only wanting the unit for a few months, the Member would not exercise its power under s. 83(1) and refuse to terminate this tenancy. Despite the tenant's request for such relief, the most that the Member was prepared to do in this case was to delay the eviction by three weeks. Fortunately for the tenant, it appears that this decision was overturned on review. The landlord then appealed the review decision to the Divisional Court. In dismissing the landlord's appeal, the Divisional Court wrote as follows:[123]

> We are of the view that the Review Decision by Member Ellacott on June 19, 2007[124] that "temporary full-time occupancy for four months does not constitute the purpose of residential occupation as contemplated by the *Residential Tenancies Act*, 2006" is correct. That conclusion is supported by case law directly on point that has held that a landlord is not entitled to evict a tenant in order to provide accommodation for his daughter on summer break from university: *Wiazek v. Armstrong*, [1994] O.J. No. 2737 (Div. Ct.). See also, *McDonald v. Smith*, [1993] O.J. 1680 (Gen. Div.). It is also an interpretation that is consistent with the intention of the legislation, which is remedial in nature and directed towards the protection of tenants, including protecting the security of tenure for tenants.

Similarly, the Board dismissed an application where the landlord stated that she wanted to have the rental unit available for use by herself, her fiancé and her mother when they occasionally visit relatives who live in the area. The landlord admitted that she did not intend to make the rental unit her usual residence and that she intended to repair and redecorate the house in order to make it easier to sell. Based upon the real substance of the transaction, the Member concluded that the landlord did not require possession of the rental unit for residential occupancy and she dismissed the application.[125]

Where there was a breakdown in the relationship between the two landlords (who were spouses) and the female landlord wished to move into the basement unit for an indeterminate period of time, relying upon the Divisional

---

[123] *MacDonald v. Richard* (2008), 2008 CarswellOnt 638 (Ont. Div. Ct.).

[124] Presumably Landlord and Tenant Board File No. EAL-00662-RV (June 19, 2007).

[125] Landlord and Tenant Board File No. SOL-00366 (March 15, 2007).

Court's decision (described above) in *MacDonald v. Richard*,[126] the Board dismissed the landlords' application.

Whether sufficient evidence has been adduced to establish that the landlord is acting in good faith is a question of fact, not law.[127] Therefore, there is no right of appeal from such a finding by the Board.

A tenant who had been evicted by a landlord who required possession for himself sought to have the order set aside because the landlord was converting the apartment into two one-bedroom apartments. The court refused to set aside the order for possession. The landlord satisfied the court of his *bona fides* and it did not matter whether the landlord required the whole or only part of the premises for his own use: *Silvani v. Neveu.*[128]

Two or more landlords of a rental unit must act together. One landlord cannot use s. 48 to the exclusion of the interests of the other landlords. In *Atkinson v. Calloo et al.*,[129] there were two owners, a husband and wife, of this house. At the time this application was filed, they were involved in a family law dispute over this property, which had been the matrimonial home. One spouse wanted to regain possession of the unit for her own use and the other spouse did not agree. The one who wanted possession unilaterally served a notice of termination upon the tenants. It was held that, on this type of application, one landlord cannot act without the knowledge and consent of the other landlord(s). The application was dismissed.

The intended use of the rental unit must be residential occupation by the person who completes the affidavit. An issue can arise as to whether or not the intended use is residential. In *Fleming v. Dileandro*,[130] the rental unit was located in the basement of the house occupied by the landlord and his spouse. The spouse, a university professor, was retiring and wished to set up a study/home office in the basement of their home. The tenant questioned whether the intended use constituted "residential occupation" within the meaning of s. 51 of the T.P.A. The Tribunal found this was consistent with residential occupation and granted the landlord's application.

Where a landlord brings such an application and the application is dismissed on its merits (rather than on a technical deficiency such as an invalid notice of termination), it has been suggested that the landlord ought not to bring a similar application against the same tenant for at least one year and only if there are compelling new facts that would overcome the doctrine of *res judicata.*[131]

---

126 (2008), 2008 CarswellOnt 638 (Ont. Div. Ct.).

127 *Lobo v. Kwan*, Div. Ct. File No. 36/03 re TSL-45882 (Ont. Div. Ct.). See Chapter 16 for more information about appeals.

128 (November 19, 1984), Doc. 407-024 (Ont. Dist. Ct.).

129 (Aug. 19, 1999), TNL-09094 (Ont. Rental Housing Trib.).

130 (June 23, 2005), TSL-72600, 2005 CarswellOnt 3277 (Ont. Rental Housing Trib.).

131 *Parker v. Wendler* (November 23, 1998), EAL-02476 (Ont. Rental Housing Trib.). Also see the discussion of *res judicata* and issue estoppel in Chapter 2.

The question also sometimes arises as to whether a corporate landlord has any right to bring an application for "personal use". Two problems are created with this type of application being brought by a corporate landlord. First, if the intended use is for the operation of a business, this does not fall within the intended purposes set out in s. 48.[132] Second, since a corporation is not a natural person, it is not capable of using a rental unit for residential occupation or of having any relatives (spouse, child, etc.) who could use the unit for residential occupation.[133]

In a British Columbia case, *Crescent Construction Corp. v. Russell*,[134] a similar section was applied permitting a corporate landlord to recover possession for its single shareholder who wanted the residential premises for his private residence. However this decision was questioned and virtually overruled in the *McInnis v. Shirlmae Enterprises Ltd.*[135] case.

A corporate landlord was refused its application for possession for its sole shareholder in *479460 Ontario Ltd. v. Lambert.*[136]

Similarly in *629576 Ontario Ltd. v. Ogg*,[137] the headnote reads:

> The section only contemplates a landlord who is a natural and not an artificial person, such as the applicant. The fact that the applicant is exclusively controlled and owned by a simple shareholder is irrelevant.

The judge also said:

> Nor is the definition landlord including legal representatives helpful. It must be restricted to human landlords and not corporate ones.[138]

However in *Megan Investments Ltd. v. Funston*,[139] the Court found that although rent was paid to the corporate owner, the sole shareholder looked after the premises and dealt with the tenants of the single family home. His application for possession for his daughter was accepted by the judge relying on the definition of "landlord" in s. 1 of the Act as "the person giving or permitting the occupation of the premises", even though the corporation was the owner and also the landlord.

The *Ogg* case, *supra*, was followed and *Megan Investments Ltd., supra*, was distinguished in *Petrozakis Corp. v. Harris*.[140] In the *Petrozakis* decision,

---

[132] *McInnis v. Shirlmae Enterprises Ltd.* (1977), 2 B.C.L.R. 391 (B.C. Co. Ct.); *Hellerman v. Dias* (1987), 60 O.R. (2d) 735 (Ont. Dist. Ct.); and *Rosati Holdings (Hamilton) Inc. v. Moore* (Aug. 26, 1998), SOL-00416 (Ont. Rental Housing Trib.).

[133] See, for example, *1461313 Ontario Limited v. Clarke* (January 17, 2002), TSL-36355 (Ont. Rental Housing Trib.).

[134] (1975), (B.C. Co. Ct.).

[135] (1977), 2 B.C.L.R. 391 (B.C. Co. Ct.).

[136] (October 22, 1981), Doc. M56437/81 (Ont. Co. Ct.).

[137] (1986), 57 O.R. (2d) 57 (Ont. Dist. Ct.).

[138] *629576 Ontario Ltd. v. Ogg* (1986), 57 O.R. (2d) 57 (Ont. Dist. Ct.) at 60 [O.R.].

[139] (1992), 25 R.P.R. (2d) 63 (Ont. Gen. Div.).

[140] (1993), 1993 CarswellOnt 3639 (Ont. Gen. Div.).

there were two shareholders; the judge noted that in *Megan Investments Ltd.* there was only one shareholder and that there was also an individual with a one-tenth interest.

In *Rodgers v. Thompson*,[141] the sole shareholder of a corporate landlord applied for his own use. The Tribunal found that the shareholder was not the landlord and, therefore, was not entitled to occupy the rental unit. Similarly, an application by a principal of one of three corporate owners was dismissed in *Megna v. Curie*.[142] In *DeMercado v. Brumm*,[143] however, the Tribunal allowed an application by a sole shareholder of a corporate landlord. Looking at the real substance of the case (s. 188) of the T.P.A., it was determined that the landlord was really this individual even though the registered owner was his corporation. His application for an order terminating the tenancy so that his daughter could live in the unit was granted.

There are two legal principles at tension in these cases. On the one hand, corporations are considered in law to be separate legal entities from the individuals who created them.[144] The corporate "veil" will only be "pierced" in very unusual circumstances. The owner of the residential complex has made a business decision to take title to the property in the name of a corporation, presumably for some legitimate business reasons (such as tax advantages or to limit personal liability). Why should such a person then be permitted to throw off the mantle of incorporation whenever it no longer suits him? That would permit the person to gain all of the advantages of incorporation but then act as if there is no corporation when it becomes inconvenient. On the other hand, there is often sympathy for an individual who is the sole controlling mind behind what is essentially a holding corporation and who genuinely wants to live (or have a relative live) in the property.[145] In addition, the definition of landlord (in s. 2 of the R.T.A.) is broad enough to allow for the possibility that there is more than one landlord and that a sole shareholder of a closely held corporation could well be considered to be a landlord (even if title to the property is held in the name of the corporation) as a person "who permits occupancy of the rental unit".

Unfortunately, the Divisional Court's efforts to clarify this issue have not been entirely successful (i.e., the Divisional Court has not been entirely consistent on this issue).

In *1461313 Ontario Limited v. Clarke*,[146] the landlord's application was dismissed for a number of reasons, including the finding that a corporate

---

141 (Oct. 1, 1998), EAL-01315-RV (Ont. Rental Housing Trib.).

142 (June 2, 2003), SOL-40528, [2003] O.R.H.T.D. No. 73 (Ont. Rental Housing Trib.).

143 (June 1, 2001), EAL-21140, [2001] O.R.H.T.D. No. 80, 2001 CarswellOnt 6060 (Ont. Rental Housing Trib.).

144 See *Russell v. Sisson* (July 25, 2001, amended July 26, 2001), TSL-31405 (Ont. Rental Housing Trib.).

145 See *Weber v. Robinson* (August 30, 1999), EAL-08202 (Ont. Rental Housing Trib.).

146 (January 17, 2002), TSL-36355 (Ont. Rental Housing Trib.).

landlord was not entitled to bring this type of application. Marsha Bielak (a 50% owner of the numbered corporation) then brought a second application in her own name (as landlord) against this tenant for use of the unit by her daughter, Sylvia Bielak, and was successful in obtaining an order (in June 2002) from the Rental Housing Tribunal terminating the tenancy. This decision, however, was overturned on appeal as the Member had failed to consider if Marsha Bielak was a privy of the numbered company, failed to weigh the evidence regarding good faith and erred in law in finding that Marsha Bielak and the numbered company were not the same parties for the purposes of the doctrine of *res judicata*. A third application was then commenced (in 2006) by Sylvia Bielak for her "own use". The application was dismissed based upon the doctrine of *issue estoppel* (i.e., these issues had already been decided in an earlier application and could not be re-litigated).[147] On appeal by the landlord, the Divisional Court held that the doctrine of *issue estoppel* could only be applied here if the landlord remained the numbered company, as the earlier decisions of the Tribunal were really about the inability of a corporation to bring this type of application. Since no evidence had been adduced by Sylvia Bielak to demonstrate that there had been any change in the ownership of the complex and since rent continued to be paid to and deposited to the credit of the numbered company, the Divisional Court was satisfied that the numbered company continued to be the landlord. As a result, the Divisional Court found that the principle of *issue estoppel* did apply and the decision of the Landlord and Tenant Board dismissing Sylvia Bialek's application was upheld. Aside from the interesting history of this case and the significance of the decision on the issue of issue estoppel, it is also noteworthy because the Divisional Court might also be seen (at paragraph 17 of the decision) to tacitly approve of the Landlord and Tenant Board's ruling that s. 51 of the T.P.A. (now s. 48 of the R.T.A.) cannot be relied upon by a corporate landlord.[148]

In a more recent case from a differently constituted panel of the Divisional Court, however, it was held that:

> Whether a sole shareholder can require possession of a rental property owned by a corporation for own use should be determined on a case-by-case basis. The consideration of the matter should include the nature of the shareholding and the discretion granted in s. 202 of the . . . Act.[149]

In this case, the Divisional Court upheld the review order from the Landlord and Tenant Board in favour of the sole shareholder of the corporate landlord

---

[147] See "Issue Estoppel" in Chapter 2.

[148] *Bielak v. Clarke* (2008), 2008 CarswellOnt 5307, 241 O.A.C. 259 (Ont. Div. Ct.).

[149] *Edward Slapsys c/o 1406393 Ontario Inc. v. Abrams*, Court File No. 80/08, June 22, 2009 (unreported), upholding Landlord and Tenant Board review order TSL-01748-RV (Feb. 1, 2008). Note that the unsuccessful tenant in this case may be seeking leave to appeal the decision of the Divisional Court to the Court of Appeal.

on the basis that this individual was also a "landlord" within the meaning of s. 2 of the R.T.A. and, therefore, was entitled, in good faith, to seek possession of the rental unit under s. 48 of the R.T.A.

In light of these decisions from the Divisional Court, it appears that the Landlord and Tenant Board will have to continue struggling with this issue,[150] especially in the case of closely held corporations and, as stated by the Divisional Court, each case will have to be decided upon its own unique facts.

The issue of a corporate landlord bringing an application for "own use" also sometimes arises in the context of a mobile home park (or land lease home[151]). In *Ben Tardiff Maisons Mobiles Ltee v. Gervais*,[152] the landlord (who lived elsewhere) wished to move into the mobile home park he owned (through a corporation) in order to have better management control. The court allowed the landlord's application for possession, being satisfied that it was "genuine", which the judge apparently considered was in "good faith". It is odd that the style of cause shows the limited company as the applicant but in the judgment, the owner of the company is described as the individual landlord and not the limited company.

In *Duke's Trailer Court Ltd. v. Block*,[153] the application was by the corporate landlord for personal possession by the controlling shareholder of the company who required the mobile home site for a mobile home so that he would be better able to monitor the mobile home park and to properly look after daily the utility building for plumbing and electrical. The court was satisfied that the application was genuine and in good faith. The judge dealt with the problem that the landlord was a corporate entity. A number of cases were discussed and the judge followed *Ben Tardiff Maisons Mobiles Ltee*, *supra*. The judge was satisfied that the controlling shareholder negotiates all leases and gives or permits the occupation of the mobile home sites. Thus the controlling shareholder in that sale comes within the definition of landlord now in s. 2 of the R.T.A.: "includes ... other person permitting occupancy of a rental unit". The judge concluded his reasons saying that otherwise it would be highly inequitable and a significant impediment to the creation of family/ corporate owned mobile home parks.

In *Kepic Estate v. Tondera*,[154] the estate of the deceased landlord brought an application for use of the unit by the daughter of the deceased landlord. It was held that, at the time the application was commenced, the landlord was

---

[150] For example, see Landlord and Tenant Board File No. TSL-17703 (Jan. 23, 2009) and Landlord and Tenant Board File No. SOL-18083 (Jan. 19, 2009).

[151] See *Chenard v. Foster* (2007), 2007 CarswellOnt 7709 (Ont. Div. Ct.), described earlier in this Chapter.

[152] (1996), 3 O.T.C. 319 (Ont. Gen. Div.).

[153] (1997), 10 R.P.R. (3d) 194 (Ont. Gen. Div.).

[154] (May 3, 2001), SOL-21879, [2001] O.R.H.T.D. No. 64, 2001 CarswellOnt 6351 (Ont. Rental Housing Trib.).

the estate and, like a corporation, the estate does not have any relatives. The application was dismissed.

Similarly, a church is also not able to bring an application under s. 48 of the R.T.A. In *Calvin Hungarian Presbyterian Church v. Owen*,[155] the church applied to terminate the tenancy on the basis that its new minister required the premises. It was held that the church could not rely on the provisions of s. 51 of the T.P.A. (now s. 48 of the R.T.A.). The Tribunal relied heavily upon the decision of the Divisional Court in *D.E.S.K. Properties Ltd. v. Skene*.[156]

(ii) Purchaser Requires Unit[157]

By s. 49(1) of the R.T.A. (formerly s. 52(1) of the T.P.A.), a landlord may, on behalf of a purchaser, give notice of termination if, in good faith, the purchaser, their spouse or a child or parent of one of them or a person who will provide care services to one of them (and who will live in the residential complex) requires possession of the rental unit for the purpose of residential occupation. There are, however, a couple of conditions. One is that the residential complex must contain no more than three residential units.[158] The other is that the landlord must have entered into an agreement of purchase and sale of the residential complex.[159]

By s. 49(2) of the R.T.A. (formerly s. 52(1.1) of the T.P.A.), a landlord who is an owner of a condominium unit and who has entered into an agreement of purchase and sale of the unit may, on behalf of a purchaser, give notice of termination if, in good faith, the purchaser, their spouse or a child or parent of one of them or a person who will provide care services to one of them (and who will live in the residential complex) requires possession of the rental unit for the purpose of residential occupation.

Notice of termination (Form N12) may be given to take effect at the end of the period of tenancy, whether weekly, monthly, or yearly, or at the end of a tenancy of a fixed term, for example two years. The notice period cannot be less than 60 days.

---

[155] (Nov. 28, 2003), EAL-37084, [2003] O.R.H.T.D. No. 142, 2003 CarswellOnt 5717 (Ont. Rental Housing Trib.).

[156] (March 7, 1983) 4 T.L.L.R. 103 (Ont. Div. Ct.).

[157] Please refer to the Board's Interpretation Guideline No. 12.

[158] In Landlord and Tenant Board File No. TSL-00597 (March 26, 2007), the landlord's application was dismissed on the basis that the residential complex contained four residential units.

[159] But this would not be so if it was an option to purchase: *1803 Renaissance v. Asseltine* (February 9, 1989), Contant J. (Ont. Dist. Ct.) – at least, not until the option is exercised; only then can the vendor landlord on behalf of the purchaser serve a notice of termination.

In *Viti v. ISC Environmental Assessment Inc.*,[160] at the end of the initial term of the tenancy the parties, through their conduct, were found to have changed the period of the tenancy so that the rent was due on the 15th day of each month (and, thus, the last day of each rental period fell on the 14th). The termination date specified in the notice of termination (Form N12) was January 31, 2006. The Member ruled that since this was not the last day of a rental period, the notice was invalid and the application was dismissed.

Having given notice of termination, the landlord may immediately commence an application for possession (s. 71). The application is in Form L2. The filing fee is $170.[161] The application cannot be commenced more than 30 days after the termination date specified in the notice of termination (s. 69(2)). The application and notice of hearing should be served on the tenant(s) at least 10 days before the hearing (Rule 10.1) and the certificate of service for the application and notice of hearing should be filed within five days of service (Rule 11.2).

The landlord selling the property may be a mortgagee who has taken possession of the unit or complex.[162] Although the *Mortgages Act* purports (in s. 46(1)) to take priority (in the case of conflict) over any other statute, the Court of Appeal ruled that the procedures for terminating a tenancy set out in the T.P.A. (including the prescribed forms and notice periods) prevailed over any conflicting provisions contained in the *Mortgages Act*.[163] This ruling would apply equally to eviction procedures under the R.T.A., the successor legislation to the T.P.A.[164]

The Board cannot make an order terminating a tenancy and evicting the tenant in an application based on notice under s. 49 (or s. 48) unless the person who requires the rental unit files with the Board an affidavit certifying that the person in good faith requires the rental unit for his or her own personal use (s. 72(1)).[165] The affidavit should be as specific as possible. Simply stating "I require the unit" may not be sufficient. The affidavit should indicate the identity of the person and their relationship to the landlord and that they require the unit for their residence (i.e., that they intend to live in the unit).

---

[160] (March 6, 2006), TNL-72846, 2006 CarswellOnt 2155, [2006] O.R.H.T.D. No. 26 (Ont. Rental Housing Trib.).

[161] Effective April 2009. From 2002 through March 2009, the fee was $150.

[162] See the section on mortgagees in possession in Chapter 3.

[163] *Canada Trustco Mortgage Co. v. Park* (2004), 72 O.R. (3d) 480, [2004] O.J. No. 3215, 2004 CarswellOnt 3184 (Ont. C.A.).

[164] See Landlord and Tenant Board File Numbers CEL-02248 (Oct. 2, 2007) and TEL-03366-RV (July 18, 2007).

[165] If the affidavit is not signed by the person who will be living in the rental unit or is not sworn, the application will be dismissed: *Akhtar v. Adamson*, (April 26, 2006), TEL-60864, [2006] O.R.H.T.D. No. 44, 2006 CarswellOnt 4415 (Ont. Rental Housing Trib.).

In *Bellows v. Gordon*,[166] although the purchaser filed a declaration, it was found that the wording used was not sufficient to satisfy the requirements of s. 70(1) of the T.P.A. (now s. 72(1) of the R.T.A.). There was insufficient evidence presented at the hearing as to the intended use of the purchaser. The landlord was also in serious breach of the landlord's obligations. For all of these reasons, the application was dismissed.

Also, although the Board cannot grant an eviction order without an affidavit being filed (s. 72(1)), the R.T.A. does not require that it *accompany* the application. Although it is advisable to file the affidavit well in advance of the hearing, a Member can permit the affidavit to be filed at the hearing.[167]

The purchaser (or other person who intends to reside in the unit) is not required to testify at the hearing. The Board may rely upon the affidavit of that person and the other evidence presented at the hearing.[168] While the affidavit may not be the best possible evidence, in some cases it may be sufficient.[169] There is a risk, however, that by not calling a key witness, the case may be weakened and may not succeed; the Board may draw an adverse inference from the absence of a crucial witness or may simply find that the applicant has failed to meet the onus of proof.[170]

Many of the issues raised in these applications are virtually the same as under s. 48 (i.e., whether the landlord is acting in good faith, whether the person in question genuinely intends to reside in the unit and so forth). I therefore refer the reader to the previous section ("Landlord Requires Unit").

One additional issue is whether there exists a genuine and binding agreement of purchase and sale. The Board's Interpretation Guideline No. 12 states as follows:

> Before a landlord may give a notice under section 49, there must be an agreement of purchase and sale to sell the residential complex. The Board may refuse an application if it is not reasonably certain that a completed sale will result from the agreement. If a term or condition of the agreement makes it uncertain that the deal will be completed, it may be appropriate to delay the application until the sale becomes more certain.
>
> The Board may also dismiss the application if the purchase is a sham created for the purpose of evicting the tenant. For example, a transfer to a family member should be examined. A sale for much less than market value may raise questions. Section 202 provides authority to look at the real nature of any transactions.

---

[166] (Dec. 8, 2000), TEL-15985, [2000] O.R.H.T.D. No. 170, 2000 CarswellOnt 6401 (Ont. Rental Housing Trib.).

[167] *Brookfield Canada Realty Inc. v. Brtnik* (Oct. 12, 1999), TNL-10075 (Ont. Rental Housing Trib.).

[168] *Walsh v. 580472 Ontario Ltd. et al.* (Nov. 6, 2002), Div. Ct. File No.: Toronto 578/02 re CEL-25335 (Ont. Rental Housing Trib.).

[169] *Lombardi v. Brenke-Leach* (Dec. 14, 2000), TNL-21991-SA, 2000 CarswellOnt 6409 (Ont. Rental Housing Trib.).

[170] *Afzalzada v. Murray* (May 18, 2001), TNL-25657 (Ont. Rental Housing Trib.).

A landlord applying based on a notice under section 49 is well advised to file with the application a copy of the agreement, together with an explanation of the circumstances of the intended sale.

In *Nela v. Kanrar et al.*,[171] during the hearing of the landlord's application, it became apparent that the landlord and the purported purchaser were personal friends and business associates. This was not an arm's-length transaction. The purchaser had not seen the property or had anyone else inspect it before making this agreement. The property had numerous serious problems and had been cited for 27 violations of health and safety regulations. The Member found the evidence of the landlord and the landlord's witnesses to be inconsistent and to be suspect. The agreement of purchase and sale was conditional upon an inspection which, if not waived within five banking days, rendered the entire agreement void. That condition had not been satisfied or waived by the purchaser. Therefore, the agreement of purchase and sale had become void. For all of these reasons, the application was dismissed. The Member went on to state that even if he had found that there was a valid, binding agreement of purchase and sale and that the landlord and purchaser were acting in good faith, he would nevertheless have refused to grant an eviction in this case because the landlord was in serious breach of his maintenance obligations.

In Landlord and Tenant Board File No. SOL-01897 (May 28, 2007), there was an agreement of purchase and sale but the original purchaser had backed out of the deal and the new purported purchaser had not executed any documents at all concerning the purchase of this property. The landlord did not testify. The purported purchaser only had to put down a $500 deposit and allegedly bought the property without ever even seeing it. Finally, the Member did not give much weight to the testimony of the purchaser as the questions that were put to him were leading ones. In these circumstances, the Member was not satisfied that the landlord had proven either the existence of a *bona fide* agreement of purchase and sale or that the purchaser was acting in good faith and the application was dismissed.

(iii) Demolition, Conversion and Renovation

A landlord may give notice of termination of a tenancy under s. 50(1) of the R.T.A. (formerly s. 53(1) of the T.P.A.) if the landlord requires possession of the rental unit in order to:

(a) demolish it;
(b) convert it to use for a purpose other than a residential premises; or
(c) do repairs or renovations to it that are so extensive that they require a building permit and vacant possession of the rental unit.

---

[171] (July 25, 2001), TSL-30516 and TSL-30517-SA (Ont. Rental Housing Trib.).

The process starts with service of a notice of termination in Form N13. The notice must be served at least 120 days before the end of a period or term (for a fixed-term tenancy).[172] If the rental unit is a mobile home or land lease home, the notice must be served at least one year in advance.[173] The date specified as the termination date must be the *last day* of a period (for a periodic tenancy) or of the term (for a fixed term tenancy).[174] If the reason given in the notice relates to repairs or renovations, the notice must also advise the tenant that the tenant has a first right of refusal (i.e., the right to move back in after the work is completed) and explain how the tenant can exercise that right.[175] As with any notice of termination, it must contain sufficient reasons and details (i.e., particulars) to be valid.[176]

A tenant who receives such a notice of termination can wait to see if the landlord actually commences an application for an eviction order and then decide whether to oppose the application. Alternatively, the tenant can make plans to vacate the rental unit on the termination date set out in the notice. Finally, the tenant has the option of ending the tenancy early, on very short notice (at least 10 days written notice).[177]

The landlord can commence the application immediately after serving the notice of termination upon the tenant; the landlord need not wait until after the termination date.[178] The termination and eviction, however, cannot be ordered to occur prior to the termination date set out in the notice of termination. The application is in Form L2 and the filing fee is $170.[179] The application cannot be commenced more than 30 days after the termination date (s. 69(2)). The application and notice of hearing must be served at least 10 days prior to the hearing (Rule 10.1). The certificate of service for the application and notice of hearing should be filed within five days after service has been effected (Rule 11.2).

In certain circumstances (discussed below), the landlord seeking to terminate the tenancy under s. 50 must provide monetary compensation to the tenant or find the tenant alternative accommodation that is acceptable to the tenant. In such circumstances, the application filed with the Board must be accompanied by evidence (by way of affidavit) that the landlord has paid the

---

172 Subsection 50(2) of the R.T.A.

173 Subsection 164(1) of the R.T.A. (formerly s. 113 of the T.P.A.).

174 Subsection 50(2) of the R.T.A. A specific date of termination must be stated, and it is not sufficient to merely state that the tenant is required to vacate 120 days after notice is given: *Dumi Construction Ltd. v. Greenspan* (1977), 15 O.R. (2d) 808 (Ont. Co. Ct.). The termination date must be the last day of a period or term: *Lypny v. Rocca* (1986), 55 O.R. (2d) 46 (Ont. Dist. Ct.), affirmed (1988), 63 O.R. (2d) 595 (Ont. Div. Ct.).

175 Subsection 50(3) of the R.T.A.

176 Subsection 43(2) of the R.T.A.

177 Subsections 50(4) and (5) of the R.T.A.

178 Section 71 of the R.T.A.

179 Effective April 2009. From 2002 through March 2009, the fee was $150.

necessary compensation required under s. 52 or 54 of the R.T.A. or has found acceptable alternative accommodation for the tenant.[180]

At the hearing of the application, the Board cannot grant the landlord's application unless it is satisfied:

1. That the landlord in good faith intends to carry out the activity on which the notice of termination was based (para. 73(a)).
2. That the landlord has obtained all necessary permits or other authority that may be required carry out the intended work or has taken all necessary steps to do so but cannot obtain the permit(s) or authority until the unit is vacant (para. 73(b)).
3. That the landlord has paid to the tenant any compensation to which the tenant may be entitled under s. 54 (s. 83(4)).
4. If the tenant has chosen to exercise a first right of refusal under s. 53(2), that the landlord has compensated the tenant in an amount equal to the rent for the amount of time the landlord estimates is required to complete the repair or renovation (s. 83(5)).

The requirement that the landlord obtain all necessary permits can sometimes cause the landlord difficulties. Nevertheless, the goal is to ensure that a tenant is not forced to move until the landlord has obtained all necessary permits to demonstrate that the landlord is ready to proceed with the proposed work.

In *Leboeuf Properties Inc. v. Meredith*,[181] the landlord required a demolition permit from the municipality in order to demolish this property, but was not able to obtain one. The municipality would not issue a demolition permit for the site until a building permit had been issued for the proposed new home to be built on the site. In this case, a building permit could not be obtained without soil tests and the soil tests demanded by the municipality could not be performed until the existing house was removed (which could not be done without a demolition permit). Notwithstanding that the landlord was acting in good faith and was caught in a "catch-22" situation, the Tribunal was forced to dismiss the application as the landlord had not complied with the requirements of para. 71(b) of the T.P.A.

To address just such situations, the wording of para. 73(b) of the R.T.A. has been drafted differently from the wording of the comparable provision previously contained in the T.P.A. (para. 71(b) of the T.P.A.). Subsection 73(b) of the R.T.A. now permits the Board to grant the landlord's application where the landlord has applied for the necessary permit(s) or other authority but cannot obtain the necessary permits (etc.) until the unit is vacant.

Also, para. 73(b) of the R.T.A., only requires the landlord to obtain "all necessary permits or other authority" that may be required to carry out the

---

[180] Paragraph 2 of s. 53, O. Reg. 516/06.

[181] (April 28, 1999), TNL-06573, 1999 CarswellOnt 5814 (Ont. Rental Housing Trib.).

proposed activity. If no permit is legally required, this provision will not pose any obstacle. For instance, in *Canada (Public Works & Government Services) v. McGrath*,[182] the rental unit was located on land that was originally expropriated by the federal government (Transport Canada) for the purpose of constructing an airport. The airport was never built but the land is still owned and operated by the federal Crown. The Tribunal held that provincial and/or municipal (by)laws and permit requirements respecting the demolition of properties cannot apply to properties located on Crown land as this would constitute an intrusion into the Crown's exclusive jurisdiction over federal Crown property. Thus, the landlord did not need to obtain a municipal demolition permit in this case.

A landlord who gives a tenant of a care home a notice of termination under s. 50 must make reasonable efforts to find appropriate alternate accommodation for the tenant.[183] Where the tenant chooses to accept that alternate accommodation, the landlord will not be required to pay compensation under s. 52 or 54.[184] If the landlord of a care home fails to make reasonable efforts to find the tenant appropriate alternate accommodation, the Board may simply refuse to grant the landlord's application.[185]

A. DEMOLITION

As for demolition, para. 50(1)(a) of the R.T.A. (formerly para. 53(1)(a) of the T.P.A.), a landlord's justification for doing so might be because the building is so old that necessary repairs or renovations would not be economically feasible, or that the building along with others owned by the landlord were to be demolished and replaced by a new housing or commercial development. Whatever the landlord's reasons or justification, the intent of the legislation is to put the onus on the landlord to prove *bona fides* or good faith (para. 73(a)).

A demolition permit must be part of the material presented to the Board on the application for termination (s. 73(b)(i)), unless it is impossible to obtain the permit until the unit is vacant (s. 73(b)(ii)). Where it is possible to obtain the permit, the landlord can serve the notice of termination and commence the application before receiving the permit, as long as it is obtained by the time of the hearing.[186]

---

[182] (Feb. 6, 2006), TEL-52097, TET-05177, 2006 CarswellOnt 2151 (Ont. Rental Housing Trib.).

[183] Subsection 146(1) of the R.T.A. (formerly subsection 98(1) of the T.P.A.).

[184] Subsection 146(2) of the R.T.A. (formerly subsection 98(2) of the T.P.A.).

[185] Since the landlord is in serious breach of the landlord's obligations under the Act (s. 83(3)) or, alternatively, because it would be unfair to grant an eviction in such circumstances (s. 83(1)).

[186] *Mississauga (City) v. Saber* (February 27, 1992), 1992 CarswellOnt 3608 (Ont. Gen. Div.).

Under the *Landlord and Tenant Act*, when the property was being sold and the purchaser in good faith intended to demolish the building, notice of termination by the landlord requiring vacant possession for the purchaser was considered valid.[187] Since s. 49 now only permits notice to be given where the purchaser requires the rental unit for the purpose of *residential occupation*, it seems unlikely that a landlord can give a valid notice under s. 49 knowing that the purchaser intends to demolish the unit, not live in it.

In *One Clarendon Inc. v. Ross*,[188] the landlord gave termination notice based on demolition (para. 53(1)(*a*) of the T.P.A.) to various tenants in the complex. The units were to be re-configured after considerable tearing down of walls. The landlord planned to rent the new units. The tenants' position was that the work represented extensive renovations, not demolition of the rental unit. The Tribunal member considered the meaning of the word "demolish", and decided that a demolition of an apartment must achieve the same result as a demolition of a building — it must cause it to disappear and change irrevocably. The work proposed by the landlord involved rearranging walls. The City Buildings Department employee who issued the building permit considered that the proposed work was basic renovations and not demolition. The Tribunal dismissed the landlord's applications.

Note that para. 50(1)(a) permits the landlord to serve a notice of termination if the landlord intends to demolish the *rental unit*. This wording has created some problems in the case of mobile homes and land lease homes where the home is owned by the tenant but the land on which it sits is rented by the tenant. In *City of Burlington v. Yox*,[189] the Tribunal dismissed the landlord's application because the notice of termination indicated that the landlord intended to demolish the site, not the land lease home on the site and, further, that the City had no right to demolish the building it did not own.

The Divisional Court has found this to be too narrow an interpretation of this paragraph. In *Bronte Creek Developments Inc. v. Murphy et al.*,[190] the landlord of a mobile home park intended to develop the site and build permanent homes. The landlord needed to remove the mobile homes so that it could blast the rock on the site and excavate. The Town had issued permits for the excavation and the building of some foundations. The applications by the landlord were dismissed at first instance and upon review before the Tribunal on the basis that the landlord was not destroying the ground but merely intending to put different types of buildings on the site and that this did not constitute demolition of the rental unit (i.e., the land). On appeal, the

---

[187] *Avro Management v. Nefsky* (1987), 59 O.R. (2d) 474 (Ont. Div. Ct.).

[188] (June 16, 1999), TSL-07790, TSL-08004, TSL-08006, TSL-08007.

[189] (Nov. 2, 1999), SOL-08815 (Ont. Rental Housing Trib.).

[190] (May 29, 2001), Div. Ct. File Nos. 1492/DV, 1491/DV re SOL-13743, SOL-13742 (Ont. Rental Housing Trib.).

Divisional Court set aside the decisions of the Member and the reviewing Member and granted the landlord's applications. The Court held that the "rental units" in question were more than just the soil beneath the homes. By altering the land and by removing the sewers, water supply and electrical service to the mobile home sites, the landlord would be demolishing the rental unit within the meaning of para. 53(1)(a) of the T.P.A.

Pursuant to s. 52 of the R.T.A., a landlord must compensate a tenant in an amount equal to three months rent[191] or offer the tenant another rental unit acceptable to the tenant if:

(a) the tenant receives notice of termination of the tenancy for the purposes of demolition or conversation to non-residential use;
(b) the residential complex in which the rental unit is located contains **at least five residential units**; and
(c) in the case of demolition, it was not ordered to be carried out under the authority of any other Act.

An issue occasionally arises as to how many units are contained within a residential complex. In *Tenants of 28 & 32 Corinth Gdns v. Forum Homes (Corinth) Inc.*,[192] there were two separate, adjacent triplexes. One corporation bought one property and a related corporation bought the other. The two properties were managed as if they were part of the one complex and, ultimately, one of the corporations ended up owning both properties. The landlord took the position that, at the time the tenants were given notice of termination for demolition, there were two separate residential complexes, each with three units and that, therefore, no compensation was required under s. 55 of the T.P.A. (now s. 52 of the R.T.A.). Looking at the real substance of the matter, the Tribunal found that the management of both of these properties and the identity of the two corporate owners was so intermingled, that the two properties became one residential complex (containing six residential units). The landlord was therefore ordered to pay to the tenants the compensation required by s. 55 of the T.P.A.

13 — LL APPLICATIONS

B. CONVERSION TO NON-RESIDENTIAL USE

Conversion of a rental unit to non-residential purposes is a permitted reason for termination of a tenancy under para. 50(1)(b) of the R.T.A. (formerly para. 53(1)(*b*) of the T.P.A.).

This may not be available for conversion from rental to condominium. It will depend on any applicable municipal by-law.

---

[191] The compensation required may be higher in the case of a mobile home or land lease home (s. 164). See Chapter 20.

[192] (May 2, 2003), TNT-03257, 2003 CarswellOnt 2640 (Ont. Rental Housing Trib.).

The conversion reason was accepted in *Cove Mobilehome Park & Sales Ltd. v. Welch*,[193] for the landlord who wished to terminate one of the mobile home sites in order to use the land in connection with snow removal. The Divisional Court did direct a new trial but only as to the landlord's *bona fides.*

Another change of use was approved in *Shippam v. Johnson*,[194] from mobile home park to seasonal trailer park with many more sites. The court also accepted the reason that the landlord could not afford to install a new water system for the limited number of mobile home sites in the park, and therefore the *Frustrated Contracts Act*[195] applied: s. 86 of Part IV, now s. 19 of the R.T.A.

A somewhat similar case is *Lypny v. Rocca.*[196] The landlord proceeded with application for possession to convert to non-residential use, s. 105(1)(*b*) of Part IV, now s. 50(1)(b) of the R.T.A., because the municipality had insisted on major structural repairs and better plumbing for the third floor apartment. The landlord satisfied the court that she could not afford the remedial work, which apparently would not be required if the premises were no longer used for living quarters.

Conversion to office space was permitted in *Canadian Slovak League v. Babic.*[197] The judge included in his order that the premises shall not be used for residential purposes for one year, stating that his authority for so ordering was in s. 113(11) of the *Landlord and Tenant Act* "to impose such terms and conditions as the judge considers appropriate," which is somewhat similar to what is now s. 204(1) of the R.T.A., and gives the Board discretion to include in an order such conditions as it considers fair in the circumstances.

Conversion by the landlord of the tenant's space to an apartment and an office for use by the landlord was turned down by the court as the notice of termination was given under s. 103, Part IV of the *Landlord and Tenant Act* for occupation by the landlord. It was pointed out by the judge that the application would succeed when made under s. 105(1)(*b*) of Part IV being conversion for a purpose other than rental residential: *Hellerman v. Dias.*[198]

Another conversion from residential rental to use by the landlord for its business was approved in *Maxbel Upholsteries Ltd. v. Dicks.*[199]

In *Haist, Re*,[200] the landlord owned and operated a business on the main floor of this complex and stored business records in the unheated basement.

---

[193] (1979), 27 O.R. (2d) 65 (Ont. Div. Ct.).

[194] (1984), 45 O.R. (2d) 307 (Ont. Co. Ct.).

[195] R.S.O. 1990, c. F.34.

[196] (1988), 63 O.R. (2d) 595 (Ont. Div. Ct.).

[197] (1988), 4 T.L.L.R. 22 (Ont. Dist. Ct.).

[198] (1987), 60 O.R. (2d) 735 (Ont. Dist. Ct.).

[199] (1989), 1989 CarswellOnt 2521 (Ont. Dist. Ct.).

[200] (Feb. 20, 2006), CEL-50308, 2006 CarswellOnt 2093, [2006] O.R.H.T.D. No. 9 (Ont. Rental Housing Trib.).

He rented out residential units located on the second and third floors. He testified that he wished to convert the third floor apartment to non-residential use as he wished to move the business records from the basement to the third floor. The tenant felt that this was a retaliatory eviction based on friction that had developed between herself and the landlord. In granting the landlord's application, the Member wrote:

> There are few relationships that do not have some periods of incidences of discontent; landlord-tenant relationships are no exception to this general rule. . . A landlord has the right to decide to use his own building according to his own whim. The requirement of the Act is that he gives proper notice and that he has an intention to convert the space to a non-residential use; his motivation for forming that intention is not relevant to my findings. The tenant has failed to prove on the balance of probabilities that the notice was given in bad faith.

While it is accurate to state that, in determining good faith, a Member need only be satisfied that the landlord's stated intention is genuine and that it need not be reasonable, I think the Member in this case goes too far if she is suggesting that motivation is completely irrelevant. The landlord's motives can be extremely relevant to considerations under s. 83 of the R.T.A. (formerly s. 84 of the T.P.A.). If, in fact, the reason the landlord brought this application is in retaliation for the tenant attempting to assert her rights, the Member would have to refuse to grant the application. The only explicit consideration the Member gave in her decision to s. 84 of the T.P.A. was with respect to delaying the eviction. Therefore it is impossible to know what consideration, if any, she gave to the provisions of s. 84(2) of the T.P.A. (currently s. 83(3) of the R.T.A.).

A somewhat unexpected judicial interpretation of the section early on permitted a landlord to give termination notice to the tenant because the landlord wished to sell and give vacant possession. This was held to be in effect a conversion for a purpose other than rental accommodation: *Cayer v. Levac*.[201]

The above case was considered in *Willroy Mines Ltd. v. Cameron*,[202] and was commented upon unfavourably by saying that sale is not a change of use. The facts were quite different. The landlord of an apartment building containing 44 suites was trying to obtain vacant possession in order to sell to a purchaser who would continue the same use, albeit with new tenants. In *Cayer and Levac*,[203] as has been said, the change of use, resulting from a sale, was from an owner of a tenant-occupied house to a purchaser who was going to occupy, which does seem to be conversion.

Cayer v. Levac was a decision of the County Court and is not binding upon the Tribunal. Given the fact that such an application could now be

---

201 (1978), 23 O.R. (2d) 526 (Ont. Co. Ct.).

202 (1983), 41 O.R. (2d) 109 (Ont. Div. Ct.).

203 (1978), 23 O.R. (2d) 526 (Ont. Co. Ct.).

brought under s. 49 of the R.T.A., it is suggested that this decision ought not to be followed.

The question sometimes arises as to whether a landlord can evict a tenant so that the unit is empty, which will make it easier to show to prospective purchasers and thereby make it easier to sell. Does wanting the unit to be vacant for a while constitute a conversion to a "use for a purpose other than residential premises"? In *Gatti v. Forsythe*,[204] the landlord wished to sell. The tenant refused to allow any realtor or prospective purchaser to inspect the premises. Notice of termination under s. 105(1)(*b*) of Part IV (*Landlord and Tenant Act*) for conversion for a purpose other than rental was accepted by the court and an order for possession granted. The judge commented:

> A landlord ... should be entitled to prepare his property for market ... [and] free from tenants whose avowed aim would be to deflect all sales efforts in order to continue their own tenancy.[205]

The judge added a condition in the order that the house was not to be occupied by another tenant until the contemplated sale was completed.

An owner of condominium units which had been rented wished to sell each unit to purchasers who would presumably occupy: *721476 Ontario Ltd. v. Asselstine*.[206] Notice of termination under s. 105(1)(*b*) of Part IV (*Landlord and Tenant Act*) was served on the tenants of the two remaining occupied units. The court distinguished *Willroy Mines Ltd. v. Cameron*,[207] as in that case the eventual use after sale would continue to be rental residential. Possession was ordered even though agreements of purchase and sale had not been entered into prior to service of the notices of termination.

Please note that caution should be exercised in trying to rely upon cases decided under the *Landlord and Tenant Act*. Under the *Landlord and Tenant Act*, a landlord could apply to terminate a tenancy if the landlord required possession for the purposes of conversion to use for a purpose "**other than *rental* residential premises**" (emphasis added). Therefore, if the property was to be sold to a purchaser who intended to live in the unit, it would no longer be a *rental* property. Under the R.T.A. (as it was under the T.P.A.), an application under para. 50(1)(b) can only be granted if the landlord requires possession of the unit to convert it to use for a purpose "**other than residential premises**". The removal of the word "rental" must be taken as intentional and purposeful. If the landlord intends to leave the unit vacant for the foreseeable future, this may be seen by the Board as a conversion to a non-residential use. If the intent is to force the tenant out in order to make it easier for someone else to move in, this is unlikely to be seen as conversion to a

---

204 (1988), 1 R.P.R. (2d) 83, 65 O.R. (2d) 449, 1988 CarswellOnt 612 (Ont. Dist. Ct.).

205 (1988), 65 O.R. (2d) 449 (Ont. Dist. Ct.) at 452 [O.R.].

206 (1988), 48 R.P.R. 260 (Ont. Dist. Ct.).

207 (1983), 41 O.R. (2d) 109 (Ont. Div. Ct.).

non-residential use. In such a case, the landlord may have to rely upon some other provision of the R.T.A., such as s. 49 (which allows a landlord to terminate a tenancy so that a purchaser can move into the rental unit).

Pursuant to s. 52 of the R.T.A., a landlord must compensate a tenant in an amount equal to three months rent[208] or offer the tenant another rental unit acceptable to the tenant if:

(a) the tenant receives notice of termination of the tenancy for the purposes of demolition or conversation to non-residential use; and
(b) the residential complex in which the rental unit is located contains **at least five residential units**.

An issue occasionally arises as to how many units are contained within a residential complex. In *Capell v. Carter*[209] the building contained six units — four commercial and two residential. The landlord wished to convert one of the residential units to commercial use. The question arose as to whether or not the tenant was entitled to compensation under s. 55 of the T.P.A. The Tribunal held that the complex only contained two *residential* units and that, therefore, the tenant was not entitled to any compensation.

In *Tenants of 28 & 32 Corinth Gdns v. Forum Homes (Corinth) Inc.*,[210] there were two separate, adjacent triplexes. One corporation bought one property and a related corporation bought the other. The two properties were managed as if they were part of the one complex and, ultimately, one of the corporations ended up owning both properties. The landlord took the position that, at the time the tenants were given notice of termination for demolition, there were two separate residential complexes, each with three units and that, therefore, no compensation was required under s. 55 of the T.P.A. (now s. 52 of the R.T.A.). Looking at the real substance of the matter, the Tribunal found that the management of both of these properties and the identity of the two corporate owners was so intermingled, that the two properties became one residential complex (containing six residential units). The landlord was therefore ordered to pay to the tenants the compensation required by s. 55 of the T.P.A.

C. MAJOR REPAIRS OR RENOVATIONS

Under para. 50(1)(c) of the R.T.A. (formerly para. 53(1)(c) of the T.P.A.), a landlord may apply to terminate a tenancy if the landlord plans to do work on the unit or complex that is so extensive as to require a building permit *and* vacant possession of the rental unit in question.

---

208 The compensation required may be higher in the case of a mobile home or land lease home (s. 164). See Chapter 20.

209 (Nov. 29, 2001), SWL-33070 (Ont. Rental Housing Trib.).

210 (May 2, 2003), TNT-03257, 2003 CarswellOnt 2640 (Ont. Rental Housing Trib.).

In *Cela Management Ltd. v. Bottlik*,[211] a building permit was not required by the municipality as the renovations did not involve structural alterations. A plumbing permit was issued to replace kitchen and bathroom fixtures. The court refused the landlord's application for possession stating that the landlord could only apply under that section if a building permit was required and a plumbing permit was not a building permit. The court also decided that vacant possession would not be required. Similarly, the landlord's application was dismissed in *Paskaleff v. Stieg*[212] on the basis that no building permit was required to perform the renovations proposed by the landlord in this case.

Pursuant to s. 53 of the R.T.A. (formerly s. 56 of the T.P.A.), a tenant who receives notice of termination of a tenancy for the purpose of repairs or renovations may, in accordance with this section, have a right of first refusal to occupy the rental unit as a tenant when the repairs or renovations are completed. A tenant who wishes to have a right of first refusal must give the landlord notice in writing before vacating the rental unit.[213] A tenant who exercises a right of first refusal may re-occupy the rental unit at a rent that is no more than what the landlord could have lawfully charged if there had been no interruption in the tenant's tenancy.[214] The tenant must inform the landlord in writing of any change of address (presumably, so that the landlord can inform the tenant when the unit is ready for occupation).[215]

The requirement for "all necessary permits" was considered in *Apogee Investments Ltd. v. Saber*.[216] The judge rather reasonably held that the obtained building permit was sufficient compliance even though further permits for plumbing and heating might be required as the work proceeded.

Some of the problems facing a landlord wishing to renovate were dealt with in *Beyer v. Absamco Developments Ltd.*[217] The case concerned tenants applying to have repairs done and rents abated. The building was to be reconstructed, and the landlord commenced the work to the great inconvenience of the tenant. The judge noted that the landlord had not yet obtained a building permit, approval from the Committee of Adjustment or approval of the plans for reconstruction (as the building had been declared an historic site under what is now the *Ontario Heritage Act*).[218]

In another case, *Albany Court Apartments Inc. v. G. Solway & Sons Ltd.*,[219] the court agreed on the need for vacant possession by referring to the chaotic conditions otherwise, plaster dust, hazardous electrical and plumbing

---

211 (1982), 136 D.L.R. (3d) 663 (Ont. Co. Ct.).

212 (1982), unreported (Ont. Co. Ct.).

213 Subsection 53(2) of the R.T.A. (formerly subsection 56(2) of the T.P.A.).

214 Subsection 53(3) of the R.T.A. (formerly subsection 56(3) of the T.P.A.).

215 Subsection 53(4) of the R.T.A. (formerly subsection 56(4) of the T.P.A.).

216 (1978), 21 O.R. (2d) 663 (Ont. Co. Ct.).

217 (1976), 12 O.R. (2d) 768 (Ont. Co. Ct.).

218 R.S.O. 1990, c. O.18.

219 (March 30, 1982), Davidson J. (Ont. Co. Ct.).

work, and the necessity for turning off these services from time to time. If the facts accepted by the judge are somewhat extreme, they are of the nature of the considerations to support the necessity for vacant possession.

In another case, the tenants offered to co-operate with the landlord, to accept inconvenience and to move from suite to suite while work was going on. The judge heard detailed evidence as to the extensive repairs and renovations and decided that vacant possession was necessary, saying that "there will be interruption of essential services and there will be dangerous conditions to persons and to property, perhaps without insurance coverage": *Kempston Grove Corp. v. Louch*.[220]

In deciding that vacant possession was not required even with extensive renovations, courts have taken into account that the tenants had not been consulted as to their willingness to stay in possession during the progress of the work, and that with reasonable co-operation of the landlord, contractor and tenant in each case, the work could be done and the accommodation continue to be sufficiently habitable: *Rocca v. Rousselle*;[221] *Lincoln Apartments Ltd. v. Houtman*;[222] *407499 Ontario Ltd. and Chevalier, Re; 407499 Ontario Ltd. and Long, Re*.[223]

Cosmetic repairs such as plastering and decorating are not the kind of extensive repair work which would require a tenant to give up possession: *Morin v. McHugh*.[224]

The *bona fide*s of the landlord were accepted by the court in *Starburst Investments Ltd. v. De Luca*,[225] where the landlord had obtained a building permit and there was evidence of the extensive nature of the renovations. The judge stated that the renovations would require vacant possession and could not be carried on while the tenant continued in occupation.

Some comfort for tenants who are being disposessed because the landlord requires vacant possession for major repairs was indicated in *Barbuto v. Kelly*,[226] in which a condition of granting vacant possession was that the landlord reimburse the tenants for improvements that had been made previously with the landlord's approval. Such relief, though, would have to be obtained by way of court action.

Pursuant to s. 54 of the R.T.A., a landlord must compensate a tenant in an amount equal to three months rent[227] or offer the tenant another rental unit

---

[220] (June 17, 1986), 1986 CarswellOnt 2992 (Ont. Dist. Ct.).

[221] (September 24, 1981) (Ont. Dist. Ct.).

[222] (November 17, 1981), Doc. M57204/81 (Ont. Co. Ct.).

[223] Both reported at (March 10, 1983), Matthews J. (Ont. Co. Ct.).

[224] (February 28, 1979), Ottawa-Carleton (Ont. Co. Ct.).

[225] (December 13, 1976) (Ont. Co. Ct.).

[226] (1990), 10 R.P.R. (2d) 48 (Ont. Dist. Ct.).

[227] The compensation required may be higher in the case of a mobile home or land lease home (s. 164). See Chapter 20.

acceptable to the tenant if the tenant receives notice of termination of the tenancy under s. 50 for the purposes of repairs or renovations and:

(a) the tenant does not give the landlord a notice that the tenant wishes to exercise a right of first refusal;
(b) the residential complex in which the rental unit is located contains **at least five residential units**; and
(c) the repair or renovation was not ordered to be carried out under the authority of the R.T.A. or any other Act.

If the tenant has given notice to the landlord of intention to exercise his or her first right of refusal (under s. 53(2)) *and* the complex contains at least five residential units, the tenant is entitled to compensation in an amount equal to the rent for the lesser of three months and the period the unit is under repair or renovation.[228]

(iv) Termination of Employment of Person Living in a Superintendent's Premises

Pursuant to s. 93 of the R.T.A. (formerly s. 68 of the T.P.A.), unless otherwise agreed, a tenancy with respect to a superintendent's premises terminates on the day on which the employment of the tenant is terminated and the tenant must vacate the premises within one week after his or her tenancy is terminated. If the tenant has not vacated within one week of the termination of his or her employment, pursuant to s. 94 of the R.T.A. (formerly s. 80 of the T.P.A.), the landlord may *then* apply to the Board for an order terminating the tenancy and for an eviction. No specific notice of termination of the tenancy need be delivered prior to delivery of the application since, by operation of law, the notice of termination of the employment automatically also terminates the tenancy. The application is in Form L2 and it must be issued and then served on the tenant, together with the notice of hearing, at least five days before the hearing (Rule 10.5(d)). The filing fee is $170.[229] The certificate of service for the application and notice of hearing should be filed within five days of effecting service (Rule 11.2).

Please refer to Chapter 3 for a much more detailed analysis of this topic.

(v) Where there is an Agreement to Terminate or the Tenant has Delivered a Notice of Termination (s. 77)

In Chapter 6, I describe in detail how and in what circumstances a landlord and tenant may agree to terminate a tenancy and how and when a

[228] Subsection 54(2) of the R.T.A. (formerly subsection 57(2) of the T.P.A.).
[229] Effective April 2009. From 2002 through March 2009, the fee was $150.

tenant can deliver a notice of termination to the landlord in order to terminate a tenancy.

If a tenant has agreed to terminate the tenancy or has served a valid notice of termination on the landlord and vacates the rental unit by the date upon which the parties agreed or as specified in the notice, no further steps need be taken by either side. If, however, the landlord is concerned that the tenant may not vacate the unit, pursuant to s. 77 of the R.T.A. (formerly s. 76 of the T.P.A.), the landlord my apply to the Board in advance of the termination date for an order terminating the tenancy and evicting the tenant (not to be enforced until after the termination date agreed upon by the parties or specified in the notice). The application is in Form L3 and it is an *ex parte* application (i.e., the tenant is not notified of the proceedings). The cost of filing this application is $170.[230] If the application is based upon a notice of termination or written agreement, a copy of the notice or agreement must be filed with the application.[231] The landlord must also file a sworn affidavit verifying the details of the agreement or notice, as the case may be (s. 77(2)). Assuming that everything is in order, the landlord will obtain an eviction order. The order can only be enforced if the tenant does not vacate the unit on the date upon which the parties agreed or as specified in the notice of termination.

Alternatively, the landlord can wait until that date to see whether or not the tenant moves out. If the tenant does not move out, the landlord can then file an application under s. 77. Such an application must be filed within 30 days of the termination date.[232]

When an *ex parte* order is issued by the Board under s. 77, a copy is forwarded to the tenant at the rental unit. If the tenant wishes to challenge the *ex parte* order, the tenant has 10 days from the date the order is issued (unless an extension is granted) in which to bring a motion to have the order set aside (Form S2).[233] Pending the hearing of that motion, the eviction order is stayed.[234] Although the Board *may* advise the sheriff of this fact, pursuant to Rule 30.1 of the Board's Rules of Practice, it is the responsibility of the party who files a set aside motion to immediately take a copy of the motion and notice of hearing to the Court Enforcement Office. This will ensure that the eviction is not enforced prior to the determination of the motion. The motion and notice of hearing must be served upon the landlord at least 48 hours prior to the time set for the hearing (Rule 10.7) and the tenant should file the certificate of service as soon as possible thereafter.

---

230 Effective April 2009. From 2002 through March 2009, the fee was $150.

231 Paragraphs 1 and 4 of s. 53, O. Reg. 516/06.

232 Subsection 77(3) of the R.T.A. See Landlord and Tenant Board File No. CEL-16338 (Feb. 9, 2009).

233 Subsection 77(6) of the R.T.A.

234 Subsection 77(7) of the R.T.A.

The R.T.A. does not list any criteria for determining whether or not an *ex parte* order ought to be set aside. Neither did the T.P.A. This created some confusion in the past as to what test, if any, ought to be met by the tenant before the tenant's motion was granted and the landlord was required to prove its case.

The revised wording of subsection 77(8) of the R.T.A. makes it clear that a hearing must be held in these cases. Presumably, this means a hearing on the merits of the landlord's original application. If the landlord cannot prove, on a balance of probabilities, that the tenant delivered a valid notice of termination or agreed to terminate the tenancy, the eviction order will be set aside and the landlord's application will be dismissed. If, on the other hand, the landlord proves its case, the Board may lift the stay and permit the existing eviction order to be enforced.

Note that under para. 77(8)(b), however, the Board retains the discretion to set aside the *ex parte* eviction order if the Board is satisfied that it would not be unfair to do so (even if the landlord has proven that the landlord was legally entitled to an eviction order). This appears to give the Board the same discretion on these set-aside motions as it normally has under s. 83 on other eviction applications.

In Landlord and Tenant Board File No. TSL-20860-SA (Jan. 26, 2009), the tenants served their landlord with a valid notice of termination because they planned to move into the condominium they were in the process of purchasing. The landlord obtained an *ex parte* eviction order based upon the notice the landlord had received from the tenants. When the tenants' real estate deal fell through, they wanted to rescind their notice and continue living in the rental unit. The landlord, however, had already signed an agreement to rent the unit to new tenants who were moving to Ontario from California. In these circumstances, the Member denied the tenants' motion to set aside the *ex parte* eviction order.

Although applications under s. 77 are meant to be resolved, primarily, as written hearings based solely upon the documents filed by the landlord, the R.T.A. recognizes that Members of the Board have discretion whether or not to grant such applications.[235] Where a Member determines that an oral hearing is required, a hearing date will be set and, pursuant to Rule 10.2 of the Board's Rules of Practice, the applicant will be asked to give the application and the notice of hearing to the tenant(s) as soon as possible but not later than 10 days before the time set for the hearing, unless otherwise directed by the Board. Some landlords have argued (under similar provisions of the T.P.A.) that there is no specific authority in the Act for a member to convert an *ex parte* procedure into an oral hearing, on notice to the tenant. I think the correct response to this is threefold. First, the Board always retains the power

---

[235] Subsection 77(4) of the R.T.A. states that the Board *may* make an order terminating the tenancy and evicting the tenant.

to control its processes and to make such orders as it deems necessary to fully and fairly adjudicate disputes that come before it; so long as the Board does not violate any express provision of the Act, there is no prohibition against the methodology that has been adopted by the Board. Second, s. 188(2) of the R.T.A. (formerly s. 175(2) of the T.P.A.) does require the applicant to serve on the other parties a copy of *any* notice of hearing issued by the Board in respect of an application. Third, where the written material filed by the landlord appears to a Member to be inadequate, the alternative to holding a *viva voce* hearing could be to simply dismiss the landlord's application at the initial stage (without providing any further opportunity to the landlord to prove its case); I doubt that landlords would find such an approach to be preferable to the one currently employed by the Board.

As pointed out in Chapter 6, an agreement to terminate need not be in writing. As long as the landlord can prove that there actually was an agreement, it will be binding upon the parties. For there to be a binding agreement, however, the terms of the agreement must be clear and unconditional and the agreement cannot have been obtained through misrepresentation or coercion (in other words, the usual laws pertaining to contracts apply). Thus, the Board has dismissed applications from landlords where there were discussions between the parties but no actual agreement to terminate the tenancy on a specific date[236] and where there was a written agreement but it was conditional (on the availability of a new rental unit) and/or was not signed by all tenants.[237]

Even where there actually was an agreement to terminate the tenancy, the Board retains discretionary powers under s. 83 to refuse to grant an eviction and/or under para. 77(8)(b) to set aside an *ex parte* order and dismiss the landlord's application. For example, the Board set aside an *ex parte* order and dismissed the landlord's application where it determined that the signature of the tenant on the agreement to terminate was forged.[238] The Board also set aside an eviction order and dismissed the landlord's application pursuant to s. 83(1) where, subsequent to the original agreement, the parties entered into an agreement to delay the termination date but the landlord failed to disclose that fact to the Board.[239] Finally, where the tenant only signed the agreement to terminate because the landlord was harassing her about non-payment of rent, the Member found it appropriate to refuse to grant an eviction pursuant to s. 83(1) of the R.T.A.[240]

Where the landlord is relying upon a notice of termination that was received from a tenant (rather than an agreement to terminate the tenancy),

---

[236] Landlord and Tenant Board File No. SOL-18030 (Jan. 13, 2009) and Landlord and Tenant Board File No. SWL-00453 (March 16, 2007).

[237] Landlord and Tenant Board File No. NOL-05945-AM and NOL-06045-AM (Jan. 23, 2009). Also see Landlord and Tenant Board File No. TNL-21335 (Feb. 2, 2009).

[238] Landlord and Tenant Board File No. SOL-00137-SA (March 7, 2007).

[239] Landlord and Tenant Board File No. CEL-00373-SA (March 9, 2007).

[240] Landlord and Tenant Board File No. NOL-00221 (March 27, 2007).

even more stringent rules apply. The notice of termination must substantially comply in form and content with the requirements set out in the R.T.A. The notice must be clear, unequivocal and unconditional. It must state a specific date for termination of the tenancy and it must be signed by all of the tenants to the unit in question.

Thus, the Board dismissed an application by a landlord under s. 77 that was based upon a notice of termination that stated "we will be moving out at the end of November" and was signed only by the spouse of the tenant.[241] Similarly, where the notice indicated that the tenant would be leaving only if she was unable to make any payments towards the rent arrears and where less than 60 days' notice was provided, the Board held that the notice was not valid and the landlord's application under s. 77 was dismissed.[242] A landlord's application was also dismissed where the notice of termination was obtained by the landlord through threats and misrepresentations.[243]

(vi) Other "No-fault" Grounds (s. 58)

The most common application filed under s. 58 of the R.T.A. (formerly s. 60 of the T.P.A.) is where a landlord seeks to terminate the tenancy and evict the tenant for persistent late payment of rent (s. 58(1)1). This subject is considered at length later in this chapter. There are, however, three other grounds for termination contained in s. 58. Although rarely used, they are worth considering further.

In each case, the process starts with service of a notice of termination in Form N8. The notice period is specified in s. 58(2): at least 28 days before the end of a period or term for a daily or weekly tenancy or at least 60 days before the end of a period or term for all other tenancies. The date specified as the termination date must be the *last day* of a period (for a periodic tenancy) or of the term (for a fixed term tenancy).[244]

As discussed in Chapter 6, s. 43(2) requires that the notice set out the "reasons and details respecting the termination". Lack of such details may

---

[241] Landlord and Tenant Board File No. TNL-20035 (Jan. 29, 2009).

[242] Landlord and Tenant Board File No. SOL-18522 (Jan. 30, 2009).

[243] Landlord and Tenant Board File No. SOL-00518 (March 26, 2007), in which the landlord attempted to enforce an unlawful term of the tenancy agreement that purported to the give the landlord absolute control over the tenant's right to share his unit with others and misrepresented the law concerning occupants (of which the landlord was aware based on a previous order from the Board on an application brought against the same landlord (File No. SOT-00022)).

[244] See *Falls Masonry Limited v. Collee et al.* (July 29, 1999), SOL-06497 (Ont. Rental Housing Trib.) in which the application was dismissed because the termination date specified in the notice of termination was May 30, 1999, which was not the last day of the month. See also *Eren v. Blott* (June 2, 1999), SOL-05873 (Ont. Rental Housing Trib.) in which the application was dismissed because the termination date chosen was several months prior to the last day of this one-year tenancy.

invalidate a notice[245] and an invalid notice cannot be saved by providing further details at the hearing. An inaccurate, vague or confusing notice may be found to be void.[246]

The landlord can commence the application after serving the notice of termination upon the tenant; the landlord need not wait until after the termination date.[247] The termination and eviction, however, cannot be ordered to occur prior to the termination date set out in the notice of termination. The application is in Form L2 and the filing fee is $170.[248] The application cannot be commenced more than 30 days after the termination date (s. 69(2)). The application and notice of hearing must be served at least 10 days prior to the hearing (Rule 10.1). The certificate of service for the application and notice of hearing should be filed within five days after service has been effected (Rule 11.2).

A. TENANT CEASES TO MEET QUALIFICATIONS FOR GOVERNMENT HOUSING

Pursuant to para. 2 of s. 58(1) of the R.T.A., a tenant ceasing to meet the qualifications for occupation of government housing is a cause for termination of the tenancy. Unlike misrepresentation of income,[249] ceasing to qualify for government housing will not result in early termination of a fixed-term tenancy.

In *Metropolitan Toronto Housing Corp. v. Gabriel*,[250] the female tenant and her son lived in subsidized housing. The father of the son moved in. The judge hearing the application was satisfied that "the tenant has ceased to meet the qualifications" for the subsidized housing (s. 110(3)(*c*) of Part IV of the *Landlord and Tenant Act*). When asked to exercise the discretion in s. 121(2) of Part IV, now s. 83 of the R.T.A., Hawkins D.C.J. commented:[251]

> As to whether it would be unfair not ... [to grant the relief] having regard to all the circumstances, that can only be directed as to whether it would be unfair to

---

245 *698077 Ontario Ltd. v. Garcia* (Aug. 3, 2000), TEL-13582, [2000] O.R.H.T.D. No. 105, 2000 CarswellOnt 4377 (Ont. Rental Housing Trib.); *Tavernier v. Morell* (June 28, 2001), EAL-21801, [2001] O.R.H.T.D. No. 91, 2001 CarswellOnt 6341 (Ont. Rental Housing Trib.); and *Pinecrest Heights v. Futi* (Sept. 6, 2000), EAL-15062, [2000] O.R.H.T.D. No. 116, 2000 CarswellOnt 4347 (Ont. Rental Housing Trib.).

246 *1255074 Ontario Inc. v. Mak* (June 10, 1999), TNL-05155-RV (Ont. Rental Housing Trib.); *Green Ash Dvpt. v. McDonald* (April 14, 1999), TNL-05851 (Ont. Rental Housing Trib.); *Cerase Holdings Ltd. v. Veres-Bafford* (March 8, 2000), TNL-13127, 2000 CarswellOnt 6435 (Ont. Rental Housing Trib.).

247 Section 71 of the R.T.A.

248 Effective April 2009. From 2002 through March 2009, the fee was $150.

249 A separate, but somewhat similar, ground for termination of the tenancy under s. 60(1).

250 (1988), 2 R.P.R. (2d) 284 (Ont. Dist. Ct.).

251 (1988), 2 R.P.R. (2d) 284 (Ont. Dist. Ct.) at 288.

> the landlord. ... Subsidized housing is a very precious commodity in this community, and those who are lucky enough to get it, in my view, ought to follow the regulations and the rules and provisions of their lease strictly.

In *Otonabee Native Homes Inc. v. Comartin*,[252] the rental unit was located in a community that was limited to occupancy for persons of Native ancestry. At the time the tenancy commenced, the tenant moved into the unit with her husband and two children. The husband and the children were of Native ancestry. Approximately 17 years later, the husband and children vacated the unit. Since the remaining tenant was not of Native ancestry, the landlord commenced an application to evict her on the basis that she no longer qualified to live in this rental unit. The Tenant argued that this constituted discrimination and was contrary to the Human Rights Code. The Member found that since the rental unit was covered by a special program designed to relieve hardship or economic disadvantage or to assist disadvantaged persons or groups to achieve or attempt to achieve equal opportunity, pursuant to subsection 14(1) of the *Code*, discrimination against the Tenant in this case based on her ancestry did not violate the *Code*.

B. EMPLOYEE NO LONGER EMPLOYED

For an employee other than one living in superintendent's premises, para. 58(1)3 of the R.T.A. (formerly para. 60(1)3 of the T.P.A.) provides for an application for possession by the employer landlord when the employment has been terminated.

Section 110(3)(*d*) of Part IV, now s. 58(1) para. 3 of the R.T.A., was applied in a case where the landlord (a golf course owner) was granted an order terminating the tenancy and evicting a golf pro from a rental unit above the pro shop because his employment at the golf course had been terminated: *Fox Glen Golf Course Ltd. v. McBride*.[253]

In *Eagleguest Golf Center Inc. v. Burch*,[254] the tenant was an employee of a company that ran a golf course. During his employment, he commenced a tenancy in a unit located on the golf course. When his employment ended, the landlord (his employer) delivered a notice of termination, relying upon para. 60(1)3 of the T.P.A. The Member who heard the case interpreted this paragraph as meaning that *if a tenancy is conditional upon the continuation of the employment,* the landlord may apply to terminate the tenancy when the employment ends. In this case, the employer never explicitly made the tenancy conditional upon the continuation of the tenant's employment. This decision was upheld upon review as being a reasonable interpretation of the paragraph in question, in light of the existing case law on point.

---

[252] (Sept. 26, 2006), TEL-62870 (Ont. Rental Housing Trib.).

[253] (April 22, 1991), Doc. 91-GD-15219 (Ont. Gen. Div.).

[254] (Feb. 26, 2002), TNL-33418-RV (Ont. Rental Housing Trib.).

C. INTERIM OCCUPANCY OF CONDOMINIUM

Section 58(1) para. 4 of the R.T.A. (formerly para 60(1)4 of the T.P.A.) refers to obtaining possession of a condominium unit when the agreement of purchase and sale has been terminated.

There can be some confusion as to the proceedings to regain possession from a purchaser of a proposed condominium unit who has gone into occupancy under an interim occupancy agreement and the offer to purchase has been terminated.

The cases referred to in Chapter 3 indicate that the courts have held that the relationship between vendor and purchaser in the interim occupancy agreement is generally that of landlord and tenant, and this latter relationship is said to be the dominant one. This is unrealistic, at least to the vendor or even the purchaser who did not contemplate the strictures on landlords under the R.T.A.

But how can possession be regained if the interim occupancy agreement results in a landlord and tenant relationship? Most interim occupancy agreements provide that upon termination of the offer to purchase, the interim occupancy agreement is likewise terminated and provide for vacant possession *forthwith*. Under the R.T.A., however, the vendor will have to provide at least 60 days notice. As a result, vendors have generally looked for ways to regain possession without relying upon the R.T.A. (and must have found them since few disputes arising from interim occupancy agreements seem to have found their way before the Tribunal/Board).

One reported decision from the Tribunal on this issue is *Lebovic Enterprises Ltd. v. Haggard*.[255] The landlord and tenants had entered into an agreement to purchase a condominium and the tenants paid a deposit to the landlord. The tenants took possession of the unit prior to the completion of that transaction and, according to the landlord, were required to make periodic payments as set out in an interim occupancy agreement. The tenants did not make these payments. As a result, the agreement of purchase and sale was terminated and the tenants refused to vacate the unit or pay the money that was owing to the landlord. The landlord commenced an application under Section 60(1) para. 4 of the T.P.A. to evict the tenants but the tenant's challenged the Tribunal's right to adjudicate a dispute arising out of an agreement of purchase and sale. The Tribunal held that it was specifically granted the jurisdiction to grant relief in such circumstances and, since the landlord had established the necessary prerequisites for the granting of relief, the Tribunal granted the landlord's application, terminated the tenancy and ordered the eviction of the tenants. Note that, although in this case the agreement of purchase and sale was terminated because of a default on the

---

[255] (May 29, 2006), TEL-61798, 2006 CarswellOnt 4385, [2006] O.R.H.T.D. No. 58 (Ont. Rental Housing Trib.).

part of the purchasers, this provision is generally considered to be a "no fault" provision because it applies regardless of why the agreement of purchase and sale is terminated (and there are many reasons why a sale may not be completed that are not the result of any "fault" on the part of the purchaser). For a more recent decision on point, see Landlord and Tenant Board File No. TEL-00235-A (released March 7, 2007 and amended on March 15, 2007).

(d) "Fault" Grounds for Termination of the Tenancy

(i) Persistent Late Payment of Rent

Paragraph 58(1)1 of the R.T.A. (formerly para. 60(1)1 of the T.P.A.) gives the Board the jurisdiction to grant an application for termination and eviction if a tenant persistently fails to pay rent on the dates it becomes due and payable.

The process starts with service of a notice of termination in Form N8. The notice period is specified in subsection 58(2): at least 28 days before the end of a period or term for a daily or weekly tenancy or at least 60 days before the end of a period or term for all other tenancies. The date specified as the termination date must be the *last day* of a period (for a periodic tenancy) or of the term (for a fixed term tenancy).[256]

As discussed in Chapter 6, s. 43(2) requires that the notice set out the "reasons and details respecting the termination". Writing "the tenant is always late in paying rent" does not provide any *details*. Lack of such details may invalidate a notice[257] and an invalid notice cannot be saved by providing further details at the hearing. An inaccurate, vague or confusing notice may

---

[256] See *Falls Masonry Limited v. Collee et al.* (July 29, 1999), SOL-06497 (Ont. Rental Housing Trib.) in which the application was dismissed because the termination date specified in the notice was May 30, 1999, which was not the last day of the month. For a similar decision, see Landlord and Tenant Board File No. TEL-00239 (March 5, 2007), in which it was determined that since the tenancy began on April 10, 2006, each rental period began on the 10th day of the month and ended on the 9th day of the following month and, therefore, a termination date of April 10, 2007 was invalid. See also *Eren v. Blott* (June 2, 1999), SOL-05873 (Ont. Rental Housing Trib.) in which the application was dismissed because the termination date chosen was several months prior to the last day of this one-year tenancy.

[257] *698077 Ontario Ltd. v. Garcia* (Aug. 3, 2000), TEL-13582, [2000] O.R.H.T.D. No. 105, 2000 CarswellOnt 4377 (Ont. Rental Housing Trib.); *Tavernier v. Morell* (June 28, 2001), EAL-21801, [2001] O.R.H.T.D. No. 91, 2001 CarswellOnt 6341 (Ont. Rental Housing Trib.); and *Pinecrest Heights v. Futi* (Sept. 6, 2000), EAL-15062, [2000] O.R.H.T.D. No. 116, 2000 CarswellOnt 4347 (Ont. Rental Housing Trib.).

be found to be void.[258] In *Ball v. Metro Capital et al.*,[259] the Divisional Court ruled that a notice of termination was void for lack of details. It stated that a tenant needs sufficient information to permit the tenant to know the case that must be met and to decide whether to dispute the allegations.

The landlord can commence the application after serving the notice of termination upon the tenant; the landlord need not wait until after the termination date.[260] The termination and eviction, however, cannot be ordered to occur prior to the termination date set out in the notice. The application is in Form L2 and the filing fee is $170.[261] The application cannot be commenced more than 30 days after the termination date (s. 69(2)). The application and notice of hearing must be served at least 10 days prior to the hearing (Rule 10.1). The certificate of service for the application and notice of hearing should be filed within five days after service has been effected (Rule 11.2).

A landlord may commence this type of application where "the tenant has persistently failed to pay rent on the date it becomes due and payable". What is meant by the word "persistent"?

One view is that to "persist" in something means to continue in the face of some objection or opposition. In other words, it means more than merely being frequently late in paying the rent. It means frequently paying the rent late despite warnings from the landlord that this is not acceptable. If this is the interpretation that is adopted, then silence or acquiescence by the landlord will be fatal to such an application.[262] The rent will have been paid *consistently* late, but not *persistently* late. In *Cottam v. Smith*,[263] the Court of Appeal did not consider late payment of rent to be default by the tenant because for some time the rent had been accepted at a later date than the due date.

In *Schneider and DuFresne et al.*,[264] the landlord's application was for arrears and persistent late payment of rent. The Tribunal was satisfied as to the amount of arrears and the persistent late paying. The Tribunal noted the number of late payments from October 1983 and in particular after 1998 when the landlord made it clear that she could not and would not accept late payment. She was retired and had mortgage payments to make. The Tribunal stated that the T.P.A. did not have a definition or guideline for persistent late payment and quoted *Webster's New Collegiate Dictionary*'s meaning of

---

[258] *1255074 Ontario Inc. v. Mak* (June 10, 1999), TNL-05155-RV (Ont. Rental Housing Trib.); *Green Ash Dvpt. v. McDonald* (April 14, 1999), TNL-05851 (Ont. Rental Housing Trib.); *Cerase Holdings Ltd. v. Veres-Bafford* (March 8, 2000), TNL-13127, 2000 CarswellOnt 6435 (Ont. Rental Housing Trib.).

[259] (Dec. 19, 2002), Div. Ct. File No. 48/02 (Ont. Div. Ct.), re (Dec. 10, 2001), TNL-31297 (Ont. Rental Housing Trib.).

[260] Section 71 of the R.T.A.

[261] Effective April 2009. From 2002 through March 2009, the fee was $150.

[262] See, for example, *Koski v. Sigurdson* (May 10, 2005) NOL-11504 (Ont. Rental Housing Trib.).

[263] [1947] O.W.N. 880 (Ont. C.A.).

[264] (April 1, 1999), EAL-04538, EAL-04986 (Ont. Rental Housing Trib.).

"persistent" as "continuing or inclined to persistent", and went on to state that the number of occasions and length of time must in each case be considered. The Tribunal ordered termination of the tenancy and eviction.

The alternative view is that every tenant contracts to pay rent on or before a certain day and that the landlord need not remind the tenant of this obligation. If the tenant repeatedly fails to pay the rent on time, this is sufficient grounds for termination of the tenancy without any further warnings to the tenant. This is the interpretation adopted by the Divisional Court with respect to similar provisions under the *Landlord and Tenant Act.* In *Oxford Square Investments v. Pickens*,[265] the Divisional Court held the landlord is not required to warn a tenant that late payments are unacceptable. Whether or not the rent payments are persistently late does not depend upon whether the landlord put the tenant on notice of the possible consequences. The Court went on to indicate, however, that the silence or acquiescence of the landlord may be relevant to the tenant's request for relief from forfeiture and a determination of whether or not it would be unjust to terminate the tenancy.

Yet another approach is to consider whether it can be implied from the conduct of the parties that the due date for rent has been changed (in which case, the rent may not be late at all).

It has been held that being late on two occasions in a 12-month period does not constitute being persistently late in paying rent.[266]

The Board will also consider when payments are actually made by the tenants and will not allow the landlord's accounting procedures to create a false impression of persistent lateness. For example, if a tenant misses one (and only one) rent payment and the landlord applies all subsequent rent payments to the previous month's rent (as opposed to the month to which the tenant intended that the payment be applied), this will create the impression that the tenant is one month late in paying his or her rent, every single month. A fairer description of the situation would be to say that the tenant is on time with all rent payments, with the exception of the one payment that was missed.[267]

On a few occasions courts have adjourned the application respecting persistent late payment and made an order that if there is another late payment the landlord may, on short notice, obtain an order terminating the lease: *Manufacturers Life Property Corp. v. Senkow*.[268] The same result was achieved by the Rental Housing Tribunal using a combination of ss. 84 and 77 of the T.P.A. Where a tenant had been persistently late in paying rent but had otherwise been a good tenant and assured the Tribunal that, henceforth, she would be able and willing to pay the rent on time, it became quite common

[265] (1977) 16 O.R. (2d) 590 (Ont. Div. Ct.).

[266] *1059815 Ontario Inc. v. Higgins*, (April 3, 2000) EAL-12929 (Ont. Rental Housing Trib.).

[267] *Moro v. Sykes*, (September 27, 1999) TSL-13076 (Ont. Rental Housing Trib.).

[268] (1990), 75 O.R. (2d) 254 (Ont. Div. Ct.).

for Members to exercise their discretion (under s. 84(1)) to refuse to grant an eviction but only on the condition that the tenant would pay the rent on time for the next six months (or such other number of months that the Member found to be appropriate — usually in the range of 6 to 12 months). The Member would then include a term in the order that stated that if the tenant failed to comply with that condition, the landlord was entitled to apply, pursuant to s. 77 of the T.P.A., without notice to the tenant, for an order terminating the tenancy and evicting the tenant. This gave the tenant one last chance but assured the landlord of obtaining a quick eviction order (without a hearing) if the tenant did not comply with the conditions imposed by the Tribunal. The Landlord and Tenant Board retains the same discretionary powers under what are now ss. 83 and 78 of the R.T.A. and I would expect that, where appropriate, the Board will continue the practice described above.

An application based upon persistent late payment of rent may be combined with other applications, most commonly an application based upon non-payment of rent. If the tenant pays all of the arrears prior to the hearing, this stays the part of the application based upon non-payment of rent but not the part of the application grounded upon persistent late payment of rent.[269]

In *Singh and McCarthy*,[270] the rent was paid late on eight occasions during the year before the landlord's application. The Tribunal granted the landlord's application based upon the tenant's persistent late payment, saying that "the tenant has exhibited a flagrant disregard of his obligation to pay the rent on the first day of each month".

13 — LL APPLICATIONS

(ii) *Non-payment of Rent*

For a general review of issues about rent and rent deposits, please see Chapters 7 and 8.

Pursuant to s. 59(1) of the R.T.A. (formerly s. 61(1) of the T.P.A.), a landlord may give the tenant notice of termination of the tenancy if the tenant fails to pay rent lawfully owing under a tenancy agreement. The notice is in Form N4. The notice of termination may not take effect earlier than:

(a) the 7th day after the notice is given, in the case of a daily or weekly tenancy; and
(b) the 14th day after the notice is given, in all other cases.

As explained in Chapter 6, if the notice of termination is not given at least the required minimum number of days in advance of the termination

---

269 *Manufacturers Life Property Corp. v. Senkow* (1990), 75 O.R. (2d) 254 (Ont. Div. Ct.).

270 (Feb. 4, 1999), SOL-02808 (Ont. Rental Housing Trib.).

date, the notice will be void (and the Board has no power to save such a defective notice by abridging the usual time requirements).[271]

The notice of termination must set out the amount of rent due and must specify that the tenant may avoid the termination of the tenancy by paying, on or before the termination date specified in the notice, the rent due as set out in the notice and any additional rent that has become due under the tenancy agreement as at the date of payment by the tenant.[272] The notice will be invalid if it lacks this information.[273]

The notice of termination becomes void if, before the day the landlord applies to the Board for an order terminating the tenancy and evicting the tenant based on the notice, the tenant pays:

(a) the rent that is in arrears under the tenancy agreement; and
(b) the additional rent that would have been due under the tenancy agreement as at the date of payment by the tenant had the notice of termination not been given.[274]

Since the tenant has the right to pay the amounts set out in the notice in order to render it void, the notice of termination must be both accurate and clear.[275] It cannot be misleading or confusing.[276]

One problem that often arises is that landlords apply money to the oldest debt first. Therefore if the tenant pays the full rent for February but there was $50 owing from January, the landlord may apply $50 from the cheque received in February to pay off the debt from January and then apply the rest of the money towards the rent owing for February. From the landlord's perspective, there is now $50 owing for February. The tenant, however, knows that the full amount was paid in February. If the landlord's N4 notice of termination only refers to $50 owing for February, this can create confusion. It can, in fact, invalidate the notice of termination.[277] To avoid this type of confusion, it has been suggested that the landlord should consider attaching to the N4 an accounting of rents charged and paid back to the last "zero" balance.[278]

---

[271] See, for example, Landlord and Tenant Board File No. CEL-00450 (March 7, 2007) and Landlord and Tenant Board File No. CEL-00452 (March 7, 2007).

[272] Subsection 59(2) of the R.T.A. (formerly subsection 61(2) of the T.P.A.).

[273] *Cory v. Carmo* (1978), 19 O.R. (2d) 340 (Ont. Dist. Ct.).

[274] Subsection 59(3) of the R.T.A. (formerly subsection 61(3) of the T.P.A.).

[275] Landlord and Tenant Board File No. EAL-00047 (March 1, 2007); Landlord and Tenant Board File No. TSL-19538 (Jan. 7, 2009); Landlord and Tenant Board File No. SOL-00616 (March 23, 2007).

[276] Landlord and Tenant Board File No. TSL-00013 (Feb. 20, 2007); Landlord and Tenant Board File No. TEL-00737 (March 30, 2007).

[277] *RESREIT v. Kurfurst* (Sept. 8, 1999), TNL-06999 (Ont. Rental Housing Trib.) and *Metcap Living Management Inc. v. Carrera* (March 10, 2006), TEL-57764-RV (Ont. Rental Houisng Trib.).

[278] *RESREIT v. Kurfurst* (Sept. 8, 1999), TNL-06999 (Ont. Rental Housing Trib.).

This type of application is always combined with an application for compensation for the arrears of rent under s. 87 (discussed earlier in this chapter).

Note that the only type of debt that can be claimed in the N4 notice of termination is for unpaid rent.[279] Pursuant to s. 1 of the R.T.A.:

> **"rent"** includes the amount of any consideration paid or given or required to be paid or given by or on behalf of a tenant to a landlord or the landlord's agent for the right to occupy a rental unit and for any services and facilities and any privilege, accommodation or thing that the landlord provides for the tenant in respect of the occupancy of the rental unit, whether or not a separate charge is made for services and facilities or for the privilege, accommodation or thing, but **"rent"** does not include,
>
> (a) an amount paid by a tenant to a landlord to reimburse the landlord for property taxes paid by the landlord with respect to a mobile home or a land lease home owned by a tenant, or
>
> (b) an amount that a landlord charges a tenant of a rental unit in a care home for care services or meals.

Other amounts that may be owing to the landlord (for utilities,[280] other charges,[281] damages, etc.) cannot be included on this form (Form N4).[282] The landlord also cannot include in a Form N4 arrears previously ordered by the Board.[283]

If the tenant does not pay all of the rent owing to the landlord by the termination date set out in the notice, then the landlord may commence an application for arrears of rent, compensation, NSF fees and administrative charges,[284] termination of the tenancy, eviction and the costs of the application. The application is in Form L1 and the filing fee is $170.[285] The earliest

13 — LL APPLICATIONS

---

[279] See Chapter 7 for a full description of what is, and is not, included in the definition of the word "rent".

[280] For example, in Landlord and Tenant Board File No. SOL-19061 (Feb. 17, 2009), it was held that the Form N4 was void because, in addition to rent, the landlord included a claim for payment of a water bill (and administrative fees in excess of the amount permitted under O. Reg. 516/06).

[281] For example, an extra charge of $50 per month for the summer months for costs related to use of an air conditioner (which is legal, but is not "rent"): Landlord and Tenant Board File No. SWL-21818 (Jan. 13, 2009).

[282] See Rule 8.9(c) of the Board's Rules of Practice (Appendix 7) and Landlord and Tenant Board File No. SWL-23237 (Feb. 12, 2009).

[283] Landlord and Tenant Board File No. TEL-20767 (Feb. 18, 2009).

[284] Subsection 87(5) of the R.T.A. (formerly subsection 86(4) of the T.P.A.). Note that, pursuant to s. 17 of O. Reg. 516/06, administrative fees for NSF cheques cannot exceed $20 per cheque.

[285] Effective April 2009. From 2002 through March 2009, the fee was $150.

date such an application may be filed is on the day following the termination date specified on the notice.[286]

A time limit is not set out in the R.T.A. for this type of application; the N4 never expires.[287] Nevertheless, if a landlord purports to file an L1 application based upon an old Form N4, the Member will wonder why the landlord waited so long to commence an application. The Member will likely want to see detailed financial records to ascertain whether the balance owing to the landlord for rent was ever nil between the date the N4 was served upon the tenant and the date the application was filed. If so, the notice of termination would have become void (pursuant to s. 59(3)) and could not form the basis of an L1 application. Even if the notice did not become void, the Board may find it to be an abuse of process for the landlord not to have issued a new notice that accurately informed the tenant of the current total arrears of rent owing to the landlord and how that total was calculated.

The application and notice of hearing must be served upon the tenant at least 10 days prior to the hearing (Rule 10.1). The certificate of service for the application and notice of hearing should be filed within five days after service has been effected (Rule 11.2).

When there is an application for possession for non-payment of rent and the property is sold after notice of termination has been given, the purchaser of the property can proceed with the application for possession and obtain an order for termination: *P.J. Construction Ltd. v. Dunn*.[288]

How the Form L1 is completed is very important. Section 1 of Part 4 of the application form has only three rows in which to show how the arrears of rent are calculated. If rent is owed for more than three rental periods, what do you do? My suggestion is to group several rental periods together. The Board's Form L1 instruction booklet also recommends this but makes it clear that the third row should always contain the most recent rent information and should relate to only one rental period. In a complicated situation, it is acceptable to attach a ledger or account summary to the Form L1 but the information must still be summarized by completing the table in Section 1 of Part 4 (within the three rows provided). Let's take a concrete example to illustrate these points.

Let's say that the rent is $1,000 per month, due on the first day of each month, and that in 2007 the tenant paid $500 in January, $800 in February, $1000 in March, $950 in April, $850 in May and the landlord is filing an L1

---

[286] Subsection 74(1) of the R.T.A. (formerly subsection 72 (1) of the T.P.A.). If the landlord files the application on the termination date, it will likely be dismissed as contravening s. 74(1) of the *Act*. It is *possible*, however, that a Member might allow the application to proceed but for arrears only and not for an order terminating the tenancy: Landlord and Tenant Board File No. TNL-00276 (March 12, 2007).

[287] There may, however, be limitation periods established by the *Limitations Act*, 2002, S.O. 2002, and the *Real Property Limitations Act*, R.S.O. 1990. See footnote 7.

[288] (1987), 1987 CarswellOnt 2948 (Ont. Dist. Ct.).

application with the Board in May 2007. Section 1 of Part 4 of the Form L1 should be completed as follows:

Rent Period		Rent Charged $	Rent Paid $	Rent Owing $
From: (dd/mm/yyyy)	To: (dd/mm/yyyy)			
01/01/2007	31/01/2007	1,000.00	500.00	500.00
01/02/2007	30/04/2007	3,000.00	2,750.00	250.00
01/05/2007	31/05/2007	1,000.00	850.00	150.00
		Total Rent Owing $		900.00

The Board's software is designed to allow only three lines of input so it makes things much easier for the Board staff if you organize the information to fit into three lines. You may also wish to attach a month-by-month breakdown to show the details for the months that have been "lumped together". This will be especially important if the rent has changed during the period in question. If the application is also for an order terminating the tenancy, it is absolutely critical that the rental period in which the termination date falls be left on its own (i.e., that rental period should have its own row) and that it not be combined on the form with any other rental period. Finally, please note that you can claim the rent for the entire rental period even if filing the application in the middle of the period or if the notice of termination (when seeking termination) falls in the middle of the rental period. If the application is just for arrears of rent (without termination), a landlord is entitled to claim for the entire rental period as the rent was due at the beginning of the period. If the application also seeks an order terminating the tenancy, the Board's software will make the necessary adjustments and calculate the arrears of rent up to the date of termination.

Sometimes the landlord starts out seeking both an order terminating the tenancy (and evicting the tenant) *and* an order for arrears of rent. In fact, such a combined application was, by far, the most common type of application received by the Rental Housing Tribunal. Where the landlord has made an error in the notice of termination that renders it void, the landlord may choose to withdraw the entire application or may choose to proceed under s. 87 to obtain an order for arrears of rent (without an order terminating the tenancy). The landlord should be aware that, in such circumstances, the landlord cannot later seek to evict the tenant based on arrears of rent owing for the same time period covered by the order issued under s. 87. The landlord has elected to forego the right to seek an eviction based upon those arrears. If what the landlord really wants is to end the tenancy, the landlord should withdraw the entire application and start from "scratch" with a new notice of termination.

Even after the application has been commenced, the tenant will have opportunities to pay the amounts owing and avoid eviction. This is discussed in detail in Chapter 14. In brief, the application is automatically discontinued if, before the Board issues the eviction order, the tenant pays the landlord:

(a) the rent that is in arrears under the tenancy agreement;
(b) the additional rent that would have been due under the tenancy agreement as at the date of payment by the tenant had the notice of termination not been given; and
(c) the landlord's application fee ($170, effective April 2009).[289]

If the tenant does not pay the amounts required prior to the issuance of an eviction order issued as a result of the arrears of rent, unless the eviction order is made enforceable immediately, the tenant will still have an opportunity to bring the tenancy into good standing.[290]

Under the R.T.A., a tenant also has one opportunity to save the tenancy even after the eviction order becomes enforceable (but before it is actually enforced).[291] If, however, the tenant has already taken advantage of such an opportunity during the tenancy, the eviction order will reflect this fact and inform the tenant that the tenant is not entitled to make another motion under subsection 74(11) during the remainder of the tenancy.[292]

When an order is granted as a result of an application made under ss. 59 and 87, the Board determines the total amount owing based upon the arrears of rent owing up to the termination date, any NSF cheque charges or related administrative charges, daily compensation owing from the day after the termination date onwards (for each day the tenant remains in possession of the unit) and any costs ordered by the Board, less the rent deposit and any interest owing thereon.[293] The eviction order must specify the total amount owing (and how that amount is calculated) and inform the tenant and the landlord that the order will become void if, before the order becomes enforceable, the tenant pays to the landlord or to the Board the amount required under s. 74(4).[294] If the tenant pays all amounts required by the order, the tenant may apply (by *ex parte* motion) for a notice or an order declaring that the eviction order is void. There is also a method by which a landlord can challenge this. See Chapter 14 for a detailed analysis of the provisions of s. 74.

Note that when bringing an application before the Board on the basis of arrears of rent, in addition to preparing to prove its own case, the landlord should also try to anticipate and prepare for the issue(s) that the tenant may raise at the hearing, either under s. 82 or s. 83 of the R.T.A. This topic is discussed further in Chapter 16.

---

[289] Subsection 74(2) of the R.T.A. (formerly subsection 72(2) of the T.P.A.).

[290] *Dean v. Grohal* (1980), 27 O.R. (2d) 643 (Ont. Div. Ct.).

[291] Under subsection 74(11) of the R.T.A. This new provision is discussed further in Chapter 14.

[292] Paragraph 74(3)(c) of the R.T.A.

[293] Subsections 87(3), (4) and (5) of the R.T.A.

[294] Subsection 74(3) of the R.T.A.

(iii) Illegal Act

Under s. 61(1) of the R.T.A. (formerly s. 62(1) of the T.P.A.), a landlord may give a tenant notice of termination of the tenancy if the tenant or another occupant of the rental unit commits an illegal act or carries on an illegal trade, business or occupation or permits a person to do so in the rental unit or the residential complex.

The notice of termination is Form N6. Normally, the notice period is a minimum of 20 days but if it is a "second notice"[295] then the notice period is 14 days and if the illegal act or trade involves a drug-related offence, the notice period is reduced to 10 days.[296]

The grounds for the application shall be set out in the notice and there must be adequate reasons and details.[297] Lack of specificity can render the notice of termination void.[298] The tenant must know the exact nature of the alleged offence(s) so that a defence can be prepared. The landlord must not only describe the conduct but state with precision in the notice of termination and at the hearing why the conduct is illegal (i.e., state precisely which provision of which statute has been violated).[299]

If the illegal act, trade or business is related to drugs, please refer to the Board's Interpretation Guideline 9 for definitions of some of the relevant terms such as "illegal drugs", "possession", "production", "trafficking", and "possession for the purposes of trafficking". Remember that the landlord will have to prove exactly what controlled substance was found on the premises. For example, the fact that something "appeared" to be a marijuana plant or that powder or pills were seized by the police or that "drug paraphernalia" was discovered in the unit will usually not be sufficient without actual evidence verifying the exact nature of the substance in question. A lab analysis from the police would usually suffice. The opinion of a police officer may not be sufficient.[300]

---

[295] I.e., an earlier notice under s. 62, 64 or 67 of the R.T.A. had been given to the tenant within the previous six months and that notice was "cured" by the tenant complying within seven days of receiving that earlier notice.

[296] Subsections 61(2) and (3) of the R.T.A.

[297] Subsection 43(2) of the R.T.A. Also see *Ball v. Metro Capital et al.* (Dec. 19, 2002), Div. Ct. File No. 48/02, re (Dec. 10, 2001), TNL-31297 (Ont. Rental Housing Trib.) and Chapter 6 for a discussion about notices of termination.

[298] *Peel Living v. Lannon* (Feb. 16, 2005), CEL-41229, 2005 CarswellOnt 1286 (Ont. Rental Housing Trib.); and Landlord and Tenant Board File No. CEL-15785 (Jan. 16, 2009).

[299] *Local 1005 Community Homes Inc. v. Lamarche* (Sept. 20, 1999), SOL-07881 (Ont. Rental Housing Trib.).

[300] Circumstantial evidence relating to possession of illegal drugs for the purposes of trafficking, however, was found to be sufficient proof in Landlord and Tenant Board File No. EAL-13599 (Jan. 19, 2009) and in Landlord and Tenant Board File No. TNL-00833 (March 19, 2007).

An application to evict a tenant for illegal conduct can be commenced immediately after service of the notice of termination (s. 71); the landlord does not need to wait until after the termination date specified in the notice of termination. The application is in Form L2 and the filing fee is $170.[301] The landlord must commence the application within 30 days of the termination date or the notice of termination will become void (ss. 46 and 69(2)). If the application is based upon a "second notice", the earlier ("first") notice of termination and proof of service must be filed with the application (s. 53 of O. Reg. 516/06). The application and notice of hearing must be served at least five days prior to the hearing in the case of the alleged production of or trafficking in an illegal drug (Rule 10.5(c)(i)) or at least 10 days prior to the hearing for all other illegal acts (Rule 10.1). The certificate of service for the application and notice of hearing should be filed with the Board within five days after service has been effected (Rule 11.2) or, if that is not possible, it should be filed at the beginning of the hearing (Rule 11.3).

The Board need not adjourn the matter until the conclusion of any criminal trial that may be pending. Since there is a different standard of proof at a criminal trial than in an application before the Board, the outcome of the criminal case is often not determinative; also, there is often a pressing need to proceed with the eviction hearing promptly and criminal proceedings can take months or years.[302] Section 75 of the R.T.A. (formerly s. 73 of the T.P.A.) provides that the Board may issue an order terminating a tenancy and evicting a tenant whether or not the tenant or other person has been convicted of an offence related to an illegal act, trade, business or occupation. In fact, an application may be filed in the absence of any criminal charges and may be continued even when such charges have been withdrawn.

In *Wellesley Developments (Brockville) Ltd. and Metzger*,[303] the Tribunal proceeded with the hearing and did not grant a stay pending the outcome of the criminal proceedings. The Tribunal ordered termination and eviction. Similarly, in *Ottawa-Carleton Regional Housing Authority v. Dimario*,[304] a landlord's application for possession because the tenant was alleged to have committed a criminal act, trafficking in heroin, was not stayed until the disposition of the criminal proceedings.

In the *Dimario* case, the court confirmed that the standard of proof in landlord and tenant proceedings is that of civil proceedings — proof upon a balance of probabilities. The Divisional Court has confirmed that the standard of proof remains a "balance of probabilities" but has suggested that, in cases

---

[301] Effective April 2009. From 2002 through March 2009, the fee was $150.

[302] *Toronto Community Housing Corp. v. Davis* (2005), 2005 CarswellOnt 4573 (Ont. Div. Ct.); also see *Toronto Community Housing Corp. v. Greaves* (May 29, 2003), TNL-41859, 2003 CarswellOnt 6367 (Ont. Rental Housing Trib.), reversed (2004), 2004 CarswellOnt 5311 (Ont. Div. Ct.), additional reasons at (2005), 195 O.A.C. 159 (Ont. Div. Ct.).

[303] (May 19, 1999), EAL-05654 (Ont. Rental Housing Trib.).

[304] (1987), 68 O.R. (2d) 581 (Ont. Dist. Ct.).

involving allegations of criminal conduct, the degree of proof required to meet this balance of probabilities is somewhat higher.[305] The Supreme Court of Canada, however, has recently disapproved of such an approach and has reaffirmed, once and for all, that:

> . . . in civil cases there is only one standard of proof and that is proof on a balance of probabilities. . . In all civil cases, the [trier of fact] must scrutinize the relevant evidence with care to determine whether it is more likely than not that an alleged event occurred.[306]

The evidence presented, however, must be sufficient to meet this standard of proof. Hearsay evidence (i.e., the landlord testifying about what other tenants told him) and video recordings showing the tenants having frequent and numerous guests was considered insufficient to prove that the tenants were dealing drugs from the residential complex.[307]

The fact that a person has been charged with an offence is not proof that they have committed an illegal act, even on a balance of probabilities.[308] Conversely, if the police have investigated the allegations and have declined to lay any charges, while not determinative, this may well be a factor considered by the Board in favour of the tenant.[309]

The term "illegal" is presumably intended to mean in breach of the Criminal Code, provincial laws or municipal by-laws. However if the word "illegal" is considered as somewhat synonymous with "not authorized" as in some dictionaries, then an illegal act could include the commission of a breach of a term of a lease, for example, the myriad regulations to be observed by tenants appended to most apartment leases, but would not apply to the omission to do something required of a tenant. Another example of a breach of covenant by a tenant which might be considered as illegal under this subsection would be the carrying on of business by a tenant in the premises when the lease specifically prohibits the use of the premises for that purpose.

Having a dog kennel business in contravention of municipal by-law was found to be an "illegal act" in *James v. Sharp*,[310] and the Tribunal ordered termination of the tenancy and eviction.

Changing the locks without the consent of the landlord was in breach of s. 93 of Part IV (*Landlord and Tenant Act*). It was therefore an illegal act. It

---

[305] See *Bogey Construction Ltd. v. Boileau* (2002), 2002 CarswellOnt 5865, [2002] O.J. No. 1575 (Ont. Div. Ct.) and *Toronto Community Housing Corp. v. Kamara* (February 21, 2005), TSL-67926 (Ont. Rental Housing Trib.).

[306] *F.H. v. McDougall* (2008), [2008] S.C.J. No. 54 (S.C.C.), at para. 49. Also see the discussion of "Standard of Proof" in Chapter 16.

[307] Landlord and Tenant Board File No. SWL-22663 (Jan. 16, 2009).

[308] *Red Lake Non-Profit Housing v. Parker et al.* (June 24, 1999), NOL-01433 (Ont. Rental Housing Trib.).

[309] *Mattis v. Bouey* (November 7, 2003), SOL-44693 (Ont. Rental Housing Trib.).

[310] (April 7, 1999), TEL-04390 (Ont. Rental Housing Trib.).

led to an order terminating the lease and for possession in *Swansea Village Co-op. Inc. v. Balcerzak.*[311] It was an ongoing problem with the tenant, and so was not trivial or an isolated incident. The court said that an illegal act under the section does not have to be criminal or quasi-criminal. One judge, although not dissenting, pointed out that a breach of statute does not automatically give the right to evict. The illegal act must have the potential to affect the character of the premises or disturb the reasonable enjoyment of the landlord or other tenants.

As the R.T.A. deals with altering the locks specifically in another section, it would likely not be considered an "illegal act" within the meaning of s. 61 of the R.T.A. when a tenant alters the locks without the consent of the landlord.

Note that the illegal act must take place within the residential complex. The fact that the tenant may have committed an illegal act away from the residential complex is not grounds for termination of the tenancy.

In *Ontario Housing Corporation v. Wigley*,[312] the illegal act allegedly took place at the swimming pool located near the apartment building but leased by the City of Toronto's Department of Parks and Recreation. The presiding judge found as a fact that the pool did not form part of the residential complex. As a result, the landlord's application was dismissed.

In *Shawana and Gervais, Re*,[313] the tenant's boyfriend had threatened the landlady's husband with a tire iron. He was charged with possession of an offensive weapon. The judge held that the tenant was not a party to the alleged offence and that the offence did not relate to the tenancy. Therefore it was not an "illegal act" within the meaning of s. 107(1)(*b*) of Part IV (*Landlord and Tenant Act*).

A somewhat similar section in the *English Rent Act, 1968*, c. 23, was considered in *Abrahams v. Wilson.*[314] The tenant had been convicted of possession of cannabis resin. The court refused the landlord's application for possession. There was no mention in the conviction of where the offence took place. The court said that evidence should have been called in the landlord's application for possession as to what actually transpired in the criminal court. The judgment also stated that it was necessary to show the tenant had used the premises for committing the offence.

Under the T.P.A., where it was not the tenant but an occupant, subtenant or guest of the tenant who allegedly committed an illegal act, it had to be proven that the tenant *permitted* this or, at the very least, was wilfully blind concerning the illegal activities in question. This has been changed somewhat under the R.T.A. Under the new wording of this section, a tenancy can now

---

[311] (1988), 63 O.R. (2d) 741 (Ont. Div. Ct.).

[312] Co. Ct., Judicial District of York, June 22, 1979 (unreported).

[313] (December 6, 1982), Collins J. (Ont. Dist. Ct.).

[314] [1971] 2 All E.R. 1114 (C.A.).

be terminated based upon the illegal conduct of an occupant of the rental unit, even if the tenant was unaware of the conduct. If the allegation is that a person permitted on the premises (i.e., not the tenant or an occupant of the unit) committed the illegal act, it must still be proven that the tenant or occupant *permitted* the illegal conduct.

In *Ecuhome Corporation v. Thofane*,[315] the tenant permitted guests to use crack cocaine, although he claimed *he* did not use cocaine. A police officer's evidence was very persuasive. The tenancy was terminated and eviction ordered.

In *3414493 Canada Inc. v. Hunter*,[316] a subtenant had turned the apartment into a marijuana greenhouse. The landlord was unaware of the subtenancy. The landlord discovered the illegal conduct (when water began leaking into the unit below) and brought an application to terminate the tenancy. The evidence supported the tenant's contention that he was unaware of the subtenant's activities within the unit and that he had not permitted this conduct. The landlord took the position that the tenant "must have known" about these activities but offered no evidence to support this assertion. The application was dismissed.

In *Nepean Housing Corp. v. Clostre*,[317] the tenant's son allegedly illegally entered another unit and stole some property. The application was dismissed because there was no evidence that the tenant *permitted* her son to commit this illegal act. Similarly, in *DeBlois v. Reed*,[318] the application was dismissed because the evidence did not persuade the Member that the tenant permitted his son to commit the alleged break-ins (nor did the evidence reveal wilful blindness on the part of the tenant towards his son's activities).

In both *3414493 Canada Inc. v. Hunter*[319] and *Nepean Housing Corp. v. Clostre*,[320] it was an occupant who had committed the illegal act but the applications were dismissed for lack of evidence that the tenant had permitted the conduct in question. Had these cases been heard under the R.T.A., the result in each case may well have been different. Under the current wording of s. 51, a landlord no longer need prove that the tenant permitted the illegal conduct of an *occupant* to be entitled to an order terminating the tenancy.

Where the conduct in question is that of a guest (rather than an occupant), the landlord will still need to prove that the tenant *permitted* the illegal conduct. In Landlord and Tenant Board File No. NOL-00159 (March 1,

---

[315] (June 3, 1999), TSL-07213 (Ont. Rental Housing Trib.).

[316] (Aug. 25, 1998), TSL-00474 (Ont. Rental Housing Trib.).

[317] (April 13, 2000), EAL-12228, [2000] O.R.H.T.D. No. 58, 2000 CarswellOnt 6365 (Ont. Rental Housing Trib.).

[318] (Aug. 11, 2001), NOL-05235, NOL-05460, [2001] O.R.H.T.D. No. 111, 2001 CarswellOnt 6332 (Ont. Rental Housing Trib.).

[319] (Aug. 25, 1998), TSL-00474 (Ont. Rental Housing Trib.).

[320] (April 13, 2000), EAL-12228, [2000] O.R.H.T.D. No. 58, 2000 CarswellOnt 6365 (Ont. Rental Housing Trib.).

2007), the landlord was unable to adduce any evidence to demonstrate that the tenants had been aware of (or had been willfully blind towards) the fact that their guests possessed controlled substances.

Note that if the person alleged to have committed the illegal act is a minor, the courts have held that the hearing before the Tribunal (now the Board) may proceed, although it may be advisable to take steps to avoid disclosure of the identity of the young person.[321]

In another illegal act case, a tenant broke into some other apartments. Though an isolated occurrence, the rights of the other tenants were violated. The tenant had a lengthy criminal record. Termination and possession were ordered: *Peel Non-Profit Housing Corp. v. Hogarth.*[322] The case was further appealed only with respect to exercising the discretion whether or not to grant the landlord's application for possession. The Court of Appeal refused to further consider the discretion exercised by the Divisional Court: *Peel Non-Profit Housing Corp. v. Hogarth.*[323]

In *Toronto Community Housing Corp. v. Clarke*,[324] the Tribunal found that the tenant had brandished a knife and uttered death threats against her neighbour's son. Notwithstanding that the tenant committed this illegal act, failed to attend the hearing before the Tribunal, failed to appear at the police station as required (resulting in a warrant being issued for her arrest) and apparently fled the country, the Member nevertheless exercised her discretion under s. 84(1) of the T.P.A. (now s. 83(1) of the R.T.A.) and refused to evict this tenant.

In *Toronto Community Housing Corp. v. Daniels*,[325] a tenant was found to have uttered a death threat to another tenant of the complex, thereby committing an illegal act and seriously impairing the safety of other persons in the complex. The Tribunal granted the landlord's application for termination of the tenancy and for an eviction order.

Possession of drugs and a shooting incident were sufficient for termination in *1011 Lansdowne Avenue Holdings Ltd. v. Ellington*,[326] without waiting for the hearing of the criminal charges. Here again the judge referred

---

[321] *Santokie v. Ontario Rental Housing Tribunal* (2000), TNL-17684, 141 O.A.C. 118, 2000 CarswellOnt 4992 (Ont. Div. Ct.), affirmed (2002), 156 O.A.C. 128 (Ont. C.A.). The Board should consider whether it is appropriate to exclude the public from the proceedings, seal the Board's file and alter the order sufficiently to shield the identity of the offender. See also *Trenton Non Profit Housing Corporate v. Rowe* (May 18, 2005), EAL-48925 (Ont. Rental Housing Trib.), in which the application was heard in camera and the file was sealed pursuant to s. 9(1)(b) of the *Statutory Powers Procedure Act* in order to protect the identity of certain alleged young offenders.

[322] (1989), 68 O.R. (2d) 617 (Ont. Div. Ct.), affirmed (1990), 72 O.R. (2d) 702 (Ont. C.A.).

[323] (1990), 72 O.R. (2d) 702 (Ont. C.A.).

[324] (March 22, 2006), TNL-74083, 2006 CarswellOnt 2139, [2006] O.R.H.T.D. No. 27 (Ont. Rental Housing Trib.).

[325] (June 28, 2006), TSL-82047, [2006] O.R.H.T.D. No. 114 (Ont. Rental Housing Trib.).

[326] (1990), 14 R.P.R. (2d) 209 (Ont. Gen. Div.).

to s. 107(1)(*c*) of Part IV (*Landlord and Tenant Act*) that the reasonable enjoyment of the premises by the landlord and other tenants was another factor although it was not stated as a reason in the landlord's notice of termination under s. 107(1)(*b*) of Part IV or application for possession under s. 113 of Part IV.

Possession of drugs *per se* was a sufficient reason for termination in *Metropolitan Toronto Housing Authority v. Cole*.[327] The trial judge dismissed the application, but the Divisional Court said there was other evidence which supported trafficking, which had the potential to affect the character of the premises and to disturb the reasonable enjoyment of the landlord and the tenants. Possession of drugs without the other evidence would not likely be a sufficient "illegal act".

Although tenants have been evicted for drug-related offences, both the courts and the Rental Housing Tribunal were generally lenient (i.e., granted relief from forfeiture) in cases of mere possession of small amounts of marijuana for personal use (especially if used for medical purposes).[328]

Although tenants have been evicted for drug-related offences, the Tribunal was generally lenient (i.e., granted relief from forfeiture under s. 84 of the T.P.A.) in cases of mere possession of small amounts of marijuana for personal use, especially if used for medical purposes.[329]

Where the tenant has been selling or otherwise trafficking in illegal drugs, however, the Board is less likely to show leniency. In *Toronto Community Housing Corp. v. Tenant*,[330] the tenant admitted selling drugs within the residential complex. Despite having been a long-standing tenant who suffered from a number of medical conditions, the Member found that the interests of the other tenants in the complex outweighed those of this one tenant. Instead of denying the eviction, the Member exercised his discretion under s. 84 of the T.P.A. by delaying the eviction for approximately six weeks.

The Divisional Court has recently confirmed that a distinction ought to be made between mere possession of an illegal drug for personal use and possession for the purpose of trafficking. The distinction is presumably based upon the fact that personal use is unlikely to affect the character of the premises or disturb others whereas trafficking in drugs is likely to impact the

---

[327] (February 17, 1993), Doc. 90-LT-9719 (Ont. Div. Ct.).

[328] See *Metropolitan Toronto Housing Authority v. Krosney*, November 15, 1991, Ontario Court of Justice (unreported); *Benniger v. Hilcox* (Jan. 10, 2001), SWL-23413 (Ont. Rental Housing Trib.); *Toronto Community Housing Corporation v. Sturge* (Nov. 22, 2001), TSL-31750, [2001] O.R.H.T.D. No. 142, (Ont. Rental Housing Trib.); and *South Hastings Non-Profit Housing and Curran* (June 25, 1999), EAL-06239 (Ont. Rental Housing Trib.).

[329] *Benniger v. Hilcox* (Jan. 10, 2001), SWL-23413 (Ont. Rental Housing Trib.); *Toronto Community Housing Corporation v. Sturge* (Nov. 22, 2001), TSL-31750, [2001] O.R.H.T.D. No. 142, (Ont. Rental Housing Trib.); and *South Hastings Non-Profit Housing and Curran* (June 25, 1999), EAL-06239 (Ont. Rental Housing Trib.).

[330] (July 18, 2006), TEL-61885 (Ont. Rental Housing Trib.).

residential complex as a whole. In *Toronto Community Housing Corp. v. Norton*,[331] the Divisional Court noted that the Member who originally heard the case found that the tenant committed one act of possession. The Member failed to address the issue of whether one act of possession in the parking lot would affect the character of the premises or the reasonable enjoyment of other tenants or the landlord. The Court found that this was an error in law and, as a result, set aside the Tribunal's decision and dismissed the landlord's application.

In addition to drug-related offences, the types of illegal acts or businesses for which the Tribunal was prepared to terminate a tenancy include:

1. Having a dog kennel business in contravention of municipal by-law;[332]
2. Committing assaults and uttering threats;[333]
3. Committing sexual assault;[334]
4. Possession of a handgun without a licence, possession of a handgun knowing that the serial number had been removed, possession of ammunition for this gun and assaulting a police officer;[335]
5. Subletting the unit and charging the subtenants more rent in total than the tenant was being charged by the landlord;[336] and
6. Constructing a self-contained bedroom in a storage area without the knowledge of the landlord, without getting a building permit and without complying with the Building Code and Fire Code.[337]

In *Metropolitan Toronto Housing Authority v. St. Louis*,[338] there was an altercation between two tenants and one tenant came at the other with a knife. In the order issued at first instance, the Member included the following conditions:

(a) before going ahead with eviction, the Housing Authority must find for the tenant another apartment in another building that it operates;
(b) if the tenant refuses the new accommodation, an eviction order may be enforced; and

---

[331] (2006), [2006] O.J. No. 2711, 2006 CarswellOnt 2500 (Ont. Div. Ct.).

[332] *James and Sharp* (April 7, 1999), TEL-04390 (Ont. Rental Housing Trib.).

[333] *Ottawa Non-Profit Housing Corp. v. Mesfin* (December 30, 1996), Doc. Ottawa 104852/96 (Ont. Gen. Div.).

[334] *Options Bytown v. Norquay* (Aug. 3, 2000), EAL-14904, 2000 CarswellOnt 4346 (Ont. Rental Housing Trib.).

[335] *Toronto Community Housing Corp., Re* (January 10, 2006), TEL-53443, [2006] O.R.H.T.D. No. 3, 2006 CarswellOnt 2094 (Ont. Rental Housing Trib.).

[336] *Sutton Place Grande Ltd. v. Hammer* (2002), 2002 CarswellOnt 1531, 159 O.A.C. 350 (Ont. Div. Ct.).

[337] *Samuel Property Management Ltd. v. Nicholson* (2002), 2002 CarswellOnt 3004, 3 R.P.R. (4th) 66 (Ont. C.A.) re TSL-22331, TSL-24516.

[338] (June 9, 1999), TEL-02124 RV (Ont. Rental Housing Trib.).

(c) the two tenants must stay away from each other.

On review, the Tribunal confirmed that, based on s. 190(1) of the T.P.A. (now s. 204 of the R.T.A.), the Member who originally heard the case was limited only by fairness in the circumstances.

In *London Cambridge Developments Ltd. v. Bogaert*,[339] the tenant, a recovering paedophile, was bound by the terms of his recognizance to avoid living in any "house, apartment or trailer where persons under the age of 16 years reside". Although no children resided in the rental unit with the tenant, the unit was located within a 35-unit residential complex that housed many children. The question was whether or not the tenant breached the terms of his recognizance and, thereby, committed an illegal act that justified his eviction from the building. The Tribunal found that the term "apartment" did not mean "apartment building" but, rather, the apartment unit of the tenant. Consequently, the landlord had failed to prove that the tenant committed an illegal act. The application was dismissed.

Not every illegal act, even if proven, will justify termination of the tenancy. For instance, in *1343892 Ontario Inc. v. Macdonald*,[340] the Tribunal found that constructing a deck on this mobile home site without a building permit and threatening the landlord's employee constituted "illegal acts" by the tenant within the meaning of s. 62 of the T.P.A. Nevertheless, in the circumstances of this particular case, it was felt that termination of the tenancy was not appropriate and the Member exercised his discretion under s. 84 of the T.P.A. (now s. 83 of the R.T.A.) and refused to grant an eviction.

The Board may only have the jurisdiction to consider the illegal act(s) specifically identified in the notice of termination and will generally not consider any other alleged illegal acts.[341]

If the illegal act, trade, business or occupation is one described in clause 61(2)(a) of the R.T.A. (i.e., related to the production of or trafficking in illegal drugs), subject to the Board's discretion to delay the eviction (under clause 83(1)(b)), the eviction order will request that the sheriff expedite the enforcement of the order.[342]

(iv) Misrepresentation of Income

A landlord may seek to terminate the tenancy of a tenant if the rental unit is one of the types described in paras. 1, 2 , 3 or 4 of s. 7(1) of the R.T.A., and the tenant has knowingly and materially misrepresented his or her income

[339] (March 5, 1999), SWL-05244 (Ont. Rental Housing Trib.).

[340] (Sept. 19, 2001), SOL-25170, [2001] O.R.H.T.D. No. 129 (Ont. Rental Housing Trib.).

[341] *DU Chapter House Ltd. v. Poirier* (December 3, 1998), TSL-03969 (Ont. Rental Housing Trib.).

[342] Section 84 of the R.T.A.

or that of other members of his or her family occupying the unit (s. 60(1) of the R.T.A.).[343] In essence, a tenant who has been given subsidized rent or who has been allowed to pay a lower rent based upon poor financial circumstances, but who has lied about income, forfeits the right to continue living in such accommodations.

The first step will be serving the tenant(s) with the notice of termination (Form N6). It must be served at least 20 days prior to the termination date if it is a "first" notice,[344] or at least 14 days in advance if the notice is given within six months of the tenant voiding an earlier notice of termination given under ss. 62, 64 or 67 of the R.T.A.[345] The notice must set out the details of the grounds for termination.[346] There is no provision for the tenant to remedy false statements as to income.

The application can be commenced immediately (s. 71); the landlord does not need to wait until after the termination date specified in the notice of termination. The application is in Form L2 and the filing fee is $170.[347] The landlord must commence the application within 30 days of the termination date or the notice of termination will become void (ss. 46 and 69(2)). If the application is based upon a "second notice", the earlier ("first") notice of termination and proof of service must be filed with the application (s. 53 of O. Reg. 516/06). The application and notice of hearing must be served at least ten days prior to the hearing (Rule 10.1). The certificate of service for the application and notice of hearing should be filed with the Board within five days after service has been effected (Rule 11.2) or, if that is not possible, it should be filed at the beginning of the hearing (Rule 11.3).

A few points about the wording of s. 60(1) are worth noting. First, a *material* misrepresentation must be proven. A minor difference between the actual and reported income that would have little impact on the calculation of the rent will not be considered material. Second, it must be proven that the misrepresentation was deliberate; this type of application can only be granted if the Board is satisfied that the landlord has proven that the tenant made the misrepresentation *knowingly*. Unless the tenant admits this, it will have to be inferred from some very strong circumstantial evidence. Third, while many landlords have drafted their leases to require tenants to report their income and that of any other members of their household, s. 60(1) only refers to misrepresentation with respect to the income of the tenant or members of the tenant's *family* who occupy the rental unit. Under this provision of the R.T.A., a landlord cannot evict a tenant for misrepresenting or failing to disclose the income of non-family members who occupy the rental unit.

---

[343] Formerly s. 62(2) of the T.P.A.

[344] Subsection 60(2) of the R.T.A.

[345] Section 68 of the R.T.A.

[346] Subsection 43(2) of the R.T.A.

[347] Effective April 2009. From 2002 through March 2009, the fee was $150.

Since an allegation of misrepresentation of income is tantamount to an allegation of fraud, the degree of proof required *may* be higher than in most other cases. As the Honourable Mr. Justice Sharpe stated:[348]

> It is clear that in such a case, although this is a civil matter and the proof is on the balance of probabilities, the burden none the less must take into account the seriousness of the allegation that has been made and that the proof must be commensurate with the seriousness of the allegation.

The Supreme Court of Canada, however, has recently disapproved of such an approach and has reaffirmed, once and for all, that:

> . . . in civil cases there is only one standard of proof and that is proof on a balance of probabilities. . . In all civil cases, the [trier of fact] must scrutinize the relevant evidence with care to determine whether it is more likely than not that an alleged event occurred.[349]

In addition to seeking to terminate the tenancy, the landlord may also apply for an order for the payment of rent the tenant would have been required to pay if the tenant had not misrepresented his or her income or that of other members of his or her family (s. 90). This type of application is usually combined with the request for termination of the tenancy but it can be brought as a separate application, so long as the application is made while the tenant is in possession of the rental unit.

In *Greater Sudbury Housing Corporation v. Dupont*,[350] a tenant received a single support payment of a few hundred dollars from her estranged spouse which she failed to disclose to her landlord. In the circumstances, the Tribunal refused to evict the tenant but ordered her to pay the rent owed because of the rent adjustment that resulted from her receiving this payment.

The tenant's lease was terminated for misrepresentation of income in *Nipissing & Parry Sound Districts Housing Authority v. Tremblay*,[351] where after the common-law husband moved into the unit his income was not reported as part of the family income to the landlord. The opposite result was held at about the same time in *London Housing Authority v. Hanson*,[352] in which the judge decided that the word "family" only included persons having a blood or marital tie with the tenant. It is suggested that the former cited decision is more in line with the present-day status of common-law relationships.

---

[348] *Homes First Society Interchurch Corporation v. Baignauth*, unreported, Court File No. 97-LT-137845, October 9, 1997 (O.C. G.D.) at p. 2.

[349] *C. (R.) v. McDougall* (2008), [2008] S.C.J. No. 54 (S.C.C.) (at para. 49). Also see the discussion of "Standard of Proof" in Chapter 16.

[350] (November 23, 2001), NOL-06077 (Ont. Rental Housing Trib.).

[351] (1979), 23 O.R. (2d) 566 (Ont. Dist. Ct.).

[352] Middlesex (Co. Ct.).

In *Stoney Creek Community Services Corporation v. Mousa et al.*,[353] the male tenant failed to provide a financial statement and tax returns. Relying upon the *Nipissing*[354] decision, the Tribunal Member inferred that this tenant had tried to conceal from the landlord a material increase in his income. The landlord, however, had already obtained an order for the arrears of rent and was only seeking termination of the tenancy. By the time the case came before the Tribunal, the male tenant had vacated the unit. There was no evidence that the female tenant had participated in, or was aware of, the other tenant's attempt to conceal his income. She was on social assistance and had three young children. The landlord waited over a year before commencing eviction proceedings. Evicting the remaining tenant and her children from housing of last resort would cause them great hardship. In these circumstances, the Member refused to terminate the tenancy (which was the only relief being sought) and dismissed the landlord's application.

As for what is income, it was pointed out in *Ontario Housing Corp. v. Timmins*,[355] that income required to be reported is usually considered as income from employment, business or property, and in this case did not include a pension to the tenant from the Workmen's Compensation Board for impairment of earning capacity.

In *Tiago et al. v. Tinimint Housing Non-profit Inc.*,[356] it was alleged that the tenants misrepresented their income in a rent-geared-to-income situation and that, consequently, they owed substantial arrears of rent. The Tribunal allowed the landlord to produce evidence concerning the financial records of the tenants and their closely held corporations. Based upon this evidence, the Member ruled in favour of the landlord. The tenants appealed. The Divisional Court held that, under s. 188 of the T.P.A. (now s. 202 of the R.T.A.), the Tribunal had every right to consider the financial circumstances of the tenants' corporations as well as their personal financial records. The appeal was dismissed.

A failure to provide regular income statements to the landlord was held not to constitute deliberate misrepresentation of income in *Ottawaska Housing Corporation v. Bromilow*[357] and in *Kanata Baptist Place v. Ouimet*.[358] A different view was expressed in Landlord and Tenant Board File No. CEL-13867 (Jan. 21, 2009), in which it was held that a delay of about one year in reporting a material change in the financial circumstances of the tenants (and members of their family living in the unit) amounted to misrepresentation. The Member was not prepared to refuse to evict the tenants but did delay the

---

353 (July 7, 1999), SOL-06347 (Ont. Rental Housing Trib.).

354 (1979), 23 O.R. (2d) 566 (Ont. Dist. Ct.).

355 (1982), 136 D.L.R. (3d) 78 (Ont. C.A.).

356 Div. Ct. File No. 02-BN-12223 and 02-BN-8911 re CEL-28530 and CEL-24823.

357 (Dec. 8, 1998), EAL-02512 (Ont. Rental Housing Trib.).

358 (Sept. 8, 2000), EAL-14606, EAL-15107, [2000] O.R.H.T.D. No. 118, 2000 CarswellOnt 4341 (Ont. Rental Housing Trib. .

eviction by about three months. A similar approach was adopted in Landlord and Tenant Board File No. SOL-18598 (Feb. 12, 2009) and Landlord and Tenant Board File No. SOL-18601 (Feb. 12, 2009).

In *Metropolitan Toronto Housing Co. Ltd. v. Botelho*,[359] the tenant had misrepresented his income over three years. However, the Tribunal Member exercised his discretion under s. 84 of the T.P.A. (now s. 83 of the R.T.A.) and refused to order termination. The order did require the tenant pay to the landlord the difference between the rent that had been paid and the rent that ought to have been paid ($6,442.58). One can only wonder how the tenant would manage to pay the deficiency in rent.

In *Beaucagte & Associates Property Mgmt v. Isaac*,[360] it was found that the tenant had not *knowingly* misrepresented her income. The Member found the tenant's explanation for her delay in filing relevant documentation to be both reasonable and credible. The Member also rejected the landlord's unfounded assumptions about the tenant's understanding of the landlord's procedures.

In considering whether it would be unfair to the landlord, in another case, the court referred to the public interest, that is, the number of people who are on waiting lists for this type of subsidized rental accommodation: *Ottawa-Carleton Regional Housing Authority v. Levesque*.[361]

(v) *Impaired Safety*

A landlord may seek to terminate the tenancy of a tenant if an act or omission of the tenant, another occupant of the rental unit or a person permitted in the residential complex by the tenant seriously impairs or has seriously impaired the safety of any person, so long as the act or omission occurs in the residential complex (s. 66(1) of the R.T.A.).[362] Remember that under the definition of "residential complex" (s. 2) this would include the common areas and facilities and, presumably, would cover events that occur anywhere on the grounds around the building (as long as the grounds are part of the same property and form part of the complex). It does not, however, cover conduct that occurs on *commercial* premises owned by the landlord, even if commercial space has the same municipal address as the residential complex.[363] Note also that the impairment of safety must be *serious*.

The notice of termination must be in Form N7 and must be given at least ten days prior to the termination date set out in the notice.[364] The application

---

359 (Dec. 2, 1998), TNL-02417 (Ont. Rental Housing Trib.).

360 (November 21, 2003), NOL-09947 (Ont. Rental Housing Trib.).

361 (December 4, 1985), Doc. 4999/85 (Ont. Dist. Ct.).

362 Formerly section 65 of the T.P.A.

363 Landlord and Tenant Board File No. EAL-07388 (Feb. 27, 2008).

364 Subsection 66(2) of the R.T.A.

can be commenced as soon as the notice of termination has been served (s. 71); the landlord does not need to wait until after the termination date specified in the notice of termination. The application is in Form L2 and the filing fee is $170.[365] The landlord must commence the application within 30 days of the termination date or the notice of termination will become void (ss. 46 and 69(2)). The application and notice of hearing must be served at least five days prior to the hearing (Rule 10.5(c)(iv)). The certificate of service for the application and notice of hearing should be filed with the Board within five days after service has been effected (Rule 11.2) or, if that is not possible, it should be filed at the beginning of the hearing (Rule 11.3).

As discussed in Chapter 6, the notice of termination must contain particulars of the conduct for which the landlord is seeking to terminate the tenancy; failure to provide sufficient details will invalidate the notice.[366] The tenant is not entitled to an opportunity to correct the problem.

A tenant will be held accountable for conduct of another occupant of the rental unit or a person permitted in the residential complex by the tenant. According to the Divisional Court, there is no defence of "due diligence".[367]

A rather obvious case about the safety of tenants being seriously impaired by the action of another tenant is *Trustco and Kingston, Re.*[368] In this case, the tenant was doing some repairs himself and the furnace was left in a dangerous state. Also, cans of fuel oil were left about. The landlord's application for possession was granted.

Each case will turn upon its own facts. In general, mere threats or abusive or offensive communications will not be considered to seriously impair the safety of others.[369] Such conduct may, however, constitute valid grounds for termination of the tenancy on the basis of an illegal act or interference with the reasonable enjoyment of other tenants or the lawful rights of the landlord.

A tenant cannot be held responsible under this section for the conduct of persons the tenant did not allow into the complex. In *Booth v. Snider*,[370] a person was "stalking" the tenant and posed a potential danger to the landlord and his family, who lived above this basement unit. It was held that the tenant, as an innocent victim who did not invite this person into the complex, could

---

365 Effective April 2009. From 2002 through March 2009, the fee was $150.

366 Subsection 43(2) of the R.T.A. Also see *Ball v. Metro Capital* (December 19, 2002), Doc. 48/02 (Ont. Div. Ct.), re (Dec. 10, 2001), TNL-31297 (Ont. Rental Housing Trib.).

367 *Harris et al. v. Toronto Community Housing Corp.*, 2009 CanLII 34989.

368 (1985), 32 A.C.W.S. (2d) 450 (Ont. Dist. Ct.).

369 *Ontario Housing Corp. v. Dube* (Oct. 28, 1998), SWL-01073 (Ont. Rental Housing Trib.); *Estate of Maurice Zajac v. Halberstadt et al.* (Nov. 5, 1998), TSL-03491 (Ont. Rental Housing Trib.); Landlord and Tenant Board File No. CEL-15450 (Jan. 9, 2009). However, see Landlord and Tenant Board File No. TSL-20395 / TSL-14056 (Jan. 8, 2009) where a tenancy was terminated primarily because the tenant had seriously impaired the safety of the landlord and other tenants but uttering threats of bodily harm.

370 (March 23, 2000), TNL-13842, 2000 CarswellOnt 6436 (Ont. Rental Housing Trib.).

not be said to have seriously impaired the safety of others in the complex by any act or omission.

In *Metropolitan Toronto Housing Authority v. McCarthy*,[371] the tenant struck another tenant in an altercation in the complex. The landlord brought an application to evict the alleged aggressor on the basis that he had seriously impaired the safety of the other tenant. The respondent's evidence was that he was acting in self-defence. This was accepted and the application was dismissed.

The evidence, however, need not be sufficient to meet a criminal standard of proof. If the circumstantial evidence is sufficient to prove, on a balance of probabilities, that there has been a serious impairment of safety, that is sufficient. Thus, in Landlord and Tenant Board File No. SOL-18534 (Feb. 2, 2009), where there was a history of animosity between the tenant and another individual and the tenant was overheard to be in an argument with this individual and was then found standing over his beaten body, even though no one actually witnessed the assault, the presiding Member was satisfied that it had been proven, on a balance of probabilities, that the tenant had assaulted the other person and thereby had seriously impaired his safety.

Given the nature of this type of application, it will be rare for the presiding Member to exercise discretion under s. 83(1) as that would be tantamount to saying, "Yes, you are seriously impairing the safety of others but I am going to allow you to remain in the building anyway." There will be, however, unusual cases where the Member will find it appropriate to grant relief from forfeiture.

In *Gateway Properties v. Bloom*,[372] the tenant endangered others by throwing objects from his balcony. Because he suffered from mental illness, was receiving treatment, was being closely monitored and had a supportive family, the Member felt that the danger of future incidents was small and the Member exercised her discretion under s. 84(1) of the T.P.A. (now s. 83(1) of the R.T.A.) and refused to grant an eviction.

In Landlord and Tenant Board File No. CEL-14165 (Jan. 16, 2009), the tenant's 14-year-old son endangered another young resident boy by shooting him in the leg with a wooden skewer, using a home-made sling shot. There were no serious injuries and it was an isolated incident. Although this did constitute a serious impairment of safety, in all of the circumstances of this case, subject to certain conditions, the Member exercised her discretion and refused to terminate this tenancy.

In *Kroner v. Cudmore*,[373] the tenant deliberately smashed a window in his second-storey unit, sending shards of glass falling to the parking lot below, and then jumped through the window. Although the tenant was taken into

---

[371] (Aug. 30, 2000), TNL-18577, 2000 CarswellOnt 6444 (Ont. Rental Housing Trib.).

[372] (Feb. 5, 1999), TNL-03614 (Ont. Rental Housing Trib.).

[373] (June 16, 2006), SWL-81842, [2006] O.R.H.T.D. No. 66 (Ont. Rental Housing Trib.).

custody for psychiatric observation on the day of the incident, no evidence was tendered at the hearing that the tenant suffered from a mental illness. The Member found that this conduct seriously impaired the safety of others in the complex and granted the landlord's application to terminate the tenancy and evict the tenant.

In *646730 Ontario Inc. v. Gaal*,[374] there was a small accidental fire in the tenant's kitchen. There was no property damage and there were no injuries. The tenant's smoke alarm was activated but the fire department did not need to attend. In the circumstances, the Tribunal was not satisfied that the actions of the tenant seriously impaired the safety of other persons in the residential complex.

Similarly, in *Peel Housing Corp. v. Anderson*,[375] the tenant also accidentally started a fire but this fire caused damage to the unit. The Member who heard this case was satisfied that the fire did seriously impair the safety of others in the complex but he exercised his discretion under s. 84(1) of the T.P.A. to refuse to grant an eviction, on certain terms (including paying for the damage over a period of time).

In Landlord and Tenant Board File No. SOL-18242 (Jan. 20, 2009), the landlord sought to evict the tenant on the basis that she repeatedly left cooking unattended on the stove. No fire had ever occurred, however, and the landlord was only able to present hearsay evidence to support its case. The Member found that the landlord had failed to meet its burden of proof and the application was dismissed.

In *Toronto Community Housing Corp. v. Singh*,[376] however, the tenant not only started a fire through careless smoking, but then removed the smoke alarm so that others in the building would not be alerted to this fact. Eventually the tenant did go into the hallway and pulled the fire alarm but the Member ruled that this was not an appropriate case in which to refuse to grant an eviction. The Member did, however, delay the eviction by approximately five weeks.

Similarly, a tenancy was terminated where, among other things, the tenants disconnected the smoke detector, handled lit cigarettes carelessly in the unit, allowed guests to congregate on the fire escape and placed objects in the common area entry door to prevent it from locking (thereby breaching the security of the complex).[377]

In *London & Middlesex Housing Corp. v. Burrill*,[378] it was determined (in the absence of the tenant since the tenant failed to attend the hearing) that

---

[374] (March 28, 2002), SOL-30533 (Ont. Rental Housing Trib.).

[375] (May 20, 2004), CEL-36643, 2004 CarswellOnt 2201 (Ont. Rental Housing Trib.).

[376] (June 26, 2006), TEL-61542, 2006 CarswellOnt 4384, [2006] O.R.H.T.D. No. 78 (Ont. Rental Housing Trib.).

[377] Landlord and Tenant Board File Nos. NOL-05945 and NOL-06045 (Jan. 23, 2009).

[378] (June 20, 2006), SWL-81597, 2006 CarswellOnt 4411, [2006] O.R.H.T.D. No. 68 (Ont. Rental Housing Trib.).

the tenant scaled a wall and broke into another tenant's unit, got into a fight with the occupant, left that unit and then threw stones at windows of that unit. The Member held that this conduct seriously impaired the safety of other tenants in the complex and ordered the immediate eviction of the tenant.

In Landlord and Tenant Board File No. TEL-07722 (November 29, 2007), the tenant shared a bathroom (and possibly other common areas) with other tenants of the complex and their guests. The tenant in question was operating a tattoo business out of his unit. By failing to comply with health and safety standards, working in unsanitary conditions and improperly disposing of needles, razor blades and other materials, the tenant put his clients, other tenants and their guests at serious risk of contracting blood-borne illnesses, including HIV. Despite a warning and an order from a local health inspector, the tenant continued these activities and the landlord commenced an application to terminate the tenancy on the grounds that the tenant seriously impaired the safety of others in the complex. The application was granted and the tenant's request for relief under s. 83(1) of the R.T.A. was denied.

In Landlord and Tenant Board File No. TEL-00016 (Feb. 19, 2007), it was held that by leaving his window open a crack (for fresh air) and smoking occasionally in his unit, the tenant had not seriously impaired the safety of other persons within the residential complex.

When an application of this type is granted, it is usually made enforceable immediately or within a few days since the continued presence of the tenant in the complex usually puts others at risk. The standard wording contained in orders issued under s. 66 instructs the Sheriff to enforce these evictions in priority to all others.[379] Again, this is to avoid unnecessary delay in the enforcement of these orders.

Something new under the R.T.A. is the ability to obtain an eviction order that is effective *earlier* than the date of termination set out in the notice of termination.[380] Thus, in an emergency situation, a landlord could (at least theoretically) serve the notice of termination for impaired safety in the morning, commence the application later that day, request an expedited hearing (within 24 or 48 hours), serve the application and notice of hearing on the tenant, attend the hearing and, if successful, obtain an eviction order that could be filed with the Sheriff and enforced prior to the termination date specified in the notice of termination. Theoretically, this could all be done in less than one week. Such a case would be truly exceptional and I would offer the following suggestions for landlords who might find such a truncated process appealing. First, if the situation is dangerous enough to warrant such expedited proceedings, intervention by the Board may not be enough to offer any real protection; police intervention should also be considered. Second, such expedited proceedings should only be sought in the most serious cases;

[379] Section 84 of the R.T.A.

[380] Paragraph 80(2)(b) of the R.T.A.

the Board is likely to deal with any abuse of this process quite harshly. Third, if the landlord truly needs to have the eviction order enforced quickly, the usual direction to the Sheriff (i.e., to enforce the order in priority to others) will probably not suffice and the landlord should request that the order instruct the Sheriff to enforce the eviction *on a particular date* and *without any further notice to the tenant* (see Chapter 17).

If the impairment of safety is alleged to have resulted from the presence, control or behaviour of an animal, then special provisions apply (see s. 76). This is discussed in detail towards the end of this chapter under the heading, "Applications Based upon the Presence of an Animal."

It has been held that the presence of dog feces at the rental unit did not constitute a serious impairment of safety.[381] On the other hand, a tenancy was terminated where the tenants repeatedly used their aggressive dog as a weapon to intimidate and attack the landlord and other tenants.[382]

(vi) Undue Damage

A. TYPICAL CASE

Pursuant to s. 62(1) of the R.T.A. (formerly s. 63(1) of the T.P.A.), a landlord can terminate a tenancy if the tenant, another occupant of the rental unit or a person whom the tenant permits in the residential complex wilfully or negligently causes undue damage to the rental unit or the residential complex.

The notice of termination is Form N5. Normally, the notice period is a minimum of 20 days but if it is a "second notice"[383] then the notice period is 14 days.[384]

The grounds for the application shall be set out in the notice and must contain adequate reasons and details (particulars of damage must be specified).[385]

In cases where a tenant has allegedly damaged the rental unit or the residential complex (but not so much to justify a fast-track notice under s. 63), para. 62(2)(c) of the R.T.A. provides the tenant with a number of options. These are reflected in Part C of Form N5 as follows:

If this notice is for Reason #1 [damage], you can correct the problem by:

---

[381] Landlord and Tenant Board File No. TEL-19265 (Jan. 8, 2009).

[382] Landlord and Tenant Board File No. SOL-00467 (March 21, 2007).

[383] I.e., an earlier notice under s. 62, 64 or 67 of the R.T.A. had been given to the tenant within the previous six months and that notice was "cured" by the tenant complying within seven days of receiving that earlier notice.

[384] Subsection 68(2) of the R.T.A.

[385] Subsection 43(2) of the R.T.A. Also see *Ball v. Metro Capital et al.* (Dec. 19, 2002), Div. Ct. File No. 48/02, re (Dec. 10, 2001), TNL-31297 (Ont. Rental Housing Trib.) and Chapter 6 for a discussion about notices of termination.

- repairing the damaged property,
- paying me $______________, which is the reasonable cost of repairing the damaged property,
- replacing the damaged property if it is not reasonable to repair it,
- paying me $______________, which is the reasonable cost or replacing the damaged property, if it is not reasonable to repair it, or
- making arrangements satisfactory to me to either,
  - repair or replace the damaged property, or
  - pay me the reasonable cost of repairing or replacing the damaged property.

If the landlord strikes out or omits any of these options or fails to insert an estimate for the cost of repair/replacement, it has been found to invalidate the notice of termination.[386]

If the tenant complies within seven days, the notice of termination is void.[387] If the tenant does not comply within the seven days, the landlord can then proceed with an application to the Board.

The application must be filed no earlier than the eighth day after service of the notice of termination (s. 70(1)) and no later than 30 days after the specified termination date (ss. 46 and 69(2)). The application is in Form L2 and the filing fee is $170.[388] If the application is based upon a "second notice", the earlier ("first") notice of termination and proof of service must be filed with the application (s. 53 of O. Reg. 516/06). The application and notice of hearing must be served at least 10 days prior to the hearing (Rule 10.1). The certificate of service for the application and notice of hearing should be filed with the Board within five days after service has been effected (Rule 11.2).

As part of this application, the landlord may also apply to the Board for an order for compensation if a tenant, another occupant of the rental unit or a person whom the tenant permits in the residential complex wilfully or negligently causes undue damage to the rental unit or the residential complex and the tenant is in possession of the rental unit (s. 89).

As discussed earlier in this chapter,[389] the landlord must prove the exact nature of the damage, the reasonable cost of repairing the damage or of replacing the damaged property (where it cannot be repaired), that the damage was caused wilfully or negligently by the tenant, another occupant of the rental unit or a person whom the tenant permits in the residential complex and that the damage was "undue" — that is, more than the usual deterioration

[386] *Fisher Kay Ltd. v. Bowen* (Sept. 17, 1999), TNL-09813, 1999 CarswellOnt 5803 (Ont. Rental Housing Trib.); *Clarke et al. v. Roach et al.* (Oct. 26, 1998), TEL-01660 (Ont. Rental Housing Trib.); and *Guillaume v. Beveridge et al.* (January 20, 1999), TSL-04155 (Ont. Rental Housing Trib.).

[387] Subsection 63(3) of the T.P.A.

[388] Effective April 2009. From 2002 through March 2009, the fee was $150.

[389] See the section entitled "Compensation for Damage to the Unit/Complex".

or "wear and tear" expected to occur over time from normal use of the premises.

Termination was granted for undue damage was in *Balfe v. Alderman*,[390] when the tenant smashed several windows. The tenant failed to repair or pay the cost of repairs estimated by the landlord. The court ordered that the tenancy be terminated and that a writ of possession be issued.

A tenant did some repairs himself without the approval of the landlord. This included rewiring and makeshift plumbing and heating, and in particular leaving the furnace in a dangerous state. The tenancy was terminated: *Tristao v. Klingspon*.[391]

Vandalism of elevators led to termination in *Parc IX Ltd. v. McCorry*.[392] It was no answer that the vandalism had ceased. The repairs had not been done or payment made for repairs within seven days as provided by s. 107(1) of Part IV of the *Landlord and Tenant Act*.

Lack of cleanliness of the tenant's apartment and the tenant's children marking on the corridor walls with crayons were each considered as possible grounds for termination in *Ontario Housing Corp. v. Danicki*.[393] The judge, however, decided there was insufficient evidence.

Significantly altering the interior structure of a rental unit, without the consent of the landlord has been held to constitute both undue damage and substantial interference with a lawful, right, privilege and interest of the landlord.[394] In *Srivastava v. Campbell et al.*,[395] the tenants rented a house. Without the knowledge or consent of the landlord, they erected a partition in the basement, removed a bar, removed carpeting on the main floor and in the basement, damaged flooring, knocked down a fence on the property and damaged the lawn by parking vehicles on the lawn. This was all held to be undue damage (and grounds for termination of the tenancy). Tenants have also been held responsible where the manner in which they have installed a satellite dish has caused undue damage to the rental unit.[396]

In Landlord and Tenant Board File No. TSL-01010 (February 25, 2008), it was held that lingering odours left by smoking within a unit can constitute undue damage. In this case, the landlord rented furnished units to executives seeking short-term, smoke-free accommodations. It was a term of the tenancy

---

[390] (April 2, 1976) (Ont. Co. Ct.).

[391] (August 26, 1985), Scott J. (Ont. Dist. Ct.).

[392] (January 6, 1988), Doc. M155031/87 (Ont. Dist. Ct.).

[393] (October 4, 1979), Doc. M28317/79 (Ont. Co. Ct.).

[394] *Toronto Community Housing Corp. v. Borys* (July 4, 2002), TEL-28626, [2002] O.R.H.T.D. No. 79 (Ont. Rental Housing Trib.).

[395] (May 26, 1999), TNL-07066 (Ont. Rental Housing Trib.).

[396] See *Parkview Management v. Dehas* (Sept. 27, 2001), EAL-22575, [2001] O.R.H.T.D. No. 126, 2001 CarswellOnt 6317 (Ont. Rental Housing Trib.). There is no liability under s. 87, however, where the installation of the satellite dish has not caused any damage to the rental unit: *Kitchener Alliance Community Homes Inc. v. Brine* (Dec. 16, 2002), SWL-43674, 2002 CarswellOnt 5027 (Ont. Rental Housing Trib.).

agreement that the tenant would not smoke and would not permit smoking within the rental unit. The tenant breached this term. It was found that, in order to restore the unit to its original condition, the unit would have to be repainted and the furnishings would have to be cleaned or replaced at considerable cost to the landlord. It was held that cigarette smoke had caused undue damage to the rental unit and also held that the tenant's breach of the no-smoking provisions of the tenancy agreement constituted substantial interference in the lawful rights of the landlord. Consequently, the tenancy was terminated and the tenant was ordered to pay the landlord $10,000 in compensation. In a March 8, 2008, article, Bob Aaron of the *Toronto Star* newspaper hailed this decision as affirming the right of landlords to include a non-smoking clause in a residential lease.

Other cases where tenants have been held responsible for having caused "undue damage" include the following:

- Negligently blocking the toilet with duct tape and sponges, resulting in a flood that caused damage that cost $1,669.50 to repair;[397]
- Negligently blocking the toilet with paper towels, resulting in a flood that caused damage to the ceiling in the unit below;[398]
- Negligently disposing of solid food waste down the sink drain, causing a blockage that could only be resolved by having the plumber remove sections of the wall and floor to replace the drain (which cost $851.25 to repair);[399]
- Modifying the electrical wiring in the rental unit without the approval or knowledge of the landlord and without being properly licensed (and which cost $1,255.25 to repair);[400]
- Negligently driving a car into the canopy pillars of the residential complex, damaging the concrete (which cost over $2,000 to repair);[401]
- Damaging the door frame around the door to the rental unit by using a knife (or similar tool) to gain entry to the unit when the tenant forgot her keys and was locked out;[402]
- Negligently leaving a candle unattended near an open window, which started a fire that caused over $800 in damage;[403]
- Negligently allowing her dog to repeatedly urinate and defecate on

13 — LL APPLICATIONS

[397] Landlord and Tenant Board File No. SWL-00140 (March 9, 2007).

[398] Landlord and Tenant Board File No. SOL-18510 (Jan. 21, 2009). In this case, the tenant was ordered to pay the cost of snaking out the toilet (to clear the clog) but not the cost of repairing the unit below because the landlord failed to bring any documentary evidence as to the cost of those repairs.

[399] Landlord and Tenant Board File No. NOL-05944 (Jan. 9, 2009).

[400] Landlord and Tenant Board File No. TSL-18048 (Jan. 9, 2009).

[401] Landlord and Tenant Board File No. CEL-15417 (Jan. 16, 2009).

[402] Landlord and Tenant Board File No. SWL-22272 (Jan. 19, 2009).

[403] Landlord and Tenant Board File No. SWL-22272 (Jan. 19, 2009).

the deck and urinate on the living room carpet and allowing her children to, among other things, make holes in the walls and doors of the unit, resulting in $1,900 worth of damage;[404]

- Improperly installing a locking mechanism on a door to the unit and erecting (without the Landlord's consent) a makeshift carport.[405]

If the allegation is that someone other than the tenant caused the damage in question, the landlord must prove that the person is either an occupant of the rental unit or that they were permitted into the residential complex by the tenant. In Landlord and Tenant Board File No. SOL-18167 (Jan. 13, 2009), the landlord established that the person who caused the damage was known to the tenant but not that the tenant permitted them into the complex. In fact, the evidence showed that this person smashed a window and forced his way into the complex. Consequently, the landlord's application was dismissed.

Finally, tenants have been held responsible for damage done by their children. In *Pezzente v. Malik*,[406] the tenants were held responsible for allowing their children to write and draw on the walls of the rental unit. In *Tellier v. Boddy*,[407] the tenants were held liable (and evicted) for damage done to the exterior of the property when the tenants allowed their children to play soccer and hockey near the building despite the repeated requests of the landlord that this not be permitted. In holding the parents responsible, the Member took some comfort from the provisions of the *Parental Responsibility Act, 2000*, S.O. 2000, c. 4.[408]

B. FAST-TRACK

Where the damage is caused deliberately or results from a use that is inconsistent with use of the unit or complex as a residential premises (and the damage is likely to be extensive), instead of proceeding under s. 62 of the R.T.A., the landlord can now choose to follow the expedited procedures set out in s. 63 of the R.T.A.

There are a few important differences to note about proceeding under s. 63 (as opposed to s. 62):

---

[404] Landlord and Tenant Board File No. CEL-15458 (Jan. 9, 2009).

[405] Landlord and Tenant Board File No. TEL-19533 / TET-01718 (Jan. 14, 2009).

[406] (Sept. 14, 2000), TNL-19048, 2000 CarswellOnt 6445 (Ont. Rental Housing Trib.).

[407] (May 26, 2006), SWL-79869, [2006] O.R.H.T.D. No. 48 (Ont. Rental Housing Trib.).

[408] See Appendix 15. Pursuant to the *Parental Responsibility Act*, a person whose property has been damaged, destroyed or stolen by a minor (a person under 18 years of age) may bring a claim for damages in the Small Claims Court against the minor's parent(s). Under the *Parental Responsibility Act*, victims need prove only: (1) that the child caused the property damage or loss; (2) that the defendant(s) are the parent(s) of the child; and (3) the amount of the damage. The burden then shifts to the young person's parent(s) to establish why they should not be found liable for the losses suffered as a result of their child's conduct.

1. the tenant has no chance to void the notice of termination (by repairing, replacing or paying);
2. the tenant only receives 10 days notice of the termination date;
3. the tenant only receives five days notice of the hearing; and
4. the eviction can be ordered to take place even before the termination date specified in the notice of termination.

Section 63 applies where the tenant, another occupant of the unit or a person whom the tenant permits in the residential complex:

(a) wilfully causes undue damage[409] to the rental unit or the residential complex; or

(b) uses the rental unit or the residential complex in a manner that is inconsistent with use as a residential premises and that causes or can reasonably be expected to cause damage that is significantly greater than the damage that is required in order to give a notice of termination under clause 63(1)(a) or subsection 62(1).

The notice of termination is Form N7. The notice period is a minimum of 10 days.[410] The grounds for the application shall be set out in the notice and there must be adequate reasons and details (particulars of damage must be specified).[411] The application can be filed as soon as the notice of termination has been served (s. 71) but no later than 30 days after the specified termination date (ss. 46 and 69(2)).[412] The application is in Form L2 and the filing fee is $170.[413] The application and notice of hearing must be served at least five days prior to the hearing (Rule 10.5(c)(ii)). The certificate of service for the application and notice of hearing should be filed with the Board within five days after service has been effected (Rule 11.2), or if that is not possible, it should be filed at the beginning of the hearing (Rule 11.3).

As part of this application, the landlord may also apply to the Board for an order for compensation if a tenant, another occupant of the rental unit or a person whom the tenant permits in the residential complex wilfully or negligently causes undue damage to the rental unit or the residential complex and the tenant is in possession of the rental unit (s. 89).

13 — LL APPLICATIONS

---

409 See the section of this chapter entitled "Compensation for Damage to the Unit/Complex" for a discussion of what constitutes "undue" damage.

410 Subsection 63(1) of the R.T.A.

411 Subsection 43(2) of the R.T.A. Also see *Ball v. Metro Capital et al.* (Dec. 19, 2002), Div. Ct. File No. 48/02, re (Dec. 10, 2001), TNL-31297 (Ont. Rental Housing Trib.) and Chapter 6 for a discussion about notices of termination.

412 The application will be dismissed if it is filed more than 30 days after the termination date specified in the notice of termination. See, for example, Landlord and Tenant Board File No. TSL-20511 (Jan. 14, 2009).

413 Effective April 2009. From 2002 through March 2009, the fee was $150.

As discussed earlier in this chapter,[414] the landlord must prove the exact nature of the damage, the reasonable cost of repairing the damage or of replacing the damaged property (where it cannot be repaired), that the damage was caused by the tenant, another occupant of the rental unit or a person whom the tenant permits in the residential complex and that the damage was "undue" — that is, more than the usual deterioration or "wear and tear" expected to occur over time from normal use of the premises. Also, the landlord must either prove that the damage was caused "wilfully" or that extensive damage has resulted or is likely to result from the use of the unit or complex for a purpose that is inconsistent with residential use.

In Landlord and Tenant Board File No. SWL-01196 (April 4, 2007), guests at the tenant's party caused damage to the residential complex by throwing an object or objects through the entrance glass door, smashing a hole in the stairwell wall, smashing in the steel door at the rear of the property and puncturing a mahogany door. The tenant admitted responsibility for the damage but, by the time of the hearing (approximately six weeks after the incident), had still not repaired the damage or paid the landlord for the cost of repairs. The Vice-chair found that the tenant's guests wilfully damaged the residential premises and granted the landlord's request for an order terminating the tenancy and for the amount required to repair the damage ($846.34). Since there was no ongoing damage or risk of damage, the Vice-chair declined to further expedite the eviction and delayed enforcement of the eviction order by one week.

In Landlord and Tenant Board File No. TSL-05881,[415] the landlord was apparently having difficulty with the manner in which some people were using the garbage chute, especially at night. The landlord placed a security camera in the area and had the door locked in the evenings. One tenant repeatedly damaged the lock on the door giving access to the garbage chute and the security camera overlooking the area. The landlord applied to terminate the tenancy for an illegal act and wilful damage (under s. 63 of the R.T.A.). Although the tenant was 77 years old and had lived in this social housing complex for 14 years, the adjudicator refused to grant relief from forfeiture under s. 83 and an eviction was ordered.

Since this is a new provision under the R.T.A., there are few cases yet decided that can give guidance as to how the relevant terms will be interpreted. Please refer to the analysis of typical eviction applications based on damage (above) and the earlier section of this chapter entitled "Compensation for Damage to the Unit/Complex" for a review of cases decided under the predecessor legislation (which may also provide some assistance in interpreting s. 63 of the R.T.A.).

---

[414] See the section entitled "Compensation for Damage to the Unit/Complex".

[415] (December 31, 2007).

Under para. 63(1)(a) of the R.T.A., the landlord must prove that the damage was caused wilfully. In Landlord and Tenant Board File No. NOL-00137 (March 19, 2007), the tenant allegedly left a window open a bit (presumably for fresh air). Unfortunately, the air in North Bay in January is not only fresh but, typically, also very cold. The water in a radiator near the window froze, thereby bursting the radiator pipes and causing a flood. The tenant denied leaving the window open. The Member held that even if he found that the tenant had left the window open, there was absolutely no evidence that the tenant had done so deliberately with the willful intent to cause damage to the residential complex. For this reason, the landlord's application was dismissed.

Under para. 63(1)(b) of the R.T.A., the landlord must prove three things:

1. that the tenant uses the rental unit or complex in a manner that is inconsistent with use as residential premises;
2. that the inconsistent use caused or can reasonably be expected to cause damage; and
3. that the amount of damage is significantly greater than the amount that would be required to give the tenant a notice to terminate the tenancy for damage under ss. 62(1) or 63(1)(a) of the *Act*.

In Landlord and Tenant Board File No. SOL-14390 (August 11, 2008), the Member dismissed the landlord's application on the basis that the damage caused by the tenant was not significant enough to have justified the landlord using the "fast-track" type of application.

Where the damage was caused wilfully and is significantly greater than would normally be needed to justify an eviction, the Board can even order that the eviction take place earlier than the termination date specified in the notice of termination (para. 80(2)(a)). Similarly, where the landlord can show that extensive damage has resulted or is likely to result from the use of the unit or complex for a purpose that is inconsistent with residential use, an early eviction can be ordered (para. 80(2)(b)).

Subject to the Board's discretion to delay the eviction (under clause 83(1)(b)), an eviction order made under s. 63 will request that the sheriff expedite the enforcement of the order.[416]

Thus, in an emergency situation, a landlord could (at least theoretically) serve the notice of termination under s. 63 in the morning, commence the application later that day, request an expedited hearing (within 24 or 48 hours), serve the application and notice of hearing on the tenant, attend the hearing and, if successful, obtain an eviction order that could be filed with the sheriff and enforced prior to the termination date specified in the notice of termination. Theoretically, this could all be done in less than one week. Such a case would be truly exceptional and I would offer the following

[416] Section 84 of the R.T.A.

suggestions for landlords who might find such a truncated process appealing. First, if the tenant is wilfully causing extensive damage to the property, that is probably an offence and police intervention should also be considered. Second, such expedited proceedings should only be sought in the most serious cases; the Board is likely to deal with any abuse of this process quite harshly. Third, if the landlord truly needs to have the eviction order enforced quickly, the usual direction to the sheriff (i.e., to enforce the order in priority to others) will probably not suffice and the landlord should request that the order instruct the sheriff to enforce the eviction *on a particular date* and *without any further notice to the tenant* (see Chapter 17).

(vii) Interference with Reasonable Enjoyment, etc.

A. TYPICAL CASE

Pursuant to s. 64(1) of the R.T.A. (also s. 64(1) of the T.P.A.), a landlord may give a tenant notice of termination of the tenancy if the conduct of the tenant, another occupant of the rental unit or a person permitted in the residential complex by the tenant is such that it:

1. Substantially interferes with the reasonable enjoyment of the residential complex for all usual purposes by the landlord or another tenant; or
2. Substantially interferes with another lawful right, privilege or interest of the landlord or another tenant.

Special provisions apply if the interference is alleged to have resulted from the presence, control or behaviour of an animal (see s. 76). This is discussed in detail towards the end of this Chapter under the heading, "Applications Based upon the Presence of an Animal."

In Landlord and Tenant Board File No. TSL-00452 (March 1, 2007), the landlord complained that the tenant was rude to her and that the smell emanating from the tenant's kitty litter box was overwhelming and permeated the house. The Member did not find that this interference with the landlord's enjoyment was "substantial" and, therefore, dismissed the landlord's application.

In Landlord and Tenant Board File No. SOL-18432 (Jan. 22, 2009), the tenant had five cats and a rabbit. The pets would often get loose into the common areas of the complex and other tenants complained of the smell coming from the tenant's unit. The tenant agreed to reduce the number of pets she kept and the Member exercised her discretion and refused to grant an eviction, upon certain terms.

The first step will be serving the tenant(s) with a notice of termination, which is in Form N5. It must be served at least 20 days prior to the termination date if it is a "first" notice, or at least 14 days in advance if the notice is given within six months of the tenant voiding an earlier notice of termination given under s. 62, 64 or 67. The notice must set out the details of the grounds for termination (para. 64(2)(b))[417] and must give the tenant seven days to stop the conduct or activity or correct the omission set out in the notice (para. 64(2)(c)). The seven-day period begins on the day after service of the notice (Rule 4.1).[418]

If the tenant does comply within that seven-day period, the notice of termination is void (s. 64(3)). If the tenant does not comply, the landlord may commence an application in Form L2.

The application must be filed no earlier than the eighth day after service of the notice (s. 70(1)) and no later than 30 days after the specified termination date (ss. 46 and 69(2)). The application is in Form L2 and the filing fee is $170.[419] If the application is based upon a "second notice", the earlier ("first") notice of termination and proof of service must be filed with the application (s. 53 of O. Reg. 516/06). The application and notice of hearing must be served at least 10 days prior to the hearing (Rule 10.1). The certificate of service for the application and notice of hearing should be filed with the Board within five days after service has been effected (Rule 11.2).

What occurs during the seven days immediately following service of the notice of termination is crucial. If the tenant complies, the matter is at an end (although the landlord will retain the right to serve a "second notice" if there is a subsequent breach of one or more of ss. 60, 61, 62, 64 or 67 in the six months following the voiding of the "first notice").[420] To be successful on an application under s. 64 (based upon a "first notice"), the landlord will need to demonstrate that the disruptive conduct did not stop during that seven-day period.

Thus, where a landlord is alleging that the tenant is interfering with the landlord's efforts to enter the unit to show it to prospective purchasers, it is important that the landlord again try to gain entry during the seven-day period to demonstrate whether or not the tenant continued to prevent such entry. In *Furtney v. Margaris*,[421] the Tribunal dismissed just such an application by

[417] If no terms are stated in the notice it will be defective: *Lugano View Ltd. v. Grannum* (1988), 64 O.R. (2d) 468 (Ont. Div. Ct.). Also see Landlord and Tenant Board File No. TEL-19422, in which the Form N5 was found to be invalid as it lacked sufficient details concerning the alleged misconduct (including dates and times).

[418] See *Gamble v. Doucette* (Dec. 11, 2000), TNL-21987, 2000 CarswellOnt 6408 (Ont. Rental Housing Trib.).

[419] Effective April 2009. From 2002 through March 2009, the fee was $150.

[420] A second notice cannot be "cured". See the discussion of this topic later in this chapter under the heading, "Application based upon a Second Notice of Termination under Sections within six months".

[421] (Sept. 27, 2000), CEL-12782, 2000 CarswellOnt 4580 (Ont. Rental Housing Trib.).

the landlord as the landlord had failed to make any effort to gain entry to the unit during the relevant seven-day period.[422]

The act or omission in question must also be capable of being "cured".

In *Carere et al. v. Balgrove*,[423] most of the complaints listed in the notice of termination were, in fact, conclusions of law and not conduct that could be discontinued by the tenant. It was found that this invalidated the notice.

In *Liberatore "In Trust" v. McClure*,[424] the tenant's 17-year-old son suffered from an intestinal disease that resulted in offensive odours emanating from the unit. It bothered other tenants and made it difficult for the landlord to find workers willing to enter the unit when repairs were required. The Member held that the word "conduct", as used in s. 64, implies conscious behaviour and not the results of a medical condition over which the occupant has no control. The application was dismissed. One would also imagine that this might be a case in which the landlord would be required to accommodate the special needs of this tenant and her son (under the *Human Rights Code*) and where the Tribunal might, in any event, have exercised its discretion to grant relief from forfeiture.

The fact that the tenant has seven days to stop the conduct does not mean that the conduct can continue for six days and stop on the seventh. Even one repetition of the conduct described in the notice of termination during the relevant seven-day period is sufficient grounds for an application under s. 64.[425]

In order to justify termination of the tenancy, the interference must be *substantial*. In making this assessment, it was said in *Murray v. Kerton*[426] that the court should look at the nature of the tenant's conduct, its duration, extent and seriousness and whether the complaints were made by other tenants. In order for a landlord to be successful one would expect that the landlord would have to satisfy the Board that the tenant had been warned previously and yet continued the disturbances, and that the complaints by the other tenants were quite serious. In *Sebok and Keeble, Re*,[427] the judge commented that the type of conduct by a tenant to warrant termination of a tenancy is hard to determine, and went on to state that "substantially" must be something more than the minor adjustments and annoyances that must be accepted where persons occupy adjoining apartments or flats; also, the conduct of the tenant must not have been provoked by the landlord, and finally the landlord cannot have permitted such conduct over a period of time without objection and then seek to serve notice of termination.

---

[422] Also see *Carere et al. v. Balgrove* (Nov. 24, 2000), TNL-18384 (Ont. Rental Housing Trib.).

[423] (Nov. 24, 2000), TNL-18384 (Ont. Rental Housing Trib.).

[424] (Nov. 2, 2000), SWL-20429, 2000 CarswellOnt 4426 (Ont. Rental Housing Trib.).

[425] *Silvershade Rental Prop v. Johnston* (March 19, 2003), NOL-08606-RV, 2003 CarswellOnt 1531 (Ont. Rental Housing Trib.).

[426] (1997), 15 R.P.R. (3d) 300 (Ont. Gen. Div.).

[427] (August 6, 1976) (Ont. Co. Ct.).

The landlord must prove that the conduct of the tenant(s) substantially interfered with the *reasonable* enjoyment of the residential complex of the landlord for all *usual* purposes. This adds an objective component to the analysis. The Board must decide not just whether the landlord or other tenants have been disturbed by the conduct in question but also whether their reaction to the conduct in question was *reasonable*. A certain amount of annoyance is to be expected in a multi-unit building. A tenant should not be evicted because they have a hyper-sensitiveor intolerant neighbour.

In *Farenga v. Pipke*,[428] the landlord sought to evict the tenants because the sounds of their children playing in the unit were disturbing the landlord. The Member found that the behaviour of the tenants' children was reasonable and foreseeable. The landlord was aware that the tenants had two small children when they moved them from the basement of this complex to the unit above the landlord's residence. The transmission of sound was related more to the age and structure of the building than to any improper conduct on the part of the tenants or their children. The landlord's application was dismissed.

In *Elizabeth Manor Apartments v. Commisso*,[429] the landlord sought to re-open an application based upon an alleged breach on an earlier order. It was alledged that the tenant was disturbing the tenant in the unit above his by making excessive "noise". The Member found that the tenant was not doing anything out of the ordinary, that the reality of older buildings is that sound travels more easily between units and that the complaining tenant was a particularly sensitive individual. The landlord's request was denied.

In dismissing the landlord's application in *Gilindo Marcocchio Ltd. v. Anonychuk*,[430] the Member held that it was to be expected that tenants within this building might hear sounds of talking, occasional arguments, walking and so forth coming from nearby units and that the conduct of the tenant in question had not been *unreasonable*.

Conduct that has been held to violate s. 64 of the R.T.A. (or similar provisions under the previous legislation)[431] includes the following:

- persisting in blocking a ramp and driveway with outdoor furniture[432]
- refusing to remove a garden utility shed from the balcony of this eighth floor unit so that the landlord could effect necessary repairs to the balcony and exterior walls of the complex[433]

---

428 (October 28, 1998), SWQL-02173 (Ont. Rental Housing Trib.).

429 (May 5, 2003), TSL-42034 (Ont. Rental Housing Trib.).

430 (May 17, 2002) TSL-40332 (Ont. Rental Housing Trib.).

431 Section 64 of the *Tenant Protection Act, 1997*, S.O. 1997, c. 24 and s. 107(1)(c) of the *Landlord and Tenant Act*, R.S.O. 1990, c. L.7.

432 *Mountbriar Building Corp. (Toronto) v. Da Rosa* (October 15, 1976), Doc. M2839 (Ont. Co. Ct.).

433 *Alet Management Ltd. v. Ruus* (November 18, 1982), Doc. M72035/82 (Ont. Co. Ct.).

- deliberately attracting a large number of pigeons to the balcony[434]
- preventing the landlord from spraying all the units in order to effectively deal with an insect infestation[435]
- frequently disturbing other tenants with excessive noise caused by (amongst other things): a stereo and musical instruments; [436] a television played at high volumes and late at night; [437] door slamming;[438] loud arguments;[439] loud parties;[440] hollering from the balcony;[441] visitors constantly running up and down the stairs and smoking in the hallways[442]
- operating a C.B. radio that interfered with the television and radio reception of other tenants[443]
- significantly altering the interior structure of the unit without the consent of the landlord[444]
- blocking access to the unit and attempting to "scare off" potential purchasers of the condominium unit[445]
- being verbally abusive towards, and attempting to intimidate, other tenants[446]
- engaging in activities in the unit that created noxious odours[447]
- removing appliances from the unit and refusing to return them[448]

---

434 *Nefibo Inc. v. Robinson* (June 13, 2003), SWL-49257, [2003] O.R.H.T.D. No. 84, 2003 CarswellOnt 2637 (Ont. Rental Housing Trib.).

435 *Blatt Holdings Ltd. v. Stumpf* (September 24, 1982), Hughes, Galligan, O'Leary J. (Ont. Div. Ct.), *Blatt Holdings Ltd. and Stein, Re.* (July 22, 1976) (Ont. Co. Ct.) and *Egrose Apartments Inc. v. Bonenfant* (Oct. 7, 1998), TEL-0173 (Ont. Rental Housing Trib.).

436 *Harmer v. Karszmarzyk* (December 1, 1981), Salhany Co. Ct. J. (Ont. Co. Ct.).

437 *Graham and Hedden, Re* (May 10, 1982), Griffiths J. (Ont. Co. Ct.).

438 *Berhold Investments Ltd. v. Fall* (1982), 35 O.R. (2d) 338 (Ont. Div. Ct.).

439 *H&R Property Management Ltd. v. Bock* (May 17, 2001), TNL-25314 (Ont. Rental Housing Trib.).

440 Landlord and Tenant Board File No. EAL-13934 (Feb. 13, 2009).

441 *King Shopping Plaza (London) Ltd. v. Schweitzer* (July 7, 1986), Doc. Halton DCOM 1167/86 (Ont. Dist. Ct.).

442 Landlord and Tenant Board File No. NOL-05996 (Feb. 17, 2009).

443 *Mastercraft Construction Co. v. Baldwin* (1978), 20 O.R. (2d) 346 (Ont. Co. Ct.).

444 *Toronto Community Housing Corp. v. Borys* (July 4, 2002), TEL-28626, [2002] O.R.H.T.D. No. 79 (Ont. Rental Housing Trib.).

445 *Leo et al. v. Tal et al.* (Feb. 16, 2001), TNL-21398 (Ont. Rental Housing Trib.).

446 *Windsor-Essex County Housing Corp. v. Dube* (Oct. 28, 1998), SWL-01073 (Ont. Rental Housing Trib.).

447 *Mantler Management Ltd. v. Sqeireq* (Jan. 27, 2003), TNL-43054, 2003 CarswellOnt 1565 (Ont. Rental Housing Trib.). The landlord's application was granted even though the landlord could not actually "catch the tenant in the act" and was not able to prove exactly what was causing the fumes that were emanating from this rental unit.

448 *Smulski v. Premont* (May 4, 2006), EAL-56419, [2006] O.R.H.T.D. No. 56, 2006 CarswellOnt 4432 (Ont. Rental Housing Trib.).

- harassing and making false accusations against the property managers[449]
- using the rental unit exclusively for the business purpose of subletting the unit on a short-term basis (one day or less) to "escorts", thereby compromising the security of the building and interfering with the reasonable enjoyment of other tenants (by constantly permitting strangers to enter the complex) and substantially interfering with the lawful rights of the landlord by negatively affecting the character of the complex, thus impeding the landlord's ability to attract good, long-term tenants for other units in the complex[450]

Excessive loud music, threatening actions, abusive language and other complaints substantially interfered with the reasonable enjoyment of the landlord and his family and an order for termination and possession was granted: *Ble v. Adomeit*.[451]

In *Jantro Corp. v. Lazarevic*,[452] Conant D.C.J. stated:

> Family living in multi-unit complexes requires concern and consideration for others, particularly when a tenant is aware there is a noise problem emanating from her apartment. Here, this [consideration] was not shown and, in my view it would be unfair to the neighbours and the landlord if termination were not given.

Cooking odours are not infrequently the subject of complaints in multi-unit dwellings. In *Stansbury v. Chatterjee*,[453] the landlord sought to evict the tenants because of complaints of cooking odours emanating from their rental unit that other tenants found to be "gross, terrible and obnoxious". The Public Health Department inspected and found no unusual activity taking place; it was simply that the tenants use spices and cooking methods that might be unfamiliar to their neighbours. In dismissing the landlord's application, the Member wrote as follows:

> "substantial interference" must be behaviour which is beyond the minor adjustments and annoyances that must be accepted where persons occupy adjoining apartments. That is to say, that the impugned behaviour, which causes the interference, cannot be behaviour that arises in the usual course of occupation of residential premises, but rather the behaviour must be "antisocial".
>
> . . . Clearly, cooking using methods that are familiar to you may result in smells that "wet" the appetite, yet to others may be repulsive. But such smells can not and must not, in this case, be considered as being anything beyond the typical smells that one must endure and accept when one lives in an apartment building.

---

449 Landlord and Tenant Board File No. SWL-22233 (Jan. 27, 2009).

450 Landlord and Tenant Board File Nos. TNL-02285 and TNL-01415, (May 31, 2007).

451 (1987), 1987 CarswellOnt 3533 (Ont. Dist. Ct.).

452 (1990), 11 R.P.R. (2d) 244 (Ont. Dist. Ct.) at 250 [R.P.R.].

453 (November 8, 1999), SOL-08895 (Ont. Rental Housing Trib.).

Such applications might now also give rise to a defence of constructive discrimination contrary to the *Ontario Human Rights Code* (see Chapter 15).

Smoking is another issue that seems to come up frequently. In *Harding v. Atkinson*,[454] the landlord complained and applied to the Tribunal about the tenant in the upper floor smoking and causing her an allergic reaction and seriously interfering with her reasonable enjoyment. The Tribunal dismissed the application as there was no evidence to substantiate the allergic reaction.

In *Vanderlinden and McConnell*,[455] the landlord complained about the tenant smoking in her unit as it had been a term of the lease (i.e., the tenant had agreed) that she would not smoke in the unit. The landlord's complaint *per se* was *not* enough to support a finding of serious interference with the landlord's reasonable enjoyment. A tenant generally has the right to smoke in his or her own home and the landlord failed to adduce sufficient evidence of harm. The landlord succeeded in obtaining an order terminating the tenancy, however, based upon arrears of rent. Presumably the arrears were paid (and the tenancy was not terminated) because the parties were back before the Tribunal on another application about smoking only one month later.[456] This time, the landlord brought better evidence of the effect of smoke on her and the reason for the "no smoking" provision in the tenancy agreement. The landlord was 74 years old, with a heart condition. The second-hand smoke was adversely affecting the health of the landlord. In these circumstances, the Member held that the tenant had seriously interfered with the reasonable enjoyment of the landlord and terminated the tenancy.

In *Feaver v. Davidson*,[457] the Tenant smoked in the basement with the knowledge of the landlord. The landlord then moved into the main level of this house (above the tenant) and was disturbed by the smoke. The landlord tried modifying the ventilation system but to no avail. Ultimately, the landlord brought an application to evict the tenant for substantially interfering in the landlord's reasonable enjoyment of the unit. The Member found that although the tenant had a *prima facie* right to smoke in his unit that right had limits when it seriously interfered in the reasonable enjoyment of persons living in other parts of the building. The Member ordered the tenant to cease smoking in the complex. Note that had this case been commenced under the R.T.A., it would likely have proceeded under the new fast-track procedures available under s. 65 of the R.T.A.

In Landlord and Tenant Board File No. TSL-01010 (February 25, 2008), the landlord rented furnished units to executives seeking short-term, smoke-free accommodations. It was a term of the tenancy agreement that the tenant would not smoke and would not permit smoking within the rental unit. The

---

[454] (May 6, 1999), TEL-04742 (Ont. Rental Housing Trib.).
[455] (April 21, 1999), TEL-05045 (Ont. Rental Housing Trib.).
[456] *Vanderlinden v. McConnell* (May 17, 1999), TEL-05320 (Ont. Rental Housing Trib.).
[457] (July 21, 2003), TSL-52189, 2003 CarswellOnt 4189 (Ont. Rental Housing Trib.).

tenant breached this term. It was held that the tenant's breach of the no-smoking provisions of the tenancy agreement constituted substantial interference in the lawful rights of the landlord (as well as the lingering smell having caused undue damage). For breach of the no-smoking provision, for interfering with the landlord's efforts to show the unit to prospective buyers and for causing smoke damage, the tenancy was terminated and the tenant was ordered to pay the landlord $10,000 in compensation. In a March 8, 2008, article, Bob Aaron of the *Toronto Star* newspaper hailed this decision as affirming the right of landlords to include a non-smoking clause in a residential lease.

Smoking in the rental unit has been, at least in part, grounds for terminating the tenancy (on the basis that the second-hand smoke and resulting odour substantially interfered with the reasonable enjoyment of other tenants and/or the landlord) in the following cases: Landlord and Tenant Board File No. TNL-00798 (March 19, 2007); Landlord and Tenant Board File No. NOL-00301 (March 26, 2007); Landlord and Tenant Board File No. SWL-00438 (March 16, 2007); and Landlord and Tenant Board File No. CEL-15596 (Jan. 21, 2009).

Pursuant to s. 36 of the R.T.A., a tenant shall not harass, obstruct, coerce, threaten or interfere with the landlord. There is no *specific* recourse section for a breach of s. 36. The landlord can seek relief under s. 64 if the landlord's reasonable enjoyment of the residential complex is substantially interfered with, or if there is substantial interference with any other lawful right, privilege or interest of the landlord.

In *Joshi v. 922859 Ontario Inc.*,[458] the landlord was prevented by the tenant from entering part of the basement premises of which the landlord had retained and had exclusive possession. The landlord required some of his personal records when he was seeking employment. The tenant continued to refuse the landlord entry and was abusive. The judge said the tenant's attitude was high-handed, and substantially interfered with the landlord's quiet enjoyment of his premises. Termination was ordered of the tenant's lease with solicitor and client costs.

Landlord's are sometimes of the view that the breach by the tenant of a covenant contained in the tenancy agreement ought to give rise to the right to terminate the tenancy. Many landlords include standard rules as part of their lease forms and landlords want to be able to enforce those rules. Except in very unusual circumstances, the breach by a tenant of a rule or other covenant of the tenancy agreement will not be so fundamental that it allow the landlord to treat the tenancy as at an end. A landlord may attempt to terminate the tenancy as a result of the breach of a term of the tenancy agreement under s. 64. It should be remembered, however, that a landlord is

[458] (1997), 1997 CarswellOnt 1772 (Ont. Gen. Div.).

only entitled to relief under s. 64 if the interference with a lawful right, privilege or interest of the landlord is *substantial*!

A perfect example of this is the issue surrounding the installation by tenants of satellite dishes. Most high-rise apartments have rules prohibiting the installation of satellite dishes. When a tenant signs the standard tenancy agreement, the tenant is agreeing to abide by such a rule. Typically, no explanation for the rule is given. Nevertheless, more and more tenants seem to be installing them on their balconies.

When a landlord discovers that a tenant has installed a satellite dish, the landlord may commence an application based on undue damage (s. 62 or s. 63), substantial interference with the lawful rights of the landlord (s. 64 or s. 65) or impaired safety (s. 66). Usually, the application will be based upon s. 62 or s. 64, or both. If the application is based upon s. 62, the landlord will have to demonstrate that the installation of the dish has actually caused undue damage to the building. Tenants have begun erecting satellite dishes in such a way that they are affixed to a pole inserted into a heavy base and not to the building itself — in this way, there is no damage to the building.

If the application is based upon s. 64, the landlord will have to prove that the breach of the landlord's rule against satellite dishes (assuming there is such a rule) substantially interferes with the lawful rights of the landlord. It may be that the landlord has an exclusive contract with a cable provider that prohibits the installation of satellite dishes or the landlord may have legitimate concerns about the safety of having satellite dishes hanging from the building or there may even be legitimate aesthetic considerations but, whatever the reason, the landlord should come to the hearing prepared to adduce evidence to demonstrate that the interference is *substantial*.

In *Parkview Management v. Dehas*,[459] the landlord was successful in demonstrating that it had a substantial interest in alterations to the building that could create safety risks or maintenance problems; the tenants were ordered to remove the satellite dish, failing which the landlord could apply under s. 77 of the T.P.A. (now s. 78 of the R.T.A.) for an *ex parte* eviction order. A similar decision was made in *Marguerita Residence Corp. v. Kelly*.[460] The landlord was unsuccessful in *Kitchener Alliance Community Homes Inc. v. Brine*.[461]

The same considerations applied under the *Landlord and Tenant Act*. In *411 Duplex Avenue (Berkshire House) v. Baker*,[462] the tenant had enclosed the balcony without the landlord's consent. This was in breach of the lease, but that in itself was not a ground for termination, unless this substantially

---

459 (Sept. 27, 2001), EAL-22575, [2001] O.R.H.T.D. No. 126, 2001 CarswellOnt 6317 (Ont. Rental Housing Trib.).

460 (Oct. 19, 2001), EAL-23117, [2001] O.R.H.T.D. No. 136, 2001 CarswellOnt 6319 (Ont. Rental Housing Trib.).

461 (Dec. 16, 2002), SWL-43674, 2002 CarswellOnt 5027 (Ont. Rental Housing Trib.).

462 (1990), 10 R.P.R. (2d) 27 (Ont. Dist. Ct.).

interfered with the reasonable enjoyment of the premises by the landlord or other tenants, s. 107(1)(*c*) of Part IV, or the tenant's conduct had seriously impaired the safety or other *bona fide* and lawful right of any other tenant, s. 107(1)(*d*) of Part IV. The evidence did not support either ground for termination.

Similarly, where the rules of the landlord prohibit a tenant from having a washer or dryer in her unit, on an application to evict the tenant under s. 64, the landlord will have to demonstrate that the presence of the appliance in question substantially interferes in the lawful rights of the landlord. In *Sky Top Developments Limited v. Linton*,[463] the landlord was able to prove that the plumbing in the building could not handle such appliances in the units. The Vice-chair allowed the tenant time in which to remove the washing machine, failing which the landlord could apply under s. 77 of the T.P.A. (now s. 78 of the R.T.A.) for an *ex parte* eviction order.

In a 2005 decision, the Divisional Court ruled that the Tribunal erred in finding that it did not have jurisdiction to determine if a breach of the tenancy agreement by the tenant substantially interfered with the lawful rights of the landlord.[464] The Court went on to suggest that if the tenant had agreed to provide the landlord with rent payments by way of pre-authorized direct debit from the tenant's bank account and then failed to fulfill that obligation, this may well merit termination of the tenancy under s. 64(1) of the T.P.A. The matter was remitted to the Tribunal for a new hearing. Note that, under the R.T.A., it is now illegal for a landlord to insist on payment by pre-authorized direct debit.[465]

B. FAST-TRACK

Some of the most difficult and volatile situations arise in smaller buildings where the landlord and tenant each have their own units but are living under the same roof. This is most commonly seen in private homes, duplexes and triplexes. When the R.T.A. was being drafted, it was felt that a landlord whose enjoyment of his or her own home was being adversely affected by the conduct of a tenant should have recourse to a more streamlined eviction process. Thus, where the substantial interference of the landlord's reasonable enjoyment or substantial interference with another lawful right, privilege or interest of the landlord occurs in a building containing not more than three residential units and the landlord resides in one of those units, the landlord may rely upon the provisions of s. 65 of the R.T.A. (rather than s. 64).

---

463 (Feb. 1, 1999), TEL-01294-RV (Ont. Rental Housing Trib.).

464 *Stanbar Properties Limited v. Rooke* (Nov. 9, 2005), Div. Ct. File No. 04-212DV, Hamilton.

465 Paragraph 108(b) of the R.T.A. For more information about approved methods of paying rent, please see Chapter 7.

There are a few important differences to note about proceeding under s. 65 (as opposed to s. 63):

1. the tenant has no chance to void the notice of termination;
2. the tenant only receives 10 days notice of the termination date; and
3. the tenant only receives five days notice of the hearing.

The notice of termination is Form N7. The notice period is a minimum of 10 days.[466] The grounds for the application shall be set out in the notice and there must be adequate reasons and details (particulars of damage must be specified).[467] The application can be filed as soon as the notice of termination has been served (s. 71) but no later than 30 days after the specified termination date (ss. 46 and 69(2)). The application is in Form L2 and the filing fee is $170.[468] The application and notice of hearing must be served at least five days prior to the hearing (Rule 10.5(c)(iii)). The certificate of service for the application and notice of hearing should be filed with the Board within five days after service has been effected (Rule 11.2), or if that is not possible, it should be filed at the beginning of the hearing (Rule 11.3).

In all other respects, the application will proceed in the same manner as under s. 64 of the R.T.A. (discussed in the previous section of this chapter). Since the general principles are the same, cases decided under s. 64 of the R.T.A. (and its predecessor) will be relevant under s. 65 as well.

Subject to the Board's discretion to delay the eviction (under clause 83(1)(b)), an eviction order made under s. 65 will request that the sheriff expedite the enforcement of the order.[469]

Special provisions apply if the interference is alleged to have resulted from the presence, control or behaviour of an animal (see s. 76). This is discussed in detail towards the end of this Chapter under the heading, "Applications Based upon the Presence of an Animal."

In Landlord and Tenant Board File No. SOL-00054 (Feb. 16, 2007), the landlord alleged that the failure of the tenants to properly supervise and control their "pit bull" dog substantially interfered with the landlord's reasonable enjoyment of the building. The Member restricted the landlord to presenting evidence only in regard to incidents for which particulars were provided in the notice of termination. With respect to those issues (related to the tenants' dog), the Member was not satisfied that the landlord had met his burden of proof and the application was dismissed.

The erratic and sometimes dangerous behaviour of the tenant concerned the Landlord, who lived in the small building with his wife and newborn

---

[466] Subsection 65(1) of the R.T.A.

[467] Subsection 43(2) of the R.T.A. Also see *Ball v. Metro Capital et al.* (Dec. 19, 2002), Div. Ct. File No. 48/02, re (Dec. 10, 2001), TNL-31297 (Ont. Rental Housing Trib.) and Chapter 6 for a discussion about notices of termination.

[468] Effective April 2009. From 2002 through March 2009, the fee was $150.

[469] Section 84 of the R.T.A.

child. The Member found that the conduct in question substantially interfered with the reasonable enjoyment of the landlord and granted an order terminating the tenancy. The Member did, however, grant the tenant almost two months to find new accommodations.[470]

In Landlord and Tenant Board File No. TNL-19302 (Jan. 23, 2009), the tenants were found to have caused excessive and ongoing noise by playing their television loudly in the middle of the night and by arguing with each other in a "loud and profane manner". This conduct adversely affected the landlord and another tenant of the complex. The Member found that the noise disturbances were extensive and serious and that the tenants continued this conduct throughout the tenancy (until they received the application). Consequently, the tenancy was terminated and the tenants were given approximately one week in which to vacate the unit. In this order, the Member also suggested that, in cases such as this, the following factors ought to be considered:

- The nature of the tenant's conduct
- Whether the conduct is unusual or part of the normal activities of daily living
- The extent and seriousness of the problem
- Complaints of other tenants
- Whether the offending tenant was warned about the conduct and, if so, whether the conduct continued after the warnings were given
- Whether the landlord provoked the conduct
- Whether the landlord condoned or permitted the behaviour over a period of time
- Whether there are any circumstances that warrant granting relief from eviction

(viii) Overcrowding

Pursuant to s. 67(1) of the R.T.A. (formerly s. 66(1) of the T.P.A.), a landlord may give a tenant notice of termination of the tenancy if the number of persons occupying the rental unit on a continuing basis results in a contravention of health, safety or housing standards required by law.

A couple of points about this subsection are worth noting. First, it does *not* permit a landlord to evict the tenants simply because there are more people living in the rental unit than the number to which the parties originally agreed. A tenant need not ask permission from a landlord to bring in a roommate, get married or have children. This section is meant to deal with situations where the number of occupants creates a health or safety hazard. For instance, the Toronto Property Standards By-law sets the maximum

[470] Landlord and Tenant Board File No. TSL-00166 (Feb. 26, 2007).

number of persons living in a habitable room at one person for each nine square metres of habitable room floor area. There are also provisions concerning the minimum amount of space required for a sleeping area, depending upon the number of persons.

The second point is that s. 67(1) only applies to the number of persons occupying the rental unit on a *continuing* basis. It is not meant to deal with temporary guests. To be successful on this type of application, a landlord will need to prove the number of people who live in the rental unit on a continuing basis, the dimensions of the unit and the rooms within the unit and the provisions of the relevant health, safety or housing standards that have allegedly been breached.[471] Perhaps the best evidence would come from a health inspector or property standards officer who had actually attended at the unit.

The first step will be serving the tenant(s) with a notice of termination, which is in Form N5. It must be served at least 20 days prior to the termination date if it is a "first" notice, or at least 14 days in advance if the notice is given within six months of the tenant voiding an earlier notice of termination given under s. 62, 64 or 67. The notice must set out the details of the grounds for termination (para. 64(2)(b))[472] and must give the tenant seven days to stop the conduct or activity or correct the omission set out in the notice (para. 64(2)(c)). The seven-day period begins on the day after service of the notice (Rule 4.1).[473]

If the tenant does comply within that seven-day period, the notice of termination is void (s. 64(3)). If the tenant does not comply, the landlord may commence an application.

The application must be filed no earlier than the eighth day after service of the notice (s. 70(1)) and no later than 30 days after the specified termination date (ss. 46 and 69(2)). The application is in Form L2 and the filing fee is $170.[474] If the application is based upon a "second notice", the earlier ("first") notice of termination and proof of service must be filed with the application (s. 53 of O. Reg. 516/06). The application and notice of hearing must be served at least 10 days prior to the hearing (Rule 10.1). The certificate of service for the application and notice of hearing should be filed with the Board within five days after service has been effected (Rule 11.2).

This cause for termination was dealt with in *Miguardi and Nugent, Re*.[475] The tenants had allowed another family to move in with them in breach of the municipal by-law. Order for termination was refused because the other family moved out within seven days of the notice to the tenants. The judge

---

[471] *Sanna v. Maidment* (April 20, 1999), TEL-04782 (Ont. Rental Housing Trib.).

[472] If no terms are stated in the notice it will be defective: *Lugano View Ltd. v. Grannum* (1988), 64 O.R. (2d) 468 (Ont. Div. Ct.).

[473] See *Gamble v. Doucette* (Dec. 11, 2000), TNL-21987, 2000 CarswellOnt 6408 (Ont. Rental Housing Trib.).

[474] Effective April 2009. From 2002 through March 2009, the fee was $150.

[475] (November 1, 1982), Matthews J. (Ont. Co. Ct.).

also commented that they were "guests". That would not likely be an answer if the guests were there for an overly long time.

In *Canyon Towers v. Branitsky*,[476] the North York Housing Standards By-law as to the number of occupants per square feet of habitable space permitted in an apartment was the basis for terminating the tenancy by reference to s. 107(1)(*e*) of Part IV.

In *Lee, Re*,[477] the landlord received notice from the county advising that her rental property was not zoned for multiple dwellings. The presence of two rental units in the building constituted a contravention of the zoning by-laws. The landlord sought to evict the tenants on the basis that the number of persons living in the unit on a continuing basis is more than permitted by housing standards. The problem here was not that too many people were living in either of these two units. Rather, it was the presence of two dwellings within the building. Since it was the landlord's act of dividing this property into two units that created the problem and not any contravention of the Act by the tenants, the landlord's application was dismissed.

(ix) *Applications Based upon a Second Notice of Termination Within Six Months*

As previously indicated, a tenant has an opportunity to void a Form N5 when the complaint of the landlord concerns undue damage to the rental unit or residential complex (s. 62), interference with the reasonable enjoyment of other tenants or with the lawful rights of the landlord (s. 64) or overcrowding (s. 67). If, within six months after the first notice becomes void, the tenant contravenes the provisions of one or more of ss. 60 (misrepresentation of income), 61 (illegal act, etc.), 62 (undue damage), 64 (interference with reasonable enjoyment) or 67 (too many persons living in unit), other than a situation involving the production of or trafficking in an illegal drug, the landlord may serve another notice of termination (either Form N5 or N6). This "second" notice generally has a shorter notice period (14 days) and indicates that the tenant does not have any right to void the notice by compliance (s. 68(1)).

Note that a "second" notice can *only* be given if the first notice became void "as a result of the tenant's compliance with the terms of that notice" (para. 68(1)(a)).[478] If the first notice was not voided as a result of compliance,

---

[476] (1989), 1989 CarswellOnt 2437 (Ont. Dist. Ct.).

[477] (June 15, 2006), SOL-67557, 2006 CarswellOnt 4421 (Ont. Rental Housing Trib.).

[478] *Aldea v. Bleiweis* (May 11, 2000), TNL-15790, [2000] O.R.H.T.D. No. 69, 2000 CarswellOnt 4512 (Ont. Rental Housing Trib.), *Bosomworth v. Shirley* (March 31, 2006), Doc. SOL-63194-RV, 2006 CarswellOnt 2147 (Ont. Rental Housing Trib.) and *Concord Pacific Property Inc. v. Hope*, (April 12, 2006), TEL-60237, 2006 CarswellOnt 4414, [2006] O.R.H.T.D. No. 45 (Ont. Rental Housing Trib.).

the landlord should commence an application based upon that first notice. If it is too late (i.e., if the first notice has become void because the landlord did not commence an application within 30 days of the termination date set out in the first notice), the landlord will have to start again with another "first" (i.e., curable) notice.

After serving the "second" notice of termination, the landlord may immediately file an application (the landlord need not wait until after the termination date).[479] The application must be accompanied by a copy of the notice just served along with a certificate of service as well as a copy of the "first" notice of termination that was served within the preceding six months and a certificate of service for that notice as well.[480]

In *Cobblestone Property Management Ltd. v. Shobbrook*,[481] the tenant complied with the first notice (Form N5) and stopped making noise. The tenant then discovered that her vehicle had been damaged. In an effort to discover who may have caused this damage, she distributed notes to the other tenants in the building asking that anyone with information about the incident contact her. The landlord then served a second notice of termination based upon the allegation that distributing these notes substantially interfered with the reasonable enjoyment and commenced an application to evict the tenant. The Tribunal found that the first notice had been voided through compliance and that there was no evidence that the conduct referred to in the second notice substantially interfered with the reasonable enjoyment of other tenants. The application was, therefore, dismissed with costs to the tenant in the amount of $300.

(x) Applications Based upon the Presence of an Animal

As a result of s. 14 of the R.T.A. (formerly s. 15 of the T.P.A.), a landlord cannot ban animals from the residential complex. "No pet" provisions in tenancy agreements have no legal effect. Even if a tenant agrees not to have any pets and states that he or she does not have any pets, it does not mean that the tenant will not soon acquire one. For the most part, pet owners are responsible tenants who do not create any problems for their landlords or their neighbours. There are, however, bound to be exceptions — cases where the mere presence of an animal of a particular species causes a neighbour to have a severe allergic reaction or cases where irresponsible conduct by a pet owner results in serious interference with the reasonable enjoyment of other tenants or with the landlord's rights or results in serious impairment of the safety of other persons in the residential complex.

---

479 Section 71 of the R.T.A.

480 Paragraphs 1 and 3 of s. 53, O. Reg. 516/06.

481 (July 14, 2006), TEL-62461, [2006] O.R.H.T.D. No. 98 (Ont. Rental Housing Trib.).

According to s. 76(1) of the R.T.A., if an application based on a notice of termination under s. 64 (substantial interference), s. 65 (substantial interference – fast track) or s. 66 (impaired safety) is grounded on the presence, control or behaviour of an animal in or about the residential complex, the Board shall not make an order terminating the tenancy and evicting the tenant without being satisfied that the tenant is keeping an animal and that,

(a) subject to s. 76(2), the past behaviour of an animal of that species has substantially interfered with the reasonable enjoyment of the residential complex for all usual purposes by the landlord or other tenants;
(b) subject to s. 76(3), the presence of an animal of that species has caused the landlord or another tenant to suffer a serious allergic reaction; *or*
(c) the presence of an animal of that species or breed is inherently dangerous to the safety of the landlord or the other tenants.

Subsection 76(2) provides that the Board shall not make an order terminating the tenancy and evicting the tenant relying on clause 76(1)(a) if it is satisfied that the animal kept by the tenant did not cause or contribute to the substantial interference.

Subsection 76(3) provides that the Board shall not make an order terminating the tenancy and evicting the tenant relying on clause 76(1)(b) if it is satisfied that the animal kept by the tenant did not cause or contribute to the allergic reaction.

All in all, this makes applications concerning animals substantially more complex. At the risk of oversimplifying these provisions, I would summarize s. 76 as follows: the landlord must demonstrate that the interference, serious allergic reaction or serious impairment of safety is created by a particular type (species) of animal, that the particular animal kept by the tenant is of that species and that the animal in question is, in fact, the source of the problem.

Situations I have seen that can lead to eviction include the following: a dog that barked continuously after the tenants left (apparently as a result of separation anxiety), thereby disturbing others; a tenant who allowed her dog to repeatedly urinate and defecate on the apartment balcony; and having a large dog that lunged at other tenants in the elevator.

In *Effort Trust Company v. Miller et al.*,[482] the tenants left their dog unattended for long periods of time. The dog barked a lot and was allowed to use the balcony for defecating and urinating. This substantially interfered with the reasonable enjoyment of other tenants, especially the tenants of the unit with the balcony immediately below this one. As a result, the Tribunal granted the landlord's application to terminate this tenancy.

---

[482] (June 22, 2004), SOL-49554 (Ont. Rental Housing Trib.).

Similarly, in Landlord and Tenant Board File No. NOL-06088 (Feb. 3, 2009), the tenancy was terminated because of the constant barking of the tenant's dog, which was substantially interfering with the reasonable enjoyment of the landlord and the landlord's children (who lived in the unit above the tenant's).

In *Carvalho et al. v. Gibson et al.*,[483] the presence of the tenants' dog substantially interfered with the landlords' reasonable enjoyment of the residential complex because it caused a serious allergic reaction in one of the landlords. The tenants were not willing to remove the dog from the premises so the Tribunal terminated this tenancy (but gave the tenants more than two months to find new accommodations).

In *Denewood Apartments v. Dodds*,[484] three dogs barked excessively and substantially interfered with the enjoyment of three separate tenants during the day and interrupted their sleep at night.

The leading case has been *Kay v. Parkway Forest Development*.[485] The Divisional Court gave guidance on interpreting "substantially interferes with reasonable enjoyment" of others. It is a question of fact after considering the nature of the conduct complained of, duration, extent, seriousness, nature of premises, the complaints, undue barking, and the reasonable expectations and feelings of the other tenants.

The big dog cases may continue to influence the Tribunal. They are *Greymac Mortgage Corp. v. Bailey*;[486] *Metropolitan Toronto Housing Authority v. Lewis*;[487] *O'Shanter Development Co. v. Chomyn*.[488] In these cases there was evidence of tenants being frightened, dogs not on a leash, undue barking and defecating in and outside the premises.

In *Sylvan Court Apartments Ltd. v. Darling*,[489] the tenant's "pit bull" type dog attacked the superintendent, causing serious injuries. The tenant was found to have failed to properly control her dog. Referring to s. 5.1 of the *Dog Owners Liability Act, 2005*, the Member found that the conduct of the tenant seriously impaired the safety of other persons within the residential complex and, as a result, granted the landlord's application to evict the tenant.

Sometimes an eviction is not necessary if the tenant is willing to take appropriate steps to rectify the situation. In *Maria Fernanda Non Profit Housing of Ontario v. Terrazas*,[490] the tenants' dog charged at and frightened the assistant superintendent. This was an isolated incident. The parties jointly suggested some solutions that were adopted by the Tribunal and incorporated

---

[483] (March 12, 2002), SOL-29918 (Ont. Rental Housing Trib.).

[484] (May 21, 1993), Doc. Toronto 93-LT-51329 (Ont. Gen. Div.).

[485] (1982), 35 O.R. (2d) 329 (Ont. Div. Ct.).

[486] (October 2, 1985), Doc. M117188/85 (Ont. Dist. Ct.).

[487] (December 30, 1986), Doc. M135405/86 (Ont. Dist. Ct.).

[488] (1987), 4 T.L.L.R. 279 (Ont. Dist. Ct.).

[489] (May 3, 2006), TEL-61029, 2006 CarswellOnt 4383 (Ont. Rental Housing Trib.).

[490] (May 27, 1999), TNL-07383, 1999 CarswellOnt 5816 (Ont. Rental Housing Trib.).

into its order. The tenants were to have their dog complete an obedience training course within nine months and keep their dog on a lead (not to exceed six feet in length) and muzzled whenever outside their unit but within the residential complex.

In summary, tenants with pets will be protected from eviction if their pets are well-behaved, kept on a leash, have not caused any harm, are not inherently dangerous and do not cause *serious* allergic reactions.

(xi) Breach of a Term of an Order or Mediated Agreement (s. 78)

Where parties have successfully negotiated a settlement of their dispute with the assistance of a Tribunal/Board mediator, a written agreement will result. If the application was one seeking to terminate the tenancy, then the mediated settlement can contain conditions which, if breached, can give the landlord the right to apply, under s. 78 of the R.T.A. (formerly s. 77 of the T.P.A.), without notice to the tenant, for an order terminating the tenancy (and any other relief available under s. 78).

Where the parties are unwilling or unable to enter into a mediated agreement, the matter will proceed to a hearing before a Member of the Board. If the parties agree or if the presiding Member deems it appropriate not to grant an eviction order, the Member retains the power to impose conditions and to include in his or her order a provision allowing enforcement of those conditions under s. 78.

Note that the mediated agreement or order must specifically refer to s. 78 in order for the landlord to be able to rely thereon.

This may be a way to allow a tenant one further opportunity to save his or her tenancy while imposing conditions that actually have some "teeth".

In *Sky Top Developments Limited v. Linton*,[491] the lease prohibited the tenant from having a washer/dryer in her unit and the evidence indicated that the building's plumbing could not handle such appliances in the units. The Vice-chair found that the presence of a washing machine in the tenant's unit did substantially interfere in the lawful rights of the landlord but wished to allow the tenant the option of remaining in the unit. The Vice-chair allowed the tenant time in which to remove the washing machine, but provided that the landlord could apply for an order terminating the tenancy, pursuant to s. 77 of the T.P.A., if the tenant failed to comply with this condition.

Similarly, in *Waterloo (Regional Municipality) Waterloo (Region Housing) v. Cluney*,[492] the tenant could have been evicted for possession of marijuana. Since the tenant required the marijuana for medical reasons, the Member exercised his discretion and refused to grant an eviction on the condition

[491] (Feb. 1, 1999), TEL-01294-RV (Ont. Rental Housing Trib.).

[492] (Feb. 4, 2005), SWL-66940, 2005 CarswellOnt 1280 (Ont. Rental Housing Trib.).

that, for the rest of the tenancy, the tenant not grow, cultivate or produce marijuana in the rental unit. The order expressly provides for enforcement under s. 77 of the T.P.A. if the tenant breaches that condition.

My review of the cases that have been released by the Landlord and Tenant Board shows that a great number of "contested" landlord applications are now being settled by way of consent orders that contain conditions concerning future behaviour of the tenant (repayment of arrears, the timing of rent payments where tardiness is an issue, the cessation of conduct that has been annoying the landlord or other tenants in the building, etc.). The consequence for a breach of these conditions by the tenant is invariably stated in the order to be that, pursuant to s. 78, upon breach, the landlord may apply to the Board, without notice to the tenant (*ex parte*), for an order terminating the tenancy and for such other relief as is available under s. 78. Of course, many cases may also be settled by way of mediated agreements but, since those agreements are not made public, it is difficult to know what proportion of parties who have reached a settlement prefer to have the terms of their agreement embodied in an order. Even where the landlord objects (i.e., the parties have not reached an agreement), the Board Member may (and often does) grant relief under s. 83(1) of the R.T.A. and refuse to evict the tenant, on the condition that the tenant comply with certain terms, again with specific reference to the consequences under s. 78 should the tenant fail to comply with those terms.

As indicated above, if the tenant does not meet the specified terms of the order or mediated settlement, the landlord can apply to the Board, without notice to the tenant, for an order terminating the tenancy and evicting the tenant (s. 78 of the R.T.A.). The application is Form L4. There is no charge for this type of application. The application must be commenced within 30 days after the breach of the condition by the tenant (s. 78(5)) and the application must be accompanied by an affidavit that contains a copy of the mediated agreement or order and the information described in subsection 78(4).[493]

In Landlord and Tenant Board File No. SOL-00033 (March 27, 2007), the landlord's application was dismissed on the basis that the landlord filled the application more than 30 days after the breach in question.

Normally, these applications are decided on an *ex parte* basis, on the strength of the written material filed (i.e., there is no hearing). Members retain the discretion, however, to refer such matter to a hearing. If that occurs, the landlord must serve a copy of the application, affidavit and notice of hearing upon the tenant at least 10 days before the hearing (Rule 10.2) and file the certificate of service within five days after effecting service (Rule 11.2).

In order to be able to rely upon s. 78, the following criteria must be met:

---

[493] Subsection 78(2) of the R.T.A.

1. The landlord previously applied to the Board for an order terminating the tenancy or evicting the tenant;
2. An order or a settlement mediated under s. 194 with respect to the previous application imposed conditions on the tenant;
3. Among the conditions imposed by the order or settlement were conditions that, if not met by the tenant, would give rise to the same grounds for terminating the tenancy as were claimed in the previous application;
4. The order or settlement provided that the landlord could apply under s. 78 if the tenant did not meet the conditions described above; and
5. The tenant has not met those conditions.

The criterion that seems to give landlords the most difficulty is the third one listed above (i.e., the condition that is breached must have been one that could have given rise in the original application to an order terminating the tenancy). In other words, if the original application was based upon non-payment of rent, the condition must relate to the payment of rent. If the original application was based upon interference with the enjoyment of other tenants, the condition must relate to conduct that could disturb other tenants. If the original application was based upon safety concerns, the conditions in the order or mediated agreement must also relate to safety concerns.

In *Lai v. Tanrikulu*,[494] the parties mediated an application to evict the tenants for persistent late payment of rent. The mediated agreement called for certain payments to be made to the landlord by way of post-dated cheques. The landlord filed an *ex parte* application for eviction under s. 77 of the T.P.A. when the tenant failed to provide the post-dated cheques. The landlord's application was dismissed because the failure to provide post-dated cheques could not give rise to the same reasons for terminating the tenancy as were claimed in the original application.

Similarly, if the tenant complies with all conditions but does not pay the costs of the original application, the landlord cannot seek to evict the tenant for failing to pay the costs. Failing to pay the costs of the application, by itself, would not be grounds to terminate the tenancy.[495] The landlord could, of course, request that the original application be re-opened if the landlord acts quickly.

In *Direct Properties Inc. v. Legault*,[496] the landlord originally commenced an application to terminate the tenancy for undue damage and substantial interference. The application was resolved through mediation. The parties agreed, amongst other things, that the tenant would vacate the unit by a

13 — LL APPLICATIONS

---

494 (March 11, 1999), TNL-05920 (Ont. Rental Housing Trib.).

495 *150 Culford Road Apts v. Fernandes* (June 28, 2000), TNL-15988-RV, [2000] O.R.H.T.D. No. 90, 2000 CarswellOnt 4510 (Ont. Rental Housing Trib.).

496 (Oct. 5, 2000), TEL-15200, [2000] O.R.H.T.D. No. 137, 2000 CarswellOnt 4450 (Ont. Rental Housing Trib.).

specified date. The tenant did not comply with that term. Instead of filing an application under s. 76 of the T.P.A. (based upon an agreement to terminate the tenancy) or requesting to re-open the application (under what is now Rule 13.13), the landlord filed an application under s. 77 of the T.P.A. The application was dismissed because the grounds (failing to vacate the unit upon the date agreed) were not the same as in the original application (undue damage and substantial interference).

As indicated, it is an *ex parte*[497] application — no notice need be served on the tenant. The landlord must include with the application a copy of the order or agreement and an affidavit setting out the conditions which have not been met (s. 78(2) of the R.T.A.). If the original application included a claim for arrears of rent and the order or settlement required the tenant to pay rent then, in addition to seeking to terminate the tenancy, a landlord can also apply under s. 78(3) for payment of arrears of rent and the amount of any compensation payable under s. 86 or 103. The affidavit filed by the landlord must then contain additional information about the current arrears, any amounts received from the tenant, the rent deposit (if any) and any NSF cheque charges (subsection 78(4)).

If the Board finds that the landlord is entitled to an order under s. 78(1), the Board may make an order terminating the tenancy and evicting the tenant (s. 78(6)) and may order any monetary relief to which the landlord may be entitled under ss. 78(7).

In *Toronto Housing Company Inc. v. Stewart*,[498] the landlord brought an application based upon the tenant's alleged interference with the reasonable enjoyment of the landlord and the other tenants. The tenant continued his disruptive intimidation and threats. Pursuant to s. 77 of the T.P.A., the landlord applied for, and was granted, an order terminating the tenancy and evicting the tenant.

When the tenant receives the *ex parte* eviction order, the tenant has ten days from the date the order was issued in which to file a motion to have that order set aside (s. 78(9)). Where such a motion is filed, execution of the order is automatically stayed (ss. 78(10)) but the tenant should ensure that the sheriff receives a copy of the motion and is aware that the order cannot be enforced until the disposition of the tenant's motion. A quick date will be set for the hearing of the tenant's motion. Subsection 78(11) of the R.T.A. requires that a hearing be held on the relevant issues. The Board should not invent its own "test" but should follow the requirements of s. 78. The Board will have to consider whether there was a failure to meet the conditions in the original order or mediated agreement and, if there was a breach of the conditions, whether those conditions properly give rise to relief under s. 78.

---

[497] At least, unless and until the Board orders otherwise.

[498] (June 1, 1999), TSL-09545-SA (Ont. Rental Housing Trib.).

There may be a dispute over whether or not the tenant has complied with the condition(s) contained in the order or mediated settlement. Where there has clearly been a breach of a valid condition giving rise to rights under s. 78, the usual result will be the issuance of an order terminating the tenancy and evicting the tenant.

In the case of a mediated agreement or consent order, the failure of the Board to enforce such terms would undermine the settlement process. Landlords would likely be reluctant to enter into agreements with tenants if those agreements will not later be honoured by the Board through enforcement under s. 78.[499]

In the case of a non-consent order that is breached, the tenant has already been shown leniency by the Tribunal/Board (in as much as an eviction could have been ordered at the original hearing but, instead, the tenant was given an opportunity to save his or her tenancy as long as he or she complied with the conditions imposed by the Member and this relief was granted over the objection of the landlord). On the hearing of the tenant's motion to set aside the *ex parte* order, a Member is likely to be very reluctant to grant a further indulgence in such circumstances.

In *Southridge Apartments v. Hastings*,[500] the tenant breached the terms of a mediated agreement but then brought a motion to set aside the resulting eviction order obtained by the landlord. The Member hearing the motion did set aside the *ex parte* order but, notwithstanding the age of the tenant and the length of her tenancy, would do no more than delay the eviction. On appeal by the tenant, the Divisional Court approved of the approach taken by the Member.

Nevertheless, Members do retain the discretionary power to refuse to grant an eviction order (pursuant to s. 83(1) of the R.T.A.) where it would be unfair to do otherwise.[501] In fact, the Divisional Court held that where a Member hears a tenant's motion to set aside an *ex parte* order, it is a reversible error for the Member not to provide the tenant an opportunity to adduce evidence and make submissions concerning relief from forfeiture.[502]

For example, if the landlord prevents the tenant from fulfilling the conditions of the agreement or order, granting the landlord's request to evict the tenant would amount to an abuse of the Board's process. In *Metropolitan Toronto Housing Authority v. Figueira*,[503] the Member found several miti-

[499] See the discussion in *Homes First Society, Re* (March 27, 2006), TSL-79209-SA, 2006 CarswellOnt 2125 (Ont. Rental Housing Trib.). Also see Landlord and Tenant Board File No. SOL-00735 (March 27, 2007) and Landlord and Tenant Board File No. TSL-00429-SA (March 5, 2007).

[500] (2007), 2007 CarswellOnt 777 (Ont. Div. Ct.).

[501] *San Ardo Apartments v. Donald* (Feb. 10, 1998), TSL-06112-SA (Ont. Rental Housing Trib.).

[502] *Forest Hill Gates v. Wolch* (2007), 2007 CarswellOnt 1864 (Ont. Div. Ct.).

[503] (May 8, 2000), TEL-11585-SA, 2000 CarswellOnt 4368 (Ont. Rental Housing Trib.).

gating factors that warranted granting relief (which the Member acknowledged is highly exceptional in such cases). These included the following factors: the breach was minor, there was compliance after that breach, the tenant had made the unit his home for a number of years, the tenant was unsophisticated, the tenant did not cause any other problems, and the tenant would likely have difficulty finding comparable alternate accommodations for the same rent. The tenant's motion was granted and the landlord's application was dismissed.

This discretionary power has now been explicitly recognized in para. 78(11)(b) of the R.T.A., which provides that, even where the landlord has proven that it was entitled to the *ex parte* order in question, the Board may nevertheless set aside that order if the Board is satisfied, having regard to all of the circumstances, that it would not be unfair to set aside the order. Thus, in every case, whether or not the alleged breach has been proven, the Member must provide an opportunity for the parties to adduce evidence and make submissions on the issue of whether or not such relief ought to be granted. As a result, tenants who have failed to comply with the terms of a mediated agreement or order may have a somewhat increased chance under the R.T.A. of being shown leniency, depending upon the circumstances.

Where the tenant cannot offer any reasonable explanation for the breach and/or is unable or unwilling to comply with any new terms, no further relief will be granted to the tenant.[504] Thus, despite sympathetic facts, no relief was granted in Landlord and Tenant Board File No. SOL-18327-SA because of the substantial arrears of rent that had accumulated and the fact that the tenant had no plan or means of repaying this debt.

One Member has summed up the policy considerations as follows:

> I am of the view that under the Act the general intention is that the Board has an obligation to uphold and enforce mediated agreements that landlords and tenants voluntarily enter into. If it does not enforce those agreements, then there is little incentive for people to enter into mediation. I believe that paragraph 78(11)(b) was primarily intended to address the situation where after the mediated agreement was entered into, something unanticipated happed which was beyond the tenant's control that made it impossible for the tenant to comply with the agreement.[505]

In this case, the Member found that the breach resulted from the tenant's carelessness rather than circumstances beyond the tenant's control and that,

---

[504] See, for example, Landlord and Tenant Board File No. EAL-00195-SA (March 8, 2007); Landlord and Tenant Board File No. EAL-14123-SA (Jan. 30, 2009); Landlord and Tenant Board File No. EAL-00660-SA (March 28, 2007); Landlord and Tenant Board File No. TNL-19419-SA (Jan. 9, 2009); Landlord and Tenant Board File No. TNL-19739-SA (Jan. 12, 2009); and Landlord and Tenant Board File No. TNL-19745-SA (Jan. 13, 2009).

[505] Landlord and Tenant Board File No. TSL-21372-SA (Feb. 6, 2009).

together with a long history of non-payment, made it unfair to grant any further relief to the tenant (other than a delay in lifting the stay).

On the other hand, where the breach is relatively minor or resulted from circumstances beyond the control of the tenant or was contributed to by the conduct of the landlord or where it would otherwise not be unfair to do so, the Board may exercise its discretion and grant further relief, either by refusing the eviction (with or without new terms and conditions) or by delaying the eviction.[506]

In Landlord and Tenant Board File No. TEL-05888-SA (Oct. 5, 2007), the tenant was required by an earlier order of the Board (TEL-04661 issued on August 9, 2007) to pay certain amounts to the landlord on August 31, 2007, and September 1, 2007. The tenant misunderstood these terms and believed that he could pay both amounts on September 1, 2007. He approached the landlord on September 1, 2007, with a cheque for the full amount that was due on August 31 and September 1. The landlord refused to accept the cheque and insisted on cash. The tenant said that this would take a few days and the landlord agreed. On September 4, 2007, the landlord commenced an *ex parte* application for an eviction order under s. 78 based upon the alleged breach of the terms of order TEL-04661. Later that day, the tenant offered the cash payment the landlord had requested and the landlord accepted it without mentioning that an eviction application had been commenced. When the tenant received a copy of the eviction order, he brought a motion to have it set aside. Based on these facts, the Member found that it would not be unfair to set aside the *ex parte* eviction order and granted the tenant's motion pursuant to s. 78(11)(b) of the R.T.A.

In Landlord and Tenant Board File No. TNL-19541 (Jan. 19, 2009), the tenant entered into a mediated agreement with the landlord in September 2008 that called for repayment of arrears of rent. The tenant defaulted in a payment that was due in late October 2008. The landlord filed an application pursuant to s. 78 and the matter was sent to hearing and the parties appeared before the Board on January 5, 2009. At that time, the amount owing to the landlord was less than $500. The Member noted that the tenant had suffered a serious accident and was off work for three months, that this tenancy was

[506] Relief was given in Landlord and Tenant Board File No. TNL-21642-SA (Jan. 22, 2009) because, by the time of the hearing, all amounts owing to the landlord had been paid but for $90. Similarly, the landlord's motion was dismissed in Landlord and Tenant Board File No. SOL-17966 (Jan. 13, 2009) where, by the time of the hearing, only $20 remained outstanding. In Landlord and Tenant Board File No. EAL-00558-SA (March 28, 2007), the *ex parte* order was set aside and the landlord's application was dismissed where, by the time of the hearing, all amounts owing to the landlord had been paid (albeit, not exactly at the times specified in mediated agreement). For more recent examples of cases in which relief was granted despite a breach of mediated agreement, see Landlord and Tenant Board File Nos.: NOL-06350 (Feb. 19, 2009), CEL-15206-SA (Feb. 12, 2009), and SWL-22698-SA (Feb. 5, 2009).

in its third year, and that the tenant had a two-year old daughter. In the circumstances, the Member exercised his discretion under s. 83(1) and refused to grant an eviction, but ordered the tenant to pay the arrears (as well as rent that would be coming due) by March 1, 2009 (again, with a s. 78 clause should there be a further breach).

In Landlord and Tenant Board File No. TNL-00600 (March 22, 2007), the tenants entered into a mediated agreement with the landlord in February 2007 that called for repayment of arrears of rent. The tenants defaulted in a payment (although the tenants had paid $820 of the $950 that they were supposed to pay during that period). The landlord filed an application pursuant to s. 78 and the matter was sent to hearing on March 20, 2007. At that time, the amount owing to the landlord was about $1,500. The Member noted that the tenant who appeared at the hearing was a single mother of a four-year-old child, was the only source of income for the household and was unexpectedly and temporarily laid off from her job. In the circumstances, the Member exercised her discretion under s. 83(1) and refused to grant an eviction, but ordered the tenant to pay the arrears (as well as rent that would be coming due) over a period of about three weeks (again, with a s. 78 clause should there be a further breach).

It should also be remembered that on set-aside motions, even when finding in favour of the landlord (i.e. denying the set-aside motion) and allowing enforcement of the *ex parte* eviction order, the Board has the discretionary power to delay the lifting of the stay on that order and, thereby, delay the eviction.[507] This power comes from para. 78(11)(c) of the R.T.A., which provides that the Board can order that the stay be lifted immediately or "on a future date specified in the order".

Finally, note that a tenant has no right to rely upon the provisions of s. 82 in a hearing being held under s. 78 of the R.T.A.; the tenant cannot raise his/her own complaints at such a hearing because the hearing of the motion to set aside an *ex parte* order is not "the hearing of an application by a landlord under s. 69 for an order terminating a tenancy and evicting the tenant based on a notice of termination under s. 59 (i.e., for arrears of rent)."

[507] For examples where the Board has issued an order that the lifting of the stay be delayed, see: Landlord and Tenant Board File No. SOL-00961-SA (April 12, 2007); Landlord and Tenant Board File No. SOL-00131-SA (March 9, 2007); Landlord and Tenant Board File No. SOL-00620-SA (March 26, 2007); Landlord and Tenant Board File No. SWL-00046-SA (March 9, 2007); Landlord and Tenant Board File No. TEL-00045-SA (Feb. 26, 2007); Landlord and Tenant Board File No. EAL-13587-SA (Jan. 20, 2009); Landlord and Tenant Board File No. TSL-21372-SA (Feb. 6, 2009); Landlord and Tenant Board File No. TNL-19140-SA (Feb. 5, 2009); Landlord and Tenant Board File No. TNL-21640-SA (Feb. 5, 2009); Landlord and Tenant Board File No. TNL-22495-SA (Feb. 23, 2005).

14

Relief for Tenants (or "How to Avoid Being Evicted")

1. INTRODUCTION

The *Residential Tenancies Act, 2006* (R.T.A.) provides considerable rights to tenants that would not otherwise exist under the common law of contracts. For instance, s. 15 of the R.T.A. relieves a tenant from having to pay accelerated rent when there has been default in the payment of rent or in the observance of any obligation of the tenant. If the tenant pays up the arrears of rent or performs any outstanding obligations, and pays any expenses incurred by the landlord, the tenant will not be required to pay accelerated rent, regardless of what terms the landlord may have written into the tenancy agreement. Furthermore, a landlord cannot interfere with or withhold the supply of vital services to the rental unit (s. 21). The ancient remedy of distress[1] has also been abolished (s. 40 of the R.T.A.). Although actual and proper distress may not have been a commonly used remedy of landlords, the threat of distress has been a very serious concern for tenants, and illegal distress against tenants who did not know the statutory requirements for landlords had been of even greater concern.

Perhaps the most important protection for tenants, however, is in relation to the concept of security of tenure. As stated by one Ontario judge:[2]

> A tenancy agreement, by statute, creates somebody's home. To put someone out of their home must call for clear and compelling circumstances that it is no longer possible for the arrangements to continue.

[1] Distress was the right given to a landlord to distrain, i.e., seize without legal process the goods and chattels of a tenant who is in default in payment of rent.

[2] *Langford v. Phipps and Gilpin*, unreported, file no. 7620/92 commenced at London, p. 9 as quoted in *Paderewski Society v. Ficyk* (September 16, 1998), SOL-00857 (Ont. Rental Housing Trib.).

A tenancy cannot be terminated except in strict accordance with the R.T.A. (s. 37(1)) and even where a landlord has valid grounds to terminate a tenancy, the tenant may still be able to avoid eviction. This chapter explains how.

2. VOIDING A NOTICE TO TERMINATE (FORM N5) BY COMPLIANCE

In some cases, the R.T.A. provides that a tenant can avoid termination of the tenancy by correcting the problem that gives rise to the notice of termination. The grounds for termination to which this principle applies are: undue damage to the unit or complex (s. 62); interference with the reasonable enjoyment of other tenants or with a lawful right, privilege or interest of the landlord (s. 64); and overcrowding of the unit (s. 67). In such circumstances, the prescribed notice of termination (Form N5), advises the tenant that the notice of termination will automatically become void if the tenant, within seven days after receiving the notice, complies with the conditions set out in Part C of the notice (i.e., if the tenant rectifies the problem).[3]

In the case of damage to the unit or the complex, the tenant has the option of: (1) making the repairs to the satisfaction of the landlord; (2) paying the reasonable costs of necessary repairs; (3) replacing the damaged property (if it cannot reasonably be repaired); (4) paying the reasonable costs of replacing the damaged property (if it cannot reasonably be repaired); or (5) making arrangements satisfactory to the landlord for any of the above. In order to void the notice of termination, the tenant may choose any of the above options. Altering the form by deleting any of the three options will invalidate the notice.[4] It should be noted, however, that there is no such right to void the notice where it is given under s. 63 rather than s. 62 (i.e., where the landlord is alleging that the damage is wilful or there is a risk of damage that is significantly greater than that required to give a notice under s. 62).

In the case of interference with the enjoyment of other tenants or with the rights of the landlord, the tenant must, within seven days, stop the conduct or activity or correct the omission set out in the notice of termination. Substantial compliance with the notice is not sufficient; if there is a single repetition of the alleged conduct in the seven days following service of the notice of termination, the notice will not become void.[5] For the notice of termination to be valid, the conduct or omission described therein must be capable of being "cured"; the notice must contain specific allegations about

---

[3] Subsections 62(3), 64(3) and 67(3) of the R.T.A.

[4] *Fisher Kay Ltd. v. Bowen et al.* (Sept. 17, 1999), TNL-09813 (Ont. Rental Housing Trib.).

[5] *Silvershade Rental Prop. v. Johnston* (March 19, 2003), NOL-08606-RV, 2003 CarswellOnt 1531 (Ont. Rental Housing Trib.).

inappropriate conduct and not merely conclusions of law.[6] Also, the tenant must be given an opportunity to correct the problem. If, for example, the landlord alleges that the tenant is preventing the landlord from gaining access to the unit, the landlord should, during the seven-day period following service of the notice of termination (Form N5) attempt once again to gain entry to the unit (with proper advance notice in writing, if required) to demonstrate whether or not the tenant continued, during the relevant period, to obstruct entry to the unit.[7] It should be noted, however, that there is no such right to void a Form N7 notice of termination.[8] In the case of overcrowding, the tenant must, during the relevant seven-day period, reduce the number of people living in the unit to a number that complies with health, safety and housing standards.

Of course, a notice of termination (Form N5) can only be voided as described above if it is the first notice of this type that the tenant has received with respect to this rental unit in the last six months. If the tenant has already voided a notice of termination under s. 62, 64 or 67 within the last six months and the landlord is serving a second notice of termination for a breach of s. 60, 61, 62, 64 or 67 of the Act, the tenant has no statutory right to void this second notice of termination.[9]

3. VOIDING A NOTICE TO TERMINATE (FORM N4) BY PAYMENT

Pursuant to s. 59(3) of the R.T.A. (formerly s. 61 of the T.P.A.), the notice of termination (for non-payment of rent) is void if, before the day the landlord applies to the Board for an order terminating the tenancy and evicting the tenant (for non-payment of rent), the tenant pays:

(a) the rent that is in arrears under the tenancy agreement; and
(b) the additional rent that would have been due under the tenancy agreement as at the date of payment by the tenant had notice of termination not been given.

Essentially, this means that the tenant can void the notice of termination (Form N4) by paying to the landlord all of the rent owing to the landlord.

---

[6] *Carere et al. v. Blagrove* (Nov. 24, 2000), TNL-18384, 2000 CarswellOnt 6443 (Ont. Rental Housing Trib.).

[7] *Carere et al. v. Blagrove* (Nov. 24, 2000), TNL-18384, 2000 CarswellOnt 6443 (Ont. Rental Housing Trib.) and *Furtney v. Margaris* (Sept. 27, 2000), CEL-12782, 2000 CarswellOnt 4580 (Ont. Rental Housing Trib.).

[8] I.e., a Form N7 given under s. 65 rather than s. 64 (i.e., where the landlord is alleging that the tenant is substantially interfering with the landlord's reasonable enjoyment, where the landlord lives in the complex and the complex has three or fewer residential units).

[9] See s. 68 of the R.T.A. A second notice cannot be voided through compliance.

Once the landlord has been paid all the rent that is due, the matter does not need to proceed to the Board.

For s. 59(3) to apply, the payment must be made by the day prior to the day the landlord files an L1 application based upon the notice of termination in question. In order to bring the tenancy into good standing (and void the Form N4), the tenant must pay all arrears set out in the notice plus the rent for any subsequent rental period that has come due. The tenant is entitled to rely upon the information contained in the notice of termination. Therefore, if the amounts that are contained (or that ought to be contained) in the notice of termination are incorrect, confusing or missing, the notice may be found to be invalid.[10]

Tenants should be cautious about relying upon this provision too often. Although it is true that, by waiting until a landlord has served a Form N4 and then paying the rent arrears to the landlord before the deadline contained in that form, a tenant can gain additional time (often two weeks or more) in which to pay the rent without any monetary penalty, it is also true that a tenancy can be terminated for persistent late payment of rent (even when there is no money owing to the landlord). Tenants who are experiencing difficulty meeting all of their financial obligations need to make paying the rent a priority. By persistently paying rent late (without the consent of the landlord), a tenant puts his or her tenancy in jeopardy.

4. VOIDING AN EVICTION ORDER (BASED UPON ARREARS OF RENT) BY PAYING ALL AMOUNTS OWING (s. 74)

(a) General

Once the landlord has filed an application based upon the Form N4 notice of termination (for non-payment of rent), it is too late for the tenant to rely upon s. 59(3). The tenant, however, still has some time in which to pay off the debt and save the tenancy.

After the landlord has commenced an L1 application but prior to the issuance of an order by the Board, pursuant to s. 74(2) of the R.T.A., the tenant can have the application automatically discontinued by paying to the landlord or to the Board:

(a) the rent that is in arrears under the tenancy agreement;
(b) the additional rent that would have been due under the tenancy

[10] In *Montreal Trust Co. v. Khaper* (Feb. 1, 2002), CEL-22701 (Ont. Rental Housing Trib.), the notice was found to be invalid as it did not set out the amount of rent due; the fact that the applicant was a mortgagee in possession and may not have known the lawful rent was no excuse.

agreement as at the date of payment by the tenant had notice of termination not been given; and

(c) the landlord's application fee.

It is important to note that, pursuant to s. 74(2), the landlord's L1 application is automatically discontinued if the amounts paid are sufficient to comply with s. 74(2) **as of the date of payment**. In Landlord and Tenant Board File No. SWL-04015 (July 10, 2007), the tenant paid all amounts necessary to comply with s. 74(2) on June 29, 2007. On July 3, 2007, the landlord attended the hearing and argued that an order should be issued by the Board as the tenant had not yet paid rent for July. The Member (correctly) pointed out that the application had been discontinued on June 29, 2007, by operation of s. 74(2). Technically, there was no longer an application for the Member to hear. This interpretation, which I believe is the correct one, is supported by the review decision in Landlord and Tenant Board File No. SWL-20489-RV (Jan. 7, 2009).

If the tenant does not pay these amounts prior to the hearing, and at the hearing, the Board finds in favour of the landlord, an order will be issued by the Board terminating the tenancy and ordering payment of the arrears of rent and other specified amounts.[11]

Although an order that is issued after a hearing can be made effective immediately, this is relatively rare. Under the T.P.A., the Rental Housing Tribunal's unofficial practice was to make a hearing order effective on the 11th day after the day the order was issued. Only time will tell whether the Landlord and Tenant Board will adopt a similar approach. The date an eviction order "takes effect" is the date upon which the order may be filed with the Court Enforcement Office (sheriff) for enforcement of the eviction. If the "effective date" is some time after the date the order is issued, this will afford the tenant *another* opportunity to save the tenancy (pursuant to s. 74(4) of the R.T.A.). In such a case, the order must set out the amount or amounts that must be paid by the tenant to avoid eviction and the deadline for payment (s. 74(3)). The order will also state that the payment can be made either to the landlord or to the Board.

If the landlord's application is not based exclusively upon arrears of rent (i.e., if the L1 application is combined with another type of application) and a termination is ordered based upon grounds other than, or in addition to, arrears of rent, the tenant will not be able to rely on s. 74 to avoid eviction.[12]

The rights under s. 59(3), 74(2) and 74(4) of the R.T.A. to save the tenancy by payment of the amounts owing to the landlord also existed under

---

[11] Under s. 87 the Board can award to the landlord arrears of rent, compensation for use of the unit after the termination date set out in the notice of termination and NSF cheque charges. The Board can also award the application fee and any other costs it deems appropriate.

[12] *Machado v. Maltais* (Oct. 4, 2001), TEL-21789-VOS, [2001] O.R.H.T.D. No. 130, 2001 CarswellOnt 6292 (Ont. Rental Housing Trib.).

the T.P.A. What is new under the R.T.A. is right of a tenant, **once per tenancy,** to save the tenancy by paying all amounts owing (plus the sheriff's fees) *after* the eviction order has been filed with the sheriff but prior to the actual enforcement of that order.[13]

In the early days of the Rental Housing Tribunal, the fact that eviction orders based upon arrears of rent were voidable created some confusion. Occasionally, when the sheriff would try to enforce the order, a tenant would claim that the amount set out in the order had been paid in full. Some tenants would even file with the Court Enforcement Office an affidavit to this effect. Some Court Enforcement Offices were reluctant to evict tenants in the face of such assertions.

Notwithstanding their reluctance, a Court Enforcement Office never had statutory authority to refuse to enforce an order of the Tribunal; an eviction order from the Tribunal has the same effect as a Writ of Possession issued by the Court; the same is true for orders of the Landlord and Tenant Board.[14] In *Orlando v. Duquette*,[15] the Divisional Court made it clear that a sheriff must enforce an eviction order and has no discretion to exercise in this regard. The sheriff has no authority to accept an affidavit or any other evidence from a tenant. Unless the Tribunal (now the Board) or a court orders otherwise, an eviction order must be enforced.

While the government wanted to send a clear message to the Court Enforcement Offices that they must enforce eviction orders issued by the Tribunal, it recognized that a process was needed to resolve disputes over whether or not such orders had been voided by payment. In 2000, s. 72 of the T.P.A. was amended to add such a process. This process has been carried forward and expanded under the R.T.A.

(b) Payment Before Eviction Order Becomes Enforceable

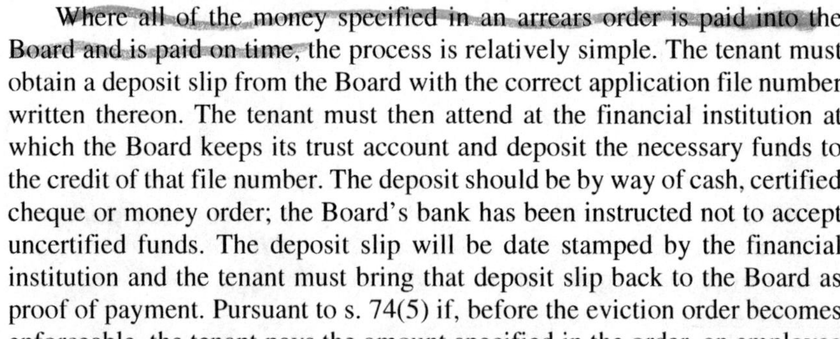

Where all of the money specified in an arrears order is paid into the Board and is paid on time, the process is relatively simple. The tenant must obtain a deposit slip from the Board with the correct application file number written thereon. The tenant must then attend at the financial institution at which the Board keeps its trust account and deposit the necessary funds to the credit of that file number. The deposit should be by way of cash, certified cheque or money order; the Board's bank has been instructed not to accept uncertified funds. The deposit slip will be date stamped by the financial institution and the tenant must bring that deposit slip back to the Board as proof of payment. Pursuant to s. 74(5) if, before the eviction order becomes enforceable, the tenant pays the amount specified in the order, an employee

[13] Subsections 74(11) and (12) of the R.T.A.

[14] Section 85 of the T.P.A. (now s. 85 of the R.T.A.).

[15] (2000), 2000 CarswellOnt 2690, 50 O.R. (3d) 412 (Ont. S.C.J.).

of the Board shall issue a notice to the tenant and the landlord acknowledging that the eviction order is void under s. 74(4) of the Act. The Board will then make arrangements to have the funds forwarded to the landlord (although this may take several weeks). If the eviction order has been filed by the landlord with the sheriff's office, it will be necessary to provide the sheriff with a copy of the notice from the Board to prove that the eviction order is void. It is the tenant's responsibility to do so.[16]

Where some or all of the money specified in an arrears order is paid directly to the landlord, the process is a bit more complex. Pursuant to s. 74(6) of the R.T.A., the tenant must file a motion, without notice to the landlord, for an order determining that the tenant has paid the full amount due under s. 74(4) and confirming that the eviction order is void. Such a motion must be accompanied by an affidavit setting out the details of any payments made to the landlord and should have attached any supporting documents upon which the tenant relies.[17] The motion material will be placed before a Member (in chambers) who will have to decide the motion solely based upon the affidavit and supporting documentation. The Member will generally not provide the tenant with an opportunity to provide additional documents or information and the Member does not have the power to refer the matter to a hearing.[18] Thus, the affidavit and supporting documentation must be clear and convincing or the motion will fail and the eviction will proceed.

The more common mistakes made by tenants on such motions include failing to provide sufficient details about payments and failing to include supporting documentation (such as copies of cheques, receipts and bank records). Payments made into the Board are easy to prove; all that is required is the deposit slip from the Board's bank showing the date and amount of the deposit. More detail is required for payments allegedly made to the landlord; specifics are required as to the date, time and method of each payment as well as the amount of each payment. Tenants should also realize that they cannot include any payments that were made prior to the date the order was issued. Presumably, all such payments were already taken into account by the Member who issued the eviction order. If what the tenant is really doing is attacking the validity of the order, then the tenant must seek to have the order overturned. Otherwise, the tenant must show that the amounts required by the order have been paid in full between the date the order was issued and the date upon which the landlord was entitled to file the order with the sheriff. Payments made before that period do not count! Payments made after the order is filed with the sheriff may be relevant under subsection 74(11) but not on a motion brought under s. 74(6).

[16] Rule 30 of the Board's Rules of Practice.

[17] Subsection 74(7) of the R.T.A.

[18] Subsection 74(8) of the R.T.A.

If the tenant's motion is denied (for instance, because the amount paid was insufficient or it was paid too late), an order will be issued to this effect and the Member will direct that any money paid into the Board by the tenant be refunded to the tenant.

If, however, the Member is satisfied that, based upon the motion material filed, the tenant has proven on a balance of probabilities that the necessary amounts have been paid at the right time to void the eviction order, the Member will issue an order declaring that the eviction order is void, and if any money has been paid into the Board, directing that such money be paid by the Board to the landlord. If the eviction order has been filed by the landlord with the sheriff's office, it will be the tenant's responsibility[19] to provide the sheriff with a copy of the new order from the Board (the "voiding order") to prove that the eviction order is void and to stop the eviction from proceeding.

What if the landlord disagrees with this new *ex parte* order (the "voiding order")? Pursuant to s. 74(9) of the R.T.A., within 10 days after such an order is issued, the landlord may, on notice to the tenant, make a motion to the Board to have the order set aside. The landlord must give a copy of the motion and the notice of hearing to the tenant at least 48 hours before the time set for the hearing.[20] The Board will then hold a hearing at which both the landlord and tenant will have an opportunity to adduce evidence and make submissions (s. 74(10)). If at the end of the hearing, the Member is satisfied that the tenant paid the full amount due under s. 74(4) before the eviction order became enforceable, the Member shall refuse to set aside the *ex parte* order made under s. 74(6). If, however, the Member is satisfied that the tenant did not pay the full amount required or did not pay it before the eviction order become enforceable, the Member shall issue an order setting aside the *ex parte* order made under s. 74(6) and shall confirm that the eviction order is *not* void.

In *Ramdeen v. Badwa*,[21] the landlord brought a motion to have the voiding order obtained by the tenants set aside. At the hearing of this motion, the Member found that the tenants had fabricated documents in order to make it appear that amounts had been paid to the landlord that were not, in fact, paid. A representative of the Ministry's Investigation and Enforcement Branch testified at this hearing that the tenants had submitted documents to the Tribunal on three previous occasions that turned out to be fraudulent and misleading. Since previous fines/costs of up to $1,000 appeared not to deter the tenants from continuing to file false and misleading documents with the Tribunal, the Member granted the landlord's motion (i.e., set aside the voiding

---

[19] Rule 30.3 of the Board's Rules of Practice.

[20] Rule 10.7 of the Board's Rules of Practice. Failure to comply with this Rule may result in dismissal or adjournment of the motion (Rule 10.8).

[21] (February 27, 2006), TEL-58129-SV, 2006 CarswellOnt 2096, [2006] O.R.H.T.D. No. 20 (Ont. Rental Housing Trib.).

order) and ordered the tenants to pay to the Tribunal $5,000 for its costs of the proceeding.[22]

One might assume that the Board has little discretion on such motions. The Member is not being asked to grant an eviction; rather, the Member is merely required to make factual findings in order to determine whether a previously issued eviction order has or has not become void. The Member, therefore, cannot rely upon the provisions of s. 83 (described in the next section of this chapter).[23] Either the full amount was paid or it was not. Either it was paid on time or it was not. If the goal of this process is efficiency and certainty, there is no room and no express authority under s. 74 for the exercise of any discretion on the part of Members to, in effect, prevent the eviction of tenants who have not strictly complied with the provisions of that section of the Act.

Nevertheless, the Board has the power to prevent an abuse of its process[24] and in appropriate circumstances, may refuse to set aside a voiding order even where the full amount required under s. 74(4) has not been paid (or has not been paid on time). Sometimes, certainty and efficiency must yield to fairness and decency. If the full amount is paid but is paid a few minutes late, is the Board obliged to allow the eviction to proceed? If the payment is 18 cents short, should a family be forcibly removed from their home?

This latter situation arose in *41-51 Brookwell Drive Ltd. v. Daniel*.[25] In order to void the eviction order, the tenant had to pay $1,184.18. She paid $1,184.00 — 18 cents short. The tenant filed an *ex parte* motion for an order declaring the eviction order to be void. Although, technically, the full amount had not been paid, the Tribunal issued an order declaring the eviction order void. The landlord brought a motion to set aside that voiding order. It was argued on behalf of the landlord that the Tribunal had no discretion in this matter and that either the correct amount was paid (and paid on time) or it was not. The Member agreed that he had no power to grant relief under s. 84 of the T.P.A. (now s. 83 of the R.T.A.) as it was not an application for eviction. Nevertheless, the Member refused to set aside the voiding order, concluding that it was not the intention of the legislature to have families evicted for mistakenly short-changing a landlord by a few pennies. In essence, the Member read into s. 72 of the T.P.A. (now s. 74 of the R.T.A.) a provision that substantial compliance is sufficient. In the alternative, the Member found

[22] Note that under the Tribunal's Rules of Procedure, the usual maximum that can be awarded for Tribunal costs is $500, but Members retain the power to waive this usual limit in exceptional circumstances.

[23] *Geiger, Re* (Feb. 21, 2006), TEL-57314-SV, 2006 CarswellOnt 2095, [2006] O.R.H.T.D. No. 19 (Ont. Rental Housing Trib.).

[24] Under s. 23 of the *Statutory Powers Procedure Act*. See the section on "Preventing Abuse of Process" in Chapter 2.

[25] (July 30, 2003), TNL-47186-SV, [2003] O.R.H.T.D. No. 106, 2003 CarswellOnt 4258 (Ont. Rental Housing Trib.).

that it would bring the administration of justice into disrepute to allow the tenant to be evicted in such circumstances. The landlord's motion could therefore be viewed as an abuse of the Tribunal's process since the result would be contrary to the public interest. The Member did not accept the landlord's argument that the public's interest in having certainty and finality in such matters overrode the public's interest in ensuring that justice prevails. I am not aware of any cases in which this precedent has been followed.

Similarly, where the tenants had the money available to give to the landlord prior to the deadline set out in the order but the landlord instructed the tenants to hold the cash so that he could pick up the money from them but he failed to do so until two days after the deadline, the Tribunal granted the tenants' *ex parte* motion to void the eviction order.[26]

In *Goldcrest Properties Inc., Re*,[27] the tenant was attempting to pay the amount needed to void the order by making a series of payments to the landlord. The landlord added up all of the payments made and advised the tenant in a written receipt that there remained a balance of $86. In fact, the landlord made an error in its calculations and $136 was actually owing at the time. The tenant paid to the landlord, before the eviction order became enforceable, the $86 it had advised the tenant was needed to void the order. Notwithstanding that the tenant was $50 short of paying the full amount ordered, the Tribunal granted the tenant's motion to void the eviction order, stating that it would be unfair to refuse in circumstances where the tenant relied upon the landlord's representation.[28]

Where, however, it is the tenant's own fault that payment was received late by the landlord, the Tribunal was not prepared to make such an exception.[29]

(c) Payment After Eviction Order Becomes Enforceable (NEW)

Pursuant to s. 74(11) of the R.T.A., a tenant may make a motion, on notice to the landlord, to set aside an eviction order (based solely upon arrears of rent) if, after the order becomes enforceable *but before it is executed*, the tenant pays an amount to the Board and files an affidavit sworn by the tenant

---

[26] *Idris v. Autenrieth* (Jan. 5, 2006), CEL-48224-VO, 2006 CarswellOnt 2142 (Ont. Rental Housing Trib.).

[27] (July 21, 2006), SWL-81881-VO, 2006 CarswellOnt 9157 (Ont. Rental Housing Trib.).

[28] Although the Member states in her decision that she relies upon "the principles of equity", since the Tribunal lacks the equitable jurisdiction of a court, it would probably have been preferable for the Member to have relied upon the concept of abuse of process and the fact that, had the Tribunal denied the tenant's motion in these circumstances, it would have brought the administration of justice into disrepute.

[29] *Plewes v. Higenell* (Dec. 14, 2005), CEL-48844-SV, 2005 CarswellOnt 7823 (Ont. Rental Housing Trib.).

stating that the amount, together with any amounts previously paid to the landlord, is at least the sum of the following amounts:

1. The amount of rent that is in arrears under the tenancy agreement;
2. The amount of additional rent that would have been due under the tenancy agreement as at the date of payment by the tenant had notice of termination not been given;
3. The amount of NSF cheque charges charged by financial institutions to the landlord in respect of cheques tendered to the landlord by or on behalf of the tenant, as allowed by the Board in an application by the landlord under s. 87;
4. The amount of administration charges payable by the tenant for the NSF cheques, as allowed by the Board in an application by the landlord under s. 87; and
5. The costs ordered by the Board.

Such a motion can only be brought by a tenant if the tenant has never previously brought this type of motion during this tenancy.[30]

Although subsection 74(11) refers to an amount being paid "to the Board", according to a recent amendment (July 5, 2007) to the Board's Interpretation Guideline #11, the tenant may pay the amount required to be paid under the subsection to the landlord, to the Board, or in part to both. This interpretation avoids the "absurd result" of refusing to void an order and allowing a tenant to be evicted where the tenant paid the full amount required, but simply paid part of that amount directly to the landlord. This interpretation was accepted in Landlord and Tenant Board File No. TS-14313-SA (August 8, 2008).

The eviction order is stayed when a motion under s. 74(11) is received by the Board and shall not be enforced during the stay.[31] It is the tenant's responsibility, however, to notify the Court Enforcement Office of the stay to ensure that the eviction order is not enforced pending the outcome of the motion.[32]

The Board will then hold a hearing at which both the landlord and tenant will have an opportunity to adduce evidence and make submissions. The Board will make enquiries as to the amounts paid and the method and timing of such payments. The Board will also accept evidence from the landlord with respect to any non-refundable amounts paid by the landlord under the *Administration of Justice Act* (i.e., the fees charged by the Court Enforcement Office) for the purpose of enforcing the eviction order. If some or all of the payments have been made by a non-certified cheque or cheques, the hearing

[30] Subsection 74(12) of the R.T.A.

[31] Subsection 74(13) of the R.T.A.

[32] Rule 30 of the Board's Rules of Practice.

of the motion may have to be delayed to ensure that the cheques in question are honoured by the bank (see Interpretation Guideline #11).

If, at the end of the hearing, the Member is satisfied that the tenant paid the full amount due under subsection 74(11) after the order became enforceable but before it was executed, the Member shall issue an order declaring the order is void. If the Board determines that the landlord has incurred any non-refundable amounts under the *Administration of Justice Act* for the purpose of enforcing the eviction order, the Board will specify in its order the amount that the tenant must pay related to such an expense and state that its order (voiding the eviction order) is not effective unless the tenant pays the specified amount into the Board by a date specified in the order and an employee of the Board issues a notice under subsection 74(16).[33] If the tenant does not pay the specified amount into the Board by the date specified in the order, the stay of the eviction order ceases to apply and the order may be enforced.[34]

If, at the end of the hearing, the Member is satisfied that the tenant has not paid the full amount due under subsection 74(11), the Member shall issue an order lifting the stay of the eviction order (i.e., allowing the eviction to proceed).[35] In addition, if the Board determines that the landlord has incurred any non-refundable amounts under the *Administration of Justice Act* for the purpose of enforcing the eviction order, the Board may make an order that the tenant pay such amount to the landlord.[36]

In Landlord and Tenant Board File No. TNL-06006-SA (January 18, 2008), the tenant brought a motion for a declaration that the eviction order was voided as a result of the tenant having paid all amounts required under s. 74(11). At the time the tenant swore an affidavit stating that the necessary payment had been made, he had not yet actually delivered the funds to the landlord. The Member could have simply denied the motion based upon the tenant having filed a false or misleading affidavit. The Member, however, went on to find that, once the uncertified cheque in question had been delivered to the landlord, it still would not constitute payment until it "cleared" (five business days later). The Member cites no authority for the proposition that payment by cheque is not deemed to be made until at least five business days after it is received by the payee. As of the date of the hearing, the cheque had not yet cleared but it was scheduled to clear within a few days. The Member could simply have adjourned the hearing to see if the cheque cleared. Instead, the Member dismissed the motion because, as of the date of the hearing, the amounts required had not yet been "paid" to the landlord (as this Member understood that term). Assuming the cheque did clear a few days

---

33 Subsection 74(15) of the R.T.A.

34 Subsection 74(17) of the R.T.A.

35 Paragraph 74(14)(b) of the R.T.A.

36 Subsection 74(18) of the R.T.A.

later, the tenant would not have been able to file a new motion before the Board because, pursuant to s. 74(11), this type of motion can only be brought once during a tenancy. The tenant would have had to file a request for a review of the order denying his motion. To avoid this harsh result in the future, tenants should consider paying the necessary amount by cash or certified funds into the Board itself. In that way, there should be no question as to when the money was paid or whether it was received on time.

In Landlord and Tenant Board File No. TSL-06312-VO (November 13, 2007), the tenant tendered $300 in cash to the landlord on the last day permitted under an eviction order (prior to the order becoming "enforceable"). By operation of s. 74(4), this would have been sufficient to void the order. The landlord, however, wished to ensure that the tenant could not do this again in the future so the landlord refused to accept the payment. As a result, the order became enforceable and the landlord decided to proceed with the eviction. The tenant again tendered payment and the landlord again rejected it (even though no additional costs had yet been incurred by the landlord). The landlord then filed the eviction order with the Sheriff. The tenant was forced to bring a motion under s. 74(11) and paid an amount into the Board that did not include the Sheriff's fees. The tenant objected to being forced to pay the Sheriff's fees since the eviction order was effectively voided when payment was tendered before the order became enforceable. The landlord argued that the Member had no discretion in this regard and that the eviction order could not now be voided under s. 74(11) without the Sheriff's fees being reimbursed by the tenant. The Member found that the fees paid to the Sheriff by the landlord were not paid "for the purpose of enforcing the order" as the landlord ought to have accepted the money when it was originally tendered, *before* the landlord incurred any Sheriff fees. The Member granted the tenant's motion and declared that the eviction order had been voided (and forced the landlord to absorb the Sheriff's fees). While I agree with the fairness of the result, I think that this is an unnecessarily complicated way of getting there. It would have been more accurate to simply state that, by refusing to accept the cash payment tendered before the eviction order became enforceable, the landlord's subsequent filing of the eviction order with the Sheriff and the consequences that flowed therefrom constituted an abuse of process. The Member would then have been within her jurisdiction to make whatever orders were necessary to prevent such abuse. Alternatively, the Member could have issued an order declaring that the order had become void when the money was first offered to the landlord, pursuant to s. 74(4).

In Landlord and Tenant Board File Number TSL-09947-SA (April 25, 2008), it was found that the tenant's affidavit contained inaccuracies concerning the amounts that had been paid. Since the amounts that were actually paid were sufficient to comply with s. 74(11) of the R.T.A., however, the Member set aside the eviction order but awarded costs of the motion against the tenant.

5. THE PROVINCIAL RENT BANK PROGRAM

The vast majority of evictions in Ontario are based upon the failure of tenants to pay their rent. If a tenant is experiencing a short-term economic crisis, it may be possible for the landlord and tenant to work out a repayment schedule. If the landlord is unwilling to negotiate, the tenant may face eviction if he or she is unable to quickly come up with some cash.

In an effort to assist low-income tenants, the provincial government set up a "rent bank" program. A rent bank is a short-term mechanism through which low-income tenants (who are not on welfare and are not living in subsidized housing) may apply to receive financial assistance to address short-term rent arrears.

According to the Ministry of Municipal Affairs and Housing, since it began in 2004, the program provided $18.8 million to help 13,200 households avoid eviction.

Although widely considered to be one of the most cost-effective methods of preventing homelessness, the future of this program is now uncertain. In late April 2008, the Ministry announced that the program had run out of money and would not be funded for 2008-2009. For more information, please refer to the Ministry's website at *www.mah.gov.on.ca* or contact the Landlord and Tenant Board.

Tenants with outstanding utility bills can still obtain assistance through the government's Energy Emergency Fund, administered by the Ministry of Community and Social Services.

6. RELIEF FROM FORFEITURE

(a) General

Equitable relief for tenants was primarily for relief against forfeiture when a landlord was seeking to forfeit a lease and regain possession. The landlord's claim for forfeiture was based on the tenant wrongfully continuing in possession without paying the rent or failing to remedy breaches of his covenants in the lease. Generally speaking, relief against forfeiture would be granted if the tenant paid up the arrears and the landlord's costs, or remedied the breaches of covenants. The result would be to put the lease back in good standing.

Equitable relief was provided for in Part IV of the *Landlord and Tenant Act*[37] by the terms of s. 113(1)(*g*), by which the judge may grant "relief against forfeiture on such terms and conditions as the judge may decide", and in s.

---

[37] In this instance, and hereinafter, the phrase "Part IV" refers to Part IV of the *Landlord and Tenant Act*, R.S.O. 1990, c. L.7.

113(11) the judge "may impose such terms and conditions as the judge considers appropriate".

Under the T.P.A., the Rental Housing Tribunal had broad powers to try to ensure just results. Many of these powers have been retained (and, in some cases, enhanced) under the R.T.A. For instance, the Board has very flexible remedies for lack of repair, illegal entry, changing locks, withholding supply of vital services, substantial interference, and harassment, including the power "to make any other order that it considers appropriate" (ss. 30 and 31 of the R.T.A.). By s. 204(1) of the R.T.A. (formerly s. 190(1) of the T.P.A.), "the Board may include in an order whatever conditions it considers fair in the circumstances." Also, consider s. 10 of the *Interpretation Act*,[38] which provides that:

> Every Act shall be deemed to be remedial, whether its immediate purport is to direct the doing of any thing that the Legislature deems to be for the public good or to prevent or punish the doing of any thing that it deems to be contrary to the public good, and shall accordingly receive such fair, large and liberal construction and interpretation as will best ensure the attainment of the object of the Act according to its true intent, meaning and spirit.

The closest provision in the current legislation to s. 113 of the *Landlord and Tenant Act* is s. 83 of the R.T.A. (formerly s. 84 of the T.P.A.). By s. 83(1)(*a*), the Board may refuse to grant an application unless satisfied, having regard to all the circumstances it would be unfair to refuse. Alternatively, by s. 83(1)(*b*), the Board may order that the enforcement of the order for eviction be postponed for a period of time. Finally, s. 83(3) prohibits retaliatory evictions.

(b) Waiver

At common law, accepting rent from a tenant who is in breach of his or her obligations has been held to constitute a waiver of the landlord's right to forfeiture of the lease. In *Chernec v. Smith*,[39] it was stated that the acceptance of rent falling due after there was a right of forfeiture, waived the right of forfeiture. This was so even if the acceptance of the rent was conditional and without prejudice to the prior right of forfeiture. In *Central Estates (Belgravia) Ltd. v. Woolgar (No. 2)*,[40] acceptance of rent by a clerk in the landlord's office, after knowledge of the right of forfeit, was held to waive the forfeiture even though the tenant knew the landlord intended to forfeit the lease. The court stated the landlord's intention was immaterial. The acceptance of rent was an unequivocal act recognizing the continuation of the tenancy.

---

[38] R.S.O. 1990, c. I.11.

[39] [1946] O.W.N. 513 (Ont. C.A.).

[40] [1972] 3 All E.R. 610 (Eng. C.A.).

After serving a notice for early termination for cause, a landlord served a further notice for a rent increase. This had been held to be an unequivocal waiver of the notice of termination in *Aaron Construction Ltd. v. Kelley*.[41] But subsequently this case was overruled by the Divisional Court in *Nicholson v. Michalas*.[42] The court's reasoning was that the notice of rent increase was only to maintain the integrity of the rent structure of the premises within the applicable rent review, and there was no waiver in law or by intention of the landlord.

However to alleviate this, s. 112(2) of Part IV of the *Landlord and Tenant Act* permitted a landlord to continue receiving rent or compensation for use and occupation after a notice of termination without it being treated as a waiver of the notice unless the parties agreed that the notice was waived.

The payment of the arrears of rent and in fact rent for three months after an order for termination had been made, along with the judge finding that there was a verbal assurance by the landlord that the tenant could stay on, all together amounted to waiver of forfeiture. The outstanding writ for possession was set aside: *Coutoulakis and Lines*.[43]

In another case decided under the *Landlord and Tenant Act*, even though the tenant had been evicted, relief from forfeiture by reason of waiver was granted. The landlord had continued threatening the tenant with a writ of possession obtained earlier for arrears of rent which the tenant then paid, and which payment was accepted by the landlord. The landlord subsequently increased the rent twice (within the permitted range) and then, for subsequent arrears of rent, the landlord had the sheriff exercise the old writ for possession and evicted the tenant. The court granted relief from forfeiture and held first, that using the stale writ of possession was an abuse of the process of the court, secondly, that within the meaning of s. 112(2) of Part IV the acceptance of rent was either a waiver of the writ of possession, or had effected a reinstatement of the tenancy, or the creation of a new tenancy. The writ of possession was set aside, the landlord was ordered to let the tenant back into possession, and the judge ordered damages of $100 to recompense the tenant for alternative accommodation: *Toronto Apt. Bldgs. Co. v. Griffiths*.[44]

Currently, ss. 45 and 103(2) of the R.T.A. offer some protection to a landlord who wishes to collect money from a tenant or otherwise deal with the tenancy without necessarily being seen as waiving breaches by the tenant. Section 45 states as follows:

> Unless a landlord and tenant agree otherwise, the landlord does not waive a notice of termination, reinstate a tenancy or create a new tenancy,

---

[41] (1982), 35 O.R. (2d) 244 (Ont. Co. Ct.).

[42] (1988), 64 O.R. (2d) 238 (Ont. Div. Ct.).

[43] (October 27, 1982), Doc. CCOM8043/83 (Ont. Co. Ct.).

[44] (1982), 1982 CarswellOnt 1900 (Ont. Co. Ct.).

(a) by giving the tenant a notice of rent increase; or
(b) by accepting arrears of rent or compensation for the use or occupation of a rental unit after,
   (i) the landlord or the tenant gives a notice of termination of the tenancy,
   (ii) the landlord and the tenant enter into an agreement to terminate the tenancy, or
   (iii) the Board makes an eviction order or an order terminating the tenancy.

Subsection 103(2) of the R.T.A. states as follows:

> A landlord does not create a tenancy with an unauthorized occupant of a rental unit by accepting compensation for the use and occupation of the rental unit, unless the landlord and the unauthorized occupant agree otherwise.

In all other cases of action or inaction by a landlord, any unequivocal act whereby the landlord recognizes the continuing relationship of landlord and tenant after the cause of forfeiture, will be treated as a waiver of the right to forfeit: *Central Estates (Belgravia) Ltd. v. Woolgar (No. 2)*.[45]

In Landlord and Tenant Board File Nos. SOL-18125-SA / SOL-17038 (Feb. 18, 2009), the parties agreed that the tenancy would be terminated and the tenants would vacate the rental unit on December 31, 2008. The landlord obtained an *ex parte* order to this effect. The landlord had collected no rent for December since the landlord assumed that it would be covered by the rent deposit and the tenant would be leaving at the end of that month. On January 2, 2009, the landlord discovered that the tenant had not vacated the rental unit. The landlord accepted $800 from the tenant and took steps to have the eviction order enforced. It was the landlord's position that he was entitled to apply that money towards the rent owing for December. The tenant's position was that, by accepting rent, the landlord had agreed to create a new tenancy. The Member found as a fact that there had been no agreement to reinstate the tenancy or create a new tenancy and that, pursuant to s. 45 of the R.T.A., absent such an agreement, the landlord is not deemed to have reinstated the tenancy or to have created a new tenancy simply by accepting arrears of rent or compensation for use or occupation of the rental unit.

Note that, to avoid confusion, in a case such as this where there were no arrears of rent owing to the landlord, what the landlord should have done was to treat December as the last month of the tenancy (since there was an order from the Board terminating the tenancy as of December 31) and to apply the rent deposit towards the rent owing for that month. Then, starting in January 2009, the tenant would owe *compensation* for each day that the tenant remained in possession of the unit and any money tendered by the tenant should explicitly have been applied towards such *compensation* and should not have been accepted as payment of *rent* (which implies that the tenancy is continuing).

---

45 [1972] 3 All E.R. 610 (Eng. C.A.).

Just as there is now some protection against a landlord being seen to waive its rights, there is also some protection for tenants.

First, subject only to s. 194,[46] a provision in a tenancy agreement inconsistent with the R.T.A. or the regulations is void (s. 4 of the R.T.A.). Second, even s. 194 of the R.T.A. has limits.

Many applications are successfully mediated at the Board (formerly the Tribunal). The Board derives its statutory authority to mediate disputes from s. 194 of the R.T.A. Subsection 194(2) of the R.T.A. provides that a settlement mediated under s. 194 may contain provisions that contravene any provision of the R.T.A. This ability to mediate terms that contravene the Act is limited. One type of limitation is set out expressly in s. 194(3) of the Act (i.e., the amount of rent increase that can be mediated is limited). Another type of limitation is with respect to the jurisdiction of the Board. The parties cannot dictate how a Member will exercise his or her powers under the Act. In particular, the parties cannot limit the power of a member to grant relief under s. 83 (formerly s. 84 of the T.P.A.).

Section 83 can become relevant to mediated settlements in the following fashion. More often than not, the terms of a mediated settlement will specifically be made enforceable by reference to s. 78 of the Act. Section 78 of the R.T.A. (formerly s. 77 of the T.P.A.) provides a mechanism whereby a landlord can obtain an *ex parte* eviction order upon the breach by the tenant of certain types of terms in a mediated settlement. Section 78 also provides a mechanism whereby a tenant can seek to have such an order set aside. When that occurs, a hearing will take place to determine whether or not the tenant has breached the terms of the mediated agreement. During such a hearing, if it is determined that a breach has occurred and the landlord is seeking an eviction order, the Board must consider whether granting relief under s. 83 of the Act is appropriate. In the past, some landlords, concerned that the Tribunal might be too lenient with such tenants, attempted to include in mediated agreements a term whereby the tenant purported to waive (in advance) any right to rely upon the provisions of s. 84 (now s. 83) should the tenant breach the terms of the agreement and should the matter come before a Member of the Tribunal. The Tribunal held that such a term is either void or unenforceable as the parties have no right to oust or usurp the jurisdiction of the Tribunal.[47] Presumably, the Board will adopt a similar approach.

---

[46] Section 194 of the R.T.A. permits parties to a settlement, mediated by the Board, to agree to terms that are inconsistent with the *Act*.

[47] *Crestview Investments Corp. v. Ali* (May 8, 2003), TSL-50528-SA, 2003 CarswellOnt 2634 (Ont. Rental Housing Trib.).

(c) Subsection 83(1)

Pursuant to s. 83(1) of the R.T.A. (formerly s. 84(1) of the T.P.A.), upon an application for an order evicting a tenant or subtenant, the Board may, despite any other provision of the R.T.A. or the tenancy agreement:

(a) refuse to grant the application unless satisfied, having regard to all the circumstances, that it would be unfair to refuse; or
(b) order that the enforcement of the order or eviction be postponed for a period of time.

On every eviction application that proceeds to a hearing, the Board must review the circumstances and consider whether or not it should exercise its powers under subsection 83(1).[48]

Even if a subtenant was not a party to the original application (i.e., the application by the landlord to evict the head tenant), the subtenant may well have the right to seek to be added as a party to the application and to ask the Board to grant relief under s. 83 (whether or not the head tenant participates in the hearing).[49]

In general terms, in deciding whether to exercise his or her discretion and delay or deny an eviction (be it absolutely or subject to compliance with specified terms), the presiding Member must consider all of the circumstances to determine whether it would be unfair to grant relief to the tenant. Factors that have recently been considered by the Landlord and Tenant Board include (but are not limited to) the following:

1. the grounds for termination;
2. the potential risk posed to other tenants in the complex and the landlord by the continuation of the tenancy;
3. the past conduct of the tenant, including the explanation for the breach of the *Act* and the tenant's efforts (if applicable) to rectify the problems identified in the notice of termination;[50]
4. whether such relief has previously been granted to the tenant;

---

[48] Subsection 83(2) of the R.T.A.

[49] See *Baker v. Hayward* (1977), 78 D.L.R. (3d) 762 (Ont. C.A.) in which the Ontario Court of Appeal held to this effect under similar provisions of the *Landlord and Tenant Act*. See also s. 187 of the R.T.A. (formerly s. 174 of the T.P.A.).

[50] For example, if all the arrears have been paid and the only amount owing by the time of the hearing is the landlord's filing fee, a Member may well refuse to terminate the tenancy: Landlord and Tenant Board File No. CEL-00488 (March 16, 2007). Not surprisingly, a Board Member will be less likely to exercise his/her discretion in favour of a tenant who has made little effort to rectify the problem: Landlord and Tenant Board File No. SOL-00750 (March 30, 2007) and Landlord and Tenant Board File No. NOL-05970 (Jan. 23, 2009).

5. the duration of the tenancy;[51]
6. the likelihood that the conduct that formed the basis of the landlord's application will be repeated if the tenancy is allowed to continue;[52]
7. the potential harm that will be caused to the tenant (and members of the tenant's household, especially young children) by an eviction (or by an *immediate* eviction);[53]
8. the past conduct of the landlord;[54]
9. the potential harm to the landlord if the tenancy is not terminated or is not terminated immediately;[55] and

---

[51] Where the tenancy is of short duration, typically fewer leniencies will be shown: Landlord and Tenant Board File No. CEL-00426 (March 7, 2007) and Landlord and Tenant Board File No. SOL-00750 (March 30, 2007). Where the tenancy is of considerable duration (especially where it has previously been a good tenancy), there is a much greater chance that the Member will grant some relief to the tenant: Landlord and Tenant Board File No. SOL-00489 (March 22, 2007); Landlord and Tenant Board File No. SOL-00042 (Feb. 22, 2007); and Landlord and Tenant Board File No. TNL-20354 (Jan. 21, 2009).

[52] If it is obvious that there is no reasonable prospect that the tenant has the ability or inclination to correct the problem (such as pay the rent or pay the rent on time), the Board is unlikely to grant an indulgence: Landlord and Tenant Board File No. CEL-00426 (March 7, 2007); Landlord and Tenant Board File No. SOL-00268 (March 7, 2007).

[53] See, for example, Landlord and Tenant Board File No. CEL-00683 (March 20, 2007), in which the Member indicates in her order that the fact that the tenants have children is one of the factors she considered under s. 83. Similarly, a Member cites as the grounds for granting relief the fact that the tenant is a single parent with four minor children: Landlord and Tenant Board File No. CEL-00537 (March 20, 2007). In Landlord and Tenant Board File No. SOL-00505 (March 22, 2007), the Member delays the eviction by about three weeks on the basis that the tenant has three children and requires some additional time to pay the money owing or find alternative accommodations. Serious health issues that make it difficult or dangerous for the tenant to move are also relevant considerations: Landlord and Tenant Board File No. TEL-00636 (March 20, 2007). Inability to find alternative housing should also be considered; the Board may be reluctant to evict a tenant from "housing of last resort", which would effectively leave the tenant homeless: Landlord and Tenant Board File No. SOL-18687 (Jan. 27, 2009). If the tenants have already had several months to find alternate accommodations, this can also be taken into consideration: Landlord and Tenant Board File No. TEL-00543 / TET-00063 (March 19, 2007).

[54] See, for example, Landlord and Tenant Board File No. CEL-00683 (March 20, 2007), in which the Member was influenced by the landlord's unprofessional conduct (failing to keep records, failing to issue receipts, using his seven-year-old daughter to act as his agent in dealings with the tenants, etc.).

[55] Relief under s. 83(1) ought to be refused if the prejudice to the landlord outweighs the prejudice to the tenant. For example, where the tenants owed substantial arrears of rent (over $6,000) and the landlords were homeless and were expecting a baby and desperately required the unit for their own occupation, the Member felt that the prejudice to the landlords in delaying the eviction outweighed the potential prejudice to the tenant and her school-aged children in having to relocate: Landlord and Tenant Board File No. SWL-21685 (Jan. 15, 2009).

10. the conduct of the parties before the Board.[56]

A recent example of a case that encompasses many of the above-noted factors is found in Landlord and Tenant Board File No. TNL-15221 (Jan. 30, 2009). This was an application by the landlord to terminate the tenancy for non-payment of rent. The parties previously attended at the Board on this application and, in July 2008, entered into a mediated agreement.

Unfortunately, the tenant was unable to abide by the terms of that agreement and missed a payment. The landlord requested that the application be re-opened. It was undisputed that, by the time this case came back before the Board, the tenant owed the landlord almost $5,000. In considering whether to grant relief under s. 83(1) to this tenant, the Member wrote as follows:

> I have taken into consideration the long tenancy, the fact that there are children involved in the tenancy, the work related accident which resulted in financial hardship because of some delays and mix up with the employment insurance agency, the other Tenant's inability to carry the rent by herself with earnings from a part time Wal-Mart job, and the sign of sincere commitment to maintain this tenancy by paying off $2,000 of the balance at the hearing.

Having considered all of this, the Member granted the tenant's request and refused to grant an eviction, but on terms that established a repayment schedule that would put the tenancy back into good standing within about six weeks (subject to termination of the tenancy pursuant to s. 78 of the R.T.A., should the tenant fail to comply with the terms of the order).

(i) *Refusal of Eviction*

To put the wording of para. 83(1)(a) somewhat more affirmatively, a tenant has the opportunity to persuade or satisfy the Board that the tenant's rights should be protected and that it would not be unfair to the landlord to deny the landlord possession of the unit.

Although the Board's power under s. 83(1) is discretionary, that discretion must be exercised in a reasonable fashion. To understand how this power will be used, it is helpful to examine the following: judicial decisions made under similar provisions of the *Landlord and Tenant Act*, decisions rendered by the Rental Housing Tribunal with respect to the identical provision under

[56] See, for example, Landlord and Tenant Board File No. CEL-01002 (March 30, 2007), in which the Member refuses to grant relief to the tenant based on the tenant's "unreasonable requests" and "his conduct in the hearing room". Also see Landlord and Tenant Board File No. EAL-00242 (March 16, 2007), in which it can be inferred that the Member felt that the tenant was attempting to mislead the Board (by alleging that certain payments were made to the landlord but then failing to comply with a direction of the Member to file the documents that the tenant stated were available to corroborate the tenant's story).

the T.P.A. (s. 84(1)), the Landlord and Tenant Board's Interpretation Guideline (No. 7) and decisions that have been released by the Board.

The Rental Housing Tribunal's Interpretation Guideline on Relief from Eviction originally stated that, "The Tribunal has no responsibility to consider these issues unless they are raised by the tenant."[57] Although the onus of raising any defence generally falls upon the respondent, the Tribunal was criticized by the Divisional Court on a number of occasions for not explicitly stating in its decisions whether or not relief under s. 84 of the T.P.A. was considered where the circumstances of the case clearly demanded such a consideration.[58] An unsophisticated and unrepresented tenant may not refer to the relevant provision by section number but may say to the adjudicator things like, "It's not fair" or "I've lived here for ten years" or "This is the first problem I've ever had with the landlord" or "It will never happen again" or the tenant may ask of the Member, "Isn't there anything you can do to help me?" The tenant may be too intimidated to speak during the hearing and may need to be invited or prompted to make submissions. Under the T.P.A., there was a growing recognition that, in deciding whether or not to grant an eviction order, Members had to take positive steps to ensure they had sufficient information to make a reasoned decision about whether or not it would be unfair to refuse to grant an eviction.[59]

This obligation on Members has now been reflected in subsection 83(2) of the R.T.A., which provides that, if a hearing is held, the Board shall not grant the application (for an order evicting a tenant) unless it has reviewed the circumstances and considered whether or not it should exercise its powers under subsection 83(1).[60] Because consideration of relief under s. 83(1) is mandatory, some Board Members have developed the practice, even where no tenant has appeared at the hearing, of asking landlords if they are aware of any circumstances that would make it unfair to grant an eviction.

As previously indicated, Members take into account numerous factors in deciding whether or not to exercise their discretion under s. 83(1), including: the grounds for termination; the potential risk posed to other tenants by the continuation of this tenancy; the past conduct of the tenant; the duration of the tenancy; the likelihood that the conduct that formed the basis of the landlord's application will be repeated if the tenancy is allowed to continue;

---

[57] Although the Tribunal's Guideline did recognize that a Member may raise such issues on his or her own initiative.

[58] See *Luray Investments Limited v. Recine-Pynn* (1999), 1999 CarswellOnt 3055 (Ont. Div. Ct.) and *Toronto Community Housing Corp. v. Greaves* (2004), 2004 CarswellOnt 5311 (Ont. Div. Ct.), overturning (May 29, 2003), TNL-41859, 2003 CarswellOnt 6367 (Ont. Rental Housing Trib.).

[59] See, for example, *Forest Hill Gates v. Wolch* (2007), 2007 CarswellOnt 1864 (Ont. Div. Ct.) in which it was held that the failure of the Tribunal member to have afforded the tenant an opportunity to address this issue constituted a denial of natural justice.

[60] I.e., the discretionary power to refuse to grant the eviction or to delay the eviction.

the potential harm that will be caused to the tenant (and members of the tenant's household) by an eviction; the conduct of the landlord; and the interests of the landlord.

With respect to the grounds for termination and the potential risk posed to other tenants, obviously illegal acts and conduct that has seriously impaired the safety of others is likely to weigh heavily against the granting of relief under s. 83(1). The Board will consider the seriousness of the conduct, whether the tenant or someone on the premises committed the act and whether the Board can be satisfied it will not happen again.

When a tenant was involved in drug trafficking, relief from forfeiture was not granted: *Ottawa-Carleton Regional Housing Authority v. Calbeck*.[61]

In another drug trafficking case, it was the son who was charged; the judge felt sorry for the mother and granted relief from forfeiture provided that the son vacated the apartment. The judge added the condition that if the son moved back into the apartment or visited and had drugs in his possession, the landlord could move *ex parte* to terminate the lease and for possession of the unit: *Ottawa-Carleton Regional Housing Authority v. Daley*.[62]

In *South Hastings Non-Profit Housing Corporation and Curran*,[63] the landlord served notice of termination for the illegal act of growing marijuana. The tenant admitted doing so and pleaded in writing to the Tribunal to let her continue as a tenant. The Tribunal, applying s. 190 of the T.P.A. (now s. 204 of the R.T.A.), dismissed the landlord's application for possession with the condition that no other illegal act would be committed or permitted. As the Tribunal said, the eviction asked for by the Housing Authority would cause undue hardship for the tenant and her family. Neither the tenant nor the public interest which provides financial assistance to the Housing Authority would be well served by evicting her. If it happened again her tenancy would be terminated.

In *Windsor Construction Co. Ltd. and Quispe*,[64] the tenant's boyfriend was involved in a fist fight with the boyfriend of the tenant's daughter. Later, the daughter's boyfriend returned and caused damage to the complex by breaking a window in the lobby area. The Tribunal held the tenant responsible for the conduct of persons she permitted into the complex but the eviction was made conditional so that if the daughter moved out of the unit by a specified date, the order would become void.

In *1343892 Ontario Inc. v. Macdonald*,[65] it was held by the Tribunal that where the illegal acts are relatively minor it is appropriate to exercise discretion under s. 84(1) of the T.P.A. in favour of the tenant and to refuse to grant

---

[61] (1989), 1989 CarswellOnt 2548 (Ont. Dist. Ct.).

[62] (1990), 1990 CarswellOnt 1931 (Ont. Gen. Div.).

[63] (June 25, 1999), EAL-06239 (Ont. Rental Housing Trib.).

[64] (Feb. 10, 1999), TNL-04198 (Ont. Rental Housing Trib.).

[65] (Sept. 19, 2001), SOL-25170, [2001] O.R.H.T.D. No. 129 (Ont. Rental Housing Trib.).

an eviction. This case involved an isolated threat made in the heat of the moment (and the addition by the tenant of a deck to a mobile home without first obtaining the consent of the landlord). The Tribunal refused to grant an eviction based upon these facts.

In *Toronto Community Housing Corporation v. Sturge*,[66] the tenant illegally possessed a small amount of marijuana. He used it for medical purposes. His conduct did not disturb or threaten anyone else. In these circumstances, the Member found it appropriate to grant relief from eviction. Similarly, in *Waterloo (Regional Municipality) Waterloo (Region Housing) v. Cluney*,[67] the tenant was found to have been in possession of marijuana in the rental unit. The tenant required the marijuana for medical reasons. The Member exercised his discretion and refused to grant an eviction on the condition that, for the rest of the tenancy, the tenant not grow, cultivate or produce marijuana in the rental unit.

In *Peel Housing Corp. v. Anderson*,[68] the tenant accidentally started a fire in the unit. The Member exercised his discretion under s. 84(1) of the T.P.A. and refused to grant an eviction upon certain terms (including requiring the tenant to pay the landlord, in installments, for the damage to the premises).

In *Gateway Properties v. Bloom*,[69] the tenant endangered others by throwing a drill from his balcony. Since the tenant suffered from schizophrenia, was receiving treatment, was being closely monitored and had a supportive family, the Member felt that the danger of future incidents was not great. The Member was likely also influenced by the fact that the tenancy had existed for 23 years. The Member exercised her discretion under s. 84(1) of the T.P.A. and refused to grant an eviction.

This last case brings to mind the Divisional Court's ruling in *Walmer Developments v. Wolch*,[70] wherein the Court held that the Tribunal (now the Board) has an obligation in relevant cases to consider under s. 84(1) of the T.P.A. (now s. 83(1) of the R.T.A.) what efforts, if any, a landlord has made to accommodate a tenant's disability so that the tenant will no longer be in breach of the tenant's obligations. Members must be alert to a landlord's duty to accommodate under the *Ontario Human Rights Code* and the relevance of these issues to a Member's decision with respect to whether or not to grant relief from forfeiture. A full discussion of this topic can be found in Chapter 15.

The impact of an eviction can be particularly severe on those for whom finding alternative accommodations will be very difficult. This is clearly a relevant consideration in the case of tenants who live in subsidized and rent-

---

[66] (Nov. 22, 2001), TSL-31750, [2001] O.R.H.T.D. No. 142 (Ont. Rental Housing Trib.).

[67] (Feb. 4, 2005), SWL-66940, 2005 CarswellOnt 1280 (Ont. Rental Housing Trib.).

[68] (May 20, 2004), CEL-36643, 2004 CarswellOnt 2201 (Ont. Rental Housing Trib.).

[69] (Feb. 5, 1999), TNL-03614 (Ont. Rental Housing Trib.).

[70] (2003), 230 D.L.R. (4th) 372, 67 O.R. (3d) 246, 2003 CarswellOnt 3325, (Ont. Div. Ct.) (re TSL-39032).

geared-to-income housing, which is often considered housing of last resort. A tenant evicted from such housing may well end up living in a shelter or on the street. Members are aware of this sad fact and may be more inclined to consider exercising their discretion to grant relief from forfeiture in such cases.

In *Metropolitan Toronto Housing Co. v. Gabriel*,[71] the judge granted possession against a tenant who was benefiting from such accommodation while not disclosing increased income as required by s. 107(1)(*f*) of Part IV of the *Landlord and Tenant Act*.

On the other hand, in *Peel Non-Profit Housing Corp. v. McNamara*,[72] the tenant in subsidized housing had not made full disclosure of income, and the trial judge said:[73]

> [The discretion] ought to be based on a full review of all the equities between the parties ... and to weigh the impact that refusal to evict would have (a) on the landlord, (b) on the tenant and (c) . . . [for subsidized housing] on the public interest.

In the *McNamara* case, the judge sympathized with the tenant's plight and refused possession. The case went on appeal to the Divisional Court and that court refused to interfere with the discretion exercised by the trial judge. The court did elaborate on the discretion saying that:[74]

> [The discretion] is not a two-part test where the judge must first look at the tenant's circumstances and consider relief from forfeiture and then look at the landlord's circumstances and determine whether it would be unfair to him. It is a one-part test that must consider all circumstances. ... the issue of unfairness [is] a matter at large.

Section 84(1) of the T.P.A. was applied by the Tribunal sympathetically for the tenant of subsidized housing in *Stoney Creek Community Services Corp. v. Monsa*.[75] The Tribunal was satisfied that the tenant "had knowingly and materially misrepresented income" (s. 62(2)). The Tribunal considered s. 84(1). The tenant was on social assistance and had three young children. The Member stated in the order, "It would be extremely difficult if not impossible for her to find alternative suitable affordable accommodation." The Tribunal referred to other pro and con reported cases, and for this case considered the effect that refusal to evict would have (a) on the landlord, (b) on the tenant, and (c) on the public interest. As the Tribunal said, "There is no evidence that an eviction would serve the landlord's interests or the public's interests." The application for eviction was dismissed.

---

71 (1988), 2 R.P.R. (2d) 284 (Ont. Dist. Ct.).

72 (1990), 74 O.R. (2d) 450 (Ont. Dist. Ct.), affirmed (1991), 2 O.R. (3d) 414 (Ont. Div. Ct.).

73 (1990), 74 O.R. (2d) 450 (Ont. Dist. Ct.) at 454-455.

74 (1991), 2 O.R. (3d) 414 (Ont. Div. Ct.) at 415.

75 (July 7, 1999), SOL-06347 (Ont. Rental Housing Trib.).

In *Minto Management Limited v. Pellerin,*[76] the tenant's guest brought stolen goods into the rental unit, with the knowledge of the tenant. In exercising his discretion and refusing to evict this tenant, the Member wrote as follows:

> I am not convinced that the Tenant's poor discretion and decision making at such a young age should result in losing her opportunity to have the substantial benefit of socially assisted housing. When I consider all of the circumstances, especially the impact on the Tenant and her infant of losing her social housing benefits, her lack of a prior record of such incidents, and her young age, I am persuaded that it would be unfair in this instance to grant the landlord's application for eviction.

In *Peel Housing Corp. v. Akomah,*[77] despite her own best efforts, the tenant could not pay the rent in full and on time. The Member ruled that to deny the landlord's application, after the forbearance and genuine efforts of the landlord to accommodate the tenant, would be "tantamount to saying that a public houser does not have the benefit of the Tenant Protection Act." The Member noted that there are "many many families waiting for this accommodation" and that it is not wrong for the landlord to attempt to manage this "valued housing stock". In the end, the Member could not in good conscience deny the eviction but, instead, postponed the eviction for approximately three months.

As illustrated by the above-noted cases, the impact of an eviction upon the tenant and members of the tenant's household will not always be the most important factor. The interests of the tenant must be weighed against the interests of the other tenants in the complex and the legitimate interests of the landlord.

For example, in *Metropolitan Toronto Housing Authority v. Hewitt,*[78] the tenant had permitted an illegal act (the possession and trafficking of drugs). The tenant was a mother of two young children and was pregnant. In refusing to grant relief from eviction, Conant J. stated:

> Although mindful of the effect upon the tenant ... the protection and well-being of the whole area with such a large child population, in my view, should take precedence over that of the tenant.

In *Blatt Holdings Ltd. and Stein, Re,*[79] the judge considered the tenant's request for relief from forfeiture, but turned it down because "the conduct of the tenant has had little regard for the interest of the other tenants". Since the tenant would not permit the fumigating of her apartment it was held that it

[76] (July 26, 1999), EAL-06524 (Ont. Rental Housing Trib.).

[77] (Dec. 9, 2004), CEL-41187, 2004 CarswellOnt 5460 (Ont. Rental Housing Trib.).

[78] (1990), 9 R.P.R. (2d) 36 (Ont. Dist. Ct.).

[79] (July 22, 1976), (Ont. Co. Ct.).

would be unfair to the other tenants to refuse the landlord's application for possession.

In Landlord and Tenant Board File No. TSL-00840 (May 10, 2007), a tenant in government housing committed or permitted several serious criminal acts in the residential complex (including drug dealing, prostitution and assault with an axe), thereby seriously impairing the safety and substantially interfering with the reasonable enjoyment of other tenants in the complex. The representative for the tenant argued that to evict the tenant from this type of housing was tantamount to capital punishment. The presiding Member strongly disagreed with this proposition and indicated that the interests of the offending tenant had to be weighed against the rights of the other, innocent tenants who have no realistic opportunity to move elsewhere. The tenant showed no remorse and failed to recognize how his conduct might be affecting others within the complex. The Member delayed enforcement of the eviction by 21 days but was not prepared to grant any other relief to this tenant.

Of course, one of the factors to be considered in cases where the application is based upon the conduct of the tenant, is whether that conduct is likely to be repeated in the future. One indicator of future behaviour is how the tenant has behaved in the past. A relatively long tenancy with no previous history of misconduct will certainly weigh in the tenant's favour. The Board is much less likely to show leniency to a tenant who has repeatedly breached his or her obligations under the tenancy agreement and the Act or who shows no remorse and seems to feel entitled to continue the conduct in question.

In *Mountbriar Building Corp. (Toronto) v. Da Rosa*,[80] the judge took into account the tenant's aggressive attitude in continuing to do what was complained about by the other tenants.

By way of contrast, in *Harmer v. Karszmarzyk*,[81] although the judge determined there had been substantial interference with the enjoyment of other tenants by loud stereo music late at night, the judge exercised discretion under s. 121(2)(*a*) of Part IV of the *Landlord and Tenant Act* and refused to order termination of the lease as the judge was "convinced that the tenant should be given a further opportunity to desist from her activities".

Even though a landlord is proceeding for possession after a second notice to the tenant for substantially interfering with the reasonable enjoyment of other tenants, s. 107(1)(*c*) of Part IV (now s. 68(1) of the R.T.A.), a judge, if satisfied that the tenant now understands her responsibility to the other tenants, may grant relief from forfeiture: *Cameron v. Parkins*.[82]

Another factor the Board will consider is whether such discretionary relief has previously been granted to the tenant. A tenant who has already been given an opportunity to save his or her tenancy will not likely be given

---

[80] (October 15, 1976), Doc. M2839 (Ont. Co. Ct.).

[81] (December 1, 1981), Salhany Co. Ct. J. (Ont. Co. Ct.).

[82] (January 11, 1984), Doc. LT 380/33 (Ont. Co. Ct.).

further opportunities unless the tenant was prevented from fulfilling his or her obligations by circumstances that were unforeseeable and completely beyond the control of the tenant.

Thus where a tenant was granted relief under s. 84(1) of the T.P.A. and was given an opportunity to bring the tenancy back into good standing and then missed subsequent payments required by the earlier order, the Tribunal declined to exercise any further discretion in favour of that tenant.[83] As one Member put it:[84]

> Termination on a breach of section 77 [of the T.P.A.] should not be refused lightly. The discretion one might apply in the original application is markedly narrowed the second time around. Coming close to complying with the original order will, in a large majority of the applications, be insufficient to rescue the tenant.

The courts have taken into account all of the relevant circumstances including any breaches of covenants by the tenant both past and still existing, and persistent late payment of rents: *Jeans West Unisex Ltd. v. Hung*.[85] In *Shiloh Spinners v. Harding*,[86] the court stated that seldom should wilful breaches by a tenant be relieved against, and the continuous disregard by the tenant of his obligations were such that relief should not be granted. On the other hand, where the tenant had acted in good faith, relief was granted: *Lippman v. Yick*.[87]

In practical terms, it is difficult to make hard and fast rules about how best to balance the interests of landlords and tenants when considering whether, and how, to grant relief from eviction under s. 83(1). The Divisional Court has explicitly rejected a two-step analysis in the *McNamara* decision (supra). Clearly, then, prejudice to the landlord does not trump hardship to the tenant. *All* of the relevant circumstances must be considered, the relative interests of all parties and persons who will be affected by the order must be weighed and the Board must render the decision it considers to be most just in the circumstances.

---

[83] *Eleven Elkhorn Investments Limited v. White* (Sept. 3, 2003), TNL-47670-RV (Ont. Rental Housing Trib.). Also see *Southridge Apartments v. Hastings* (2007), 2007 CarswellOnt 777 (Ont. Div. Ct.).

[84] *Metropolitan Toronto Housing Authority v. Figueira* (May 8, 2000), TEL-11585-SA, 2000 CarswellOnt 4368 (Ont. Rental Housing Trib.). Interestingly, despite this pronouncement, the Member refused to evict the tenant for a breach of a previous order because the breach was minor, there were no subsequent breaches, the tenant was unsophisticated, the tenant had lived in this unit without incident for many years, future problems with this tenancy were unlikely and the tenant would not be able to find suitable alternative housing that he could afford (this was housing of last resort).

[85] (1975), 9 O.R. (2d) 390 (Ont. H.C.).

[86] [1973] 1 All E.R. 90 (U.K. H.L.).

[87] [1953] O.R. 514 (Ont. H.C.).

In the case of a superintendent, for instance, because the superintendent took the position knowing that upon termination of her employment she would have to vacate the unit within one week and because the residential complex often cannot be properly maintained without a superintendent on-site, the interests of the landlord and the other tenants of the complex will usually outweigh the interests of a superintendent whose employment has been terminated.[88]

The Board can also use its power under s. 83(1) to relieve the tenant of the consequences of the tenant's own improvident conduct. In *Cencourse Project Inc. v. Leach*,[89] the tenant, who was distraught over an incident in the building, gave the landlord a notice of termination. Shortly thereafter she sought legal advice and attempted to rescind the notice. The landlord took the position that once the notice of termination had been given by the tenant, she had no right to change her mind. The landlord brought an application to terminate the tenancy and evict the tenant. Since the application was without notice to the tenant, the landlord was successful in obtaining an *ex parte* eviction order. The tenant then brought a motion to set aside that order. The tenant's motion was granted and the Tribunal refused (pursuant to s. 84(1) of the T.P.A.) in these circumstances to grant an eviction.

The landlord's conduct may be relevant to the Board's consideration of whether or not it is unfair to the landlord to refuse to grant an eviction. Take, for example, an application by a landlord based upon the landlord's stated desire to live in the rental unit. The case law indicates that the landlord need not act reasonably in choosing this unit out of all possible units, only that the landlord's desire to live in the unit must be genuine (sincere). The availability of other rental units in the same building cannot, in the absence of other evidence, support a finding that the landlord is acting in bad faith.[90] The availability of other suitable units, however, can be a significant factor in deciding whether or not to refuse to grant the requested eviction order pursuant to s. 83(1). In essence, this was the reasoning behind the decision in *Horst v. Beingessner*;[91] the Tribunal refused to grant an eviction on the basis that the requested order would cause hardship for the tenant and that other vacant units were available in the complex.

Similarly, if the landlord is in breach of the landlord's obligations under the tenancy agreement or the R.T.A., this may be relevant to how the Board decides to exercise its discretion. Serious breaches will result in automatic refusal of an eviction order as a result of s. 83(3), described in detail below.

[88] *Stewart-Kerr Properties Ltd. v. Fitzgerald* (1979), 25 O.R. (2d) 374 (Ont. Co. Ct.).

[89] (July 28, 2003), SWL-47347-SA, 2003 CarswellOnt 4160 (Ont. Rental Housing Trib.).

[90] *Salter v. Beljinac* (2001), 201 D.L.R. (4th) 744, 43 R.P.R. (3d) 114, 148 O.A.C. 291, 2001 CarswellOnt 2494, [2001] O.J. No. 2792 (Ont. Div. Ct.). Also see *Cohen v. Klein* (May 11, 2001), TNL-17189(2), [2001] O.R.H.T.D. No. 66, 2001 CarswellOnt 6410 (Ont. Rental Housing Trib.).

[91] (November 14, 2002), SWL-43648, 2002 CarswellOnt 5019 (Ont. Rental Housing Trib.).

Smaller breaches, though not necessarily serious enough to invoke the protection of s. 83(3), may still be relevant under s. 83(1).

Finally, under the T.P.A., Members struggled with the issue of whether they could or should look behind the rent charged by landlords in rent-geared-to-income housing, the subsidies provided to (or withdrawn from) tenants in social housing and determinations by landlords as to tenants' eligibility for, or the amount of, any prescribed form of housing assistance. For instance, in *Kingston & Frontenac Housing Corporation v. Rumney et al.*,[92] the Member reviewed the process by which the landlord decided to revoke the tenants' rent subsidy and found that the landlord's process was so flawed that it would be unfair in the circumstances to terminate the tenancy (for arrears of rent). The reviewing Member exercised his discretion under what was then s. 84(1) of the T.P.A. and refused to grant an eviction. Note, however, that a new provision of the R.T.A. (s. 203) now prohibits the Landlord and Tenant Board from *making a determination or reviewing the decisions* concerning a tenant's eligibility for rent-geared-to-income assistance or the amount of rent payable in such situations or eligibility for, or the amount of, any prescribed form of housing assistance. Given the broad language of s. 203 of the R.T.A., it appears that this prohibition also extends to considerations under s. 83(1) of the R.T.A. and it is no longer appropriate for the Board to engage in the type of analysis that was done in *Kingston & Frontenac Housing Corporation v. Rumney et al.*[93]

(ii) Terms and Conditions

Subsection 204(1) of the R.T.A. (formerly s. 190(1) of the T.P.A.) states that, "The Board may include in an order whatever conditions it considers fair in the circumstances." This grants Members of the Board considerable freedom to add to their orders conditions that will ensure a just result. The only limit (other than that the conditions must not exceed the Member's jurisdiction or be contrary to public policy) is the imagination of the adjudicator. This is particularly useful in conjunction with ss. 83 and 78 of the Act; where appropriate, a Member can exercise their discretion under s. 83(1) by refusing to grant an eviction but issuing an order that imposes upon the tenant strict terms (such as a repayment schedule) and stating in the order that if those terms are breached then the landlord may apply to the Board, without further notice to the tenant, for an order terminating the tenancy pursuant to s. 78 of the R.T.A.[94]

---

[92] (Juune 6, 2005), EAL-46520-RV (Ont. Rental Housing Trib.).

[93] (June 6, 2005), EAL-46520-RV (Ont. Rental Housing Trib.).

[94] The provisions of s. 78 can only be invoked where the terms that have been breached are of the same nature that gave rise to the original application. See Chapter 13.

In *Preview Technologies Inc. v. Black*,[95] for instance, instead of evicting the tenant for arrears of rent, the Member set out a repayment schedule, ordered that all payments be made by guaranteed funds and provided that if any of the payments were missed, the landlord could apply for an *ex parte* eviction order pursuant to s. 77 of the T.P.A. (now s. 78 of the R.T.A.). Similar terms were imposed in *Eastdale Ltd. v. Boudreault*.[96]

In *Metropolitan Toronto Housing Authority v. Davis*,[97] where both parties agreed that the tenant should have time to repay the rent arrears but where both the income and the rent (geared to income) were uncertain, the Member simply ordered that the debt be repaid within six months (failing which the landlord could apply for an *ex parte* eviction order) but without setting out a rigid repayment schedule.

The adjudicator can also impose terms to help ensure the conduct will not be repeated or that the tenant take steps to rectify the problem.

For instance, in *Mastercraft Construction Co. v. Baldwin*,[98] the tenant was using a C.B. radio which annoyed other tenants. The order for relief from forfeiture was made effective provided the tenant desisted and removed the antenna within two weeks of the hearing.

In *Sietsma v. Smith*,[99] the tenant's un-neutered male cats were creating a problem by spraying and creating offensive odours. The Member refused to evict the tenant on the condition that she either remove the cats from the unit or have them neutered and that she also not allow any other cats into the unit.

In *Silva v. Moiser*,[100] the tenant created a fire hazard by allowing debris to accumulate in the rental unit. Instead of evicting the tenant, the Member gave the tenant three weeks to clean out the unit, pass an inspection by the local Fire Marshall and then co-operate with the landlord inspecting the unit every two months for a one-year period (to ensure that the unit remained free of combustible debris). If the tenant failed to comply with any of these terms, the landlord was permitted to apply for an *ex parte* eviction order pursuant to s. 77 of the T.P.A. (now s. 78 of the R.T.A.).

In Landlord and Tenant Board File No. TEL-00091 (Feb. 22, 2007), the problem was excessive noise coming from the rental unit. The Vice-chair granted relief to the tenant under s. 83(1) (i.e., refused to grant an eviction) but then put the tenant "on probation" with respect to noise for a six-month period with a provision that, should the problem be repeated during that time, the landlord could apply to the Board, without notice to the tenant, for an order terminating the tenancy and evicting the tenant in accordance with s. 78 of the R.T.A.

---

[95] (December 16, 2003), TSL-57311 (Ont. Rental Housing Trib.).

[96] (December 16, 2003), TSL-57065 (Ont. Rental Housing Trib.).

[97] (February 8, 2001), TNL-23016 (Ont. Rental Housing Trib.).

[98] (1978), 20 O.R. (2d) 346 (Ont. Co. Ct.).

[99] (April 17, 2003), SOL-39582 (Ont. Rental Housing Trib.).

[100] (November 15, 2002), TEL-31602 (Ont. Rental Housing Trib.).

Where such conditional relief is most commonly seen is in applications based upon persistent late payment of rent.[101] As was stated by the Ontario Court of Appeal in *Rexdale Investments Ltd. v. Gibson*:[102]

> [T]here is no good reason to refuse such relief when the landlord can be made whole by money payments and terms can be imposed ... to require regularity in making payments on the due dates.

Where the rent has been persistently paid late, but the tenant has announced his or her willingness and ability to pay the rent on time in the future, the Board can exercise its discretion under s. 83(1) and refuse to grant an eviction at this time, on condition that the rent be paid on time for the next *x* number of rental periods. The Board can include, as one of the conditions, that during that specified period, all amounts will be paid by way of guaranteed funds.[103] By incorporating by reference the provisions of s. 78 of the R.T.A. (formerly s. 77 of the T.P.A.), such an order can have real "teeth"; a breach of the order will enable the landlord to obtain an eviction order very quickly and without further expense or notification to the tenant.

In *Portree Properties Ltd. v. Vanoostrum*,[104] the Tribunal exercised its discretion and refused to evict the tenant for persistent late payment of rent. The tenant, who had made an assignment in bankruptcy, had resided in the premises for four years and there were no arrears of rent at the time the application was heard.

Where, however, there is no reasonable prospect that the tenant will be able to pay her rent on time, it is not an appropriate case in which to deny the eviction (notwithstanding that the tenant presented a sympathetic case on behalf of herself and her six children).[105] The Tribunal did, however, utilize its power under para. 84(1)(b) of the T.P.A. (now para. 83(1)(b) of the R.T.A.) to delay the eviction for one month.

Many Members are reluctant to evict tenants from social housing because it is considered to be the housing of last resort. As a result, some Members have become very creative in the conditions they impose. In *Metropolitan Toronto Housing Authority v. St. Louis*,[106] the tenant seriously impaired the safety of another tenant by approaching the other tenant, in a threatening manner, while holding a knife. The Member granted the landlord's eviction application, on the condition that landlord offer her a unit in another of its

---

[101] *Cormier v. Norman* (1989), 9 R.P.R. (2d) 164 (Ont. Dist. Ct.).

[102] [1967] 1 O.R. 251 (Ont. C.A.) at 254.

[103] Landlord and Tenant Board File No. TNL-19884 (Jan. 13, 2009).

[104] (Nov. 25, 2003), TSL-56260, [2003] O.R.H.T.D. No. 143, 2003 CarswellOnt 5710 (Ont. Rental Housing Trib.).

[105] *Postdam Townhouses Limited v. Brown* (July 30, 2001), TNL-28362 (Ont. Rental Housing Trib.). See also *Greater Sudbury Housing Corporation v. Jire*, (December 5, 2002), NOL-07776-RV (Ont. Rental Housing Trib.).

[106] (January 11, 1999), TEL-02124 (Ont. Rental Housing Trib.).

buildings (in a different residential complex) before proceeding with enforcement of the eviction order.

(iii) Delay of Eviction

Where the Board is not convinced that the eviction should be refused outright, it still retains the discretion to "order that the enforcement of the order of eviction be postponed for a period of time" under para. 83(1)(b) of the R.T.A. (formerly para. 84(1)(b) of the T.P.A.). Note that under this paragraph, the Board need not even specifically consider whether it would be unfair to the landlord to delay the eviction. Nevertheless, I would suggest that a similar balancing of interests is warranted.

In *Tarsitano v. Duff*,[107] the judge took into account the elderly tenant's very poor health and the difficulty of obtaining other suitable accommodation and ordered that the issue of the writ of possession be delayed for five months.

In *Cassan v. Gagne*,[108] the judge ordered that the writ of possession should not be issued for three and one-half months to enable the tenants to find other accommodation.

In *City of Ottawa Non Profit Housing v. Munroe*,[109] although the landlord proved that the tenant had committed several illegal acts, including assault upon another tenant, because of the poor health of the tenant and his special housing needs, the eviction was delayed approximately one month.

In *Greater Sudbury Housing Corporation v. Jire*,[110] the tenant was persistently late in paying his rent. In this case, there was a long history of problems with the tenancy, including persistent late payment of rent. Despite the promises of the tenant to begin paying on time, the Member found that the tenant would likely not be able to keep these promises and that this was not an appropriate case in which to refuse to grant the requested eviction. Instead, the Member delayed the eviction by approximately two months.

In Landlord and Tenant Board File No. TSL-04977 (Aug. 21, 2007), the landlord, an 89-year-old woman, required the basement unit for a person who would be providing care services to the landlord. Given that the landlord currently had some caregiving assistance and that the basement tenant had been living in the unit for 18 years, at the request of the tenant, the presiding Member delayed the eviction for two months to permit the tenant time in which to find alternate accommodations.

In practice, delaying the eviction is a much more common form of relief than an outright refusal by the Board to grant an eviction. It is done by Members routinely and, often, little explanation is provided in the order.

---

[107] (1988), 50 R.P.R. 225 (Ont. Dist. Ct.).
[108] (1987), 63 O.R. (2d) 198 (Ont. Dist. Ct.).
[109] (March 23, 1999), EAL-0449 (Ont. Rental Housing Trib.).
[110] (December 5, 2002), NOL-07776-RV (Ont. Rental Housing Trib.).

There are a few recent examples in which there has actually been some discussion of the rationale for granting this relief.

In Landlord and Tenant Board File No. TEL-00013 (Feb. 28, 2007), the Member considered that the tenant was a single mother of six children who, until recently, had been working but was having difficulty finding new employment. The Member delayed the eviction by approximately one month to allow the tenant some time to find suitable alternate accommodations.

In Landlord and Tenant Board File No. TEL-00053 (Feb. 21, 2007), the tenants indicated that they expected to receive money from a class-action lawsuit. The Vice-chair delayed the eviction by a couple of weeks in order to give the tenants the opportunity of borrowing sufficient funds (using the expected payout from the lawsuit as security for the loan) to repay their debt to the landlord.

In Landlord and Tenant Board File No. TSL-16923 (Jan. 12, 2009), the tenant had lived in the unit for about 15 years. She was a single mother with a disability whose sole source of income was disability benefits from the Ontario Disability Support Program (ODSP). The tenant had lost much of her money recently in some criminal scam. The tenant's mother had recently passed away and the tenant chose to use her remaining money to pay for her mother's funeral rather than paying her rent. The tenant hoped to repay the landlord from money she was expecting to inherit from her mother's estate and from additional financial assistance she was expecting from ODSP. Over the objection of the landlord, the Member decided to delay the eviction by about six weeks in order to give the tenant an opportunity to pay off the debt she owed to the landlord and save the tenancy.

The Board's practice of making eviction orders (issued following a hearing) enforceable 11 days after the date of issuance, is itself a postponement of the eviction order.[111] Since postponing evictions by 11 days has become routine, Members do not even see a need to explain such delays in their orders, as they do not see it as an exercise of their discretion. Nevertheless, all parties should bear in mind that *any* delay of the eviction is, in reality, a matter of discretion on the part of the Board and should not be taken for granted.

Finally, where a lengthy delay is being considered, the Member should also consider what conditions ought to be included in the order to ensure the landlord is paid rent or compensation pending the eviction. The goal of a postponement of an eviction should be to assist the tenant without causing undue prejudice or harm to the landlord.

---

[111] In all likelihood, this 11-day delay originated in the software used by Rental Housing Tribunal staff for the issuance of default orders and was then transported into the process of creating draft hearing orders as well.

(d) Subsection 83(3)

By s. 83(3) of the R.T.A. (formerly s. 84(2) of the T.P.A.), the Tribunal *shall* refuse to order termination and eviction if satisfied that:

(a) the landlord is in serious breach of the landlord's responsibilities under this Act or of any material covenant in the tenancy agreement;
(b) the reason for the application being brought is that the tenant has complained to a governmental authority of the landlord's violation of a law dealing with health, safety, housing or maintenance standards;
(c) the reason for the application being brought is that the tenant has attempted to secure or enforce his or her legal rights;
(d) the reason for the application being brought is that the tenant is a member of a tenants' association or is attempting to organize such an association; or
(e) the reason for the application being brought is that the rental unit is occupied by children and the occupation by the children does not constitute overcrowding.

To summarize, the R.T.A. prohibits landlords from obtaining eviction orders where: (1) the landlord is in serious breach of the landlord's obligations; (2) the eviction application is retaliatory; or (3) the application is being brought because of the presence of children in the rental unit. The onus is upon the tenant to establish the facts necessary for a ruling under s. 83(3). If the tenant is able to satisfy the Board that one of the conditions listed under s. 83(3) exists, then the Board *must* refuse to grant an eviction; it has no discretion in this regard. Where such issues are raised during the course of the hearing, the Board's order should make it explicit that due consideration was given to the relevant portion(s) of s. 83(3). This is true whether or not the tenant specifically refers to this section by number.[112] Such an explicit analysis is even required where the tenant fails to attend the hearing altogether but the landlord's own evidence refers to facts that put into question whether the landlord's application is retaliatory in nature.[113]

[112] See *Kuzyk v. SK Properties* (November 22, 2001), Doc. 106/01, 2001 CarswellOnt 6074 (Ont. S.C.J.) (re TSL-18855) in which the Court found that the Member had erred by, among other things, failing to specifically deal in the order with the tenant's assertion that the landlord had brought the application because of the tenant's involvement in a tenants' association.

[113] *Sutherland v. Lamontagne* (Mrach 3, 2008), Court File No. DV-756-07 (Ont. Div. Ct.), unreported.

(i) *Serious Breach by the Landlord (s. 83(3)(a))*

Pursuant to para. 83(3)(a) of the R.T.A. (formerly s. 84(2) of the T.P.A.), the Board shall refuse to order termination and eviction if satisfied that the landlord is in serious breach of the landlord's responsibilities under the Act or of any material covenant in the tenancy agreement.

A couple of points about how this section is worded are worth noting. First, it is phrased in the present tense. It does not say that an eviction shall be refused if the landlord *has been* in serious breach of the landlord's responsibilities. An eviction should only be refused if the landlord *is* in serious breach (i.e., at the time of the hearing), not if the landlord has been in serious breach at some point in the past[114] or if there is the potential that the landlord may be in serious breach at some point in the future.[115] Second, the breach by the landlord must be *serious*. While this does not necessarily mean that it must be so fundamental a breach that, for instance, the unit is uninhabitable, it must be more than a minor annoyance. It has been held by the Divisional Court that whether or not a breach is "serious" is a question of fact, not law;[116] consequently, there may be no right to appeal such a finding.[117] Also, the test under para. 83(3)(a) is different than under s. 20 (and s. 29(1)1); therefore, the Board may not delay the hearing of the landlord's (eviction) application until the resolution of a tenant's application concerning alleged breaches of the landlord's maintenance obligations.[118]

I shall now review some relevant court, Tribunal and Board decisions in which this issue has been considered.

By s. 121(3)(*a*) of Part IV (*Landlord and Tenant Act*), the judge was directed to refuse an application for possession where he or she is satisfied that the landlord is in breach of responsibilities under the Act or a material covenant in the lease.[119] In *Victoria Park Community Homes Inc. v. Buzza*,[120] the judge refused the landlord's application for termination of a lease for non-

---

[114] *Dang v. Deon* (March 9, 2000), CEL-09846-RV, [2000] O.R.H.T.D. No. 41 (Ont. Rental Housing Trib.); *Campbell v. Workman* (March 10, 2006), TNL-72870, 2006 CarswellOnt 2156, [2006] O.R.H.T.D. No. 26 (Ont. Rental Housing Trib.); and *Puterbough v. Canada (Public Works & Government Services)*, [2007] O.J. No. 748, 55 R.P.R. (4th) 189, 2007 CarswellOnt 2222 (Ont. Div. Ct.), additional reasons at (2007), 2007 CarswellOnt 7645 (Ont. Div. Ct.). To hold otherwise would mean that a landlord who has been in serious breach of the landlord's responsibilities in the past would *never* be able to evict a tenant, even if the problem was rectified and the landlord's recent conduct had been exemplary.

[115] *Chenard v. Foster* (2007), 2007 CarswellOnt 7709 (Ont. Div. Ct.).

[116] *Meredith v. Leboeuf Properties Inc.* (2000), 2000 CarswellOnt 165 (Ont. Div. Ct.).

[117] Under s. 210 of the R.T.A. (formerly s. 196 of the T.P.A.).

[118] *Glimjem Holdings v. Weidenfeld* (December 16, 2002), TNL-41312-SA, 2002 CarswellOnt 5012 (Ont. Rental Housing Trib.). Having the two applications heard together (for the sake of efficiency and consistency) is preferable but not always practical.

[119] See Chapter 5.

[120] (1975), 10 O.R. (2d) 251 (Ont. Co. Ct.).

payment of rent as the landlord "was unconscionably in breach of [the obligation] to repair".

In *Rocca v. Rousselle*,[121] the landlord's application for termination based on extensive repairs requiring vacant possession was refused because the landlord consistently failed to keep the premises in repair.

In *Pinarski v. Rowe*,[122] the landlord's request for an order evicting the tenant was denied on the basis that the landlord was in serious breach of his maintenance obligations. The Member came up with a list of about 40 items that required repair. This finding was based upon the testimony of the parties as well as an inspection of the premises conducted by the Member and a Tribunal mediator, conducted at the request of both parties.

In *Lacombe v. Duval*,[123] lack of potable water was considered to be a "serious" breach within the meaning of para. 84(2)(a). The Member also held that, if the breach is cured shortly before the hearing, the Tribunal can still consider the nature and duration of that breach in considering whether to grant discretionary relief under s. 84(1) of the T.P.A.

A similar issue of water quality was dealt with in the case of *Sage v. Wellington (County)*.[124] The landlord brought an application to evict the tenants because the landlord intended to convert the unit to a non-residential use. The tenants had lived in the unit since 1990 and opposed the application based on, amongst other things, the landlord's failure to address the issue of the contaminated well-water. The Member hearing the case found that since the tenants did not convince him that the water supply was unsafe at all times, this was not a *serious* breach within the meaning of s. 84(2)(*a*) of the T.P.A. On appeal, the Divisional Court ruled that it was wrong for the Member to use the word "convince" as it suggests a higher standard of proof than "on a balance of probabilities". The Divisional Court also held that the Member's interpretation of the word "serious" was wrong in law. In the opinion of the Court, water quality is a very serious matter and the failure of the landlord to deal with the contaminated well water was a serious breach of the landlord's obligations. The tenants' appeal was granted and the eviction order quashed.

In *Agius v. Banks et al.*,[125] on a landlord's application based upon non-payment of rent, the tenants alleged that the landlord was failing to properly maintain the unit and that the landlord had been harassing the tenants. The

---

[121] (September 24, 1981), (Ont. Dist. Ct.).

[122] (Feb. 12, 2002), TEL-24430 & TEL-24850-SA (Ont. Rental Housing Trib.). The tenant brought two of his own applications and was awarded an abatement of rent. The Member ordered the tenant to pay the small balance that remained owing to the landlord after the rent abatement was deducted from the amounts the tenant otherwise owed to the landlord for rent and damage to the property.

[123] (June 28, 2002), EAL-26736, EAL-28533, and EAT-03340, [2002] O.R.H.T.D. No. 74 (Ont. Rental Housing Trib.).

[124] (2005), 2005 CarswellOnt 7833 (Ont. Div. Ct.) (re SWL-59763).

[125] (July 22, 1998), TSL-00338 (Ont. Rental Housing Trib.).

Member found that the maintenance problems were not serious enough to invoke para. 84(2)(a) of the T.P.A., and that while some of the conduct of the landlord was bizarre, the tenant was not harassed.

In *Campbell v. Workman*,[126] the landlord applied to terminate the tenancy on the basis that the property had been sold and the purchaser intended to reside in the unit. Shortly before the landlord delivered the notice of termination, the tenant had obtained an order against the landlord. Although that order found that the landlord had breached certain provisions of the Act, there was no specific finding that those breaches were serious within the meaning of s. 84(2)(a) of the T.P.A. (now s. 83(3)(a) of the R.T.A.) or that those breaches continued up to present (i.e., there was no evidence that the landlord was currently in serious breach of any provision of the Act or of the tenancy agreement). The Vice-chair was satisfied that this application was *bona fide* and that it had not been brought in retaliation. He therefore granted the application.

In *Canada (Public Works & Government Services) v. McGrath*,[127] the landlord applied for an order to terminate the tenancy and evict the tenants because the landlord intended to demolish the rental unit. One of the defences raised by the tenants was that the landlord was in serious breach of its maintenance obligations with respect to the rental unit and that, as a result, the Tribunal had to refuse to grant an eviction. The tenants also brought their own applications concerning the condition of the unit and the conduct of the landlord. With respect to maintenance, there was no question that the landlord was in breach of its obligations and the Vice-chair awarded an abatement of $1,500 with respect to the landlord's failure to properly repair and maintain the rental unit. The real question was whether those breaches were so serious that the Tribunal had to refuse to grant the eviction. The Vice-chair found that although it was problematic that the landlord had failed to replace the furnace, to rectify the mould problem, to repair the flooring, to paint the interior and exterior of the house, to repair deteriorated concrete on the front porch, to address water seepage in the basement and to repair or replace windows, these problems did not pose an immediate risk to the tenants' health and safety and did not significantly impact on the tenants' ability to reside in the rental unit in its current condition. Therefore, he concluded that the landlord was not in *serious* breach of its maintenance obligations.

In Landlord and Tenant Board File No. NOL-00165 (March 8, 2007), the landlord applied to terminate the tenancy for non-payment of rent. The tenants attended the hearing and, pursuant to s. 82 of the R.T.A., raised as an issue the fact that there had not been adequate heat in the unit for more than

---

[126] (March 10, 2006), TNL-72870, 2006 CarswellOnt 2156, [2006] O.R.H.T.D. No. 26 (Ont. Rental Housing Trib.).

[127] (Feb. 6, 2006), TEL-52097, TET-05177, 2006 CarswellOnt 2151 (Ont. Rental Housing Trib.).

two years. In addition to awarding a rent abatement to the tenants, the Board found the landlord's failure to ensure an adequate supply of heat constituted a serious breach of the landlord's maintenance responsibilities and, pursuant to s. 83(3)(a) of the *Act*, the Board refused to grant an order terminating this tenancy.

The Divisional Court has made a distinction between serious maintenance problems (i.e., a serious defect or deficiency) and a serious breach of the landlord's maintenance obligations. In *Puterbough v. Canada (Public Works & Government Services)*,[128] the landlord rented out 300 homes on land previously expropriated for an airport that was never built. The homes were 50 to 100 years old and some required extensive repairs. The landlord decided that it was not economical to effect repairs to some of the buildings – that it made more sense to demolish the worst buildings. With respect to those buildings, the landlord sought orders from the Rental Housing Tribunal to terminate the tenancies and evict the tenants so that the demolitions could proceed. The tenants of those premises opposed eviction on grounds that the landlord was in serious breach of its maintenance and repair obligations. The Tribunal granted most but not all of the landlord's applications. Three tenants appealed the eviction orders granted against them. The landlord appealed two cases where the Tribunal refused to evict the tenants on the basis that the landlord was in serious breach of its maintenance obligations. All five appeals were heard together.

The Divisional Court held that the term "serious breach", in the context of the landlord's obligations under ss. 24, 25 and 26 of the T.P.A. (now ss. 20, 21 and 22 of the R.T.A.), means more than the rental premises being in poor condition and in need of significant work:

> To accept the Tenants' strict liability interpretation would reduce eviction to an option rarely available to a landlord despite the structure being old and in need of extensive and costly repairs and the property being of insignificant value. Such an interpretation could require a landlord to make significant capital improvements to rental property simply to get permission to evict the tenants and demolish the premises. That flies in the face of common sense. In short, a serious breach of the landlord's responsibilities is not established simply by the rental premises being in need of extensive repairs.[129]

The Court found that a more pragmatic, balanced and contextual approach must be adopted in deciding such cases – one that takes into account such factors as the length of time during which the deficiency existed, the causal connection between the landlord's failure to repair and the resulting deficiency, the absence of any efforts on the part of the landlord to deal with the deficiency and the severity of the health and safety risks produced by the

---

[128] (2007), [2007] O.J. No. 748, 55 R.P.R. (4th) 189, 2007 CarswellOnt 2222 (Ont. Div. Ct.), additional reasons at (2007), 2007 CarswellOnt 7645 (Ont. Div. Ct.).

[129] At paragraph 21 of the decision (cited above).

deficiency. The Divisional Court dismissed the appeals brought by the tenants (i.e., those eviction orders were allowed to stand) and granted the two appeals brought by the landlord (and referred those two cases back to the Tribunal for reconsideration).[130]

Paragraph 83(3)(a) of the R.T.A. is *not* restricted to breaches by a landlord of the landlord's *maintenance* obligations (although that is the most common complaint). For instance, in *Leo v. Tal,*[131] the landlord's failure to pay the tenant $1,200 in interest on the rent deposit was found to be a serious breach of the landlord's responsibilities under the *Tenant Protection Act.*

(ii) Retaliatory Application (s. 83(3)(b), (c), (d))

By s. 83(3) of the R.T.A. (formerly s. 84(2) of the T.P.A.), the Board *shall* refuse to order termination and eviction if satisfied that:

(b) the reason for the application being brought is that the tenant has complained to a governmental authority of the landlord's violation of a law dealing with health, safety, housing or maintenance standards;
(c) the reason for the application being brought is that the tenant has attempted to secure or enforce his or her legal rights;
(d) the reason for the application being brought is that the tenant is a member of a tenants' association or is attempting to organize such an association.

Collectively, these have been referred to as "retaliatory applications" because they are commenced by a landlord in retaliation for the tenant's attempt to assert his or her legal rights as a tenant.

Under similar provisions of the *Landlord and Tenant Act*, it was sufficient (in order to refuse to grant an eviction) if the court was satisfied that the improper motives of the landlord were "a reason" for the commencement of the application.[132] By way of contrast, paras. (b), (c) and (d) of s. 83(3) of the R.T.A. use the phrase "the reason" [for the application]. The Divisional Court has stated that this change demonstrates that the legislature intends to bar

---

[130] Presumably, if the Tribunal/Board follows the Court's direction and applies a pragmatic, balanced, contextual approach and makes a finding of fact that the landlord *is* in serious breach of its obligations, the Divisional Court will not then interfere since it has previously held that such a finding is a question of fact, not a question of law: *Meredith v. Leboeuf Properties Inc.* (2000), 2000 CarswellOnt 165 (Ont. Div. Ct.).

[131] (April 12, 2000), TNL-12557 and TNT-00872, [2000] O.R.H.T.D. Nos. 56 and 57 (Ont. Rental Housing Trib.).

[132] *Metzendorf v. Thomas* (July 22, 1976), (Ont. Co. Ct.) and *Chin v. Lawson* (1986), (sub nom. *Chin v. Hunt*) 17 O.A.C. 267 (Ont. Div. Ct.).

evictions only where the landlord's sole or primary reason for commencing the eviction application is retaliatory.[133]

A landlord will rarely admit that an eviction application was commenced as a retaliatory measure and, in the absence of such an admission, it is impossible to prove with absolute certainty what was in the mind of the landlord at the time the application was filed. This makes it difficult for the tenant to satisfy his or her onus of proof. Usually, the reason for the landlord's application must be inferred from the sequence of events. If, for example, the tenant tries to assert his or her rights and that effort is immediately followed by the commencement of the landlord's application, this will certainly lead to a strong inference that the landlord's application is retaliatory. The credibility of the parties and their past conduct will also be of some assistance in determining these issues. Since the chronology and the credibility of the parties are typically both very important in such cases, any relevant documents that a party can produce that contain dates may assist the Board in determining an accurate sequence of events.

In *Delic v. Brown*,[134] the tenant had successfully defended an eviction application brought by the landlord and obtained an order for an abatement of rent (due to maintenance concerns), ordering the landlord to effect repairs and for costs. The landlord then almost immediately commenced an application to terminate the tenancy because his sons purportedly wished to live in the unit. Although the presiding Member believed that the landlord's sons would move in if they had the chance, she found that the reason the application had been brought by the landlord was because the tenant attempted to enforce his legal rights. As a result, the application was dismissed.

In *Blatt Holdings Ltd. and Stein, Re*,[135] the tenant alleged that it was retaliatory eviction by the landlord because she had complained to the police about the noise from construction work of a new building being erected nearby for the landlord. The judge held that the tenant's complaint may have been an annoyance to the landlord, but that the real reason for the landlord taking action to terminate the lease was that the tenant had refused to have her apartment fumigated as had been requested by the other tenants, and her refusal was conduct that substantially interfered with the reasonable enjoyment of the other tenants.

When a tenant refused to agree to an increase in rent which could not be lawfully supported it was held to be retaliatory eviction for the landlord thereafter to apply ostensibly for possession for himself. By refusing to agree to the illegal increase in rent, the court stated that the tenant had quite properly

---

[133] *MacNeil et al. v. 976445 Ontario Ltd.*, (May 2005), Doc. 04-1464 (Stratford) and 04-1465 (London) – Appeal No. A1296 (Ont. Div. Ct.) (re SWL-58901).

[134] (August 5, 1998), CEL-00335 (Ont. Rental Housing Trib.).

[135] (July 22, 1976) (Ont. Co. Ct.).

"attempted to secure or enforce his legal rights": s. 121(3)(*c*) of Part IV, *Yarmuch v. Lynchek.*[136]

In another case under a similar section of the Newfoundland *Landlord and Tenant (Residential Tenancies) Act, 1973*[137] the landlord's application for termination was refused and the notice of termination was held to be retaliatory because the notice was given following the tenant signing a petition protesting a proposed rent increase and appearing at the rent review hearing: *Oceanic Development & Construction Co. v. Strickland.*[138]

In *Rocca v. Rousselle*,[139] the other reason that the judge turned down the landlord's application for termination was that the application was "to counter-attack the tenant as a result of complaints by him to the municipal authorities for the landlord's violation of the municipal health and safety standards by-law".

It may sometimes be difficult for the Board to be satisfied that the landlord's application was brought as a retaliatory eviction for one of the above listed reasons. In other words, "Was retaliation the landlord's *predominant* motive for giving the notice to terminate and applying for possession?"

In *Netherton Properties Ltd. v. Perrier*,[140] the landlord's application for possession was refused when the court was satisfied that the landlord's application for possession was retaliation for the tenant asking for rent review.

Similar relief was given to a tenant who was served with a presumably valid notice of termination, but the court was satisfied that the landlord was applying for possession because the tenant had challenged the landlord's attempt to increase the rent illegally: *Chin v. Lawson.*[141] The Divisional Court pointed out that once it is determined that there is retaliatory eviction, s. 121(3)(*c*) of Part IV, there is no discretion and the judge "shall" refuse the landlord's application for possession.

These defences for a tenant are likely to be more applicable when a tenant has been involved in trying to have the landlord repair or fulfill other obligations such as housing standards by-laws, and the landlord then applies for possession.

Where the landlord applied for possession and the tenant subsequently notified the municipality about non-repair and a work order was issued, the tenant complained that notice to terminate was retaliatory. The court did not accept that argument and terminated the lease: *Maxbel Upholsteries Ltd. v. Dicks.*[142]

---

[136] (June 11, 1984), Doc. 14293/84 (Ont. Dist. Ct.).

[137] S.N. 1973, c. 54, s. 15(7) [as am. S.N. 1981, c. 16, s. 2].

[138] (1981), 35 Nfld. & P.E.I.R. 228 (Nfld. Dist. Ct.).

[139] (September 24, 1981), (Ont. Dist. Ct.).

[140] (1977), 3 Alta. L.R. (2d) 248 (Alta. T.D.).

[141] (sub nom. *Chin v. Hunt*) (1986), 17 O.A.C. 267 (Ont. Div. Ct.).

[142] (November 3, 1989), Doc. York M187070 (Ont. Dist. Ct.).

A tenant's defence to an application for possession based on lack of repairs and failure to comply with a municipal work order for structural changes was not accepted by the court as retaliatory eviction as in s. 121(3)(*b*) of Part IV. There were special circumstances and the Divisional Court was satisfied that the elderly landlady was financially unable to make the required changes for continued residential use and had applied for possession in order to convert the premises to non-residential: *Lypny v. Rocca.*[143]

In *MacNeil et al. v. 976445 Ontario Ltd.*,[144] the landlord ran a mobile home site. The landlord incurred ever-increasing expenses to provide safe water and septic systems to its tenants. It had an ongoing dispute with one set of tenants in particular. Ultimately, the landlord decided to convert the site to a non-residential use and provided the appropriate notices to all tenants. The Tribunal held that the landlord was acting in good faith and, notwithstanding the history of animosity with a few tenants, the landlord's main reason for closing the site was not retaliatory. On appeal to the Divisional Court, the Tribunal's decision was upheld.

In Landlord and Tenant Board File No. SOL-18674 (Feb. 20, 2009), the tenants gave the landlord an itemized list of needed repairs. When the landlord refused to do any repairs the tenants called the Electrical Safety Authority and the local fire department and property standards department. The landlord then served the tenants with a notice that he required the unit for his own use. The landlord's application was dismissed because it was found that the landlord was not acting in good faith and that the reason for the application being brought was because the tenants had complained to a government authority about the maintenance problems.

(iii) Presence of Children (s. 83(3)(e))

The Board shall also refuse the landlord's application if it is brought because the premises are occupied by children, s. 83(3)(*e*) of the R.T.A., provided the occupation by children does not constitute overcrowding[145] and the premises are suitable for children.

(e) Subsections 83(4) and 83(5) – Relief When Compensation Has Not Been Paid

In certain situations, the landlord must pay compensation to a tenant who is being forced to temporarily or permanently leave his or her rental unit.

---

[143] (1988), 63 O.R. (2d) 595 (Ont. Div. Ct.).

[144] (May 2005), Doc. 04-1464 (Stratford) and 04-1465 (London) – Appeal No. A1296 (Ont. Div. Ct.) (re SWL-58901).

[145] Overcrowding relates to the number of persons permitted in residential premises on a continuing basis according to any applicable housing standards by-law.

A landlord may plan to demolish the unit or complex or to convert the rental unit to a use for a purpose other than residential premises. A landlord may also need to do repairs or renovations that are so extensive it is not feasible for the tenant to remain in the rental unit during the work. In such circumstances, the landlord will serve upon the tenant a notice of termination (under s. 50). In most cases, if the residential complex contains at least five units, the landlord is required to compensate such a tenant by paying the tenant an amount equal to three months rent (ss. 52 and 54). A tenant may also be entitled to compensation where the tenant agrees to move out during the repairs or renovations but is exercising a first right of refusal (s. 54(2)) or where a tenant is losing his or her home as a result of severance (s. 55). The compensation required may be higher in the case of a mobile home or land lease home (s. 164).[146]

Pursuant to ss. 83(4) and 83(5) of the R.T.A. (formerly ss. 84(3) and 84(4) of the T.P.A.), the Board shall not issue an eviction order until the landlord complies with the above-noted provisions and pays the tenant any compensation to which the tenant is entitled.

(f) Setting Aside *Ex Parte* Orders

Pursuant to s. 77 of the R.T.A., where the landlord and tenant have agreed to terminate the tenancy or where the tenant has delivered a notice of termination to the landlord, the landlord may apply to the Board, without notice to the tenant (*ex parte*), for an order terminating the tenancy and evicting the tenant (not earlier than the date agreed upon or set out in the notice). The landlord can bring this application in advance so that the landlord will have the order ready to go should the tenant not leave on the date specified in the notice or in their agreement or the landlord can wait and see what happens and only then bring an application if the tenant remains in the rental unit after that date. When the tenant receives the eviction order, the tenant may file a motion to have that order set aside. At that motion, even where the landlord has proven that there was a valid agreement to terminate the tenancy or that the tenant did deliver a valid notice of termination, the Board may nevertheless exercise its discretion under para. 77(8)(b) and set aside the *ex parte* eviction order if the Board is satisfied, having regard to all the circumstances, that it would not be unfair to do so.

Similarly, even where a landlord has proven that the tenant has breached a condition of a mediated agreement or an order of the Board and that the landlord is entitled to an eviction order pursuant to s. 78(1) of the Act, on hearing a motion by the tenant brought under s. 78(9), the Board retains the discretionary power under para. 78(11)(b) to set aside the *ex parte* eviction

---

[146] See Chapter 20.

order if the Board is satisfied, having regard to all the circumstances, that it would not be unfair to do so.[147]

In Landlord and Tenant Board File No. SOL-01024-SA (April 20, 2007), the tenant entered into a mediated agreement to pay off arrears of rent on specified dates. He missed a payment and the landlord obtained an *ex parte* eviction order based upon this breach. The tenant then filed a motion to have that order set aside. He was a social assistance recipient who paid monthly rent of $139.00. He made arrangements to have the Ontario Disability Support Plan make payments directly to the landlord and proposed a new repayment schedule to the Board. In these circumstances, the Board set aside the *ex parte* order and issued a new order setting out a revised repayment schedule and indicating that if the tenant defaults on any of the payments set out in the order, the landlord may seek another *ex parte* order pursuant to s. 78.

In Landlord and Tenant Board File No. TEL-05888-SA (Oct. 5, 2007), the tenant was required by an earlier order of the Board (TEL-04661 issued on August 9, 2007) to pay certain amounts to the landlord on August 31, 2007, and September 1, 2007. The tenant misunderstood these terms and believed that he could pay both amounts on September 1, 2007. He approached the landlord on September 1, 2007, with a cheque for the full amount that was due on August 31 and September 1. The landlord refused to accept the cheque and insisted on cash. The tenant said that this would take a few days and the landlord agreed. On September 4, 2007, the landlord commenced an *ex parte* application for an eviction order under s. 78 based upon the alleged breach of the terms of order TEL-04661. Later that day, the tenant offered the cash payment the landlord had requested and the landlord accepted it without mentioning that an eviction application had been commenced. When the tenant received a copy of the eviction order, he brought a motion to have it set aside. Based on these facts, the Member found that it would not be unfair to set aside the *ex parte* eviction order and granted the tenant's motion pursuant to s. 78(11)(b) of the R.T.A.

On such motions, even when finding in favour of the landlord (i.e. denying the set-aside motion) and allowing enforcement of the *ex parte* eviction order, the Board has the discretionary power to <u>delay</u> the lifting of the stay on that order and, thereby, delay the eviction. This power comes from paras. 77(8)(c) and 78(11)(c) of the R.T.A., which provide that the Board can order that the stay be lifted immediately or "on a future date specified in the order". See Landlord and Tenant Board File No. SOL-00961-SA (April 12, 2007) for an example of a case where the Board granted such relief.

Since the Board has the power to grant relief from forfeiture on a motion to set aside an *ex parte* order made under s. 77 or 78 of the R.T.A., the

[147] See Chapter 13 ("Breach of a Term of an Order or Mediated Agreement (s. 78)") for a further discussion of this topic.

Member hearing such a motion has the duty to provide the parties with an opportunity to adduce evidence and make submissions on whether, having regard to all of the circumstances, it would be unfair to set aside the eviction order. The failure to provide the parties with such an opportunity is a reversible procedural error.[148]

(g) Preventing Abuses of Process

In the vast majority of cases, where a landlord has obtained an eviction order and enforced that order through the Court Enforcement Office (sheriff), the Tribunal will consider the matter to be at an end and will not intervene. It has been held, however, that where it would amount to an abuse of process to allow a landlord to enforce an eviction order, the Board has the power to put a tenant back into possession, even after the sheriff has enforced the eviction order: *Metropolitan Toronto Housing Authority v. Ahmed.*[149] Examples of such an abuse of process might include cases where the landlord obtains an eviction order from the Board through fraud or enforces an eviction order after it has been overturned (on review), has become void (as a result of the tenant making all payments required by s. 74 of the Act) or its enforcement has been stayed[150] (e.g., pending the hearing of a set aside motion or review).

After the *Ahmed* decision was issued, the T.P.A. was amended to specifically grant Members the power to put tenants back into possession where there has been an "illegal lockout" (i.e., where the landlord has locked the tenant out of the rental unit without the assistance of the sheriff, without going through a formal eviction process and, frequently, without obtaining an eviction order). These provisions have been carried forward into the R.T.A.

Where the landlord *has* obtained an eviction order from the Board and *has* used the sheriff to enforce that order (i.e., where there does not appear to be an "illegal lockout"), the *Ahmed* decision may still be of use where, for reasons such as the ones suggested above, it would constitute an abuse of process to permit the landlord to successfully evict the tenant. This has been confirmed by the Divisional Court in the case of *Kwak v. Marinecorp Mgt. Inc.*[151] in which, although there is no specific reference to the *Ahmed* decision,

---

[148] See *Kingston & Frontenac Housing Corporation v. Rumney et al.* (June 6, 2005), EAL-46520-RV (Ont. Rental Housing Trib.) and *Forest Hill Gates v. Wolch* (2007), 2007 CarswellOnt 1864 (Ont. Div. Ct.).

[149] (2001), 2001 CarswellOnt 1347 (Ont. Div. Ct.) (re TNL-06552).

[150] See *Commvesco Levinson Viner Group v. Pershaw* (Oct. 11, 2001), EAL-23388-RV and EAT-03169, [2001] O.R.H.T.D. No. 134 (Ont. Rental Housing Trib.) in which the *Ahmed* decision was followed. It was found to be an abuse of process for the landlord to have enforced an eviction order that was stayed. The landlord was ordered to allow the tenant back into possession (upon certain terms).

[151] (2007), 2007 CarswellOnt 4335 (Ont. Div. Ct.).

the Court comes to the same conclusion. In the absence of an abuse of process, however, the Board will have no jurisdiction to put a tenant back into possession once an eviction order has been duly enforced.[152]

In *Kwak v. Marinecorp Mgt. Inc.*,[153] the tenant provided a series of post-dated rent cheques to the landlord but inadvertently missed providing a cheque for April. The landlord applied for and, because the tenant did not file a Dispute, obtained an eviction order based upon the arrears for April. The landlord, however, chose not to enforce the eviction order at that time. The landlord cashed the cheques for May and June and the tenant offered on several occasions to pay to the landlord the arrears and costs but the landlord ignored these offers and, instead, filed the eviction order with the Sheriff at the end of June. Consequently, the tenant was evicted. The tenant then filed a motion with the Tribunal for an order to reinstate the tenancy on the basis that, in these circumstances, it was an abuse of process for the landlord to enforce the eviction order. The Tribunal granted the tenant's motion (on the condition that the arrears and costs be paid) and ordered that the landlord permit the tenant back into possession of the unit. The landlord appealed that decision to the Divisional Court on a number of grounds, including the argument that the Tribunal lacked the jurisdiction to make the order it did (i.e., it lacked the statutory authority to set aside an eviction order once it had been enforced). In finding in favour of the tenant and dismissing the appeal, the Divisional Court wrote as follows: "it appears to us that s. 23(1) of the *Statutory Powers Procedures Act* permits the tribunal to make an order of this sort in order to prevent an abuse of the process of the tribunal which the Member found had occurred and with which finding we concur."

(h) *Courts of Justice Act*

Section 98 of the *Courts of Justice Act*[154] provides that a court "may grant relief against penalties and forfeitures, on such terms as to compensation or otherwise as are considered just." In at least one case, a judge has held that the court retains the power to grant relief from forfeiture to a residential tenant under this provision and that this power was in addition to the Tribunal's powers under s. 84 of the T.P.A. (now s. 83 of the R.T.A.).

In *Dovale v. Metropolitan Toronto Housing Authority*,[155] the tenant brought a set-aside motion before the Tribunal. The motion was denied with the order reading, in part:

---

[152] Landlord and Tenant Board File No. TSL-19648-RV (Feb. 26, 2009).

[153] (2007), 2007 CarswellOnt 4335 (Ont. Div. Ct.).

[154] R.S.O. 1990, c. C.43.

[155] (2001), 2001 CarswellOnt 400, 53 O.R. (3d) 181 (Ont. S.C.J.) (re TNT-01377 and TNL-18225-SA).

> It was not reasonable for the Tenant to fail to check her mail for almost two months . . . the conduct of the Tenant was tantamount to evading service or being willfully blind. Such conduct cannot be regarded as reasonable . . . The Tenant has failed to prove, on a balance of probabilities, that she was denied a reasonable opportunity to participate in the proceedings. The Tenant has failed to prove that the Landlord has abused the Tribunal's processes.

The Tenant did not file an appeal of this order. Instead, she brought an application to the Superior Court seeking relief there. Madam Justice Molloy agreed that a hearing to set aside a default order under the T.P.A. must be conducted in two stages (the Tenant must first demonstrate that he or she was denied a reasonable opportunity to participate and then, if they pass that hurdle, the Tribunal can consider the merits of the application) and approved of the Tribunal's ruling that relief under s. 84 of the T.P.A. could not be considered by the Tribunal unless the set-aside motion was granted. Justice Molloy considered this to be a flaw in the T.P.A. She ruled that the Superior Court retains the authority under s. 98 of the *Courts of Justice Act* to grant relief from forfeiture where, as here, the Tenant could not succeed on a set-aside motion but could demonstrate compassionate grounds for relief from forfeiture. I am not aware of any cases in which this precedent has been followed. Now that the default process has been eliminated under the R.T.A. and Members are required to consider granting relief from forfeiture in all eviction applications and on motions to set aside *ex parte* eviction orders, judges may be more reluctant to intervene (except by way of appeal or judicial review applications).

7. EXPIRATION OF AN EVICTION ORDER

When the T.P.A. was first enacted, there was no automatic expiry date for eviction orders. Unfortunately, this created a situation that was open to abuse by landlords. A landlord could obtain an eviction order and then hold it "over the head" of a tenant for the remainder of the tenancy. An unscrupulous landlord could use the ever-present threat of eviction in order to extort the tenant. The tenant would know that, at the smallest provocation, the landlord could file the eviction order with the sheriff and have the tenant evicted, even if the grounds upon which the order had been issued had long ago been rectified.

In 2000, s. 83.1 was added to the T.P.A. to address these concerns. This provision has been carried forward into the R.T.A. as s. 81. This section provides that, "An order of the Board evicting a person from a rental unit expires six months after the day on which the order takes effect if it is not filed within those six months with the sheriff who has territorial jurisdiction where the rental unit is located." Words to this effect are now included in all eviction orders.

Note that the six-month period begins to run on the first day that the order can be filed with the sheriff for enforcement; the six month period does *not* begin on the day the order is issued. If enforcement of the eviction is delayed this will also delay the expiration of the order. If, however, the landlord has not filed the order within six months from the date the eviction became enforceable, the landlord will have forever lost the right to rely upon that order to seek an eviction.

Any order for the payment of money or for relief other than eviction remains enforceable beyond this six-month period and is not affected by s. 81.

15

Human Rights Issues In Rental Housing

1. INTRODUCTION

(a) What is the *Human Rights Code*?

The Ontario *Human Rights Code*[1] (the "*Code*") is quasi-constitutional legislation that has primacy over all other legislation in Ontario, unless the other legislation specifically states that it applies despite the *Code*.[2] Thus, the Ontario *Human Rights Code* applies to residential landlords and tenants in Ontario, including those governed by the *Residential Tenancies Act, 2006*[3] (R.T.A.). Where the provisions of the R.T.A. and those of the *Human Rights Code* conflict, the provisions of the *Code* take priority.[4]

The purpose of the *Code*, as stated in its Preamble, is to create:

> [A] climate of understanding and mutual respect for the dignity and worth of each person so that each person feels a part of the community and able to contribute fully to the development and well-being of the community and the Province.

The Preamble also recognizes that it is public policy in Ontario:

> [T]o recognize the dignity and worth of every person and to provide for equal rights and opportunities without discrimination.

The *Code* attempts to achieve these aims by prohibiting certain specified types of discrimination or harassment.

[1] R.S.O. 1990, c. H.19, as amended.

[2] Subsection 47(2) of the *Code*.

[3] S.O. 2006, c. 17.

[4] See s. 47 of the *Human Rights Code* and s. 3 of the R.T.A. (formerly s. 2 of the T.P.A.).

(b) Recent Amendments to the *Human Rights Code*

On December 20, 2006, the *Human Rights Code Amendment Act, 2006*[5] (Bill 107) received Royal Assent. The changes introduced by Bill 107 came into effect on June 30, 2008. Although the substance of the *Code* remained largely intact, there were significant changes to the procedures for seeking resolution to a complaint of harassment or discrimination.

Every claimant now has the right to file an application for a hearing *directly* with the Human Rights Tribunal of Ontario. Publicly-funded legal, investigative and support services are available to assist claimants. There is no cost to file an application and the time to file a claim has been increased from 6 to 12 months.

The Human Rights Commission no longer processes human rights complaints (since applicants now apply directly to the Human Rights Tribunal). The Human Rights Commission, however, will still play an important role in preventing discrimination and promoting and advancing human rights in Ontario. The Human Rights Commission has been given enhanced independence; it has the right to launch its own applications, hold public enquiries and intervene in any application before the Human Rights Tribunal (with the consent of the applicant/claimant). The Commission is also able to promote human rights and prevent discrimination by engaging in proactive measures such as public education, policy development, research and analysis.

(c) 2007 Housing Consultation

The Human Rights Commission considers the right to adequate and affordable housing and the elimination of discrimination in rental housing to be important human rights issues in Ontario at this time. Concerned that there is insufficient affordable housing and widespread discrimination taking place in rental housing, in the summer and fall of 2007, the Commission held a public consultation on discrimination in rental housing. Almost 130 organizations and over 100 individuals took part in consultation meetings held across the province and the Commission also received numerous written submissions from groups and individuals. In the spring of 2008, the Ontario Human Rights Commission issued its report based upon this consultation.[6]

The Commission made a number of recommendations for action by various levels of government. It also specifically made the following two recommendations with respect to the Landlord and Tenant Board and the *Residential Tenancies Act*:

---

[5] S.O. 2006, c. 30.

[6] The Consultation Paper, Background Papers, Report ("Right at Home") and Summary Report can be obtained in person from the Human Rights Commission in a number of formats as well as being available online at *www.ohrc.on.ca*.

1. That decision makers, including service managers and the Landlord and Tenant Board (LTB), develop accommodation policies and procedures in accordance with the Commission's recently revised *Guidelines on Developing Human Rights Policies and Procedures*. Such policies should clearly provide a process for dealing with accommodation issues like language interpretation and extensions to deadlines.
2. That the *Code*, the *Residential Tenancies Act* (RTA) and the *Social Housing Reform Act* be interpreted and applied by tribunals, service managers and other decision-makers in a manner consistent with the *Code* and the *International Covenant on Economic, Social and Cultural Rights* (ICESCR). For example, that the LTB consider the fundamental importance of housing and apply the *Code* principle of accommodation to the point of undue hardship when considering whether to evict a tenant with a mental illness for having interfered with the reasonable enjoyment of rental premises.

(d) Role of the Landlord and Tenant Board

For the first five years of the Rental Housing Tribunal's existence, human rights issues were generally thought to be outside of the jurisdiction of the Tribunal.[7] That all changed when the Divisional Court issued its decision in 2003 in *Walmer Developments v. Wolch*.[8] This decision shall be discussed further below.

Based on the decision in *Walmer Developments v. Wolch*,[9] and subsequent decisions from the courts (including the Supreme Court of Canada), it is now clear that the Landlord and Tenant Board must interpret and enforce the provisions of the R.T.A. in a manner consistent with the objectives of the Ontario *Human Rights Code*. The Landlord and Tenant Board must also ensure that its actions, policies and procedures do not result in discrimination against individuals, contrary to the provisions of the *Code*.

Given their relative positions of power, the human rights of a tenant (or occupant or guest) — rather than those of a landlord — are more likely to be violated and this chapter will focus on the rights of tenants under the *Code*.

---

[7] See, for example, *Paramount Property Management v. Heafey* (May 2, 2002), EAL-27897, [2002] O.R.H.T.D. No. 35 (Ont. Rental Housing Trib.).

[8] (2003), 230 D.L.R. (4th) 372, 67 O.R. (3d) 246, 2003 CarswellOnt 3325, (Ont. Div. Ct.) (re TSL-39032).

[9] (2003), 230 D.L.R. (4th) 372, 67 O.R. (3d) 246, 2003 CarswellOnt 3325, (Ont. Div. Ct.) (re TSL-39032).

2. FREEDOM FROM DISCRIMINATION AND HARASSMENT IN HOUSING

(a) What is Discrimination in Rental Housing?

Discrimination is the result, whether or not that result was intended, of treating a person unequally by imposing unequal burdens or denying benefits. Discrimination in rental housing can take many forms and can occur at any stage. There can be discrimination based upon the types of tenants for which a landlord advertises. There can be discrimination in the process through which the landlord chooses whether or not to offer a tenancy to a potential tenant and any special terms imposed by the landlord on particular applicants. There can be discrimination against particular tenants during their tenancy. The failure of the landlord to make the complex accessible or to permit necessary alterations to a unit or the complex to accommodate a tenant's needs based upon disability can constitute discrimination. A landlord's decision to terminate a particular tenancy may also be evidence of discrimination if that decision is based upon a ground prohibited under the *Human Rights Code*.

(b) What is "Harassment" Under the *Code*?

According to the definition contained in s. 10 of the *Human Rights Code*, "harassment" means engaging in a course of vexatious comment or conduct that is known or ought reasonably to be known to be unwelcome.

(c) Relevant Provisions of the *Code*

Section 9 of the *Code* provides that, "No person shall infringe or do, directly or indirectly, anything that infringes a right under this Part." Section 11 of the *Code* prohibits constructive discrimination and imposes a duty to accommodate the needs of persons in order to avoid violating their human rights.

Section 1 of the *Code* provides that, "Every person has a right to equal treatment with respect to services, goods and facilities, without discrimination because of race, ancestry, place of origin, colour, ethnic origin, citizenship, creed, sex, sexual orientation, age, marital status, family status or disability."

Subsection 2(1) of the *Human Rights Code* provides that, "Every person has a right to equal treatment with respect to the occupancy of accommodation, without discrimination because of race, ancestry, place of origin, colour, ethnic origin, citizenship, creed, sex, sexual orientation, age, marital status, family status, disability or the receipt of public assistance."

Subsection 2(2) of the *Code* provides that, "Every person who occupies accommodation has a right to freedom from harassment by the landlord or agent of the landlord or by an occupant of the same building because of race, ancestry, place of origin, colour, ethnic origin, citizenship, creed, age, marital status, family status, disability or the receipt of public assistance."[10]

Not only is it contrary to the *Code* to discriminate against persons identified by a prohibited ground of discrimination, it is also contrary to the *Code* to discriminate against any person because of relationship, association or dealings with such persons (s. 12 of the *Code*).

Similar to clause 5(i) of the R.T.A., shared accommodations are exempt from s. 2 of the *Code*. The rights under s. 2 of the *Code* do not extend to a person living in a dwelling in which the owner or his or her family reside if the occupant or occupants of the residential accommodation are required to share a bathroom or kitchen facility with the owner or family of the owner (s. 21(1) of the *Code*).

Also, if you compare the language in s. 2(1) and 2(2), you will note that sex does not appear in s. 2(2) of the *Code*. This is because it is not considered a violation of human rights to set up accommodations designed specifically for one gender (s. 21(2) of the *Code*).[11]

Pursuant to s. 21(3) of the *Code*, the right under s. 2 to equal treatment with respect to the occupancy of residential accommodation without discrimination is not infringed if a landlord uses in the prescribed manner income information, credit checks, credit references, rental history, guarantees or other similar business practices prescribed in O. Reg. 290/98 (as amended).

Every 16- or 17-year-old person who has withdrawn from parental control has a right to equal treatment with respect to occupancy of and contracting for accommodation without discrimination because the person is less than 18 years old (s. 4(1) of the *Code*). A contract for accommodation entered into by a 16- or 17-year-old person who has withdrawn from parental control is enforceable against that person as if the person were 18 years old (s. 4(2) of the *Code*).

Every person who occupies accommodation has a right to freedom from harassment because of sex by the landlord or agent of the landlord or by an occupant of the same building (s. 7(1) of the *Code*). A person also has a right to be free from a sexual solicitation or advance made by a person in position to confer, grant or deny a benefit and to be free from a reprisal or threat of reprisal for the rejection of such a sexual solicitation or advance (s. 7(3) of the *Code*).

---

[10] Note that it is one of the recommendations contained in the 2008 report of the Ontario Human Rights Commission ("Right at Home") that the *Code* be amended to also explicitly list gender identity and sexual orientation as prohibited grounds of discrimination and harassment.

[11] See *Bowley v. McMenemy* (May 3, 1999), SWT-00495 (Ont. Rental Housing Trib.) in which it was not found to be unreasonable for the landlord to refuse to consent to a sublet from a female tenant to a male when all of the other tenants sharing the apartment were female.

(d) Constructive Discrimination

Although discrimination may be direct, it is perhaps just as common for discrimination to occur indirectly, often, unintentionally. *Constructive* discrimination is where seemingly neutral rules, procedures, qualifications or factors that may not be directly discriminatory, may nonetheless have an adverse and disproportionate effect or impact on a person or group protected under the *Code*. Constructive discrimination is prohibited by s. 11 of the *Code* unless:

1. it is specifically permitted by some other express provision of the *Code*; or
2. the landlord (in the case of residential rental accommodations) can prove that the requirement, qualification or factor imposed by the landlord is reasonable and *bona fide* in the circumstances **and** that the needs of the group of which the person adversely affected is a member cannot be accommodated without undue hardship on the landlord, considering the cost, outside sources of funding, if any, and health and safety requirements.

The Ontario Court of Appeal has held that it does not amount to discrimination, however, to hold a disabled tenant financially responsible for damage caused by the tenant to the rental unit as a result of his disability. In *Eskritt v. MacKay*,[12] the court wrote as follows (at paragraphs 2 and 3):

> The appellants submit that the trial judge erred in awarding the respondents amounts on account of damage occasioned as a result of Mr. McKay's disability. We reject this submission. The trial judge made a finding of fact that the damage caused to the respondents' premises were beyond reasonable wear and tear. This finding was available on the evidence.
>
> The *Human Rights Code* does not obviate a disabled person's responsibility to pay for damage to a landlord's premises extending beyond reasonable wear and tear. The appellants have produced no authority to that effect and, in our view, that is not the intent of the *Human Rights Code*.

(e) Examples of Discrimination in Rental Housing

The Ontario Human Rights Commission has provided on its website the following examples of situations that might be discriminatory in the context of rental housing:

- Advertising "adult only" buildings that exclude families with chil-

[12] (2008), 2008 CarswellOnt 5165 (Ont. C.A.), reversed (2008), 2008 CarswellOnt 5165 (Ont. C.A.).

dren or young people over 16 who have "withdrawn from parental control"

- Constructing buildings that are not suitable for people of all ages and abilities
- Saying to a racialized person that an apartment is rented but continuing to show it to White applicants
- Applying neutral rules that act as barriers to access, for example, a rule that only applicants with income above a set amount can rent a unit
- Not responding to a tenant's requests for disability-related changes to a unit or a building (i.e., not accommodating to the point of undue hardship)
- Making harassing statements or failing to address discriminatory comments and conduct by others, including other tenants
- Not allowing a same-sex couple the same benefits as other tenants, for example, a right to automatic renewal of a lease
- Asking tenants to remove religious displays from their front doors
- Calling the police very often because a tenant has a mental illness
- Targeting for eviction people who are not citizens or who speak languages other than English

In *Williams v. Strata Plan LMS 768*,[13] the British Colombia Human Rights Tribunal held that it was discriminatory for a landlord to have installed a security system that required tenants to go to the front door of the complex to let a visitor in during certain hours of the night. Although the landlord was justified in being concerned about building security, the complainant was an elderly person with a number of medical conditions that might prevent her from going down to the front door to admit guests or medical attendants. The Tribunal ordered the landlord to return to the old "buzz-in" system. The Tribunal found that the landlord had failed in its duty to accommodate this tenant in that it refused to even investigate what it might do to address her legitimate concerns.

In *Ganser v. Rosewood Estates Condominium Corporation*,[14] the Alberta Human Rights Panel found the Condominium Corporation's decision to be discriminatory when it took away the complainant's parking space because she did not own a vehicle. The complainant had several disabilities that left her visually impaired and limited her ability to stand and walk. The complainant's parking space was near the building entrance. Caregivers and other guests upon whom the complainant relied for transportation to and from daily activities and medical appointments used her space to pick her up and drop

[13] (2003), 46 C.H.R.R. D/326 (B.C. Human Rights Trib.).

[14] (2002), 42 C.H.R.R. D/264 (Alta. Human Rights Bd. of Inquiry).

her off. The Panel also found that no efforts had been made by the Condominium Corporation to accommodate the needs of the complainant.

In *Matthews v. Westphal Mobile Home Court Ltd.*,[15] the Nova Scotia Human Rights Board of Inquiry held that a decision to refuse to allow a tenant to build a shed on a mobile home lot to store his scooter was discriminatory. Without such a shed, he could not continue to reside in the mobile home. There was no evidence presented that the landlord had made any attempt to accommodate the tenant.

In *Eagleson Co-operative Homes Inc. v. Theberge*,[16] members of this co-op were required to perform two hours' volunteer work each month. The appellant, a member of this co-op, provided the co-op with a doctor's written opinion that she was incapable of performing volunteer work. She refused to provide further particulars demanded by the co-op concerning her disability. The co-op applied for and obtained a writ of possession under the *Co-operative Corporations Act*. The appellant successfully appealed this eviction to the Divisional Court. The Divisional Court found that eviction was unfair in the circumstances and that it violated the Ontario *Human Rights Code*; there was *prima facie* discrimination against the appellant based upon her disability and there was no evidence of any attempt by the co-op to accommodate her particular situation.

Other examples are described later in this Chapter.

3. DISCRIMINATION IN THE SELECTION OF TENANTS

It is important to realize that human rights issues concerning discrimination in the selection of tenants likely will <u>not</u> be brought before the Landlord and Tenant Board for two reasons. First, the discrimination will have occurred prior to the commencement of the tenancy and such conduct will, therefore, be outside the time period that can properly be considered by the Board. Second, prospective tenants who have suffered from such discrimination will likely not be accepted as tenants and no tenancy will be created (which means that the Board will, once again, lack jurisdiction). Such issues will usually have to be brought before the Ontario Human Rights Tribunal. There may be some exceptions, however, to this general rule. One example would be where a landlord accepts a person as a tenant but the landlord imposes into the tenancy agreement discriminatory terms (such as requiring payment of many months' rent in advance or additional security not normally required by this landlord from others). In such a case, after the commencement of the tenancy, the tenant, upon discovering the discriminatory nature of the special terms insisted upon by the landlord, could bring an application before the Landlord

---

[15] (2005), 55 C.H.R.R. D/312 (N.S. Bd. of Inquiry).

[16] (2006), 218 O.A.C. 321, 274 D.L.R. (4th) 359, 2006 CarswellOnt 5334 (Ont. Div. Ct.).

and Tenant Board[17] and, in the context of that hearing, the Landlord and Tenant Board could consider what relief under the RT.A. would be appropriate for any violation of the *Human Rights Code*.

A landlord is specifically prohibited from discriminating against a person on the basis of their age. Thus, if a 16- or 17-year-old person who has withdrawn from parental control applies as a prospective tenant, that person has the right to be treated by the landlord in the same manner as any other applicant. This right is specifically protected by s. 4 of the *Code*.

Though clearly contrary to the *Code*, discrimination based upon age and/or family status continues to be quite common in Ontario. For instance, it is common to see advertising promoting "adult only" or "seniors only" or "lifestyle" rental housing.

It is interesting to note that the Ontario *Human Rights Code* only prohibits discrimination based upon one or more of the characteristics (race, gender, age, etc.) specifically listed within the *Code*. Therefore, it is not a violation of the *Code* for a landlord to discriminate against a person based upon some other characteristic, such as the person owning a pet,[18] being a smoker or having a criminal record.[19] It is an open question as to whether it is discriminatory to insist on a police background check for a prospective tenant.

In *Otonabee Native Homes Inc., Re*,[20] the rental unit was located in a community that was limited to occupancy for persons of Native ancestry. At the time the tenancy commenced, the tenant moved into the unit with her husband and two children. The husband and the children were of Native ancestry. Approximately 17 years later, the husband and children vacated the unit. Since the remaining tenant was not of Native ancestry, the landlord commenced an application to evict her on the basis that she no longer qualified to live in this rental unit. The tenant argued that this constituted discrimination and was contrary to the *Code*. The Member found that since the rental unit was covered by a special program designed to relieve hardship or economic disadvantage or to assist disadvantaged persons or groups to achieve or

---

[17] Based upon harassment, obstruction or interference (contrary to s. 23 of the R.T.A.), substantial interference with the tenant's reasonable enjoyment (contrary to s. 22 of the R.T.A.) or the illegal collection or retention of money (contrary to Part VII of the R.T.A.).

[18] If, however, the "pet" is necessary to assist a prospective tenant in relation to a disability, then a refusal based on the pet would clearly contravene the *Code*.

[19] In its draft policy on "Mental Health Discrimination and Police Record Checks", the Human Rights Commission has made a distinction between police record checks (which may reveal both convictions and any records related to non-criminal contact between police and an individual) and criminal record checks (that will only reveal any convictions registered against the person). The Commission recommends that, barring unusual circumstances, criminal record checks should be sufficient to address most legitimate concerns about safety and security and thereby avoid further stigmatizing persons with mental illness who have committed no crimes but may have come into contact with the police from time to time as a result of their disability.

[20] (Sept. 26, 2006), 2006 CarswellOnt 9164, TEL-62870 (Ont. Rental Housing Trib.).

attempt to achieve equal opportunity, pursuant to s. 14(1) of the *Code*, discrimination against the Tenant in this case based on her ancestry did not violate the *Code*.

Many landlords apply a standard guideline that a tenant applicant should be spending no more than 25-35 percent of his or her income on rent. According to the Ontario Human Rights Commission, recipients of public assistance and other low-income individuals have been particularly affected by the application of such rent-to-income ratios and minimum income requirements. The Divisional Court seemed to approve of the use by landlords of rent/income ratios in selecting prospective tenants as long as this was considered in conjunction with other criteria.[21] Two later decisions of the Ontario Board of Inquiry, however, now put into question that interpretation.[22]

Pursuant to s. 21(3) of the *Code*, the right under s. 2 to equal treatment with respect to the occupancy of residential accommodation without discrimination is not infringed if a landlord uses, in the prescribed manner, income information, credit checks, credit references, rental history, guarantees or other similar business practices prescribed in O. Reg. 290/98 (as amended).[23] This Regulation specifically reaffirms that none of these assessment tools may be used in an arbitrary manner to screen out prospective tenants based on prohibited grounds. The criteria must be used in a *bona fide* and non-discriminatory fashion. According to the Ontario Human Rights Commission's Background Paper,[24]

> Where income information, credit checks, credit references, rental history or guarantees are being applied in a fashion that creates systemic barriers to persons identified by a *Code* ground, the landlord will be required to show that it is a *bona fide* requirement – that is, that the criteria could not be applied in a non-discriminatory fashion without creating undue hardship for the landlord.

For instance, the Commission has suggested that the practice of some landlord's requiring co-signors or guarantors merely because an applicant is in receipt of social assistance may be a violation of the *Code*.[25] Similarly, the Commission has suggested that a landlord's request for first and last month's rent also has the potential to "constructively discriminate against those in receipt of public assistance, as well as other members of disadvantaged groups

---

[21] *Kearney v. Bramalea Ltd.* (2001), 2001 CarswellOnt 256, [2001] O.J. No. 297 (Ont. Div. Ct.).

[22] *Schaaf v. M & R Property Management Ltd.* (2000), [2000] O.H.R.B.I.D. No. 13, 2000 CarswellOnt 5601 (Ont. Bd. of Inquiry) and *Sinclair v. Morris A. Hunter Investments Ltd.* (2001), [2001] O.H.R.B.I.D. No. 24, 2001 CarswellOnt 5620 (Ont. Bd. of Inquiry).

[23] Section 10 of the R.T.A.. The full text of O. Reg. 290/98 made under the *Human Rights Code* is reproduced in Appendix 12.

[24] *Human Rights and Rental Housing in Ontario – Background Paper*, March 28, 2007, p. 49.

[25] *Human Rights and Rental Housing in Ontario – Background Paper*, March 28, 2007, p. 49.

protected by the *Code*, who frequently have lower incomes and will often be unable to generate such resources".[26]

Obviously, unless the residential complex is specifically exempted from the application of the *Human Rights Code*, it is a violation of the *Code* for a landlord to refuse to rent to a person on the grounds of the applicant's race, colour, ancestry, creed (religion), place of origin, ethnic origin, citizenship, sex (including pregnancy and gender identity), sexual orientation, age, marital status, family status, disability and/or receipt of public assistance or the person's association with someone who the landlord finds objectionable on one or more of the same grounds. Unfortunately, such discrimination is not uncommon.

In *Richards v. Waisglass*,[27] a Board of Inquiry found that the respondent discriminated against the complainant, a Black woman, because of her race when he refused to rent her an apartment. According to the Commission's Background Paper, studies in the U.S. and Canada reveal that Black persons find it more difficult to acquire rental accommodations. There is also evidence of linguistic profiling and, since September 11, 2001,[28] increased complaints of discrimination in housing against persons identified as, or perceived to be, Muslim, Arab and South Asian.[29] In Canada, there is also an unfortunate history of discrimination against Aboriginals. In *Flamand v. DGN Investments*,[30] a Tribunal found that the landlord violated the *Code* by refusing to rent an apartment to the complainant when he found out that she was of Aboriginal ancestry.

Recent immigrants and refugees are also frequently victims of discrimination. Such persons may be required to pay their rent up to 12 months in advance or may be required to provide exorbitant security deposits, despite such practices being illegal.[31] Insisting on a rental history or credit history from <u>all</u> prospective tenant applicants may seem like a neutral practice, but it effectively excludes from consideration most new immigrants and refugees (who, as new arrivals to the country, will not have available such histories) and, thus, may well constitute constructive discrimination under the *Code*.[32] In *Ahmed v. 177061 Canada Ltd.*,[33] a Board of Inquiry found that even through the *Code* permits landlords to request income information, rental history and

---

[26] *Human Rights and Rental Housing in Ontario – Background Paper*, March 28, 2007, p. 45. See *Garbett v. Fisher* (1996), 25 C.H.R.R. D/379 (Ont. Bd. of Inquiry) and *Larson v. Graham* (1999), 35 C.H.R.R. D/382 (B.C. Human Rights Trib.).

[27] (1994), 24 C.H.R.R. D/51 (Ont. Bd. of Inquiry).

[28] The date of the attack on the World Trade Center in New York City, commonly referred to as "9-11".

[29] *Human Rights and Rental Housing in Ontario – Background Paper*, March 28, 2007, pp. 24 and 25.

[30] (2005), 52 C.H.R.R. D/142 (Ont. Human Rights Trib.).

[31] *Human Rights and Rental Housing in Ontario – Background Paper*, March 28, 2007, p. 28.

[32] *Human Rights and Rental Housing in Ontario – Background Paper*, March 28, 2007, p. 28.

[33] (2002), 43 C.H.R.R. D/379 (Ont. Bd. of Inquiry).

credit checks and references under certain circumstances, the landlord's tenant-selection policy was discriminatory in that it assumed a connection between the absence of a credit rating and the likelihood of a rental default.

Similarly, requirements for rental and employment histories are "likely to have an adverse effect on women who have taken time out of the workforce to raise children, provide care-giving for others, who are leaving abusive relationships or otherwise attempting to establish and support themselves independently".[34]

Discrimination may occur on the basis of the sex (including pregnancy and gender identity) of the person applying to become a tenant. This is often combined with discrimination on the basis of marital and/or family status. A landlord may decide that they do not wish to rent to a person of a particular gender or to a single parent (usually a single mother). In *Conway v. Koslowski*,[35] an Ontario Board of Inquiry found that the respondent discriminated against the complainant by refusing to rent a house to her in part because there was no man in her family to do the yardwork. In *Schaaf v. M & R Property Management Ltd.*,[36] the superintendent refused to rent to the complainant and her roommate because of the landlord's preference to rent to married couples. In *Booker v. Floriri Village Investments Inc.*,[37] an Ontario Board of Inquiry found that the complainant was discriminated against because she was a single parent and the superintendent expressed a preference for married couples since this was a "family building".[38]

Some landlords may be reluctant to rent to someone because that person's "lifestyle" offends the landlord's religious views. For example, in *Matyson v. Provost*,[39] the respondents would not rent to common-law couples because it offended their religious beliefs. A Saskatchewan Board of Inquiry found that, while the landlords' freedom of religion was protected under both the Canadian *Charter of Rights and Freedoms* and the Saskatchewan *Human Rights Code*, once the respondents decided to make rental accommodations available to the public they had an obligation to do so in a non-discriminatory manner.

Discrimination in the selection of tenants may also be based upon disability. In *Yale v. Metropoulos*[40] the respondent landlord refused to even show the apartment to a prospective tenant when the landlord discovered that she was blind.

---

[34] *Human Rights and Rental Housing in Ontario – Background Paper*, March 28, 2007, p. 31.

[35] (1993), 19 C.H.R.R. D/253 (Ont. Bd. of Inquiry).

[36] (2000), 38 C.H.R.R. D/251 (Ont. Bd. of Inquiry).

[37] (1989), 11 C.H.R.R. D/44 (Ont. Bd. of Inquiry).

[38] See also *St. Hill v. VRM Investments Ltd.* (2004), 2004 HRTO 1 (Ont. Human Rights Trib.) in which the landlord refused to rent to prospective tenants with children.

[39] (1987), 9 C.H.R.R. D/4623 (Sask. Bd. of Inquiry).

[40] (1992), 20 C.H.R.R. D/45 (Ont. Bd. of Inquiry).

Discrimination is also common against recipients of public assistance. There are many cases where rental housing has simply been denied to such persons. For example, in *Willis v. David Anthony Philips Properties*,[41] a Board of Inquiry found that the owner wrongfully discriminated against the complainant by refusing to rent accommodations to her because she was on social assistance. In another case,[42] the landlord was found to have violated the *Code* by refusing to rent to a single mother who was receiving social assistance.

4. ACCOMODATING TENANTS[43]

(a) Duty to Accommodate

Landlords have a duty to accommodate tenants where required to prevent discrimination, including those tenants who are disabled and those receiving social assistance. Pursuant to s. 11 of the *Human Rights Code*, constructive discrimination is prohibited unless:

1. it is specifically permitted by some other express provision of the *Code*; or
2. the landlord (in the case of residential rental accommodations) can prove that the requirement, qualification or factor imposed by the landlord is reasonable and *bona fide* in the circumstances **and** that the needs of the group of which the person adversely affected is a member cannot be accommodated without undue hardship on the landlord, considering the cost, outside sources of funding, if any, and health and safety requirements.

The duty of the landlord is to accommodate up to the point of undue hardship.

The duty to accommodate arises most commonly in cases of discrimination based upon disability. For that reason, the focus in this Chapter will be upon accommodation of the needs of persons with disabilities. Nevertheless, one should bear in mind that the duty to accommodate arises in *any* case of constructive discrimination based upon any of the grounds identified in the *Code*, not exclusively discrimination based upon disability. For instance, reasonable accommodation of a person receiving social assistance may require a landlord to waive the usual requirement of paying a rent deposit.

Under the Ontario *Human Rights Code*,[44] "disability" means:

(a) any degree of physical disability, infirmity, malformation or disfig-

[41] (1987), 8 C.H.R.R. D/3847 (Ont. Bd. of Inquiry).

[42] *Kostanowicz v. Zarubin* (1994), 28 C.H.R.R. D/55 (Ont. Bd. of Inquiry).

[43] And other occupants of the rental unit and guests of tenants or other occupants.

[44] Subsection 10(1) of the *Code*.

urement that is caused by bodily injury, birth defect or illness and, without limiting the generality of the foregoing, includes diabetes mellitus, epilepsy, a brain injury, any degree of paralysis, amputation, lack of physical co-ordination, blindness or visual impairment, deafness or hearing impairment, muteness or speech impediment, or physical reliance on a guide dog or other animal or on a wheelchair or other remedial appliance or device,

(b) a condition of mental impairment or a developmental disability,

(c) a learning disability, or a dysfunction in one or more of the processes involved in understanding or using symbols or spoken language,

(d) a mental disorder, or

(e) an injury or disability for which benefits were claimed or received under the insurance plan established under the *Workplace Safety and Insurance Act, 1997*.

(b) Responsibilities of Person with a Disability

According to the Human Rights Commission, a person with disability is required to do the following:[45]

- advise the accommodation provider (i.e., landlord) of the disability (although not necessarily details of the disability);
- make her or his needs known to the best of his or her ability, preferably in writing, in order that the person responsible for accommodation may make the requested accommodation;
- answer questions or provide information regarding relevant restrictions or limitations, including information from health care professionals, where appropriate, and as needed;
- participate in discussions regarding possible accommodation solutions;
- co-operate with any experts whose assistance is required to manage the accommodation process or when information is required that is unavailable to the person with a disability;
- meet agreed-upon benchmarks once accommodation is provided;[46]
- work with the accommodation provider on an ongoing basis to manage the accommodation process; and
- discuss his or her disability only with persons who need to know.

---

[45] Ontario Human Rights Commission, *Policy and Guidelines on Disability and the Duty to Accommodate*, pp. 23 and 24.

[46] Note: this relates more to employment situations where the employee with a disability, when accommodated, should be able to meet agreed-upon performance and job standards. This condition probably does not apply to rental housing situations.

A tenant who intends to complain about the failure of a landlord to accommodate that tenant's disability, will need to be able to prove that he or she complied with all of the obligations set out above. It is a "two-way street". A landlord cannot be expected to accommodate a tenant if the landlord is unaware of the existence of a problem, the specific needs of the tenant and possible solutions that are available.

In *Bathurst-Vaughan Mall Limited v. Eini*,[47] a tenant appealed from the decision of the Landlord and Tenant Board on the grounds that the Board did not embark upon an inquiry as to whether the landlord made any effort to accommodate the tenant's disability (mental illness) as it may have impacted upon her ability to pay rent on time. The Divisional Court dismissed the tenant's appeal because there was no evidence on the record that at any time during the tenancy did the tenant advise the landlord of her disability and request accommodation; on the contrary, her first mention of disability was at the hearing.

(c) Responsibilities of Landlord

Once a landlord is made aware that a tenant[48] requires accommodation, the landlord has a duty to accommodate the person on the basis of three general principles: (1) respect for dignity; (2) individualization; and (3) integration and full participation.[49]

The accommodation must be provided in a manner that most respects the dignity of the person. Dignity includes consideration of how accommodation is provided and the individual's own participation in the process. For instance, the dignity of a tenant who uses a wheelchair requires that he or she be able to access the building through the same entrance as all other tenants, and that he or she not be expected to enter via a loading dock or garbage room simply because a ramp may already be in place in such locations.

According to the Human Rights Commission:[50]

> There is no set formula for accommodating people with disabilities. Each person's needs are unique and must be considered afresh when an accommodation request is made. A solution may meet one person's requirements but not another's.

Thus, it is important for the person with a disability to state clearly what sort of accommodation they require and to participate and co-operate in the plan-

---

[47] (2009), 2009 CarswellOnt 470 (Ont. Div. Ct.).

[48] Or occupant or, potentially, a guest of the tenant or an occupant.

[49] Ontario Human Rights Commission, *Policy and Guidelines on Disability and the Duty to Accommodate*, pp. 12 to 16.

[50] Ontario Human Rights Commission, *Policy and Guidelines on Disability and the Duty to Accommodate*, p. 14.

ning and implementation of an accommodation that is suitable to their specific needs.

Finally, landlords should seek not only to ensure that existing tenants with special needs are accommodated in such a way that they can fully participate in and enjoy the same daily activities as other tenants but landlords also need to consider designing and building residential complexes that feature barrier-free and inclusive designs and removing barriers from existing buildings.

In *North Bay Community Housing Initiatives v. Huthcinson*,[51] the tenant suffered from paranoid schizophrenia and would, from time to time, yell in response to voices he was hearing. This disturbed other tenants of this complex, all of whom were also struggling with mental health disabilities. The Tribunal found that the landlord had failed to take all reasonable steps necessary to accommodate this tenant and that evicting him from this complex would be too great a hardship. The landlord's application was dismissed.

Once aware of a tenant's need for accommodation, a landlord must take steps to accommodate that tenant to the point that the discrimination has been eliminated. The only exceptions are:

1. rental housing provided or governed under legislation that is specifically exempt from the *Human Rights Code*;
2. situations that are otherwise specifically exempted by a provision of the *Code* itself; and
3. situations where the necessary accommodation cannot be made without undue hardship on the landlord, considering the cost, outside sources of funding, if any, and health and safety requirements.

Courts and human rights tribunals have been loathe to make it too easy for service providers to avoid the duty to accommodate by reliance upon the "undue hardship" defence. For this reason, the *Ontario Human Rights Code* has restricted this defence to a consideration of only three factors (cost, outside sources of funding and health/safety requirements) and these three criteria have been interpreted narrowly.

It is not sufficient for a landlord to demonstrate that the requested accommodation will result in higher costs. The costs must be quantifiable, must be shown to be related to the accommodation and, most importantly, must be so substantial that they would alter the essential nature of the enterprise or be so significant that they would substantially affect its viability.[52] The financial costs of the accommodation may include:

- capital costs (such as the installation of a ramp);

---

[51] (September 25, 2005), NOL-13823 (Ont. Rental Housing Trib.).

[52] Ontario Human Rights Commission, *Policy and Guidelines on Disability and the Duty to Accommodate*, pp. 30 and 31.

- operating costs (such as increased insurance premiums);
- costs incurred as a result of restructuring that are necessitated by the accommodation; and
- any other quantifiable costs incurred directly as a result of the accommodation.

For the purposes of determining whether a financial cost would alter or jeopardize the landlord's business, consideration will be given to the following:[53]

- the ability of the landlord to recover the costs of accommodation in the normal course of business;
- the availability of any grants, subsidies or loans from the federal, provincial or municipal government or from non-government sources that could offset the costs of accommodation;
- the ability of the landlord to spread the cost over a period of time by doing the work in phases;
- the ability of the landlord to distribute the costs of accommodation throughout the whole operation;
- the ability of the landlord to amortize or depreciate capital costs associated with the accommodation; and
- the ability of the landlord to deduct from the costs of accommodation any savings that may be available as a result of the accommodation (including the value of potential benefits the landlord may enjoy as a result of the accommodation such as tax deductions, an increase in the resale value of the property and/or an increase in the potential pool of tenants the landlord may attract to the residential complex).

The most common factor landlords will rely upon in arguing that an accommodation would impose undue hardship is cost. It is important to remember, however, that cost is but one of three factors that must be considered. Another factor is the availability of outside sources of funding. The individual who requires accommodation may have available funds that could assist in providing housing accommodation. There may also be government programs that would help defray the cost of, for example, making an apartment building more accessible. The availability of such funds would make such accommodation more affordable and, therefore, more palatable to a landlord. It will also make it more difficult for a landlord to successfully argue that the cost of the requested accommodation would impose an undue hardship upon the landlord.

The final considerations are any applicable health and safety requirements. The landlord should not, in the process of accommodating the needs

[53] Ontario Human Rights Commission, *Policy and Guidelines on Disability and the Duty to Accommodate*, pp. 31 and 32.

of one tenant, put at serious risk that tenant or others within the complex or be forced to expose itself to potential liability for violation of relevant health and safety standards. Accommodation will only be excused as imposing an undue hardship where the risk posed by making the requested accommodation is both serious and real. Consideration would have to be given to the nature of the risk, the severity of the potential risk, the probability of real harm and the scope of the risk (i.e., how many people are potentially affected).

5. ROLE OF THE LANDLORD AND TENANT BOARD

(a) Jurisdiction

As previously stated in this Chapter, for the first five years of the Rental Housing Tribunal's existence, human rights issues were generally thought to be outside of the jurisdiction of the Rental Housing Tribunal.[54] That all changed when the Divisional Court issued its decision in 2003 in *Walmer Developments v. Wolch.*[55]

In *Walmer Developments v. Wolch,* the landlord applied to evict a tenant who suffered from schizophrenia on the grounds that she was substantially interfering with the reasonable enjoyment of other tenants in the complex. Primarily, the complaints were about her screaming and shouting in the common areas and throwing garbage in the halls. This only occurred occasionally when the tenant was off her medication. After a number of adjournments, the hearing proceeded and the tenancy was terminated by the Ontario Rental Housing Tribunal. The reasons given in the order were sparse and do not refer to the *Human Rights Code* although it was apparently an issue that had been raised at the hearing. The Member apparently did not consider the implications of the fact that the tenant was a person with a disability. The tenant requested a review of the eviction order but that request was denied on the basis that it was "not a serious error for a member not to apply the Human [Rights] Code." The tenant then appealed to the Divisional Court.

The Divisional Court reviewed the law in this area, including a couple of earlier decisions of the Rental Housing Tribunal. In *Longo Properties Limited v. Clarke*,[56] the Rental Housing Tribunal refused to evict a tenant for making "unnecessary noise" that evidence showed was involuntary and caused by the tenant's mental illness. The Member wrote: "The duty not to discriminate includes in it a duty to accommodate persons with a disability unless such accommodation is economically or in some other way not fea-

[54] See, for example, *Paramount Property Management v. Heafey* (May 2, 2002), EAL-27897, [2002] O.R.H.T.D. No. 35 (Ont. Rental Housing Trib.).

[55] (2003), 230 D.L.R. (4th) 372, 67 O.R. (3d) 246, 2003 CarswellOnt 3325, (Ont. Div. Ct.) (re TSL-39032).

[56] (2002), TSL-35686-SA (Ont. Rental Housing Trib.).

sible. It is incumbent on the Tribunal to consider the Human Rights Code if it affects a tenant in their housing needs." Similarly, in *Ottawa Housing Corp. v. Mongeon*,[57] the Member wrote (at para. 14):

> [T]he Human Rights Code is an important expression of the public's values and it is reasonable to question the fairness of a legal outcome that appears to violate rights guaranteed by the Code. Therefore, in applications for eviction, the Tribunal should consider whether a person might be accommodated within the meaning of subsection 11(2) of the Human Rights Code.

Following the principles enunciated by the Supreme Court of Canada in the case of *Rizzo & Rizzo Shoes Ltd., Re*,[58] the Divisional Court in *Walmer Developments v. Wolch* concluded as follows:

> [T]he ORHT [Ontario Rental Housing Tribunal] is bound by the legislation to comply with section 17 [of the T.P.A.] in full in its decision-making and in particular when exercising its discretion under section 84 [of the T.P.A.] as to whether it would be unfair to the landlord not to evict a person suffering from a disability. The ORHT must consider whether any disruption in the enjoyment of other tenants may be sufficiently alleviated by a reasonable accommodation of the disabled tenant without undue hardship to the landlord.

Since the tenant's family had, during the intervening period, taken steps to minimize the risk of a repetition of the tenant's objectionable conduct, the Divisional Court was content to grant the tenant's appeal, quash the Tribunal's orders and dismiss the landlord's application, upon certain terms.

In *Werbeski v. Ontario (Director of Disability Support Program, Ministry of Community & Social Services)*,[59] the Supreme Court of Canada has confirmed that a tribunal with jurisdiction to decide issues of law also has jurisdiction to determine whether any provision of the legislation regulated by the tribunal violates the *Human Rights Code*. Contrary to the position taken by the Ontario Court of Appeal, the majority of the Supreme Court of Canada held that such a tribunal cannot decline to hear an issue related to the *Code* (by referring the matter to another forum such as the Human Rights Commission) unless the tribunal's empowering statue specifically grants the tribunal the authority to decline such jurisdiction.

The issue of human rights can arise in proceedings before the Landlord and Tenant Board in four ways.

---

[57] (May 9, 2002), EAL-28086, [2002] O.R.H.T.D. No. 36 (Ont. Rental Housing Trib.).

[58] [1998] 1 S.C.R. 27 (S.C.C.).

[59] (2005), (sub nom. *Tranchemontagne v. Disability Support Program (Ont.)*) 2005 CarswellOnt 1015 (S.C.C.), reversed (2006), (sub nom. *Tranchemontagne v. Ontario (Director, Disability Support Program)*) 2006 CarswellOnt 2350 (S.C.C.). Also see the decision of the Supreme Court of Canada in *Werbeski v. Ontario (Director of Disability Support Program, Ministry of Community & Social Services)*, (sub nom. *Tranchemontagne v. Ontario (Director, Disability Support Program)*) [2006] 1 S.C.R. 513, 2006 SCC 14 (S.C.C.).

First, a tenant may bring an application before the Board to complain about harassment or discriminatory conduct by the landlord or by other tenants (where such conduct is brought to the attention of the landlord and the landlord has either condoned this harassment or has failed to take reasonable steps to stop it). This can include both actual harassment and more passive discrimination, such as ignoring requests for repairs and maintenance from certain tenants who, for prohibited reasons, the landlord has decided to treat poorly. The conduct about which the tenant is complaining may, on its own, constitute a violation of provisions of the R.T.A.[60] or may constitute an aggravating factor that would warrant the granting of greater relief to the tenant and/or a more severe penalty to the landlord under s. 31 of the R.T.A.

Second, a landlord may be seeking to evict a tenant because the tenant's conduct (or that of a member of their household) has tended to annoy (i.e., substantially interfere with the reasonable enjoyment of) or endanger others within the residential complex. The tenant may wish to demonstrate that the conduct in question was the result of a disability that the landlord has an obligation to accommodate. An example would be a tenant with a mental disorder who, periodically, yells loudly within the rental unit; the problem might be resolved by better sound-proofing of the unit. Alternatively, a tenant may assert that the landlord's standard rules and/or policies constructively discriminate against the tenant. An example may be where a tenant has been asked to remove a religious article from her door on the basis that it is the landlord's policy that no religious items may be displayed outside of a rental unit. In Judaism, for instance, it is a requirement to attach a religious item (a mezuzah)[61] to the doorframe and the blanket application of the landlord's policy in my example would have the effect of precluding observant Jews from taking up residence within the complex.

Third, where a tenant is facing eviction, the tenant can raise at the hearing before the Landlord and Tenant Board the fact that the tenant has a disability and that the landlord failed to accommodate the tenant's needs as factors to be considered by the Board in deciding whether, pursuant to s. 83 of the R.T.A. (formerly s. 84 of the T.P.A.), the Board must refuse to evict the tenant or whether the Board ought to exercise its discretionary power and choose to refuse to grant or to delay the requested eviction.

Fourth, a party (usually the tenant) may allege that a provision of the R.T.A. (or regulations thereunder) or a rule, practice or procedure of the Landlord and Tenant Board itself contravenes the *Ontario Human Rights Code* (most likely on the basis that it constructively discriminates against the

---

[60] Such as harassment, obstruction or interference (contrary to s. 23 of the R.T.A.), substantial interference with the tenant's reasonable enjoyment (contrary to s. 22 of the R.T.A.) or the illegal collection or retention of money (contrary to Part VII of the R.T.A.).

[61] A *mezuzah* is a piece of parchment (usually contained in a decorative case) inscribed with specified Hebrew verses from the Torah.

person on a prohibited ground) and, therefore, is of no effect. Such allegations are rare. Although one Member's decision is not, strictly speaking, binding upon the rest of the Board, a determination by a Member that part of the legislation is contrary to the *Human Rights Code* carries significant implications. A Board Member may, therefore, wish to consider requiring the person who is raising such an allegation to notify the office of the Attorney-General for Ontario to see if that office wishes to intervene in the proceeding and make submissions on the issue.

The Landlord and Tenant Board has recently developed an Interpretation Guideline[62] on human rights issues in the context of proceedings before the Board. Reference should be made to that Guideline in any case before the Board where human rights violations have been or may be raised as an issue or where a party to the proceeding requires special accommodations by the Board in order to have access to or to be able to meaningfully participate in the Board's proceedings.

(b) Choice of Forum

A person with a potential human rights complaint must decide whether to have the issue dealt with before the Human Rights Tribunal or as part of another administrative proceeding. The choice may be affected by: (1) what other issues, if any, need to be adjudicated; (2) the scope of remedies available; (3) the cost; and (4) the time it will take to get a decision. Only the Human Rights Tribunal can grant the remedies provided for in the *Human Rights Code*. Once a human rights issue has been adjudicated, there is (usually) no "second kick at the can". Thus, if a person chooses to raise a human rights issue before the Landlord and Tenant Board, that person may well be precluded from later bringing the same issue before the Human Rights Tribunal (s. 45.1 of the *Code*). That is, however, a matter that is within the discretion of the Human Rights Tribunal.[63]

(c) Onus of Proof

As a general proposition, a Member of the Board should rely upon the parties to bring forward human rights issues and the Member should not raise such issues on his or her own motion.

---

[62] Interpretation Guideline No. 17, released on October 15, 2009. See Appendix 8.

[63] See, for example, *Carlos v. 1174364 Ontario Ltd. et al.*, 2008 HRTO 403 in which the Landlord and Tenant Board considered the alleged sexual harassment of the tenant in the context of an application before it but the Human Rights Tribunal nevertheless allowed the tenant to proceed with a human rights complaint before it, based on the same facts, because the Human Rights Tribunal was not satisfied that the Landlord and Tenant Board had "appropriately dealt with" the human rights aspect of the alleged harassment.

Where a person raises an allegation of a breach of the *Human Rights Code*, the onus will be upon that person to prove, on a balance of probabilities, that they have been subjected to discrimination or harassment on grounds prohibited under the *Code*. It is important to remember that a person must present cogent evidence if they wish to prove that they are a member of a protected group. It will rarely be sufficient for a tenant to simply claim to have a disability. The Human Rights Commission takes the position that a person with a disability does not need to provide details about the disability to the party from whom accommodation is being sought. While a person is entitled to privacy, given the serious consequences that can flow from a finding of a breach of the *Human Rights Code*, better evidence will usually be required than a bald and unsubstantiated assertion by a tenant that they have a disability. It may not be necessary to identify the exact disability, but the tenant should be prepared to adduce written or oral evidence from a doctor or other health practitioner confirming that the tenant has a disability and indicating the type of accommodation required by the tenant.

Once a *prima facie* case has been established by the tenant, if the landlord wishes to rely upon a defence available under *Code*, the evidentiary onus will then be upon the landlord. If it is a case of constructive discrimination, the landlord will first have to prove that the requirement, qualification or factor imposed by the landlord is *reasonable* and *bona fide* in the circumstances (s. 11 of the *Code*). Only if the landlord passes that hurdle, can the landlord then attempt to prove that the accommodation requested by the tenant would cause the landlord undue hardship. According to the Human Rights Commission:[64]

> The evidence adduced by the landlord of hardship must be objective, real, direct, and, in the case of cost, quantifiable. The person responsible for accommodation must provide facts, figures, and scientific data or opinion to support a claim that the proposed accommodation in fact causes undue hardship. A mere statement, without supporting evidence, that the cost or risk is "too high" based on impressionistic views or stereotypes will not be sufficient.

In *Vanwyngaarden v. Cummings*,[65] the tenant suffered from Tourette's syndrome, which resulted in his experiencing severe involuntary physical tics that caused substantial interference to the tenants who lived in the unit above this tenant's unit. The landlord argued that accommodation was not feasible because of the cost but this defence was rejected by the Rental Housing Tribunal as the landlord had failed to adduce any objective and quantifiable evidence as to the actual cost associated with viable alternatives and how those costs represented an undue hardship for this landlord.

---

[64] Ontario Human Rights Commission, *Policy and Guidelines on Disability and the Duty to Accommodate*, at p. 29.

[65] [2006] File No. EAL-47938 and EAT-06934 (Ont. Rental Housing Trib. .

(d) Remedies

Where the Landlord and Tenant Board finds that there has been a breach of the *Code*, the Board only has the jurisdiction to grant such relief as specifically given to the Board under the *Residential Tenancies Act*. The Board has no authority to grant any of the remedies set out in the *Ontario Human Rights Code*.

(e) Cases

From its decision in *Walmer Developments v. Wolch*,[66] the Divisional Court made it clear that, in appropriate circumstances, the Rental Housing Tribunal (now the Landlord and Tenant Board) has an obligation to consider what efforts, if any, a landlord had made to accommodate a tenant in deciding whether or not to grant relief from forfeiture (under s. 84 of T.P.A., now s. 83 of the R.T.A.).

In *Hillhurst Park Apartments v. Wolstat*,[67] it was held that the tenant's persistent lateness in paying rent was contributed to by a neurological condition. Based upon this fact as well as upon the fact that the tenancy had lasted 30 years and upon the failure of the landlord to prove that receiving the rent late created undue hardship for the landlord, the Member exercised his discretion under s. 84 of the T.P.A. and refused to grant an eviction (or make any other order in favour of the landlord).

In *Campanaro v. Dixon*,[68] the tenant was found to have a disability because of "multiple chemical sensitivies". Despite the fact that the Board Member found that the landlord genuinely required the rental unit for personal use, the Board exercised its discretion under s. 83 of the R.T.A. and refused to grant an eviction because of the difficulties this tenant would have in finding suitable alternate accommodations. The Member held that granting the requested eviction in this case would amount to discrimination.

In *Longo Properties Limited v. Clarke*,[69] the landlord sought to evict the tenant because there were complaints from other tenants about excessive noise from this tenant's unit. At the original hearing, the tenant failed to attend. The presiding member nevertheless refused to grant the eviction but granted an order to the landlord permitting the landlord to file a new application for an eviction order, without notice to the tenant (under s. 77 of the T.P.A.), if the tenant created "unnecessary noise". There were further incidents and the landlord applied for and received an *ex parte* eviction order.

---

[66] (2003), 230 D.L.R. (4th) 372, 67 O.R. (3d) 246, 2003 CarswellOnt 3325 (Ont. Div. Ct.) (re TSL-39032).

[67] (June 17, 2005), TNL-66758, 2005 CarswellOnt 3275 (Ont. Rental Housing Trib.).

[68] [2007] SWL-02844 (L.T.B.).

[69] (February 20, 2002), TSL-35686-SA (Ont. Rental Housing Trib.).

The tenant suffered from a mental illness that caused her to hallucinate. It is at these times that she made the noise that disturbed other tenants. On a motion to set aside the *ex parte* eviction order, the Tribunal found that since the noise was involuntary, it was not "unnecessary" and that the landlord's application and the conditions contained in the Tribunal's previous order constructively discriminated against this tenant. The tenant's motion was granted and the *ex parte* eviction order was set aside.

In *Vanwyngaarder v. Cummings*,[70] the landlord sought to evict a tenant for disturbing other tenants. The tenant suffered from Tourette's syndrome and had little, if any, control over the noises he made. The Member adjourned the hearing so that the landlord could learn more about the tenant's condition and what reasonable accommodations might be possible. The landlord failed to take reasonable steps to comply with the Member's direction or to fulfill his obligations to accommodate this tenant. Consequently, the landlord's application was dismissed.

If the Board does not make it explicit in its order that it has considered human rights issues in its deliberations as to whether or not to grant relief from forfeiture (where the facts clearly call for such analysis), the Divisional Court may well quash the Board's decision and order a new hearing.

In *McKenzie v. Supportive Housing in Peel*,[71] the appellant tenant allegedly assaulted the spouse of the superintendent. The tenant had been diagnosed with a form of schizophrenia. The Tribunal's eviction order does not specifically refer to the tenant's condition or what efforts, if any, the landlord made to accommodate her. The order also does not indicate whether the member took into consideration the landlord's duty to accommodate when deciding not to grant relief to the tenant under s. 84 of the T.P.A. Since it was not clear from the record whether the Member turned his mind to the relevant issue, the matter was remitted back to the Tribunal for reconsideration. After a new hearing, the Tribunal ultimately determined that the landlord had made reasonable efforts to accommodate the tenant and granted the landlord's application. An appeal of this order was dismissed by the Divisional Court as raising no issues of law.[72]

In *Girard v. Soluri*,[73] the landlord applied for an order to terminate this tenancy because the tenant, who suffered from a psychiatric condition, was allegedly disturbing other tenants of the complex by playing her radio or television very loudly and by screaming in her unit. The Tribunal explicitly recognizes in its decision its obligation to consider what efforts, if any, the landlord made to accommodate the needs of this tenant so as to allow her to

---

[70] (January 3, 2006), EAL-47938 and EAT-06934 (Ont. Rental Housing Trib.).

[71] (2005), 2005 CarswellOnt 1561 (Ont. Div. Ct.).

[72] *McKenzie v. Supportive Housing in Peel* (2006), 2006 CarswellOnt 1556, [2006] O.J. No. 1019 (Ont. Div. Ct.).

[73] (February 27, 2006), SOL-62764, 2006 CarswellOnt 2145, [2006] O.R.H.T.D. No. 14 (Ont. Rental Housing Trib.).

remain in the complex but not disturb other tenants. The landlord failed to adduce any evidence concerning any of the three relevant critera: (1) cost; (2) outside sources of funding; and (3) health and safety requirements. The landlord had made no effort to investigate whether additional soundproofing would ameliorate the situation. As a result, the landlord failed to prove that the needs of the tenant could not be accommodated without undue hardship on the landlord. Consequently, the Vice-chair exercised her discretion under s. 84(1) of the T.P.A. (now s. 83(1) of the R.T.A.) and refused to terminate this tenancy.

Similarly, in Landlord and Tenant Board File No. NOL-00453, the Board found that the landlord's efforts to assist a disabled tenant (by delaying the eviction process and engaging in a dialogue with the tenant) were good first steps by the landlord but were insufficient (without further action) to satisfy the landlord's duty under the *Human Rights Code* to accommodate the tenant's needs.

On the other hand, in *Canadian Mental Health Association v. Warren*,[74] the Rental Housing Tribunal found that the landlord had made reasonable efforts to accommodate the tenant as the landlord had made numerous compromises and settlements, had participated in a process whereby a team attempted to develop a strategy for resolving the disturbances created by this tenant, had assigned caseworker after caseworker to deal with the needs of the tenant and had changed the smoke detectors in the tenant's unit to "less sensitive" types. The Rental Housing Tribunal found these efforts to be sufficient to have met the landlord's duty of accommodation.

Similarly, in *Drewlo Holdings Inc. v. Todd*,[75] the Rental Housing Tribunal found the landlord's efforts to accommodate the tenant to have been adequate. The tenant's conduct was disturbing other tenants in the residential complex. The tenant's conduct resulted from a mental disorder. The landlord attempted to arrange for the tenant to receive assistance from members of her family, members of a local support group and a member of the clergy who the tenant knew and trusted. These efforts failed and, for the sake of the other tenants, the landlord felt compelled to seek to terminate this tenancy. In the circumstances, the Member concluded that the landlord had met its obligation to attempt to accommodate the tenant and that it would be unfair to the other tenants of the complex to refuse to grant the requested eviction.

In *Toronto Community Housing Corp. v. West*,[76] the tenant, a developmentally impaired person, created a serious fire hazard by allowing boxes, clothing, garbage and other waste to accumulate in the rental unit, thereby seriously impairing the safety of all the tenants in the complex. The Tribunal

---

[74] File No. TEL-40151 (Ont. Rental Housing Trib.), aff'd [2004] Div. Ct. File No. 278/04 (Ont. Div. Ct.).

[75] File No. SWL-79765 (Ont. Rental Housing Trib.).

[76] (August 3, 2005), TEL-51896 (Ont. Rental Housing Trib.).

member gave the tenant five months in which to rectify the problem, failing which the landlord could apply (under s. 77 of the T.P.A.) for an eviction order.

In Landlord and Tenant Board File No. TSL-00166 (Feb. 26, 2007) , the tenant rented a basement apartment in the landlord's home. The tenant suffered from an unspecified mental illness that caused erratic behaviour including angry outbursts, various fire safety violations and leaving the door to the complex unlocked at night. The landlord and his wife and young child were concerned about their safety and brought an application to terminate this tenancy on the basis that the tenant's conduct substantially interfered in the landlord's reasonable enjoyment of the house. In the year prior to commencing the eviction application, the landlord had attempted to accommodate the needs of the tenant by working with him and with the tenant's mother, who was a personal friend of the landlord. The Member considered the landlord's duty under the *Ontario Human Rights Code* to accommodate the tenant and found that the landlord's previous efforts had been reasonable. The Member granted the landlord's application but, pursuant to s. 83(1) of the R.T.A., delayed the eviction by approximately two months to give the tenant additional time in which to find alternate accommodations.

In Landlord and Tenant Board File No. SOT-00795 (Feb. 7, 2008) , the tenant had been diagnosed with multiple sclerosis (MS), which made it difficult for him to walk more than short distances. For longer journeys, he possessed an electric scooter. The tenant was having some difficulty, however, getting his scooter in and out of his rental unit because he had no way to keep the door ajar. The tenant brought an application seeking an order from the Landlord and Tenant Board that would force the landlord to install an automated door opener on the door to his unit. The landlord suggested that there might be a less expensive solution to the problem. Since the landlord had failed to take any steps to accommodate the tenant, the Member granted a modest abatement of rent (15% of the rent for a three-month period) but agreed with the landlord that a simple and inexpensive solution (such as a door-stop or wedge) would be adequate in this case to accommodate the needs of the tenant. On this issue, the Member wrote as follows:

> [T]he accommodation process is a shared responsibility of the parties. The Tenant has to participate by advising of his needs and suggesting reasonable solutions. However, the Tenant does not dictate the solution. He has an obligation to accept reasonable accommodations. He can not expect a perfect solution. If the Tenant can be accommodated by a less expensive solution, the Landlord is free to choose that option. If the reasonable accommodation is refused, the Landlord's duty to accommodate has been discharged.

Where it has been established that the landlord's conduct has constructively discriminated against a tenant who has a disability, the landlord must adduce evidence as to the landlord's efforts to satisfy the duty upon the landlord to accommodate the tenant. In Landlord and Tenant Board File No. SOL-73477-RV (March 19, 2007), no such evidence was adduced by the landlord, yet the Member hearing the application granted the landlord's application to evict the tenant. Upon review of that decision by another Member of the Board, the original eviction order was overturned and the reviewing Member granted the tenant relief from forfeiture (on certain terms) under s. 83 of the R.T.A.

Whether or not a landlord has made reasonable efforts to accommodate a tenant is a question of fact, not law, and the Divisional Court has recognized that there is no right to appeal a decision of the Tribunal (Board) on a question of fact.[77] Nevertheless, parties have attempted to raise human rights issues on appeal.

In *Connelly v. Mary Lambert Swale Non-Profit Homes*,[78] the tenant, who was addicted to drugs, was found to have converted the rental unit into a "crack house" (used for the purposes of drug trafficking). The tenant was evicted because of this conduct. On appeal, the tenant argued that the Tribunal erred in law in failing to recognize his drug addiction as a disability and failing to explicitly consider the *Ontario Human Rights Code* in its decision as to whether to grant relief from forfeiture. The Divisional Court noted that the tenant had not raised these issues before the Tribunal at the initial hearing. The Divisional Court agreed that the appellant's addiction must be considered a disability. The Court noted, however, that there was an important distinction between the appellant's addiction-disability and his decision to deal drugs from his apartment. Quoting from the decision of the Supreme Court of Canada in *Renaud v. Central Okanagan School District No. 23*,[79] the Divisional Court noted that:

> To facilitate the search for an accommodation, the complainant must do his or her part as well . . . Thus in determining whether the duty of accommodation has been fulfilled the conduct of the complainant must be considered.

The Court found that in these circumstances, no accommodation was possible. In the face of overwhelming evidence, the appellant continued to deny that he was dealing drugs or causing any problems for his neighbours. In dismissing the appeal, the Court wrote as follows:

> We reject any suggestion there is an obligation on the respondent to permit the tenant to operate a crack house in order to accommodate his disability. We

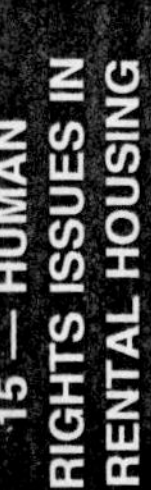

---

[77] *Warren v. Canadian Mental Health Association* (2004), 2004 CarswellOnt 2372 (Ont. Div. Ct.) (re TEL-40151). Also see *McKenzie v. Supportive Housing in Peel* (2006), 2006 CarswellOnt 1556, [2006] O.J. No. 1019 (Ont. Div. Ct.), citing *Renaud v. Central Okanagan School District No. 23*, (sub nom. *Central Okanagan School District No. 23 v. Renaud*) [1992] 2 S.C.R. 970 (S.C.C.) at p. 18.

[78] (2007), 2007 CarswellOnt 7838 (Ont. Div. Ct. .

[79] [1992] 2 S.C.R. 910 at para. 50.

> conclude that such an attempt at accommodation would be an undue hardship to the respondent by substantially interfering with the rights of other tenants.

In Landlord and Tenant Board File No. TEL-12889 (October 31, 2008), a tenant who was permitted access to the landlord's computer was found to have used it to access child pornography. As a result, the police were notified and they obtained and executed a search warrant. As a result of this search of the tenant's unit, charges were laid and the tenant was convicted of, among other things, possession of child pornography. The landlord commenced proceedings to evict the tenant on the basis that he had committed an illegal act within the residential complex. The tenant argued that his "disability" entitled him to accommodation. The Vice-chair found that the psychiatric evidence that the tenant has a "sexual preference" for young persons (hebephilia) did not justify, on a balance of probabilities, a finding that the tenant had a disability within the meaning of the *Human Rights Code*. Similarly, the Vice-chair found that the tenant had not established, on a balance of probabilities, that the tenant had schizophrenia. In addition, there was no evidence to support a finding that the illegal acts of possession of child pornography and sexual assault were directly caused by schizophrenia. In the alternative, if the tenant did suffer a disability within the meaning of the *Human Rights Code*, given the likelihood that the tenant would re-offend, the Vice-chair held that accommodation would result in undue hardship to the landlord. The tenancy was terminated but eviction was delayed by one month.

In Landlord and Tenant Board File No. TSL-16589 (October 2, 2008), the residential complex housed persons who have mental illnesses. The tenant, who had a disability because of mental illness, had assaulted other tenants in the residential complex. The Member found that the tenant's conduct seriously impaired the safety of other tenants in the residential complex. The Member found, however, that there had been no further incidents for two months prior to the hearing, the assaults were at the lower end of the spectrum, the tenant was remorseful and, to the date of the hearing, the landlord's attempts at accommodation within the meaning of the *Human Rights Code* were minimal. The Member found that the tenant's actions resulted from the tenant's disability. Having considered the landlord's duty to accommodate to the point of undue hardship, the Member issued a conditional order continuing the tenancy and requiring the tenant to refrain from assaulting anyone in the residential complex for 12 months. In the event of a future assault by the tenant within the 12-month period from the date of the order, the landlord could apply to the Board under s. 78 of the R.T.A. for termination and eviction.

16

Proceedings Before the Landlord and Tenant Board

1. INTRODUCTION

Where a dispute arises between a landlord and a tenant or where a party wishes to pursue his or her rights under the terms of a tenancy agreement or under the provisions of the *Residential Tenancies Act, 2006*, (R.T.A.), the matter must be brought before the Landlord and Tenant Board.[1] This Chapter will describe the process of bringing an application before the Board. The following topics will be discussed: serving a notice upon the other party, commencing an application, preparing for a hearing, negotiation and mediation, adjournments, the hearing, the standard of proof, orders and reasons and how to challenge a Board decision by way of internal review, appeal or judicial review.

The Board is required to adopt the most expeditious method of determining the questions arising in a proceeding that affords to all persons directly affected by the proceeding an adequate opportunity to know the issues and be heard on the matter.[2] Pursuant to Rule 2.2 of the Board's Rules of Practice, the presiding Member may decide the procedure to be followed for an application, may make specific procedural directions or orders at any time and may impose such conditions as are appropriate and fair.

Pursuant to Rule 1.5 of the Board's Rules of Practice, a Member may also waive or vary a Rule where appropriate. This rule is authorized by s. 4(2) of the *Statutory Powers Procedure Act*. A party is entitled to present reasons why any Rule should be waived in the particular circumstances of that case. In most cases, a Rule will not be waived by a Member without inviting and considering submissions from all parties. Pursuant to Rule 1.5,

---

1 As long as the type of dispute and amounts in dispute are within the jurisdiction of the Board (see Chapter 2).

2 Section 183 of the R.T.A. and Rule 1.1 of the Board's Rules of Practice.

however, the following Rules cannot be waived by a Member: (1) those concerning the computation of time (Rule 4.5); (2) those concerning the confidentiality required in mediations (Rules 13.17 to 13.21);[3] and (3) those concerning the issuance of Orders and Reasons (Rule 26).

The procedural powers of the Board (to add and remove parties, to join and sever applications, to amend applications, to permit withdrawal of applications, to extend and shorten certain time periods, to control the proceedings and prevent abuses of its processes, to order disclosure, to compel and accept evidence, to order or permit payment of money into the Board, to conduct pre-hearing conferences and to stay proceedings) are described in detail in Chapter 2. Other topics covered in Chapter 2 include: the nature of the Board; the jurisdiction of the Board; the Board's investigative, inquisitorial and remedial powers; principles of natural justice; *res judicata*; choice of forum; applications to determine whether the R.T.A. applies in a particular situation; and access to Board decisions. It is highly recommended that you read Chapter 2 before reading this Chapter.

For applications not seeking termination of a tenancy, the usual steps for commencing an application are as follows:

1. Complete the appropriate application form(s), file it with the Board (along with any other documents that are required)[4] and pay the filing fee (if any);
2. The Board will give the application a file number, date stamp it and issue a notice of hearing;
3. The applicant must serve the application and notice of hearing on all other parties;
4. Pursuant to s. 189 of the R.T.A., the Board will also notify the respondent(s) that an application has been made and provide the file number, the date of hearing and contact information for the Board (ss. 54 and 55 of O. Reg. 516/06);
5. The applicant must then file a certificate of service with the Board as proof of service;
6. The hearing will proceed on the date set out in the notice of hearing.

For applications seeking termination of a tenancy (other than *ex parte* applications under ss. 77 and 78), the usual steps for commencing an application are as follows:

1. Serve a notice of termination on the respondent(s) and complete a certificate of service;

---

[3] See Rule 13.22 of the Board's Rules of Practice.

[4] For certain types of applications, the application must be accompanied by additional documentation. See, for example, subsection 72(1) of the R.T.A., ss. 22 and 53 of O. Reg. 516/06 and Rule 19 of the Board's Rules of Practice.

2. At the appropriate time,[5] complete the appropriate application form(s) and file it with the Board, along with a copy of the notice of termination and a certificate of service to prove service of the notice of termination[6] and any other documents that are required[7] and pay the filing fee (if any);
3. The Board will give the application a file number, date stamp it and issue a notice of hearing;
4. The applicant must serve the application and notice of hearing on all other parties;
5. Pursuant to s. 189 of the R.T.A., the Board will also notify the respondent(s) that an application has been made and provide the file number, the date of hearing and contact information for the Board (ss. 54 and 55 of O. Reg. 516/06);
6. The applicant must then file a certificate of service with the Board as proof of service;
7. The hearing will proceed on the date set out in the notice of hearing.

In addition to other methods of filing documents with the Board, s. 213 of the R.T.A. provides that a document referred to in the R.T.A. and specified in the regulations or the Rules may be dealt with electronically (this includes being "signed", filed and received electronically) as long as it is done in accordance with the procedures established by the Board.

2. NOTICES OF TERMINATION

Not all applications to the Board involve a request to terminate a tenancy. If the applicant is not seeking to terminate a tenancy, no notice of termination need be served. In such cases, filing an application will be the first step in the process of bringing an issue before the Board.

Where a landlord or tenant wants to end a tenancy, however, unless they have reached an agreement, the party seeking to terminate the tenancy must usually serve a notice of termination on the other party. In such cases, this is the first step in the process. The notice must be in the correct form, contain the required information, be signed, be served in the proper manner and in sufficient time prior to the date set for termination and that date must also comply with the requirements of the R.T.A. The notice of termination is a highly technical document; it is crucial that this step be done right as an error

[5] Certain types of applications cannot be filed until after the termination date set out in the notice of termination and most applications must be commenced within 30 days of the termination date or the notice of termination will automatically become void.

[6] Paragraph 1 of s. 53, O. Reg. 516/06.

[7] For certain types of applications, the application must be accompanied by additional documentation. See, for example, subsection 72(1) of the R.T.A., ss. 22 and 53 of O. Reg. 516/06 and Rule 19 of the Board's Rules of Practice.

may not be detected until months later at the hearing. The Board has no power to cure most defects in a notice of termination and an error in the notice or in the timing[8] or manner of service will usually result in dismissal of the application.

In Chapter 6, the following topics are discussed in great detail: the form and content of notices of termination; service of the notice; the importance of timing; the different types of notices of termination; and the required notice periods. Please refer to Chapter 6 for a more thorough analysis of issues arising from notices of termination.

Pursuant to s. 46(1) of the R.T.A., a notice of termination becomes void 30 days after the termination date specified in the notice unless: (a) the tenant vacates the rental unit before that time; or (b) the landlord applies for an order terminating the tenancy and evicting the tenant before that time. The only exception to this is a notice of termination for non-payment of rent (Form N4), which has no "expiry" date (s. 46(2)).

Thus, with the exception of the Form N4, all notices of termination become void at the end of 30 days after the termination date named in the notice if the landlord has not commenced an application to terminate the tenancy and evict the tenant by then. Certain types of notices can *also* become void if the tenant resolves the problem identified in the notice. Such notices can be thought of as being "curable".[9] These include notices of termination based upon non-payment of rent (Form N4), undue damage (Form N5), interfering with reasonable enjoyment (Form N5) and having too many people living in the unit (Form N5).

3. SERVICE OF DOCUMENTS

(a) Methods of Service

Permitted methods of service of documents are set out in s. 191 of the R.T.A. and in Rule 5 of the Board's Rules of Practice. Pursuant to s. 191(1) of the R.T.A., a notice or document is sufficiently given to a person (other than the Board):

(a) by handing it to the person;
(b) if the person to be served is a landlord, handing it to an employee of the landlord (who is exercising authority in respect of the residential complex to which the notice or document relates);
(c) if the person to be served is a tenant (or subtenant or occupant), by handing it to an apparently adult person in the rental unit;

---

[8] See s. 56 of O. Reg. 516/06.

[9] At least on the first notice. See Chapter 6.

(d) by leaving it in the mail box where mail is ordinarily delivered to the person;
(e) if there is no mail box, by leaving it at the place where mail is ordinarily delivered to the person;
(f) by sending it by mail to the last known address where the person resides or carries on business; or
(g) by any other means allowed in the Rules.

Rule 5.1 also permits a notice to be given to another person by any of the following methods:

(a) by courier to that person;
(b) if there is a fax machine where the person carries on business or in the residence of the person, by fax;
(c) for service on a person who *occupies* the rental unit, by placing it under the door of the unit or through a mail slot in the door;
(d) for service on a tenant of a notice under section 27 of the Act (i.e., notice to enter the rental unit), by any permitted method of service or posting it on the door of the rental unit;
(e) if the document is an application or was created after the application was filed, by hand delivery, mail, courier or fax to the representative; or
(f) if the document is an application or was created after the application was filed, by any method directed or permitted by the Board in writing.

Note that, except for a notice to enter the unit under s. 27 of the R.T.A., no other document can be served by posting the document on the door to the rental unit. This was a common method of service under the *Landlord and Tenant Act* but, with only the one stated exception, this type of service has been prohibited since June 1998 (when the T.P.A. came into effect). A landlord that posts a notice of termination on a tenant's door may not only find that it is an invalid method of service but that he may have exposed himself to allegations of harassment by the tenant and potential liability should the tenant choose to commence an application against the landlord or should the Investigation & Enforcement Unit choose to prosecute the landlord for a provincial offence under ss. 233 through 237 of the R.T.A.

Rule 5.2 also gives a Member the power to give written directions to a party, either on his or her own initiative or on that party's request, regarding one or both of the following: (1) who shall be served with the application or any other document; and (2) how an application or document shall be served. Finally, if a document is given to another person by a method other than an approved method, if it is proven that the contents of the document actually came to the attention of the person for whom it was intended within the required time period, service will be considered valid.[10] For example, improper service was accepted when the Tribunal was satisfied that the notice did come to the attention of the tenant: *H. & R. Property Management and Kutusa.*[11]

For most methods of service, a document is deemed to be served on the same date it is delivered. This is not true, however, for service by mail or courier. A notice or document given by mail shall be deemed to have been given on the fifth day after mailing;[12] a notice or document given by Xpresspost is deemed to be given by mail (not by courier).[13] If a notice or document is delivered to another person by courier, it is deemed to be given on the day following the day it was given to the courier but, if that is a non-business day, it is deemed to be given on the next business day.[14] Notwithstanding these presumptive rules, if a party can prove that the document was actually received earlier than the date of deemed service, the Board will find that it was served on that earlier date.[15] Similarly, the presumption that a document was received five days after it was mailed can be rebutted if a party can prove that the document was actually received on a later date.[16]

(b) Timing of Service of Notice of Termination

See Chapter 6.

(c) Timing of Service of the Application and Notice of Hearing

An applicant who files an application with the Board shall give the other parties to the application (i.e., any other applicants, the respondents and any other parties) a copy of the application and any notice of hearing issued by the Board within the time set out in the Board's Rules of Practice.[17]

---

[10] Subsection 191(2) of the R.T.A.

[11] (June 4, 1999), TNL-07551 (Ont. Rental Housing Trib.).

[12] Subsection 191(3) of the R.T.A.

[13] Rule 5.4 of the Board's Rules of Practice.

[14] Rule 5.3 of the Board's Rules of Practice.

[15] Rule 5.6 of the Board's Rules of Practice.

[16] *Monty Enterprises, Re* (September 11, 2006), Doc. TNL-79397-SA, 2006 CarswellOnt 9167 (Ont. Rental Housing Trib.).

[17] Subsections 188(1) and (2) of the R.T.A. and Rule 10.6 of the Board's Rules of Practice. Pursuant to s. 6(1) of the *Statutory Powers Procedure Act,* a tribunal is usually required to notify respondents about a hearing but the Landlord and Tenant Board, through its Rules, has placed this responsibility upon the applicant. The Board, however, will notify the respondent(s) that an application has been made and provide the file number, the date of hearing and contact information for the Board (pursuant to s. 189 of the R.T.A. and ss. 54 and 55 of O. Reg. 516/06).

For most applications, the applicant must give a copy of the application and the notice of hearing to each respondent as soon as possible but not later than **10 days** before the hearing date (Rule 10.1).

For an application under s. 77 or 78 of the *Act*, which is sent to a hearing by a Member who decides that it ought not to proceed on an *ex parte* basis, the applicant must give a copy of the application and the notice of hearing to the respondent as soon as possible but not later than **10 days** before the time set for the hearing, unless otherwise directed by the Board (Rule 10.2). Ordinarily, an application under s. 77 (eviction based on a tenant's notice to vacate or an agreement of the parties to terminate the tenancy) or s. 78 (eviction based on a tenant's breach of a mediated settlement or an order) will result in an order without a hearing. For these applications, the landlord is not required to give the application to the tenant in most cases. However, if the Member reviewing the application believes it should proceed to a hearing (see notes to Rule 10.2), the applicant will be asked to give the application and a notice of hearing to the tenant respondents. According to the usual service rules, at least 10 days notice must be given by the landlord to the tenant, but the Member may direct more or less notice depending on the circumstances.

Where an order is issued under s. 206(1)[18] and a party files a request to re-open the application under subsection 206(4) or 206(5), the party who files the request must give a copy of the request to re-open the application and the notice of hearing to the other parties as soon as possible but not later than five days before the hearing (Rule 10.3).

For applications filed under ss. 126 (above-guideline rent increase), 132 (application to vary a rent reduction) or 148 (to transfer a tenancy from a care home), the applicant must give a copy of the application and notice of hearing to the respondent(s) as soon as possible but not later than 30 days before the hearing date (Rule 10.4). The Board recognizes that respondents need a reasonable amount of time to prepare for the hearing for these kinds of applications.

Other types of applications need to be heard more quickly.

For applications filed by a tenant or former tenant under s. 29(1) and made solely or in part under para. 5 (illegal lockout), the applicant must give a copy of the application and the notice of hearing to the respondent as soon as possible but not later than **five days** before the hearing date (Rule 10.5(a)).

A former tenant must give a copy of the application and notice of hearing to the respondent not less than **five** days before the hearing where the application is related to the disposition of the tenant's property that was left in the

[18] I.e., where an application based upon arrears of rent was resolved by the parties requesting a consent order prior to the hearing and the order was issued in accordance with that request.

rental unit.[19] Of course, a Member retains the power to shorten this time period in cases of real urgency (Rule 15).

Similarly, the minimum notice period is **five** days in cases where the landlord is seeking to terminate the tenancy under clause 61(2)(a),[20] s. 63,[21] s. 65,[22] s. 66[23] or s. 94 of the R.T.A.[24]

A party who brings a motion to set aside a default order (issued under the T.P.A.), an *ex parte* order, an order under subsection 74(3), or an order under subsection 74(8), must give a copy of the motion and the notice of hearing to the other party(ies) **at least 48 hours** before the time set for the hearing (Rule 10.7).

Pursuant to Rule 10.8, if a party fails to give the notice of hearing and application or motion to any other party(ies) in accordance with these Rules the Member may:

(a) proceed with the hearing if the Member finds that the other party(ies) suffered no prejudice whatsoever as a result of the party's failure to serve the documents or to serve them on time;
(b) adjourn the hearing to give the other party(ies) an adequate opportunity to prepare for the hearing; or
(c) dismiss the application or motion if the Member finds that the party deliberately failed to serve the documents in accordance with these Rules.

A Member may proceed with the application or motion if convinced that the party(ies) who were not served, or not served on time, have consented to proceed with the hearing without further delay. The only other situation in which the hearing should proceed on the scheduled date is where the Member is convinced that the other party(ies) had sufficient time after they knew the details of the application or motion to prepare for the hearing.

The power to dismiss the application or motion should only be used in extraordinary circumstances. This would include a situation in which the party who filed the application or motion, or their agent, appears to have deliberately failed to serve the documents, or to serve them on time.

In most cases, an adjournment will be the appropriate way to resolve a party's failure to serve the documents according to these Rules.

The Member may also determine that any delay caused by the failure of the party who filed the application or motion to serve the other party(ies)

---

[19] I.e., under subsection 41(6) of the R.T.A. (Rule 10.5(b)).

[20] I.e., based on an illegal act related to the production or trafficking of an illegal drug (Rule 10.5(c)(i)).

[21] I.e., fast-track eviction for undue damage (Rule 10.5(c)(ii)).

[22] I.e., fast-track eviction for interference with the reasonable enjoyment of the landlord (Rule 10.5(c)(iii)).

[23] I.e., impaired safety (Rule 10.5(c)(iv)).

[24] I.e., superintendent's premises (Rule 10.5(d)).

promptly, without an appropriate reason, is unreasonable conduct as defined in the Interpretation Guideline (No. 3) on "Costs".

(d) Proof of Service

A party must file with the Board a certificate of service in the form approved by the Board in the circumstances set out in the Rules.[25] The certificate of service is evidence of what was served, when, how and upon whom. It must be signed by the person who actually delivered the documents and that person may later be called as a witness if the certificate of service is challenged. If a party is concerned that the other party may later deny receiving the documents in question, the documents should probably be served in person, a witness should be present and the recipient can be asked to sign a receipt.

Once an applicant has served the application and notice of hearing upon the respondent, the applicant must file with the board a certificate of service signed by the individual who actually delivered the documents (Rule 11.1).

The best practice is to serve the application and notice of hearing as quickly as possible, and file the certificate as soon as possible thereafter. According to Rule 11.2, the applicant must file any necessary certificate of service within five days after the application and notice of hearing are served. Nevertheless, if the applicant fails to file the certificate of service before the hearing, the applicant may (pursuant to rule 11.3) prove service of the application and notice of hearing by:

(a) filing a certificate of service at the beginning of the hearing; or
(b) by calling as a witness at the hearing the individual who gave the application and notice of hearing to the other party to the application.

If the respondent does not appear at the hearing, it will be important for the applicant to bring a certificate of service of the application and notice of hearing, or provide a witness to testify about the service; otherwise, the Member may not grant the application.

A Member may also direct any party to an application to file a certificate of service with respect to *any* document which was given in relation to the proceedings (Rule 11.4). Not only the application and notice of hearing must be served on another party. For most types of eviction applications, the landlord must have earlier served a notice of termination. Also, the Rules require notice to be given to another party in various circumstances. In any of these situations, the Member may require a certificate of service to be filed before taking any action that would result from the service of that document.

---

[25] Subsection 188(3) of the R.T.A.

4. THE APPLICATION

An application shall be filed with the Board in the form approved by the Board, shall be accompanied by the prescribed information and shall be signed by the applicant.[26] An applicant may give an agent written authorization to sign an application and, if the applicant does so, the Board may require the agent to file a copy of the authorization.[27]

The parties to an application are the landlord and any tenants or other persons directly affected by the application.[28] The Board may add or remove parties as the Board considers appropriate.[29]

The Board will now screen the documents filed by the applicant and may reject defective applications or point out potential problems with the documents that have been filed (Rule 8). For a more detailed description of this "pre-screening" process, please refer to Chapter 2.

An applicant will sometimes have a choice of more than one type of application that may seem appropriate. A tenant, for instance, may have complaints about the condition of the unit *and* about the conduct of the landlord. The tenant could file a T6 application concerning the maintenance issues or a T2 application about the landlord's conduct, or both. A tenant may combine several applications into one application.[30] Also, two or more tenants of the same complex may together file one application as long as each tenant applying signs the application.[31]

A landlord, on the other hand, may have several potential grounds upon which to seek to terminate a tenancy; the tenant's conduct may interfere with the enjoyment of others and the tenant may owe rent to the landlord and the tenant may persistently pay rent late. A landlord may combine several applications relating to a given tenant into one application (so long as the landlord does not combine an application for a rent increase with any other application).[32]

How, then, does an applicant decide which applications to file with the Board and whether to combine different types of applications? Usually, it is a question of strategy, best decided by those with considerable experience appearing before the Board. Several factors must be considered.[33]

Three related factors are complexity, delay and expense. Some cases are, by their nature, more complex and more difficult to prove. Allegations of illegal conduct, for instance, usually require calling several witnesses, in-

---

[26] Subsection 185(1) of the R.T.A.
[27] Subsection 185(2) of the R.T.A.
[28] Subsection 187(1) of the R.T.A.
[29] Subsection 187(2) of the R.T.A.
[30] Subsection 186(1) of the R.T.A.
[31] Subsection 186(2) of the R.T.A.
[32] Subsection 186(3) of the R.T.A.
[33] Some of these are discussed in the Board's Interpretation Guideline No. 10.

cluding police officers. The exact offence will have to be proven and, if the tenant did not commit the offence himself, it will have to be proven that the tenant permitted the illegal conduct. A complex case involving numerous witnesses may need to be scheduled on its own (as a "special") instead of in a normal hearing "block". If more than one day is required for the hearing, the hearing will often take several months to complete (as the Board rarely schedules several consecutive days of hearing for the same matter). Thus complex cases often result in considerable delay and additional expense.

Similarly, some notices of termination require more notice than others. If the type of notice of termination chosen is one that cannot take effect until the end of the tenancy and there is another eight months left in the tenancy, this will clearly result in considerable delay, even if the order is granted very quickly (as the eviction cannot be enforced until after the termination date).

Furthermore, some grounds for termination can be "cured". For instance, an application for arrears of rent will be discontinued if the tenant pays all amounts claimed (plus the landlord's filing fee). If what the landlord wants more than anything else is to end the tenancy, the landlord may wish to choose another type of application such as termination for persistent late payment of rent. This latter type of application cannot be "cured" but it takes longer (i.e., the notice period is longer) and there is a good chance that a Member may grant relief to the tenant under s. 83 and permit the continuation of the tenancy (on certain terms). The landlord could also combine the two types of applications but this will require the service of two different notices of termination and the filing of two different applications (that can be combined) and will likely result in a hearing that will be more complex than if the landlord had chosen just one ground for seeking termination of the tenancy.

Whether or not to combine applications is also a difficult decision. On the one hand, a person is expected to bring forward all of their issues in one proceeding. If they fail to do so, they may be *estopped* from commencing subsequent applications.[34] On the other hand, combining several different types of applications may only serve to unduly complicate and lengthen the proceedings. Board hearings are meant to be summary in nature. By failing to restrict the claim to one or two serious issues, the hearing can become a long and unfocused affair.

The decision as to the type and number of applications to file is really a judgment call, based upon the facts of the particular case at hand and one's experience before the Board. In my view, it is generally better to restrict an application to one main issue and to bring forward all facts relevant to that issue. For instance, if a tenant is complaining about the condition of the

---

[34] On the basis that the filing of multiple, consecutive applications can represent an abuse of the Board's process. See the discussion in Chapter 2 on *res judicata* and, in particular, abuse of process by re-litigation.

building, the tenant should bring forward *all* maintenance concerns about which the tenant is aware at the time the application is filed. If there is another discrete issue that will not unduly complicate the proceeding (such as the failure of the landlord to pay interest on the rent deposit), the tenant could combine a T1 application with the T6 application. As a general proposition, however, an applicant should avoid combining multiple applications unless the issues are related.

5. PREPARING FOR THE HEARING

(a) General

Hearings are not just about who is right and who is wrong, but about proving you are right and persuading the adjudicator to grant the order you are requesting. Hearings are, therefore, about presenting the best possible evidence and persuading the adjudicator you are right and that the relief you are seeking is reasonable and within the power of the Board to grant.

If you are an applicant (or represent one), hopefully you carefully researched the law *before* commencing an application and came to the conclusion you are legally entitled to the relief being claimed. If the relief you were hoping for is not within the jurisdiction of the Board to grant (such as forcing the respondent to apologize), the application will be a waste of everyone's time and money. If you are the respondent (or represent the respondent), you must also research the law before the date of the hearing to understand what issues may be relevant at the hearing.

If you require legal advice or the assistance of a legal representative, this should also be arranged well in advance of the hearing. A person who fails to diligently pursue their right to legal representation may be denied an adjournment if they later claim they are not prepared to proceed on the date scheduled for the hearing.

The next and probably most important step in preparing for the hearing is gathering the evidence you will need. You will need originals (if possible) or clear photocopies (where the original is not available) of all documents relevant to the issues in dispute. This may include correspondence, notices that were posted in the building, notices from government officials, the tenancy agreement, receipts, cheque stubs, banking and other financial records, photographs or videotaped evidence, and so forth. Banks, government organizations and other large institutions often require several weeks to retrieve records so it is important to begin gathering all necessary documents well before the date set for the hearing.

If you want a witness to testify at the hearing, you must arrange for them to attend the hearing. Keep in mind that hearings before the Board are meant to be summary in nature and, in most cases, only the parties themselves testify (i.e., there are no other witnesses). You should try to keep the number of witnesses to the minimum number necessary to adequately present your case.

If you believe your witness will not attend the hearing voluntarily, you can ask the Board to issue a **summons** which requires that person to appear. Also, some government employees (like inspectors) require you to serve them with a summons before they can attend a hearing. If you think a summons may be needed, you should read the Board's information pamphlet on "Summons" and follow the procedures set out in Rule 23 of the Board's Rules of Practice.

A summons is a document issued by the Board at the request of a party, requiring a person to attend a hearing as a witness. A summons can also require the witness to bring with them any specified documents. It is important that you request a summons as soon as you become aware that one is necessary. If you want the Board to issue a summons, you should complete a request for summons form and file it with the Board. This form is available from a Board office in your area or from the Board's website (www.ltb.gov.on.ca). If you are a lawyer or paid agent, you should also file a draft summons with your request (ready to be signed by a Member). Be sure to explain how the testimony of the witness will be relevant and important to the case and be sure to include a complete list of any documents you believe to be in the possession of the witness that you require the witness to produce at the hearing.

When a request for a summons is filed, a Board Member will decide whether or not to grant the request. The power to issue a summons is derived from s. 12 of the *Statutory Powers Procedure Act*. The Board Member will only issue a summons if they are convinced by your written request that the testimony of the witness or the documents the witness can produce will be relevant to the issues in the application and admissible at a hearing.

You are responsible for ensuring that a copy of the summons is **personally** served on the witness.[35] The summons can be served by you or you can have it served by someone else. The summons must be handed directly to the witness. It cannot be mailed or faxed to the witness or left with any other person.

If a witness does not attend the hearing, you may need to prove that the witness was in fact properly served with the summons.

The person who served the summons on the witness should prepare an **affidavit**, swearing or affirming that a copy of the summons was personally served on the witness. A copy of the summons should be attached to the affidavit. You can obtain an affidavit form at a Board office in your area or from the Board's website at www.ltb.gov.on.ca. The completed Affidavit must be sworn before a Commissioner of Oaths or a Notary Public. A Com-

---

[35] Subsection 12(3) of the *Statutory Powers Procedure Act*.

missioner of Oaths is available at most Board offices to administer oaths and affirmations for affidavits relating to Board applications.

A witness is entitled to a fee for attending the hearing.[36] The fees are the same as those paid in the Superior Court of Justice (currently, $50 per day plus a travel allowance and in some cases, an accommodation allowance).[37] When serving the witness with a copy of the summons, inform him that he is entitled to fees. The fees, however, do not have to be paid until the witness actually attends the hearing.

If a witness who has been properly served with a summons fails to attend the hearing, the witness may be found to be in contempt, arrested and brought before the Superior Court of Justice.[38]

Note that a Member of the Board or person employed as a mediator by the Board cannot be compelled to give testimony or produce documents in a civil proceeding (including hearings before the Board) with respect to matters that come to his or her knowledge in the course of exercising his or her duties under this Act.[39]

(b) Implications of Section 82

As discussed in Chapter 1, one of the new rights of tenants under the R.T.A. is the right of a tenant to raise, at an application commenced by the landlord with respect to arrears of rent,[40] any issue the tenant wishes (s. 82) and to be granted the same relief as if the tenant had commenced his or her own application.

From a tenant's point of view, this is a good thing because it allows a tenant to raise issues at the hearing scheduled by the landlord without having to commence a separate application and without having to schedule a separate hearing on another date. If the landlord is in breach of the landlord's obligations under the R.T.A. or the tenancy agreement, it permits the tenant to raise the issue not only as a defence to the landlord's application (under s. 83 of the R.T.A., if it is an eviction application), but also in order to obtain a remedial order from the Board. Thus, even where it is found that the tenant owes the landlord (for example) $1,000 in rent, it may be found that the tenant is entitled to an abatement of rent and/or compensation in the amount of $1,500, in which case the landlord's application based upon arrears of rent will be dismissed and an order will be issued that the landlord pay to the

---

[36] Subsection 12(3.1) of the *Statutory Powers Procedure Act*.

[37] See Appendix B to the Board's Rules of Practice.

[38] Sections 12 and 13 of the *Statutory Powers Procedure Act*.

[39] Section 175 of the R.T.A.

[40] Either an eviction application (Form L1) brought under ss. 59 and 69 of the R.T.A. (subsection 82(1)) or an application for arrears of rent without an eviction (Form L9) brought under s. 87 of the R.T.A. (subsection 87(2)).

tenant the balance owing to the tenant after one amount is set-off as against the other. In this example, the landlord would be ordered to pay the tenant $500.

A tenant will need to come to the hearing prepared to present cogent evidence to support his or her allegations. Mere assertions without corroborating evidence (photographs, documents, independent witnesses, etc.) will likely be insufficient. Also, recall that if the complaint is about the condition of the unit or the complex, in deciding the appropriate remedy (and, in particular, whether an abatement of rent is warranted), the Board must consider whether the tenant advised the landlord of the alleged breaches before applying for relief to the Board (s. 30(2)). The tenant must therefore be prepared to present convincing evidence that the landlord was advised of the problems and that the landlord failed to take adequate steps to investigate and correct the problems within a reasonable period of time. The best evidence of notice to the landlord would be copies of written complaints to the landlord with a date stamp or other written acknowledgement of receipt from the landlord.[41]

In fact, based on past experience, the most common issue likely to be raised by tenants under s. 82 will be complaints about maintenance. Knowing this, landlords can take certain steps to better prepare themselves to deal with maintenance issues that arise at the hearing of an L1 or L9 application.

First, landlords should implement a system for regularly inspecting the common areas of a residential complex. A landlord should have staff keep careful and detailed written records of any maintenance problems in the building. Common areas should be routinely inspected. A report should be generated from each such inspection so that there is a record of the condition of the building as of the date of the inspection. Photographs can be taken and kept on file. If the landlord receives any notice of a problem from a municipal, regional or provincial authority, records should be kept of the work that was required, the work that was done (and when), and if possible, written confirmation from the authority that the work done was satisfactory.

Second, landlords should implement a system for periodically inspecting the rental units. Since landlords are now permitted to enter rental units to inspect their condition (on 24 hours notice — clause 27(1)4 of the R.T.A.), landlords should probably have each unit inspected at least once or twice per year. A written inspection report should be produced and, if possible, the tenant should be asked to sign (and date) an acknowledgement that the inspection report is accurate and/or to list any of the tenant's maintenance concerns not already identified in the report. If the tenant acknowledges that

---

[41] See Landlord and Tenant Board File No. SOL-01316 (April 27, 2007), in which the Member was not convinced, in the absence of any documentation, that the tenants had advised the landlord of two of the three maintenance problems raised by the tenants at the hearing of the landlord's application to evict the tenants for non-payment of rent.

the unit is in good condition, the tenant will have difficulty, one or two months later, alleging that the unit has been unfit for a substantial period of time. Similarly, if the tenant only identifies one or two problems on the inspection report, it will be difficult for that tenant to be taken seriously if he or she presents the Member at the hearing with a long list of maintenance complaints.

Third, landlords should implement and maintain a system whereby all maintenance complaints must be submitted to the landlord in writing (in a form approved by the landlord) and the landlord should date stamp all such forms it receives.[42] Some landlords use a form that is in triplicate so that the tenant can keep one copy, the landlord keeps one copy for its records and a third copy goes to the superintendent or property manager for investigation and action. If the landlord's record-keeping is meticulous and the tenant cannot produce any copies of such work requests, the Board may well believe the landlord that it never received any complaints from this tenant.

Fourth, landlords should consider inspecting the rental unit (on proper notice) to ascertain its condition just before the landlord serves a Form N4 or shortly before the hearing so that, if necessary, the landlord can call a witness to testify about the current condition of the unit.

Fifth, landlords should bring to the hearing all records related to maintenance/repairs that were requested or done in the unit for *at least* the last 12 months preceding the hearing.

Sixth, landlords should review a tenant's entire file to see if other issues have arisen in the previous 12-month period that are likely to be raised by the tenant under s. 82 at the hearing of the landlord's L1 or L9 application.

If a landlord who has commenced an application based upon arrears of rent is aware of some other issue that has been upsetting the tenant (i.e., not related to maintenance), the landlord should come to the hearing prepared to deal with such issues. Any relevant documents should be brought to the hearing (just in case) and key witnesses should either be present or available to come to the hearing on short notice should they be needed.

In Landlord and Tenant Board File No. SOL-01316 (April 27, 2007), the property manager was on hand to testify about the maintenance issues raised by the tenants and brought documentation (letters from a pest control company that had attended at the unit on three occasions in the preceding year). All this convinced the Member that the tenants had obstructed the landlord's reasonable efforts to address the presence of pests in the rental unit. As a result, the tenants were denied any relief.

If the tenant raises an issue that could not reasonably have been anticipated by the landlord or to which the landlord cannot adequately respond on

---

[42] This avoids the possibility of a tenant completing a form, not actually submitting it to the landlord and then claiming that it had been submitted but that the landlord failed to take any action.

the date set for the original hearing, the landlord may have to request an adjournment.[43]

Finally, many landlords who commence an L1 application (for arrears of rent, compensation, termination of the tenancy and eviction) do not realistically expect to collect the money that is owed by the tenant. In such cases, where the tenant raises an issue at the hearing pursuant to s. 82 of the R.T.A., the landlord might be prepared to negotiate with the tenant and reduce the amount of arrears being claimed (or, possibly, waive any claim for money), on the condition that the tenant consent to an order terminating the tenancy (and evicting the tenant). This would avoid the risk of a long, contested hearing and the possibility of an adjournment and would provide the certainty of an order that is virtually unassailable.[44]

If the parties do reach an agreement and it is intended to finally resolve all issues arising from the tenancy (other than issues related to the enforcement of the order to which they are consenting), the parties should also consider obtaining a full and final release from the other (or a mutual release) to ensure that neither party can later make a claim against the other. For instance, in one case, a landlord inserted into the Form N11 (Agreement to Terminate the Tenancy) a clause stating that, "This settles all matters arising out of the tenancy . . ." After the tenant vacated the unit, the tenant brought an application against the landlord for harassment and serious interference with the tenant's reasonable enjoyment. The presiding Member found that the tenant was bound by the release and was, therefore, barred from commencing any proceedings concerning the tenancy. The tenant's application was dismissed.

6. NEGOTIATION AND MEDIATION

Landlords and tenants are always free to negotiate a settlement of any dispute that may arise between them. It is often a good idea for people to attempt to work out an amicable settlement on terms they can both accept. Compromising is frequently better than proceeding through to the end of a hearing because a settlement is less adversarial, is faster, cheaper and more certain. Although most people assume they are in the right and will succeed at a hearing, every application has a loser and at least half of the people who think they will win are unpleasantly surprised by the Board's decision. A negotiated settlement allows the parties to retain some control over the outcome and, while a person may not get everything they want, at least they will get some of what they wanted if they can make a deal.

If the parties are able to resolve their dispute before an application is commenced, the Board will usually not become involved in the matter.

---

43 See Interpretation Guideline No. 1.

44 See the discussion on consent orders in "Orders and Reasons" below.

Where the application concerns arrears of rent,[45] the parties can sign a written settlement (typically, a repayment schedule) and file it with the Board before the hearing has commenced. The Board can then incorporate the terms of this settlement into a consent order (prior to the date set for the hearing).[46] Such an order, however, cannot include any provision for termination of the tenancy or even termination in the event of a breach of any terms of the agreement. The most that can happen is that, upon a breach of the agreement by the tenant, the landlord may request that the application be re-opened and a new hearing date be set. Either party can also seek to have the consent order set aside on the basis that the agreement was only obtained through misrepresentation or coercion. The request to re-open the application must be filed within 30 days of the alleged breach of the order (s. 206(6) of the R.T.A.) or, if there is an allegation of coercion or misrepresentation, within 30 days of the date of the order (s. 206(5)). According to the note under Rule 10.3, the hearing will be scheduled "promptly"; presumably, this suggests that the matter will be given priority and the hearing will be expedited. The request to re-open and the notice of hearing must be served on the other party(ies) as soon as possible but not less than five days before the hearing (Rule 10.3).

In my view, landlords are not likely to take advantage of this provision for the following reasons: (1) the consent order is, for all intents and purposes, unenforceable; (2) the hearing will be more complex (i.e., more issues will need to be resolved) and the onus upon the landlord will be twofold as the landlord will have to prove a breach of the agreement before there can even be a hearing of the merits of the landlord's original application; and (3) notwithstanding the Board's stated intention to schedule such matters promptly, there is the risk that the hearing may be substantially delayed. Therefore, there is little, if any, advantage to the landlord making a deal with the tenant and obtaining an order in accordance with s. 206 of the R.T.A. A landlord who wishes to negotiate with the tenant would likely be better off waiting until the day of the hearing and then entering into a mediated agreement or a consent order *at* the hearing.

If an application has been commenced and then the parties reach a settlement on their own prior to the commencement of the hearing, the parties may want their agreement to be reflected, in whole or in part, in an order from the Board. In such a case, a party may file a copy of the written settlement agreement with the Member at the beginning of the hearing (Rule 14.1).

The Member may hear evidence or submissions to determine whether the request to include terms of the agreement in an order is proper and whether the terms of the agreement are in accordance with the provisions of the Act

---

[45] Either an application under s. 69 for an order terminating the tenancy and evicting the tenant based on a notice of termination under s. 59 or an application for payment of arrears of rent, or both.

[46] Section 206 of the R.T.A.

(Rule 14.2). You will recall that parties cannot contract out of the R.T.A. and cannot waive their rights under the Act. If the Member is satisfied that the request to include terms of the agreement in the order is proper and that the terms of the agreement appear to be in accordance with the provisions of the Act, an order may be issued in accordance with the agreement or, with the consent of the parties, as the Member otherwise sees fit (Rule 14.2).

The Member cannot include in the order any term which the Act would not permit to be included in the order for this particular type of application (Rule 14.2). For instance, the Board cannot order the payment of rent where the application brought by the landlord is about alleged damage to the rental unit. Similarly, the Board cannot order the tenant to pay arrears of rent to the landlord if the application was commenced by the tenant and there has been no application filed by the landlord.

Once an application has been commenced, however, landlords and tenants often have difficulty dealing with each other directly. There may be some animosity between the parties and mutual feelings of mistrust. One or more of the parties may be ignorant of their respective rights and obligations under the law. One party may feel they are at a disadvantage in negotiations because the other party is more experienced, has greater assets and/or has legal representation.

To facilitate settlement by parties, the Board provides mediation services. The authority of the Board to mediate disputes arises from s. 194 of the R.T.A. Participating in mediation is voluntary. The Board encourages parties to attempt to resolve their disputes through mediation, but a party is not obliged to enter into negotiations.[47] The rules and procedures related to mediation are found in Rule 13 of the Board's Rules of Practice.

Mediation is a process whereby a neutral third party, a Mediator, attempts to assist the parties in identifying their interests and in devising ways of satisfying those interests which are agreeable to all parties (Rule 13.1). A Mediator will describe the process to the parties and may explain the provisions of the R.T.A., regulations, Rules and Interpretation Guidelines, relevant case law or practices of the Board (Rule 13.4). A Mediator will not offer a personal opinion or give advice to either party to the mediation regarding the merits of the application (Rule 13.5). The Mediator may meet with all of the parties together, or separately. A Mediator does not make any decisions about the case.

A Mediator does not decide who is right or wrong — that is for a Member to decide if the matter proceeds to a hearing. Interest-based mediation is about what the parties *want*. If a tenant wants to end the tenancy early and the landlord also wants to have the tenant leave, they have something in common and should be able to work out an agreement (it may just be a matter of

---

[47] Except where a landlord applies to move a tenant out of a care home (s. 148(3) of the R.T.A.). In such applications, mediation is mandatory (see Chapter 21).

working out when the tenancy will end and what one party or the other is willing to offer to make the deal attractive to the other side). For mediation to succeed it doesn't matter who is at fault; what matters is what the parties really want and what they are prepared to give up in order to get what they want. Sometimes, all a person wants is validation or an apology. Mediators are skilled in discovering the parties' underlying interests and in helping them to reach a compromise that will allow them both to achieve at least some of their goals.

Mediation has a fairly high success rate and is often worth trying. Even where it does not fully resolve the application, the exchange of information that occurs during the mediation process often helps clear up misunderstandings, reduce the number of issues (and, thereby, reduce the length of the hearing), and give each side some idea of the evidence upon which the other side intends to rely.[48] It also gives the parties an opportunity to get information from an objective, neutral third party who is knowledgeable about the R.T.A. and the decisions of the Board and who can provide a bit of a "reality check". For instance, a tenant who brings an application about the disturbance caused by balcony repairs may believe he or she will receive a 100% abatement of rent if successful at the hearing; a Mediator can explain to such a tenant that, under the regulations, the most the tenant is likely to receive in such a situation is a 25% abatement of rent.[49] Once the tenant's expectations become more realistic, the possibility of reaching a settlement is greatly enhanced.

The advantages of mediation[50] can be summarized as follows:

1. Mediators help balance any inequality in the bargaining power of the parties;
2. Mediators assist the parties by providing important information and insight into the law and the procedures of the Board;
3. Mediators help parties move past merely blaming each other and begin discussing their desires and possible solutions to their mutual problems;
4. A settlement mediated by the Board may contain provisions that contravene the provisions of the R.T.A.; and
5. A mediated settlement results in a written agreement that is enforceable by the Board.

From a landlord's point of view, if the issue is arrears of rent, it may also be advantageous to first try reaching an agreement with the tenant for the following additional reasons. If a settlement is reached with respect to the

---

48 Since there is no formal discovery process, the disclosure obtained through mediation can be quite informative.

49 See Chapter 11.

50 I.e., the advantages of mediation over negotiation directly between the parties, without the assistance of a neutral third party.

repayment of the arrears and is incorporated into a mediated agreement or consent order that permits the landlord to resort to s. 78 of the R.T.A. in the event of a breach, this may give the landlord two additional advantages. First, should the tenant breach the agreement/order and then seek to have the *ex parte* eviction order set aside, the tenant will not be able to raise other issues at the resulting hearing under s. 82 of the R.T.A. (since the hearing is being conducted under s. 78, not under s. 69 or s. 87). Second, the Board will be less inclined to provide relief under s. 83 to a tenant who has already been given an opportunity to repay the rent that is admittedly owing and who could not live up to a repayment schedule that was negotiated by the tenant.

Despite s. 3(1) of the R.T.A., a settlement mediated by the Board may contain terms that contravene any provision of the R.T.A.[51] This allows the parties greater flexibility to craft innovative solutions to their conflicts. Where such a provision is to be included in a mediated agreement, the Mediator is required to take special care to explain to each party the effect of such a provision before the party signs the agreement (Rule 13.3).

The Rental Housing Tribunal held, however, that the power of parties to agree (through mediation) to terms inconsistent with the Act did not permit parties to oust the jurisdiction of the Tribunal.

In *Crestview Investment Corp. v. Ali*,[52] the landlord commenced an eviction application against the tenant but the landlord and tenant were able to reach a mediated settlement of the issues in dispute. The mediated agreement contained a provision under s. 77 of the T.P.A. (now s. 78 of the R.T.A.) that permitted the landlord to obtain an *ex parte* eviction order if the tenant breached certain terms of the mediated agreement. The landlord was concerned that, in such circumstances, the tenant might bring a motion to set aside the *ex parte* order and ask the Tribunal to exercise its discretion under s. 84(1) of the T.P.A. (now s. 83 of the R.T.A.). The landlord therefore insisted on adding a clause to the mediated agreement, indicating that the agreement was final and that, upon a breach by the tenant of the mediated agreement, the tenant waived any right to request relief under s. 84 of the T.P.A. As the landlord predicted, the tenant breached the agreement, brought a motion to have the landlord's *ex parte* order set aside and requested relief under s. 84. On the set-aside motion, the landlord argued that the Tribunal was not entitled to grant relief under s. 84 because the tenant had in the agreement waived any right to such relief and the parties are, pursuant to s. 181(2) of the T.P.A. (now s. 194(2) of the R.T.A.), entitled to include in a mediated agreement terms that are inconsistent with the Act. The Member hearing the set-aside motion disagreed with this interpretation of s. 181(2). He found that the parties do not have the power to oust the jurisdiction of the Tribunal and that such a provision is contrary to public policy and unenforceable.

---

[51] Subsection 194(2) of the R.T.A.

[52] (May 8, 2003), TSL-50528-SA, 2003 CarswellOnt 2634 (Ont. Rental Housing Trib.).

Where the parties are unable to resolve their dispute through mediation, they will return to the hearing room and their hearing will proceed as scheduled (time permitting). If the parties are able to resolve their dispute, the Mediator will usually assist the parties by preparing a written agreement for them to sign (Rule 13.7). The parties will each get a copy of the signed agreement but no copy will be kept in the Board's file. What occurs in or results from mediation is confidential and ought not to be disclosed to a Member of the Board.[53] The provisions concerning confidentiality of the mediation process and agreements that result therefrom are found in Rules 13.17 through 13.22.

If the agreement resolves all the issues raised by the application, the Mediator will close the file (Rule 13.9). If part of the agreement involves the payment of money that has been paid by one of the parties into the Board, the Mediator has the authority to order the release of those funds (Rule 13.8). If a settlement resolves only some of the issues raised in an application, the remaining issues will be decided through a hearing (Rule 13.10). If the parties cannot reach a full settlement but can agree on some facts that may expedite the hearing, the Mediator can assist the parties in preparing a written "Agreed Statement of Facts" to be presented to the Member at the hearing (Rule 13.11).

Where the parties do reach an agreement through mediation, the agreement will be reduced to writing and all parties (or their legal representatives) will be asked to sign the agreement. The parties will each receive a copy of the agreement but a copy will *not* be retained in the Board's file. The mediator will usually assist in the preparation of this document. It is crucial that all parties carefully review the written agreement to ensure that it accurately reflects the terms of their settlement. Misunderstandings or omissions can later lead to further litigation.

If the parties do reach an agreement and it is intended to finally resolve all issues arising from the tenancy (other than enforcement of the order to which they are consenting), the parties should also consider obtaining a full and final release from the other (or a mutual release) to ensure that neither party can later make a claim against the other.

In *Clement v. Varga*,[54] the tenants brought an application based upon the landlord's alleged breaches of her maintenance obligations. The landlord brought a motion to have this application dismissed on the basis that the issues raised therein had already been resolved when the parties reached a mediated agreement of a prior application brought by the landlord for arrears of rent. It was impossible for the Member to know what may have been

---

[53] Except to the extent that the parties jointly request an order on consent or there is a dispute over the mediated agreement that comes before a Member on a request to re-open or under s. 78.

[54] (May 16, 2006), SWT-07504-IN, [2006] O.R.H.T.D. No. 39 (Ont. Rental Housing Trib.).

discussed during the earlier mediation process so he had to rely on the written terms of the mediated agreement. That agreement said that the parties had resolved all issues set out in the landlord's application (for arrears of rent). The agreement made no mention of any issues concerning maintenance. If the parties' intention was to settle *all* issues between them up to that point in time (including mould-related maintenance issues), that could have been set out expressly in the agreement. Since the agreement only referred to the landlord's application concerning arrears of rent, the Member ruled that the tenants were not barred from proceeding with their maintenance application. This case illustrates the importance of careful drafting when it comes to settlement agreements.

What happens if a party does not live up to the terms of the mediated agreement? How is such an agreement enforced? It depends. If the application in question was an eviction application, if the agreement contains a s. 78 clause and if the term that was breached is one for which relief can be granted under s. 78, then the landlord may file an application under s. 78 and obtain an eviction order very quickly, without notice to the tenant, based upon the affidavit evidence filed by the landlord along with the application.[55] No further attendance before a Member is required.[56] Where there has been a breach of the terms of a mediated agreement, the innocent party may also request that the application be "re-opened" in accordance with Rule 13.13 of the Board's Rules of Practice.

A request to re-open an application must identify the alleged breach of the agreement, and must be filed, together with a copy of the agreement, within one year of the date the agreement was signed (Rule 13.15). The person requesting that the application be re-opened shall give a copy of their request and the notice of hearing to all other parties to the application at least five days before the hearing (Rule 13.16).

A party to a mediated agreement may also request that the application be re-opened on the basis that, during the mediation, the other party coerced them or deliberately made false or misleading representations which had a material effect on the agreement (Rule 13.14). This is often difficult to prove since there will be no record (other than the mediated agreement) as to what was discussed during the mediation, and the mediator cannot be compelled to testify (s. 175 of the R.T.A.). The fact that a party later changes his or her mind about the deal that was made is not sufficient grounds to set aside the settlement and re-open the original application.[57]

---

[55] See Chapter 13 for a detailed discussion of the process of bringing an application under s. 78.

[56] Unless the tenant files a motion to have the *ex parte* order set aside, in which case there will be a hearing of the tenant's motion.

[57] *Hall v. Gelly* (Aug. 17, 2006), SOT-05718, [2006] O.R.H.T.D. No. 106 (Ont. Rental Housing Trib.).

Where a request to re-open an application has been made, a hearing will be scheduled so that a Member can ascertain whether the conditions set out in Rule 13.13 or 13.14, as the case may be, have been proven. If the request to re-open the application is granted, the mediated agreement ceases to have any effect and cannot be enforced by either party.[58] The Board then proceeds to hear the original application as if there had never been a settlement.

7. ADJOURNMENTS

Pursuant to s. 21 of the *Statutory Powers Procedure Act*, the Board has the power to adjourn a hearing on its own motion or where it is shown to the satisfaction of the Board that the adjournment is required to permit an adequate hearing to be held.

Where all the parties to an application agree to the rescheduling of a hearing, the Board will usually grant the request of the parties. Nevertheless, the Board retains the discretion to refuse such a request.[59] A party who requests the rescheduling of a hearing must obtain the consent of all other parties, whether or not the notice of hearing and application have been served on the respondent(s).[60] Hopefully, this Rule (12.2) will prevent situations like the one in *Wiernak Estate v. Majid*.[61]

In *Wiernak Estate v. Majid*,[62] the applicant commenced an application but never served the application or notice of hearing on the respondent. The applicant had adjourned the hearing on three previous occasions. On the fourth request for an adjournment, it was held that adjournments are not automatic, that prejudice is presumed to result from delay and that an applicant should serve the respondent promptly and be prepared to proceed on the date set for the hearing. The request for another adjournment was denied and the case was dismissed.

The Board's Interpretation Guideline No. 1 sets out the procedures to be followed by a party who is seeking to reschedule or adjourn a hearing. Whenever possible, the request should be made in writing to the Board, well in advance of the hearing date. The party requesting the adjournment should attempt to obtain the consent of the other parties to the application and should indicate what dates, if any, the parties prefer for the rescheduled hearing.

When a request for an adjournment is made on the day of the hearing, it should be made in person by the party seeking the adjournment or by another

---

[58] *Mueller v. Urry* (July 27, 2000), TEL-09669-RV, TET-00874-RV, 2000 CarswellOnt 4508 (Ont. Rental Housing Trib.).

[59] Rule 12.1.

[60] Rue 12.2.

[61] (Nov. 17, 2000), TNL-18663, [2000] O.R.H.T.D. No. 157 (Ont. Rental Housing Trib.).

[62] *Ibid.*

person authorized to act as that party's agent.[63] If the request is opposed, the Member will weigh the prejudice that might be suffered by each party, while bearing in mind the public interest in resolving the case expeditiously. A request for a short adjournment to retain legal representation will generally be permitted, provided the party can demonstrate having made reasonable efforts to retain a lawyer or agent before the hearing.[64] An adjournment may also be granted to permit a party to file a related application or to permit two (or more) related applications to be heard together.

As previously discussed in this Chapter ("Preparing for the Hearing"), mustering the best possible evidence is crucial to success. In Landlord and Tenant Board File No. CEL-03686, the landlord was seeking to evict the tenant for abandoning an infant in the rental unit (which could constitute both an illegal act and serious impairment of the safety of a person in the complex). The tenant's defence was that she left another adult in the unit with the infant. The police had investigated the matter. As the applicant, the landlord had to present its evidence first. The landlord called as witnesses a representative of the landlord and the police officer who was now in charge of the investigation. The first witness had third- or fourth-hand information about what occurred on the day in question. The police officer who testified similarly had no first-hand information as that officer did not attend at the complex on the day in question and only became involved in the case subsequently. The landlord knew the names of the officers who actually attended at the rental unit on the day in question but chose not to summons them to the hearing. After the landlord purported to close its case, it requested an adjournment so that it could call these two officers as witnesses. No reasonable explanation was given for having failed to summons them in the first place. The tenant opposed the adjournment on the grounds that the tenant's witnesses would soon be out of the country and would be unavailable for the foreseeable future. The Member weighed the prejudice to both parties and, ultimately, denied the landlord's request for an adjournment. The tenant and her witnesses then testified. Unlike the landlord's witnesses, they had first-hand knowledge of the events in question and, if found to be credible, their testimony would likely be given greater weight. The landlord again requested an adjournment in order to call the two other police officers in reply, arguing that the landlord could not have anticipated the tenant's defence. The Member found that the

---

[63] See *Mascherin v. James* (Feb. 7, 2002), TET-02271, [2002] O.R.H.T.D. No. 21 (Ont. Rental Housing Trib.).

[64] See Interpretation Guideline No. 1 and *Doherty v. Minto Developments Inc.* (November 19, 2003), Doc. 02-DV-000820 (Ont. Div. Ct.) (re EAL-31684) in which the Divisional Court found that it was a reversible error for the Tribunal to refuse the tenant, in the circumstances, additional time in which to retain counsel. Although it is a matter of discretion, that discretion must be exercised in a reasonable fashion that ensures fairness to all parties. Also see *Toronto-Dominion Bank v. Couto* (March 3, 2006), SWL-78675-IN, [2006] O.R.H.T.D. No. 33 (Ont. Rental Housing Trib.).

landlord was aware of the tenant's defence before the hearing commenced and could reasonably have made arrangements to have the additional officers available to testify at the hearing. This request for an adjournment was, once again, denied.

The Board recognizes that a landlord may not be prepared to respond to an issue that is raised for the first time at the hearing (pursuant to s. 82 of the R.T.A.). Interpretation Guideline No. 1 provides that,

> Where the tenant raises issues under s. 82 that the landlord could not reasonably have anticipated and cannot address at the hearing with a short recess, the landlord may request an adjournment to another date for the purpose of investigating the tenant's allegations and obtaining relevant evidence.

A tenant, however, should be prepared on the date set for the hearing of the landlord's application to raise any issues the tenant wishes to bring forward under s. 82. Where a tenant requested an adjournment to consider whether or not he wanted to raise any issues under s. 82, that request was denied.[65]

The Board recognizes that a landlord may not be prepared to respond to an issue that is raised for the first time at the hearing (pursuant to s. 82 of the R.T.A.). Interpretation Guideline No. 1 provides that, "Where the tenant raises issues under s. 82 that the landlord could not reasonably have anticipated and cannot address at the hearing with a short recess, the landlord may request an adjournment to another date for the purpose of investigating the tenant's allegations and obtaining relevant evidence."

The Member may impose such conditions[66] to the granting of the adjournment as the Member deems appropriate, including: (1) awarding the legal costs needlessly incurred (costs "thrown away") by the other party for a legal representative to prepare and attend before the Board (since the matter is being adjourned); (2) ordering that some money be paid into the Board in the interim; (3) ordering disclosure of documents or information; and (4) making the next date "peremptory" upon the person requesting the adjournment (i.e., the hearing will proceed on the next date whether or not the party is ready).

8. THE HEARING

(a) Types of Hearings

Pursuant to s. 183 of the R.T.A., the Board is required to adopt the most expeditious method of determining the questions arising in a proceeding that affords to all persons directly affected by the proceeding an adequate opportunity to know the issues and be heard on the matter. The natural assumption

---

[65] Landlord and Tenant Board File No. SOL-03369 (July 9, 2007).

[66] Section 204 of the R.T.A.

is that all hearings will be oral (i.e., a face-to-face hearing that resembles a courtroom trial). The vast majority of cases that proceed to a hearing before the Board are, in fact, adjudicated by way of oral hearings. In some circumstances, however, it may be difficult, impractical or unnecessary to hold a face-to-face hearing.

If the parties live in a more remote location, for instance, they might have to wait a long time for a hearing and the Board may not want to send an adjudicator to such a location to hear only one case. If the matter is a technical one that relies exclusively on documentation, it may be unnecessary for the Member to hear testimony and again, the Board or the parties may find it undesirable to hold an oral hearing. In cases like these, the law permits hearings to be held electronically or in writing, as long as certain criteria have been met.[67]

The Board may conduct an electronic hearing on its own initiative or at the request of one of the parties (Rule 21). An electronic hearing is a hearing held by conference call, video conferencing or some other means of electronic technology permitting persons to hear one another. Since the Board has created a brochure specifically dealing with telephone hearings, it is reasonable to assume that the Board anticipates conducting more of this type of hearing than did the Rental Housing Tribunal under the T.P.A. In fact, during the first six months of 2009, the Board conducted a pilot project to expand the use of telephone and video conferencing technologies for mediation and hearings in the counties of Bruce, Grey, Haldimand/Norfolk and Huron as well as in the district of Thunder Bay.

An electronic hearing will not be held unless all parties, the Member and the witnesses can hear each other at all times.[68] If the hearing is only meant to deal with procedural issues, the Board can proceed with an electronic hearing even if one of the parties objects.[69] If the hearing will deal with substantive issues, a party has the right to object (Rule 21.2) and the Board will not hold the hearing electronically if the party satisfies it that holding an electronic rather than an oral hearing is likely to cause the party significant prejudice.[70] In deciding whether or not to hold an electronic hearing, the Member may consider any relevant factors (including those listed in Rule 21.1). The Board can direct that a party arrange for the facilities or equipment necessary for the electronic hearing and can order that the party pay any associated expenses (Rule 21.3).

The Board may also conduct a written hearing on its own initiative or at the request of one of the parties (Rule 22). In a written hearing, the parties are required to file their evidence and make their submissions to the Board

---

[67] See ss. 5.1, 5.2 and 5.2.1 of the *Statutory Powers Procedure Act*.

[68] Subsection 5.2(4) of the *Statutory Powers Procedure Act*.

[69] Subsection 5.2(3) of the *Statutory Powers Procedure Act*.

[70] Subsection 5.2(2) of the *Statutory Powers Procedure Act* and Rule 20.1.

in writing. The Board then makes a decision based on the evidence and submissions filed without holding a meeting between the parties. Written hearings are not suitable for applications where facts may be in dispute or credibility is an issue. In deciding whether or not to hold a written hearing, the Member may consider any relevant factors (including those listed in Rule 22.1).

If the hearing is only meant to deal with procedural issues, the Board can proceed with a written hearing even if one of the parties objects.[71] If the hearing will deal with substantive issues, a party has the right to object (Rule 22.2). Normally, a tribunal will not hold a written hearing where a party can demonstrate a good reason for not doing so.[72] Also, the law normally requires each party to serve on the other parties every document that is filed with the tribunal.[73] The drafters of the R.T.A. felt this would be too onerous in certain types of applications where there would be too many documents or too many parties to make this practical.

For applications under s. 132 (application to vary a rent reduction), 133 (application by a tenant to reduce rent as a result of a reduction in taxes) or para. 1 only of s. 126(1) (an application to increase rents above the guideline based solely upon an extraordinary increase in municipal taxes and/or utilities), the Board may proceed with a written hearing even if a party objects.[74] For such applications, the parties are also not required to serve every document on the other parties.[75] The document filing procedures are set out in Rule 22.4 of the Board's Rules of Practice.

(b) Recording Proceedings

The Board is required to compile a record of any proceeding in which a hearing has been held. Such a record shall include the application, notice of hearing, any interlocutory orders made by the Board, all documentary evidence filed with the Board and the decision of the Board (and reasons, if any have been given).[76] The Board is *not* required by law to make a recording of

---

[71] Subsection 5.1(2.1) of the *Statutory Powers Procedure Act*.

[72] Subsection 5.1(2) of the *Statutory Powers Procedure Act*.

[73] Subsection 5.1(3) of the *Statutory Powers Procedure Act*.

[74] See s. 184(2) of the R.T.A., which exempts these specific types of applications from s. 5.1(2) of the *Statutory Powers Procedure Act*.

[75] See Rule 22.5 and subsection 184(3) of the R.T.A., which exempts these specific types of applications from s. 5.1(3) of the *Statutory Powers Procedure Act*. The applicant is required to serve a copy of the application and notice of written hearing on each respondent no later than 20 days after the notice of written hearing is issued (Rule 22.4(1)).

[76] Section 20 of the *Statutory Powers Procedure Act*.

the hearing.[77] Nevertheless, the Board does attempt to record all of its hearings.

Where the Board records the hearing, the recording will form part of the record and any party may request a copy of the recording upon payment of the required fee (Rule 25.2). The deadline for a party to request a copy of a recording is ten years from the date the hearing was recorded (Rule 25.3).[78]

In the past, the quality of the recordings made by the Rental Housing Tribunal was unreliable. The Tribunal started off with an audio cassette recording system and then began to use digital recording. Despite the Tribunal's efforts, many recordings were found to be inaudible, unintelligible or missing. This was the subject of considerable criticism from appellate judges who often found it difficult to decide the merits of an appeal in the absence of a transcript of the proceedings.

In *Longhouse Village (Thunder Bay) Inc. v. Smolcec*,[79] the Tribunal's recordings of the hearing were apparently either lost or destroyed. The Court found that the absence of the transcript of the original hearing hindered the appellant tenant's ability to properly advance his grounds for appeal and the Court's ability to assess the validity of his claims. The Court found that to deny the appeal in such circumstances would amount to a denial of natural justice. The Court remitted the matter back to the Tribunal for a new hearing. A similar decision was rendered by the Divisional Court in *Saleh v. 1269805 Ontario Inc.*[80] and in *Swire v. Walleye Trailer Park Ltd.*[81]

In *McKenzie v. Supportive Housing in Peel*,[82] the Tribunal granted an eviction order on the basis that the tenant assaulted the spouse of the superintendent. The tenant, however, was diagnosed with a form of schizophrenia, which is a factor the Tribunal ought to have considered under both s. 84 of the T.P.A. and the *Human Rights Code*. Since the Tribunal's eviction order does not specifically refer to the tenant's condition and what efforts, if any, the landlord made to accommodate her or whether these issues were considered by the member as part of the s. 84(1) analysis and *since no tape recording or transcript of the proceedings was available*, the matter was remitted back to the Tribunal for reconsideration.

In *Cymbalski v. Alcorn*,[83] the appellant raised issues about the conduct of the proceedings at the Rental Housing Tribunal and comments made by

---

[77] *D'Andrade et al. v. Cheng* (August 20, 2001), Doc. Toronto 103/01 & 104/01(Ont. Div. Ct.) (re TSL-24815 and TSL-26497).

[78] After ten years, the Board may destroy the recording (Rule 25.4). Note that prior to December 2008, the Board's Rules only required the Board to retain copies of its recordings for one year.

[79] (2001), 2001 CarswellOnt 688, [2001] O.J. No. 875 (Ont. Div. Ct.).

[80] (February 18, 2002), Doc. 404/01 (Ont. Div. Ct.) (re TSL-27813).

[81] (2001), 2001 CarswellOnt 2832 (Ont. Div. Ct.).

[82] (2005), 2005 CarswellOnt 1561 (Ont. Div. Ct.).

[83] (March 9, 2006), Doc. Newmarket DC 05-075497-00, 209 O.A.C. 47 (Ont. Div. Ct.).

the Member. No transcript or recording was available for the proceedings due to a mechanical malfunctioning of the recording equipment. In the absence of such a record, the Divisional Court decided that it could not fairly assess these issues. The court set aside the decision of the Member and directed that the matter be remitted to the Tribunal to be reheard before a different Tribunal Member. The Divisional Court also pointed out that "on at least five occasions this Court has commented unequivocally, and expressed grave concerns about the failure to properly record proceedings before the Tribunal" and that "this failure to report the proceedings may well prevent this Court from fulfilling, in a meaningful way, its appellate functions." Similar sentiments were expressed by the Divisional Court in *Nimmo v. Toronto Housing Co.*[84]

Perhaps the harshest criticism to date from the Divisional Court can be found in the case of *Lepori v. Jackson.*[85] The Tribunal's recording of the hearing in this case was inaudible so that it was not possible to have a transcript prepared. The Court took the opportunity to express in its decision its frustration with what it perceived to be an ongoing problem with the Tribunal's recordings and made the following comments (at paras. 5 and 6):

> This Court is frequently advised by counsel who appear on appeals from orders of the Tribunal that proceedings are not always recorded and, even when they are, it is not always possible to obtain a reliable transcript showing what occurred.
>
> Accordingly, we take this opportunity to express our view that, despite the absence of any statutory requirement that all hearings of the Tribunal be recorded, it would be wise for the Tribunal to record all hearings in a manner that makes it possible for parties to obtain accurate and reliable transcripts for use in appeals. Without such transcripts, it will continue to be necessary for some applications to be remitted to the Tribunal for new hearings when appeals cannot properly be determined without them. Such new hearings add considerable cost and delay to a process that should be both affordable and expedient and should not become necessary only because the Tribunal does not take the necessary steps to record its proceedings effectively.

In *Wamboldt v. Wellman,*[86] the Divisional Court again commented upon the poor quality of the Tribunal's recordings and the effect of an incomplete transcript on the Divisional Court's ability to assess the merits of an appeal in which it is alleged that there was a denial of natural justice in the manner in which the original hearing was conducted:

> The state of the transcript of the May 16, 2006 hearing is entirely unsatisfactory as it is replete with references to "inaudible". In this regard, we add our voices to what is becoming an altogether too common refrain from this Court respecting

---

[84] [2002] O.J. No. 3450.

[85] (2005), 2005 CarswellOnt 2910 (Ont. Div. Ct.).

[86] (2007), 2007 CarswellOnt 8328 (Ont. Div. Ct.), at paras.42 and 43.

the state of the record of ORHT proceedings: *Cymbalski v. Alcorn*, [2006] O.J. No. 971 (Ont. Div. Ct.) at para. 8-19; *Manpel v. Greenwin Property Management Inc.*, [2005] O.J. No. 3079 (Ont. Div. Ct.) at para. 9.

Because of the inability of the appellants to fully present relevant evidence to the tribunal on account of the tribunal's ruling, and having regard to the state of the transcript, we are not in a position to do anything other than remit the matter to the ORHT with this judgment pursuant to s. 196(4)(b) of the *Act*.

In *Stanoulis v. Lykakim Holdings Ltd*,[87] the Divisional Court concluded that providing the parties (upon request) with a complete record (*including a complete, audible recording of the proceedings*) was part and parcel of the Board's obligation to provide reasons for its decision. In the absence of both a complete recording of the proceedings and adequate written reasons from the Board Member, the Divisional Court found that meaningful appellate review was impossible and it was forced to remit the matter back to the Board for a new hearing.

In a few decisions, lack of a recording (or an audible recording) was not found to be sufficient grounds to permit an appeal on the particular facts of those cases.[88] Where the hearing order contains extensive reasons for the decision or where the issue on appeal is a question of the correct interpretation of a statutory provision, the lack of a recording may not be as significant to the determination of the appeal and may not, in and of itself, justify ordering a new hearing. Nevertheless, the Divisional Court has made its feelings on this issue very clear and it is up to the Landlord and Tenant Board to implement a better system for recording its proceedings than it utilized when it was known as the Rental Housing Tribunal.

In the meantime, a party does have the right to request the Board's permission to make his or her own recording of the proceedings.[89] The only way to get an *accurate* recording is to retain the services of a professional court reporter (a "verbatim" reporter). Any party may bring a verbatim reporter at their own expense for the purpose of creating a transcript, provided that the party notifies the Board in advance (Rule 25.5). Obviously, hiring a court reporter is quite expensive and will likely only be done in exceptional cases.

---

[87] (2008), 2008 CarswellOnt 2629 (Ont. Div. Ct.).

[88] *Karrum Properties Inc. v. Yolanda Enterprises Ltd.* (2001), [2001] O.J. No. 5417, 2001 CarswellOnt 1839 (Ont. Div. Ct.), upheld on appeal (2002), 2002 CarswellOnt 3483 (Ont. C.A.) and *D'Andrade et al. v. Cheng* (August 20, 2001), Doc. Toronto 103/01 & 104/01 (Ont. Div. Ct.) (re TSL-24815 and TSL-26497).

[89] Rule 25.1 of the Board's Rules of Practice.

(c) What to Expect on the Day of the Hearing[90]

As with any tribunal, the best way to learn about what to expect is to actually attend some hearings. This is true for legal professionals as well as for lay persons. Knowing the tribunal and being familiar with the expectations and predilections of the decision-makers is often the key to success. It is highly recommended that those who have not previously appeared before the Landlord and Tenant Board take some time, a week or two before their own hearing, to observe one or two hearing blocks in order to become familiar with how hearings are conducted at the Board.

Unless the matter is an application by a landlord under s. 126 (an above-guideline rent increase application) or has been set up as a special appointment, an application will usually be scheduled in the same hearing "block" as many other cases. A hearing block is usually scheduled to last for either half a day or a whole day. Just because the notice of hearing says that your hearing will begin at a specific time does not mean that your case will actually be heard at that time; that is the time that the hearing block will commence and there is no way to predict when your case will be called within that block of time. If you do not show up on time, your case may be dealt with in your absence!

Whatever time is set out in the notice of hearing, you should show up at least 30 minutes prior to the time shown on the notice of hearing. This will give you time to find the Board's office and find the correct hearing room (as there are often hearings taking place in several rooms at the same time). Tenants who wish to speak to duty counsel should show up well before the hearing is scheduled to commence so that they can obtain some advice without risking being late for the hearing. If you are sending someone on your behalf, that person should have written authorization signed by you to prove to the Board that he or she has the authority to speak on your behalf.[91] Remember, though, if that person does not have first-hand knowledge of the relevant facts, they will not make a very convincing witness (if they are allowed to testify at all).

When you arrive for your hearing, you must sign your name on a "sign-in" sheet. This is proof you attended the hearing. You may then proceed to

---

[90] Please refer to the Board's pamphlets entitled, "Important Information About Your Hearing" and "Important: Your Hearing Today".

[91] In *Gillespie v. Barriault* (May 4, 2006), CEL-52590, 2006 CarswellOnt 4430, [2006] O.R.H.T.D. No. 53 (Ont. Rental Housing Trib.), the person who purported to appear on behalf of the applicant did not have written authorization and, as a consequence, the application was dismissed. A better solution might have been to allow the representative to file written authorization after the hearing or to adjourn the hearing to permit the applicant to attend in person or to provide her representative with such a written authorization. Nevertheless, this case illustrates the danger of an agent appearing before the Tribunal/Board without signed authorization.

the room where your hearing will be held. Except for rare cases, hearings are held in public.

At the beginning of the hearing block, the presiding Member will introduce himself or herself, explain the process to the parties present and give instructions as to how the Member expects people to act during the hearing. Typically, the Member will then "vet" the list, by seeing which matters can be dealt with quickly.

Under the T.P.A., the Rules of the Tribunal required Members to wait at least 30 minutes to give missing parties some extra time to show up. This is no longer the case! Since parties are instructed to show up at least 30 minutes prior to the commencement of the hearing, a Member can proceed immediately at the scheduled time, whether or not the parties are present.

If you are present but have to leave the hearing room for some reason, you must ensure that the Member knows that you are present and agrees that he or she will wait for you to return before calling your case. If you do not advise the Member and simply leave the hearing room (to negotiate, make a telephone call, go to the bathroom, get legal advice, etc.), the case may proceed in your absence!

Before the hearing block commences or during the course of the block, you may have the opportunity to discuss the possibility of settling your case either through direct negotiations with the other party, the party's representative or with the assistance of a Board mediator. The Board encourages parties to explore the possibility of settlement, even on the day of the hearing, but the parties should remember two things: (1) let the Member know what is going on so the case is not called while you are out of the room; and (2) if the negotiations go late into the hearing block, there may be insufficient time left for the Board to hear your case (if negotiations fail to bring about a settlement) and your case may then have to be rescheduled.

The cases do not proceed in the order in which they appear on the list posted outside the hearing room. The Member decides the order in which to hear the cases. When it is time for your hearing, the Board Member will call the file number and the names of the parties and/or the address of the rental unit. You may then come forward to sit at the desk at the front of the room.

Usually, the Member will deal first with any cases in which the applicant wishes to withdraw the application or in which the parties have reached an agreement and are requesting an order on consent (often this will simply be an agreement by the parties to adjourn the hearing to another date but it can also include situations where the parties are jointly requesting a final order on certain terms).

The Member may then ask if there are any requests for adjournments that are opposed and may proceed to hear and determine such contested adjournment requests.

The Member may then begin to deal with unopposed matters — cases where one side or the other has not attended the hearing. If the missing party is the applicant and the Board has not received any communication from the applicant requesting that the matter be delayed or adjourned, the Board will usually treat the application as abandoned and will dismiss the application (and possibly order costs against the applicant). If the missing party is the respondent and the Board has not received any communication for the respondent requesting that the matter be delayed or adjourned, the Board may proceed to hear the case in the absence of the respondent. The applicant must still prove his or her case so there will still be a hearing; it will just be a much shorter hearing where only the applicant presents evidence and has the opportunity to make submissions. If the applicant has followed the correct procedures and is able to prove everything that he or she is required to prove, the Board will grant the application. Since the application is unopposed, the hearing is usually quite short. Some Members, however, prefer to leave the unopposed matters to later in the hearing block to give the missing party additional time (in case they were unavoidably delayed). This is a matter for the discretion of the presiding Member.

Also, given the elimination of the default process, all cases will now have to proceed to a hearing. Therefore, many more uncontested arrears applications will now have to be dealt with in person. The Board has hired additional staff and is developing procedures for dealing with such matters expeditiously. Landlords should be sure to bring up-to-date information about any additional rent that has become due or payments that have been made since the application was filed.

The Member will then usually proceed to hear the contested matters (where both the applicant and respondent are present and are ready to proceed with their hearing). The Member determines how a particular hearing will be conducted. Usually, Board hearings are extremely quick and informal.

For example, in the case of an application for arrears of rent, the Member may ask the landlord to explain how much rent is owed and (going month-by-month) explain how that figure was calculated. The Member may then turn to the tenant and say, "Is that correct?" If the tenant answers "Yes" then the Member may say to the tenant, "Why have you not paid your rent? What is going on?" The tenant will then have an opportunity to explain and the Member may then take submissions from both sides as to the order they are both seeking. The entire hearing may only last five or ten minutes.

In more complex cases and cases in which material facts are in dispute, the hearing may be much more formal. In more formal hearings, the order of the proceeding is as follows:

1. **Opening statements** by the parties or their representatives (applicant first). This is an opportunity for each party to sum up their case in a *few* sentences — to tell the adjudicator what the case is about without going into detail.
2. **Evidence is introduced by the applicant** through the applicant and

witnesses. Evidence usually consists of testimony and documents. Each witness gives evidence which may be taken under oath or affirmation and, when finished, the opposing side has the right to cross-examine them. If new issues come up during cross-examination, the witness may be re-examined by the party who called the witness. A witness may also be questioned at any time by the Member.

3. **The respondent now has an opportunity to present his or her evidence** (in the same manner as the applicant).
4. If new issues were raised by the respondent, the applicant may be allowed to call **rebuttal evidence**.
5. Once all the evidence has been introduced, the parties (first the applicant and then the respondent) or their representatives will be allowed to make **submissions**. This is an opportunity for each party to sum up the evidence, make arguments about how the law should be interpreted and applied to the facts of the case and indicate the order the party wishes the Board to make.

Where there are two or more related applications or where the tenant is raising issues pursuant to s. 82 of the R.T.A., the Member will have to decide the manner in which the hearing shall proceed so that the various issues raised by the parties can be dealt with in a fair and efficient manner.

The Member will then render a decision. The decision is often given orally by the Member at the conclusion of the hearing but the Member can "reserve" his or her decision to take some time to think about the matter. In either case, the Member will issue a written decision (the order), usually within a few days of the conclusion of the hearing. If a party has requested it, or if the Member feels it is appropriate, the Order may be accompanied or followed by detailed written reasons.

The decision of the Member is not final until it is in writing. Although very unusual, it is possible for the final written decision to be different from what was announced orally at the conclusion of the hearing. In such circumstances, the Member should provide reasons as to why the order does not reflect the decision announced orally at the hearing.

9. STANDARD OF PROOF

The standard of proof in proceedings before the Landlord and Tenant Board is the civil standard of proof, a "balance of probabilities". The phrase "on a balance of probabilities" is incapable of precise definition and adjudicators and judges who have tried to do so invariably find themselves being criticized on appeal. For instance, where an adjudicator wrote that the tenants had failed to "convince" him the water supply was unsafe, the Divisional Court overturned the decision because the use of the word "convince" suggested that the Member may have been applying a higher standard of proof than a balance of probabilities.[92] In very basic terms (and at the risk of falling into the same trap of trying to define this concept), I would say that a fact has been proven on a balance of probabilities when it has been proven more likely to be true than not.

Until recently, it was believed that "proof on a balance of probabilities" did not mean the same thing in every case. Several courts suggested that the civil standard of proof could be thought of as being a sliding scale, rather than a particular point on that scale. Based on decisions from the Supreme Court of Canada and the English Court of Appeal,[93] the Divisional Court adopted the approach that proof of criminal conduct, requires a higher degree of probability. The test remained the same (i.e., it remains proof on a balance of probabilities and not the higher, criminal standard of proof beyond a reasonable doubt) but the degree of probability required was increased when there was an allegation of criminal or quasi-criminal conduct in the context of an administrative proceeding.[94]

In *Bogey Construction Ltd. v. Boileau*,[95] the Rental Housing Tribunal granted an eviction order based upon the landlord's allegation that the tenant had committed an illegal act in breaking into the mail boxes of the other tenants. The Member wrote, "On a balance of probabilities, I find that the tenant . . . has committed an illegal act, as described by the landlord in this application." Given the very general language used by the Member, the Divisional Court doubted whether the Member was aware of or had applied the correct standard. The appeal was therefore granted and a new hearing was ordered before a different Member of the Tribunal.

The Supreme Court of Canada, however, has recently disapproved of such an approach and has reaffirmed, once and for all, that:

> [I]n civil cases there is only one standard of proof and that is proof on a balance of probabilities. . . In all civil cases, the [trier of fact] must scrutinize the relevant evidence with care to determine whether it is more likely than not that an alleged event occurred.[96]

In this decision, the Supreme Court of Canada has specifically stated that there is no heightened standard of proof or need for greater scrutiny of the evidence in civil cases where criminal or morally blameworthy conduct is alleged. The same careful scrutiny is required in all civil cases and the standard

---

[92] *Sage v. Wellington (County)* (2005), 2005 CarswellOnt 7833 (Ont. Div. Ct.).

[93] *Continental Insurance Co. v. Dalton Cartage Ltd.* (1982), 131 D.L.R. (3d) 559 (S.C.C.) at 563 and *Bater v. Bater*, [1950] 2 All E.R. 458 (Eng. C.A.) at 459.

[94] See the discussion of this issue in *London & Middlesex Housing Corp. v. Vineski* (June 21, 2006), SWL-81599, [2006] O.R.H.T.D. No. 70 (Ont. Rental Housing Trib.).

[95] (2002), 2002 CarswellOnt 5865, [2002] O.J. No. 1575 (Ont. Div. Ct.).

[96] *C. (R.) v. McDougall* (2008), [2008] S.C.J. No. 54 (S.C.C.) at para. 49.

of proof remains the same. Until the Supreme Court of Canada has occasion to revisit this issue, this is the last word on this subject.[97]

10. ORDERS AND REASONS

In order to perform its function, Members of the Landlord and Tenant Board must not only be able to adjudicate disputes between landlords and tenants but must be able to issue orders to control its processes, protect the rights of parties, and grant relief to a deserving party. Such orders must be enforceable.

Pursuant to s. 19(1) of the *Statutory Powers Procedure Act*, a certified copy of a tribunal's decision or order in a proceeding may be filed in the Superior Court of Justice by the tribunal or by a party and on filing shall be deemed to be an order of that court and enforceable as such. On receiving a certified copy of the tribunal's order for the payment of money, the sheriff shall enforce the order as if it were an execution issued by the Court.[98] Similarly, an eviction order has the same effect and will be enforced in the same manner as a writ of possession.[99] Thus, an order from the Board can be enforced in the same manner as an order from the Superior Court of Justice.

From a practical perspective, however, the order must contain sufficient details to be enforceable. In *Rizzi v. Roberts*,[100] the Rental Housing Tribunal ordered that the tenant remove the personal property stored outside in the yard and that upon failure to do so by April 15th, 2006, the landlord could file for eviction pursuant to s. 77 of the T.P.A. (now s. 78 of the R.T.A.). On appeal by the tenant, the Divisional Court held that this order was "too vague or uncertain as to be capable of enforcement and could be interpreted to include all of the tenant's goods which might normally be stored in the yard such as a snow blower or the family car". Rather than remitting the matter back to the Tribunal, the Divisional Court amended the Tribunal's order to make it more specific and gave the tenant additional time in which to remove the goods listed in the amended order.

Prior to making a final decision, a Member may find it appropriate to issue an interim order. The authority to make interim orders is derived from s. 16.1 of the *Statutory Powers Procedure Act*. The Board may impose such

---

[97] And decisions of the Landlord and Tenant Board that adopted the approach recommended in *Bogey*, such as File No. EAL-13599 (Jan. 19, 2009) and EAL-13160 (Jan. 19, 2009), ought not to be followed as they run contrary to the approach mandated by the highest court in the country.

[98] Subsection 19(3) of the *Statutory Powers Procedure Act*.

[99] Section 85 of the R.T.A. See Chapter 17 for a thorough discussion of the enforcement of eviction orders.

[100] (2007), 2007 CarswellOnt 1889 (Ont. Div. Ct.).

conditions as it deems appropriate on an interim order and the interim order need not be accompanied by reasons.[101]

The Board must give its final decision and order, if any, in writing. The Board shall also give reasons in writing for a final decision, if requested by a party.[102] An order is usually mailed to the parties and their representatives (if any) but the Board can send an order by any method directed or permitted by the Member.[103]

As a general rule, the Board does not provide written reasons for its decisions. According to Rule 26.2 of the Board's Rules of Practice, if a party wishes the Member to issue written reasons for the order, the party must make the request orally at the hearing or in writing within 30 days after the order is issued. Even where a party does not request reasons, a Member is required to issue reasons: if the Member departs from an interpretation guideline,[104] if the order has been appealed,[105] or if the order is under review and the Member considering the review considers it to be necessary to have reasons in order to assess the merits of the request for review.[106]

Even where a party does not specifically request reasons, if the decision can have a significant impact on a party, reasons ought to be provided.[107]Where the Tribunal awarded $2,000 in damages for the tenant's property that was illegally disposed of by the landlord but failed to give any explanation as to how it arrived at this figure, on appeal by the tenants, the Divisional Court found that the lack of any reasons constituted an error in law and allowed the tenants to decide whether they wished to return to the Tribunal for a new hearing on this issue or whether they preferred to pursue this part of their claim by way of court action.[108]

Where reasons are provided, they must be intelligible to the parties and must permit for meaningful appellate review.[109] The reasons must be considered as a whole and in the context of the record (pleadings, exhibits, transcripts, etc.). To merely recite the facts and baldly state conclusions is not the same as explaining the reasoning behind those conclusions. On this basis alone (i.e., lack of sufficient reasons), a decision can be overturned on appeal.[110]

---

[101] Subsections 16.1(2) and (3) of the *Statutory Powers Procedure Act.*

[102] Subsection 17(1) of the *Statutory Powers Procedure Act.*

[103] Rule 26.1 of the Board's Rules of Practice.

[104] Rule 26.3 of the Board's Rules of Practice.

[105] Rule 26.5 of the Board's Rules of Practice.

[106] Rule 26.4 of the Board's Rules of Practice

[107] *Baker v. Canada (Minister of Citizenship & Immigration)*, [1999] 2 S.C.R. 817 (S.C.C.); *Megens v. Ontario Racing Commission* (2003), 64 O.R. (3d) 142 (Ont. Div. Ct.), additional reasons at (2003), 2003 CarswellOnt 3481 (Ont. Div. Ct.), varied (2004), 185 O.A.C. 349 (Ont. C.A.).

[108] *Natarelli v. Sheikh* (2007), 2007 CarswellOnt 889 (Ont. Div. Ct.).

[109] *R. v. Sheppard*, [2002] 1 S.C.R. 869 (S.C.C.).

[110] *Stanoulis v. Lykakim Holdings Ltd.* (2008), 2008 CarswellOnt 2629 (Ont. Div. Ct.).

The Board may include in an order whatever conditions it considers fair in the circumstances.[111] This is a broad power that allows Members to craft orders that will achieve the intended results. This might involve issuing an interim order requiring a landlord to perform certain repairs or to allow a tenant back into a rental unit and then bringing the matter back before the same Member to see what further relief ought to be granted (depending on whether the landlord complied with the interim order). It might also involve the combined use of ss. 83(1) and 78 of the R.T.A. Where appropriate, a Member can exercise his/her discretion under s. 83(1) by refusing to grant an eviction but issue an order that imposes upon the tenant strict terms (such as a repayment schedule or requiring or prohibiting certain types of conduct[112]) and stating in the order that if those terms are breached then the landlord may apply to the Board, without further notice to the tenant, for an order terminating the tenancy pursuant to s. 78 of the R.T.A.[113]

Take, for example, the case of a tenant who has been persistently late in paying rent, but who has otherwise been a good tenant and assures the Board that, henceforth, she is able and willing to pay the rent on time. Under the T.P.A., it became a common practice in such cases for Members to exercise their discretion (under s. 84(1) of the T.P.A. — now s. 83(1) of the R.T.A.) to refuse to grant an eviction but only on the condition that the tenant shall pay the rent on time for the next six months (or such other number of months that the Member finds appropriate — usually in the range of 6 to 12 months). The Member then included a term in the order that states that if the tenant fails to comply with that condition, the landlord is entitled to apply, pursuant to s. 77 of the T.P.A . (now s. 78 of the R.T.A.), without notice to the tenant, for an order terminating the tenancy and evicting the tenant.[114] This gave the tenant one last chance but assured the landlord of obtaining a quick eviction order (without a hearing) if the tenant did not comply with the condition(s) imposed by the Tribunal. My review of the decisions that have been released by the Landlord and Tenant Board suggests that this practice has continued under the R.T.A.

Similarly, it is quite common for Members of the Board on L1 (arrears of rent) eviction applications to refuse to grant an eviction but to create a repayment plan in the order, along with a term which permits the landlord (pursuant to s. 78) to bring an *ex parte* application to terminate the tenancy (and for any outstanding arrears) should the tenant miss any of the required

---

[111] Subsection 204(1) of the R.T.A. (Formerly subsection 190(1) of the T.P.A.).

[112] See, for example, Landlord and Tenant Board File Nos. TSL-19140 / TSL-19176 (Jan. 26, 2009) and Landlord and Tenant Board File No. EAL-14114 (Jan. 23, 2009).

[113] The provisions of s. 78 can only be invoked where the terms that have been breached are of the same nature that gave rise to the original application. See Chapter 13.

[114] The *ex parte* application process under s. 78 is described in detail in Chapter 13.

payments. Such an order can also stipulate that payments are to be made in a specified manner (for example, by way of guaranteed funds).[115]

In one case, a Member made it a condition of granting relief under s. 83 of the R.T.A. (i.e., a condition of refusing to grant the eviction sought by the landlord) that the tenant complete an alcohol withdrawal program. On appeal, the Divisional Court pointed out that, pursuant to s. 204 of the R.T.A., the Board may impose such conditions as it deems fair in the circumstances and that, since the tenant was permitted to stay in the unit, the Court also found the condition to be fair and dismissed the appeal.[116]

The only *caveat* (or words of caution) concerning a Member's power in this regard is that the terms and conditions need to be clear, enforceable and within the jurisdiction of the Member.

An example of an order that is beyond the power of a Member would be to issue a final order but purport to remain seized of the matter. Occasionally, a Member will place a condition in an order and indicate that, if that condition is breached, the applicant may bring the matter back before the same Member.[117] I can find no statutory or common law authority for such an approach. If it is an *interim* order that does not fully dispose of the issues in dispute, that is a different matter; clearly in such a case the Member retains jurisdiction over the matter. Once a *final* order is issued, however, the Member is *functus*. The Rules concerning a request to re-open an application (Rules 13.13 – 13.16) relate *only* to mediated agreements. The Board has no power, other than through its review process, to reconsider an application once a final order has been issued.[118]

Examples of confusing orders would be ones that provide for more than one eviction date[119] or that permit an eviction to occur on an unspecified date, to be determined solely within the discretion of the landlord (should the landlord determine that a term of the order has been breached).[120] The former (orders with more than one eviction date) may present difficulties with enforcement and the latter do not permit for any oversight by the Board (such as would exist if the order had included reference to s. 78).

---

115 See, for example, Landlord and Tenant Board File No. SOL-19285 (Feb. 23, 2009).

116 *Beboning v. Wigwamen Inc.* (2008), 2008 CarswellOnt 6995 (Ont. Div. Ct.). The Court also found this issue to be moot since the program in question terminated in May 2007.

117 See, for example, Landlord and Tenant Board File No. TNL-20451 (Jan. 23, 2009) and Landlord and Tenant Board File No. TNL-21130 (Jan. 26, 2009).

118 *Oates v. Colonia Treuhand Limited* (Jan. 22, 2002), TET-02035-RV, [2002] O.R.H.T.D. No. 11 (Ont. Rental Housing Trib.).

119 See, for example, Landlord and Tenant Board File No. EAL-13976 (Jan. 23, 2009) and Landlord and Tenant Board File Nos. NOL-05982 / NOT-00938 (Jan. 13, 2009).

120 See, for example, Landlord and Tenant Board File No. SWL-00785 (March 30, 2007) and Landlord and Tenant Board File No SOL-00692 (March 28, 2007).

The Board may also include in an interim or final decision an order that one party pay the other party's costs of the proceeding (or a step in the proceeding) or the Board's costs.[121]

Parties sometimes request that the Board issue orders "on consent". In fact, under the R.T.A., this is becoming increasingly common. This typically happens where the parties have reached an agreement and they desire an order that reflects that agreement. There are two important things to know about such consent orders.

The first is that the presiding Member has the discretion to decide whether or not to grant any order, notwithstanding the agreement of the parties. If a Member determines that the order requested is outside of his or her jurisdiction, the Member may decline to grant the order requested and may suggest that the parties content themselves with a mediated agreement. The Member may also wish to satisfy himself or herself that the parties (especially any unrepresented parties) fully understand the implications of the order being requested and are freely consenting thereto.

For instance, on an arrears application a landlord may request an order (purportedly with the consent of the tenant) requiring the tenant to make specified payments by specified dates and, upon default of any of the payments, permitting the landlord to immediately file that order with the sheriff and to have the tenant evicted. Many Members consider this type of order to be problematic as it provides for no oversight by the Board and, potentially, no avenue for the tenant to challenge the landlord's assertion that there was a breach of the terms of that order. For this reason, a Member may well refuse to issue such an order and instead, issue an order with the same payment schedule but include a "s. 78 clause" in the order. In the event of a breach of the order, this will permit the landlord to apply to the Board, without notice to the tenant, for an order terminating the tenancy (and for monetary relief) but will ensure that the landlord files an affidavit to establish the breach and will provide a mechanism whereby the tenant can challenge the *ex parte* order.[122]

The second point worth noting about consent orders is that the courts will almost never overturn such an order, even if the result might have been different had a hearing been held on the merits of the application.[123] As long

---

[121] Subsections 204(2), (3) and (4) of the R.T.A. and Rule 27 of the Board's Rules of Practice. See the discussion in Chapter 2 of the Board's power to award costs.

[122] See *Boardwalk General Partnership v. Ready* (July 26, 2006), SWL-82124, [2006] O.R.H.T.D. No. 86 (Ont. Rental Housing Trib.) and *Cambridge Non-Profit Housing Corp., Re* (June 7, 2006), SWL-81146-SA, 2006 CarswellOnt 4410, [2006] O.R.H.T.D. No. 63 (Ont. Rental Housing Trib.).

[123] *Torgis v. Brajovic* (January 14, 2002), Doc. 01-BN-2696 (Ont. Div. Ct.) (re CEL-16579); *Belz v. Mernick* (1999), 1999 CarswellOnt 1656, [1999] O.J. No. 1940 (Ont. C.A.); *Laboissiere et al. v. Butler*, Doc. 03-DV-000927 (Ont. Div. Ct.) (re EAL-33322); *Berbatovci v. Crescent Village* (July 25, 2002), Doc. 428/02 (Ont. Div. Ct.) (re TNL-27783); *Carlson*

as the matter involved a residential tenancy and was apparently within the jurisdiction of the Board to adjudicate, the fact that there may have been procedural errors (such as an invalid notice of termination) will not constitute valid grounds for appeal of a consent order. A consent order can only be set aside on grounds such as mistake, misrepresentation, fraud or other grounds that would invalidate a contract.[124] The fact that one person was ignorant of his or her rights or that the parties did not possess equal bargaining power is not sufficient justification for overturning a consent order. In fact, pursuant to s. 133 of the *Courts of Justice Act*, no appeal lies from a consent order without first obtaining leave from the court.[125] There is a public interest in the finality of Board decisions and, absent coercion or fraud, the court will not save a person from making what may have been, in retrospect, a bad deal.

Even where the original application did not seek termination of the tenancy or in cases where termination was being sought but the notice of termination is void (and, therefore, cannot form the basis for a termination of the tenancy), the parties can nevertheless agree to terminate the tenancy and request a consent order on the basis of that agreement.

Also, if the original application was based upon arrears of rent, under normal circumstances, the tenant(s) would have the opportunity (and the statutory right) to pay the amounts ordered and void the eviction order. Where both parties agree, however, the order can be structured so that the termination of the tenancy is based upon the agreement of the parties (rather than being grounded on the arrears application) and, thus, the termination is stated to be "non-voidable" or "non-remedial". It appears that the Board is prepared to issue orders of this nature.[126]

11. REVIEWS

(a) Authority of the Board to Review its Decisions

Pursuant to s. 209 of the R.T.A., except where the Act provides otherwise, and subject to s. 21.2 of the *Statutory Powers Procedure Act,* an order of the Board is final and binding. Section 21.2 of the *Statutory Powers Procedure Act* permits a tribunal to create procedures for reviewing its own decisions.

---

v. Kaneff Properties Ltd. (2002), 2002 CarswellOnt 338 (Ont. Div. Ct.) (re CEL-14794); and *Lockhart et al. v. Nistrap Dev. Corp.*, Doc. 695/03 (Ont. Div. Ct.) (re TEL-38506) in which the Court wrote, "there is no appeal from a consent order."

124 *Torgis v. Brajovic* (January 14, 2002), Doc. 01-BN-2696 (Ont. Div. Ct.) (re CEL-16579).

125 *Morgan v. Whing* (2009), 2009 CarswellOnt 2927 (Ont. Div. Ct.).

126 See, for example: Landlord and Tenant Board File No. SWL-21978 (Jan. 13, 200); Landlord and Tenant Board File No. TSL-20116 (Jan. 13, 2009); Landlord and Tenant Board File No. TSL-20647 (Jan. 27, 2009); Landlord and Tenant Board File No. SWL-22541 (Jan. 26, 2009); Landlord and Tenant Board File No. SWL-21840 (Jan. 12, 2009); and Landlord and Tenant Board File No. SWL-21724 (Jan. 27, 2009).

The Landlord and Tenant Board has created just such a review process and the details are set out in Rule 29 of the Board's Rules of Practice. The Board also has an Interpretation Guideline (No. 8) to assist in understanding the review process.

(b) Purpose

The purpose of Rule 29 is to permit the Board to correct serious errors (legal or factual) that may be contained in its orders or to make such orders as are required to prevent a miscarriage of justice. Minor clerical errors contained in an order can be corrected through a different process.[127]

According to the Board's Interpretation Guideline (No. 8), a serious error may include one of the following:

1. an error of jurisdiction;
2. an error of procedure which prejudiced a party;[128]
3. an error of fact which was material to the decision and which was clearly an unreasonable finding considering the evidence that was before the Member;[129]
4. an error of fact which is material to the decision which is demonstrated by new evidence which was not before the Member, so long as the Member reviewing the order is satisfied that there is sufficient reason why the evidence was not presented in the original hearing;[130]

---

[127] See "Correcting Errors" in Chapter 2.

[128] For instance, not allowing a party sufficient time at the hearing to fully present his evidence: *Sheppard v. Suraski* (April 21, 2006), TST-08126-RV-RV, 2006 CarswellOnt 4424, [2006] O.R.H.T.D. No. 42 (Ont. Rental Housing Trib.).

[129] A review, however, is not meant to give the losing party an opportunity to re-argue the case simply because they are unhappy with the original result. If the party requesting the review is alleging that the Member who originally heard the case has made an error in fact, it must be demonstrated that there was essentially no evidence upon which the Member could reasonably have made the findings of fact contained in the order. A reviewing Member will not lightly interfere with findings of fact made at the original hearing. See Landlord and Tenant Board File No. SOL-16969-RV (Jan. 21, 2009); Landlord and Tenant Board File Nos. CET-01659-RV and CEL-14573-RV (Jan. 12, 2009); and Landlord and Tenant Board File Nos. TNL-11016-RV and TNT-00598-RV (Jan. 9, 2009).

[130] Where a party seeks to introduce new evidence, the reviewing Member should enquire as to why this evidence was not presented at the original hearing. Failure to do so may be considered to be a valid ground for appeal: *Wamboldt v. Wellman* (2007), 2007 CarswellOnt 8328 (Ont. Div. Ct.). Also see Landlord and Tenant Board File No. SWL-20850-RV (Feb. 10, 2009), in which it was found that the evidence the tenant sought to introduce at the review hearing had been available at the time of the original hearing but was accepted by the reviewing Member anyway as it was *also* relevant to the tenant's allegation that the landlord had obtained the original order through false and misleading documents (an allegation that the reviewing Member found to be unsubstantiated, even in light of the "new" evidence tendered by the tenant).

5. an error in law;[131]
6. an error in applying discretion allowed by the law which is unreasonable.[132]

The review process is meant to be faster and less expensive than an appeal to the Divisional Court and, unlike an appeal, the Board can consider errors of fact (and not just errors in law). It is *not* meant, however, to provide an unsuccessful party a "second kick at the can" simply because they are unhappy with the result of the first hearing. Nor will the Board allow respondents to abuse the review process for the purpose of delaying enforcement of the original order.

Pursuant to subsection 209(2) of the R.T.A., it is now explicit in the Act that the Board may also exercise its power to review a decision if a party was "not reasonably able to participate in the proceeding". Since this is the same "test" that was mandated for motions under s. 192(4) of the T.P.A. to set aside a default order, it may be helpful to consider how the Rental Housing Tribunal interpreted this phrase.

In such cases, the onus will be upon that person to provide a good explanation for their failure to participate in the hearing.[133] The Board will have to take a "hard look" at the explanation provided. The Tribunal generally found that difficulty reading or understanding English, being too busy to respond, failing to read the application and notice of hearing or failing to read them with care were not sufficient excuses.[134]

Where, however, the Tribunal was convinced that the application and notice of hearing did not actually come to the attention of the respondent in time for the respondent to participate, the Tribunal found that this was proof that the respondent was not reasonably able to participate in the proceeding.

---

[131] See *Toor et al. v. Franco et al.* (May 1, 2001), TNL-25146-RV (Ont. Rental Housing Trib.). A reviewing Member will not, however, overturn a reasonable interpretation of the law: *Gavriline v. Westwood Management International* (Dec. 24, 1999), TNT-00573-RV (Ont. Rental Housing Trib.).

[132] Great deference is shown in the area of a Member's exercise of discretionary powers. A reviewing Member is loathe to second-guess the Member who originally heard all of the evidence and will only intervene if the original Member exercised (or refused to exercise) his/her discretion in an unreasonable manner. For this reason, challenges to the manner in which a Member exercised his or her discretion (for example, the amount of rent abatement the Member chose to award) are rarely successful. See Landlord and Tenant Board File No. CET-01659-RV and CEL-14573-RV (July 12, 2009) and Landlord and Tenant Board File No. EAL-12848-RV (Jan. 13, 2009).

[133] *Boardwalk General Partnership v. Miskokoman* (March 16, 2006), SWL-75304-RV, [2006] O.R.H.T.D. No. 6 (Ont. Rental Housing Trib.) at para. 11: "The purpose of a review is not to allow those who fail to attend tribunal proceedings though properly served to re-litigate matters they failed to contest when they had the opportunity."

[134] See *Oliver v. Canadian Apartment Management Inc.* (Dec. 1, 1998), TSL-03547-SA (Ont. Rental Housing Trib.) and *Metropolitan Toronto Housing Authority v. Newell* (Sept. 16, 1998), TNL-00737-SA, 1998 CarswellOnt 6067 (Ont. Rental Housing Trib.).

Additional situations in which it was found by the Tribunal that a tenant was "not reasonably able to participate in the proceeding" include the following:

- where the respondents did not understand the documents served by the applicant because the respondents could not read English;[135]
- where the respondent failed to appreciate the need for filing a dispute because the notice of hearing itself was confusing and difficult to understand;[136]
- where the parties (through their respective representatives) were involved in negotiations and the respondent simply forgot to file a dispute;[137] and
- where the dispute was filed on time but, inadvertently, with the wrong file number written thereon.[138]

Under the T.P.A., the Tribunal generally adopted a fairly liberal approach towards motions to set aside default orders. The time limits for responding to applications were very short (five days), some of the forms were confusing, many tenants were unsophisticated and the consequences to tenants of being denied a hearing could be devastating. Members generally preferred to decide cases upon their merits rather than upon technicalities.[139]

The Landlord and Tenant Board may not be as generous in overturning decisions on review (based upon a party's assertion that they were not reasonably able to participate in the proceeding) for several reasons:

1. A respondent will have more difficulty establishing that no notice of the proceeding was received. Not only must the applicant provide proof that the application and notice of hearing were served upon the respondent, but the Board itself will also have sent out a notice to the respondent. A bald assertion that "I never got anything in the mail" may not be believed.
2. The time limits have been lengthened. A respondent may have many weeks between being served with the application and notice of hearing and the date of the hearing itself. There should be plenty of time in which to obtain information from the Board or duty counsel or otherwise seek assistance in understanding the documents that have been received.
3. The forms, especially the notice of hearing, have been simplified

---

135 *Bauer v. Maeng et al.* (March 24, 1999), NOL-00916-SA (Ont. Rental Housing Trib.).

136 *Trailridge Crescent Apts. v. Jagnarine* (Oct. 17, 2003), TEL-38278-SA, [2003] O.R.H.T.D. No. 128, 2003 CarswellOnt 4020 (Ont. Rental Housing Trib.).

137 *Montgomery et al. v. 737259 Ontario Ltd.* (October 13, 1999), Doc. 1031 (re SWT-00253-SA).

138 *Fischer et al. v. Anastasopoulos*, Doc. 00-2455-DV (Ont. Div. Ct.) (re SOL-17404).

139 *O'Rourke v. Judge* (Sept. 21, 1999), EAL-08454 (Ont. Rental Housing Trib.).

and make clear the possible consequences of failing to attend the hearing.

The idea that fewer orders will be set aside under the current legislation than was the case under the T.P.A. seems to be supported by the currently available evidence. First, early statistics released by the Board indicate that very few requests for review are being filed.[140] Second, from a review of the cases released by the Board, it appears that the Board is taking a harder look at any tenant's claim that they were not reasonably able to participate in the proceedings. For instance, in Landlord and Tenant Board File Nos. SWL-03592-RV and SWT-00325-RV, the tenant failed to attend her own application as well as one commenced by the landlord. She had attended an earlier hearing and agreed to adjourn the hearing to a date to be set in late June but failed to contact the Board to confirm that date. The tenant then moved out of the unit but did not provide a new address to the landlord or to the Board. She did provide an e-mail address but failed to check her messages. The hearing proceeded on June 28, 2007, in her absence. In July, she discovered what had happened and filed a request to review the orders that were issued in both files. The requests for review proceeded to a hearing but were denied. The Member wrote as follows:

> The Tenant is responsible for ensuring that the Board has her current contact information, and for following up with the Board in a timely fashion if she does not receive information that she is expecting to receive. . . Neither the Board, nor the Landlord, nor the Landlord's representative is obligated to chase the Tenant.

Similarly, in Landlord and Tenant Board File No. SWT-01796-RV (Jan. 13, 2009), the landlord's explanation for failing to attend the hearing (despite being aware of it) was not accepted. In this case, the tenants had brought an application against the landlord alleging harassment, substantial interference with the tenants' reasonable enjoyment, failure to comply with the landlord's maintenance obligations, illegal entry into the rental unit and, ultimately, an illegal lock-out. The landlord admitted receiving notice of the hearing but, in a request for review, the landlord requested that the existing order be cancelled and a new hearing be held on the basis that the landlord had not been able to participate in the original hearing. The explanation given for the landlord's failure to attend the hearing was that the landlord had already addressed the maintenance issue raised by the tenants and, therefore, believed that there were no issues that required a hearing. Not surprisingly, the request for review was denied.

The Landlord and Tenant Board has set aside a hearing order and conducted a new hearing on the basis that a party had been unable to participate in the hearing in the following situations:

---

[140] Early statistics indicate that reviews are filed in less than 1% of all cases.

- Where the landlord was unable to attend the hearing due to illness and her representative was unable to attend due to heavy traffic;[141]
- Where the reviewing Member was satisfied that although the application and notice of hearing were properly sent by the landlord to the tenants in the mail, the tenants did not actually receive these documents;[142]
- Where the tenant was unable to attend the original hearing for medical reasons;[143] and
- Where the tenant relied upon the advice of the landlord that she need not attend the hearing.[144]

Where a tenant has not been misled by the landlord, however, the tenant's failure to attend the hearing may be fatal to any subsequent attack by the tenant of the resulting order. In Landlord and Tenant Board File No. SWL-21133-RV (Feb. 12, 2009), the landlord's representative advised the tenant that the landlord would be seeking a "standard" order for arrears of rent that would provide the tenant with 11 days in which to pay the arrears and avoid eviction. The landlord's representative also indicated that the landlord would not seek to enforce the eviction order if the tenant could make some payments towards the debt and work out a satisfactory repayment plan. The tenant chose not to attend the hearing. The landlord obtained a "standard" order and attempted to work with the tenant to work out a mutually agreeable plan. About a month after the order was issued, when the tenant failed to make any payments, the landlord filed the order with the Sheriff and sought to have the order enforced. The tenant filed a request for review of the eviction order, claiming that she had been unable to participate in the original hearing because the landlord duped her into not attending. The tenant's request for review was heard and dismissed. The reviewing Member held that this was not a case where a tenant was misled about her rights or about the order that the landlord would be seeking. The tenant did have a reasonable opportunity to participate but chose not to do so.

The Landlord and Tenant Board has recently clarified its position with respect to when a party will be considered to have not reasonably been able to participate in the proceedings. Please refer to the Board's Interpretation Guideline No. 8 (see Appendix 8), but recall that the Board's Interpretation Guidelines are not binding upon its Members.

When the Rental Housing Tribunal was first created, only Vice-chairs (or specific Members selected by the Chair) conducted reviews. This system soon resulted in a "bottle-neck"; there were not enough "Review Officers" to efficiently deal with all of the requests for review and there was a danger

[141] Landlord and Tenant Board File No. CEL-16032-RV (Feb. 20, 2009).
[142] Landlord and Tenant Board File No. SOL-17992-RV (Feb. 13, 2009).
[143] Landlord and Tenant Board File No. SOL-18305-RV (Feb. 11, 2009).
[144] Landlord and Tenant Board File No. CEL-14491-RV (Feb. 13, 2009).

that tenants who had no valid grounds for a review could exploit this weakness in the system as a way of delaying their eviction. For this reason, it was decided that any Member or Vice-chair of the Tribunal could review the decision of any other Member or Vice-Chair and every effort was made to ensure that requests for review were dealt with promptly. This system continues under the new legislation.

On a request for review, the Board will generally not interfere in the decision of the Member who originally heard the case if it involved the *reasonable* exercise of discretion or a *reasonable* interpretation of the law, even if the reviewing Member might have made a different decision in the circumstances. The Board will also not lightly interfere with a decision that is based upon the Member's assessment of the credibility of the parties. Members show considerable deference to each other in such areas.[145]

The review process is also not meant to deal with clerical errors contained in an order (including errors in the name of a party or the address of the rental unit) as there is a different process for this (see Rule 28).

A request for review of an interim order will not be entertained. There is only a right to request a review of an order or decision that finally disposes of an application (Rule 29.1).[146]

(c) Who Can Request the Review of a Decision?[147]

A party to an order may request that it be reviewed. In fact, *any* person affected by the order (whether named as a party or not) has the right to request a review of the decision. Finally, a Vice-chair can initiate a review on his or her own initiative.

(d) Time Limit

A request for review must be made to the Board within 30 days of the issuance of the order (or, if the order is amended, within 30 days of the date the amended order is issued).[148] This time limit can be extended if a Member deems it appropriate.[149] The longer a person waits to request the review, however, the greater the suspicion with which it will be viewed. If, for instance, a tenant does not file a request for review until the day before the sheriff is scheduled to enforce an eviction order, the Member considering the

---

[145] See, for example, Landlord and Tenant Board File No. SWL-20850-RV (Feb. 10, 2009).

[146] *Morris v. Axes Investments Inc. et al.* (May 2, 2000), TNT-01062-RV (Ont. Rental Housing Trib.).

[147] See Rule 29.1 of the Board's Rules of Practice.

[148] Rules 29.3 and 29.4 of the Board's Rules of Practice.

[149] Rule 15 of the Board's Rules of Practice.

request for review may well wonder whether the request is being made in good faith.

(e) Procedure

A request to review an order must be made in writing and must be signed by the person making the request (Rule 29.5). It must include the Board's order number, the address of the rental unit or residential complex concerned, the name, address and telephone number of the person requesting the review, detailed reason why the order should be reviewed and the remedy requested (Rule 29.6). This must be accompanied by the filing fee of $50 (Rule 29.5).[150] The parties to the review are the parties to the order being reviewed, the person requesting the review and any other person added to the proceedings by the Board (Rule 29.8). If the review was initiated by a Vice-chair of the Board, the Vice-chair is not a party to the proceeding (Rule 29.8).

A request for review does not automatically stay enforcement of the order under review. For instance, a tenant could be evicted while waiting for a review of the eviction order. If a person wants to ensure that the order under review is not enforced until the review has been decided, the person must specifically request this relief in the request for review. The person must set out what prejudice they may suffer if the order is not stayed pending the decision regarding the review (Rule 29.7). Of course, a Member can also stay the order (or revoke a stay) on his or her own initiative (Rule 29.12). If a stay is granted, an interim order to this effect will be granted by the Board and it is the responsibility of the person who requested the stay to immediately deliver the interim order to the Court Enforcement Office (Rule 30.4).

Members may not review their own orders or any order with regard to an application for which the Member issued an interim order, except an interim order that stays the order under review (Rule 29.9). Once a request for review has been received by the Board and the appropriate fee has been paid, the matter will be referred to a Member (other than the one who issued the order in question) for consideration. This initial perusal (sometimes referred to as a "preliminary review" or "paper review") is very important because the Member will decide at this stage whether or not there appears to be sufficient merit in the request to permit the matter to proceed to a review hearing. The Member may deny the request for review at this preliminary stage without holding a hearing (Rule 29.10). That is why it is crucial to include in the request for review full and detailed reasons for the request.[151]

---

150 This is a reduction from the $75 fee charged for a review by the Rental Housing Tribunal.

151 See *Niknejad v. Vaez* (Nov. 9, 1999), TNL-10996-RV (Ont. Rental Housing Trib.) and Landlord and Tenant Board File Number TNL-09252-RV (May 27, 2008) for examples of cases in which a request for review was denied at the preliminary stage because the request

Rule 29.2 states that, "A request for review of an order must provide sufficient information to support a preliminary finding that the order may contain a serious error or that a serious error may have occurred in the proceedings."

If the Member concludes that the person requesting the review has failed to demonstrate that there may be a serious error in the order or that there may have been a serious error in the proceedings, the request for review will be denied; a Decision on Request for Review (i.e., the denial of the request) will be mailed by the Board to all parties.[152]

If the Member determines the order may contain a serious error or that a serious error may have occurred in the proceedings, a date will be scheduled to hold a full review hearing (Rules 29.11). The Board will advise the person who requested the review what steps, if any, that person needs to take to serve a copy of the request for review and notice of the review hearing upon the other parties; the Board may itself serve the other parties.

If there has also been an appeal (to the Divisional Court) of the order in question, then the Board will also have to order that the automatic stay of that order (under subsection 25(1) of the *Statutory Powers Procedure Act*) be lifted so that the review hearing can proceed (Rules 29.11(b) and (c)).

The review hearing may be made conditional upon the requesting person complying with certain conditions that may be set out in an interim order. If, for instance, a tenant is seeking a review of an eviction order based upon arrears of rent and admits owing some or all of the money to the landlord but is alleging there is some other serious error in the order or in the process, the Board may well order that the tenant pay some or all of the arrears into the Board by a specified date as a condition of proceeding with a full review hearing. If the tenant fails to comply with such a condition, the review hearing will be cancelled (and any stay of the original order will be lifted).[153]

Normally, the review hearing will be conducted by the same Member who conducted the preliminary review as that Member will be familiar with the relevant issues. The Member who conducts the review decides which issues require a hearing. The issues may be some or all of the issues that were raised in the request for review or can be any other issue which the Member believes should be reviewed (Rules 29.17 and 29.18). Although the review hearing is usually held in person (i.e., an oral hearing), the presiding Member can also decide to conduct the review by way of an electronic or written hearing (Rule 29.15). At the conclusion of a review hearing, the Member

---

itself did not set out *in detail* (i.e., did not specify) what serious error was made in the order or in the proceedings.

152 See *Leith Hill Property Rentals Inc. v. Sethi et al.* (Aug. 8, 2000), TNL-17743-RV (Ont. Rental Housing Trib.).

153 See *Royal Bank of Canada v. Chambers* (March 24, 2000), TNL-14082-RV (Ont. Rental Housing Trib.) and *Royal Bank of Canada v. Chambers* (March 30, 2000), TNL-14082-RV (Ont. Rental Housing Trib.); and *Farkas and Mollon* (Sept. 3, 1999), SOL-06564-RV (Ont. Rental Housing Trib.).

may confirm, vary, suspend or cancel the order under review, and lift any stay if necessary.[154] Also, pursuant to s. 182 of the R.T.A., if the Member does find that the request for review has merit, he or she can also order that the Board refund the fee that was paid to file the request for review.

If the original order is quashed, the Board will usually hold a new hearing of the original application on the spot. On the review hearing, the onus of proof is upon the person requesting the review (to demonstrate a serious error in the order or in the proceedings). If the review is successful, the original order is quashed and a new hearing is held; the onus will now be upon the applicant to prove his or her case all over again. The parties should come to the review hearing prepared to argue the original application in the event that the original order is cancelled.

The parties should also be prepared for the possibility that, if a new hearing is held, the outcome could be worse for them. Take, for example, the case where a landlord is fined $2,000 and seeks a review of that decision on the basis that the landlord did not receive notice of the original hearing and was, therefore, denied an opportunity to participate in the original hearing. If the landlord's request for review is successful and a new hearing is held, the Member could decide that the appropriate fine ought to be $10,000. The landlord would have, to coin a phrase, "won the battle but lost the war." People sometimes assume they can only do better on a review. This is a dangerous and erroneous assumption.

(f) Subsequent Requests for Review

Generally, a person can only make *one* request for review and cannot request a review of the review decision (Rule 29.20). The Board may review an order which has previously been reviewed, or may review a review order, if the request is made by another party upon different grounds or is made by a Vice-chair of the Board (Rule 29.21).

Under a rule identical to Rule 29.20, the Rental Housing Tribunal was, for a time, refusing to even accept for consideration a subsequent request for review from the same person who had previously filed a request for review. In *Toronto Housing Co. v. Sabrie*,[155] the Divisional Court was quite critical of the Tribunal's approach, writing as follows (at paras. 30 through 33):

> It was within the tribunal's power, under its necessarily incidental power and its rules, to grant a remedy for the denial of natural justice. The tribunal, however, refused even to consider whether there was sufficient independent credible evidence of a denial of natural justice to warrant a rehearing. The tribunal did so on

---

[154] Section 21.2 of the *Statutory Powers Procedure Act* and Rule 29.19 of the Board's Rules of Practice.

[155] (2003), 2003 CarswellOnt 384, 168 O.A.C. 363 (Ont. Div. Ct.).

> the basis of an inflexible policy set out in Rule 27.18 that a further review request would never even be considered.
>
> The policy is understandable and its application in some cases may cause no problem. Finality is important to the landlord, the tenant, and to the public interest in the fair allocation of a scarce public resource. It would be wrong to open the floodgates to repeated reconsideration requests. An inflexible rule of the kind applied here makes sense in terms of administrative efficiency because it spares the resources required to screen groundless and frivolous requests.
>
> But administrative convenience, although important, should not be achieved at the potential cost of real injustice where there is independent credible evidence, as here, of a denial of natural justice.
>
> The tribunal declined even to consider the threshold issue, whether it was appropriate to entertain a further review request in order to cure a denial of natural justice. The tribunal, by its inflexible application of the policy in Rule 27.18 against further reviews, improperly fettered its discretion and declined jurisdiction.

In light of this decision, it would seem that subsequent requests for review should be put before a Member or Vice-chair of the Board who can then decide whether extraordinary circumstances may exist that would warrant waiving Rule 29.20. According to the Divisional Court, rejecting such requests at the counter or without considering the facts of the particular case, is itself a denial of natural justice.

12. APPEALS

(a) Right of Appeal

Pursuant to subsection 210(1) of the R.T.A. (formerly subsection 196(1) of the T.P.A.), any person affected by an order of the Board may appeal the order to the Divisional Court within 30 days after being given the order, but only on a question of law. A person appealing an order under this section must give to the Board any documents relating to the appeal (s. 210(2)).

The Board is entitled to participate in the appeal if it wishes (s. 210(3)). The Court may also grant others (such as representatives from landlord or tenant advocacy groups) permission to intervene in the proceedings as an added party or as a friend of the court.[156]

The Divisional Court may decline to hear an appeal if the appellant has not first attempted to have the order reconsidered through the Board's review process. It is therefore recommended that any person intending to appeal a Board order also file a request for review with the Board. If the review is successful, the appeal will be unnecessary. If the review is unsuccessful, the

---

156 Rule 13.03 of the Rules of Civil Procedure. See *1162994 Ontario Inc. v. Bakker* (2004), [2004] O.J. No. 2565, 2004 CarswellOnt 869 (Ont. C.A.) (re SWL-40290).

party who filed the notice of appeal can add to the appeal a request to have the Divisional Court consider the review order as well.

(b) Time Limit

As previously stated, the time limit for commencing an appeal is 30 days (s. 210(1)). The appeal process is governed by Rule 61 of the Rules of Civil Procedure.

This time limit may be extended in extraordinary circumstances by the Court but the person seeking such an extension must show a firm intention from the beginning to appeal the decision and a reasonable explanation must be given for the delay.[157]

In *Garside v. Jane Oak Apartments Inc.*,[158] the tenant was granted an extension of time to appeal on terms that the appeal be perfected by a fixed date and that full rent be paid until the appeal, and further that if the tenant failed to pay rent on time the landlord could apply to a single judge of the Divisional Court to dissolve the order extending the time, and so make effective the District Court judge's order terminating the lease and ordering possession.

In *Sarafian v. Sherlock*,[159] the tenant's request for an extension of time in which to appeal an eviction order was denied. The order was issued on October 21, 2005, after two adjournments at the request of the tenant. It was uncontested that the tenant had paid no rent from July 2005 onwards. The eviction was enforced on November 28, 2005. The appeal was filed on or about December 20, 2005. In denying the tenant's motion for an extension of time, Chapnik J. noted that "the legislation's underlying policy is to provide expeditious adjudication in Landlord/Tenant matters" and that "the appeal does not appear to be meritorious".

Similarly, in *Habte-Mariam v. Toronto Community Housing Corp.*,[160] the tenant sought leave for late filing of a notice of appeal (about four months late). Although the Divisional Court was satisfied that the tenant had intended to appeal and did not do so in a timely manner because of misinformation and inexperience, the Court nevertheless denied the tenant leave to file the appeal late as it raised no questions of law as required by s. 196 of the T.P.A.

Once a notice of appeal has been filed, the appellant has a limited time in which to "perfect" the appeal (which, amongst other things, usually involves filing a transcript of the original hearing). If the appellant does not perfect the appeal in the time allotted, the Registrar of the Divisional Court

---

[157] *Grand River Conservation Authority v. Hargreaves* (2004), 2004 CarswellOnt 1703, [2004] O.J. No. 1777 (Ont. S.C.J.).

[158] (1987), 27 O.A.C. 308 (Ont. Div. Ct.).

[159] (2006), 2006 CarswellOnt 292 (Ont. Div. Ct.).

[160] (2006), 2006 CarswellOnt 4689 (Ont. Div. Ct.).

may dismiss the appeal for delay. If the appellant still wishes to pursue the appeal, he or she will then be forced to bring a motion to have the Registrar's order set aside. The factors considered by the Court on such a motion are: evidence of a *bona fide* intent to pursue the appeal, the length and explanation for the delay, prejudice to the other party not compensable by costs and the merits of the appeal.[161]

(c) Automatic Stay

An appeal from an order of the Board operates as an automatic stay of that order (i.e., it cannot be enforced) unless the Board or the Divisional Court orders otherwise.[162] The Board's power to lift this stay was confirmed by the Divisional Court in *J. Edwin Brown Holdings v. Rousson et al.*[163] The Board, though, is likely to be reluctant to proceed with a hearing in the face of a pending appeal. It will be a matter for the exercise of discretion of the presiding Member and such discretion will not be interfered with lightly.[164]

(d) Question of Law

An appeal only lies to the Divisional Court on a question of law.[165] It is, therefore, crucial for the appellant to identify an error in the Board's interpretation of the law (including errors with respect to the Board's jurisdiction) or an error in the process that is so serious that it amounts to an error in law. Factual findings of the Board Member are not subject to review by the Court. Whether or not there is *any* evidence upon which the Board could reach a finding of fact is a question of law. What inference can or should be drawn from some evidence is, at best, a question of mixed fact and law.[166]

An appeal that fails to allege an error in law can be quashed prior to the hearing of the merits of the appeal by way of motion brought by the respondent

---

[161] *Miller Manufacturing & Development Co. v. Alden* (1979), [1979] O.J. No. 3109, 1979 CarswellOnt 461 (Ont. C.A.), *Campitelli v. Ontario (Municipal Board)* (2000), [2000] O.J. No. 4185, 2000 CarswellOnt 4008 (Ont. Div. Ct.), *Clydesdale v. Natoli* (2001), 2001 CarswellOnt 4123 (Ont. Div. Ct.) and *Gates v. Wolch* (2006), 2006 CarswellOnt 1273, [2006] O.J. No. 1911, [2006] O.J. No. 1912 (Ont. Div. Ct.) re TSL-68491.

[162] Subsection 25(1) of the *Statutory Powers Procedure Act*.

[163] Doc. Ottawa 00-DV-000967 (Ont. Div. Ct.) (re EAT-04040).

[164] *Kobayashi v. Pezim et al.* (Oct. 29, 2001), TNL-28254-RV (Ont. Rental Housing Trib.).

[165] Subsection 196(1) of the T.P.A.

[166] *Jemiola v. Firchuk* (2005), 2005 CarswellOnt 7363 (Ont. Div. Ct.) citing with approval: *Meredith v. Leboeuf Properties Inc.* (2000), [2000] O.J. No. 209 (Ont. Div. Ct.); *Longhouse Village (Thunder Bay) Inc. v. Smolcec* (2001), 143 O.A.C. 137 (Ont. Div. Ct.).

before a single judge of the Divisional Court.[167] Otherwise, such an appeal shall be dismissed when it is heard in the normal course.[168] An appeal cannot be used to attempt to re-litigate issues of fact.[169]

Where there was evidence upon which the Board could base its decision and the issue is characterized by the Court as a pure question of fact, the Court will not interfere.[170] For instance, whether or not the landlord gave a notice of termination in good faith (for "own use") was held to be a question of fact, not law.[171] Similarly, the Court held that the Tribunal's findings that a landlord's efforts to accommodate a tenant with a disability were reasonable and that further attempts to accommodate the tenant would cause undue hardship for the landlord were questions of fact, not law, and that there was, therefore, no right to appeal those findings.[172]

Where there is conflicting evidence presented at the hearing and the Member considers and weighs that evidence, the Divisional Court will generally not intervene. In *Kazor v. Kavalir*,[173] the Court wrote the following:

> The appellant argues that the Tribunal misconstrued the evidence before it and ought to have found that there was a landlord & tenant relationship between the parties. There was conflicting evidence before the Tribunal and it is not the function of this Court to re-weigh the evidence. Section 196 of the Tenant Protection Act limits appeals to this Court to questions of law only. No error of law has been shown. The appeal is dismissed.

Similarly, in *Great Union Holdings Ltd. v. Palovick*,[174] the tenant appealed an order of the Rental Housing Tribunal terminating his tenancy on the basis that he had seriously impaired the safety of other persons in the complex and dismissing the tenant's applications. The landlord brought a

---

[167] See, for example: *Dresar v. Kyle* (2008), 2008 CarswellOnt 962 (Ont. Div. Ct.); *Carinci v. Gartner* (2007), 2007 CarswellOnt 1370 (Ont. Div. Ct.); *Hornstein v. Royal Bank* (2007), 2007 CarswellOnt 2413 (Ont. Div. Ct.); *Seleanu v. Devgan* (2007), 2007 CarswellOnt 918 (Ont. Div. Ct.); *1145084 Ontario Inc. v. Katyal* (2007), 2007 CarswellOnt 4639 (Ont. Div. Ct.); *Karpuchin v. Lancelotte* (2007), 2007 CarswellOnt 3520 (Ont. Div. Ct.); and *Jayaraj v. Nguyen* (2009), 2009 CarswellOnt 1408 (Ont. Div. Ct.).

[168] See, for example: *Great Union Holdings Ltd. v. Palovick* (2007), 2007 CarswellOnt 1062, 221 O.A.C. 255 (Ont. Div. Ct.); *Nemmour v. Wieland* (2007), 2007 CarswellOnt 4645 (Ont. Div. Ct.); *Basur v. Harpantidis* (2006), 2006 CarswellOnt 7540 (Ont. Div. Ct.); and *Scalzo v. Turtledove Management Corp.* (2009), 2009 CarswellOnt 1676 (Ont. Div. Ct.).

[169] See, for example: *Jayaraj v. Nguyen* (2009), 2009 CarswellOnt 1408 (Ont. Div. Ct.); and *Scalzo v. Turtledove Management Corp.* (2009), 2009 CarswellOnt 1676 (Ont. Div. Ct.).

[170] *Tsui v. St. Joseph Apartments Ltd.* (1989), [1989] O.J. No. 139, 1989 CarswellOnt 1640 (Ont. Div. Ct.). See also *Basur v. Harpantidis*, 2006 CarswellOnt 7540 (Ont. Div. Ct..

[171] *Kwan v. Lobo* (2003), 2003 CarswellOnt 5139 (Ont. Div. Ct.). See also *Shieff v. Cooper* (2008), 2008 CarswellOnt 172 (Ont. Div. Ct.).

[172] *Warren v. Canadian Mental Health Association* (2004), 2004 CarswellOnt 2372 (Ont. Div. Ct.) (re TEL-40151).

[173] (March 10, 2004), Doc. 69203/03 (Ont. Div. Ct.) (re CEL-32376).

[174] (2007), 2007 CarswellOnt 1062 (Ont. Div. Ct.).

motion to have the hearing of the appeal expedited and heard by a single judge of the Divisional Court and this motion was granted. On the hearing of the merits of the appeal, Justice T.A. Platana found that the tenant was challenging the Tribunal's findings of fact but had not actually alleged any errors in law. Consequently, the appeal was dismissed.

The Divisional Court has also ruled that there is no appeal from a finding of whether or not a landlord's breach of the landlord's obligations was "serious" within the meaning of para. 84(2)(a) of the T.P.A. (now para. 83(3)(a) of the R.T.A.). It was held that this was a question of fact (or, at best, mixed fact and law) and not a question of law.[175]

The Divisional Court has held that it has no jurisdiction to review a finding of the Board as to whether there has been substantial interference in reasonable enjoyment as this is, at best, a question of mixed fact and law.[176]

Where, however, the Divisional Court has strongly disagreed with the Member's decision under para. 84(2)(a) of the T.P.A., it has found that the Member's interpretation of the word "serious" was wrong in law.

In *Sage v. Wellington (County)*,[177] the landlord brought an application to evict the tenants because the landlord intended to convert the unit to a non-residential use. The tenants had lived in the unit since 1990 and opposed the application based on, amongst other things, the landlord's failure to address the issue of the contaminated well-water. The Member hearing the case found that since the tenants did not convince him that the water supply was unsafe at all times, this was not a *serious* breach within the meaning of para. 84(2)(a). On appeal, the Divisional Court ruled that it was wrong for the Member to use the word "convince" as it suggests a higher standard of proof than "on a balance of probabilities". The Court also held that the Member's interpretation of the word "serious" was wrong in law. Water quality is a very serious matter and the failure of the landlord to deal with the contaminated well water was a serious breach of the landlord's obligations. The appeal was granted and the order terminating the tenancy and evicting the tenants was quashed.

Similarly, in *Puterbough v. Canada (Public Works & Government Services)*[178] the Divisional Court was prepared to overturn the decision of the Tribunal where that decision was based on what the Divisional Court found to be a flawed interpretation of the term "serious breach". For a more detailed analysis of this case, please refer to the discussion of s. 83(3) of the R.T.A. found in Chapter 14.

---

175 *Meredith v. Leboeuf Properties Inc.* (2000), 2000 CarswellOnt 165, [2000] O.J. No. 209 (Ont. Div. Ct.).

176 *Zouhar v. Salford Investments Ltd.* (2008), 2008 CarswellOnt 3302 (Ont. Div. Ct.).

177 (2005), 2005 CarswellOnt 7833 (Ont. Div. Ct.) (re SWL-59763).

178 (2007), 2007 CarswellOnt 2222, 55 R.P.R. (4th) 189, [2007] O.J. No. 748 (Ont. Div. Ct.), additional reasons at (2007), 2007 CarswellOnt 7645 (Ont. Div. Ct.).

If a party simply forgets to attend the hearing, this does not constitute an error in law. The party will have to bear the consequences of his or her own negligence and that of his or her representative.[179]

In a case where a question arises as to whether or not a landlord has taken reasonable measures to accommodate the needs of a person in order to avoid violating their human rights, what constitutes "reasonable" measures (to accommodate the person) is a question of fact and will not be subject to appeal.[180]

Some issues must be raised at first instance (i.e. at the original hearing) or the party who knew or ought to have known of the relevant facts and who ought to have raised the issue at the original hearing will be taken to have waived any objection (estoppel by waiver) and will be barred from raising that issue on appeal. Two examples of this are allegations of bias[181] and questions with respect to the jurisdiction of the Board.[182]

(e) Appeals Brought for Improper Purposes

An appeal can take many months, sometimes more than a year, to complete. This delay, coupled with the fact that an appeal automatically stays execution of the order under appeal, creates the risk that a person will file an appeal solely (or primarily) for the purpose of delay. Abuse of the court process by a litigant, including the filing of an appeal as a stratagem to delay eviction, should not be condoned.[183] Where a respondent will be severely prejudiced by delay or believes that the appeal is just a stalling tactic, the

---

179 *Mandache et al. v. Dron* (September 20, 2004), Doc. 02/007 DV (Ont. Div. Ct.) (re SOT-02023).

180 *McKenzie v. Supportive Housing in Peel* (2006), 2006 CarswellOnt 1556, [2006] O.J. No. 1019 (Ont. Div. Ct.), citing *Renaud v. Central Okanagan School District No. 23*, (sub nom. *Central Okanagan School District No. 23 v. Renaud*) [1992] 2 S.C.R. 970 (S.C.C.) (at p. 18). Also see *Warren v. Canadian Mental Health Assn.* (2004), 2004 CarswellOnt 2372 (Ont. Div. Ct.) (re TEL-40151).

181 See, for example: *Authorson (Litigation Guardian of) v. Canada (Attorney General)* (2002), [2002] O.J. No. 2050, 161 O.A.C. 1, 32 C.P.C. (5th) 357, 2002 CarswellOnt 1724 (Ont. Div. Ct.), additional reasons at (2002), 2002 CarswellOnt 2939 (Ont. Div. Ct.); *Stabile v. Milani Estate* (2002), [2002] O.J. No. 3833 (Ont. S.C.J.), additional reasons at (2002), 2002 CarswellOnt 3293 (Ont. S.C.J.), affirmed (2004), 2004 CarswellOnt 831 (Ont. Div. Ct.); *Suguitan (Re)* (2006), [2006] O.J. No. 360 (Ont. S.C.J.); *Metrin Mechanical Contractors Ltd. v. Big H Construction Inc.* (2001), [2001] O.J. No. 3387 (Ont. S.C.J.); *Southridge Apartments v. Hastings* (2007), 2007 CarswellOnt 777 (Ont. Div. Ct.); *Canada (Human Rights Commission) v. Taylor* (1990), [1990] S.C.J. No. 129 (S.C.C.); and *U.F.C.W. v. Rol-Land Farms Ltd.* (2008), 235 O.A.C. 172 (Ont. Div. Ct.), additional reasons at (2008), 2008 CarswellOnt 3707 (Ont. Div. Ct.). See Chapter 2 for a more detailed discussion of the topic of "bias" in administrative proceedings.

182 *Kaiman v. Graham* (2009), 2009 CarswellOnt 378 (Ont. C.A.).

183 *Haley v. Morra* (2000), [2001] O.J. No. 134 (Ont. Div. Ct.) and *Minto Yorkville Inc. v. Trattoria Fieramosca Inc.* (1997), [1997] O.J. No. 5247 (Ont. Div. Ct.).

onus is upon the respondent to bring a motion before a judge of the Divisional Court to ask for interim relief (such as an order that the rent be paid to the landlord or into Court pending the outcome of the appeal[184]) or for an order quashing the appeal. The Divisional Court has been more receptive to such motions in recent years as there appears to be a growing awareness of the potential for abuse inherent in the system.

In *Karpuchin v. Lancelotte*,[185] the landlord brought a motion to quash the tenants' appeal on the basis that they had failed to raise any question of law and that the appeal was frivolous and vexatious. The tenants requested an adjournment of the motion. The motion was adjourned for one month, on the condition that by the commencement of the motion, the tenants pay five months' rent into court and file proof of ordering a transcript of the proceedings. The tenants failed to comply with either condition. Their request for a further adjournment was denied and the appeal was quashed with costs of $600 awarded to the landlord.

Being granted an automatic stay, a tenant must proceed with the appeal procedure expeditiously. Failure to order the transcript of the evidence until the last day and other delaying tactics were strongly criticized in *Belmont Property Management v. Evelyn*.[186] In his decision Rosenberg J. said:[187]

> In my view the Court should send a clear message to counsel that the tenant, having received the benefit of the stay pending disposition of the appeal, has an obligation in good faith to pursue the appeal and not to use the type of tactics used here to delay the day of reckoning as long as possible.

In a somewhat unusual decision of a Divisional Court justice, the landlord's motion to quash the appeal for the tenant's delay was refused but the tenant was ordered to pay security for costs of the appeal. The tenant had delayed perfecting the appeal. The tenant's credibility was in question, rent arrears were over $12,000 and there was evidence that the tenant had a long record of delinquent accounts: *Soundtrack Audio-Visual Recording Studios of Canada Inc. v. Beecroft Partnership*.[188] Although the tenant in the style of cause is described as a corporation, it was the individual in occupation who was appealing. The Divisional Court ordered that if the rent and security for costs were not paid into court the landlord could apply *ex parte* for an order

---

[184] See, for example, *Hughes v. Transglobe Property Management Services Inc.* (2009), 2009 CarswellOnt 585 (Ont. Div. Ct.), in which a judge of the Divisional Court may order it a condition of hearing the tenant's appeal that the tenant pay the landlord (and file with the Court proof of payment) some outstanding rent and also ongoing rent as it came due until the date set for the hearing of the appeal. Also see *Costa v. Masterson*, 2009 CarswellOnt 3568 (Ont. Div. Ct.).

[185] (2007), 2007 CarswellOn 3250 (Ont. Div. Ct.).

[186] (1991), 16 R.P.R. (2d) 11 (Ont. Div. Ct.).

[187] (1991), 16 R.P.R. (2d) 11 at 15 (Ont. Div. Ct.).

[188] (1992), 1992 CarswellOnt 2374 (Ont. Div. Ct.).

striking the appeal, and so proceed to enforce the order terminating the lease and for a writ of possession. A similar order was issued more recently by the Divisional Court in the case of *Princess Apartments v. Pohvalynskyi.*[189]

In *Taylor v. Reisenecker,*[190] the landlord filed an appeal from a decision of the Tribunal but failed to diligently pursue this appeal. Finally, the Registrar intervened and ordered that the landlord file a transcript in order to perfect the appeal. The landlord failed to do so by the deadline set by the Registrar. The transcript was not filed until two years after the notice of appeal was served and filed. In the intervening period, the property had been severely damaged in a fire and the property had been sold (despite the tenant's alleged right of first refusal). The tenant brought a motion to dismiss the appeal for delay and, in the circumstances of this case, the motion was granted.

In *Portree Properties Ltd. v. Dunbar,*[191] the Tribunal had granted an eviction order based upon the evidence of the tenants' neighbours that they were repeatedly disturbed by noise coming from the tenants' rental unit. The tenants filed an appeal but failed to perfect their appeal within a reasonable period of time. The landlord brought a motion to quash the appeal. The tenants requested an adjournment of the motion. Justice O'Driscoll concluded that the Tribunal's findings about the disturbance created by noise coming from the tenants' unit was "a finding of fact based on the evidence of neighbouring tenants" and that the appeal involved no question of law or of mixed law and fact. He concluded as follows, "As far as I can see, there is no merit to this appeal and the notice of appeal and stay order are simply instruments to stave off the ultimate day on which the Tenants will be required to vacate the premises." The motion was granted, the appeal was quashed and the tenants were ordered to pay the landlord's costs of the motion. The Divisional Court has made similar orders in *Niazi Holdings Inc. v. Jaupaj,*[192] *Haley v. Morra,*[193] *Klymko v. Lem,*[194] *Hornstein v. Royal Bank,*[195] *1145084 Ontario Inc. v. Katyal,*[196] and *Seleanu v. Devgan.*[197]

In *Pompey v. Metcap Living Management Inc.,*[198] the landlord had originally brought an application before the Landlord and Tenant Board to evict the tenant for non-payment of rent. The tenant consented to the Board issuing an order terminating the tenancy and for arrears of rent but delaying enforcement of that order to allow the tenant some time to pay the arrears of rent and

---

[189] (2006), 2006 CarswellOnt 2456 (Ont. Div. Ct.).
[190] (2006), [2006] O.J. No. 4326, 2006 CarswellOnt 6679 (Ont. Div. Ct.).
[191] (2005), 2005 CarswellOnt 2376 (Ont. Div. Ct.).
[192] (2000), 2000 CarswellOnt 5125 (Ont. Div. Ct.).
[193] (2000), 2000 CarswellOnt 5043 (Ont. Div. Ct.).
[194] (2000), 2000 CarswellOnt 5068 (Ont. Div. Ct.).
[195] (2007), 2007 CarswellOnt 2413 (Ont. Div. Ct.).
[196] (2007), 2007 CarswellOnt 4639 (Ont. Div. Ct.).
[197] (2007), 2007 CarswellOnt 918 (Ont. Div. Ct.).
[198] (2007), 2007 CarswellOnt 6892 (Ont. Div. Ct.).

thereby void the order. After the order became enforceable, the tenant attempted to bring a motion before the Board to have that order set aside under s. 74(11) on the basis that all amounts required under that subsection had been paid. The tenant, however, withdrew that motion before it could be decided. The tenant then brought a motion to a judge of the Divisional Court for an extension of the time to file an appeal of the eviction order. That motion was rejected. The tenant then filed a second motion under s. 74(11) at the Board to have the eviction order set aside but that motion was dismissed by the Board on the basis that only one such motion may be brought per tenancy. The tenant then filed an appeal of the Board's order dismissing his motion under s. 74(11). The landlord brought a motion before a judge of the Divisional Court to have the appeal quashed on the basis that it was devoid of merit and constituted an abuse of process. The tenant failed to appear at the motion. In these circumstances, Justice K. Swinton agreed both that the appeal was devoid of merit and that it represented an abuse of process. Accordingly, the landlord's motion was granted and the tenant's appeal was quashed.

In *Chong v. Castiglione*,[199] the appeal appeared to have little, if any, merit but the tenant indicated he was able to pay all of the arrears in rent owing to the landlord. When nothing was paid to the landlord, the landlord brought a motion to request that the stay be lifted. Lane J. ordered that if the arrears and the costs of the motion were not paid within two weeks, the stay was lifted and the landlord could proceed at that time to enforce the eviction order.

In *O'Regan v. Commvesco Levinson-Viner Group*,[200] the landlord brought a motion to quash the tenant's appeal of a Tribunal order terminating this tenancy. The grounds for the appeal were that the Member allegedly misapprehended the evidence presented at the hearing, failed to properly apply the provisions of s. 84(2) of the T.P.A. (now s. 83(3) of the R.T.A.) or failed to properly exercise her discretion under s. 84(1) of the T.P.A. (now s. 83(1) of the R.T.A.). Justice Lalonde summarized the relevant law as follows (at p. 5):

> *National Life Assurance Co. of Canada v. McCoubrey*, [1926] S.C.R. 277 at P. 283 has established that where there is no proper question of law raised and an appeal is manifestly devoid of merit, i.e. where there is no prospect of finding an error by the trial judge which could lead to success on the appeal, it may properly be quashed on a motion to quash.
>
> The *National Life Assurance* case also stands for the proposition that were an appeal lacks merit, every court of justice has an inherent jurisdiction to prevent such abuse of its own procedure. An appeal having a manifest lack of substance as would bring it within the character of vexatious proceedings designed merely to delay should not be entertained.

---

[199] (2005), 2005 CarswellOnt 7048 (Ont. Div. Ct.).

[200] (2006), 2006 CarswellOnt 5398, [2006] O.J. No. 3528 (Ont. Div. Ct.).

> The Divisional Court in *Jemiola v. Firchuck*, [2005] O.J. No. 6085, 2005 CarswellOnt 7363 (Ont. Div. Ct. Dec. 02, 2005), at p. 4 decided that the factual findings of the Tribunal are not subject to review. Whether or not there is any evidence is a question of law. What inferences can or should be drawn from some evidence is, at best, a question of mixed fact and law. The jurisdiction of the Divisional Court is limited to questions of law. . .
>
> The decision in *Longhouse Village (Thunder Bay) Inc. v. Smolcec* (2001), 143 O.A.C. 137 (Ont. Div. Ct.), p. 6-7 and s. 84, *Tenant Protection Act, 1997* have settled the question that the application of s. 84 of the Tenant Protection Act is not strictly a jurisdictional issue, but fall within the expertise of the Tribunal. Once the Tribunal has made its findings under s. 84, a court on appeal will afford the Tribunal a great deal of deference. The standard of review to be applied when involving findings of the Tribunal under s. 84 is that of 'patently unreasonable'.

In this case, Justice Lalonde found that there was ample evidence upon which the Tribunal Member could base her decision and that there was nothing patently unreasonable about her decisions concerning whether or not to grant relief under s. 84 of the T.P.A. Since the Member did not misapprehend the evidence and there were no questions of law involved, the appeal was quashed and the landlord was awarded its costs of the motion, fixed in the amount of $1,500.

In *Cannata v. Applegate*,[201] the landlord brought a motion to quash the tenant's appeal as being devoid of merit. The tenant failed to attend the hearing of this motion. In granting the landlord's motion, Justice Chapnik wrote as follows:

> The arrears are substantial. The tenant is essentially living rent-free in the premises. She appears to be playing games with the landlord and the system.

In addition to quashing the appeal and lifting the stay on the eviction order, the Divisional Court also awarded the landlord costs in the amount of $5,200 payable forthwith.

In *Falconer v. Manufacturers Life Insurance Co.*,[202] two eviction orders were granted by the Landlord and Tenant Board against the tenant, one based upon persistent late payment of rent and the other based upon substantial arrears in rent (approximately $7,000) that had accrued. The tenant requested a review of the order based upon persistent late payment of rent but this request was denied. The tenant brought a motion to void the eviction order based upon arrears of rent but this motion was also denied because the cheque used by the tenant to purportedly pay the landlord was drawn upon a closed bank account (and, therefore, it was dishonoured). The tenant appealed to the Divisional Court the eviction order based upon arrears of rent and the order dismissing his motion to have that order declared void. The landlord brought

---

[201] (2006), [2006] O.J. No. 2683, 2006 CarswellOnt 2750 (Ont. Div. Ct.).

[202] (2008), 2008 CarswellOnt 1275 (Ont. Div. Ct.).

a motion to quash the tenant's appeal. At the request of the tenant, the landlord's motion was adjourned several times. Eventually, the Court proceeded in the tenant's absence, granted the landlord's motion quashing the appeal for being completely devoid of merit and an abuse of process and awarded to the landlord its costs, fixed in the amount of $15,000.00.

In *Martino v. Mohammad*,[203] however, the landlord's motion to quash the tenant's appeal was not granted. Justice Then was not persuaded that the appeal as presented was entirely devoid of merit and the issue of whether the Member's conduct gave rise to a reasonable apprehension of bias (which issue was raised by the tenant on review but was not dealt with in the Tribunal's review order) constituted questions of law. Quoting from *Schmidt v. Toronto Dominion Bank*,[204] Justice Then pointed out that the landlord still had the option of attempting to secure (through the usual channels) an early date for the hearing of the appeal if the landlord felt that the appeal was devoid of merit. For the reasons set out above, the landlord's motion was dismissed but, largely because the tenant had still not ordered the transcript of the Tribunal proceedings, no costs were awarded to the tenant.

In *Wismer Markham Developments Inc. v. MacDonald*,[205] the landlord brought a motion to quash the tenant's appeal and lift the stay of the eviction order. Although the order under appeal was a "consent" order, the tenant alleged that the Member erred in failing to ascertain whether the tenant's consent was voluntarily given and whether the Tribunal had the jurisdiction to grant the order it did. Although there was little doubt that the tenant's appeal was a delay tactic to extend his tenancy, Justice Fuerst held that it was not appropriate to quash the appeal since it was not possible to conclude that the appeal was completely devoid of merit. Instead of quashing the appeal, Justice Fuerst made an interim order requiring the tenant to pay into the court five months rent (some of the rent that was in arrears) and to continue paying rent into court as it came due until the appeal was resolved. It was also ordered that the appeal be perfected within a couple of weeks. Finally, the interim order provided that if the tenant breached any of the terms of interim order, the landlord could immediately apply, without notice to the tenant, for an order quashing the appeal and lifting the stay of the eviction order.

In *Scalzo v. Turtledove Management Corp.*,[206] the landlord brought a motion to quash an appeal. The landlord had given the tenant notice of termination in order to do major renovations/repairs to the unit and had, pursuant to ss. 83(4) and 54 of the R.T.A., paid the tenant compensation equal to three months of rent. The landlord argued that the tenant could not keep this money while, at the same time, seeking to have the eviction order

---

[203] (2006), [2006] O.J. No. 3158, 2006 CarswellOnt 4725 (Ont. Div. Ct.).

[204] (1995), 24 O.R. (3d) 1 (Ont. C.A.) at p. 3.

[205] (2006), [2006] O.J. No. 1374, 2006 CarswellOnt 2076 (Ont. Div. Ct.).

[206] (2008), 2008 CarswellOnt 3576 (Ont. Div. Ct.).

set aside. Justice Lederman was not satisfied that the appeal was completely devoid of merit. Rather than quash the appeal, he allowed the appeal to proceed but on the condition that the compensation be reimbursed to the landlord pending the disposition of the appeal.

In *Park v. Chau*,[207] the landlord brought a motion to quash the tenant's appeal on the basis that it was without merit. At the hearing of that motion, the tenant consented to an order adjourning the motion *sine die* to be brought back on not less than seven days' notice on the condition that the tenant perfect the appeal on a strict timeline and continue paying rent pending the hearing on the merits of the appeal. When the tenant failed to comply with the terms of this consent order, the landlord brought the motion back and obtained an order quashing the appeal. The tenant then brought a motion to set aside that order. As a condition to hearing the tenant's motion, Justice Kiteley ordered that the tenant pay a substantial sum to the landlord within 48 hours (by certified funds) and provide an affidavit confirming that a transcript had been ordered and indicating when it would be available. If these conditions were met, a stay would be issued and the tenant was then ordered to continue paying rent on the first of each month pending the outcome of the motion. If the tenant failed to comply with these terms, no stay would be issued and the landlord would be free to enforce the original eviction order.

In *Bank of Montreal v. Weidenfeld*,[208] the Bank of Montreal (the "Bank"), as mortgagee in possession, sought to show the premises to prospective purchasers. The tenant refused to allow entry into the premises and stopped paying rent. The tenant demanded that the Bank pay him a rental fee for having a "For Sale" sign on the front lawn and for each entry into the unit. The Bank commenced proceedings to terminate the tenancy and evict the tenant for substantial interference with its lawful rights (i.e., for refusing to allow the Bank to show the unit) and for failing to pay rent. The Board found that the Bank was a landlord by virtue of being a mortgagee in possession, granted the Bank's application and issued and eviction order. The tenant then filed a request for review and was able to drag that process out for several months before an order was issued upholding the original eviction order. The tenant then filed an application for judicial review. Eventually, the tenant withdrew that application but, instead, filed an appeal to the Divisional Court, citing numerous grounds for the appeal. The landlord brought a motion to quash the appeal as being devoid of merit and brought for improper purposes. By the time this motion was heard, the tenant owed approximately $8,000 in arrears of rent and the market value of the property had dropped by about $60,000.

---

[207] (2008), 2008 CarswellOnt 1454 (Ont. Div. Ct.).

[208] (2008), 2008 CarswellOnt 3016 (Ont. Div. Ct.).

Justice M. Fuerst acknowledged that quashing an appeal is a power that should seldom be exercised but was satisfied that this was a proper case in which to do so. Justice Fuerst found that most of the grounds listed by the tenant raised questions of fact, not law. For instance, whether a mortgagee is a mortgagee in possession is a question of fact. Other grounds were either frivolous or stood no chance of success on appeal. In granting the Bank's motion (and awarding costs to the Bank in the amount of $8,000), Justice Fuerst wrote as follows:

> This is an appeal that is manifestly devoid of merit. I am satisfied that it is nothing more than an artifice to prolong Mr. Weidenfeld's rent-free stay in the property, to the Bank's ultimate detriment. The record of Mr. Weidenfeld's dealings with the Bank . . .make it clear that he has not acted and is not acting in good faith. Even when ordered by the Board to pay money in trust, he refused. He has used the legal process to extend his tenancy and avoid eviction, while paying no rent to the Bank for almost a year. I am satisfied that he launched this appeal for no purpose other than to obtain an automatic stay of eviction so that he could remain in the property indefinitely at no expense to himself, while continuing to deny the Bank the access to which it is entitled.
>
> Abuse of the court process by a litigant, including the filing of an appeal as a stratagem to delay eviction, should not be condoned: *Haley v. Morra* (2000), [2001] O.J. No. 134 (Ont. Div. Ct.); *Minto Yorkville Inc. v. Trattoria Fieramosca Inc.*, [1977] O.J. No. 5247 (Ont. Div. Ct.).

In *Toronto Community Housing Corp. v. Jilks*,[209] Lax J. found that the appeal raised no question of law, was manifestly devoid of merit and was commenced for the purpose of delay and to avoid eviction. On motion by the landlord, the appeal was quashed and the certificate of stay vacated. Costs were fixed against the tenant in the amount of $1,750.

Where it appears that the appeal has been filed as a delaying tactic and is not being diligently pursued by the appellant, the responding party may be well advised to bring a motion to quash the appeal. A typical response from such appellants seems to be to ask the Court to adjourn the motion so that the appellant can retain counsel. In such cases, the Divisional Court will take a hard look at both the merits of the appeal and what efforts, if any, the appellant has made to retain counsel *prior* to the date scheduled for the hearing of the motion. Recent cases demonstrate that, unless the appellant can advance a very compelling argument, it is likely that the request for an adjournment will be denied and that the appeal will be quashed.[210]

Pursuant to s. 81 of the R.T.A., an eviction order cannot be enforced more than six months after the date it becomes effective (see Chapter 17). Consequently, if, by filing an appeal, a tenant is able to delay enforcement

---

[209] (2008), 2008 CarswellOnt 4166 (Ont. Div. Ct.).

[210] *Gateway Properties v. Frants* (2006), 2006 CarswellOnt 3232 (Ont. Div. Ct.) and *Deans v. James Garden Apartments* (2005), 2005 CarswellOnt 7728 (Ont. Div. Ct.).

of an eviction order by at least six months, even if the landlord is ultimately successful on the appeal, the landlord may have difficulty enforcing the original eviction order. Thus, in such situations, the landlord may need to request that the Divisional Court grant its own writ of possession[211] or amend the original order so that it remains enforceable.

(f) Standard of Review

The standard of review is the degree of deference which the appellate court will give to the decision of an administrative tribunal. In deciding the amount of deference to show a tribunal, the court will consider the presence of a privative clause, the expertise of the tribunal, the purpose of the legislation and nature of the issue being raised on appeal. Much (perhaps too much) has been written about the "standard of review analysis" and the Supreme Court of Canada has, over time, attempted to elucidate numerous tests. The most recent approach was described by the Supreme Court of Canada in the *Dunsmuir* case.[212]

In general, if the court decides to show deference to an administrative tribunal, the court will only overturn the tribunal's decision where that decision is found by the court to have been "unreasonable". A court conducting a review for reasonableness inquires into the qualities that make a decision reasonable. Reasonableness is concerned mostly with the existence of justification, transparency and intelligibility within the decision-making process and with whether the decision falls within a range of possible, acceptable outcomes that are defensible in respect of the facts and the law.

Where the court indicates that the test is one of "correctness", it is showing little (if any) deference to the tribunal and is essentially taking the position that the court is in as good a position as the tribunal to come to the "correct" decision. When applying the correctness standard, a reviewing court will undertake its own analysis of the question and decide whether it agrees with the determination of the decision maker; if not, the court will substitute its own view and provide the correct answer.

An exhaustive analysis is not required in every case to determine the proper standard of review. Courts must first ascertain whether the jurisprudence has already determined in a satisfactory manner the degree of deference to be accorded to a decision maker with regard to a particular category of

---

[211] As was done in *Bakardjiev v. MacLean* (2008), 2008 CarswellOnt 5587 (Ont. Div. Ct.). See, however, *Tal v. Koor* (2009), 2009 CarswellOnt 2923 (Ont. Div. Ct.), in which it was held that, once the appeals had been abandoned and/or dismissed for delay, the Divisional Court lacked jurisdiction to amend the original eviction orders to extend the time for the enforcement of those orders.

[212] *New Brunswick (Board of Management) v.* Dunsmuir, (sub nom. *Dunsmuir v. New Brunswick*), [2008] 1 S.C.R. 190 (S.C.C.).

question. If that inquiry proves unfruitful, in order to identify the proper standard of review, the court must analyze the following factors: the presence or absence of a privative clause; the expertise of the tribunal; the purpose of the legislation; and nature of the issue being raised on appeal.

In appeals from decisions of the Landlord and Tenant Board, it is difficult to predict how appellate courts will apply the post-*Dunsmuir* standard of review analysis as they were not entirely consistent on this issue prior to the *Dunsmuir* decision. Nevertheless, based upon the decisions to date, my analysis suggests the following:

1. In cases where a Member has clearly turned his or her mind to an issue, considered the evidence presented and exercised a **discretionary power** that was clearly within his or her jurisdiction (such as whether or not to grant relief from forfeiture), the courts will generally defer to the Member who heard the case unless the exercise of discretion was unreasonable.[213]
2. Where the appeal of a decision of the Tribunal or Board turns on a **mixed question of fact and law**, in some cases the Divisional Court has applied the test of "reasonableness"[214] while in other cases it has indicated that it has no jurisdiction to intervene at all.[215]
3. In cases where the facts are not in dispute and the question turns upon the interpretation of a statute, regulation or common law principle (i.e., **a pure question of law**), the appellate courts have been much less deferential and have usually applied the test of "correctness".[216]

---

[213] *Longhouse Village (Thunder Bay) Inc. v. Smolcec* (2001), [2001] O.J. No. 875, 2001 CarswellOnt 688, 143 O.A.C. 137, 32 Admin. L.R. (3d) 72 (Ont. Div. Ct.). See *Toronto Community Housing Corp. v. Jilks* (2008), 2008 CarswellOnt 4166 (Ont. Div. Ct.), in which Lax J. stated that, given the Member's findings of fact against the tenants, it was neither unreasonable nor patently unreasonable for the Member to exercise her discretion to refuse to grant relief from eviction. Lax J. stated that "There is no basis to interfere with her exercise of discretion, which is to be accorded deference." See also *Goodman v. Menyhart* (2009), 2009 CarswellOnt 2205 (Ont. Div. Ct.), in which the Court found that there was no basis to interfere with the Board Member's discretionary decision on the costs of the hearing and *Caputo v. Newberg*, 2009 CanLII 32908 (Ont. Div. Ct.).

[214] *Paul Bunyan Trailer Camp Ltd. v. McCormick* (1999), 1999 CarswellOnt 5466, (sub nom. *McCormick v. Paul Bunyan Trailer Camp Ltd.*) [1999] O.J. No. 5784, 22 R.P.R. (4th) 305 (Ont. Div. Ct.).

[215] *Zouhar v. Salford Investments Ltd.* (2008), 2008 CarswellOnt 3302 (Ont. Div. Ct.).

[216] *Samuel Property Management Ltd. v. Nicholson* (2002), [2002] O.J. No. 3571, 2002 CarswellOnt 3004, 3 R.P.R. (4th) 66, (sub nom. *Nicholson v. Samuel Property Management Ltd.*) 217 D.L.R. (4th) 292, 61 O.R. (3d) 470 (Ont. C.A.); *Dollimore v. Azuria Group Inc.* (2001), 2001 CarswellOnt 4042, 152 O.A.C. 57 (Ont. Div. Ct.); *Norberry Residences v. Cox* (2002), [2002] O.J. No. 747, 2002 CarswellOnt 5753 (Ont. Div. Ct.); *Karrum Properties Inc. v. Aveiro* (2001), [2001] O.J. No. 5417 (Ont. Div. Ct.); *Sage v. Wellington (County)* (2005), 2005 CarswellOnt 7833, 19 C.E.L.R. (3d) 210 (Ont. Div. Ct.). Note that in a recent decision following the release of the Supreme Court of Canada's decision in *New Brunswick*

4. In determining whether the appellant received a fair hearing, however, there is no need for the appellate court to apply any particular standard of review; if there was a denial of natural justice, the tribunal's decision will be quashed.[217]

Although appellate courts and parties who appear before such courts often spend a lot of time arguing about the proper standard of review, the "bottom line" is that an appellate court will often overturn a tribunal decision with which it strongly disagrees, regardless of the standard of review that the court is purporting to apply.

(g) Examples

Appeals have been granted in the following instances:

- the Member gave no reasons for finding that the tenant had committed an illegal act in the face of a dispute with another tenant where self-defence was raised;[218]
- the Member rejected evidence on the basis of lack of credibility without explaining the basis for finding that the evidence was not credible;[219]
- the absence of an audible recording of the proceedings so prejudiced the appellant that the court felt that it had no alternative but to grant the appeal and order a new hearing;[220]
- the Member failed to specifically consider the issues raised under s. 84(2) of the T.P.A. by the tenant and the issue of whether it was appropriate to grant relief to the tenant under s. 84(1) of the T.P.A.;[221]

(Board of Management) v. Dunsmuir, (sub nom. *Dunsmuir v. New Brunswick*), [2008] 1 S.C.R. 190 (S.C.C.), the Ontario Divisional Court has held that on an appeal from a decision of the Landlord and Tenant Board on a pure question of law, the applicable standard of review remains correctness: *Darragh v. Normar Developments Inc.* (2008), [2008] O.J. No. 2586 (Ont. S.C.J.) and *Goodman v. Menyhart* (2009), 2009 CarswellOnt 2205 (Ont. Div. Ct.).

[217] *Davidson v. Bagla* (2006), 2006 CarswellOnt 6171 (Ont. Div. Ct.); *Baker v. Canada (Minister of Citizenship & Immigration*, [1999] 2 S.C.R. 817 (S.C.C.) at para 18-28; *Manpel v. Greenwin Property Management* (2005), [2005] O.J. No. 3079 (Ont. Div. Ct.), additional reasons at (2005), 48 R.P.R. (4th) 212 (Ont. Div. Ct.); and *London (City) v. Ayerswood Development Corp.* (2002), [2002] O.J. No. 4859 (Ont. C.A.) at para. 10.

[218] *Toronto Community Housing Corp. v. Greaves* (2004), 2004 CarswellOnt 5311, [2004] O.J. 5112 (Ont. Div. Ct.), additional reasons at (2005), 2005 CarswellOnt 820 (Ont. Div. Ct.).

[219] *Bell v. Peel Living* (January 27, 2005), Doc. 03-BN-12624 (Ont. Div. Ct.) in which the tenant alleged that she was absent from the hearing due to illness, there was no evidence to the contrary but the Member apparently rejected this explanation without saying why.

[220] *Swire v. Walleye Trailer Park Ltd.* (2001), 2001 CarswellOnt 2832 (Ont. Div. Ct.) and *Cymbalski v. Alcorn* (2006), 209 O.A.C. 47 (Ont. Div. Ct.) (March 9, 2006), Doc. Newmarket DC-05-075497-00 (Ont. Div. Ct.) (re TNL-63305).

[221] *Luray Investments Ltd. v. Recine-Pynn* (1999), 126 O.A.C. 303 (Ont. Div. Ct.).

- the Member failed to specifically deal in the order with the tenant's assertion that the landlord had brought the application because of the tenant's involvement in a tenants' association (which was relevant under s. 84(2) of the T.P.A.) and failed to reconvene the hearing when new issues arose by way of post-hearing submissions;[222]
- the Member refused to consider documentary evidence that was submitted during the hearing and which formed part of the record;[223]
- the landlord was not given a meaningful opportunity to defend the allegations made against him by the tenants because: the Member refused to grant an adjournment in order to permit the landlord time to retain counsel and prepare a defence (the landlord had only had 48 hours' notice of the hearing); the Member frequently interrogated the landlord and interrupted his cross-examination of witnesses; and the Member refused to accept into evidence audiotapes that may well have affected the outcome of the hearing solely on the basis that listening to the tapes would take too long;[224]
- the Member failed to deal with a jurisdictional issue that arose during the hearing (i.e., whether the rental unit was subject to the Act) and made rulings without any evidentiary basis to support them.[225]
- the Member misinterpreted the law by finding that he could not grant relief for any period earlier than one year immediately preceding the date upon which the order was issued.[226]

When it comes to s. 83 of the R.T.A. (formerly s. 84 of the T.P.A.), it is always a live issue that a Member must consider whether or not specifically raised as an issue by the tenant and the Member should indicate in the order that relief from forfeiture was considered and the relevant facts that influenced the Member to grant or to refuse to grant such relief. It is not sufficient, however, for the Member to simply recite in the order that he or she has considered the matter. The Member must have provided the parties with an opportunity to present evidence and make submissions relevant to the issue of whether it is appropriate in the circumstances of the particular case to grant relief from forfeiture and the Member should recite the relevant facts and reasons (even if briefly) for granting or denying such relief. The failure of a Member to do so may well result in the Divisional Court ordering a new hearing, as occurred in the case of *Forest Hill Gates v. Wolch*.[227]

---

222 *Kuzyk v. SK Properties* (2001), 2001 CarswellOnt 6074 (Ont. S.C.J.) (re TSL-18855).

223 *Manafa v. Rickerby* (2005), 206 O.A.C. 254 (Ont. Div. Ct.) (January 21, 2005), Doc. 169/04 (Ont. Div. Ct.) (re TET-03885 and TEL-42276).

224 *Davidson v. Bagla* (2006), 2006 CarswellOnt 6171 (Ont. Div. Ct.), overturning Tribunal orders CET-04405-RV (Dec. 14, 2004) and CET-04405 (Nov. 10, 2004).

225 *Davidson v. Bagla* (2006), 2006 CarswellOnt 6171 (Ont. Div. Ct.), overturning Tribunal orders CET-04405-RV (Dec. 14, 2004) and CET-04405 (Nov. 10, 2004).

226 *Goodman v. Menyhart* (2009), 2009 CarswellOnt 2205 (Ont. Div. Ct.)

227 (2007), 2007 CarswellOnt 1864 (Ont. Div. Ct.).

Appeals have been dismissed where:

- it was implicit that the Member turned his or her mind to the relevant issues and the failure of the Member to grant discretionary relief under s. 84(1) of the T.P.A. was not unreasonable in the circumstances;[228]
- the Tribunal failed to provide a French interpreter;[229]
- the issue raised by the appellant on appeal (i.e. whether the landlord complied with s. 8 of the T.P.A.) had not been raised by the appellant at the original hearing and there was no reasonable explanation for this failure;[230]
- the absence of a recording of the proceedings did not prejudice the appellant;[231]
- the Divisional Court agreed with the Board's interpretation of s. 203 of the R.T.A. (prohibiting the Board from making determinations or reviewing decisions concerning elegibility for rent geared to income assistance or the amount of geared to income rent payable under the Social Housing Reform Act);[232] and
- the party failed to raise the issue of jurisdiction at the original hearing.[233]

With respect to consent orders,[234] the Divisional Court will generally uphold such orders because a consent order can only be set aside "on grounds such as mistake, misrepresentation, fraud or other grounds that would invalidate a contract."[235] There is a heavy onus upon the person seeking to set aside a consent order to prove that it ought not to be allowed to stand. In *Lockhart et al. v. Nistrap Dev. Corp.*,[236] the Divisional Court went so far as to write, "There is no appeal from a consent order." This may have been

---

228 *Patridge v. Borris-Brown* (2005), 2005 CarswellOnt 6951 (Ont. Div. Ct.), *Vescio Investments Inc. v. Robinson* (March 6, 2002), Doc. 278/01 (Ont. Div. Ct.) (re TNL-24633) and *Hornstein v. Royal Bank* (2007), 2007 CarswellOnt 2413 (Ont. Div. Ct.).

229 *Karrum v. Yolanda Enterprises Ltd.* (2001), [2001] O.J. No. 5417, 2001 CarswellOnt 1839 (Ont. Div. Ct.), upheld on appeal (2002), 2002 CarswellOnt 3483 (Ont. C.A.) (re TSL-12922).

230 *Higgins v. Yi* (2007), 2007 CarswellOnt 2077 (Ont. Div. Ct.).

231 *Karrum v. Yolanda Enterprises Ltd.* (2001), [2001] O.J. No. 5417, 2001 CarswellOnt 1839 (Ont. Div. Ct.), upheld on appeal (2002), 2002 CarswellOnt 3483 (Ont. C.A.) (re TSL-12922) and *Longhouse Village (Thunder Bay) Inc. v. Smolcec* (2001), 2001 CarswellOnt 688, [2001] O.J. No. 875 (Ont. Div. Ct.).

232 *Peel Housing Corp. v. Ellis* (2009), 2009 CarswellOnt 693 (Div. Ct.).

233 *Kaiman v. Graham* (2009), 2009 CarsellOnt 378 (Ont. C.A.).

234 A consent order is an order issued by the Tribunal/Board at the joint request of the parties, on terms to which the parties have agreed.

235 *Torgis v. Brajovic* (January 14, 2002), Doc. 01-BN-2696 (Ont. Div. Ct.) (re CEL-16579).

236 Doc. 695/03 (Ont. Div. Ct.) (re TEL-38506). See also *Belz v. Mernich* (1999), [1999] O.J. No. 1940, 1999 CarswellOnt 1656 (Ont. C.A.) and *Laboissiere et al. v. Butler*, Doc. 03-DV-000927 (Ont. Div. Ct.) (re EAL-33322).

overstating things but it is true that, pursuant to s. 133 of the *Courts of Justice Act*, no appeal lies from a consent order without first obtaining leave from the court.[237]

(h) Powers of Divisional Court

Pursuant to s. 210(4) of the R.T.A., on an appeal, the Divisional Court may affirm, rescind, amend[238] or replace the decision or order or may remit the matter back to the Board with the opinion of the Divisional Court. The Court may make any other order that it considers proper (s. 210(5)); this includes relief from forfeiture.[239] It also includes any order for costs that it considers proper (and costs will typically be awarded at the scale usually granted in proceedings before the Divisional Court and not the extremely modest costs that are granted by the Tribunal/Board).[240] At Divisional Court, costs awarded on a motion (e.g., a motion to quash an appeal) are typically in the $500 to $750 range and costs awarded to the successful party at the end of a full appeal hearing are typically between $1,500 and $4,500.

13. JUDICIAL REVIEW

An application for judicial review involves a different process than an appeal. In very broad terms, where there already exists a statutory right of appeal, judicial review is an alternate method by which a party can seek relief where an administrative tribunal has exceeded its jurisdiction. Also, through judicial review, a party can seek to have the court intervene *before* the resolution of a particular case that is before a tribunal where the tribunal's process is so clearly flawed that it ought not to be allowed to continue. Judicial review has been used very rarely in relation to decisions of the Ontario Rental Housing Tribunal and the Landlord and Tenant Board, probably because there are other ways to obtain a reconsideration of a decision (internal review by the Board itself and a statutory right of appeal to the Divisional Court on questions of law).

When a person files an application for judicial review, the *Judicial Review Procedure Act*[241] requires the Board to file with the Court a record of the proceedings (including a copy of any audio recording of the hearing). The

---

237 *Morgan v. Whing* (2009), 2009 CarswellOnt 2927 (Ont. Div. Ct. .

238 See, for example, *Rizzi v. Roberts* (2007), 2007 CarswellOnt 1889 (Ont. Div. Ct.), discussed in detail earlier in this Chapter.

239 *Ontario Housing Corp. v. Jarvis* (1990), 1990 CarswellOnt 2338 (Ont. Div. Ct.).

240 Subsection 210(5) of the R.T.A.

241 R.S.O. 1990, c. J.1.

reviewing court then looks at the record of proceedings to determine whether there has been an error of law on the face of the record.[242]

Unlike an appeal, an application for judicial review does not operate as an automatic stay.[243]

The Supreme Court of Canada has held that courts should not intervene on an application for judicial review where the applicant has not availed himself or herself of internal rights of appeal.[244] Thus, where the person applying for judicial review of a Board decision does not attempt to utilize the Board's internal review process (under Rule 29) and fails to exercise their statutory right of appeal on a question of law pursuant to s. 210 of the R.T.A., the application for judicial review may be dismissed.[245]

One instance where a party might seek a judicial review is where an interim decision of the Board might, if incorrect, result in a hearing that is so fundamentally flawed that it would be wrong (and a waste of everyone's time and money) to let the matter proceed any further.

In *Metropolitan Toronto Housing Authority v. Godwin,*[246] the Member was faced with the prospect of hearing evidence from 312 tenants in this multi-tenant application. In an interim order, she indicated her intention to hear "representative" evidence from eleven of the tenants rather than hearing from each and every tenant named as a party to the application. The landlord brought a judicial review application to challenge this procedural order on the basis that the interim order prevented the landlord from hearing the evidence of all of the applicants and denied the landlord the chance to cross-examine them. The Divisional Court granted the landlord's request for judicial review and quashed the Tribunal's interim order. The Court of Appeal subsequently overturned the order of the Divisional Court and restored the interim decision of the Tribunal. The Court of Appeal noted that the purpose of the *Tenant Protection Act, 1997* is to encourage speedy, fair and efficient access to justice in residential tenancy matters, that the Act is tenant-centred and that a liberal approach should govern the interpretation of the T.P.A. It held that the Tribunal did have the jurisdiction to control its process and to make the challenged order.

In *Santokie v. Toronto Housing Co. Inc.*,[247] the case involved an allegation of wrongdoing on the part of the tenant's minor child. The Tribunal adjourned

---

242 *Sedlezky v. Jeffrey* (2005), 2005 CarswellOnt 1566 (Ont. Div. Ct.) (re SWT-06014).

243 Subsection 25(2) of the *Statutory Powers Procedure Act.*

244 *Harelkin v. University of Regina*, [1979] 2 S.C.R. 561 (S.C.C.).

245 *Sedlezky v. Jeffrey* (2005), 2005 CarswellOnt 1566 (Ont. Div. Ct.) (re SWT-06014).

246 (2002), 2002 CarswellOnt 2051, 161 O.A.C. 57 (Ont. C.A.), overturning the decision of the Div. Ct., reported at (2000), 2000 CarswellOnt 3223 (re interim order TST-01206 issued March 10, 2000).

247 (2000), (*sub nom. Santokie v. Ontario Rental Housing Tribunal*) 141 O.A.C. 118, 2000 CarswellOnt 4992 (Ont. Div. Ct.), affirmed (2002), 2002 CarswellOnt 596, 156 O.A.C. 128 (Ont. C.A.) (re TNL-17684).

the case to be heard on a later date. In the interim, tenant's counsel sought a judicial review, arguing that it offended the *Young Offenders Act* (now the *Youth Criminal Justice Act*, S.C. 2002, c. 1) for the Tribunal to proceed with the hearing because the identity of the tenant's child might become known. The Divisional Court was prepared to hear this matter by way of judicial review. Ultimately, the Court ruled that the Tribunal may hear such cases.

The current judicial attitude seems to support an administrative tribunal's inherent right to control its process and to be somewhat creative in issuing orders that assist the tribunal in hearing its cases efficiently and in preventing abuses of its process.[248]

Courts are also extremely reluctant to interfere with an interim or interlocutory order of an administrative tribunal. The Ontario Court of Appeal has stated that,

> it is trite law that the court will only interfere with a preliminary ruling made by an administrative tribunal where the tribunal never had jurisdiction or has irretrievably lost it.[249]

So the court will usually intervene only if a tribunal has exceeded its jurisdiction or if there has been a denial of natural justice or there is likely to be a fundamental failing of justice if the tribunal matter is allowed to proceed.[250]

In *Hennick v. Toronto Community Housing Corp.*,[251] the tenant refused the landlord access to her unit to upgrade the fire alarm system on the basis that in 1996, the parties had agreed to a consent order in which the landlord agreed not to enter the unit during her tenancy in order to upgrade the heating system. The landlord brought an application to evict the tenant alleging that the tenant's conduct substantially interfered with the lawful rights of the landlord. As a preliminary matter, the tenant argued that the landlord was *estopped* from seeking to gain entry to her unit because of the terms of the 1996 order (i.e., she relied on the principle of *issue estoppel*). The Tribunal ruled that the issues currently before it were not identical to those raised in the earlier court proceeding and that the landlord was not precluded from bringing this application. The tenant then brought an application for judicial review of this preliminary ruling by the Tribunal. The Divisional Court ruled that this matter was within the jurisdiction of the Tribunal and that there was

---

248 *Volfson v. Royal & SunAlliance Insurance Co. of Canada* (2005), 2005 CarswellOnt 5232, [2005] O.J. No. 4523 (Ont. Div. Ct.), additional reasons at (2006), 2006 CarswellOnt 244 (Ont. Div. Ct.).

249 *Howe v. Institute of Chartered Accountants (Ontario)* (1994), 19 O.R. (3d) 483 (Ont. C.A.), leave to appeal refused (1995), 21 O.R. (3d) xvi (note) (S.C.C.).

250 *Gage v. Ontario* (Attorney General) (1992), 90 D.L.R. (4th) 537 (Ont. Div. Ct.) and *Sears Canada Inc. v. Ontario (Regional Coroner, Southwest Region)* (1997), (sub nom. *Sears Canada Inc. v. Southwest Region Regional Coroner*) 102 O.A.C. 60 (Ont. Div. Ct.).

251 (2006), 2006 CarswellOnt 6875 (Ont. Div. Ct.) (October 19, 2006), Doc. Toronto 37/06 (Ont. Div. Ct.) (unreported) re TSL-74879.

no concern here of a denial of natural justice. Furthermore, the Court pointed out that, should the Tribunal err in its interpretation of the law, the tenant still retained a statutory right of appeal. In these circumstances, the Court was not prepared (on a judicial review application) to interfere with the Tribunal's preliminary ruling.

17

Enforcing an Eviction Order

1. WHAT IS ENFORCEMENT?

An eviction order is an order that permits the landlord to take back possession of the rental unit. If the tenant will not obey the order (will not leave voluntarily), the landlord may have no alternative but to force the tenant out. This can lead to ugly and potentially violent confrontations between landlords and tenants. In order to reduce the chance of things getting out of hand, the law requires the landlord to use the Court Enforcement Office (Sheriff) to enforce all eviction orders. An eviction order from the Board has the same effect and shall be enforced in the same manner as a writ of possession issued by a court.[1] Enforcement of an eviction order, therefore, involves filing the order with the Court Enforcement Office and then following the prescribed procedures for having the Sheriff attend at the rental unit to assist the landlord in taking possession of the unit. The details of that process will be described later in this chapter.

2. WHEN CAN AN EVICTION ORDER BE ENFORCED?

An eviction can be enforced when the order says it can be filed with the Court Enforcement Office. That is the date that the order for eviction is "effective".

Pursuant to s. 80(1) of the *Residential Tenancies Act, 2006* (R.T.A.), if the eviction order is based upon a notice of termination, the order of the Board evicting the tenant may not be effective earlier than the date of termination set out in the notice of termination. There are, however, two exceptions to this general rule. Pursuant to s. 80(2) of the R.T.A., the Board has the power to make the eviction order effective on a date *earlier* than the termination date set out in the notice of termination if:

[1] Section 85 of the *Residential Tenancies Act, 2006*.

1. the order is made on an application based upon a notice of termination under clause 63(1)(a)[2] and the Board determines that the damage caused was significantly greater than the damage that was required by that clause in order to give the notice of termination; or
2. the order is made on an application based on a notice of termination under clause 63(1)(b)[3] or subsection 66(1).[4]

Under the *Tenant Protection Act, 1997* (T.P.A.), the Members of the Rental Housing Tribunal developed the practice of making eviction orders effective on the 11th day after the orders were issued. Although this was a statutory requirement for default orders, there was no such requirement for orders issused following a hearing. Nevertheless, unless safety was a factor, Members would typically not make the eviction effective until some date in the future.

An eviction order cannot be filed for enforcement prior to the date indicated in the order. There is also a deadline for filing such an order. An eviction order must be filed with the Sheriff who has territorial jurisdiction where the rental unit is located within six months of the date it becomes effective or it automatically expires (s. 81 of the R.T.A.).

3. PROCEDURE

The landlord must ascertain which Sheriff has territorial jurisdiction where the rental unit is located. The Board can be of assistance in this regard.

For illustration purposes, I will describe the enforcement process for the City of Toronto. The process may vary in different parts of the province. You should always consult with your local Sheriff's Office to find out how eviction orders are enforced in your area.

Once the eviction order becomes effective, the landlord must attend the Sheriff's Office to file the order for enforcement. It is probably best to file a certified copy (obtainable from the Board) rather than the original order as the landlord may require the original order later for collection purposes. In Toronto, the Sheriff's Office is located on the 19th Floor at 393 University Avenue (416-327-5600). The landlord will be required to pay $315 plus a mileage charge (which varies depending upon the distance from the courthouse to the rental unit). The landlord will also have to complete an eviction information request sheet.

Depending upon how busy the Sheriff's Office is and the time of year, execution of an eviction order in Toronto may take two to three weeks or

[2] Wilfully causing undue damage.

[3] Use that is inconsistent with a residential premises and that has caused or is likely to cause significant damage.

[4] Seriously impairing the safety of others within the residential complex.

longer. The Sheriff's Office will then mail a notice to the tenant. That notice will state that the tenant must vacate the rental unit by noon of a particular date (two to three weeks in the future). The landlord is required to check on that date to see whether or not the tenant has vacated the rental unit. If the tenant has not vacated the rental unit, the landlord must telephone the Sheriff's Office to request that the eviction proceed.

Once the Sheriff receives this call from the landlord, the Sheriff will arrange a date and time to meet the landlord at the rental unit within the next couple of days. The Sheriff's Office will need to know if the tenant is potentially dangerous or if there are any dangerous animals present. If any such danger exists, the Sheriff may arrange to have the police and/or to have Animal Control present. If the landlord is not able to change the lock himself, he may wish to arrange to have a locksmith present so that, once entry has been gained to the unit and the tenant has been evicted, the locks can be changed to ensure that the tenant does not re-enter the unit.

Once the Sheriff's Office sends out the notice to the tenant, the enforcement of the eviction has begun and the $315 filing fee becomes *non-refundable*. If the tenant heeds the Sheriff's notice (and vacates the rental unit) and the Sheriff is not required to actually attend at the rental unit, the Sheriff will only refund the mileage charge (usually about $3 to $18).

Unless otherwise ordered by a Court or the Board, the Sheriff *must* enforce an eviction order. Before the additions of ss. 72(4) through 72(10) of the T.P.A. (now ss. 74(4) through 74(10) of the R.T.A.), there was no clear procedure for a determination of whether or not an eviction order based upon arrears of rent had been voided through payment of the amounts ordered. Sheriffs were sometimes faced with tenants who swore (by way of affidavit) that the correct amounts had been paid and some Sheriffs refused to enforce an eviction order in such circumstances. The Divisional Court has made it clear that Sheriffs do not have any discretion in this regard and must enforce eviction orders.[5]

4. URGENT EVICTIONS

Just as Sheriffs have no discretion about whether or not to enforce an eviction order, they have no discretion about when to enforce an eviction order if *specifically* ordered to enforce the order on a particular date or in priority to all other eviction orders.

In cases where the basis for the termination of the tenancy is involvement in illegal drug activities (under s. 61(1)), undue damage to the rental unit or residential complex (under s. 63), interference with the reasonable enjoyment of the landlord who also lives in the complex and where the unit has three or

---

[5] *Orlando v. Duquette* (2000), 2000 CarswellOnt 2690 (Ont. S.C.J.).

fewer units (under s. 65), or serious impairment of safety (under s. 66), subject to the exercise of the Board's power to delay the eviction,[6] the Board shall include in the eviction order a request that the Sheriff expedite the enforcement of the order. Nevertheless, there will likely still be some delay (a week or so) before the landlord will actually be able to recover possession of the unit.

In very rare cases, such as where the continuation of the tenancy poses *substantial and immediate* risk to the health or safety of the landlord or other tenants in the complex or where there is an imminent risk of substantial damage to the unit or the complex, the Board may wish to order that the tenant be evicted very quickly. In such circumstances, the Board can specify in the order that the eviction is to be enforced by the Sheriff *on a particular date*,[7] without any further notice to the tenant and in priority to all other eviction orders. A landlord should not ask for the inclusion of such terms unless there exist extraordinary circumstances that warrant an immediate eviction.

5. ONE LAST CHANCE TO SAVE THE TENANCY

Under the T.P.A., a tenant who was being evicted **for non-payment of rent** had the opportunity to pay the full amount owing (plus any costs ordered by the Tribunal) up to (but not including) the date the eviction order could be filed with the Sheriff's Office. That right continues to exist under the R.T.A. (see s. 74) but it has been expanded so that, **once per tenancy,** the tenant can save the tenancy by paying all amounts owing plus the Sheriff's fees after the order has been filed with the Sheriff, but prior to the actual enforcement of the eviction order.[8] For more details concerning the relevant provisions, please refer to Chapter 14.

6. WHAT HAPPENS ON THE DAY OF THE EVICTION?

If the eviction order has not been cancelled or stayed by a subsequent order from the Board or from an appellate court, the landlord may proceed with the eviction as scheduled. The landlord arranges to meet the Sheriff at the rental unit. If the tenant has not vacated the rental unit by the time the Sheriff arrives, the landlord and Sheriff will typically knock on the door and hope the tenant co-operates. If not, the Sheriff (with the help of the landlord) will open the door to the rental unit (with force if necessary), the tenant will

---

[6] The Board retains discretion under clause 83(1)(b) of the R.T.A. to delay the eviction and s. 84 specifically states that it is subject to clause 83(1)(b).

[7] As opposed to the usual eviction order which indicates that the eviction can be enforced any time after a particular date.

[8] See ss. 74(11) through (18) of the R.T.A.

be escorted out of the complex and the tenant will be prevented from re-entering the rental unit (usually by changing the locks to the unit).

If any pets are left behind in the unit, it is the landlord's responsibility to deal with them (i.e., to make arrangements to have them properly cared for by Animal Control).

Although the landlord may allow the tenant some time to remove his or her possessions (see the next part of this chapter), there is a risk to the landlord in allowing the tenant access to the unit. An eviction order can only be enforced once. Once the Sheriff has enforced the order and has left, if the landlord allows the tenant back inside the rental unit, the tenant could try to remain in the unit and claim that a new tenancy has been created. In my view, a tenant who tries to take advantage of a landlord's good nature in this way is no more than a trespasser and should be treated as such. Nevertheless, there is the danger that the police will refuse to intervene in a landlord and tenant matter and the landlord's rights under the eviction order would have been exhausted once the Sheriff enforced the order. Even if the landlord were able to obtain a new eviction order, it would likely take several weeks and considerably more time, money and aggravation. The landlord may, therefore, wish to consider moving the tenant's property to a storage facility within or near the residential complex.

7. WHAT HAPPENS TO THE TENANT'S PROPERTY AFTER THE EVICTION?

Where the landlord actually has to enforce an eviction order to regain possession of the rental unit, the landlord may not sell, retain or otherwise dispose of the tenant's property during the 72 hours immediately following the enforcement of the eviction order.[9] During that time period, the landlord must make the evicted tenant's property available to be retrieved at a location close to the rental unit during the prescribed hours within that 72 hours.[10] Pursuant to s. 46 of O. Reg. 516/06, the landlord must make an evicted tenant's property available between the hours of 8 a.m. and 8 p.m. If the tenant has not collected his or her property within the stated 72-hour period, the landlord is then free to sell, retain for the landlord's own use or otherwise dispose of the property left behind by the evicted tenant.

A landlord and a tenant may agree to terms other than those set out in s. 41 with regard to the disposal of the tenant's property.[11] To avoid misunderstandings, it is suggested that any such agreement be in writing.

---

[9] Subsection 41(2) of the R.T.A.

[10] Subsection 41(3) of the R.T.A.

[11] Subsection 41(5) of the R.T.A.

As long as the landlord follows these rules, the landlord will not be liable to any person for selling, retaining, or otherwise disposing of the property in accordance with s. 41 of the R.T.A.[12]

See Chapter 18 for a more detailed discussion of this topic.

8. IS THERE ANY WAY A TENANT CAN LEGALLY REGAIN POSSESSION ONCE AN EVICTION ORDER HAS BEEN ENFORCED?

Normally, **once an eviction order has been enforced**, unless the landlord agrees to allow the tenant to move back into the rental unit, there is no way for a tenant to legally regain possession of the unit. There is one exception to this rule. If the landlord obtained the eviction order through misrepresentation, enforced the order when the landlord knew or ought to have known that the order had been stayed by a subsequent order of the Board or by operation of law or where the eviction would otherwise constitute an abuse of process, the Board retains jurisdiction (under s. 23 of the *Statutory Powers Procedure Act*) to put a tenant back into possession. The Divisional Court has confirmed that the Tribunal (now the Landlord and Tenant Board) has the power to put a tenant back into possession even after the Sheriff has enforced an eviction order.[13] This is an extraordinary remedy which has been used very rarely. Nevertheless, the Board does retain this discretionary power to prevent an abuse of its process.

---

[12] Subsection 41(4) of the R.T.A.

[13] *Metropolitan Toronto Housing Authority v. Ahmed* (2001), 2001 CarswellOnt 1347 (Ont. Div. Ct.) (re TNL-06552); followed in *Commvesco Levinson Viner Group v. Pershaw* (Oct. 11, 2001), EAL-23388-RV and EAT-03169, [2001] O.R.H.T.D. No. 134 (Ont. Rental Housing Trib.).

18

Disposing of Abandoned Property

1. INTRODUCTION

In non-residential tenancies, landlords are often permitted to seize a tenant's property for default in payment of rent or for other breaches of the tenant's obligations. The government felt that such a remedy was generally not appropriate for residential tenancies and, therefore, distress was abolished as a remedy in Part IV of the *Landlord and Tenant Act*. That prohibition was continued under the *Tenant Protection Act* (T.P.A.) and has been carried forward into the *Residential Tenancies Act* (R.T.A.).[1]

However, a few situations allow a landlord to deal with personal property left in a rental unit or residential complex. Where a tenancy has been terminated and the tenant does not retrieve his or her property within 72 hours after the enforcement of an eviction order, the landlord may, pursuant to s. 41 of the R.T.A.,[2] sell, retain or otherwise dispose of the tenant's property. Similarly, a landlord may dispose of property in a rental unit that a tenant has abandoned (pursuant to s. 42 of the R.T.A.[3]) if the landlord first obtains an order from the Board or provides proper notification to the tenant and to the Board. Finally, where the sole tenant of a rental unit has died, the landlord may immediately remove any property that is unsafe or unhygienic and, after 30 days, may sell, retain for the landlord's own use or otherwise dispose of any other property still remaining in the rental unit (s. 92 of the R.T.A.[4]). Each of these topics will be discussed in greater detail below.[5]

---

[1] Section 40 of the R.T.A.

[2] Formerly s. 42 of the T.P.A.

[3] Formerly s. 79 of the T.P.A.

[4] Formerly s. 50 of the T.P.A.

[5] The reader may also wish to refer to the Board's pamphlet entitled, "Disposal of Abandoned Property".

It is important to note that, during the time that a landlord is required to keep the tenant's property available for retrieval, the landlord becomes the bailee of that property. That is, the landlord has a duty to take care of the property and may be liable to the tenant for any damage that results from the landlord's negligence in this regard.[6]

2. UPON DEATH OF TENANT (s. 92)

Upon the death of the sole tenant, the landlord may need to immediately dispose of any of the tenant's property that is within the rental unit (or elsewhere in the residential complex) that is unsafe or unhygienic. Paragraph 92(1)(a) of the R.T.A. permits the landlord to do this. Recall, however, that if the tenant has a spouse who also lives in the unit, that spouse may be deemed to be a tenant even if not listed on the tenancy agreement.[7]

Until the tenancy is terminated by either the passage of time[8] or by agreement,[9] the landlord must preserve any property of the deceased tenant that is in the rental unit or the residential complex (other than property that is unsafe or unhygienic).[10] The landlord must also afford the executor or administrator of the tenant's estate (or, if there is no executor or administrator, a member of the tenant's family) reasonable access to the rental unit and the residential complex for the purpose of removing the tenant's property.

Once the tenancy has been terminated, the landlord may sell, retain for the landlord's own use or otherwise dispose of property of a tenant who has died that is in a rental unit and in the residential complex in which the rental unit is located. In other words, unless the landlord and the tenant's estate have agreed otherwise, the estate has only 30 days in which to remove from the residential complex all of the property of the deceased tenant.

After that 30-day period, the landlord can deal with the tenant's property as the landlord sees fit, subject to two further conditions. First, if the landlord has retained any of the tenant's property for the landlord's own use, the person who speaks on behalf of the estate of the deceased tenant has six months in which to demand the return of this property and, if the demand is made in time, the landlord must comply with that demand and return the

---

[6] See *Mputa v. Wright* (2004), [2004] O.J. No. 6055 (Ont. S.C.J.) and *Cruickshank v. Mobal Khan Enterprises* (2002), [2002] O.J. No. 3355 (Ont. S.C.J.).

[7] See Chapter 3, "Protection of the Spouse of a Tenant".

[8] The tenancy is deemed to be terminated 30 days after the death of the tenant (s. 91(1) of the R.T.A., formerly s. 49(1) of the T.P.A.).

[9] Pursuant to s. 92(5) of the R.T.A. (formerly s. 50(5) of the T.P.A.), a landlord and the executor or administrator of a deceased tenant's estate may agree to terms other than those set out in s. 92 of the R.T.A. with regard to the termination of the tenancy and disposal of the tenant's property.

[10] Paragraph 91(2)(a) of the R.T.A. (formerly para. 49(2)(a) of the T.P.A.).

property to the tenant's estate.[11] Second, the person who speaks on behalf of the estate of the deceased tenant has six months in which to demand what is, in essence, an accounting of the proceeds from the sale of any of the tenant's property by the landlord. The landlord may first apply any such proceeds to cover the landlord's reasonable out of pocket expenses for moving, storing, securing or selling the property. The landlord may then apply any remaining amounts towards any arrears of rent owed by the deceased tenant. Any sale proceeds that exceed the amount necessary to cover the landlord's reasonable expenses and outstanding arrears of rent must be paid by the landlord to the estate.[12]

As long as the landlord follows these rules, the landlord will not be liable to any person for selling, retaining, or otherwise disposing of the property in accordance with s. 92(1) of the R.T.A. (formerly s. 50(1) of the T.P.A.).[13]

Note that ss. 91 and 92 of the R.T.A. do not apply in the case of a tenant in a mobile home where the home was owned by the deceased tenant at the time of his or her death.[14] In such cases, the estate assumes the tenancy agreement after the tenant's death and the tenancy continues until it is terminated in accordance with the R.T.A. (see Chapter 20).

3. WHEN UNIT ABANDONED (s. 42)

Pursuant to para. 39(a) of the R.T.A. (formerly para. 41(a) of the T.P.A.), a landlord can recover possession of a rental unit where the tenant has abandoned the unit. The concept of abandonment was discussed in Chapter 13; it involves a situation in which the tenant voluntarily leaves the rental unit with the express or implied intention to not return. Where there are no arrears of rent, the unit *cannot* be considered to be "abandoned".[15]

The tenant may leave behind some personal property in the rental unit or in the residential complex. Where the tenant leaves behind a lot of personal property, this may be an indication that the tenant still intends to return. In such circumstances, the Board may not be convinced that the unit has, in fact, been abandoned and may decline to issue an order terminating the tenancy (under s. 79 of the R.T.A.). It is not uncommon, however, for a tenant who abandons a rental unit to abandon some personal property as well. The provisions for dealing with such property are contained in s. 42 of the R.T.A. (formerly s. 79 of the T.P.A.).

---

[11] Subsection 92(4) of the R.T.A. (formerly subsection 50(4) of the T.P.A.).

[12] Subsection 92(3) of the R.T.A. (formerly subsection 50(3) of the T.P.A.).

[13] Subsection 92(2) of the R.T.A. (formerly subsection 50(2) of the T.P.A.).

[14] Section 163 of the R.T.A. (formerly section 112 of the T.P.A.).

[15] Subsection 2(3) of the R.T.A. (formerly para. 5 of s. 1, O. Reg. 194/98, made under the T.P.A.).

First, if the tenant has abandoned the rental unit, the landlord may immediately dispose of any unsafe or unhygienic items.

A landlord who wishes to deal with other personal property left behind by a tenant who has abandoned the rental unit must either obtain an order from the Board terminating the tenancy under s. 79 of the R.T.A. or provide notice of the landlord's intention to dispose of the property.[16] Obtaining an order from the Board that terminates the tenancy (under s. 79) is probably the safer course for the landlord who will then have the added protection of an order. Nevertheless, the landlord also has the option of simply giving written notice to the tenant and to the Board of the landlord's intention to dispose of the property.

Once an order under s. 79 has been issued or the landlord has given the proper notice (in accordance with clause 42(1)(b)), the tenant has 30 days in which to notify the landlord that he or she intends to collect the property.[17] During this period, the landlord must co-operate and make the property available to the tenant at a reasonable time and reasonably close to the rental unit.[18] The landlord may not be willing to allow the tenant to enter the rental unit or possibly even the residential complex. This may be for security reasons or out of fear that the tenant may attempt to take back possession of the rental unit. Some landlords, therefore, will move a tenant's goods to a secure, neutral location near, but not at, the residential complex. It is permissible for the landlord to require the tenant to pay the landlord for any outstanding arrears of rent and any reasonable out of pocket expenses incurred by the landlord in moving, storing or securing the tenant's property before allowing the tenant to collect the property.[19]

If 30 days have passed since an order was issued under s. 79 or since the landlord gave the notice referred to in clause 42(1)(b), the landlord may sell, retain for the landlord's own use or otherwise dispose of any items (other than those disposed of immediately because they were unsafe or unhygienic).[20] The tenant, however, has up to six months to seek an accounting of any proceeds received by the landlord from the sale of the tenant's property. The landlord is entitled to apply those proceeds first to cover the landlord's reasonable out of pocket expenses for moving, storing, securing or selling the property and any arrears of rent; if the sale proceeds exceed that sum, upon demand by the tenant, the landlord must pay the excess amount to the tenant.[21]

As long as the landlord follows these rules, the landlord will not be liable to any person for selling, retaining, or otherwise disposing of the property in

---

[16] Subsection 42(1) of the R.T.A. (formerly subsection 79(1) of the T.P.A.).

[17] Subsection 42(4) of the R.T.A. (formerly subsection 79(4) of the T.P.A.).

[18] Subsection 42(5) of the R.T.A. (formerly subsection 79(5) of the T.P.A.).

[19] Subsection 42(6) of the R.T.A. (formerly subsection 79(6) of the T.P.A.).

[20] Subsection 42(3) of the R.T.A. (formerly subsection 79(3) of the T.P.A.).

[21] Subsection 42(7) of the R.T.A. (formerly subsection 79(7) of the T.P.A.).

accordance with s. 42 of the R.T.A.[22] Otherwise, a landlord may be liable to the tenant.[23]

4. MOBILE HOMES AND LAND LEASE HOMES

A tenant's mobile home (or home in a land lease community) may be considered abandoned if the tenant has vacated the unit where:

(i) the tenant gave the landlord a notice to terminate the tenancy or the landlord gave the tenant a notice to terminate the tenancy; or
(ii) the landlord and tenant agreed to terminate the tenancy; or
(iii) the Board has issued an order which terminates the tenancy; or
(iv) the landlord applied to the Board for an order terminating the tenancy because the unit was abandoned (under s. 79) and the Board has issued such an order.[24]

In such circumstances, the landlord must follow the procedures set out in s. 162 of the R.T.A. Please see Chapter 20 for further details.

5. IN ALL OTHER CIRCUMSTANCES (s. 41)

Section 41 of the R.T.A. (formerly s. 42 of the T.P.A.) applies if the premises are vacated as a result of:

(a) a notice of termination,
(b) an agreement between the parties to terminate the tenancy,
(c) the tenant of superintendent's premises voluntarily leaving the unit when his or her employment ends (s. 93(2)), or
(d) an order of the Board terminating the tenancy or evicting the tenant.

With respect to a rental unit that has been vacated as a result of (1) a notice of termination, (2) the landlord and tenant agreeing to terminate the tenancy, or (3) the tenant vacating the superintendent's premises within one week of the termination of the tenancy, the landlord is free to sell, retain for the landlord's own use or otherwise dispose of property in the rental unit or in the residential complex. In other words, the landlord is free to do as the

[22] Subsection 42(8) of the R.T.A. (formerly subsection 79(8) of the T.P.A.).

[23] *Scioscia v. Dawood* (1991), 1991 CarswellOnt 1680 (Ont. Gen. Div.) in which the landlord thought the tenant had abandoned the apartment and re-entered and disposed of the tenant's property; damages were awarded.

[24] Subsection 162(1) of the R.T.A. (formerly subsection 111(1) of the T.P.A.). Note that, pursuant to s. 152(2) of the R.T.A., Part X of the R.T.A. applies equally to tenancies in land lease communities and in mobile home parks.

landlord wishes with goods left behind by a tenant who vacates the rental unit without enforcement of an eviction order.[25]

Where the landlord actually has to enforce an eviction order in order to regain possession of the rental unit, the landlord may not sell, retain or otherwise dispose of the tenant's property before 72 hours have elapsed after the enforcement of the eviction order.[26] This is an increase from the 48 hour-period formerly required under the T.P.A. During that 72-hour period, the landlord must make the evicted tenant's property available between the hours of 8 a.m. and 8 p.m.[27] If the tenant has not collected his or her property within the stated 72-hour period, the landlord is then free to sell, retain for the landlord's own use or to otherwise dispose of the property left behind by the evicted tenant.

A landlord and a tenant may agree to terms other than those set out in s. 41 with regard to the disposal of the tenant's property.[28] To avoid misunderstandings, it is suggested that any such agreement be in writing.

As long as the landlord follows these rules, the landlord will not be liable to any person for selling, retaining, or otherwise disposing of the property in accordance with s. 41 of the R.T.A.[29]

6. REMEDIES AND THE EXPANDED JURISDICTION OF THE LANDLORD AND TENANT BOARD

Obviously, very specific rules describe the circumstances in which a landlord can sell, keep or dispose of property left behind in the rental unit or elsewhere in the residential complex. Failure to follow the strict procedures set out in the R.T.A. leaves the landlord potentially liable to the tenant in civil proceedings and subject to prosecution for an offence under s. 234 of the R.T.A. or even for an offence under the *Criminal Code.* Until such time as the landlord is legally entitled to dispose of the tenant's property, the landlord is a bailee of that property, meaning that the landlord has an obligation to take reasonable care of the property while it is in the landlord's possession.[30] The landlord can be liable for the loss of, or damage to, that property.[31] Correctly following the procedures set out in the R.T.A. will help protect a landlord from such liability.

---

[25] Subsection 41(1) of the R.T.A. See, for example, Landlord and Tenant Board File No. TET-01828 (Feb. 19, 2009).

[26] Subsection 41(2) of the R.T.A.

[27] Subsection 41(3) of the R.T.A. and s. 46 of O. Reg. 516/06.

[28] Subsection 41(5) of the R.T.A.

[29] Subsection 41(4) of the R.T.A.

[30] *Cruickshank v. Mobal Khan Enterprises* (2002), 2002 CarswellOnt 2811 (Ont. S.C.J.).

[31] *Gottlieb v. Duo Group Investments Inc.* (1989), 1989 CarswellOnt 3042 (Ont. Prov. Ct.) and *Macfarlane v. Pop* (December 16, 1983), Salhany J. (Ont. Co. Ct.) in which it was held that

In *Martin v. Voyer*,[32] the tenant had been evicted but had left property in a leased storage locker. The landlord retained the goods. The tenant sued and succeeded.

In *Clatney v. Genova*,[33] the tenant was arrested and taken into custody. He gave his key to his girlfriend. She removed some of her belongings and moved out. The landlord demanded she hand over the key, which she did. The landlord treated the unit as abandoned (despite the tenant's belongings still being there and his being removed against his will), changed the lock to the unit and disposed of the tenant's property. About one year later, the tenant commenced an application for illegal entry, etc. The Divisional Court ruled that the landlord could not in these circumstances treat the unit as abandoned and that the landlord ought to have obtained an order from the Tribunal if the landlord wished to regain possession of the unit. Since the landlord had not obtained an order from the Tribunal and had not provided proper notice to the tenant of the landlord's intention to dispose of the property, the landlord was held liable.

One of the more difficult problems that sometimes arises, is a dispute over the conduct of the parties during the 72-hour period following an eviction (s. 41).

Sometimes, the landlord places restrictions on the time of day during which the tenant is permitted to retrieve the property, or fails to allow the tenant the full time period or attempts to exercise some sort of lien on the property (i.e., use it as leverage to get money allegedly owed by the tenant).[34] In *Duke and Visser*,[35] the landlord did not give the tenants the 48 hours required by s. 42(2) of the T.P.A. to remove all of their goods. The Tribunal found that to be interference with the tenant and ordered the landlord to pay an administrative fine of $750 to the Tribunal. Further, the Tribunal ordered the landlord to make available to the tenants their remaining goods.

Sometimes a dispute arises as to when the 48-hour period (now a 72-hour period) actually commences and ends.[36] Sometimes the landlord and tenant agree to a time for the tenant to retrieve the property outside that 48-hour period and then the landlord breaches that agreement.[37]

Landlords, tenants and some Members of the Rental Housing Tribunal *assumed* that the Tribunal had the jurisdiction to intervene and provide some

18 — ABANDONED PROPERTY

---

a landlord who moves abandoned chattels to an unsafe place was a gratuitous bailee and liable for his negligence.

32 (1984), 31 Man. R. (2d) 1 (Man. Co. Ct.).

33 (2005), [2005] O.J. No. 1285, 2005 CarswellOnt 1552 (Ont. Div. Ct.).

34 *Walters et al. v. Visconti* (Dec. 21, 2001), TNT-02194-RV, [2001] O.R.H.T.D. No. 152 (Ont. Rental Housing Trib.).

35 (October 22, 1999), SWT-00872 (Ont. Rental Housing Trib.).

36 *Krall and Snook v. Soroka* (Jan. 5, 2001), SWT-01885 (Ont. Rental Housing Trib.).

37 *Natarelli v. Sheikh* (April 29, 2005), CET-04866, 2005 CarswellOnt 3280 (Ont. Rental Housing Trib.), reversed in part (2007), 2007 CarswellOnt 889 (Ont. Div. Ct.).

sort of remedy if a landlord did not comply with the landlord's statutory obligation to make the tenant's property available. After all, what sense is there in providing a right, without providing a corresponding remedy — a way to enforce that legal right?

According to the Divisional Court, however, the Tribunal did *not* have the jurisdiction to enforce the provisions of s. 42 of the T.P.A. In *Lombard v. Lorini*,[38] the landlord obtained an eviction order from the Tribunal and had the order enforced (i.e., the tenant was evicted). The tenant sought relief from the Tribunal in a number of ways, including commencing an application against the landlord on the basis that, by failing to comply with s. 42(3) of the T.P.A. (i.e., failing to make the tenant's property available for retrieval for 48 hours after the eviction), the landlord had substantially interfered with her reasonable enjoyment of the rental unit for all usual purposes or that this also amounted to harassment, obstruction or interference. On this issue, the Divisional Court dismissed the tenant's appeal for the following reasons (emphasis added):

> As for the events which occur between the landlord and the tenant, after termination of the tenancy, we agree that there is no jurisdiction in the Tribunal to consider such disputes save and except as set out in section 32 of the T.P.A.
>
> Section 32 refers to "a tenant" or "former tenant" in relation to misconduct occurring *during the tenancy* but to which the tenant may not be able to seek redress until after vacating the premises. In each instance, however, the referenced misconduct occurs during the tenancy.
>
> In our view any remedy available to a tenant in circumstances such as these is to bring an action for damages against the landlord and not the Tribunal under section 32.

Members of the Tribunal were bound to follow this decision. Thus, a tenant who felt that the landlord did not comply with the requirements of s. 42 of the T.P.A. had to commence court proceedings as the Tribunal lacked jurisdiction to provide any relief for events that occurred after the enforcement of an eviction order.[39]

This problem has been rectified by the inclusion in s. 41 of the R.T.A. of remedies for a landlord's breach of this provision. If, on an application by a former tenant, the Landlord and Tenant Board determines that a landlord has breached an obligation under subsection 41(2) or (3), the Board may, pursuant to s. 41(6) of the R.T.A., do one or more of the following:

---

[38] (May 17, 2001), 2001 CarswellOnt 5380 (Ont. Div. Ct.), re TEL-06893, TET-00615.

[39] See *St. Kitts v. Murjay Construction Ltd. et al.* (Feb. 27, 2003), TNT-02877 (Ont. Rental Housing Trib.).

1. order that the landlord not breach the obligation again;
2. order that the landlord return to the former tenant property of the former tenant that is in the possession or control of the landlord;
3. order that the landlord pay a specified sum to the former tenant for,
   i. the reasonable costs that the former tenant has incurred or will incur in repairing or, where repairing is not reasonable, replacing property of the former tenant that was damaged, destroyed or disposed of as a result of the landlord's breach, and
   ii. other reasonable out-of-pocket expenses that the former tenant has incurred or will incur as a result of the landlord's breach;
4. order that the landlord pay to the Board an administrative fine not exceeding the greater of $10,000 and the monetary jurisdiction of the Small Claims Court;
5. make any other order that it considers appropriate.

One of the few cases dealing with s. 41 of the R.T.A. is Landlord and Tenant Board File No. EAT-01586 (Jan. 7, 2009). In this case, the parties had previously appeared before the Board and agreed to terminate the tenancy. A consent order was issued. The tenant, however, failed to vacate the unit by the date agreed upon so the landlords filed the consent order and had the Sheriff enforce the eviction. On the date the Sheriff arrived (November 20, 2008), the tenant requested one more day in which to move. The landlords agreed and the Sheriff returned the following day (November 21) and evicted the tenant. The landlords moved the tenant's items into the garage next to the rental home. The tenant, however, did not return to the rental unit within 72 hours to retrieve his personal property. The tenant brought an application under s. 41 of the R.T.A. for a declaration that the landlords had breached their obligations under s. 41 and for compensation for alleged damage to his property. Given that the tenant had stayed for almost a month beyond the date the tenant had agreed to vacate the unit and had failed to retrieve his property in a timely manner, the Member was not terribly sympathetic to the tenant and was not satisfied that the tenant had proven any part of his claim. The tenant's application was dismissed in its entirety.

In a more recent case,[40] despite reasonable efforts on the part of the tenant, he was unable to contact the landlord and gain possession of his personal property during the 72-hour period immediately following his eviction. He then brought an application under s. 41 of the R.T.A. Under the circumstances, the presiding Vice-chair ordered the landlord not to sell, retain or otherwise dispose of the tenant's property and to make it available on a specified date for retrieval by the tenant.

Please refer to Chapter 12 for a description of how a former tenant can go about enforcing his or her rights under s. 41 of the R.T.A.

[40] Landlord and Tenant Board File No. TST-02275 (Feb. 12, 2009).

19

Penal Sanctions[1]

1. INTRODUCTION

(a) General

Relief is available to landlords and tenants, both under the *Residential Tenancies Act, 2006* (R.T.A.) and by way of court action (for breach of contract, negligence, intentional torts, etc.) for breaches of their respective obligations. These obligations may exist under the common law, under the R.T.A. or under the terms of the tenancy agreement. In addition to such remedies, however, breaches of the R.T.A. can also result in prosecution of the offender. Sections 233 through 239 of the R.T.A. (formerly s. 206 of the *Tenant Protection Act* (T.P.A.)) create a number of offences with which a person may be charged and prosecuted under the *Provincial Offences Act*.[2]

The process typically starts when a complaint is made to the Investigation and Enforcement Unit of the Ministry of Municipal Affairs and Housing.[3] The Unit will investigate the complaint. It may determine that there has been no violation of the R.T.A. If a violation of the R.T.A. does appear to have occurred, the investigator may try to convince the offender to cease the conduct in question or take such steps as are necessary to resolve the problem. If, however, such informal requests go unheeded or if the breach is a very

19 — PENAL SANCTIONS

[1] I would like to thank the Investigation and Enforcement Unit of the Ministry of Municipal Affairs and Housing for its continued cooperation and assistance in providing the information necessary to keep this chapter up-to-date. In order to ensure the privacy of the defendants and complainants, the Unit has chosen to withhold the names of all parties involved. I will therefore refer to cases by the date and location of the trial and, where known, the name of the presiding Justice of the Peace. Anyone requiring more information about a particular case should consult directly with the Investigation and Enforcement Unit or with the Court before which the case was heard.

[2] R.S.O. 1990, c. P.33.

[3] The Unit can be contacted by telephone at 416-585-7214 or, outside the Greater Toronto Area, at 1-888-772-9277 (toll free). It is located at 777 Bay Street, 12th Floor, Toronto ON M5G 2E5.

serious one, the Unit may then decide to have charges laid and to proceed with a prosecution.

(b) Purpose

As with all such provisions, the goal of ss. 233 – 239 of the R.T.A. is both punishment and deterrence. The "victim" receives no compensation as a result of a conviction. The offender is punished by having to pay a fine. It is also hoped that such convictions will discourage both this offender (specific deterrence) and others who learn about the conviction (general deterrence) from committing similar offences in the future.

(c) Onus

There is the standard of proof as in criminal cases[4] (i.e., the prosecutor must prove all elements of the offence beyond a reasonable doubt).

Since the standard of proof is lower at the level of the Landlord and Tenant Board,[5] it is possible to have the court, on a prosecution, reach a different conclusion than the Board on the same evidence. In a case heard in Brampton on July 3, 2007, Justice of the Peace Florence found that the prosecution had failed to prove "beyond a reasonable doubt" that the landlord had illegally locked the tenant out of the rental unit despite an earlier finding to the contrary by the Rental Housing Tribunal; the Tribunal's decision, however, was made under a less onerous standard of proof.

If part of the offence (the *mens rea*) requires knowledge, then it must be proven that the accused knew of (or was wilfully blind about) the conduct in question. For instance, there can only be a conviction under ss. 233 and 235 of the R.T.A. (formerly ss. 206(1) and (3) of the T.P.A.) where it has been proven that the landlord "knowingly" engaged in certain conduct.

(d) Types of Offences

The types of conduct that can result in prosecution under the R.T.A. relate primarily to breaches of statutory requirements under the R.T.A. or to contraventions of certain types of orders relating to the maintenance and safety of the residential complex.

---

4 *R. v. Poulin*, [1973] 2 O.R. 875 (Ont. Prov. Ct.).

5 I.e., proof on a balance of probabilities (see "Standard of Proof" in Chapter 16).

(e) Attempts

Pursuant to s. 236 of the R.T.A. (formerly s. 206(4) of the T.P.A.), it is not only an offence if a person actually commits any of the offences referred to in ss. 233, 234 and 235 of the R.T.A. (formerly ss. 206 (1), (2) and (3) of the T.P.A.), but also if a person knowingly *attempts* to commit any of those offences.

In a case heard in Toronto on December 2, 2004, before Justice of the Peace Kowarsky, the landlord was convicted of (amongst other things) knowingly *attempting* to unlawfully recover possession of the rental unit. A total fine of $4,000 was imposed (of which $1,000 related to the attempt to unlawfully recover possession of the unit).

In a case heard in Kingston on July 7, 2005, before Justice of the Peace Hickling, the landlord was convicted of knowingly *attempting* to obtain possession of the rental unit improperly by giving notice to terminate in bad faith. Counsel for the landlord gave written notice of termination to the tenant on the basis that the landlord required the rental unit for himself. This was not true. The tenant refused to move and, ultimately, the landlord withdrew the application it had commenced based upon this notice. The landlord pleaded guilty and was fined $1,500.

In a case heard in St. Catharines on July 10, 2003, before Justice of the Peace Cowan, the defendant pleaded guilty to (amongst other things) attempting to illegally raise the tenant's monthly rent from $300 to $400 (the tenant refused to pay the illegal rent increase so it remained an *attempt*). The Court fined the landlord $800 for attempting to unlawfully increase the rent.

In a case heard in St. Catharines on June 17, 2005, before Justice of the Peace O'Hara, the landlord pleaded guilty to, amongst other things, knowingly attempting to charge rent in an amount greater than permitted. The landlord purported to increase the monthly rent from $550 to $600 without proper notice and in an amount that exceeded the guideline. The Court accepted the joint submission on penalty and imposed a fine of $500 with respect to the attempt to charge an illegal rent increase (a further $2,250 in fines was imposed for interference with the supply of vital services).

In a case heard in Windsor on March 12, 2007, before Justice of the Peace E. Neilson, the landlord served the tenants with an eviction order purportedly issued by the Ontario Rental Housing Tribunal. The tenants contacted the Tribunal and discovered that the order was not genuine. The landlord was charged with and pleaded guilty to one count of knowingly *attempting* to unlawfully recover possession of the rental unit. Her Worship accepted the joint submission with respect to penalty and imposed a fine of $1,000.

(f) Limitation Period

Pursuant to s. 239 of the R.T.A. (formerly s. 206(8) of the T.P.A.), no proceeding shall be commenced respecting an offence under clause 234(v) of the R.T.A. (i.e., furnishing false or misleading information) more than two years after the date on which the facts giving rise to the offence came to the attention of the Minister. It may not become immediately apparent that information a person has furnished[6] is false or misleading. The limitation period for this offence, therefore, does not begin to run until the government actually discovers that the information provided is false or misleading.

For all other offences under the R.T.A., the limitation period is two years from the date on which the offence was, or is alleged to have been, committed (s. 239(2) of the R.T.A.).

(g) Evidence

The usual rules of evidence that apply to a trial under the *Provincial Offences Act* apply to prosecutions under the R.T.A. Section 240 of the R.T.A. (formerly s. 207 of the T.P.A.), however, does contain some special provisions designed to make it easier for prosecutors to adduce documentary evidence and to prove who created or signed such documents.

(h) Penalties and Factors Considered on Sentencing

A person, other than a corporation, convicted of an offence under the R.T.A. is liable to a fine of not more than $25,000 (s. 238(1) of the R.T.A.). This is a substantial increase from the maximum fine provided for individuals under the T.P.A. ($10,000). A corporation is liable on conviction to a fine of not more than $100,000 (s. 238(2) of the R.T.A.). This amount is double the maximum corporate fine that was permitted under the T.P.A. ($50,000). A director or officer of a corporation can be held responsible for the actions of the corporation if he or she knowingly concurred in the offence (s. 237 of the R.T.A., formerly s. 206(5) of the T.P.A.).

In any case where a fine is imposed, the government will automatically add a "victim fine surcharge" to the amount ordered by the court. The money collected under this program is used to maintain and expand services to victims of crime. Where the fine is less than $1,000, the surcharge is a set rate which amounts to approximately 20% of the fine amount. For fines over

---

[6] I.e., furnished in any material filed in any proceeding under the R.T.A. or provided to the Board, an employee or official of the Board, an inspector, an investigator, the Minister or a designate of the Minister.

$1,000, the surcharge is 25% of the actual fine amount. The amounts referred to in the case summaries that follow do not include the victim fine surcharge.

Where a fine is imposed, the Court has discretion to decide how long the convicted person has to pay the fine. Typically, a person is given from one to six months in which to pay the fine. In cases where it can otherwise cause undue financial hardship or the court is inclined to show some leniency, the courts have been known to allow up to one year (or, in rare circumstances, up to two years) for payment of a fine.

Section 238 of the R.T.A. (formerly subsections (6) and (7) of s. 206 of the T.P.A.) establishes the *maximum* fine (per charge) that can be imposed upon conviction. The amount of the fine actually imposed can, therefore, vary significantly. Although the amount of the fine (within the limits imposed by statute) is a matter within the discretion of the presiding judge or justice of the peace, certain factors tend to influence the size of the fine imposed.

Mitigating factors (i.e., factors that tend to reduce the size of the fine) include the following: where the defendant is an individual with limited financial means; where the defendant is an individual who is relatively unsophisticated and unfamiliar with the relevant provisions of the R.T.A.; where the defendant has no prior convictions under the R.T.A. (or its predecessor legislation); where the defendant co-operated with the prosecutor by pleading guilty at the earliest opportunity, thereby avoiding unnecessary delay and the expense of a contested trial; where the defendant shows remorse and is unlikely to re-offend; where the "victim" was partially responsible for the events that led to the offence; and where the Board has already punished the defendant landlord by granting to the tenant an abatement of rent and/or ordering an administrative fine against the landlord.

Aggravating factors (i.e., factors that tend to increase the size of the fine) include the following: where the defendant has substantial financial means and will likely be undeterred unless a substantial fine is imposed; where the defendant is a sophisticated and experienced individual or corporation; where the defendant has previously been convicted of offences under the R.T.A. (or its predecessor legislation); where the defendant pleaded not guilty and insisted on a full trial; where the defendant shows no remorse and is likely to re-offend; where the conduct in question was not an isolated incident but formed part of a pattern of misconduct; where the conduct was particularly egregious or offensive; where the victim was a vulnerable individual; and where the conduct, if not sufficiently punished, would tend to bring the administration of justice into disrepute (such as filing false or misleading documents in order to gain an unwarranted advantage in Tribunal/Board proceedings).

Often, the prosecutor and defendant are able to work out a plea bargain in which, in exchange for the defendant pleading guilty to at least one of the charges, the prosecutor will agree to do one or more of the following: (1) withdraw other charges; (2) withdraw some or all of the charges against a co-accused; and/or (3) agree to make a joint submission with respect to the amount of the fine and/or the amount of time in which the fine must be paid. Since the defendant has agreed to co-operate, the fine recommended by the prosecutor will usually be considerably less than what might otherwise have been imposed upon conviction following a full hearing. Joint submissions with respect to the amount of the fine are *usually* accepted by the judge or justice of the peace. While plea bargaining may have resulted in the more efficient processing of cases and in a greater number of convictions, it may also have resulted in fines that are smaller than one might expect given the very serious nature of some of the charges.

(i) Recent Developments

In reviewing the results of prosecutions over the last few years, I have noted a few trends or developments that bear further examination.

The first noteworthy development is an apparent increase in the number of trials that are being adjourned (or carried over) as there is insufficient time to start (or complete) the hearing on the date originally set for the trial. This problem of delay caused by lack of judicial resources has become systemic in provincial offences courts throughout the province (especially in the larger urban centres). As a result of such delays, there is a risk that we may begin to see more *Charter* challenges. For further discussion of this issue, please refer to the next section of this Chapter, "Trial within a Reasonable Period of Time".

Another development is represented by a case heard in Whitby on August 17, 2007. When Justice of the Peace Solomon discovered that the agent appearing for the accused was not licensed under the *Law Society Act*, he barred the agent from the courtroom as not being competent to represent the defendant (*per* s. 50(3) of the *Provincial Offences Act*), declared a mistrial and ordered a new trial. Given the recent changes to the *Law Society Act* (whereby, as of May 1, 2008, paralegals must now be licensed with the Law Society of Upper Canada), justices of the peace at provincial offences courts may regularly begin to scrutinize whether agents who appear before the court to represent defendants are actually licensed to do so.

Finally, I note, with some concern, that the courts *continue* to impose fines that are too small to have any deterrent effect. Clearly the Legislature was signalling that it expected larger fines to be imposed when, with the enactment of the R.T.A., the maximum fine (per charge) for an individual was increased to $25,000 (compared to $10,000 under the T.P.A.) and the maximum fine (per charge) for a corporation was increased to $100,000 (compared to $50,000 under the T.P.A.). Despite this clear signal, many justices of the peace continue to impose fines for serious offences that are so small that, not only is it unlikely to act as a deterrent, it may even *encourage* parties to resort to self-help measures (rather than following the procedures set out in the R.T.A.) since taking the law into one's own hands is faster, cheaper and there appears to be little risk, even if convicted of an offence under the Act.

(j) Trial Within a Reasonable Period of Time

Section 11(b) of the *Canadian Charter of Rights and Freedoms* provides that an accused person is entitled to a trial within a reasonable period of time. Where this right has been violated, the accused person may bring a motion to have the charge(s) stayed, pursuant to s. 24(1) of the *Charter*.

In deciding whether the delay in bringing an accused to trial has been unreasonable, the court must consider a number of factors: (1) the length of the delay; (2) the explanation for the delay (which includes an analysis of the extent to which the delay is attributable to the conduct of the prosecution and to systemic or institutional problems such as lack of judicial resources); (3) wavier by the accused; and (4) prejudice to the accused.[7]

My review of prosecutions in 2007, 2008 and the first half of 2009 of offences under the R.T.A. (and the T.P.A.) suggests that there has been an increase in the number of trials that are being adjourned (or carried over) due to institutional delays. This problem of delay caused by lack of judicial resources has become systemic in provincial offences courts throughout the province (especially in the larger urban centres). As a result of such delays, there is a risk that we may begin to see more *Charter* challenges. Examples of successful *Charter* challenges follow.

In a case heard in Barrie on November 5, 2007, before Justice of the Peace Wilson, the defendant landlord was charged with two counts of unlawfully recovering possession of a rental unit contrary to s. 206(2)4 of the T.P.A. (now s. 234(w) of the R.T.A.) and two counts of knowingly interfering with a tenant's reasonable enjoyment of the rental unit contrary to s. 206(3) of the T.P.A. (now s. 235(1) of the R.T.A.). The hearing was adjourned numerous times for various reasons (some of which were attributable to the accused but most of which were attributable to the prosecution and/or the court). Although each delay, on its own, would not be considered to be outside the acceptable range, the cumulative "institutional" delay exceeded 24 months. The accused brought a motion to stay the charges as a result of a breach of his constitutional right to trial within a reasonable period of time and the motion was granted.

In a case heard in Peterborough on March 12, 2008, before Justice of the Peace Joni Glover, counsel for the defendant brought a motion to have the charge stayed on the basis that the defendant's right to a speedy trial under the *Charter* had been denied. The Information in this matter was sworn on

19 — PENAL SANCTIONS

[7] *R. v. Askov* (1990), [1990] S.C.J. No. 106 (S.C.C.).

August 14, 2006. The court was closed on the first return date, resulting in a delay of three months. When the matter could eventually be spoken to, a pre-trial date was set three months later. Due to lack of judicial resources and difficulties in coordinating the schedules of the prosecutor and defence counsel, the pre-trial could not proceed as scheduled and did not actually take place until March 2008. The trial could not be set until at least three months later. In total, the systemic delay in this case was 16 months.[8] Although each delay, on its own, would not be considered to be outside the acceptable range, the cumulative effect of the numerous delays had the effect of denying the accused a trial within a reasonable period of time.[9] Her Worship noted that the nature of the matter itself was not intrinsically complicated and the offence itself did not rise above the standard for a regulatory offence – it could not be considered in the category of "serious". Her Worship was satisfied that the defendant had been prejudiced by the delay by having this matter "over his head" and by the fact that the memory of witnesses concerning the facts surrounding the offence was likely to have "dimmed" over time. Consequently, the defendant's motion for a stay of the proceedings was granted.

The rest of this chapter is devoted to an examination of specific offences under the R.T.A., examples of cases in which a person has been convicted under the various provisions being examined (or similar provisions under the T.P.A.) and the amount or range of the fines imposed.

2. ILLEGAL CHANGE OF LOCKS AND UNLAWFUL RECOVERY OF POSSESSION

Pursuant to s. 233(b) of the R.T.A. (formerly para. 206(1)2 of the T.P.A.) it is an offence to knowingly alter or cause to be altered the locking system on any door giving entry to a rental unit or the residential complex in a manner that contravenes s. 24 or 35 of the R.T.A. (formerly s. 23 of the T.P.A.).

Section 24 of the R.T.A. provides that a landlord "shall not alter the locking system on a door giving entry to a rental unit or residential complex or cause the locking system to be altered during the tenant's occupancy of the rental unit without giving the tenant replacement keys."

Section 35 of the R.T.A. provides that a tenant "shall not alter the locking system on a door giving entry to a rental unit or residential complex or cause

[8] This period does not include delays related to the neutral "intake" period or attributable to the accused (or his counsel).

[9] In very general terms, a "reasonable period of time" for simple provincial offences to get to trial is considered to be in the range of 8 to 12 months (not including the "intake" period): *R. v. Meisner* (2003), [2003] O.J. No. 1948 (Ont. S.C.J.) at para. 71, affirmed (2004), 2004 CarswellOnt 3791 (Ont. C.A.); *R. v. Morin* (1992), 1992 CarswellOnt 75 (S.C.C.) at para. 50; *R. v. Jaggernauth* (2004), [2004] O.J. No. 4204 (Ont. S.C.J.) at para. 31; and *R. v. Currie* (2004), [2004] O.J. No. 5893 (O.C.J.) at para. 25.

the locking system to be altered during the tenant's occupancy of the rental unit without the consent of the landlord."

Thus, s. 233(b) of the R.T.A. applies equally to both landlords and tenants. There are few examples, however, of tenants being convicted of this offence.

In a case involving a condominium unit,[10] the tenant changed the lock to the unit door upon being advised that the landlord intended to show the unit to prospective purchasers. Two months later, as a result of a Tribunal order, the landlord was given a key to the unit. The tenant was charged with one count of knowingly altering the locking system on the door to the rental unit without the consent of the landlord (contrary to para. 206(1)2 of the T.P.A.) and one count of knowingly hindering, obstructing or interfering with the landlord in the exercise of securing the landlord's right to enter the rental unit. The tenant was convicted and fined $500 per count for a total penalty of $1,000.

In a case heard in Brampton on November 1, 2005, before Justice of the Peace Farnham, the defendant tenant entered a plea of guilty to knowingly altering or causing to be altered the locking system on the door giving entry to the basement unit without the landlord's permission. The tenant fell into arrears and the landlord obtained a termination order against the tenant in October 2004. The order was stayed as the tenant filed an appeal to Divisional Court. The tenant then stopped paying rent. The tenant had complained about lack of maintenance so the landlord gave notice of his intention to enter the unit on November 22, 2004, to undertake any necessary repairs. When the landlord attended at the property on that date, he discovered that the locks to the unit had been changed. The landlord was never able to obtain a key to the new lock. The Court imposed a fine of $1,500.

In a case heard in Toronto on January 19, 2006, before Justice of the Peace Yamanaka, a tenant was convicted of altering the locking system on the door to the rental unit. The tenant moved into Room 3 on January 1, 2005. In April 2005 the tenant agreed to move to Room 1. The tenant then changed his mind. Instead of moving, he removed the door to Room 3, replaced it with a new door and lock and refused to provide the landlord with a key to the new lock. The tenant was convicted and fined $500.

In a case heard in Toronto on February 9, 2006, before Justice of the Peace, D. Keilty, a tenant was convicted of one count of knowingly altering the locking system on the door to the rental unit. When the door to the unit was damaged, the tenant repaired the door and replaced the lock but failed to provide the landlord with a key. The tenant ignored several requests by the landlord for a key to the new lock. His Worship fined the tenant $250.

Where a tenant altered the lock on the door to the rental unit without the consent of the landlord and then refused to provide the landlord with a key

---

[10] Heard in Toronto on May 14, 2004, before Justice of the Peace Gettlich.

to the altered lock, the tenant was charged with and convicted of an offence under para. 206(1)2 of the T.P.A. and was fined $1,000.[11] In a similar case heard under clause 233(b) of the R.T.A.,[12] the two tenants were convicted and each was fined $2,500 (for a total fine of $5,000).

The vast majority of prosecutions under this paragraph involve a charge against a landlord for altering the locking system as part of an illegal lockout (where the landlord takes back possession of the unit without execution of an eviction order). Often, the charge of altering the locks will be combined with a charge of unlawfully recovering possession (s. 234(w) of the R.T.A., formerly para. 206(2)4 of the T.P.A.).

There was a conviction for the landlord changing the locks in *R. v. Horsford*[13] and of the property manager of the landlord in *R. v. Smith.*[14]

Although locking a tenant out of the rental unit is one of the worst things a landlord can do to a tenant, the fines imposed thus far have been surprisingly light. Typically, the fines have ranged from $500 to $2,000. These relatively small fines tend to reflect the fact that the defendant landlord often co-operates by pleading guilty and that the landlord may have already been punished by the Tribunal.

One somewhat disturbing trend is the apparent willingness of the courts to consider the conduct of the tenant preceding the lockout. An accused landlord will often explain how the tenant was not paying rent or was otherwise causing the landlord difficulties. Some justices of the peace seem to be willing to consider this as a mitigating factor. Personally, I believe that this sends the wrong message to landlords. Such self-help measures must be deterred. Imposing small fines and putting the victim on trial does not further this aim.

The risk is that a small fine may be seen by landlords more as a license than as a penalty. Many landlords would happily pay $500 to get rid of a troublesome tenant. Fortunately, some justices seem to understand this and have been imposing more substantial fines.

The following are some examples of successful prosecutions for knowingly altering the locks and/or unlawfully recovering possession.

In a case heard in Richmond Hill on January 31, 2005, before Justice of the Peace J. Oates, the corporate defendant pleaded guilty to knowingly altering the locks to the door to the rental unit. The tenant moved into the unit in November 2002. She started to experience maintenance problems and on July 2, 2003, she informed the landlord that she would be withholding July's rental payment. The landlord then commenced an application based upon non-payment of rent and was successful in obtaining an eviction order.

---

[11] Heard in Whitby on June 5, 2006, before Justice of the Peace A. Romagnoli.

[12] Heard in St. Catharines on October 9, 2008, before Justice of the Peace Donna J. Cowan.

[13] (1991), 1991 CarswellOnt 3432 (Ont. Prov. Ct.).

[14] (1983), 4 T.L.L.R. 335 (Ont. Prov. Ct.).

The order was filed with the Sheriff's Office. The sheriff posted a notice to vacate the unit by September 2, 2003. On September 1, 2003, when the tenant arrived home she found that the lock had been changed and discovered her belongings had been strewn across the yard. She was not provided with a replacement key. His Worship accepted the joint submission agreed upon between the prosecutor and the agent for the defendant and imposed a fine of $1,200.

In a case heard in Hamilton on February 4, 2005, before Justice of the Peace Stevely, the defendant landlord was convicted of one count of knowingly altering the locks and one count of unlawfully recovering possession of the unit. The tenant, who had fallen into arrears, had been injured and was unable to walk up the stairs to his unit. He was living at a cousin's home until his injuries healed. While he was away from the unit, the landlord changed the locks (and would not provide a replacement key unless the arrears were paid). The Court imposed a fine of $1,000 on the first count (altering locks) and suspended the passing of sentence on the second count (unlawfully taking possession of the unit). Of course, had the landlord waited just one more day, the sheriff would have enforced the eviction order and the landlord could have avoided prosecution!

In a Brampton case,[15] the landlord received six separate notices from the tenants that they intended to vacate the premises (all with different termination dates). While they were away on vacation, the manager of the complex took it upon herself to have the locks on the unit door changed, effectively evicting the tenants from their unit. The landlord pleaded guilty and, based upon a joint submission on penalty, the Court fined the corporate landlord $1,500.

In a case heard in Wawa on November 4, 2003, before Justice of the Peace Forth, the two defendant landlords were each charged with one count of unlawfully recovering possession of the rental unit, one count of knowingly altering the locks and one count of knowingly seizing the property of the tenant without legal process. In January 2003, the tenant held back the rent since he had been without heat. The landlords changed the locks on January 21, 2003, and then about a week later removed the door completely and put the tenant's belongings on the front lawn. Each landlord was fined $500 per count, for a total penalty of $3,000.

In a case heard in Kitchener on March 21, 2005, before Justice of the Peace Bruinwood, the defendant corporate landlord pleaded guilty to unlawfully recovering possession of a rental unit. On July 27, 2004, the tenants gave the landlord a notice to vacate their unit by September 30, 2004. On September 15, 2004, the tenants discovered that new tenants were living in their unit and their possessions that had been in the rental unit had been

---

[15] Heard in Brampton on August 7, 2001, before Justice of the Peace M. Biss.

discarded. The Court accepted the plea agreement and imposed the suggested fine of $2,000 against the landlord.

In a case heard in Toronto on April 20, 2006, before Justice of the Peace Wilson, the tenant returned home to find the door to his unit torn off its hinges and many personal items missing. When he returned the next day to collect the remaining items, he found them thrown around the outside deck. Both the corporate owner of the complex and the individual acting as landlord were charged with one count of knowingly altering or causing to be altered the locking system on the door and one count of knowingly interfering with the tenant's reasonable enjoyment of his rental unit. His Worship imposed a fine against the corporation of $6,000 per count and against the individual of $1,500 per count for a total fine of $15,000.

In a similar case, heard in Toronto on August 24, 2006, before Justice of the Peace Conacher, a vulnerable tenant (who was on a number of medications) who had fallen into arrears returned home to discover that the landlord had removed the door to the rental unit. Despite the intervention of police and the Investigation and Enforcement Unit, the landlord refused to replace the door. The tenant continued to live in the unit for two weeks without a door until the tenant returned home to discover that the doorway had been blocked by a piece of plywood screwed to the doorframe. The tenant managed to unscrew the board and regain access to the unit, but within 48 hours, the landlord had nailed the board back into place. At that point, the tenant finally gave up and did not attempt to regain possession. Both the corporate landlord and the individual in charge were charged with two counts of unlawfully recovering possession of the rental unit and one count of interfering with the tenant's reasonable enjoyment of her rental unit. The individual in charge was only convicted on the charge of interfering with the tenant's reasonable enjoyment and was fined $2,500. The corporate defendant was convicted of all three counts and was fined $5,000 per count. Thus, the court imposed a total fine in this case of $17,500.

In a case heard in Lindsay on October 27, 2006, before Justice of the Peace Jackson, the corporate landlord and its director plead guilty to one count each of knowingly altering the locks to the residential complex without giving the tenant a key, knowingly altering the locks to the rental unit without giving the tenant a key, unlawfully recovering possession of the rental unit and knowingly interfering with the tenant's reasonable enjoyment. The sole director was fined $500 per count and the company was fined $1,000 per count for a total penalty of $6,000.

In a case heard in Toronto on January 19, 2007, before Justice of the Peace Frederick, the defendant landlord plead guilty to one count of knowingly altering or causing to be altered the locking system on the door giving entry to the basement rental unit without giving the tenants a replacement key (contrary to s. 206(1)2 of the T.P.A.) and one count of knowingly seizing property of the tenant without legal process (contrary to s. 206(1)7 of the

T.P.A.). His Worship imposed a fine of $750 per count for a total penalty of $1,500.

In a case heard in Brampton on February 6, 2007, before Justice of the Peace Jackson, the landlord sold the house and advised the tenant that the tenant had to move out immediately so that the new owner could move in. The tenant came home the next day to find that his possessions had been removed and, shortly thereafter, the locks were changed. The landlord was convicted of one count of harassment, one count of knowingly altering the locking system and one count of unlawfully recovering possession of the unit and was fined $1,000 per count, for a total fine of $3,000.

In a case heard in Woodstock on February 7, 2007, before Justice of the Peace McMahon, the corporate landlord changed the locks to the unit and refused to give the tenant keys unless he signed an agreement to permanently remove his pet (dog) from the unit. The landlord plead guilty and, upon a joint submission, was ordered to pay a fine of $1,500.

In a case heard in St. Catherines on April 12, 2007, before Justice of the Peace Froese, the landlord was upset that the tenant had a guest in her unit after 11:00 p.m. The next day, while the tenant was away, the landlord changed the locks and refused to allow the tenant back into the unit. The tenant's father was allowed to retrieve her clothes. The landlord returned the rent that had been paid. The defendant landlord entered a plea of guilty and His Worship accepted a joint submission and imposed a fine of $750.

In a case heard in Toronto on April 19, 2007, before Justice of the Peace Frederick, the landlord was able to get the police to evict the tenant without an order from the Rental Housing Tribunal. On an application by the former tenant, the Rental Housing Tribunal ordered the landlord to refund the rent deposit and interest and pay $3,000 for out-of-pocket and moving expenses. The landlord was also charged with one count of knowingly altering the locking system contrary to s. 206(1)2 of the T.P.A. and a second count of knowingly attempting to recover possession of the rental unit without due process contrary to s. 206(4) of the T.P.A. In exchange for the landlord pleading guilty to the first charge, the second one was withdrawn. By the time of the trial, the landlord had paid all amounts ordered by the Rental Housing Tribunal. On sentencing, the landlord was able to rely upon his compliance with the Tribunal's order and his co-operation in the prosecution (by pleading guilty) as mitigating factors. Her Worship accepted the joint submission with respect to penalty and imposed a fine of $800.

In a case heard in Whitby on July 20, 2007, before Justice of the Peace Johnson, the defendant landlord entered a plea of guilty to one count of unlawfully recovering possession of the room occupied by the tenant, contrary to s. 206(2)4 of the T.P.A. (now s. 234(w) of the R.T.A.). The tenant of this rooming house developed a personal relationship with the landlord but they each maintained their own unit. After approximately two and a half years, the relationship soured and the tenant returned home one day to find her access to her unit blocked and all her possessions gone. The tenant was forced to move. Only after the tenant obtained an order from the Rental Housing Tribunal against the landlord did the landlord give the tenant access to her property. It took another year before the landlord paid the tenant the monetary compensation that had been ordered by the Tribunal ($923). Although the prosecutor sought a higher penalty, His Worship imposed a fine of only $100, giving the defendant six months within which to pay the fine. In sentencing, His Worship noted that the defendant had come forward to plead guilty and that he was convinced that the landlord had "learned his lesson". One can only wonder what lesson the landlord learned from this experience. One might also wonder, were His Worship to return home from court one day to find that someone had illegally entered his home and taken all of his belongings, whether he would still think it sufficient to punish the thieves with a $100 penalty.

Another example of a surprisingly low penalty comes from a case that was heard in Owen Sound on August 8, 2007, before Justice of the Peace R.T. Gray. The landlords wished to end this tenancy. Rather than following the procedures required under the T.P.A., they simply changed the locks and placed the tenant's property at the curb at the end of the driveway (but behind a locked gate). In assessing the amount of the fine, His Worship took into account the following mitigating circumstances:

1. the landlords had to spend thousands of dollars to eliminate a potential health hazard (which, I take it, may have been created by the tenants although this is not entirely clear from the prosecutor's summary);
2. the landlord had already been ordered by the Landlord and Tenant Board to pay an administrative fine of $500 and damages to the tenant in the amount of $2,000 and both amounts had been paid;
3. the property was subsequently destroyed in suspicious circumstances (an arson investigation was ongoing);
4. the landlords owned no other rental properties and indicated that they would not be renting property in the future (and, thus, there was no need for specific deterrence).

In these circumstances, His Worship assessed a fine of $800.

Yet another example of a small fine comes from a case that was heard in Simcoe on October 25, 2007, before Justice of the Peace MacDonald. The tenant had fallen into arrears and was in the process of looking for cheaper accommodations. One day, she returned home to find that the locks had been changed. The landlord not only refused to let her back into the unit, but also refused to return her possessions until all the rent arrears had been paid. Eventually, through mediation at the Landlord and Tenant Board, the tenant did retrieve her belongings. In order to address both specific and general deterrence, a substantial fine was sought by the prosecutor. Counsel for the defendant argued that sentence should be suspended considering that the defendant had shown remorse by entering a plea at an early opportunity and that the defendant had indeed "learned his lesson". Despite the prosecutor's concerns about deterrence and the message that would be sent by a light fine, His Worship imposed a fine of only $800.

In the case cited above, His Worship seems to have been influenced by the argument that even though the landlord obtained an order against the tenant for $2,900 in arrears of rent, it was unlikely that the landlord would be able to collect on that debt. Does this mean that the courts are willing to administer only a "slap on the wrist" to landlords who illegally lock out tenants who owe rent? I certainly hope not since non-payment of rent is the most common type of dispute that arises in residential tenancies and I would prefer to think that provincial offences courts want to encourage compliance with the eviction procedures set out in the R.T.A. rather than encouraging a free-for-all where landlords can adopt the most expedient and cost-effective method of removing delinquent tenants (i.e., through illegal means) without any fear of significant repercussions.

In a case heard in Whitby on October 24, 2007, before Justice of the Peace G. Ryan, the defendant landlord pleaded guilty to one count of unlawfully recovering possession of the rental unit. As a result of an order from the Rental Housing Tribunal, the landlord had already been ordered to compensate the former tenant and pay an administrative fine of $500. His Worship accepted a joint submission with respect to penalty and imposed a fine of $1,200.

In a case heard in Woodstock on March 6, 2008, before Justice of the Peace R. Gaye, the defendant landlord pleaded guilty to one count of an illegal lockout contrary to clause 233(b) of the R.T.A. When the tenant fell into arrears, she agreed to vacate the unit on June 18, 2007. On June 14, 2007, the tenant moved all the large items from the unit. When she returned to the unit on June 16, 2007, to collect the rest of her possessions, she found that the lock had been changed. Prior to sentencing, the landlord made the tenant's possessions available to her. His Worship imposed a fine of $1,000, giving the defendant landlord 12 months within which to pay the fine.

In a case heard in Hamilton on April 8, 2008, before Justice of the Peace Wendy Casey, both the landlord and his paralegal were charged with one count of altering the locks without providing the tenant with a replacement key and one count of unlawfully recovering possession of the unit. The landlord pleaded guilty to both counts. Since the landlord showed remorse, pleaded guilty, was unsophisticated and inexperienced, relied entirely upon his agent to give him sound advice and to follow the procedures required by the R.T.A. and since it was the agent who orchestrated the changing of the locks, the landlord was given a suspended sentence. Unlike the landlord, the other defendant (i.e., the paralegal in question) chose to fight the charge laid against him, and his trial is pending. This case should, however, serve to put legal representatives on notice that they may have to bear personal responsibility should they, in purporting to provide legal services to the landlord, commit an offence under the R.T.A.

In a case heard in Windsor on May 13, 2008, before Justice of the Peace Angela Renaud, the landlord was convicted of one count of changing the locks (without providing the tenant with replacement keys) and one count of unlawfully recovering possession of the rental unit. Following a full trial, Her Worship imposed a fine of $1,500 on the first count and $1,000 on the second, for a total penalty of $2,500.

In a case heard in Toronto on June 5, 2008, before Justice of the Peace Mary Anne Ross Hendriks, the landlord pleaded guilty to one count of changing the locks (without providing the tenant with replacement keys), contrary to clause 233(b) of the R.T.A. The tenant returned home one day to find that the landlord had changed the locks. Despite the intervention of the Investigation and Enforcement Unit, the landlord refused to allow the tenant access to the unit or to return to the tenant his possessions. The landlord took the position that the tenant was dangerous and a thief. The Landlord and Tenant Board ordered the landlord to pay $2,425 in compensation to the tenant. Prior to entering a plea, the landlord paid the amount ordered by the Board. Her Worship imposed a fine of $2,000 and gave the defendant 15 days in which to pay the fine.

In a case heard in Brantford on June 17, 2008, before Justice of the Peace Daniele D'Ignazio, the landlord wanted to get rid of the tenant and his girlfriend. First, she cut the supply of electricity to the unit. The tenant and his girlfriend were forced to move into a motel for a couple of days while looking for other, more permanent accommodations. When they returned to the unit to retrieve their possessions, they discovered that the locks had been changed and that many of their possessions had been thrown out onto the street. The tenant had to obtain assistance from the police to forcibly gain access to the unit in order to retrieve the rest of his personal effects. Upon application by the tenant, the Ontario Rental Housing Tribunal ordered an abatement of rent of $350 and restitution of $1,500. On conviction of withholding a vital service and illegally recovering possession of the unit, His Worship imposed a total fine of $5,000 ($2,500 for the lockout and $2,500 for cutting the supply of electricity).

In a case heard in Toronto on April 17, 2009, following an *ex parte* trial before His Worship, Justice of the Peace Mark Conacher, one of two defendant landlords was convicted of knowingly altering or causing to be altered the locking system on the door giving entry to the rental unit without giving the tenant a replacement key, unlawfully recovering possession of a rental unit and entering the rental unit where such entry was not permitted – *Residential Tenancies Act, 2006*. She was fined a total of $6,000. Given the other landlord's minimal involvement in the incident, he was convicted on the first two counts but given a suspended sentence.

In a case heard in Toronto on February 25, 2009, on the return date before His Worship, Justice of the Peace Peter W. Wilson, one of the landlords entered a plea of guilty and was fined $1,000 on count #1 (knowingly altering or causing to be altered the locking system on the door giving entry to the rental unit without giving the tenants a replacement key) and $1500 on count #3 (knowingly seizing property of the tenants without legal process), for a total fine of $2,500. This was in addition to the order from the Landlord and Tenant Board requiring the landlord to pay the tenants restitution of over $7,700 and to pay an administrative fine of $350.

One example of a successful prosecution where the size of the fines may be large enough to actually have the deterrent effect contemplated by the legislature is a case heard in Hamilton (on July 8, August 22 and October 1, 2008) before Justice of the Peace Hugh Brown. In this case, a corporate landlord owned two residential complexes. The director and controlling mind of that corporation used another of his corporations to act as the property manager for these two complexes (he was also the director of this second corporation). This individual personally oversaw the management of these complexes. If a tenant fell into arrears or otherwise displeased this individual, he would cut off the supply of electricity to that tenant's unit. He did this to tenants of several different units. With respect to at least two units, he also illegally changed the locks, seized their property and refused to give keys to the tenants or return their property. On application by a number of tenants to the Landlord and Tenant Board, the tenants were awarded abatements of their rent and the individual landlord was ordered to pay an administrative fine. Nine charges were laid against each of the two corporations and against the individual directing them. Of those nine charges, six proceeded to trial. All three defendants entered a plea of "not guilty" but all were found to be guilty on all six charges. Each corporation was fined $5,000 per count (i.e. each corporation was fined $30,000) and the director was fined $2,500 per count (he was fined $15,000), for a total penalty of $75,000.

3. INTERFERENCE WITH VITAL SERVICES

Pursuant to s. 233(a) of the R.T.A. (formerly para. 206(1)3 of the T.P.A.), it is an offence for anyone to knowingly withhold the reasonable supply of a vital service, care service or food, or deliberately interfere with the supply in contravention of s. 21 of the R.T.A. (formerly s. 25 of the T.P.A.). This was the most commonly prosecuted offence under the T.P.A.[16] and this also appears to be the case under the R.T.A. On conviction, fines under the T.P.A.

---

[16] Over 70 convictions for this offence occurred under the T.P.A.

tended to be in the range of $500 to $2,000 per count[17] for individuals and somewhat larger amounts for corporate defendants. Under the R.T.A., the fines imposed have increased slightly with fines tending to be in the range of $1,000 to $3,000 per count for individuals. Larger penalties have been awarded against corporate defendants[18] and individuals whose conduct has been particularly blameworthy. The fine imposed by the Court may be reduced if the offender has already been ordered to pay a fine by the Board/ Tribunal under s. 31 of the R.T.A. (formerly s. 35 of the T.P.A.).[19]

Under the T.P.A., "vital service" meant "fuel, hydro, gas or hot or cold water".[20] This sometimes created problems for the Enforcement Branch when the landlord was supplying fuel, hydro or gas to the unit but, nevertheless, adequate heat was not being provided to the unit. Consequently, the definition of "vital service" has now been amended to include: hot or cold water, fuel, electricity, gas or *heat*.[21] Heat must now be provided between September 1 and June 15[22] so that the room temperature at 1.5 metres above floor level and one metre from exterior walls in all habitable space and in any area intended for normal use by tenants (including recreation rooms and laundry rooms but excluding locker rooms and garages) is at least 20 degrees Celsius.[23] Where, however, the tenant can control the heat within the unit and is able to maintain a minimum temperature of 20 degrees Celsius, the landlord

---

[17] If there has been more than one interruption to the service or more than one service interrupted, the offender may be charged separately for *each* violation of this paragraph and, on conviction, will be fined separately for each count. Therefore, if both hot water and electricity are cut off on two separate occasions, the person responsible might be charged with four separate counts of this offence. If the Court decides to impose a fine of $500 per count, the total fine would be $2,000. See, for example, the case heard in London on February 20, 2003, before Justice of the Peace E. Stevens in which the defendant was convicted of all five counts with which the defendant had been charged and was fined $500 per count (a total fine of $2,500). In a case heard in Hamilton on February 20, 2007, before Justice of the Peace Ross, two defendants were convicted of two counts of knowingly withholding or deliberately interfering with the reasonable supply of gas and were each fined $1,000 on each count (for a total penalty of $4,000).

[18] See, for example, the cases heard in Hamilton (July 8, August 22 and October 1, 2008) before Justice of the Peace Hugh Brown and heard in Guelph (October 1, 2008) before Justice of the Peace Michael A. Cuthbertson in which the corporate defendants were fined $5,000 per count.

[19] For instance, in a case heard in Windsor on July 21, 2003, before Justice of the Peace L. Murphy, His Worship imposed only a suspended sentence, likely because the Tribunal had already imposed an administrative fine against the landlord in the amount of $4,000. Similarly, in a case heard in St. Catharines on May 17, 2002, before Justice of the Peace G. Radojcic, the fine recommended by the prosecutor and imposed by the Court was $1,500 as the landlord had already been fined $2,000 by the Tribunal (for the same interruption of services).

[20] Subsection 1(1) of the T.P.A.

[21] Section 2 of the R.T.A.

[22] Subsection 4(1) of O. Reg. 516/06.

[23] Subsection 4(2) of O. Reg. 516/06.

will not have committed any offence if the tenant chooses to keep the unit cooler than that.[24]

Typically, in these cases, the supply of gas, electricity or (less frequently) water is cut off because the landlord has failed to pay the utility bills. This may be due to severe financial hardship on the part of the landlord that has nothing to do with the rental unit. Alternatively, the landlord may state that, since the tenant was not paying his or her rent, there was insufficient money to pay the utility bills. Sometimes the landlord deliberately stops the supply of gas, electricity or water in retaliation against the tenant or in an effort to drive the tenant out of the rental unit (without having to go through the normal eviction procedures).

If the interruption only lasted a short time or was the result of unexpected financial difficulties experienced by the landlord, the Court may show some leniency when deciding the amount of the fine. The time of year may also be taken into account; cutting the supply of heat to the rental unit in the dead of winter is likely to be treated as a more serious matter than interrupting the supply of gas in July or August.[25] A heavier fine is also likely to be imposed if the defendant has previously been convicted of the same offence.

In a case heard in St. Catharines on June 12, 2003, before Justice of the Peace O'Hara, the defendant landlord pleaded guilty to three counts of knowingly withholding or deliberately interfering with the reasonable supply of a vital service (gas), contrary to s. 206(1) para. 3 of the T.P.A. (now s. 233(a) of the R.T.A.). In August of 2002, the utility company disconnected the supply of gas to the small residential complex owned by the landlord due to non-payment of the account. For almost an entire year, the tenants were without gas to heat their water or fuel their stove. The service had still not been restored when this matter came to trial in June 2003. The landlord had been convicted of the same offence in July 2002 and was fined $500. This time, the Court imposed a fine of $1,000 per count for a total penalty of $3,000.

In a case heard in Kitchener on September 21, 2006, before Justice of the Peace Johnson, the landlord was convicted of one count of knowingly withholding or deliberately interfering with the reasonable supply of electricity. The Electrical Safety Authority (ESA) inspected the premises and found conditions that posed serious hazards. It ordered that work be done to rectify the problems. After numerous attempts to get the landlord to comply with the order, the ESA ordered the electricity to be disconnected on April 28, 2005. The tenant remained in the unit (without electricity) until September 2, 2005. The Court imposed a fine of $2,000.

---

[24] Subsection 4(3) of the O. Reg. 516/06.

[25] Bear in mind, however, that lack of natural gas may not only affect heat but, frequently, will also impact on the supply of hot water to the rental unit and an adequate supply of hot water is required throughout the year.

In a case heard in Hamilton on September 21, 2006, before Justice of the Peace Stevely, the defendant landlord entered a plea of guilty to two counts of deliberately interfering with the reasonable supply of gas to the complex. In exchange for pleading guilty, three additional charges against this defendant were withdrawn as well as charges against a second defendant. On or about June 8, 2006, the supply of gas was disconnected by Union Gas because the gas account was in arrears. The interruption in the supply of gas left all of the tenants without the supply of hot water. His worship accepted the joint submission and imposed a fine of $1,500 per count, for a total fine of $3,000.

In a case heard in Belleville on October 18, 2006, before Justice of the Peace Ross, the corporate defendant entered a plea of guilty to one count of knowingly withholding the reasonable supply of a vital service (gas). In exchange, the charge against the registered owner of the property was withdrawn. The company was fined $1,750.

In a case heard in Brantford on March 13, 2007, before Justice of the Peace Boon, the gas supply was disconnected in May 2006 due to arrears on the account. Despite an order from the Rental Housing Tribunal, the supply of gas was still not restored by the time the tenant vacated the unit in January 2007. A corporation and two individuals were charged with one court of knowingly withholding or deliberately interfering with the reasonable supply of gas to the rental unit. All three defendants were convicted and his Worship imposed a fine of $8,000 for the corporate defendant and $2,000 for each individual, for a total penalty of $12,000.

In a case heard in Hamilton on March 20, 2007, before Justice of the Peace Ross, the gas supply was disconnected to the residential complex due to non-payment of the account. The tenants were without gas for approximately two weeks. Charges were laid with respect to five affected units but, since the complainants from two of the units failed to attend the hearing, the prosecution only proceeded with three of the charges against a corporate defendant and an individual defendant. His Worship fined the corporate defendant $10,000 per count and fined the individual defendant $2,000 per count, for a total penalty of $36,000.

In a case heard in Blenheim on June 26, 2007, before Justice of the Peace Nielson, the defendants were convicted of two counts of knowingly withholding gas (the service was disconnected due to non-payment of the account) on two occasions for a total of approximately two-and-a-half months. Her Worship imposed a fine of $4,000 on each count for the defendant corporation and $750 on each count for the individual defendant, for a total penalty of $9,500.

In a case heard in Sault Ste. Marie on February 14, 2008, before Justice of the Peace Nichols, a corporate landlord was charged with ten counts of interfering with the supply of hot water contrary to clause 233(a) of the R.T.A. The gas supply to the complex was disconnected due to non-payment of the account. As a result, tenants in many units were without hot water for about one month. Her Worship was "appalled" that the tenants were unable to wash or clean with hot water during the offence period and imposed a fine of $5,000 per count for a total penalty of $50,000.

In a case heard in Burlington on February 19, 2008, before Justice of the Peace O'Halloran, two individuals were convicted of interfering with the supply of gas. The supply was disconnected due to outstanding arrears and was not reconnected until about five weeks later when the property was sold to new owners. Her Worship imposed a fine of $3,000 against each defendant (the former owners) for a total penalty of $6,000.

In a case heard in Ottawa on December 4, 2008, before Justice of the Peace Richard C.P. Sculthorpe, the tenant had no heat for November 2007, December 2007, January 2008 and February 2008. Eventually, service was restored, but not by the landlord. It was restored when the uncle of the tenant put the gas account into his own name. The landlord was convicted of one count of interfering with the reasonable supply of a vital service and was fined $5,000.

Note that in the preceding six cases, the defendants failed to attend the hearing and the hearing proceeded in their absence (*ex parte*). In such cases, the courts have apparently been much more willing to impose substantial fines. By way of contrast, in a case heard in St. Catharines on December 21, 2007 (under the R.T.A.), before Justice of the Peace Froese, the gas had been disconnected for approximately two-and-a-half months (due to non-payment of the gas account) before the tenant finally gave up and moved out of the rental unit. The defendant landlord appeared in court, pleaded guilty, was fined $1,000 and was given 12 months within which to pay the fine. In other cases where the defendant has attended the trial and entered a guilty plea, the typical fines imposed have generally been in the range of $1,000 to $2,000 per count.[26] Thus, it is clearly a better strategy for defendants to respond to, rather than ignore, these types of proceedings.

Also note that the landlord is not the only one who can be convicted under the R.T.A. Sections 233 and 234 of the R.T.A. make it an offence for "*a person*" to have engaged in the conduct described therein. In the T.P.A., the comparable paragraph used the phrase "*any person*" rather than "*a person*" and it is unclear to me what, if anything, was intended by this change.

[26] Based on the following cases: one heard in Haileybury on April 3, 2008, before Justice of the Peace Theodore A. Hodgins; another heard in Sarnia on May 2, 2008, before Justice of the Peace Donna Phillips; another heard in Toronto on May 16, 2008, before Justice of the Peace Cesar De Moraisôther heard in St.Catharines on June 20, 2008, before Justice of the Peace Straughan; another heard in St. Catharines on June 26, 2008, before Justice of the Peace Shelly; another heard in St. Catharines on September 19, 2008, before Justice of the Peace Moira A. Moses; another heard in Guelph on October 1, 2008, before Justice of the Peace Michael A. Cuthbertson; another heard in Simcoe on October 23, 2008, before Justice of the Peace Catherine G. Woron; and, finally, a case heard in Brockville on November 13, 2008, before Justice of the Peace Jack Chiang.

In a case heard in Hamilton on January 3, 2003, before Justice of the Peace W. Casey, the landlord *and the superintendent* were jointly charged with two counts of knowingly withholding or interfering in the supply of a vital service (gas). Both defendants were convicted on both counts and each was fined $750 per count (for a total fine of $3,000). However, it is clear from the legislators' choice of language that it is not just landlords and their employees or agents who are potentially liable to prosecution under ss. 233 and 234 of the R.T.A. Were that the intention, those sections would have said so explicitly (as is the case in s. 235 of the R.T.A.).

4. INTERFERENCE BY TENANT WITH RIGHTS OF LANDLORD

Pursuant to s. 233(j) of the R.T.A. (formerly para. 206(1)6 of the T.P.A.), it is an offence for a tenant to knowingly harass, hinder, obstruct or interfere with a landlord in the exercise of: (i) securing a right or seeking relief under the R.T.A. or in the court; or (ii) participating in a proceeding under the R.T.A.

In one case, the tenant prevented the landlord from showing the unit to prospective purchasers.[27] The dispute was taken before the Tribunal. Pending a final determination of the issue by the Tribunal, the tenant continued to prevent access to the rental unit. In these circumstances, the tenant pleaded guilty and the prosecutor recommended a suspended sentence. The Court accepted this recommendation.

In another case involving a condominium unit,[28] the tenant changed the lock to the unit door upon being advised that the landlord intended to show the unit to prospective purchasers. It took two months and a Tribunal order before the landlord was able to obtain a key to the unit. The tenant was charged with one count of knowingly altering the locking system on the door to the rental unit without the consent of the landlord and one count of knowingly hindering, obstructing or interfering with the landlord in the exercise of securing the landlord's right to enter the rental unit. The tenant was convicted and fined $500 per count for a total penalty of $1,000.

In a somewhat similar case,[29] the tenants repeatedly refused the landlord to access the rental unit to show it to potential purchasers who had come to view the property, despite having been given adequate notice in advance. This effectively prevented the landlord from selling this house. Eventually the landlord had the tenants evicted for rent arrears exceeding $4,000. His Worship fined one tenant $5,000 and the other $2,500, for a total penalty of $7,500.

---

[27] Heard in Brampton on October 9, 2001, before Justice of the Peace M. Nadkarni.

[28] Heard in Toronto on May 14, 2004, before Justice of the Peace Gettlich.

[29] Heard in Brampton on November 7, 2006, before Justice of the Peace Farnham.

In a case heard in Newmarket on January 8, 2008, before Justice of the Peace K. Walker, it was found that the former tenant had prevented the landlords on four occasions from showing the rental unit to prospective purchasers. The landlords were not able to access the unit until after an eviction order was issued by the Board. The tenant was convicted of one count of knowingly harassing, hindering, obstructing or interfering with the landlord in the exercise of the landlord's right to enter the rental unit and was fined $2,500.

In a similar case,[30] the former tenant had on at least three occasions refused to allow the landlord entry into the rental unit (a single-family home) in order to show it to a potential purchaser and, on another occasion, refused to allow the landlord to enter the unit in order to determine its state of repair. The defendant was convicted of two counts under subclause 233(j)(i) of the R.T.A. and was fined $3,000 per count (a total penalty of $6,000).

Another case in which a tenant refused to permit the landlord to enter the unit in order to conduct an inspection was heard in St. Catharines on October 9, 2008, before Justice of the Peace Donna J. Cowan. On entering a plea of guilty, the defendant was fined $1,000.

Where a tenant repeatedly prevented the landlord from entering the rental unit to perform repairs, despite being provided with adequate notice and being urged by the police to co-operate, the tenant was convicted of knowingly hindering, obstructing or interfering with the landlord in the exercise of securing his right to enter the unit and was fined $3,000.[31] The Court indicated that the fine might well have been greater had damage resulted to the unit because of the tenant's conduct.

In a similar case heard in Richmond Hill on April 20, 2007, before Justice of the Peace Clark, the former tenant was fined $2,000. A tenant was also convicted of an offence under subclause 233(j)(i) of the R.T.A. where he prevented the landlord from entering his unit as part of an effort to eradicate a pest infestation (which required treatment of the entire residential complex).[32]

19 — PENAL SANCTIONS

5. DISTRESS (UNLAWFUL SEIZURE OF GOODS)

Pursuant to s. 233(d) of the R.T.A. (formerly para. 206(1)7 of the T.P.A.), it is an offence to knowingly seize any property of the tenant in contravention of s. 40 of the R.T.A. (formerly s. 31 of the T.P.A.). Section 40 of the R.T.A. states that no landlord shall, without legal process, seize a tenant's property

[30] Heard in Thunder Bay on August 29, 2008, before Justice of the Peace Raymond Zuliani.

[31] Heard in Peterborough on March 20, 2006, before Justice of the Peace Hiscox.

[32] This case was heard in Toronto on February 22, 2008, before Justice of the Peace Ross. Given the tenant's limited financial means, however, only a small penalty was imposed (a total fine of $300).

for default in the payment of rent or for the breach of any other obligation of the tenant (i.e., there is no right of distress in the case of residential tenancies).

I am aware of only two cases of a successful prosecution under para. 206(1)7 of the T.P.A. (and none yet under s. 233(d) of the R.T.A.)

In one case,[33] after an eviction order was enforced, the tenant wanted to retrieve her property from her (former) rental unit and storage unit. The tenant was told she could remove her possessions from the rental unit but not from the storage unit. The police were contacted and tried to convince the landlord to allow the tenant to remove her belongings but he refused. The landlord was charged with an offence under para. 206(1)7 of the T.P.A. He pleaded guilty. On the joint submission of the defendant and the prosecutor, the Court imposed a fine of $750.

In a more recent case,[34] the landlord brought an application to evict the tenant for non-payment of rent. An order was issued by the Tribunal for the payment of the arrears but, because of a defect in the notice of termination, the request for an order terminating the tenancy and evicting the tenant was denied. About 11 days later, when the tenant did not pay the arrears ordered, the landlord removed the tenant's property from the unit and threw it all into the City Dump. The landlord was convicted on one count of knowingly interfering with the tenant's reasonable enjoyment of the rental unit, one count of knowingly harassing the tenant and one count of knowingly seizing property of a tenant without legal process, contrary to s. 206(1)7 of the T.P.A. (and none yet under s. 233(d) of the R.T.A.)

6. FAILURE TO COMPLY WITH SECTIONS 52, 54 and 55

Pursuant to s. 233(f) of the R.T.A. (formerly para. 206(1)10 of the T.P.A.), it is an offence to knowingly recover possession of a rental unit without complying with the requirements of ss. 52, 54 and 55 of the R.T.A. (formerly ss. 55, 57 and 58 of the T.P.A.). These sections require a landlord to compensate a tenant in an amount equal to three months rent or offer the tenant another unit acceptable to the tenant, in certain circumstances, where the landlord purports to terminate the tenancy because the unit is to be demolished or converted to non-residential use (s. 52), is going to be extensively repaired or renovated (s. 54) or is located in a complex that is created as a result of a severance (s. 55).

In a case heard in Toronto on December 15, 2005, before Justice of the Peace Hunt, the defendant corporation was convicted of one count of knowingly recovering possession of a rental unit without complying with the requirements of s. 57 of the T.P.A. (now s. 54 of the R.T.A.). The complainant

---

[33] Heard in Peterborough on September 12, 2005, before Justice of the Peace C. Young.

[34] Heard in Whitby on May 1, 2006, before Jutice of the Peace Solomon.

tenant, aware that he was entitled to three months compensation, withheld his rent. Each time, the landlord served him with a notice of termination for non-payment of rent and the tenant backed down and paid the rent. Then the landlord served on all the tenants of the complex a notice advising that no compensation would be paid because of the "exemption provided by legislation". Under s. 57 of the T.P.A., an exemption is provided where the residential complex contains fewer than five residential units or where the repair or renovation was ordered to be carried out under the authority of the T.P.A. or any other Act. Neither exemption applied in this case. The dispute then came before the Tribunal; the Tribunal found that the landlord did owe three months compensation to the tenants. More than two years later, the landlord had still not paid the compensation ordered by the Tribunal. On sentencing, His Worship noted the need for both specific and general deterrence commenting on the history and deceptiveness of the corporation in its refusal to pay the compensation fairly owing to the tenant. The defendant corporation was fined $20,000.

In a case heard in Cambridge on January 19, 2007, before Justice of the Peace M. Cuthbertson, the defendant corporate landlord and the president/director both entered a plea of guilty to two counts of knowingly recovering possession of a rental unit without complying with s. 57 of the T.P.A. The tenants of this retirement home were given notice that they had to vacate their units so that the building could undertake extensive renovations. Contrary to the Act, the tenants who chose not to move into another of the landlord's complexes were not paid the required compensation equal to three months of rent. His Worship fined the corporation $5,000 per count and the principal $500 per count for a total penalty of $11,000.

In a case heard in Goderich on December 6, 2007, before Justice of the Peace Campbell, the defendant corporation entered a plea of guilty to six counts of knowingly recovering possession of a rental unit without complying with s. 52 of the R.T.A. (contrary to s. 233(f) of the *Act*). This complex was a care home facility with approximately 21 rooms. The landlord advised the tenants that the facility was closing down and that they would have to vacate. The landlord did not provide the required 120 days' notice nor were the tenants offered alternate accommodation or any form of compensation as required by s. 52 of the R.T.A. His Worship accepted the joint submission on sentencing and imposed a fine of $5,000 per count, for a total penalty of $30,000.

7. FURNISHING FALSE OR MISLEADING INFORMATION

Pursuant to s. 234(v) of the R.T.A. (formerly para. 206(2)1 of the T.P.A.), it is an offence for anyone to furnish false or misleading information in any material in any proceeding under the R.T.A. (formerly the T.P.A.) or in any material provided to the Board (formerly the Tribunal), an employee or official of the Board, an inspector, an investigator, the Minister or a designate of the Minister. This was the second most commonly prosecuted offence under the T.P.A.[35] but the number of prosecutions for this offence appears to have declined a bit under the R.T.A. Prosecutions under this paragraph have attracted some of the larger fines. On conviction, fines have ranged from a low of $250 per count to as much as $10,000, with typical penalties being in the range of $2,000 to $6,000 per charge. Clearly the courts consider this to be a very serious offence.

Any person can be charged with this offence. It can be a landlord, an employee of the landlord, a tenant, someone acting on behalf of a landlord or tenant, a witness or someone with no connection to the landlord or the tenant.

With respect to this type of offence, there have only been a handful of convictions of landlords and persons acting on behalf of landlords.

In a case heard in Toronto on January 9, 2002, before Justice of the Peace G. Lau, the former property manager of a landlord pleaded guilty to three counts of furnishing false or misleading information in the supporting documentation filed in the landlord's application to increase rents above the guideline (under s. 138 of the T.P.A.). He manufactured or "doctored" invoices to justify an above-guideline rent increase based upon capital expenditures that the landlord had never actually incurred (or had not incurred in the amounts claimed or in respect of the residential complex in question). The defendant was fined a total of $8,500.

In another case,[36] the defendant superintendent entered a plea of guilty to two counts of furnishing false and misleading information in material filed in a proceeding before the Rental Housing Tribunal. The superintendent had taken cash rental payments from two tenants and diverted the money to his own use. He intended to replace the money before the landlord evicted the tenants for non-payment of rent. He therefore filed Disputes on behalf of the tenants in order to "buy more time" in which to replace the funds. He made it appear that the tenants themselves had filed these disputes. The Court imposed a penalty of $1,000 per count for a total fine of $2,000.

In a case heard in Peterborough on June 19, 2003, the defendant landlord was found guilty of filing documents with the Tribunal as part of an application to terminate a tenancy in which it was alleged that the tenant had failed to pay their rent for two months and that the tenant had not provided the landlord with a rent deposit. Both statements were false. The Court com-

---

[35] Over 55 convictions for this offence occurred under the T.P.A.

[36] Heard originally in Ottawa on November 28, 2002, before Justice of the Peace R. Sculthorpe but adjourned for sentencing to May 22, 2003, at which time Justice of the Peace Rozon allowed the defendant to be arraigned again, accepted his plea of guilty and then took submissions on sentencing.

mented that this was a blatant attempt to mislead the Tribunal and fined the landlord the amount that he had claimed was owed in his application ($3,000).

In a case heard in Orillia on March 28, 2006, the defendant landlord was found guilty of, amongst other things, furnishing false or misleading information to the Tribunal. In support of the landlord's *ex parte* application to the Tribunal to terminate a tenancy, the landlord filed a notice, allegedly signed by the tenant, stating that she was vacating the unit. The Tribunal relied upon this notice and granted the landlord's eviction application. The tenant later denied having signed the notice in question and a forensic document examiner confirmed that the signature was not that of the tenant. The landlord entered a plea of guilty and the Court imposed a fine of $2,000 based upon the falsification of the notice (and a further fine of $500 related to the withholding of electricity).

In a case heard in London on September 5, 2006, the defendant landlord was convicted of furnishing false or misleading information in material filed in a proceeding under the T.P.A. The landlord and tenant had agreed that the tenant would be given one month's free rent at the end of the tenancy. The landlord did not disclose this to the Tribunal and wrongly claimed that rent was in arrears for the last rental period. Her Worship, Justice of the Peace Rogers imposed on the landlord a fine of $1,000 on the false information charge (and a further $500 for charging rent in an amount greater than permitted).[37]

In a case heard in Toronto on May 17, 2007, before Justice of the Peace F. Cresswell, the defendant landlord was convicted of four counts of furnishing false or misleading information in material provided to the Ontario Rental Housing Tribunal, one count of receiving an unlawful security deposit and one count of knowingly interfering with the tenant's reasonable enjoyment. When the tenant raised maintenance concerns, the landlord falsified a notice of termination purportedly received from the tenant and obtained an *ex parte* eviction order based upon that notice. That order was set aside and the tenant brought her own application. During that hearing, the landlord filed two other false documents and made a false statement about a third document (a cheque that the landlord alleged he did not cash). His Worship imposed a total penalty of $9,700, of which $9,000 was related to the false documents/statements of the landlord.

In a case heard in Toronto on October 25, 2007, before Justice of the Peace Camposano, the landlord entered a plea of guilty to one count of furnishing false or misleading information in material provided to the Ontario Rental Housing Tribunal. In order to obtain an eviction order, the landlord filed an agreement to terminate the tenancy, purportedly signed by the tenant.

[37] It appears that this decision was appealed by the landlord. The appeal was scheduled to be heard in London on November 15, 2007, before His Honour, Judge G. Pockele. The defendant landlord failed to appear and the appeal was dismissed as abandoned.

In fact, the agreement had not been signed by the tenant. Her Worship accepted the joint submission with respect to the penalty and imposed a fine of $1,000.

Finally, in a case heard in St. Catharines on May 16, 2008, before Justice of the Peace Bruce Phillips, the owner of a residential complex pleaded guilty to one count of altering the locking system without giving the tenant a key (an illegal lockout) and one count of trying to mislead the Rental Housing Tribunal. At a hearing before the Tribunal, the landlord tried to argue that the premises were exempt from the *Act* on the basis that she lived in the complex and shared a kitchen or bathroom with the tenant. When asked to provide proof that she resided in the complex, she produced an old driver's licence showing her residence as being at the complex in question. The landlord, however, was aware that this licence had been replaced by a more recent one that reflected that she had informed the Ministry of Transportation that she had moved to a different address. The landlord was fined $1,500 for her attempt to mislead the Tribunal. Had she not entered a guilty plea, the fine would likely have been substantially higher.

The vast majority of charges laid under para. 206(2)1 of the T.P.A. (now s. 234(v) of the R.T.A.), have been laid against tenants who have filed false documents in order to avoid or delay an imminent eviction. Such documents include forged receipts, altered negotiable instruments and falsified bank records. Tenants have furnished such falsified documents as part of their dispute, during the original hearing or in proceedings in which the tenants were seeking to have the eviction order set aside, cancelled or declared void (or at least to delay the enforcement of the eviction order).[38]

The prosecutor may need to obtain evidence from a forensic document examiner in order to prove that the document has been altered or that a signature has been forged or transferred from another document. Such evidence tends to carry great weight.

In a case heard in St. Catharines on August 17, 2001, before Justice of the Peace C. Straughan, a tenant was convicted of two counts of furnishing false and misleading information. During a hearing in which the landlord was seeking to evict the tenant for non-payment of rent, the tenant filed two receipts allegedly signed by the landlord. The landlord denied signing these receipts or receiving the money in question. Based upon the expert evidence of a forensic document examiner from The Centre for Forensic Sciences, the Court was satisfied that the receipts had not, in fact, been signed by the landlord and that the tenant had manufactured these documents. The defen-

---

[38] A tenant may bring an *ex parte* motion to have an eviction order declared void as a result of the tenant paying all amounts ordered therein by the stated deadline. A tenant can also request a review of the eviction order filed on the basis that the original order contains serious errors of fact and may request that the eviction be stayed pending the hearing of the review.

dant was convicted on both counts and was fined $2,000 on each count (for a total fine of $4,000).

In a similar case heard in Brampton on August 5, 2003, before Justice of the Peace S. Spadafora, the two defendant tenants were each fined $2,500 for falsifying a receipt allegedly signed by the landlord (the landlord's signature had, in fact, been recreated using a colour ink jet printer). In other cases where tenants have manufactured false evidence of rental payments, Courts have imposed fines of anywhere from a few hundred dollars up to several thousand dollars. Recently, the fines have become quite large.[39]

In a case heard in Toronto on September 1, 2005, before Justice of the Peace Europa, a tenant was found guilty of two counts of filing falsified documents in support of a request for review. His worship imposed a fine of $2,000 per count for a total penalty of $4,000.

In a case heard in Bracebridge on March 2, 2006, before Justice of the Peace Robillard, a tenant was convicted of one count of filing falsified documents in support of a motion to set aside an eviction order. The tenant manufactured receipts to make it appear that the landlord had been paid all the money owing. Ultimately, the Tribunal concluded that the receipts were forgeries. Her Worship imposed a fine of $2,000.

One tenant altered a deposit slip to make it appear that the tenant had paid $450 into the Tribunal's trust account rather than the actual figure of $150. Subsequently, the tenant falsified another deposit slip. The tenant was charged and convicted of two counts of furnishing false information to the Tribunal and was fined a total of $4,000.[40]

Although fines for this type of offence in the range of $1,000 to $2,000 (per count) are quite common,[41] it is not unusual to see much higher penalties being imposed.

In a case heard in Whitby on November 21, 2005, before Justice of the Peace McIlwain, the tenant was convicted of one count of furnishing false or misleading information in material filed in a proceeding. In an affidavit filed in support of the tenant's motion to void an eviction order for arrears of rent, the tenant swore payment was made to the landlord by cheque on August 7, 2004. She submitted a copy of the duplicate cheque as proof of payment. This was not actually the cheque that had been given to the landlord in August.

---

[39] Although, exceptions have been made where the accused has no ability to pay a substantial fine. See the case heard in Brampton on December 6, 2005, before Justice of the Peace Fallon in which the defendant was only fined $700 because the tenant pleaded guilty and because of her limited ability to pay a fine.

[40] Heard in Ottawa on July 14, 2006, before Justice of the Peace K. Miller.

[41] For more recent examples, see the following cases: January 23, 2007, in Barrie, before Justice of the Peace Pussari; February 8, 2007, in Toronto, before Justice of the Peace Camposano; March 28, 2007, in Toronto, before Justice of the Peace Keilty; May 1, 2007, in Brampton, before Justice of the Peace Fallon; June 21, 2007, in Toronto, before Justice of the Peace Bubba.

The cheque that was given in August was returned by the bank as the account had been frozen and there were insufficient funds in the account to cover the cheque. His Worship imposed the maximum penalty of $10,000.

In another case of a falsified receipt heard in Whitby on November 28, 2005, His Worship, Justice of the Peace Norton imposed a fine of $5,000. A few days later in a similar case heard in Toronto,[42] the Court imposed a fine of $6,000.

Another case worth noting is one heard in Toronto on September 21, 2006, before Justice of the Peace V.N. Bubba. The case is interesting because it involved a repeat offender. In March 2005, this tenant pleaded guilty to two counts of filing false information and was fined a total of $3,000. Within less than a year, she was again facing eviction for rental arrears and again falsified financial records (a bank statement and a receipt purportedly signed by the landlord) in order to try to avoid eviction. An expert determined that the bank statement had been created by computer manipulation and that the landlord's signature on the receipt had been traced from an earlier application. For both specific and general deterrence, His Worship imposed a fine of $5,000 on each count, for a total penalty of $10,000. Unbelievably, in a case heard in Toronto on March 22, 2007, before Justice of the Peace Quon, this same defendant was convicted for a third time of filing falsified documents with the Tribunal (one count). This time, she was fined $8,000.

In a case heard in Hamilton on March 2, 2007, before Justice of the Peace L. Ross, in order to avoid eviction, the tenant filed an affidavit stating that the landlord had been paid in full, despite knowing that the two cheques that had been provided to the landlord would be dishonoured by the tenant's bank (for insufficient funds). Her Worship imposed a fine of $7,500.

In a case heard in Barrie on January 22, 2008, before Justice of the Peace Norton, the defendant was convicted of two counts of furnishing false or misleading information to the Landlord and Tenant Board. When facing eviction for arrears of rent, the defendant tenant filed a motion to void an eviction order together with an affidavit is support of that motion. The affidavit contained false information (alleging more had been paid than was the case) and altering a receipt from the landlord to make it appear as if $1,850 had been paid to the landlord whereas the original receipt showed that $850 had been paid. His Worship fined the defendant $3,000 on each count for a total penalty of $6,000.

In another case where a former tenant falsified records of a purported payment in order to try to avoid eviction, she was convicted and fined $4,000.[43] In a similar case heard in Kitchener on July 25, 2008, Justice of the

---

42 Heard December 1, 2005, before Justice of the Peace Ralph.

43 Heard in Hamilton on April 4, 2008, before Justice of the Peace Don M. Stevely. Note that this same tenant had been convicted of a similar offence only two years earlier and had been fined $7,500 in that earlier case. This begs the question as to whether these prosecutions are

Peace Gordon Chaput fined each of the two defendants $3,000. Similarly, where a former tenant falsified rent receipts, she was convicted and fined $3,500.[44]

It is, therefore, clear that the Courts take such matters very seriously, imposing fines for even one count of this offence that are beginning to approach the maximum end of the permitted range. While I think it is appropriate that the Courts severely punish those who seek to subvert the administrative justice system by deliberately filing false and misleading documents, I cannot help but wonder what message it sends when the Courts impose the maximum permitted penalty for misleading the Tribunal/Board but only a relatively small fine for locking a tenant out of their home or forcing them out by cutting off the supply of heat, electricity or water.

8. ILLEGAL ENTRY

Pursuant to s. 234(a) of the R.T.A. (formerly para. 206(2)2 of the T.P.A.), it is an offence to enter a rental unit where such entry is not permitted by s. 26, 27 or 142 of the R.T.A. (formerly ss. 20, 21 or 94 of the T.P.A.) or to enter without first complying with the requirements of those sections.

The following are examples of cases in which a landlord was convicted for illegally entering the tenant's unit.

In a case heard in Toronto on June 7, 2002, before Justice of the Peace McNish, the evidence showed that, on a number of occasions, the landlord walked into the tenant's unit unannounced and without prior notice or any legal justification. She claimed she needed to use the telephone or was checking that everything was in order. The landlord was charged under para. 206(2)2 of the T.P.A. and pleaded guilty. On sentencing, the Court accepted the joint submission with respect to penalty and fined the landlord $500.

In a case heard in Sudbury on April 11, 2006, before Justice of the Peace D. Lafleur, the landlord entered a plea of guilty to one count of entering the rental unit without complying with the requirements of s. 20 or 21 of the T.P.A. The tenant discovered that the landlord frequently entered the rental unit without any prior notification. On July 1, 2005, the tenant awakened to find the defendant landlord in her unit and then he refused to leave for 30 minutes. Her Worship accepted the joint submission and imposed a fine of $1,000 for the illegal entry and a further $1,000 for altering the locks without providing a replacement key to the tenant (for a total penalty of $2,000).

In another case,[45] the landlord and tenant got into a heated argument about the payment of utility charges. The police had to be called to the scene.

---

acting as much of a deterrent to this particular individual and makes one wonder why, on a second conviction, the fine was not greater than it had been on a first conviction.

[44] Heard in Hamilton on April 8, 2008, before Justice of the Peace Wendy Casey.

[45] Heard in Toronto on June 22, 2006, before Justice of the Peace Keilty.

During the course of this argument, one of the tenants stated that she would be moving out at the end of January 2005. On January 31, 2005, without any prior notification and without permission, the landlord entered the rental unit to see if the tenant had vacated; the landlord returned and entered the unit again after midnight. The landlord was charged with two counts of illegal entry and two counts of harassment. In exchange for entering a guilty plea to one count of illegal entry, the other three charges were withdrawn and the Prosecutor and the defendant agreed upon a fine of $1,000. His Worship imposed the fine accordingly.

In a case heard in Brampton on December 5, 2006, before Justice of the Peace Frederickson, the defendant landlord pleaded guilty to three counts of entering the basement rental unit where such entry was not permitted. On many occasions when the tenant returned home, he would find the heater and the lights turned off. The tenant set up a video camera and began to capture images of the landlord entering the unit to turn off lights and appliances. The landlord had consulted with the police and fire departments and had been advised to enter the unit and turn off the heater. Due to this and the fact that the landlord was a pensioner with limited financial means, a relatively light fine was imposed.

In a case heard in Whitby on August 13, 2007, before Justice of the Peace Read, the tenant was in the process of moving out over a period of time. He asked his cousins to stay in the unit to keep it secure. The landlord concluded that the tenant was trying to unlawfully transfer possession of the unit to his cousins, entered the unit without consent and without notice, ejected the tenant's cousins and changed the locks. Several charges were laid against the landlord as a result but, in exchange for pleading guilty to illegally entering the unit, the other charges were dropped. The Ontario Rental Housing Tribunal already awarded the tenant $4,000 in compensation and fined the landlord $1,000 and these amounts had been paid by the time of this trial. His Worship took this into account and only imposed a further fine of $1,000.

9. FAILURE TO DO WORK

A landlord who fails to comply with health, safety, housing and maintenance standards may face prosecution at the instance of the government authority responsible for ensuring compliance with the relevant standards.[46] In addition, the Ministry of Municipal Affairs & Housing (Investigation & Enforcement Unit) has authority to commence a provincial prosecution pursuant to s. 234 of the R.T.A.

Pursuant to s. 234(y) of the R.T.A. (formerly subpara. 206(2)3, item i. of the T.P.A.), it is an offence for a person to contravene an order of the

[46] The Fire Marshall, the Electrical Safety Association, the Technical Standards and Safety Association, the municipal or regional Health Department, and so forth.

Board (formerly Tribunal) that orders a landlord to do specified repairs or other work within a specified time. Obviously, this requires orders from the Board/Tribunal to be very *specific* about the work that must be done and the date by which the work must be completed.

Fines imposed for this offence have tended to be in the range of $500 to $1,500 (per count).[47] The relatively small fines may reflect that the required repairs were relatively minor in nature, that the landlord had done most of the work by the time of the trial, or that the Tribunal/Board already granted some relief to the tenants. Although the Court will sometimes take into account the ability of the landlord to pay a substantial fine,[48] the Court must balance this with the need for general deterrence.[49]

Given the length of time it takes to prosecute these matters and the relatively light fines being imposed, deterrence may be better achieved if Board Members adopt the approach I have suggested in Chapter 11 (under the heading "Remedies — Order Landlord to Do Repairs"). This involves the issuance of an interim order requiring that the landlord do specified work by a specified date and then requiring the parties to return before the same Member. When the parties return before the Member at the resumed hearing, the Member will receive evidence as to the work done in the intervening period. While a Member cannot impose a fine under s. 30 of the R.T.A. (formerly s. 34 of the T.P.A.), the Member's final decision as to the type and amount of relief to be awarded to the tenant will certainly be influenced by whether or not the landlord has complied with the Member's earlier (interim) order. In addition, if it is a serious breach, the Member can issue an order prohibiting a rent increase until the work is done. Such orders from the Board may well have a greater deterrent effect on landlords than the risk of prosecution under s. 234 of the R.T.A.

Pursuant to s. 234(t) of the R.T.A. (formerly para. 206(2)17 of the T.P.A.), it is also an offence for a person to fail to comply with any or all of the items contained in a work order issued under s. 225 of the R.T.A. (formerly s. 155 of the T.P.A.). Only five convictions are recorded under this paragraph. Four have resulted in fines of less than $1,000.

---

[47] See, for example the following cases: January 11, 2007, in Toronto, before Justice of the Peace Bubba; January 12, 2007, in Richmond Hill, before Justice of the Peace Oates; July 26, 2007, in Toronto, before Justice of the Peace Stethem; May 27, 2008, before Justice of the Peace Joanna T. Opalinski; October 17, 2008, in St. Catharines, before Justice of the Peace Carollyn A. Straughan; and May 28, 2009, in Peterborough, before Justice of the Peace Michael O'Toole.

[48] As in a case heard in Brantford on September 7, 2004, before Justice of the Peace C. Boon, in which the fine was reduced to $600 in consideration of the landlord's difficult financial circumstances.

[49] As in the case heard in Hamilton on March 1, 2002, before Justice of the Peace Stevely, in which a fine of $1,000 was imposed for the failure to do relatively "minor" work ordered by the Tribunal in an effort to send the message to landlords that they must comply with repair orders issued by the Tribunal.

In a case heard in Perth on July 3, 2007, before Justice of the Peace Doelman, at the complaint of a tenant, a property standards inspector attended at the complex and issued a work order outlining 27 deficiencies and requiring that these deficiencies be rectified by a specified date. A re-inspection after that date found that none of the items contained in the work order had been completed. The landlord pleaded guilty to one count of failing to comply with the work order and was fined $1,500.

Mitigating factors that have been considered by the courts include the following: the fact that the maintenance problems were relatively minor in nature;[50] the fact that the ordered repairs were completed prior to trial (albeit after the deadline imposed in the work order);[51] and, the fact that the landlord pleaded guilty, was not a "commercial" landlord and had no previous record.[52]

10. OFFENCES RELATED TO SECURITY DEPOSITS

Four offences are related to security deposits. It is an offence for a landlord to:

(a) Require or receive a security deposit from a tenant contrary to section 105 of the R.T.A. (i.e., for purposes other than as a rent deposit, in an amount that exceeds the rent for one rental period, or that is demanded at a time other than at the commencement of the tenancy);[53]
(b) Fail to pay to the tenant annual interest on the rent deposit;[54]
(c) Fail to apply the rent deposit towards the rent for the last month of the tenancy;[55] and
(d) Fail to repay an amount received as a rent deposit as required by subsection 107(1) or (2).[56]

With respect to this last offence, there have been a few successful prosecutions. Section 118.1 of the T.P.A. (now s. 107 of the R.T.A.) was added to deal with situations were a prospective tenant provides a deposit to a landlord and then the landlord cannot or will not deliver vacant possession of the unit to the prospective tenant. It may be because the tenant currently in the unit has failed to vacate the unit or because the unit is not ready for occupancy (if it is being constructed, renovated or repaired) or simply because

[50] A case heard in Sturgeon Falls on January 20, 2003, before Justice of the Peace Lecouteur.
[51] A case heard in Penetanguishene on November 22, 2001, before Justice of the Peace G. Maurice.
[52] A case heard in Walkerton on September 4, 2001, before Justice of the Peace R. Gay.
[53] Section 234(d) of the R.T.A. (formerly para. 206(2)10 of the T.P.A.).
[54] Section 234(e) of the R.T.A. (formerly para. 206(2)11 of the T.P.A.).
[55] Section 234(f) of the R.T.A. (formerly para. 206(2)12 of the T.P.A.).
[56] Section 234(g) of the R.T.A. (formerly para. 206(2)12.1 of the T.P.A.).

the landlord has changed his or her mind about allowing the prospective tenant to move in. If the landlord fails to return the tenant's money, in addition to the landlord's potential liability to the tenant in proceedings before the Landlord and Tenant Board or in court, the landlord may also be charged with an offence under s. 234(g) of the R.T.A.

In a case heard in Welland on April 5, 2004, before Justice of the Peace C. Staughan, the defendant landlord pleaded guilty to failing to repay a rent deposit. The tenants had entered into an agreement to rent a single-family home and paid a deposit of $600. At the time the tenants were to move into the home, they were advised that it was not yet available. The tenants demanded the return of their deposit. The money was not returned. The tenants obtained a judgment for this amount from the Small Claims Court. On this prosecution, Her Worship fined the landlord $600.

In a case heard in Brantford on April 6, 2005, before Justice of the Peace P. Welch, the defendant landlord was convicted of failing to repay a rent deposit. On February 12, 2004, the tenants provided a rent deposit of $725 to the landlord. Subsequently, the landlord informed the tenant that the landlord had decided not to rent to the tenant and would not be providing a refund of her deposit. His Worship imposed a fine of $1,000.

In a case heard in Toronto on August 11, 2005, before Justice of the Peace Saab, the defendant landlord was convicted of failing to repay a rent deposit contrary to s. 206(2) para. 12.1 of the T.P.A. The tenant provided a total deposit of $1,890. The landlord then informed her that he had decided not to rent to her. Despite his promises to reimburse the deposit, he never did. Her worship imposed a fine of $4,000.

In a case heard in Toronto on June 14, 2007, before Justice of the Peace Avrich-Skapinker, the landlord collected first and last month's rent from a prospective tenant, then refused to let the tenant move in and returned only one-half of the money. The Rental Housing Tribunal ordered that the deposit (i.e., the balance of the funds being held by the landlord) be returned. The landlord failed to comply. The landlord was then charged and convicted of failing to repay the rent deposit and was fined $1,500. In a similar case heard in St. Catharines on September 13, 2007, before Justice of the Peace Legatt, the two landlords were fined $1,500 and $1,000, respectively.

In more recent cases, substantial fines have been awarded against landlords who have failed or refused to return rent deposits.

In a case heard in Cornwall on February 17, 2009, noting the need for both specific and general deterrence, Justice of the Peace Linda Leblanc fined the corporate defendant $7,500 and fined the sole officer and director of the corporation $2,500, for a total penalty of $10,000.

In a case heard in Churchill on February 18, 2009, before Justice of the Peace Tina Molinari, no one appeared on behalf of the defendant corporation and, following a hearing, it was convicted. Noting the need for both specific and general deterrence, Justice of the Peace Molinari imposed a fine of $25,000 upon the corporate defendant.

In a case heard in Brantford on March 24, 2009, the defendant was convicted following an *ex parte* trial before Her Worship, Justice of the Peace Catherine Woron. Her Worship noted the need for both specific and general deterrence and imposed a fine of $3,000.

Most other convictions related to security deposits have been made under para. 206(2)10 of the T.P.A. (now s. 234(d) of the R.T.A.) and, invariably, result from landlords collecting excessive rent deposits or deposits for things other than rent (such as "damage deposits"). Fines for this offence have tended to be in the range of $2,000 to $3,000. The following are a few examples of successful prosecutions under para. 206(2)10 of the T.P.A.

In a case heard in Toronto on March 13, 2001, before Justice of the Peace A. Napier, two defendants were charged with collecting a deposit in an amount that contravened s. 117 of the T.P.A. (now s. 105 of the R.T.A.). The defendants were the landlord and the real estate broker (a corporation) that had acted on behalf of both the landlord and the tenant with respect to the creation of this tenancy. The defendants required and received a security deposit of five months' rent. Judgment was reserved until May 16, 2001. Both defendants were convicted. The relatively unsophisticated landlord was fined $100 but the real estate company was fined $10,000.

In another Toronto case,[57] the defendant's rental agent (on instructions from the property manager) required and received a security deposit of six months' rent in addition to first and last months' rent. The Court imposed a fine of $2,000.

In a case heard in Orangeville on March 10, 2003, before Justice of the Peace Scarlett, the corporate defendant pleaded guilty to this offence. The landlord (through its sole corporate officer and director) required and received from the tenants a security deposit of four months' rent in addition to first and last months' rent. The landlord pleaded guilty and Her Worship accepted the joint submission on penalty and imposed a fine of $2,000.

In a similar case in London, the Court imposed a find of $3,000.[58] The higher fine may reflect the fact that the corporate defendant in this case did not plead guilty and insisted on a full trial. The landlord in this case also tried to argue that it was entitled to an additional four months rent under the provision of the *Human Rights Code* that permits a landlord to obtain a "guarantee for the rent" and which, it was argued, takes priority over any conflicting provisions of the T.P.A. Her Worship found that this pre-paid rent constituted a security deposit and not a guarantee.[59]

---

[57] Heard in Toronto on January 10, 2003, before Justice of the Peace J. Cottrell.

[58] Heard in London on October 15, 2003, before Justice of the Peace M. Ryan-Brode.

[59] A similar argument was rejected by the Tribunal in *2960 Don Mills Rd. Apts. v. Hitchcock* (October 3, 2001), TNL-27583-RV, 2001 CarswellOnt 6310 (Ont. Rental Housing Trib.),

In a case heard in Kingston on June 2, 2005, before Justice of the Peace Hickling, the corporate landlord pleaded guilty to the offence of receiving an excessive rent deposit. In January 2004, the tenant agreed to rent an apartment from this landlord for $785 per month. Shortly before the tenancy was to commence, the landlord informed the tenant that because she was unemployed, she would need to have someone act as her guarantor or she would have to provide a bank draft in the amount of $5,495 to cover the rent for seven months. She did provide the required amount and moved into the unit. Her Worship accepted the joint submission on penalty and imposed a fine of $3,000.

In a case heard in Brampton on September 6, 2005, before Justice of the Peace S. Fallon, the corporate defendant landlord pleaded guilty to one count of requiring or receiving a security deposit contrary to s. 206(2) para. 10 of the T.P.A. Upon entering an agreement to lease one of the landlord's rental units, the tenants (who were recent immigrants to Canada) were told that they were required to pay the full year's rent ($12,378) in advance in order to secure the lease. The tenants were advised that since they had no jobs or a credit rating, the pre-payment would be required. A complaint was filed upon the expiry of the lease. On sentencing, the Court was advised that the landlord was a small family-owned corporation with one residential complex in Toronto and that the corporation no longer requires (or accepts) pre-paid rent. The Court accepted the joint submission on penalty and imposed a fine of $2,500.

In a case heard in Peterborough on March 20, 2006, before Justice of the Peace H.W. Peter Hiscox, the defendant landlord was convicted of collecting a $400 security deposit in addition to the permitted rent deposit. Despite an order from the Tribunal requiring the landlord to refund this security deposit to the tenants, the landlord refused to do so. His Worship fined the landlord $2,400.

In a case heard in London on November 17, 2008, before Justice of the Peace Jacob W. Bruinewood, the landlord had collected a pet/damage deposit in the amount of $2,000. As a result of an order of the Landlord and Tenant Board, the tenants had already been reimbursed the $2,000 in question. The landlord pleaded guilty, was convicted and was fined $750.

Similarly, in a case heard in Sarnia on October 10, 2008, before Justice of the Peace John H. Caroll, the landlord had collected a $20 key deposit and a $100 damage deposit (in addition to first and last months' rent). After the tenant moved out, she requested the return of the key and damage deposits. Initially, her requests were ignored. After the intervention of the Investigation and Enforcement Unit, the funds were returned to her. The landlord pleaded

overturning (July 12, 2001), TNL-27583, (Ont. Rental Housing Trib.), referring to TNT-01688 (Ont. Rental Housing Trib.) For further discussion of this issue, please see Chapter 8.

guilty to one count of requiring a deposit larger than permitted by law and was fined $375.

In a case heard in Burlington on March 27, 2006, before Justice of the Peace Mills, the corporate defendant pleaded guilty to one count of failing to pay annually to the tenant interest on the rent deposit. His Worship accepted the joint submission of the prosecutor and the defendant and imposed a fine of $500. Since this case, a few other landlords have been convicted of failing to pay interest on rent deposits and the fines have typically ranged from $100 to $500 (at least in the cases where the interest has been paid prior to the trial and where the landlord co-operates by pleading guilty).[60]

One of the more significant cases to be decided recently was heard in Newmarket on October 10, 2008, before Justice of the Peace Douglas W. Clark. The owner of a single-family dwelling hired an agent to find a suitable tenant. The agent found a prospective tenant but then discovered that this prospective tenant was unemployed. The owner advised the agent that, if the prospective tenant paid one year's rent in advance, he could rent the property and he would get a reduction in the monthly rent (down from $2,400 to $2,000). The agent instructed the tenant to make the funds payable to his corporation. The tenant paid first and last months' rent and a further, separate payment of $20,000 to the corporation in question. The tenant took possession of the property. Within about six weeks, the tenant was advised that the owner had not been making the mortgage payments and the mortgagee was looking to the tenant to pay monthly rent directly to the bank. Since the tenant had already paid the rent for a year, he refused to pay the bank. The bank made an application to the Landlord and Tenant Board seeking to have the tenant evicted for non-payment of rent. The Board found in the tenant's favour and dismissed the bank's application.

Charges were then laid against the owner, her agent and the corporation in question. The owner failed to appear at the trial. The agent appeared on behalf of himself and the corporation. He argued that the $20,000 was "pre-paid rent" and did not fall within the definition of "security deposit". He also argued that the corporation was not involved with this tenancy – it was merely a "banking convenience". The Court found that pre-paid rent is a form of security deposit and that the corporation was involved in the unlawful transaction. All three defendants were convicted. The corporation was fined $10,000 and both individuals were fined $2,500 (for a total penalty of $15,000).

---

[60] See the following cases: January 23, 2007, in Barrie, before Justice of the Peace Pussari; March 28, 2007, in Richmond Hill, before Justice of the Peace Hartt; May 8, 2007, in Toronto, before Justice of the Peace Quon; and June 25, 2007, in Burlington, before Justice of the Peace B. Quinn.

11. FAILURE TO PROVIDE RECEIPT

Pursuant to s. 234(h) of the R.T.A. (formerly para. 206(2)13 of the T.P.A.), it is an offence to fail to provide a tenant *or former tenant* with a receipt, upon request (as required by s. 109 of the R.T.A., formerly s. 120 of the T.P.A.). Note that the section has been amended to permit a former tenant to demand a receipt for amounts that had been paid to the landlord during the tenancy.

The following are examples of two cases where a landlord was convicted of failing to provide a receipt.

In a case heard in Whitby on November 25, 2002, before Justice of the Peace C. Dube, the relationship between the landlord and the two tenants had become antagonistic and the landlord refused to provide rent receipts to the tenants. Even after the Investigation and Enforcement Unit intervened, the landlord still refused to provide receipts to the tenants. The tenants subsequently moved out, one tenant leaving two months of rent unpaid and leaving the premises in shambles. The landlord pleaded guilty. The Court accepted the joint submission on penalty and imposed a fine of $250.

In a case heard in Burlington on April 18, 2006, before Justice of the Peace P. Bonas, the defendant corporate property manager entered a plea of guilty to one count of failing to provide a rent receipt to a tenant. In exchange for this plea, the charge against both the director of the management company and the corporate owner of the residential complex were withdrawn. The property manager had taken the position that the tenant's cancelled cheques were her receipts and refused to provide receipts, even after intervention by the Investigation and Enforcement Unit. Finally, in court, the property manager provided a receipt to the tenant. His Worship imposed a fine of $2,000.

In a case heard in Kingston on June 28, 2007, before Justice of the Peace Hickling, the defendant corporate landlord and the property manager were convicted of one count of failing to provide a tenant with a receipt. The defendants refused to provide receipts despite numerous requests from the tenant and repeated intervention attempts by the Investigation and Enforcement Unit. The corporation was fined $1,000 and the property manager was fined $500.

In general, where rent receipts are withheld until the intervention of the Investigation and Enforcement Unit but are provided by the time of the trial, the Court has tended to impose fines of $500 or less.[61]

---

[61] See the case heard in St. Thomas on June 29, 2007, before Justice of the Peace Obokata, the case heard in Sarnia on October 10, 2008, before Justice of the Peace John H. Caroll, the case heard in Peterborough on November 24, 2008, before Justice of the Peace Joni E. Glover, and the case heard in St. Catharines on November 27, 2008, before Justice of the Peace Richard E. Bisson.

12. CHARGING ILLEGAL RENT

Pursuant to s. 234(x) of the R.T.A. (formerly para. 206(2)14 of the T.P.A.), charging rent in an amount greater than permitted under the Act is an offence

In a case heard June 14, 2002, in Toronto before Justice of the Peace Europa, the landlord pleaded guilty to, amongst other things, charging a rent in an amount greater than permitted. When the tenant's brother moved into the rental unit, the landlord charged the tenant an extra $175. When the tenant later failed to pay the extra rent, the landlord locked her out of the rental unit. The Court imposed a fine of $200 for the illegal rent increase.

In a case heard in London on September 5, 2006, before Justice of the Peace Rogers, the evidence showed that the landlord had purported to raise the rent by $50 per month, despite the fact that the landlord did not provide any written notice that would permit such a rent increase. The landlord was convicted of charging rent in an amount greater than permitted, contrary to s. 206(2)14 of the T.P.A. and was fined $500.

13. HARASSING OR INTERFERING WITH THE REASONABLE ENJOYMENT OF THE TENANT

Pursuant to s. 235(1) of the R.T.A. (formerly s. 206(3) of the T.P.A.), it is an offence for any landlord or superintendent, agent or employee of the landlord to knowingly harass a tenant or interfere with a tenant's reasonable enjoyment of a rental unit or the residential complex in which it is located. This is, however, not meant to apply to disturbance created by repairs, maintenance and capital improvements unless it is reasonable to believe:

(a) that the date or time when the work is done or the manner in which it is carried out is intended to harass the tenant or interfere with the tenant's reasonable enjoyment; or
(b) that the repairs, maintenance or capital improvements were carried out without reasonable regard for the tenant's right to reasonable enjoyment.[62]

In a case heard in Toronto on May 26, 2003, before Justice of the Peace Chandhoke, this corporate landlord pleaded guilty to one count under s. 206(3) of the T.P.A. Over two years, the landlord had brought eight applications against the tenant, all but one of which were dismissed. The landlord refused to allow the tenant to park his car on the property and did not provide the tenant with a key to the mailbox. The Tribunal had awarded the tenant an

[62] Subsection 235(2) of the R.T.A. (formerly subsection 206(3.1) of the T.P.A.).

abatement of $500. The Court accepted the joint submission on penalty and imposed a fine of $3,500.

In a case heard in Burlington on February 23, 2004, before Justice of the Peace Lina Mills, the defendant landlord pleaded guilty to an offence under s. 206(3) of the T.P.A.. The landlord prevented the tenant from parking in his designated parking space, had the tenant's mail marked "return to sender" and removed the tenant's refrigerator and stove. The tenant moved one month later. Her Worship accepted the joint submission on penalty and imposed a fine of $500.

In a case heard in Toronto on December 2, 2004, before Justice of the Peace Kowarsky, the landlord was found guilty of, amongst other things, knowingly interfering with the tenant's reasonable enjoyment of the residential complex. After a number of incidents between the landlord and tenant, the tenant returned home one day to find that the lock had been changed and the landlord refused to provide a key to the tenant. Often the tenant was forced to wait outside in the cold until the landlord would allow him into his unit. Eventually, the tenant moved out. The Court fined the landlord a total of $4,000, of which $1,000 related to the offence under s. 206(3) of the T.P.A.

In a case heard[63] in Brampton on December 7, 2004, before Justice of the Peace L. Debartol, the landlord was convicted of knowingly interfering with the tenant's reasonable enjoyment of the rental unit. The landlord had removed the door to the tenant's basement unit and then later replaced the door but refused to put a lock on it. About two weeks later, the gas to the unit was disconnected, leaving the tenant and her infant child without heat or hot water. The Court imposed of fine of $500 for the offence under s. 206(3) of the T.P.A. (and a further $2,500 for the interference with the supply of gas to the rental unit).

In a rather bizarre case, a municipal law enforcement officer determined that by adding a rental unit into the house in question, the landlords were in violation of a municipal by-law which designated this property as a single family dwelling. The landlords removed the tenant's bedroom and kitchen so that, by the time the inspector returned, it appeared that the property had been converted back to a single family dwelling. The landlords had told the tenant that, once the inspection had been completed, the kitchen and bedroom would be reinstalled but this did not occur and the tenant vacated the house. The landlords were charged with knowingly interfering with the tenant's reasonable enjoyment of the unit, contrary to s. 206(3) of the T.P.A. The case was heard in Brampton on May 2, 2006, before Justice of the Peace Farnham. The landlords pleaded guilty and the Court accepted the joint submission that an appropriate fine in this case would be $2,000.

---

[63] Re-heard, since this was a new trial ordered by Judge Rosmay on January 9, 2004, after a successful appeal launched by the defendant landlord following the landlord's conviction by Justice of the Peace Lawlor at a trial held in Brampton on February 5, 2002.

Equally strange is the case heard in Hamilton on April 17, 2007, before Justice of the Peace Ross, in which the landlord removed the stove and refrigerator from the unit and refused to return them until the tenant paid the arrears of rent that were owing. The landlord pleaded guilty to one count of knowingly interfering with a tenant's reasonable enjoyment of the rental unit. Her Worship accepted the joint submission with respect to penalty and imposed a fine of $2,500, giving the defendant six months within which to pay the fine.

In a case heard in Toronto,[64] the landlord had brought an application to evict the tenants so that a purchaser could reside in the rental unit. During the hearing before the Landlord and Tenant Board, the landlord became irate and stormed out the hearing room. When the tenants returned home that evening, they found a hole in their living room wall, approximately three feet in diameter. The landlord had clearly caused this damage in his anger and he refused, for over a month, to repair the damage. His Worship convicted the landlord of knowingly interfering with the tenants' reasonable enjoyment and, upon the landlord pleading guilty, imposed a fine of $1,000.

14. FAILING TO MAKE AN EVICTED TENANT'S PROPERTY AVAILABLE FOR RETRIEVAL

Pursuant to s. 234(b) of the R.T.A. (formerly para. 206(2)4.1 of the T.P.A.), it is an offence if a person fails to make an evicted tenant's property available for retrieval in accordance with subsection 41(3) of the R.T.A. (formerly subsection 42(3) of the T.P.A.).

Under the T.P.A., the landlord had to make the evicted tenant's property available for retrieval for 48 hours. Under the R.T.A., that time period has been extended to 72 hours and it has been clarified in the regulations that, during that 72-hour period, the property must be available between 8 a.m. and 8 p.m. (see Chapter 18).

A tenant who owed a substantial amount of rent (over $7,000) to the landlord was evicted by way of enforcement of an order from the Rental Housing Tribunal. Once the order had been enforced by the Sheriff's Office, the landlord refused to allow the tenant to retrieve her property, purporting to exercise a lien of that property. The tenant brought an application to the Tribunal. The Tribunal fined the landlord $5,000, awarded the tenant a substantial abatement of rent and ordered that the former tenant's property be returned to her.[65] The landlord ignored that order. The landlord was then

---

[64] On April 18, 2008, before Justice of the Peace Milan Then.

[65] Although it is not clear that the Tribunal actually had the jurisdiction to grant relief for events that occurred after enforcement of an eviction order: *Lorini v. Lombard* (2001), 2001 CarswellOnt 5380 (Ont. Div. Ct.) (May 17, 2001), Doc. 694/99 (Ont. Div. Ct.), re TEL-06893, TET-00615. This is discussed further in Chapter 18. Note, however, that under the

prosecuted under paragraph 206(2)4.1 of the T.P.A. The case was heard in Brampton on April 4, 2006, before Justice of the Peace Spadafora. His worship imposed the maximum penalty (as it then was under the T.P.A.) of $10,000, finding that the landlord's actions were high-handed and that he took advantage of a vulnerable tenant.

15. NEW OFFENCES UNDER THE R.T.A.

The following new offences have been added under the *Residential Tenancies Act*:

1. failure to give a new tenant the required notice that sets out the lawful rent to be charged or giving false information in the notice where there is an order preventing a rent increase (OPRI);[66]
2. failure to provide information on the total cost of utilities in accordance with subsection 128(2);[67]
3. doing anything to prevent a tenant of a care home from obtaining care services from a person of the tenant's choice contrary to clause 147(a);[68] and
4. interfering with the provision of care services to a tenant of a care home contrary to clause 147(b).[69]

There have not yet been any prosecutions of these new offences.

R.T.A., the Board has been given clear statutory authority to grant relief in such circumstances (see subsection 41(6) of the R.T.A.).

[66] Clause 234(i) of the R.T.A.

[67] Clause 234(k) of the R.T.A.

[68] Clause 234(n) of the R.T.A.

[69] Clause 234(o) of the R.T.A.

20

Mobile Homes and Land Lease Homes

1. INTRODUCTION

(a) Definition of Mobile Home

A "mobile home" is defined in s. 2 of the *Residential Tenancies Act, 2006*[1], as any dwelling that is designed to be made mobile and that is being used as a **permanent** residence.

"Mobile home park" in s. 2 means the land on which mobile homes are located and includes the rental units and the land, structures, services and facilities of which the landlord retains possession and that are intended for the common use of other mobile home owners as tenants of the landlord.

A mobile home park may have a mix of dwellings manufactured without wheels and trailers manufactured with wheels. The fact that a trailer may not meet certain safety standards does not mean that it does not meet the definition of "mobile home".[2] If, however, the trailer is not used as a permanent residence, it cannot be considered a "mobile home" within the meaning of the R.T.A.[3]

"Rental unit", as defined in s. 2, includes a site for a mobile home that is used or intended for use as rented residential premises. This is true even if the mobile home on the site is owned by the tenant of the site.[4] Thus, where the tenant owns the home, the rental unit is not the home itself; rather, it is the site upon which the home is located.

---

[1] S.O. 2006, c. 17 (hereinafter referred to as the R.T.A.).

[2] See *Spera v. 1435509 Ontario Inc.* (Jan. 3, 2002), SOT-01952 (Ont. Rental Housing Trib.) in which the Rental Housing Tribunal found that the trailer was a mobile home as it was used by the tenant as his permanent residence.

[3] *Fraser v. Ellison* (Feb. 9, 1999), EAL-02654 (Ont. Rental Housing Trib.), upheld on appeal to the Divisional Court.

[4] Subsection 2(4) of the R.T.A.

For the purposes of Part X of the R.T.A., reference to a "tenant's mobile home" shall be interpreted to be a reference to a mobile home owned by the tenant and situated within a mobile home park of the landlord with whom the tenant has a tenancy agreement.

As many mobile homes have become affixed to the ground because of plumbing, landscaping or additions built with the landlord's consent, the mobile home has become virtually a bungalow, and so the question should be addressed as to whether such a mobile home is still mobile. The definition of mobile home in the R.T.A. refers to any dwelling unit designed to be mobile and being used as a permanent residence.

If a landlord can terminate the lease of the site for any of the causes in the R.T.A., what then happens to the mobile home permanently affixed to the land? The question was considered in Newfoundland in *Cook v. Doyle*.[5] The court stated:

> [To] evict these tenants who would necessarily have to leave their residences which are now permanently affixed to the land would, ... in law constitute an unjust enrichment and benefit to the [landlord].

The court relied on *Nicholson v. St. Denis* (1976), 8 O.R. (2d) 315, a leading case on the subject of unjust enrichment.

This, of course, presumes that what has been affixed to the land can never be detached. Unjust enrichment will only result if: (1) the tenant is forced to leave behind valuable property; (2) the tenant is not permitted or is not able to retrieve that property; and (3) the landlord need never account for the value of that property.

Fears of unjust enrichment are largely unfounded in my view for several reasons. First, mobile homes are designed to be mobile. Although it may take a bit of work, most mobile homes can be driven or towed from the site. Leaving the property behind is more of a concern in the case of land lease homes but even these can sometimes be moved *en masse*, albeit at considerable expense. Second, the tenant is given time under the R.T.A. to remove his or her property. Third, the landlord cannot dispose of the tenant's property without first providing written notice to the tenant and allowing the tenant an opportunity to retrieve the property. Even after that, for up to six months the tenant can request either the return of the property or the proceeds from the sale thereof (less the landlord's actual expenses and any arrears of rent owing to the landlord).

(b) Definition of Land Lease Home

A "land lease home" is defined in s. 2 of the R.T.A. as, "a dwelling, other than a mobile home, that is a permanent structure, where the owner of the dwelling leases the land used or intended for use as the site for the dwelling."

[5] (1985), 51 Nfld. & P.E.I.R. 234 (Nfld. Dist. Ct.) at 239.

A "land lease community" means the land on which one or more occupied land lease homes are situate and includes the rental units and the land, structures, services and facilities of which the landlord retains possession and that are included for the common use and enjoyment of the tenants of the landlord.[6]

"Rental unit", as defined in s. 2, includes a site on which there is a land lease home that is used or intended for use as rented residential premises. This is true, even if the land lease home on the site is owned by the tenant of the site.[7] Thus, where the tenant owns the home, the rental unit is not the home itself; rather, it is the site upon which the home is located.

In *Graham v. Barker*,[8] a religious group owned a tract of land and permitted the members of its group to build homes on the land. The members did not pay "rent" for the right to use the land. Two of the members decided that they wanted to sell their home and move away. They did not want to be restricted to their original agreement to only sell to other members since they could get a better price on the open market. They applied to the Rental Housing Tribunal for a determination as to whether the part of the T.P.A. dealing with land lease homes applied to this property. The Member held that this was not a land lease home as there was no actual or implied tenancy agreement between the parties concerning the renting of the land.

(c) Application of the R.T.A.

Unless specifically exempted, rented sites or dwellings in a mobile home park or land lease community are covered by most of the same provisions of the R.T.A. that apply to other types of residential rental units. In addition, some rules in the R.T.A. apply only to mobile home parks and land lease communities. These special rules are generally contained in Part X of the R.T.A.

In interpreting a provision of the R.T.A. with regard to mobile home parks and land lease communities, if a provision in Part X conflicts with a provision in another Part of the Act, the provision in Part X applies.[9]

Although many of the provisions in Part X refer only to mobile homes,[10] the provisions are equally meant to apply to land lease homes. Subsection 152(2) of the R.T.A. specifically provides that Part X applies with necessary modifications with respect to tenancies in land lease communities, as if the tenancies were in mobile home parks.

[6] Section 2 of the R.T.A.

[7] Subsection 2(4) of the R.T.A.

[8] (March 4, 2003) NOT-00747, [2003] O.R.H.T.D. No. 33 (Ont. Rental Housing Trib.).

[9] I.e., the provisions of Part X of the Act are paramount with respect to mobile homes and land lease homes: s. 3(3) of the R.T.A.

[10] Subsection 152(1) of the R.T.A. provides that Part X applies with respect to tenancies in mobile home parks.

An issue often arises in the context of such rented premises as to whether or not the *Act* applies at all. A party (usually the landlord) may wish to argue that the R.T.A. does not apply. More often than not, such an argument will be based upon the provisions of s. 5(a) of the R.T.A. (formerly s. 3(a) of the *Tenant Protection Act, 1997*[11]) which states that the Act does not apply with respect to living accommodation:

(1) intended to be provided to the travelling or vacationing public; or
(2) occupied for a seasonal or temporary period in a hotel, motel or motor hotel, resort, lodge, tourist camp, cottage or cabin establishment, inn, campground, trailer park, tourist home, bed and breakfast vacation establishment or vacation home.

Where the units were found to be trailers intended for seasonal use in a trailer park, the Act was held not to apply.[12]

According to the Divisional Court, since a land lease community is not specifically listed in s. 5(a) as one of the types of establishments exempt from the Act, if it can be established that the unit is a land lease home, s. 5(a) may have no application.[13] Therefore, where it is found that a premises better fits the definition of land lease home than living accommodation in a cottage establishment, it will be held that the Act applies to the unit.[14]

In *Pietens v. Lighthouse Cove Trailer Park*,[15] most of the residents of this trailer park lived there year-round in winterized trailers while others spent the winter months in warmer climes. They all identified their homes in the park as their permanent residences in Canada. The onus was upon the landlord to establish that these units were exempt from the Act. The Member found that the first part of s. 3(a) of the T.P.A. (living accommodation intended to be provided to the travelling or vacationing public) did not apply in this case. With respect to the tenants who lived in their homes year-round, the Act obviously did apply as they did not occupy the unit for a "seasonal or temporary period." For the "snowbirds", it was a more difficult decision. The Member did not directly deal with the question of whether or not these tenants occupied the living accommodation for a seasonal or temporary period. Instead, the Member considered the definition of "mobile home" and concluded that the homes were being used (even by the "snowbirds") as permanent residences. The Member therefore concluded that the Act applied to all of the units in question.

---

[11] S.O. 1997, c. 24 (hereinafter referred to as the T.P.A.).

[12] *McCormick v. Paul Bunyan Trailer Camp Ltd.*, [1999] O.J. No. 5784 (Ont. Div. Ct.), followed in *Hadlow v. MSV Holdings* (Aug. 28, 2002) CET-02677, [2002] O.R.H.T.D. No. 106 (Ont. Rental Housing Trib.).

[13] *Moss v. Jackson*, [2002] O.J. No. 933 (Ont. Div. Ct.).

[14] *Putnam v. Grand River Conservation Authority* (April 1, 2005) SWT-05672, SWT-05673, SWT-04384 and SWT-04385, [2005] O.R.H.T.D. No. 12 (Ont. Rental Housing Trib.).

[15] (July 4, 2006) SWT-07140, [2006] O.R.H.T.D. No. 72 (Ont. Rental Housing Trib.).

For other cases concerning the interpretation and application of similar provisions, please see "Vacation and Seasonal Accommodations" in Chapter 4.

In *North York General Hospital Foundation v. Armstrong*,[16] the "hospital" owned parcels of land that its predecessor had leased to a number of tenants for seventy years. The tenants owned the houses located on these parcels. The tenants alleged that the landlord was refusing to allow them to assign their tenancies (making it impossible for them to sell their interests) in an effort to force the tenants to purchase the parcels of land at a price set by the landlord. The landlord commenced an application for a determination by the Tribunal as to whether the T.P.A. (or specific provisions thereof) applied to the land in question. The Tribunal reviewed all of the relevant facts and concluded that this constituted a land lease community (and that the structures thereon were land lease homes) and that the premises were governed by the provisions of the Act relevant to such communities. The relevant provisions included ss. 103, 105(1) and 108 of the T.P.A. which, when read together, led the Member to the inescapable conclusion that the tenants, as owners of land lease homes, had the right to sell or lease their homes without the landlord's consent. The landlord appealed the Tribunal's decision to the Divisional Court. In a lengthy decision, the Court upheld the Tribunal's decision and dismissed the appeal. On a further appeal, the Court of Appeal also dismissed the landlord's appeal and found that these were land lease homes and that the Act applied.[17]

One creative landlord attempted to come up with a way to exempt a mobile home park from the *Tenant Protection Act*. In *Parsons v. Twin Elm Estates Ltd.*,[18] the landlord realized that the definition of "tenant" in the Act excluded a person who has the right to occupy the rental unit by virtue of being a shareholder of a corporation that owns the residential complex. The landlord organized the business such that a corporation owned the park and special corporate shares were issued to tenants that gave them the right to occupy sites within the park. However, the landlord also entered into tenancy agreements with the tenants and charged them rent. The reviewing Member found that the real substance of the relationship was one of landlord and tenant and that the Act did apply.

[16] (2004), 15 R.P.R. (4th) 295 (Ont. Div. Ct.), affirmed 34 R.P.R. (4th) 173 (Ont. C.A.) (re TNL-26391).

[17] *North York General Hospital Foundation v. Armstrong*, 2005 CarswellOnt 3953, [2205] O.J. No. 3627 (Ont. C.A.). The Court of Appeal went on, however, to also answer a question that was not originally before the Tribunal: Does the landlord of a land lease community or a mobile home park have the right to withhold consent to a potential assignment of a rental unit (the site) to a specific assignee? The Court of Appeal answered this question in the affirmative. This is discussed later in this chapter under the heading "Assignment of the Site".

[18] (Feb. 15, 2000) SWT-00300-RV, [2000] O.R.H.T.D. No. 32 (Ont. Rental Housing Trib.).

In a case with some similarities to *Parsons v. Twin Elm Estates Ltd.*, the Landlord and Tenant Board came to a different conclusion. In Landlord and Tenant Board File No. SWT-00135 (October 26, 2007), this campground was owned by a non-profit, non-share corporation. Each tenant was a "member" of the corporation with full voting rights. Each member paid the same annual membership dues. Membership granted the right to exclusive use of a site for the member's trailer. The Board found that there was no landlord and tenant relationship here and that it was the intent of the corporation to provide recreational facilities to its members, not residential premises. Hence, it was held that the *Residential Tenancies Act* did not apply.

Where the Act applies, the Landlord and Tenant Board will have exclusive jurisdiction to resolve disputes arising from the tenancy. If, for instance, a dispute arises over the property taxes collected by the landlord of a mobile home park or land lease community, the dispute must be resolved by the Board and not in Small Claims Court.[19]

2. PARK/COMMUNITY RULES

A landlord may establish rules for a mobile home park or land lease community. Where the landlord does establish such rules, the landlord must: (1) provide a written copy of the rules to each tenant; and (2) inform each tenant in writing of any change to the rules.[20] Until the landlord complies with these requirements, the tenant's obligation to pay rent is suspended and the landlord cannot require the tenant to pay rent.[21] After the landlord has complied with these requirements, however, the landlord may require the tenant to pay any rent that was withheld by the tenant.[22]

This is analogous to the tenant's rights under s. 12 of the R.T.A. (formerly s. 8 of the T.P.A.) and cases decided under these provisions may be of some assistance in interpreting s. 154 of the R.T.A. (see Chapter 5).

3. INFORMATION ABOUT PROPERTY ASSESSMENT

Since municipal property taxes are based not just on the value of the land but also on the value of any building located thereon, such taxes can become a contentious issue in mobile home parks and land lease communities.

If the landlord and tenant agree that the rent charged shall include all property taxes, the tenant does not need to have any additional information.

---

19 *Walleye Trailer Park Ltd. v. Swire*, [2001] O.J. No. 3227 (Div. Ct.).

20 Subsection 154(1) of the R.T.A.

21 Subsection 154(2) of the R.T.A.

22 Subsection 154(3) of the R.T.A.

Where, however, the tenant is obliged to pay the landlord an amount to reimburse the landlord for property taxes paid by the landlord with respect to a mobile home or land lease home owned by the tenant, the landlord must promptly provide the tenant with a copy of any information the landlord obtains from the Municipal Property Assessment Corporation with respect to the value of the home for assessment purposes.[23] If a landlord has not made reasonable efforts in the previous 12 months to obtain this information or has otherwise failed to comply with these requirements, the tenant's obligation to pay the landlord an amount to reimburse the landlord for such property taxes is suspended (until the landlord does comply).[24]

4. TENANT'S RIGHT TO SELL

(a) General

A tenant has the right to sell or lease his or her mobile home or land lease home without the landlord's consent.[25] A landlord may act as the tenant's agent in negotiations to sell or lease the home if the landlord has written authority to do so[26] but any term of the tenancy agreement that purports to force the tenant to use the landlord as an agent for the sale of the home is void.[27]

Although a tenant may sell his or her home without the consent of the landlord, unless the purchaser intends to remove the home from its current site, the purchaser will also need to obtain an assignment of the tenancy of that site. If the landlord is unwilling to cooperate in the assignment, this can have serious consequences upon a tenant's ability to sell his or her home and can lead to complex legal proceedings. This topic will be discussed under the heading "Assignment of the Site".

(b) Landlord's Right of First Refusal

Sometimes a landlord of a mobile home park or land lease community wishes to have the right to prohibit a tenant from selling the tenant's mobile home or land lease home without first offering to sell it to the landlord. No such right automatically exists under the provisions of the R.T.A. To create such a right, a landlord must insert an express provision into the tenancy agreement granting the landlord this "right of first refusal".[28]

---

[23] Subsection 155(1) of the R.T.A.

[24] Subsections 155(2), (3) and (4) of the R.T.A.

[25] Subsection 156(1) of the R.T.A.

[26] Subsection 156(2) of the R.T.A.

[27] Subsection 156(3) of the R.T.A.

[28] Subsection 157(1) of the R.T.A.

Where the tenancy agreement provides the landlord with a right of first refusal, if the tenant receives an acceptable offer to purchase the home, the tenant must advise the landlord of the offer and give the landlord at least 72 hours to match the offer (i.e., to agree to purchase the home at the same price and subject to the same terms and conditions as the third party's offer).[29]

If a provision of the tenancy agreement gives the landlord not only a right of first refusal but also purports to permit the landlord to purchase the home at a price lower than the one contained in a prospective purchaser's offer, the landlord may exercise a right of first refusal but only if the landlord matches the offer. The provision that purports to permit the landlord to purchase the home at a preferred (i.e., lower) price is void.[30]

(c) Advertising

A tenant of a mobile home park or land lease community may wish to advertise that their home is for sale. A landlord of such a facility may wish to restrict the manner in which such advertising can be done but there is nothing in the R.T.A. that directly speaks to this issue except s. 158.

According to s. 158 of the R.T.A., a landlord cannot prevent a tenant who owns the home from placing in the window of the home a sign that the home is for sale unless:

1. the prohibition applies to all tenants;
2. the landlord provides a bulletin board for the purpose of placing "for sale" advertisements;
3. the bulletin board is provided to all tenants in the park/community free of charge; and
4. the bulletin board is placed in a prominent place and is accessible to the public at all reasonable times.

5. ASSIGNMENT OF THE SITE

When a tenancy is *assigned*, it means that a new person is assuming all of the tenant's rights and responsibilities under an existing tenancy agreement. This topic is discussed in greater detail in Chapter 3. There are, however, some special provisions (primarily s. 159 of the R.T.A.) relating to the assignment of a mobile home or land lease home which are considered below.

The precursor to the current provision (s. 159 of the R.T.A) was s. 108 of the T.P.A. Section 108 of the T.P.A. dealt with a tenant's right, upon the sale of the tenant's mobile home or land lease home, to assign the tenancy of the site to the purchaser of the home. Some believed that s. 108 removed any

---

[29] Subsections 157(2) and (3) of the R.T.A.

[30] Subsection 157(4) of the R.T.A.

right of a landlord to refuse consent to an assignment of the site in such circumstances. They argued that this was a reasonable interpretation since few purchasers would be willing to wait until the ultimate resolution of a dispute between the vendor/tenant and landlord about the reasonableness of the landlord's refusal to consent to the proposed assignment.

In a 2005 decision, however, the Ontario Court of Appeal held that s. 108 of the T.P.A. eliminated the landlord's right to refuse consent to an assignment "in principle" but did not restrict the landlord's right to refuse to consent to a "specific assignment".[31] The Court held that, in its view, this interpretation of s. 108 of the T.P.A.:

> achieves the appropriate balance between the rights of the homeowner and the rights of the landlord because it eliminates the landlord's right to withhold its consent generally to any assignment of the rental unit, but preserves the landlord's right to assess whether a potential assignee is an appropriate tenant.[32]

This left the practical problem of whether a landlord could frustrate a potential sale of a mobile home or land lease home by unreasonably refusing consent to an assignment to the purchaser. After all, the purchaser may only be interested in purchasing the home if it can be used in its current location. If the purchaser cannot obtain an assignment of the site, the purchaser may not be able or willing to use the structure and, therefore, may not be interested in completing the transaction.

Since the landlord has the right to refuse consent to an assignment to a particular purchaser (or prospective purchaser), the question may arise as to whether the landlord's withholding of the consent was reasonable.

In *Eickmeier v. 395321 Ontario Ltd. (c.o.b. Silver Creek)*,[33] the Member found it reasonable that the landlord withheld consent to an assignment of this mobile home site until the tenant complied with existing work orders and made the home habitable. The Member also found it reasonable for the landlord to reject the particular proposed assignees who had insufficient income to "carry" the home and had poor credit histories.

---

[31] *North York General Hospital Foundation v. Armstrong*, [2005] O.J. No. 3627, 2005 CarswellOnt 3953, at para. 56. Also see *Moss v. Wilson*, (May 23, 2003), EAL-34116, EAL-34117-SA and EAL-34118, [2003] O.R.H.T.D. No. 68 (Ont. Rental Housing Trib.); *Foster v. Laventure* (March 8, 2005), EAL-46290, EAL-46287, EAT-06268 and EAT-06269, [2005] O.R.H.T.D. No. 10 (Ont. Rental Housing Trib.); and *Eickmeier v. 395321 Ontario Ltd. (c.o.b. Silver Creek)*, (Aug. 23, 2001), CET-01857-RV, [2001] O.R.H.T.D. No. 113 (Ont. Rental Housing Trib.).

[32] *North York General Hospital Foundation v. Armstrong*, [2005] O.J. No. 3627, 2005 CarswellOnt 3953, at para. 56 (Ont. C.A.).

[33] (Aug. 23, 2001), CET-01857-RV, [2001] O.R.H.T.D. No. 113 (Ont. Rental Housing Trib.).

In *Foster v. Laventure*,[34] the Member found it reasonable that the landlord rejected a potential assignee who would not complete the landlord's forms and who refused, in advance, to pay an extra $50 per month to rent the site even though such an increase was permitted under the T.P.A. (as it is under the R.T.A.).

The R.T.A. preserves the landlord's right to refuse consent to an assignment of the site to the purchaser of the home located on that site but it changes the previous law in two ways.

First, it places the onus upon the landlord to object. The usual procedure under s. 98 of the R.T.A. requires the tenant to commence an application if the tenant wishes to challenge the landlord's refusal to consent to an assignment. Under s. 159 of the R.T.A., it is the landlord who must commence an application with the Board if the landlord objects to the proposed assignee.[35] The landlord must set out in the application the landlord's grounds for refusing consent.[36] Since it is the landlord who must commence the application, presumably the onus is upon the landlord to prove, on a balance of probabilities, that the landlord's grounds for refusing consent are reasonable.

Second, there is a tight deadline for making this application. The landlord must apply to the Board within 15 days after the tenant asks the landlord to consent to the assignment.[37] If the landlord fails to apply within this time limit (and if that time limit has not been extended by the Board[38]), the landlord shall be deemed to have consented to the assignment.[39]

If the landlord commences the application on time but, following a hearing, the Board determines that the landlord's grounds for refusing consent are not reasonable, the landlord shall be deemed to have consented to the assignment.[40]

Hopefully, the Board will be able to deal with these applications expeditiously. Any substantial delay may well put the sale of the mobile home or land lease home in jeopardy and allow an unscrupulous landlord to achieve indirectly what the landlord is prohibited from doing directly.

---

[34] (March 8, 2005), EAL-46290, EAL-46287, EAT-06268 and EAT-06269, [2005] O.R.H.T.D. No. 10 (Ont. Rental Housing Trib.).

[35] Subsections 159(1) and (2) of the R.T.A.

[36] Subsection 159(3) of the R.T.A.

[37] Subsection 159(2) of the R.T.A.

[38] Subsection 190(1) of the R.T.A.

[39] Subsection 159(4) of the R.T.A.

[40] Subsection 159(4) of the R.T.A.

6. RESTRAINT OF TRADE PROHIBITED

A landlord cannot restrict the right of a tenant to purchase goods or services from the person of his or her choice, except to the extent that the landlord may set reasonable standards for mobile home equipment.[41]

7. LANDLORD'S ADDITIONAL MAINTENANCE OBLIGATIONS

All of the general rules about maintenance and repair which apply to other tenants and landlords (described in Chapter 11) also apply to mobile home parks and land lease communities.

Pursuant to s. 161 of the R.T.A., in addition to fulfilling its obligations under s. 20 of the R.T.A., the landlord of a mobile home park or land lease community has these *additional* responsibilities:

(a) removing or disposing of garbage or ensuring the availability of a means of removing or disposing of garbage in the park/community at reasonable intervals;
(b) maintaining the park/community in a good state of repair;
(c) removing snow from park/community roads;
(d) maintaining the water supply, sewage disposal, fuel, drainage and electrical systems in the park/community in a good state of repair;
(e) maintaining the park/community grounds and all buildings, structures, enclosures and equipment intended for the common use of tenants in a good state of repair; and
(f) repairing damage to a tenant's property, if the damage is caused by the wilful or negligent conduct of the landlord.

The landlord will still be expected to comply with any health, safety, housing or maintenance standards applicable to the site. If there are no municipal property standards, the provincial standards (set out in O. Reg. 517/06) will apply. These standards, amongst other things, require a landlord to: maintain a supply of potable water and water pressure sufficient for normal household use; maintain adequate water and pressure for fire fighting; maintain roads free of potholes, snow and other obstructions, and control dust on them; and, empty sewage holding tanks.

Maintenance of roads in a good state of repair in mobile home parks was enforced by court order in *Guillemette v. Kingsway Villa Ltd.*[42]

20 — MOBILE AND LAND LEASE HOMES

---

[41] Section 160 of the R.T.A. Theoretically, a landlord could also set standards for equipment to be used on or attached to a land lease home but, practically speaking, this is less likely to become an issue.

[42] (1991), 1991 CarswellOnt 2079 (Ont. Gen. Div.).

A tenant or former tenant may apply (under para. 29(1)1 of the R.T.A.) to the Board for relief as a result of a breach of the landlord's obligations under s. 161. The tenant only has one year to commence the application from the date of the breach by the landlord (s. 29(2)) and, in determining the appropriate remedy (if any) to grant, the Board must consider whether the tenant or former tenant advised the landlord of the alleged breaches (s. 39(2)). The list of possible remedies is contained in s. 30(1) of the R.T.A. (see Chapter 11).

For complete lack of repair, *Lacey v. Shaughnessy Brothers Investments Ltd.*[43] tells a full story. Adequate disposal of garbage was not available, the roads were in poor shape and the grounds and structures for common use were in poor repair. Court orders to comply were disregarded. The judge said there was total failure by the landlord and there would be 100% abatement gradually reduced as the landlord complied. Punitive damages of $200 were awarded as well as solicitor and client costs.

A somewhat similar lack of repair and proper services in a mobile home park is in *Plachta v. Minnie.*[44] The landlord of a mobile home park wanted to close it down and convert the property to vacant land. His application was according to s. 105(1)(*b*) of Part IV (now s. 50(1)(*b*) of the R.T.A.). The court accepted the genuineness of the landlord's intention, noting that the reasonableness, economical or otherwise, was not to be considered. However, the application was refused based in the counter-claim of the tenants that the judge should not grant termination and possession as it would be unfair: Part IV, s. 121 (now s. 83 of the R.T.A.). The landlord had allowed the park to deteriorate: roads were not properly maintained, garbage was not disposed of, plumbing and electrical were left in disrepair, water was not potable. As in *Lacey, supra*, abatement was ordered of 20%, the estimate of the trial judge was the difference between the fair value of the premises if they had been repaired and the fair value in the present state. The judge ordered repairs and ordered the landlord to have the water supply properly working as to quantity, quality and pressure, to repair the roads, remove snow soon after a snowfall, then sand the roads, to replace outdoor lights, and to promptly and regularly remove garbage. The judge refused the landlord's application for termination of the tenancy. Costs were awarded to the successful tenant.

Note that the extra responsibilities under s. 161 of the R.T.A. relate to the condition of the park or community. The landlord of a mobile home park and land lease community is responsible for the condition of the site that is rented, the surrounding grounds and the common services and facilities. Such a landlord is generally not responsible for the condition of the mobile home or land lease home.

---

[43] (1993), 1993 CarswellOnt 1968 (Ont. Gen. Div.).

[44] (1994), 1994 CarswellOnt 3277 (Ont. Gen. Div.).

If the owner of a mobile home or land lease home rents that home (and sublets the site) to someone else, that owner becomes the landlord of the new occupant and has all of the maintenance obligations of a landlord. There will be no contractual relationship between the occupant of the home and the landlord of the park/community.

8. DISPOSAL OF THE TENANT'S HOME AND PERSONAL PROPERTY

(a) On Termination of the Tenancy

Where the owner of a mobile home or land lease home rents their home to someone else, although the owner is the tenant of the site upon which the home stands, he or she becomes the landlord of the person who is renting the home. Arguably, when that person vacates the rental unit but leaves behind some personal possessions, the owner of the home (as a landlord) can rely upon the usual provisions dealing with disposition of abandoned property (ss. 40 and 41 of the R.T.A.).[45] However, different provisions apply between the owner of the home and the landlord of the mobile home park or land lease community.

Unlike other types of tenancies, in the case of a mobile home or land lease home, what is being rented by the owner of the home is a piece of land, not the building that sits on that land. Therefore, the landlord of the mobile home park or land lease community has no statutory right to enter into the mobile home or land lease home. The landlord may, however, have to deal with the mobile home (or the land lease home) if the tenant vacates the unit but leaves the home behind.

If the tenant has vacated the home in accordance with a notice of termination, an agreement to terminate the tenancy or an order of the Board terminating the tenancy or declaring that the rental unit has been abandoned by the tenant (under s. 79 of the R.T.A.), then the landlord must follow the procedures set out in s. 162 of the R.T.A. before disposing of the home.

In the circumstances set out above, the landlord must first notify the tenant (by registered mail and by notice published in a local newspaper) of the landlord's intention to dispose of the home.[46] After waiting 60 days, if the landlord has not received a claim from the tenant, the landlord may then proceed to sell, retain for the landlord's own use or dispose of the home.[47] If the tenant does make a claim for the home within this 60-day period, the landlord can refuse to return the home until the tenant has paid to the landlord

[45] See Chapter 18.

[46] Subsection 162(2) of the R.T.A.

[47] Subsection 162(3) of the R.T.A.

any arrears of rent and any reasonable expenses incurred by the landlord with respect to the home.[48]

If, within six months of the day the notices were given to the tenant, the tenant makes a claim for a home which the landlord has already sold, the landlord must pay to the tenant the proceeds from the sale, less an amount needed to cover the landlord's reasonable out-of-pocket expenses incurred with respect to the home and any arrears of rent of the tenant.[49]

If, within six months of the day the notices were given to the tenant, the tenant makes a claim for a home which the landlord has retained for the landlord's own use, the landlord must return the home to the tenant.[50] However, the landlord can refuse to return the home until the tenant has paid to the landlord any arrears of rent owed to the landlord by the tenant and any reasonable expenses incurred by the landlord with respect to the home.[51]

If a landlord complies with these provisions, the landlord will not be liable to any person for selling, retaining or otherwise disposing of a tenant's mobile home or land lease home.[52] Where, however, the landlord fails to follow the correct procedures, the landlord may be held civilly[53] and, potentially, criminally liable.

In *Morawski Estate v. Twin Elm Estates Ltd.*,[54] the tenant owned a mobile home in the landlord's mobile home park. Although she hadn't used the home for a few years, she continued to pay rent for the use of the site. When the tenant passed away, the landlord contacted her estate and requested that the home be removed. After several attempts to elicit a response from the estate, the landlord took the position that the property had been abandoned and sold the home. Eventually, the estate trustee commenced an action against the landlord for recovery of the proceeds of the sale. In dismissing this action, the court found that the landlord was reasonable in believing the property had been abandoned (by the estate). The court also held that, although the landlord did not strictly comply with all notice requirements set out in what were ss. 111 and 112 of the T.P.A. (now ss. 162 and 163 of the R.T.A.), the notices sent by the landlord to the estate substantially complied with the requirements of the Act, the estate failed to respond and, in those circumstances, the landlord was entitled to take the actions it did.

---

48 Subsection 162(6) of the R.T.A.

49 Subsection 162(4) of the R.T.A.

50 Subsection 162(5) of the R.T.A.

51 Subsection 162(6) of the R.T.A.

52 Subject only to the landlord's obligation to return the home or the proceeds from its sale if the tenant makes a claim within six months of the landlord's notice: s. 162(7) of the R.T.A.

53 In a case in which the landlord wrongfully removed a mobile home from the mobile home park, he was ordered to return it and do any necessary repairs of damage caused in the removal: *Jackowski Estate v. Cedar Grove Mobile Home Park Ltd* (February 18, 1982), Doc. Peel 6764/81 (Ont. Co. Ct.), decided under Part IV of the *Landlord and Tenant Act*, s. 128(1)(*f*).

54 [2004] O.J. NO. 5699 (Ont. S.C.J.).

(b) Where Home Abandoned

A tenant's mobile home (or home in a land lease community) may be considered abandoned if the tenant has vacated the unit where:

(i) the tenant gave the landlord a notice to terminate the tenancy or the landlord gave the tenant a notice to terminate the tenancy; or
(ii) the landlord and tenant agreed to terminate the tenancy; or
(iii) the Board has issued an order which terminates the tenancy; or
(iv) the landlord applied to the Board for an order terminating the tenancy because the unit was abandoned (under s. 79) and the Board has issued such an order.[55]

In such circumstances, the landlord must follow the procedures set out in s. 162 of the R.T.A. (described above).

(c) On Death of the Owner

Normally, on the death of the sole tenant of a rental unit, the tenancy is deemed to terminate 30 days after the death of the tenant and the landlord's obligations with respect to the unit and the property within the rental unit are set out in ss. 91 and 92 of the R.T.A.

In the case of a mobile home or land lease home **owned by the tenant**, however, ss. 91 and 92 of the R.T.A. do not apply (pursuant to s. 163 of the R.T.A.). The tenancy of the site is *not* automatically terminated and the landlord is *not* entitled to dispose of the contents of the unit. Presumably, this means that the landlord will have to deal with the estate of the deceased tenant with respect to the termination or continuation of the tenancy and with respect to the disposition of the home. If, however, the estate takes no action with respect to the property and fails to respond to notices from the landlord, the landlord may be able to treat the unit as having been abandoned.[56]

In *Sama Parks Ltd. v. Solmes*,[57] Mary Solmes owned a mobile home and lived in the home. Ronald Solmes was listed as an occupant. When Mary died, the landlord sought to evict Ronald as an unauthorized occupant. The Member held that since the tenancy did not automatically terminate 30 days after Mary's death, since her estate continued the tenancy and since the definition of "tenant" includes "the tenant's heirs, assigns and personal representatives", there had not been a *transfer* of occupancy of the unit at all. Therefore, it could not be considered an *unauthorized* transfer of occupancy. The landlord's application was dismissed.

---

[55] Subsection 162(1) of the R.T.A. (formerly subsection 111(1) of the T.P.A.).

[56] See *Morawski Estate v. Twin Elm Estates Ltd.*, [2004] O.J. NO. 5699 (Ont. S.C.J.), discussed earlier in this chapter.

[57] (January 15, 2001), TEL-15764 (Ont. Rental Housing Trib.).

9. TERMINATION FOR DEMOLITION, CONVERSION OR REPAIRS

A landlord may give notice of termination for demolition, conversion or extensive repairs: s. 50 of the R.T.A. (formerly s. 53 of the T.P.A.). The date for termination in such cases must *usually* be at least 120 days after the date the notice is given to the tenant. In the case of a mobile home or land lease home **that is owned by the tenant**, however, the minimum notice period is one year (*not* the usual 120 days).[58] The date for termination must be the day a period of the tenancy ends or, where the tenancy is for a fixed term, the end of the term.

If a notice of termination is given under s. 50 of the R.T.A. with respect to a tenancy agreement between the landlord and a tenant who owns a mobile home or land lease home and the tenant is entitled to compensation under s. 52, 54 or 55, the amount of the compensation shall, despite those sections, be equal to the lesser of the following amounts:[59]

1. One year's rent.
2. $3,000 or the prescribed amount,[60] whichever is greater.

In *Cove Mobilehome Park & Sales Ltd. v. Welch*,[61] the landlord applied for conversion of a mobile home site for purpose of snow removal pursuant to Part IV of the *Landlord and Tenant Act*, s. 105(1)(*b*) (now s. 50(1)(*b*) of the R.T.A.). The trial judge had decided that was not a use for a purpose within the meaning of the section. The Divisional Court determined otherwise and that it was "conversion" to a non-residential use within the meaning of the section but sent the case back for further evidence as to the genuineness of the landlord's intention.

Termination and possession for conversion was granted in *Lavoie v. Hall*,[62] when the landlord was required by a work order by the Ministry of Housing, Maintenance and Standards, on the direction of the Fire Marshall, to provide a fire route across the mobile home site of the tenant. Another factor was that the tenant had built an addition to this mobile home without the approval of the landlord which interfered with the widening of the fire route. The effect of the termination and possession was that the lease of the mobile home site would revert to the landlord and that mobile home site would no longer be available for leasing.

Another conversion case is *Plachta v. Minnie*,[63] in which the landlord wished to discontinue the mobile home park as the operating expenses were

---

[58] Subsection 164(1) of the R.T.A.

[59] Subsection 164(2) of the R.T.A.

[60] There currently is no other "prescribed amount" set out in the regulations.

[61] (1979), 27 O.R. (2d) 65 (Ont. Div. Ct.).

[62] (1994), 1994 CarswellOnt 2875 (Ont. Gen. Div.).

[63] (1994), 1994 CarswellOnt 3277 (Ont. Gen. Div.).

more than the income, and to leave the land vacant. The court was sympathetic for the landlord's genuine intent which would have been sufficient to grant the application; however, the application was refused as the landlord was in violation of his responsibilities for the proper upkeep of the mobile home park and also because the tenants had sought to enforce their legal rights.

In *Bronte Creek Developments Inc. v. Murphy et al.*,[64] the landlord intended to convert the mobile home park to another use. The landlord gave the tenants notices to terminate the tenancies based upon the landlord's intention to "demolish" the rental units. Technically, nothing was being demolished (although some sites might have been excavated). The landlord had obtained all necessary permits. The Court found in favour of the landlord and ruled that the notices of termination the landlord had given to the tenants were valid.

10. RENT AND OTHER CHARGES

(a) Rent Increase Permitted on Assignment of Site

Normally, where a tenancy is assigned, the assignee "steps into the shoes" of the former tenant.[65] Thus, the landlord is not permitted to treat it as a new tenancy and cannot increase the rent unless it has been at least 12 months since the last increase[66] and the landlord has served a notice of rent increase at least 90 days in advance.[67]

Where, however, a tenancy agreement for a site for a mobile home or land lease home is assigned and the assignee purchases or enters into an agreement to purchase the former tenant's home, s. 95(8) of the R.T.A. does not apply and, immediately upon the assignment, the landlord may increase the rent payable for the site. The amount of rent increase cannot exceed the greater of:

(a) $50 per month; and
(b) the amount, including the guideline, that the landlord would have been entitled to take as a rent increase under an order under subsection 126(10) of the Act before the first anniversary of the commencement of the new tenancy had the former tenant remained the tenant.[68]

Thus, if the landlord obtained an order for an above-guideline rent increase that was to take effect after but within one year of the assignment, the

[64] (May 29, 2001), Doc. 1492/DV, 1491/DV (Ont. Div. Ct.) (re SOL-13743 and SOL-13742).
[65] Subsection 95(8) of the R.T.A.
[66] Section 119 of the R.T.A.
[67] Section 116 of the R.T.A. (subject to the exceptions listed in s. 117).
[68] Section 165 of the R.T.A. and s. 50 of O. Reg. 516/06.

landlord can proceed to take that increase immediately upon the assignment of the tenancy.

(b) Permitted Charges

In addition to being able to charge rent, a landlord of a mobile home park or land lease community can also charge (pursuant to s. 166 of the R.T.A.) for its reasonable out-of-pocket expenses incurred with regard to the following:

1. The entry of a mobile home into a mobile home park;
2. The exit of a mobile home from a mobile home park;
3. The installation of a mobile home in a mobile home park;
4. The removal of a mobile home from a mobile home park; and
5. The testing of water or sewage in a mobile home park.

Although, theoretically all five types of charges also apply to land lease communities, as a practical matter, land lease homes are rarely moved and only the water/sewage testing charge is likely to become an issue in a land lease community.

Since the Act permits a landlord to levy charges for water and sewage testing, it is not necessary for the parties to have specifically agreed to such charges within the tenancy agreement.[69]

Similarly, since the Act permits such charges, it does not matter whether the landlord incurs these expenses because it is required to do so by the government.[70]

In *New Country Investors Ltd., Re*,[71] the landlord brought an application to terminate the tenancy and evict the tenants because the tenants: (1) failed to pay rent and membership fees (arrears of rent); and (2) refused to pay water testing charges and property taxes as calculated by the landlord (interference with the rights of the landlord). With respect to the first issue, the Member held that membership fees do not constitute "rent" and since the landlord included such fees as part of the arrears on the notice of termination, this rendered the notice invalid (and was fatal to the application). With respect to the property taxes, the previous landlord had included this in the rent and did not charge separately. The Member held that the new landlord could not unilaterally change these terms. With respect to the cost of water testing, the Member found that the landlord was entitled to charge for its reasonable out-of-pocket expenses incurred with regard to the testing of the water (which included the cost of the labour of employees devoted to this testing) but that

---

[69] *Campbell v. Maytown Inc.*, [2005] O.J. No. 5948 (Ont. Div. Ct.).

[70] *Campbell v. Maytown Inc.*, [2005] O.J. No. 5948 (Ont. Div. Ct.).

[71] (July 20, 2006) SOL-46391, [2006] O.R.H.T.D. No. 94, 2006 CarswellOnt 9166 (Ont. Rental Housing Trib.).

the landlord had not properly allocated these costs amongst the tenants and, therefore, dismissed the application (with suggestions as to how the costs might be better allocated).

Where the landlord decided to upgrade the water supply system, this cost could not properly be passed on to the tenants as "the testing of water".[72]

(c) Exemption from Usual "Cap" on Rent Increase Above Guideline Based upon Certain Types of Capital Expenditures

Under subsection 126(11) of the R.T.A., a rent increase above the guideline based upon capital expenditures cannot exceed 3% per year over a maximum period of three years (see Chapter 9).

If the landlord of a mobile home park or a land lease community is forced by the government to carry out "infrastructure work", the Board may disregard the usual restrictions in subsection 126(11) and may "determine the number of years over which the rent increase justified by that capital expenditure may be taken."[73]

The term "infrastructure work" is defined in subsection 167(2) of the Act as work with respect to roads, water supply, fuel, sewage disposal, drainage, electrical systems and other "prescribed services and things" provided to the mobile home park (or land lease community). The "prescribed services and things" are listed in s. 51 of O. Reg. 516/06 as including: work with respect to fire hydrants and related systems, poles for telephone service, walkways, garbage storage and disposal areas, fencing, retaining walls and flood control systems.

Thus, if a landlord of a mobile home park or a land lease community is required by the federal, provincial or municipal government (or an agency of any of them) to carry out "infrastructure work" and the total cost, if passed on to the tenants, would result in an above-guideline increase exceeding 9% (the usual "cap"), instead of losing the difference, the landlord can request that the increase be applied over how ever many years it takes for the landlord to be fully compensated for the cost of this work.

(d) Collecting Municipal or Local Services Taxes

The landlord of a mobile home park or land lease community is required to collect the taxes for the mobile home or land lease home owned by the tenant. This money is turned over by the landlord to the municipal government or local services board that provides services to the community. The landlord

---

72 *Sanderson v. Bohusz* (Sept. 4, 2002) SWT-03292, [2002] O.R.H.T.D. No. 93 (Ont. Rental Housing Trib.).

73 Subsection 167(1) of the R.T.A.

does not keep this money. It is not considered part of the "rent."[74] Any increase in taxes for the tenant's dwelling is not considered a rent increase.

If the landlord has had to pay this money (i.e., property taxes with respect to the mobile home or land lease home owned by the tenant) out of its own funds, it is entitled to be reimbursed by the tenant.[75]

The amount of taxes for the tenant's mobile home or land lease home will reflect the assessed valued of the dwelling. However, the tax assessment notice issued to a landlord does not separate the assessed value for the site and the home situated on it. As a result, a landlord must apportion the taxes between the site and the dwelling, and bill each tenant for their property taxes. If a tenant believes that the taxes they have been charged by the landlord are based on an improper apportionment or breakdown of the combined assessed value of the site and the dwelling, the tenant can file an application with the Board claiming that part of the tax payment was money collected illegally by the landlord.[76]

11. RENTING A MOBILE HOME OR LAND LEASE HOME FROM THE OWNER

If the owner of a mobile home or land lease home wants to rent the home, they can do so. Since, however, the home sits on land that is being rented through an agreement with the landlord of the mobile home park or land lease community, the owner of the home must sublet the site rental agreement. The landlord's consent to a sublet of the site rental agreement is required, but the landlord cannot refuse to consent without a good reason.

In a sublet, the site rental agreement between the landlord and the original tenant remains in effect. The original tenant must continue to pay the site rent (and taxes) to the landlord, and comply with all other tenant duties.

The original tenant who owns the home also becomes a landlord to the person who is renting the home; that person is a tenant of the building and a subtenant of the site on which it stands. If there are maintenance or repair problems within the home itself which require attention, these will likely be the responsibility of the original tenant in the role as a landlord.

If there are problems with site maintenance or with services or facilities in the park or community, these should be reported by the occupant to the

---

[74] See the definition of "rent" in s. 2 of the R.T.A. Also see *Hearst Trailer Park v. Guilbault*, (Feb. 25, 2002) NOL-06722, [2002] O.R.H.T.D. No. 26 (Ont. Rental Housing Trib.) and Landlord and Tenant Board File No. CEL-14835 (Feb. 10, 2009).

[75] Paragraph 9 of s. 17, O. Reg. 516/06.

[76] The tenant should *not* file a claim in Small Claims Court as the Board has exclusive jurisdiction over such matters: *Walleye Trailer Park Ltd. v. Swire*, [2001] O.J. No. 3227 (Div. Ct.).

original tenant (the owner of the home) who should, in turn, report the problems to the landlord of the park or community.

For further details concerning the sublet of a rental unit, please refer to Chapter 3.

21

Care Homes

1. INTRODUCTION

Like other rental residential premises, a unit within a care home is also subject to the *Residential Tenancies Act*[1] unless otherwise specifically exempted by provisions of the R.T.A. In general terms, all of the usual provisions of the R.T.A. are presumed to apply to a unit in a care home. However, special provisions related to care homes are contained in Part IX of the R.T.A. as well as some specific exemptions from the R.T.A. that will be discussed in detail in this chapter. In interpreting a provision of the R.T.A. with regard to a care home, if a provision in Part IX conflicts with a provision in another Part of the Act, the provision in Part IX applies.[2]

2. DEFINITIONS

In s. 2 of the R.T.A., a "care home" is defined as a residential complex that is occupied or intended to be occupied by persons for the purpose of receiving care services, whether or not receiving the services is the primary purpose of the occupancy. In s. 1 of O. Reg. 516/06, this definition is further explained as follows:

> One or more rental units that form part of a residential complex are care homes for the purpose of the definition of "care home" in subsection 2(1) of the Act if the rental units are occupied or intended to be occupied by persons for the purpose of receiving care services, whether or not receiving care services is the primary purpose of the occupancy.
>
> [This] applies even if a third party rents the rental unit from the landlord and provides or arranges to provide both the rental unit and care services to the tenant.

---

[1] *Residential Tenancies Act, 2006*, S.O. 2006, c. 17 (R.T.A.).

[2] I.e., the provisions of Part IX of the Act are paramount with respect to care homes: s. 3(2) of the R.T.A.

"Care services" are defined in s. 2 of the R.T.A. as:

- health care services;
- rehabilitative or therapeutic services; or
- services that provide assistance with the activities of daily living.

The term "rehabilitative" was defined in *Keith Whitney Homes Society v. Payne*[3] as "restoration of the individual to his or her greatest potential whether physically, mentally, socially or vocationally"; and "therapeutic" is defined by the Shorter Oxford English Dictionary as "to treat medically, pertaining to the healing of disease".

Pursuant to s. 2(1) of O. Reg. 516/06, care services include:

- Nursing care
- Administration and supervision of medication prescribed by a medical doctor
- Assistance with feeding
- Bathing assistance
- Incontinence care
- Dressing assistance
- Assistance with personal hygiene
- Ambulatory assistance
- Personal emergency response service

If provided along with one or more of the services listed above, care services can also include:[4]

- Recreational or social activities
- Housekeeping
- Laundry services
- Assistance with transportation

In short, a care home is one or more rental units in a residential complex where it is intended that the occupant(s) will receive care services as outlined above.

In the situation of a boarding house, the landlord will typically provide not only a room but also meals, and sometimes, housekeeping services. A boarding house is **not** a care home as defined by the Act unless the landlord also provides any of the prescribed care services.

---

[3] (1992), 9 O.R. (3d) 186 (Ont. Gen. Div.).

[4] Subsection 2(2) of O. Reg. 516/06.

3. APPLICATION OF THE R.T.A.

Although many care homes will be subject to the R.T.A., some homes and buildings where care is provided to residents will **not** be covered by the R.T.A. These include:

(a) nursing homes (now called "long term care centres");[5]
(b) private or public hospitals;[6]
(c) municipal homes for the aged or rest homes;[7]
(d) most residential homes for persons with a developmental disability;[8]
(e) accommodation occupied by persons while in custody or confinement;[9]
(f) living accommodation in a care home occupied by a person for the purpose of receiving short-term respite care;[10]
(g) a home or building where the main reason the person lives there is to receive rehabilitation or therapy and where:
  (i) the parties have agreed in advance that:
    (A) the person will live in the home or building for a specified period of time; **or**
    (B) the person's right to live there will end when the rehabilitation or therapy goals for the person have been met;

  and

  (ii) the accommodation is intended to be provided for no more than a one-year period.[11]

4. CREATING THE TENANCY

Because of the potential vulnerability of prospective tenants seeking to move into a care home, the R.T.A. requires special procedures be followed.

For instance, whereas most tenancy agreements can be written, oral or implied,[12] in the case of care homes, the tenancy agreement for each and

---

5 Paragraph 5(e) of the R.T.A.
6 Paragraph 5(e) of the R.T.A.
7 Paragraph 5(e) of the R.T.A.
8 Paragraph 5(e) of the R.T.A. Such premises that are not completely exempt from the R.T.A. will likely be partially exempt under the provisions of s. 6 of the R.T.A.
9 Paragraph 5(d) of the R.T.A.
10 Paragraph 5(l) of the R.T.A.
11 Paragraph 5(k) of the R.T.A. See *Barrie v. Matt Talbot House Division of St. Michael's Halfway Houses* (Jan. 29, 2004), TST-06105 and TST-06106, [2004] O.R.H.T.D. No. 8 (Ont. Rental Housing Trib.), discussed in Chapter 4, for an interesting case dealing with an identical provision under the T.P.A.
12 See the definition of "tenancy agreement" in s. 2(1) of the R.T.A.

every tenant must be in writing.[13] That agreement must set out what has been agreed to with respect to care services and meals and the charges for them.[14] If, on an application by a tenant, the Board determines that the landlord has not complied with these requirements, the Board may award the tenant an abatement of rent.[15]

Furthermore, before entering into a new tenancy agreement with a new tenant in a care home, the landlord must give to the new tenant an information package containing the following information:[16]

1. a list of the different types of accommodation provided and the alternative packages of care services and meals available as part of the total charge;
2. the charges for the different types of accommodation and for the alternative packages of care services and meals;
3. minimum staffing levels and qualifications of staff;
4. details of the emergency response system, if any, or a statement that there is no emergency response system;
5. a list and fee schedule of the additional services and meals available from the landlord on a user pay basis; and
6. internal procedures, if any, for dealing with complaints, including a statement as to whether tenants have any right of appeal from an initial decision, or a statement that there is no internal process for dealing with complaints.

Until the landlord provides the information package required by law, the landlord cannot give a notice of rent increase or a notice of increase of a charge for providing care services or meals.[17]

Finally, every tenancy agreement relating to the tenancy of a tenant in a care home shall contain a statement that the tenant has the right to consult a third party with respect to the agreement and to cancel the agreement within five days after the agreement has been entered into.[18] Thus, the tenant has five days to cancel the tenancy agreement by **written notice** to the landlord.[19]

5. TENANT PRIVACY

The general rules about a tenant's right to privacy and a landlord's right to enter a rental unit (set out in ss. 25 through 27 of the R.T.A.) apply equally

[13] Subsection 139(1) of the R.T.A.
[14] Subsection 139(2) of the R.T.A.
[15] Subsection 139(3) of the R.T.A.
[16] Subsection 140(1) of the R.T.A. and s. 47 of O. Reg. 516/06.
[17] Subsection 140(2) of the R.T.A.
[18] Subsection 141(1) of the R.T.A.
[19] Subsection 141(2) of the R.T.A.

to care homes. The landlord of a care home may also be entitled to enter a tenant's room or unit without any advance notice if the rental agreement requires a landlord to check on the condition of the tenant[20] or to provide care. However, a tenant whose tenancy agreement contains a provision requiring the landlord to regularly check the condition of the tenant may unilaterally revoke that provision by written notice to the landlord.[21]

6. ASSIGNMENT/SUBLETTING

The usual provisions concerning a tenant's right to assign or sublet his or her unit are contained in Part VI of the R.T.A. Section 143 contains a specific provision concerning a rental unit in a care home: a landlord may withhold consent to an assignment or subletting of a rental unit in a care home if the effect of the assignment or subletting would be to admit a person to the care home contrary to the admission requirements or guidelines set by the landlord.

7. EXTERNAL CARE PROVIDERS

Although, by definition, the landlord of a care home will typically provide care services to its tenants, the government was concerned that such a landlord might try to restrict a tenant's ability to have someone other than the landlord provide alternate or supplementary care services. Section 147 of the R.T.A. states that the landlord must not do anything to prevent a tenant from obtaining additional care services from an external care provider or interfere with the provision of additional care services by an external care provider of the tenant's choice. Violation of these provisions is an offence under s. 234 of the R.T.A.[22]

8. TRANSFERRING THE TENANT

Pursuant to s. 148 of the R.T.A. (formerly s. 99 of the T.P.A.), a landlord may apply to the Board for an order transferring a tenant out of a care home and evicting the tenant if,

(a) the tenant no longer requires the level of care provided by the landlord; or
(b) the tenant requires a level of care that the landlord is not able to provide.

---

[20] Subsection 142(1) of the R.T.A.
[21] Subsection 142(2) of the R.T.A.
[22] Clauses 234(n) and (o) of the R.T.A.

The expression "no longer requires the level of care provided by the landlord" includes circumstances where the tenant has repeatedly and substantially withdrawn from participation in some or all of the care services provided by the landlord that are set out in the tenancy agreement, and the tenant is not receiving substantially equivalent community based services.[23]

On an application to transfer the tenant out of a care home, the Board may only issue such an order, however, if it is satisfied that appropriate alternate accommodations are available for the tenant **and** that the level of care that the landlord is able to provide when combined with the community based services provided to the tenant in the care home cannot meet the tenant's care needs.[24]

As was the case under the T.P.A., mediation in *these* cases is mandatory.[25] If a dispute arises between the landlord and the tenant concerning the transfer of the tenant out of the care home, the Board cannot make an order until mediation has taken place and the Board can dismiss the landlord's application if the landlord fails to participate in that mediation.[26]

No notice of termination is required in these circumstances. The landlord must serve a copy of the application (Form L7) and notice of hearing upon the tenant and then file proof of service as soon as possible. Under the T.P.A., only five days' notice was required. The minimum notice has now been increased in these situations to 30 days.[27]

9. RENT AND CHARGES FOR CARE SERVICES

By the definition contained in s. 2 of the R.T.A., rent is the consideration paid for the right to occupy the rental unit but it does not include an amount that a landlord charges a tenant of a rental unit in a care home for care services or meals. Therefore, unpaid charges for care services or meals will not constitute arrears of rent. A landlord that is owed money only for care services or meals will have no right to apply to the Board for an order for either the payment of the outstanding sums or for termination of the tenancy based upon this debt.

The usual rent provisions contained in Part VII of the R.T.A. generally apply to units in a care home. Of course, this is not true of premises that are partially exempt from the R.T.A. pursuant to the provisions of s. 6(2) of the R.T.A.

---

[23] Section 49 of O. Reg. 516/06.

[24] Subsection 148(2) of the R.T.A.

[25] Subsection 148(3) of the R.T.A. In all other types of cases, participation in mediation is voluntary.

[26] Subsection 148(4) of the R.T.A.

[27] Rule 10.4 of the Board's Rules of Practice.

If there is more than one tenancy agreement for a rental unit in a care home (where, for instance, more than one tenant shares the unit and each tenant has his or her own separate agreement), the provisions of Part VII apply, subject to subsection 6(2), with respect to each tenancy agreement as if it were an agreement for a separate rental unit.[28]

In *Hall v. Howie*,[29] the landlord operated a care home. He did not provide the required information package to the tenant and continually increased the rent and other charges without providing prior written notice as required by the *Tenant Protection Act*. The landlord was ordered to repay more than $5,500 to the tenant and the Member also referred the matter to the Investigations and Enforcement Unit.

The usual provisions concerning at least 90 days written notice of rent increase apply in care homes as well.[30] In a care home, however, a similar notice must also be provided where the landlord wishes to increase a charge for providing a care service or meals to a tenant.[31] The notice must be in writing in the approved form.[32] An increase in a charge for a care service or meals is void if the landlord has not given the notice required by s. 150 of the R.T.A. and the landlord must give a new notice before the landlord can take the increase.[33]

Notwithstanding s. 134(1) of the R.T.A., it is not illegal for a landlord to charge for the provisions of care services or meals as long as the landlord complies with ss. 140 and 150 of the R.T.A.[34] Similarly, although a tenant cannot generally charge more to a subtenant than the tenant himself is paying to the landlord, that does not prohibit the tenant of a unit in a care home (or person acting on behalf of the tenant) from charging a subtenant for the provision of care services or meals.[35]

10. TERMINATING THE TENANCY

(a) Termination by the Tenant

Notwithstanding the *usual* amount of notice that a tenant must give to a landlord (under s. 44 of the R.T.A.), a tenant of a care home may terminate

---

[28] Section 149 of the R.T.A.

[29] (Feb. 16, 2006), SOT-05210, 2006 CarswellOnt 2150, [2006] O.R.H.T.D. No. 16 (Ont. Rental Housing Trib.).

[30] Section 116 of the R.T.A.

[31] Section 150 of the R.T.A.

[32] Subsection 150(2) of the R.T.A.

[33] Subsection 150(3) of the R.T.A.

[34] Subsection 151(1) of the R.T.A.

[35] Subsection 151(2) of the R.T.A.

a tenancy at any time by giving at least 30 days notice of termination to the landlord.[36]

A tenant who terminates the tenancy under s. 145(1) of the R.T.A. (i.e., on 30 days' notice) can also require the landlord to stop providing care services and meals prior to the termination date by giving 10 days' notice[37] and the tenant has no obligation to pay for such services thereafter.[38]

Of course, a landlord and tenant are also free to agree to terminate a tenancy at any time pursuant to s. 37(3) of the R.T.A.[39]

(b) Termination on Death of Sole Tenant

If the tenant dies, and there is no other tenant of the same rental unit, the tenancy will be deemed to be terminated 30 days after the date of the tenant's death. During that 30-day period, the landlord has certain obligations concerning the deceased tenant's property within the complex and the tenant's estate will have certain rights as well. The usual provisions apply (see Chapters 6 and 18). One unique provision that only applies to care homes, however, is that the estate of the tenant has no obligation to pay for care services and meals that would otherwise have been provided under the tenancy agreement more than 10 days after the death of the tenant.[40]

(c) Termination by the Landlord

(i) General

Most of the usual provisions of the R.T.A. apply to tenancies in care homes. Therefore, the usual grounds for termination by a landlord also apply. However, a few special considerations regarding this type of tenancy are described below.

(ii) Termination Based on Agreement

A landlord may apply (without notice) under s. 77 of the R.T.A. to the Board for an order terminating the tenancy on the basis that the tenant agreed to terminate the tenancy or on the basis that the tenant delivered to the landlord a signed notice of termination.

---

[36] Subsection 145(1) of the R.T.A.

[37] Subsection 145(2) of the R.T.A.

[38] Subsection 145(3) of the R.T.A.

[39] See "Termination by Agreement" in Chapter 6. Also see Landlord and Tenant Board File No. SOT-00249 (June 21, 2007).

[40] Subsection 145(4) of the R.T.A.

Normally, such an agreement or notice is void if it was created at the commencement of the tenancy.[41] This is not necessarily so in the case of a rental unit in a care home. Pursuant to s. 7 of O. Reg. 516/06, subsections 37(4) and (5) of the R.T.A. do not apply to a rental unit in a care home <u>if</u>:

(a) the rental unit is occupied for the purpose of receiving rehabilitative or therapeutic services agreed upon by the tenant and the landlord;
(b) the period of occupancy agreed to by the tenant and the landlord is no more than four years;
(c) the tenancy agreement stipulates that the tenancy may be terminated and the tenant evicted when the objectives of the services have been met or will not be met;[42] **and**
(d) the unit is subject to an agreement for the provision of housing services between the landlord and a service manager as defined in the *Social Housing Reform Act, 2000.*

In cases where all of these conditions are met, the landlord may bring an application under s. 77, relying upon the agreement contained in the tenancy agreement and the "termination date specified in the agreement" shall be the earlier of the following dates:[43]

1. The last day of the period of occupancy originally agreed to by the tenant and the landlord; and
2. the day that is 60 days after the day the tenant received notice from the landlord that the objectives of the services have been met or will not be met.

(iii) Termination Based on s. 144

Pursuant to s. 144(1) of the R.T.A., a landlord may, by notice, terminate the tenancy of a tenant in a care home if:

(a) the rental unit was occupied solely for the purpose of receiving rehabilitative or therapeutic services agreed upon by the tenant and the landlord;
(b) no other tenant of the care home occupying a rental unit solely for the purpose of receiving rehabilitative or therapeutic services is permitted to live there for longer than four years;[44] and
(c) the period of tenancy agreed to has expired.

---

[41] See subsections 37(4) and (5) of the R.T.A.

[42] I.e., if the tenant has repeatedly and substantially withdrawn from participation in the services (subsection 7(3) of O. Reg. 516/06).

[43] Subsection 7(2) of O. Reg. 516/06.

[44] Section 48 of O. Reg. 516/06.

The length of notice required shall be in accordance with s. 44 of the R.T.A. and must be the day a period of the tenancy ends or, where the tenancy is for a fixed term, the end of the term.[45]

(iv) Termination Based on Demolition, Conversion or Repairs

A landlord who gives a tenant of a care home a notice of termination under s. 50 of the R.T.A. must make reasonable efforts to find appropriate alternate accommodation for the tenant.[46] Where the tenant chooses to accept that alternate accommodation, the landlord will not be required to pay compensation under s. 52 or 54 of the R.T.A.[47] If the landlord of a care home fails to make reasonable efforts to find the tenant appropriate alternate accommodation, the Board may simply refuse to grant the landlord's application.[48]

---

[45] Subsection 144(2) of the R.T.A.

[46] Subsection 146(1) of the R.T.A. (formerly subsection 98(1) of the T.P.A.).

[47] Subsection 146(2) of the R.T.A. (formerly subsection 98(2) of the T.P.A.). Although subsection 146(2) refers to compensation under ss. 52 and 64, this is clearly a typographical error as it ought to say "sections 52 and 54".

[48] Since the landlord is in serious breach of the landlord's obligations under the Act (s. 83(3)) or, alternatively, because it would be unfair to grant an eviction in such circumstances (s. 83(1)).

Appendix 1

Feldman's Quick Reference Guide

	TYPE OF APPLICATION	SECT.	P.
A.	**BY LANDLORD OR TENANT (MISC.)**		
	Application to determine if R.T.A. applies	9	871
	Motion to set aside default order (transitional)	242(2) R.T.A. and 192(2) T.P.A.	872
	To determine whether arrears order has been voided by payment (*ex parte*)	74(6)	873
	Landlord's motion to set aside voiding order	74(9)	874
B.	**BY LANDLORD**		
(i)	**Termination/Eviction Applications**		
	For possession by the landlord, etc.	48, 69	875
	For possession by purchaser, etc.	49, 69	876
	For demolition, conversion, repairs or renovations	50, 69	877
	For persistent late payment of rent	58(1)1, 69	878
	For ceasing to qualify for social housing	58(1)2, 69	879
	For non-payment of rent	59, 69, 74, 87	880
	For illegal act or business	61(1), 68, 69, 75, 84	881
	For misrepresentation of income	60(1), 68, 69, 75, 90	883
	For undue damage (typical case)	62(1), 68, 69, 70, 89	885
	For undue damage (fast-track) - NEW	63(1), 68, 69, 70, 80, 84, 89	887
	For substantial interference with reasonable enjoyment or other rights of landlord or other tenants (typical case)	64(1), 68, 69, 76	889
	For substantial interference with reasonable enjoyment or other rights of landlord or other tenants (fast-track) - NEW	65(1), 68, 69, 76, 84	890
	For impairment of safety	66, 69, 76, 80, 84	891
	For overcrowding	67, 68, 69, 70	892
	Based on agreement or tenant's notice	77	893
	For breach of a mediated agreement or order	78	894
	For abandonment of the rental unit	79	895
	On termination of the employment of a person occupying superintendent's premises	93, 94	896
	Unauthorized occupant	100	897

(ii)	**Applications Where the Landlord is Not Seeking to Terminate the Tenancy**		
	Tenant alter locks	35	898
	Payment of arrears of rent	87, 88	899
	Compensation for undue damage		900
C.	**BY TENANT**		
(i)	**General Applications**		
	Landlord unreasonably withheld consent to an assignment or sublet	95, 96, 97, 98	901
	Landlord failed to repair or maintain property	20, 29(1)1, 30, 161	902
	Landlord entered unit illegally	25, 26, 27, 29(1)6, 31	903
	Landlord altered locks without providing a key	24, 29(1)5, 31	904
	Landlord withheld vital service, etc.	21, 29(1)2, 31	905
	Landlord interfered with reasonable enjoyment	22, 29(1)3, 31	906
	Landlord harassed (etc.) tenant	23, 29(1)4, 31	907
	Landlord's notice of termination was given in bad faith	57	908
	Landlord disposed of tenant's property within 72 hours of eviction or failed to make evicted tenant's property available for retrieval - NEW	41	909
	Motion to set aside order based on alleged agreement or tenant's notice of termination	77(6)	910
	Motion to set aside order based upon alleged breach of agreement or order	78(9)	911
(ii)	**Rent Applications**		
	Rent reduction because of reduction or discontinuance in services	130	912
	Payment of money collected/retained illegally	135	913

Application to determine if R.T.A. applies

SECTION(S) - 9

FORM(S)	COMMENTS
Application (Form A1)	
Notice of Hearing	– issued by board
Certificate of Service	- A1 and Notice of Hearing must be served at least 10 days before hearing (Rule 10.1) - file within five days of service (Rule 11.2)

TO BE PROVEN BY APPLICANT
- varies

DEFENCES TO CONSIDER
- n/a

TYPICAL ORDER SOUGHT
A declaration that:

1. The R.T.A. does/does not apply to the rental unit; or
2. Particular provisions of the T.P.A. do/do not apply to the rental unit.
3. Costs (application fee and other legal expenses).

Motion to set aside default order (transitional)

SECTION(S) - 242(2) of the R.T.A., 192(2) of the T.P.A.

FORM(S)	COMMENTS
Motion (Form S1)	- filed within 10 days after order issued
Notice of Hearing	- issued by Board
Certificate of Service	- Motion and Notice of Hearing must be served at least 48 hours before time set for hearing (Rule 6.8 of the Tribunal's Rules; analogous to Rule 10.7 of the Board's Rules)

TO BE PROVEN BY RESPONDENT (MOVING PARTY)

1. Respondent was not reasonably able to participate in the proceeding

DEFENCES TO CONSIDER

- n/a

TYPICAL ORDER SOUGHT

1. Set aside default order and hear the application on its merits
2. If the motion is granted, even though the proceeding will then be determined by the Board under the provisions of the T.P.A., s. 83 of the R.T.A. must be considered.

Note: This is a transitional provision that will only apply to applications that were commenced under the T.P.A. (i.e., before January 31, 2007) as there will be no default orders issued under the R.T.A.

To determine whether arrears order has been voided by payment (*ex parte*)

SECTION(S) - 74(6)

FORM(S)	COMMENTS
Motion	- must be filed before the eviction order becomes enforceable
Affidavit	- must accompany Motion (s. 74(7))

TO BE PROVEN BY RESPONDENT (MOVING PARTY)

1. All amounts required to be paid have been paid by the deadline set out in the order.

DEFENCES TO CONSIDER

- n/a

TYPICAL ORDER SOUGHT

1. Declaration that eviction order is void.
2. Direction to have any money that was paid into the Board released to the landlord.

Note: Motion can only be granted or denied upon the documents filed. The Member has no discretion to refer the matter to a hearing (s. 74(8)).

Landlord's motion to set aside voiding order

SECTION(S) - 74(9)

FORM(S)	COMMENTS
Motion (Form S3)	- must be filed within 10 days after voiding order is issued
Notice of Hearing	- issued by Board
Certificate of Service	- Motion and Notice of Hearing must be served at least 48 hours before time set for hearing (Rule 10.7)

TO BE PROVEN BY APPLICANT (MOVING PARTY)

1. The tenant did not pay all amounts required by the effective date of the order.

DEFENCES TO CONSIDER

- n/a

TYPICAL ORDER SOUGHT

1. Landlord will seek an order setting aside the voiding order and declaring that the eviction order remains in effect and may be enforced.

Termination for possession by landlord, etc.

SECTION(S) - 48(1), 69

FORM(S)	COMMENTS
Notice of Termination (Form N12)	- must be complete and accurate - termination date must be end of period/term
Certificate of Service (for Form N12)	- N12 must be served at least 60 days prior to termination date set out in notice
Application (Form L2)	- can be commenced immediately after Notice of Termination served (s. 71) - cannot be commenced more than 30 days after termination date (s. 69(2))
Affidavit	- by person who wants to live in unit (s. 72(1))
Notice of Hearing	- issued by Board
Certificate of Service (for L2 and Notice of Hearing)	- L2 and Notice of Hearing must be served at least 10 days before hearing (Rule 10.1) - file within five days of service (Rule 11.2)

TO BE PROVEN BY APPLICANT

1. The landlord, their spouse or a child or parent of one of them or a person who will provide care services to one of them (and who will live in the residential complex),
2. in good faith,
3. requires possession of the rental unit for the purpose of residential occupation.

If (and only if) the landlord is relying on a right to occupy in a tenancy agreement, then the landlord must also demonstrate that the building contains no more than four residential units OR the person who wants to live in the unit has previously been a genuine occupant of the premises (s. 72(2)).

DEFENCES TO CONSIDER

1. Defective Notice of Termination or other procedural errors.
2. Landlord has failed to prove all necessary elements.
3. Relief under s. 83.

TYPICAL ORDER SOUGHT

1. Terminate the tenancy effective not earlier than the termination date set out in the Notice of Termination (s. 80(1)) and order eviction.
2. Costs (application fee and other legal expenses).

Termination for possession by purchaser, etc.

SECTION(S) - 49(1), 69

FORM(S)	COMMENTS
Notice of Termination (Form N12)	- must be complete and accurate - termination date must be end of period/term
Certificate of Service (for Form N12)	- N12 must be served at least 60 days prior to termination date set out in notice
Application (Form L2)	- can be commenced immediately after Notice of Termination served (s. 71) - cannot be commenced more than 30 days after termination date (s. 69(2))
Affidavit	- by person who wants to live in unit (s. 72(1))
Notice of Hearing	- issued by Board
Certificate of Service (for L2 and Notice of Hearing)	- L2 and Notice of Hearing must be served at least 10 days before hearing (Rule 10.1) - file within five days of service (Rule 11.2)

TO BE PROVEN BY APPLICANT

1. The landlord of a residential complex that contains no more than three residential units,
2. has entered into an agreement of purchase and sale of the residential complex, and
3. the purchaser in good faith,
4. requires possession of the complex or a unit in it for residential occupation,
5. by the purchaser, the purchaser's spouse or a child or parent of one of them or a person who will provide care services to one of them (and who will live in the residential complex).

Note: Under s. 49(2) there are similar provisions for a condominium unit (but no restriction based on the number of units).

DEFENCES TO CONSIDER

1. Defective notice or other procedural errors.
2. Landlord has failed to prove all necessary elements.
3. Relief under s. 83.

TYPICAL ORDER SOUGHT

1. Terminate the tenancy (and evict) effective not earlier than the termination date set out in the Notice of Termination (s. 80(1)).
2. Costs (application fee and other legal expenses).

Termination for demolition, conversion, repairs or renovations

SECTION(S) - 50(1), 69

FORM(S)	COMMENTS
Notice of Termination (Form N13)	- must be complete and accurate - termination date must be end of period/term
Certificate of Service (for the Form N13)	- N13 must be served at least 120 days prior to termination date set out in notice (at least one year in advance for a mobile home or land lease home— s. 164)
Application (Form L2)	- can be commenced immediately after Notice of Termination served (s. 71) - cannot be commenced more than 30 days after termination date (s. 69(2))
Notice of Hearing	- issued by Board
Certificate of Service (for L2 and Notice of Hearing)	- L2 and Notice of Hearing must be served at least 10 days before hearing (Rule 10.1) - file within five days of service (Rule 11.2)

TO BE PROVEN BY APPLICANT

1. The landlord requires possession of the unit in order to
2. demolish it, convert it to a non-residential use, or do extensive repairs or renovations that require a building permit and vacant possession.
3. landlord in good faith intends to carry out activity (s. 73(a)), and
4. the landlord has obtained all necessary permits or other authority to carry out the intended work or has taken all necessary steps to do so but cannot obtain the permit(s) or authority until the unit is vacant (s. 73(b)).

Note: Under *some* circumstances, the landlord must pay the tenant compensation, find the tenant alternative accommodation or offer the tenant first right of refusal (ss. 52, 53 and 54). In such circumstances, the landlord must file proof of compliance (s. 53 of O. Reg. 516/06).

DEFENCES TO CONSIDER

1. Defective notice or other procedural errors.
2. Landlord has failed to prove all necessary elements.
3. Relief under subsections 83(1), (2), (3), **(4) and (5)**.
4. In a care home, landlord has not made reasonable efforts to find appropriate alternate accommodation for the tenant (s. 146).

TYPICAL ORDER SOUGHT

1. Terminate the tenancy (and evict) effective not earlier than the termination date set out in the Notice of Termination (s. 80(1)).
2. Costs (application fee and other legal expenses).

Termination for persistent late payment of rent

SECTION(S) - 58(1)1, 69

FORM(S)	COMMENTS
Notice of Termination (Form N8)	- must contain reasons and **details** (s. 43) - termination date must be end of period/term
Certificate of Service (for the Form N8)	- N8 must be served at least 28 days for daily/weekly tenancies or 60 days for all other tenancies before termination date
Application (Form L2)	- can be commenced immediately after Notice of Termination served (s. 71) - cannot be commenced more than 30 days after termination date (s. 69(2))
Notice of Hearing	- issued by Board
Certificate of Service (for L2 and Notice of Hearing)	- L2 and Notice of Hearing must be served at least 10 days before hearing (Rule 10.1) - file within five days of service (Rule 11.2)

TO BE PROVEN BY APPLICANT

1. The tenant has persistently failed to pay rent on the date it becomes due and payable.

DEFENCES TO CONSIDER

1. Defective notice or other procedural errors.
2. Landlord has failed to prove all necessary elements.
3. Relief under s. 83.

TYPICAL ORDER SOUGHT

1. Terminate the tenancy effective not earlier than the termination date set out in the Notice of Termination (s. 80(1)) and order eviction.
2. Costs (application fee and other legal expenses).

Termination because tenant ceases to qualify for social housing

SECTION(S) - 58(1)2, 69

FORM(S)	COMMENTS
Notice of Termination (Form N8)	- must contain reasons and **details** (s. 43) - termination date must be end of period/term
Certificate of Service (for the Form N8)	- N8 must be served at least 28 days for daily/weekly tenancies or 60 days for all other tenancies before termination date
Application (Form L2)	- can be commenced immediately after Notice of Termination served (s. 71) - cannot be commenced more than 30 days after termination date (s. 69(2))
Notice of Hearing	- issued by Board
Certificate of Service (for L2 and Notice of Hearing)	- L2 and Notice of Hearing must be served at least 10 days before hearing (Rule 10.1) - file within five days of service (Rule 11.2)

TO BE PROVEN BY APPLICANT

1. The rental unit falls within paragraph 7(1)1,2,3 or 4; and
2. the tenant has ceased to meet the qualifications required for occupancy of the unit.

DEFENCES TO CONSIDER .

41. Defective notice or other procedural errors.
2. Landlord has failed to prove all necessary elements.
3. Relief under s. 83.

TYPICAL ORDER SOUGHT

1. Terminate the tenancy effective not earlier than the termination date set out in the Notice of Termination (s. 80(1)) and order eviction.
2. Costs (application fee and other legal expenses).

Early termination for non-payment of rent

SECTION(S) - 59(1), 69, 74, 87

FORM(S)	COMMENTS
Notice of Termination (Form N4)	- must be complete and accurate
Certificate of Service (for the Form N4)	- N4 must be served at least seven days for daily/ weekly tenancies or 14 days for all other tenancies prior to the termination date
Application (Form L1)	- cannot be commenced until the day after the termination date set out in the notice (s. 74(1)) - no upper time limit set out in R.T.A.
Notice of Hearing	- issued by Board
Certificate of Service (for L1 and Notice of Hearing)	- L1 and Notice of Hearing must be served at least 10 days before hearing (Rule 10.1) - file within five days of service (Rule 11.2)

TO BE PROVEN BY APPLICANT

1. The tenant has failed to pay
2. rent
3. lawfully owing under a tenancy agreement, and
4. the tenant was in possession of the rental unit when the application was commenced (s. 87(1)(b)).

DEFENCES TO CONSIDER

1. Defective notice or other procedural errors.
2. The Notice of Termination was void before the application was commenced because all the rent due was paid (s. 59(3)).
3. The application was discontinued by operation of s. 74(2) because all amounts required were paid to the landlord before an eviction order was issued.
4. Landlord has failed to prove all necessary elements.
5. Relief under s. 83.
6. Tenant can raise own issue(s) pursuant to s. 82.

TYPICAL ORDER SOUGHT

1. Terminate the tenancy (and evict) effective not earlier than the termination date set out in the Notice of Termination (s. 80(1)).
2. Payment of rent arrears, NSF charges, daily compensation for use of the unit after the termination date and the costs, less the deposit and interest thereon.

Early termination for illegal act or business

SECTION(S) - 62(1), 68, 69, 75, 84

FORM(S)	COMMENTS
Notice of Termination (Form N6)	- must contain reasons and details (s. 43) - no right to remedy a breach of s. 61(1)
Certificate of Service (for the Form N6)	- N6 must be served at least 10 days in advance if related to drug offences - for other matters, at least 20 days notice is required if it is a first notice - at least 14 days notice must be provided if the N6 is being given within six months of the tenant voiding an earlier notice given under s. 62, 64 or 67
Original Notice of Termination and Certificate of Service	- **if the current application is based upon a "second" notice** within six months, the landlord must also file a copy of the original Notice of Termination and proof of service of that notice (s. 53 of O. Reg. 516/06)
Application (Form L2)	- can be commenced immediately after Notice of Termination served (s. 71) - cannot be commenced more than 30 days after termination date (s. 69(2))
Notice of Hearing	- issued by Board
Certificate of Service (for L2 and Notice of Hearing)	- L2 and Notice of Hearing must be served at least 10 days before hearing for most offences (Rule 10.1) or at least five days before the hearing in the case of the production of or trafficking in an illegal drug (Rule 10.5(c)(i)) - file within five days of service (Rule 11.2)

TO BE PROVEN BY APPLICANT

1. The tenant or another occupant of the rental unit committed an illegal act or carried on an illegal trade, business or occupation
2. or permitted a person to do so
3. in the rental unit or the residential complex.

DEFENCES TO CONSIDER

1. Defective notice or other procedural errors.
2. Landlord has failed to prove all necessary elements.
3. Relief under s. 83.

TYPICAL ORDER SOUGHT

1. Terminate the tenancy effective not earlier than the term. date set out in the Notice of Termination (s. 80(1)) and order eviction.

2. Direct sheriff to enforce the eviction in priority to other eviction orders and, possibly, on a specific date set by the Board (s. 84).
3. Costs (application fee and other legal expenses).

Early termination for misrepresentation of income

SECTION(S) - 60(1), 68, 69, 75, 90

FORM(S)	COMMENTS
Notice of Termination (Form N6)	- must contain reasons and details (s. 43) - no right to remedy a breach of s. 60(1)
Certificate of Service (for the Form N6)	- for "first notice", N6 must be served at least 20 days before termination date - if the N6 is being given within six months of the tenant voiding an earlier notice under s. 62 (undue damage), 64 (interference with reasonable enjoyment) or 67 (overcrowding), the N6 must be served at least 14 days before the termination date
Original Notice of Termination and Certificate of Service	**- if the current application is based upon a "second" notice** within six months, the landlord must also file a copy of the original Notice of Termination and proof of service of that notice (s. 53 of O. Reg. 516/06)
Application (Form L2)	- can be commenced immediately after Notice of Termination served (s. 71) - if seeking termination of the tenancy, L2 cannot be commenced more than 30 days after termination date (s. 69(2))
Notice of Hearing	- issued by Board
Certificate of Service (for L2 and Notice of Hearing)	- L2 and Notice of Hearing must be served at least 10 days before hearing (Rule 10.1) - file within five days of service (Rule 11.2)

TO BE PROVEN BY APPLICANT

1. The rental unit falls within para. 7(1)1,2, 3 or 4 and
2. the tenant has knowingly
3. and materially
4. misrepresented his or her income or the income of other members of his or her family occupying the rental unit.

DEFENCES TO CONSIDER

1. Defective notice or other procedural errors.
2. Landlord has failed to prove all necessary elements.
3. Relief under s. 83.

TYPICAL ORDER SOUGHT

1. Terminate the tenancy effective not earlier than the term. date set out in the Notice of Termination (s. 80(1)) and order eviction.

2. Direct sheriff to enforce the eviction in priority to other eviction orders, and, possibly, on a specific date set by the Board (s. 84).
3. Costs (application fee and other legal expenses).

Early termination for undue damage (typical case)

SECTION(S) - 62(1), 68, 69, 70, 89

FORM(S)	COMMENTS
Notice of Termination (Form N5)	- must contain reasons and details (s. 43) - tenant has seven days to void the notice (s. 62(2), (3))
Certificate of Service (for the Form N5)	- for "first notice", N5 must be served at least 20 days before termination date - if the N5 is being given within six months of the tenant voiding an earlier notice under s. 62, 64 or 67, the N5 must be served at least 14 days before the termination date
Original Notice of Termination and Certificate of Servicew	- **if the current application is based upon a "second" notice** within six months, the landlord must also file a copy of the original Notice of Termination and proof of service of that notice (s. 53 of O. Reg. 516/06)
Application (Form L2)	- if seeking termination, application must be commenced on or after the eighth day after service of the Notice of Termination but not more than 30 days after termination date (s. 69(2) and 70)
Notice of Hearing	- issued by Board
Certificate of Service (for L2 and Notice of Hearing)	- L2 and Notice of Hearing must be served at least 10 days before hearing (Rule 10.1) - file within five days of service (Rule 11.2)

TO BE PROVEN BY APPLICANT

1. The tenant, another occupant of the unit or a person whom the tenant permits in the residential complex
2. wilfully or negligently
3. caused undue damage
4. to the rental unit or the residential complex
5. and the tenant was in possession of the unit at the time the application was commenced (s. 89).

DEFENCES TO CONSIDER

1. Defective notice or other procedural errors.
2. Landlord has failed to prove all necessary elements.
3. Relief under s. 83.

TYPICAL ORDER SOUGHT

1. Terminate the tenancy (and evict) effective not earlier than the termination date set out in the Notice of Termination (s. 80(1)).

APP. 1 — FELDMAN'S QRG

2. Payment of compensation for the damage (s. 89).
3. Costs (application fee and other legal expenses).

Early termination for undue damage (fast-track)

SECTION(S) - 63(1), 68, 69, 70, 80, 84, 89

FORM(S)	COMMENTS
Notice of Termination (Form N7)	- must contain reasons and details (s. 43) - tenant has no right to void this notice (s. 63(2))
Certificate of Service (for the Form N7)	- N5 must be served at least 10 days before termination date
Application (Form L2)	- can be commenced immediately after Notice of Termination served (s. 71) - if seeking termination of the tenancy, L2 cannot be commenced more than 30 days after termination date (s. 69(2))
Notice of Hearing	- issued by Board
Certificate of Service (for L2 and Notice of Hearing)	- L2 and Notice of Hearing must be served at least five days before hearing (Rule 10.5(c)(ii)) - file within five days of service (Rule 11.2)

TO BE PROVEN BY APPLICANT

1. The tenant, another occupant of the unit or a person whom the tenant permits in the residential complex
2. wilfully
3. causes undue damage
4. to the rental unit or the residential complex
5. and the tenant was in possession of the unit at the time the application was commenced (s. 89).

OR

1. The tenant, another occupant of the unit or a person whom the tenant permits in the residential complex
2. uses the rental unit or the residential complex in a manner that is inconsistent with use as residential premises
3. and that causes or can reasonably be expected to cause damage that is significantly greater than the damage that is required in order to give a Notice of Termination under 63(1)(a) or 62(1)
4. and the tenant was in possession of the unit at the time the application was commenced (s. 89).

DEFENCES TO CONSIDER

1. Defective notice or other procedural errors.
2. Landlord has failed to prove all necessary elements.
3. Relief under s. 83.

TYPICAL ORDER SOUGHT

1. Terminate the tenancy (and evict). In appropriate circumstances, the eviction can be effective *earlier* than the termination date set out in the Notice of Termination (s. 80(2)).
2. Payment of compensation for the damage (s. 89).
3. Costs (application fee and other legal expenses).
4. Direct sheriff to enforce the eviction in priority to other eviction orders, and, possibly, on a specific date set by the Board (s. 84).

Early termination for substantial interference with reasonable enjoyment or other rights of landlord or other tenants (typical case)

SECTION(S) - 64(1), 68, 69, 76

FORM(S)	COMMENTS
Notice of Termination (Form N5)	- must contain reasons and details (s. 43) - tenant has seven days to void the notice (s. 64(3))
Certificate of Service (for the Form N5)	- for "first notice", N5 must be served at least 20 days before termination date - if the N5 is being given within six months of the tenant voiding an earlier notice under s. 62, 64 or 67, the N5 must be served at least 14 days before the termination date
Original Notice of Termination and Certificate of Service	- **if the current application is based upon a "second" notice** within six months, the landlord must also file a copy of the original Notice of Termination and proof of service of that notice (s. 53 of O. Reg. 516/06)
Application (Form L2)	- can be commenced on the eighth day after service of the notice but not more than 30 days after termination date (if seeking termination)
Notice of Hearing	- issued by Board
Certificate of Service (for L2 and Notice of Hearing)	- L2 and Notice of Hearing must be served at least 10 days before hearing (Rule 10.1) - file within five days of service (Rule 11.2)

TO BE PROVEN BY APPLICANT

1. The conduct of the tenant, another occupant of the unit or a person whom the tenant permits in the residential complex
2. substantially interferes with the reasonable enjoyment of the residential complex for all usual purposes by the landlord or another tenant, or
3. substantially interferes with another lawful right, privilege or interest of the landlord or another tenant.

Note: If based on presence or behaviour of an animal, see s. 76.

DEFENCES TO CONSIDER

1. Defective notice or other procedural errors.
2. Landlord has failed to prove all necessary elements.
3. Relief under s. 83.

TYPICAL ORDER SOUGHT

1. Terminate the tenancy (and evict) effective not earlier than the termination date set out in the Notice of Termination (s. 80(1)).
2. Costs (application fee and other legal expenses).

Early termination for substantial interference with reasonable enjoyment or other rights of landlord or other tenants (fast-track)

SECTION(S) - 65(1), 68, 69, 76, 84

FORM(S)	COMMENTS
Notice of Termination (Form N7)	- must contain reasons and details (s. 43) - tenant has no right to void notice (s. 65(3))
Certificate of Service (for the Form N7)	- N5 must be served at least 10 days before termination date
Application (Form L2)	- can be commenced immediately after Notice of Termination served (s. 71) - if seeking termination of the tenancy, L2 cannot be commenced more than 30 days after termination date (s. 69(2))
Notice of Hearing	- issued by Board
Certificate of Service (for L2 and Notice of Hearing)	- L2 and Notice of Hearing must be served at least five days before hearing (Rule 10.5(c)(iii)) - file within five days of service (Rule 11.2)

TO BE PROVEN BY APPLICANT

1. The landlord resides in the same building as the tenant and the building contains not more than three residential units;
2. the conduct of the tenant, another occupant of the unit or a person whom the tenant permits in the residential complex
3. substantially interferes with the reasonable enjoyment of the residential complex for all usual purposes by the landlord or another tenant or
4. substantially interferes with another lawful right, privilege or interest of the landlord or another tenant.

Note: If based on presence or behaviour of an animal, see s. 76.

DEFENCES TO CONSIDER

1. Defective notice or other procedural errors.
2. Landlord has failed to prove all necessary elements.
3. Relief under s. 83.

TYPICAL ORDER SOUGHT

1. Terminate the tenancy (and evict) effective not earlier than the termination date set out in the Notice of Termination (s. 80(1)).
2. Costs (application fee and other legal expenses).
3. Direct sheriff to enforce the eviction in priority to other eviction orders and, possibly, on a specific date set by the Board (s. 84).

Early termination for serious impairment of safety

SECTION(S) - 66, 69, 76, 80, 84

FORM(S)	COMMENTS
Notice of Termination (Form N7)	- must contain reasons and details (s. 43)
Certificate of Service (for the Form N7)	- must be served at least 10 days before termination date set out in notice
Application (Form L2)	- can be commenced immediately after Notice of Termination served (s. 71) - cannot be commenced more than 30 days after termination date (s. 69(2))
Notice of Hearing	- issued by Board
Certificate of Service (for L2 and Notice of Hearing)	- L2 and Notice of Hearing must be served at least five days before hearing (Rule 10.5(c)(iv)) - file within five days of service (Rule 11.2)

TO BE PROVEN BY APPLICANT

1. An act or omission of the tenant, another occupant of the unit or a person permitted in the complex by the tenant
2. seriously impairs or has seriously impaired the safety
3. of any person, and
4. the act or omission occurs in the residential complex.

Note: If based on presence or behaviour of an animal, see s. 76.

DEFENCES TO CONSIDER

1. Defective notice or other procedural errors.
2. Landlord has failed to prove all necessary elements.
3. Relief under s. 83.

TYPICAL ORDER SOUGHT

1. Terminate the tenancy (and evict). In appropriate circumstances, the eviction can be effective *earlier* than the termination date set out in the Notice of Termination (s. 80(2)).
2. Costs (application fee and other legal expenses).
3. Direct sheriff to enforce the eviction in priority to other eviction orders and, possibly, on a specific date set by the Board (s. 84).

Early termination for "overcrowding"

SECTION(S) - 67, 68, 69, 70

FORM(S)	COMMENTS
Notice of Termination (Form N5)	- must contain reasons and details (s. 43) - tenant has seven days to void the notice (s. 67(3))
Certificate of Service (for the Form N5)	- for "first notice", N5 must be served at least 20 days before termination date - if the N5 is being given within six months of the tenant voiding an earlier notice under s. 62, 64 or 67, the N5 must be served at least 14 days before the termination date
Original Notice of Termination and Certificate of Service	- **if the current application is based upon a "second" notice** within six months, the landlord must also file a copy of the original Notice of Termination and proof of service of that notice (s. 53 of O. Reg. 516/06)
Application (Form L2)	- can be commenced on the eighth day after service of the notice but not more than 30 days after termination date
Notice of Hearing	- issued by Board
Certificate of Service (for L2 and Notice of Hearing)	- L2 and Notice of Hearing must be served at least 10 days before hearing (Rule 10.1) - file within 5 days of service (Rule 11.2)

TO BE PROVEN BY APPLICANT

1. The number of persons occupying the rental unit
2. on a continuing basis
3. results in a contravention of health, safety or housing standards.

DEFENCES TO CONSIDER

1. Defective notice or other procedural errors.
2. Landlord has failed to prove all necessary elements.
3. Relief under s. 83.

TYPICAL ORDER SOUGHT

1. Terminate the tenancy effective not earlier than the termination date set out in the Notice of Termination (s. 80(1)) and order eviction.
2. Costs (application fee and other legal expenses).

Early termination based on agreement or notice to terminate from the tenant (*ex parte*)

SECTION(S) - 77

FORM(S)	COMMENTS
Application (Form L3)	- can be commenced up to 30 days after the termination date specified in the agreement or notice (s. 77(3))
Affidavit	- verifying the agreement or Notice of Termination (s. 77(2)), with details and a copy of the notice or agreement (if written) attached (s. 53 of O. Reg. 516/06)
Certificate of Service	- normally, none required as this is an *ex parte* application - if, however, a Member refers the matter to a hearing, unless otherwise directed by the Board, the applicant must serve a copy of the L4 and Notice of Hearing on the respondent at least 10 days before the hearing (Rule 10.2) and must file the COS within five days of service (Rule 11.2)

TO BE PROVEN BY APPLICANT

1. Notice of Termination was served by the tenant or the parties reached an agreement to terminate the tenancy.
2. the notice or agreement was not entered into at the same time as the tenancy was created or as a condition of entering into the tenancy (s. 37(4) and (5)).

Note 1 – some post-secondary institutions may be exempt from s. 37
Note 2 – an *agreement* can be oral but a *notice* must be in writing

DEFENCES TO CONSIDER

1. Applicant has failed to prove all necessary elements.
2. Relief under s. 83.

TYPICAL ORDER SOUGHT

1. Terminate the tenancy effective not earlier than the termination date specified in the notice or agreement (s. 77(5)).
2. Application fee (if the order is made *after* the termination date).
3. Compensation for use and occupation of the unit by the tenant after the termination date (s. 86) — this is rarely requested.

Early termination for breach of a mediated agreement or order (*ex parte*)

SECTION(S) - 78

FORM(S)	COMMENTS
Application (Form L4)	- can be commenced up to 30 days after the tenant's breach of a condition described in subparagraph 78(1)2.i (s. 78(5))
Affidavit	- attach a copy of the mediated agreement or order (s. 78(4)) - set out tenant's alleged breach (s. 78(2)) - the affidavit must contain additional financial information if the landlord is also seeking payment of arrears of rent and compensation
Certificate of Service	- normally, none required - if, however, a Member refers the matter to a hearing, unless otherwise directed by the Board, the applicant must serve a copy of the L4 and Notice of Hearing on the respondent at least 10 days before the hearing (Rule 10.2) and file the Certificate of Service within five days of service (Rule 11.2)

TO BE PROVEN BY APPLICANT

1. There was a previous application for an order terminating the tenancy or evicting the tenant,
2. which was resolved (without termination) by a mediated agreement or an order that imposed conditions on the tenant;
3. those conditions specifically provided for relief under s. 78 if there was a breach by the tenant, and
4. the terms that have been breached would give rise to the same grounds for termination as were claimed in the previous application.

DEFENCES TO CONSIDER

1. Landlord has failed to prove all necessary elements.
2. Landlord is responsible for the breach or the breach is so minor that granting the application would be contrary to public policy.
3. Relief under s. 83.

TYPICAL ORDER SOUGHT

1. Terminate the tenancy and evict the tenant
2. If the original application was based on arrears of rent, the landlord can seek an order for rent, NSF fees, compensation, etc.

Early termination where tenant has abandoned the rental unit

SECTION(S) - 79

FORM(S)	COMMENTS
Application (Form L2)	- can be commenced at any time
Notice of Hearing	- issued by Board
Certificate of Service	- L2 and Notice of Hearing must be served at least 10 days before hearing (Rule 10.1) - file within five days of service (Rule 11.2)

TO BE PROVEN BY APPLICANT

1. The tenant has abandoned the unit.

Note: if the rent is being paid, the unit cannot be considered abandoned (s. 2(3)).

TYPICAL ORDER SOUGHT

1. Terminate the tenancy.
2. Costs (application fee and other legal expenses).

Early termination of the tenancy on termination of the employment of a person occupying superintendent's premises

SECTION(S) - 93, 94

FORM(S)	COMMENTS
Application (Form L2)	- cannot be commenced until at least eight days after termination of the employment
Notice of Hearing	- issued by Board
Certificate of Service (for L2 and Notice of Hearing)	- L2 and Notice of Hearing must be served at least five days before hearing (Rule 10.5(d)) - file within five days of service (Rule 11.2)

TO BE PROVEN BY APPLICANT

1. The tenant occupies superintendent's premises,
2. the tenant's employment related to the residential complex has been terminated, and
3. the tenant has not vacated the unit within seven days of the termination of the employment.

DEFENCES TO CONSIDER

1. Procedural errors.
2. Landlord has failed to prove all necessary elements.
3. The landlord and tenant have agreed that the usual presumptive termination date (one week after termination of employment) would not apply (s. 93(1)).
4. Relief under s. 83.

TYPICAL ORDER SOUGHT

1. Terminate the tenancy and order eviction.
2. Costs (application fee and other legal expenses).

Unauthorized occupant

SECTION(S) - 100

FORM(S)	COMMENTS
Application (Form A2)	- must be commenced within 60 days of landlord discovering the unauthorized transfer of occupancy
Notice of Hearing	- issued by Board
Certificate of Service (for A2 and Notice of Hearing)	- A2 and Notice of Hearing must be served at least 10 days before hearing (Rule 10.1) on tenant and occupant - file within five days of service (Rule 11.2)

TO BE PROVEN BY APPLICANT

1. The tenant has transferred the occupancy of the unit
2. other than by an assignment under s. 95 or a sublet under s. 97.

DEFENCES TO CONSIDER

1. Procedural errors.
2. Landlord has failed to prove all necessary elements.
3. The landlord let more than 60 days go by and the landlord is now deemed to accept the occupant as a new tenant (s. 104(4)).
4. The landlord and the occupant have entered into a tenancy agreement.
5. Relief under s. 83.

TYPICAL ORDER SOUGHT

1. Termination of the tenancy (NEW)
2. Eviction of the unauthorized occupant.
3. Application fee.
4. Daily compensation for use and occupation of the unit (s. 100(3)) — rarely requested.
5. NSF cheque charges (s. 100(4)).

Tenant has altered the locks

SECTION(S) - 35

FORM(S)	COMMENTS
Application (Form L8)	
Notice of Hearing	- issued by Board
Certificate of Service (for L8 and Notice of Hearing)	- L8 and Notice of Hearing must be served at least 10 days before hearing (Rule 10.1) - File within five days of service (Rule 11.2)

TO BE PROVEN BY APPLICANT

1. The tenant has altered the locking system on a door giving entry to the rental unit or residential complex or has caused the locking system to be altered,
2. during the tenant's occupancy of the rental unit,
3. without the consent of the landlord.

DEFENCES TO CONSIDER

1. Procedural errors.
2. Landlord has failed to prove all necessary elements.

TYPICAL ORDER SOUGHT

1. The tenant shall provide the landlord with keys or pay the landlord the reasonable out of pocket expenses necessary to change the locking system.
2. Costs (application fee and other legal expenses).

Payment of arrears of rent (without seeking termination of the tenancy based on the arrears)

SECTION(S) - 87, 88

FORM(S)	COMMENTS
Application (Form L9)	- provide detailed calculations
Notice of Hearing	- issued by Board
Certificate of Service (for L1 and Notice of Hearing)	- L9 and Notice of Hearing must be served at least 10 days before hearing (Rule 10.1) -file within five days of service (Rule 11.2)

TO BE PROVEN BY APPLICANT

1. The tenant has not paid
2. rent
3. lawfully required under the tenancy agreement, and
4. the tenant was in possession of the rental unit when the application was filed.

DEFENCES TO CONSIDER

1. Procedural errors.
2. Landlord has failed to prove all necessary elements.
3. The amounts being charged are not rent or are not legal.
4. The landlord has failed to take reasonable steps to minimize its losses in accordance with s. 16.
5. The amount claimed by the landlord exceeds the amount permitted in accordance with the provisions of s. 88.
6. Tenant can raise own issue(s) pursuant to s. 82 and 87(2),

TYPICAL ORDER SOUGHT

1. Payment of arrears of rent.
2. Payment of NSF cheque charges.
3. If the tenancy has otherwise been terminated, payment of compensation for use and occupation of the unit after the termination has taken effect.
4. Costs (application fee and other legal expenses).

Compensation for undue damage (without termination of the tenancy)

SECTION(S) - 89

FORM(S)	COMMENTS
Application (Form L2)	- provide details
Notice of Hearing	- issued by Board
Certificate of Service (for L2 and Notice of Hearing)	- L2 and Notice of Hearing must be served at least 10 days before hearing (Rule 10.1) - file within five days of service (Rule 11.2)

TO BE PROVEN BY APPLICANT

1. The tenant or a person whom the tenant permits in the residential complex,
2. wilfully or negligently,
3. caused undue damage
4. to the rental unit or the residential complex, and
5. the tenant is in possession of the rental unit.

DEFENCES TO CONSIDER

1. Procedural errors.
2. Landlord has failed to prove all necessary elements.

TYPICAL ORDER SOUGHT

1. The tenant shall pay compensation for the reasonable costs that the landlord has incurred or will incur for the repair of or, where repairing is not reasonable, the replacement of the damaged property.
2. Costs (application fee and other legal expenses).

Landlord unreasonably withheld consent to an assignment or sublet

SECTION(S) - 95, 96, 97, 98

FORM(S)	COMMENTS
Application (Form A2)	- by tenant or former tenant - must be filed within one year of conduct
Notice of Hearing	- issued by Board
Certificate of Service (for A2 and Notice of Hearing)	- A2 and Notice of Hearing must be served at least 10 days before hearing (Rule 10.1) -file within five days of service (Rule 11.2)

TO BE PROVEN BY APPLICANT

1. The landlord *arbitrarily or unreasonably* withheld consent to a request for assignment to a specific person or to a request to sublet to a specific person.

Note 1: Certain types of housing cannot be assigned/sublet (see subsections 95(9), 97(6), 7(1), 8(2)).

Note 2: If care home, see s. 143.

Note 3: If the assignment is on the site on which a mobile home or land lease home rests and the assignment is in furtherance of a sale of the home, see s. 165.

DEFENCES TO CONSIDER

1. Applicant has failed to prove all necessary elements.
2. Tenant failed to pay charges for reasonable expenses to investigate potential assignee or subtenant.
3. This type of housing cannot be assigned/sublet.

TYPICAL ORDER SOUGHT

1. Pursuant to s. 98(3) of the R.T.A., an order to:
   a. authorize the requested assignment/sublet;
   b. authorize an alternate assignment/sublet;
   c. terminate the tenancy; and/or
   d. award an abatement of rent.
2. Costs (application fee and other legal expenses).
3. If the Board authorizes an assignment or sublet, it can impose terms and conditions (s. 98(4)).
4. If the Board terminates the tenancy (at the tenant's request), the order will permit the landlord to evict the tenant if the tenant does not vacate the unit by the specified date (s. 98(6)) — NEW.

Landlord failed to repair or maintain property

SECTION(S) - 20, 29(1)1, 30 and 161(additional maintenance responsibilities for mobile home parks and land lease communities)

FORM(S)	COMMENTS
Application (Form T6)	- by tenant or former tenant - must be filed within one year of alleged breach
Notice of Hearing	- issued by Board
Certificate of Service (for T6 and Notice of Hearing)	- T6 and Notice of Hearing must be served at least 10 days before hearing (Rule 10.1) - file within five days of service (Rule 11.2)

TO BE PROVEN BY APPLICANT

1. The landlord failed to provide and maintain the complex in a good state of repair and fit for habitation, and/or
2. The landlord failed to comply with health, safety, housing and maintenance standards.

DEFENCES TO CONSIDER

1. Procedural errors.
2. Tenant has failed to prove all necessary elements.
3. Tenant never informed landlord of problem(s).
4. Landlord took reasonable steps to fix the problem(s).
5. Tenant obstructed repairs.
6. Tenant caused the damage.

TYPICAL ORDER SOUGHT

1. Pursuant to para. 29(1)1, a declaration that landlord breached its obligations under s. 20(1) or s. 161 (N.B. — this is a prerequisite to obtaining relief under s. 30).
2. Under s. 30, an order for one or more of the following:
   a. Termination of the tenancy;
   b. An abatement of rent;
   c. Authorizing work done by the tenant and ordering the landlord to reimburse the tenant for the cost of that work;
   d. The cost of repairing or replacing damaged property;
   e. Reasonable out-of-pocket expenses;
   f. An order prohibiting a rent increase (OPRI) until specified work has been completed — NEW;
3. Costs (application fee and other legal expenses).

Landlord entered unit illegally

SECTION(S) - 25, 26, 27, 29(1)6, 31

FORM(S)	COMMENTS
Application (Form T2)	- by tenant or former tenant - must be filed within one year of alleged conduct
Notice of Hearing	- issued by Board
Certificate of Service (for T2 and Notice of Hearing)	- T2 and Notice of Hearing must be served at least 10 days before hearing (Rule 10.1) - file within five days of service (Rule 11.2)

TO BE PROVEN BY APPLICANT

1. The landlord, superintendent or agent
2. entered the unit
3. at a time or in a manner other than permitted under ss. 26 or 27.

DEFENCES TO CONSIDER

1. Procedural errors.
2. Tenant has failed to prove all necessary elements.

TYPICAL ORDER SOUGHT

1. Relief under s. 31(1); and
2. If the tenant moved as a result, relief under s. 31(2).

Landlord altered locks without providing a key

SECTION(S) - 24, 29(1)5, 31

FORM(S)	COMMENTS
Application (Form T2)	- by tenant or former tenant - must be filed within one year of alleged conduct
Notice of Hearing	- issued by Board
Certificate of Service (for T2 and Notice of Hearing)	- T2 and Notice of Hearing must be served at least five days before hearing (Rule 10.5) - a Member can shorten this time (Rule 15) - file Certificate of Service within five days od service (Rule 11.2)

TO BE PROVEN BY APPLICANT

1. The landlord, superintendent or agent
2. altered the locking system
3. on a door giving entry to a rental unit or the residential complex
4. or caused such an alteration
5. during the tenant's occupancy of the rental unit
6. without giving the tenant replacement keys.

DEFENCES TO CONSIDER

1. Tenant has failed to prove all necessary elements.

TYPICAL ORDER SOUGHT

1. Relief under s. 35(1).
2. If the tenant moved as a result, relief under s. 31(2).
3. If the unit is still vacant, an order putting the tenant back into possession of the unit pursuant to s. 31(3), (4) and (5).

Landlord withheld vital service, etc.

SECTION(S) - 21, 29(1)2, 31

FORM(S)	COMMENTS
Application (Form T2)	- by tenant or former tenant - must be filed within one year of alleged conduct
Notice of Hearing	- issued by Board
Certificate of Service (for T2 and Notice of Hearing)	- T2 and Notice of Hearing must be served at least 10 days before hearing (Rule 10.1) -file within five days of service (Rule 11.2)

TO BE PROVEN BY APPLICANT

1. The landlord, superintendent or agent
2. withheld the reasonable supply
3. of a vital service, care service or food
4. that the landlord is obliged to provide under the tenancy agreement or
5. deliberately interfered with the reasonable supply of any vital service, care service or food.

DEFENCES TO CONSIDER

1. Procedural errors.
2. Tenant has failed to prove all necessary elements.

TYPICAL ORDER SOUGHT

1. Relief under s. 31(1).
2. If the tenant moved as a result, relief under s. 31(2).

Landlord substantially interfered with reasonable enjoyment

SECTION(S) - ss.22, 29(1)3, 31 of R.T.A. and s. 8 of O. Reg. 516/06

FORM(S)	COMMENTS
Application (Form T2)	- by tenant or former tenant - must be filed within one year of alleged conduct
Notice of Hearing	- issued by Board
Certificate of Service (for T2 and Notice of Hearing)	- T2 and Notice of Hearing must be served at least 10 days before hearing (Rule 10.1) -file Certificate of Service within five days of service (Rule 11.2)

TO BE PROVEN BY APPLICANT

1. The landlord, superintendent or agent
2. has substantially interfered with
3. the reasonable enjoyment of the rental unit or residential complex in which the unit is located
4. for all usual purposes
5. by the tenant or a member of his or her household.

DEFENCES TO CONSIDER

1. Procedural errors.
2. Tenant has failed to prove all necessary elements.
3. If the disturbance is caused by repairs and the landlord has complied with requirements set out in s. 8(4) of O. Reg. 516/06, no abatement can be granted.
4. If the disturbance is caused by repairs and the landlord has not complied with all requirements, 25% is the maximum abatement the tenant can expect unless there are very unusual circumstances (s. 8(6) of O. Reg. 516/06).

TYPICAL ORDER SOUGHT

1. Relief under s. 35(1), subject to s. 8 of O. Reg. 516/06.
2. If the tenant moved as a result, relief under s. 31(2).

Landlord harassed tenant

SECTION(S) - 23, 29(1)4, 31

FORM(S)	COMMENTS
Application (Form T2)	- by tenant or former tenant - must be filed within one year of alleged conduct
Notice of Hearing	- issued by Board
Certificate of Service (for T2 and Notice of Hearing)	- T2 and Notice of Hearing must be served at least 10 days before hearing (Rule 10.1) - file Certificate of Service within five days of service (Rule 11.2)

TO BE PROVEN BY APPLICANT

1. The landlord, superintendent or agent
2. has harassed, obstructed, coerced, threatened or interfered with the tenant
3. during the tenant's occupancy of the rental unit.

Note: Once commenced, this type of application cannot be withdrawn by the tenant without the Board's permission (s. 200(3)).

DEFENCES TO CONSIDER

1. Procedural errors.
2. Tenant has failed to prove all necessary elements.

TYPICAL ORDER SOUGHT

1. Relief under s. 31(1).
2. If the tenant moved as a result, relief under s. 31(2).

Landlord's Notice of Termination was given in bad faith

SECTION(S) - 57

FORM(S)	COMMENTS
Application (Form T5)	- by former tenant - must be filed within one year of alleged conduct
Notice of Hearing	- issued by Board
Certificate of Service (for T5 and Notice of Hearing)	- T5 and Notice of Hearing must be served at least 10 days before hearing (Rule 10.1) -file Certificate of Service within five days of service (Rule 11.2)

TO BE PROVEN BY APPLICANT

1. A notice under s. 48 (landlord's own use), s. 49 (purchaser's use) or s. 50 (renovation, demolition, etc.)
2. was given in bad faith;
3. the tenant vacated the unit
4. as a result of the notice or as a result of an application to or order made by the Board based on that notice,
5. but, within a reasonable time, the unit was not occupied by the person identified in the Notice of Termination or the demolition/renovation/conversion described in the notice was not done by the landlord.

DEFENCES TO CONSIDER

1. Procedural errors.
2. Tenant has failed to prove all necessary elements.

TYPICAL ORDER SOUGHT

1. Relief under s. 57(3).

Landlord disposed of tenant's property within 72 hours of eviction or failed to make evicted tenant's property available for retrieval

SECTION(S) - 41

FORM(S)	COMMENTS
Application (Form T2)	- by former tenant
Notice of Hearing	- issued by Board
Certificate of Service (for T2 and Notice of Hearing)	- T2 and Notice of Hearing must be served at least five days before hearing (Rule 10.5(b)) -file Certificate of Service within five days of service (Rule 11.2)

TO BE PROVEN BY APPLICANT

1. The former tenant's landlord has breached an obligation
2. under subsection 41(2) or
3. under subsection 41(3)

DEFENCES TO CONSIDER

1. Procedural errors.
2. Tenant has failed to prove all necessary elements.

TYPICAL ORDER SOUGHT

1. Relief under s. 41(6).

Motion to set aside *ex parte* order based on alleged agreement or tenant's Notice of Termination

SECTION(S) - 77(6)

FORM(S)	COMMENTS
Application (Form S2)	- must be filed within 10 days after order is issued - the eviction order is stayed pending the outcome of the motion (s. 77(7))
Notice of Hearing	- issued by Board
Certificate of Service (for S2 and Notice of Hearing)	- unless otherwise directed by the Board, the moving party must serve a copy of the S2 and Notice of Hearing at least 48 hours before the time set for the hearing (Rule 10.7)

TO BE PROVEN BY MOVING PARTY
Nothing. The onus is upon the Applicant.

Given the wording of s. 77(8), it appears that where such a motion is filed, the Board must immediately proceed to hear the merits of the eviction application. There is no "test" that the moving party need satisfy. Therefore, the onus will remain on the original applicant to prove that there was an agreement to terminate the tenancy or that the tenant delivered a Notice of Termination.

TYPICAL ORDER SOUGHT

1. If the Board is satisfied after hearing all of the evidence that the landlord and tenant did not enter into an agreement to terminate the tenancy or that the tenant did not give the landlord Notice of Termination **or** if the Board determines that it would be fair in the circumstances to grant relief to the tenant, the Board shall set aside the *ex parte* eviction order (paras. 77(8)(a) and (b)).
2. Otherwise, the Board shall lift the stay and permit the eviction order to be enforced either immediately or on a future date specified in the order (para. 77(8)(c)).

Motion to set aside *ex parte* order based on alleged breach of agreement or order

SECTION(S) - 78(9)

FORM(S)	COMMENTS
Application (Form S2)	- must be filed within 10 days after order is issued - the eviction order is stayed pending the outcome of the motion (s. 78(10))
Notice of Hearing	- issued by Board
Certificate of Service (for S2 and Notice of Hearing)	- unless otherwise directed by the Board, the moving party must serve a copy of the S2 and Notice of Hearing at least 48 hours before the time set for the hearing (Rule 10.7)

TO BE PROVEN BY MOVING PARTY
Nothing. The onus is upon the Applicant.

Given the wording of s. 77(8), it appears that where such a motion is filed, the Board must immediately proceed to hear the merits of the eviction application. There is no "test" that the moving party need satisfy. Therefore, the onus will remain on the original applicant to prove that there was an agreement to terminate the tenancy or that the tenant delivered a Notice of Termination.

TYPICAL ORDER SOUGHT

1. If the Board is satisfied after hearing all of the evidence that the conditions set out in subsection 78(1) have not been satisfied **or** if the Board determines that it would be fair in the circumstances to grant relief to the tenant, the Board shall set aside the *ex parte* eviction order (paras. 78(11)(a) and (b)).
2. Otherwise, the Board shall lift the stay and permit the eviction order to be enforced either immediately or on a future date specified in the order (para. 78(11)(c)).

Application for rent reduction because of reduction or discontinuance in services

SECTION(S) - 130

FORM(S)	COMMENTS
Application (Form T3)	- by tenant or former tenant - must be filed within one year of alleged reduction or discontinuance of a service/facility
Notice of Hearing	- issued by Board
Certificate of Service (for T3 and Notice of Hearing)	- T3 and Notice of Hearing must be served at least 10 days before hearing (Rule 10.1) - file Certificate of Service within five days of service (Rule 11.2)

TO BE PROVEN BY APPLICANT

1. There has been a reduction or discontinuance in services or facilities provided
2. in respect of the rental unit or the residential complex.

DEFENCES TO CONSIDER

1. See s. 39 of O. Reg. 516/06.
2. The tenant has not correctly calculated the value of the service or facility.

TYPICAL ORDER SOUGHT

1. A determination that the landlord has reduced or discontinued a service or facility.
2. Temporary or permanent rent reduction and/or rent rebate.

Application for payment of money collected or retained illegally

SECTION(S) - 135

FORM(S)	COMMENTS
Application (Form T1)	- by prospective tenant, tenant or former tenant - must be filed within one year after the person collected or retained money in contravention of the Act
Notice of Hearing	- issued by Board
Certificate of Service (for T1 and Notice of Hearing)	- T1 and Notice of Hearing must be served at least 10 days before hearing (Rule 10.1) -file Certificate of Service within five days of service (Rule 11.2)

TO BE PROVEN BY APPLICANT

1. The landlord, superintendent or agent has collected amounts (for rent, rent increase, security deposit or other charges) that are not legally permitted, or
2. Amounts (for such things as rent, a rent deposit or interest thereon) have been illegally retained by the landlord, superintendent or agent.

DEFENCES TO CONSIDER

1. Section 134 prohibits additional charges unless specifically permitted. The prescribed, permitted additional charges are set out in s. 17 of O. Reg. 516/06.
2. Expiration of limitation period.

TYPICAL ORDER SOUGHT

1. A determination that the landlord has illegally collected or retained money, contrary to s. 135 of the R.T.A.
2. A rebate of the money collected or retained.
3. Costs (application fee and other legal expenses).

Appendix 2

Residential Tenancies Act, 2006

An Act to revise the law governing residential tenancies

S.O. 2006, c. 17 [ss. 137, 138, 254 not in force at date of publication.] as am. S.O. 2006, c. 17, s. 261; 2006, c. 32, Sched. C, s. 56, Sched. E, s. 7(4), (5); 2006, c. 35, Sched. C, s. 118; 2007, c. 8, s. 226 [Not in force at date of publication.]; 2007, c. 13, s. 48; 2008, c. 14, s. 58 [s. 58(1)-(4) conditions not yet satisfied, (5) not in force at date of publication.]

Her Majesty, by and with the advice and consent of the Legislative Assembly of the Province of Ontario, enacts as follows:

Part I — Introduction

1. Purposes of Act — The purposes of this Act are to provide protection for residential tenants from unlawful rent increases and unlawful evictions, to establish a framework for the regulation of residential rents, to balance the rights and responsibilities of residential landlords and tenants and to provide for the adjudication of disputes and for other processes to informally resolve disputes.

2. (1) Interpretation — In this Act,

"Board" means the Landlord and Tenant Board; (*"Commission de la location immobilière"*)

"care home" means a residential complex that is occupied or intended to be occupied by persons for the purpose of receiving care services, whether or not receiving the services is the primary purpose of the occupancy; (*"maison de soins"*)

"care services" means, subject to the regulations, health care services, rehabilitative or therapeutic services or services that provide assistance with the activities of daily living; (*"services en matière de soins"*)

"guideline", when used with respect to the charging of rent, means the guideline determined under section 120; (*"taux légal"*)

"land lease community" means the land on which one or more occupied land lease homes are situate and includes the rental units and the land, structures, services and facilities of which the landlord retains possession and that are intended for the common use and enjoyment of the tenants of the landlord; (*"zone résidentielle à baux fonciers"*)

"land lease home" means a dwelling, other than a mobile home, that is a permanent structure where the owner of the dwelling leases the land used or intended for use as the site for the dwelling; (*"maison à bail foncier"*)

"landlord" includes,

(a) the owner of a rental unit or any other person who permits occupancy of a rental unit, other than a tenant who occupies a rental unit in a residential complex and who permits another person to also occupy the unit or any part of the unit,
(b) the heirs, assigns, personal representatives and successors in title of a person referred to in clause (a), and
(c) a person, other than a tenant occupying a rental unit in a residential complex, who is entitled to possession of the residential complex and who attempts to enforce any of the rights of a landlord under a tenancy agreement or this Act, including the right to collect rent; (*"locateur"*)

"Minister" means the Minister of Municipal Affairs and Housing; (*"ministre"*)

"Ministry" means the Ministry of Municipal Affairs and Housing; (*"ministère"*)

"mobile home" means a dwelling that is designed to be made mobile and that is being used as a permanent residence; (*"maison mobile"*)

"mobile home park" means the land on which one or more occupied mobile homes are located and includes the rental units and the land, structures, services and facilities of which the landlord retains possession and that are intended for the common use and enjoyment of the tenants of the landlord; (*"parc de maisons mobiles"*)

"municipal taxes and charges" means taxes charged to a landlord by a municipality and charges levied on a landlord by a municipality and includes taxes levied on a landlord's property under Division B of Part IX of the *Education Act* and taxes levied on a landlord's property in unorganized territory, but **"municipal taxes and charges"** does not include,

(a) charges for inspections done by a municipality on a residential complex related to an alleged breach of a health, safety, housing or maintenance standard,

(b) charges for emergency repairs carried out by a municipality on a residential complex,

(c) charges for work in the nature of a capital expenditure carried out by a municipality,

(d) charges for work, services or non-emergency repairs performed by a municipality in relation to a landlord's non-compliance with a by-law,

(e) penalties, interest, late payment fees or fines,

(f) any amount spent by a municipality under subsection 219(1) or any administrative fee applied to that amount under subsection 219(2), or

(g) any other prescribed charges; (*"redevances et impôts municipaux"*)

"non-profit housing co-operative" means a non-profit housing co-operative under the *Co-operative Corporations Act*; (*"coopérative de logement sans but lucratif"*)

"person", or any expression referring to a person, means an individual, sole proprietorship, partnership, limited partnership, trust or body corporate, or an individual in his or her capacity as a trustee, executor, administrator or other legal representative; (*"personne"*)

"prescribed" means prescribed by the regulations; (*"prescrit"*)

"regulations" means the regulations made under this Act; (*"règlements"*)

"rent" includes the amount of any consideration paid or given or required to be paid or given by or on behalf of a tenant to a landlord or the landlord's agent for the right to occupy a rental unit and for any services and facilities and any privilege, accommodation or thing that the landlord provides for the tenant in respect of the occupancy of the rental unit, whether or not a separate charge is made for services and facilities or for the privilege, accommodation or thing, but **"rent"** does not include,

(a) an amount paid by a tenant to a landlord to reimburse the landlord for property taxes paid by the landlord with respect to a mobile home or a land lease home owned by a tenant, or

(b) an amount that a landlord charges a tenant of a rental unit in a care home for care services or meals; (*"loyer"*)

"rental unit" means any living accommodation used or intended for use as rented residential premises, and **"rental unit"** includes,

(a) a site for a mobile home or site on which there is a land lease home used or intended for use as rented residential premises, and

(b) a room in a boarding house, rooming house or lodging house and a unit in a care home; (*"logement locatif"*)

"residential complex" means,

(a) a building or related group of buildings in which one or more rental units are located,

(b) a mobile home park or land lease community,

(c) a site that is a rental unit,

(d) a care home, and,

includes all common areas and services and facilities available for the use of its residents; (*"ensemble d'habitation"*)

"residential unit" means any living accommodation used or intended for use as residential premises, and **"residential unit"** includes,

(a) a site for a mobile home or on which there is a land lease home used or intended for use as a residential premises, and

(b) a room in a boarding house, rooming house or lodging house and a unit in a care home; (*"habitation"*)

"Rules" means the rules of practice and procedure made by the Board under section 176 of this Act and section 25.1 of the *Statutory Powers Procedure Act*; (*"règles"*)

"services and facilities" includes,

(a) furniture, appliances and furnishings,

(b) parking and related facilities,

(c) laundry facilities,

(d) elevator facilities,

(e) common recreational facilities,

(f) garbage facilities and related services,

(g) cleaning and maintenance services,

(h) storage facilities,

(i) intercom systems,

(j) cable television facilities,

(k) heating facilities and services,

(l) air-conditioning facilities,

(m) utilities and related services, and

(n) security services and facilities; (*"services et installations"*)

"spouse" means a person,

(a) to whom the person is married, or

(b) with whom the person is living in a conjugal relationship outside marriage, if the two persons,

(i) have cohabited for at least one year,

(ii) are together the parents of a child, or

(iii) have together entered into a cohabitation agreement under section 53 of the *Family Law Act*; (*"conjoint"*)

"subtenant" means the person to whom a tenant gives the right under section 97 to occupy a rental unit; (*"sous-locataire"*)

"superintendent's premises" means a rental unit used by a person employed as a janitor, manager, security guard or superintendent and located in the residential complex with respect to which the person is so employed; (*"logement de concierge"*)

"tenancy agreement" means a written, oral or implied agreement between a tenant and a landlord for occupancy of a rental unit and includes a licence to occupy a rental unit; (*"convention de location"*)

"tenant" includes a person who pays rent in return for the right to occupy a rental unit and includes the tenant's heirs, assigns and personal representatives, but **"tenant"** does not include a person who has the right to occupy a rental unit by virtue of being,

> (a) a co-owner of the residential complex in which the rental unit is located, or
>
> (b) a shareholder of a corporation that owns the residential complex; (*"locataire"*)

"utilities" means heat, electricity and water; (*"services d'utilité publique"*)

"vital service" means hot or cold water, fuel, electricity, gas or, during the part of each year prescribed by the regulations, heat. (*"service essentiel"*)

(2) Interpretation, sublet — For the purposes of this Act, a reference to subletting a rental unit refers to the situation in which,

> (a) the tenant vacates the rental unit;
>
> (b) the tenant gives one or more other persons the right to occupy the rental unit for a term ending on a specified date before the end of the tenant's term or period; and
>
> (c) the tenant has the right to resume occupancy of the rental unit after that specified date.

(3) **Interpretation, abandoned** — For the purposes of this Act, a tenant has not abandoned a rental unit if the tenant is not in arrears of rent.

(4) **Rental unit, clarification** — A rented site for a mobile home or a land lease home is a rental unit for the purposes of this Act even if the mobile home or the land lease home on the site is owned by the tenant of the site.

3. (1) Application of Act — This Act applies with respect to rental units in residential complexes, despite any other Act and despite any agreement or waiver to the contrary.

(2) Conflicts, care homes — In interpreting a provision of this Act with regard to a care home, if a provision in Part IX conflicts with a provision in another Part of this Act, the provision in Part IX applies.

(3) Conflicts, mobile home parks and land lease communities — In interpreting a provision of this Act with regard to a mobile home park or a land lease community, if a provision in Part X conflicts with a provision in another Part of this Act, the provision in Part X applies.

(4) Conflict with other Acts — If a provision of this Act conflicts with a provision of another Act, other than the *Human Rights Code*, the provision of this Act applies.

4. Provisions conflicting with Act void — Subject to section 194, a provision in a tenancy agreement that is inconsistent with this Act or the regulations is void.

5. Exemptions from Act — This Act does not apply with respect to,

(a) living accommodation intended to be provided to the travelling or vacationing public or occupied for a seasonal or temporary period in a hotel, motel or motor hotel, resort, lodge, tourist camp, cottage or cabin establishment, inn, campground, trailer park, tourist home, bed and breakfast vacation establishment or vacation home;

(b) living accommodation whose occupancy is conditional upon the occupant continuing to be employed on a farm, whether or not the accommodation is located on that farm;

(c) living accommodation that is a member unit of a non-profit housing co-operative;

(d) living accommodation occupied by a person for penal or correctional purposes;

(e) living accommodation that is subject to the *Public Hospitals Act*, the *Private Hospitals Act*, the *Community Psychiatric Hospitals Act*, the *Mental Hospitals Act*, the *Homes for the Aged and Rest Homes Act*, the *Nursing Homes Act*, the *Ministry of Correctional Services Act*, the *Charitable Institutions Act* or the *Child and Family Services Act* or is listed in Schedule 1 to Regulation 272 of the Revised Regulations of Ontario, 1990 made under the *Developmental Services Act*;

Proposed Amendment — 5(e)

(e) living accommodation that is subject to the *Public Hospitals Act*, the *Private Hospitals Act*, the *Community Psychiatric Hospitals Act*, the *Mental Hospitals Act*, the *Long-Term Care Homes Act 2007*, the *Ministry of Correctional Services Act or the Child and Family Services Act* or is listed in Schedule 1 to Regulation 272 of the Revised Regulations of Ontario, 1990 made under the *Developmental Services Act*;

2007, c. 8, s. 226 [Not in force at date of publication.]

Proposed Amendment — Conditional Amendment — 5(e)

If on the day S.O. 2008, c. 14, s. 58(1) [Not in force at date of publication.] is in force and S.O. 2007, c. 8, s. 226 [Not in force at date of publication.] is not in force, clause 5(e) is replaced by the following:

(e) living accommodation that is subject to the *Public Hospitals Act*, the *Private Hospitals Act*, the *Community Psychiatric Hospitals Act*, the *Mental Hospitals Act*, the *Homes for the Aged and Rest Homes Act*, the *Nursing Homes Act*, the *Ministry of Correctional Services Act*, the *Charitable Institutions Act* or the *Child and Family Services Act* or is a facility that was,

(i) established under the *Developmental Services Act* before that Act was repealed by section 63 of the *Services and Supports to Promote the Social Inclusion of Persons with Developmental Disabilities Act, 2008*, and

(ii) listed in Schedule 1 to Regulation 272 of the Revised Regulations of Ontario, 1990 (General) made under the *Developmental Services Act*;

2008, c. 14, s. 58(1) [Conditions not yet satisfied.]

Proposed Amendment — Conditional Amendment — 5(e)

If on the day S.O. 2008, c. 14, s. 58(3) [Not in force at date of publication.] is in force and S.O. 2007, c. 8, s. 226 [Not in force at date of publication.] is not in force, clause 5(e) as re-enacted by S.O. 2008, c. 14, s. 58(1) is replaced by the following:

(e) living accommodation that is subject to the *Public Hospitals Act*, the *Private Hospitals Act*, the *Community Psychiatric Hospitals Act*, the *Mental Hospitals Act*, the *Homes for the Aged and Rest Homes Act*, the *Nursing Homes Act*, the *Ministry of Correctional Services Act*, the *Charitable Institutions Act or the Child and Family Services Act*;

2008, c. 14, s. 58(1) [Conditions not yet satisfied. Amended 2008, c. 14, s. 58(3). Conditions not yet satisfied.]

Proposed Amendment — Conditional Amendment — 5(e)

On the later of the coming into force of S.O. 2008, c. 14, s. 58(2) [Not in force at date of publication.] and S.O. 2007, c. 8, s. 226 [Not in force at date of publication.], clause 5(e) is replaced by the following:

(e) living accommodation that is subject to the *Public Hospitals Act*, the *Private Hospitals Act*, the *Community Psychiatric Hospitals Act*, the *Mental Hospitals Act*, the *Long-Term Care Homes Act, 2007*, the *Ministry of Correctional Services Act* or the *Child and Family Services Act* or is a facility that was,

(i) established under the *Developmental Services Act* before that Act was repealed by section 63 of the *Services and Supports to Promote the Social Inclusion of Persons with Developmental Disabilities Act, 2008*, and

(ii) listed in Schedule 1 to Regulation 272 of the Revised Regulations of Ontario, 1990 (General) made under the *Developmental Services Act*;

2008, c. 14, s. 58(2) [Conditions not yet satisfied.]

Proposed Amendment — Conditional Amendment — 5(e)

On the later of the coming into force of S.O. 2008, c. 14, s. 58(4) [Not in force at date of publication.] and S.O. 2007, c. 8, s. 226 [Not in force at date of publication.], clause 5(e) as re-enacted by S.O. 2008, c. 14, s. 58(2) is replaced by the following:

(e) living accommodation that is subject to the *Public Hospitals Act*, the *Private Hospitals Act*, the *Community Psychiatric Hospitals Act*, the *Mental Hospitals Act*, the *Long-Term Care Homes Act, 2007*, the *Ministry of Correctional Services Act* or the *Child and Family Services Act*;

2008, c. 14, s. 58(2) [Conditions not yet satisfied. Amended 2008, c. 14, s. 58(4). Conditions not yet satisfied.]

(f) short-term living accommodation provided as emergency shelter;

(g) living accommodation provided by an educational institution to its students or staff where,

(i) the living accommodation is provided primarily to persons under the age of majority, or all major questions related to the living accommodation are decided after consultation with a council or association representing the residents, and

(ii) the living accommodation does not have its own self-contained bathroom and kitchen facilities or is not intended for year-round occupancy by full-time students or staff and members of their households;

(h) living accommodation located in a building or project used in whole or in part for non-residential purposes if the occupancy of the living accommodation is conditional upon the occupant continuing to be an employee of or perform services related to a business or enterprise carried out in the building or project;

(i) living accommodation whose occupant or occupants are required to share a bathroom or kitchen facility with the owner, the owner's spouse, child or parent or the spouse's child or parent, and where the owner, spouse, child or parent lives in the building in which the living accommodation is located;

(j) premises occupied for business or agricultural purposes with living accommodation attached if the occupancy for both purposes is under a single lease and the same person occupies the premises and the living accommodation;

(k) living accommodation occupied by a person for the purpose of receiving rehabilitative or therapeutic services agreed upon by the person and the provider of the living accommodation, where,

(i) the parties have agreed that,

(A) the period of occupancy will be of a specified duration, or

(B) the occupancy will terminate when the objectives of the services have been met or will not be met, and

(ii) the living accommodation is intended to be provided for no more than a one-year period;

(l) living accommodation in a care home occupied by a person for the purpose of receiving short-term respite care;

(m) living accommodation in a residential complex in which the Crown in right of Ontario has an interest, if,

(i) the residential complex was forfeited to the Crown in right of Ontario under the *Civil Remedies Act, 2001*, the *Prohibiting Profiting from Recounting Crimes Act, 2002* or the *Criminal Code* (Canada), or

(ii) possession of the residential complex has been or may be taken in the name of the Crown under the *Escheats Act*; and

(n) any other prescribed class of accommodation.

2007, c. 13, s. 48

6. Other exemptions — (1) Homes for special care, developmental services — Paragraphs 6, 7 and 8 of subsection 30(1) and sections 51, 52, 54, 55, 56, 104, 111 to 115, 117, 119 to 134, 136, 140 and 149 to 167 do not apply with respect to,

(a) accommodation that is subject to the *Homes for Special Care Act*; or

(b) accommodation that is subject to the *Developmental Services Act* but is not listed in Schedule 1 to Regulation 272 of the Revised Regulations of Ontario, 1990 made under that Act.

Proposed Amendment — 6(1)(b)

(b) accommodation that is a supported group living residence under the *Services and Supports to Promote the Social Inclusion of Persons with Developmental Disabilities Act, 2008*.

2008, c. 14, s. 58(5) [Not in force at date of publication.]

(2) Rules relating to rent — Sections 104, 111, 112, 120, 121, 122, 126 to 133, 165 and 167 do not apply with respect to a rental unit if,

(a) it was not occupied for any purpose before June 17, 1998;

(b) it is a rental unit no part of which has been previously rented since July 29, 1975; or

(c) no part of the building, mobile home park or land lease community was occupied for residential purposes before November 1, 1991.

7. (1) Exemptions related to social, etc., housing — Paragraphs 6, 7 and 8 of subsection 30(1), sections 51, 52, 54, 55, 56 and 95 to 99, subsection 100(2) and sections 101, 102, 104, 111 to 115, 117, 120, 121, 122, 126 to 133, 140, 143, 149, 150, 151, 159, 165 and 167 do not apply with respect to a rental unit described below:

1. A rental unit located in a residential complex owned, operated or administered by or on behalf of the Ontario Mortgage and Housing Corporation, the Government of Canada or an agency of either of them.

2. A rental unit in a residential complex described in paragraph 1 whose ownership, operation or management is transferred under the *Social Housing Reform Act, 2000* to a service manager or local housing corporation as defined in that Act.

3. A rental unit located in a non-profit housing project or other residential complex, if the non-profit housing project or other residential complex was developed or acquired under a prescribed federal, provincial or municipal program and continues to operate under,

i. Part VI of the *Social Housing Reform Act, 2000*,

ii. an operating agreement, as defined in the *Social Housing Reform Act, 2000*, or

iii. an agreement made between a housing provider, as defined in the *Social Housing Reform Act, 2000*, and one or more of,

A. a municipality,

B. an agency of a municipality,

C. a non-profit corporation controlled by a municipality, if an object of the non-profit corporation is the provision of housing,

D. a local housing corporation, as defined in the *Social Housing Reform Act, 2000*, or

E. a service manager, as defined in the *Social Housing Reform Act, 2000*.

4. A rental unit that is a non-member unit of a non-profit housing co-operative.

5. A rental unit provided by an educational institution to a student or member of its staff and that is not exempt from this Act under clause 5(g).

6. A rental unit located in a residential complex owned, operated or administered by a religious institution for a charitable use on a non-profit basis.

(2) Exemption re 12-month rule — Section 119 does not apply with respect to,

(a) a rental unit described in paragraph 1, 2, 3 or 4 of subsection (1) if the tenant occupying the rental unit pays rent in an amount geared-to-income due to public funding; or

(b) a rental unit described in paragraph 5 or 6 of subsection (1).

(3) Exemption re notice of rent increase — Sections 116 and 118 do not apply with respect to increases in rent for a rental unit due to increases in the tenant's income if the rental unit is as described in paragraph 1, 2, 3 or 4 of subsection (1) and the tenant pays rent in an amount geared-to-income due to public funding.

(4) Exception, subs. (1), par. 1 — Despite subsection (1), the provisions of this Act set out in that subsection apply with respect to a rental unit described in paragraph 1 of that subsection if the tenant occupying the rental unit pays rent to a landlord other than the Ontario Mortgage and Housing Corporation, the Government of Canada or an agency of either of them.

(5) Same, subs. (1), par. 2 — Despite subsection (1), the provisions of this Act set out in that subsection apply with respect to a rental unit described in paragraph 2 of that subsection if the tenant occupying the rental unit pays rent to a landlord other than a service manager or local housing corporation as defined in the *Social Housing Reform Act, 2000* or an agency of either of them.

(6) Same, subs. (1), par. 5 — Despite subsection (1), the provisions of this Act set out in that subsection apply with respect to a rent increase for rental units described in paragraph 5 of that subsection if there is a council or association representing the residents of those rental units and there has not been consultation with the council or association respecting the increase.

2006, c. 32, Sched. E, s. 7(4), (5)

8. (1) Rent geared-to-income — If a tenant pays rent for a rental unit in an amount geared-to-income due to public funding and the rental unit is not a rental unit described in paragraph 1, 2, 3 or 4 of subsection 7(1), paragraph 6 of subsection 30(1) and Part VII do not apply to an increase in the amount geared-to-income paid by the tenant.

(2) Same, assignment, subletting — Sections 95 to 99, subsection 100(2), sections 101 and 102, subsection 104(3) and section 143 do not apply to a tenant described in subsection (1).

9. (1) Application to determine issues — A landlord or a tenant may apply to the Board for an order determining,

(a) whether this Act or any provision of it applies to a particular rental unit or residential complex;

(b) any other prescribed matter.

(2) Order — On the application, the Board shall make findings on the issue as prescribed and shall make the appropriate order.

PART II — TENANCY AGREEMENTS

10. Selecting prospective tenants — In selecting prospective tenants, landlords may use, in the manner prescribed in the regulations made under the *Human Rights Code*, income information, credit checks, credit references, rental history, guarantees, or other similar business practices as prescribed in those regulations.

11. (1) Information to be provided by landlord — If a tenancy agreement is entered into, the landlord shall provide to the tenant information relating to the rights and responsibilities of landlords and tenants, the role of the Board and how to contact the Board.

(2) Form — The information shall be provided to the tenant on or before the date the tenancy begins in a form approved by the Board.

12. Tenancy agreement — (1) Name and address in written agreement — Every written tenancy agreement entered into on or after June 17, 1998 shall set out the legal name and address of the landlord to be used for the purpose of giving notices or other documents under this Act.

(2) Copy of tenancy agreement — If a tenancy agreement entered into on or after June 17, 1998 is in writing, the landlord shall give a copy of the agreement, signed by the landlord and the tenant, to the tenant within 21 days after the tenant signs it and gives it to the landlord.

(3) Notice if agreement not in writing — If a tenancy agreement entered into on or after June 17, 1998 is not in writing, the landlord shall, within 21 days after the tenancy begins, give to the tenant written notice of the legal name and address of the landlord to be used for giving notices and other documents under this Act.

(4) Failure to comply — Until a landlord has complied with subsections (1) and (2), or with subsection (3), as the case may be,

(a) the tenant's obligation to pay rent is suspended; and

(b) the landlord shall not require the tenant to pay rent.

(5) After compliance— After the landlord has complied with subsections (1) and (2), or with subsection (3), as the case may be, the landlord may require the tenant to pay any rent withheld by the tenant under subsection (4).

13. (1) Commencement of tenancy — The term or period of a tenancy begins on the day the tenant is entitled to occupy the rental unit under the tenancy agreement.

(2) Actual entry not required — A tenancy agreement takes effect when the tenant is entitled to occupy the rental unit, whether or not the tenant actually occupies it.

14. "No pet" provisions void — A provision in a tenancy agreement prohibiting the presence of animals in or about the residential complex is void.

15. Acceleration clause void — A provision in a tenancy agreement providing that all or part of the remaining rent for a term or period of a tenancy or a specific sum becomes due upon a default of the tenant in paying rent due or in carrying out an obligation is void.

16. Minimize losses — When a landlord or a tenant becomes liable to pay any amount as a result of a breach of a tenancy agreement, the person entitled to claim the amount has a duty to take reasonable steps to minimize the person's losses.

17. Covenants interdependent — Except as otherwise provided in this Act, the common law rules respecting the effect of a serious, substantial or fundamental breach of a material covenant by one party to a contract on the obligation to perform of the other party apply with respect to tenancy agreements.

18. Covenants running with land — Covenants concerning things related to a rental unit or the residential complex in which it is located run with the land, whether or not the things are in existence at the time the covenants are made.

19. Frustrated contracts — The doctrine of frustration of contract and the *Frustrated Contracts Act* apply with respect to tenancy agreements.

PART III — RESPONSIBILITIES OF LANDLORDS

20. (1) Landlord's responsibility to repair — A landlord is responsible for providing and maintaining a residential complex, including the rental units in it, in a good state of repair and fit for habitation and for complying with health, safety, housing and maintenance standards.

(2) Same — Subsection (1) applies even if the tenant was aware of a state of non-repair or a contravention of a standard before entering into the tenancy agreement.

21. (1) Landlord's responsibility re services — A landlord shall not at any time during a tenant's occupancy of a rental unit and before the day on which an order evicting the tenant is executed, withhold the reasonable supply of any vital service, care service or food that it is the landlord's obligation to supply under the tenancy agreement or deliberately interfere with the reasonable supply of any vital service, care service or food.

(2) Non-payment — For the purposes of subsection (1), a landlord shall be deemed to have withheld the reasonable supply of a vital service, care service or food if the landlord is obligated to pay another person for the vital service, care service or food, the landlord fails to pay the required amount and, as a result of the non-payment, the other person withholds the reasonable supply of the vital service, care service or food.

22. Landlord not to interfere with reasonable enjoyment — A landlord shall not at any time during a tenant's occupancy of a rental unit and before the day on which an order evicting the tenant is executed substantially interfere with the reasonable enjoyment of the rental unit or the residential complex in which it is located for all usual purposes by a tenant or members of his or her household.

23. Landlord not to harass, etc. — A landlord shall not harass, obstruct, coerce, threaten or interfere with a tenant.

24. Changing locks — A landlord shall not alter the locking system on a door giving entry to a rental unit or residential complex or cause the locking system to be altered during the tenant's occupancy of the rental unit without giving the tenant replacement keys.

25. Privacy — A landlord may enter a rental unit only in accordance with section 26 or 27.

26. Entry without notice — (1) Entry without notice, emergency, consent — A landlord may enter a rental unit at any time without written notice,

(a) in cases of emergency; or

(b) if the tenant consents to the entry at the time of entry.

(2) **Same, housekeeping** — A landlord may enter a rental unit without written notice to clean it if the tenancy agreement requires the landlord to clean the rental unit at regular intervals and,

(a) the landlord enters the unit at the times specified in the tenancy agreement; or

(b) if no times are specified, the landlord enters the unit between the hours of 8 a.m. and 8 p.m.

(3) **Entry to show rental unit to prospective tenants** — A landlord may enter the rental unit without written notice to show the unit to prospective tenants if,

(a) the landlord and tenant have agreed that the tenancy will be terminated or one of them has given notice of termination to the other;

(b) the landlord enters the unit between the hours of 8 a.m. and 8 p.m.; and

(c) before entering, the landlord informs or makes a reasonable effort to inform the tenant of the intention to do so.

27. (1) Entry with notice — A landlord may enter a rental unit in accordance with written notice given to the tenant at least 24 hours before the time of entry under the following circumstances:

1. To carry out a repair or replacement or do work in the rental unit.

2. To allow a potential mortgagee or insurer of the residential complex to view the rental unit.

3. To allow a person who holds a certificate of authorization within the meaning of the *Professional Engineers Act* or a certificate of practice within the meaning of the *Architects Act* or another qualified person to make a physical inspection of the rental unit to satisfy a requirement imposed under subsection 9(4) of the *Condominium Act, 1998.*

4. To carry out an inspection of the rental unit, if,

   i. the inspection is for the purpose of determining whether or not the rental unit is in a good state of repair and fit for habitation and complies with health, safety, housing and maintenance standards, consistent with the landlord's obligations under subsection 20(1) or section 161, and

   ii. it is reasonable to carry out the inspection.

5. For any other reasonable reason for entry specified in the tenancy agreement.

(2) Same — A landlord or, with the written authorization of a landlord, a broker or salesperson registered under the *Real Estate and Business Brokers Act, 2002*, may enter a rental unit in accordance with written notice given to the tenant at least 24 hours before the time of entry to allow a potential purchaser to view the rental unit.

(3) Contents of notice — The written notice under subsection (1) or (2) shall specify the reason for entry, the day of entry and a time of entry between the hours of 8 a.m. and 8 p.m.

28. Entry by canvassers — No landlord shall restrict reasonable access to a residential complex by candidates for election to any office at the federal, provincial or municipal level, or their authorized representatives, if they are seeking access for the purpose of canvassing or distributing election material.

29. (1) Tenant applications — A tenant or former tenant of a rental unit may apply to the Board for any of the following orders:

1. An order determining that the landlord has breached an obligation under subsection 20(1) or section 161.

2. An order determining that the landlord, superintendent or agent of the landlord has withheld the reasonable supply of any vital service, care service or food that it is the landlord's obligation to supply under the tenancy agreement or deliberately interfered with the reasonable supply of any vital service, care service or food.

3. An order determining that the landlord, superintendent or agent of the landlord has substantially interfered with the reasonable enjoyment of the rental unit or residential complex for all usual purposes by the tenant or a member of his or her household.

4. An order determining that the landlord, superintendent or agent of the landlord has harassed, obstructed, coerced, threatened or interfered with the tenant during the tenant's occupancy of the rental unit.

5. An order determining that the landlord, superintendent or agent of the landlord has altered the locking system on a door giving entry to the rental unit or the residential complex or caused the locking system to be altered during the tenant's occupancy of the rental unit without giving the tenant replacement keys.

6. An order determining that the landlord, superintendent or agent of the landlord has illegally entered the rental unit.

(2) Time limitation — No application may be made under subsection (1) more than one year after the day the alleged conduct giving rise to the application occurred.

30. (1) Order, repair, comply with standards — If the Board determines in an application under paragraph 1 of subsection 29(1) that a landlord has breached an obligation under subsection 20(1) or section 161, the Board may do one or more of the following:

1. Terminate the tenancy.

2. Order an abatement of rent.

3. Authorize a repair or replacement that has been or is to be made, or work that has been or is to be done, and order its cost to be paid by the landlord to the tenant.

4. Order the landlord to do specified repairs or replacements or other work within a specified time.

5. Order the landlord to pay a specified sum to the tenant for,

i. the reasonable costs that the tenant has incurred or will incur in repairing or, where repairing is not reasonable, replacing property of the tenant that was damaged, destroyed or disposed of as a result of the landlord's breach, and

ii. other reasonable out-of-pocket expenses that the tenant has incurred or will incur as a result of the landlord's breach.

6. Prohibit the landlord from charging a new tenant under a new tenancy agreement an amount of rent in excess of the last lawful rent charged to the former tenant of the rental unit, until the landlord has,

i. completed the items in work orders for which the compliance period has expired and which were found by the Board to be related to a serious breach of a health, safety, housing or maintenance standard, and

ii. completed the specified repairs or replacements or other work ordered under paragraph 4 found by the Board to be related to a serious breach of the landlord's obligations under subsection 20(1) or section 161.

7. Prohibit the landlord from giving a notice of a rent increase for the rental unit until the landlord has,

i. completed the items in work orders for which the compliance period has expired and which were found by the Board to be related to a serious breach of a health, safety, housing or maintenance standard, and

ii. completed the specified repairs or replacements or other work ordered under paragraph 4 found by the Board to be related to a serious breach of the landlord's obligations under subsection 20(1) or section 161.

8. Prohibit the landlord from taking any rent increase for which notice has been given if the increase has not been taken before the date an order under this section is issued until the landlord has,

i. completed the items in work orders for which the compliance period has expired and which were found by the Board to be related to a serious breach of a health, safety, housing or maintenance standard, and

ii. completed the specified repairs or replacements or other work ordered under paragraph 4 found by the Board to be related to a serious breach of the landlord's obligations under subsection 20(1) or section 161.

9. Make any other order that it considers appropriate.

(2) **Advance notice of breaches** — In determining the remedy under this section, the Board shall consider whether the tenant or former tenant advised the landlord of the alleged breaches before applying to the Board.

31. (1) Other orders re s. 29 — If the Board determines that a landlord, a superintendent or an agent of a landlord has done one or more of the activities set out in paragraphs 2 to 6 of subsection 29(1), the Board may,

(a) order that the landlord, superintendent or agent may not engage in any further activities listed in those paragraphs against any of the tenants in the residential complex;

(b) order that the landlord, superintendent or agent pay a specified sum to the tenant for,

(i) the reasonable costs that the tenant has incurred or will incur in repairing or, where repairing is not reasonable, replacing property of the tenant that was damaged, destroyed or disposed of as a result of the landlord, superintendent or agent having engaged in one or more of the activities listed in those paragraphs, and

(ii) other reasonable out-of-pocket expenses that the tenant has incurred or will incur as a result of the landlord, superintendent or agent having engaged in one or more of the activities listed in those paragraphs;

(c) order an abatement of rent;

(d) order that the landlord pay to the Board an administrative fine not exceeding the greater of $10,000 and the monetary jurisdiction of the Small Claims Court;

(e) order that the tenancy be terminated;

(f) make any other order that it considers appropriate.

(2) **Same** — If in an application under any of paragraphs 2 to 6 of subsection 29(1) it is determined that the tenant was induced by the conduct of the landlord, the superintendent or an agent of the landlord to vacate the rental unit, the Board may, in addition to the remedies set out in subsection (1), order that the landlord pay a specified sum to the tenant for,

(a) all or any portion of any increased rent which the tenant has incurred or will incur for a one-year period after the tenant has left the rental unit; and

(b) reasonable out-of-pocket moving, storage and other like expenses which the tenant has incurred or will incur.

(3) Order, s. 29(1), par. 5 — If the Board determines, in an application under paragraph 5 of subsection 29(1), that the landlord, superintendent or agent of the landlord has altered the locking system on a door giving entry to the rental unit or the residential complex, or caused the locking system to be altered, during the tenant's occupancy of the rental unit without giving the tenant replacement keys, and if the Board is satisfied that the rental unit is vacant, the Board may, in addition to the remedies set out in subsections (1) and (2), order that the landlord allow the tenant to recover possession of the rental unit and that the landlord refrain from renting the unit to anyone else.

(4) Effect of order allowing tenant possession — An order under subsection (3) shall have the same effect, and shall be enforced in the same manner, as a writ of possession.

(5) Expiry of order allowing tenant possession — An order under subsection (3) expires,

(a) at the end of the 15th day after the day it is issued if it is not filed within those 15 days with the sheriff who has territorial jurisdiction where the rental unit is located; or

(b) at the end of the 45th day after the day it is issued if it is filed in the manner described in clause (a).

32. Eviction with termination order — If the Board makes an order terminating a tenancy under paragraph 1 of subsection 30(1) or clause 31(1)(e), the Board may order that the tenant be evicted, effective not earlier than the termination date specified in the order.

PART IV — RESPONSIBILITIES OF TENANTS

33. Tenant's responsibility for cleanliness — The tenant is responsible for ordinary cleanliness of the rental unit, except to the extent that the tenancy agreement requires the landlord to clean it.

34. Tenant's responsibility for repair of damage — The tenant is responsible for the repair of undue damage to the rental unit or residential complex caused by the wilful or negligent conduct of the tenant, another occupant of the rental unit or a person permitted in the residential complex by the tenant.

35. (1) Changing locks — A tenant shall not alter the locking system on a door giving entry to a rental unit or residential complex or cause the locking system to be altered during the tenant's occupancy of the rental unit without the consent of the landlord.

(2) Landlord application — If a tenant alters a locking system, contrary to subsection (1), the landlord may apply to the Board for an order determining that the tenant has altered the locking system on a door giving entry to the rental unit or the residential complex or caused the locking system to be altered during the tenant's occupancy of the rental unit without the consent of the landlord.

(3) **Order** — If the Board in an application under subsection (2) determines that a tenant has altered the locking system or caused it to be altered, the Board may order that the tenant provide the landlord with keys or pay the landlord the reasonable out-of-pocket expenses necessary to change the locking system.

36. **Tenant not to harass, etc.** — A tenant shall not harass, obstruct, coerce, threaten or interfere with a landlord.

PART V — SECURITY OF TENURE AND TERMINATION OF TENANCIES

Security of Tenure

37. (1) **Termination only in accordance with Act** — A tenancy may be terminated only in accordance with this Act.

(2) **Termination by notice** — If a notice of termination is given in accordance with this Act and the tenant vacates the rental unit in accordance with the notice, the tenancy is terminated on the termination date set out in the notice.

(3) **Termination by agreement** — A notice of termination need not be given if a landlord and a tenant have agreed to terminate a tenancy.

(4) **When notice void** — A tenant's notice to terminate a tenancy is void if it is given,

(a) at the time the tenancy agreement is entered into; or

(b) as a condition of entering into the tenancy agreement.

(5) **When agreement void** — An agreement between a landlord and tenant to terminate a tenancy is void if it is entered into,

(a) at the time the tenancy agreement is entered into; or

(b) as a condition of entering into the tenancy agreement.

(6) **Application of subss. (4) and (5)** — Subsections (4) and (5) do not apply to rental units occupied by students of one or more post-secondary educational institutions in a residential complex owned, operated or administered by or on behalf of the post-secondary educational institutions.

(7) **Same** — Subsections (4) and (5) do not apply to rental units in a residential complex with respect to which the landlord has entered into an agreement with one or more post-secondary educational institutions providing,

(a) that the landlord, as of the date the agreement is entered into and for the duration of the agreement, rents the rental units which are the subject of the agreement only to students of the institution or institutions;

(b) that the landlord will comply with the maintenance standards set out in the agreement with respect to the rental units which are the subject of the agreement; and

(c) that the landlord will not charge a new tenant of a rental unit which is a subject of the agreement a rent which is greater than the lawful rent being charged to the former tenant plus the guideline.

(8) Same — The maintenance standards set out in the agreement and referred to in clause (7)(b) shall not provide for a lower maintenance standard than that required by law.

(9) Same — If the landlord breaches any of clauses (7)(a), (b) and (c), the agreement referred to in subsection (7) is terminated and the exemption provided by subsection (7) no longer applies.

(10) Same — The landlord shall be deemed to have not breached the condition in clause (7)(a) if,

(a) upon a tenant ceasing to be a student of a post-secondary educational institution that is a party to the agreement with the landlord, the landlord takes action to terminate the tenancy in accordance with an agreement with the tenant to terminate the tenancy or a notice of termination given by the tenant; or

(b) a tenant sublets the rental unit to a person who is not a student of a post-secondary educational institution that is a party to the agreement with the landlord.

(11) Same — Either party to an agreement referred to in subsection (7) may terminate the agreement on at least 90 days written notice to the other party and, upon the termination of the agreement, the exemption provided by subsection (7) no longer applies.

38.(1) Deemed renewal where no notice — If a tenancy agreement for a fixed term ends and has not been renewed or terminated, the landlord and tenant shall be deemed to have renewed it as a monthly tenancy agreement containing the same terms and conditions that are in the expired tenancy agreement and subject to any increases in rent charged in accordance with this Act.

(2) Same — If the period of a daily, weekly or monthly tenancy ends and the tenancy has not been renewed or terminated, the landlord and tenant shall be deemed to have renewed it for another day, week or month, as the case may be, with the same terms and conditions that are in the expired tenancy agreement and subject to any increases in rent charged in accordance with this Act.

(3) Same — If the period of a periodic tenancy ends, the tenancy has not been renewed or terminated and subsection (2) does not apply, the landlord and tenant shall be deemed to have renewed it as a monthly tenancy, with the same terms and conditions that are in the expired tenancy agreement and subject to any increases in rent charged in accordance with this Act.

39. Restriction on recovery of possession — A landlord shall not recover possession of a rental unit subject to a tenancy unless,

(a) the tenant has vacated or abandoned the unit; or

(b) an order of the Board evicting the tenant has authorized the possession.

40. Distress abolished — No landlord shall, without legal process, seize a tenant's property for default in the payment of rent or for the breach of any other obligation of the tenant.

41. (1) Disposal of abandoned property if unit vacated — A landlord may sell, retain for the landlord's own use or otherwise dispose of property in a rental unit or the residential complex if the rental unit has been vacated in accordance with,

(a) a notice of termination of the landlord or the tenant;

(b) an agreement between the landlord and the tenant to terminate the tenancy;

(c) subsection 93(2); or

(d) an order of the Board terminating the tenancy or evicting the tenant.

(2) Where eviction order enforced — Despite subsection (1), where an order is made to evict a tenant, the landlord shall not sell, retain or otherwise dispose of the tenant's property before 72 hours have elapsed after the enforcement of the eviction order.

(3) Same — A landlord shall make an evicted tenant's property available to be retrieved at a location close to the rental unit during the prescribed hours within the 72 hours after the enforcement of an eviction order.

(4) Liability of landlord — A landlord is not liable to any person for selling, retaining or otherwise disposing of a tenant's property in accordance with this section.

(5) Agreement — A landlord and a tenant may agree to terms other than those set out in this section with regard to the disposal of the tenant's property.

(6) Enforcement of landlord obligations — If, on application by a former tenant, the Board determines that a landlord has breached an obligation under subsection (2) or (3), the Board may do one or more of the following:

1. Order that the landlord not breach the obligation again.

2. Order that the landlord return to the former tenant property of the former tenant that is in the possession or control of the landlord.

3. Order that the landlord pay a specified sum to the former tenant for,

   i. the reasonable costs that the former tenant has incurred or will incur in repairing or, where repairing is not reasonable, replacing property of the former tenant that was damaged, destroyed or disposed of as a result of the landlord's breach, and

ii. other reasonable out-of-pocket expenses that the former tenant has incurred or will incur as a result of the landlord's breach.

4. Order that the landlord pay to the Board an administrative fine not exceeding the greater of $10,000 and the monetary jurisdiction of the Small Claims Court.

5. Make any other order that it considers appropriate.

42. (1) Disposal of property, unit abandoned — A landlord may dispose of property in a rental unit that a tenant has abandoned and property of persons occupying the rental unit that is in the residential complex in which the rental unit is located in accordance with subsections (2) and (3) if,

(a) the landlord obtains an order terminating the tenancy under section 79; or

(b) the landlord gives notice to the tenant of the rental unit and to the Board of the landlord's intention to dispose of the property.

(2) Same — If the tenant has abandoned the rental unit, the landlord may dispose of any unsafe or unhygienic items immediately.

(3) Same — The landlord may sell, retain for the landlord's own use or otherwise dispose of any other items if 30 days have passed after obtaining the order referred to in clause (1)(a) or giving the notice referred to in clause (1)(b) to the tenant and the Board.

(4) Tenant's claim to property — If, before the 30 days have passed, the tenant notifies the landlord that he or she intends to remove property referred to in subsection (3), the tenant may remove the property within that 30-day period.

(5) Same — If the tenant notifies the landlord in accordance with subsection (4) that he or she intends to remove the property, the landlord shall make the property available to the tenant at a reasonable time and at a location close to the rental unit.

(6) Same — The landlord may require the tenant to pay the landlord for arrears of rent and any reasonable out-of-pocket expenses incurred by the landlord in moving, storing or securing the tenant's property before allowing the tenant to remove the property.

(7) Same — If, within six months after the date the notice referred to in clause (1)(b) is given to the tenant and the Board or the order terminating the tenancy is issued, the tenant claims any of his or her property that the landlord has sold, the landlord shall pay to the tenant the amount by which the proceeds of sale exceed the sum of,

(a) the landlord's reasonable out-of-pocket expenses for moving, storing, securing or selling the property; and

(b) any arrears of rent.

(8) No liability — Subject to subsections (5) and (7), a landlord is not liable to any person for selling, retaining or otherwise disposing of the property of a tenant in accordance with this section.

Notice of Termination—General

43. (1) Notice of termination — Where this Act permits a landlord or tenant to give a notice of termination, the notice shall be in a form approved by the Board and shall,

(a) identify the rental unit for which the notice is given;

(b) state the date on which the tenancy is to terminate; and

(c) be signed by the person giving the notice, or the person's agent.

(2) Same — If the notice is given by a landlord, it shall also set out the reasons and details respecting the termination and inform the tenant that,

(a) if the tenant vacates the rental unit in accordance with the notice, the tenancy terminates on the date set out in clause (1)(b);

(b) if the tenant does not vacate the rental unit, the landlord may apply to the Board for an order terminating the tenancy and evicting the tenant; and

(c) if the landlord applies for an order, the tenant is entitled to dispute the application.

44. Period of notice — (1) **Period of notice, daily or weekly tenancy** — A notice under section 47, 58 or 144 to terminate a daily or weekly tenancy shall be given at least 28 days before the date the termination is specified to be effective and that date shall be on the last day of a rental period.

(2) Period of notice, monthly tenancy — A notice under section 47, 58 or 144 to terminate a monthly tenancy shall be given at least 60 days before the date the termination is specified to be effective and that date shall be on the last day of a rental period.

(3) Period of notice, yearly tenancy — A notice under section 47, 58 or 144 to terminate a yearly tenancy shall be given at least 60 days before the date the termination is specified to be effective and that date shall be on the last day of a yearly period on which the tenancy is based.

(4) Period of notice, tenancy for fixed term — A notice under section 47, 58 or 144 to terminate a tenancy for a fixed term shall be given at least 60 days before the expiration date specified in the tenancy agreement, to be effective on that expiration date.

(5) Period of notice, February notices — A tenant who gives notice under subsection (2), (3) or (4) which specifies that the termination is to be effective on the last day of February or the last day of March in any year shall be deemed to have given at least 60 days notice of termination if the notice is given not later than January 1 of that year in respect of a termination which is to be effective on the last day of

February, or February 1 of that year in respect of a termination which is to be effective on the last day of March.

45. Effect of payment — Unless a landlord and tenant agree otherwise, the landlord does not waive a notice of termination, reinstate a tenancy or create a new tenancy,

(a) by giving the tenant a notice of rent increase; or

(b) by accepting arrears of rent or compensation for the use or occupation of a rental unit after,

(i) the landlord or the tenant gives a notice of termination of the tenancy,

(ii) the landlord and the tenant enter into an agreement to terminate the tenancy, or

(iii) the Board makes an eviction order or an order terminating the tenancy.

46. (1) Where notice void — A notice of termination becomes void 30 days after the termination date specified in the notice unless,

(a) the tenant vacates the rental unit before that time; or

(b) the landlord applies for an order terminating the tenancy and evicting the tenant before that time.

(2) Exception — Subsection (1) does not apply with respect to a notice based on a tenant's failure to pay rent.

Notice by Tenant

47. Tenant's notice to terminate, end of period or term — A tenant may terminate a tenancy at the end of a period of the tenancy or at the end of the term of a tenancy for a fixed term by giving notice of termination to the landlord in accordance with section 44.

Notice by Landlord at End of Period or Term

48. (1) Notice, landlord personally, etc., requires unit — A landlord may, by notice, terminate a tenancy if the landlord in good faith requires possession of the rental unit for the purpose of residential occupation by,

(a) the landlord;

(b) the landlord's spouse;

(c) a child or parent of the landlord or the landlord's spouse; or

(d) a person who provides or will provide care services to the landlord, the landlord's spouse, or a child or parent of the landlord or the landlord's spouse, if the person receiving the care services resides or will reside in the building, related group of buildings, mobile home park or land lease community in which the rental unit is located.

(2) Same — The date for termination specified in the notice shall be at least 60 days after the notice is given and shall be the day a period of the tenancy ends or, where the tenancy is for a fixed term, the end of the term.

(3) Earlier termination by tenant — A tenant who receives notice of termination under subsection (1) may, at any time before the date specified in the notice, terminate the tenancy, effective on a specified date earlier than the date set out in the landlord's notice.

(4) Same — The date for termination specified in the tenant's notice shall be at least 10 days after the date the tenant's notice is given.

49. (1) Notice, purchaser personally requires unit — A landlord of a residential complex that contains no more than three residential units who has entered into an agreement of purchase and sale of the residential complex may, on behalf of the purchaser, give the tenant of a unit in the residential complex a notice terminating the tenancy, if the purchaser in good faith requires possession of the residential complex or the unit for the purpose of residential occupation by,

(a) the purchaser;

(b) the purchaser's spouse;

(c) a child or parent of the purchaser or the purchaser's spouse; or

(d) a person who provides or will provide care services to the purchaser, the purchaser's spouse, or a child or parent of the purchaser or the purchaser's spouse, if the person receiving the care services resides or will reside in the building, related group of buildings, mobile home park or land lease community in which the rental unit is located.

(2) Same, condominium — If a landlord who is an owner as defined in clause (a) or (b) of the definition of "owner" in subsection 1(1) of the *Condominium Act, 1998* owns a unit, as defined in subsection 1(1) of that Act, that is a rental unit and has entered into an agreement of purchase and sale of the unit, the landlord may, on behalf of the purchaser, give the tenant of the unit a notice terminating the tenancy, if the purchaser in good faith requires possession of the unit for the purpose of residential occupation by,

(a) the purchaser;

(b) the purchaser's spouse;

(c) a child or parent of the purchaser or the purchaser's spouse; or

(d) a person who provides or will provide care services to the purchaser, the purchaser's spouse, or a child or parent of the purchaser or the purchaser's spouse, if the person receiving the care services resides or will reside in the building, related group of buildings, mobile home park or land lease community in which the rental unit is located.

(3) Period of notice — The date for termination specified in a notice given under subsection (1) or (2) shall be at least 60 days after the notice is given and shall be the day a period of the tenancy ends or, where the tenancy is for a fixed term, the end of the term.

(4) Earlier termination by tenant — A tenant who receives notice of termination under subsection (1) or (2) may, at any time before the date specified in the notice, terminate the tenancy, effective on a specified date earlier than the date set out in the landlord's notice.

(5) Same — The date for termination specified in the tenant's notice shall be at least 10 days after the date the tenant's notice is given.

50. (1) Notice, demolition, conversion or repairs — A landlord may give notice of termination of a tenancy if the landlord requires possession of the rental unit in order to,

(a) demolish it;

(b) convert it to use for a purpose other than residential premises; or

(c) do repairs or renovations to it that are so extensive that they require a building permit and vacant possession of the rental unit.

(2) Same — The date for termination specified in the notice shall be at least 120 days after the notice is given and shall be the day a period of the tenancy ends or, where the tenancy is for a fixed term, the end of the term.

(3) Same — A notice under clause (1)(c) shall inform the tenant that if he or she wishes to exercise the right of first refusal under section 53 to occupy the premises after the repairs or renovations, he or she must give the landlord notice of that fact in accordance with subsection 53(2) before vacating the rental unit.

(4) Earlier termination by tenant — A tenant who receives notice of termination under subsection (1) may, at any time before the date specified in the notice, terminate the tenancy, effective on a specified date earlier than the date set out in the landlord's notice.

(5) Same — The date for termination specified in the tenant's notice shall be at least 10 days after the date the tenant's notice is given.

51. (1) Conversion to condominium, security of tenure — If a part or all of a residential complex becomes subject to a registered declaration and description under the *Condominium Act, 1998* or a predecessor of that Act on or after June 17, 1998, a landlord may not give a notice under section 48 or 49 to a person who was a tenant of a rental unit when it became subject to the registered declaration and description.

(2) Proposed units, security of tenure — If a landlord has entered into an agreement of purchase and sale of a rental unit that is a proposed unit under the *Condominium Act, 1998* or a predecessor of that Act, a landlord may not give a notice under section 48 or 49 to the tenant of the rental unit who was the tenant on the date the agreement of purchase and sale was entered into.

(3) **Non-application** — Subsections (1) and (2) do not apply with respect to a residential complex if no rental unit in the complex was rented before July 10, 1986 and all or part of the complex becomes subject to a registered declaration and description under the *Condominium Act, 1998* or a predecessor of that Act before the day that is two years after the day on which the first rental unit in the complex was first rented.

(4) **Assignee of tenant not included** — Despite subsection 95(8), a reference to a tenant in subsection (1), (2) or (5) does not include a person to whom the tenant subsequently assigns the rental unit.

(5) **Conversion to condominium, right of first refusal** — If a landlord receives an acceptable offer to purchase a condominium unit converted from rented residential premises and still occupied by a tenant who was a tenant on the date of the registration referred to in subsection (1) or an acceptable offer to purchase a rental unit intended to be converted to a condominium unit, the tenant has a right of first refusal to purchase the unit at the price and subject to the terms and conditions in the offer.

(6) **Same** — The landlord shall give the tenant at least 72 hours notice of the offer to purchase the unit before accepting the offer.

(7) **Exception** — Subsection (5) does not apply when,

(a) the offer to purchase is an offer to purchase more than one unit; or

(b) the unit has been previously purchased since that registration, but not together with any other units.

52. **Compensation, demolition or conversion** — A landlord shall compensate a tenant in an amount equal to three months rent or offer the tenant another rental unit acceptable to the tenant if,

(a) the tenant receives notice of termination of the tenancy for the purposes of demolition or conversion to non-residential use;

(b) the residential complex in which the rental unit is located contains at least five residential units; and

(c) in the case of a demolition, it was not ordered to be carried out under the authority of any other Act.

53. (1) **Tenant's right of first refusal, repair or renovation** — A tenant who receives notice of termination of a tenancy for the purpose of repairs or renovations may, in accordance with this section, have a right of first refusal to occupy the rental unit as a tenant when the repairs or renovations are completed.

(2) **Written notice** — A tenant who wishes to have a right of first refusal shall give the landlord notice in writing before vacating the rental unit.

(3) Rent to be charged — A tenant who exercises a right of first refusal may reoccupy the rental unit at a rent that is no more than what the landlord could have lawfully charged if there had been no interruption in the tenant's tenancy.

(4) Change of address — It is a condition of the tenant's right of first refusal that the tenant inform the landlord in writing of any change of address.

54. (1) Tenant's right to compensation, repair or renovation — A landlord shall compensate a tenant who receives notice of termination of a tenancy under section 50 for the purpose of repairs or renovations in an amount equal to three months rent or shall offer the tenant another rental unit acceptable to the tenant if,

(a) the tenant does not give the landlord notice under subsection 53(2) with respect to the rental unit;

(b) the residential complex in which the rental unit is located contains at least five residential units; and

(c) the repair or renovation was not ordered to be carried out under the authority of this or any other Act.

(2) Same — A landlord shall compensate a tenant who receives notice of termination of a tenancy under section 50 for the purpose of repairs or renovations in an amount equal to the rent for the lesser of three months and the period the unit is under repair or renovation if,

(a) the tenant gives the landlord notice under subsection 53(2) with respect to the rental unit;

(b) the residential complex in which the rental unit is located contains at least five residential units; and

(c) the repair or renovation was not ordered to be carried out under the authority of this or any other Act.

55. Tenant's right to compensation, severance — A landlord of a residential complex that is created as a result of a severance shall compensate a tenant of a rental unit in that complex in an amount equal to three months rent or offer the tenant another rental unit acceptable to the tenant if,

(a) before the severance, the residential complex from which the new residential complex was created had at least five residential units;

(b) the new residential complex has fewer than five residential units; and

(c) the landlord gives the tenant a notice of termination under section 50 less than two years after the date of the severance.

56. Security of tenure, severance, subdivision — Where a rental unit becomes separately conveyable property due to a consent under section 53 of the *Planning Act* or a plan of subdivision under section 51 of that Act, a landlord may not give a notice under section 48 or 49 to a person who was a tenant of the rental unit at the time of the consent or approval.

57. (1) Former tenant's application where notice given in bad faith — The Board may make an order described in subsection (3) if, on application by a former tenant of a rental unit, the Board determines that,

(a) the landlord gave a notice of termination under section 48 in bad faith, the former tenant vacated the rental unit as a result of the notice or as a result of an application to or order made by the Board based on the notice, and no person referred to in clause 48(1)(a), (b), (c) or (d) occupied the rental unit within a reasonable time after the former tenant vacated the rental unit;

(b) the landlord gave a notice of termination under section 49 in bad faith, the former tenant vacated the rental unit as a result of the notice or as a result of an application to or order made by the Board based on the notice, and no person referred to in clause 49(1)(a), (b), (c) or (d) or 49(2)(a), (b), (c) or (d) occupied the rental unit within a reasonable time after the former tenant vacated the rental unit; or

(c) the landlord gave a notice of termination under section 50 in bad faith, the former tenant vacated the rental unit as a result of the notice or as a result of an application to or order made by the Board based on the notice, and the landlord did not demolish, convert or repair or renovate the rental unit within a reasonable time after the former tenant vacated the rental unit.

(2) Time limitation — No application may be made under subsection (1) more than one year after the former tenant vacated the rental unit.

(3) Orders — The orders referred to in subsection (1) are the following:

1. An order that the landlord pay a specified sum to the former tenant for,

   i. all or any portion of any increased rent that the former tenant has incurred or will incur for a one-year period after vacating the rental unit, and

   ii. reasonable out-of-pocket moving, storage and other like expenses that the former tenant has incurred or will incur.

2. An order for an abatement of rent.

3. An order that the landlord pay to the Board an administrative fine not exceeding the greater of $10,000 and the monetary jurisdiction of the Small Claims Court.

4. Any other order that the Board considers appropriate.

(4) Previous determination of good faith — In an application under subsection (1), the Board may find that the landlord gave a notice of termination in bad faith despite a previous finding by the Board to the contrary.

58. (1) Notice at end of term or period, additional grounds — A landlord may give a tenant notice of termination of their tenancy on any of the following grounds:

1. The tenant has persistently failed to pay rent on the date it becomes due and payable.

2. The rental unit that is the subject of the tenancy agreement is a rental unit described in paragraph 1, 2, 3 or 4 of subsection 7(1) and the tenant has ceased to meet the qualifications required for occupancy of the rental unit.

3. The tenant was an employee of an employer who provided the tenant with the rental unit during the tenant's employment and the employment has terminated.

4. The tenancy arose by virtue of or collateral to an agreement of purchase and sale of a proposed unit within the meaning of the *Condominium Act, 1998* in good faith and the agreement of purchase and sale has been terminated.

(2) Period of notice — The date for termination specified in the notice shall be at least the number of days after the date the notice is given that is set out in section 44 and shall be the day a period of the tenancy ends or, where the tenancy is for a fixed term, the end of the term.

Notice by Landlord Before End of Period or Term

59. (1) Non-payment of rent — If a tenant fails to pay rent lawfully owing under a tenancy agreement, the landlord may give the tenant notice of termination of the tenancy effective not earlier than,

(a) the 7th day after the notice is given, in the case of a daily or weekly tenancy; and

(b) the 14th day after the notice is given, in all other cases.

(2) Contents of notice — The notice of termination shall set out the amount of rent due and shall specify that the tenant may avoid the termination of the tenancy by paying, on or before the termination date specified in the notice, the rent due as set out in the notice and any additional rent that has become due under the tenancy agreement as at the date of payment by the tenant.

(3) Notice void if rent paid — The notice of termination is void if, before the day the landlord applies to the Board for an order terminating the tenancy and evicting the tenant based on the notice, the tenant pays,

(a) the rent that is in arrears under the tenancy agreement; and

(b) the additional rent that would have been due under the tenancy agreement as at the date of payment by the tenant had notice of termination not been given.

60. (1) Termination for cause, misrepresentation of income — A landlord may give a tenant notice of termination of the tenancy if the rental unit is a rental unit described in paragraph 1, 2, 3 or 4 of subsection 7(1) and the tenant has knowingly and materially misrepresented his or her income or that of other members of his or her family occupying the rental unit.

(2) Notice — A notice of termination under this section shall set out the grounds for termination and shall provide a termination date not earlier than the 20th day after the notice is given.

61. (1) Termination for cause, illegal act — A landlord may give a tenant notice of termination of the tenancy if the tenant or another occupant of the rental unit commits an illegal act or carries on an illegal trade, business or occupation or permits a person to do so in the rental unit or the residential complex.

(2) Notice — A notice of termination under this section shall set out the grounds for termination and shall provide a termination date not earlier than,

(a) the 10th day after the notice is given, in the case of a notice grounded on an illegal act, trade, business or occupation involving,

(i) the production of an illegal drug,

(ii) the trafficking in an illegal drug, or

(iii) the possession of an illegal drug for the purposes of trafficking; or

(b) the 20th day after the notice is given, in all other cases.

(3) Definitions — In this section,

"illegal drug" means a controlled substance or precursor as those terms are defined in the *Controlled Drugs and Substances Act* (Canada); (*"drogue illicite"*)

"possession" has the same meaning as in the *Controlled Drugs and Substances Act* (Canada); (*"possession"*)

"production" means, with respect to an illegal drug, to produce the drug within the meaning of the *Controlled Drugs and Substances Act* (Canada); (*"production"*)

"trafficking" means, with respect to an illegal drug, to traffic in the drug within the meaning of the *Controlled Drugs and Substances Act* (Canada). (*"trafic"*)

62. (1) Termination for cause, damage — A landlord may give a tenant notice of termination of the tenancy if the tenant, another occupant of the rental unit or a person whom the tenant permits in the residential complex wilfully or negligently causes undue damage to the rental unit or the residential complex.

(2) Notice — A notice of termination under this section shall,

(a) provide a termination date not earlier than the 20th day after the notice is given;

(b) set out the grounds for termination; and

(c) require the tenant, within seven days,

(i) to repair the damaged property or pay to the landlord the reasonable costs of repairing the damaged property, or

(ii) to replace the damaged property or pay to the landlord the reasonable costs of replacing the damaged property, if it is not reasonable to repair the damaged property.

(3) Notice void if tenant complies — The notice of termination under this section is void if the tenant, within seven days after receiving the notice, complies with the requirement referred to in clause (2)(c) or makes arrangements satisfactory to the landlord to comply with that requirement.

63. (1) Termination for cause, damage, shorter notice period — Despite section 62, a landlord may give a tenant notice of termination of the tenancy that provides a termination date not earlier than the 10th day after the notice is given if the tenant, another occupant of the rental unit or a person whom the tenant permits in the residential complex,

(a) wilfully causes undue damage to the rental unit or the residential complex; or

(b) uses the rental unit or the residential complex in a manner that is inconsistent with use as residential premises and that causes or can reasonably be expected to cause damage that is significantly greater than the damage that is required in order to give a notice of termination under clause (a) or subsection 62(1).

(2) Notice — A notice of termination under this section shall set out the grounds for termination.

(3) Non-application of s. 62(2) and (3) — Subsections 62(2) and (3) do not apply to a notice given under this section.

64. (1) Termination for cause, reasonable enjoyment — A landlord may give a tenant notice of termination of the tenancy if the conduct of the tenant, another occupant of the rental unit or a person permitted in the residential complex by the tenant is such that it substantially interferes with the reasonable enjoyment of the residential complex for all usual purposes by the landlord or another tenant or substantially interferes with another lawful right, privilege or interest of the landlord or another tenant.

(2) Notice — A notice of termination under subsection (1) shall,

(a) provide a termination date not earlier than the 20th day after the notice is given;

(b) set out the grounds for termination; and

(c) require the tenant, within seven days, to stop the conduct or activity or correct the omission set out in the notice.

(3) Notice void if tenant complies — The notice of termination under subsection (1) is void if the tenant, within seven days after receiving the notice, stops the conduct or activity or corrects the omission.

65. (1) Termination for cause, reasonable enjoyment of landlord in small building — Despite section 64, a landlord who resides in a building containing not more than three residential units may give a tenant of a rental unit in the building notice of termination of the tenancy that provides a termination date not earlier than the 10th day after the notice is given if the conduct of the tenant, another occupant of the rental unit or a person permitted in the building by the tenant is such that it substantially interferes with the reasonable enjoyment of the building for all usual purposes by the landlord or substantially interferes with another lawful right, privilege or interest of the landlord.

(2) Notice — A notice of termination under this section shall set out the grounds for termination.

(3) Non-application of s. 64(2) and (3) — Subsections 64(2) and (3) do not apply to a notice given under this section.

66. (1) Termination for cause, act impairs safety — A landlord may give a tenant notice of termination of the tenancy if,

(a) an act or omission of the tenant, another occupant of the rental unit or a person permitted in the residential complex by the tenant seriously impairs or has seriously impaired the safety of any person; and

(b) the act or omission occurs in the residential complex.

(2) Same — A notice of termination under this section shall provide a termination date not earlier than the 10th day after the notice is given and shall set out the grounds for termination.

67. (1) Termination for cause, too many persons — A landlord may give a tenant notice of termination of the tenancy if the number of persons occupying the rental unit on a continuing basis results in a contravention of health, safety or housing standards required by law.

(2) Notice — A notice of termination under this section shall,

(a) provide a termination date not earlier than the 20th day after the notice is given;

(b) set out the details of the grounds for termination; and

(c) require the tenant, within seven days, to reduce the number of persons occupying the rental unit to comply with health, safety or housing standards required by law.

(3) Notice void if tenant complies — The notice of termination under this section is void if the tenant, within seven days after receiving the notice, sufficiently reduces the number of persons occupying the rental unit.

68. (1) Notice of termination, further contravention — A landlord may give a tenant notice of termination of the tenancy if,

(a) a notice of termination under section 62, 64 or 67 has become void as a result of the tenant's compliance with the terms of the notice; and

(b) within six months after the notice mentioned in clause (a) was given to the tenant, an activity takes place, conduct occurs or a situation arises that constitutes grounds for a notice of termination under section 60, 61, 62, 64 or 67, other than an activity, conduct or a situation that is described in subsection 61(1) and that involves an illegal act, trade, business or occupation described in clause 61(2)(a).

(2) Same — The notice under this section shall set out the date it is to be effective and that date shall not be earlier than the 14th day after the notice is given.

Application by Landlord — After Notice of Termination

69. (1) Application by landlord — A landlord may apply to the Board for an order terminating a tenancy and evicting the tenant if the landlord has given notice to terminate the tenancy under this Act or the *Tenant Protection Act, 1997.*

(2) Same — An application under subsection (1) may not be made later than 30 days after the termination date specified in the notice.

(3) Exception — Subsection (2) does not apply with respect to an application based on the tenant's failure to pay rent.

70. No application during remedy period — A landlord may not apply to the Board for an order terminating a tenancy and evicting the tenant based on a notice of termination under section 62, 64 or 67 before the seven-day remedy period specified in the notice expires.

71. Immediate application — Subject to section 70 and subsection 74(1), a landlord who has served a notice of termination may apply immediately to the Board under section 69 for an order terminating the tenancy and evicting the tenant.

72. (1) Landlord or purchaser personally requires premises — The Board shall not make an order terminating a tenancy and evicting the tenant in an application under section 69 based on a notice of termination under section 48 or 49 unless the landlord has filed with the Board an affidavit sworn by the person who personally requires the rental unit certifying that the person in good faith requires the rental unit for his or her own personal use.

(2) Same — The Board shall not make an order terminating a tenancy and evicting the tenant in an application under section 69 based on a notice of termination under section 48 or 49 where the landlord's claim is based on a tenancy agreement or occupancy agreement that purports to entitle the landlord to reside in the rental unit unless,

(a) the application is brought in respect of premises situate in a building containing not more than four residential units; or

(b) one or more of the following people has previously been a genuine occupant of the premises:

(i) the landlord,

(ii) the landlord's spouse,

(iii) a child or parent of the landlord or the landlord's spouse, or

(iv) a person who provided care services to the landlord, the landlord's spouse, or a child or parent of the landlord or the landlord's spouse.

73. Demolition, conversion, repairs — The Board shall not make an order terminating a tenancy and evicting the tenant in an application under section 69 based on a notice of termination under section 50 unless it is satisfied that,

(a) the landlord intends in good faith to carry out the activity on which the notice of termination was based; and

(b) the landlord has,

(i) obtained all necessary permits or other authority that may be required to carry out the activity on which the notice of termination was based, or

(ii) has taken all reasonable steps to obtain all necessary permits or other authority that may be required to carry out the activity on which the notice of termination was based, if it is not possible to obtain the permits or other authority until the rental unit is vacant.

74. (1) Non-payment of rent — A landlord may not apply to the Board under section 69 for an order terminating a tenancy and evicting the tenant based on a notice of termination under section 59 before the day following the termination date specified in the notice.

(2) Discontinuance of application — An application by a landlord under section 69 for an order terminating a tenancy and evicting the tenant based on a notice of termination under section 59 shall be discontinued if, before the Board issues the eviction order, the Board is satisfied that the tenant has paid to the landlord or to the Board,

(a) the amount of rent that is in arrears under the tenancy agreement;

(b) the amount of additional rent that would have been due under the tenancy agreement as at the date of payment by the tenant had notice of termination not been given; and

(c) the landlord's application fee.

(3) Order of Board — An order of the Board terminating a tenancy and evicting the tenant in an application under section 69 based on a notice of termination under section 59 shall,

(a) specify the following amounts:

(i) the amount of rent that is in arrears under the tenancy agreement,

(ii) the daily amount of compensation that must be paid under section 86, and

(iii) any costs ordered by the Board;

(b) inform the tenant and the landlord that the order will become void if, before the order becomes enforceable, the tenant pays to the landlord or to the Board the amount required under subsection (4) and specify that amount; and

(c) if the tenant has previously made a motion under subsection (11) during the period of the tenant's tenancy agreement with the landlord, inform the tenant and the landlord that the tenant is not entitled to make another motion under that subsection during the period of the agreement.

(4) Payment before order becomes enforceable — An eviction order referred to in subsection (3) is void if the tenant pays to the landlord or to the Board, before the order becomes enforceable,

(a) the amount of rent that is in arrears under the tenancy agreement;

(b) the amount of additional rent that would have been due under the tenancy agreement as at the date of payment by the tenant had notice of termination not been given;

(c) the amount of NSF cheque charges charged by financial institutions to the landlord in respect of cheques tendered to the landlord by or on behalf of the tenant, as allowed by the Board in an application by the landlord under section 87;

(d) the amount of administration charges payable by the tenant for the NSF cheques, as allowed by the Board in an application by the landlord under section 87; and

(e) the costs ordered by the Board.

(5) Notice of void order — If, before the eviction order becomes enforceable, the tenant pays the amount specified in the order under clause (3)(b) to the Board, an employee of the Board shall issue a notice to the tenant and the landlord acknowledging that the eviction order is void under subsection (4).

(6) Determination that full amount paid before order becomes enforceable — If, before the eviction order becomes enforceable, the tenant pays the amount due under subsection (4) either in whole to the landlord or in part to the landlord and in part to the Board, the tenant may make a motion to the Board, without notice to the landlord, for an order determining that the tenant has paid the full amount due under subsection (4) and confirming that the eviction order is void under subsection (4).

(7) Evidence — A tenant who makes a motion under subsection (6) shall provide the Board with an affidavit setting out the details of any payments made to the landlord and with any supporting documents the tenant may have.

(8) No hearing — The Board shall make an order under subsection (6) without holding a hearing.

(9) Motion by landlord — Within 10 days after an order is issued under subsection (6), the landlord may, on notice to the tenant, make a motion to the Board to have the order set aside.

(10) Order of Board — On a motion under subsection (9), the Board shall hold a hearing and shall,

(a) if satisfied that the tenant paid the full amount due under subsection (4) before the eviction order became enforceable, refuse to set aside the order made under subsection (6);

(b) if satisfied that the tenant did not pay the full amount due under subsection (4) before the eviction order became enforceable but that the tenant has since paid the full amount, refuse to set aside the order made under subsection (6); or

(c) in any other case, set aside the order made under subsection (6) and confirm that the eviction order is not void under subsection (4).

(11) Payment after order becomes enforceable — A tenant may make a motion to the Board, on notice to the landlord, to set aside an eviction order referred to in subsection (3) if, after the order becomes enforceable but before it is executed, the tenant pays an amount to the Board and files an affidavit sworn by the tenant stating that the amount, together with any amounts previously paid to the landlord, is at least the sum of the following amounts:

1. The amount of rent that is in arrears under the tenancy agreement.

2. The amount of additional rent that would have been due under the tenancy agreement as at the date of payment by the tenant had notice of termination not been given.

3. The amount of NSF cheque charges charged by financial institutions to the landlord in respect of cheques tendered to the landlord by or on behalf of the tenant, as allowed by the Board in an application by the landlord under section 87.

4. The amount of administration charges payable by the tenant for the NSF cheques, as allowed by the Board in an application by the landlord under section 87.

5. The costs ordered by the Board.

(12) Exception — Subsection (11) does not apply if the tenant has previously made a motion under that subsection during the period of the tenant's tenancy agreement with the landlord.

(13) Motion under subs. (11) stays eviction order — An order under subsection (3) is stayed when a motion under subsection (11) is received by the Board and shall not be enforced under this Act or as an order of the Superior Court of Justice during the stay.

(14) Order of Board — Subject to subsection (15), if a tenant makes a motion under subsection (11), the Board shall, after a hearing,

(a) make an order declaring the order under subsection (3) to be void, if the tenant has paid the amounts set out in subsection (11); or

(b) make an order lifting the stay of the order under subsection (3), if the tenant has not paid the amounts set out in subsection (11).

(15) Enforcement costs — If, on a motion under subsection (11), the Board determines that the landlord has paid any non-refundable amount under the *Administration of Justice Act* for the purpose of enforcing the order under subsection (3), the Board shall specify that amount in the order made under clause (14)(a) and shall provide in the order that it is not effective unless,

(a) the tenant pays the specified amount into the Board by a date specified in the order; and

(b) an employee of the Board issues a notice under subsection (16).

(16) Notice of payment — If subsection (15) applies to an order made under clause (14)(a) and the tenant pays the amount specified in the order into the Board by the date specified in the order, an employee of the Board shall issue a notice to the tenant and the landlord acknowledging that the eviction order is void.

(17) Failure to pay — If subsection (15) applies to an order made under clause (14)(a) and the tenant does not pay the amount specified in the order into the Board by the date specified in the order, the stay of the order under subsection (3) ceases to apply and the order may be enforced.

(18) Order for payment — If the Board makes an order under clause (14)(b), the Board may make an order that the tenant pay to the landlord any non-refundable amount paid by the landlord under the *Administration of Justice Act* for the purpose of enforcing the order under subsection (3).

75. Illegal act — The Board may issue an order terminating a tenancy and evicting a tenant in an application referred to under section 69 based on a notice of termination under section 61 whether or not the tenant or other person has been convicted of an offence relating to an illegal act, trade, business or occupation.

76. (1) Application based on animals — If an application based on a notice of termination under section 64, 65 or 66 is grounded on the presence, control or behaviour of an animal in or about the residential complex, the Board shall not make an order terminating the tenancy and evicting the tenant without being satisfied that the tenant is keeping an animal and that,

(a) subject to subsection (2), the past behaviour of an animal of that species has substantially interfered with the reasonable enjoyment of the residential complex for all usual purposes by the landlord or other tenants;

(b) subject to subsection (3), the presence of an animal of that species has caused the landlord or another tenant to suffer a serious allergic reaction; or

(c) the presence of an animal of that species or breed is inherently dangerous to the safety of the landlord or the other tenants.

(2) Same — The Board shall not make an order terminating the tenancy and evicting the tenant relying on clause (1)(a) if it is satisfied that the animal kept by the tenant did not cause or contribute to the substantial interference.

(3) Same — The Board shall not make an order terminating the tenancy and evicting the tenant relying on clause (1)(b) if it is satisfied that the animal kept by the tenant did not cause or contribute to the allergic reaction.

Application by Landlord — No Notice of Termination

77. (1) Agreement to terminate, tenant's notice — A landlord may, without notice to the tenant, apply to the Board for an order terminating a tenancy and evicting the tenant if,

(a) the landlord and tenant have entered into an agreement to terminate the tenancy; or

(b) the tenant has given the landlord notice of termination of the tenancy.

(2) Same — The landlord shall include with the application an affidavit verifying the agreement or notice of termination, as the case may be.

(3) Same — An application under subsection (1) shall not be made later than 30 days after the termination date specified in the agreement or notice.

(4) Order — On receipt of the application, the Board may make an order terminating the tenancy and evicting the tenant.

(5) Same — An order under subsection (4) shall be effective not earlier than,

(a) the date specified in the agreement, in the case of an application under clause (1)(a); or

(b) the termination date set out in the notice, in the case of an application under clause (1)(b).

(6) Motion to set aside order — The respondent may make a motion to the Board, on notice to the applicant, to have the order under subsection (4) set aside within 10 days after the order is issued.

(7) Motion stays order — An order under subsection (4) is stayed when a motion to have the order set aside is received by the Board and shall not be enforced under this Act or as an order of the Superior Court of Justice during the stay.

(8) Order of Board — If the respondent makes a motion under subsection (6), the Board shall, after a hearing,

(a) make an order setting aside the order under subsection (4), if,

(i) the landlord and tenant did not enter into an agreement to terminate the tenancy, and

(ii) the tenant did not give the landlord notice of termination of the tenancy;

(b) make an order setting aside the order under subsection (4), if the Board is satisfied, having regard to all the circumstances, that it would not be unfair to do so; or

(c) make an order lifting the stay of the order under subsection (4), effective immediately or on a future date specified in the order.

78. (1) Application based on previous order, mediated settlement — A landlord may, without notice to the tenant, apply to the Board for an order terminating a tenancy or evicting the tenant if the following criteria are satisfied:

1. The landlord previously applied to the Board for an order terminating the tenancy or evicting the tenant.

2. A settlement mediated under section 194 or order made with respect to the previous application,

   i. imposed conditions on the tenant that, if not met by the tenant, would give rise to the same grounds for terminating the tenancy as were claimed in the previous application, and

   ii. provided that the landlord could apply under this section if the tenant did not meet one or more of the conditions described in subparagraph i.

3. The tenant has not met one or more of the conditions described in subparagraph 2 i.

(2) Same — The landlord shall include with the application a copy of the settlement or order and an affidavit setting out what conditions of the settlement or order have not been met and how they have not been met.

(3) Order for payment — In an application under subsection (1), the landlord may also request that the Board make an order for payment under subsection (7) if the following criteria are satisfied:

1. The landlord applied for an order for the payment of arrears of rent when the landlord made the previous application described in paragraph 1 of subsection (1).

2. A settlement mediated under section 194 or order made with respect to the previous application requires the tenant to pay rent or some or all of the arrears of rent.

(4) Affidavit — If the landlord makes a request under subsection (3), the affidavit included with the application under subsection (2) must also provide the following information:

1. The amount of any additional arrears of rent arising after the date of the settlement or order.

2. The amount of NSF cheque charges, if any, claimed by the landlord that were charged by financial institutions after the date of the settlement or order in respect of cheques tendered to the landlord by or on behalf of the tenant, to the extent the landlord has not been reimbursed for the charges.

3. The amount of NSF administration charges, if any, claimed by the landlord in respect of NSF cheques tendered by or on behalf of the tenant after the date of the settlement or order, to the extent the landlord has not been reimbursed for the charges.

4. If a settlement was mediated under section 194 with respect to the previous application,

i. the amount and date of each payment made under the terms of the settlement and what the payment was for,

ii. the amount of arrears of rent payable to the landlord under the terms of the settlement,

iii. the amount of NSF cheque charges payable to the landlord under the terms of the settlement,

iv. the amount of NSF administration charges payable to the landlord under the terms of the settlement, and

v. the amount that the terms of the settlement required the tenant to pay to the landlord as reimbursement for the fee paid by the landlord for the application referred to in paragraph 1 of subsection (1).

5. The amount of any rent deposit, the date it was given and the last period for which interest was paid on the rent deposit.

(5) Time for application — An application under this section shall not be made later than 30 days after a failure of the tenant to meet a condition described in subparagraph 2 i of subsection (1).

(6) Order terminating tenancy — If the Board finds that the landlord is entitled to an order under subsection (1), the Board may make an order terminating the tenancy and evicting the tenant.

(7) Order for arrears — If an order is made under subsection (6) and the landlord makes a request under subsection (3), the Board may order the payment of the following amounts:

1. The amount of any compensation payable under section 86.

2. The amount of arrears of rent that arose after the date of the settlement or order referred to in paragraph 2 of subsection (3).

3. Such amount as the Board may allow in respect of NSF cheque charges claimed by the landlord that were charged by financial institutions, after the date of the settlement or order referred to in paragraph 2 of subsection (3), in respect of cheques tendered by or on behalf of the tenant and for which the landlord has not been reimbursed.

4. Such amount as the Board may allow in respect of NSF administration charges claimed by the landlord that were incurred after the date of the settlement or order referred to in paragraph 2 of subsection (3) in respect of NSF cheques tendered by or on behalf of the tenant and for which the landlord has not been reimbursed, not exceeding the amount per cheque that is prescribed as a specified amount exempt from the operation of section 134.

5. If a settlement was mediated under section 194 with respect to the previous application,

i. the amount of arrears of rent payable under the terms of the settlement that has not been paid,

ii. the amount payable under the terms of the settlement in respect of NSF cheque charges that were charged by financial institutions in respect of cheques tendered by or on behalf of the tenant and for which the landlord has not been reimbursed,

iii. the amount payable under the terms of the settlement in respect of NSF administration charges for which the landlord has not been reimbursed, not exceeding the amount per cheque that is prescribed as a specified amount exempt from the operation of section 134, and

iv. the amount payable under the terms of the settlement as reimbursement for the fee paid by the landlord for the previous application, to the extent that the amount payable did not exceed that fee and to the extent that the amount payable has not been paid.

(8) Credit for rent deposit — In determining the amount payable by the tenant to the landlord, the Board shall ensure that the tenant is credited with the amount of any rent deposit and interest on the deposit that would be owing to the tenant on the termination of the tenancy.

(9) Motion to set aside order — The respondent may make a motion to the Board, on notice to the applicant, to have an order under subsection (6), and any order made under subsection (7), set aside within 10 days after the order made under subsection (6) is issued.

(10) Motion stays order — An order under subsection (6) or (7) is stayed when a motion to have the order set aside is received by the Board and shall not be enforced under this Act or as an order of the Superior Court of Justice during the stay.

(11) Order of Board — If the respondent makes a motion under subsection (9), the Board shall, after a hearing,

(a) make an order setting aside the order under subsection (6), and any order made under subsection (7), if any of the criteria set out in subsection (1) are not satisfied;

(b) make an order setting aside the order under subsection (6), and any order made under subsection (7), if the Board is satisfied, having regard to all the circumstances, that it would not be unfair to set aside the order under subsection (6); or

(c) make an order lifting the stay of the order under subsection (6), and any order made under subsection (7), effective immediately or on a future date specified in the order.

79. **Abandonment of rental unit** — If a landlord believes that a tenant has abandoned a rental unit, the landlord may apply to the Board for an order terminating the tenancy.

Eviction Orders

80. (1) **Effective date of order** — If a notice of termination of a tenancy has been given and the landlord has subsequently applied to the Board for an order evicting the tenant, the order of the Board evicting the tenant may not be effective earlier than the date of termination set out in the notice.

(2) **Exception, notice under s. 63 or 66** — Despite subsection (1), an order evicting a tenant may provide that it is effective on a date specified in the order that is earlier than the date of termination set out in the notice of termination if,

(a) the order is made on an application under section 69 based on a notice of termination under clause 63(1)(a) and the Board determines that the damage caused was significantly greater than the damage that was required by that clause in order to give the notice of termination; or

(b) the order is made on an application under section 69 based on a notice of termination under clause 63(1)(b) or subsection 66(1).

81. **Expiry date of order** — An order of the Board evicting a person from a rental unit expires six months after the day on which the order takes effect if it is not filed within those six months with the sheriff who has territorial jurisdiction where the rental unit is located.

82. (1) **Tenant issues in application for non-payment of rent** — At a hearing of an application by a landlord under section 69 for an order terminating a tenancy and evicting a tenant based on a notice of termination under section 59, the Board shall permit the tenant to raise any issue that could be the subject of an application made by the tenant under this Act.

(2) **Orders** — If a tenant raises an issue under subsection (1), the Board may make any order in respect of the issue that it could have made had the tenant made an application under this Act.

83. (1) **Power of Board, eviction** — Upon an application for an order evicting a tenant, the Board may, despite any other provision of this Act or the tenancy agreement,

(a) refuse to grant the application unless satisfied, having regard to all the circumstances, that it would be unfair to refuse; or

(b) order that the enforcement of the eviction order be postponed for a period of time.

(2) Mandatory review — If a hearing is held, the Board shall not grant the application unless it has reviewed the circumstances and considered whether or not it should exercise its powers under subsection (1).

(3) Circumstances where refusal required — Without restricting the generality of subsection (1), the Board shall refuse to grant the application where satisfied that,

(a) the landlord is in serious breach of the landlord's responsibilities under this Act or of any material covenant in the tenancy agreement;

(b) the reason for the application being brought is that the tenant has complained to a governmental authority of the landlord's violation of a law dealing with health, safety, housing or maintenance standards;

(c) the reason for the application being brought is that the tenant has attempted to secure or enforce his or her legal rights;

(d) the reason for the application being brought is that the tenant is a member of a tenants' association or is attempting to organize such an association; or

(e) the reason for the application being brought is that the rental unit is occupied by children and the occupation by the children does not constitute overcrowding.

(4) No eviction before compensation, demolition or conversion — The Board shall not issue an eviction order in a proceeding regarding termination of a tenancy for the purposes of demolition, conversion to non-residential rental use, renovations or repairs until the landlord has complied with section 52, 54 or 55, as the case may be.

(5) No eviction before compensation, repair or renovation — If a tenant has given a landlord notice under subsection 53(2) and subsection 54(2) applies, the Board shall not issue an eviction order in a proceeding regarding termination of the tenancy until the landlord has compensated the tenant in accordance with subsection 54(2).

84. Expedited eviction order — Subject to clause 83(1)(b), the Board shall, in an order made under section 69 based on a notice given under subsection 61(1) that involves an illegal act, trade, business or occupation described in clause 61(2)(a) or based on a notice given under section 63, 65 or 66, request that the sheriff expedite the enforcement of the order.

85. Effect of eviction order — An order evicting a person shall have the same effect, and shall be enforced in the same manner, as a writ of possession.

Compensation for Landlord

86. Compensation, unit not vacated — A landlord is entitled to compensation for the use and occupation of a rental unit by a tenant who does not vacate the unit after his or her tenancy is terminated by order, notice or agreement.

87. (1) Application — A landlord may apply to the Board for an order for the payment of arrears of rent if,

(a) the tenant has not paid rent lawfully required under the tenancy agreement; and

(b) the tenant is in possession of the rental unit.

(2) Tenant issues — Section 82 applies, with necessary modifications, to an application under subsection (1).

(3) Compensation, overholding tenant — If a tenant is in possession of a rental unit after the tenancy has been terminated, the landlord may apply to the Board for an order for the payment of compensation for the use and occupation of a rental unit after a notice of termination or an agreement to terminate the tenancy has taken effect.

(4) Amount of arrears of rent or compensation — In determining the amount of arrears of rent, compensation or both owing in an order for termination of a tenancy and the payment of arrears of rent, compensation or both, the Board shall subtract from the amount owing the amount of any rent deposit or interest on a rent deposit that would be owing to the tenant on termination.

(5) NSF cheque charges — On an application by a landlord under this section, the Board may include the following amounts in determining the total amount owing to a landlord by a tenant in respect of a rental unit:

1. The amount of NSF cheque charges claimed by the landlord and charged by financial institutions in respect of cheques tendered to the landlord by or on behalf of the tenant, to the extent the landlord has not been reimbursed for the charges.

2. The amount of unpaid administration charges in respect of the NSF cheques, if claimed by the landlord, that do not exceed the amount per cheque that is prescribed as a specified payment exempt from the operation of section 134.

88. (1) Arrears of rent when tenant abandons or vacates without notice — If a tenant abandons or vacates a rental unit without giving notice of termination in accordance with this Act and no agreement to terminate has been made or the landlord has not given notice to terminate the tenancy, a determination of the amount of arrears of rent owing by the tenant shall be made in accordance with the following rules:

1. If the tenant vacated the rental unit after giving notice that was not in accordance with this Act, arrears of rent are owing for the period that ends on the earliest termination date that could have been specified in the notice, had the notice been given in accordance with section 47, 96 or 145, as the case may be.

2. If the tenant abandoned or vacated the rental unit without giving any notice, arrears of rent are owing for the period that ends on the earliest termination date that could have been specified in a notice of termination had the tenant, on the date that the landlord knew or ought to have known that the tenant had abandoned or vacated the rental unit, given notice of termination in accordance with section 47, 96 or 145, as the case may be.

(2) **Where landlord has given notice under s. 48, 49 or 50** — If a notice of termination has been given by the landlord under section 48, 49 or 50 and the tenant vacates the rental unit before the termination date set out in the notice without giving a notice of earlier termination or after giving a notice of earlier termination that is not in accordance with subsection 48(3), 49(4) or 50(4), as the case may be, a determination of the amount of arrears of rent owing by the tenant shall be made as if arrears of rent are owing for the period that ends on the earlier of the following dates:

1. The date that is 10 days after,

   i. the date the tenant gave notice of earlier termination, if the tenant vacated the rental unit after giving a notice of earlier termination that was not in accordance with subsection 48(3), 49(4) or 50(4), as the case may be, or

   ii. the date the landlord knew or ought to have known that the tenant had vacated the rental unit, if the tenant vacated the rental unit without giving a notice of earlier termination.

2. The termination date set out in the landlord's notice of termination.

(3) **New tenancy** — Despite subsections (1) and (2), if the landlord enters into a new tenancy agreement with a new tenant with respect to the rental unit, the tenant who abandoned or vacated the rental unit is not liable to pay an amount of arrears of rent that exceeds the lesser of the following amounts:

1. The amount of arrears of rent determined under subsection (1) or (2).

2. The amount of arrears of rent owing for the period that ends on the date the new tenant is entitled to occupy the rental unit.

(4) **Minimization of losses** — In determining the amount of arrears of rent owing under subsections (1), (2) and (3), consideration shall be given to whether or not the landlord has taken reasonable steps to minimize losses in accordance with section 16.

89. (1) Compensation for damage — A landlord may apply to the Board for an order requiring a tenant to pay reasonable costs that the landlord has incurred or will incur for the repair of or, where repairing is not reasonable, the replacement of damaged property, if the tenant, another occupant of the rental unit or a person whom the tenant permits in the residential complex wilfully or negligently causes undue damage to the rental unit or the residential complex and the tenant is in possession of the rental unit.

(2) **Same** — If the Board makes an order requiring payment under subsection (1) and for the termination of the tenancy, the Board shall set off against the amount

required to be paid the amount of any rent deposit or interest on a rent deposit that would be owing to the tenant on termination.

90. Compensation, misrepresentation of income — If a landlord has a right to give a notice of termination under section 60, the landlord may apply to the Board for an order for the payment of money the tenant would have been required to pay if the tenant had not misrepresented his or her income or that of other members of his or her family, so long as the application is made while the tenant is in possession of the rental unit.

Death of Tenant

91. (1) Death of tenant — If a tenant of a rental unit dies and there are no other tenants of the rental unit, the tenancy shall be deemed to be terminated 30 days after the death of the tenant.

(2) Reasonable access — The landlord shall, until the tenancy is terminated under subsection (1),

(a) preserve any property of a tenant who has died that is in the rental unit or the residential complex other than property that is unsafe or unhygienic; and

(b) afford the executor or administrator of the tenant's estate, or if there is no executor or administrator, a member of the tenant's family reasonable access to the rental unit and the residential complex for the purpose of removing the tenant's property.

92. (1) Landlord may dispose of property — The landlord may sell, retain for the landlord's own use or otherwise dispose of property of a tenant who has died that is in a rental unit and in the residential complex in which the rental unit is located,

(a) if the property is unsafe or unhygienic, immediately; and

(b) otherwise, after the tenancy is terminated under section 91.

(2) Same — Subject to subsections (3) and (4), a landlord is not liable to any person for selling, retaining or otherwise disposing of the property of a tenant in accordance with subsection (1).

(3) Same — If, within six months after the tenant's death, the executor or administrator of the estate of the tenant or, if there is no executor or administrator, a member of the tenant's family claims any property of the tenant that the landlord has sold, the landlord shall pay to the estate the amount by which the proceeds of sale exceed the sum of,

(a) the landlord's reasonable out-of-pocket expenses for moving, storing, securing or selling the property; and

(b) any arrears of rent.

(4) Same — If, within the six-month period after the tenant's death, the executor or administrator of the estate of the tenant or, if there is no executor or administrator, a member of the tenant's family claims any property of the tenant that the landlord has retained for the landlord's own use, the landlord shall return the property to the tenant's estate.

(5) Agreement — A landlord and the executor or administrator of a deceased tenant's estate may agree to terms other than those set out in this section with regard to the termination of the tenancy and disposal of the tenant's property.

Superintendent's Premises

93. (1) Termination of tenancy — If a landlord has entered into a tenancy agreement with respect to a superintendent's premises, unless otherwise agreed, the tenancy terminates on the day on which the employment of the tenant is terminated.

(2) Same — A tenant shall vacate a superintendent's premises within one week after his or her tenancy is terminated.

(3) No rent charged for week — A landlord shall not charge a tenant rent or compensation or receive rent or compensation from a tenant with respect to the one-week period mentioned in subsection (2).

94. Application to Board — The landlord may apply to the Board for an order terminating the tenancy of a tenant of superintendent's premises and evicting the tenant if the tenant does not vacate the rental unit within one week of the termination of his or her employment.

PART VI — ASSIGNMENT, SUBLETTING AND UNAUTHORIZED OCCUPANCY

95. (1) Assignment of tenancy — Subject to subsections (2), (3) and (6), and with the consent of the landlord, a tenant may assign a rental unit to another person.

(2) Landlord's options, general request — If a tenant asks a landlord to consent to an assignment of a rental unit, the landlord may,

(a) consent to the assignment of the rental unit; or

(b) refuse consent to the assignment of the rental unit.

(3) Landlord's options, specific request — If a tenant asks a landlord to consent to the assignment of the rental unit to a potential assignee, the landlord may,

(a) consent to the assignment of the rental unit to the potential assignee;

(b) refuse consent to the assignment of the rental unit to the potential assignee; or

(c) refuse consent to the assignment of the rental unit.

(4) Refusal or non-response — A tenant may give the landlord a notice of termination under section 96 within 30 days after the date a request is made if,

(a) the tenant asks the landlord to consent to an assignment of the rental unit and the landlord refuses consent;

(b) the tenant asks the landlord to consent to an assignment of the rental unit and the landlord does not respond within seven days after the request is made;

(c) the tenant asks the landlord to consent to an assignment of the rental unit to a potential assignee and the landlord refuses consent to the assignment under clause (3)(c); or

(d) the tenant asks the landlord to consent to an assignment of the rental unit to a potential assignee and the landlord does not respond within seven days after the request is made.

(5) Same — A landlord shall not arbitrarily or unreasonably refuse consent to an assignment of a rental unit to a potential assignee under clause (3)(b).

(6) Same — Subject to subsection (5), a landlord who has given consent to an assignment of a rental unit under clause (2)(a) may subsequently refuse consent to an assignment of the rental unit to a potential assignee under clause (3)(b).

(7) Charges — A landlord may charge a tenant only for the landlord's reasonable out-of-pocket expenses incurred in giving consent to an assignment to a potential assignee.

(8) Consequences of assignment — If a tenant has assigned a rental unit to another person, the tenancy agreement continues to apply on the same terms and conditions and,

(a) the assignee is liable to the landlord for any breach of the tenant's obligations and may enforce against the landlord any of the landlord's obligations under the tenancy agreement or this Act, if the breach or obligation relates to the period after the assignment, whether or not the breach or obligation also related to a period before the assignment;

(b) the former tenant is liable to the landlord for any breach of the tenant's obligations and may enforce against the landlord any of the landlord's obligations under the tenancy agreement or this Act, if the breach or obligation relates to the period before the assignment;

(c) if the former tenant has started a proceeding under this Act before the assignment and the benefits or obligations of the new tenant may be affected, the new tenant may join in or continue the proceeding.

(9) Application of section — This section applies with respect to all tenants, regardless of whether their tenancies are periodic, fixed, contractual or statutory, but does not apply with respect to a tenant of superintendent's premises.

96. (1) Tenant's notice to terminate, refusal of assignment — A tenant may give notice of termination of a tenancy if the circumstances set out in subsection 95(4) apply.

(2) Same — The date for termination specified in the notice shall be at least a number of days after the date of the notice that is the lesser of the notice period otherwise required under this Act and 30 days.

97. (1) Subletting rental unit — A tenant may sublet a rental unit to another person with the consent of the landlord.

(2) Same — A landlord shall not arbitrarily or unreasonably withhold consent to the sublet of a rental unit to a potential subtenant.

(3) Charges — A landlord may charge a tenant only for the landlord's reasonable out-of-pocket expenses incurred in giving consent to a subletting.

(4) Consequences of subletting — If a tenant has sublet a rental unit to another person,

(a) the tenant remains entitled to the benefits, and is liable to the landlord for the breaches, of the tenant's obligations under the tenancy agreement or this Act during the subtenancy; and

(b) the subtenant is entitled to the benefits, and is liable to the tenant for the breaches, of the subtenant's obligations under the subletting agreement or this Act during the subtenancy.

(5) Overholding subtenant — A subtenant has no right to occupy the rental unit after the end of the subtenancy.

(6) Application of section — This section applies with respect to all tenants, regardless of whether their tenancies are periodic, fixed, contractual or statutory, but does not apply with respect to a tenant of superintendent's premises.

98. (1) Tenant application — A tenant or former tenant of a rental unit may apply to the Board for an order determining that the landlord has arbitrarily or unreasonably withheld consent to the assignment or sublet of a rental unit to a potential assignee or subtenant.

(2) Time limitation — No application may be made under subsection (1) more than one year after the day the alleged conduct giving rise to the application occurred.

(3) Order re assignment, sublet — If the Board determines that a landlord has unlawfully withheld consent to an assignment or sublet in an application under subsection (1), the Board may do one or more of the following:

1. Order that the assignment or sublet is authorized.

2. Where appropriate, by order authorize another assignment or sublet proposed by the tenant.

3. Order that the tenancy be terminated.

4. Order an abatement of the tenant's or former tenant's rent.

(4) Same — The Board may establish terms and conditions of the assignment or sublet.

(5) Same — If an order is made under paragraph 1 or 2 of subsection (3), the assignment or sublet shall have the same legal effect as if the landlord had consented to it.

(6) Eviction with termination order — If an order is made terminating a tenancy under paragraph 3 of subsection (3), the Board may order that the tenant be evicted, effective not earlier than the termination date specified in the order.

99. Tenant's notice, application re subtenant — The following provisions apply, with necessary modifications, with respect to a tenant who has sublet a rental unit, as if the tenant were the landlord and the subtenant were the tenant:

1. Sections 59 to 69, 87, 89 and 148.
2. The provisions of this Act that relate to applications to the Board under sections 69, 87, 89 and 148.

100. (1) Unauthorized occupancy — If a tenant transfers the occupancy of a rental unit to a person in a manner other than by an assignment authorized under section 95 or a subletting authorized under section 97, the landlord may apply to the Board for an order terminating the tenancy and evicting the tenant and the person to whom occupancy of the rental unit was transferred.

(2) Time limitation — An application under subsection (1) must be made no later than 60 days after the landlord discovers the unauthorized occupancy.

(3) Compensation — A landlord who makes an application under subsection (1) may also apply to the Board for an order for the payment of compensation by the unauthorized occupant for the use and occupation of the rental unit, if the unauthorized occupant is in possession of the rental unit at the time the application is made.

(4) Application of s. 87(5) — Subsection 87(5) applies, with necessary modifications, to an application under subsection (3).

101. (1) Overholding subtenant — If a subtenant continues to occupy a rental unit after the end of the subtenancy, the landlord or the tenant may apply to the Board for an order evicting the subtenant.

(2) Time limitation — An application under this section must be made within 60 days after the end of the subtenancy.

102. Compensation, overholding subtenant — A tenant may apply to the Board for an order for compensation for use and occupation by an overholding subtenant after the end of the subtenancy if the overholding subtenant is in possession of the rental unit at the time of the application.

103. (1) Compensation, unauthorized occupant — A landlord is entitled to compensation for the use and occupation of a rental unit by an unauthorized occupant of the unit.

(2) Effect of payment — A landlord does not create a tenancy with an unauthorized occupant of a rental unit by accepting compensation for the use and occupation of the rental unit, unless the landlord and unauthorized occupant agree otherwise.

104. Miscellaneous new tenancy agreements — (1) **Assignment without consent** — If a person occupies a rental unit as a result of an assignment of the unit without the consent of the landlord, the landlord may negotiate a new tenancy agreement with the person.

(2) Overholding subtenant — If a subtenant continues to occupy a rental unit after the end of the subtenancy and the tenant has abandoned the rental unit, the landlord may negotiate a new tenancy agreement with the subtenant.

(3) Lawful rent — Sections 113 and 114 apply to tenancy agreements entered into under subsection (1) or (2) if they are entered into no later than 60 days after the landlord discovers the unauthorized occupancy.

(4) Deemed assignment — A person's occupation of a rental unit shall be deemed to be an assignment of the rental unit with the consent of the landlord as of the date the unauthorized occupancy began if,

(a) a tenancy agreement is not entered into under subsection (1) or (2) within the period set out in subsection (3);

(b) the landlord does not apply to the Board under section 100 for an order evicting the person within 60 days of the landlord discovering the unauthorized occupancy; and

(c) neither the landlord nor the tenant applies to the Board under section 101 within 60 days after the end of the subtenancy for an order evicting the subtenant.

PART VII — RULES RELATING TO RENT

General Rules

105. (1) Security deposits, limitation — The only security deposit that a landlord may collect is a rent deposit collected in accordance with section 106.

(2) Definition — In this section and in section 106,

"security deposit" means money, property or a right paid or given by, or on behalf of, a tenant of a rental unit to a landlord or to anyone on the landlord's behalf to be held by or for the account of the landlord as security for the performance of an obligation or the payment of a liability of the tenant or to be returned to the tenant upon the happening of a condition.

106. (1) Rent deposit may be required — A landlord may require a tenant to pay a rent deposit with respect to a tenancy if the landlord does so on or before entering into the tenancy agreement.

(2) Amount of rent deposit — The amount of a rent deposit shall not be more than the lesser of the amount of rent for one rent period and the amount of rent for one month.

(3) Same — If the lawful rent increases after a tenant has paid a rent deposit, the landlord may require the tenant to pay an additional amount to increase the rent deposit up to the amount permitted by subsection (2).

(4) Qualification — A new landlord of a rental unit or a person who is deemed to be a landlord under subsection 47(1) of the *Mortgages Act* shall not require a tenant to pay a rent deposit if the tenant has already paid a rent deposit to the prior landlord of the rental unit.

(5) Exception — Despite subsection (4), if a person becomes a new landlord in a sale from a person deemed to be a landlord under subsection 47(1) of the *Mortgages Act*, the new landlord may require the tenant to pay a rent deposit in an amount equal to the amount with respect to the former rent deposit that the tenant received from the proceeds of sale.

(6) Interest — A landlord of a rental unit shall pay interest to the tenant annually on the amount of the rent deposit at a rate equal to the guideline determined under section 120 that is in effect at the time payment becomes due.

(7) Deduction applied to rent deposit — The landlord may deduct from the amount payable under subsection (6) the amount, if any, by which the maximum amount of the rent deposit permitted under subsection (2) exceeds the amount of the rent deposit paid by the tenant and the deducted amount shall be deemed to form part of the rent deposit paid by the tenant.

(8) Transition — Despite subsection (6), the first interest payment that becomes due under subsection (6) after the day this subsection comes into force shall be adjusted so that,

(a) the interest payable in respect of the period ending before the day this subsection comes into force is based on the annual rate of 6 per cent; and

(b) the interest payable in respect of the period commencing on or after the day this subsection comes into force shall be based on the rate determined under subsection (6).

(9) Deduction of interest from rent — Where the landlord has failed to make the payment required by subsection (6) when it comes due, the tenant may deduct the amount of the payment from a subsequent rent payment.

(10) Rent deposit applied to last rent — A landlord shall apply a rent deposit that a tenant has paid to the landlord or to a former landlord in payment of the rent for the last rent period before the tenancy terminates.

107. (1) Rent deposit, prospective tenant — A landlord shall repay the amount received as a rent deposit in respect of a rental unit if vacant possession of the rental unit is not given to the prospective tenant.

(2) Exception — Despite subsection (1), if the prospective tenant, before he or she would otherwise obtain vacant possession of the rental unit, agrees to rent a different rental unit from the landlord,

(a) the landlord may apply the amount received as a rent deposit in respect of the other rental unit; and

(b) the landlord shall repay only the excess, if any, by which the amount received exceeds the amount of the rent deposit the landlord is entitled to receive under section 106 in respect of the other rental unit.

108. Post-dated cheques, etc. — Neither a landlord nor a tenancy agreement shall require a tenant to,

(a) provide post-dated cheques or other negotiable instruments for payment of rent; or

(b) permit automatic debiting of the tenant's account at a financial institution, automatic charging of a credit card or any other form of automatic payment for the payment of rent.

109. (1) Receipt for payment — A landlord shall provide free of charge to a tenant or former tenant, on request, a receipt for the payment of any rent, rent deposit, arrears of rent or any other amount paid to the landlord.

(2) Former tenant — Subsection (1) applies to a request by a former tenant only if the request is made within 12 months after the tenancy terminated.

General Rules Governing Amount of Rent

110. Landlord's duty, rent increases — No landlord shall increase the rent charged to a tenant for a rental unit, except in accordance with this Part.

111. (1) Landlord not to charge more than lawful rent — No landlord shall charge rent for a rental unit in an amount that is greater than the lawful rent permitted under this Part.

(2) Lawful rent where discounts offered — The lawful rent is not affected by,

(a) a discount in rent at the beginning of, or during, a tenancy, that consists of up to three months rent in any 12-month period, if the discount is provided in the form of rent-free periods and meets the prescribed conditions;

(b) a discount in rent at the beginning of, or during, a tenancy, of up to 2 per cent of the rent that could otherwise be lawfully charged for a rental period, if the discount is provided for paying rent on or before the date it is due and the discount meets the prescribed conditions; or

(c) a prescribed discount.

(3) Same — Subject to subsection (2), where a landlord offers a discount in rent at the beginning of, or during, a tenancy, the lawful rent shall be calculated in accordance with the prescribed rules.

(4) Lawful rent where higher rent for first rental period — Where the rent a landlord charges for the first rental period of a tenancy is greater than the rent the landlord charges for subsequent rental periods, the lawful rent shall be calculated in accordance with the prescribed rules.

112. Lawful rent when this section comes into force — Unless otherwise prescribed, the lawful rent charged to a tenant for a rental unit for which there is a tenancy agreement in effect on the day this section comes into force shall be the rent that was charged on the day before this section came into force or, if that amount was not lawfully charged under the *Tenant Protection Act, 1997*, the amount that it was lawful to charge on that day.

113. Lawful rent for new tenant — Subject to section 111, the lawful rent for the first rental period for a new tenant under a new tenancy agreement is the rent first charged to the tenant.

114. (1) Notice to new tenant, order under par. 6, 7 or 8 of s. 30(1) in effect — If an order made under paragraph 6, 7 or 8 of subsection 30(1) is in effect in respect of a rental unit when a new tenancy agreement relating to the rental unit is entered into, the landlord shall, before entering into the new tenancy agreement, give to the new tenant written notice about the lawful rent for the rental unit in accordance with subsection (3).

(2) Same — If an order made under paragraph 6, 7 or 8 of subsection 30(1) takes effect in respect of a rental unit after a new tenancy agreement relating to the rental unit is entered into but before the tenancy agreement takes effect, the landlord shall, before the tenancy agreement takes effect, give to the new tenant written notice about the lawful rent for the rental unit in accordance with subsection (3).

(3) Contents of notice — A notice given under subsection (1) or (2) shall be in the form approved by the Board and shall set out,

(a) information about the order made under paragraph 6, 7 or 8 of subsection 30(1);

(b) the amount of rent that the landlord may lawfully charge the new tenant until the prohibition in the order made under paragraph 6, 7 or 8 of subsection 30(1) ends;

(c) the amount of rent that the landlord may lawfully charge the new tenant after the prohibition in the order made under paragraph 6, 7 or 8 of subsection 30(1) ends;

(d) information about the last lawful rent charged to the former tenant; and

(e) such other information as is prescribed.

(4) Order takes effect after tenancy agreement — If an order made under paragraph 6, 7 or 8 of subsection 30(1) takes effect in respect of a rental unit after a new tenancy agreement relating to the rental unit takes effect, the landlord shall promptly give to the new tenant written notice about the lawful rent for the rental unit in accordance with subsection (5), unless the order was made on the application of the new tenant.

(5) Contents of notice — A notice given under subsection (4) shall be in the form approved by the Board and shall set out,

(a) information about the order made under paragraph 6, 7 or 8 of subsection 30(1); and

(b) such other information as is prescribed.

115. (1) Application by new tenant — A new tenant who was entitled to notice under section 114 may apply to the Board for an order,

(a) determining the amount of rent that the new tenant may lawfully be charged until the prohibition in the order made under paragraph 6, 7 or 8 of subsection 30(1) ends;

(b) determining the amount of rent that the new tenant may lawfully be charged after the prohibition in the order made under paragraph 6, 7 or 8 of subsection 30(1) ends; and

(c) requiring the landlord to rebate to the new tenant any rent paid by the new tenant in excess of the rent that the tenant may lawfully be charged.

(2) Time for application — No order shall be made under subsection (1) unless the application is made not later than one year after the new tenancy agreement takes effect.

(3) Failure to comply with s. 114 — If, in an application under subsection (1), the Board finds that the landlord has not complied with section 114, the Board may order the landlord to pay to the Board an administrative fine not exceeding the greater of $10,000 and the monetary jurisdiction of the Small Claims Court.

(4) Information to be filed — If an application is made under subsection (1), the landlord shall file with the Board information as prescribed within the time prescribed.

(5) Application of s. 135 — Section 135 does not apply to a new tenant with respect to rent paid by the new tenant in excess of the rent that the tenant could lawfully be charged if an application could have been made under subsection (1) for an order requiring the rebate of the excess.

Notice of Rent Increase

116. (1) Notice of rent increase required — A landlord shall not increase the rent charged to a tenant for a rental unit without first giving the tenant at least 90 days written notice of the landlord's intention to do so.

(2) Same — Subsection (1) applies even if the rent charged is increased in accordance with an order under section 126.

(3) Contents of notice — The notice shall be in a form approved by the Board and shall set out the landlord's intention to increase the rent and the amount of the new rent.

(4) Increase void without notice — An increase in rent is void if the landlord has not given the notice required by this section, and the landlord must give a new notice before the landlord can take the increase.

117. (1) Compliance by landlord, no notice required — Despite section 116 but subject to subsections (3) and (4), if an order was issued under paragraph 6 of subsection 30(1) and a new tenancy agreement was entered into while the order remained in effect, no notice of rent increase is required for the landlord to charge an amount that the landlord would have been entitled to charge in the absence of the order.

(2) Same — Despite section 116 but subject to subsections (3) and (4), if an order was issued under paragraph 8 of subsection 30(1), no notice of rent increase is required for the landlord to take a rent increase that the landlord would have been entitled to take in the absence of the order.

(3) Limitation — Subsections (1) and (2) apply only where the landlord,

(a) has completed the items in work orders for which the compliance period has expired and which were found by the Board to be related to a serious breach of a health, safety, housing or maintenance standard; and

(b) has completed the specified repairs or replacements or other work ordered under paragraph 4 of subsection 30(1) found by the Board to be related to a serious breach of the landlord's obligations under subsection 20(1) or section 161.

(4) Effective date — The authority under subsection (1) or (2) to take an increase or charge an amount without a notice of rent increase is effective on the first day of the rental period following the date that the landlord completed,

(a) the items in work orders for which the compliance period has expired and which were found by the Board to be related to a serious breach of a health, safety, housing or maintenance standard; and

(b) the specified repairs or replacements or other work ordered under paragraph 4 of subsection 30(1) found by the Board to be related to a serious breach of the landlord's obligations under subsection 20(1) or section 161.

(5) Date of annual increase — In determining the effective date of the next lawful rent increase under section 119,

(a) an amount charged under subsection (1) shall be deemed to have been charged at the time the landlord would have been entitled to charge it if the order under paragraph 6 of subsection 30(1) had not been issued; and

(b) an increase taken under subsection (2) shall be deemed to have been taken at the time the landlord would have been entitled to take it if the order under paragraph 8 of subsection 30(1) had not been issued.

118. Deemed acceptance where no notice of termination — A tenant who does not give a landlord notice of termination of a tenancy under section 47 after receiving notice of an intended rent increase under section 116 shall be deemed to have accepted whatever rent increase would be allowed under this Act after the landlord and the tenant have exercised their rights under this Act.

12-Month Rule

119. (1) 12-month rule — A landlord who is lawfully entitled to increase the rent charged to a tenant for a rental unit may do so only if at least 12 months have elapsed,

(a) since the day of the last rent increase for that tenant in that rental unit, if there has been a previous increase; or

(b) since the day the rental unit was first rented to that tenant, if clause (a) does not apply.

(2) Exception — An increase in rent under section 123 shall be deemed not to be an increase in rent for the purposes of this section.

Guideline

120. (1) Guideline increase — No landlord may increase the rent charged to a tenant, or to an assignee under section 95, during the term of their tenancy by more than the guideline, except in accordance with section 126 or 127 or an agreement under section 121 or 123.

(2) Guideline — The guideline for a calendar year is the percentage change from year to year in the Consumer Price Index for Ontario for prices of goods and services as reported monthly by Statistics Canada, averaged over the 12-month period that ends at the end of May of the previous calendar year, rounded to the first decimal point.

(3) Publication of guideline — The Minister shall determine the guideline for each year in accordance with subsection (2) and shall have the guideline published in *The Ontario Gazette* not later than August 31 of the preceding year.

(4) Transition — The guideline for the calendar year in which this section comes into force shall be deemed to be the guideline established for that year under the *Tenant Protection Act, 1997.*

(5) Same — If this section comes into force on or after September 1 in a calendar year, the guideline for the following calendar year shall be deemed to be the guideline established for the following year under the *Tenant Protection Act, 1997.*

Agreements to Increase or Decrease Rent

121. (1) Agreement — A landlord and a tenant may agree to increase the rent charged to the tenant for a rental unit above the guideline if,

(a) the landlord has carried out or undertakes to carry out a specified capital expenditure in exchange for the rent increase; or

(b) the landlord has provided or undertakes to provide a new or additional service in exchange for the rent increase.

(2) **Form** — An agreement under subsection (1) shall be in the form approved by the Board and shall set out the new rent, the tenant's right under subsection (4) to cancel the agreement and the date the agreement is to take effect.

(3) **Maximum increase** — A landlord shall not increase rent charged under this section by more than the guideline plus 3 per cent of the previous lawful rent charged.

(4) **Right to cancel** — A tenant who enters into an agreement under this section may cancel the agreement by giving written notice to the landlord within five days after signing it.

(5) **Agreement in force** — An agreement under this section may come into force no earlier than six days after it has been signed.

(6) **Notice of rent increase not required** — Section 116 does not apply with respect to a rent increase under this section.

(7) **When prior notice void** — Despite any deemed acceptance of a rent increase under section 118, if a landlord and tenant enter into an agreement under this section, a notice of rent increase given by the landlord to the tenant before the agreement was entered into becomes void when the agreement takes effect, if the notice of rent increase is to take effect on or after the day the agreed to increase is to take effect.

122. (1) **Tenant application** — A tenant or former tenant may apply to the Board for relief if the landlord and the tenant or former tenant agreed to an increase in rent under section 121 and,

(a) the landlord has failed in whole or in part to carry out an undertaking under the agreement;

(b) the agreement was based on work that the landlord claimed to have done but did not do; or

(c) the agreement was based on services that the landlord claimed to have provided but did not do so.

(2) **Time limitation** — No application may be made under this section more than two years after the rent increase becomes effective.

(3) **Order** — In an application under this section, the Board may find that some or all of the rent increase above the guideline is invalid from the day on which it took effect and may order the rebate of any money consequently owing to the tenant or former tenant.

123. (1) **Additional services, etc.** — A landlord may increase the rent charged to a tenant for a rental unit as prescribed at any time if the landlord and the tenant agree that the landlord will add any of the following with respect to the tenant's occupancy of the rental unit:

1. A parking space.

2. A prescribed service, facility, privilege, accommodation or thing.

(2) Application — Subsection (1) applies despite sections 116 and 119 and despite any order under paragraph 6 of subsection 30(1).

124. Coerced agreement void — An agreement under section 121 or 123 is void if it has been entered into as a result of coercion or as a result of a false, incomplete or misleading representation by the landlord or an agent of the landlord.

125. Decrease in services, etc. — A landlord shall decrease the rent charged to a tenant for a rental unit as prescribed if the landlord and the tenant agree that the landlord will cease to provide anything referred to in subsection 123(1) with respect to the tenant's occupancy of the rental unit.

Landlord Application for Rent Increase

126. (1) Application for above guideline increase — A landlord may apply to the Board for an order permitting the rent charged to be increased by more than the guideline for any or all of the rental units in a residential complex in any or all of the following cases:

1. An extraordinary increase in the cost for municipal taxes and charges or utilities or both for the residential complex or any building in which the rental units are located.

2. Eligible capital expenditures incurred respecting the residential complex or one or more of the rental units in it.

3. Operating costs related to security services provided in respect of the residential complex or any building in which the rental units are located by persons not employed by the landlord.

(2) Interpretation — In this section,

"extraordinary increase" means extraordinary increase as defined by or determined in accordance with the regulations.

(3) When application made — An application under this section shall be made at least 90 days before the effective date of the first intended rent increase referred to in the application.

(4) Information for tenants — If an application is made under this section that includes a claim for capital expenditures, the landlord shall make information that accompanies the application under subsection 185(1) available to the tenants of the residential complex in accordance with the prescribed rules.

(5) Rent chargeable before order — If an application is made under this section and the landlord has given a notice of rent increase as required, until an order authorizing the rent increase for the rental unit takes effect, the landlord shall not require the tenant to pay a rent that exceeds the lesser of,

(a) the new rent specified in the notice; and

(b) the greatest amount that the landlord could charge without applying for a rent increase.

(6) Tenant may pay full amount — Despite subsection (5), the tenant may choose to pay the amount set out in the notice of rent increase pending the outcome of the landlord's application and, if the tenant does so, the landlord shall owe to the tenant any amount paid by the tenant exceeding the amount allowed by the order of the Board.

(7) Eligible capital expenditures — Subject to subsections (8) and (9), a capital expenditure is an eligible capital expenditure for the purposes of this section if,

(a) it is necessary to protect or restore the physical integrity of the residential complex or part of it;

(b) it is necessary to comply with subsection 20(1) or clauses 161(a) to (e);

(c) it is necessary to maintain the provision of a plumbing, heating, mechanical, electrical, ventilation or air conditioning system;

(d) it provides access for persons with disabilities;

(e) it promotes energy or water conservation; or

(f) it maintains or improves the security of the residential complex or part of it.

(8) Exception — A capital expenditure to replace a system or thing is not an eligible capital expenditure for the purposes of this section if the system or thing that was replaced did not require major repair or replacement, unless the replacement of the system or thing promotes,

(a) access for persons with disabilities;

(b) energy or water conservation; or

(c) security of the residential complex or part of it.

(9) Same — A capital expenditure is not an eligible capital expenditure with respect to a rental unit for the purposes of this section if a new tenant entered into a new tenancy agreement in respect of the rental unit and the new tenancy agreement took effect after the capital expenditure was completed.

(10) Order — Subject to subsections (11) to (13), in an application under this section, the Board shall make findings in accordance with the prescribed rules with respect to all of the grounds of the application and, if it is satisfied that an order permitting the rent charged to be increased by more than the guideline is justified, shall make an order,

(a) specifying the percentage by which the rent charged may be increased in addition to the guideline; and

(b) subject to the prescribed rules, specifying a 12-month period during which an increase permitted by clause (a) may take effect.

(11) Limitation — If the Board is satisfied that an order permitting the rent charged to be increased by more than the guideline is justified and that the percentage increase justified, in whole or in part, by operating costs related to security services and by eligible capital expenditures is more than 3 per cent,

> (a) the percentage specified under clause (10)(a) that is attributable to those costs and expenditures shall not be more than 3 per cent; and
>
> (b) the order made under subsection (10) shall, in accordance with the prescribed rules, specify a percentage by which the rent charged may be increased in addition to the guideline in each of the two 12-month periods following the period specified under clause (10)(b), but that percentage in each of those periods shall not be more than 3 per cent.

(12) Serious breach — Subsection (13) applies to a rental unit if the Board finds that,

> (a) the landlord,
>
> > (i) has not completed items in work orders for which the compliance period has expired and which are found by the Board to be related to a serious breach of a health, safety, housing or maintenance standard,
> >
> > (ii) has not completed specified repairs or replacements or other work ordered by the Board under paragraph 4 of subsection 30(1) and found by the Board to be related to a serious breach of the landlord's obligations under subsection 20(1) or section 161, or
> >
> > (iii) is in serious breach of the landlord's obligations under subsection 20(1) or section 161; and
>
> (b) the rental unit is affected by,
>
> > (i) one or more items referred to in subclause (a)(i) that have not been completed,
> >
> > (ii) one or more repairs or replacements or other work referred to in subclause (a)(ii) that has not been completed, or
> >
> > (iii) a serious breach referred to in subclause (a)(iii).

(13) Same — If this subsection applies to a rental unit, the Board shall,

> (a) dismiss the application with respect to the rental unit; or
>
> (b) provide, in any order made under subsection (10), that the rent charged for the rental unit shall not be increased pursuant to the order until the Board is satisfied, on a motion made by the landlord within the time period specified by the Board, on notice to the tenant of the rental unit, that,
>
> > (i) all items referred to in subclause (12)(a)(i) that affect the rental unit have been completed, if a finding was made under that subclause,
> >
> > (ii) all repairs, replacements and other work referred to in subclause (12)(a)(ii) that affect the rental unit have been completed, if a finding was made under that subclause, and

(iii) the serious breach referred to in subclause (12)(a)(iii) no longer affects the rental unit, if a finding was made under that subclause.

(14) Order not to apply to new tenant — An order of the Board under subsection (10) with respect to a rental unit ceases to be of any effect on and after the day a new tenant enters into a new tenancy agreement with the landlord in respect of that rental unit if that agreement takes effect on or after the day that is 90 days before the first effective date of a rent increase in the order.

127. Two ordered increases — Despite clause 126(11)(b), if an order is made under subsection 126(10) with respect to a rental unit and a landlord has not yet taken all the increases in rent for the rental unit permissible under a previous order pursuant to clause 126(11)(b), the landlord may increase the rent for the rental unit in accordance with the prescribed rules.

Reductions of Rent

128. (1) Utilities — If the Board issues an order under subsection 126(10) permitting an increase in rent that is due in whole or in part to an extraordinary increase in the cost of utilities,

(a) the Board shall specify in the order the percentage increase that is attributable to the extraordinary increase; and

(b) the Board shall include in the order a description of the landlord's obligations under subsections (2) and (3).

(2) Information for tenant — If a landlord increases the rent charged to a tenant for a rental unit pursuant to an order described in subsection (1), the landlord shall, in accordance with the prescribed rules, provide that tenant with information on the total cost of utilities for the residential complex.

(3) Rent reduction — If a landlord increases the rent charged to a tenant for a rental unit pursuant to an order described in subsection (1) and the cost of utilities for the residential complex decreases by more than the prescribed percentage in the prescribed period, the landlord shall reduce the rent charged to that tenant in accordance with the prescribed rules.

(4) Application — This section ceases to apply to a tenant of a rental unit in respect of a utility if the landlord ceases to provide the utility to the rental unit in accordance with this Act or an agreement between the landlord and that tenant.

129. Capital expenditures — If the Board issues an order under subsection 126(10) permitting an increase in rent that is due in whole or in part to eligible capital expenditures,

(a) the Board shall specify in the order the percentage increase that is attributable to the eligible capital expenditures;

(b) the Board shall specify in the order a date, determined in accordance with the prescribed rules, for the purpose of clause (c); and

(c) the order shall require that,

(i) if the rent charged to a tenant for a rental unit is increased pursuant to the order by the maximum percentage permitted by the order and the tenant continues to occupy the rental unit on the date specified under clause (b), the landlord shall, on that date, reduce the rent charged to that tenant by the percentage specified under clause (a); and

(ii) if the rent charged to a tenant for a rental unit is increased pursuant to the order by less than the maximum percentage permitted by the order and the tenant continues to occupy the rental unit on the date specified under clause (b), the landlord shall, on that date, reduce the rent charged to that tenant by a percentage determined in accordance with the prescribed rules that is equal to or lower than the percentage specified under clause (a).

130. (1) Reduction in services — A tenant of a rental unit may apply to the Board for an order for a reduction of the rent charged for the rental unit due to a reduction or discontinuance in services or facilities provided in respect of the rental unit or the residential complex.

(2) Same, former tenant — A former tenant of a rental unit may apply under this section as a tenant of the rental unit if the person was affected by the discontinuance or reduction of the services or facilities while the person was a tenant of the rental unit.

(3) Order re lawful rent — The Board shall make findings in accordance with the prescribed rules and may order,

(a) that the rent charged be reduced by a specified amount;

(b) that there be a rebate to the tenant of any rent found to have been unlawfully collected by the landlord;

(c) that the rent charged be reduced by a specified amount for a specified period if there has been a temporary reduction in a service.

(4) Same — An order under this section reducing rent takes effect on the day that the discontinuance or reduction first occurred.

(5) Same, time limitation — No application may be made under this section more than one year after a reduction or discontinuance in a service or facility.

131. (1) Municipal taxes — If the municipal property tax for a residential complex is reduced by more than the prescribed percentage, the lawful rent for each of the rental units in the complex is reduced in accordance with the prescribed rules.

(2) Effective date — The rent reduction shall take effect on the date determined by the prescribed rules, whether or not notice has been given under subsection (3).

(3) Notice — If, for a residential complex with at least the prescribed number of rental units, the rents that the tenants are required to pay are reduced under subsection (1), the local municipality in which the residential complex is located shall, within the prescribed period and by the prescribed method of service, notify the landlord and all of the tenants of the residential complex of that fact.

(4) Same — The notice shall be in writing in a form approved by the Board and shall,

(a) inform the tenants that their rent is reduced;

(b) set out the percentage by which their rent is reduced and the date the reduction takes effect;

(c) inform the tenants that if the rent is not reduced in accordance with the notice they may apply to the Board under section 135 for the return of money illegally collected; and

(d) advise the landlord and the tenants of their right to apply for an order under section 132.

(5) Same — A local municipality that gives a notice under this section shall, on request, give a copy to the Board or to the Ministry.

132. (1) Application for variation — A landlord or a tenant may apply to the Board under the prescribed circumstances for an order varying the amount by which the rent charged is to be reduced under section 131.

(2) Same — An application under subsection (1) must be made within the prescribed time.

(3) Determination and order — The Board shall determine an application under this section in accordance with the prescribed rules and shall issue an order setting out the percentage of the rent reduction.

(4) Same — An order under this section shall take effect on the effective date determined under subsection 131(2).

133. (1) Application, reduction in municipal taxes — A tenant of a rental unit may apply to the Board for an order for a reduction of the rent charged for the rental unit due to a reduction in the municipal taxes and charges for the residential complex.

(2) Order — The Board shall make findings in accordance with the prescribed rules and may order that the rent charged for the rental unit be reduced.

(3) Effective date — An order under this section takes effect on a date determined in accordance with the prescribed rules.

Illegal Additional Charges

134. (1) Additional charges prohibited — Unless otherwise prescribed, no landlord shall, directly or indirectly, with respect to any rental unit,

(a) collect or require or attempt to collect or require from a tenant or prospective tenant of the rental unit a fee, premium, commission, bonus, penalty, key deposit or other like amount of money whether or not the money is refundable;

(b) require or attempt to require a tenant or prospective tenant to pay any consideration for goods or services as a condition for granting the tenancy or continuing to permit occupancy of a rental unit if that consideration is in addition to the rent the tenant is lawfully required to pay to the landlord; or

(c) rent any portion of the rental unit for a rent which, together with all other rents payable for all other portions of the rental unit, is a sum that is greater than the rent the landlord may lawfully charge for the rental unit.

(2) Same — No superintendent, property manager or other person who acts on behalf of a landlord with respect to a rental unit shall, directly or indirectly, with or without the authority of the landlord, do any of the things mentioned in clause (1)(a), (b) or (c) with respect to that rental unit.

(3) Same — Unless otherwise prescribed, no tenant and no person acting on behalf of the tenant shall, directly or indirectly,

(a) sublet a rental unit for a rent that is payable by one or more subtenants and that is greater than the rent that is lawfully charged by the landlord for the rental unit;

(b) collect or require or attempt to collect or require from any person any fee, premium, commission, bonus, penalty, key deposit or other like amount of money, for subletting a rental unit, for surrendering occupancy of a rental unit or for otherwise parting with possession of a rental unit; or

(c) require or attempt to require a person to pay any consideration for goods or services as a condition for the subletting, assignment or surrender of occupancy or possession in addition to the rent the person is lawfully required to pay to the tenant or landlord.

Money Collected Illegally

135. (1) Money collected illegally — A tenant or former tenant of a rental unit may apply to the Board for an order that the landlord, superintendent or agent of the landlord pay to the tenant any money the person collected or retained in contravention of this Act or the *Tenant Protection Act, 1997*.

(2) Prospective tenants — A prospective tenant may apply to the Board for an order under subsection (1).

(3) Subtenants — A subtenant may apply to the Board for an order under subsection (1) as if the subtenant were the tenant and the tenant were the landlord.

(4) Time limitation — No order shall be made under this section with respect to an application filed more than one year after the person collected or retained money in contravention of this Act or the *Tenant Protection Act, 1997*.

136. (1) Rent deemed lawful — Rent charged one or more years earlier shall be deemed to be lawful rent unless an application has been made within one year after the date that amount was first charged and the lawfulness of the rent charged is in issue in the application.

(2) Increase deemed lawful — An increase in rent shall be deemed to be lawful unless an application has been made within one year after the date the increase was first charged and the lawfulness of the rent increase is in issue in the application.

(3) s. 122 prevails — Nothing in this section shall be interpreted to deprive a tenant of the right to apply for and get relief in an application under section 122 within the time period set out in that section.

PART VIII — SMART METERS AND APPORTIONMENT OF UTILITY COSTS

Unproclaimed Text — 137, 138

137. (1) Smart meters — In this section,

"smart meter" has the same meaning as in the *Electricity Act, 1998*.

(2) Interruption in supply — A landlord who has the obligation under a tenancy agreement to supply electricity may interrupt the supply of electricity to a rental unit when a smart meter is installed if,

(a) the smart meter is installed by a person licensed under the *Ontario Energy Board Act, 1998* to install smart meters;

(b) the supply of electricity is interrupted only for the minimum length of time necessary to install the smart meter; and

(c) the landlord provides adequate notice to the tenant in accordance with the prescribed rules.

(3) Termination of obligation to supply electricity — Subject to subsection (4), if a smart meter is installed in respect of a rental unit by a person licensed under the *Ontario Energy Board Act, 1998* to install smart meters, a landlord who has the obligation under a tenancy agreement to supply electricity to the rental unit may, without the consent of the tenant, terminate that obligation by,

(a) providing adequate notice of the termination of the obligation to the tenant in accordance with the prescribed rules; and

(b) reducing the rent, in accordance with the prescribed rules, by an amount that accounts for the cost of electricity consumption and related costs.

(4) Limitation — A landlord shall not terminate an obligation to supply electricity under subsection (3) earlier than 12 months, or such longer period as may be prescribed, after the installation of the smart meter.

(5) Information for prospective tenants — If a smart meter is installed in respect of a rental unit, the landlord shall, before entering into a tenancy agreement with a prospective tenant for the unit, provide the prospective tenant with the following information:

1. the most recent information available to the landlord for a 12-month period from the Smart Metering Entity, as defined in the *Electricity Act, 1998*, concerning electricity consumption in the rental unit.

2. If the rental unit was vacant during any part of the period to which the information referred to in paragraph 1 applies, a statement of the period that the rental unit was vacant.

3. Such other information as is prescribed.

(6) Other circumstances where information required — A landlord shall, before entering into a tenancy agreement with a prospective tenant for a rental unit, provide the prospective tenant with the information referred to in subsection (5) in such other circumstances as are prescribed.

(7) Electricity conservation obligations — If a smart meter is installed in respect of a rental unit, the landlord shall,

(a) ensure that any appliances provided for the rental unit by the landlord satisfy the prescribed requirements relating to electricity conservation;

(b) ensure that other aspects of the rental unit satisfy the prescribed requirements relating to electricity conservation; and

(c) ensure that other prescribed requirements relating to electricity conservation are complied with.

(8) Tenant's application — A tenant or a former tenant of a rental unit may apply to the Board in the prescribed circumstances for an order determining whether the landlord has breached an obligation under subsection (7).

(9) Order — If the Board determines in an application under subsection (8) that a landlord has breached an obligation under subsection (7), the Board may do one or more of the following:

1. Terminate the tenancy.

2. Order an abatement of rent.

3. Authorize a repair or replacement that has been or is to be made, or work that has been or is to be done, and order its cost to be paid by the landlord to the tenant.

4. Order the landlord to do specified repairs or replacements or other work within a specified time.

5. Make any other order that it considers appropriate.

(10) Advance notice of breaches — In determining the remedy under subsection (9), the Board shall consider whether the tenant or former tenant advised the landlord of the alleged breaches before applying to the Board.

(11) Eviction with termination order — If the Board makes an order terminating a tenancy under paragraph 1 of subsection (9), the Board may order that the tenant be evicted, effective not earlier than the termination date specified in the order.

(12) Determination re capital expenditures — For the purpose of section 126, a capital expenditure is not an eligible capital expenditure if,

(a) a smart meter was installed in respect of a residential complex before the capital expenditure was made;

(b) the capital expenditure failed to promote the conservation of electricity; and

(c) the purpose for which the capital expenditure was made could reasonably have been achieved by making a capital expenditure that promoted the conservation of electricity.

138. (1) Apportionment of utility costs — A landlord of a building containing not more than six rental units who supplies a utility to each of the rental units in the building may, without the consent of the tenants, charge each tenant a portion of the cost of the utility in accordance with the prescribed rules if,

(a) the landlord provides adequate notice to the tenants in accordance with the prescribed rules; and

(b) the rent for each rental unit is reduced in accordance with the prescribed rules.

(2) Not a service — If a landlord charges a tenant a portion of the cost of a utility in accordance with subsection (1) or with the consent of the tenant, the utility shall not be considered a service that falls within the definition of "rent" in subsection 2(1).

(3) Termination of tenancy prohibited — If a landlord charges a tenant a portion of the cost of a utility in accordance with subsection (1) or with the consent of the tenant, the landlord shall not serve a notice of termination under section 59 or make an application to the Board for an order under section 69 or 87 if the notice or application is based on the tenant's failure to pay the utility charge.

(4) Information for prospective tenants — If a landlord charges tenants a portion of the cost of a utility, the landlord shall, before entering into a tenancy agreement with a prospective tenant, provide the prospective tenant with the following information:

1. The portion of the cost of the utility that is applicable to the rental unit that would be occupied by the prospective tenant, expressed as a percentage of the total cost of the utility.

2. The total cost of the utility for the building in the most recent 12-month period for which the landlord has information on the cost of the utility.

3. If any part of the building was vacant during any part of the period to which the information referred to in paragraph 2 applies, a statement of which part of the building was vacant and of the period that it was vacant.

4. Such other information as is prescribed.

(5) Utility conservation obligations — If a landlord charges tenants a portion of the cost of a utility, the landlord shall,

(a) ensure that any appliances provided by the landlord satisfy the prescribed requirements relating to conservation of the utility; and

(b) ensure that other aspects of the rental unit and building satisfy the prescribed requirements relating to conservation of the utility.

(6) Tenant's application — A tenant or a former tenant of a rental unit may apply to the Board in the prescribed circumstances for an order determining whether the landlord has breached an obligation under subsection (5).

(7) Order — If the Board determines in an application under subsection (6) that a landlord has breached an obligation under subsection (5), the Board may do one or more of the following:

1. Terminate the tenancy.

2. Order an abatement of rent.

3. Authorize a repair or replacement that has been or is to be made, or work that has been or is to be done, and order its cost to be paid by the landlord to the tenant.

4. Order the landlord to do specified repairs or replacements or other work within a specified time.

5. Make any other order that it considers appropriate.

(8) Advance notice of breaches — In determining the remedy under subsection (7), the Board shall consider whether the tenant or former tenant advised the landlord of the alleged breaches before applying to the Board.

(9) Eviction with termination order — If the Board makes an order terminating a tenancy under paragraph 1 of subsection (7), the Board may order that the tenant be evicted, effective not earlier than the termination date specified in the order.

(10) Determination re capital expenditures — For the purpose of section 126, a capital expenditure is not an eligible capital expenditure if,

(a) the landlord charged tenants a portion of the cost of a utility before the capital expenditure was made;

(b) the capital expenditure failed to promote the conservation of the utility; and

(c) the purpose for which the capital expenditure was made could reasonably have been achieved by making a capital expenditure that promoted the conservation of the utility.

PART IX — CARE HOMES

Responsibilities of Landlords and Tenants

139. (1) Agreement required — There shall be a written tenancy agreement relating to the tenancy of every tenant in a care home.

(2) Contents of agreement — The agreement shall set out what has been agreed to with respect to care services and meals and the charges for them.

(3) Compliance — If, on application by a tenant, the Board determines that subsection (1) or (2) has not been complied with, the Board may make an order for an abatement of rent.

140. (1) Information to tenant — Before entering into a tenancy agreement with a new tenant in a care home, the landlord shall give to the new tenant an information package containing the prescribed information.

(2) Effect of non-compliance — The landlord shall not give a notice of rent increase or a notice of increase of a charge for providing a care service or meals until after giving the required information package to the tenant.

141. Tenancy agreement: consultation, cancellation — (1) **Tenancy agreement: right to consult** — Every tenancy agreement relating to the tenancy of a tenant in a care home shall contain a statement that the tenant has the right to consult a third party with respect to the agreement and to cancel the agreement within five days after the agreement has been entered into.

(2) Cancellation — The tenant may cancel the tenancy agreement by written notice to the landlord within five days after entering into it.

142. (1) Entry to check condition of tenant — Despite section 25, a landlord may enter a rental unit in a care home at regular intervals to check the condition of a tenant in accordance with the tenancy agreement if the agreement requires the landlord to do so.

(2) Right to revoke provision — A tenant whose tenancy agreement contains a provision requiring the landlord to regularly check the condition of the tenant may unilaterally revoke that provision by written notice to the landlord.

143. Assignment, subletting in care homes — A landlord may withhold consent to an assignment or subletting of a rental unit in a care home if the effect of the assignment or subletting would be to admit a person to the care home contrary to the admission requirements or guidelines set by the landlord.

144. (1) Notice of termination — A landlord may, by notice, terminate the tenancy of a tenant in a care home if,

(a) the rental unit was occupied solely for the purpose of receiving rehabilitative or therapeutic services agreed upon by the tenant and the landlord;

(b) no other tenant of the care home occupying a rental unit solely for the purpose of receiving rehabilitative or therapeutic services is permitted to live there for longer than the prescribed period; and

(c) the period of tenancy agreed to has expired.

(2) Period of notice — The date for termination specified in the notice shall be at least the number of days after the date the notice is given that is set out in section 44 and shall be the day a period of the tenancy ends or, where the tenancy is for a fixed term, the end of the term.

145. (1) Termination, care homes — Despite section 44, a tenant of a care home may terminate a tenancy at any time by giving at least 30 days notice of termination to the landlord.

(2) Care services and meals — A tenant who terminates a tenancy under subsection (1) may require the landlord to stop the provision of care services and meals before the date the tenancy terminates by giving at least 10 days notice to the landlord.

(3) Same — The tenant has no obligation to pay for care services and meals that would otherwise have been provided under the tenancy agreement after the date the landlord is required to stop the provision of care services and meals under subsection (2).

(4) Same — The estate of a tenant has no obligation to pay for care services and meals that would otherwise have been provided under the tenancy agreement more than 10 days after the death of the tenant.

146. (1) Notice of termination, demolition, conversion or repairs — A landlord who gives a tenant of a care home a notice of termination under section 50 shall make reasonable efforts to find appropriate alternate accommodation for the tenant.

(2) Same — Sections 52 and 64 do not apply with respect to a tenant of a care home who receives a notice of termination under section 50 and chooses to take alternate accommodation found by the landlord for the tenant under subsection (1).

147. External care providers — A landlord shall not,

(a) do anything to prevent a tenant of a care home from obtaining care services from a person of the tenant's choice that are in addition to care services provided under the tenancy agreement; or

(b) interfere with the provision of care services to a tenant of a care home, by a person of the tenant's choice, that are in addition to care services provided under the tenancy agreement.

Transferring Tenancy

148. Transferring tenancy — (1) **Application** — A landlord may apply to the Board for an order transferring a tenant out of a care home and evicting the tenant if,

(a) the tenant no longer requires the level of care provided by the landlord; or

(b) the tenant requires a level of care that the landlord is not able to provide.

(2) Order — The Board may issue an order under clause (1)(b) only if it is satisfied that,

(a) appropriate alternate accommodation is available for the tenant; and

(b) the level of care that the landlord is able to provide when combined with the community based services provided to the tenant in the care home cannot meet the tenant's care needs.

(3) Mandatory mediation — If a dispute arises, the dispute shall be sent to mediation before the Board makes an order.

(4) Same — If the landlord fails to participate in the mediation, the Board may dismiss the landlord's application.

Rules Related to Rent and Other Charges

149. Rent in care home — If there is more than one tenancy agreement for a rental unit in a care home, the provisions of Part VII apply, subject to subsection 6(2), with respect to each tenancy agreement as if it were an agreement for a separate rental unit.

150. (1) Notice of increased charges — A landlord shall not increase a charge for providing a care service or meals to a tenant of a rental unit in a care home without first giving the tenant at least 90 days notice of the landlord's intention to do so.

(2) Contents of notice — The notice shall be in writing in the form approved by the Board and shall set out the landlord's intention to increase the charge and the new charges for care services and meals.

(3) Effect of non-compliance — An increase in a charge for a care service or meals is void if the landlord has not given the notice required by this section, and the landlord must give a new notice before the landlord can take the increase.

151. (1) Certain charges permitted — Nothing in subsection 134(1) limits the right of a landlord to charge a tenant of a rental unit in a care home for providing care services or meals to the tenant so long as the landlord has complied with the requirements of sections 140 and 150.

(2) Same — Nothing in subsection 134(3) limits the right of a tenant or a person acting on behalf of a tenant to charge a subtenant of a rental unit in a care home for providing care services or meals to the subtenant.

PART X — MOBILE HOME PARKS AND LAND LEASE COMMUNITIES

General

152. (1) Application — This Part applies with respect to tenancies in mobile home parks.

(2) Same; land lease communities — This Part applies with necessary modifications with respect to tenancies in land lease communities, as if the tenancies were in mobile home parks.

153. Interpretation — A reference in this Part to a tenant's mobile home shall be interpreted to be a reference to a mobile home owned by the tenant and situated within a mobile home park of the landlord with whom the tenant has a tenancy agreement.

Responsibilities of Landlords and Tenants

154. (1) Park rules — If a landlord establishes rules for a mobile home park,

(a) the landlord shall provide a written copy of the rules to each tenant; and

(b) the landlord shall inform each tenant in writing of any change to the rules.

(2) Failure to comply — Until a landlord has complied with clause (1)(a) or (b), as the case may be,

(a) the tenant's obligation to pay rent is suspended; and

(b) the landlord shall not require the tenant to pay rent.

(3) After compliance — After the landlord has complied with clause (1)(a) or (b), as the case may be, the landlord may require the tenant to pay any rent withheld by the tenant under subsection (2).

155. (1) Information about property assessment — If a tenant is obligated to pay a landlord an amount to reimburse the landlord for property taxes paid by the landlord with respect to a mobile home owned by the tenant and the landlord obtains information from the Municipal Property Assessment Corporation with respect to the value of the mobile home for assessment purposes, the landlord shall promptly provide the tenant with a copy of that information.

(2) Suspension of tenant's obligation to pay — A tenant's obligation to pay the landlord an amount to reimburse the landlord for property taxes paid by the landlord with respect to a mobile home owned by the tenant is suspended, and the landlord shall not require the tenant to pay that amount, if,

(a) the landlord has failed to comply with subsection (1) with respect to the most recent information obtained by the landlord from the Municipal Property Assessment Corporation; or

(b) the landlord has not, in the previous 12 months, obtained written information from the Municipal Property Assessment Corporation with respect to the value of the mobile home for assessment purposes.

(3) **Exception** — Clause (2)(b) does not apply if the landlord has made reasonable efforts in the previous 12 months to obtain written information from the Municipal Property Assessment Corporation with respect to the value of the mobile home for assessment purposes but has been unable to obtain the information.

(4) **After compliance** — The landlord may require the tenant to pay any amount withheld by the tenant under subsection (2) after,

(a) complying with subsection (1), if clause (2)(a) applied; or

(b) obtaining written information from the Municipal Property Assessment Corporation with respect to the value of the mobile home for assessment purposes and complying with subsection (1), if clause (2)(b) applied.

156. (1) **Tenant's right to sell, etc.** — A tenant has the right to sell or lease his or her mobile home without the landlord's consent.

(2) **Landlord as agent** — A landlord may act as the agent of a tenant in negotiations to sell or lease a mobile home only in accordance with a written agency contract entered into for the purpose of beginning those negotiations.

(3) **Same** — A provision in a tenancy agreement requiring a tenant who owns a mobile home to use the landlord as an agent for the sale of the mobile home is void.

157. (1) **Landlord's right of first refusal** — This section applies if a tenancy agreement with respect to a mobile home contains a provision prohibiting the tenant from selling the mobile home without first offering to sell it to the landlord.

(2) **Same** — If a tenant receives an acceptable offer to purchase a mobile home, the landlord has a right of first refusal to purchase the mobile home at the price and subject to the terms and conditions in the offer.

(3) **Same** — A tenant shall give a landlord at least 72 hours notice of a person's offer to purchase a mobile home before accepting the person's offer.

(4) **Landlord's purchase at reduced price** — If a provision described in subsection (1) permits a landlord to purchase a mobile home at a price that is less than the one contained in a prospective purchaser's offer to purchase, the landlord may exercise the option to purchase the mobile home, but the provision is void with respect to the landlord's right to purchase the mobile home at the lesser price.

158. Advertising a sale — (1) **For sale signs** — A landlord shall not prevent a tenant who owns a mobile home from placing in a window of the mobile home a sign that the home is for sale, unless the landlord does so in accordance with subsection (2).

(2) **Alternative method of advertising a sale** — A landlord may prevent a tenant who owns a mobile home from placing a for sale sign in a window of a mobile home if all of the following conditions are met:

1. The prohibition applies to all tenants in the mobile home park.

2. The landlord provides a bulletin board for the purpose of placing for sale advertisements.

3. The bulletin board is provided to all tenants in the mobile home park free of charge.

4. The bulletin board is placed in a prominent place and is accessible to the public at all reasonable times.

159. (1) Assignment — If a tenant has sold or entered into an agreement to sell the tenant's mobile home and the tenant asks the landlord to consent to the assignment of the site for the mobile home to the purchaser of the mobile home,

(a) clause 95(3)(c) does not apply; and

(b) the landlord may not refuse consent to the assignment unless, on application under subsection (2), the Board determines that the landlord's grounds for refusing consent are reasonable.

(2) Time for application — The landlord may apply to the Board, within 15 days after the tenant asks the landlord to consent to the assignment, for a determination of whether the landlord's grounds for refusing consent are reasonable.

(3) Contents of application — The landlord shall set out in the application the landlord's grounds for refusing consent.

(4) Deemed consent — If the landlord does not apply to the Board in accordance with subsections (2) and (3), or the Board determines that the landlord's grounds for refusing consent are not reasonable, the landlord shall be deemed to have consented to the assignment.

160. (1) Restraint of trade prohibited — A landlord shall not restrict the right of a tenant to purchase goods or services from the person of his or her choice, except as provided in subsection (2).

(2) Standards — A landlord may set reasonable standards for mobile home equipment.

161. Responsibility of landlord — In addition to a landlord's obligations under section 20, a landlord is responsible for,

(a) removing or disposing of garbage or ensuring the availability of a means for removing or disposing of garbage in the mobile home park at reasonable intervals;

(b) maintaining mobile home park roads in a good state of repair;

(c) removing snow from mobile home park roads;

(d) maintaining the water supply, sewage disposal, fuel, drainage and electrical systems in the mobile home park in a good state of repair;

(e) maintaining the mobile home park grounds and all buildings, structures, enclosures and equipment intended for the common use of tenants in a good state of repair; and

(f) repairing damage to a tenant's property, if the damage is caused by the wilful or negligent conduct of the landlord.

Termination of Tenancies

162. (1) Mobile home abandoned — This section applies if,

(a) the tenant has vacated the mobile home in accordance with,

(i) a notice of termination of the landlord or the tenant,

(ii) an agreement between the landlord and tenant to terminate the tenancy, or

(iii) an order of the Board terminating the tenancy or evicting the tenant; or

(b) the landlord has applied for an order under section 79 and the Board has made an order terminating the tenancy.

(2) Notice to tenant — The landlord shall not dispose of a mobile home without first notifying the tenant of the landlord's intention to do so,

(a) by registered mail, sent to the tenant's last known mailing address; and

(b) by causing a notice to be published in a newspaper having general circulation in the locality in which the mobile home park is located.

(3) Landlord may dispose of mobile home — The landlord may sell, retain for the landlord's own use or dispose of a mobile home in the circumstances described in subsection (1) beginning 60 days after the notices referred to in subsection (2) have been given if the tenant has not made a claim with respect to the landlord's intended disposal.

(4) Same — If, within six months after the day the notices have been given under subsection (2), the tenant makes a claim for a mobile home which the landlord has already sold, the landlord shall pay to the tenant the amount by which the proceeds of sale exceed the sum of,

(a) the landlord's reasonable out-of-pocket expenses incurred with respect to the mobile home; and

(b) any arrears of rent of the tenant.

(5) Same — If, within six months after the day the notices have been given under subsection (2), the tenant makes a claim for a mobile home which the landlord has retained for the landlord's own use, the landlord shall return the mobile home to the tenant.

(6) Same — Before returning a mobile home to a tenant who claims it within the 60 days referred to in subsection (3) or the six months referred to in subsection (5), the landlord may require the tenant to pay the landlord for arrears of rent and any reasonable expenses incurred by the landlord with respect to the mobile home.

(7) No liability — Subject to subsection (4) or (5), a landlord is not liable to any person for selling, retaining or otherwise disposing of a tenant's mobile home in accordance with this section.

163. Death of mobile home owner — Sections 91 and 92 do not apply if the tenant owns the mobile home.

164. (1) Termination under s. 50 — If a notice of termination is given under section 50 with respect to a tenancy agreement between the landlord and a tenant who owns a mobile home, the date for termination specified in the notice shall, despite subsection 50(2), be at least one year after the date the notice is given and shall be the day a period of the tenancy ends or, where the tenancy is for a fixed term, the end of the term.

(2) Same — If a notice of termination is given under section 50 with respect to a tenancy agreement between the landlord and a tenant who owns a mobile home and the tenant is entitled to compensation under section 52, 54 or 55, the amount of the compensation shall, despite those sections, be equal to the lesser of the following amounts:

1. One year's rent.
2. $3,000 or the prescribed amount, whichever is greater.

Rules Related to Rent and Other Charges

165. Assignment of existing tenancy agreement — Despite subsection 95(8), if a tenancy agreement for a site for a mobile home is assigned and the assignee purchases or enters into an agreement to purchase the former tenant's mobile home, the landlord may increase the rent payable by the assignee under the tenancy agreement by not more than the prescribed amount.

166. Entrance and exit fees limited — A landlord shall not charge for any of the following matters, except to the extent of the landlord's reasonable out-of-pocket expenses incurred with regard to those matters:

1. The entry of a mobile home into a mobile home park.
2. The exit of a mobile home from a mobile home park.
3. The installation of a mobile home in a mobile home park.
4. The removal of a mobile home from a mobile home park.
5. The testing of water or sewage in a mobile home park.

167. (1) Increased capital expenditures — If the Board finds that a capital expenditure is for infrastructure work required to be carried out by the Government of Canada or Ontario or a municipality or an agency of any of them, despite subsection

126(11), the Board may determine the number of years over which the rent increase justified by that capital expenditure may be taken.

(2) **Definition** — In this section,

"infrastructure work" means work with respect to roads, water supply, fuel, sewage disposal, drainage, electrical systems and other prescribed services and things provided to the mobile home park.

PART XI — THE LANDLORD AND TENANT BOARD

168. (1) **Board** — The Ontario Rental Housing Tribunal is continued under the name Landlord and Tenant Board in English and Commission de la location immobilière in French.

(2) **Board's jurisdiction** — The Board has exclusive jurisdiction to determine all applications under this Act and with respect to all matters in which jurisdiction is conferred on it by this Act.

169. (1) **Composition** — The members of the Board shall be appointed by the Lieutenant Governor in Council.

(2) **Remuneration and expenses** — The members of the Board who are not public servants employed under Part III of the *Public Service of Ontario Act, 2006* shall be paid the remuneration fixed by the Lieutenant Governor in Council and the reasonable expenses incurred in the course of their duties under this Act, as determined by the Minister.

(3) **Public servant members** — Members of the Board may be persons who are employed under Part III of the *Public Service of Ontario Act, 2006*.

2006, c. 35, Sched. C, s. 118

170. (1) **Chair and vice-chair** — The Lieutenant Governor in Council shall appoint one member of the Board as Chair and one or more members as vice-chairs.

(2) **Same** — The Chair may designate a vice-chair who shall exercise the powers and perform the duties of the Chair when the Chair is absent or unable to act.

(3) **Chair, chief executive officer** — The Chair shall be the chief executive officer of the Board.

171. Quorum — One member of the Board is sufficient to conduct a proceeding under this Act.

172. Conflict of interest — The members of the Board shall file with the Board a written declaration of any interests they have in residential rental property, and shall be required to comply with any conflict of interest guidelines or rules of conduct established by the Chair.

173. Expiry of term — Despite section 4.3 of the *Statutory Powers Procedure Act*, if the term of office of a member of the Board who has participated in a hearing expires before a decision is given, the term shall be deemed to continue for four weeks, but only for the purpose of participating in the decision and for no other purpose.

174. Power to determine law and fact — The Board has authority to hear and determine all questions of law and fact with respect to all matters within its jurisdiction under this Act.

175. Members, mediators not compellable — No member of the Board or person employed as a mediator by the Board shall be compelled to give testimony or produce documents in a civil proceeding with respect to matters that come to his or her knowledge in the course of exercising his or her duties under this Act.

176. (1) Rules and Guidelines Committee — The Chair of the Board shall establish a Rules and Guidelines Committee to be composed of the Chair, as Chair of the Committee, and any other members of the Board the Chair may from time to time appoint to the Committee.

(2) Committee shall adopt rules — The Committee shall adopt rules of practice and procedure governing the practice and procedure before the Board under the authority of this section and section 25.1 of the *Statutory Powers Procedure Act.*

(3) Committee may adopt guidelines — The Committee may adopt non-binding guidelines to assist members in interpreting and applying this Act and the regulations made under it.

(4) Means of adoption — The Committee shall adopt the rules and guidelines by simple majority, subject to the right of the Chair to veto the adoption of any rule or guideline.

(5) Make public — The Board shall make its rules, guidelines and approved forms available to the public.

177. Information on rights and obligations — The Board shall provide information to landlords and tenants about their rights and obligations under this Act.

178. Employees — Employees may be appointed for the purposes of the Board in accordance with the regulations.

179. Professional assistance — The Board may engage persons other than its members or employees to provide professional, technical, administrative or other assistance to the Board and may establish the duties and terms of engagement and provide for the payment of the remuneration and expenses of those persons.

180. Reports — (1) **Annual report** — At the end of each year, the Board shall file with the Minister an annual report on its affairs.

(2) Further reports and information — The Board shall make further reports and provide information to the Minister from time to time as required by the Minister.

(3) Tabled with Assembly — The Minister shall submit any reports received from the Board to the Lieutenant Governor in Council and then shall table them with the Assembly if it is in session or, if not, at the next session.

181. (1) Board may set, charge fees — The Board, subject to the approval of the Minister, may set and charge fees,

(a) for making an application under this Act or requesting a review of an order under section 21.2 of the *Statutory Powers Procedure Act*;

(b) for furnishing copies of forms, notices or documents filed with or issued by the Board or otherwise in the possession of the Board; or

(c) for other services provided by the Board.

(2) Same — The Board may treat different kinds of applications differently in setting fees and may base fees on the number of residential units affected by an application.

(3) Make fees public — The Board shall ensure that its fee structure is available to the public.

182. Fee refunded, review — The Board may refund a fee paid for requesting a review of an order under section 21.2 of the *Statutory Powers Procedure Act* if, on considering the request, the Board varies, suspends or cancels the original order.

PART XII — BOARD PROCEEDINGS

183. Expeditious procedures — The Board shall adopt the most expeditious method of determining the questions arising in a proceeding that affords to all persons directly affected by the proceeding an adequate opportunity to know the issues and be heard on the matter.

184. (1) SPPA applies — The *Statutory Powers Procedure Act* applies with respect to all proceedings before the Board.

(2) Exception — Subsection 5.1(2) of the *Statutory Powers Procedure Act* does not apply with respect to an application under section 132 or 133 or an application solely under paragraph 1 of subsection 126(1).

(3) Exception — Subsection 5.1(3) of the *Statutory Powers Procedure Act* does not apply to an application under section 126, 132 or 133.

185. (1) Form of application — An application shall be filed with the Board in the form approved by the Board, shall be accompanied by the prescribed information and shall be signed by the applicant.

(2) Application filed by representative — An applicant may give written authorization to sign an application to a person representing the applicant under the authority of the *Law Society Act* and, if the applicant does so, the Board may require such representative to file a copy of the authorization.

2006, c. 17, s. 261(3)

186. (1) Combining applications — A tenant may combine several applications into one application.

(2) Same — Two or more tenants of a residential complex may together file an application that may be filed by a tenant if each tenant applying in the application signs it.

(3) Same — A landlord may combine several applications relating to a given tenant into one application, so long as the landlord does not combine an application for a rent increase with any other application.

187. (1) Parties — The parties to an application are the landlord and any tenants or other persons directly affected by the application.

(2) Add or remove parties — The Board may add or remove parties as the Board considers appropriate.

188. Service — (1) **Service of application** — An applicant to the Board shall give the other parties to the application a copy of the application within the time set out in the Rules.

(2) Service of notice of hearing — Despite the *Statutory Powers Procedure Act*, an applicant shall give a copy of any notice of hearing issued by the Board in respect of an application to the other parties to the application.

(3) Certificate of service — A party shall file with the Board a certificate of service in the form approved by the Board in the circumstances set out in the Rules.

189. (1) Notice by Board — Where an application is made to the Board, the Board shall notify the respondent in writing that an application has been made and, where possible, shall provide the respondent with information relating to the hearing and such other information as is prescribed.

(2) Exception — Subsection (1) does not apply in the circumstances prescribed.

190. (1) Board may extend, shorten time — The Board may extend or shorten the time requirements related to making an application under section 126, subsection 159(2) or section 226 in accordance with the Rules.

(2) Same — The Board may extend or shorten the time requirements with respect to any matter in its proceedings, other than the prescribed time requirements, in accordance with the Rules.

191. (1) How notice or document given — A notice or document is sufficiently given to a person other than the Board,

(a) by handing it to the person;

(b) if the person is a landlord, by handing it to an employee of the landlord exercising authority in respect of the residential complex to which the notice or document relates;

(c) if the person is a tenant, subtenant or occupant, by handing it to an apparently adult person in the rental unit;

(d) by leaving it in the mail box where mail is ordinarily delivered to the person;

(e) if there is no mail box, by leaving it at the place where mail is ordinarily delivered to the person;

(f) by sending it by mail to the last known address where the person resides or carries on business; or

(g) by any other means allowed in the Rules.

(2) When notice deemed valid — A notice or document that is not given in accordance with this section shall be deemed to have been validly given if it is proven that its contents actually came to the attention of the person for whom it was intended within the required time period.

(3) Mail — A notice or document given by mail shall be deemed to have been given on the fifth day after mailing.

192. (1) How notice or document given to Board — A notice or document is sufficiently given to the Board,

(a) by hand delivering it to the Board at the appropriate office as set out in the Rules;

(b) by sending it by mail to the appropriate office as set out in the Rules; or

(c) by any other means allowed in the Rules.

(2) Same — A notice or document given to the Board by mail shall be deemed to have been given on the earlier of the fifth day after mailing and the day on which the notice or the document was actually received.

193. Time — Time shall be computed in accordance with the Rules.

194. (1) Board may mediate — The Board may attempt to mediate a settlement of any matter that is the subject of an application or agreed upon by the parties if the parties consent to the mediation.

(2) Settlement may override Act — Despite subsection 3(1) and subject to subsection (3), a settlement mediated under this section may contain provisions that contravene any provision under this Act.

(3) Restriction — The largest rent increase that can be mediated under this section for a rental unit that is not a mobile home or a land lease home or a site for either is equal to the sum of the guideline and 3 per cent of the previous year's lawful rent.

(4) Successful mediation — If some or all of the issues with respect to an application are successfully mediated under this section, the Board shall dispose of the application in accordance with the Rules.

(5) Hearing — If there is no mediated settlement, the Board shall hold a hearing.

195. (1) Money paid to Board — Where the Board considers it appropriate to do so, the Board may, subject to the regulations,

> (a) require a respondent to pay a specified sum into the Board within a specified time; or
>
> (b) permit a tenant who is making an application for an order under paragraph 1 of subsection 29(1) to pay all or part of the rent for the tenant's rental unit into the Board.

(2) Rules re money paid — The Board may establish procedures in the Rules for the payment of money into and out of the Board.

(3) No payment after final order — The Board shall not, under subsection (1), authorize or require payments into the Board after the Board has made its final order in the application.

(4) Effect of failure to pay under cl. (1)(a) — If a respondent is required to pay a specified sum into the Board within a specified time under clause (1)(a) and fails to do so, the Board may refuse to consider the evidence and submissions of the respondent.

(5) Effect of payment under cl. (1)(b) — Payment by a tenant under clause (1)(b) shall be deemed not to constitute a default in the payment of rent due under a tenancy agreement or a default in the tenant's obligations for the purposes of this Act.

196. (1) Board may refuse to proceed if money owing — Upon receiving information that an applicant owes money to the Board as a result of having failed to pay any fine, fee or costs,

> (a) if the information is received on or before the day the applicant submits an application, an employee of the Board shall, in such circumstances as may be specified in the Rules, refuse to allow the application to be filed;
>
> (b) if the information is received after the application has been filed but before a hearing is held, the Board shall stay the proceeding until the fee, fine or costs have been paid and may discontinue the application in such circumstances as may be specified in the Rules;
>
> (c) if the information is received after a hearing with respect to the application has begun, the Board shall not issue an order until the fine, fee or costs have been paid and may discontinue the application in such circumstances as may be specified in the Rules.

(2) Definition — In subsection (1),

"fine, fee or costs" does not include money that is paid in trust to the Board pursuant to an order of the Board and that may be paid out to either the tenant or the landlord when the application is disposed of.

197. (1) Where Board may dismiss — The Board may dismiss an application without holding a hearing or refuse to allow an application to be filed if, in the opinion of the Board, the matter is frivolous or vexatious, has not been initiated in good faith or discloses no reasonable cause of action.

(2) Same — The Board may dismiss a proceeding without holding a hearing if the Board finds that the applicant filed documents that the applicant knew or ought to have known contained false or misleading information.

198. Joinder and severance of applications — (1) **Applications joined** — Despite the *Statutory Powers Procedure Act*, the Board may direct that two or more applications be joined or heard together if the Board believes it would be fair to determine the issues raised by them together.

(2) Applications severed — The Board may order that applications that have been joined be severed or that applications that had been ordered to be heard together be heard separately.

199. Application severed — The Board may order that an application be severed and each severed part dealt with as though it were a separate application under this Act if,

(a) two or more applications are combined under section 186 in the application;

(b) the application is made by more than one tenant under subsection 186(2); or

(c) the Board believes it would be appropriate to deal separately with different matters included in the application.

200. Amendment and withdrawal of applications — (1) **Amend application** — An applicant may amend an application to the Board in accordance with the Rules.

(2) Withdraw application — Subject to subsection (3), an applicant may withdraw an application at any time before the hearing begins.

(3) Same, harassment — An applicant may withdraw an application under paragraph 4 of subsection 29(1) only with the consent of the Board.

(4) Same — An applicant may withdraw an application after the hearing begins with the consent of the Board.

201. (1) Other powers of Board — The Board may, before, during or after a hearing,

(a) conduct any inquiry it considers necessary or authorize an employee of the Board to do so;

(b) request a provincial inspector or an employee of the Board to conduct any inspection it considers necessary;

(c) question any person, by telephone or otherwise, concerning the dispute or authorize an employee of the Board to do so;

(d) permit or direct a party to file additional evidence with the Board which the Board considers necessary to make its decision;

(e) view premises that are the subject of the hearing; or

(f) on its own motion and on notice to the parties, amend an application if the Board considers it appropriate to do so and if amending the application would not be unfair to any party.

(2) Same — In making its determination, the Board may consider any relevant information obtained by the Board in addition to the evidence given at the hearing, provided that it first informs the parties of the additional information and gives them an opportunity to explain or refute it.

(3) Same — If a party fails to comply with a direction under clause (1)(d), the Board may,

(a) refuse to consider the party's submissions and evidence respecting the matter regarding which there was a failure to comply; or

(b) if the party who has failed to comply is the applicant, dismiss all or part of the application.

(4) Parties may view premises with Board — If the Board intends to view premises under clause (1)(e), the Board shall give the parties an opportunity to view the premises with the Board.

202. Findings of Board — In making findings on an application, the Board shall ascertain the real substance of all transactions and activities relating to a residential complex or a rental unit and the good faith of the participants and in doing so,

(a) may disregard the outward form of a transaction or the separate corporate existence of participants; and

(b) may have regard to the pattern of activities relating to the residential complex or the rental unit.

203. Determinations related to housing assistance — The Board shall not make determinations or review decisions concerning,

(a) eligibility for rent-geared-to-income assistance as defined in the *Social Housing Reform Act, 2000* or the amount of geared-to-income rent payable under that Act; or

(b) eligibility for, or the amount of, any prescribed form of housing assistance.

204. (1) Conditions in order — The Board may include in an order whatever conditions it considers fair in the circumstances.

(2) Order re costs — The Board may order a party to an application to pay the costs of another party.

(3) Same — The Board may order that its costs of a proceeding be paid by a party or the party's paid representative.

(4) Same — The amount of an order for costs shall be determined in accordance with the Rules.

(5) Same — Subsections (2) to (4) apply despite section 17.1 of the *Statutory Powers Procedure Act*.

2006, c. 17, s. 261(4)

205. (1) Order payment — The Board may include in an order the following provision:

> "The landlord or the tenant shall pay to the other any sum of money that is owed as a result of this order."

(2) Payment of order by instalments — If the Board makes an order for a rent increase above the guideline and the order is made three months or more after the first effective date of a rent increase in the order, the Board may provide in the order that if a tenant owes any sum of money to the landlord as a result of the order, the tenant may pay the landlord the amount owing in monthly instalments.

(3) Same — If an order made under subsection (2) permits a tenant to pay the amount owing by instalments, the tenant may do so even if the tenancy is terminated.

(4) Same — An order providing for monthly instalments shall not provide for more than 12 monthly instalments.

206. (1) Agreement to settle matter — Where a landlord has made an application under section 69 for an order terminating a tenancy and evicting the tenant based on a notice of termination under section 59 or an application for payment of arrears of rent, or both, the Board may make an order including terms of payment without holding a hearing if,

(a) the parties have reached a written agreement resolving the subject-matter of the application;

(b) the agreement has been signed by all parties; and

(c) the agreement is filed with the Board before the hearing has commenced.

(2) Contents of order — In an order under subsection (1), the Board may, based on the agreement reached by the parties, order,

(a) payment of any arrears and NSF cheque charges or related administration charges that are owing;

(b) payment of the fee paid by the landlord for the application to the Board; and

(c) payment of any rent that becomes due during the period in which the arrears are required to be paid.

(3) Restriction — In an order under subsection (1), the Board shall not order that the tenancy be terminated or include a provision allowing for an application under section 78.

(4) Request by landlord — A landlord may file a request to reopen the application if the tenant fails to comply with the terms of the order and shall, in the request, indicate which terms were not complied with and the manner in which the tenant failed to meet the terms of the order.

(5) Request by landlord or tenant — A landlord or tenant may file a request to reopen the application within 30 days after the order was made on the basis that the other party coerced them or deliberately made false or misleading representations which had a material effect on the agreement and the order issued under subsection (1).

(6) Timing — A request under subsection (4) shall not be made later than 30 days after a failure of the tenant to meet a term of the order.

(7) Copy of request, notice of hearing — The party filing the request must give the other parties to the application a copy of the request to reopen the application and the notice of hearing within the time set out in the Rules.

(8) Condition — If a request to reopen is made under subsection (4), the Board shall not proceed to hear the merits of the application unless the Board is satisfied that the tenant failed to comply with a term of the order.

(9) Same — If a request to reopen is made under subsection (5), the Board shall not proceed to hear the merits of the application unless the Board is satisfied that there was coercion or deliberate false or misleading representations which had a material effect on the agreement and the order issued under subsection (1).

207. Monetary jurisdiction; deduction of rent; interest — **(1) Monetary jurisdiction of Board** — The Board may, where it otherwise has the jurisdiction, order the payment to any given person of an amount of money up to the greater of $10,000 and the monetary jurisdiction of the Small Claims Court.

(2) Same — A person entitled to apply under this Act but whose claim exceeds the Board's monetary jurisdiction may commence a proceeding in any court of competent jurisdiction for an order requiring the payment of that sum and, if such a proceeding is commenced, the court may exercise any powers that the Board could have exercised if the proceeding had been before the Board and within its monetary jurisdiction.

(3) Same — If a party makes a claim in an application for payment of a sum equal to or less than the Board's monetary jurisdiction, all rights of the party in excess of the Board's monetary jurisdiction are extinguished once the Board issues its order.

(4) Minimum amount — The Board shall not make an order for the payment of an amount of money if the amount is less than the prescribed amount.

(5) Order may provide deduction from rent — If a landlord is ordered to pay a sum of money to a person who is a current tenant of the landlord at the time of the order, the order may provide that if the landlord fails to pay the amount owing, the tenant may recover that amount plus interest by deducting a specified sum from the tenant's rent paid to the landlord for a specified number of rental periods.

(6) Same — Nothing in subsection (5) limits the right of the tenant to collect at any time the full amount owing or any balance outstanding under the order.

(7) Post-judgment interest — The Board may set a date on which payment of money ordered by the Board must be made and interest shall accrue on money owing only after that date at the post-judgment interest rate under section 127 of the *Courts of Justice Act*.

208. (1) Notice of decision — The Board shall send each party who participated in the proceeding, or the person who represented the party, a copy of its order, including the reasons if any have been given, in accordance with section 191.

(2) Same — Section 18 of the *Statutory Powers Procedure Act* does not apply to proceedings under this Act.

2006, c. 17, s. 261(5)

209. (1) Order final, binding — Except where this Act provides otherwise, and subject to section 21.2 of the *Statutory Powers Procedure Act*, an order of the Board is final and binding.

(2) Power to review — Without limiting the generality of section 21.2 of the *Statutory Powers Procedure Act*, the Board's power to review a decision or order under that section may be exercised if a party to a proceeding was not reasonably able to participate in the proceeding.

210. (1) Appeal rights — Any person affected by an order of the Board may appeal the order to the Divisional Court within 30 days after being given the order, but only on a question of law.

(2) Board to receive notice — A person appealing an order under this section shall give to the Board any documents relating to the appeal.

(3) **Board may be heard by counsel** — The Board is entitled to be heard by counsel or otherwise upon the argument on any issue in an appeal.

(4) **Powers of Court** — If an appeal is brought under this section, the Divisional Court shall hear and determine the appeal and may,

(a) affirm, rescind, amend or replace the decision or order; or

(b) remit the matter to the Board with the opinion of the Divisional Court.

(5) Same — The Divisional Court may also make any other order in relation to the matter that it considers proper and may make any order with respect to costs that it considers proper.

211. Board may appeal Court decision — The Board is entitled to appeal a decision of the Divisional Court on an appeal of a Board order as if the Board were a party to the appeal.

212. Substantial compliance sufficient — Substantial compliance with this Act respecting the contents of forms, notices or documents is sufficient.

213. Electronic documents — Any document referred to in this Act and specified in the regulations or in the Rules may be created, signed, filed, provided, issued, sent, received, stored, transferred, retained or otherwise dealt with electronically if it is done in accordance with the regulations or the Rules.

214. (1) Contingency fees, limitation — No agent who represents a landlord or a tenant in a proceeding under this Act or who assists a landlord or tenant in a matter arising under this Act shall charge or take a fee based on a proportion of any amount which has been or may be recovered, gained or saved, in whole or in part, through the efforts of the agent, where the proportion exceeds the prescribed amount.

(2) Same — An agreement that provides for a fee prohibited by subsection (1) is void.

PART XIII — MUNICIPAL VITAL SERVICES BY-LAWS

215. Definition — In this Part,

"vital services by-law" means a by-law passed under section 216.

216. (1) By-laws respecting vital services — The council of a local municipality may pass by-laws,

(a) requiring every landlord to provide adequate and suitable vital services to each of the landlord's rental units;

(b) prohibiting a supplier from ceasing to provide the vital service until a notice has been given under subsection 217(1);

(c) requiring a supplier to promptly restore the vital service when directed to do so by an official named in the by-law;

(d) prohibiting a person from hindering, obstructing or interfering with or attempting to hinder, obstruct or interfere with the official or person referred to in subsection 218(1) in the exercise of a power or performance of a duty under this section or sections 217 to 223;

(e) providing that a person who contravenes or fails to comply with a vital services by-law is guilty of an offence for each day or part of a day on which the offence occurs or continues;

(f) providing that every director or officer of a corporation that is convicted of an offence who knowingly concurs in the commission of the offence is guilty of an offence;

(g) authorizing an official named in the by-law to enter into agreements on behalf of the local municipality with suppliers of vital services to ensure that adequate and suitable vital services are provided for rental units.

(2) Exception — A vital services by-law does not apply to a landlord with respect to a rental unit to the extent that the tenant has expressly agreed to obtain and maintain the vital services.

(3) Contents of vital services by-law — A vital services by-law may,

(a) classify buildings or parts of buildings for the purposes of the by-law and designate the classes to which it applies;

(b) designate areas of the local municipality in which the by-law applies;

(c) establish standards for the provision of adequate and suitable vital services;

(d) prohibit a landlord from ceasing to provide a vital service for a rental unit except when necessary to alter or repair the rental unit and only for the minimum period necessary to effect the alteration or repair;

(e) provide that a landlord shall be deemed to have caused the cessation of a vital service for a rental unit if the landlord is obligated to pay the supplier for the vital service and fails to do so and, as a result of the non-payment, the vital service is no longer provided for the rental unit.

217. (1) Notice by supplier — A supplier shall give notice of an intended discontinuance of a vital service only if the vital service is to be discontinued for the rental unit because the landlord has breached a contract with the supplier for the supply of the vital service.

(2) Same — The notice shall be given in writing to the clerk of the local municipality at least 30 days before the supplier ceases to provide the vital service.

218. (1) Inspection — An official named in a vital services by-law or a person acting under his or her instructions may, at all reasonable times, enter and inspect a building or part of a building with respect to which the by-law applies for the purpose of determining compliance with the by-law or a direction given under subsection 221(1).

(2) Same — Despite subsection (1), the official or person shall not enter a rental unit,

(a) unless he or she has obtained the consent of the occupier of the rental unit after informing him or her that he or she may refuse permission to enter the unit; or

(b) unless he or she is authorized to do so by a warrant issued under section 231.

219. (1) Services by municipality — If a landlord does not provide a vital service for a rental unit in accordance with a vital services by-law, the local municipality may arrange for the service to be provided.

(2) Lien — The amount spent by the local municipality under subsection (1) plus an administrative fee of 10 per cent of that amount shall, on registration of a notice of lien in the appropriate land registry office, be a lien in favour of the local municipality against the property at which the vital service is provided.

(3) Not special lien — Subsection 349(3) of the *Municipal Act, 2001* and subsection 314(3) of the *City of Toronto Act, 2006* do not apply with respect to the amount spent and the fee, and no special lien is created under either subsection.

(4) Certificate — The certificate of the clerk of the local municipality as to the amount spent is proof, in the absence of evidence to the contrary, of the amount.

(5) Interim certificate — Before issuing a certificate referred to in subsection (4), the clerk shall send an interim certificate by registered mail to the registered owner of the property that is subject to the lien and to all mortgagees or other encumbrancers registered on title.

2006, c. 32, Sched. C, s. 56(4)

220. Appeal — An affected owner, mortgagee or other encumbrancer may, within 15 days after the interim certificate is mailed, appeal the amount shown on it to the council of the local municipality.

221. (1) Payments transferred — If the local municipality has arranged for a vital service to be provided to a rental unit, an official named in the vital services by-law may direct a tenant to pay any or all of the rent for the rental unit to the local municipality.

(2) Effect of payment — Payment by a tenant under subsection (1) shall be deemed not to constitute a default in the payment of rent due under a tenancy agreement or a default in the tenant's obligations for the purposes of this Act.

222. (1) Use of money — The local municipality shall apply the rent received from a tenant to reduce the amount that it spent to provide the vital service and the related administrative fee.

(2) Accounting and payment of balance — The local municipality shall provide the person otherwise entitled to receive the rent with an accounting of the rents received for each individual rental unit and shall pay to that person any amount remaining after the rent is applied in accordance with subsection (1).

223. (1) Immunity — No proceeding for damages or otherwise shall be commenced against an official or a person acting under his or her instructions or against an employee or agent of a local municipality for any act done in good faith in the performance or intended performance of a duty or authority under any of sections 215 to 222 or under a by-law passed under section 216 or for any alleged neglect or default in the performance in good faith of the duty or authority.

(2) Same — Subsection (1) does not relieve a local municipality of liability to which it would otherwise be subject.

PART XIV — MAINTENANCE STANDARDS

224. Prescribed standards and complaints — (1) **Application of prescribed standards** — The prescribed maintenance standards apply to a residential complex and the rental units located in it if,

(a) the residential complex is located in unorganized territory;

(b) there is no municipal property standards by-law that applies to the residential complex; or

(c) xthe prescribed circumstances apply.

(2) Minister to receive complaints — The Minister shall receive any written complaint from a current tenant of a rental unit respecting the standard of maintenance that prevails with respect to the rental unit or the residential complex in which it is located if the prescribed maintenance standards apply to the residential complex.

(3) Complaints to be investigated — Upon receiving a complaint respecting a residential complex or a rental unit in it, the Minister shall cause an inspector to make whatever inspection the Minister considers necessary to determine whether the landlord has complied with the prescribed maintenance standards.

(4) Cost of inspection — The Minister may charge a municipality and the municipality shall pay the Minister for the cost, as prescribed, associated with inspecting a residential complex in the municipality, for the purposes of investigating a complaint under this section and ensuring compliance with a work order under section 225.

(5) Same — If a municipality fails to make payment in full within 60 days after the Minister issues a notice of payment due under subsection (4), the notice of payment may be filed in the Superior Court of Justice and enforced as if it were a court order.

225. (1) Inspector's work order — If an inspector is satisfied that the landlord of a residential complex has not complied with a prescribed maintenance standard that applies to the residential complex, the inspector may make and give to the landlord a work order requiring the landlord to comply with the prescribed maintenance standard.

(2) Same — The inspector shall set out in the order,

(a) the municipal address or legal description of the residential complex;

(b) reasonable particulars of the work to be performed;

(c) the period within which there must be compliance with the terms of the work order; and

(d) the time limit for applying under section 226 to the Board for a review of the work order.

226. (1) Review of work order — If a landlord who has received an inspector's work order is not satisfied with its terms, the landlord may, within 20 days after the day the order is issued, apply to the Board for a review of the work order.

(2) Order — On an application under subsection (1), the Board may, by order,

(a) confirm or vary the inspector's work order;

(b) rescind the work order, if it finds that the landlord has complied with it; or

(c) quash the work order.

PART XV — ADMINISTRATION AND ENFORCEMENT

227. Duties of Minister — The Minister shall,

(a) monitor compliance with this Act;

(b) investigate cases of alleged failure to comply with this Act; and

(c) where the circumstances warrant, commence or cause to be commenced proceedings with respect to alleged failures to comply with this Act.

228. Delegation — The Minister may in writing delegate to any person any power or duty vested in the Minister under this Act, subject to the conditions set out in the delegation.

229. Investigators and inspectors — The Minister may appoint investigators for the purpose of investigating alleged offences and may appoint inspectors for the purposes of sections 224 and 225.

230. (1) Inspections — Subject to subsection (6), an inspector may, at all reasonable times and upon producing proper identification, enter any property for the purpose of carrying out his or her duty under this Act and may,

(a) require the production for inspection of documents or things, including drawings or specifications, that may be relevant to the inspection;

(b) inspect and remove documents or things relevant to the inspection for the purpose of making copies or extracts;

(c) require information from any person concerning a matter related to the inspection;

(d) be accompanied by a person who has special or expert knowledge in relation to the subject-matter of the inspection;

(e) alone or in conjunction with a person possessing special or expert knowledge, make examinations or take tests, samples or photographs necessary for the purposes of the inspection; and

(f) order the landlord to take and supply at the landlord's expense such tests and samples as are specified in the order.

(2) Samples — The inspector shall divide the sample taken under clause (1)(e) into two parts and deliver one part to the person from whom the sample is taken, if the person so requests at the time the sample is taken and provides the necessary facilities.

(3) Same — If an inspector takes a sample under clause (1)(e) and has not divided the sample into two parts, a copy of any report on the sample shall be given to the person from whom the sample was taken.

(4) Receipt — An inspector shall provide a receipt for any documents or things removed under clause (1)(b) and shall promptly return them after the copies or extracts are made.

(5) Evidence — Copies of or extracts from documents and things removed under this section and certified as being true copies of or extracts from the originals by the person who made them are admissible in evidence to the same extent as and have the same evidentiary value as the originals.

(6) Where warrant required — Except under the authority of a warrant issued under section 231, an inspector shall not enter any room or place actually used as a dwelling without requesting and obtaining the consent of the occupier, first having informed the occupier that the right of entry may be refused and entry made only under the authority of a warrant.

231. (1) Warrant — A provincial judge or justice of the peace may at any time issue a warrant authorizing a person named in the warrant to enter and search a building, receptacle or place if the provincial judge or justice of the peace is satisfied by information on oath that there are reasonable grounds to believe that an offence has been committed under this Act and the entry and search will afford evidence relevant to the commission of the offence.

(2) Seizure — In a warrant, the provincial judge or justice of the peace may authorize the person named in the warrant to seize anything that, based on reasonable grounds, will afford evidence relevant to the commission of the offence.

(3) Receipt and removal — Anyone who seizes something under a warrant shall,

(a) give a receipt for the thing seized to the person from whom it was seized; and

(b) bring the thing seized before the provincial judge or justice of the peace issuing the warrant or another provincial judge or justice to be dealt with according to law.

(4) Expiry — A warrant shall name the date upon which it expires, which shall be not later than 15 days after the warrant is issued.

(5) Time of execution — A warrant shall be executed between 6 a.m. and 9 p.m. unless it provides otherwise.

(6) Other matters — Sections 159 and 160 of the *Provincial Offences Act* apply with necessary modifications with respect to any thing seized under this section.

232. (1) Protection from personal liability — No proceeding for damages shall be commenced against an investigator, an inspector, a member of the Board, a lawyer for the Board or an officer or employee of the Ministry or the Board for any act done in good faith in the performance or intended performance of any duty or in the exercise or intended exercise of any power under this Act or for any neglect or default in the performance or exercise in good faith of such a duty or power.

(2) Crown liability — Despite subsections 5(2) and (4) of the *Proceedings Against the Crown Act*, subsection (1) does not relieve the Crown of any liability to which it would otherwise be subject.

PART XVI — OFFENCES

233. Offences requiring knowledge — A person is guilty of an offence if the person knowingly,

(a) withholds the reasonable supply of a vital service, care service or food or interferes with the supply in contravention of section 21;

(b) alters or causes to be altered the locking system on any door giving entry to a rental unit or the residential complex in a manner that contravenes section 24 or 35;

(c) restricts reasonable access to the residential complex by political candidates or their authorized representatives in contravention of section 28;

(d) seizes any property of the tenant in contravention of section 40;

(e) fails to afford a tenant a right of first refusal in contravention of section 51 or 53;

(f) recovers possession of a rental unit without complying with the requirements of sections 52, 54 and 55;

(g) coerces a tenant to sign an agreement referred to in section 121;

(h) harasses, hinders, obstructs or interferes with a tenant in the exercise of,

(i) securing a right or seeking relief under this Act or in a court,

(ii) participating in a proceeding under this Act, or

(iii) participating in a tenants' association or attempting to organize a tenants' association;

(i) harasses, coerces, threatens or interferes with a tenant in such a manner that the tenant is induced to vacate the rental unit;

(j) harasses, hinders, obstructs or interferes with a landlord in the exercise of,

(i) securing a right or seeking relief under this Act or in a court, or

(ii) participating in a proceeding under this Act;

(k) obtains possession of a rental unit improperly by giving a notice to terminate in bad faith; or

(l) coerces a tenant of a mobile home park or land lease community to enter into an agency agreement for the sale or lease of their mobile home or land lease home or requires an agency agreement as a condition of entering into a tenancy agreement.

234. Other offences — A person is guilty of an offence if the person,

(a) enters a rental unit where such entry is not permitted by section 26, 27 or 142 or enters without first complying with the requirements of section 26, 27 or 142;

(b) fails to make an evicted tenant's property available for retrieval in accordance with subsection 41(3);

(c) gives a notice to terminate a tenancy under section 48 or 49 in contravention of section 51;

(d) requires or receives a security deposit from a tenant contrary to section 105;

(e) fails to pay to the tenant annually interest on the rent deposit held in respect of their tenancy in accordance with section 106;

(f) fails to apply the rent deposit held in respect of a tenancy to the rent for the last month of the tenancy in contravention of subsection 106(10);

(g) fails to repay an amount received as a rent deposit as required by subsection 107(1) or (2);

(h) fails to provide a tenant or former tenant with a receipt in accordance with section 109;

(i) fails to provide the notice in the form required under section 114 or gives false information in the notice;

(j) requires a tenant to pay rent proposed in an application in contravention of subsection 126(5);

(k) fails to provide information on the total cost of utilities in accordance with subsection 128(2);

(l) charges or collects amounts from a tenant, a prospective tenant, a subtenant, a potential subtenant, an assignee or a potential assignee in contravention of section 134;

(m) gives a notice of rent increase or a notice of increase of a charge in a care home without first giving an information package contrary to section 140;

(n) does anything to prevent a tenant of a care home from obtaining care services from a person of the tenant's choice contrary to clause 147(a);

(o) interferes with the provision of care services to a tenant of a care home contrary to clause 147(b);

(p) increases a charge for providing a care service or meals to a tenant in a care home in contravention of section 150;

(q) interferes with a tenant's right under section 156 to sell or lease his or her mobile home;

(r) restricts the right of a tenant of a mobile home park or land lease community to purchase goods or services from the person of his or her choice in contravention of section 160;

(s) charges an illegal contingency fee in contravention of subsection 214(1);

(t) fails to comply with any or all of the items contained in a work order issued under section 225;

(u) obstructs or interferes with an inspector exercising a power of entry under section 230 or 231 or with an investigator exercising a power of entry under section 231;

(v) furnishes false or misleading information in any material filed in any proceeding under this Act or provided to the Board, an employee or official of the Board, an inspector, an investigator, the Minister or a designate of the Minister;

(w) unlawfully recovers possession of a rental unit;

(x) charges rent in an amount greater than permitted under this Act; or

(y) contravenes an order of the Board that,

(i) orders a landlord to do specified repairs or replacements or other work within a specified time, or

(ii) orders that a landlord, a superintendent or an agent of a landlord may not engage in any further activities listed in paragraphs 2 to 6 of subsection 29(1) against any of the tenants in a residential complex.

235. (1) Harassment, interference with reasonable enjoyment — Any landlord or superintendent, agent or employee of the landlord who knowingly harasses a tenant or interferes with a tenant's reasonable enjoyment of a rental unit or the residential complex in which it is located is guilty of an offence.

(2) Exception — For the purposes of subsection (1), the carrying out of repairs, maintenance and capital improvements does not constitute harassment or interference with a tenant's reasonable enjoyment of a rental unit or the residential complex in which it is located unless it is reasonable to believe,

(a) that the date or time when the work is done or the manner in which it is carried out is intended to harass the tenant or interfere with the tenant's reasonable enjoyment; or

(b) that the repairs, maintenance or capital improvements were carried out without reasonable regard for the tenant's right to reasonable enjoyment.

236. Attempts — Any person who knowingly attempts to commit any offence referred to in section 233, 234 or 235 is guilty of an offence.

237. Directors and officers — Every director or officer of a corporation who knowingly concurs in an offence under this Act is guilty of an offence.

238. (1) Penalties — A person, other than a corporation, who is guilty of an offence under this Act is liable on conviction to a fine of not more than $25,000.

(2) Same — A corporation that is guilty of an offence under this Act is liable on conviction to a fine of not more than $100,000.

239. (1) Limitation — No proceeding shall be commenced respecting an offence under clause 234(v) more than two years after the date on which the facts giving rise to the offence came to the attention of the Minister.

(2) Same — No proceeding shall be commenced respecting any other offence under this Act more than two years after the date on which the offence was, or is alleged to have been, committed.

240. Evidence (1) Proof of filed documents — The production by a person prosecuting a person for an offence under this Act of a certificate, statement or document that appears to have been filed with or delivered to the Board by or on behalf of the person charged with the offence shall be received as evidence that the certificate, statement or document was so filed or delivered.

(2) Proof of making — The production by a person prosecuting a person for an offence under this Act of a certificate, statement or document that appears to have been made or signed by the person charged with the offence or on the person's behalf shall be received as evidence that the certificate, statement or document was so made or signed.

(3) Proof of making, Board or Minister — The production by a person prosecuting a person for an offence under this Act of any order, certificate, statement or document, or of any record within the meaning of section 20 of the *Statutory Powers Procedure Act*, that appears to have been made, signed or issued by the Board, the Minister, an employee of the Board or an employee of the Ministry, shall be received as evidence that the order, certificate, statement, document or record was so made, signed or issued.

(4) True copies — Subsections (1) to (3) apply, with necessary modifications, to any extract or copy of a certificate, statement, document, order or record referred to in those subsections, if the extract or copy is certified as a true extract or copy by the person who made the extract or copy.

PART XVII — REGULATIONS

241. (1) Regulations — The Lieutenant Governor in Council may make regulations,

1. prescribing circumstances under which one or more rental units that form part of a residential complex, rather than the entire residential complex, are care homes for the purposes of the definition of "care home" in subsection 2(1);

2. prescribing services that are to be included or not included in the definition of "care services" in subsection 2(1);

3. prescribing charges not to be included in the definition of "municipal taxes and charges" in subsection 2(1);

4. prescribing persons that are to be included or are not to be included in the definition of "tenant" in subsection 2(1) and exempting any such persons from any provision of the Act specified in the regulation;

5. prescribing, for the purposes of the definition of "vital service" in subsection 2(1), the part of each year during which heat is a vital service;

6. prescribing classes of accommodation for the purposes of clause 5(n);

7. prescribing federal, provincial or municipal programs for the purpose of paragraph 3 of subsection 7(1);

8. providing that specified provisions of this Act apply with respect to any specified housing project, housing program, rental unit, residential complex or other residential accommodation or any class of them;

9. exempting any housing project, housing program, rental unit, residential complex or other residential accommodation or any class of them from any provision of this Act;

10. prescribing grounds of an application for the purposes of clause 9(1)(b);

11. respecting the rules for making findings for the purposes of subsection 9(2);

12. prescribing for the purposes of section 22, paragraph 3 of subsection 29(1) and subsection 31(1),

    i. standards and criteria to be applied by the Board in determining if a landlord, superintendent or agent of a landlord has substantially interfered with the reasonable enjoyment of a rental unit or residential complex in carrying out maintenance, repairs or capital improvements to the unit or complex, and

ii. criteria to be applied by the Board in determining whether to order an abatement of rent under subsection 31(1) when a landlord, superintendent or agent of a landlord is found to have substantially interfered with the reasonable enjoyment of a rental unit or residential complex in carrying out maintenance, repairs or capital improvements to the unit or complex and rules for calculating the amount of the abatement;

13. prescribing the hours during which a landlord is required to make an evicted tenant's property available to be retrieved under subsection 41(3);

14. prescribing conditions applicable to discounts referred to in clause 111(2)(a) or (b);

15. prescribing discounts for the purpose of clause 111(2)(c);

16. prescribing rules for the purpose of subsection 111(3) for calculating the lawful rent which may be charged where a landlord provides a tenant with a discount in rent at the beginning of, or during, a tenancy, and prescribing different rules for different types of discounts;

17. prescribing rules for the purpose of subsection 111(4) for the calculation of lawful rent where the rent a landlord charges for the first rental period of a tenancy is greater than the rent the landlord charges for any subsequent rental period;

18. prescribing the circumstances under which lawful rent for the purposes of section 112 will be other than that provided for in section 112 and providing the lawful rent under those circumstances;

19. prescribing information to be included in a notice under clause 114(3)(e);

20. prescribing information to be filed and the time in which it is to be filed for the purposes of subsection 115(4);

21. respecting rules for increasing or decreasing rent charged for the purposes of sections 123 and 125;

22. prescribing services, facilities, privileges, accommodations and things for the purposes of paragraph 2 of subsection 123(1);

23. defining or describing the method for determining what constitutes "extraordinary increase" for the purpose of section 126;

24. prescribing rules governing making information available under subsection 126(4);

25. prescribing the rules for making findings for the purposes of subsection 126(10);

26. prescribing rules governing the time period to be specified in an order under clause 126(10)(b);

27. prescribing rules for the purpose of clause 126(11)(b);

28. prescribing rules for the purposes of section 127;

29. prescribing rules for the purposes of subsection 128(2);

30. prescribing a percentage, a period and rules for the purposes of subsection 128(3);

31. prescribing rules governing the determination of the date to be specified in an order under clause 129(b);

32. prescribing rules governing the determination of the percentage by which rent is required to be reduced under subclause 129(c)(ii);

33. prescribing the rules for making findings for the purposes of subsection 130(3);

34. prescribing percentages and rules for the purposes of subsection 131(1);

35. prescribing rules for the purposes of subsection 131(2);

36. prescribing a number of rental units, a period and methods of service for the purposes of subsection 131(3);

37. prescribing circumstances for the purposes of subsection 132(1);

38. prescribing a period of time for the purposes of subsection 132(2);

39. prescribing rules for the purposes of subsection 132(3);

40. prescribing the rules for making findings for the purposes of subsection 133(2) and for determining the effective date for an order under subsection 133(3);

41. exempting specified payments from the operation of section 134;

42. prescribing rules governing the provision of notice for the purposes of clause 137(2)(c);

43. prescribing rules governing the provision of notice for the purposes of clause 137(3)(a);

44. prescribing rules governing the reduction of rent for the purposes of clause 137(3)(b);

45. prescribing a period for the purposes of subsection 137(4);

46. prescribing information to be provided to a prospective tenant for the purposes of paragraph 3 of subsection 137(5);

47. prescribing other circumstances for the purposes of subsection 137(6);

48. prescribing requirements for the purposes of clauses 137(7)(a), (b) and (c);

49. prescribing circumstances in which a tenant may apply to the Board under subsection 137(8);

50. prescribing rules governing charging tenants a portion of the cost of a utility for the purposes of subsection 138(1);

51. prescribing rules governing the provision of notice for the purposes of clause 138(1)(a);

52. prescribing rules governing the reduction of rent for the purposes of clause 138(1)(b);

53. prescribing information to be provided to a prospective tenant for the purposes of paragraph 4 of subsection 138(4);

54. prescribing requirements for the purposes of clauses 138(5)(a) and (b);

55. prescribing circumstances in which a tenant may apply to the Board under subsection 138(6);

56. prescribing the information that shall be contained in an information package for the purposes of section 140;

57. prescribing a period for the purpose of clause 144(1)(b);

58. prescribing an amount for the purposes of paragraph 2 of subsection 164(2);

59. prescribing an amount for the purposes of section 165;

60. prescribing services and things for the purposes of section 167;

61. respecting the appointment, including the status, duties and benefits, of employees of the Board for the purposes of section 178;

62. prescribing information to be filed with an application to the Board for the purposes of subsection 185(1);

63. prescribing information to be provided under subsection 189(1);

64. prescribing circumstances for the purposes of subsection 189(2);

65. prescribing time requirements that cannot be extended or shortened for the purposes of subsection 190(2);

66. restricting the circumstances in which the Board may, under section 195, require a person to make a payment into the Board;

67. governing the management and investment of money paid into the Board, providing for the payment of interest on money paid into the Board and fixing the rate of interest so paid;

68. prescribing forms of housing assistance for the purposes of clause 203(b);

69. prescribing an amount for the purposes of subsection 207(4);

70. governing electronic documents for the purposes of section 213, including specifying the types of documents that may be dealt with electronically for the purposes of that section, regulating the use of electronic

signatures in such documents and providing for the creating, filing, providing, issuing, sending, receiving, storing, transferring and retaining of such documents;

71. prescribing an amount for the purposes of subsection 214(1);

72. prescribing maintenance standards for the purposes of section 224;

73. prescribing other criteria for determining areas in which maintenance standards apply for the purposes of clause 224(1)(c);

74. respecting the amount or the determination of the amount the Minister may charge a municipality for the purposes of subsection 224(4), including payments to inspectors, overhead costs related to inspections and interest on overdue accounts;

75. making a regulation made under paragraph 25, 26, 66 or 67 applicable, with necessary modifications, to an application to which subsection 242(6) or (7) applies, and providing that the regulation applies despite any regulations made under the *Tenant Protection Act, 1997*;

76. defining "serious" as it is used in any provision of this Act and defining it differently for different provisions;

77. defining any word or expression used in this Act that has not already been expressly defined in this Act;

78. prescribing any matter required or permitted by this Act to be prescribed.

(2) Same — A regulation made under subsection (1) may be general or particular in its application.

PART XVIII — TRANSITION

242. (1) Applications made under *Tenant Protection Act, 1997* — Despite the repeal of the *Tenant Protection Act, 1997* but subject to the other provisions of this section, that Act shall be deemed to be continued in force for the purpose only of continuing and finally disposing of applications that were made under that Act before that Act was repealed, including any appeals, motions or other steps in those applications.

(2) Default orders — Sections 177 and 192 of the *Tenant Protection Act, 1997* do not apply to an application referred to in subsection 192(1) of that Act unless, before that Act was repealed, an order was made with respect to the application without holding a hearing.

(3) Powers on eviction applications — Section 83 of this Act applies, with necessary modifications, and section 84 of the *Tenant Protection Act, 1997* does not apply, to an application made under the *Tenant Protection Act, 1997* before that Act was repealed for an order evicting a tenant, unless the final order in the application was made before that Act was repealed.

(4) Eviction orders for arrears of rent — If, pursuant to subsection (1), subsections 72(4) to (10) of the *Tenant Protection Act, 1997* apply to an eviction order, subsections 74(11) to (18) of this Act also apply, with necessary modifications, to the eviction order.

(5) Eviction and other orders for arrears of rent — Section 82 of this Act applies, with necessary modifications, to an application by a landlord under section 69 of the *Tenant Protection Act, 1997* for an order terminating a tenancy and evicting a tenant based on a notice of termination under section 61 of that Act, and to an application by a landlord under subsection 86(1) of that Act, unless the final order in the application was made before that Act was repealed.

(6) Breach of landlord's responsibility to repair — Section 195 of this Act applies, with necessary modifications, and section 182 of the *Tenant Protection Act, 1997* does not apply, to an application made under subsection 32(1) of that Act before it was repealed for an order determining that a landlord breached the obligations under subsection 24(1) or 110(1) of that Act, unless a final order was made under subsection 34(1) or 110(3) of that Act before it was repealed.

(7) Application for above guideline increase — Subsections 126(12) and (13) of this Act apply, with necessary modifications, to an application made under section 138 of the *Tenant Protection Act, 1997*, unless a final order was made under subsection 138(6) or (10) of that Act before it was repealed.

243. Proceedings before other bodies under earlier legislation — Section 223 of the *Tenant Protection Act, 1997* continues to apply, despite the repeal of that Act.

244. Orders, etc., under former Act — Subject to section 242, a reference in this Act to an order, application, notice, by-law or other thing made, given, passed or otherwise done under a provision of this Act includes a reference to an order, application, notice, by-law or thing made, given, passed or done under the corresponding provision of the *Tenant Protection Act, 1997*.

245. (1) Information from former Rent Registry — The Board shall provide any information it received under subsection 157(3) of the *Tenant Protection Act, 1997* to members of the public on request.

(2) Application — Subsection (1) does not apply after the first anniversary of the date this section comes into force.

246. Use of certain forms — Despite the repeal of the *Tenant Protection Act, 1997*, the form of a notice of rent increase, notice of increased charges in a care home or notice of termination that could have been used under that Act may be used for the corresponding purpose under this Act any time within two months after this section comes into force.

Part XIX — Other Matters

Amendments to Other Acts

247. Commercial Tenancies Act — Section 2 of the *Commercial Tenancies Act* is amended by striking out "*Tenant Protection Act, 1997*" and substituting "*Residential Tenancies Act, 2006*".

248. Condominium Act, 1998 — (1) Subsection 4(2) of the *Condominium Act, 1998* is amended by striking out "*Tenant Protection Act, 1997*" and substituting "*Residential Tenancies Act, 2006*".

(2) Subsection 4(3) of the Act is amended by striking out "Part III of the *Tenant Protection Act, 1997*" and substituting "Part V of the *Residential Tenancies Act, 2006*".

(3) Subsection 80(7) of the Act is amended by striking out "*Tenant Protection Act, 1997*" at the end and substituting "*Residential Tenancies Act, 2006*".

(4) Subsection 80(10) of the Act is amended by striking out "Sections 100, 101, 102, 114, 115 and 116 and Part VI of the *Tenant Protection Act, 1997*" at the beginning and substituting "Sections 149, 150, 151, 165, 166 and 167 and Part VII of the *Residential Tenancies Act, 2006*".

(5) Subsection 165(7) of the Act is amended by striking out "*Tenant Protection Act, 1997*" and substituting "*Residential Tenancies Act, 2006*".

249. Consumer Protection Act, 2002 — Clause 2(2)(g) of the *Consumer Protection Act, 2002* is amended by striking out "*Tenant Protection Act, 1997*" at the end and substituting "*Residential Tenancies Act, 2006*".

250. Co-operative Corporations Act — (1) Subsection 171.7(1) of the *Co-operative Corporations Act* is amended by striking out "*Tenant Protection Act, 1997*" and substituting "*Residential Tenancies Act, 2006*".

(2) Subsection 171.7(2) of the Act is amended by striking out "*Tenant Protection Act, 1997*" and substituting "*Residential Tenancies Act, 2006*".

251. Education Act — Section 257.13.1 of the *Education Act* is amended by striking out "section 136 of the *Tenant Protection Act, 1997*" at the end and substituting "section 131 of the *Residential Tenancies Act, 2006*".

252. Mortgages Act — (1) Section 27 of the *Mortgages Act* is amended by striking out "section 118 of the *Tenant Protection Act, 1997*" and substituting "section 106 of the *Residential Tenancies Act, 2006*".

(2) The definition of "landlord" in section 44 of the Act is amended by striking out "subsection 1(1) of the *Tenant Protection Act, 1997*" at the end and substituting "subsection 2(1) of the *Residential Tenancies Act, 2006*".

(3) The definition of "rental unit" in section 44 of the Act is amended by striking out "subsection 1(1) of the *Tenant Protection Act, 1997*" at the end and substituting "subsection 2(1) of the *Residential Tenancies Act, 2006*".

(4) The definition of "residential complex" in section 44 of the Act is amended by striking out "subsection 1(1) of the *Tenant Protection Act, 1997*" at the end and substituting "subsection 2(1) of the *Residential Tenancies Act, 2006*".

(5) The definition of "tenancy agreement" in section 44 of the Act is amended by striking out "subsection 1(1) of the *Tenant Protection Act, 1997*" at the end and substituting "subsection 2(1) of the *Residential Tenancies Act, 2006*".

(6) The definition of "tenant" in section 44 of the Act is amended by striking out "subsection 1(1) of the *Tenant Protection Act, 1997*" at the end and substituting "subsection 2(1) of the *Residential Tenancies Act, 2006*".

(7) Subsection 47(3) of the Act is amended by striking out "*Tenant Protection Act, 1997*" and substituting "*Residential Tenancies Act, 2006*".

(8) Subsection 48(1) of the Act is amended by striking out "*Tenant Protection Act, 1997*" at the end and substituting "*Residential Tenancies Act, 2006*".

(9) Clause 51(1)(b) of the Act is amended by striking out "*Tenant Protection Act, 1997*" at the end and substituting "*Residential Tenancies Act, 2006*".

(10) Subsection 53(1) of the Act is amended by striking out "section 51 of the *Tenant Protection Act, 1997*" and substituting "section 48 of the *Residential Tenancies Act, 2006*".

(11) Subsection 53(2) of the Act is amended by striking out "section 51 of the *Tenant Protection Act, 1997*" at the end and substituting "section 48 of the *Residential Tenancies Act, 2006*".

(12) Subsection 53(5) of the Act is amended by striking out "section 43 of the *Tenant Protection Act, 1997*" and substituting "section 43 of the *Residential Tenancies Act, 2006*".

(13) Subsection 53(6) of the Act is amended by striking out "section 51 of the *Tenant Protection Act, 1997*" and substituting "section 48 of the *Residential Tenancies Act, 2006*".

(14) The French version of subsection 53(7) of the Act is amended by striking out "d'éviction" and substituting "d'expulsion".

(15) Subsection 53(7) of the Act is amended by striking out "section 69 of the *Tenant Protection Act, 1997*" at the end and substituting "section 69 of the *Residential Tenancies Act, 2006*".

(16) Section 57 of the Act is amended by striking out "section 178 of the *Tenant Protection Act, 1997*" at the end and substituting "section 191 of the *Residential Tenancies Act, 2006*".

253. Personal Health Information Protection Act, 2004 — Subparagraph 4 ii of the definition of "health information custodian" in subsection 3(1) of the *Personal*

Health Information Protection Act, 2004 is amended by striking out "*Tenant Protection Act, 1997*" at the end and substituting "*Residential Tenancies Act, 2006*".

Unproclaimed Text — 254

254. Private Security and Investigative Services Act, 2005 — Clause 9(1)(c) of the *Private Security and Investigative Services Act, 2005* is repealed and the following substituted:

(c) an eviction under the *Residential Tenancies Act, 2006*.

255. Real Estate and Business Brokers Act, 2002 — Clause 5(1)(j) of the *Real Estate and Business Brokers Act, 2002* is amended by striking out "*Tenant Protection Act, 1997*" and substituting "*Residential Tenancies Act, 2006*".

256. Residential Complex Sales Representation Act — The definition of "residential complex" in section 1 of the *Residential Complex Sales Representation Act* is amended by striking out "*Tenant Protection Act, 1997*" at the end and substituting "*Residential Tenancies Act, 2006*".

257. Social Housing Reform Act, 2000 — (1) The definition of "landlord" in section 2 of the *Social Housing Reform Act, 2000* is amended by striking out "*Tenant Protection Act, 1997*" at the end and substituting "*Residential Tenancies Act, 2006*".

(2) Subsection 86(7) of the Act is amended by striking out "Sections 127 and 128 of the *Tenant Protection Act, 1997*" at the beginning and substituting "Sections 116 and 118 of the *Residential Tenancies Act, 2006*".

258. *Tenant Protection Act, 1997*, amendments — (1) Section 135 of the *Tenant Protection Act, 1997* is repealed and the following substituted:

Increase Based on *Rent Control Act, 1992*

135. (1) Increase based on *Rent Control Act, 1992* — If, on or after May 3, 2006, a landlord increased rent under this section, as it read on that day,

(a) any amount collected by the landlord from the tenant in excess of the amount that the landlord would otherwise have been authorized to collect shall be deemed to be money the landlord collected in contravention of this Act; and

(b) any amount referred to in clause (a) that was charged or collected by the landlord before the day the *Residential Tenancies Act, 2006* received Royal Assent shall be deemed to have been charged and collected on the day that Act received Royal Assent.

(2) Same — Subsection (1) does not apply if notice of the rent increase was given in accordance with this Act before May 3, 2006.

(2) The Act is amended by adding the following section:

139.1 Reduction: capital expenditures — If an application is made under section 138 on or after May 3, 2006, an order is issued under subsection 138(6) or (10), and the order permits an increase in rent that is due in whole or in part to capital expenditures,

(a) the Tribunal shall specify in the order the percentage increase that is attributable to the capital expenditures; and

(b) the order shall require that,

(i) if the rent charged to a tenant for a rental unit is increased pursuant to the order by the maximum percentage permitted by the order, and the tenant continues to occupy the rental unit on the 15th anniversary of the first day of the time period ordered under subsection 138(6), the landlord shall, on that anniversary, reduce the rent charged to that tenant by the percentage specified under clause (a); and

(ii) if the rent charged to a tenant for a rental unit is increased pursuant to the order by less than the maximum percentage permitted by the order, and the tenant continues to occupy the rental unit on the 15th anniversary of the first day of the time period ordered under subsection 138(6), the landlord shall, on that anniversary, reduce the rent charged to that tenant by the lesser of,

(A) the percentage increase that was charged to the tenant pursuant to the order, and

(B) the percentage specified under clause (a).

259. *Tenant Protection Act, 1997*, repeal — The *Tenant Protection Act, 1997* is repealed.

260. Toronto Islands Residential Community Stewardship Act, 1993 — (1) Subsection 9(20) of the *Toronto Islands Residential Community Stewardship Act, 1993* is amended by striking out "*Tenant Protection Act, 1997*" and substituting "*Residential Tenancies Act, 2006*".

(2) Subsection 28(5) of the Act is amended by striking out "_Tenant Protection Act, 1997_" and substituting "*Residential Tenancies Act, 2006*".

(3) Subsection 33(1) of the Act is amended by striking out "_Tenant Protection Act, 1997_" and substituting "*Residential Tenancies Act, 2006*".

Access to Justice Act, 2006 (Bill 14)

261. *Access to Justice Act, 2006* (Bill 14) — (1) This section applies only if Bill 14 (*An Act to promote access to justice by amending or repealing various Acts and by enacting the Legislation Act, 2006*), introduced on October 27, 2005, receives Royal Assent.

(2) References in this section to provisions of Bill 14 are references to those provisions as they were numbered in the first reading version of the Bill and, if

Bill 14 is renumbered, the references in this section shall be deemed to be references to the equivalent renumbered provisions of Bill 14.

(3) On the later of the day subsection 185(2) of this Act comes into force and the day subsection 2(6) of Schedule C to Bill 14 comes into force, subsection 185(2) of this Act is repealed and the following substituted:

> **(2) Application filed by representative** — An applicant may give written authorization to sign an application to a person representing the applicant under the authority of the *Law Society Act* and, if the applicant does so, the Board may require such representative to file a copy of the authorization.

(4) On the later of the day subsection 204(3) of this Act comes into force and the day subsection 2(6) of Schedule C to Bill 14 comes into force, subsection 204(3) of this Act is amended by striking out "a paid agent or counsel to a party" and substituting "the party's paid representative".

(5) On the later of the day subsection 208(1) of this Act comes into force and the day subsection 2(6) of Schedule C to Bill 14 comes into force, subsection 208(1) of this Act is amended by striking out "the party's counsel or agent" and substituting "the person who represented the party".

Commencement and Short Title

262. (1) Commencement — Subject to subsections (2), (3), (4) and (5), this Act comes into force on a day to be named by proclamation of the Lieutenant Governor.

(2) Same — If a proclamation under subsection (1) names a date for the coming into force of section 137 that is earlier than the date section 2 of Schedule B to the *Energy Conservation Responsibility Act, 2006* comes into force, section 137 comes into force on the date section 2 of Schedule B to that Act comes into force.

(3) Same — Sections 258 and 261, this section and section 263 come into force on the day this Act receives Royal Assent.

(4) Same — Sections 247 to 253, 255, 256, 257 and 260 come into force on the same day that section 259 comes into force.

(5) Same — Section 254 comes into force on the later of the following days:

1. The day section 259 comes into force.

2. The day subsection 9(1) of the *Private Security and Investigative Services Act, 2005* comes into force.

263. Short title — The short title of this Act is the *Residential Tenancies Act, 2006*.

Appendix 3

Ont. Reg. 516/06 — General

made under the ***Residential Tenancies Act, 2006***

O. Reg. 516/06, as am. O. Reg. 561/06 (Fr.)

Part I — Interpretation and Exemptions

1. (1) Definition of "care home" — One or more rental units that form part of a residential complex are care homes for the purpose of the definition of "care home" in subsection 2(1) of the Act if the rental units are occupied or intended to be occupied by persons for the purpose of receiving care services, whether or not receiving the care services is the primary purpose of the occupancy.

(2) Subsection (1) applies even if a third party rents the rental unit from the landlord and provides or arranges to provide both the rental unit and care services to the tenant.

2. Definition of "care services" — (1) As part of health care services, rehabilitative services, therapeutic services and services that provide assistance with the activities of daily living, the following are included in the definition of "care services" in subsection 2(1) of the Act:

1. Nursing care.
2. Administration and supervision of medication prescribed by a medical doctor.
3. Assistance with feeding.
4. Bathing assistance.
5. Incontinence care.
6. Dressing assistance.
7. Assistance with personal hygiene.
8. Ambulatory assistance.
9. Personal emergency response services.

(2) The following services are included in the definition of "care services" in subsection 2(1) of the Act if they are provided along with any service set out in subsection (1):

1. Recreational or social activities.
2. Housekeeping.

3. Laundry services.

4. Assistance with transportation.

3. Definition of "tenant" — (1) If a tenant of a rental unit dies and the rental unit is the principal residence of the spouse of that tenant, the spouse is included in the definition of "tenant" in subsection 2(1) of the Act unless the spouse vacates the unit within the 30-day period described in subsection 91(1) of the Act.

(2) If a tenant vacates a rental unit without giving a notice of termination under the Act and without entering into an agreement to terminate the tenancy, and the rental unit is the principal residence of the spouse of that tenant, the spouse is included in the definition of "tenant" in subsection 2(1) of the Act.

(3) Subsection (2) does not apply if any one or more of the following criteria are satisfied:

1. The rental unit is in a building containing not more than three residential units and the landlord resides in the building.

2. The spouse vacates the rental unit no later than 60 days after the tenant vacated the rental unit.

3. The tenant who vacated the rental unit was not in arrears of rent and the spouse fails to advise the landlord, before an order is issued under section 100 of the Act, that he or she intends to remain in the rental unit.

4. The tenant who vacated the rental unit was in arrears of rent, the landlord gives the spouse a notice in a form approved by the Board within 45 days after the date the tenant vacated the unit, and the spouse fails, within 15 days after receiving the notice,

   i. to advise the landlord that he or she intends to remain in the rental unit, or

   ii. to agree in writing with the landlord to pay the arrears of rent.

5. The tenant who vacated the rental unit was in arrears of rent, the landlord does not give the spouse a notice referred to in paragraph 4 within 45 days after the date the tenant vacated the unit, and the spouse fails, before an order is issued under section 100 of the Act,

   i. to advise the landlord that he or she intends to remain in the rental unit, or

   ii. to agree in writing with the landlord to pay the arrears of rent.

(4) Subsections (1) and (2) do not apply to,

(a) a rental unit described in section 7 of the Act;

(b) a rental unit that is in a care home to which Part IX of the Act applies; or

(c) a rental unit to which section 6 of this Regulation applies.

4. Definition of "vital service" — (1) For the purpose of the definition of "vital service" in subsection 2(1) of the Act, September 1 to June 15 is prescribed as the part of the year during which heat is a vital service.

(2) For the purposes of subsection (1), heat shall be provided so that the room temperature at 1.5 metres above floor level and one metre from exterior walls in all habitable space and in any area intended for normal use by tenants, including recreation rooms and laundry rooms but excluding locker rooms and garages, is at least 20 degrees Celsius.

(3) Subsection (2) does not apply to a rental unit in which the tenant can regulate the temperature and a minimum temperature of 20 degrees Celsius can be maintained by the primary source of heat.

5. Prescribed programs — The following federal, provincial or municipal programs are prescribed for the purposes of paragraph 3 of subsection 7(1) of the Act:

1. Non-Profit Low Rental Housing Program established under the *National Housing Act* (Canada).

2. Non-Profit 2% Write-Down Non-Profit Housing Program established under the *National Housing Act* (Canada).

3. Non-Profit Full Assistance Housing Programs administered before January 1, 2001 by the Ministry, not including the Municipal Non-Profit Housing Program, but including,

   i. JobsOntario Homes,

   ii. The Ontario Non-Profit Housing Program (P-3000),

   iii. The Ontario Non-Profit Housing Program (P-3600),

   iv. The Ontario Non-Profit Housing Program (P-10,000),

   v. Homes Now, and

   vi. Federal/Provincial Non-Profit Housing Program (1986–1993).

4. Municipal Non-Profit Housing Program (1978–1985).

5. Municipal Assisted Housing Program (Toronto Housing Company).

6. Urban Native Fully Targeted Housing Program established under the *National Housing Act* (Canada).

7. Urban Native 2% Write-Down and Additional Assistance Program established under the *National Housing Act* (Canada).

6. Exemptions from certain provisions — (1) Section 8, paragraphs 6, 7 and 8 of subsection 30(1), sections 51, 52, 54, 55, 56 and 95 to 99, subsection 100(2) and sections 101, 102, 104, 111 to 115, 117, 120, 121, 122, 126 to 133, 140, 143, 149, 150, 151, 159, 165 and 167 of the Act do not apply to rental units that meet the criteria set out in subsection (2) and that were developed or acquired under the following initiatives:

1. Canada-Ontario Affordable Housing Program—Rental and Supportive Housing.

2. Canada-Ontario Affordable Housing Program—Northern Housing.

3. Residential Rehabilitation Assistance Program.

4. Supporting Communities Partnership Initiative.

5. Municipal capital facility by-laws for housing or other council-approved municipal housing programs.

(2) Subsection (1) applies to a rental unit described in that subsection if,

(a) the unit is subject to an agreement related to the provision of housing services between the landlord and one or more of,

(i) a municipality,

(ii) an agency of a municipality,

(iii) a non-profit corporation controlled by a municipality, if an object of the non-profit corporation is the provision of housing,

(iv) a local housing corporation, as defined in the *Social Housing Reform Act, 2000*, or

(v) a service manager as defined in the *Social Housing Reform Act, 2000*;

(b) the unit is identified as a subsidized unit that was developed or acquired under an initiative listed in subsection (1), and as being subject to an agreement described in clause (a), in,

(i) the tenancy agreement, or

(ii) a written notice that was given by the landlord to the tenant, if the tenancy agreement was entered into before January 31, 2007; and

(c) the tenant, at the time the tenancy agreement was entered into, was on or was eligible to be on a social housing waiting list.

(3) Section 8, paragraphs 6, 7 and 8 of subsection 30(1), sections 51, 52, 54, 55, 56 and 95 to 99, subsection 100(2) and sections 101, 102, 104, 111 to 115, 117, 120, 121, 122, 126 to 133, 140, 143, 149, 150, 151, 159, 165 and 167 of the Act do not apply to rental units that were developed or acquired, and that continue to operate, under the Rural and Native Rental Housing Program established under the *National Housing Act* (Canada).

(4) Section 119 of the Act does not apply to a rental unit that is exempt under subsection (1) or (3) if the tenant occupying the unit pays rent in an amount geared-to-income due to public funding.

(5) Sections 116 and 118 of the Act do not apply to increases in rent for a rental unit due to increases in the tenant's income if the rental unit is exempt under subsection

(1) or (3) and the tenant pays rent in an amount geared-to-income due to public funding.

(6) Paragraph 2 of subsection 58(1) and subsection 60(1) of the Act apply to a rental unit described in subsection (1) or (3) of this section, even though the rental unit is not a rental unit described in paragraph 1, 2, 3 or 4 of subsection 7(1) of the Act.

7. Rental unit in care home — (1) Subsections 37(4) and (5) of the Act do not apply to a rental unit in a care home if,

(a) the rental unit is occupied for the purpose of receiving rehabilitative or therapeutic services agreed upon by the tenant and the landlord;

(b) the period of occupancy agreed to by the tenant and the landlord is no more than four years;

(c) the tenancy agreement stipulates that the tenancy may be terminated and the tenant evicted when the objectives of the services have been met or will not be met; and

(d) the unit is subject to an agreement for the provision of housing services between the landlord and a service manager as defined in the *Social Housing Reform Act, 2000*.

(2) If a landlord makes an application under subsection 77(1) of the Act and the application is based on a notice or agreement to which, pursuant to subsection (1), subsections 37(4) and (5) of the Act do not apply, the expression "the termination date specified in the agreement or notice" in subsection 77(3) of the Act means the earlier of the following dates:

1. The last day of the period of occupancy referred to in clause (1)(b).

2. The day that is 60 days after the day the tenant received notice from the landlord that the objectives of the services have been met or will not be met.

(3) For greater certainty, for the purposes of clause (1)(c) and subsection (2), the objectives of the services will not be met if the tenant has repeatedly and substantially withdrawn from participation in the services.

PART II — MATTERS RELATING TO RENT

8. Reasonable enjoyment during repairs — (1) **Definition** — In this section,

"work" means maintenance, repairs or capital improvements carried out in a rental unit or a residential complex.

(2) For the purposes of section 22, paragraph 3 of subsection 29(1) and subsection 31(1) of the Act, this section applies to the Board in making a determination,

(a) as to whether a landlord, superintendent or agent of a landlord, in carrying out work in a rental unit or residential complex, substantially interfered with the reasonable enjoyment of the unit or complex for all usual purposes by a tenant or former tenant, or by a member of the household of a tenant or former tenant; and

(b) whether an abatement of rent is justified in the circumstances.

(3) In making a determination described in subsection (2),

(a) the Board shall consider the effect of the carrying out of the work on the use of the rental unit or residential complex by the tenant or former tenant, and by members of the household of the tenant or former tenant; and

(b) the Board shall not determine that an interference was substantial unless the carrying out of the work constituted an interference that was unreasonable in the circumstances with the use and enjoyment of the rental unit or residential complex by the tenant or former tenant, or by a member of the household of the tenant or former tenant.

(4) If the Board finds that the landlord, superintendent or agent of the landlord, in carrying out work in a rental unit or residential complex, substantially interfered with the reasonable enjoyment of the unit or complex for all usual purposes by a tenant or former tenant, or by a member of the household of a tenant or former tenant, the Board shall not order an abatement of rent if all of the following conditions are satisfied:

1. The landlord gave notice to the tenant or former tenant at least 60 days before the commencement of the work, or, in cases of emergency, as soon as was reasonable in the circumstances, concerning the work to be carried out.

2. The landlord gave notice to any prospective tenant of a rental unit at the first opportunity to do so before the landlord entered into a new tenancy agreement with that tenant.

3. The notice describes the nature of the work to be carried out, the expected impact on tenants and members of their households and the length of time the work is expected to take.

4. The notice was reasonably accurate and comprehensive in the circumstances at the time it was given.

5. If there was a significant change in the information provided under paragraph 3, the landlord provided to the tenant or former tenant an update to the notice in a timely manner.

6. The work,

i. is necessary to protect or restore the physical integrity of the residential complex or part of it,

ii. is necessary to comply with maintenance, health, safety or other housing related standards required by law,

iii. is necessary to maintain a plumbing, heating, mechanical, electrical, ventilation or air conditioning system,

iv. provides access for persons with disabilities,

v. promotes energy or water conservation, or

vi. maintains or improves the security of the residential complex.

7. If required under the *Building Code Act, 1992*, a permit was issued in respect of the work.

8. The work was carried out at reasonable times, or if a municipal noise control by-law was in effect, during the times permitted under the noise control by-law.

9. The duration of the work was reasonable in the circumstances.

10. The landlord took reasonable steps to minimize any interference resulting from noise associated with the work.

(5) If the Board finds that the landlord, superintendent or agent of the landlord, in carrying out work in a rental unit or residential complex, substantially interfered with the reasonable enjoyment of the unit or complex for all usual purposes by a tenant or former tenant, or by a member of the household of a tenant or former tenant, and an abatement of rent is not prohibited under subsection (4), the Board shall consider the following in determining whether it is appropriate to order an abatement of rent and the amount of the abatement:

1. The nature, duration and degree of interference with the reasonable enjoyment of the rental unit or residential complex that was caused by the carrying out of the work.

2. Whether the tenant or former tenant is responsible for any undue delay in the carrying out of the work.

3. The steps taken by the landlord during the work to minimize interference with the reasonable enjoyment of the rental unit or residential complex.

4. Whether the tenant or former tenant took advantage of any service provided by the landlord or arrangement made by the landlord that would minimize interference with the reasonable enjoyment of the rental unit or residential complex.

5. Whether a failure to carry out the work could, within a reasonable period of time, reasonably be expected to result in,

i. interference with the reasonable enjoyment of the rental unit or residential complex for all usual purposes by a tenant or member of his or her household,

ii. a reduction or discontinuation of a service or facility,

iii. damage or additional damage to the rental unit, the residential complex or anything in the unit or complex,

iv. a risk to any person's health or personal safety, or

v. a breach of section 20 or section 161 of the Act by the landlord.

(6) Except as permitted under subsection (7), no abatement of rent shall exceed 25 per cent of the monthly rent for each month or part of a month during which there was substantial interference with the reasonable enjoyment of the rental unit or residential complex for all usual purposes by the tenant or former tenant, or by a member of the household of the tenant or former tenant.

(7) The Board may order an abatement of rent that exceeds 25 per cent of the monthly rent for a rental unit if,

(a) the Board considers a larger abatement to be warranted in the circumstances because the interference with the reasonable enjoyment of the rental unit or residential complex far exceeded the level that would normally be expected, taking into consideration all of the relevant circumstances; and

(b) the Board is satisfied that,

(i) the work is not work described in paragraph 6 of subsection (4),

(ii) the work was carried out at unreasonable times or at a time that is not permitted under any applicable noise control by-law,

(iii) the work was carried out in a manner that contravened a condition or requirement of a building permit issued under the *Building Code Act, 1992*,

(iv) the work was carried out over a period of time far in excess of the amount of time that normally would be required, after taking into consideration any exceptional circumstances beyond the control of the landlord, including weather-related delays, delays in obtaining necessary government approvals or permits and delays caused by market shortages of suitable goods or services or qualified labour at reasonable costs, or

(v) the landlord refused to take reasonable steps during the work to minimize interference with the reasonable enjoyment of the rental unit or residential complex for all usual purposes by the tenant or former tenant, or by a member of the household of the tenant or former tenant.

(8) The Board shall not order an abatement of rent that exceeds 100 per cent of the monthly rent for each month or part of a month during which the Board determines that the work substantially interfered with the reasonable enjoyment of the rental unit or residential complex for all usual purposes by the tenant or former tenant, or by a member of the household of the tenant or former tenant.

9. Receipt — A document constitutes a receipt for the purposes of section 109 of the Act if it includes, at a minimum,

(a) the address of the rental unit to which the receipt applies;

(b) the name of the tenants to whom the receipt applies;

(c) the amount and date for each payment received for any rent, rent deposit, arrears of rent, or any other amount paid to the landlord and shall specify what the payment was for;

(d) the name of the landlord of the rental unit; and

(e) the signature of the landlord or the landlord's authorized agent.

10. Prescribed conditions under s. 111(2)(a) and (b) of the Act — (1) The following conditions are prescribed for the purpose of clause 111(2)(a) of the Act:

1. The discount must be provided for in a written agreement.

2. If the rent is paid monthly and the discount is equal to the rent for one month or less, the entire discount must be taken during one rental period.

3. If the rent is paid monthly and the discount is equal to the rent for a period greater than one month but not more than two months, the discount equal to the rent for one month must be taken during one rental period and the balance within one other rental period.

4. If the rent is paid monthly and the discount is equal to the rent for a period greater than two months but not more than three months, the discount equal to the rent for two months must be taken for two rental periods and the balance within one other rental period.

5. If the rent is paid daily or weekly, the discount must be taken in periods that are at least one week in duration.

(2) The only condition prescribed for the purpose of clause 111(2)(b) of the Act is that the discount must be provided for in a written or oral agreement.

11. Prescribed discounts under s. 111(2)(c) of the Act — (1) The following discounts are prescribed for the purposes of clause 111(2)(c) of the Act:

1. A discount provided for in a written agreement, if the total amount of the discount that is provided during the first eight months of the 12-month period does not exceed the rent for one month.

2. A discount provided for in a written agreement, if,

   i. the total amount of the discount that is provided in the 12-month period does not exceed the rent for two months,

   ii. the total amount of the discount that is provided in the first seven months of the 12-month period does not exceed the rent for one month, and

   iii. any discount that is provided in the last five months of the 12-month period is provided in only one of those months and does not exceed the rent for one month.

3. A discount provided under a tenancy agreement that operates under the Strong Communities Housing Allowance Program—Toronto Pilot, if the landlord sets out the discounted rent and the undiscounted rent in the written tenancy agreement and in a written notice to the tenant accompanying any notice of rent increase given to the tenant under section 116 of the Act.

(2) In this section,

"the 12-month period" means,

(a) the 12-month period following the commencement of the tenancy,

(b) the 12-month period following any rent increase taken after the 12-month period described in clause (a), other than a rent increase taken under section 123 of the Act, or

(c) where clauses (a) and (b) do not apply, the 12-month period following the most recent anniversary of a rent increase taken in accordance with section 116 of the Act or, where no rent increase has been taken in accordance with section 116 of the Act, the commencement of the tenancy.

12. Calculation of lawful rent — (1) The rules set out in this section apply in calculating lawful rent under subsection 111(3) of the Act.

(2) The lawful rent for any rental period in the 12-month period shall be calculated in the following manner:

1. Add the sum of the rents that are actually charged or to be charged in each of the rental periods in the 12-month period to the largest eligible discount determined under subsection (6).

2. Divide the amount determined under paragraph 1 by the number of rental periods in the 12-month period.

3. Add to the amount determined under paragraph 2 any rent increases under section 123 of the Act and subtract from that amount any rent decreases under section 125 of the Act.

(3) Despite subsection (2), if a landlord provides a discount in rent that is greater than 2 per cent of the rent that could otherwise be lawfully charged for a rental period for paying rent on or before the date it is due, the lawful rent shall be calculated by dividing the discounted rent by 0.98.

(4) Despite subsections (2) and (3), if the landlord provides a discount in rent described in clause 111(2)(b) of the Act and the landlord also provides another discount, other than a discount described in clause 111(2)(a) or (c) of the Act, the lawful rent for any rental period in the 12-month period shall be calculated in the following manner:

1. Add the sum of the rents that are actually charged or to be charged in each of the rental periods in the 12-month period to the sum of the discounts described in clause 111(2)(b) of the Act actually provided or to be provided to the tenant during the 12-month period.

2. Add the amount determined under paragraph 1 to the largest eligible discount determined under subsection (6).

3. Divide the amount determined under paragraph 2 by the number of rental periods in the 12-month period.

4. Add to the amount determined under paragraph 3 any rent increases under section 123 of the Act and subtract from that amount any rent decreases under section 125 of the Act.

(5) Despite subsections (2) and (3), if the landlord provides a discount in rent that is greater than 2 per cent of the rent that could otherwise be lawfully charged for a rental period for paying rent on or before the date it is due, and the landlord also provides another discount in rent, other than a discount described in clause 111(2)(a) or (c) of the Act, the lawful rent for any rental period in the 12-month period shall be calculated in the following manner:

1. Divide the discounted rent by 0.98.

2. Multiply the amount determined under paragraph 1 by the number of rental periods in the 12-month period and add the result to the largest eligible discount determined under subsection (6).

3. Divide the amount determined under paragraph 2 by the number of rental periods in the 12-month period.

4. Add to the amount determined under paragraph 3 any rent increases under section 123 of the Act and subtract from that amount any rent decreases under section 125 of the Act.

(6) For the purpose of this section, the largest eligible discount shall be determined in accordance with the following rules:

1. In the case of a discount that is provided for in a written agreement, the largest eligible discount is the largest of the following amounts:

   i. The lesser of the following amounts:

      A. The sum of the discounts in rent during the first eight months of the 12-month period.

      B. The rent for one month.

   ii. The largest discount in rent during any month in the last five months of the 12-month period, plus the lesser of the following amounts:

      A. The sum of the discounts in rent during the first seven months of the 12-month period.

      B. The rent for one month.

   iii. The largest discount in rent during any month in the 12-month period, if,

      A. the rent is paid monthly, and

      B. the largest discount in rent during any month in the 12-month period is equal to the rent for less than one month.

   iv. The sum of the largest discount in rent during any month in the 12-month period and the second-largest discount in rent during any month in the 12-month period, if,

A. the rent is paid monthly,

B. the largest discount in rent during any month in the 12-month period is equal to the rent for one month, and

C. the second-largest discount in rent during any month in the 12-month period is equal to the rent for less than one month.

v. The sum of the largest discount in rent during any month in the 12-month period, the second-largest discount in rent during any month in the 12-month period, and the third-largest discount in rent during any month in the 12-month period, if,

A. the rent is paid monthly,

B. the largest discount in rent during any month in the 12-month period and the second-largest discount in rent during any month in the 12-month period are both equal to the rent for one month, and

C. the third-largest discount in rent during any month in the 12-month period is equal to the rent for less than one month.

vi. The rent for three months, if,

A. the rent is paid monthly, and

B. the largest discount in rent during any month in the 12-month period, the second-largest discount in rent during any month in the 12-month period, and the third-largest discount in rent during any month in the 12-month period are all equal to the rent for one month.

vii. The lesser of the following amounts, if the rent is paid daily or weekly:

A. The sum of the discounts in rent provided in the form of rent-free weeks during the 12-month period.

B. The rent for 13 weeks.

2. In the case of a discount that is not provided for in a written agreement, the largest eligible discount is the largest discount in rent in one rental period in the 12-month period.

(7) Despite subsection (2), if a tenancy agreement operates under the Strong Communities Housing Allowance Program—Toronto Pilot, and the landlord does not comply with paragraph 3 of subsection 11(1), the lawful rent shall be the undiscounted rent that was permitted under the Act at the time when the tenancy agreement began to operate under the Program.

(8) In this section,

"the 12-month period" has the same meaning as in section 11.

13. Higher rent charged in first rental period — If the rent a landlord charges for the first rental period of a tenancy is greater than the rent the landlord charges for subsequent rental periods in the 12-month period beginning on the day the tenancy commenced, the lawful rent for each rental period in that 12-month period shall be calculated in the following manner:

1. Add all the rents actually charged or to be charged by the landlord during the 12-month period.
2. Subtract from that sum the rent for the first rental period.
3. Divide the amount determined under paragraph 2 by a number equal to the number of rental periods in the 12-month period minus 1.

14. Exclusions from calculation of rent — For the purpose of calculating lawful rent under sections 12 and 13, the rent actually charged or to be charged does not include,

(a) amounts which cannot be lawfully charged for a reason other than the operation of section 12 or 13;

(b) rent increases under section 123 of the Act during the 12-month period defined in subsection 11(2) of this Regulation; or

(c) rent decreases under section 125 of the Act during the 12-month period defined in subsection 11(2) of this Regulation.

15. Material to be filed — If an application is made by a new tenant under subsection 115(1) of the Act, the landlord shall file with the Board, at or before the hearing, an affidavit sworn by the landlord setting out the last lawful rent charged to the former tenant and any available evidence in support of the affidavit.

16. Prescribed services, facilities, etc. — (1) The following services, facilities, privileges, accommodations or things are prescribed for the purposes of subsection 123(1) and section 125 of the Act:

1. Cable television.
2. Satellite television.
3. An air conditioner.
4. Extra electricity for an air conditioner.
5. Extra electricity for a washer or dryer in the rental unit.
6. Blockheater plug-ins.
7. Lockers or other storage space.
8. Heat.
9. Electricity.
10. Water or sewage services, excluding capital work.

11. Floor space.

12. Property taxes with respect to a site for a mobile home or a land lease home.

(2) If there is an agreement under subsection 123(1) or section 125 of the Act, the maximum increase in rent or minimum decrease in rent shall be the actual cost to the landlord of the service, facility, privilege, accommodation or thing, other than floor space, that is the subject of the agreement or, where the actual cost to the landlord cannot be established or where there is no cost to the landlord, a reasonable amount based on the value of the service, facility, privilege, accommodation or thing.

(3) If the agreement under subsection 123(1) or section 125 of the Act is to provide or cease to provide floor space, the maximum increase in rent or minimum decrease in rent shall be proportionate to the change in floor space.

(4) If an amount determined in accordance with subsection (3) would be unreasonable given the nature and quality of the floor space added or taken away, the maximum increase in rent or minimum decrease in rent shall be a reasonable amount based on the nature and quality of the floor space and the amount of the change in the floor space.

(5) Despite subsections (2), (3) and (4), where a service, facility, privilege, accommodation or thing was provided in accordance with a previous agreement under section 123 of the Act, section 132 of the *Tenant Protection Act, 1997*, section 46 of the *Rent Control Act, 1992* or subsection 96(4) of the *Residential Rent Regulation Act*, the minimum decrease in rent on ceasing to provide the service, facility, privilege, accommodation or thing shall be equal to,

(a) the most recent amount of the separate charge for the service, facility, privilege, accommodation or thing; or

(b) where there is no separate charge, the increase in rent which the landlord took when the service, facility, privilege, accommodation or thing was first provided, adjusted by the percentage increase in the rent being charged for the rental unit from the date the service, facility, privilege, accommodation or thing was first provided to the date the landlord ceased to provide it.

17. Exemptions from s. 134 of the Act — The following payments are exempt from section 134 of the Act:

1. Payment for additional keys, remote entry devices or cards requested by the tenant, not greater than the direct costs.

2. Payment for replacement keys, remote entry devices or cards, not greater than the direct replacement costs, unless the replacement keys, remote entry devices or cards are required because the landlord, on the landlord's initiative, changed the locks.

3. Payment of a refundable key, remote entry device or card deposit, not greater than the expected direct replacement costs.

4. Payment of NSF charges charged by a financial institution to the landlord.

5. Payment of an administration charge, not greater than $20, for an NSF cheque.

6. Payment by a tenant or subtenant in settlement of a court action or potential court action or an application or potential application to the Board.

7. Payment to a landlord or tenant of a mobile home park or land lease community at the commencement of a tenancy as consideration for the rental of a particular site.

8. Payment of a charge not exceeding $250 for transferring, at the request of the tenant,

i. between rental units to which subsection 6(1) or (3) of this Regulation applies, if the rental units are located in the same residential complex, or

ii. between rental units in a residential complex that is described in paragraph 1, 2, 3 or 4 of subsection 7(1) of the Act.

9. Payment of an amount to reimburse the landlord for property taxes paid by the landlord with respect to a mobile home or a land lease home owned by the tenant.

Part III — Application for Rent Increases Above Guideline

18. Definitions — (1) In the Act and in this Part,

"capital expenditure" means an expenditure for an extraordinary or significant renovation, repair, replacement or new addition, the expected benefit of which extends for at least five years including,

(a) an expenditure with respect to a leased asset if the lease qualifies as determined under subsection (2), and

(b) an expenditure that the landlord is required to pay on work undertaken by a municipality, local board or public utility, other than work undertaken because of the landlord's failure to do it,

but does not include,

(c) routine or ordinary work undertaken on a regular basis or undertaken to maintain a capital asset in its operating state, such as cleaning and janitorial services, elevator servicing, general building maintenance, grounds-keeping and appliance repairs, or

(d) work that is substantially cosmetic in nature or is designed to enhance the level of prestige or luxury offered by a unit or residential complex;

"incurred" means, in relation to a capital expenditure,

(a) the payment in full of the amount of the capital expenditure, other than a holdback withheld under the *Construction Lien Act*,

(b) if the expenditure relates to a lease, the assumption, when the lease commences, of the obligations under it, or

(c) if the expenditure relates to work undertaken by a municipality, local board or public utility, when the work is completed;

"physical integrity" means the integrity of all parts of a structure, including the foundation, that support loads or that provide a weather envelope and includes, without restricting the generality of the foregoing, the integrity of,

(a) the roof, exterior walls, exterior doors and exterior windows,

(b) elements contiguous with the structure that contribute to the weather envelope of the structure, and

(c) columns, walls and floors that support loads.

(2) For the purposes of the definition of "capital expenditure" in subsection (1), a lease qualifies if substantially all the risks and benefits associated with the leased asset are passed to the lessee and, when the lease commences, any one or more of the following is satisfied:

1. The lease provides that the ownership of the asset passes to the lessee at or before the end of the term of the lease.

2. The lease provides that the lessee has an option to purchase the asset at the end of the term of the lease at a price that is less than what the market value of the asset will be at that time.

3. The term of the lease is at least 75 per cent of the useful life of the asset, as determined in accordance with section 27 but without regard to any part of section 27 that prevents the useful life from being determined to be less than 10 years.

4. The net present value of the minimum lease payments is at least 90 per cent of the asset's fair market value at the commencement of the lease where the net present value is determined using the interest rate determined under section 20.

19. Definitions — (1) In this Part,

"base year" means,

(a) when determining rent increases due to an extraordinary increase in the cost for municipal taxes and charges, the last completed calendar year immediately preceding the day that is 90 days before the effective date of the first intended rent increase referred to in the application,

(b) when determining rent increases due to an extraordinary increase in the cost for utilities or due to operating costs related to security services, the annual accounting period of one year in length chosen by the landlord which is most recently completed on or before the day that is 90 days before the effective date of the first intended rent increase referred to in the application;

"local board" means a "local board" as defined in the *Municipal Affairs Act*;

"reference year" means the 12-month period immediately preceding the base year.

(2) Despite clause (b) of the definition of "base year" in subsection (1), if an order has previously been issued with respect to the residential complex under section 126 of the Act in which relief was granted for an extraordinary increase in costs for utilities or for operating costs related to security services, the base year shall begin and end on the same days of the year as the base year used in the previous order.

20. Interest rate — The interest rate for the purposes of subsection 18(2) and subsection 26(6) is the chartered bank administered conventional five-year mortgage interest rate on the last Wednesday of the month before the month in which the application is made, as reported by the Bank of Canada.

21. Factor to be applied — (1) The factor to be applied for the purposes of paragraph 6 of subsection 29(2), paragraph 3 of subsection 29(3) and paragraph 2 of subsection 30(2) is determined by dividing the total rents of the rental units in the residential complex that are subject to the application and are affected by the operating cost by the total rents of the rental units in the residential complex that are affected by the operating cost.

(2) For the purpose of subsection (1), the rent for a rental unit that is vacant or that is otherwise not rented shall be deemed to be the average rent charged for the rental units in the residential complex.

22. Material to accompany application — (1) An application under section 126 of the Act must be accompanied by the following material:

1. If the application is based on an extraordinary increase in the cost for municipal taxes and charges or utilities or both,

   i. evidence of the costs for the base year and the reference year and evidence of payment of those costs, and

   ii. evidence of all grants, other forms of financial assistance, rebates and refunds received by the landlord that effectively reduce those costs for the base year or the reference year.

2. If the application is based on capital expenditures incurred,

   i. evidence of all costs and payments for the amounts claimed for capital work, including any information regarding grants and assistance from any level of government and insurance, resale, salvage and trade-in proceeds,

   ii. details about each invoice and payment for each capital expenditure item, in the form approved by the Board, and

iii. details about the rents for all rental units in the residential complex that are affected by any of the capital expenditures, in the form approved by the Board.

3. If the application is based on operating costs related to security services, evidence of the costs claimed in the application for the base year and the reference year and evidence of payment of those costs.

(2) Despite subsection (1), if any of the following material is unavailable at the time the application is made under section 126 of the Act but becomes available before the end of the hearing, the material must be provided to the Board before or during the hearing:

1. Evidence described in subparagraph 1 ii of subsection (1).

2. Information concerning grants and assistance referred to in paragraph 2 of subsection (1).

3. Information concerning insurance, resale, salvage and trade-in proceeds referred to in paragraph 2 of subsection (1).

(3) An application under section 126 of the Act must be accompanied by two additional photocopies of the application, by two additional photocopies of the material that accompanies the application under subsection (1), and by a compact disc containing the material that accompanies the application under subsection (1) in portable document format.

(4) If material is provided to the Board under subsection (2), it must be accompanied by two additional photocopies of the material and by an updated compact disc containing the material that accompanied the application under subsection (1) and the material provided under subsection (2) in portable document format.

(5) A landlord does not have to provide a compact disc under subsection (3) or (4) if,

(a) the residential complex to which the application relates contains six or fewer residential units and the residential complex is located in a rural or remote area; and

(b) the landlord cannot reasonably provide the compact disc.

(6) Subsections (3), (4) and (5) do not apply if the application referred to in subsection (1) is not based on capital expenditures.

23. Information for tenants — (1) The rules set out in this section apply for the purposes of subsection 126(4) of the Act.

(2) Upon the request of a tenant subject to the application, the landlord shall provide the tenant with a compact disc containing the material provided to the Board under subsections 22(1) and (2) in portable document format, for a charge of not more than five dollars.

(3) Instead of providing the compact disc referred to in subsection (2), the landlord and the tenant may agree that the landlord will provide the tenant with,

(a) a photocopy of the material provided under subsections 22(1) and (2), for no more than the landlord's reasonable out-of-pocket costs for the photocopying; or

(b) an e-mail of the material provided under subsections 22(1) and (2) in portable document format, at no charge to the tenant.

(4) Despite subsection (2), if a landlord does not provide the Board with a compact disc pursuant to subsection 22(5), the landlord shall, upon the request of the tenant, provide the tenant with a photocopy of the material provided under subsections 22(1) and (2), for a charge of not more than five dollars.

(5) If the landlord has an office in or close to the residential complex, the landlord shall, during normal business hours and at no charge, make a photocopy of the material provided under subsections 22(1) and (2) available for viewing by tenants subject to the application.

(6) The landlord shall, in the application, inform every tenant subject to the application of the ways in which a tenant may obtain access under this section to the material provided under subsections 22(1) and (2).

24. Determination of capital expenditures, operating costs — (1) In determining the amount of any capital expenditures or the amount of operating costs in an application under section 126 of the Act, the Board shall,

(a) include any goods and services tax and provincial sales tax paid by the landlord in respect of the capital expenditures or operating costs;

(b) exclude any penalties, interest or other similar charges for late payment of any amount paid by the landlord in respect of the capital expenditures or operating costs;

(c) exclude any amount that has already been included in calculating the amount of a capital expenditure or operating cost in the same application or for which the landlord has obtained relief in a previous order under the Act or under the *Tenant Protection Act, 1997*; and

(d) subtract the amount of all grants, other forms of financial assistance, rebates and refunds received by the landlord that effectively reduce the operating costs.

(2) If a residential complex forms part of a larger project, the operating costs for the project and the amount of capital expenditures which benefit both the residential complex and the other parts of the project shall be allocated between the residential complex and the other parts of the project in accordance with one or more of the following factors:

1. The area of each part of the project.

2. The market value of each part of the project.

3. The revenue generated by each part of the project.

(3) If the allocation of operating costs and capital expenditures in accordance with subsection (2) would be unreasonable considering how much of the costs and expenditures are attributable to each part of the project, the operating costs and capital expenditures shall be allocated among the parts of the project in reasonable proportions according to how much of the costs and expenditures are attributable to each part of the project.

25. Non-arm's length transaction — (1) If the landlord incurs a cost arising out of a transaction that is not an arm's length transaction, the Board shall consider only that part of the landlord's cost that is less than or equal to the costs that would arise from a similar market transaction.

(2) In this section,

"arm's length" means the persons involved are not related persons;

"control" means direct or indirect ownership or control either alone or with a related person of,

(a) more than 50 per cent of the issued share capital of a corporation having full voting rights under all circumstances, or

(b) issued and outstanding share capital of a corporation in an amount that permits or may permit the person to direct the management and policies of the corporation;

"family", in relation to a person, means,

(a) the person's spouse,

(b) the parents or other ancestors or the children or other descendants of the person or the person's spouse,

(c) the brothers and sisters of the person or the person's spouse, and the children and other descendants of those brothers and sisters,

(d) the aunts and uncles of the person and the person's spouse and the children and other descendants of those aunts and uncles,

(e) the spouses of the person's sons and daughters;

"related person", where used to indicate a relationship with any person, includes,

(a) a member of the family of such person,

(b) an employer or employee of such person,

(c) a partner of such person,

(d) a trust or estate in which such person has a beneficial interest,

(e) a trust or estate in which such person serves as a trustee or in a similar capacity,

(f) a trust or estate in which persons related to such person, as otherwise determined under this definition, have a beneficial interest,

(g) a corporation controlled by such person,

(h) a corporation controlled by such person and persons related to such person, or

(i) a corporation controlled by a person related to such person;

"similar market transaction" means an arm's length transaction that occurs or may reasonably be expected to occur under the same or comparable terms and conditions and in the same general geographic location.

(3) In this section, one corporation is related to another corporation if,

(a) one of the corporations is controlled by the other corporation;

(b) both of the corporations are controlled by the same person or group of related persons each member of which is related to every other member of the group;

(c) each of the corporations is controlled by one person and the person who controls one of the corporations and the person who controls the other corporation are related persons;

(d) one of the corporations is controlled by one person and that person is related to any member of a group of related persons that controls the other corporation;

(e) one of the corporations is controlled by one person and that person is related to each member of an unrelated group that controls the other corporation;

(f) any member of a group of related persons that controls one of the corporations is related to each member of an unrelated group that controls the other corporation; or

(g) each member of an unrelated group that controls one of the corporations is a related person to at least one member of an unrelated group that controls the other corporation.

26. Findings related to capital expenditures — (1) The rules set out in this section apply to the Board in making findings relating to capital expenditures.

(2) A rent increase shall not be ordered in respect of a capital expenditure unless the work was completed during the 18-month period ending 90 days before the effective date of the first intended rent increase referred to in the application.

(3) The value of the landlord's own labour in carrying out the work involved in the capital expenditure is equal to the amount of time spent multiplied by a rate of pay that is reasonable given the landlord's experience and skill in the type of work done but,

(a) if the amount of time spent exceeds the amount of time that would be reasonable given the landlord's experience and skill, the latter amount of time shall be used in the calculation of the value of the landlord's own labour;

(b) only that part of the value of the landlord's own labour that does not exceed the amount a person in the business of doing such work would charge shall be considered; and

(c) the value of the landlord's own labour does not include any amount with respect to the management and administration of the work involved in the capital expenditure.

(4) The cost of a leased asset is the fair market value of the leased asset at the commencement of the lease.

(5) The amount of a capital expenditure is calculated as follows:

1. Add the following amounts:

i. The purchase prices.

ii. The cost of any leased assets.

iii. The installation, renovation and construction costs.

iv. The value of the landlord's own labour as determined under subsection (3).

2. Subtract from the amount determined under paragraph 1 any grant or other assistance from any level of government and any insurance, salvage, resale or trade-in proceeds related to the work undertaken or the item purchased.

(6) For each rental unit that is subject to the application, the percentage rent increase that is justified by capital expenditures shall be determined in accordance with the following rules.

1. Determine which capital expenditures affect the unit.

2. For each capital expenditure that affects the unit, multiply the amount of the capital expenditure determined under subsection (5) by the rent for the unit, and divide that result by the sum of the rents for all rental units in the residential complex that are affected by the capital expenditure.

3. If the Board is of the opinion that the amount determined under paragraph 2 for a capital expenditure does not reasonably reflect how the unit is affected by the capital expenditure,

i. paragraph 2 does not apply, and

ii. the Board shall determine an amount by another method that, in the opinion of the Board, better reflects how the unit is affected by the capital expenditure.

4. Add the amounts determined under paragraph 2 or 3, as the case may be, for all of the capital expenditures that affect the unit.

5. Amortize the amount determined under paragraph 4 over the weighted useful life of the capital expenditures that affect the unit, as determined in paragraph 6, in equal monthly instalments of blended principal and interest.

6. The weighted useful life of all capital expenditures that affect the unit shall be determined in accordance with the following rules:

i. For each capital expenditure that affects the unit,

A. divide the amount determined under paragraph 2 or 3, as the case may be, for the capital expenditure by the amount determined under paragraph 4, and

B. multiply the amount determined under sub-subparagraph A by the useful life of the capital expenditure, as determined under section 27.

ii. Add the results determined under sub-subparagraph i B for all capital expenditures that affect the unit and round to the nearest full year.

7. The amortization under paragraph 5 shall be calculated using the interest rate determined under section 20.

8. The percentage rent increase that is justified for the unit by capital expenditures is determined by dividing the amortized amount determined under paragraph 5 by the monthly rent for the unit, and multiplying the result by 100.

27. Useful life of work or thing — (1) The useful life of work done or a thing purchased shall be determined from the Schedule subject to the following rules:

1. Where the useful life set out in Column 2 of the Schedule is less than 10 years, the useful life of work done or a thing purchased shall be deemed to be 10 years.

2. If, when a thing is purchased, it has previously been used, the useful life of the thing shall be determined taking into account the length of time of that previous use.

3. If the work done or thing purchased does not appear in the Schedule, the useful life of the work or thing shall be determined with reference to items with similar characteristics that do appear in the Schedule.

4. Despite paragraphs 2 and 3, for the purposes of making a finding under this section, the useful life of work done or a thing purchased shall not be determined to be less than 10 years.

(2) If the useful life of work done or a thing purchased cannot be determined under subsection (1) because the work or thing does not appear in the Schedule and no item with similar characteristics appears in the Schedule, the useful life of the work or thing shall be what is generally accepted as the useful life of such work or thing but in no case shall the useful life be determined to be less than 10 years.

28. Municipal taxes or charges and utilities, extraordinary increase — (1) An increase in the cost of municipal taxes and charges or utilities is extraordinary if it is greater than the guideline plus 50 per cent of the guideline.

(2) For the purposes of subsection (1), the guideline is the guideline for the calendar year in which the effective date of the first intended rent increase referred to in the application falls.

(3) Despite subsection (1), if the guideline is less than zero, any increase in the cost of municipal taxes and charges or utilities is deemed to be extraordinary.

29. Rules — (1) The rules set out in this section apply to the Board in making findings related to extraordinary increases in the cost for municipal taxes and charges or utilities or both.

(2) Subject to subsection (4), the amount of the allowance for an extraordinary increase in the cost for municipal taxes and charges is calculated as follows:

1. Adjust the reference year costs for municipal taxes and charges by the guideline plus 50 per cent of the guideline determined in accordance with subsection 28(2).

2. If municipal taxes and charges for a tax year are increased as a result of an appeal of a tax assessment, add to the base year costs for municipal taxes and charges the amount of the increase resulting from the appeal.

3. If a tax notice respecting the reference year municipal taxes and charges is issued on or after November 1 in the base year, add to the base year costs for municipal taxes and charges the amount, if any, by which the reference year municipal taxes and charges exceed the municipal taxes and charges for the year preceding the reference year.

4. If a tax notice respecting the reference year municipal taxes and charges is issued on or after November 1 in the base year and if the reference year municipal taxes and charges are increased as a result of an appeal of a tax assessment, the amount of the increase resulting from the appeal,

   i. shall be included in determining the amount by which the reference year municipal taxes and charges exceed the municipal taxes and charges for the year preceding the reference year for the purpose of paragraph 3, and

   ii. shall not be added under paragraph 2.

5. Subtract the reference year costs for municipal taxes and charges, as adjusted under paragraph 1, from the base year costs for municipal taxes and charges, as adjusted under paragraphs 2, 3 and 4.

6. Multiply the amount determined in paragraph 5 by the factor determined under section 21.

(3) The amount of the allowance for an extraordinary increase in the cost for utilities shall be calculated as follows:

1. Adjust the reference year costs for each of heat, electricity and water by the guideline plus 50 per cent of the guideline determined in accordance with subsection 28(2).

2. Subtract the amount determined in paragraph 1 for heat from the base year costs for heat and do the same for electricity and water.

3. Multiply the amount determined in paragraph 2 for heat by the factor for heat determined under section 21 and do the same for electricity and water.

4. Add together the amounts determined under paragraph 3.

(4) The amount of the adjusted base year utility costs shall be calculated as follows:

1. Multiply the reference year costs for each of heat, electricity and water by 50 per cent of the guideline determined in accordance with subsection 28(2).

2. Subtract the amount determined under paragraph 1 for heat from the base year costs for heat and do the same for electricity and water.

3. Add together the amounts determined under paragraph 2.

(5) Despite section 28, if the guideline is less than zero per cent, for the purposes of the calculations in subsections (2), (3) and (4) the guideline is deemed to be zero per cent.

(6) An increase in municipal taxes and charges as a result of an appeal of a tax assessment shall not be considered under subsection (2) if the application for the rent increase was filed more than 12 months after the decision on the appeal was issued.

30. Operating costs related to security services — (1) This section applies to the Board when making findings respecting operating costs related to security services.

(2) The amount of the allowance for operating costs related to security shall be calculated as follows:

1. Subtract the operating costs for security services in the reference year from the operating costs for security services in the base year.

2. Multiply the amount determined under paragraph 1 by the factor determined under section 21.

(3) The Board shall exclude from the calculation under subsection (2) any operating costs for security services that are no longer being provided to the tenant at the time the application is heard.

31. Calculation of percentage rent increase — The percentage rent increase above the guideline for each rental unit that is the subject of the application shall be calculated in the following manner:

1. Divide the amount of each allowance determined under subsection 29(2), subsection 29(3) and section 30 by the total rents for the rental units that are subject to the application and are affected by the operating cost.

2. If the Board is of the opinion that the amount determined under paragraph 1 for an allowance does not reasonably reflect how the rental units that are subject to the application are affected by the operating cost to which the allowance relates,

   i. paragraph 1 does not apply in respect of the allowance, and

   ii. the Board shall determine an amount by another method that, in the opinion of the Board, better reflects how the rental units that are subject to the application are affected by the operating cost to which the allowance relates.

3. Determine the percentage that each allowance referred to in paragraph 1 represents of the total rents for the rental units that are subject to the application and are affected by the operating cost by multiplying each of the amounts determined under paragraph 1 or 2, as the case may be, by 100.

4. Subject to paragraph 5, add together the percentages determined under paragraph 3 for each allowance referred to in paragraph 1 that relates to an operating cost that affects the rental unit.

5. In performing the addition required by paragraph 4, do not include the percentage determined under paragraph 3 for the allowance determined under subsection 29(3) if that percentage is less than 0.50.

6. Add the percentage determined under paragraph 4 and the percentage determined under paragraph 8 of subsection 26(6).

32. When rent increase may be taken — (1) Subject to section 33 of this Regulation, if the Board orders a rent increase for a rental unit under subsection 126(10) of the Act, that rent increase may only be taken within 12 months of the first intended rent increase referred to in the application for a rental unit in the residential complex.

(2) Subject to section 33 of this Regulation, the rent increases provided for under subsection 126(11) of the Act may only be taken during the subsequent 12-month periods which begin and end on the same days of the year as the 12-month period referred to in subsection (1).

(3) Despite subsection (1), if the unit is subject to clause 126(13)(b) of the Act, the rent charged for the rental unit shall not be increased before the date specified by the Board under clause 126(13)(b) of the Act, and the increase may only be taken within 12 months after that date.

(4) Despite subsection (2), if the unit is subject to clause 126(13)(b) of the Act, the rent increases provided for under subsection 126(11) of the Act may only be taken during the subsequent 12-month periods which begin and end on the same days of the year as the 12-month period referred to in subsection (3).

33. When rent increase may be taken — (1) If an order with respect to a rental unit that increases the lawful rent is made under section 126 of the Act with respect to capital expenditures or operating costs for security services before the time for taking any rent increases under one or more previous orders has expired, the landlord may annually increase the lawful rent being charged by no more than the guideline rent increase plus 3 per cent of the previous lawful rent, until such time as no rent increase with respect to capital expenditures or operating costs related to security services ordered under section 126 of the Act remains to be taken.

(2) If a landlord fails to take a rent increase in accordance with subsection (1) in any 12-month period in which the landlord was entitled to take such a rent increase, the landlord may not take that rent increase in any subsequent time period.

(3) If a landlord takes a rent increase in accordance with subsection (1) that is less than the amount the landlord was entitled to take, the landlord may not take the amount of the rent increase which the landlord failed to take in any subsequent time period.

(4) This section does not prevent a landlord from increasing the rent charged by more than 3 per cent of the previous lawful rent charged with respect to an extraordinary increase in the cost for municipal taxes and charges or utilities or both in accordance with an order under subsection 126(10) of the Act.

34. Sequence—components of the increase — For the purpose of making determinations under section 36 and subsection 38(2) of this Regulation, the following rules apply if a landlord was permitted to increase the rent pursuant to an order under subsection 126(10) of the Act based on more than one of the grounds in subsection 126(1) of the Act but the increase taken by the landlord was less than the maximum increase permitted by the order:

1. The increase taken by the landlord shall be deemed to have been taken for municipal taxes and charges, up to the percentage set out in the order for municipal taxes and charges.

2. If the increase taken by the landlord was greater than the percentage set out in the order for municipal taxes and charges, the balance of the increase shall be deemed to have been taken for eligible capital expenditures, up to the percentage set out in the order for eligible capital expenditures.

3. If the increase taken by the landlord was greater than the sum of the percentages set out in the order for municipal taxes and charges and for eligible capital expenditures, the balance of the increase shall be deemed to have been taken for utilities, up to the percentage set out in the order for utilities.

4. If the increase taken by the landlord was greater than the sum of the percentages set out in the order for municipal taxes and charges, for eligible capital expenditures and for utilities, the balance of the increase shall be deemed to have been taken for operating costs related to security services.

PART IV — REDUCTIONS IN RENT—UTILITIES AND CAPITAL EXPENDITURES

35. Utilities — (1) If the Board has issued an order under subsection 126(10) of the Act permitting an increase in rent that is due in whole or in part to an extraordinary increase in the cost of utilities, and the landlord has taken the increase in whole or in part, the landlord shall provide, in a form approved by the Board, information to a tenant who was subject to the order and continues to reside in the unit to which the order applied in accordance with the rules set out in this section.

(2) The information shall be provided on or before the anniversary of the first effective date of the rent increase set out in the order each year for five years following the first effective date.

(3) The information shall include,

(a) the total amount of the adjusted base year utility costs for the residential complex or building as set out in the order;

(b) the current utility costs;

(c) if the amount in clause (b) is less than the amount in clause (a), the determinations made under section 36; and

(d) if applicable, the percentage and dollar amount of the rent reduction and the date it takes effect.

(4) Subsection (1) ceases to apply to a tenant if the landlord has provided the tenant with rent reductions under subsection 128(3) of the Act and the total amount of those reductions is equal to the lesser of the following amounts:

1. The amount of the increase permitted under subsection 126(10) of the Act that is set out in the order as related to utilities.

2. The amount of the increase taken for utilities, as determined under section 34.

(5) Upon the request of a tenant who was subject to the order, the landlord shall provide a compact disc containing all utility bills used to justify current utility costs in portable document format.

(6) The landlord is only required to provide the information requested under subsection (5) upon a request made by the tenant within two years from the date the information under this section was given.

(7) The information referred to in subsection (5) shall be provided for a charge of not more than five dollars.

(8) Instead of providing the compact disc referred to in subsection (5), the landlord and the tenant may agree that the landlord will provide the tenant with,

(a) a photocopy of the information required under subsection (5), for no more than the landlord's reasonable out-of-pocket costs for the photocopying; or

(b) an e-mail of the information required under subsection (5) in portable document format at no charge to the tenant.

(9) A landlord does not have to provide a compact disc under subsection (5) if,

(a) the residential complex to which the application relates contains six or fewer residential units and the residential complex is located in a rural or remote area;

(b) the landlord cannot reasonably provide the compact disc; and

(c) that landlord provides the tenant with a photocopy of the information required under subsection (5), for a charge of not more than five dollars.

(10) In this section and section 36,

"current utility costs" means,

(a) the costs covering the most recent of the subsequent 12-month periods which begin and end on the same days of the year as the base year used in the previous order, multiplied, where applicable, by the allocation factor determined under subsection 24(2) or (3) and set out in the order, or

(b) the amount determined in accordance with subsection (11), if,

(i) the landlord no longer provides one or more utilities to the residential complex or to other parts of a larger project that the residential complex forms part of, and

(ii) an allocation factor was determined under section 24(2) or (3) and set out in the order.

(11) The amount referred to in clause (b) of the definition of "current utility costs" in subsection (10) shall be determined in accordance with the following rules:

1. If the landlord no longer provides one or more utilities to all or part of the non-residential portions of the project,

i. multiply the total base year utility costs for the project as set out in the order by the percentage that was set out in the order for each utility that the landlord no longer provides to all or part of the non-residential portions of the project,

ii. subtract the allocation factor determined under subsection 24(2) or (3) and set out in the order from 1, and

iii. for each utility that the landlord no longer provides to all or part of the non-residential portions of the project, multiply the amount determined under subparagraph i by the amount determined under subparagraph ii.

2. If the landlord no longer provides one or more utilities to part of the non-residential portions of the project, the landlord shall, for each of those utilities, modify the amount determined under subparagraph 1 iii to reflect the proportion of the non-residential portion of the project to which he or

she still provides the utility, in a manner consistent with the original methodology used to apportion the costs under subsection 24(2) or (3), as described in the order.

3. If the landlord no longer provides one or more utilities to all or part of the residential portions of the project, for each of those utilities,

i. multiply the total base year utility costs for the project as set out in the order by the percentage that was set out in the order for the utility,

ii. multiply the amount determined in subparagraph i by the allocation factor determined in subsection 24(2) or (3) and set out in the order, and

iii. multiply the amount determined under subparagraph ii by the number of rental units for which the landlord no longer provides the utility divided by the total number of rental units for which the landlord provided the utility at the time the increase was ordered.

4. Add the following amounts:

i. The utility costs covering the most recent of the subsequent 12-month periods which begin and end on the same days of the year as the base year used in the previous order.

ii. The amounts determined under subparagraph 1 iii, if any, for utilities that the landlord no longer provides to all the non-residential portions of the project.

iii. The amounts determined under paragraph 2, if any, for utilities that the landlord no longer provides to part of the non-residential portions of the project.

iv. The amounts determined under subparagraph 3 iii, if any, for utilities that the landlord no longer provides to all or part of the residential portions of the project.

5. Multiply the amount determined under paragraph 4 by the allocation factor determined in subsection 24(2) or (3) and set out in the order.

6. Subtract from the amount determined under paragraph 5 the sum of the amounts determined under subparagraph 3 iii, if any, for utilities that the landlord no longer provides to all or part of the residential portions of the project.

36. Rent reductions under s. 128(3) of the Act — (1) The following rules apply in determining the amounts of rent reductions under subsection 128(3) of the Act:

1. Subtract the current utility costs from the adjusted base year utility costs as set out in the order.

2. If the amount determined in paragraph 1 is zero or less, no rent reduction is required.

3. If the amount determined in paragraph 1 is greater than zero,

i. divide the amount determined in paragraph 1 by the allowance that justified the increase that was set out in the order, and

ii. multiply the amount from subparagraph i by the percentage increase in rent for utilities that was set out in the order.

4. Despite paragraph 1, if a reduction in utility costs was previously determined in accordance with this subsection, the determination in paragraph 1 shall be made by subtracting the current utility costs from the utility costs used to justify the previous rent reduction.

(2) Despite subsection (1), the following rules apply in determining the amounts of rent reductions under subsection 128(3) of the Act if, in accordance with the Act or an agreement between the landlord and the affected tenants, the landlord ceases to provide one or more utilities to one or more rental units in the residential complex:

1. Subject to paragraphs 5 and 6, multiply the adjusted base year utility costs by the percentage that was set out in the order for each utility.

2. Subject to paragraph 6, multiply the allowance that justified the increase that was set out in the order by the percentage that was set out in the order for each utility.

3. The following rules apply to a rental unit to which the landlord has not ceased to provide any utilities:

i. Calculate the sum of the amounts determined under paragraph 1.

ii. If the amounts of one or more previous rent reductions were determined under this paragraph for the rental unit, subtract from the amount determined under subparagraph i the sum of all determinations previously made under subparagraph iii for the rental unit.

iii. Subtract the current utility costs from the amount determined under subparagraph i or, if subparagraph ii applies, from the amount determined under subparagraph ii.

iv. Calculate the sum of the amounts determined under paragraph 2.

v. If the amount determined under subparagraph iii is zero or less, no rent reduction is required.

vi. If the amount determined under subparagraph iii is greater than zero, the amount of the rent reduction under subsection 128(3) of the Act shall be determined in accordance with the following rules:

A. Divide the amount determined under subparagraph iii by the amount determined under subparagraph iv.

B. Multiply the amount determined under sub-subparagraph A by the percentage increase in rent for utilities that was set out in the order.

4. The following rules apply to a rental unit to which the landlord has ceased to provide one or more utilities:

i. Calculate the sum of the amounts determined under paragraph 1 for the utilities that the landlord still provides to the rental unit.

ii. If the amounts of one or more previous rent reductions were determined under this paragraph for the rental unit, subtract from the amount determined under subparagraph i the sum of all determinations previously made under subparagraph iv.

iii. If the amounts of one or more previous rent reductions were determined under paragraph 3 for the rental unit, subtract the amount determined in accordance with the following rules from the amount determined under subparagraph i or, if subparagraph ii applies, from the amount determined under subparagraph ii:

A. Calculate the sum of all amounts previously determined under subparagraph 3 iii for the rental unit.

B. Calculate the sum of the percentages that were set out in the order for the utilities that the landlord has not ceased to provide to the rental unit.

C. Multiply the amount determined under sub-subparagraph A by the percentage determined under sub-subparagraph B.

iv. Subtract the portion of the costs in the current utility costs attributable to the utilities no longer provided to the rental unit by the landlord from the current utility costs.

v. Subtract the amount determined under subparagraph iv from,

A. the amount determined under subparagraph i, if neither subparagraph ii nor subparagraph iii applies,

B. the amount determined under subparagraph ii, if subparagraph ii applies and subparagraph iii does not apply, or

C. the amount determined under subparagraph iii, if subparagraph iii applies.

vi. Calculate the sum of the amounts determined under paragraph 2 for the utilities that the landlord still provides to the rental unit.

vii. For each utility set out in the order that is still provided to the rental unit by the landlord, multiply the percentage that was set out in the order for the utility by the percentage increase in rent for utilities that was set out in the order.

viii. If the amount determined under subparagraph v is zero or less, no rent reduction is required.

ix. If the amount determined under subparagraph v is greater than zero, the amount of the rent reduction under subsection 128(3) of the Act shall be determined in accordance with the following rules:

A. Divide the amount determined under subparagraph v by the amount determined under subparagraph vi.

B. Multiply the amount determined under sub-subparagraph A by the sum of the percentages determined under subparagraph vii.

x. Despite subparagraph ix, if the amount determined under subparagraph v is greater than zero and the sum of the percentages of any previous rent reductions arising from the same order is less than the sum of the percentages determined under subparagraph vii, the amount of the rent reduction under subsection 128(3) of the Act shall be determined by subtracting from the amount determined under sub-subparagraph ix B the sum of the percentages of the previous rent reductions arising from the same order.

xi. Despite subparagraph ix, no rent reduction is required if the amount determined under subparagraph v is greater than zero and the sum of the percentages of any previous rent reductions arising from the same order is equal to or greater than the sum of the percentages determined under subparagraph vii.

5. If one or more rent reductions were previously determined in accordance with subsection (1), the reference in paragraph 1 to the adjusted base year utility costs shall be deemed to be a reference to the current utility costs used to determine the most recent of the previous rent reductions in accordance with subsection (1).

6. If a utility is no longer provided by the landlord to one or more rental units, the references in paragraphs 1 and 2 to the percentage that was set out in the order for that utility shall be deemed to be a reference to the percentage that was set out in the order for that utility multiplied by the number of rental units to which the landlord still provides the utility divided by the number of rental units to which the landlord provided the utility at the time of the application.

(3) Despite subsections (1) and (2), if the amount of a rent reduction determined under those subsections, expressed as a percentage of the current rent, is less than 0.50, no rent reduction is required.

(4) Despite subsections (1) and (2), if the amount of a rent reduction determined under those subsections, expressed as a percentage of the current rent, is 0.50 or more, the rent reduction shall be reduced, if necessary, so that the sum of the rent reduction and any previous rent reductions arising from the same order does not exceed the lesser of the following amounts:

1. The amount of the increase permitted under subsection 126(10) of the Act that is set out in the order as related to utilities.

2. The amount of the increase taken for utilities, as determined under section 34 of this Regulation.

(5) A rent reduction determined under this section takes effect on the first anniversary, on or after the latest date for providing information under subsection 35(2), of the date the increase permitted by the order was taken.

(6) If the date that a rent reduction takes effect under subsection (5) is the same as the date on which a rent increase takes effect, the rent reduction shall be deemed to take effect immediately before the rent increase.

37. Prescribed percentage, period — (1) The prescribed percentage for the purposes of subsection 128(3) of the Act is the percentage decrease in utility costs that results in a percentage decrease in rent of 0.50 per cent or more as determined under subsections 36(1) and (2) of this Regulation.

(2) The prescribed period for the purposes of subsection 128(3) of the Act is the most recent 12-month period which begins and ends on the same days of the year as the base year used in the previous order.

38. Rules for prescribing a date for the purpose of s. 129 of the Act — (1) The rules for determining a date for the purpose of clause 129(c) of the Act are as follows:

1. If the unit is subject to an order issued under subsection 126(10) of the Act and subsection 126(13) of the Act does not apply, the date shall be the day immediately before the anniversary, in the year determined by adding the weighted useful life as determined under paragraph 6 of subsection 26(6) of this Regulation to the year in which the landlord took the increase, of the date the landlord took the increase.

2. Despite paragraph 1, if a landlord was entitled to take an increase under clause 126(10)(b) of the Act but only took an increase or increases under clause 126(11)(b) of the Act, the date shall be the day immediately before the anniversary, in the year determined by adding the weighted useful life as determined under paragraph 6 of subsection 26(6) of this Regulation to the year that contains the first effective date set out in the order, of the first effective date set out in the order.

3. If the unit is subject to an order issued under subsection 126(10) of the Act, and was subject to subsection 126(13) of the Act, the date shall be the day immediately before the anniversary, in the year determined by adding the weighted useful life as determined under paragraph 6 of subsection 26(6) of this Regulation to the year that contains the first effective date set out in the order, of the first effective date set out in the order.

(2) The rules to determine the percentage for the purpose of subclause 129(c)(ii) of the Act are as follows:

1. If an order was issued by the Board under subsection 126(10) of the Act permitting an increase in rent that is due in whole to eligible capital expen-

ditures, the percentage reduction shall be equal to the percentage increase taken by the landlord.

2. If an order was issued by the Board under subsection 126(10) of the Act permitting an increase in rent that is due only in part to eligible capital expenditures, the percentage reduction shall be the percentage for eligible capital expenditures as determined under section 34 of this Regulation.

Part V — Reductions in Rent—Services and Taxes

39. Rules relating to reduction in services — (1) The rules set out in this section apply in respect of making findings relating to a reduction of the rent charged under section 130 of the Act based on a discontinuance or reduction in services or facilities.

(2) If a service or facility is discontinued and the discontinuance was reasonable in the circumstances, the rent shall be reduced by an amount that is equal to what would be a reasonable charge for the service or facility based on the cost of the service or facility to the landlord or, if the cost cannot be determined or if there is no cost, on the value of the service or facility, including the cost to the tenant or former tenant of replacing the discontinued service or facility.

(3) If a service or facility is discontinued and the discontinuance was not reasonable in the circumstances, the rent shall be reduced by an amount that takes into account the following matters:

1. The value of the service or facility, including the cost to the tenant or former tenant of replacing the discontinued service or facility.

2. The effect of the discontinuance on the tenant or former tenant.

(4) The amount of the rent reduction determined under subsection (3) shall not be less than the amount of the reduction that would have been required under subsection (2) had the discontinuance been reasonable.

(5) Despite subsections (2), (3) and (4), if a service or facility was previously provided to the tenant or former tenant under an agreement under section 123 of the Act, section 132 of the *Tenant Protection Act, 1997*, section 46 of the *Rent Control Act, 1992* or subsection 96(4) of the *Residential Rent Regulation Act*, the reduction in rent on discontinuing the service or facility shall be equal to,

(a) the most recent amount of the separate charge for the service or facility; or

(b) where there is no separate charge, the increase in rent that the landlord took when the service or facility was first provided, adjusted by the percentage increase in rent being charged for the rental unit from the date the service or facility was first provided to the date the landlord discontinued the service or facility.

(6) If a service or facility is reduced, the amount of the reduction of rent shall be a reasonable proportion, based on the degree of the reduction of the service or facility, of the amount of the reduction in rent that would have been determined under subsections (2) to (5) had the service or facility been discontinued.

(7) If the discontinuance or reduction is temporary and its duration is reasonable, taking into account the effect on the tenant or former tenant, there shall be no reduction of rent.

40. Application of ss. 24 and 25 — Sections 24 and 25 of this Regulation apply with necessary modifications to an application to the Board by a tenant under section 130 or 133 of the Act.

41. Reduction of municipal taxes — (1) For the purpose of subsection 131(1) of the Act, the prescribed percentage is 2.49 per cent.

(2) For the purpose of section 131 of the Act,

"municipal property tax" means taxes charged to a landlord by a municipality and includes taxes levied on a landlord's property in unorganized territory and taxes levied under Division B of Part IX of the *Education Act*, but does not include,

(a) charges for inspections done by a municipality on a residential complex related to an alleged breach of a health, safety, housing or maintenance standard,

(b) charges for emergency repairs carried out by a municipality on a residential complex,

(c) charges for work in the nature of a capital expenditure carried out by a municipality,

(d) charges for work, services or non-emergency repairs performed by a municipality in relation to a landlord's non-compliance with a by-law,

(e) penalties, interest, late payment fees or fines,

(f) any amount spent by a municipality under subsection 219(1) of the Act or any administrative fee applied to that amount under subsection 219(2) of the Act, or

(g) any other charges levied by the municipality.

(3) If the lawful rent for the rental units in a residential complex is to be reduced under subsection 131(1) of the Act, the reduction in rent shall be determined as follows:

1. Determine the percentage by which the municipal property tax for the residential complex in the year has been reduced from the municipal property tax for the residential complex in the previous year.

2. Determine the percentage by which the rent is to be reduced by multiplying the percentage determined under paragraph 1 by 20 per cent for properties that fall under the multi-residential property class as defined in section 4 of Ontario Regulation 282/98 (*General*) made under the *Assessment Act*, and 15 per cent otherwise.

(4) The prescribed date for the purposes of subsection 131(2) of the Act is December 31 of any year in which the municipal property tax reduction takes effect.

(5) The prescribed number of rental units for the purpose of subsection 131(3) of the Act is seven.

(6) The period within which notification of a rent reduction must be given for the purpose of subsection 131(3) of the Act is,

(a) between June 1 and September 15 for landlords; and

(b) between October 1 and December 15 for tenants.

(7) When the notice under subsection 131(3) of the Act is served on the landlord, it shall be addressed to the landlord or to the owner of the property for tax purposes and when it is served on the tenants, the notice for each tenant shall be addressed to the tenant or occupant of the tenant's rental unit.

(8) The notice under subsection 131(3) of the Act shall be served,

(a) by handing it to the person;

(b) if the person is a landlord, by handing it to an employee of the landlord exercising authority in respect of the residential complex to which the notice relates;

(c) if the person is a tenant, by handing it to an apparently adult person in the rental unit;

(d) by leaving it in the mail box where mail is ordinarily delivered to the person;

(e) if there is no mail box, by leaving it at the place where mail is ordinarily delivered to the person; or

(f) by sending it by mail, by courier or by facsimile to the last known address where the person resides or carries on business.

42. Application for variance — (1) For the purpose of subsection 132(1) of the Act, a person may apply to the Board for an order varying the rent reduction determined under section 131 of the Act if,

(a) other charges that are in addition to the municipal property tax and that are not set out in clauses (a), (b), (c), (d), (e) and (f) of the definition of "municipal property tax" in subsection 41(2) were levied upon the landlord by the municipality in the base year;

(b) the percentage of the rent charged in the residential complex that the municipal property tax comprises is not 20 per cent for properties that fall under the multi-residential property class as defined in section 4 of Ontario Regulation 282/98 (*General*) made under the *Assessment Act*, and 15 per cent otherwise;

(c) there is an error in the notice of rent reduction with respect to the amount by which the municipal property tax is reduced or the amount by which the rent is to be reduced; or

(d) the municipal property tax is increased or decreased during the period from the day the notice of rent reduction was issued to March 31 of the year following the date the rent reduction takes effect.

(2) An application referred to in subsection (1) shall be made,

(a) if a notice of the rent reduction is required to be given under subsection 131(3) of the Act, on or before the later of,

(i) 90 days following the day on which the person who will be the applicant is given the notice of rent reduction, and

(ii) March 31 in the year following the year in which the rent reduction takes effect;

(b) if a notice of the rent reduction is not required to be given under subsection 131(3) of the Act, on or before the later of,

(i) 90 days following the day on which the tax notice effecting the reduction in the municipal property tax and forming the basis of the rent reduction is issued, and

(ii) March 31 in the year following the year in which the rent reduction takes effect.

43. Determination by Board — (1) **Definitions** — In this section,

"base year" means the calendar year in which the rent reduction takes effect;

"reference year" means the calendar year immediately preceding the base year.

(2) The Board shall make a determination in respect of an application under clause 42(1)(a), (c) or (d) in the following manner:

1. Calculate the actual decrease, if any, in the municipal taxes and charges from the reference year to the base year.

2. Determine the percentage rent decrease for a rental unit that is subject to the application,

i. if the total of the annual rents is not proven by the landlord or the tenant, in accordance with paragraphs 1 and 2 of subsection 41(3), and

ii. otherwise, by dividing the amount determined under paragraph 1 by the total of the annual rents for all of the rental units in the residential complex and multiplying that quotient by 100.

(3) The Board shall make a determination in respect of an application under clause 42(1)(b) in the following manner:

1. Calculate the actual decrease, if any, in the municipal taxes and charges from the reference year to the base year.

2. Determine the percentage rent decrease for a rental unit that is subject to the application by dividing the amount determined under paragraph 1 by the total of the annual rents for all of the rental units in the residential complex and multiplying that quotient by 100.

44. Information to be filed with application — The following shall be filed with an application under section 132 of the Act:

1. Evidence of the amount of municipal taxes in the reference year and in the base year.

2. If the application is made under clause 42(1)(a), evidence of the other charges levied by the municipality in the reference year and in the base year.

3. If the application is made under clause 42(1)(b), evidence of the rents charged for the residential complex.

4. If notice of a reduction of rent has been given under subsection 131(3) of the Act, a copy of that notice.

45. Reduction in municipal taxes and charges — (1) **Definitions** — In this section,

"base year" means the last completed calendar year immediately preceding the day on which an application under section 133 of the Act is filed with the Board;

"reference year" means the calendar year immediately preceding the base year.

(2) For the purpose of this section, the adjusted costs for municipal taxes and charges for the base year shall be calculated in the following manner:

1. If municipal taxes and charges for a tax year are decreased as a result of an appeal of a tax assessment, subtract from the base year costs for municipal taxes and charges the amount of the decrease resulting from the appeal.

2. If a tax notice respecting the reference year municipal taxes and charges is issued on or after November 1 in the base year,

i. subtract from the base year costs for municipal taxes and charges the amount, if any, by which the municipal taxes and charges for the year preceding the reference year exceed the reference year municipal taxes and charges, and

ii. if the reference year municipal taxes and charges are decreased as a result of an appeal of a tax assessment, the amount of the decrease resulting from the appeal shall be taken into account in determining the amount by which the municipal taxes and charges for the year preceding the reference year exceed the reference year municipal taxes and charges for the purpose of subparagraph i, and shall not be subtracted under paragraph 1.

3. A decrease in municipal taxes and charges as a result of an appeal of a tax assessment shall not be considered under paragraph 1 or 2 if,

i. the decrease is for a tax year before 1996, or

ii. the application for the rent reduction was filed more than 12 months after the decision on the appeal was issued.

(3) The following are prescribed as the rules for making findings on an application for a reduction in rent due to a reduction in the municipal taxes and charges for the residential complex:

1. If the reduction in municipal taxes and charges takes effect in the base year, the amount of the allowance is the amount by which the costs for the reference year exceed the costs for the base year.

2. Otherwise, the amount of the allowance is the amount by which the costs for the base year exceed the adjusted costs for the base year.

(4) The percentage rent decrease for a rental unit that is subject to an application under section 133 of the Act shall be calculated in the following manner:

1. Divide the amount of the allowance determined under subsection (3) by the total of the annual rents for the rental units in the residential complex.

2. Multiply the amount determined under paragraph 1 by 100.

(5) If the landlord or the tenant does not prove the total of the annual rents for the rental units in the residential complex, the percentage rent decrease shall be calculated in the following manner:

1. Divide the amount of the allowance determined under subsection (3) by the reference year costs.

2. Multiply the amount determined under paragraph 1 by 20 for properties that fall under the multi-residential property class as defined in section 4 of Ontario Regulation 282/98 (*General*) made under the *Assessment Act*, and 15 otherwise.

(6) A rent reduction order made under section 133 of the Act takes effect on the first day of the first rental period that commences on or after the date the application was filed with the Board.

PART VI — GENERAL

46. Hours for retrieval of property — For the purposes of subsection 41(3) of the Act, a landlord shall make an evicted tenant's property available between the hours of 8 a.m. and 8 p.m.

47. Contents of information package — The information package referred to in section 140 of the Act must contain the following information:

1. List of the different types of accommodation provided and the alternative packages of care services and meals available as part of the total charge.

2. Charges for the different types of accommodation and for the alternative packages of care services and meals.

3. Minimum staffing levels and qualifications of staff.

4. Details of the emergency response system, if any, or a statement that there is no emergency response system.

5. List and fee schedule of the additional services and meals available from the landlord on a user pay basis.

6. Internal procedures, if any, for dealing with complaints, including a statement as to whether tenants have any right of appeal from an initial decision, or a statement that there is no internal procedure for dealing with complaints.

48. Care homes — The prescribed period for the purposes of clause 144(1)(b) of the Act is four years.

49. Interpretation — For the purpose of clause 148(1)(a) of the Act, the expression "no longer requires the level of care provided by the landlord" includes circumstances where the tenant has repeatedly and substantially withdrawn from participation in some or all of the care services provided by the landlord that are set out in the tenancy agreement, and the tenant is not receiving substantially equivalent community based services.

50. Mobile homes — For the purpose of section 165 of the Act, the prescribed amount is the greater of,

(a) $50 per month; and

(b) the amount, including the guideline, that the landlord would have been entitled to take as a rent increase under an order under subsection 126(10) of the Act before the first anniversary of the commencement of the new tenancy had the former tenant remained the tenant.

51. Interpretation — For the purpose of section 167 of the Act, the definition of **"infrastructure work"** includes work with respect to fire hydrants and related systems, poles for telephone service, walkways, garbage storage and disposal areas, fencing, retaining walls and flood control systems.

PART VII — BOARD — ADMINISTRATION AND POWERS

52. Employees — Employees of the Board shall be appointed under the *Public Service Act*.

53. Information to accompany application — An application to the Board must be accompanied by the following information:

1. If the application is with respect to a notice of termination on any ground, a copy of the notice of termination and a certificate of service of the notice of termination, if notice was given by the landlord.

2. If the application is with respect to a notice of termination for demolition, conversion repair or severance, in addition to the information required by paragraph 1, evidence, where required, that the landlord paid the necessary compensation required under section 52, 54 or 55 of the Act or found acceptable alternative accommodation for the tenant.

3. If the application is with respect to a notice of termination due to a second contravention in six months, in addition to the information required by paragraph 1, a copy of the original notice of termination and a copy of the certificate of service of the original notice of termination.

4. If the application is made under section 77 of the Act with respect to an agreement to terminate the tenancy, a copy of the agreement.

5. If the application is with respect to a review of a work order under section 226 of the Act, a copy of the work order.

54. Board notice — (1) The following information shall be included in the notice set out in subsection 189(1) of the Act:

1. The Board's file number for the application.

2. Where scheduled, the date of the hearing.

3. Contact information for the Board.

(2) An application filed under section 77 or 78 of the Act is prescribed for the purposes of subsection 189(2) of the Act.

55. Service of notice — Where an application is scheduled to be heard within seven days of the application being filed, the Board shall send the notice referred to in section 189 of the Act to the respondent by courier service or, where courier service to the rental unit is not available, the Board shall attempt to contact the respondent by telephone and send the notice by mail.

56. Restriction on altering time requirements — The following are time requirements that the Board may not extend or shorten under subsection 190(2) of the Act:

1. All time requirements related to notice requirements for terminating tenancies.

2. All deadlines for filing applications, other than those which the Board is expressly permitted to extend or shorten under subsection 190(1) of the Act.

3. The 24-hour notice required under subsection 27(1) of the Act.

4. The 72-hour period referred to in subsection 41(2) of the Act.

5. The six-month periods referred to in subsections 42(7), 92(3) and (4) and 162(4) and (5) of the Act.

6. The 30-day period referred to in subsection 46(1) of the Act.

7. The period described in subsection 77(5) of the Act during which an eviction order is not effective.

8. The period described in subsection 80(1) of the Act, subject to subsection 80(2) of the Act, during which an eviction order is not effective.

9. The 30-day period referred to in subsection 91(1) of the Act.

10. The seven-day period referred to in clause 95(4)(d) of the Act.

11. The 60-day period referred to in subsection 104(3) of the Act.

12. The 90-day notice period required by sections 116 and 150 of the Act.

13. The 12-month period referred to in subsection 119(1) of the Act.

14. The five-day period in which an agreement to increase the rent charged may be cancelled under subsection 121(4) of the Act.

15. The six-day period referred to in subsection 121(5) of the Act.

16. The one-year period after which rent and rent increases shall be deemed to be lawful under subsections 136(1) and (2) of the Act.

17. The five-day period in which a tenancy agreement may be cancelled, as described in section 141 of the Act.

18. The 10-day period referred to in subsection 145(2) of the Act.

19. The 30-day period referred to in subsection 206(6) of the Act.

20. The 60-day period referred to in paragraph 2 of subsection 3(3) of this Regulation.

21. The 45-day periods referred to in paragraphs 4 and 5 of subsection 3(3) of this Regulation.

57. Financial matters — (1) The Board may establish bank accounts in the name of the Board into which it may place money paid to the Board.

(2) The Board may invest money paid to the Board in investments in which the Minister of Finance may invest public money under section 3 of the *Financial Administration Act*.

(3) The Board may employ a trust corporation to make the investments or to act as a custodian of the securities purchased as investments.

(4) Money paid into the Board shall bear interest at the rate of 0.25 per cent per year, compounded semi-annually.

58. Prescribed amount — The amount prescribed for the purpose of subsection 207(4) of the Act is five dollars.

59. Filings in electronic format — (1) If the Board permits an application to be filed in an electronic format by electronic means, **"sign"** for the purposes of subsections 185(1) and (2) and 186(2) of the Act means to type one's name on the application, and **"signed"** and **"signs"** have a corresponding meaning.

(2) If the Board permits an application to be filed in an electronic format by electronic means, "shall be accompanied by the prescribed information" in subsection 185(1) of the Act shall be interpreted as requiring the mailing, faxing or delivery of the prescribed information such that it is received by the Board, or is deemed under the Act to have been given to the Board, within five days following the day on which the application was filed electronically with the Board.

60. Contingency fees — For the purpose of section 214 of the Act, the allowed amount of a contingency fee charged by an agent of a landlord or tenant is 10 per cent of the amount that has been or may be recovered, gained or saved, in whole or in part, over a one-year period through the efforts of the agent.

Part VIII — Other Matters

61. Transition — Section 32 of this Regulation applies with necessary modifications to an application to which subsection 242(7) of the Act applies despite any regulation made under the *Tenant Protection Act, 1997*.

62. Revocation — Ontario Regulation 194/98 is revoked.

63. Commencement — This Regulation comes into force on January 31, 2007.

Schedule [1]

Useful Life of Work Done or Thing Purchased

The number in square brackets has been editorially added by Carswell.

Column 1		**Column 2**
Work done or thing purchased		**Useful life in years**
Sitework		
1.	Fences	
	i. Concrete	20
	ii. Steel, Chain Link	15
	iii. Metal, Wrought Iron	25
	iv. Wood	15
2.	Landscaping	
	i. Dead Tree Removal	20
	ii. New Trees	20
	iii. Shrub Replacement	15
	iv. Sodding	10

Column 1		Column 2
Work done or thing purchased		**Useful life in years**
3.	Parking Lot, Driveways and Walkways	
	i. Asphalt	15
	ii. Concrete	15
	iii. Gravel	10
	iv. Interlocking Brick	20
	v. Repairs	5
Concrete		
1.	Curbs and Patio Slabs	15
2.	Foundation Walls	20
3.	Garage Concrete Floor (Slab) and Rebar Repairs	10
4.	Retaining Walls	25
5.	Stairs and porches	10
6.	Balcony Slabs	10
Masonry		
1.	Chimney	
	i. Masonry (Brick, Block)	20
	ii. Metalbestos Type	15
	iii. Repairs, Masonry	15
2.	Masonry	
	i. Repairs, Tuck Pointing	15
	ii. Replacement	20
3.	Sandblasting	25
Metals		
1.	Balcony Railings, Steel	15
Wood and plastics		
1.	Balcony Railings, Wood	10
2.	Decks and Porches	20
3.	Retaining Walls, Wood	15
Thermal and Moisture Protection		
1.	Caulking	10
2.	Eavestrough and Downpipes	
	i. Aluminium, Plastic	15
	ii. Galvanized	20
3.	Garage Conc. Floor, Waterproofing	

Column 1		**Column 2**
Work done or thing purchased		**Useful life in years**
	i. Membrane	15
	ii. Sealer	5
4.	Insulation	20
5.	Metal Flashing	
	i. Aluminium	25
	ii. Galvanized, Painted	15
	iii. Steel, Prefinished	10
6.	Roof	
	i. Cedar Shakes	25
	ii. Clay Tiles	25
	iii. Built Up	15
	iv. Inverted four-ply	20
	v. Metal Panels	25
	vi. Sarnafil	25
	vii. Single ply	20
	viii. Slate	25
	ix. Sloped (Asphalt Shingles)	15
	x. Repairs	5
7.	Siding	
	i. Asphalt Shingles	15
	ii. Cedar	25
	iii. Cedar Shakes	25
	iv. Insulated Panel, Aluminium	25
	v. Steel	25
	vi. Masonite	20
	vii. Plywood	10
	viii. Stucco	20
8.	Soffits and Fascia	
	i. Aluminium	25
	ii. Gypsum	15
	iii. Plywood	20
	iv. Pre-finished Steel	25
	v. Vinyl	25
	vi. Wood	15

Column 1		Column 2
Work done or thing purchased		**Useful life in years**
9.	Waterproofing, Above Ground	15
Doors and Windows		
1.	Aluminium Storm Doors and Windows	15
2.	Doors	
	i. Aluminium, Steel	20
	ii. Patio	20
	iii. Wood	20
3.	Garage Door and Operator	10
4.	Lock Replacement, Building	20
5.	Window Framing	
	i. Aluminium	20
	ii. Wood	15
Finishes		
1.	Carpets	
	i. Common Areas	10
	ii. Ensuite	10
2.	Flooring	
	i. Asphalt	10
	ii. Ceramic Tile	10
	iii. Hardwood	20
	iv. Linoleum	10
	v. Marble	25
	vi. Parquet	20
	vii. Quarry Tile	10
	viii. Restaining	5
	ix. Rubber Tiles x. Sanding	20 5
	xi. Vinyl Tile	10
3.	Gypsum Board	
	i. Repairs	5
	ii. Replacement	20
4.	Marble Wall Panels	25
5.	Mirror Panels	10
6.	Painting	

Column 1		Column 2
Work done or thing purchased		**Useful life in years**
	i. Exterior: Walls, Trim, Balconies	5
	ii. Interior: Common Areas, Ensuite	10
7.	Panelling	20
8.	Suspended Ceilings	
	i. Fibre	15
	ii. Metal	25
9.	Wallcovering, Vinyl	10
Specialties		
1.	Bicycle Racks	10
2.	Building, Storage/Service	20
3.	Lockers	
	i. Recreational	15
	ii. Storage	15
4.	Mailboxes	15
5.	Playground Equipment (Swings, etc.)	10
6.	Satellite Dish	10
7.	Saunas	
	i. Heaters	10
	ii. Walls	15
8.	Steel Television Antennae	15
9.	Swimming Pool	
	i. Above Ground	10
	ii. Ceramic Tile	15
	iii. Concrete	20
	iv. Heater	10
	v. Painting	5
	vi. Pump, Filter	15
	vii. Vinyl	15
10.	Whirlpool, Jacuzzi	15
Equipment		
1.	Backhoe	10
2.	Dehumidifiers	10
3.	Floor Polishers	
	i. Commercial	15

Column 1		Column 2
Work done or thing purchased		**Useful life in years**
	ii. Domestic	5
4.	Front End Loader	10
5.	Garbage Bins, Boxes	10
6.	Garbage Compactors	15
7.	Garbage Disposers	5
8.	Garbage Huts	
	i. Metal	20
	ii. Wood	15
9.	Humidifiers	10
10.	Incinerator	15
11.	Metal Scaffold	20
12.	Power Lawnmower	10
13.	Snow Blower	10
14.	Tractors, Small	10
15.	Trucks, Pick-up and Delivery	10
16.	Vacuums, Commercial	10
Furnishings		
1.	Appliances	
	i. Clothes Dryer	15
	ii. Dishwasher	10
	iii. Microwave	10
	iv. Refrigerator	15
	v. Stove	15
	vi. Washing Machine	15
2.	Cabinets, Counters: Bath, Kitchen	25
3.	Drapes	10
4.	Furniture	
	i. Couches	10
	ii. Folding Chairs and Tables	10
	iii. Office	10
5.	Pictures	15
6.	Venetian Blinds	10
Conveying Systems		
1.	Elevators	

Column 1		Column 2
Work done or thing purchased		**Useful life in years**
	i. Electrical Controls	15
	ii. Interior Wall Panels	15
	iii. New Installation	20
	iv. Mechanical Retrofit (Cable System)	15
Mechanical		
1.	Heating, ventilation and air conditioning	
	i. Boilers	
	A. Gas Fired Atmospheric	15
	B. Hot Water	15
	C. Insulation	25
	D. Retubing	20
	E. Steam	25
	ii. Central System (air conditioning)	15
	iii. Chiller	25
	iv. Cooling Tower	25
	v. Corridor System	15
	vi. Exhaust and Supply Fans	20
	vii. Fan Coil Units	20
	viii. Furnace	
	A. Electric, Forced Air	25
	B. Oil, Gas, Forced Air	25
	C. Oil, Gas, Wall or Floor	20
	ix. Heat Exchanger	15
	x. Heat Pumps	15
	xi. Heating System	
	A. Electric	10
	B. Hot Air	15
	C. Hot Water	25
	D. Steam	10
	xii. Hot Water Tanks	
	A. Commercial	20
	B. Domestic	25
	xiii. Sanitary Exhaust	
	A. Central System	20

Column 1		Column 2
Work done or thing purchased		**Useful life in years**
	B. Individual System	15
	xiv. Stair Pressurization Fans	20
	xv. Units (Air Conditioners)	
	A. Incremental	15
	B. Sleeve, Window	10
2.	Mechanical	
	i. Culvert (Metal, Concrete)	25
	ii. Drains, Stacks (Plastic)	20
	iii. Lawn Sprinklers (Underground)	10
	iv. Plumbing Fixtures	
	A. Faucets	10
	B. Tubs, Toilets, Sinks	15
	v. Pumps	
	A. Booster, Circulating	25
	B. Fire, Jockey	15
	C. Sump	15
	vi. Risers	25
	vii. Sanitary System	25
	viii. Septic Tank and Tile Bed	20
	ix. Storm System	25
	x. Valves, Access Doors, Fittings, etc.	15
	xi. Water Softener	15
	xii. Water Treatment	20
	xiii. Wells and Water System	20
Electrical		
1.	Electric Heating Cables (Garage Ramp)	10
2.	Emergency Lighting (Battery Operated)	15
3.	Emergency System	
	i. Lighting	20
	ii. Generator	25
4.	Fire Extinguishers	10
5.	Fire System (Alarms, Smoke Detectors)	15
6.	Intercom	15
7.	Light Fixtures	

Column 1		Column 2
Work done or thing purchased		**Useful life in years**
	i. Exterior	15
	ii. Interior: Common Areas, Ensuite	10
8.	Panel and Distribution	15
9.	Power Line	25
10.	Rewiring	25
11.	Street Lighting	15
12.	Surveillance System	
	i. Cameras	15
	ii. Monitors	15
	iii. Switchers	15
13.	Switches and Splitters	25
14.	Temperature Control	
	i. Electric	
	A. Indoor	15
	B. Outdoor	15
	ii. Pneumatic	20
15.	Transformer	25

Ont. Reg. 517/06 — Maintenance Standards

made under the *Residential Tenancies Act, 2006*

O. Reg. 517/06

Part I — Interpretation and Application

1. Definitions — In this Regulation,

"exterior common areas" includes roads, pathways, parking areas, garbage storage areas, grounds for the use of tenants and, in a mobile home park or land lease community, the sites on which homes are situated; (*"aires communes extérieures"*)

"guard" means a barrier, that may or may not have openings through it; (*"garde-corps"*)

"habitable space" means a room or area used or intended to be used for living, sleeping, cooking or eating purposes and includes a washroom. (*"local habitable"*)

2. Maintenance standards and compliance — (1) This Regulation prescribes the maintenance standards for the purposes of subsection 224(1) of the Act.

(2) Except as otherwise provided, the landlord shall ensure that the maintenance standards in this Regulation are complied with.

3. Good workmanship — All repairs to and maintenance of a rental unit or residential complex shall be carried out in a manner and with the materials that are accepted as good workmanship in the trades concerned.

4. Municipal property standards by-laws applicable to exterior — If there is a municipal property standards by-law applicable only to the exterior of residential complexes or rental units, the maintenance standards in this Regulation that relate to the exterior of residential complexes or rental units do not apply to the residential complexes or rental units in the municipality that are subject to the by-law, but the maintenance standards in this Regulation that relate to the interior of residential complexes or rental units do apply to them.

Part II — Structural Elements

5. Maintenance — The structural elements in a residential complex shall be maintained in a sound condition so as to be capable of safely sustaining their own weight and any load or force that may normally be imposed.

6. Structural soundness, etc. — (1) Every floor of a basement, cellar or crawl space, and every slab at ground level, foundation wall, wall and roof shall be structurally sound, weathertight and damp-proofed and shall be maintained so as to reasonably protect against deterioration, including that due to weather, fungus, dry rot, rodents, vermin or insects.

(2) The site upon which a residential complex is situated shall be graded and drained to prevent the ponding of water on the surface, the erosion of soil and the entrance of water into a building or structure.

7. Roofs — (1) Every roof shall be watertight.

(2) The roof and any cornice flashing, fascia, soffit, coping, gutter, rainwater leader, vent or other roof structure,

(a) shall be maintained to properly perform their intended function; and

(b) shall be kept clear of obstructions, hazards and dangerous accumulations of snow and ice.

8. Retaining walls, guards and fences — Retaining walls, guards and fences in exterior common areas shall be maintained in a structurally sound condition and free from hazards.

PART III — UTILITIES AND SERVICES

Plumbing

9. Maintenance — (1) Plumbing and drainage systems in a residential complex, and their appurtenances, shall be maintained free from leaks, defects and obstructions and adequately protected from freezing.

(2) A residential complex shall be provided with a means of sewage disposal.

(3) The means of sewage disposal shall be maintained in a good state of repair.

10. Required fixtures — (1) Subject to subsections (2), (3) and (4), every rental unit shall contain the following fixtures:

1. A toilet.
2. A kitchen sink.
3. A washbasin.
4. A bathtub or shower.

(2) Subsection (1) does not apply to rental units that share a fixture described in paragraph 1, 2 or 4 of subsection (1) if no more than two rental units share the fixture and access to the fixture from each rental unit is possible without,

(a) passing through another rental unit;

(b) travelling along an unheated corridor; or

(c) travelling outside the building containing the rental units.

(3) Subsection (1) does not apply to a boarding house or lodging house if,

(a) there is at least one toilet, one washbasin and one bathtub or shower for every five rental units;

(b) all tenants have access to a kitchen sink; and

(c) all fixtures mentioned in clauses (a) and (b) are available in each building containing rental units.

(4) Subsection (1) does not apply to a residential complex or rental unit that has never been provided with piped water.

(5) The fixtures required by this section shall be maintained in a good state of repair and in a safely operable condition and shall be supplied with a supply of potable water sufficient for normal household use at a flow and pressure sufficient for the intended use of the fixtures.

11. Hot and cold running water — (1) Every kitchen sink, washbasin, bathtub and shower shall be provided, by safe equipment, with hot and cold running water.

(2) The ordinary temperature of the hot water provided must be at least 43 degrees Celsius.

12. Washroom requirements — (1) Every washroom shall be enclosed and shall have,

(a) a water-resistant floor; and

(b) a door that can be,

(i) secured from the inside, and

(ii) opened from the outside in an emergency.

(2) The walls and ceiling around a bathtub or shower shall be water-resistant.

(3) In subsection (1),

"washroom" means an area containing a toilet, urinal, bathtub, shower or washbasin.

13. Toilets and urinals — No toilet or urinal shall be located in a room used for or intended to be used for sleeping or preparing, consuming or storing food.

Electrical

14. Supply of electrical power — (1) A supply of electrical power shall be provided to all habitable space in a residential complex.

(2) The wiring and receptacles necessary to provide electrical power shall be maintained free of conditions dangerous to persons or property.

(3) Every kitchen shall have outlets suitable for a refrigerator and a cooking appliance.

(4) If a rental unit has a meter for electricity for the purpose of billing the tenants of that rental unit, the meter shall be properly maintained and kept accessible to the tenants.

(5) This section does not apply to a residential complex that has never been connected to an electrical power system.

Heating

15. Maintenance of room temperature — (1) Heat shall be provided and maintained so that the room temperature at 1.5 metres above floor level and one metre from exterior walls in all habitable space and in any area intended for normal use by tenants, including recreation rooms and laundry rooms but excluding locker rooms and garages, is at least 20 degrees Celsius.

(2) Subsection (1) does not apply to a rental unit in which the tenant can regulate the temperature and a minimum temperature of 20 degrees Celsius can be maintained by the primary source of heat.

(3) Every residential complex shall have heating equipment capable of maintaining the temperature levels required by subsection (1).

(4) No rental unit shall be equipped with portable heating equipment as the primary source of heat.

(5) Only heating equipment approved for use by a recognized standards testing authority shall be provided in a room used or intended for use for sleeping purposes.

16. Fuel and utilities — (1) Fuel supplied to a residential complex or rental unit shall be supplied continuously in adequate quantities.

(2) Utilities supplied to a residential complex or rental unit shall be supplied continuously.

(3) The supply of fuel and utilities may be interrupted for such reasonable period of time as may be required for the purpose of repair or replacement.

(4) Subsections (1) and (2) do not apply if the tenancy agreement makes the tenant responsible for the supply of fuel or utilities and the supply has been discontinued because of arrears in payment.

17. Maintenance of heating systems — Heating systems, including stoves, heating appliances, fireplaces intended for use, chimneys, fans, pumps and filtration equipment, shall be maintained in a good state of repair and in a safely operable condition.

18. Air supply and fuel storage — (1) A space that contains heating equipment that burns fuel shall have a natural or mechanical means of supplying the air required for combustion.

(2) If heating equipment burns solid or liquid fuel, a storage place or receptacle for the fuel shall be provided in a safe place and maintained in a safe condition.

Lighting and Ventilation

19. Artificial lighting — (1) Adequate artificial lighting shall be available at all times in all rooms, stairways, halls, corridors, garages, and basements of a residential complex that are accessible to tenants.

(2) Artificial lighting shall be provided in exterior common areas to permit these areas to be used or passed through safely, and to provide security.

(3) Subsections (1) and (2) do not apply to a residential complex that has never been connected to an electrical power system.

(4) Artificial lighting that has been installed in outbuildings normally used by tenants, including garages, shall be kept in operable condition.

(5) Artificial lighting shall be maintained in a good state of repair.

20. Ventilation — All habitable space shall be provided with natural or mechanical means of ventilation that is adequate for the use of the space.

21. Smoke, gases and toxic fumes — (1) Chimneys, smoke-pipes, flues and gas vents shall be kept clear of obstructions and maintained so as to prevent the escape of smoke and gases into a building containing one or more rental units.

(2) Parking garages shall be maintained so as to prevent the accumulation of toxic fumes and the escape of toxic fumes into a building containing one or more rental units.

22. Rooms that require windows — (1) Subject to subsections (2) and (3), every bedroom, living room and dining room shall have a window (which may be part of a door) to the outside of the building.

(2) A window is not required in a dining room if it has artificial lighting.

(3) A window is not required in a living room or dining room if,

(a) there is an opening in a dividing wall to an adjoining room;

(b) the adjoining room has a window to the outside; and

(c) the total window area of the adjoining room is at least 5 per cent of the combined floor areas of the living room or dining room and the adjoining room.

23. Doors, windows and skylights — (1) Every existing opening in the exterior surface of a building designed for a door or window shall be equipped with a door or window capable of performing the intended function.

(2) Doors, windows and skylights shall be maintained so that,

(a) they are weathertight; and

(b) any damaged or missing parts are repaired or replaced.

PART IV — SAFETY AND SECURITY

24. Guards — (1) Guards shall be installed and maintained wherever,

(a) there is a vertical drop of more than 600 millimetres (including along the open sides of stairs, ramps, balconies, mezzanines and landings); and

(b) they would be required for a newly constructed or renovated area under the building code made under the *Building Code Act, 1992.*

(2) A guard required by subsection (1) shall provide reasonable protection from accidental falls for any person on the premises.

25. Window safety devices — (1) This section applies with respect to every window in a rental unit that is in a storey above the storey that has,

(a) its floor closest to ground level; and

(b) its ceiling more than 1.8 metres above average ground level.

(2) At the request of the tenant, each window referred to in subsection (1) shall be equipped with a safety device to prevent any part of the window from opening so as to admit a sphere greater than 100 millimetres in diameter.

(3) The safety device required by subsection (2) shall not make the window incapable of being opened by an adult without a key or the use of tools.

26. Exterior common areas — (1) Exterior common areas shall be maintained in a condition suitable for their intended use and free of hazards and, for these purposes, the following shall be removed:

1. Noxious weeds as defined in the regulations to the *Weed Control Act.*

2. Dead, decayed or damaged trees or parts of such trees that create an unsafe condition.

3. Rubbish or debris, including abandoned motor vehicles.

4. Structures that create an unsafe condition.

5. Unsafe accumulations of ice and snow.

(2) An inoperative motor vehicle or trailer that has remained in an exterior common area for more than a reasonable amount of time shall be removed.

(3) Wells and holes in exterior common areas shall be filled or safely covered and the wells shall also be protected from contamination.

27. Abandoned refrigerators, etc. — (1) An abandoned or inoperable icebox, refrigerator or freezer shall not be left in a common area unless it is awaiting removal.

(2) An icebox, refrigerator or freezer that is awaiting removal shall have all its doors removed.

28. Surface of driveways, etc. — Driveways, ramps, parking garages, parking areas, paths, walkways, landings, outside stairs and any similar area shall be maintained to provide a safe surface for normal use.

29. Locking windows and doors — (1) Every window and exterior door, including a balcony door, that is capable of being opened and that is accessible from outside a rental unit or a building containing a rental unit shall be equipped so that it can be secured from the inside.

(2) At least one entrance door in a rental unit shall be capable of being locked from outside the rental unit.

(3) If a rental unit-to-vestibule communication system together with a vestibule door locking release system is provided, it shall be maintained in a good state of repair and in a safely operable condition.

(4) Parking areas that are intended to be secured, shared locker rooms and shared storage rooms shall be provided with doors equipped with security devices that prevent access to persons other than the landlord and tenants.

(5) A mail delivery slot that enters directly into a rental unit, and any similar opening for deliveries, shall be located and maintained to prevent access to any door's or window's locking or securing mechanisms.

(6) Subsection (5) does not apply with respect to a mail delivery slot or other opening that has been sealed.

(7) Mail boxes provided by the landlord shall be properly maintained and capable of being secured.

Part V — Mobile Home Parks and Land Lease Communities

30. Application — (1) Sections 31 to 36 apply to mobile home parks and land lease communities.

(2) The other sections of this Regulation also apply to mobile home parks and land lease communities.

31. Water supply — (1) A supply of potable water and water pressure that are sufficient for normal household use shall be available for each rental unit in a mobile home park or land lease community.

(2) An adequate supply of water and adequate water pressure shall be available for fire fighting.

(3) Fire hydrants owned by the landlord shall be regularly tested and maintained and kept free from accumulations of snow and ice.

32. Roads — (1) Roads within a mobile home park or land lease community shall be,

(a) kept free of holes and cleared of snow and obstructions;

(b) maintained to control dust; and

(c) kept passable.

(2) Excavations made for repairs shall be filled in and the ground returned to its previous condition.

33. Mailboxes — Mailboxes and the approaches to them shall be kept free of snow and other obstructions.

34. Distance between mobile homes — Where the distance between mobile homes is three metres or more, that distance shall not be reduced to less than three metres through the addition of a deck or ramp or by any other means, unless a lesser distance provides an adequate degree of fire safety.

35. Sewage — (1) Sewage holding tanks in a mobile home park or land lease community shall be emptied whenever necessary.

(2) Sewage connections and other components of a sewage system shall be provided in a mobile home park or land lease community and shall be permanently secured to prevent a discharge of sewage.

(3) In subsection (2),

"sewage system" means a municipal sanitary sewage system or a private sewage disposal system and includes a sewage system as defined in the building code made under the *Building Code Act, 1992* and a sewage works as defined in the *Ontario Water Resources Act*.

36. Electrical supply — Electrical supply and connections in a mobile home park or land lease community supplied by the landlord shall be maintained free of conditions dangerous to persons or property.

PART VI — GENERAL MAINTENANCE

37. Floors, etc. — Every floor, stair, veranda, porch, deck, balcony, loading dock and every structure similar to any of them, and any covering, guard or surface finishing shall be maintained in a good state of repair.

38. Cabinets, etc. — Every cabinet, cupboard, shelf and counter top provided by the landlord of a rental unit shall be maintained in a structurally sound condition, free from cracks and deterioration.

39. Walls and ceilings — (1) Interior cladding of walls and ceilings shall be maintained free from holes, leaks, deteriorating materials, mould, mildew and other fungi.

(2) A protective finish shall be applied to all repairs made to walls and ceilings.

40. Appliances — (1) Appliances supplied by the landlord of the rental unit shall be maintained in a good state of repair and in a safely operable condition.

(2) In subsection (1),

"appliances" includes refrigerators, stoves, clothes washers, clothes dryers, dishwashers and hot water tanks.

41. Heat loss — Those portions of a residential complex used for human habitation, including common areas, shall be maintained to minimize heat loss through air infiltration.

42. Locker and storage rooms — Locker and storage rooms shall be kept free of dampness and mildew.

43. Elevators — Elevators intended for use by tenants shall be properly maintained and kept in operation except for such reasonable time as may be required to repair or replace them.

44. Common areas — (1) All interior common areas and exterior common areas shall be kept clean and free of hazards.

(2) For the purpose of subsection (1),

"interior common areas" includes laundry rooms, garbage rooms, corridors, lobbies, vestibules, boiler rooms, parking garages, storage areas and recreation rooms.

45. Garbage — (1) In a building containing more than one rental unit, one or more suitable containers or compactors shall be provided for garbage.

(2) Garbage in a container or compactor provided in accordance with subsection (1) shall be stored and either placed for pick-up or regularly disposed of so as not to cause a risk to the health or safety of any person.

(3) A container or compactor provided in accordance with subsection (1) shall be maintained in a clean and sanitary condition, shall be accessible to tenants and shall not obstruct an emergency route, driveway or walkway.

46. Rodents, etc. — (1) A residential complex shall be kept reasonably free of rodents, vermin and insects.

(2) The methods used for exterminating rodents and insects shall be in accordance with applicable municipal or provincial law.

(3) Openings and holes in a building containing one or more rental units shall be screened or sealed to prevent the entry of rodents, vermin, insects and other pests.

47. Interior doors — Every existing interior door shall be maintained so that it is capable of performing its intended function and any damaged or missing parts shall be repaired or replaced.

PART VII — INSPECTION CHARGES

48. Inspection charge — The Minister may charge a municipality $265 for each inspection made under subsection 224(3) of the Act or to ensure compliance with a work order under section 225 of the Act.

49. Invoice — The Minister shall send an invoice to the municipality requiring the payment of one or more charges and the invoice shall specify for each charge the date of the inspection, the address of the residential complex inspected and the date by which the municipality must pay.

PART VIII — REVOCATION AND COMMENCEMENT

50. Revocation — Ontario Regulation 198/98 is revoked.

51. Commencement — This Regulation comes into force on January 31, 2007.

Appendix 4

Forms, Office Locations and Contact Information for the Landlord and Tenant Board

Forms

A complete selection of current Landlord and Tenant Board Forms can be found on the CD included with this text. Forms are changed periodically, however, and it is always advisable to ensure that the form you are using is up to date by visiting the website of the Landlord and Tenant Board at *http://www.ltb.gov.on.ca*.

Office Locations

Regional Office Locations and Fax Numbers

Regional Offices have Customer Service Representatives available during regular business hours. Customer Service Representatives can provide you with information about the Board and the law. Applications and supporting documents may be filed in person, by mail, or by fax to any Regional Office below.

Hamilton
Southern Regional Office
119 King Street West, 6th Floor
Hamilton, Ontario L8P 4Y7
Fax No. 905-521-7870 or 1-866-455-5255

London
Southwestern Regional Office
150 Dufferin Avenue, Suite 400
London, Ontario N6A 5N6
Fax No. 519-679-7290 or 1-888-377-8813

Mississauga
Central Regional Office
3 Robert Speck Parkway, Suite 520
Mississauga, Ontario L4Z 2G5
Fax No. 905-279-7286 or 1-888-322-2841

Ottawa
Eastern Regional Office
255 Albert Street, 4th Floor
Ottawa, Ontario K1P 6A9
Fax No. 613-787-4024 or 1-888-377-8805

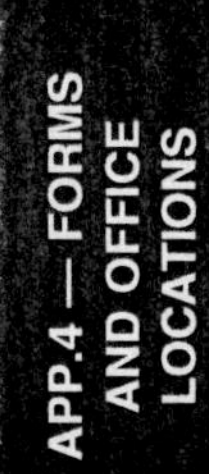

Sudbury
Northern Regional Office
199 Larch Street, Suite 301
Sudbury, Ontario P3E 5P9
Fax No. 705-564-4118 or 1-866-410-1399

Toronto
Toronto South Regional Office
79 St. Clair Avenue East, Suite 212
Toronto, Ontario M4T 1M6
Fax No. 416-326-9838

Toronto
Toronto North Regional Office
47 Sheppard Avenue East, Suite 700
Toronto, Ontario M2N 5X5
Fax No. 416-314-9567

Toronto East
Durham Regional Office
2275 Midland Avenue, Unit 2
Toronto, Ontario M1P 3E7
Fax No. 416-314-8649 or 1-888-377-8808

ServiceOntario Office Locations

Below is a list of **ServiceOntario** offices. You can file applications and supporting documents in person at any of these locations. If you want to file documents by mail or fax, you must send them to one of the Regional Offices listed above.

The offices in this list do not have Board staff working behind the counters. They cannot provide you with information about the law, but they can accept documents on behalf of the Landlord and Tenant Board.

Changes to the ServiceOntario Process: Note that as of Monday, September 28, 2009, the way ServiceOntario Centres (SOCs) deal with Landlord and Tenant Board (LTB) applications and documents submitted to them has changed.

The key changes are:

- in most cases the original applications and documents filed at the SOC will be sent to the LTB by courier each day, rather than being sent by fax (urgent, time-sensitive documents will be sent by fax in addition to the originals being sent by courier),
- SOC staff will complete a Document Tracking Form to record the receipt of applications and documents; the original will be sent with the documents submitted to the LTB and a copy of the form will be given to the client for their records,
- fees to be paid by credit card, certified cheque, money order or bank draft will be processed by the LTB; only debit and cash will be processed at the SOC,

- the LTB will send a completed Notice of Hearing package (including a copy of the application) directly to the applicant by mail or fax – there will be no need to return to the SOC to pick it up.

Important: Clients must indicate on the Payment and Scheduling Information Form of their application whether they wish to receive the Notice of Hearing packages from the LTB by mail or fax. Although "Pick up at a ServiceOntario location" is an option on the Payment and Scheduling Information Form, it is no longer an option offered by the LTB. The form will be amended in the future.

ServiceOntario/Government Information Centres

Atikokan
108 Saturn Avenue

Aurora
50 Bloomington Road West

Aylmer
615 John Street North

Bancroft
50 Monck Street

Barrie
34 Simcoe Street

Belleville
Century Place Mall, 199 Front Street

Blind River
62 Queen Avenue

Brampton
7765 Hurontario Street

Brockville
7 King Street West

Chapleau
190 Cherry Street

Chatham
Civic Centre, 315 King Street West

Cochrane
143 Fourth Avenue

Cornwall
127 Sydney Street

Dryden
479 Government Road, Main Floor

Elliot Lake
50 Hillside Drive North

Espanola
148 Fleming Street, Suite 2

Fort Frances
922 Scott Street

Geraldton
208 Beamish Avenue West

Goderich
38 North Street, Main Floor

Gore Bay
35 Meredith Street

Guelph
1 Stone Road West, Main Floor

Hawkesbury
692 Main Street East

Hearst
613 Front Street

Huntsville
207 Main Street West

Ignace
Corner of Highways 17 and 599

Iroquois Falls
260 Main Street

Kanata
580 Terry Fox Drive, Main Floor

Kapuskasing
122 Government Road West

Kemptville
10 Campus Drive

Kenora
810 Robertson Street, Suite 104

Kingston
Ontario Government Centre, Beechgrove Complex, 51 Heakes Lane, Main Floor

Kirkland Lake
10 Government Road East

Kitchener
City Hall, Main Floor, 200 King Street West

Lindsay
322 Kent Street West

Manitouwadge
40 Manitou Road

Marathon
Peninsula Square, Centre Block, 52 Peninsula Road, Suite 105

Minden
Highway 35 By-pass

Moosonee
Ontario Government Building, 34 Revillion Road North

New Liskeard
280 Armstrong Street

Nipigon
Ontario Government Building, 5 Wadsworth Drive

North Bay
447 McKeown Avenue, Suite 111

Oakville
Halton Region Administrative Centre, 1151 Bronte Road

Ottawa
110 Laurier Avenue West

Owen Sound
1400 1st Avenue West

Parry Sound
7 Bay Street

Pembroke
400 Pembroke Street East

Peterborough
Ontario Government Building, 300 Water Street, Main Floor

Rainy River
408 Atwood Avenue

Red Lake
Heritage Centre (Museum), 51A Highway 105

Renfrew
316 Plaunt Street South

Sarnia
Bayside Mall, 150 Christina Street North

Sault Ste. Marie
70 Foster Drive, Suite 110, Main Lobby

Simcoe
50 Frederick Hobson VC Drive, Suite 201

Sioux Lookout
62 Queen Street

St. Catharines
301 St. Paul Street East

Stratford
5 Huron Street

Sturgeon Falls
94 King Street, Unit 8

Terrace Bay
1004 Hwy 17

Thunder Bay
435 South James Street, Suite 114

Timmins (South Porcupine)
Ontario Government Building, Highway 101 East

Toronto (Central)
777 Bay Street, Suite M212 Market Place

Toronto (Downsview)
3737 Chesswood Drive

Tweed
255 Metcalf Street

Wawa
48 Mission Road

Whitby
590 Rossland Road East

Windsor
400 City Hall Square East, Suite 205, 2nd Floor

Contact the Landlord and Tenant Board by Telephone

You can call the **Landlord and Tenant Board** (the Board) at **416-645-8080** from within the Toronto calling area, or toll-free at **1-888-332-3234** from outside Toronto, and speak to a Customer Service Representative.

Customer Service Representatives are available Monday to Friday, except holidays, from 8:30 a.m. to 5:00 p.m. They can provide you with *information* about the *Residential Tenancies Act* and the Board's processes; they cannot provide you with legal advice. You can also access the Board's automated information menu at the same numbers listed above 24 hours a day, 7 days a week.

Appendix 5

PRINCIPLES OF CONDUCT FOR MEMBERS OF THE LANDLORD AND TENANT BOARD

Members of the Board are committed to the following principles:

1. A Member will approach every hearing with an open mind with respect to every issue.
2. A Member will listen carefully to the submissions of the parties and their representatives.
3. A Member will at all times show respect for the parties and their representatives and witnesses, and for the hearing process itself, through his or her demeanour, timeliness, dress, and conduct.
4. A Member will demonstrate a high degree of sensitivity to issues of gender, ability, race, language, culture and religion which may affect the conduct of a hearing and assessment of credibility.
5. A Member will endeavour to conduct all hearings expeditiously, commencing at the appointed time and preventing unnecessary delay, while ensuring that all parties have a fair opportunity to present their evidence and argument.
6. A Member will conduct a hearing in a firm but courteous manner and should likewise require courteous behaviour from hearing participants. The Member will promote mutual respect among hearing participants, and will not allow unprofessional, sexist, racist, ethnocentric or inappropriate religious comment or contemptuous conduct.
7. A Member will permit parties and agents to present their evidence and arguments without undue interruption from other participants or the Member him / herself.
8. A Member will attempt to ensure that parties who are unrepresented are not unduly disadvantaged at the hearing, although he or she cannot advise or take the side of an unrepresented party.
9. A Member will not communicate directly or indirectly with any party, witness or representative in respect of a proceedings outside of a hearing or pre-hearing conference, except in the presence of all parties and their representatives. He or she will behave in a manner that ensures parties view the Member as impartial towards all participants and representatives.
10. A Member will decide each case in good faith to the best of his or her ability. The prospect of disapproval from any person, institution, media representative or community will not deter the Member from making the

decision which he or she believes is correct based on the law and the evidence.

11. A Member accepts responsibility for the accuracy and correctness of his or her Orders and Reasons.
12. A Member is responsible for ensuring that all decisions are rendered promptly. Written reasons for decisions will be prepared without undue delay.
13. A Member will consider any Interpretation Guidelines and relevant Board decisions on a question at issue before him or her, although neither are binding. A Member is not required by law to follow a Guideline or its reasoning, but must be prepared to explain clearly in the reasons why he or she does not find a Guideline or previous decision relevant or why he or she has adopted different reasoning. The Member will give due weight to the need for a degree of consistency in the interpretation of the law.

Appendix 6

MEDIATOR'S CODE OF ETHICS AND PROFESSIONAL CONDUCT

1. Preamble

The purpose of this Code of Ethics and Professional Conduct is to serve as a guide for Board mediators. As well, it is intended to inform the mediating participants about a Board mediator's professional responsibilities and, in general, to promote public confidence in mediation as a process for resolving disputes.

Mediation is a process in which an impartial third party facilitates communication and negotiation and promotes voluntary decision making by the parties.

Mediators of the Landlord and Tenant Board shall make every effort to ensure that participants in mediation are afforded the highest quality service which is prompt, flexible and reasonable.

A mediator will provide a means of dispute resolution which is neutral, fair to all participants, confidential, collaborative and which promotes empowerment of the participants.

In order to fulfill this mandate, a mediator subscribes to the following Code of Ethics and Professional Conduct and undertakes to abide by the terms set out here.

2. Mediator's Role

A Board mediator's role is to facilitate a voluntary resolution of a dispute in an impartial manner by:

- promoting good faith communication between the participants
- encouraging the participants to identify and convey their interests to each other
- assisting the participants to assess information presented
- informing the participants about their rights and responsibilities or referring the participants to specialized advice, where appropriate
- encouraging participants to consider settlement options thoroughly and ensuring that proposed terms of settlement do not impugn the integrity of the process
- ensuring potential or actual power imbalances among participants are addressed

3. *Principle of Self-Determination*

A Board mediator believes that it is of fundamental and primary importance to the dispute resolution process that the participants are empowered so as to enable them to negotiate their own voluntary, considered, uncoerced agreement.

A Board mediator shall conduct a mediation based on the principle of party self-determination. Self-determination is the act of coming to a voluntary decision in which each party makes a free and informed choice as to process and outcome.

4. *Impartiality*

A Board mediator will not allow personal or socio-economic biases to compromise the process. A mediator shall conduct the mediation in an impartial and even-handed manner. If a mediator cannot conduct a process that is free from favouritism, bias or prejudice, then they will withdraw.

A mediator shall avoid conduct that gives the appearance of partiality toward any of the participants.

A mediator shall not provide advice to any participant. Where appropriate, a mediator will recommend that participants seek independent advice. Any information provided by a mediator in mediation shall be presented in a fair and impartial manner.

5. *Conflict of Interest*

A Board mediator shall disclose any actual or perceived conflict of interest as soon as they become aware of it and will withdraw unless the participants consent to the mediator continuing.

A mediator shall not act in a manner which would raise legitimate questions about the integrity of the mediator or the mediation process.

6. *Confidentiality*

A Board mediator shall not disclose information provided by a participant in confidence or obtained through the mediation process, either meeting together or separately, except with the express consent of that participant or where law or public policy requires.

A mediator shall ensure his or her mediation notes and documents are properly stored during mediation and disposed of after mediation.

Confidentiality shall not be construed to limit effective reporting for monitoring, training and evaluating with respect to the mediation program.

7. *Quality of the Process*

A Board mediator shall conduct a mediation in accordance with this Code of Ethics and Professional Conduct and in a manner that promotes diligence, timeliness, safety, party participation and mutual respect among the participants.

A mediator shall ensure that the participants are fully informed about the purpose of mediation, the nature of the process and the alternatives to mediation.

A mediator shall demonstrate a high level of professionalism in a manner that will withstand public scrutiny.

A mediator shall terminate mediation if:

- a participant requests that the process be terminated
- a participant is using the process inappropriately or not in good faith
- in the mediator's opinion the mediation is counter-productive or it is unlikely to settle after best efforts have been made
- proposals for settlement undermine the participants' or the public's trust in the process of mediation or the Board
- a settlement is unlikely to take place within a reasonable amount of time

A mediator will exercise good judgment in using efficient and effective case management practices.

A mediator is committed to and assumes responsibility for providing a level of service to participants that is of high professional standards.

A Board mediator and the Board recognize that there is a joint responsibility and duty to improve the practice of mediation and improve the mediator's professional skills and abilities through lifelong learning, self-evaluation, critical analysis and adherence to established standards and accepted principles.

Appendix 7

LANDLORD AND TENANT BOARD RULES OF PRACTICE*

Rules of Practice made under: the *Residential Tenancies Act, 2006* and the *Statutory Powers Procedure Act*

Table of Contents

These documents are subject to change without notice. The most current versions of the documents are available from the Landlord and Tenant Board at *www.LTB.gov.on.ca*.

Introduction

Legislation:

Subsection 176(2) of the Residential Tenancies Act, 2006 ('the RTA')
Section 25.1 of the Statutory Powers Procedure Act ('the SPPA')

Subsection 176(2) of the RTA requires the Board to "adopt rules of practice and procedure" governing its practice and procedure, as permitted by section 25.1 of the Statutory Powers Procedure Act. Subsection 176(5) states that the Board must make its rules available to the public.

Section 25.1 of the SPPA provides that "a tribunal may make rules governing the practice and procedure before it".

NOTE:

The Rules are set out in**bold** face. The commentary in italics is to assist the parties in understanding the application of the Rules and some of the procedures of the Board. Questions regarding the Rules may be directed to the Board by calling 1-888-332-3234, or 416-645-8080 from within the greater Toronto area.

Release Date: January 31, 2007

Rule 1 — General Rules

Legislation:

Section 4 of the *Statutory Powers Procedure Act* ('the SPPA')
Section 183 of the *Residential Tenancies Act, 2006* ('the RTA')

1.1 These Rules will be interpreted broadly to produce the fairest and most expeditious resolution of the application.

Under section 183 of the RTA, the Board shall adopt the most expeditious method of determining the questions arising in an application that affords to all parties directly affected by it an adequate opportunity to know the issues and to be heard on the matter. It is important that the Rules should be interpreted and applied in a manner that is consistent with the RTA.

1.2 Where a provision of the RTA or the SPPA, or of a regulation under either of them, applies directly to a particular issue, that provision will determine the issue, regardless of any Rule to the contrary.

If there is any situation in which one of these Rules would produce one result, but a specific provision of the RTA, the regulations or the SPPA would produce a different result, the legislation or regulations would apply. In other words, the RTA, the SPPA and the regulations prevail over these Rules.

1.3 Where something is not provided for in these Rules, the practice may be decided by referring to a similar provision in these Rules.

These Rules cannot deal with every situation. This Rule contemplates that a Member would seek guidance from other Rules on analogous subjects in deciding how to proceed.

1.4 No defect in an application, a document created after the application was filed, or in a step taken in the proceedings after the application was filed, will make the application invalid unless the rights of another party are substantially prejudiced by the defect, and the prejudice cannot be remedied.

If any part of a proceeding is tainted by a procedural error, this should not prevent the Board from determining the case on its merits. The same is true if there is a flaw in the application or any other document created for the purpose of the application. However, this Rule does not allow a Member to disregard any defect in a document created before the application was filed (e.g., a notice of rent increase or a notice of termination) or a step taken before that date (e.g., the service of such a notice). Further, this Rule would not apply if the error was detrimental to another party's rights in a significant way, and could not be remedied. If there is prejudice claimed on both sides, it is up to the Member to weigh the prejudice and balance the rights of the parties. This Rule is similar to a rule of the civil courts.

1.5 A Member may waive a Rule where appropriate, provided that the Rule does not have a non-waiver provision. If a Member waives a Rule, the Member shall give reasons for waiving the Rule in the order or decision. Rules that have a non-waiver provision, such as Rules 4.5, 13.22 and 26.6, may not be waived.

There will be situations where a Rule that is appropriate in most situations would not be fair or just in a specific case. For that reason, a party may request that a Rule be waived, or a Member may waive a Rule on his or her own initiative. For example, a Member may waive a Rule for the purpose of accommodating a party in accordance with the Human Rights Code. In most cases, a Rule would not be waived without inviting and considering submissions from the parties. This Rule is authorized by subsection 4(2) of the SPPA.

Despite this Rule, Rules 4.5, 13.22 and 26.6 may not be waived.

1.6 After the application is filed, a party may waive service by the Board or by another party of a Notice of Hearing or any other document.

Under subsection 4(1) of the SPPA, a party may waive any procedural requirement of the "governing legislation". This Rule deals with only some of the procedural requirements to which subsection 4(1) would apply. It deals with a situation such as scheduling the hearing of a set aside motion, which will be heard very quickly if the landlord agrees to waive service of the Notice of Hearing. There are other rules in the RTA and in the Rules which require the Board to give a document to a party after the application has begun. Parties are allowed to waive service of these documents because they wish to expedite the proceedings or because they have been advised of them at the hearing or by telephone.

Amended October 15, 2009

Rule 2 — Initiative of the Board

Legislation:

Sections 16.1, 23 and 25.1 of the Statutory Powers Procedure Act ('the SPPA')

A number of rules in the SPPA give a Member the initiative to take procedural steps without a request from a party. For example, under section 16.1, the Member may make any interim decision or order in the proceedings, and impose conditions on the decision or order. Under section 23, a Member may make orders or directions which are proper to prevent abuse of its process.

2.1 Members may exercise any of their powers under these Rules or under the RTA on their own initiative or at the request of a party.

If a Rule applies to a case, it need not be raised by a party. The Member may decide on his or her own to apply the Rule.

2.2 The Member may decide the procedure to be followed for an application and may make specific procedural directions or orders at any time and may impose such conditions as are appropriate and fair.

Members should make procedural directions or orders to assist the parties and bring the proceedings to a fair and expeditious conclusion. The Member may decide that a procedural ruling should be made only with specific conditions, so long as those conditions are fair to all parties. For example, an adjournment may be granted, but the Member may require that the respondent pay a sum of money into the Board, or order that one party pay another party's costs, or direct that there may not be an adjournment of the next hearing date, except in the most extraordinary circumstances.

Release Date: January 31, 2007

Rule 3 — Communications with the Board

3.1 A party shall not attempt to speak directly to a Member outside a hearing.

The principle is that no party should give any evidence or submissions to a decision-maker, except in the presence of the other parties at a hearing to avoid the perception of bias. As such, any communication with the Board will have to be through an employee of the Board.

3.2 The Member may direct a party or representative communicating with the Board to provide a copy or notice of the communication to each other party.

In some cases, a communication with the Board should be disclosed to the other party. For example, if a party tells Board staff that an adjournment will be requested in advance of the hearing, they may be ordered to tell the other party.[The party should use one of the methods of service permitted by section 191 of the RTA or Rule 5.1, unless the Member specifies another method.]

Release Date: January 31, 2007

Rule 4 — Computation of Time

Legislation:

Section 193 of the Residential Tenancies Act, 2006 ('the RTA')
Sections such as 44, 59, 77 and 116 have deadlines for certain actions

Related Rules:

Many Rules have deadlines for which it is necessary to count days.

Section 193 of the RTA provides that: "Time shall be computed in accordance with the Rules." It is important that parties understand the way in which the Board will count days in order to know the deadlines for giving documents to other parties such as applications and motions, and filing other documents with the Board, etc. These Rules are also important for landlords to understand since they apply to deadlines not related to an application, such as the time for giving a notice of termination or a notice of rent increase.

4.1 Subject to Rule 1.2, the time between two events is computed by excluding the day on which the first event occurs and including the day on which the second event occurs.

For example, if a landlord is counting 14 days that are required between the date a notice of termination will be given to a tenant, and the date of termination to be set out in the notice, they would not count the date the notice will be given (the "first event") but will include the proposed date of termination (the "second event"). All weekend days and other holidays are counted. Thus, a notice given on the 10th of the month could be effective as early as the 24th.

"Business Days" and "Non-Business Days"

4.2 The following days are referred to as "non-business days" in these Rules:

> **(a) Saturday or Sunday;**
>
> **(b) a day proclaimed by the Governor General or Lieutenant Governor as a public holiday;**
>
> **(c) New Year's Day, Family Day, Good Friday, Easter Monday, Victoria Day, Canada Day, the civic holiday in August, Labour Day, Thanksgiving Day, Remembrance Day, Christmas Day and Boxing Day;**
>
> **(d) if New Year's Day, Canada Day or Remembrance Day fall on a Saturday or Sunday, the following Monday; and**
>
> **(e) if Christmas Day falls on a Saturday or Sunday, then the following Monday and Tuesday, and if on a Friday, then the following Monday.**

A "business day" is a day that the Board is open to the public for the filing of documents and conducting its business. This definition of "non-business days" is provided to assist the understanding of the following Rules.

4.3 If the time limit for filing a notice or document falls on a non-business day, the notice or document may be filed on the next business day.

For example, the deadline for filing a motion to set aside an ex parte order is ten days after the date the order is issued. Where the 10-day deadline falls on a Saturday or Sunday, the motion may be filed on the following Monday.

4.4 A notice or document may be given to another person on a non-business day and, in the case of a notice, it may become effective on a non-business day.

A party is permitted to give a document to another party on a non-business day. For example, a notice may be served on a Saturday, and days are counted from the Sunday. If the days counted to compute the effective date of a notice were to end on a Sunday, it would be effective on that day, even though it is a non-business day. This is somewhat different than the rules of court, but they recognize that some documents given under the RTA do not relate to proceedings, but to such situations as giving a notice of termination or a notice of rent increase.

4.5 Despite Rule 1.5, Rules 4.1 to 4.4 may not be waived or varied.

Rule 1.5 allows a Member to waive or vary any of these Rules in the circumstances of the application. However, the Rules concerning computation of time cannot be waived by the Member in any circumstances.

Amended December 08, 2008

Rule 5 — Serving a Document on Another Party

Legislation:

Section 191 of the Residential Tenancies Act, 2006 ('the RTA')

Related Rules:

Rules 4.1 to 4.5 (Computation of Time)
Rules 10.1 to 10.8 (Serving the Application or Motion & Notice of Hearing)
Rules 11.1 to 11.4 (Certificates of Service)

Section 191 of the RTA provides that a party may give another person a document by various means listed in subsection (1), including handing it to the person, mailing it to them, leaving it in a mail box or a place where mail is ordinarily delivered. It refers to giving a document to a "person" rather than a "party" because it includes all documents mentioned in the RTA, such as notices of termination and rent increase, which are not related to applications when they are given. Clause 191(1)(g) deems "any other means allowed in the Rules" to be sufficient service of the document.

These Rules also set out when a document is considered to have been given to another person, depending upon the method of service used. For service by mail, subsection 191(3) of the RTA provides that service is effective five days after mailing.

Other Permitted Methods of Service

5.1 A person may give a notice or document to another person by any of the following methods:

(a) by courier to that person;

(b) if there is a fax machine where the person carries on business or in the residence of the person, by fax;

(c) for service on a person who occupies the rental unit, by placing it under the door of the unit or through a mail slot in the door;

(d) for service on a tenant of a notice under section 27of the RTA, by any permitted method of service or posting it on the door of the rental unit;

(e) if the document is an application or was created after the application was filed, by hand delivery, mail, courier or fax to the representative for a party; or

(f) if the document is an application or was created after the application was filed, by any method directed or permitted by the Board in writing.

Where a notice or document is given by a method other than the methods of service permitted by subsection 191(1) of the RTA or this rule, that notice or document will be deemed to have been validly given if it is proven that the information in the notice or document came to the attention of the person for whom it was intended.

Board Permitting Other Methods of Service

5.2 A Member may give written directions to a party, either on his or her own initiative or on that party's request, regarding one or both of the following:

(a) who shall be served with the application or any other document; or

(b) how an application or document shall be served.

If a party is unsure about how the requirements of the RTA should be interpreted in a particular case, they may ask in writing for a Member to issue written directions. The party may also want directions because they have had difficulty in serving documents on another party according to the methods permitted by the RTA and these Rules. Such a party may ask in writing that a Member issue written directions to serve the documents by another method, as permitted by Rule 5.1. Finally, the Member may, on their own initiative, direct service on additional parties who should have been served or direct the method of service if there has been some problem to date.

Using Courier Delivery

5.3 If a notice or document is delivered to another person by courier, it is deemed to be given on the day following the day it was given to the courier but, if that is a non-business day, it is deemed to be given on the next business day.

This Rule recognizes that couriers usually deliver documents the next day. If the party who mailed the document can prove that the other party received it earlier than the deemed date, see Rule 5.6. For example, if a party paid for "same day" courier service, and the delivery occurred on the same day the document was given to the courier, it would be found to be given that day.

Using Xpresspost

5.4 A notice or document given by Xpresspost is deemed to be given by mail.

Although Xpresspost is marketed as a courier-like service, a notice or document given by this method is deemed to be given by mail. Subsection 191(3) of the RTA specifies that a notice or document that is given by mail is deemed to have been given on the fifth day after mailing.

Using Fax

5.5 If a notice or document is given to another person by fax, it will be found to be given on the date imprinted on the fax.

If a fax is received by 11:59 P.M. on Monday, it will be found to have been given on Monday. After midnight, it will be found to be given on Tuesday.

Earlier Receipt

5.6 If the person who gave a notice or document to another person can prove that the person received it on an earlier date than the date deemed by the RTA or these Rules, the Board will find that it was given on the earlier date.

This Rule would apply if, at a hearing, the date of service is an issue. If the other party admits receiving the document earlier than five days after mailing, this would be accepted. If the party who gave the document can show in some other way that the other party received it earlier, the earlier date may be accepted.

Release Date: January 31, 2007

Rule 6 — Filing Documents with the Board

Legislation:

Subsection 192(1) of the *Residential Tenancies Act, 2006* ('the RTA')

Related Rules:

Rules 4.1 to 4.5 (Computation of Time)

Subsection 192(1) of the RTA states that: **A***A notice or document is sufficiently given to the Board,*

> *(a) by hand delivering it to the Board at the appropriate office as set out in the Rules;*
>
> *(b) by sending it by mail to the appropriate office as set out in the Rules; or*
>
> *(c) by any other means allowed in the Rules."*

6.1 A document may be delivered in person to any Board office or to a ServiceOntario Centre that accepts service on behalf of the Board.

For example, an application may be filed in person with the Toronto South Regional Office, even if the address to which it relates falls within the area that is the responsibility of the Toronto North Regional Office. The offices at which filing is permitted include all Board offices.

A document delivered to a ServiceOntario Centre that accepts service on behalf of the Board is considered filed under section 185 (under the authority of clause 192(1)(c) of the RTA). A ServiceOntario Centre is an office of the Ontario government which provides a wide range of general information about many ministries in one location.

To determine if a ServiceOntario Centre accepts service on behalf of the Board, call 416-326-1234 or toll free at 1-800-267-8097. This information is also available online at www.Ontario.ca.

6.2 A document that is filed by mail, courier or fax shall be sent to the Regional Office responsible for the area in which the residential complex referred to in the document is located.

A party should send a document to the Board office that is processing or will process the application. Sending the document to any other office is sufficient according to Rule 6.3, but the best practice is to send it to the correct office, avoiding possible delays or filing errors. This Rule recognizes courier and fax as acceptable methods of filing under clause 192(1)(c) of the RTA.

6.3 A document is sufficiently given if sent by mail, courier or fax to any other office of the Board, but not to a ServiceOntario Centre.

While the best practice, as contemplated by Rule 6.2, is to file documents with the office responsible for their processing, the Board will forward the documents to the responsible Regional Office as quickly as possible if they are sent to another office. Documents should not, however, be sent by mail, courier or fax to a ServiceOntario Centre.

When a Document is Considered Received

6.4 If a party files a document by mail addressed to a Board office, it is deemed to be filed on the fifth day following the day it was mailed or, if that is a non-business day, the next business day.

Subsection 192(2) of the RTA provides that a notice or document given by mail to the Board shall be deemed to have been given on the fifth day after mailing or, if earlier, the date it is actually received. A Member may not waive a provision in the RTA. For example, if a document was mailed to the Board on the 7th of the month, but was not delivered until the 20th, it is considered received on the 12th.

This Rule clarifies that the five days is computed taking into account whether or not the fifth day is a business day. A business day is a day that is not a weekend day or statutory holiday (see Rule 4.2). In the example, if the 12th was a Saturday, the document would be considered filed on the 14th (Monday). However, if the document was actually received earlier, it would be found to be received on the earlier date (see subsection 192(2) of the RTA).

6.5 If a document is filed by fax into a Board office, it will be considered received on the date imprinted by the fax machine.

For example, if a document was received by fax at 11:59 P.M. on March 3rd, it will be considered to be received on March 3rd. However, it is the responsibility of the person filing the document to ensure that the fax transmission was in fact received by the Board. No faxes should be sent to ServiceOntario Centres.

Amended October 15, 2009

Rule 7 — French Language Services

Legislation:

The French Language Services Act (the "FLSA")
The FLSA sets out general requirements for the provision of French language services in the province of Ontario. This Rule sets out the Board's practice regarding its provision of these services.

7.1 Parties are entitled to communicate with and receive services from the Board in French where:

(a) the rental unit that is the subject of an application is located in a designated area of the province as set out in the Schedule to the French Language Services Act; or

(b) the party making the request for French language services resides in a designated area.

7.2 Where a party is entitled to French language services, hearings can proceed in both French and English, or fully in French if all parties in attendance consent.

With the assistance of an interpreter, parties may participate in a Board hearing in both French and English. In some cases, however, all of the parties may be capable and willing to proceed solely in French.

7.3 Where a party is entitled to French language services, they must inform the Board in writing as soon as possible before the hearing that they require French language services at the hearing.

It is important for parties who intend to request French language services at a Board hearing to do so as quickly as possible, so that the necessary arrangements can be made for an interpreter.

7.4 Where a party makes a request at a hearing for French language services, the Member presiding at the hearing will decide how to proceed.

Where a party fails to request French language services until the day of the hearing, it will be up to the Member to decide whether or not to adjourn the hearing to a later date so that arrangements can be made for an interpreter.

7.5 Where a party is entitled to and requests French language services, the Board will book and pay for the service of an interpreter.

Where a party qualifies for and requests French language services, the Board will make the necessary arrangements for the services of an interpreter and pay the related costs.

7.6 Where a party is entitled to and requests French language services at a hearing, the Board will attempt to schedule a French-speaking Member within a reasonable time to preside at the hearing.

7.7 Where a French-speaking Member cannot be scheduled to hear a matter within a reasonable time, the Board may schedule an English-speaking Member and arrange for the services of an interpreter at the hearing.

When a party makes a request for French language services at a hearing, the Board attempts to schedule a French-speaking Member. However, it is not always possible to provide this level of service within a reasonable time from the date the application was filed. In such cases, the Board will schedule an English-speaking Member and will ensure that an interpreter is present to assist the parties and the Member.

7.8 The Board will provide all of its correspondence and decisions in French to a party who is entitled to and has requested French language services.

Where a party has requested French language services, the Board will ensure that the party receives all correspondence initiated by the Board with respect to the application in French, including a French translation of the Member's decision.

7.9 The Board will not translate documents that are filed by parties or their representatives from French to English, nor from English to French.

7.10 Where a document is filed in either English or French, the Member may order the person to also provide it in the other language, translated by a qualified translator at the person's expense, if the Member considers it necessary for the fair determination of the matter.

Where a Member determines that it is necessary for a party to provide a translation of a document they have filed, the Member should consider that the services of a certified translator can be quite costly. Where a party uses the services of an uncertified translator, however, the Member may need to determine whether the translation is adequate.

Release Date: January 31, 2007

Rule 8 — Application Screening Rules

Legislation:

Section 185 of the Residential Tenancies Act (the "RTA")

Staff of the Landlord and Tenant Board will check applications when they are filed and inform the applicant if the application is incomplete, or if they note any errors that may potentially invalidate the application; the applicant will decide how they want to proceed.

Although staff will review applications, it is always the applicant's responsibility to ensure that their application is complete, accurate and in compliance with the RTA. Ultimately it will be up to the Member hearing the application to decide whether or not the application is valid.

Applications that will be Refused

8.1 Where the RTA requires an application, other than an application made under section 126, to be accompanied by prescribed information, staff will not accept the application if the prescribed information is not filed at the same time.

Subsection 185(1) of the RTA requires that an application be accompanied by the prescribed information. If the prescribed information is not filed along with the application, the application is not properly filed and it will be returned.

The only exception is for applications for an above guideline rent increase, made under section 126 of the RTA. Staff will not check these applications for the required information before the application is filed. The process staff will follow is set out in Rules 8.5.1 and 8.5.2 below.

8.2 Staff will not accept a landlord's application for compensation for arrears, damages and/or misrepresentation of income where the landlord has indicated that the tenant is not in possession of the rental unit.

An application for the payment of arrears (s.87), compensation for damages (s.89) and compensation for misrepresentation of income (s.90) can only be made to the Board if the tenant is still in possession of the rental unit at the time the application is filed.

8.3 Staff will not accept an application to terminate the tenancy and evict the tenant for non-payment of rent if the application is being filed on or before the termination date in the landlord's notice of termination.

The RTA states that an application to terminate a tenancy and evict a tenant cannot be made until the day following the termination date specified in the notice. If the application is filed on or before the termination date, it will be returned to the landlord and the landlord informed of the earliest date that they can file the application.

8.4 Staff will not accept an application to terminate the tenancy and evict the tenant based on a notice of termination under section 62, 64 or 67 of the RTA if the application is made before the seven-day remedy period specified in the notice expires.

Where a notice of termination gives the tenant a seven-day period to remedy the notice, the application to terminate the tenancy and evict the tenant cannot be made before the 8th day. An application that is filed before the seven-day remedy period expires will be returned.

8.5 Staff will not accept an application to terminate the tenancy and evict the tenant if it is filed later than 30 days after the termination date specified in the notice, unless it is an application based on the tenant's failure to pay rent.

Applications for an Above Guideline Rent increase (s.126 of the RTA)

8.5.1 Staff will check an application made under section 126 to ensure that the landlord has included the following:

- **(i) a completed application Form L5 - Application for a Rent Increase Above the Guideline Order;**
- **(ii) if the application includes a claim under s.126(1)1:**
  - **(a) a completed Schedule 1- Details of Operating Costs**
  - **(b) supporting documents**
- **(iii) if the application includes a claim under s.126(1)2:**
  - **(a) three copies of a completed Schedule 2 - Details of Capital Expenditures;**
  - **(b) three copies of a completed "Information about Rental Units in the Complex" form**

(c) three copies of completed "Capital Expenditures: Additional Details" forms

(d) two additional copies of the L5 application form

(e) three copies of any supporting documents for the application

(f) a compact disk containing the information filed with the application in portable document format

(iv) if the application includes a claim under s.126(1)3

(a) a completed Schedule 1- Details of Operating Costs

(b) supporting documents

Although staff will check the application to ensure that the necessary forms have been filled out and that supporting documents have been filed, they will not check to confirm that there are supporting documents for each cost claimed, nor will they confirm any of the amounts claimed by the landlord against the supporting documents. Further, staff will not check for calculation errors.

8.5.2 If the information listed in Rule 8.5.1 is missing from an application made under section 126 of the RTA, staff will send the applicant a letter that:

(i) lists the information that is missing, and

(ii) informs the applicant that a hearing will not be scheduled until the missing information is received.

After a landlord files an application for an above guideline rent increase, staff will check the application to ensure that the information set out in Rule 8.5.1 has been filed. If anything is missing, staff will let the applicant know in writing. The Board will not schedule a hearing for an application for an above guideline rent increase until all the required material has been filed.

Applications with Potential Errors

8.6 Unless the application is made under section 126 of the RTA, staff will inform the applicant of any information that is missing or that may be inaccurate and give them an opportunity to correct or complete the information before the application is considered "filed."

These errors include errors or incomplete information in the name and address of the parties and rental unit; not clearly indicating which grounds are being applied for; clerical errors in calculating the amounts claimed in the application and the application not being signed.This rule does not apply to applications for an above guideline rent increase. The process Board staff will follow for this type of application is set out in Rules 8.5.1 and 8.5.2 above.

8.7 (a) If there is a potential error which may invalidate the Notice of Termination, staff will contact the applicant and ask them how they wish to proceed.

(b) Staff will return an application by mail if the applicant does not inform the Board how they wish to proceed within one business day from the time they were contacted.

If a landlord filed an application by fax, mail or courier and an error is noted that could invalidate the Notice of Termination, staff will call the landlord to inform them of this error and ask them how they wish to proceed. If staff are unable to reach the landlord, they will leave a message explaining the error and asking that the landlord contact the Board by the end of the following business day. Staff will also inform the landlord that if they do not do so, the application will be returned.

8.8 If the notice of termination specifies a termination date that is not at least the number of days required by the RTA for that type of notice, this error is considered to potentially invalidate the notice.

For example, if a termination notice is given for nonpayment of rent, the termination date for a daily or weekly tenancy must be at least 7 days and 14 days for monthly or yearly tenancies. These types of timeframes cannot be extended by the Board and thus, if the landlord has specified a termination date that is less than the number of days required, the notice would be invalid.

8.9 In addition to rule 8.8, other errors that potentially invalidate a notice of termination for non-payment of rent given under section 59 of the RTA may include:

(a) Failing to identify the tenant of the rental unit;

(b) Failing to identify the rental unit;

(c) Indicating an amount other than rent in the total amount the tenant owes;

(d) Indicating inconsistent amounts that the tenant owes within the notice;

(e) Incorrectly calculating the amounts the tenant owes (in the table explaining how the arrears owing were calculated);

(f) Failing to sign or fill in the landlord's or agent's name in the signature field of the notice form;

(g) Failing to provide contact information for the landlord or agent.

8.10 Errors that could potentially invalidate a notice of termination for reasons other than nonpayment of rent under the RTA may include:

(a) Failing to identify the tenant of the rental unit;

(b) Failing to identify the rental unit;

(c) Failing to indicate the reason for termination on a notice form that has more than one reason;

(d) Failing to provide any details in the notice of termination where the form requires details explaining the reason to be provided;

(e) Failing to give complete information in the notice as to how the tenant can remedy the problem where the notice of termination is under section 62, 64 or 67 of the RTA;

(f) Failing to sign or fill in the landlord's or agent's name in the signature field of the notice form;

(g) Failing to provide contact information for the landlord or agent.

8.11 Notwithstanding Rules 8.6 to 8.10, it will always be the applicant's decision whether or not to make any changes to the application or file it as is.

8.12 Notwithstanding Rules 8.1 to 8.10, the applicant is ultimately responsible for ensuring that the application is complete, accurate and in compliance with the RTA.

Amended December 08, 2008

Rule 9 — Refusing to Accept or Proceed with an Application

Legislation:

Section 196 of the Residential Tenancies Act (the "RTA")

Where the Board learns of an applicant's failure to pay any fine, fee or costs payable to the Board on or before the date that person submits a new application, section 196 of the RTA states that staff may refuse to accept the application "in such circumstances as may be specified in the Rules". This Rule defines the circumstances where such refusal is appropriate.

Where the Board learns of an applicant's failure to pay any fee, fine or costs before a hearing has been held, the RTA states that the proceeding shall be stayed until the fee, fine or costs have been paid. Where the Board learns of the applicant's failure to pay after a hearing has been held, the order shall not be issued until the fee, fine or costs have been paid.

In addition to these provisions, the RTA allows a Board Member to discontinue an application "in such circumstances as may be specified in the Rules". These Rules establish those circumstances.

9.1 If an applicant has failed to pay to the Board any fine, fee or costs, staff shall refuse to accept any new application from that person until the fine, fee or costs have been paid unless the issues raised in the new application are of an urgent nature.

Although the RTA enables Board staff to refuse to accept a new application from an applicant who has failed to pay a fee, fine or costs to the Board, if the new application appears urgent staff will accept it. An application might be viewed as urgent if, for example, it deals with conduct which seriously impairs the safety of the landlord or other tenants or if it has been filed in an attempt to regain entry into a rental unit where the locks have been changed illegally.

9.2 With respect to Rule 9.1, applications pursuant to section 69 for an order terminating a tenancy and evicting a tenant due to rent arrears and applications pursuant to section 87 for an order for payment of rent arrears are not urgent.

9.3 Where an employee of the Board has accepted an application pursuant to Rule 9.1, a Member may determine that the issues raised in the application are not sufficiently urgent to have justified accepting it, and:

> **(a) shall stay the proceeding,**
>
> **(b) shall inform the parties by notice that the applicant must pay the full amount owing by a specified date, not later than 15 days after the notice is issued, and**
>
> **(c) may discontinue the application if the full payment is not made by the specified date.**

Although staff may accept a new application from an applicant who owes money to the Board in accordance with Rule 9.1, a Member may find that the issues are not urgent. The Member may make this finding with or without inviting submissions from the parties. Where the Member finds that the application should not have been accepted, they will stay the proceeding and give the applicant a deadline by which to pay the outstanding monies. Where the applicant fails to pay by the deadline, the Member may discontinue the application.

9.4 Where the Board learns that the applicant has failed to pay a fine, fee or costs before a hearing is commenced, a Board Member shall inform the parties by notice that:

> **(a) the proceeding is stayed,**
>
> **(b) a hearing will not be held unless the applicant pays the fee, fine or costs by a specified date not later than 15 days after the notice is issued, and**
>
> **(c) the application may be discontinued if the full payment is not made by the specified date.**

This Rule limits the amount of time the Board will hold on to a pending application once it is learned that the applicant owes money to the Board as a result of their failure to pay a fine, fee or costs. The impact of the applicant's failure to pay, on both the Board and the respondent, is such that reasonable measures must be taken promptly to ensure that the outstanding debt is satisfied before the application can proceed.

9.5 Where a hearing is commenced and the Board learns, before the hearing is completed or before an order is issued, that the applicant has failed to pay a fine, fee or costs, the Board Member hearing the application:

> **(a) shall stay the proceeding,**
>
> **(b) shall inform the parties by notice that the hearing will not conclude or an order will not be issued unless the applicant pays the full amount**

owing by a specified date, not later than 15 days after the notice is issued, and

(c) may discontinue the application if the full payment is not made by the specified date.

Because an adjournment may result in a hearing being held over a number of days, it is possible that the Board will learn that an applicant owes money to the Board after the hearing has begun but before it is completed. In such cases, the Board Member will stay the proceeding and give the applicant a deadline to pay the outstanding fee, fine or costs and may discontinue the application where the full amount is not paid by the specified deadline.

9.6 Where an applicant has failed to pay an outstanding fine, fee or costs by the deadline specified by the Board Member, the Member may discontinue the application without refunding the filing fee unless discontinuing the application would be inappropriate in the particular circumstances.

The deadline specified by the Member provides the applicant with a reasonable amount of time to pay the outstanding fine, fee or costs to the Board. Although the Member may discontinue the application where full payment is not received by the deadline, the Member may decide that this would be inappropriate in light of the circumstances of the applicant(s) or respondent(s).

Release Date: January 31, 2007

Rule 10 — Serving the Application or Motion & the Notice of Hearing

Legislation:

Subsections 188(1) and (2) of the Residential Tenancies Act, 2006, ('the RTA')
Subsection 6(1) of the Statutory Powers Procedure Act ('the SPPA')

Related Rules:

Rules 4.1 to 4.5 (Computation of Time)
Rules 5.1 to 5.6 (Serving a Document on Another Party)
Rules 11.1 to 11.4 (Certificates of Service)

Subsection 188(1) of the RTA states that *"An applicant to the Board shall give the other parties to the application a copy of the application within the time set out in the Rules". Subsection 188(2) of the RTA requires the applicant to serve the Notice of Hearing on the respondent. Subsection 6(1) of the SPPA requires that the parties be "given reasonable notice of the hearing ..."*

The Board may set a deadline for the applicant to serve (give) the Notice of Hearing and application or motion on the respondent(s). This is to ensure that the respondent will have adequate time to prepare for the hearing.

The rules for serving these documents are set out in Rules 5.1 to 5.4. In most cases, it is expected that the applicant will serve these documents on the respondent as soon as they have filed the application or motion and received the Notice of Hearing from the Board. However, if there is a delay in serving these documents, the applicant must have regard to these Rules.

An explanation of how to count days under the RTA is set out in Rules 4.1 to 4.5.

These Rules do not apply where an application is resolved by written hearing.

10.1 For any type of application under the RTA other than those mentioned in Rules 10.2, 10.3, 10.4 and 10.5, the applicant must give a copy of the application and the Notice of Hearing to the respondent as soon as possible but not later than ten days before the hearing date.

This Rule applies to applications such as, a tenant's rebate application, a harassment application or an application filed together by the tenants of more than one unit.

10.2 For an application under section 77 or 78 of the RTA which proceeds to a hearing, the applicant must give a copy of the application and the Notice of Hearing to the respondent as soon as possible but not later than ten days before the time set for the hearing, unless otherwise directed by the Board.

Ordinarily, an application under section 77 (eviction based on a tenant's notice to vacate or an agreement of the parties to terminate the tenancy) or section 78 (eviction based on a tenant's breach of the settlement of a previous eviction application) will result in an order without a hearing. For these applications, the landlord is not required to give the application to the tenant in most cases. However, if the Member reviewing the application believes it should proceed to a hearing, the applicant will be asked to give the application and a Notice of Hearing to the tenant respondents. The usual rule is that ten days notice must be given by the landlord to the tenant, according to the usual service rules, but the Member may direct more or less notice depending on the circumstances.

10.3 Where an order is issued under section 206(1) and a party files a request to re-open the application under subsection 206(4) or 206(5), the party who files the request must give a copy of the request to re-open the application and the Notice of Hearing to the other parties as soon as possible but not later than five days before the hearing date.

When a request is filed to re-open an application that has been resolved by consent order, the hearing is scheduled promptly. As a result, the usual 10-day service of the request and notice of hearing do not apply.

10.4 For applications filed under sections 126, 132 or 148, the applicant must give a copy of the application and the Notice of Hearing to the respondent(s) as soon as possible but not later than 30 days before the hearing date.

The time to hearing is longer for certain applications than others. For example, an application to increase the rent above the guideline, an application to vary the amount of a rent reduction, or an application to transfer a tenant out of a care home. The Board recognizes that respondents may need more time to prepare for the hearing for this kind of application.

10.5 For applications filed under the following sections of the RTA, the applicant must give a copy of the application and the Notice of Hearing to the respondent as soon as possible but not later than five days before the hearing date:

> **(a) subsection 29(1), made solely or in part under paragraph 5**
>
> **(b) subsection 41(6)**
>
> **(c) section 69, based on notice given under:**
>
> > **(i) subsection 61(1) that involves an illegal act, trade, business or occupation described in clause 61(2)(a),**
> >
> > **(ii) section 63,**
> >
> > **(iii) section 65, or**
> >
> > **(iv) section 66.**
>
> **(d) section 94.**

This rule applies to applications to the Board to deal with serious and time-sensitive matters such as the illegal lock-out of a tenant, the retrieval of property after the enforcement of an eviction by the Sheriff and the eviction of a tenant whose conduct may affect the safety of other tenants and the landlord. It also applies to applications to terminate the tenancy of a tenant of a superintendent's unit when their employment has ended. This is important to ensure that a landlord is able to provide accommodation to the new superintendent in a timely manner. Whenever possible, a hearing on these types of application will be scheduled within seven days of the receipt of the application. As a result, the applicant will be required to give these documents to the respondent at least five days before the hearing.

If an applicant believes that the matter should be heard more quickly, they can ask the Board to shorten the time for serving these documents under Rule 15.

10.6 If there is more than one applicant, the applicant who files the application with the Board must give a copy of the Notice of Hearing to the other applicants.

If there are several applicants, it is the responsibility of the applicant who files the application, and receives the Notice of Hearing, to give it to the other applicants. This should be done as quickly as possible to avoid any need to reschedule or adjourn the hearing.

10.7 A party who brings a motion to set aside an ex parte order, an order under subsection 74 (3), or an order under subsection 74(8) must give a copy of the motion and the Notice of Hearing to the other party(ies) at least 48 hours before the time set for the hearing, unless otherwise directed by the Board.

Where the Board issues an ex parte order, the respondent may file a motion to set aside the order within ten days of the date it was issued. Where the Board issues an order under subsection 74(8) to void an eviction order, the respondent/landlord also has ten days to file the set-aside motion. A tenant can also make a motion under subsection 74(11) to void an eviction order after the order becomes enforceable but before it is executed, provided the tenant files a sworn affidavit stating that the required amounts have been paid to the landlord and the Board.

The usual rule is that the party bringing the motion must give 48 hours notice to the other party(ies) by any of the permitted methods of service. However, the Member may direct the party bringing the motion to give more or less notice depending on the circumstances.

10.7.1 A landlord who files a motion under s.126(13)(b) must give a copy of the motion and the Notice of Hearing to the tenant(s) affected by the motion, at least 10 days before the time set for the hearing, unless otherwise directed by the Board.

Under s.126(13)(b) of the RTA, a Member can order that an increase justified in an Above Guideline Increase Application be deferred until the landlord has completed required repairs. The order will include a date by which the repairs must be completed. Once the landlord has completed the required repairs they must file a motion with the Board by the deadline set out in the order. A hearing will be scheduled and the landlord will have to serve the Notice of Hearing, along with a copy of the motion, on the tenants affected by the motion.

10.8 If a party fails to give the Notice of Hearing and application or motion to any other party(ies) in accordance with these Rules the Member may:

> **(a) proceed with the hearing if the Member finds that the other party(ies) suffered no prejudice whatsoever as a result of the party's failure to serve the documents or to serve them on time;**
>
> **(b) adjourn the hearing to give the other party(ies) an adequate opportunity to prepare for the hearing; or**
>
> **(c) dismiss the application or motion if the Member finds that the party deliberately failed to serve the documents in accordance with these Rules.**

A Member may proceed with the application or motion if convinced that the party(ies) who were not served, or not served on time, have consented freely and without pressure from the party who filed the application or motion to proceed then with the hearing. The only other situation in which the hearing should proceed on the scheduled date is where the Member is convinced that the other party(ies) had sufficient time after they knew the details of the application or motion to prepare for the hearing.

The power to dismiss the application or motion should only be used in extraordinary circumstances. This would include a situation in which the party who filed the application or motion, or their agent, appears to have deliberately failed to serve the documents, or to serve them on time.

In most cases, an adjournment will be the appropriate way to resolve a party's failure to serve the documents according to these Rules.

The Member may also determine that any delay caused by the failure of the party who filed the application or motion to serve the other party(ies) promptly, without an appropriate reason, is unreasonable conduct as defined in the Guideline on "Costs".

Amended December 08, 2008

Rule 11 — Certificates of Service

Legislation:

Subsection 188(3) of the *Residential Tenancies Act, 2006* ('the RTA')

Related Rules:

Rules 4.1 to 4.5 (Computation of Time)
Rules 5.1 to 5.6 (Serving a Document on Another Party)
Rules 10.1 to 10.8 (Serving the Application or Motion & Notice of Hearing)

Section 188 of the RTA provides that the applicant shall give the other parties to the application a copy of the application and a copy of the Notice of Hearing issued by the Board for the application. Subsection (3) provides that a party shall file a Certificate of Service in the form approved by the Board in the circumstances set out in these Rules.

11.1 The applicant must file with the Board a Certificate of Service signed by the individual who gave the application and Notice of Hearing to another party.

The Certificate of Service is a document in which an individual declares that they have given a copy of the application and Notice of Hearing to a respondent, or a document to another person (e.g., notice of termination). Thus, the certificate may only be completed by the individual who served the documents (e.g., applicant, property manager, superintendent, process server, friend, etc.). The applicant may not sign the certificate if they were not the individual who gave the documents. The individual must state when and how the documents were served. In some cases, more than one Certificate of Service will be filed for the same application, because there may have been more than one respondent. However, the individual may certify to serving more than one individual on the same date in the same certificate if they were served in the same manner.

The best practice is to serve the application and Notice of Hearing as quickly as possible, and file the certificate right after. If the respondent does not appear at the hearing, it will be important for the applicant to prove that the application and Notice of Hearing were served; otherwise, the Member may not make an order.

11.2 The applicant shall file any necessary Certificate of Service within five days after the application and Notice of Hearing are served.

Prompt filing of the Certificate of Service is important to ensure that the file is complete for the hearing day. Thus, failure to file a certificate may result in an order for costs against the applicant or their representative, even if the applicant is successful in the application.

11.3 If the applicant does not file the Certificate of Service before the hearing, the applicant may prove service of the application and Notice of Hearing by:

(a) filing a Certificate of Service at the beginning of the hearing; or

(b) by calling as a witness at the hearing the individual who gave the application and Notice of Hearing to the other party to the application.

The applicant is expected in all cases to file the Certificate of Service as soon as they have given the application and Notice of Hearing, well in advance of the hearing. However, where this is not possible, the applicant may prove the service of the documents in two ways. A certificate may be filed at the start of the hearing. The applicant may also bring the individual who served the documents to the hearing, and call them as a witness if service is questioned.

Of course, the party who was allegedly served may challenge the facts in a Certificate of Service and give evidence that they were not served, or were served on a different date or in a different way. The Member may also have questions about the statements made in the certificate or given by a witness at the hearing.

11.4 A Member may direct any party to an application to file a Certificate of Service with respect to any document which was given in relation to the proceedings.

Not only the application and Notice of Hearing must be served on another party. For most types of eviction application, the landlord must have earlier served a notice of termination. Also, these Rules require notice to be given to another party in various circumstances. In any of these situations, the Member may require a Certificate of Service to be filed before taking any action that would result from the service of that document.

Amended October 15, 2009

Rule 12 — Rescheduling a Hearing

Legislation:

Section 183 of the *Residential Tenancies Act* (the RTA)

12.1 Where, prior to a hearing, all parties to an application agree to having the hearing of the application rescheduled, the Board may reschedule the hearing, and the original hearing shall be cancelled.

Before a party makes a request to the Board for a hearing to be rescheduled, they must contact the other parties and obtain their consent. The rescheduling request must include confirmation that the consent of the other parties has been obtained. Where the other parties do not agree to the rescheduling, the issue may be raised at the originally scheduled hearing. [See Interpretation Guideline 1, "Adjourning and Rescheduling Hearings" for additional information about making a request.]

In exceptional cases, the Board may refuse a request even where all the parties agree to the rescheduling. This might be the case where, for example, the request appears to be an attempt to delay the process.

12.2 A party who requests the rescheduling of a hearing must obtain the consent of all other parties, whether or not the notice of hearing and application have been served on the respondent(s).

Although the requestor must obtain the consent of all parties before making the rescheduling request, it is not a requirement that the application and notice of hearing be served before the rescheduling request is made. Where the applicant realizes, before they serve these documents, that they need to reschedule the hearing, the applicant will have to explain to the respondent that they have filed an application against them.

12.3 The Board may reschedule a hearing on its own initiative and the original hearing shall be cancelled.

It may be necessary from time to time for the Board to reschedule a hearing on its own initiative. In such cases, the parties and their representatives will be notified.

Amended October 15, 2009

Rule 13 — Mediation by the Board

Legislation:

Sections 74, 78, 148, 175,194 and 195 of the *Residential Tenancies Act* (the "RTA")

Related Rules:

Rule 14 (Settlements Reached Without Board Mediation)

The RTA gives special recognition to mediation of applications which is conducted by Mediators employed by the Board. Section 194 of the RTA permits the Board to attempt to mediate a settlement of any matter that is the subject of an application or agreed upon by the parties, if the parties consent to the mediation (except mandatory mediation under section 148 of the RTA for care home "transfers"). If a mediation is conducted by a Board Mediator, the agreement may include provisions that contravene the RTA. There is, however, a limitation on agreements reached through Board mediation, since negotiated rent increases cannot exceed 3% above the annual guideline.

Subparagraph 78(1)2.i of the RTA provides that the conditions imposed on the tenant in the order or mediated settlement described in paragraph 78(1)2 include only those conditions which, if not met by the tenant, would give rise to the same reasons for terminating the tenancy under the RTA as were claimed in the previous application. Thus, a term of settlement which is a condition for future termination without notice to the tenant must meet two tests; it must be the same reason that was raised in the eviction application that was settled and the reason must be one recognized by the RTA. For this reason, mediated settlements of eviction applications based only on rental arrears will not allow for a section 78 application based on late payment of future rents, once the arrears and costs have been paid.

The RTA provides that these Rules will set out the way in which the Board will dispose of an application if a Board mediated agreement resolves some or all of the issues raised by an application. If there is no mediated settlement, the Board is required to hold a hearing.

Mediators will not mediate agreements intended to modify an order of the Board, such as an agreement with terms that impose conditions on the enforceability of the order. A Board order is a final disposition of an application and as such, these types of agreements, commonly referred to as "side agreements" will not be mediated.

Pursuant to subsection 194(1) of the RTA, the Board may only mediate landlord and tenant disputes when an application has been made to the Board. The Board may decide not to mediate an application where there is little chance of success, where it will cause undue delay, or where there are minimal potential benefits.

When the parties to an application agree, a Board mediation may deal with and resolve issues which are not included in that application to satisfy the interests of the parties and to make more effective and long lasting agreements.

The Conduct of Board Mediations

13.1 A Mediator shall assist the parties in identifying their interests and in devising ways of satisfying those interests which may be agreeable to all parties.

Mediators are expected to elicit from each party their positions and interests relating to the issues. Mediators will assist the parties in focussing on their interests so as to find potential solutions to satisfy those interests.

13.2 If a Mediator ends a mediation before an agreement is reached between the parties, the application shall proceed to a hearing.

A Mediator may terminate a mediation for a number of reasons. It may become obvious that the mediation will be unsuccessful in settling the issues raised by the parties, or will take an unreasonable amount of time before a settlement becomes possible. One of the parties may become disorderly and refuse to follow the Mediator's requests to act in an orderly manner. A party may be attempting to delay the resolution of the application. A party may be badgering the other party or using inappropriate methods to obtain concessions, or misrepresent the facts, the law or the rules or practices of the Board. In any of these cases, the Mediator may bring the mediation to an end and send the parties to a hearing. Any settlement that the parties reach without the Mediator will be subject to Rules 14.1 to 14.3.

13.3 A Mediator shall explain to any party involved in a mediation the effect of any provision of the proposed agreement which may be inconsistent with the RTA or regulations before the party signs the agreement.

There may be disputes between parties to an application in which a resolution may involve an inconsistency with the rights and obligations set out in the RTA. It may be in the interests of both parties to make such an agreement. However, Board mediators will not allow a party to give up their rights under the RTA without that party being aware of what they are giving up. The degree of explanation necessary will depend on factors such as whether the party is represented at the mediation session and the nature of the contravention. The explanation may be given in the presence of all parties or in individual "caucuses" with parties.

13.4 A Mediator may describe to the parties to the mediation, the provisions of the RTA, regulations, Rules, Guidelines, relevant case law or practices of the Board.

As many parties are not represented by a lawyer or agent, they will often be unfamiliar with the procedures for a mediation or a hearing. It is proper for a Mediator to answer questions about those procedures or inform the parties about the provisions of the RTA, the regulations, a Guideline or a past decision of the Courts, former Tribunal, or the Board which appears to be relevant.

13.5 A Mediator shall not offer a personal opinion or give advice to either party to the mediation regarding the merits of the application.

The role of a Mediator is to remain neutral, while assisting the parties to come to a settlement. They are an impartial facilitator of the discussions between the parties. They do not decide the case, nor express their personal opinion about the fairest outcome, if the case were adjudicated. In this role, it is not proper to give an opinion regarding the merits of the application or any other issue raised by the parties.

Representative's Authority at a Mediation

13.6 A representative who wishes to participate in a mediation without the party they represent shall do one of the following:

> **(a) file an agency authorization signed by the party specifically authorizing them to enter into a settlement on the party's behalf;**
>
> **(b) if the representative is a lawyer entitled to practice in Ontario, give assurances that the party has authorized them to enter into a settlement on the party's behalf; or**
>
> **(c) indicate that they have the verbal authorization to act on behalf of the absent party and obtain the consent of the other participating parties and the Mediator to mediate with such an authorization.**

It is crucial to any settlement discussions in a mediation that all participants have authority to make an agreement. It is not satisfactory if a deal is reached, but a representative must have it ratified later by the party they represent. This leads to situations in which a representative can seek a settlement, and then use the client's approval as a means of trying to obtain better terms. However, if the circumstances are acceptable to the other party and the Mediator, the mediation may be conducted with the participation of the representative, even without written agency authorization. The representative must give assurances that the party has authorized them to enter into a settlement on the party's behalf. The representative must also be prepared to either sign the resulting mediated settlement as the party's authorized agent, or give consent to the terms of the settlement before a Member of the Board in the event of a joint submission for an Order of the Board on consent. If the representative is a lawyer, it is assumed that they would not misrepresent their instructions from the client, since they are subject to discipline by the Law Society.

Settlement Agreements

13.7 A Mediator may prepare a written agreement based on the parties' settlement.

This Rule recognizes that Mediators may involve themselves to the extent of assisting the parties to draft their agreement since the Board believes this helps to ensure that the parties understand their respective rights and responsibilities and promotes the clear and objective wording of agreements between parties, especially where one or both are not represented.

The Mediator will tell the parties that a written mediated agreement will not result in an order of the Board. The written agreement may be structured to provide virtually everything which could be contained in an order, including the possibility of re-opening the application according to these Rules if any party does not carry out their obligations under the agreement within one year. The written agreement may also allow for a new application for eviction being filed by the landlord without notice to the tenant pursuant to section 78 of the RTA if the tenant does not carry out specified obligations under the agreement.

13.8 If a party has paid money into the Board, the Mediator shall direct payment out of the funds in accordance with the agreement of the parties.

Under the terms of the RTA, the Board may establish procedures in its rules for the payment of money into and out of the Board. This Rule deals with any situation in which a party has either voluntarily paid money into the Board or was directed to pay money into the Board. It is important that the funds held by the Board are dealt with, and the mediated agreement must address this. If there is a full settlement, the parties must agree how much will be paid to each party. The Mediator will then use their signing authority in respect of the Board account to ensure that this agreement is carried out properly. If there is only a partial settlement, this issue may be one of those which proceeds to the hearing to be decided by the Member.

Disposing of an Application

13.9 If a written mediated settlement resolves the issues raised by an application the Mediator shall dispose of the application.

When all of the issues with respect to an application are successfully mediated and a mediated agreement is signed by each of the parties, the Mediator will dispose of the application by updating the Board's electronic records to reflect that the application was resolved by means of mediation. If mediation results in a joint submission for an order of the Board on consent, the resulting order will dispose of the application.

Section 148 of the RTA (care home transfers), provides that mediation is mandatory and that the Board may dismiss the landlord's application where the landlord fails to participate in the mediation. As a result, the Mediator must advise the Member hearing the application that mediation has been attempted, and when applicable, where the landlord has failed to participate in the mediation. The Mediator may advise the Member orally or in writing.

Partial Settlement Reached Through Board Mediation

13.10 If mediation results in the resolution of some but not all of the issues raised in the application, the Mediator may present a joint submission to the Board respecting the resolved issues, leaving the unresolved issues to be decided at the hearing in accordance with the RTA.

The parties may be able to resolve only one or some of the issues raised in the application. The Mediator will explain to the parties that the hearing of the unresolved issues in the application will proceed and an order will be issued, but the Member will not usually question the parties' agreement regarding the issues which have been settled through a Board mediation. So that the Member is clear about which issues are left to be resolved by the hearing, the Mediator may present, either orally or in writing in the form of a Joint Submission, those issues which were settled. A copy of the mediated agreement for these issues shall not be presented.

13.11 If the issues in the application are not resolved through mediation but the parties have agreed on some of the facts, a Mediator may assist the parties in preparing an "Agreed Statement of Facts" which shall be presented to the Member at the hearing.

There may be situations where the parties cannot resolve the application through mediation but they do agree to some of the facts. In such cases, and if the parties agree, the Mediator can draft an "Agreed Statement of Facts" for the parties to sign. It facilitates the hearing if the Member can be told which facts are not in dispute.

13.12 A mediated settlement of procedural matters only may result in an interim agreement being signed by the parties and this agreement will be kept as part of the Board's record. Such interim agreements will not be subject to the confidentiality provisions of Rule 13.20.

If the mediation takes place before the date of the hearing, the parties may agree to sign an interim agreement on procedural matters. Such interim agreements may include terms such as rescheduling the hearing to a different date, disclosure of issues, and payment in/out. Interim agreements must contain a provision where each party agrees to have a copy of the interim agreement placed on the Board's record for consideration by the Member when the application is decided at a hearing.

Re-opening the Application

13.13 Either party to an agreement resulting from mediation by the Board may request in writing that the application be re-opened due to the failure of the other party to meet any of the terms of the written mediated agreement.

If a party does not comply with any term of a written mediated agreement, the other party may ask to re-open the original application. A party may ask for an application to be re-opened if either monetary or non-monetary items were not complied with.

However, since the Member hearing the re-opening can only consider issues properly raised in the application, it may not be useful to ask to re-open if the part of the agreement which was breached relates to something outside the application (e.g., brought up at the mediation). Also, as the Member is limited to ordering remedies permitted by the RTA, re-opening for a breach of a provision of the agreement that could not be ordered may not have the desired effect.

This right to request re-opening of the application exists whether or not the agreement provides for the re-opening of the application. A hearing will be scheduled, but the Board may attempt to mediate a request to re-open if the parties consent.

13.14 Either party to an agreement resulting from mediation by the Board may request in writing that the application be re-opened on the basis that, during the mediation, the other party coerced them or deliberately made false or misleading representations which had a material effect on the agreement.

If a party claims that the mediation which resolved the application was affected by another party's coercion or misrepresentation of material facts, the application may be re-opened to review that issue. The first issue at the hearing will be whether there was any coercion, misrepresentation or the furnishing of misleading information. The seriousness of these allegations makes it unlikely that mediation of the request to re-open will be attempted as it would not likely be successful.

13.15 A request to re-open an application must state the alleged breach of the agreement and must be filed, with a copy of the agreement, within one year of the date the agreement was signed. However, with the consent of each party at the time of the signing of the agreement, the parties may agree to a longer re-opening period.

It is essential for the party requesting the re-opening of the application to file the agreement and set out in the request what part of the agreement was not met by the other party, and how it was not met. The request must be filed within one year of the date the agreement was signed. In some limited cases, for example, where there is an extended repayment period, the parties may agree at the time of the signing of the mediated agreement to a longer re-opening period. If the request is filed late, it must be accompanied by a request to extend the time for filing, explaining why it was late.

The procedural rules in the RTA and these Rules regarding applications apply with respect to a re-opened application. In deciding the re-opened application, the Member will usually take into consideration the terms of the agreement which were already met by each party, in deciding what remedies are then appropriate.

13.16 The person requesting that the application be re-opened shall give a copy of their request and the notice of hearing to all other parties to the application at least five days before the hearing.

Since the application is being re-opened, a hearing will be scheduled when the request is filed. A notice of hearing will be given to the party making the request. As with any application, it is their responsibility to advise the other party by giving them a copy of the notice of hearing. They must also give the other party a copy of their request (and, if applicable, a copy of the request for an extension of time). These documents must be served using one of the permitted methods of service (see Rules 5.1 to 5.2) at least five days before the scheduled hearing date.

Confidentiality of the Mediation Process

13.17 Anything said in a Board mediation and any offer to settle the application will be confidential and, where no agreement is reached, may not be used by one party against another in the same or any other proceedings.

It is essential to the mediation process that all parties trust that what they say in the mediation in order to try to settle the case is confidential and will not be used against them later in the hearing or in other Board or Court proceedings. A party should feel free to make any statement of fact or suggest that a fact in dispute may be true in the mediation without fear that it will be used as an admission (that is, the other party must still prove the fact if there is a hearing). Similarly, parties must be able to make and discuss offers to settle, without concern that the other party will raise those offers at the hearing.

By the same principle, parties should be able to make written proposals to settle, or draft proposed agreements. If the mediation does not result in a complete settlement, the document should not be used by one party against another later (whether or not the document was expressly "without prejudice").

13.18 Board Mediators shall not reveal information obtained in mediation to any other persons, including Board Members.

Board Mediators must respect the confidentiality of the mediation process.

13.19 Notwithstanding Rule 13.18, Board Mediators may discuss the issues raised and offers of settlement in collegial discussions for professional development purposes without revealing the names of the parties or other specifics about a case that may reveal the names of the parties.

13.20 Except where the parties agree otherwise, copies of any Board mediated agreements are confidential and:

> **(a) are the property of the parties; and**
>
> **(b) any signed copy which has come into the possession of the Mediator will be returned to the parties or destroyed.**

The Mediator will normally assist the parties in setting out in writing the terms of their agreement. However, the signed copies of the agreement belong to each party, and any copies in the possession of the Mediator will be destroyed. Signed copies which are given to the Mediator for any reason will be returned to the party for whom they were intended. It is the intention of the Board to preserve the interest of the parties in maintaining confidentiality regarding the terms of their agreements.

13.21 Unless the Mediator is required by law to disclose information provided during a mediation, any information provided to the Mediator:

> **(a) will not be disclosed to any other party without the consent of the party who provided it;**
>
> **(b) will not be retained by the Board; and**
>
> **(c) if it is a document, will be returned to the party who provided it,**

unless the party who provided it asks that it be placed on the application file.

The information may have been provided verbally or in the form of documents. A document provided to a Mediator will be returned to the party who submitted it after the mediation is terminated, and no copy will be retained in the application file (unless the party requested it to be filed). However, some documents received during a mediation are intended to be evidence or submissions to be placed in the application, and will be considered if there is a hearing because the mediation is not successful.

Permission to give the documents or information to other parties would normally be obtained when the information was provided, but could be obtained later. Permission will always be obtained before the information or document is shared with other parties. Permission can be given by the party regarding specified information or documents in writing or orally (noted in the file).

Under section 175 of the RTA, a Member or Mediator cannot be compelled to give testimony or produce documents in a civil proceeding if the information came to their knowledge in the course of their duties under the RTA. This means that a Mediator cannot be called to a hearing of the Board or a Court to report what was said at a mediation session or in separate discussions with any party.

However, in extraordinary cases, the evidence of a Mediator may be compelled in Court (such as at a criminal trial, where the public interest requires the evidence). It is also possible that information will have to be produced to a member of the public under the provisions of the Freedom of Information and Protection of Privacy Act. Further, the Board recognizes that it has an obligation to advise appropriate officials if any potential criminal act or intention is revealed in the course of the mediation.

13.22 Despite Rule 1.5, Rules 13.17 to 13.21 may not be waived or varied.

Rule 1.5 allows a Member to waive or vary any of these Rules in the circumstances of the application. However, the Rules concerning confidentiality of the mediation process cannot be waived or varied by the Member in any circumstances.

Release Date: January 31, 2007

Rule 14 — Settlements Reached Without Board Mediation

Legislation:

Section 3 of the *Residential Tenancies Act* (the "RTA")
Section 206 of the RTA
Section 4.1 of the *Statutory Powers Procedure Act* (the "SPPA")

Related Rules:

Rule 13 (Mediation by the Board)

There will be cases in which the parties, between themselves, resolve an application without any assistance from a Mediator employed by the Board. They may also retain the services of a private mediator or any other person to assist them in settling the dispute between them. These Rules deal with the consequences of such an agreement.

Section 3 of the RTA provides that the Act applies, regardless of any agreement or waiver to the contrary. Thus, parties may only settle an application by agreeing to terms or conditions which are consistent with the legislation. Section 4.1 of the SPPA permits an order to be issued without a hearing, on the consent of the parties, so long as the Act under which the order is issued permits this. The power to issue a "consent order" under the RTA is restricted by section 3, in that no order may include terms which contravene the Act. This is further confirmed by subsection 194(2) of the RTA which allows a settlement to contain provisions which contravene the Act, but only where it was mediated by the Board.

If the parties settle the issues raised by the application, and part of the agreement is that the application will be withdrawn, the applicant may withdraw the application without the consent of the Board at any time prior to the commencement of the hearing (subject to the provisions of subsection 200(3) of the RTA). However, if any term of the agreement to settle is not in accordance with the Act, the fact that the parties agreed to it will not prevent the applicant from applying again or affect the result of any subsequent application.

If the parties settle the application, and part of the agreement is that an order should be issued in accordance with what the parties have agreed, these Rules will apply.

14.1 If the parties have settled an application without mediation by the Board, and all parties request that some or all of the terms of their agreement be made part of an order, a party may file the agreement at the beginning of the hearing.

A party may file an agreement to settle or "minutes of settlement" before the hearing date, but all of the parties should still attend the hearing. If a party files the agreement at the hearing, this should be done before any evidence is heard. The Member will then review the agreement in accordance with Rule 14.2.

14.2 If the Member is satisfied that the terms of the agreement:

(a) are in accordance with the provisions of the RTA, and

(b) do not include any term which the RTA would not permit to be ordered for the application,

an order may be issued in accordance with the agreement or, with the consent of the parties, another order may be issued that would be more appropriate, based on what the parties have agreed to and in compliance with this Rule.

Parties to an application may settle issues that are beyond the scope of the application in their agreement. Or, their settlement may include terms that would normally not be included in an order for that type of application.

The Member will ask the parties any questions necessary to satisfy themselves that the parties fully appreciate the consequences of their agreement and that it was voluntarily settled. This will be difficult in some cases without understanding all of the facts of the case. Nevertheless, in view of section 3 of the RTA, the Member should ensure that the parties' agreement is not inconsistent with any provision of the Act. In some cases, they may ask for evidence to confirm this.

If the Member believes that another order would be appropriate, based on the basic principles that the parties have agreed to, the Member may ask whether the parties consent to that order. If the Member decides not to adopt the agreed terms within an order, and the parties do not agree to any variation proposed by the Member, the hearing on the merits of the application will proceed, unless the applicant wishes to withdraw the application (and, if required, permission to withdraw is granted, such as in a harassment application).

14.3 If the parties to an application have settled, or are close to a settlement of the issues between them, they may request that a Board Mediator facilitate a mediated settlement of the application before the Board.

Only settlements resulting from mediation by the Board will dispose of the application without an order. Settlement of the issues raised by an application without the assistance of a Board Mediator may result in an agreement, but an order in accordance with the agreement will only be issued if the terms are not inconsistent with the Act.

If the parties have already settled some or all of the issues between them and approach a Board Mediator, the Mediator may agree to conduct a mediation with them in accordance with Rule 13. This will include eliciting from each party their interests and whether the terms they have already agreed to satisfy those interests.

The special provisions for settlements mediated by the Board recognizes that Mediators employed by the Board will have a role in ensuring that the mediation is fair and the parties realize what they may be giving up, if they are agreeing to settlements that may contravene the Act. If the parties have settled the application themselves or through an outside mediator, the Board cannot be sure that the parties were aware of their rights.

14.4 Rules 14.1 through 14.3 do not apply to agreements made under s.206 of the RTA.

Under section 206 of the RTA the Board may issue an order on consent without holding a hearing if the parties submit an agreement. In these cases, it is not necessary for the parties to appear before a Member at a hearing.

Amended July 5, 2007

Rule 15 — Extending and Shortening Time

Legislation:

Section 190 of the *Residential Tenancies Act, 2006* ('the RTA')

Related Rules:

Rule 13.15 (Mediation by the Board: Re-opening Applications)
Rule 30.1 (Order Void or Stayed)
Rule 29.3 - 29.4 (Review of Orders: Time for Making a Request)

Regulation:

Section 56 of Ontario Regulation 516/06

The RTA and the Board's Rules of Practice establish a number of deadlines for filing applications and other documents with the Board, and for serving documents to other parties. Subsection 190(1) of the RTA specifically authorizes the Board to extend or shorten the time for making an application under: section 126 (to increase the rent above guideline), subsection 159(2) (for a determination that the landlord's grounds for refusing consent to an assignment of a mobile home site are reasonable), and/or section 226 (to review a provincial work order). Subsection 190(2) permits the Board to extend or shorten time for other matters in proceedings in accordance with these Rules.

15.1 Subject to section 56 of O. Reg. 516/06, a party may make a request to extend or shorten time.

For example, a party may file a motion to set aside an ex parte order after the deadline if they submit a request for an extension of time when filing the motion. Under subsection 77(7) of the RTA, an ex parte order is stayed if a motion to set aside the order is received by the Board. When a motion is filed late, it will not stay the order unless a Member decides to extend the time for filing the motion. It is important to determine as quickly as possible whether the extension of time is granted.

A party may also request an extension of time where a Member has allowed a party to file a document by a certain date, and the party realizes that they may have difficulty meeting the deadline. In this case, the party should make the request for extension of time as soon as they become aware of the need for it.

A party may make a request to shorten the time requirement to serve a Notice of Hearing or for other procedural matters. However, the Board has no authority to extend or shorten those time requirements which are specified under the regulations (see section 56), such as notice requirements for terminating tenancies or the 12 month deeming rule for rent to be lawful under subsection 119(1) of the RTA.

A request pursuant to this Rule may include a request to extend the time to either request reasons or request a review of an order (see Rule 15.6 commentary).

15.2 A request to extend or shorten time must be in writing and must set out the reasons why additional time is requested.

Where a document is filed after the deadline, it is up to the party making the request to set out in writing the reasons why additional time is necessary. Documents, except for applications made under section 126, subsection 159(2) or section 226, will not be accepted without a written request for an extension of time.

15.3 Where the request to extend or shorten time is related to a document in a party's possession, the document must be filed along with the request.

For example, if a party is filing a request to review an order more than 30 days after the order was issued, the party must file the request to extend time along with the review request. This will avoid delays in processing the document if the request to extend or shorten time is granted.

15.4 Where the Board has denied a party's request to extend or shorten time, no subsequent request from the same party to extend or shorten the same time requirement will be considered.

Where a party has sought an extension of time (or an abridgement of time, as the case may be) to do a particular thing, such as file a set aside motion, a Member will decide whether or not to grant the request. If the request is denied, the same party may not file another request seeking the same remedy, even if different reasons are set out in the subsequent request.

15.5 A Member may extend or shorten the time for filing a document without obtaining or considering submissions from the other parties to the application.

It may be prejudicial to a party to delay the decision on the request to extend or shorten time by seeking submissions from the other parties to the application. In many cases, it will be necessary to decide the issue based only on the reasons given in the request. However, a Member may seek submissions from the other parties before deciding the issue.

15.6 A Member shall consider the following factors in deciding whether to extend or shorten any time requirement under the RTA or these Rules:

(a) the length of the delay, and the reason for it;

(b) any prejudice a party may experience;

(c) whether any potential prejudice may be remedied;

(d) whether the request is made in good faith; and

(e) any other relevant factors.

The Board has the discretion to extend or shorten a time period set out in the RTA or the Rules, or refuse such a request. In most cases, the request will be to extend time, and the length of the delay requested is very relevant. So too are the reasons that the party explains as the need for the extension.

If the extension causes little or no prejudice to other parties, a close examination of the reason for and length of the extension will be less important.

Although subsection 190(2) of the RTA authorizes the Board to extend or shorten time requirements in accordance with these Rules, the regulations limit which time requirements under the RTA may be extended.

For example, a party may request an extension of time to file a request for review because they have requested reasons within a reasonable time, and those reasons were not issued in time to review those reasons and file the request for a review of the order within the 30 days prescribed by this rule.

15.7 A document for which a request to extend or shorten time is required is deemed not to be received until the request has been made and granted.

If the request to extend or shorten time is denied, the document will be returned to the party who submitted it, as the document will not be considered to have been accepted by the Board.

15.8 If the request to extend or shorten time is granted, the document will be deemed to have been received on the date on which the party filed it.

15.9 Rules 15.7 and 15.8 do not apply to applications made under section 126, subsection 159(2) and section 226 of the RTA.

A request to extend or shorten time made on an application filed under section 126(for an above guideline increase), subsection 159(2) (for a determination that the landlord's grounds for refusing consent to an assignment of a mobile home site are reasonable) or section 226 (to review a work order) is typically handled as a preliminary matter at the hearing. In order to schedule a hearing, the application must be accepted.

Amended July 5, 2007

Rule 16 — Amending Applications

Legislation:

Section 200 and subsection 201(1) of the *Residential Tenancies Act, 2006* ('the RTA')

Subsection 200(1) of the RTA permits an applicant to amend an application in accordance with the Rules.

Subsection 201(1) also permits the Board to amend an application on its own motion and on notice to the parties where the Board considers it appropriate and as long as to do so would not be unfair to any party.

16.1 An applicant who wishes to amend the application before the hearing shall:

(a) file the written request for the amendment and an amended application;

(b) give a copy of the documents to all other parties;

(c) file a certificate of service for the request and the amended application.

The applicant should give written notice of the amendment to the Board and the respondent(s) as soon as possible after the need for the amendment becomes known. The applicant should give this notice by filing both:

- *a written request describing the amendment requested, and*
- *a copy of the application marked "Amended" at the top of the first page, and clearly showing the requested amendment at the appropriate place in the application in a way that the respondent will understand it, initialling the changes. (Usually the applicant will photocopy the application, and highlight the amendment on this copy.)*

The applicant must give a copy of the written request and the amended application to each respondent. This should be given using one of the methods of service permitted by section 191 of the RTA and Rules 5.1 to 5.6. A certificate of service must be filed to prove that the documents were given to each respondent.

The applicant must decide whether the amendment is so minor that it should be raised at the beginning of the hearing, or whether notice should be given earlier to the respondents. The best practice is to give notice of the requested amendment to each respondent and the Board as much before the hearing as possible. The applicant must still convince the Member that the amendment is proper.

16.2 When an applicant files a request to amend an application, staff of the Board will process the amended application and, if necessary, issue a new Notice of Hearing. The decision about whether or not to grant the requested amendment will be made by a Member.

When an amended application is filed, staff will process it according to the usual application filing procedures. Where the amendment affects the information that appears on the Notice of Hearing, a new notice will be issued. The decision about whether or not to grant the amendment will be made by the Member at the hearing.

16.3 If a new Notice of Hearing is required, the hearing date in the new notice will remain the same as the existing Notice of Hearing unless the applicant has consent of all parties to reschedule. If a new Notice of Hearing is issued, the applicant must give a copy to each respondent.

If there no consent to reschedule and there is insufficient time for the applicant to provide the required amount of service of the new Notice of the Hearing, the matter will proceed as originally scheduled and it will be up to the Member at the hearing or who otherwise decides the application, to deal with any issues raised as a result of the insufficient service.

If a new Notice of Hearing is issued, the applicant should give it to the other parties using one of the methods of service permitted by section 191 of the RTA and Rules 5.1 to 5.6. A certificate of service must be filed to prove that the notice was given to each respondent.

16.4 A Member shall decide whether to permit an amendment taking into consideration the following factors:

> **(a) whether the amendment was requested as soon as the need for it was known, if that was important in the circumstances;**
>
> **(b) any prejudice a party may experience as a result of the amendment;**
>
> **(c) whether the amendment is significant enough to warrant any delay that may be caused by the amendment;**
>
> **(d) whether the amendment is necessary and was requested in good faith; and**
>
> **(e) any other relevant factors.**

The Board has the discretion to accept an amendment of an application, or refuse to permit it. Some amendments are necessary because they correct mistakes which are so significant that, without them, the respondent would not understand what they were to answer, or the hearing would deal with the wrong issues. Other amendments are less significant (e.g., a minor up-dating of information, or addition of information that does not change the relief requested). The Member should consider the need for the amendment, balancing this against any delay in requesting it (notifying the respondents) and any prejudice the respondents will suffer if they must respond to it. The Member may consider any other relevant factor when deciding the application.

The decision to accept or reject a proposed amendment will be made by the Member at the start of the hearing, and rarely if ever in advance.

16.5 Where the parties to an application resolve the application through mediation conducted by the Board and the parties agree to the requested amendment, the application will be considered amended.

For example, if the applicant has named a child of the tenant as one of the tenants in the application and both the applicant and respondent agree that the child's name should be removed from the application, the Mediator will make note of this amendment in the Board's file. In this case, the parties would not be required to appear before a Member to have a decision made on the amendment to the application.

Release Date: January 31, 2007

Rule 17 — Withdrawing an Application

Legislation:

Section 200 of the *Residential Tenancies Act, 2006* ('the RTA')

Related Rules:

Rule 22 (Written Hearings)

Subsection 200(2) of the RTA allows an applicant to withdraw an application without the consent of the Board if the request is made before the hearing begins. Subsection 200(4) provides that, once the hearing starts, the applicant may only withdraw the application with the consent of a Member. However, under subsection 200(3), a tenant who applies under paragraph 4 of subsection 29(1) of the RTA may not withdraw an application at any stage without the consent of the Board.

When a Hearing Begins

17.1 For the purposes of subsection 200(2) of the RTA, an oral or electronic hearing has begun when the parties first appear before a Member, even if the appearance is only to deal with a preliminary matter.

It is important to be certain when a hearing has begun in order to ascertain whether or not a Member's consent is required before an application can be withdrawn. Note that this definition of when a hearing has begun only applies for the purposes of determining whether or not consent is required, and does not necessarily mean that the Member who heard the preliminary matter is seized with the application.

17.2 For the purposes of subsection 200(2) of the RTA, a written hearing has begun when the respondents' deadline to file responses has passed.

When an application is being resolved by written hearing, deadlines are established for respondents to file responses to the application, and for the applicant to reply to those responses (see Rule 22.4).

Applicant's Responsibility to Notify Respondents

17.3 An applicant who withdraws an application shall promptly notify the Board and each other party.

It is the responsibility of the applicant to notify each respondent that the hearing has been cancelled because of the withdrawal, even if the Notice of Hearing has not been served.The best practice is for the applicant to notify the Board and the other party or parties in writing of the withdrawal of the application. However, the Board will accept verbal notice of a withdrawal.

Amended July 5, 2007

Rule 18 — Severing an Application

Legislation:

Section 199 of the *Residential Tenancies Act* (the "RTA")

18.1 Where an application is created as the result of the severing of another application, any procedural requirements that were satisfied, or procedural issues resolved in the original application continue to apply to the severed application, unless a Member decides otherwise.

This Rule ensures that a party's rights are not prejudiced in situations where the Board determines that an application will be severed into a number of separate applications. For example, if the Member dealing with the original application grants a party's request to close the file to the public, the party who made the request would not have to make this request again where another application was created as a result of severing. However, a Member could determine that because of the severing, the issues raised which lead to the closing of the original file are now not applicable to all of the applications, and those applications where public access is no longer an issue could be opened to the public.

Release Date: January 31, 2007

Rule 19 — Disclosure Rules

Legislation:

Section 5.4 of the *Statutory Powers Procedure Act* ('the SPPA')

Under section 5.4 of the SPPA, a tribunal may, at any stage of its proceedings up to the end of the hearing, make orders for the exchange of documents, the exchange of reports of expert witnesses, the provision of particulars and any other form of disclosure. The tribunal must adopt rules of practice in order to use this authority but cannot use these powers to require the production of privileged information.

Disclosure may be useful to facilitate a better hearing, especially if proper consideration is given to the type of proceedings, the knowledge of the parties about procedures, and the desire for an expeditious and fair procedure.

Note that the powers set out in these rules are in addition to the power the Board has to conduct inquiries or direct parties to file additional evidence as set out in s.201 of the RTA. Further discussion of the Board's powers under s.201 may be found in the Board's Guideline 13 - Other Powers of the Board.

19.1 (1) A Member may, at any stage of the proceeding, before the hearing has been completed, direct or order a party to disclose and exchange documents or any other material relevant to the proceeding, within the time and according to the method that the Member directs or orders.

(2) A Member shall not direct or order the disclosure of privileged information.

(3) A party who breaches an order or direction for disclosure may not rely on the evidence that was not disclosed as directed or ordered, unless otherwise ordered.

The rules of natural justice provide parties with the right to know the case that they must meet at a hearing and the right to disclosure from an opposing party of all documents or other material relevant to the issues in the hearing. The scope of disclosure includes documents or other material that might enable the other party to advance its case or to damage the case of the adversary.

The Board strongly encourages cooperation from parties in voluntarily disclosing and exchanging all relevant documents or other material, before or on the day of the hearing. Where necessary, a Member will make an order or issue a direction, in order to assist a party in obtaining disclosure in a manner that ensures a fair hearing.

19.2 A landlord who applies for an above guideline rent increase based on paragraphs 1 or 3 of subsection 126(1) shall be prepared to disclose at the hearing the rent for each rental unit in the residential complex, and the date that rent was established for a new tenant under section 113 of the RTA or last increased for an existing tenant.

On an application for an above guideline rent increase based on an extraordinary increase in the cost for municipal taxes and charges or utilities or both, or based on operating costs related to security services the landlord does not have to file a detailed list of rents for all the rental units in the residential complex. They should, however, bring such a list to the hearing in case the total rent information for the complex is disputed by the tenant or questioned by the Member. In addition to the rent information (total rent charged for each unit, before any discounts, as of the month the application is made), the landlord should be prepared to give evidence as to the date that rent was established: if the rent was set for a new tenant, the date is when the tenancy began; if the rent was the result of an increase for an existing tenant, the date is when the rent last increased.

Where a landlord makes an application for a rent increase above the guideline based on capital expenditures incurred, they are required by paragraph 22(1)2 of O.Reg. 516/06 to file a detailed list of rents, among other materials, with the application.

Amended December 08, 2008

Rule 20 — Pre-Hearing Conferences

Legislation:

Section 5.3 of the *Statutory Powers Procedure Act* ('the SPPA')

Under section 5.3 of the SPPA, a Board may direct the parties to attend a pre-hearing conference. The Board must adopt rules of practice in order to be able to use this authority. The purpose of a conference is to discuss the preparations for the hearing and the hearing itself, including attempts to define and narrow the issues in dispute, disclose potential evidence and witness lists, and discuss the possibilities of mediation.

Generally speaking, the Board will direct a conference to be held only where it is anticipated that there will be a lengthy hearing of one or more days, and the hearing could be shortened or made more effective as a result of a pre-hearing conference.

Direction to Attend

20.1 A Member may direct a pre-hearing conference to be held to consider any or all of the following:

> **(a) which issues will be dealt with at the hearing and whether these can be clarified or simplified;**
>
> **(b) whether any facts or evidence may be agreed upon by the parties;**
>
> **(c) the dates by which any steps in the proceeding are to be taken or begun;**
>
> **(d) the estimated duration of the hearing; and**
>
> **(e) any other matter that may assist in the just and most expeditious disposition of the application.**

A Member or staff member may conduct the pre-hearing conference, but it may only be held at the direction of a Member. There are various issues which could be considered. For example, the parties could make submissions concerning whether a party should be added or removed, the date by which any step should be taken or begun, the order of proceedings at the hearing and the estimated length of the hearing.

A pre-hearing conference is intended to deal with procedural issues, to the largest degree possible by consensus among the parties. However, where necessary, the conference may result in recommendations or, if a Member presided, a procedural order or direction.

Release Date: January 31, 2007

Rule 21 — Electronic Hearings

Legislation:

Section 5.2 of the *Statutory Powers Procedure Act* (the "SPPA")

Under subsection 5.2(2) of the SPPA, a tribunal may hold an electronic hearing rather than an "oral hearing" (a face to face hearing, or a hearing in person). "Electronic hearing" means a hearing held by conference call, video conferencing or some other means of electronic technology permitting persons to hear one another. An electronic hearing should not be held unless all parties, the Member and the witnesses can hear each other at all times.

According to subsection 5.2(2) of the SPPA, a tribunal will not hold an electronic hearing if a party satisfies it that holding an electronic hearing instead of an oral hearing is likely to cause the party significant prejudice.

When to Hold an Electronic Hearing

21.1 In deciding whether to hold an electronic hearing, the Board may consider any relevant factors, including:

(a) the number of parties to the proceeding;

(b) the suitability of the electronic technology for the subject matter of the hearing;

(c) whether the nature of the evidence is appropriate for an electronic hearing, including whether credibility is in issue and the extent to which facts are in dispute;

(d) the extent to which the matters in dispute are questions of law;

(e) the convenience of the parties; and

(f) the cost, efficiency and timeliness of proceedings.

Electronic hearings are most appropriate in cases in which there are few issues of fact to be decided, there will be few witnesses, and they are not likely to be cross-examined. However, cases with some factual issues can be heard electronically. This kind of hearing is well suited to dealing with submissions on procedural and legal issues.

There may be logistics which would make an electronic hearing difficult or unworkable, such as lack of facilities for viewing videos, no way of viewing photographs, or the lack of a fax machine to view documents that should be exchanged during the hearing.

In some cases, an electronic hearing on an early date may be preferred by the parties, and it may also be more convenient than travelling to a hearing facility and spending more time. In many cases, an electronic hearing will result in less public expense and will permit an earlier resolution of the application. This is not to say that the Board will hold most hearings electronically, but this option may be used in appropriate cases.

21.2 A party to an electronic hearing who objects to the type of hearing shall file an objection in writing with the Board by the date set out in the notice of electronic hearing, setting out how an electronic hearing would cause them significant prejudice.

For an electronic hearing (unlike a written hearing) a party's objection will not automatically convert the hearing into an oral one. It will be up to the Member who reviews the submissions to decide whether the electronic hearing would significantly prejudice the party who objects. The Member may, without hearing from the other parties, decide to convert the hearing to an oral hearing (a hearing in person) or to continue with the electronic hearing because there is no significant prejudice. The Member may also decide to invite submissions from the other parties before deciding this question.

Conditions for an Electronic Hearing

21.3 If directed by the Board, the party specified in the direction may be required to arrange for the facilities or equipment necessary for the electronic hearing, including paying any associated expenses.

Where an electronic hearing is scheduled at the request of a party, the Member may require that party to pay all or part of the cost of providing the necessary facilities.

Procedural directions specific to individual hearings could, for example, identify who will be responsible for setting up electronic hearings and paying for facilities, and in which locations video-conferences can be held. Usually conference calls will be arranged by and paid for by the Board, but one or more parties may be required to pay the costs of video-conferences.

Release Date: January 31, 2007

Rule 22 — Written Hearings

Legislation:

Section 5.1 of the *Statutory Powers Procedure Act* (the "SPPA")
Subsections 184(2) & (3) of the *Residential Tenancies Act* (the "RTA")

Related Rules:

Rule 17 (Withdrawing an Application)
Rule 21 (Electronic Hearings)

Under section 5.1 of the SPPA, the Board may hold a written hearing rather than an "oral hearing" (a face to face hearing) or an "electronic hearing" (held by conference call, video conferencing or some other means of electronic technology permitting persons to hear one another). In a written hearing, the parties are required to file their evidence and make submissions to the Board in writing. The Board makes a decision based on the evidence and submissions filed without holding an oral hearing.

Written hearings are inexpensive and easy to arrange. However, they may not be suitable for applications where facts may be in dispute or credibility is an issue.

Subsection 5.1(2) of the SPPA as amended on February 14, 2000, sets out that if a party satisfies the Board that there is a good reason not to hold a written hearing, the Board will not do so. However, subsection 184(2) of the RTA sets out that if the application was made under sections 132 or 133 or if it was made solely under paragraph 1 of subsection 126(1) of the RTA, subsection 5.1(2) of the SPPA does not apply. For applications which relate to municipal property taxes or utilities, parties are not invited to make submissions regarding whether or not the application should be resolved by written hearing.

Subsection 5.1(3) of the SPPA sets out that in a written hearing, all parties are entitled to receive every document that the Board receives in a proceeding. However, under subsection 184(3) of the RTA applications related to municipal property taxes or rent increases above the guideline are exempt from this provision. As a result, the requirement for all parties to receive every document that the Board receives does not apply to applications under sections 126, 132 and 133. For these applications, the applicant is required to serve only the application and notice of hearing on the other parties. As well, the Board is not required to send copies of the documents filed with respect to an application to the parties.

If a party wants to review the documents, they can do so by requesting to view the application file at a Board office. Also, if the application was filed under section 126 and includes a claim for capital expenditures, landlords are required to make extra efforts to give tenants access to the supporting documents for the application. Additional information on these requirements may be found in the Board's Guideline 14 - Above Guideline Rent Increase Applications.

When to Hold a Written Hearing

22.1 In deciding whether to hold a written hearing, the Board may consider any relevant factors, including:

> **(a) the suitability of a written hearing format considering the subject matter of the hearing;**
>
> **(b) whether the nature of the evidence is appropriate for a written hearing, including whether credibility is in issue and the extent to which facts are in dispute;**
>
> **(c) the extent to which the matters in dispute are questions of law;**
>
> **(d) the convenience of the parties;**
>
> **(e) the ability of the parties to participate in a written hearing; and**
>
> **(f) the cost, efficiency and timeliness of proceedings.**

The Board may schedule a written hearing if the application was made under sections 132 (an application to vary the amount of a rent reduction) or 133 (an application for a rent reduction for municipal taxes) or if it was made solely under paragraph 1 of subsection 126(1) of the RTA (an application for an above guideline rent increase due to increased municipal taxes or utilities). The evidence (in these applications) is generally straightforward and objective and in most cases parties will not dispute the facts or need to test credibility. As a result, these applications are ideally suited for written hearings.

The Board may schedule written hearings for other applications such as applications to increase the rent above the guideline ***not*** based solely on the ground of increased taxes or utilities, or if a written hearing was requested by the applicant. However, a written hearing ***may*** not always be appropriate, for example, where credibility is an issue, and the Board will schedule an oral or electronic hearing instead.

22.2 A party who objects to a written hearing shall file an objection in writing with the Board no later than 27 days after the notice of written hearing is issued, setting out why the party believes the application should not be resolved by a written hearing.

The 27 day period for objecting will be set out in the notice of written hearing. If a party files an objection within the 27 day deadline, the Board will consider whether to convert the hearing to either an oral or an electronic hearing. However, if the application was made under sections 132 or 133 or if it was made solely under paragraph 1 of subsection 126(1) of the RTA, the Board can proceed with the written hearing despite a party's objection. A 27 day period for objecting will not be set out in the notice of written hearing for these applications.

22.3 Whenever appropriate, the Board may continue a written hearing as:

(a) an oral hearing;

(b) an electronic hearing, after considering any objections made under Rule 21.2.

In some cases, a Member may decide after beginning a written hearing that an oral or an electronic hearing would be more appropriate. For example, the Member may decide that oral submissions are necessary to resolve facts in dispute. The Member may convert the written hearing to an oral or electronic hearing without inviting submissions from the parties. If the Member is considering an electronic hearing, and is aware of any objections to an electronic hearing, the Member will consider the objections before making the decision. Provisions for objecting to electronic hearings are set out in Rule 21.2.

Document Filing Procedure

22.4(1) The applicant shall serve a copy of the application and the notice of written hearing on each respondent no later than 20 days after the notice of written hearing is issued.

(2) If the application was made for an increase above the guideline under section 126 of the RTA, and if a party wishes to respond, they shall do so by filing a response with the Board no later than 50 days after the notice of written hearing is issued.

(3) For all other applications, if a party wishes to respond, they shall do so by filing a response with the Board no later than 34 days after the notice of written hearing is issued.

(4) A response shall:

(a) set out the party's submissions;

(b) set out any remedy or other relief requested; and

(c) be accompanied by the evidence that explains or supports the response.

(5) If the application was made for an increase above the guideline under section 126 of the RTA, the applicant may reply to a response by filing a reply with the Board no later than 65 days after the notice of written hearing is issued.

(6) For all other applications, the applicant may reply to a response by filing a reply with the Board no later than 41 days after the notice of written hearing is issued.

In a written hearing, respondents to the application are entitled to respond to the evidence and submissions made by the applicant. Applicants are entitled to reply to any responses. The deadlines for responding, and for replying to responses are set out in the notice of written hearing. If the respondent or applicant responds or replies after the deadline for doing so has expired, the Member may decide not to consider the response or reply.

Pursuant to subsection 5.1(3) of the SPPA, all parties to the application being resolved by a written hearing are entitled to receive copies of any document filed with the Board. Therefore, the applicant and respondents are required to serve a copy of any document they file with the Board in a written hearing on the other parties to the application. However, in accordance with subsection 184(3) of the the RTA, applications that are limited to claims regarding taxes or rent increases above the guideline are exempt from this provision.

22.5 If the application was made under sections 126, 132 or 133 of the RTA, then parties to the application are not required to serve copies of any documents filed with respect to the application on the other parties to the application, except as required by subsection 126(4) and the related regulations and Rule 22.4, sub rule (1).

Subsection 184(3) of the RTA states that if the application was made under sections 126, 132 or 133 then, subsection 5.1(3) of the SPPA does not apply. This means that for these applications, parties are not required to serve copies of the documents they file with the Board on the other parties (other than the requirement for the applicant to serve the application and the notice of hearing on the other parties).

Certificate of Service

22.6 The applicant must file with the Board a certificate of service according to Rule 11.1 no later than 25 days after the notice of written hearing is issued.

22.7 If the applicant fails to file the certificate of service by the date set out in Rule 22.6 the Board may dismiss the application.

Rule 11.1 requires an applicant to file a certificate of service demonstrating that they have given a copy of the application and the notice of hearing to the other parties to the application. The deadline for filing the certificate of service will be set out in the notice of written hearing.

Amended July 5, 2007

Rule 23 — Requiring a Witness to Attend a Hearing

Legislation:

Section 12 of the *Statutory Powers Procedure Act* (the "SPPA")

Section 12 of the SPPA permits the Board to issue a summons to require a witness to attend a hearing and give sworn or unsworn evidence and to produce documents, records, and things which are relevant and admissible.

23.1 Any Member may sign a summons to a witness.

This Rule clarifies that the Chair is not required to sign a summons, nor will it always be the Member who eventually hears the case. Since the RTA does not address who may issue a summons, clause 12(2)(b) of the SPPA provides the Chair will do so. The Rule allows any Member to sign the summons.

23.2 An applicant who requests the issuance of a summons to a witness shall provide a written request to the Board, stating the necessity and relevance of the summons. This request shall be made promptly after the applicant becomes aware of the need for the summons.

If a Member is satisfied by the written request that the evidence sought will be relevant and will likely be admissible, the Member will issue a summons. It is preferable that the summons be issued as soon before the hearing as possible so that it can be served on the witness in time to allow them to arrange to attend the hearing. The written request should set out the following:

- *the name of the witness and their address for service;*
- a summary of the evidence to be given by the witness;
- *an explanation of why the evidence of the witness would be relevant and necessary; and*
- details of any documents or things which the witness should be required to bring to the hearing.

If the party requesting the summons is represented by a lawyer or paid agent, the request should be accompanied by a drafted summons, ready to be signed by a Member.

23.3 A respondent who requests the issuance of a summons to a witness shall provide a written request, stating the necessity and relevance of the summons, promptly after being served with the notice of hearing.

The timing of making the request (same contents as listed under Rule 23.2) is different for a respondent since they do not become aware of the application until the notice of hearing is served on them by the applicant. Again, it is preferable to file the request as early as possible so that the summons may be served by the respondent on the witness as much before the hearing as possible.

23.4 The issuance or refusal to issue a summons may be reviewed by the Member presiding at the hearing.

In some cases, the Board may choose not to decide whether to issue a summons until the start of the hearing, after hearing the requesting party's explanation, and asking any questions. In other cases, where a summons has been issued before the hearing, the Member conducting the hearing may decide that the summons should be cancelled or amended, or if the witness is present, they may be excused from remaining. For example, the Member may decide that some of the documents which the witness was required to bring to the hearing will have no relevance to the facts in issue, and excuse that some were not produced.

23.5 The party who requested the summons shall be responsible for serving the summons on the witness, paying any associated expenses and fees, and enforcing the summons.

Subsection 12(3) of the SPPA requires that the summons be "served personally" on the witness, which means handing it to the person. The rules for serving by mail or leaving it with another person, etc. do not apply. Where a person fails to appear at a hearing pursuant to a summons, a party may seek to have the summons enforced pursuant to section 12 of the SPPA. Section 12 provides that a judge of the Superior Court of Justice may issue a warrant against a person if the judge is satisfied that the person was served with a summons, the person failed to participate, attend or to remain in attendance in accordance with the summons, and the person's attendance or participation is material to the ends of justice. A party seeking to enforce a summons is encouraged to seek legal advice.

23.6 If the witness attends the hearing, the party who requested the summons shall pay to the witness the fees and allowances set out in the Tariff which is Appendix "B" of these Rules.

A witness need not be paid until they attend the hearing.

23.7 A person effecting personal service of a summons need not produce the original signed document or have it in their possession.

Although there are many permitted methods of serving an application and notice of hearing, there is only one way to serve a summons. "Personal service" means handing the document to the potential witness (a specific individual, never a company, partnership, etc.), or at least approaching the individual and offering it to them. This Rule makes it clear that the person will be serving a copy of the summons and does not even need to take the signed original with them. This Rule is based on R16.02(2) of the Rules of Civil Procedure for the Courts.

Amended October 15, 2009

Rule 24 — Restricting Public Access to the Hearing

Legislation:

Section 9 of the *Statutory Powers Procedure Act* ('the SPPA')

Under section 9 of the SPPA, a hearing shall be open to the public except where matters involving public security may be disclosed or where:

> *"intimate financial or personal matters or other matters may be disclosed at the hearing of such a nature, having regard to the circumstances, that the desirability of avoiding disclosure thereof in the interests of any person affected or in the public interest, outweighs the desirability of adhering to the principle that hearings be open to the public...".*

The public will have access to all Board hearings, unless otherwise ordered by a Member. In rare circumstances, a Member will be satisfied that the hearing must be closed in accordance with section 9 of the SPPA. For example, this may occur if there will be medical evidence in a hearing, such as one dealing with a care home transfer application (section 148 of the RTA).

The Board's position on public access is as follows: Hearings will be open to the public unless the Member believes that there is sufficient reason to deny the public access. While hearings are open to the public, the application file is not. This means that while a member of the public can attend a Board hearing, they will not be given access to the file. Only parties and their representatives can be given access to the file.

24.1 If an applicant wishes the hearing to be closed, they shall file with the application a written request explaining the reasons for the request, and give a copy to each respondent.

The Board must know as soon as possible that a request to close the hearing will be made so that it can make any special arrangements required to prevent public access to the hearing. It is important that the applicant explain the basis of the request because otherwise a Member may decide special arrangements are not required.

24.2 If a respondent wishes the hearing to be closed, they shall notify the Board in writing promptly, and shall explain in the notice the reasons for the request.

The respondent should notify the Board as soon as possible after being served with the application. This will allow it to make any special arrangements required to prevent public access to the hearing. If the respondent does not provide an explanation of why the hearing should be closed, a Member might decide special arrangements are not required.

24.3 If a Member decides that all or part of the hearing should be closed to the public, the Member may:

> **(a) decide which persons who are not parties may be present at the closed portions of the hearing;**
>
> **(b) direct any persons who will be present at the hearing to file an undertaking to maintain confidentiality;**

(c) issue an order for the parties and a copy for the public in which any personal information related to the closed portion of the hearing is severed.

Once the Member has heard the submissions of the parties at the start of the hearing, the Member may decide that the evidence and submissions on one or more particular issues should be heard while excluding the public. The Member might also conclude that the entire hearing should be closed to the public. Of course, it is also possible that the request will be unsuccessful and the hearing will be open.

If the hearing will be closed, this Rule authorizes the Member to include specific directions about how the proceedings will be conducted. For example, during the portion of the hearing to be closed to the public, the Member can specify who should be in the hearing room. In a particularly sensitive case, those present can be required by the Member to sign an undertaking not to disclose what took place during the closed portion of the hearing. Further, the Member may decide to issue a "public" copy of the order, and the reasons if they are issued, in which references to the closed portion of the hearing are removed, although the parties would receive the complete order and reasons, if issued.

Release date: January 31, 2007

Rule 25 — Recording of Proceedings

Legislation:

Subsection 9(2) and section 20 of the *Statutory Powers Procedure Act* (the "SPPA")

These Rules explain the practices of the Board regarding its own recording of hearings, as well as that by parties, journalists and other persons. Subsection 9(2) of the SPPA permits the Board to make orders or directions at an oral or electronic hearing to maintain order, and provides for certain actions which may be taken against a person who disobeys the Board's instructions.

25.1 Subject to Rule 25.5, no person shall make a visual or audio recording of any part of the proceeding unless authorized by the Member before or at the beginning of the hearing.

This Rule is intended to apply to parties, their agents, journalists or other persons. The Member may impose conditions on the recording to protect the integrity of the hearing.

25.2 If the Board records the hearing, the recording will form part of the record and any party may request a copy of the recording upon payment of the required fee.

The Board will record a hearing if circumstances permit. Accordingly, most Board hearings will be recorded. If requested, the Board will do a search for an audio recording of the hearing, and will provide a copy of a hearing recorded, for a fee. No guarantee of the existence or quality of a recording can be provided. Recordings made by the Board are not transcribed, but pursuant to section 20 of the SPPA, they are part of the "record" for the purposes of review of an order or for appeal.

25.3 The deadline for a party to request a copy of a recording of a hearing is ten years from the date the hearing was recorded.

This deadline is established because per Rule 25.4, the Board may dispose of any recording of a hearing ten years after the hearing was recorded.

25.4 The Board may erase or otherwise dispose of a recording of a hearing if ten years have passed since the hearing was recorded.

The Board reserves the right to dispose of any recording of a hearing ten years after it was made. However the Board may, if it chooses, retain a recording for a longer period of time if one of the hearings on it is still pending with the Board or with the Courts.

25.5 Any party may bring a verbatim reporter at their own expense for the purpose of creating a transcript, provided that the party notifies the Board in advance.

In particular cases, a party will wish to have a transcript of the hearing. As the Board will not produce transcripts, the party would have to arrange for their own professional reporter (e.g. a court reporter) to be present at the hearing. As long as the party advises the Board in advance, the Member will permit this. The reporter must, of course, be sufficiently experienced to properly record the hearing and not disrupt it. The Board will not pay for the reporter's fees or expenses.

Amended December 08, 2008

Rule 26 — Orders and Reasons

Legislation:

Section 208 of the *Residential Tenancies Act, 2006* (the "RTA")
Section 17 of the *Statutory Powers Procedure Act* the "SPPA")

At the end of a hearing, the Member will adjourn the hearing pending the issuance of an order.

In view of subsection 17(1) of the SPPA, the written order is the official decision of the Board. The written order (and reasons, if issued) have legal status and are enforceable.

26.1 The Board shall send a copy of any order and/or reasons to each party to the application:

(a) by ordinary mail to the last known address of each party;

(b) by ordinary mail to the representative of the party; or

(c) by any other method directed or permitted by the Member.

The usual practice will be to mail a certified copy of the order to all parties and their representatives, not only to those who participated in the hearing. Generally, copies will not be sent by fax, although they may be picked up for a fee at the responsible Regional Office. However, occasionally special circumstances will arise, and the Board may arrange a different method of service. Although in general copies of the order will be certified, orders that are not certified may be sent in cases such as above guideline rent increase applications.

26.2 If a party wishes the Member to issue written reasons for the order, the party must make the request:

> **(a) orally at the hearing, or**
>
> **(b) in writing within 30 days after the order is issued, and the Member shall issue their reasons promptly. However, if the Member has already issued the written reasons the Member shall deny the request.**

Subsection 17(1) of the SPPA requires a tribunal to issue written reasons for its orders upon the request of any party. The Board will exercise its authority to issue reasons on its own initiative in some cases, and will issue reasons when requested under this Rule. However, in most cases, written reasons will not be issued. Parties who intend to request a review of an order or appeal it are encouraged to ask for written reasons as soon as possible after the order is issued.

A party who only wishes reasons if they are not successful (the order does not give them the relief they are seeking) may ask at the hearing for reasons to be issued under those conditions.

26.3 Despite Rule 26.2, a Member shall give reasons for departing from a guideline whether or not reasons are requested.

Interpretation Guidelines are intended to assist the parties in understanding the Board's usual interpretation of the law and to promote consistency in decision-making. A Member's reasons for not following a guideline should be clearly explained in the decision.

26.4 If an order is reviewed under section 21.2 of the Statutory Powers Procedure Act, and a Member determines that it is necessary to have reasons, the Member who issued the order under review shall issue reasons promptly, without having regard to the content of the request for a review of the order.

Many review requests (see Rule 29) can be decided without reasons, so a Member is only required to write reasons if a Member who is conducting the preliminary review or review hearing determines that reasons are necessary. See the commentary to Rule 15.1 and 15.6.

26.5 If an order has been appealed and the Member who issued the order is requested to issue reasons, the Member shall issue reasons promptly without having regard to the content of the appeal.

For an appeal, reasons, if requested, should be issued quickly in order to have a complete record available for the Divisional Court, and to allow the parties to understand the decision they are appealing. (Note: Under subsection 210(2) of the RTA a party who appeals an order must give copies of the Notice of Appeal and any other appeal documents to the Board.)

26.6 Despite Rule 1.5, Rule 26 cannot be waived.

Amended July 5, 2007

Rule 27 — Ordering Costs to a Party or Board Costs

Legislation:

Sections 74, 78, 182, 206 and subsections 204(2) to (4) of the *Residential Tenancies Act, 2006* (the "RTA")

Interpretation Guideline:

Guideline #3 Costs

Subsection 204(2) of the RTA gives the Board the discretion to order one party to pay another party's "costs" of the application. Subsection 204(3) allows the Board to order that its costs of an application be paid by a party or a paid agent or counsel to a party. The amount of an order for costs shall, according to subsection 204(4), be set in these Rules.

The Interpretation Guideline on Costs sets out the usual approach of the Board to ordering costs against a party or representative of a party. These Rules complement the approach suggested in the Guideline.

Allowing Application Fee as "costs"

27.1 If the applicant is successful, the Board may order the respondent to pay the application fee to the applicant as "costs".

This Rule will generally allow a successful applicant to obtain an order for recovery of the application fee they have paid. See Guideline # 3 - Costs regarding when an applicant should be considered to have been "successful". Note that there are some sections of the RTA that explicitly authorize or require the Board to issue an order for the payment of the application fee, or other fees, as costs. For example: sections 74, 78, 182 and 206.

27.2 Where the Board orders a party to an application to pay the costs of another party under subsection 204(2) of the RTA, representation fees shall not exceed $75 per hour for the services of a lawyer or paid agent.

This Rule sets the maximum amount which may be allowed if a Member decides it is appropriate to order one party to pay another party's "costs". The Guideline on costs suggests this is appropriate only where a party has been responsible for unreasonable conduct. It also suggests situations in which a party is not entitled to costs even if there has been unreasonable conduct by another party.

Although it may be difficult to estimate, the intention is to allow the representation fees only for the portion of the hearing that was affected by the unreasonable conduct. For example, if the Member warned the respondent's representative that an issue they raised did not seem relevant to the application, and yet they continued to pursue *the issue for an hour, the Member could order the respondent to pay the applicant $75 as costs.*

27.3 If the Member decides to allow costs related to the representative's preparation time, fees may be allowed not exceeding $75 per hour for the time spent.

The Guideline on costs suggests that preparation fees are only to be allowed in the most serious cases of unreasonable conduct. For example, if the applicant raises a totally irrelevant issue in their application, the respondent's representative may be allowed a preparation fee of up to $75 per hour for reviewing the RTA, Guidelines and any past significant decisions related to that issue.

27.4 Expenses of the Board which a party or representative may be ordered to pay shall not exceed $75 per hour for the hearing or $500 in total in respect of the proceedings as a whole.

This Rule recognizes unreasonable conduct in any stage of the proceedings will be relevant in considering the Board's costs, not just unreasonable conduct at the hearing.There are two limits on the amount ordered. First, if the unreasonable conduct affects only part of the hearing, the order shall not exceed $75 per hour. (However, there may be an order for Board costs even where the unreasonable conduct did not affect the hearing.) Second, the amount allowed in total for the proceedings cannot exceed $500, including any amount ordered for the hearing.

Amended July 5, 2007

Rule 28 — Amending an Order

Legislation:

Section 21.1 of the Statutory Powers Procedure Act ("the SPPA")

Related Rules:

Rule 15 (Extending and Shortening Time)
Rule 30 (Order Void or Stayed)

Interpretation Guidelines

Guideline 15 - Amending Orders

Section 21.1 of the SPPA allows a tribunal, at any time, to correct a typographical error, error of calculation or similar error made in its decision or order. These types of errors may be construed as clerical errors.

A clerical error may be the result of a mistake or omission made by the Board in the process of writing an order or other decision. Or, a clerical error may be an error made by a party in preparing a document which is submitted to the Board that ends up being transcribed into an order or decision. A serious error, on the other hand, such as an error of procedure or fact or an unreasonable application of discretion, would be the subject of a request for the Board to review an order (see Rule 29).

See also Guideline 15 "Amending an Order".

28.1 A party to an order or any person directly affected by it may request that an order or any other decision be amended to correct a clerical error on or before the date that is 30 days after the order or decision is issued.

This Rule permits any party to an order to request that the order or other decision be amended to correct a clerical error. It also permits any other person directly affected by a particular order or other decision to request such an amendment.

The time limit to make the request recognizes the desire of the Board that its orders be considered final within a reasonable time. A request to extend this time limit may be made under Rule 15. The Member considering such a request would consider factors such as the reason for the delay, the length of the delay, and any evidence of prejudice suffered by any person.

28.2 A Member of the Board may, upon their own initiative, amend an order or decision they have issued, in order to correct a clerical error.

This Rule permits the Board to amend an order or decision. Generally, an order or decision will only be amended if a party requests it, but in some cases a Member may initiate an amendment where they believe it is appropriate and necessary.

Form and Contents of Request

28.3 A request to amend an order or other decision to correct a clerical error shall be made in writing and shall be signed by the person making the request.

The person requesting the amendment may use the form provided by the Board, but the form is not required. A letter will be sufficient if it at least contains the information required by Rule 28.4. The form or letter must be signed by the person making the request or their representative.

28.4 A request must include: the Board's order number, the address of the rental unit or residential complex concerned and the name, address and telephone number of the person requesting the amendment, a description of the error, and the requested change.

These are minimum requirements. If the person requesting the amendment is not a party, they should explain their interest in the matter. If they are also appealing the order, applying for judicial review or asking for a review of the order (see Rule 29), this should also be noted in the request.

Assigning a Member to the Request

28.5 Subject to Rule 28.6, a request to amend an order or other decision will be considered by the Member who issued the order or decision that is the subject of the request.

The Member who issued the original order is in the best position to know the reasons for their findings and the intent of the decision. Therefore, the Member who issued the order or decision that is the subject of the request will be responsible for determining whether or not a clerical error was made in the order or decision.

28.6 Where the Member who issued the order or decision that is the subject of an amendment request is on an extended absence from the Board, the request will be considered by the regional Vice-Chair.

This might be the case, for example, where a request to amend a clerical error is received while a Member is on vacation, or some other form of leave, or where a request is received after a Member's appointment to the Board has ended.

Considering the Request

28.7 The Member who considers the request to amend an order or other decision, may:

> **(a) amend the order, without requesting submissions or holding a hearing, based solely upon the request to amend the order;**
>
> **(b) deny the amendment request, based solely upon the request to amend the order;**
>
> **(c) issue a direction letter to invite written submissions and amend the order or deny the request to amend the order after considering those submissions;**
>
> **(d) hold a hearing to determine if the order should be amended or the request to amend denied.**

Ordinarily, a Member will decide whether or not a clerical error exists in the order or decision based solely on the contents of the request, without seeking submissions from the other parties.

If the Member determines, with or without seeking submissions, that a clerical error exists in the order or decision, and that it should be amended, an amended order that clearly explains why the order is being changed and what the changes are will be sent to all parties.

Where a decision to deny the request is made without seeking submissions, the Member will send a letter to the party who made the request, explaining why the request has been denied. If a decision to deny the request is made after seeking submissions, a denial letter will be sent to all parties to the application. Where the decision to deny the request is made after a hearing has been held, an order will be sent to all parties explaining the reasons for the denial.

A member may find that it is necessary to invite submissions from other parties before making a decision.

In deciding whether or not to seek submissions, the Member should consider whether a party might be prejudiced if the order is amended.

Submissions may be requested in writing, by means of a direction letter, or at a hearing. In some cases, a Member may decide, after considering the written submissions of the parties, that it is necessary to hold a hearing to allow the parties to make further submissions or to clarify the issue(s).

Request to Stay the Order

28.8 A party may request a stay of the order by setting out in writing the prejudice they may suffer if the order is not stayed pending the decision regarding the amendment.

Generally, a stay of the order will not be necessary unless the amendment request is received late in the process and the Member is unable to deal with the request immediately. For example, if a party believes that an order for eviction due to nonpayment of rent and for the payment of arrears contains an error in the amount owing, and the amendment request is made close to the enforceable date of the order, the tenant may request that the order be stayed so that the landlord cannot enforce the eviction. A stay may also be needed if the Member decides to seek submissions on the request.

When a Member decides to stay an order, they may at the same time require the requester of the amendment to pay an amount into the Board. See the Interpretation Guideline entitled 'Payment into the Board'.

If the Board stays the order, it will ordinarily be stayed until a final decision is made regarding the amendment of the clerical error. However, the Member may at any time decide that the stay is no longer appropriate and revoke it.

28.9 A Member may, upon the request of a party or upon their own initiative, stay an order pending the resolution of a request to amend the order or may revoke a stay, without obtaining submissions from any party or holding a hearing.

The Member who considers the request to amend the order to correct a clerical error may decide to stay the order, whether or not a party asks for a stay. At a later stage, it may become apparent that the stay is no longer appropriate, and a Member would then be authorized to revoke the stay that had previously been ordered.

The reason for not obtaining submissions or holding a hearing before a stay is issued is that it is necessary that the stay be in effect as quickly as possible to protect the status quo while the amendment request is being considered. Without the stay, the order could be enforced, which may render the request meaningless. Since the amendment request will generally be dealt with within a relatively short period of time, it would unduly lengthen the proceedings to add a period of submissions.

Where an order is stayed, the person who might be adversely affected if the order were not stayed is responsible to take a copy of that order to the Court Enforcement Office (see Rule 30.4).

Consequential Amendments

28.10 If an order is amended to correct a clerical error, the Member may also amend or update other provisions of the order as necessary.

Amended July 5, 2007

Rule 29 — Review of Orders

Legislation:

Section 21.2 of the *Statutory Powers Procedure Act* (the "SPPA")
Section 181, 182, 184 and 209 of the *Residential Tenancies Act, 2006* (the "RTA")

Related Rules:

Rule 15 (Extending and Shortening Time)
Rule 26.4 (Orders and Reasons)
Rule 28 (Amending an Order)
Rule 30 (Order Void or Stayed)

Interpretation Guidelines

Guideline 8 – Review of Orders

Section 21.2 of the SPPA authorizes a tribunal which adopts rules of practice to review its own orders. The scope of and procedures for such reviews are set out in these Rules. A person affected by an order may request a review if they believe the Member made a serious error, such as an error of procedure or fact or an unreasonable application of discretion. A clerical error, on the other hand, such as a mistake made by the Board in writing an order, would be the subject of a request to amend an order (see Rule 28).

It is clear that the review of orders was a power which the Legislature contemplated for the Board. Section 184 of the RTA states that the SPPA applies to proceedings before the Board and section 209 sets out that orders of the Board are final and binding subject to the review provision of section 21.2 of the SPPA. Also, section 181(1)(a) allows the Board to charge fees for a request to review an order, and section 182 provides that the fee may be refunded in certain situations.

The following expressions are used interchangeably in these rules: "request for a review of an order", "request to review an order", and "review request".

Requests to Review an Order

29.1 A party to an order or any person directly affected by it may request a review and any Vice-Chair of the Board may initiate a review of any order or any decision which finally disposes of an application.

Any person named as a party by the order may request a review. As well, any other person directly affected by the outcome of that particular order (but not merely a similar fact situation) may request a review and thereby seek to be added as a party to the proceedings. For example, if two persons own a residential complex, but only one was named as the landlord and participated in the proceedings, the other landlord may seek a review of the order if the order affects his or her interests.

The Board expects that the parties or any other person directly affected by a particular order will exercise the opportunity to request a review of that order if they believe a serious error occurred. Generally, a Vice Chair will not consider initiating a review until the parties have exhausted their rights in this regard.

Any final order may be reviewed if there are proper grounds to do so (see the Interpretation Guideline entitled "Review of an Order"). The Board may also review any other decision which terminates the proceedings because it determined the rights of the parties in a final way. Except in extraordinary circumstances, this would not include an interim order, since it is not usually appropriate to interrupt and delay a proceeding before there is a final result.

29.2 A request for a review of an order must provide sufficient information to support a preliminary finding that the order may contain a serious error or that a serious error may have occurred in the proceedings.

A description of what is a serious error is contained in the Board's Interpretation Guideline entitled "Review of an Order".

Time for Making a Request

29.3 A request to review an order shall be made to the Board on or before the date that is 30 days after the order is issued unless the review was initiated by a Vice-Chair.

This time limit recognizes the desire of the Board that its orders should be considered final within a reasonable time. The same time period is used as that within which a party must decide whether or not appeal an order on a question of law. This will encourage parties to consider their options and act quickly.

A request to extend this time limit may be made under Rule 15. For example, if a person who alleges they should have been a party does not discover there was an order until long after it was issued, time would usually be extended to permit the request to be considered on its merits. The Member considering such a request would consider factors such as the reason for the delay, the length of the delay, and any evidence of prejudice suffered by any person.

29.4 If an order is amended, a request to review the order shall be made on or before the date that is 30 days after the amended order is issued.

For example, if the name of a party is corrected through an amending order, and the person believes the name is still incorrect, the time period of 30 days to ask for a review starts to run on the date after the amending order was issued.

Form, Contents and Parties

29.5 A review request shall be made in writing, shall be signed by the person making the request and shall be accompanied by the required fee.

The person requesting the review should use the Board-approved form. A letter will be sufficient if it is clearly identified as a request for review, and if it at least contains the information specified in Rule 29.6. The form or letter must be signed by the person making the request or their representative and must be accompanied by the required fee.

29.6 A review request must include: the Board's order number; the address of the rental unit or residential complex concerned; the name, address and telephone number of the person requesting the review; the reason, in detail, why the order should be reviewed; the remedy requested; and, where an appeal of the order has been filed with the Divisional Court, an explanation as to why the stay resulting from the appeal should be lifted for the purpose of resolving the review request.

These are minimum requirements. The form or letter used to request the review may also ask for an extension of time to file the request (see Rule 15) and/or a stay of the order during the review process (see Rule 29.7). If the person requesting the review was not a party to the original proceedings, they should explain their interest in the matter, or if they were a party who did not attend the hearing, they should explain why. If the person requesting the review is also appealing the order, applying for judicial review or asking for an amendment of the order (see Rule 28), this should also be noted in the request.

29.7 A party requesting a review of an order may also request a stay of the order by setting out in writing the prejudice they may suffer if the order is not stayed pending the decision regarding the review.

In some cases, by the time the review is completed, the issue would no longer exist if the order has already been enforced. In cases where a Member decides to stay an order pending the resolution of the review, the Member may also be concerned that a party might be prejudiced by the delay caused by the review.

For example, if an order for eviction due to arrears of rent is stayed, the landlord cannot enforce the order and re-rent the unit, and if the current tenant continues to fall behind in rental payments during the time of the review the landlord is powerless to take action. In these cases, when a Member decides to stay an order, they may at the same time require the requester of the review to pay an amount into the Board. See the Interpretation Guideline entitled "Payment into the Board".

If the Board stays the order, it will ordinarily be stayed until a final decision is made regarding the review. However, the Member may at any time decide that the stay is no longer appropriate and lift it.

29.8 The parties to the review request are the parties to the order being reviewed, the person requesting the review, and any other person added to the proceedings by the Board, but a Vice-Chair who initiated the review is not a party.

Rule 29.1 sets out that a person directly affected by the order may request a review, even if they were not a party to the original proceedings. The Member may also determine in the course of the review that a person directly affected by the proceedings should be added. See section 187 of the RTA.

Assigning a Member to the Review

29.9 A Member may not review their own orders, or any order with regard to an application for which the Member issued an interim order, except an interim order that stays the order under review.

In order to avoid possible prejudice to the party requesting the review, a review will not be conducted by the Member who issued the order.

Preliminary Decisions Regarding a Request for a Review of an Order

29.10 After a preliminary review of a request to review an order, unless the Member determines that the order may contain a serious error or that a serious error may have occurred in the proceedings, the Member shall deny the review request without a hearing.

In most cases, a Member will conduct a preliminary review of the request to review an order. In a preliminary review, a Member determines whether the request for review discloses a potential serious error in the order or in the proceeding, and whether the issues raised are within the scope of the power to review. Ordinarily, a decision in a preliminary review will be based solely on the contents of the request and the order, without seeking submissions from the other party and without holding a hearing.

The Member shall deny the request immediately if the request for review does not identify a potential serious error in the order or in the proceeding, or if the issues raised are not within the scope of the power to review. If the review request is denied, the Member will issue a decision denying the request, including a brief statement of the reasons for the decision.

29.11 **(a) If, after a preliminary review of a request to review an order, the Member determines that the order may contain a serious error or that a serious error may have occurred in the proceedings, the Member shall send the matter to a hearing for a consideration as to whether or not the request discloses a serious error in the order or proceedings.**

(b) If the matter that the Member is sending to a hearing pursuant to Rule 29.11(a) has been stayed by subsection 25(1) of the SPPA as a result of an appeal of the order to Divisional Court, the Member shall lift the stay of the order, pursuant to subsection 25(1)(b) of the SPPA, so that the Member at the hearing may determine whether or not the request discloses a serious error in the order or the proceedings.

(c) However, should the Member determine that the rights of the parties should be preserved pending the Board's decision regarding the request for a review of the order, the Member shall issue a Board stay of the order.

29.12 A Member may, upon the request of a party or upon their own initiative, without obtaining submissions or holding a hearing in that regard, stay an order or lift any stay, pending the outcome of the hearing of a review request.

The Member who conducts the preliminary review of the request to review an order when it is received may decide to stay the order, whether or not the party who made the request asked for a stay. Without the stay, the order could be enforced.

Note: where an order is stayed, the person who might be adversely affected if the order were not stayed is responsible to take a copy of that order to the Court Enforcement Office (see Rule 30.4).

At a later stage, it may become apparent that the stay ordered by the Board is no longer appropriate, in which case the Member would then lift the stay.

Where the order for which a review request has been made has also been appealed to the Divisional Court, the Member, in order to conduct a review of the order, may decide to lift the stay of proceedings that is automatically imposed by the filing of the appeal.

The reason for not obtaining submissions or holding a hearing before a stay is ordered is that it is necessary that the stay be in effect as quickly as possible to protect the status quo while the review is being determined. Since the review proceedings will generally be disposed of within a relatively short period of time, it would unduly lengthen the proceedings to add a period of submissions about such preliminary issues as the ordering or lifting of a stay.

29.13 If a Vice-Chair initiated the review, that Vice-Chair shall determine whether or not the order should be stayed at the time the review is initiated and shall issue an interim order staying the order under review, if necessary, and may lift any stay as required, pending the outcome of the review hearing.

29.14 A Vice-Chair, prior to initiating any review of an order, shall conduct a preliminary review to determine if there may be a serious error in the order or in the proceedings and, having made that determination, that Vice-Chair, another Vice-Chair or a Member shall be assigned to conduct the review hearing without any other preliminary review.

A Board initiated review shall proceed directly to the review hearing.

Type of Hearing

29.15 A Member may conduct a hearing to consider a review request, or to consider any issues to be reviewed, by way of an oral, electronic or written hearing.

An oral hearing is one conducted in the presence of the Member and any parties and representatives who appear. An electronic hearing is conducted through a conference call or through audio-visual facilities, usually with the Member, parties and representatives at two or more locations, but able to hear everything said by all of the other participants. Electronic hearings may be held under Rule 21.

In a written hearing, the parties are required to file their evidence and make submissions to the Board in writing. The Member makes a decision based on the evidence and submissions filed without holding a meeting between the parties. Written hearings may be held under Rule 22.

An oral hearing would ordinarily be held when the issues to be reviewed involve the presentation of evidence because there is alleged to be an error of fact; that is, it is alleged that there is an error as to the facts found in the order. Depending on a number of factors, such as whether credibility of witnesses will be an issue, the hearing may be conducted by conference call or in person (i.e., an electronic or an oral hearing).

Where the Member believes that the issues raised by the request are straightforward, and involve arguments based on the facts found by the Member who made the order, the Member conducting the review may decide that the review may be conducted by written hearing.

Where the party requesting the review alleges an error of natural justice, the reviewing Member could ask for written submissions regarding that issue and, if convinced there was an error, proceed to hear the application from the beginning through an oral or electronic hearing.

Decisions Resulting from a Hearing of a Request for a Review of an Order

29.16 If, after holding a hearing to determine if a review request discloses a serious error in the order or proceedings, the Member determines that there is no serious error, the Member shall dismiss the request, lift any stay and confirm the order under review.

If, after hearing from the parties, the Member determines that there is no serious error, the Member shall issue an order dismissing the request for review.

29.17 If, after holding a hearing to determine if a review request discloses a serious error in the order or proceedings, the Member determines that there is a serious error, the Member will determine the issues to be reviewed.

If the Member determines that there is a serious error, the Member will proceed to hear the issues to be reviewed.

29.18 The Member may decide that the issues to be reviewed will be:

(a) all or some of the issues raised in the request;

(b) any other issues which the Member believes should be reviewed.

When the Member considers the issues raised in the request, they may decide that all of these issues should be reviewed, with submissions from both parties. However, they may decide that only one or more of the issues are within the scope of the review, and would then limit the issues to be reviewed.

In considering the issues raised in the request and the order or decision itself, the Member may come to the preliminary conclusion that those issues will lead to a need to review other parts of the order. In addition, the Member may find that there was another possible serious error in the proceedings or in the order.

29.19 After hearing the issues to be reviewed, the Member may confirm, vary, suspend or cancel the order under review, and lift any stay if necessary.

Subsequent Requests for Review

29.20 The Board shall accept only one review request from a party, and shall not accept a subsequent request from that same party to review the resulting review order or decision.

This Rule is based on the legal principle that a matter already decided cannot be decided again by a court or tribunal. It also encompasses the concept that a party should raise all grounds for possible serious error in their request.

29.21 The Board may review an order which has previously been reviewed, or may review a review order, if the request is made by another party upon different grounds or if the review is initiated by a Vice-Chair of the Board.

The request of a party for a review will not prevent a new request from a different party, unless the request is based on grounds already decided through the other review. However, if the request is made late, the requesting party must convince the Board that this further review should be allowed to proceed. The Board reserves the right to initiate a second review or review of a review order, on its own motion, in appropriate cases.

Withdrawing a Request

29.22 If a request to withdraw a review request is made at a hearing or after an interim order has been issued, the request may be withdrawn only with the consent of the Board.

The Board recognizes a party's right to withdraw a request to review. However, if the request is made at the hearing or after an interim order has been issued, the review request may be withdrawn only if the Member consents. If the Member allows the request to be withdrawn, they will also lift the stay of the original order, if it was stayed, and order payment out, if money was paid into the Board.

29.23 A party may withdraw a review request without the consent of the Board as long as the hearing of the request has not commenced, and no interim or other order has been issued regarding the request.

Amended October 15, 2009

Rule 30 — Order Void or Stayed

Legislation:

Sections 74, 77 and 78 of the *Residential Tenancies Act, 2006*

Related Rules:

Rule 28 (Amending an Order)
Rule 29 (Review of Orders)
Rule 31 (Paying money into and out of the Board)

There are a number of situations in which an action taken by a party to a Board proceeding impacts the enforcement of a prior Board decision. For example, a respondent may file a motion to set aside an ex parte order or make the payment required to void an eviction order.

30.1 Except where a set aside motion is filed under subsection 74(9), it is the responsibility of the party who files a set aside motion to immediately take a copy of the motion and Notice of Hearing to the Court Enforcement Office.

In most cases, the automatic legal effect of filing a set aside motion after an ex parte order has been issued is to stay the order. Before the applicant is notified of the set aside motion, they may take steps to enforce the order; however, once the motion is filed, the applicant cannot enforce the order.

For an eviction order, the respondent should take the set aside motion and Notice of Hearing to the Sheriff's Office after filing the motion with the Board. For an eviction order which also orders the payment of money, the respondent should take a copy of the motion and Notice of Hearing to the Sheriff's Office and the enforcement offices of the Superior Court of Justice and the Small Claims Court.

However, where a set aside motion is filed under subsection 74(9) about an order which voids an eviction order, there is no requirement to take the motion or Notice of Hearing to the Sheriff's Office. In this case, the order that voids the eviction order remains in effect; there is nothing to be enforced pending the Board's decision on the set aside motion.

30.2 Where a notice is issued under subsection 74(5) or subsection 74(16) which acknowledges that an eviction order is void, it is the responsibility of the tenant to immediately take a copy of that notice to the Court Enforcement Office.

If a tenant has paid the full amount required to void an eviction order (based on rent arrears) to the Board, an employee of the Board will issue a notice acknowledging that the eviction order is void. Once this notice is issued the landlord cannot enforce the eviction order. As soon as the tenant receives the notice from the Board, they are responsible for taking a copy of it to the Court Enforcement Office (Sheriff).

30.3 Where an order is issued under subsection 74(6) or under clause (a) of subsection 74(14) which confirms that an eviction order is void, it is the responsibility of the tenant to immediately take a copy of that order to the Court Enforcement Office.

If a tenant has paid the full amount required to void an eviction order based on rent arrears, before the order becomes enforceable, either in whole to the landlord or in part to the landlord and in part to the Board, and then files a motion in accordance with subsections 74(6) and 74(7) for an order confirming that the order is void, the Board can issue such an order. Once this order is issued the landlord cannot enforce the eviction order. As soon as the tenant receives the order from the Board, they are responsible for taking a copy of the order to the Court Enforcement Office (Sheriff).

The same holds true, in most cases, for an order that the Board issues on a tenant's motion under subsection 74(11) if, after the order becomes enforceable, the tenant pays the amount required under subsection 74(11) to void the eviction order based on rent arrears. However, where the Board determines that the landlord has already paid a non-refundable amount to enforce the eviction order, the Board will specify that the order voiding the eviction will not be effective unless the tenant pays to the Board a specified amount, by a specified date, to cover the landlord's enforcement costs.

30.4 Where an order is issued that stays the order under consideration, it is the responsibility of the person who might be adversely affected if the order were not stayed to immediately take a copy of that order to the Court Enforcement Office.

For example, if a tenant files a request to review an eviction order and includes a request for a stay, the Board can issue such a stay under Rule 29.12. Similarly, the Board can issue a stay under Rule 28.9 related to a request to amend an order. Once the stay is issued, the landlord cannot enforce the original order. As soon as the tenant receives the order from the Board, they are responsible for taking a copy of the order to the Court Enforcement Office (Sheriff). The Board is not responsible to ensure that the Sheriff's office receives a copy of the order.

Amended July 5, 2007

Rule 31 — Paying Money Into and Out of the Board

Legislation:

Subsections 74(2) to (18) and section 195 of the *Residential Tenancies Act, 2006* (the "RTA")

Related Rules:

Rule 13.8 (Mediation by the Board: Paying Out Under an Agreement)

Subsection 74(2) of the RTA states that if the Board is satisfied that a tenant has paid the sum owing and the application fee to the Board or to the landlord before the order is issued, the application will be discontinued.

Subsection 74(4) of the RTA states that if an eviction order has been issued but, before it becomes enforceable, the tenant voluntarily pays the amount specified in the order, the eviction order is void. The amount can be paid entirely to the Board, entirely to the landlord, or in part to the Board and in part to the landlord. These Rules establish procedures for the payment out of these monies.

Further, subsection 74(11) allows a tenant to void the order after the date the order becomes enforceable but before it is enforced, by paying everything owing, including the Sheriff's fees if applicable. The tenant must file a motion and a hearing will be held to determine if the order is void. A tenant is only allowed to void an eviction order in this manner once per tenancy.

Clause 195(1)(a) of the RTA provides that the Board may require the respondent to pay a specified amount into the Board within a specified time where the Board considers it appropriate to do so. Further, under subsection 195(4), if the respondent fails to pay in as required, the Board may refuse to consider their evidence and submissions.

Clause 195(1)(b) of the RTA allows the Board to permit a tenant who has made an application about maintenance to pay some or all of their rent into the Board. Subsection 195(5) states that if such a payment is allowed, it is not considered to be arrears of rent or a breach of the tenant's obligations.

Subsection 195(2) provides that the Board may establish procedures for payment into and out of the Board through these Rules. Interpretation Guideline #2 (Payment into the Board) provides guidance as to the reasons for which a Member might require payment, as well as what the consequences might be if the respondent fails to follow such a requirement.

Arrears of Rent: Voluntary Payments Made Before an Order is Issued

31.1 If, before an order is issued, a tenant voluntarily pays money to the Board which is at least the amount required to discontinue the application under subsection 74(2) of the RTA, a Member shall:

> **(a) direct that the amount that would be required to discontinue the application be paid out to the landlord,**
>
> **(b) direct that any excess be paid to the tenant, and**
>
> **(c) order that the application is discontinued without holding a hearing.**

Where a landlord files an application to evict a tenant for non-payment of rent, and the tenant pays the rent arrears, any additional rent owing and the landlord's filing fee, the landlord's application will be discontinued and no hearing will be held. The amount that would be required to discontinue the application will be paid out to the landlord. If the tenant has paid in more than enough to discontinue the application, the extra amount will be paid back to the tenant.

Arrears of Rent: Payments Made Before an Eviction Order is Enforceable

31.2 If, after an order is issued, a tenant voluntarily pays money to the Board in accordance with subsection 74(4) of the RTA before the eviction order becomes enforceable, and the amount paid in is at least the amount that would be required to void the order according to subsection 74(4), a Regional Manager or Coordinator will:

> **(a) direct that the amount that would be required to void the order be paid to the landlord,**
>
> **(b) direct that any excess be paid to the tenant, and**
>
> **(c) issue a Notice to the parties acknowledging that the eviction order that is based on arrears of rent is void.**

After the Board has issued an eviction order in a landlord's application based on non-payment of rent, the tenant has an opportunity to void the order before the date the landlord can enforce it. Where the tenant pays into the Board an amount that is sufficient to void the eviction order, staff of the Board will issue a notice acknowledging that the eviction order is void. The staff member will also direct that the amount that the tenant has paid in that would be sufficient to void the order will be paid out to the landlord. Where the tenant has paid in more than enough to void the order, the extra amount will be paid back to the tenant.

31.3 If, after an order is issued but before it becomes enforceable, a tenant voluntarily pays money to the Board in an amount that is less than the amount that would be required to void the order according to subsection 74(4), and the tenant does not file a motion under subsection 74(6), a Regional Manager or Coordinator will:

> **(a) direct the money to be paid to the landlord, once the order has become enforceable, and**
>
> **(b) issue a Notice to the parties confirming the amount that was paid out to the landlord, and that it was not sufficient to void the order.**

Where an eviction order has been issued based on non-payment of rent, the tenant can void the order by paying the amounts owing to the landlord and/or to the Board. Where the tenant pays the whole amount to the landlord, or part to the landlord and part to the Board, the tenant can make a motion to the Board for an order determining that the full amount has been paid and that the eviction order is void.

Where the tenant pays money into the Board but it is less than the amount required to void an eviction order and the tenant does not make a motion for an order confirming that the eviction order is void, staff of the Board will issue a notice to the parties informing them that the amount the tenant paid in was not sufficient to void the order. The staff member will direct that the money that the tenant has paid into the Board will be paid out to the landlord. The notice and direction will be issued after the date the order can be enforced.

31.4 If, after an order is issued but before it becomes enforceable, a tenant voluntarily pays money to the Board in an amount that is less than the amount that would be required to void the order according to subsection 74(4), and the tenant files a motion under subsection 74(6), a Member will, at the time of issuing an order on the motion, direct payment out to the landlord of any monies paid in.

Where the tenant makes a motion to the Board for a notice confirming that the eviction order is void, but the amount that the tenant has paid in to the Board is not sufficient to void the order, the Member will direct that any monies paid into the Board will be paid out to the landlord when it issues an order on the tenant's motion.

Arrears of Rent: Payments Made After Eviction Order Enforceable

31.5 If, after an order becomes enforceable, a tenant voluntarily pays money to the Board in an amount that is at least the amount that would be required to void the order and the tenant files a motion under subsection 74(11), a Member will, at the time of issuing an order on the motion:

> **(a) direct that the amount that would be required to void the order be paid to the landlord; and**
>
> **(b) direct that any excess shall be paid to the tenant.**

Even after the date an eviction order can be enforced, a tenant has an opportunity to void the order. Where a tenant pays to the Board an amount that is sufficient to void the eviction order and makes a motion to set aside the order, the Board will issue an order declaring that the eviction order is void. The Board will, at that time, also direct that the amount that would be sufficient to void the eviction order be paid out to the landlord; any extra amount that the tenant paid into the Board will be paid out to the tenant.

31.6 If, after an order becomes enforceable, a tenant voluntarily pays money to the Board in an amount that is less than the amount that would be required to void the order, and the tenant files a motion under subsection 74(11), a Member will, at the time of issuing an order on the motion, direct the money to be paid to the landlord.

Where a tenant makes a motion to the Board to set aside an eviction order after the date the order can be enforced, and pays money to the Board, but the amount is not sufficient to void the eviction order, the Board will lift the stay of the eviction order resulting from the tenant's motion. This means that the landlord will be able to enforce the eviction order. The Board will direct that the money the tenant has paid in to the Board be paid out to the landlord.

31.7 If, after an order becomes enforceable, a tenant voluntarily pays money to the Board but does not file a motion under subsection 74(11) a Regional Manager or Coordinator will:

> **(a) direct the money to be paid to the landlord; and**
>
> **(b) issue a Notice to the parties confirming the amount that was paid out to the landlord, and that the order is not void.**

Where a tenant pays to the Board an amount to void the eviction order but does not make a motion to set aside the order, staff of the Board will direct that the money be paid out to the landlord and will issue a notice to the parties informing them of the amount that was paid. The notice will also set out that the order is not void.

Enforcement Costs Set Out in an Order Issued Under Subsection 74(14)

31.8 If a tenant pays to the Board at least the amount specified pursuant to subsection 74(15) (enforcement costs) in an order issued under subsection 74(14) by the date set out in that order, a Regional Manager or Coordinator will:

> **(a) issue a Notice acknowledging that the eviction order that is based on arrears of rent is void;**
>
> **(b) direct that the amount that would be required to void the order be paid to the landlord, and**
>
> **(c) direct that any excess shall be paid to the tenant.**

Where a tenant makes a motion to the Board to set aside an eviction order after the enforceable date in the order, a hearing will be held. The Board will determine whether the eviction order is void because the tenant has paid the required amounts and whether the landlord has paid any non-refundable enforcement fees with respect to the eviction order. Where the Board determines that the tenant has paid the required amounts and that the landlord has paid enforcement fees, the Board will issue an order setting out that the eviction order is void, provided that the tenant pays an amount into the Board to cover the enforcement fees by a specified date. Where the tenant pays that amount into the Board by the date set out in the order, staff of the Board will issue a notice acknowledging that the eviction order is void. The staff member will also direct that the amount the tenant has paid in to cover the enforcement costs will be paid out to the landlord; if the tenant has paid more than the required amount, any excess will be paid back to the tenant.

31.9 If an order is issued under subsection 74(14) that specifies an amount payable pursuant to subsection 74(15), and the tenant does not pay this specified amount into the Board by the date set out in the order, a Regional Manager or Coordinator will:

> **(a) issue a Notice confirming that the specified amount was not paid by the specified date, and that the order issued under clause (a) of subsection 74(14) is no longer stayed and may be enforced, and (b) direct that any money paid in to the Board be paid out to the landlord.**

Where the Board determines that the tenant has paid the amounts required to void an eviction order after the enforcement date, the Member can order the tenant to pay into the Board an amount to cover the costs the landlord has incurred to enforce the eviction order. Where the tenant does not pay the full amount by the deadline in the Board's order, staff of the Board will issue a notice informing the parties that the eviction order can be enforced. The staff member will also direct that any money the tenant has paid in will be paid out to the landlord.

Directed Payments:

31.10 If a respondent pays money into the Board in accordance with a direction or order of a Member, a Member will direct payment out at the time of issuing an order.

If a respondent pays money into the Board as a result of a Member's direction or order requiring them to pay in that amount, the applicant is not entitled to have the money paid out to them in advance of an order being made. The requirement to pay into the Board may have arisen because of a delay of the hearing, and was in the nature of security for payment of any amount which the Board decides should be ordered against the respondent. Thus, payment out to the applicant would be premature before the hearing is completed and an order is issued. Payment out would be in accordance with the amount determined to be owing in the order.

Payment In on Maintenance Applications

31.11 Unless the tenant's request under clause (b) of subsection 195(1) is made at the hearing, it must be in writing, and must specify:

> **(a) the amount of rent the tenant is required to pay and the date rent payments are due under the tenancy agreement;**

(b) the amount of rent the tenant wishes to pay in and the rent period(s) or portion(s) of rent period(s) covered by that amount; and

(c) the reasons why the tenant believes the Board should allow their request.

When a tenant makes an application to the Board about maintenance, they can also make a request to pay their rent into the Board. The tenant can make this request orally at the hearing. At any other point in the application process, this request must be made in writing. To make the request in writing, the tenant should use the form approved by the Board; however, a letter will be sufficient if it at least contains the information required by this rule. The form or letter must be signed by the person making the request or their representative.

31.12 If the tenant's request under clause (b) of subsection 195(1) is made before the hearing for the application starts, the request will be decided ex parte.

Where a tenant makes a request to pay their rent into the Board on a maintenance application before the start of the hearing, the Member will make a decision on the request without seeking submissions from the other parties.

31.12.1 Where the Board has denied a tenant's request to pay in under Rule 31.12, no subsequent request from the tenant to pay into the Board will be considered before the hearing for the application starts.

If a tenant asks to pay into the Board on a maintenance application before the start of the hearing, a Member will decide whether or not to grant the request. If the request is denied, the tenant may not make another such request before the start of the hearing.

31.13 If the tenant's request under clause 195(1)(b) is made after the hearing for the application starts, the Member hearing the application will decide whether or not to grant the request ex parte or after receiving submissions (oral or written) from the other parties.

For information on when the Board considers it appropriate to allow a party to pay money into the Board, see the Interpretation Guideline #2, Payment into the Board.

31.14 If a Member decides to allow the tenant to pay some or all of their rent into the Board, the Member will issue an interim order which will be sent to all parties to the application.

31.15 If a tenant pays their rent into the Board pursuant to an interim order issued under Rule 31.14, the Member will direct payment out at the time of issuing an order, or if the application is resolved by mediation, the Mediator will direct payment out under rule 13.8.

Amended July 5, 2007

Appendix A — ServiceOntario Centres

Atikokan 108 Saturn Avenue	**Dryden** 479 Government Road Main Floor	**Kapuskasing** 122 Government Road West
Aurora 50 Bloomington Road West	**Elliot Lake** 50 Hillside Drive North	**Kenora** 810 Robertson Street, Suite 104
Bancroft 50 Monck Street	**Espanola** 148 Fleming Street, Suite 2	**Kingston*** Beechgrove Complex 51 Heakes Lane, Main Floor
Barrie* 34 Simcoe Street	**Fort Frances** 922 Scott Street	**Kirkland Lake** 10 Government Road East
Belleville 199 Front Street Century Place	**Geraldton** 208 Beamish Avenue West	**Kitchener*** City Hall, Main Floor 200 King Street West
Blind River 62 Queen Avenue	**Gore Bay** 35 Meredith Street	**Lindsay** 322 Kent Street West
Brampton 7765 Hurontario Street	**Guelph** 1 Stone Road West, Main Floor	**Manitouwadge** 40 Manitou Road
Brockville 7 King Street West	**Hawkesbury** 692 Main Street East	**Marathon** Peninsula Square, Centre Block 52 Peninsula Road, Suite 105
Chapleau 190 Cherry Street	**Hearst** 613 Front Street	**Minden** Highway 35 by-pass
Chatham Civic Centre 315 King Street West	**Huntsville** 207 Main Street West	**Moosonee** **Ontario Government** **Building** **34 Revillion Road North**
Cochrane 2 3rd Avenue	**Idnace** Corner Hwy. 17 and Hwy. 599	**New Liskeard** 280 Armstrong Street

Cornwall 127 Sydney Street	**Iroquois Falls** 260 Main Street	**Toronto (Downsview)** 2680 Keele Street Building A
Nipigon Ontario Government Building 5 Wadsworth Drive	**Renfrew** 316 Plaunt Street South	**Wawa** 48 Mission Road
North Bay 447 McKeown Avenue Suite 11	**Sarnia** Bayside Mall 150 Christina Street North	**Whitby*** 590 Rossland Road East
Oakville Halton Region Administrative Centre 1151 Bronte Road	**Sault Ste. Marie** 70 Foster Drive, Main Lobby	**Windsor*** 400 City Hall Square East Suite 205
Ottawa 110 Laurier Avenue West	**Sioux Lookout** 62 Queen Street	
Owen Sound 1400 1st Avenue West	**St. Catharines*** 301 St. Paul Street	
Parry Sound 7 Bay Street	**Stratford** 5 Huron Street	
Pembroke 31 Riverside Drive	**Sturgeon Falls** 94 King Street, Unit 8	
Peterborough Ontario Government Building 300 Water Street, Main Floor	**Thunder Bay*** 435 South James Street suite 114	
Rainy River 408 Atwood Avenue	**Timmins (South Porcupine)** Ontario Government Building Highway 101 East	
Red Lake 227 Howey Street		

Notes:

* This is a co-locate office; it is staffed by Landlord and Tenant Board non-Board personnel.

Appendix B — Witness Fees

1. Tariff A: Solicitors' Fees and Disbursements Allowable Under Rule 58.05 of the Rules of Civil Procedure: Disbursements

Attendance Money Allowed pursuant to
Rule 53.04(4) of the Rules of Civil Procedure

2. Part II — Disbursements

Attendance money actually paid to a witness who is entitled to attendance money, to be calculated as follows:

Item Amount

1. Attendance allowance for each day of necessary attendance $50
2. Travel allowance, where the hearing or examination is held,
   (a) in a city or town in which the witness resides, $3.00 for each day of necessary attendance;;
   (b) within 300 kilometres of where the witness resides, 24¢ a kilometre each way between his or her residence and the place of hearing or examination;
   (c) more than 300 kilometres from where the witness resides, the minimum return airfare plus 24¢ a kilometre each way from his her residence to the airport and from the airport to the place of hearing or examination.
3. Overnight accommodation and meal allowance, where the witness resides elsewhere than the place of hearing or examination and is required to remain overnight, for each overnight $75

Appendix 8

LANDLORD AND TENANT BOARD INTERPRETATION GUIDELINES*

Table of Contents

These documents are subject to change without notice. The most current versions of the documents are available from the Landlord and Tenant Board at *www.LTB.gov.on.ca*.

INTERPRETATION GUIDELINE 1 — ADJOURNING AND RESCHEDULING HEARINGS

Interpretation Guidelines are intended to assist the parties in understanding the Board's usual interpretation of the law, to provide guidance to Members and promote consistency in decision-making. However, a Member is not required to follow a Guideline and may make a different decision depending on the facts of the case.

Section 184 of the *Residential Tenancies Act, 2006* (the RTA) provides that the *Statutory Powers Procedure Act* applies to all proceedings before the Board; and the authority to adjourn hearings is found in section 21 of the *Statutory Powers Procedure Act* which provides that:

> A hearing may be adjourned from time to time by a tribunal of its own motion or where it is shown to the satisfaction of the tribunal that the adjournment is required to permit an adequate hearing to be held.

This guideline identifies situations that may warrant the rescheduling or adjournment of a Board hearing.

Rescheduling and adjourning can be defined in the following way:

> Rescheduling involves staff setting a new date for the hearing in advance of the date originally set for it, usually confirmed by a new Notice of Hearing;
>
> Adjourning involves a Member's decision regarding when the hearing of an application will proceed and/or be completed.

General Approach of the Board

Section 183 of the RTA directs the Board to "adopt the most expeditious method of determining the questions arising in a proceeding that affords to all persons directly affected by the proceeding an adequate opportunity to know the issues and to be heard on the matter."

Parties should assume that all of their evidence and submissions will usually be heard on the date stated in the Notice of Hearing. This means that the parties should be prepared to present their evidence, call and question witnesses and make their submissions. The Board's decision will generally be made shortly afterwards.

Risks of Failing to Attend the Hearing or Prepare For It

Parties failing to appear at the hearing specified on the Notice take considerable risks. Section 7 of the *Statutory Powers Procedure Act* provides that a tribunal may proceed with a hearing in the absence of any party. In exceptional circumstances, a Member may exercise the jurisdiction to adjourn a case on the Board's motion in order to determine whether the party who did not appear will do so on a later date. However, parties should not expect such a decision.

Where an applicant fails to appear, the Member will normally proceed with the hearing, which means the applicant's case will be dismissed as abandoned, whether or not the respondent has attended.

Where the respondent fails to appear, the Member will normally proceed with the hearing, and may make a decision based on the evidence of the applicant.

Not preparing for a hearing based on the expectation that it will be postponed, even though the other party prefers to proceed, has substantial risks. If the Member decides to proceed with the hearing on the date set, the evidence presented will be considered, even if additional evidence should rightfully have been presented. Being unprepared strongly increases the risk of failure to prove one's case.

Finally, the only remedies for an incorrect order may be "review of the order" (reconsideration), judicial review or appeal; however, appeal is limited to questions of law, and both appeal and judicial review can be very expensive court procedures. It is highly advisable to deal with the application promptly at the start, rather than count on someone interceding later to reverse an order already issued.

RESCHEDULING HEARINGS

If a party realizes it will be difficult to attend a hearing or that they will not be prepared in time for a hearing, they may seek the rescheduling of the hearing date set out in the Notice of Hearing. They should request rescheduling as soon as possible after they realize it is necessary.

The Board will generally only reschedule a hearing if the party seeking the delay is able to obtain the agreement of the other party or parties (see Rule 12).

If a tenant requests rescheduling, they should deal with the landlord's representative, if there is one, or with the landlord directly. If there are multiple landlords, the agreement of each must be obtained.

When a landlord requests rescheduling, they should deal with the tenant's representative, if one exists, or with the tenant directly. If there is more than one tenant, the agreement of each must be obtained.

It is important that parties respond reasonably to requests from another party to reschedule. Although there are always a number of factors to take into account, if parties are unreasonable in their responses to requests to rescheduling, a Member may find that since rescheduling caused no prejudice to either party, the party who refused the request may be ordered to pay costs.

The party seeking the hearing's rescheduling should send or fax to the Board a written request for rescheduling indicating:

- confirmation that the other party or parties have agreed to the rescheduling;
- what dates the party requesting the rescheduling will be available (subject to the availability of a Member); and
- what dates, if any, the other party(ies) indicated they preferred for the rescheduled hearing.

This written request must be received by the Board no later than the morning of the day before the hearing and a copy should be sent to the other party(ies).

All parties should phone the Board no later than the afternoon of the day before the hearing to ensure that the written request was received, and that the hearing has in fact been rescheduled, and to what date, time and place.

In some cases, exceptional circumstances arise at the last moment (such as the death of a close family member) which prevent the party from meeting the procedures set out above. In such circumstances, the party should notify the Board by telephone as soon as they become aware of this, and inform the other party or their agent, as well. The case will remain on the list of hearings for the scheduled time, but the Member will be apprised of the telephone message and, if convinced that the circumstances are indeed exceptional, may adjourn the hearing without the party being present.

A party may request that a hearing be rescheduled because they are covered by section 1 of the *Human Rights Code*, and the Board is unable to accommodate their needs at the originally scheduled hearing. Such requests will be addressed by the Board in accordance with the Board's *Human Rights Policy*.

It may be necessary from time to time for the Board to reschedule a hearing on its own initiative. For example, the Board may determine that it is necessary to reschedule a hearing to a different date in order to ensure that a sign-language interpreter is available, if so required by one of the parties. In such cases, the parties and their representatives will be notified.

When Partial Mediation is Achieved

When a Board Mediator assists the parties in mediation and a partial settlement is reached by the parties, an interim agreement may be signed by the parties. The parties to the interim agreement may agree to reschedule the hearing to a later date for a Member to determine the unresolved issues (see Rule 13.12).

ADJOURNMENTS

Procedural Issues

If a party is unable to obtain consent to a rescheduling from the other parties in advance of the hearing date, the party or their agent must attend on the hearing date to request an adjournment from the Member. A request for an adjournment will normally be heard at the outset of the session for which the hearing is scheduled.

An adjournment is a procedural decision. If the request is made at the start of the hearing, the Member is not "seized" with the case, thus the same Member is not required to conduct the hearing on the adjourned date. However, if the request is made part way through a hearing, the Member will likely be seized with the case because they heard evidence. For instance, an applicant may discover that the respondent's case involves facts that they did not realize were going to be raised, and that evidence from a witness who is not present is necessary to counter the respondent's defence. In such a situation, the hearing must be adjourned to a time when the same Member can continue the hearing.

Balancing Rights Between the Parties

Section 183 of the RTA states that the Board should be expeditious, but should ensure that the parties are given "an adequate opportunity to know the issues and to be heard on the matter." The key question becomes how to balance the rights of the parties to ensure that matters are resolved quickly while not sacrificing their rights to a fair hearing. The determining factors a Member will weigh are very different depending on whether the parties agree to adjourn, or one party's request to adjourn is contested by one or more other parties.

Agreement to Adjourn

If the parties agree to adjourn the hearing, the Board will not interfere with this agreement in most circumstances. The hearing will be adjourned to a date set by the Board, although the parties may have an opportunity to offer some preferred dates.

However, sometimes the Member may decide it would not be in the public interest to proceed as the parties have arranged. Although the Member will not normally force the parties into a hearing immediately, the parties may be required to proceed on an earlier date than what was agreed upon.

Considerations Where There is No Agreement

Parties are generally required to make themselves available to attend scheduled hearings by making whatever arrangements are necessary. The granting of adjournments is in the discretion of the Member hearing the application. However, if the parties cannot attend the scheduled hearing and are not able to reach an agreement regarding one party's wish to adjourn the hearing, the Member should weigh the prejudice that might be suffered by each party. The Member will consider the prejudice to a party having to appear repeatedly, without a good reason for having to do so. As discussed below, if a Member grants an adjournment, certain conditions may be imposed upon either party in order to alleviate the prejudice the other party may experience as a result of the adjournment.

Therefore, when appearing before the Member the parties should present specific reasons why they would be significantly prejudiced by an adjournment. For example, a delay may economically prejudice a party or may mean a lost opportunity. There may also be aggravating circumstances, such as an urgent need for certain repairs or the continued tenancy will be a threat to other tenants' safety.

The Member is also entitled to consider the conduct of the party opposing the adjournment. For example, if that party is the applicant, and they delayed serving the application until the last day permitted by the Rules, thus giving the respondent the minimum time contemplated, the request is more likely to be granted. Also, if the party opposing the request has shown bad faith or refused to provide information about their case to the respondent which would allow them to prepare quickly for the hearing, this should weigh in favour of an adjournment.

The Member must take into account the public interest in resolving the case as soon as possible. However, the public interest in an expeditious result is greater in some types of applications than in others. A claim for eviction because the tenant threatens the safety of the landlord or other tenants should be dealt with as swiftly as possible, as should a case in which the tenant claims there is ongoing harassment by the landlord or their staff.

Adjournment to Allow Representation

Section 10 of the *Statutory Powers Procedure Act* allows parties the right to be represented by a lawyer or agent at the hearing. However, the right to representation does not automatically guarantee an adjournment. Therefore, the onus is on a party notified of a hearing and wishing to be represented and to make all reasonable efforts to find a lawyer or agent able to represent them on the date on their Notice of Hearing. Nevertheless, a short adjournment may be allowed where a representative has been retained, but is unavailable on the date set for the hearing, or where the party can demonstrate that they have made reasonable efforts to retain a lawyer or agent before the hearing but have yet been unable to do so.

Adjournment to Permit Another Application

A respondent may also request an adjournment because they have filed or will be filing an application against the applicant. This should merit an adjournment only if the respondent's application will affect the outcome of the application being considered.

Adjournment Requests Respecting Court Proceedings

Some parties seek adjournments on the basis that a Court will rule on a similar issue between other parties in the future. This would generally be an invalid reason for permitting a case to remain undecided for a long period: it would be preferable to proceed with the hearing.

Adjournment on Consent for Mediation

A party sometimes hopes that a case may be settled, and that they need more time to resolve the issues with the other party. Although the Board encourages this, and in many cases offers mediation services, a hearing should not be delayed for this purpose, unless both parties agree.

Adjournment to Prepare Case

A respondent may request an adjournment because they may not know the case they must answer. If the respondent demonstrates that the information about the applicant's claims is unclear or not detailed enough to allow them to know what evidence they must present at the hearing, this may justify an adjournment. In deciding whether the claim is sufficiently complete and clear, the Member should evaluate the application, documents filed with it and any information the respondent already had.

A party may request an adjournment to acquire evidence required to prove the facts of the case. It may be a respondent who makes this request because they have received the application too close to the hearing date (though technically "on time" according to the rules for giving applications). Also, any party who has become aware of the other party's intended evidence, and wishes to review or obtain their own evidence to refute their position may request an adjournment.

Adjournment to Prepare for Section 82

In an application by a landlord for rent arrears (section 87 of the RTA) or for termination of the tenancy for rent arrears (section 59 of RTA), section 82 permits tenants to raise any issue that could be raised in a tenant application under the RTA. Where the tenant raises issues under section 82 that the landlord could not reasonably have anticipated and cannot address at the hearing with a short recess, the landlord may request an adjournment to another date for the purpose of investigating the tenant's allegations and obtaining relevant evidence.

Adjournment to Accommodate the needs of a party

At the beginning of a hearing a party may request an adjournment to a later date on the ground that they are covered by section 1 of the Human Rights Code, and the Board is unable to accommodate their needs at the hearing. If the Member determines that it is not possible to accommodate the needs of the party at the hearing, an adjournment may be granted. Further information respecting the Board's accommodation practices can be found in the Board's *Human Rights Interpretation Guideline*.

Conditions for an Adjournment

The Member may decide that a condition should be attached to the granting of an adjournment. Examples of some conditions that may be included:

- an adjournment may be given on the condition that the party requesting it will disclose to the other party(ies) some further information about their position or a copy of evidence that the party will present to the Board when the hearing resumes;
- in a case involving a claim for the payment of money, the Member may decide that a respondent requesting an adjournment should pay the amount claimed by the applicant, or a lesser sum, into the Board as security for the payment of any order which may result from the application, or may come due before the next hearing date (see section 195 of the RTA and Guideline 3, entitled "Costs");
- the adjournment will be granted on a "peremptory" basis, which means that no further adjournment requests will be granted to the party that requested the adjournment, except in the most exceptional circumstances or where the other party consents to the subsequent adjournment request;
- a party opposing the adjournment may ask for costs incurred resulting from the adjournment and any such costs will be considered pursuant to Guideline 3 (also see subsection 204(2) of the RTA).

Amended October 15, 2009

INTERPRETATION GUIDELINE 2 — PAYMENT INTO THE BOARD

Interpretation Guidelines are intended to assist the parties in understanding the Board's usual interpretation of the law, to provide guidance to Members and promote consistency in decision-making. However, a Member is not required to follow a Guideline and may make a different decision depending on the facts of the case.

This Guideline is meant to help parties understand when a Member may: a) require a respondent to pay money into the Board and b) permit a tenant to pay all or part of their rent into the Board.

Subsection 195(1) of the Residential Tenancies Act, 2006 (the "RTA") reads as follows:

> Where the Board considers it appropriate to do so, the Board may, subject to the regulations,[1]
>
> (a) require a respondent to pay a specified sum into the Board within a specified time; or
>
> (b) permit a tenant who is making an application for an order under paragraph 1 of subsection 29(1) to pay all or part of the rent for the tenant's rental unit into the Board.

The money paid into the Board is held in a special trust account. Once the application is decided, the Member will order the money paid out to the appropriate party.

Requiring payment into the Board

A decision under paragraph 195(1)(a) would generally be made at the hearing after receiving submissions from the parties. As most cases will be heard expeditiously, orders to pay money into the Board would be most appropriate in cases where the hearing will be adjourned for some length of time.

In some cases, the amount owing may increase during the proceedings. The longer the adjournment, the more is at risk to the applicant. The applicant may want the Member to require the respondent to pay money into the Board in order to discourage the respondent from unnecessarily prolonging the proceedings.

Where the potential amount owing will increase during the proceedings, and the matter will be adjourned, the Board may require the respondent to pay into the Board:

- all or part of the amount that is owing or claimed to be owing as of the hearing date; and/or,
- the additional amount that will become owing.

[1] No regulation has been passed which affects this provision.

It is generally more appropriate to require payment into the Board of the additional amount that will become owing during the delay, because otherwise the respondent's right to dispute the application may be negatively affected.

As an alternative, the Board may require one party to make a payment directly to the other party instead of paying into the Board. However, the consequences of failing to comply in subsection 195(4) would not apply in this situation.

The applicant may want to ensure that there will be no problems collecting the amount ordered. However, in any application for the payment of money, the applicant may have problems collecting the amount ordered to be paid. If Members required money to be paid into the Board whenever a respondent wished to dispute the application, this would discourage some respondents from exercising their right to a hearing of the merits of the application. This would give an unfair advantage to parties with greater economic power, or to parties who claimed more than the amount they are owed. Therefore, it would not be appropriate to require payment into the Board for this reason.

Rules for payment in and payment out

Subsection 195(2) of the RTA states that the Board may establish rules for the payment of money into and out of the Board. The rules for payment into and out of the Board may be found in Rule 31 of the Rules of Practice, Paying Money Into and Out of the Board.

Consequences of failing to pay money into the Board

The consequences of failing to follow the requirement to pay money into the Board are set out in subsection 195(4):

> If a respondent is required to pay a specified sum into the Board within a specified time under clause (1)(a) and fails to do so, the Board may refuse to consider the evidence and submissions of the respondent.

Where the Member determines that there is no reasonable explanation for the respondent's failure to pay money into the Board, the Member may proceed with the hearing and refuse to hear the evidence and submissions of the respondent. The respondent would be entitled to be present at the hearing, to make procedural objections and to cross-examine witnesses. However, the respondent would not be entitled to present their own documents or witnesses nor to argue their case.

If the respondent can provide a reasonable explanation for their failure to comply with the requirement to pay money into the Board, the Member may proceed with the hearing and allow the respondent to participate.

Permitting payment into the Board

The Board may permit a tenant who is making an application based on a landlord's breach of the duty to repair in subsection 20(1) or section 161 to pay all or part of their rent into the Board. This request may be made at the time the tenant files the application or at the hearing. For further information see Rule 31, Paying Money Into and Out of the Board, and Guideline 5, Breach of Maintenance Obligations.

The tenant will have to satisfy the Board that special circumstances exist that justify the payment in of rent. Special circumstances may include: where the tenant does not know who to pay or how to contact the landlord; the landlord refuses to accept the rent; or where the tenancy will be terminated and it may be difficult for the tenant to enforce the order. There may be other factors and circumstances to consider.

Note that under subsection 195(5) of the RTA, when a tenant is permitted to pay into the Board, the payment is deemed not to constitute a default in the payment of rent under the tenancy agreement or the RTA.

Released Date: January 31, 2007

INTERPRETATION GUIDELINE 3 — COSTS

Interpretation Guidelines are intended to assist the parties in understanding the Board's usual interpretation of the law, to provide guidance to Members and promote consistency in decision-making. However, a Member is not required to follow a Guideline and may make a different decision depending on the facts of the case.

Generally, when someone takes another person to court, they hope that they will collect from the other party some part of their expenses of the lawsuit. The Board has a discretionary power similar to that of the Courts to order "costs". The Board may order one of the parties to pay costs to another party or may order that the Board's costs be paid by a party, a paid agent or counsel to a party. However, the Board does not want to use its power to award costs in a way which would discourage landlords and tenants from exercising their statutory rights.

Subsections 2, 3 and 4 of section 204 of the *Residential Tenancies Act, 2006* (the "RTA") provide that:

> (2) The Board may order a party to an application to pay the costs of another party.
>
> (3) The Board may order that its costs of a proceeding be paid by a party or a paid agent or counsel to a party.
>
> (4) The amount of an order for costs shall be determined in accordance with the Rules.

This Guideline sets out the Board's position on when it may be appropriate to order costs. Generally costs may be ordered where a party's conduct in the proceeding was unreasonable. Costs should not be confused with an administrative fine. An administrative fine is a remedy to be used by the Board to encourage compliance with the RTA and to deter landlords from engaging in similar activity in the future. For further information on administrative fines, see Guideline 16.

SUBMISSIONS ON REPRESENTATION COSTS AND BOARD COSTS

Before ordering a party to pay representation costs of another party or before ordering a party, agent or lawyer to pay the costs of the Board, a Member should ensure that the person who will be affected by the order for costs has an opportunity to make submissions on the matter.

However, if a party has received notice of a hearing and does not attend or if an agent or lawyer is on the record as representing a party and does not attend a hearing, a Member may proceed to make an order for costs without notifying the person affected of the intention to do so, provided that the failure to attend the hearing delayed the process unnecessarily or caused unnecessary expense to the other party.

ORDERING COSTS AGAINST A PARTY OR A PAID REPRESENTATIVE

Costs Ordered in Most Cases

In most cases, the only costs allowed will be the application fee. This should be ordered if the applicant is successful in obtaining an order which allows the relief they asked for in the application, or substantially all of that relief. This includes cases which are resolved by an order based on an application for which no notice is required (section 77 of the RTA). Where appropriate, this cost will be ordered regardless of whether or not the applicant seeks such a remedy.

It is anticipated that return of the application fee will not usually be ordered in the situations listed below:

1. Applications to increase rents above the guideline; such applications involve many respondents and it would be impractical to order costs in these cases.

2. Applications to evict tenants based on their own notice or agreement to terminate where the application is made before the date of termination.

3. Applications to evict a tenant based on a no-fault ground (e.g. a landlord application for termination of the tenancy for the landlord's own use).

Other Costs

A party who wants to claim costs in addition to the application fee should be prepared to speak to the matter and to provide support for the claim. The other party will also be allowed to make submissions on the issue.

In most cases, costs should not be allowed for the other expenses incurred by the successful party such as travel, expert reports, etc. Neither the fees of a representative for preparation time, nor hearing time, should be allowed except in the circumstances set out below.

Further Costs Where a Party's Conduct is Unreasonable

A Member has the discretion to require a party to pay, as costs, any representation or preparation expenses of another party where the conduct of the party was unreasonable. Conduct is unreasonable if it causes undue expense or delay and includes the following:

1. Bringing a frivolous or vexatious application or motion

2. Initiating an application or any procedure in bad faith

3. Taking unnecessary steps in a proceeding

4. Failing to take necessary steps, such as those required by the RTA or Rules

5. Any misconduct at the hearing or in the proceeding

6. Raising an issue which is irrelevant to the proceedings and continuing to pursue that issue after the Member has pointed out that it is irrelevant

7. Asking for adjournments or delays without justification

8. Failing to prepare adequately for the hearing

9. Acting contemptuously toward the Member or showing a lack of respect for the process or the Board

10. Failing to follow the directions of the Member or upsetting the orderly conduct of the hearing

11. Unreasonably maligning another party or slurring the character of the other party

Examples of failing to comply with the RTA or Rules would include the following situations:

- Failing to follow a procedural order or direction such as an order to serve another party with a document
- Serving another party in a way which was not appropriate
- Delaying the hearing by not taking actions required in the Rules

The amount ordered by a Member will usually be less than the actual cost since the Rules will set out maximum amounts for the Member to consider.

Generally, only fees for a representative's time spent at the hearing will be allowed. However, in some cases, a further amount for preparation time may be allowed if the unreasonable conduct led to the need for the representative to spend additional time preparing for the hearing.

Representation fees should not be allowed if the representative did not conduct themselves in a professional manner.

Generally speaking, the Member may refuse to allow representation fees if the conduct of the representative does not demonstrate an understanding of the following:

- Legislation, Regulations, Rules and Guidelines
- The position of their client
- The role of an agent appearing before a quasi-judicial Board
- Standards of proper behaviour and conduct in a hearing

Further Costs Where the Conduct of the Paid Representative of a Party is Unreasonable

A Member has the discretion to order a party to pay costs to another party where the conduct of the party's representative was unreasonable. Conduct is unreasonable if it causes undue expense or delay and includes situations listed above under the heading "Further Costs Where a Party's Conduct is Unreasonable". Unreasonable conduct may also include displaying an inadequate knowledge of the RTA and other relevant legislation.

In addition to making an award of costs, the Board may exclude from a hearing any person, other than a lawyer qualified to practice in Ontario, appearing as an agent on behalf of a party if it is found that the agent is not competent to properly represent or advise the party or does not understand and comply at the hearing with the duties and responsibilities of an advocate and adviser.

Cases Where Costs Should Not Be Allowed

As a general principle, a Member should not order costs of any kind in favour of a party if the conduct of that party was not proper. For example, if the applicant was responsible for an adjournment because they were not prepared, the Member might decide that they should not be awarded any costs. If both parties were responsible for unreasonable conduct, neither should be ordered to pay the costs to the other, although one or both may be ordered to pay the Board costs.

Amount of Costs

Rule 27 of the Board's Rules of Practice sets out the criteria for Members to consider when determining the amount of costs to order.

ORDERING THE BOARD'S COSTS

The Board expects parties and their paid representatives to act reasonably in pursuing their applications or defending their positions. This includes bringing applications only when there are substantial grounds. It also includes taking all required procedural steps, not taking unnecessary ones and acting in a courteous and orderly way at a hearing.

When a party or a paid representative acts improperly or unreasonably in a proceeding, the Board may order the party or their paid representative to pay to the Board an amount that will partly cover the expenses that the Board has incurred as a result of that conduct. If the unreasonable conduct was the fault of the party's representative, the Board will normally order that the paid representative pay the Board's costs.

Pursuant to section 196 and Rule 9, failure to pay costs ordered may result in the Board refusing to allow the filing of an application; a stay in proceedings; a delay in the issuance of an order; and/or a discontinuance of the proceeding. See Rule 9 "Refusing to Accept or Proceed with an Application" for further details.

General Approach

A Member has the discretion to order a party or a paid representative to pay the costs of the Board. This power, however, should be used sparingly. It was not the intent of the Legislature that this power should ever be used to obtain cost recovery for salaries, administration or other expenses of the Board.

In those rare situations in which a party or their representative is responsible for unreasonable conduct, this power allows the Board to accomplish two objectives:

- Recover some of the taxpayers' monies which funded the proceedings, and,

- Discourage inappropriate practices and conduct by parties and their representatives.

An award of Board costs is appropriate in cases in which the adjudicative costs to the public have been unjustifiably increased by the unreasonable conduct or omission of a party or their agent or lawyer.

Unreasonable conduct would include the situations listed above under the headings "Further Costs Where a Party's Conduct is Unreasonable" and "Further Costs Where the Conduct of the Paid Representative of a Party is Unreasonable."

Ordering Board costs is not related to which party is successful. Since the reason such costs are awarded is to encourage proper conduct, it is conceivable that a successful party who adds unnecessary steps to the proceeding or behaves inappropriately at a hearing, may have to pay the Board's expenses for part of the proceeding.

The discretion for a Member to order Board costs to be paid by an agent or lawyer would only be used where, on the balance of probabilities, it is the behaviour of the agent or lawyer and not the client which is in issue.

Ordering Party Costs and Board Costs

An order for a party to pay both the representation/preparation fees of another party and to pay the Board's costs in the same case would only be made in exceptional circumstances.

This would usually include the following:

- A case in which a party clearly and knowingly misled the Board, such as filing an inflated claim for arrears, a false certificate of service, or an altered invoice
- A case where a party was reckless or indifferent about the truthfulness of their evidence, such as stating that the other party did not serve a document which they know they received
- Situations in which the party failed to comply with directions from the Member about the orderly conduct of the hearing
- Evidence of harassment of the other party to prevent the application or defence of the application

Generally, if the party who would pay the costs has been unsuccessful, it is more appropriate to order them to pay costs to the successful party. If the party whose conduct was unreasonable was the successful party, they should be ordered to pay Board costs.

Released Date: January 31, 2007

INTERPRETATION GUIDELINE 4 — ABANDONMENT OF A RENTAL UNIT

Interpretation Guidelines are intended to assist the parties in understanding the Board's usual interpretation of the law, to provide guidance to Members and promote consistency in decision-making. However, a Member is not required to follow a Guideline and may make a different decision depending on the facts of the case.

Section 79 of the *Residential Tenancies Act, 2006* (the "RTA") states:

> If a landlord believes that a tenant has abandoned a rental unit, the landlord may apply to the Board for an order terminating the tenancy.

Although section 79 explains how the landlord may receive an order terminating the tenancy in cases where the tenant has abandoned the unit, it is not mandatory for this type of order to be issued for the landlord to treat the unit as abandoned. However, there is a substantial risk in re-renting the unit without such an order unless it is clear that the tenant has vacated and does not intend to continue the tenancy.

This Guideline is intended to provide guidance in determining if the unit has been abandoned.

When May the Unit be Considered to be Abandoned?

Abandonment is a unilateral act by the tenant to relinquish their tenancy and give up possession of the rental unit without properly giving notice of the termination to the landlord. If the landlord is not sure whether or not a rental unit has been abandoned, they may file an application for determination of this issue with the Board; however, it should be noted the Board has no jurisdiction to issue an order for rent or compensation if a tenant is no longer in possession of the rental unit (see section 87). In this case, the landlord may seek a remedy by applying to Court.

Section 2(3) of the RTA provides that a rental unit is not considered abandoned where the tenant is not in arrears of rent. Even if there is evidence of abandonment, such as the furniture being removed, the landlord cannot treat the unit as abandoned before the end of the rental period if the rent is fully paid.

Evidence of Abandonment

If there is rent due, there must still be substantial evidence of abandonment before the landlord can re-rent the unit or deal with the tenant's property that is remaining in the unit. There are circumstances where the evidence is clear. For example, the tenant may tell the landlord or the superintendent that they are moving out. The tenant may be seen in the process of moving out of the building, and later the door of the unit is found open, showing that all furniture and personal effects were removed. Provided there is no evidence to the contrary, this evidence would support a finding that the tenant has abandoned the rental unit.

The evidence may also be cumulative; there may be several indications that the tenant has left the unit. For example, a neighbour has reported that they saw the tenant moving and the tenant advised the landlord that they intended to leave, or the tenant was known to have accepted a job in another city and the mail has not been collected for a number of weeks. In such circumstances, the landlord may be justified in considering the unit to be abandoned.

The landlord should make reasonable efforts to contact the tenant to determine if they have left the unit (for example, by writing the tenant or calling them at different times each day). The landlord should give the tenant a reason to reply to a letter and should keep notes of the times and dates that they telephoned. The failure of the tenant to respond to the letters and telephone calls should be consistent with the abandonment of a unit and not with a tenant who is on vacation or out of town on business.

If the unit has been abandoned, in accordance with subsection 42(1), the landlord may dispose of any of the tenant's property found in the unit provided that one of the following conditions is met:

1. The landlord applied to the Board and obtained an order terminating the tenancy based on the abandonment of the rental unit.

OR

2. The landlord gave a notice to the tenant and to the Board stating that the landlord intends to dispose of the property if the tenant does not claim the property within 30 days of the notice being given.

If either of these conditions has been met, the landlord may immediately dispose of anything unsafe or unhygienic and, after 30 days following the issuance of the order or the giving of the notice, may dispose of any other tenant belongings. If a tenant does claim the belongings within the 30 day period, they must pay the landlord any arrears of rent and any reasonable costs of moving, storing and securing the property.

If the landlord sells the property, the tenant has 6 months - from the date of the order or from the date the landlord gave notice of their intention to dispose of the property - to claim the proceeds of the sale. The landlord is allowed to deduct from the proceeds of the sale any arrears of rent and any reasonable costs incurred in the moving, storing, securing or selling of the property.

Application to Determine if the Tenant has Abandoned the Unit

If the landlord applies to the Board under section 79, the application must be served on the tenant in accordance with section 191.

Released Date: January 31, 2007

INTERPRETATION GUIDELINE 5 — BREACH OF MAINTENANCE OBLIGATIONS

Interpretation Guidelines are intended to assist the parties in understanding the Board's usual interpretation of the law, to provide guidance to Members and promote consistency in decision-making. However, a Member is not required to follow a Guideline and may make a different decision depending on the facts of the case.

This Guideline deals with the responsibility of landlords to maintain residential complexes and rental units and with the appropriate choice of remedies.

Section 20 of the *Residential Tenancies Act, 2006* (the "RTA") states as follows:

> (1) A landlord is responsible for providing and maintaining a residential complex, including the rental units in it, in a good state of repair and fit for habitation and for complying with health, safety, housing and maintenance standards.
>
> (2) Subsection (1) applies even if the tenant was aware of a state of non-repair or a contravention of a standard before entering into the tenancy agreement.

A tenant may apply to the Board under paragraph 2 of subsection 29(1) of the RTA for an order to determine if the landlord is in breach of these obligations.[2] If the Board determines that a breach occurred, section 30 provides a number of available remedies that may be ordered, including ordering the work to be done, abatement of rent, and termination of the tenancy. The Board may also order the landlord to pay compensation to the tenant for the cost of repairing or replacing property damaged, destroyed or disposed of as a result of the landlord's breach, as well as other reasonable out-of-pocket expenses.

The Intention of the Legislation

The intention behind sections 20, 29 and 30 is to make landlords responsible for maintaining their complexes, and not to limit their obligations by transferring them by agreement to the tenant. If a tenant agreed in a lease to assume the responsibility to maintain any part of the unit or complex, beyond ordinary cleanliness and damage, this would not be enforceable.[3]

The statute should be interpreted in a way which encourages the best maintained complexes and units. The landlord is required to rectify maintenance deficiencies and

---

[2] This guideline does not discuss the additional responsibilities under section 161 for mobile home parks or land lease communities. For a mobile home park or land lease community, the landlord has additional specific responsibilities under section 161, such as garbage removal, park roads maintenance and sewage disposal, etc. Although these obligations may also be enforced under subs. 29(1), they are not specifically addressed in this Guideline.

[3] See *Fleischman v. Grossman Holdings Ltd.* (1976), 16 O.R. (2d) 746 (C.A.) regarding exclusionary clauses in leases and *Burt Dozet Management Inc. v. Goharzad* [2001] O.J. No. 695 (Div. Ct.).

meet applicable standards. When a deficiency is found, the breach of maintenance obligations will generally result in an order under section 30. In some situations, the landlord will also be ordered to compensate tenants for problems of which the landlord was aware, or could reasonably be expected to have knowledge of, but took no action to rectify.

It is not a proper defence to such an application that the landlord needs the money for other purposes, even for other repairs. If there are many repairs necessary in a complex, the Member could take into account that some work should come first, and delay an order for other repairs. However, the obligation to maintain residential premises is not subject to whether the landlord has available funds.

Obligation Extends to the Residential Complex

The residential complex extends beyond the rental unit occupied by the tenant, to include the facilities and common areas provided for tenants by the landlord. This includes the lobby, hallways, stairwells, laundry facilities, parking areas, exterior grounds, recreational facilities, etc.[4]

Any physical facilities which the landlord can be found to have rented to the tenant, or permitted the tenant to use, should be maintained by the landlord. This may include facilities not immediately adjacent to the complex, but which the landlord has specifically agreed to provide (such as a swimming pool at a nearby building, parking in a separate lot, storage elsewhere, etc.).

In *Quann v. Pajelle Investments Ltd.*,[5] it was held that:

> In our day and age, the urban lease of an apartment in a substantial building gives to the tenant a package of goods and services. Those goods and services include not only walls and ceilings but adequate heat, light, and ventilation, serviceable plumbing facilities, secure windows and doors, proper sanitation and maintenance, the rights guaranteed to the tenant ...If the duty of the landlord is not fulfilled the tenant has the right to seek relief.

A landlord may assert that they have a good program of maintenance and repair, including preventative maintenance and a system of processing complaints. This is not a release of the landlord's responsibility to respond to a real problem. It is reasonable management practice to answer maintenance requests in the order of their urgency (e.g., water leaks come before a loose wall tile), but all legitimate requests must be answered within a reasonable time.

---

[4] In *Herbold v. Pajelle Investments Ltd.*, [1976] 2 S.C.R. 520, the Supreme Court of Canada held that rented premises extend beyond the rental unit and include the facilities and common areas provided to the tenants. This has been further clarified in the TPA by the use of the terms "rental unit" and "residential complex".

[5] (1975) 7 O.R. (2d) 769 (Co.Ct.).

A Landlord's Right to Enter a Unit to Check Maintenance Issues

Paragraph 4 of subsection 27(1) the RTA permits a landlord to enter a rental unit to carry out an inspection where notice is provided 24 hours before the time the landlord intends to enter provided that:

i. The inspection is to determine whether or not the unit is in a good state of repair and fit for habitation and complies with health, safety, housing and maintenance standards consistent with the landlord's obligations under subsection 20(1) or section 161, and

ii. It is reasonable to carry out the inspection.

When Can An Application Be Made?

An application must be made by the current or former tenant within one year of the date the alleged breach occurred[6]. Counting a year from an event, such as an illegal entry, is not difficult, but a breach of a maintenance obligation or non-compliance with standards occurs over a period of time, and it is often impossible to determine when it started.

The intention behind a limitation period is that the applicant has only a certain time to bring the complaint and obtain a remedy. If the applicant leaves the issue too long, it reduces the respondent's ability to answer the allegation. A unit or complex may have numerous problems which started at various times and gradually worsened to arrive at a state of non-repair which caused the tenant to apply.

In view of the policy intent to encourage better maintenance, the Legislature cannot have intended to impose a one year limitation from the start of each breach. The breach of obligations is a continuing event. However, the tenant may not raise any item which was rectified by the landlord more than one year before the application was filed.

Rent Payment Into the Board

Clause (b) of subsection 195(1) indicates that where the Board considers it appropriate, the Board may permit a tenant who is making a maintenance application to pay some or all of their rent into the Board. Subsection 195(5) states that if such a payment is allowed, it is not considered to be arrears of rent or a breach of the tenant's obligations. As discussed in Guideline 2 "Payment Into the Board", such requests will only be granted in special circumstances.

See Rule 31, Paying Money into and Out of the Board for details on the procedures for requesting payment of rent into the Board.

What Issues Should be Permitted at the Hearing

The applicant has an obligation to set out the nature of the issues being raised, so that the respondent has the opportunity to prepare for the hearing. The items alleged to be in need of maintenance or repair or failure to meet standards should be set out on

---

[6] Subsection 29(2) of the RTA.

the application form, as should any claims for compensation for damaged, destroyed or disposed of items. If no details are set out, the application could be dismissed, or the applicant may be allowed an amendment to provide details. In some cases this will cause an adjournment to allow the landlord to prepare to meet those issues.

Even if the tenant has been specific in the application about the items which require repair or are below standards, or about compensation claims, they may try to raise further items at the hearing. The Member will have to decide whether to permit these additional items, usually after hearing the tenant's explanation of why they were not raised before, and the landlord submissions about any prejudice they may suffer in responding to the new items. The new items must have a connection with the items raised initially.

Applying the Tests to Each Item

Each item raised by the tenant which was not remedied within the last year must be considered under all the tests in section 20. For example, with a complaint of lack of heat, the Member will have to consider whether this is failing to maintain a good state of repair, whether the premises are unfit for habitation because of the lack of heat, and whether the landlord has thus failed to comply with standards. If the problem alleged by the tenant falls into any of these categories, it will justify a finding of breach of obligations.

In general, where there is a conflict between what the Member believes would be required by "good state of repair and fit for habitation" and the standard imposed by the responsible public authority, and the landlord has met the standard, the Member should not find the landlord in breach of section 20.

Good State of Repair

The landlord's obligation under section 20 to provide and maintain the premises in a good state of repair is very broad. It would include anything that was capable of being repaired. The full extent of the obligation does not depend on the tenancy agreement.

Fit for Habitation

A number of cases have also considered the meaning of "fit for habitation". *Summers v. Salford Corp.*[7] is the leading case from Britain. The Court held that if the state of disrepair is such that by ordinary use, damage may naturally be caused to the occupier, either in respect of personal injury to life or limb or injury to health, the house is considered not reasonably fit for habitation.

This phrase "fit for habitation" is not the standard expected, and should not be used to limit or qualify "good state of repair". Generally, it is enough for any part of the premises to be unfit. Examples would include infestations of rodents or vermin, bathrooms with backed-up sewage, rooms with broken windows, etc.

---

[7] [1943] 1 All E.R. 68.

Health, Safety, Housing and Maintenance Standards

Most standards are found in municipal property standards by-laws, but may also be provincial standards such as the fire code, elevator standards or the provincial standard under the RTA (see below). The tenant has the obligation to bring the standard to the attention of the Member, usually by filing a copy of the by-law, RTA or other document either before or at the hearing. However, the Member may on his or her own initiative refer to the standard.

If a notice of violation, work order or other order has been issued for this complex or unit, it represents a finding by a public official that the landlord has not complied with the standard. Once the tenant files a copy of the notice or order, a Member will be entitled to accept this as evidence of non-compliance with a standard. However, the landlord is entitled to have the issue determined by the Board if they dispute the notice or order. In such a case, the landlord must raise this dispute, file the document and bring forward evidence to prove their position.

A landlord may argue that the work order has not taken effect, and should not be considered, if the time for compliance has not yet expired. In fact, many work orders are issued after non-compliance with a standard has existed for some time. The fact that the landlord has been given more time by another authority to rectify the problem does not mean that there is no problem. The issue should not be dismissed on this basis. Of course, if the work order was the first way that the landlord discovered this problem existed, the fact that the compliance period has not yet expired for a non-urgent item may indicate a different remedy than a long-standing problem that was ignored.

A landlord may also argue that actions taken by the public authority pursuant to the work order, such as prosecution of a provincial offence, should be considered as penalty enough for the non-compliance with the standard. However, the Member must still determine whether there was non-compliance with a standard, although it may be taken into account that the landlord has paid a fine in deciding what remedy is appropriate.

If no complaint has been filed with the appropriate public authority, it is then necessary for the Board to hear evidence on the issue and come to its own conclusion. A notice of violation issued by a public authority is not necessary for a finding of a breach of section 20.

If the applicant submits that a maintenance condition does not meet a standard, but has no evidence at the hearing of the exact nature of the standard, the Member may consider the item under the other tests (good state of repair or fit for habitation). However, the landlord is entitled then to introduce the standard, and to show that they are meeting it.

Provincial Maintenance Standard

Work orders will also be issued by the Ministry of Municipal Affairs and Housing for municipalities which do not have their own property standards by-laws. These orders are authorized by the provincial maintenance standard set out in the regulations.[8]

Some tenants may wish to use the provincial maintenance standard, even though their own municipality has a property standards by-law. However, section 20 requires landlords to comply with standards and this must be read as meaning only those standards which are enforceable for that complex.

What is Not Required by This Landlord Obligation

Landlords may choose to undertake programs of preventative maintenance. However, a tenant cannot insist that their landlord undertake specific preventative maintenance work as a necessary repair.

When landlords undertake repairs, there is often a dispute between the parties about whether the repairs were properly done. The tenant has no right to insist upon a standard of perfection regarding repairs. By the same token, a landlord is not entitled to rely upon repairs that were improperly done as a complete answer to the need for repairs, especially if the repairs had no effect or resulted in a need for further repairs.

Where the Problem Has Been Repaired/Rectified

The tenant must apply within one year after the breach of obligation existed, but the fact that a problem has been rectified before the application was filed does not exclude it from consideration. However, it would appear that the cases generally support the principle that, if the landlord responded within a reasonable time, and the response was appropriate to effect the repair, no abatement or other remedy should be ordered.

Timeliness of response depends on a great number of factors, but principally on the seriousness of the state of non-repair and its possible effects on the tenant and the availability of materials and possibly contractors to do the repairs. The tenant may also be alleging that the repairs attempted by the landlord were ineffective or badly done, which has reduced the value of the unit or left the same problem unremedied. These issues must be addressed directly through evidence and decided by the Member.

Tenant Conduct that will Result in Dismissing a Claim

Section 34 of the RTA provides that the tenant is responsible for the repair of any undue damages to the rental unit or residential complex caused by the wilful or negligent conduct of the tenant, other occupants of the rental unit or persons who are permitted in the residential complex by the tenant. Thus, if the landlord alleges that the repairs requested by the tenant were in fact the tenant's responsibility, this issue must be decided by the Member.

Similarly, it may be necessary to hear evidence regarding an allegation that the tenant or persons they permitted on the premises contributed to the severity of the maintenance problem, or aggravated its repair. The tenant may have unreasonably prevented the landlord from entering the unit to assess the problem or make the repairs. In such

---

[8] O. Reg. 517/06.

a case, the repair may still be ordered to be done by the landlord or the tenant, but the tenant's conduct may result in no abatement or other remedy.

REMEDIES THAT MAY BE ORDERED

Assuming that the Member has heard the evidence and decided that there has been a breach of the landlord's obligations, there are a number of factors that should be considered before arriving at the remedy or remedies to be included in the order.

The Member should ask for submissions from the parties specifically about the remedies that are appropriate for each item. The applicant and respondent may have discussed the dispute and come to some conclusion concerning the type or amount of relief to be given, although a Member is not bound to follow a joint submission.

Whether Tenant Notified the Landlord

Subsection 30(2) of the RTA states that, in determining the remedy, the adjudicator shall consider whether the applicant advised the landlord of the alleged breaches before filing their application. If the tenant failed to notify the landlord before making the application, it does not mean that the application must be dismissed, or even that this item should be dismissed.

Although the best practice for a tenant is to notify a landlord in writing of any serious problem, this provision does not require the notice to be written. Where the tenant alleges there was oral notice, they must convince the Member through their testimony that notice was given to the landlord or an employee, and when.

However, failure to advise the landlord will affect the remedies to be ordered, unless the landlord knew about the problem already or should have known. An applicant should not be awarded less relief than another tenant if they reasonably believed other tenants had already complained or the problem should have been obvious to the landlord or their employees.

A. Order the Landlord to Do the Work

Section 30 permits the Member to order the landlord to do specified repairs or replacements or other work within a specified time.

Most tenants apply because they want the landlord to be ordered to do the repairs or replacements. Thus, where these applications are mediated or settled, the agreement will usually include the landlord's promise to do the agreed work by a certain date.

An order should be very specific about the repairs or replacements that are required and by what date. The time allowed should be realistic given the season and any other factors that may delay the work. A Member may order that a tenant can deduct an amount from future rent payments if a landlord fails to comply with the order within a specified period of time.

B. Authorize the Tenant to Do the Repairs or Replacements

Section 30 allows a Member to authorize a repair or replacement that has been or is to be made and order its cost to be paid by the landlord to the tenant.

This will be an appropriate remedy where the failure of the landlord to comply with their maintenance obligations has resulted in the tenant being forced to do the repair or replacement. For example, if a tenant has already paid to have their refrigerator repaired, the Member could authorize the repair and order the landlord to refund the tenant the cost they incurred (so long it is reasonable) by a specific date or to deduct the amount from the rent.

In general, if repairs or replacements have not been done yet, difficult repairs or replacements and those that must be done consistently with similar work in the complex should usually be done by the landlord.

Where the repairs or replacements could be properly done by the tenant, the best order may be a combination. For example, the landlord could be ordered to do specified work by a specific date, failing which, the tenant would be authorized to do the same work, and deduct a specified amount from the rent. It would usually be advisable to have evidence, through estimates, of the cost of the repairs or replacements.

Section 207 of the RTA allows the adjudicator to set out recovery provisions in the order in the event that the landlord does not pay the tenant the lump sum amount ordered.

C. Order an Abatement of Rent

Section 30 allows a Member to order an abatement of rent. This is a monetary award expressed in terms of past or future rent. It may be a lump sum payment the landlord is ordered to pay the tenant, which effectively orders the landlord to give back part of the rent paid. It may be an order to allow the tenant to pay less rent by a certain amount or percentage, or even to pay no rent, for a specified time period. It could also be a combination of these.

This remedy is not appropriate where the landlord was not aware of the problem until the application was filed, but they should be ordered to fix the problem. If the landlord has already rectified the problem, and did so within a reasonable time, an abatement is not appropriate.

There is no guidance in the RTA to assist the Member in determining the amount of an abatement of rent. In determining the amount to be ordered, the Member will consider the period of time that the problem existed and the severity of the problem in terms of its effect on the tenant.

The test should be the impact on the average tenant or the impact a reasonable person would expect this problem to have had on a tenant. If the tenant has a particular susceptibility to this particular problem, the landlord can only reasonably be liable to the tenant for more significant penalties if it can be shown that the landlord knew of the particular condition of the tenant.

This remedy should not be seen as punishment for landlord conduct or inaction. It is compensation to the tenant for the inadequate state of repair and any inconvenience or actual loss of use of the rental unit or common facilities.

Effect of the Rent Level on the Abatement

The usual approach will be to look at an abatement as a portion of the rent. In other words, a Member will assess what percentage of the package of shelter and services rented by the tenant is not available to the tenant. That will then be expressed as a dollar amount, and logically this will be greater if the rent is greater.

In a rental unit with a low rent, or a lower rent than for similar units nearby, the landlord may argue that the maintenance standard expected would be somewhat less, and there should be no abatement or a minimal one. However, it must be remembered that the RTA guarantees adequate maintenance even if the tenant accepted the unit "as is". This is what one Ontario Court Justice stated about this issue:

> It is clear from the existing jurisprudence that there is no magic formula for determining what is an appropriate amount for an abatement...And while a tenant cannot reasonably expect luxury accommodation for marginally economic rent, even at the low end of the market a tenant is entitled to certain minimum guarantees.[9]

The other side of this issue is whether a higher rent entitles a tenant to better maintenance, and thus faster repairs, a wider responsibility for repairs and higher abatements if repairs are not done. This would seem to be an expectation related to the contract, rather than a tenant protection intended by the statute. Section 20 should not be interpreted in this way.

Knowledge of the Landlord

A landlord may assert that they are not liable for the unexpected results of maintenance problems of which they were not aware or that they could not reasonably be expected to have knowledge of. This is indeed the law, as established by two Ontario Court of Appeal decisions. The Court rejected the claim for damages to a tenant who fell through rotting steps, of which the landlord was unaware.[10] However, in a similar case in which the tenant had advised the landlord of the wobbling stairs, the Court found the landlord liable for damages.[11] These were claims for "damages" but the same principle applies to abatements.

Is There Liability for Abatement During Repairs or Replacements?

In some past decisions, the Court ordered landlords to pay an abatement of rent for the period of major repairs done for the tenant's benefit. This reflects the loss of use of part of the unit or services, and from one point of view this loss was directly caused (at least in some cases) from the landlord's failure to do work earlier. The opposite viewpoint is that such an abatement is counterproductive because the landlord will not have enough funds to do the work, and will discourage landlords from doing necessary improvements.

---

[9] *Prenor Trust Company of Canada v. Karen Forrest* [1993] O.J. No. 1058 (Ont. Ct. J.).

[10] In *McQuestion v. Schneider* (1975), 8 O.R. (2d) 249 (C.A.), the Court rejected the tenant's argument that this duty to repair imposed a strict or absolute liability on the landlord.

[11] In *Dye v. McGregor* (1978), 20 O.R. (2d) 1 (C.A.), the Court found that this notice was sufficient to establish some degree of want of repair and found the landlord liable.

The Supreme Court of Canada set out the basic rule in *Herbold v. Pajelle Investments Ltd.*[12] The Court held that only in the most exceptional cases should an abatement of rent be granted for failure to provide common facilities and services during a short period required for necessary repairs and renovations. The Court noted that where there are long and important delays in providing these things which the landlord is responsible for providing, an abatement should be ordered. In *Greenbranch Investments Ltd. v. Goulborn*[13] the Court of Appeal held that repairs done by the landlord in that case did not deprive the tenants of the physical use and enjoyment of their premises.

Section 8 of O. Reg. 516/06 sets out criteria to be applied by the Board in determining whether there is substantial interference when a landlord does maintenance, repairs or capital improvements, criteria for determining whether to order an abatement of rent, and rules for calculating an abatement. These rules must be applied in an application for a finding that the landlord has substantially interfered with the reasonable enjoyment of the unit by the tenant, but they do not apply to an application for a finding that a landlord has failed to repair or maintain the unit or complex.

If a landlord has done little maintenance for an extended period, and a serious condition results that takes some time to rectify, the landlord should be responsible for the tenants' loss of use of their unit or common facilities during the repairs. However, if the landlord has a reasonable program of maintenance, including preventative maintenance, and is acting responsibly to rectify a problem that requires extensive repairs, an abatement of rent should not be ordered.

This approach imposes greater liability on landlords who do not meet their maintenance obligations, while encouraging responsible landlords to undertake major projects.

Thus, although proving that there is good maintenance of a complex will not avoid a finding that specific maintenance problems exist and must be rectified, it will affect the abatement remedy. Thus, it is only where the tenant has claimed an abatement of rent and that remedy is available that evidence of a good maintenance program should be accepted.

D. Termination of the Tenancy and Eviction of the Tenant

These remedies should be used in serious cases and only where the tenant requests them or a public authority has required the unit to be vacated. These remedies may also be ordered on consent of both parties if, for example, they both feel the relationship cannot continue.

If the rental unit is not fit for human habitation, the tenancy should be terminated. For example, if this occurred due to a disaster such as flooding, and the landlord does not wish to restore the unit immediately and make provisions such as a hotel to bridge the time, the tenancy could be terminated retroactively to the date of the flooding,

[12] [1976] 2 S.C.R. 520.

[13] [1972] O.J. No. 956 (C.A.).

with an abatement ordered from that date on (similar to compensation in the other direction).

The Member may also choose this remedy if the condition of the unit is so poor as to threaten the safety of the tenants or threaten their well-being. However, ordinarily the landlord should have had a reasonable opportunity to rectify the situation before termination is ordered.

Where an eviction of the tenant is ordered, the effective date of the eviction may not be earlier than the termination date specified in the order.

E. Order the Landlord to Pay a Specified Sum to the Tenant

The Member may order the landlord to pay the reasonable costs the tenant has or will incur to replace property where the tenant's property has been damaged, destroyed or disposed of as a result of the landlord's breach. These costs should only be awarded where repairing the property is not a reasonable alternative.

The Member may also order the landlord to pay the tenant compensation for other reasonable out-of-pocket expenses that the tenant has or will incur as a result of the landlord's breach.

F. Prohibit Rent Increases

The Member may also prohibit the landlord from:

i. charging a new tenant an amount of rent in excess of the last lawful rent charged to the former tenant;

ii. giving a notice of a rent increase; or

iii. taking any rent increase for which notice has been given if the increase has not been taken before the date of any order the member may issue under this section.

Any of these remedies may be included in an order for the period until the landlord:

i. has completed the items in work orders for which the compliance period has expired and which were found by the Board to be related to a serious breach of a health, safety, housing or maintenance standard; and

ii. has completed the specified repairs or replacements or other work ordered under paragraph 4 of section 30 found by the Board to be related to a serious breach of the landlord's obligations under section 20(1) or section 161 of the RTA.

Note that a Member must find that a landlord has not completed the items in a work order or orders relating to a "serious" breach of the relevant standard or obligation. What constitutes a serious breach is discussed under "Serious Breach of Landlord Obligations" in Guideline 7, Relief from Eviction.

G. Any Other Order that is Appropriate

Section 30 also permits the Board to make any other order that it considers appropriate.

The Board has the authority under the Statutory Powers Procedure Act to issue interim orders. This may be an appropriate remedy when the landlord has shown no inclination to do the work required, and the Member does not believe that an order to do the work will be respected. This would be especially applicable where authorizing the tenant to do the work would not be appropriate because of the nature of the repairs needed. The Member could issue an interim order assessing an abatement of rent of an appropriate amount for each month until the landlord completes the repairs. This will encourage the landlord to do the work expeditiously.

For cases in which the work should be done very quickly, the decision on the abatement could be delayed by adjourning the case for a short period, allowing the landlord to return on a later date to show the work is completed. The advantage of this approach is that it encourages the work to be done, while not putting the Member in the position of issuing a final order with conditions (which may be difficult to enforce for the tenant). Usually a date for the adjourned hearing should be set, but in appropriate cases the hearing could be adjourned without a date, allowing any party to bring it back on with seven days notice to the other parties.

Another option would be to order the landlord to do the specific repairs within a specific period, but also order that, failing the work being done within that time, the tenant may recover the appropriate amount to do the work through deductions to the rent. Alternatively, if the landlord failed to do the work by the deadline, the tenant would be entitled to a rent abatement for each rental period until the work was completed.

The Member may also combine any of the above mentioned remedies where they believe it is appropriate to do so.

Amended December 08, 2008

INTERPRETATION GUIDELINE 6 — TENANT'S RIGHTS

Interpretation Guidelines are intended to assist the parties in understanding the Board's usual interpretation of the law, to provide guidance to Members and promote consistency in decision-making. However, a Member is not required to follow a Guideline and may make a different decision depending on the facts of the case.

Under subsection 29(1) of the *Residential Tenancies Act, 2006* (the "RTA") a tenant may apply to the Board for an order determining that the landlord, superintendent or agent of the landlord:[14]

- has illegally entered the unit;
- has altered a locking system on a door giving entry to the unit or the complex, without giving the tenant replacement keys;
- has withheld or deliberately interfered with the reasonable supply of any vital service, care service or food;
- has substantially interfered with the tenant's reasonable enjoyment of the premises;
- has harassed, obstructed, coerced, threatened or interfered with a tenant.

Section 31 of the RTA sets out the remedies which the Board may include in an order if a finding is made in respect to any of these matters (referred to as the "actions").

Under subsections (1), (2) and (3), these remedies include:

- ordering the landlord, superintendent or agent not to engage in any of those actions against any of the tenants in the complex;
- ordering an abatement of rent;
- ordering the landlord to pay an administrative fine to the Board up to $10,000;
- ordering the landlord, superintendent or agent to pay compensation to the tenant for property that has been damaged, destroyed or disposed of as a result of the action;
- ordering the landlord, superintendent or agent to pay other reasonable out-of-pocket expenses that the tenant has incurred or will incur;
- where the tenant has been illegally locked out, ordering the landlord to allow the tenant to recover possession of the rental unit, and to refrain from re-renting the unit in the interim;
- terminate tenancy and order eviction (see s. 32); and/or
- making any other order it considers appropriate.

[14] For the exact text of these provisions, see the RTA.

If the conduct induced the tenant to vacate the unit, subsection (2) also permits the Board to order the landlord to pay a specified amount to the tenant as compensation for:

- increased rent the tenant incurs within 12 months, and
- reasonable moving and related expenses.

Section 8 of O. Reg. 516/06, made pursuant to section 241 of the RTA, sets out criteria to be applied by the Board in determining whether there is substantial interference when a landlord does maintenance, repairs or capital improvements; as well as criteria for determining whether to order an abatement of rent, and rules for calculating the abatement.

Subsection 31(3) permits the Board to order the landlord to allow the tenant to recover possession of the rental unit. If the landlord does not voluntarily comply with the Board's order by allowing the tenant to regain possession, the tenant can enforce the Board's order through the sheriff's office. In the case where the tenant does not regain possession, the Board's order will expire at the end of 15 days after the date it was issued if it has not been filed with the sheriff's office. Even where the tenant files the order with the appropriate sheriff's office the Board's order will expire at the end of the 45th day (see subsection 31(4) and (5) for exact wording of the RTA).

Where Notice is Given in Bad Faith

Notice of termination of the tenancy can be given by the landlord:

- for the use of the rental unit by the landlord, the landlord's spouse, child or parent of the landlord or spouse of the landlord, or for a person providing care services to the landlord or the landlord's spouse, child or parent of the landlord or spouse of the landlord (see section 48 of the RTA);
- for the use of the rental unit by the purchaser, the purchaser's spouse, child or parent of the purchaser or spouse of the purchaser, or for a person providing care services to the purchaser or the purchaser's spouse, child or parent of the purchaser or spouse of the purchaser (see section 49 of the RTA);
- for the demolition, conversion or repairs of the rental unit (see section 50 of the RTA).

Under subsection 57(1) of the RTA, a former tenant may apply to the Board for an order determining that the landlord has given notice of termination in bad faith in the circumstances found in sections 48, 49 or 50 of the RTA. The former tenant may apply if they have vacated the rental unit as a result of the notice given by the landlord or an application or as a result of an order issued by the Board based on the notice. The application must be filed by the former tenant within one year after they vacated the rental unit.

Properly Naming Respondents

It is essential that the tenant name the appropriate persons as respondents. The tenant should name the landlord as a respondent in the application as well as any other person that they believe is responsible for the issues that they are raising in their application. If a person who the tenant alleges to be responsible is not named as a party to the application, and thus has no opportunity to respond to the allegations and make submissions on the possible remedies, no remedies will be ordered against that person.

For example, if the tenant names only the landlord as a respondent, but proves that a superintendent or agent of the landlord was responsible for the action, the Board can order remedies against the landlord but cannot order remedies against the superintendent or agent personally.

If the landlord is a corporation or similar entity, the Member must determine whether the persons who engaged in the actions against the tenant were acting on behalf of the landlord. A corporation may only act through human beings: namely, its officers and employees. The corporation may also enter into a contract with an agent to act on its behalf. Thus, if the individual who engaged in the action against the tenant was an officer, employee or agent of the corporation, the corporation is responsible as the landlord and the Member may order remedies against both the individual and the corporation.

If the tenant decides early in the hearing that another respondent should have been named, the Member must consider whether the tenant should have been aware that the other respondent should have been named in the application. The hearing would have to start again from the beginning if another respondent is added by the Member. However, if the other respondent is a corporation, one of whose employees, officers or agents was at the hearing already, it might not be necessary to re-start the hearing.

Abatement Orders

If the Board determines that the landlord, superintendent or agent has violated the rights of the tenant under subsection 29(1), the Board may order any one or more of the remedies mentioned in subsection 31(1).

If the Board determines that an abatement of rent is appropriate in the circumstances, the Board will determine the amount and/or duration of the abatement. To make this determination the Board will look at factors such as:

- The respondent's intentions in doing the action complained of by the tenant;
- Whether the respondent was motivated by malice toward the tenant;
- The extent of harm that the tenant suffered as a result of the respondent's actions;
- Whether the tenant contributed to or aggravated the situation;
- The frequency or duration of the actions or events, and if a landlord has taken or permitted an action against the tenant. For instance, if it was a single action which deprived the tenant of their tenancy, such as locking the tenant out of the unit, the Board should consider this among the most serious means of harming a tenant. If the actions occurred over a period of time,

the Member should consider the number of occasions and the total period of time. The abatement may be expressed as a portion of the rent which would reflect the seriousness of the expected effects on a tenant. Normally, this would be allowed for the periods in which the actions occurred. For example, for a serious case of harassment, an abatement of twenty-five to fifty per cent of the rent may be appropriate. In cases of minor (but not trivial) harassment, an order of between five and fifteen percent abatement would be more appropriate.

When a Member finds that the respondent engaged in actions against the tenant, they should consider the effects those actions would have on an average tenant. However, if it is proven that the respondent was aware of particular circumstances of this applicant which would aggravate the effects of the actions, those circumstances should be considered. For example, cornering a person in a parking garage and raising one's voice may be annoying to most tenants; however, if the landlord knows the tenant is vulnerable and lives alone, such an incident may be seriously disturbing and may warrant a larger abatement of rent.

If a superintendent or agent is proven to have engaged in the actions, and not the landlord, an order for the landlord to pay an abatement may be made if the person who engaged in the actions was an employee, agent or officer of the landlord, whether or not acting properly under instructions from the landlord.

A superintendent or agent would not be ordered to pay an abatement of rent, since the tenant pays rent to the landlord; however, they may be ordered to pay compensation (see below under "other appropriate orders").

Orders Prohibiting Actions Against Tenants

Normally the order will direct the respondent not to engage in any of the listed activities against any tenant in the complex. This remedy may be appropriate even if there is no evidence that the landlord has engaged in similar actions against another tenant or tenants. However, in an appropriate case, the Member may order the respondent not engage in a specific activity against the applicant tenant and members of their household.

The main test in deciding whether to order this relief is whether it is in the public interest to deter this respondent from any further occurrence of actions against tenants. This is particularly true if the actions against the tenant threatened the health or safety of the tenant or a member of their household.

Orders Terminating Tenancies

There are several situations in which a tenancy may be terminated by the order.

If the tenant was induced to move out of the unit by reason of the landlord's actions, and the Member finds that moving out was reasonable in the circumstances, the tenancy should be ordered terminated, usually as of the date they vacated the unit. This will prevent the landlord from applying to the Board for any further rent from the tenant. The Member should order the landlord to refund to the tenant all rent paid pertaining to the period of time after the effective date of termination, plus the rent deposit. For example, if the termination is June 15, and June rent and a rent deposit were paid, the landlord should refund 1 1/2 months rent to the tenant. The authority for such an order is "Other Appropriate Orders" (see below).

If the tenant requests termination of the tenancy or if the parties agree, termination may be ordered. It is desirable if the parties agree on appropriate terms and timing of the termination. This would avoid unintended financial consequences to one or both of the parties. If the Board makes an order terminating the tenancy the Board may also order that the tenant be evicted.

If the tenant wants to stay in the unit, this request should be honoured unless there is clear danger to the occupants of the unit. If the health or safety of the tenant or a member of their household is threatened, the tenancy should be terminated.

If the respondent's actions put the tenant in a position that the tenancy cannot be safely continued, the request to terminate the tenancy should be granted. For example, the landlord cuts off a tenant's heat in the winter. In order not to put the tenant at a disadvantage compared to a tenant who moved out before applying, the Member might also order the respondent to pay the tenant's moving expenses, even if these have to be estimated.

Orders to Pay an Administrative Fine

An administrative fine is a remedy to be used by the Board to encourage compliance with the RTA and to deter landlords, superintendents and agents from engaging in similar actions in the future. This remedy is appropriate in serious cases where the landlord has shown a blatant disregard for the RTA and other remedies will not provide adequate deterrence and compliance.

For further information on administrative fines please see Guideline 16.

Other Appropriate Orders

The legislation allows the Board to make an order which may be appropriate, in addition to the other remedies set out in sections 30 and 31 of the RTA. Before making such an order the Member shall take into consideration the individual circumstances between the parties and will advise the parties of the order they may be considering. The Board will allow the parties an opportunity to make submissions on the order and will also consider the practicality and enforceability of the order.

Compensation for Future Rent and Moving Expenses

These remedies are limited to cases in which the applicant was induced to vacate the unit as a result of the landlord actions. For example, if the respondent's conduct was sufficient to justify a finding of serious interference with reasonable enjoyment, to a degree that would cause the average tenant to vacate, moving expenses and other reasonable out of pocket expenses can be ordered. This compensation is in addition to any abatement of rent or other remedies ordered.

The tenant may claim for "all or any portion of any increased rent which the tenant has incurred or will incur for a one year period after the tenant has left the rental unit." The first question then is whether the tenant has actually rented another unit, and what the rent for that unit is. If the rent is higher, the total amount that could be ordered is the difference over a 12 month period. However, if the tenant has rented a larger unit or a better unit, the Member would consider evidence of the rents for units in the neighbourhood similar to the unit which is subject of the application. The compensation could be limited to the lower amount.

However, the tenant is not required to make an exhaustive search of every possible rental unit. If the tenant rents a comparable unit, after a reasonable search, they should not be expected to have found the lowest rent possible. Further, the tenant cannot be expected to have rented another unit from the respondent, even at a lower rent.

In some cases, a tenant who has been forced to leave the rental unit as a result of the landlord's actions will be living in temporary accommodation at the time of hearing. The tenant may be paying little or no rent for this temporary accommodation. However, if the tenant can establish that they have found permanent accommodation after a reasonable search and intend to move into this accommodation, the tenant could make a claim for the increased rent they will incur once they move into the permanent accommodation. Such proof could include a rental application or a signed lease. However, the time limit for making such a claim is 12 months after the tenant vacated the rental unit which is the subject of the application.

In addition, the tenant may also claim "reasonable out of pocket moving, storage and other like expenses." These are costs which the tenant has already incurred which may be proven by bills or receipts, or will incur and may be proven by contracts or quotations. The term "other like expenses" would include other costs that were incurred or will be incurred in order to move into another unit, such as a fee to an apartment locating service or real estate service or expenses to move the telephone or cable service.

INTERFERENCE RESULTING FROM MAINTENANCE, REPAIRS OR CAPITAL IMPROVEMENTS

Where the landlord has substantially interfered with a tenant's reasonable enjoyment of a unit or complex while carrying out maintenance, repairs or improvements, the remedy that the Board will normally consider is an abatement of rent. It is unlikely that the Board will consider it reasonable to order the landlord to stop doing the work. However, in some cases, it may be appropriate to consider an order for payment of the tenant's out-of-pocket expenses, an order terminating the tenancy or, where the tenant has been induced to move as a result of the activity, an order for payment of increased rent and moving expenses.

Section 241 of the RTA provides the authority to make regulations that set standards and criteria to be applied where tenants claim that landlords have substantially interfered with their reasonable enjoyment of the unit or complex in carrying out maintenance, repairs or capital improvements to the unit or complex. The section also authorizes regulations establishing criteria that must be applied by the Board in determining whether to order an abatement of rent in these applications.

These standards and criteria are found in section 8 of O. Reg. 516/06. The regulation requires the Board to consider the effect of the work on the tenant's use of the unit or the complex. The Member must determine that the effect was unreasonable in the circumstances, in order to find that there has been a substantial interference with the tenant's reasonable enjoyment of the unit or complex. If it is not found that the effect on the tenant was unreasonable in the circumstances, the application will be dismissed.

If it is determined that there has been a substantial interference, the regulation provides that the Board shall not grant the remedy of an abatement of rent, regardless of the effect of the work on the tenant, if the landlord has met the ten conditions set out in the regulation.

Where it is determined that there has been substantial interference and that an abatement is not prohibited, the Board will consider the five criteria set out in the regulation in determining whether it is appropriate to order an abatement and the amount of the abatement.

Any abatement ordered will not exceed 25% of the monthly rent for any month or part of a month in which there is substantial interference unless the specific circumstances exist as set out in the regulation. In such case, the Board cannot order an abatement of rent that exceeds 100 per cent of the rent for each month or part of a month during which the Board determines that the work substantially interfered with the tenant's reasonable enjoyment of the rental unit or residential complex.

Released Date: January 31, 2007

INTERPRETATION GUIDELINE 7 — RELIEF FROM EVICTION

Interpretation Guidelines are intended to assist the parties in understanding the Board'*s usual interpretation of the law, to provide guidance to Members and promote consistency in decision-making. However, a Member is not required to follow a Guideline and may make a different decision depending on the facts of the case.*

Even though a landlord proves their case in an application to evict a tenant, the Board must review and consider the circumstances of each case to determine whether or not the eviction should be refused or delayed. In some cases, the Board must refuse the eviction. These powers are referred to as "relief from eviction".

Legislation

Section 83 of the *Residential Tenancies Act, 2006* (the "RTA") states:

(1) Upon an application for an order evicting a tenant, the Board may, despite any other provision of this Act or the tenancy agreement,

(a) refuse to grant the application unless satisfied, having regard to all the circumstances, that it would be unfair to refuse; or

(b) order that the enforcement of the order of eviction be postponed for a period of time.

(2) If a hearing is held, the Board shall not grant the application unless it has reviewed the circumstances and considered whether or not it should exercise its powers under subsection (1).

(3) Without restricting the generality of subsection (1), the Board shall refuse to grant the application where satisfied that:

(a) the landlord is in serious breach of the landlord's responsibilities under this Act or of any material covenant in the tenancy agreement;

(b) the reason for the application being brought is that the tenant has complained to a government authority of the landlord's violation of a law dealing with health, safety, housing or maintenance standards;

(c) the reason for the application being brought is that the tenant has attempted to secure or enforce his or her legal rights;

(d) the reason for the application being brought is that the tenant is a member of a tenant's association or is attempting to organize such an association; or

(e) the reason for the application being brought is that the rental unit is occupied by children and the occupation by the children does not constitute overcrowding.

General Principles

The Board has a general discretion to refuse or delay an eviction under subsection 83(1), after considering all relevant circumstances. This authority arises upon any application for an order to evict a tenant. This general discretion does not automatically arise where an application is resolved without a hearing (e.g., in the case of an ex-parte order issued pursuant to subsection 78(6) of the RTA) or where a hearing is held for another purpose (e.g., in the case of a hearing of a set aside motion under subsection 74(11) of the RTA). Where a hearing is held on an application to evict a tenant, including a hearing that the tenant does not attend, and a hearing of an application that would normally by resolved by an ex parte order but has been sent to hearing (subsection 77 (1) or 78 (1) applications), the Board must review and consider the circumstances of both parties to determine whether or not the eviction should be delayed or refused prior to granting an application. The Board must consider the circumstances whether or not the tenant requests relief from eviction, and may pose questions to the landlord and/or tenant to better understand the circumstances.

Further, subsection 83(3) provides for mandatory relief from eviction in certain situations. If the Board finds that any of clauses (a) to (e) of subsection 83(3) applies, the Board must not grant the application to evict.

DISCRETIONARY REFUSAL OF AN EVICTION

If a hearing is held, the Board must review and consider all the circumstances to determine whether or not to exercise its discretion to refuse an eviction. For example:

- in a case involving an allegation of tenant "fault" (such as eviction for arrears or illegal act), consider whether the reason is serious enough to justify eviction,
- in a case involving a landlord's allegation of interference with reasonable enjoyment, consider whether refusing to evict the tenant would result applications against the landlord by other tenants for interference with their reasonable enjoyment, or
- consider whether refusing to evict the tenant would result in an unreasonable financial hardship to the landlord.

In "having regard to all the circumstances" the Member shall consider the relevant circumstances of the tenant and landlord and the impact on other occupants in the residential complex in delaying or denying eviction. Therefore, if the tenant's request presents a possible reason for refusal, the landlord may then explain why the refusal to evict would be unfair to them or to other occupants in the residential complex.

Where the Board exercises its discretion to refuse to evict a tenant, the Board may attach conditions to such an order that one or both parties must follow.

Circumstances Justifying Discretionary Refusal

The tenant's conduct has been an important consideration in many past decisions. For example:

- If the tenant got far behind in their rent payments, but has recently made extra payments to catch up, and owes relatively little now, the discretion may be exercised in their favour.

- In a case of persistent late payment of rent, the tenant had financial problems when he became unemployed, but for months since he found another job, payment has been right on time. The eviction may be refused despite the earlier months of late payments, due to the tenant's good conduct. In such circumstances, the Member may order that on-time rent payments are to be made, by the tenant to the landlord, for a specified number of months following the hearing.

- A tenant is not excused from paying rent even if the landlord has greater financial resources (e.g., a public agency or large corporate landlord). Other relevant factors may include whether the current reason for eviction has been repeated, the impact this tenant is having on the landlord or other tenants, whether the tenant has taken positive steps to reduce or eliminate the reason for the eviction, and other indications of good faith on the part of either the landlord or the tenant.

Landlord actions or conduct which led to the eviction should also be considered. For example, if the landlord unreasonably prevented a tenant from repairing damage done by a guest or child, this would be relevant. If the landlord has excused many other tenants from a minor breach, an arbitrary eviction of one tenant for the same breach may be refused, depending on all of the other circumstances.

DISCRETIONARY DELAY OF AN EVICTION

The Board must review and consider the circumstances to determine whether or not to exercise its discretion to delay an eviction.

Although the time period is not set out in the RTA, Board orders commonly provide that a tenant has 11 days after an order for arrears of rent and termination of the tenancy is issued to pay all of the rent arrears and costs owing to the landlord. If the tenant does not make the necessary payment, the tenant can be evicted for failure to pay rent starting on the 12th day after the order is issued. This period of time takes into account such matters as the time it takes for the tenant to receive the order in the mail and acquire the rent money to pay to the landlord. Therefore, a decision of the Board to postpone the enforcement of an eviction order under clause 83(1) (b) of the RTA often means the order would provide that the order could not be filed with the Court Enforcement Office until more than 12 days after the date the order is issued.

Generally, the Member would take into account the time that it will normally take the landlord to enforce the order through the Court Enforcement Office.

Even if "all of the circumstances" did not justify refusal of the eviction, the Member may look at the same issues of unfairness to each party, and decide whether or not to delay the eviction. Eviction may appear to be unfair if no other accommodation is available to the tenant (e.g., a social housing tenant). However, a case in which the landlord is in a better financial position than the tenant does not justify refusal of the eviction. Ordinarily, the tenant's lack of resources will be considered as a reason to delay an eviction, not to refuse it. However, all circumstances must be considered.

The following are some examples that illustrate situations in which a delay may be considered:

- The tenant asserts that the market conditions in the locality are unusually "tight" and that it will take some time to find suitable accommodation.
- The tenant shows that they are affected by a severe medical condition which makes it difficult to find other accommodation, and there are no persons who can help him or her search for a vacant unit.
- The tenant's family is very large and they require at least five bedroom accommodation, similar to their current unit. There are very few such units in the local market, and none are in the current advertisements.

MANDATORY REFUSAL OF EVICTION

Mandatory refusal applies to situations which the RTA provides are serious enough to justify refusal — regardless of any other circumstances.

If a tenant raises circumstances which might fall into subsection 83(3), the Member must decide whether it applies.[15] Further, once it is found that subsection (3) applies, the Member must refuse the eviction.[16]

Serious Breach of Landlord Obligations

The Board must refuse an eviction if the landlord is in serious breach of the landlord's responsibilities under the RTA or the tenancy agreement.

Many claims are related to the landlord's maintenance obligations. A health or safety concern due to lack of repair may be serious enough to justify refusal. Conditions which deprive the tenant of the full use of the premises will usually be serious, particularly if it affects the kitchen, bathroom or sleeping areas. Members must decide whether other repair problems constitute a "serious breach" of obligations, considering the landlord's actions to resolve the problems as well. Other factors such as how long the breach was ongoing or the level of risk to the tenants may also be relevant.[17]

In cases related to the obligation to repair, the tenant's conduct may also be relevant. For example, if the tenant has never before complained to the landlord about a long-standing repair problem, they may have shown they did not consider it to be serious. Further, if the landlord was not aware or could not reasonably have been expected to be aware of the problem, the Member may find that the landlord is not in serious breach. Further, the tenant should not have contributed to the problem, such as by obstructing the landlord's repair efforts.

---

[15] See *Forgie v. Widdicombe Place* [2002] O.J. No. 2956 (Div. Ct.)

[16] See *Chin v. Hunt* (1986), 17 O.A.C. 267 (Divisional Court)

[17] *Sage v. Corporation of the County of Wellington* (April 25, 2005), London Docket No. 1471 (Div. Ct.)

In cases related to the obligation to repair, the age of the property and the landlord's intentions for the property may be factors for the Member to consider. For example, if the landlord is intending to demolish the property and the tenant was served a notice to terminate for that reason, the Member would consider these factors before deciding to refuse to evict[18].

The tenant may raise a breach of another obligation of the landlord under the RTA. For example, the RTA imposes on landlords the obligation not to illegally enter a unit, nor to harass a tenant. The Member must decide the issue and, if satisfied that the facts presented show a serious breach, they must refuse the eviction. However, mandatory refusal of eviction is generally accepted to refer to serious breaches existing at the time of the hearing, not breaches from the past that have been remedied[19].

If the tenant raises a breach of the tenancy agreement, they must present facts to show that it is a serious breach and that it relates to a significant provision of the agreement.

Even if the breach is not found to be serious and there would be no mandatory refusal, the lack of repair or other breach of obligation may still be considered. It would be one of the circumstances of unfairness to consider in deciding whether discretionary refusal is appropriate.

Retaliatory Actions by the Landlord

The Member must refuse the eviction if the reason the landlord applied for eviction is described in clause (b) to (e) of subsection 83(3) (these clauses are quoted on page 1).

The tenant would explain what actions they took which they believe caused the landlord to seek the eviction. However, the tenant has a higher onus. They must prove that the reason for the application is one of the above motivations.[20] It is difficult to prove another person's state of mind. The landlord will assert that the reason stated in the application was the reason for the application.

The tenant may try to show from the landlord's conduct that the motivation was retaliatory. For example, the tenant may be able to show that the landlord has evicted other tenants who asserted their rights. The tenant might also show that the landlord ignored the same issue that is the basis for this eviction, for other tenants. A pattern of conduct may be considered by the Board, but it may also be explained by the landlord.

Even if the tenant does not establish to the Member's satisfaction that the reason for the application was retaliation and, thus refusal is not mandatory, the facts that supported the tenant's claim could be one of the circumstances considered in deciding whether there should be discretionary refusal of the eviction.

---

[18] *Puterbough v. Canada Public Works and Government Services* (unreported decision of Divisional Court, February 12, 2007)

[19] *Ibid.*

[20] *MacNeil et al. v. 976445 Ontario Ltd.* (June 6, 2005), London Docket No. 04-1465 (Div. Ct.)

Applications Under Section 77

Under subsection 77(4) of the RTA, the Board may make an order terminating the tenancy and evicting the tenant without notice to the tenant and without a hearing (ex-parte), if the landlord has filed an application with the Board under subsection 77(1), based on either an agreement between the landlord and the tenant to terminate the tenancy or a notice of termination given by the tenant.

Decisions Made Ex Parte

An application (L3) filed by a landlord pursuant to subsection 77 (1) of the Act is generally resolved by an ex parte order issued pursuant to subsection 77 (4).

The tenant may file a motion pursuant to subsection 77(6) to set aside the ex parte order. The Board then holds a hearing to consider the tenant's motion. As a hearing concerning such a motion does not arise upon an application for an order to evict a tenant, subsection 83(1) does not apply. Instead, the Board exercises similar discretionary relief under subsection 77(8), which provides:

> If the respondent makes a motion under subsection (6), the Board shall, after a hearing,
>
> (a) make an order setting aside the order under subsection (4), if
>
> i. the landlord and tenant did not enter into an agreement to terminate the tenancy, and
>
> ii. the tenant did not give the landlord notice of termination of the tenancy;
>
> (b) make an order setting aside the order under subsection (4), if the Board is satisfied, having regard to all the circumstances, that it would not be unfair to do so; or
>
> (c) make an order lifting the stay of the order under subsection (4), effective immediately or on a future date specified in the order.

When having regard to all the circumstances, pursuant to clause 77 (8) (b) the Board should consider circumstances that occurred with regard to the signing of the agreement to terminate the tenancy and thereafter or circumstances that occurred after the giving of the notice of termination by the tenant to the landlord.

Decisions Made When a Hearing is Held

In those cases where an application filed under subsection 77(1) is sent to hearing and therefore is not decided ex parte, subsection 83(2) provides that the Board shall not grant the application unless it has reviewed the circumstances and considered whether or not it should exercise its powers under subsection (1).

With respect to the exercise of discretion under section 83, Members hearing a subsection 77(1) application will consider the circumstances that occurred with regard to the signing of the agreement to terminate and thereafter or circumstances that occurred after the giving the notice of termination.

Applications Under Section 78

Under subsections 78(6) & (7) of the RTA, the Board may issue an order evicting the tenant and ordering the tenant to pay arrears of rent without a hearing (ex-parte), if the landlord has filed an application with the Board under subsection 78(1).

Decisions Made Ex Parte

An application (L4) filed by a landlord pursuant to subsection 78 (1) of the Act is generally resolved by an ex parte order issued pursuant to subsections 78(6) & (7).

The tenant may file a motion pursuant to subsection 78(9), to set aside an ex parte order issued under subsections 78(6) & (7). The Board then holds a hearing to consider the tenant's motion. As a hearing concerning such a motion does not arise upon an application for an order to evict a tenant, subsection 83 (1) does not apply. Instead, the Board exercises similar discretionary relief under clauses 78(11) (b) & (c).

Pursuant to clause 78(11)(b) the Board may make an order setting aside the ex parte order issued if the Board is satisfied, having regard to all the circumstances, that it would not be unfair to set aside the order.

This provision gives the Members discretion to grant relief to the tenant by setting aside the ex parte order, notwithstanding the fact that the tenant has breached a condition required in the conditional order or mediated agreement.

In their consideration of this provision, Members should take into account:

- Circumstances that occurred after the date of the mediated agreement or conditional order that caused the party to be unable to meet the terms of the agreement or order. (Circumstances that occurred prior to the issuance of the conditional order or the signing of the mediated agreement should have been considered at the time the conditional order was made or the mediated agreement was signed, with respect to the previous application.)

- The circumstances of both the landlord and tenant and the impact on other occupants in the residential complex in delaying or denying eviction.

It is also important to remember that setting aside the ex parte order results in the original mediated agreement or conditional order remaining in full force and effect. In some cases, it may be impossible for the tenant to fulfill the remaining conditions contained in the mediated agreement or conditional order (i.e. the deadline for payments has now passed), and/or the parties wish to consent to new conditions.

The matter may be resolved in one of the following ways:

- The parties can consent to be bound by a new mediated agreement containing new terms or conditions, and in addition agree that the ex parte order would be set aside by order of the Member which order would also acknowledge that the L4 application had been resolved through a mediated agreement.

- The parties can consent to be bound by a new hearing order to be issued by the Member containing new terms or conditions.

- In the absence of consent, the Member can issue a new order containing new terms or conditions that are fair in the circumstances (i.e. a revised payment schedule) using the authority found in subsection 204(1)). In exercising this authority, the Member may, subject to the consideration of fairness, wish to consider ordering new conditions that are as close as possible to the original conditions imposed in the original order or mediated agreement.

If the tenant's motion to set aside the ex parte order is denied and clause 78(11)(b) has not been applied, the Board may make an order lifting the stay of the ex-parte order effective immediately or on a future date. Clause 78 (11)(c) directs the Member to lift the stay of the ex parte order, thus permitting the landlord to enforce the ex parte order. The discretion given to Members to lift the stay on a future date is similar to the relief from eviction provided by clause 83(1)(b) which gives the Member authority to postpone the enforcement of the eviction for a period of time.

In considering such relief, the Member should take into account the same criteria as set out for clause 78 (11)(b).

Decisions Made When a Hearing is Held

In those cases where an application filed under subsection 78(1) is sent to hearing for clarification, therefore is not decided ex parte, subsection 83(2) provides that the Board shall not grant the application unless it has reviewed the circumstances and considered whether or not it should exercise its powers under subsection (1).

With respect to the exercise of discretion under section 83, Members hearing a subsection 78(1) application will consider the circumstances that occurred with regard to the signing of the mediated agreement and thereafter or circumstances that occurred after the date of the hearing which resulted in the conditional order.

Amended October 15, 2009

INTERPRETATION GUIDELINE 8 — REVIEW OF AN ORDER

Interpretation Guidelines are intended to assist the parties in understanding the Board*'s usual interpretation of the law, to provide guidance to Members and promote consistency in decision-making. However, a Member is not required to follow a Guideline and may make a different decision depending on the facts of the case.*

The authority of the Board to review its own orders comes from section 21.2 of the *Statutory Powers Procedure Act* (the "SPPA") and subsection 209(2) of the *Residential Tenancies Act, 2006* (the "RTA"). Subsection 209(2) of the RTA provides that the Board's power to review a decision or order under section 21.2 of the SPPA may be exercised if a party to a proceeding was not reasonably able to participate in the proceeding. The procedures for dealing with a request to review an order are found in the Rules of Practice (see Rule 29).

This Guideline provides guidance concerning the *scope* of the power to review.

The party may ask for a review of the order if they believe the Member made a "serious error" or where they were not reasonably able to participate in the proceeding relying on section 21.2 of the SPPA, subsection 209(2) of the RTA, and Rule 29 of the Rules of Practice. Although Rule 29 permits a Vice Chair to initiate a review, the Board does not contemplate that reviews will be initiated often by a Vice Chair. The Board expects a party or a person directly affected by the Board order to make a written request for review under Rule 29 first, and not merely to request the Vice Chair to initiate a review.

If the order subject to the review request was resolved by a hearing, the review will be decided by a Member other than the Member who heard the application. Otherwise, any Member may decide the review.

What is a Serious Error?

A serious error may include one of the following:

- an error of jurisdiction (e.g., applying a provision of the RTA in a case to which it does not apply, or exercising a power outside the proper authority of the Board), whether or not it was raised at the original hearing

- an error of procedure which prejudiced a party (e.g., failing to comply with the rules of natural justice)

- if a party to a proceeding was not reasonably able to participate in the proceeding pursuant to subsection 209(2)

- an error of fact which was material to the decision, and which was clearly an unreasonable finding considering the evidence which was before the Member

- an error of fact which is material to the decision which is demonstrated by new evidence which was not before the Member (e.g., a witness who was out of the country on the day of the original hearing), so long as the Member reviewing the order is satisfied that there is a sufficient reason why the evidence was not presented in the original hearing

- an error in law, but the Board will not normally review a reasonable interpretation of the statute by a Member, even if the interpretation differs from that of the reviewing member

- an error in applying discretion allowed by the law which is unreasonable (e.g., the Member allowed remedies which were inappropriate in the circumstances or which were, in quantum or degree, beyond what would reasonably be allowed).

When is a party "not reasonably able to participate" in a proceeding?

A party may not be reasonably able to participate in a proceeding in a variety of circumstances. In *Montgomery and Turgeon* v. *737259 Ontario Ltd.*, the Divisional Court found that the phrase "being reasonably able to participate in the proceeding," as that phrase appeared in the *Tenant Protection Act, 1997*, s. 192(4), should not be interpreted so strictly as to unduly prevent the Ontario Rental Housing Tribunal or court from exercising its discretion when it is right and just to do so. In *Mandache et al. v. Dron,* also under the TPA, the Member found that the party's failure to attend a hearing as a result of their own negligence or the negligence of their paid agent did not mean the party lacked a proper opportunity to participate in the hearing. The party appealed this decision to the Divisional Court which dismissed the appeal on the basis that the appellant had not raised a question of law as required by s.196 of the TPA, this result left the Tribunal's decision undisturbed.

Consistent with this guidance, the Board may determine that a party was not reasonably able to participate in a proceeding where:

- the party did not receive the notice of hearing and the application because of the party's brief absence during the time of service (e.g., where the party was out of town, in the hospital, detained in police custody);

- the notice of hearing and other documents are served incorrectly (e.g., to the wrong address or to the incorrect individual);

- the party was physically unable to attend and did not have the opportunity to have an agent attend on his or her behalf (e.g., sudden illness);

- the party was led to believe by the other party that there was no need to respond to the application or attend the proceeding because all issues had been settled; or

- the party attended the proceeding, but the member's conduct did not allow the party to be reasonably able to participate.

These are only examples of the types of circumstances in which the Board may determine that a party was not reasonably able to participate in a proceeding. The Board would need to consider the specific circumstances of a matter to determine whether a party was not reasonably able to participate in a particular proceeding. It will usually be insufficient for a party to state they did not participate in the proceeding because they did not understand the possible consequences of the proceedings. The Board expects parties to read a notice of hearing and other documents received in relation to a matter before the Board and to seek help if they cannot understand it.

In general, an assertion that a party had not been able to attend without explaining why in the review request can result in the request for review being denied without a hearing. Accordingly, the party requesting the review must describe the specific circumstances that prevented them from participating in the proceeding. A member may consider all the circumstances that are relevant, including the party's understanding of the proceeding, as well as matters such as the actions taken by the party in preparing their case, in obtaining representation, in contacting the Board or the other party, etc. A member then determines whether, if proven at a hearing, the circumstances described in the review request may lead the Board to find that the requester was not reasonably able to participate.

What will be Reviewed?

Under Rule 29.10, a Member will conduct a preliminary review of a request to review an order without holding a hearing and determine whether or not the order may contain a serious error or a serious error may have occurred in the proceedings.

Where the Member determines that there is a possibility of a serious error affecting the result of the case, a review hearing will be held. Otherwise, the Member will issue an order dismissing the request for review.

Where a review hearing is held, a Member will hear submissions on whether or not the request for review actually discloses a serious error. Where a Member determines that no serious error occurred, the request for review will be denied.

Where a Member determines that a serious error has occurred, parties requesting a review should understand that they will not automatically obtain a full rehearing of the application, and that the review may be limited to certain issues. The hearing may proceed with one or all of the following:

1. There may be a partial or full rehearing of the matter.

2. The Member will decide what, if any, issues will be reviewed. This may be some or all of the issues set out in the request and any potential errors identified by the reviewing Member.

3. The Member may or may not hear or rehear evidence and may simply decide to hear submissions.

Not Interfering With Discretion

The Board will not interfere with the proper exercise of discretion by a Member. Discretion refers to decisions such as whether relief from eviction should be granted (see section 83) or what remedies should be ordered in a particular case. The reviewing Member should not interfere with the decision even if they may have exercised the discretion in a somewhat different way. A review is not for making minor adjustments to the discretion which was reasonable: for example, that an abatement was within the reasonable range of amounts which could have been ordered.

Error of Fact

Since a party cannot appeal an order to the Divisional Court, except on a point of law, it is important that the Board review alleged errors of fact. However, the Board may decline to review an order if the alleged error is trivial in amount or would not significantly change the result. This means that it is essential that the party requesting the review should specify in some detail not only what the error is, but how it would change the order if the Board agrees it is an error.

New Evidence

If a Member did not give proper consideration to the evidence before them, this should be reviewed. However, if the evidence was not presented by the party now making the request, the reviewing Member has a discretion to accept or refuse the new evidence. If the original Member improperly refused the evidence, it should now be admitted. If the party had no access to the evidence at the time of the hearing, and it is necessary to properly decide the case, the evidence may be permitted, allowing the other parties their respective rights.

Nevertheless there are some cases in which new evidence can be refused. If there is no reason why the evidence was not presented in the first instance, permission may be denied. Presenting a "case" in stages is inappropriate because it prejudices the other party and increases the costs and delays of proceedings. New evidence of little weight or related to issues which were not in dispute should not be accepted.

Interim Orders

A Member may make an interim order to stay the order under review upon a party's request or on their own initiative. This will prevent parties from enforcing the original order during the review, which in some cases would mean a review order would have no effect. The decision to stay the order may be further considered after submissions are heard at the review hearing. The stay may be lifted if, for example, it was requested only for delay.

Any other interim order which is appropriate may be made, such as one for disclosure, for certain work to be performed by a landlord, for payment into the Board by a landlord or tenant, etc.

Results of the Review

A request to review may be granted or denied. If the request is granted, section 21.2 of the SPPA allows the Board to "confirm, vary, suspend or cancel the decision or order." Thus, the reviewing Member may resolve the request in any of these manners:

- dismissing the original application and canceling the order;
- varying part of the original order or reasons;
- canceling the original order and replacing it with a new order; or

- confirming the original order.

Where appropriate, the reviewing Member may take into account any change in the facts of the case since the date the order was issued. For example, if any payment was made under the order or any work was done which it ordered, it would not be proper to ignore such changes. If more has been paid under an order than the review shows should have been owing, the reviewing Member may order repayment to set the matter right in accordance with the conclusions of the review order.

Under section 182 of the RTA, the reviewing member may order a refund of a fee paid for a request to review if, on considering the request, the Board varies, suspends or cancels the order.

What Happens Where an Appeal is Filed with the Divisional Court?

Where an appeal from a Board decision has been filed in the Divisional Court, the appeal operates as a stay of the matter under subsection 25(1) of the SPPA. In this circumstance, clause 25(1)(b) permits the Board to lift the stay. If a party or a person directly affected by the order has filed a request for review, the requester should include in the written request an explanation why the Board should lift the stay and consider the request for review. The lifting of the stay is a discretionary power that the Board may exercise in the appropriate situation and parties should be prepared to make submissions on it if requested by the Member. In the situation where the Board decides to proceed with the review, the Board may make an interim order lifting the stay and may include in that order any conditions that it considers appropriate. Such conditions may include preserving the status quo between the parties until the matter is finally disposed of.

Amended October 15, 2009

INTERPRETATION GUIDELINE 9 — EVICTION FOR AN ILLEGAL ACT OR BUSINESS

Interpretation Guidelines are intended to assist the parties in understanding the Board's usual interpretation of the law, to provide guidance to Members and promote consistency in decision-making. However, a Member is not required to follow a Guideline and may make a different decision depending on the facts of the case.

This Guideline deals with eviction applications under the *Residential Tenancies Act, 2006* (the "RTA") that are based on an illegal act or business. Subsection 61(1) of the RTA provides:

> 61. (1) A landlord may give a tenant notice of termination of the tenancy if the tenant or another occupant of the rental unit commits an illegal act or carries on an illegal trade, business or occupation or permits a person to do so in the rental unit or the residential complex.

Illegal act or business

The term "illegal" is not defined in the RTA but would include a serious violation of a federal, provincial or municipal law. If the illegality is trivial or technical, the act or business or occupation might not be considered serious enough to warrant eviction.

An illegal act will be serious if it has the potential to affect the character of the premises or to disturb the reasonable enjoyment of the landlord or other tenants.[21] The seriousness of this ground can be seen in the fact that there is no opportunity in section 61 for the tenant to avoid termination by rectifying the illegal act.

The fact that a tenant or another occupant may have devised a fraud in the unit, written a bad cheque or failed to file a tax return does not necessarily create a threat to the other tenants in the building or a problem for the landlord. By contrast, drug offences may bring the risk of harmful effects upon other occupants of the complex.

A contravention of the RTA would not, in itself, constitute an illegal act under section 61 of the RTA. If there is a remedy for the act elsewhere in the RTA, it would not be appropriate to evict for an illegal act. For example, a failure to pay rent would not be considered an illegal act for the purpose of section 61. Subletting or assigning the rental unit without the landlord's consent would not necessarily constitute an illegal act that justifies eviction.[22]

However, in one case the Divisional Court held that where the tenant listed her rental unit with a real estate agent and repeatedly sublet the unit to short-term occupants for a rent that greatly exceeded the lawful rent and without the landlord's consent, this pattern of activity constituted the conduct of an illegal business.[23] Such conduct is

---

[21] *Samuel Property Management Ltd. v. Nicholson* (2002), 61 O.R. (3d) 470 (C.A.), at paragraph 28, citing *Swansea Village Co-operative v. Balcerzak* (1988), 63 O.R. (2d) 741 at 745 (Div. Ct.).

[22] *Valleyview Apartments Ltd. and Estate of Max Rothbart* (1988), 65 O.R. (2d) 209 (Div. Ct.).

[23] *Sutton Place Grande Limited v. Hammer and Griffiths* [2002] O.J. No. 1792 (Div. Ct.).

contrary to section 134 of the RTA and is an offence under section 234(1) of the RTA, but those sections do not provide a remedy for the landlord.

Permitting an illegal act or business

A tenant may be evicted under section 61 if the tenant or other occupant "permits" a person to commit an illegal act in the rental unit or residential complex. It is not sufficient to prove that the tenant or other occupant allowed the person who committed the illegal act to be in the rental unit or residential complex.

A finding that the tenant or other occupant permitted an illegal act may be inferred from their knowledge of the illegal act. For instance, there may be sufficient evidence for the Member to conclude that the tenant or other occupant knew of the illegal act or was wilfully blind to the illegal act and therefore permitted it.[24]

Rental unit or residential complex

Subsection 61(1) provides that the illegal act must have occurred in the rental unit or the residential complex. The definition of "residential complex" in section 2 of the RTA includes all common areas and services and facilities available for the use of its residents. This would include areas such as the laundry room, parking lot and recreational facilities.

The fact that a tenant or other occupant has been charged with robbing the convenience store across the street would not be a ground for the landlord to evict, whereas robbing other units in the complex would be sufficient.[25]

Notice Periods

Subsection 61(2) sets out notice periods for different types of illegal acts.

> (2) A notice of termination under this section shall set out the grounds for termination and shall provide a termination date not earlier than,
>
> (a) the 10th day after the notice is given, in the case of a notice grounded on an illegal act, trade, business or occupation involving,
>
> (i) the production of an illegal drug;
>
> (ii) trafficking in an illegal drug;
>
> (iii) the possession of an illegal drug for the purposes of trafficking; or
>
> (b) the 20th day after the notice is given, in all other cases.

Subsection 61(2)(b) allows a landlord to terminate a tenancy on 20 days notice where a tenant or another occupant commits an illegal act or carries on an illegal trade, business or occupation in the rental unit or residential complex, or the tenant or

---

[24] *Grant v. Metropolitan Toronto Housing Authority* [2002] O.J. No. 1162 (Div. Ct.).

[25] *Peel Non-Profit v. Hogarth* (1990), 72 O.R. (2d) 702 (C.A.), affirming (1989), 68 O.R. (2d) 617 (Div. Ct.).

another occupant permits someone else to commit an illegal act or carry on an illegal activity in the unit or the complex.

Subsection 61(2)(a) provides a shorter 10-day notice period when the illegal activity involves the production of an illegal drug, trafficking in an illegal drug or the possession of an illegal drug for the purpose of trafficking. Further, an application to terminate a tenancy based on such a notice is processed more quickly than most other types of applications, with a shorter time to hearing due to the potentially serious implications for the landlord and other tenants.

A landlord may file an application based on an illegal act immediately after the notice of termination is given, but not later than 30 days after the termination date in the notice.

Notice Period for a Second Breach

If a landlord has given a notice of termination for damage under section 62, interference with reasonable enjoyment under section 64 or overcrowding under section 67, and the notice has become void as a result of the tenant's compliance, the landlord may give a 14-day notice instead of a 20-day notice if the tenant commits an illegal act within six months of when the first notice was given. But this does not apply if the second notice is for one of the three drug-related activities in subsection 61(2)(a) as the termination date in these cases is already a minimum of 10 days after the notice is given.

Drug offences

The drug offences in subsection 61(2) include:

(i) the production of an illegal drug;

(ii) trafficking in an illegal drug;

(iii) the possession of an illegal drug for the purposes of trafficking.

Subsection 61(3) provides the following definitions:

(3) In this section,

"illegal drug" a controlled substance or precursor as those terms are defined in the Controlled Drugs and Substances Act (Canada);

"possession" has the same meaning as in the Controlled Drugs and Substances Act (Canada);

"production" means, with respect to an illegal drug, to produce the drug within the meaning of the Controlled Drugs and Substances Act (Canada);

"trafficking" means, with respect to an illegal drug, to traffic in the drug within the meaning of the Controlled Drugs and Substances Act (Canada).

Meaning of "illegal drug"

Subsection 61(3) of the RTA states that an illegal drug means a controlled substance or precursor as those terms are defined in the Controlled Drugs and Substances Act

(CDSA). The CDSA states that a "controlled substance" refers to those substances included in Schedule I, II, III, IV or V in the CDSA (such as Cannabis or Opium), and that "precursor" refers to a substance found in Schedule VI of that Act (such as Ephedrine).

Meaning of "possession"

Subsection 61(3) of the Act states that possession has the same meaning as in the CDSA. The CDSA states that possession means possession within the meaning of subsection 4(3) of the Criminal Code. Subsection 4(3) of the Criminal Code states:

> (3) For the purposes of this Act,
>
> (a) a person has anything in possession when he has it in his personal possession or knowingly
>
> (i) has it in the actual possession or custody of another person, or
>
> (ii) has it in any place, whether or not that place belongs to or is occupied by him, for the use or benefit of himself or another person, and
>
> (b) where one of two or more persons, with the knowledge and consent of the rest, has anything in his custody or possession, it shall be deemed to be in the custody and possession of each and all of them.

Note that simple possession of a drug is not enough to attract subsection 61(2) of the RTA which deals with possession "for the purposes of trafficking." Thus, where mere possession of a drug is alleged, the landlord should give a 20-day notice under subsection 61(2)(b) instead of a 10-day notice under subsection 61(2)(a).

Meaning of "production"

Subsection 61(3) of the Act states that production means, with respect to an illegal drug, to produce the drug within the meaning of the CDSA. The CDSA states that "produce" means, in respect of a substance included in Schedule I to IV of that Act, to obtain the substance by any method or process including:

- manufacturing, synthesizing or using any means of altering the chemical or physical properties of the substance, or
- cultivating, propagating, or harvesting the substance or any living thing from which the substance may be extracted or otherwise obtained, and
- includes the offer to produce.

Meaning of "trafficking"

Subsection 61(3) of the Act states that trafficking in an illegal drug means to traffic within the meaning of the CDSA. The CDSA states that "traffic" means, in respect of a substance in Schedule I to IV, to

- sell, administer, give, transfer, transport, send or deliver the substance,

- to sell an authorization to obtain the substance, or
- to offer to do either of the above

unless they are done under the authority of the regulations to the CDSA.

Meaning of "possession for the purposes of trafficking"

The phrase "possession for the purposes of trafficking" in subsection 61(2)(iii) is not defined in the RTA or the CDSA. Subsection 5(2) of the CDSA simply states that "No person shall, for the purpose of trafficking, possess a substance included in Schedule I, II, III or IV."

In some cases, possession for the purposes of trafficking may be inferred from the surrounding circumstances. For instance, where the police find a large quantity of drugs, cash and weigh scales, the Member may be able to determine that the tenant or another occupant had possession of the drugs for the purpose of trafficking.

Burden of proof

In most Board proceedings the burden of proof is based on a "balance of probabilities" rather than "beyond a reasonable doubt" as in criminal proceedings. However, in *Bogey Construction Ltd. v. Boileau*, the Divisional Court stated that allegations of criminal conduct in a rental housing context require a higher degree of proof than a balance of probabilities.[26] The burden is not as high as proof beyond a reasonable doubt, but must be commensurate with the gravity of the allegations.

An eviction can be ordered even though the tenant or other occupant carrying on the illegal act, trade, business or occupation has not been charged with an offence relating to the illegal act.[27] Conversely, the fact that a tenant or other occupant has been charged with an offence is not necessarily proof that an illegal act was committed.[28]

Furthermore, section 75 of the RTA provides that the Board may evict a tenant for an illegal act whether or not the tenant or other person has been convicted of an offence relating to the illegal act. Therefore, there is no need for a Member to adjourn the Board proceeding until the matter has been heard by a court of competent jurisdiction.

Relief from Eviction

The Member must consider whether a termination of the tenancy may be unfair having regard to all the circumstances: see subsection 83(1)(a) of the RTA and the Guideline on "Relief from Eviction." This means there will be a two step determination: first, whether the tenant has committed an illegal act that justifies eviction; and second, whether the eviction should, nevertheless, be refused or delayed having regard to the circumstances.

---

[26] *Bogey Construction Ltd. v. Boileau* [2002] O.J. No. 1575 (Div. Ct.).

[27] *Samuel Property Management Ltd. v. Nicholson* (2002), 61 O.R. (3d) 470 (C.A.).

[28] *Greaves v. Toronto Community Housing Corporation* (December 14, 2004), Toronto Docket No. 411/03 (Div. Ct.).

In determining whether to refuse or delay an eviction, the Member should weigh the seriousness of the illegal act against factors such as: the length of the tenancy, the financial circumstances of the tenant, whether there are children living in the unit, whether there have been other problems with the tenant, whether the tenant is likely to commit the illegal act again.[29] There may be other factors to consider.

In addition, instead of terminating the tenancy the Member may impose conditions in the order pursuant to subsection 204(1) of the RTA. For example, if the tenant is keeping a dangerous animal in the rental unit, the tenant could be ordered to remove it. If the tenant is carrying on a business that is prohibited by a zoning by-law, the Member could impose a condition in the order that the tenant no longer conduct the business in the unit. If the tenant's guest committed an illegal act, relief from eviction could be considered with a condition that the tenant not permit that person into the building again. The order could provide that if the tenant does not comply with a condition specified in the order, the landlord may apply ex parte under section 78 of the RTA for eviction.

Released Date: January 31, 2007

---

[29] *Metropolitan Toronto Housing Authority v. Pennant* (1991), 81 D.L.R. (4th) 404 (Ont. Ct. Gen. Div.).

INTERPRETATION GUIDELINE 10 — PROCEDURAL ISSUES REGARDING EVICTION APPLICATIONS

Interpretation Guidelines are intended to assist the parties in understanding the Board's usual interpretation of the law, to provide guidance to Members and promote consistency in decision-making. However, a Member is not required to follow a Guideline and may make a different decision depending on the facts of the case.

This Guideline deals with interpretation questions respecting the steps required to bring an eviction application under the Residential Tenancies Act, 2006 ("the RTA") and what will be the result of failing to follow those procedures.

Adequacy of the Notice of Termination

The Notice of Termination (the Notice) is an essential step in the landlord's process of evicting a tenant[30] (except section 77 and 78 applications). The Board will not terminate a tenancy and order eviction of the tenant unless the tenant has received a valid Notice of Termination from the landlord and the landlord has successfully proved the ground claimed in the Notice at the hearing of the application.

If the document given to the tenant or the method or time of service are defective, in most cases this will result in dismissal of the application or the denial of the eviction portion of the application.

The Notice of Termination must specify a date of termination without doubt or condition. The landlord must set a date which allows at least the minimum period of Notice for that ground for eviction, or the longest period if there are several grounds set out in the same Notice. The Board has no authority to shorten the notice period required by the RTA in view of section 56 of the regulations (O. Reg. 516/06) and Rule 1.4 of the Rules of Practice. If a shorter notice period is given than is required, the application will be dismissed.

The Divisional Court of Ontario has held that an unsigned Notice of Termination may be valid, so long as the landlord's name is shown.[31] However, other requirements may not be so easily resolved. An incorrect termination date in a Notice may render it invalid.[32] For example, stating a period of time but not a specific date (e.g., "14 days" rather than "April 16, 2001") may not be sufficient.[33]

If the Notice of Termination is confusing to the degree that a reasonable person could not understand precisely what it means, a Member would find it defective.[34] For

---

[30] *Re Bransfield Construction Co. Ltd. And Cox* [1973] 3 O.R. 989 (Div. Ct.).

[31] *Darraugh Construction and Investment Ltd. v. Cain* (1988), 30 O.A.C. 1, in which the landlord's name was typed in by the landlord's solicitor.

[32] *Re Bianci and Aguanno* (1983), 42 O.R. 76 (Divisional Court).

[33] *Dumi Construction Ltd. V. Greenspan* (1977), 15 O.R. (2d) 808 (Co. Ct.).

[34] *Kuzyk v. SK Properties* (November 22, 2001), Toronto Docket No. 106/01, [2001] O.J. No. 5260 (Div. Ct.) Re: TSL-18855.

example, in some cases this might include: uncertainty about whether the landlord is the person giving the Notice, vagueness about the reason for giving the Notice[35], a lack of details about the reason, etc. A Notice which only specifies a reason which is not a ground for eviction under the RTA would be invalid; and even adding such a claim to a legitimate ground may confuse the Notice in some cases.

In the end, whether the Notice is adequate is a question of whether it communicates the necessary elements clearly enough that a tenant would be expected to understand it and the options they have. For example, Notices were found invalid which did not state the required information that the tenant need not vacate pursuant to the Notice.[36]

Adequacy of Service of the Notice of Termination

The Notice of Termination must be given to the tenant by a method set out in subsection 191(1) of the RTA and in Rule 5.1 of the Rules of Practice. If the landlord has used a different method (without specific permission through a direction signed by a Member), and the tenant does not voluntarily admit to receiving the Notice on time, an application for eviction may be dismissed. If the tenant acknowledges receipt of the Notice by the date required or if the landlord can prove that the tenant received it, this will be sufficient no matter how the Notice was served.

Substantial Compliance with Forms

Some landlords like to produce their own versions of the approved forms for Notices of Termination and Applications. These forms usually use the wording found on the Board's form and are simply intended to allow computer inputting or other convenience to the landlord. So long as the landlord's form includes the information set out for the tenant in the Board form, the different form will usually be permitted. The Member who must rule on the adequacy of such a Notice may consider whether it substantially complies with the legal requirements as expressed in the form approved by the Board, taking into consideration the points mentioned above.

However, if the landlord seeks to communicate other messages in the form which are misleading about the tenant's rights or inconsistent with the provisions of the RTA, this may cause a Member to find it defective. Information may be provided which is not misleading, is not inconsistent with the law and does not confuse the essential information in the Notice.

Oral notice of termination cannot substantially comply with a requirement to give written notice. The statutory requirement to give written Notice cannot be waived by a Member.

Giving Multiple Notices of Termination

A landlord may believe there is more than one ground for eviction, and give a Notice with more than one ground or, more likely, two Notices of Termination together. The

---

[35] *Ball v. Metro Capital Property and Lockhurst* (December 19, 2002), Toronto Docket No. 48/02 (Div. Ct.) Re: TNL-31297.

[36] *Dumi (above) and Forrest Estates Home Sales Inc. v. Gwyn* (1987) Doc. No. 131-1987 (Ont. Dist. Co.).

landlord may also find another ground for eviction while a Notice has not yet been resolved, and give another Notice for the new ground.

The RTA doesn't prohibit a landlord from starting eviction proceedings against a tenant relying on more than one ground and succeed on all or some of the grounds. For example, if the tenant is behind in the rent, and has damaged property in the complex, the landlord should be able to ask for eviction under both grounds. Sometimes the same event may give rise to more than one ground for termination, as a result the landlord may serve more than one Notice of Termination citing the same event as the reason for both of the Notices. For example, if the tenant damages the fire alarm system in the residential complex, the landlord may serve a Notice to Terminate alleging an illegal act and a second notice alleging an impairment of safety.

Although the landlord is permitted to give Notices of Termination with different termination dates, confusion to the tenant should be minimized. The Notices may be challenged on the basis that they are confusing and therefore defective. In the worst case, an application may be dismissed.

Date When Application May be Filed

In a Notice of Termination for non-payment of rent, the landlord may specify any date of termination, so long as it is at least 14 days (7 days for a weekly tenancy) after the day the notice is given to the tenant (see section 59). The landlord must then wait to apply until at least the day after the termination date specified in the Notice (see subsection 74(1)).

An eviction application based on damages, interference with reasonable enjoyment or overcrowding (sections 62, 64 or 67) may not be brought until after the seven day period for the tenant to remedy the situation has passed without the tenant complying with that remedy. For example, if the tenant paid for the damages within the seven days following the Notice being given, no application could be made. Otherwise, the tenant doesn't void the Notice and the landlord could apply on or after the 8th day after giving the Notice to the tenant.

For all other types of eviction applications (e.g., personal use, safety, illegal act, tenant's notice to vacate, etc.), the application may be filed on or after the day the Notice is given.

Under subsection 69(2), an eviction application based on any ground other than unpaid rent must be filed within 30 days after the termination date set out in the Notice of Termination; otherwise, the application will be dismissed.[37]

Completeness of the Application

It is the landlord's responsibility to ensure that their application is correct and complete.

Staff of the Board will check applications for completeness in accordance with Rule 8; however, the Board Member who will make a decision on the application will

---

[37] *Knapp v. Herauf* (June 25, 2004), Ottawa Docket No. 03-DV-947 (Div. Ct.).

ultimately determine whether or not it meets the requirements of the legislation. Where it does not, the application may be dismissed.

Other Claims That May Be Filed With An Eviction Application

An eviction application may be combined with an application for which no Notice of Termination is required. For example, a landlord may seek termination of the tenancy for an illegal act and can also apply for an order for rent arrears and/or compensation for damages caused by the tenant. In such a situation the landlord would have to give the tenant a Notice of Termination for the illegal act, but would not have to give a Notice of Termination for the rent arrears or compensation for damages. It is desirable that an application for damages be supported by estimates for the work alleged to be necessary, preferably from a reputable contractor or supplier, since a Member may refuse to issue an order for an unsupported amount. If the landlord is unsuccessful in proving the application for illegal act, but is successful in proving the rent arrears or damages, the Board will issue an order for the rent arrears or damages, but will not issue a termination of the tenancy.

In any Board order which terminates a tenancy for damages or rent arrears the Board will inquire whether the landlord is holding last month's rent from the tenant and credit the tenant with this amount.

Where a Notice of Termination Becomes Void

Subsection 59(3) provides that a Notice of Termination given for rent arrears is void if, before the day the landlord applies for eviction, the tenant pays the rent arrears and any additional rent that is be due under the tenancy agreement on the date the tenant makes the payment. The purpose of this provision is to create finality when the tenant pays the amount required to bring the rent up to date.

Thus, if the tenant pays the rent that was owed when the Notice was given, and does so before the end of the current rental period, the Notice is void. If the tenant has voided the Notice of Termination, the landlord cannot file an application with the Board based on that Notice. However, if the tenant does not pay the arrears before the end of that rental period and another rental period begins, the rent for that rental period as well as the previous arrears must be paid before the landlord applies in order to void the Notice.

For example:

> A landlord gives a Notice of Termination for Non-Payment of Rent on May 2nd, specifying that the tenant owes $800 for the rental period of May 1st to 31st, with a termination date of May16th. The earliest date that the landlord could apply to the Board is May 17th and the tenant could void the Notice by paying $800 on or before May 16th. However, if the landlord does not apply to the Board in the month of May the tenant could also void the Notice by paying $800 on or before May 31st.
>
> In the same example, if the landlord waited to give the Notice of Termination until May 20th, specifying a termination date of June 3rd, the tenant could void the Notice by paying $800 on or before May 31st. However, if the payment was

made on or after June 1st, the tenant would have to pay $1600 in order to void the Notice.

Where a Notice of Termination is given for damages, interference with reasonable enjoyment or overcrowding (sections 62, 64 or 67), and it is the first Notice within six months, the Notice is void where a tenant corrects the behaviour that led to the giving of the Notice within seven days of receiving it. If the tenant does not correct the behaviour within the seven days the landlord then has thirty days to file an application with the Board. However, if the tenant corrects the behaviour within the seven days of receiving the Notice, but within six months after the first Notice was given, once again contravenes the RTA as specified under section 68, then the landlord may give the tenant a second Notice and can apply to the Board based on the second Notice immediately after the second Notice is served.

Payment of Arrears after the Application Is Filed

If, before the hearing, the landlord receives payment from the tenant of the full arrears (see the Guideline entitled "Eviction for Failure to Pay Rent" regarding the amount required), any additional rent that is owing as of the date the tenant makes the payment, plus the application filing fee, the landlord should advise the Board so that the application may be treated as discontinued pursuant to subsection 74(2) and the hearing may be cancelled.

However, if only partial payment is made, the landlord need not advise the Board before the hearing, but should do so at the hearing.

If the landlord informs the Board of receipt of a partial payment after filing the application, any such amounts will be taken into account in issuing the order.

Payment Made after the Order Becomes Enforceable

See Guideline 11 — Eviction For Failure to Pay Rent

Multiple Landlords

If more than one landlord entered into the tenancy, and only one of them gives a Notice of Termination, they take a risk that the tenant will object to it at the hearing. The Notice may not be sufficient if any of the landlords' names are missing from the Notice, although it is sufficiently signed if any one of the landlords signs it.

The same may be true of the application. If there are multiple landlords, all should be named in the application, although one may sign it as agent for the others.

If the Notice was given by a different landlord than the applicant, this may be proper if the property has been sold and the new landlord is the applicant. However, both the purchaser and vendor should be named and sign the application if there is rent owing to each.

Multiple Tenants

If the landlord has entered into a tenancy agreement with more than one tenant, the Notice of Termination should name and be given to all tenants. This may be done in one Notice naming all the tenants. Although a Notice to a tenant may be served by giving it to any apparently adult person in the unit, if one of the tenants lives at another address, they must be served separately in accordance with the RTA and Rules of Practice.

Where there is a subtenant or assignee these persons should also be named in the Notice of Termination. However, other occupants, such as guests of the tenant, need not be named on the Notice of Termination for the landlord to obtain possession of the rental unit because the Board orders vacant possession of the rental unit, in orders terminating the tenancy.

Expiry of the Eviction Order

Under section 81 of the RTA, an order of the Board that evicts someone expires within 6 months of the date the order unless it is filed with the appropriate Court Enforcement Office before that time. This expiration provision applies notwithstanding any appeal proceeding that may be initiated in a court of competent jurisdiction. Once an eviction order expires, there is no authority to renew it, nor will the landlord be able to apply again for the same remedy for the same time period.

Released Date: January 31, 2007

INTERPRETATION GUIDELINE 11 — EVICTION FOR FAILURE TO PAY RENT

Interpretation Guidelines are intended to assist the parties in understanding the Board's usual interpretation of the law, to provide guidance to Members and promote consistency in decision-making. However, a Member is not required to follow a Guideline and may make a different decision depending on the facts of the case.

This Guideline deals with applications based on a tenant's failure to pay rent. (See also Guideline 10 on "Procedural Issues regarding Eviction Applications").

Method of Ordering Arrears[38]

If the landlord's application for termination based on arrears of rent is granted, the tenant will be ordered to pay: a) rent arrears up to the termination date in the notice of termination; and b) lump sum compensation for use of the rental unit from the termination date in the notice to the order date. The rent deposit and interest owing thereon will be deducted from the arrears and compensation in accordance with subsection 87(4) of *Residential Tenancies Act* (the "RTA"). Daily compensation will then be ordered from the order date until the tenant vacates.

If the landlord is attempting to enforce the order, the landlord has an obligation to inform the Court or the Court Enforcement Office of any rent payments the tenant made that are not reflected in the order.

If the tenant vacated the unit after the application was filed but before the date of the hearing, the tenant will be ordered to pay arrears plus compensation only up to the date they vacated, less the rent deposit and interest.

If the order does not evict the tenant but rent is found owing, the tenant may be ordered to pay arrears up to the end of the current month. The rent deposit will not be deducted from the arrears because the tenancy has not been terminated.

The determination of arrears is usually based on the principle that payments are applied to the earliest rent owing. For example, if the tenant did not pay the May rent, but paid in June, the payment for June will be applied to May leaving the June rent outstanding.

Ordering arrears of rent where the tenant has vacated the rental unit

At hearings about arrears of rent, the Member must decide if the tenant was "in possession of the rental unit" at the time the landlord filed the application with the Board.

If the tenant owes the landlord arrears of rent, the landlord can serve the tenant with a notice of termination. This notice states that the tenant must pay all of the arrears of rent by a date specified in the notice, known as a termination date. If the tenant

---

[38] For simplicity, the descriptions in this Guideline assume monthly payment of rent. If the tenancy was on a weekly or other basis, it should be adjusted accordingly.

moves out of the unit by the termination date, the tenancy will be considered terminated effective that date.[39] If the tenant terminated the tenancy by moving out of the rental unit by the termination date, the Board does not have the jurisdiction to consider an application for arrears of rent filed by the landlord, even if the tenant still owes rent to the landlord.

If the tenant does not move out by the termination date, but moves out of the rental unit before the landlord files an application with the Board requesting termination of the tenancy for non-payment of rent, the Board cannot issue such an order, even if the tenant owes arrears of rent to the landlord. Under subsection 87(1) of the *RTA*, the landlord may only apply to the Board for an order for the payment of rent if the tenant was "in possession of the rental unit" when the application was filed.

Whether or not the tenant is "in possession" of a rental unit depends, on whether the tenant exercises some "form of control over that unit as demonstrated by factors such as access to, use of, or occupation of the unit.[40] The landlord is expected to be able to provide evidence about efforts made to determine whether the tenant is still in possession of the unit. Such evidence may include:

- Whether the tenant returned keys to the landlord;
- Whether the tenant gave a notice to the landlord or it is otherwise clear that the tenant intends to move out;
- Whether utility service to the unit has been disconnected and the unit has been without gas or electricity for some time prior to the hearing;
- Whether the tenant has actually been observed moving out of the unit by the landlord or others;
- Whether the landlord has changed the locks and/or taken steps to re-rent the unit.

The existence of an unexpired lease, by itself, is not proof of "possession" under the RTA. There must be proof of actual use, control or occupancy of the rental unit by the tenant.

If evidence provided to the Member establishes that the tenant was in possession of the unit when the landlord filed the application, the Board has authority to consider the landlord's application. If the tenant is still in possession of the unit as of the hearing date, the tenant can be ordered to pay the landlord all arrears of rent and compensation owing up to that point.

In some cases, the evidence may establish that the tenant moved out of the rental unit after the application was filed, but before the hearing date. In that case, the Board's order will generally include a determination that the tenancy ended on the date the tenant moved out. Further, the order will generally: (1) end the tenancy effective the date the tenant moved out of the rental unit without ordering enforcement through

[39] See *RTA*, s. 43(2)(a).

[40] See the Ontario Court of Appeal's unanimous judgment in *1162994 Ontario Inc.* v. *Bakker, et al.*, [2004] O.J. No. 2565 (Ont. C.A.) (hereinafter "*Bakker*").

the Sheriff's Office; and (2) require the tenant to pay arrears up to the date specified in the termination notice, and lump sum compensation for use of the unit from the termination date in the notice to the date the tenancy ended. Unlike orders for arrears and termination where the tenant is in possession of the unit on the hearing date, the order would not provide the tenant with an opportunity to continue the tenancy by paying all of the arrears by a specified date. Moreover, as there is a finding that the tenancy has ended, the tenant's rent deposit and interest owing on it will be deducted from the arrears and compensation ordered to the landlord.

Arrears Less than a Rent Deposit

A notice of termination is not invalid simply because the landlord holds a rent deposit that is greater than the rent owing. The rent deposit can only be applied to the last month of the tenancy. Therefore, the landlord should not apply the deposit to the rent arrears before applying to evict the tenant.

The amount that is owed to the landlord on the order date may be a negative amount, after the deposit and interest are deducted from the rent and compensation owing to the landlord. If so, the landlord would owe money to the tenant. In that case, the Board may order the landlord to pay the tenant the amount that will be owed as of the order date. The authority for this lies in section 205 of the RTA which states that the Board may order that "The landlord or the tenant shall pay to the other any sum of money that is owed as a result of this order."

Non-Sufficient Funds Charges

Under section 87 of the RTA, where a landlord applies for an order for the payment of arrears of rent, the application may include a claim for the amount of NSF charges paid to a financial institution in respect of cheques tendered to the landlord by the tenant, plus the landlord's administrative charges in respect of those cheques. The administrative charges are limited to a maximum of $20.00 per cheque per section 17 of Regulation 516/06.

These charges, if claimed, will normally be awarded and, if the order terminates the tenancy, the tenant will have to pay these amounts in addition to the other amounts payable in order to avoid eviction. See also the section below on Amount Payable to Prevent an Eviction.

Although a landlord may apply for NSF charges, they cannot be claimed in an N4 notice of termination. Under subsection 59(3) of the RTA, a notice of termination is void if the tenant pays the arrears and the additional rent that has become owing. There is no requirement for the tenant to pay NSF charges to void the notice. Therefore, including NSF charges on an N4 will likely invalidate the notice.

Similar Charges

Other amounts may be owed to the landlord for charges permitted under the RTA or regulations, such as the cost of installing a mobile home under section 166 of the RTA, or for transferring a tenant to another unit in a social housing complex under section 17 of Regulation 516/06. Although the RTA allows a landlord to levy these charges, the RTA does not provide for their recovery in an application to the Board. A landlord should therefore not include such charges in a notice of termination or application for non-payment of rent.

Certain charges are not permitted by the RTA, even if they are set out in the tenancy agreement. This includes non-refundable key deposits, most types of administrative charges, and late payment charges in excess of what is permitted. See section 17 of Regulation 516/06.

Utilities Charges

When a landlord and tenant are entering into a tenancy agreement, they may agree that utilities will be included in the rent. In this case, the landlord is responsible for paying all utility bills and the rent would remain unchanged despite any fluctuations in these costs.

Alternatively, the landlord and tenant may agree that utilities will not be included in the rent, and that the tenant will be responsible for paying all utility costs directly to the utility company. In this case it is clear that the payment of the utility costs is not rent, and even if the landlord pays the bill because the tenant fails to, they would not be able to claim the amount as rent arrears.

However, in some cases the tenancy agreement may require the tenant to reimburse the landlord for the actual amount of the utility costs. The question that then arises is, if the tenant is in default, can the landlord include these amounts in an application for the payment of rent arrears?

In these situations, it will generally be considered that the cost of utilities is not included in the "rent", and that the landlord is acting as an agent for the utility company for the purposes of collecting payment from the tenant. If these amounts were considered to be part of the rent then any upward fluctuations in the utility charge could be considered an unlawful rent increase.

Therefore, any unpaid amounts for utilities will not be included in the calculation of arrears, although they may be a debt owing to the landlord that may be recovered through the courts.

In all cases, the Member must review the tenancy agreement. However, the definition of rent cannot be affected by the tenancy agreement in view of sections 3 and 4 of the RTA. Section 3 provides that the RTA applies despite any agreement to the contrary, and section 4 provides that any provision of the tenancy agreement inconsistent with the RTA is void.

Rent Deposits

A landlord may require a tenant to pay a rent deposit of no more than one month's rent, so long as the landlord does so on or before entering into the tenancy agreement in accordance with subsection 106(1) of the RTA. If the tenant does not provide a rent deposit, the Board cannot order the tenant to pay one. It follows that if the landlord claims a rent deposit on the notice of termination it will invalidate the notice.

The landlord may require the tenant to update the rent deposit when the rent increases so that the deposit is equal to the lawful rent for the last month: see subsection 106(3) of the RTA.

Tenant Issues

Under section 82 of the RTA, a tenant may raise any issue that could be the subject of a tenant application. If the Board determines that the tenant is entitled to money (e.g., a rent abatement or rebate), it will be deducted from any amount owing to the landlord.

May a Guarantor be Ordered to Pay Rent Arrears

There are tenancies that the landlord only accepted on the basis that a person other than the tenants would guarantee that the rent would be paid, should the tenants not be able to pay. The question is whether the Board may order a guarantor to pay rent arrears if the landlord includes them with the tenants as respondents to the application.

In most cases, the guarantor has no express right of possession and, even if they do, no one expects them to ever occupy the rental unit.

The Board will not make an order against guarantors because they are not tenants. The RTA does not authorize the Board to deal with such claims, even if they are related to the issue of rent arrears. Landlords may seek enforcement of such obligations through the courts.

Relief from Eviction

Where the Board finds there is unpaid rent, the Board must consider whether to delay or refuse the eviction under section 83 of the RTA. In some cases, refusing or delaying the eviction is discretionary; in others, refusing the eviction is mandatory. Even if the eviction claim in the application is refused or delayed, the tenant will be ordered to pay any arrears to the landlord. A payment schedule for the arrears may be imposed upon the tenant under section 204 as a condition of giving relief under section 83. See also Guideline 7 on "Relief from Eviction" for further discussion of this point.

Amount Payable to Prevent an Eviction

Section 74 of the RTA provides that a tenant may avoid an eviction in three circumstances.

Before the order is issued

Subsection 74(2) provides that if the tenant pays the landlord the full arrears, the application fee and any additional rent that is owed as of the date of payment by the tenant, before the eviction order is issued, the landlord's application will be discontinued.

After the order is issued

Under subsection 74(3), an order must specify the amount of rent arrears, the daily compensation payable and any costs ordered by the Board. The order will also set out any amount payable for NSF and administration charges. The order must also inform the tenant and the landlord that the order will become void under subsection 74(4) if the tenant pays the landlord or the Board the amount specified in the order before it is enforceable. An order is enforceable on the date the order specifies that the Court Enforcement Office (Sheriff) may give possession to the landlord.

If the tenant pays the amount specified in the order to the Board, staff of the Board will issue a notice to the landlord and tenant acknowledging that the order is void. If the tenant pays the entire amount to the landlord or part to the landlord and part to the Board, the tenant may file a motion with the Board, without notice to the landlord, asking for a Member to issue an order determining that the tenant has paid the full amount due and confirming that the order is void. Such an order will be made without holding a hearing. However, within ten days after it is issued, a landlord may, on notice to the tenant, make a motion to set the order aside. A hearing will be held to determine the landlord's set aside motion.

After the order is enforceable

Under subsection 74(11), if the tenant pays the amount specified in the order and any additional rent owing after it becomes enforceable but before it is enforced by the sheriff, the tenant may file a motion with the Board, on notice to the landlord, to set aside the eviction order. The eviction order is stayed and cannot be enforced until the Board issues an order lifting the stay.

Although subsection 74(11) refers to an amount being paid to the Board, the tenant may pay the amount required to be paid under that subsection to the landlord, to the Board, or in part to both. This interpretation is consistent with the wording in subsection 74(11) because if the tenant has paid an amount to the landlord that is sufficient to void the order, then the amount that the tenant must pay into the Board under subsection 74(11) is "$0".

This interpretation of subsection 74(11) avoids the absurd result of refusing to void an order and allowing a tenant to be evicted where the tenant paid the full amount to the landlord.

The Board will hold a hearing on the motion. If the tenant paid some or all of the amount owing to the landlord by non-certified cheque, and the landlord is concerned that the cheque may be returned NSF, the member holding the hearing can grant an adjournment or permit post-hearing submissions to allow time for the cheque to clear before making their final order.

If the Board determines that the tenant paid the arrears and any additional rent owed to the landlord as of the date of the motion hearing, any NSF and administration charges and the costs ordered by the Board, the Board will make an order declaring the eviction order to be void. However, under subsection 74(15), if the Board determines that the landlord has paid a non-refundable amount under the *Administration of Justice Act* for the purpose of enforcing the order (e.g. sheriff fees), the Board will specify that amount in the motion order and require the tenant to pay that amount into the Board by a specified date.

If the tenant pays the specified amount by the specified date, a Board employee will issue a notice to the tenant and the landlord acknowledging that the eviction order is void.

If the Board determines that the tenant did *not* pay the specified amount by the specified date, a Board employee will issue a notice stating that the stay of the order ceases to apply and the eviction order may be enforced.

A motion to void an order after it has become enforceable may be made only once during the period of the tenant's tenancy agreement with the landlord: see subsection 74(12).

Amended October 15, 2009

INTERPRETATION GUIDELINE 12 — EVICTION FOR PERSONAL USE

Interpretation Guidelines are intended to assist the parties in understanding the Board's usual interpretation of the law, to provide guidance to Members and promote consistency in decision-making. However, a Member is not required to follow a Guideline and may make a different decision depending on the facts of the case.

This Guideline deals with interpretation questions respecting eviction applications under the *Residential Tenancies Act, 2006* (the "RTA"), based on use of the rental unit by: the landlord; a family member of the landlord; or a person who provides or will provide care services to the landlord or a family member of the landlord where the person receiving the care services resides or will reside in the building. It also deals with eviction by the landlord for personal use of a unit by: a purchaser; a family member of the purchaser; or a person who provides or will provide care services to the purchaser or a family member of the purchaser if the person receiving the care services resides or will reside in the building.

A family member may be the landlord's (or purchaser's) spouse, or a child or parent of one of them. The term "spouse" includes opposite-sex couples and same-sex couples who are married or who live together in conjugal relationships outside of marriage.

For general information about eviction applications, see Guideline 10, entitled "Procedural Issues regarding Eviction Applications".

PERSONAL USE BY THE LANDLORD OR LANDLORD'S FAMILY

Section 48 of the RTA permits the landlord to give notice of termination to a tenant if the landlord, in good faith, requires the unit for residential occupation by: the landlord; the landlord's spouse; a child or a parent of either the landlord or the landlord's spouse; or a person who provides or will provide care services to the landlord or a family member of the landlord where the person receiving the care services resides or will reside in the building. The termination date in the landlord's notice of termination must be at least 60 days after the notice is given and must be the last day of a fixed term tenancy, or if there is no fixed term, on the last day of a rental period. For example, if the current month is January and the lease expires on June 30 of the same year, the termination date should be June 30. Another example may arise on a month to month lease where notice is provided to the tenant on January 20. In this scenario, the earliest the termination date on the notice can be is March 31 which is 60 days after the notice is given and on the last day of the monthly rental period.

The landlord may apply to the Board as soon as this notice has been given, but any order issued may not be effective before the termination date in the notice. During the notice period, the tenant may give the landlord ten days written notice to terminate the tenancy at an earlier date.

Requirement of Good Faith

The issue that arises in some cases is whether the landlord or a family member has a real intention to reside in the rental unit. Subsection 72(1) addresses this concern by requiring the landlord to file with the Board an affidavit sworn by the person who personally requires the rental unit certifying that the person in good faith requires the rental unit for his or her own personal use.

PERSONAL USE BY A PURCHASER OR THEIR FAMILY

Section 49 of the RTA permits the landlord to give notice of termination to a tenant if:

> (a) the landlord has entered into an agreement of purchase and sale to sell a residential complex containing no more than 3 units or a condominium unit, and
>
> (b) the purchaser, in good faith, requires possession of the complex or the unit for residential occupation by the purchaser, his or her spouse, or a child or parent of one of them.

Agreement of Purchase and Sale

Before a landlord may give a notice under section 49, there must be an agreement of purchase and sale to sell the residential complex. The Board may refuse an application if it is not reasonably certain that a completed sale will result from the agreement. If a term or condition of the agreement makes it uncertain that the deal will be completed, it may be appropriate to delay the application until the sale becomes more certain.

The Board may also dismiss the application if the purchase is a sham created for the purpose of evicting the tenant. For example, a transfer to a family member should be examined. A sale for much less than market value may raise questions. Section 202 provides authority to look at the real nature of any transactions.

A landlord applying based on a notice under section 49 is well advised to file with the application a copy of the agreement, together with an explanation of the circumstances of the intended sale.

Requirement of Good Faith

The requirement is similar to that related to section 48 (see above). The requirement relates to the genuine intention of the purchaser and the person who declares they intend to occupy the unit (see subsections 49(1) and 72(1) of the RTA).

PERSONAL USE BY A PERSON WHO PROVIDES OR WILL PROVIDE CARE SERVICES

Subsection 48(1)(d) and 49(1)(d) of the RTA permit a landlord to give notice of termination to a tenant if the landlord or purchaser, in good faith, requires the unit for residential occupation by a person who provides or will provide care services to the landlord or purchaser, or the landlord or purchaser's spouse, parent, child, or spouse's parent or child.

The person receiving the care must reside or be going to reside in the building, related group of buildings, mobile home park or land lease community in which the rental unit is located.

Under section 2 of the RTA, "care services" is defined as meaning "subject to the regulations, health care services, rehabilitative or therapeutic services or services that provide assistance with the activities of daily living".

The termination date in the notice of termination must be at least 60 days after the notice was given and must be the last day of a fixed term tenancy, or if there is no fixed term, on the last day of a rental period. The landlord may apply to the Board as soon as this notice has been given, but any order issued may not be effective before the termination date in the notice. During the notice period, the tenant may give ten days written notice to terminate the tenancy earlier.

Requirement of Good Faith

The requirement is similar to that related to section 48 (see above). The requirement relates to the genuine intention of the landlord and the person who declares they intend to occupy the unit (see subsections 48(1) and 72(1) of the RTA).

REQUIREMENT OF GOOD FAITH

The case law under the similarly worded provision of the *Tenant Protection Act* (the "TPA") indicates that the landlord must have a real or genuine desire to occupy the rented premises. Tenants may believe that the landlord's intention is not genuine or honest[41], and seek to discredit it. The Ontario Divisional Court has said that the real issue is whether the landlord is genuine in their intention to occupy the rental unit.[42]

The Divisional Court has also held that the landlord does not have to prove their good faith beyond a reasonable doubt.[43] The correct test is whether the Member believes that good faith exists on a balance of probabilities. Thus the Member must decide whether it is more likely that there is good faith than not.

A tenant may wish to prove that the same landlord gave a notice of termination for personal use of another unit earlier, obtained possession and then rented it to another tenant. This is not determinative evidence that the landlord lacks good faith in the present case[44], but it is a "similar fact" situation that may be considered, at least in weighing the landlord's evidence. Under clause 202(b) the Board shall ascertain the real substance of activities and have regard to the pattern of activities relating to the residential complex or the rental unit.

---

[41] Good faith was defined in *Semeniuk v. White Oak Stables Ltd.* (1991),27A.C.W.S. (3d)505 (B.C. C.A.) as honestly, without fraud, collusion or participation in wrong doing.

[42] *Beljinac v. Salter* [2001] O.J. No. 2792 (Div. Ct.) Re: TSL-21378. Also see Feeney v. Noble (1994), 19 O.R. (3d) 762 (Div. Ct.) in which the Court decided that this requirement does not imply a "complete bona fides (i.e., untainted by any element of bad faith and total probity)".

[43] *Kulusic v. Kennedy*, unreported Dec. 7, 1989 decision (file # 51/89) (Div. Ct.).

[44] *Re Yarmuch and Jacobson* (1985), 34 A.C.W.S. (2d) 145 (Ont. Dist. Ct.).

The evidence of the landlord should be reviewed to determine if it convinces the Member that the landlord or family member will move into the unit within a reasonable time after the unit becomes vacant. Evidence of previous problems between the current tenant and the landlord may be relevant to the genuineness of the landlord's intention to use the unit as stated in the notice. It may also be considered in reviewing requests for relief from eviction (see below).

Where a landlord provides notice to a tenant under sections 48 or 49 in bad faith and the tenant moves out of the unit as a result of the landlord notice or an application to or an order by the Board based on such a notice and no person specified under the appropriate subsection has occupied the unit within a reasonable time after the former tenant vacated the rental unit, subsection 57 of the RTA provides that the Board may make:

- An order that the landlord pay a specified sum to the tenant for all or any portion of any increased rent that the former tenant has incurred or will incur for a one-year period after vacating the rental unit, and a reasonable out-of-pocket moving, storage and other like expenses that the former tenant has incurred or will incur;
- An order for abatement of rent;
- An order that the landlord pay to the Board an administrative fine not exceeding the greater of $10,000 and the monetary jurisdiction of the Small Claims Court; or,
- Any other order that the Board considers appropriate.

The Landlord Requires the Unit -- Test to be Applied

The Ontario Divisional Court found that the reasonableness of the landlord's intention to occupy the unit was not important because the real test was the genuine want and desire for the unit.[45] In the leading case of *Kennealy v. Dunne*,[46] the English Court of Appeal stated that:

> *A landlord need not establish that his requirement of possession was reasonable, only that he bona fide wanted and genuinely had the immediate intention to occupy the premises as a residence.*

Some court cases have held that the word "requires" means wants, and not needs. Accordingly, the landlord has no obligation to prove that the unit is the only option or the best one for the person intending to occupy the unit. However, in other cases, the Court concluded from the lack of real need for the unit, and usually from other circumstances such as disputes with the tenant, that the landlord lacked good faith in their desire to evict the tenant.

The burden of proof is on the landlord. It is relevant to the good faith of the landlord's intention to occupy the unit to determine the likelihood that the intended person will move into it.

---

[45] *Beljinac v. Salter* [2001] O.J. No. 2792 (Div. Ct.) Re: TSL-21378.

[46] [1977] 2 All E.R. 16 (C.A.).

Corporate Landlords and Shareholders of a Corporation

Section 103 of the *Landlord and Tenant Act* (the "LTA") was similar in wording to section 51 of the TPA and section 48 of the RTA. Therefore, in interpreting seciton 48 of the RTA, it is approptiate to consider how courts have interpreted those provisions of the LTA and TPA.

A number of decisions denied corporations the right to use section 103 of the LTA,finding that only a human landlord could personally occupy the premises[47]. In *D.E.S.K. Properties Ltd. v. Skene*,[48] the County Court found:

> *Although in some circumstances a corporation may be regarded as a facade, the fact that the premises here are owned by a corporation prevents an Order being made under s. [103]. I am satisfied that [Mr. H.] bona fide requires possession of the apartment, but it is the corporation whose shares he owns that is the landlord, not [Mr. H.] ... A corporation and its shareholders (even where, as here, one person owns all the shares) are two separate entities.*

The landlord appealed the decision to the Divisional Court, but the appeal was dismissed.[49]

In contrast, in other instances, courts have taken a more flexible approach to the interpretation of the legislation. Courts have found that the sole shareholder of a corporation may also be a "landlord," as defined by the LTA, and may thus be entitled to use this ground for eviction for their personal occupation or that of their family member.

For example, in *Megan Investments Ltd. v. Funston*,[50] Philp J. held that where a corporation owns premises, the sole shareholder and officer may qualify as a landlord if the evidence establishes that he or she is "the person giving or permitting occupation" of the premises. In *Duke's Trailer Court Limited v. Block*,[51] Platana J. followed and extended the reasoning of Megan Investments to allow a controlling shareholder of a family held corporation to claim that he acted separately from the landlord company and was another landlord with a right of occupation.

In *Melhuish and Walsh v. 580472 Ontario Ltd. and Strelchuk*,[52] the Court found that the TPA's requirements were sufficiently met where the individual who sought to rely on the TPA was the beneficial owner of the rental unit, even though a numbered company was shown as the owner of the rental unit in the records of the land register. In support of the application, an officer of the corporate landlord swore a statutory declaration stating that the corporation is solely a trustee and holds the title to the rental unit for and on behalf of the individual, the beneficial owner. The Court found

---

[47] For example, see *629576 Ontario Ltd. v. Ogg*, (1986) 42 R.P.R. 310 (Ontario District Court, Kileen, D.C.J.).

[48] (1982) 4 TLLR 101 (Co. Ct.).

[49] See (1983) 4 TLLR 103 (Div. Ct.).

[50] [1992] O.J. No. 1290, (1992), 25 R.P.R. (2d) 63 (Ont. Gen. Div.).

[51] [1997] O.J. No. 2415, (1997), 41 O.T.C. 129, 10 R.P.R. (3d) 194 (Ont. Gen. Div.).

[52] [2002] O.J. No. 4343 (Div. Ct).

that it was clear that the individual was the beneficial owner of the premises and a landlord.

The Board is required to ascertain the real substance of all transactions relating to a residential complex or a rental unit and the good faith of the participants in making findings on an application. Where the residential complex or rental unit is owned by a corporation, the Board must examine the real substance of the facts in each case to try to determine whether the sole shareholder of a corporate landlord can seek to rely on sections 48 and 49. In Melhuish, the Court noted section 188 of the TPA, now section 202 of the RTA. Section 202 of the RTA provides:

> *In making findings on an application, the Board shall ascertain the real substance of all transactions and activities relating to a residential complex or a rental unit and the good faith of the participants and in doing so,*
>
> > *(a) may disregard the outward form of a transaction or the separate corporate existence of participants; and*
> >
> > *(b) may have regard to the pattern of activities relating to the residential complex or the rental unit.*

Consistent with the approach of the Court in Melhuish and section 202 of the RTA, the Board must examine the real substance of the particular facts of a case to identify a landlord who can rely on section 48 of the RTA.

RESTRICTION ON "CO-OWNERSHIPS"

Co-ownership involves a number of individuals owning a building through a corporation or as tenants-in-common. Subsection 72(2) applies when such a building has been marketed as single units. This method of offering a building for sale on a unit basis avoids the rules of the Condominium Act. The co-owner has no rights to the unit they are apparently buying, except by agreement with the other co-owners. Their rights respecting the unit may only be the net revenue from that unit, but may also include the right to occupy the unit.

Subsection 72(2) provides protection for tenants of units that have been sold in this way to co-owners. Even if the co-ownership agreement purports to give the "unit owner" the right to occupy the unit, they cannot do so unless they meet the test set out in either clause 72(2)(a) or 72(2)(b).

Subsection 72(2) restricts the right of such a landlord to apply for possession for landlord's or purchaser's own use. Specifically subsection 72(2) provides:

> (2) The Board shall not make an order terminating a tenancy and evicting the tenant in an application under section 69 based on a notice of termination under section 48 or 49 *where the landlord's claim is based on a tenancy agreement or occupancy agreement that purports to entitle the landlord to reside in the rental unit* unless,
>
> > *(a) the application is brought in respect of premises situate in a building containing not more than four residential units; or*

(b) one or more of the following people has previously been a genuine occupant of the premises:

(i) the landlord,

(ii) the landlord's spouse,

(iii) a child or parent of the landlord or the landlord's spouse, or

(iv) a person who provided care services to the landlord, the landlord's spouse, or a child or parent of the landlord or the landlord's spouse.

This is not a general prohibition on landlords of complexes with more than four rental units. The underlined words most commonly refer to a co-ownership situation where specific co-owners claim rights to certain units.

RELIEF FROM EVICTION

Even though the Board has found that the landlord or purchaser requires the unit in good faith, which would result in an eviction order, the Board must consider, having regard to all the circumstances, whether or not to refuse to grant the application or to postpone the eviction for a period of time. In some cases, refusing or delaying the eviction is discretionary; in others, refusing the eviction is mandatory. See Guideline 7, entitled "Relief from Eviction".

Amended December 08, 2008

INTERPRETATION GUIDELINE 13 — OTHER POWERS OF THE BOARD

Interpretation Guidelines are intended to assist the parties in understanding the Board's usual interpretation of the law, to provide guidance to Members and promote consistency in decision-making. However, a Member is not required to follow a Guideline and may make a different decision depending on the facts of the case.

Section 201 of the *Residential Tenancies Act, 2006* (the RTA) states:

Other powers of Board

201. (1) The Board may, before, during or after a hearing,

(a) conduct any inquiry it considers necessary or authorize an employee of the Board to do so;

(b) request a provincial inspector or an employee of the Board to conduct any inspection it considers necessary;

(c) question any person, by telephone or otherwise, concerning the dispute or authorize an employee of the Board to do so;

(d) permit or direct a party to file additional evidence with the Board which the Board considers necessary to make its decision;

(e) view premises that are the subject of the hearing; or

(f) on its own motion and on notice to the parties, amend an application if the Board considers it appropriate to do so and if amending the application would not be unfair to any party.

Same

(2) In making its determination, the Board may consider any relevant information obtained by the Board in addition to the evidence given at the hearing, provided that it first informs the parties of the additional information and gives them an opportunity to explain or refute it.

Same

(3) If a party fails to comply with a direction under clause (1) (d), the Board may,

(a) refuse to consider the party's submissions and evidence respecting the matter regarding which there was a failure to comply; or

(b) if the party who has failed to comply is the applicant, dismiss all or part of the application.

Parties may view premises with Board

(4) If the Board intends to view premises under clause (1) (e), the Board shall give the parties an opportunity to view the premises with the Board.

This Guideline is intended to provide guidance on powers of the Board under section 201 of the RTA. The Board does not gather evidence for or on behalf of the parties. The parties are responsible for bringing all relevant evidence and witnesses they wish the Member to consider to the hearing. However, the Board may, on its own initiative or at the request of a party, decide to exercise its discretion under section 201 to conduct an inquiry, question a person, view premises, amend an application or permit or direct a party to file additional evidence. This discretion will generally be exercised where the information at issue is relevant and necessary to the application and there is no other way to obtain the information or no other evidence that may be utilized in its place. The discretion under section 201 should be considered in light of section 171 of the RTA which states "The Board shall adopt the most expeditious method of determining the questions arising in a proceeding that affords to all persons directly affected by the proceeding an adequate opportunity to know the issues and be heard on the matter."

Each subsection is reviewed in turn.

a. Conduct any inquiry it considers necessary or authorize an employee of the Board to do so.

- There may be certain limited circumstances where a Member determines that it is necessary to instruct an employee of the Board to make an inquiry before, during or after the hearing. Where possible, the purpose of such an inquiry should be limited to clarifying or obtaining necessary information.

- Where the inquiry is to be conducted by a Board employee, the Member will provide the employee with clear direction as to the nature and scope of the inquiry in writing. The Board employee will provide the results of their inquiry to the Member in writing.

- The results of the inquiry should be provided to the parties within the time and according to the method that the Member directs or orders. The parties should be given reasonable opportunity to review and respond to any information provided.

- Examples where a Member may request a Board employee to make an inquiry include: contacting a party prior to a hearing to ascertain a party's availability for a proposed hearing date; determining the status of a related Board application; or determining when a post-hearing submission will be filed.

b. Request a provincial inspector or an employee of the Board to conduct any inspection it considers necessary.

- In special circumstances, a Member may determine that it is necessary to request an inspection because it is not possible for the parties to bring forward the necessary evidence in any other form such as photographs, inspection reports, or witnesses. For example, an inspection may be requested of a unit to determine whether or not there are appliances in the unit or if the damage alleged has occurred.

• Where a Member determines an inspection is necessary, either a provincial inspector or a Board employee will be requested to carry out the inspection.

• The Member will provide the provincial inspector or Board employee a written direction setting out the details of the inspection (e.g. unit address, time to conduct the inspection, and the purpose of the inspection). The provincial inspector or Board employee will, in turn, provide the Member with a written response describing their observations or findings.

• The results of the inspection should be provided to the parties within the time and according to the method that the Member directs or orders. The parties should be given reasonable opportunity to review and respond to any information provided.

c. Question any person, by telephone or otherwise, concerning the dispute or authorize an employee of the Board to do so.

• A Member may have some questions relating to a dispute or wish to clarify information already received. For example, the Member may be unable to read one sentence in an affidavit due to poor penmanship.

• In these types of situations where a Member wishes to question a person by telephone or otherwise concerning the dispute, the Member will usually ask a Board employee to question that person. The Member will provide the Board employee a written request setting out the issues or questions they have regarding the matter. The Board employee will provide the Member with a response to these issues and questions in writing.

• Where the Member or the staff employee has received a response to their questions, that response will be provided to the parties within the time and according to the method that the Member directs or orders. The parties should be given reasonable opportunity to review and respond to any information provided.

d. Permit or direct a party to file additional evidence with the Board which the Board considers necessary to make its decision.

• See Rule 19. Rule 19 provides disclosure rules in situations where a Member may wish to clarify the contents of an application, dispute, motion or other document filed with the Board.

• Note that subsection 201(3) provides that if a party fails to comply with such a direction, the Board may:

  • refuse to consider the party's submissions and evidence respecting the matter regarding which there was a failure to comply; or

  • the party who has failed to comply is the applicant, dismiss all or part of the application.

e. View premises that are the subject of the hearing.

• Premises will normally be viewed in special circumstances only.

• Subsection 201(4) states that if the Member intends to view premises, the Member should give the parties an opportunity to view the premises with the Member.

• In order to provide parties adequate opportunity to view premises with the Member, parties should be provided with reasonable notice of the date and time of the viewing. Where possible, the parties should be canvassed for possible dates and times for the viewing.

f. On its own motion and on notice to the parties, amend an application if the Board considers it appropriate to do so and if amending the application would not be unfair to any party.

• The Board may on its own motion consider amending an application before, during or after a hearing. For example to add a party or to remove a party.

• A Member shall decide whether or not to amend an application before, during or after a hearing taking into consideration the following factors:

• Any prejudice a party may experience as a result of the amendment

• Whether the amendment is significant enough to warrant any delay that may be caused by the amendment

• Whether the amendment is necessary

• Any other relevant factors

Subsection 201(2) provides that in making its determination, the Board may consider any relevant information obtained by the Board in addition to the evidence given at the hearing, provided that it first informs the parties of the additional information and gives them an opportunity to explain or refute it.

• Parties should be informed of any additional information under consideration by the Member within the time and according to the method that the Member directs or orders. The Member must also file any such information with the Board.

• The parties should be given reasonable opportunity to review and respond to any information provided.

Released Date: January 31, 2007

INTERPRETATION GUIDELINE 14 — APPLICATIONS FOR RENT INCREASES ABOVE THE GUIDELINE

Interpretation Guidelines are intended to assist the parties in understanding the Board's usual interpretation of the law, to provide guidance to Members and promote consistency in decision-making. However, a Member is not required to follow a Guideline and may make a different decision depending on the facts of the case.

All increases in rent are subject to the rules set out in the *Residential Tenancies Act, 2006* (the "RTA"). Subsection 126(1) of the RTA provides for applications to the Board by landlords for rent increases that are in addition to the yearly guideline increase a landlord may take. A landlord's application may include some or all of the rental units or a portion of the rental units in the residential complex.

Applications for above the guideline increases ("AGIs") in rent can be made in any or all of the following cases:

1. An extraordinary increase in the cost for municipal taxes and charges, an extraordinary increase in the cost of utilities or an extraordinary increase in the cost for both municipal taxes and utilities, for the residential complex or any building in which the rental units are located.

2. Eligible capital expenditures incurred respecting the residential complex or one or more of the rental units in it.

3. Operating costs related to security services provided in respect of the residential complex or any building in which the rental units are located by persons not employed by the landlord.

This guideline is intended to assist parties in understanding the law and procedures applicable to the various kinds of AGIs.

THE NATURE OF THE APPLICATION

Section 120 of the RTA requires the Minister to set the guideline for rent increases every year. The Board does not set the guideline and has no jurisdiction to increase or decrease the guideline.

The purpose of section 126 of the RTA is to allow landlords to apply for an increase in rent above the guideline in three specific circumstances where they have incurred expenses that are not taken into account in calculating the guideline.

Maintenance Issues:

Despite the fact that an AGI application is filed by the landlord a tenant may raise issues concerning breaches of maintenance. However, the Board is limited to considering only existing serious breaches of the landlord's maintenance obligations as set out in subsection 126(12). Further the Board is limited to the remedies that it may order if it finds that there is a serious breach. Pursuant to subsection 126 (13) of the

RTA, if the Board finds a serious breach in maintenance it shall dismiss the AGI application with respect to the affected rental unit or make an order as provided for in paragraph (b) of subsection 126 (13), that the rent not be increased for the rental unit until the landlord makes the appropriate motion with notice to the tenant and the Board permits the increase, where the landlord has not:

- completed items on work orders related to a serious breach of health, safety, housing or maintenance standards;
- completed work, repairs or replacements ordered by the Board under paragraph 4 of subsection 30 (1) of the RTA and was found by the Board to be related to serious breaches of subsection 20 (1) or section 161 of the RTA; or
- is in serious breach of subsection 20 (1) or section 161 of the RTA.

The Board cannot award a rent abatement to a tenant on an AGI order.

If the tenant believes that the landlord has breached the maintenance obligations set out in the RTA, the tenant may file their own application about maintenance whether or not the maintenance issues are raised at the AGI hearing. For further information on tenant applications for breaches of maintenance obligation see Interpretation Guideline 5: Breach of Maintenance Obligations which discusses both the landlord's maintenance obligations and the types of remedies that may be awarded on the tenant's application.

3% limitation:

Subsection 126(11) of the RTA provides that the maximum annual increase that may be allowed in an application based on capital expenditures or security services or both is 3% above the guideline. Where an application justifies more than 3%, the rent is increased by

3% in the first year and any remaining increase may be taken in subsequent years, to a maximum of two additional years at 3% per year, according to the prescribed rules in section 33 of O. Reg. 516/06.

The 3% limitation does not apply where the application is based on an increase in the cost of municipal taxes and charges, or utilities. Where an increase is justified by these categories, the landlord may take the entire increase in the first year.

Exception for Mobile Home Parks & Land Lease Communities:

Section 167 of the RTA contains an exception to subsection 126(11) where a landlord incurs a capital expenditure with regard to a mobile home park or a land lease community for "infrastructure work" as defined in subsection 167(2) and section 51 of O. Reg. 516/06, required to be carried out by the Government of Canada or Ontario or a municipality, or an agency of any of them. In these circumstances, the Board has the jurisdiction to set the number of years over which the justified rent increase may be taken.

Charging the approved rent increase:

Where a landlord has applied for an increase above the guideline, all rules regarding notices of rent increase still apply. Where a landlord has filed an AGI and gives a tenant a notice of rent increase before the Board orders such an increase, the tenant may choose to pay only the amount that the landlord could lawfully charge, without the order. If the tenant chooses to pay a higher amount and the application is unsuccessful, or the Board orders a lesser amount, the landlord owes that tenant any amount overpaid. If the AGI is successful and the tenant has not paid the amount required by the order, the tenant owes the landlord the difference between the amount paid and the amount required by the order, provided the landlord has served a proper notice of rent increase for that amount. If the Board makes the order for an above the guideline rent increase three months or more after the FED of a rent increase, s.205 of the RTA allows the Board to order that any money owing by the tenant as a result of the ordered rent increase can be paid by the tenant in monthly installments over a period of no more than 12 months.

Subsection 33(2) of O. Reg. 516/06 provides that where a landlord does not take an increase in the 12-month time period for which it is ordered, the landlord may not take the increase at a later date. The right to take that increase is therefore lost.

First Effective Date (FED) in an AGI Application:

All AGI applications must be filed at least 90 days before the effective date of the first intended rent increase that is being claimed in the application.

FILING THE APPLICATION

Because of the nature of an application to increase the rent above the guideline, much of the evidence to support the application is documentary. Section 22 of O. Reg. 516/06 provides for timely disclosure of supporting material by requiring that:

1. if the application is based on an extraordinary increase in the cost for municipal taxes and charges or utilities or both, the landlord must file with the application,

   i) Evidence of the costs claimed and proof of payment of the costs, and

   ii) Any information that effectively reduces the landlord's costs, including, but not limited to, grants, financial assistance, rebates and refunds. If the information is not available when the application is filed, the landlord continues to have an obligation to file the information, if it becomes available at any time before the hearing is completed; and

2. if the application is based on capital expenditures, the landlord must file with the application documentation,

   i) on a Board approved form, details about each invoice and payment for eachcapital expenditure item, and

ii) on a Board approved form, details about the rents for all rental units in the residential complex that are affected by any of the capital expenditures,

iii) evidence of the costs claimed and proof of payment of the costs, including any information that effectively reduces the landlord's costs, including grants and assistance from any level of government and insurance, resale, salvage and trade-in proceeds, rebates and refunds. If that information is not available when the application is filed, the landlord continues to have an obligation to file the information, if it becomes available at any time before the hearing is completed;

iv) two additional photocopies of the application and the material that accompanies the application and, a compact disc containing the material that accompanies the application in portable document format (PDF). See following for exception:

Exception to iv): a landlord does not have to provide a compact disc where the residential complex contains six or fewer residential units and the residential complex is located in a rural or remote area and the landlord cannot reasonably provide the compact disc.

A Member may refuse to allow the landlord to rely on documents that were not filed in a timely manner. The result of such a refusal will often be that the landlord is unable to prove that the claimed expense was incurred.

Where an application only relates to operating costs, a landlord must also be prepared to comply with the disclosure requirements of Rule 19.2 of the Board's Rules of Practice. That rule provides that a landlord who files an AGI must be prepared to disclose at the hearing, the rent for each unit in the complex, the date the rent was established for a new tenant and the date the rent was last increased for existing tenants.

Also, subsection 126(4) of the RTA provides that where an application includes a claim for capital expenditures, the landlord must make information that accompanies the application available to the tenants of the residential complex in accordance with the prescribed rules. Section 23 of O. Reg. 516/06 sets out the following rules related to the material referred to under subsections 22(1) and (2):

1. On the request of a tenant subject to the application, the landlord shall provide the tenant with a compact disc containing the material provided to the Board in PDF for a charge of not more than five dollars;

2. Instead of option one, the landlord and the tenant may agree that the landlord will provide the tenant with either a photocopy of the material for no more than the landlord's reasonable out-of-pocket costs for the photocopying or an email of the material in PDF, at no charge to the tenant;

3. Despite option one, if a landlord has not provided the Board with a compact disc, the landlord must, on the tenant's request, provide the tenant with a photocopy of the material provided for a charge of not more than five dollars;

4. If the landlord has an office in or close to the residential complex, the landlord must, during normal business hours and at no charge, make a photocopy of the material provided available for viewing by tenants subject to the application; and

5. The landlord must, in the application, inform every tenant subject to the application of the ways in which a tenant may obtain access under this section to the material.

WRITTEN OR ORAL HEARING

Pursuant to section 184 of the RTA, the Board generally schedules AGI applications for an oral hearing. However, section 5.1 of the Statutory Powers Procedure Act (the "SPPA") provides authority for tribunals to hold written hearings where the tribunal has made rules regarding written hearings. Rule 22 of the Board's Rules of Practice sets out the Board's procedure for written hearings.

ADJOURNMENTS

Section 21 of the SPPA gives the Board the jurisdiction to adjourn hearings, where it is shown that an adjournment is required to permit an adequate hearing to be held. Further guidance with respect to adjournments is pertained in Guideline #1.

As with all other applications, it is expected that applicants will be ready to proceed with the hearing on the date that is set for the AGI hearing and that respondents, properly served, will also be prepared to proceed.

The most common reasons given by parties requesting adjournments in AGI applications are that the landlord requires additional time to file documents or that the tenants require additional time to prepare for the hearing. Since section 22 of O. Reg. 516/06 requires the applicant to file all documentary evidence with the application, a hearing will not normally be adjourned in order to allow these documents to be filed. Instead, the hearing will proceed but the landlord will not be permitted to rely on the documents that were not properly filed.

Similarly, since landlords are required by Rule 10.4 to serve the notice of hearing in an AGI application at least 30 days before the date of the hearing, it is expected that tenants will have ample time to prepare for the hearing and to retain a representative. Hearings will therefore not be adjourned where tenants have not made reasonable efforts to take advantage of the time that they have had.

The Board reserves a substantial amount of hearing time for AGI applications. This resource of the Board cannot be recovered if the hearing is adjourned. Often, AGI applications involve a large number of tenants who may be inconvenienced if required to attend more than once. These factors will be considered when parties request adjournments.

In addition, a landlord seeking to file documents that should have been filed with the application, must seek leave to extend the time requirement for filing. The Member will consider the factors set out in Rule 15.6 in making that decision. Leave will not be granted where the reason for failure to file on time is purely neglect on the part of the applicant.

MEDIATION AND CONSENT ORDERS

As with all other applications, the Board encourages parties to AGI applications to settle the application with the assistance of one of the Board's mediators. The outcome of mediation can be 1) a mediated agreement, or 2) a consent order.

Where an AGI application is resolved by a mediated agreement and the application is with regard to a rental unit that is not a mobile home or a land lease home or a site for either, subsection 194(3) of the RTA limits the increase to an amount equal to the sum of the guideline plus 3% of the previous year's lawful rent.

It is clear that if all of the parties are in attendance and they negotiate a settlement that results in a consent order, in the absence of circumstances that render the agreement invalid, such as fraud, duress or misrepresentation, they are bound by the order. This applies even though the order is not the one that would have been made, had there been a hearing[53].

Where all of the tenants are not in attendance at the hearing, the approach of the Board is to presume that the tenants not in attendance admit the facts supported in the application. Therefore, where the application is properly filed, the tenants in attendance at the hearing and the landlord may agree to a consent order for an increase that is not greater than the evidence filed with the application would support.

An order issued on consent permitting a rent increase must specify the percentage increase that is attributed to an extraordinary increase or a capital expenditure. In the case of a rent increase due to capital expenditures the Board order must also include a date on which the rent decrease will take effect if the tenant continues to occupy the rental unit. In the case of an extraordinary increase in the costs for utilities the order must set out the adjusted base year utilities costs pursuant to subsection 29(4) of O.Reg. 516/06. These requirements flow from sections 128 and 129 of the RTA, which require that the landlord decrease the rent due to decreases in the costs of utilities and/or the elapse of the amortization period for capital expenditures, by the percentage increase allowed in the Board order.

ISSUES AT THE HEARING

(a) Taxes and Utilities

Paragraph 1 of subsection 126(1) of the RTA allows landlords to apply for an increase above the guideline if they experienced an extraordinary increase in the cost for municipal taxes and charges or utilities, or both, for the whole residential complex or any building in which the rental units are located.

Subsection 126(2) of the RTA provides that "extraordinary increase" means an extraordinary increase as defined by or determined in accordance with the regulations. Section 28 of O. Reg. 516/06 provides that an increase in the cost of municipal taxes and charges or utilities is extraordinary if it is greater than the guideline plus 50 per

---

[53] See the decisions of the Divisional Court in *Torgis v. Brajovic* (January 14, 2002) Brampton Divisional Court File No. 01-BN-2696, *Carlson v. Kaneff Properties* (January 14, 2002) Toronto Divisional Court File No. 176/01 [2002] O.J. No. 361, and *Berbatovci v. Crescent Village* (July 25, 2002) Toronto Divisional Court File No. 428/02.

cent of the guideline. The Board will use the guideline for the calendar year in which the FED for the application falls. If the guideline is less than zero, any increase in the cost of municipal taxes and charges or utilities is deemed to be extraordinary.

A landlord may choose to apply for either municipal taxes and charges or utilities, or both. If the application is for only one category, the costs for the other category are not relevant. The allowance to be included in the total justified rent increase will be determined according to the rules set out in section 29 of O. Reg. 516/06.

Section 29 of O. Reg. 516/06 allows landlords to apply for an AGI based on an increase in municipal taxes and charges as a result of an appeal of a tax assessment.

Municipal taxes and charges are defined under section 2 of the RTA and section 41 of O. Reg. 516/06. Municipal taxes and charges include:

- taxes charged to a landlord by the municipality (which include education taxes levied under Division B of Part IX of the Education Act);
- charges levied on a landlord by the municipality; and
- taxes levied on a landlord's property in unorganized territory.

However, municipal taxes and charges do not include the following:

- charges for inspections done by a municipality related to an alleged breach of a health, safety, housing or maintenance standard;
- charges for emergency repairs carried out by a municipality;
- charges for work in the nature of a capital expenditure carried out by a municipality;
- charges for services, work or non-emergency repairs performed by a municipality related to the landlord's non-compliance with a by-law;
- penalties, interest, late payment fees and fines;
- any amount spent by a municipality to arrange for vital service for a rental unit in accordance with a vital service by-law plus an administrative fee of 10 per cent of that amount; or
- any other prescribed charges under section 41 of O. Reg. 516/06.

Utilities are defined in section 1 of the RTA. They are heat, electricity and water. A landlord making a claim for an AGI based on an increase in the cost of utilities must provide the cost for each of these three utility sub-categories. As a result, a decrease in cost in one sub-category will offset an increase in another sub-category. Where the landlord fails to prove the costs in all categories, the application with regard to utilities will be dismissed.

Tenants have argued that, where a landlord experiences a temporary increase in the cost of utilities, and then there is a decrease in the following year, an order based on the increase should be denied because the result is a windfall to the landlord, since the increase, once granted, is never removed from the rent. It was argued that the Ontario Rental Housing Tribunal had the jurisdiction to take this approach based on the "real substance" of the transaction, as is required by section 188 of the Tenant Protection Act, 1997.

The Divisional Court addressed this position in its decision in *Scott Burton et al v. Leadway Apartments Ltd.*,[54] which they examined section 188 of the Tenant Protection Act, 1997 that contained similar wording to section 202 of the RTA. The Court ruled that the Ontario Rental Housing Tribunal did not have the jurisdiction to depart from the regulations in deciding this issue. The Court of Appeal subsequently denied a motion for leave to appeal that Divisional Court decision.

However, the RTA addresses situations where the cost of a utility decreases in the years following the increase order under section 126. For information on rent decreases due to decreases in utility costs see section 128 and sections 35 -37 of O. Reg. 516/06 which address rent reductions due to utility cost decreases. Such a decrease has sometimes been referred to as "costs no longer borne".

(b) Security Services

Paragraph 3 of subsection 126(1) of the RTA allows landlords to apply for an AGI based on operating costs related to security services provided in respect of the residential complex or any building in which the rental units are located. Eligible costs, however, only include services provided by persons who are not the landlord's employees. The allowance will be determined according to the rules set out in section 30 of O. Reg. 516/06.

For the application to be allowed the landlord must prove either an increase from the Reference Year to the Base Year (see subsection (c) below) or costs incurred in this category for a new service. The service must also have been provided by persons not employed by the landlord. For example, if the superintendent provides this service in addition to his/her regular duties and responsibilities, any increases in costs will not be allowed.

(c) Accounting periods for AGI Applications based on Utilities and Security Services

When landlords file AGI application based on operating costs for utilities or security services, they are required to provide the costs for the prescribed accounting periods. Section 19 of O. Reg. 516/06 sets out the accounting periods to be used for calculating an allowance for operating costs for utilities or security services. The accounting periods include a Base Year (BY) and a Reference Year (RY). The BY for operating costs for utilities or security services is the most recently completed 12-month period chosen by the landlord that ends 90 days before the effective date of the first intended rent increase (FED) applied for. The RY is the 12-month period immediately preceding the BY. If the landlord claims an extraordinary increase in the cost of utilities and security services, the accounting periods chosen for utilities must be the same as those chosen for operating costs for security services.

Where there is a prior RTA order that allowed an AGI due to an extraordinary increase in the cost of utilities or operating costs for security services, subsection 19(2) of O.

---

[54] (August 26, 2002, Toronto Divisional Court File No. 86/02)

Reg.516/06 requires that the BY for a subsequent AGI application start and end on the same days as the BY in the prior order. This rule applies even if a new landlord has purchased the residential complex, or the landlord has switched the FED in the subsequent application to a different month of the year.

(d) Capital Expenditures

Paragraph 2 of subsection 126(1) of the RTA allows landlords to apply for an AGI if they incurred eligible capital expenditures respecting the residential complex or one of the rental units in it. The amount of a capital expenditure item and the allowance will be determined according to the rules set out in sections 16 and 27 of O. Reg. 516/06.

What May be Allowed as a Capital Expenditure in an AGI Application:

In order for a capital expenditure to be allowed in an AGI application,

- it must be eligible,
- it must meet the definition set out in the regulations,
- it must have been incurred by the landlord at the time the application is filed, and
- it must have been completed within the prescribed time.

Non-Arms Length Transactions:

If a landlord incurs costs that arise from a transaction that involves related persons this would be considered by the Board as a non- arm's length transaction. In such a situation, the Board will only consider that part of the landlord's cost that is less than or equal to the cost that would arise from a similar market transaction. Section 25 of O. Reg. 516/06 defines what constitutes non- arm's length transactions.

Definition of Capital Expenditure:

Section 18 of O. Reg. 516/06 provides that capital expenditure means:

an expenditure for an extraordinary or significant renovation, repair, replacement or new addition, the expected benefit of which extends for at least five years including,

(a) an expenditure with respect to a leased asset if the lease qualifies, and

(b) an expenditure that the landlord is required to pay on work undertaken by a municipality, local board or public utility, other than work undertaken because of the landlord's failure to do it

but, does not include,

(c) routine or ordinary work undertaken on a regular basis or undertaken to maintain a capital asset in its operating state, such as cleaning and janitorial services, elevator servicing, general building maintenance, grounds-keeping and appliance repairs, or

(d) work that is substantially cosmetic in nature or is designed to enhance the level of prestige or luxury offered by a unit or residential complex

The Board will consider all of the circumstances, including the size of the complex, the nature of the work, its effect on and importance to the unit or complex, and the amount of the expenditure when determining if the expenditure is extraordinary or significant.

The period of the expected benefit is determined as of the time that the expenditure is incurred. Therefore, if a landlord incurs an expenditure on an item that is expected to last more than five years but the item does not, the landlord is not disqualified from recovery of the expenditure, for this reason alone.

Subsection 126(7) of the RTA provides that subject to subsection 126(8) and (9), a capital expenditure is an eligible capital expenditure for the purposes of this section if,

- it is necessary to protect or restore the physical integrity of the residential complex or part of it;
- it is necessary to comply with subsection 20(1) or clauses 161(a) to (e);
- it is necessary to maintain the provision of a plumbing, heating, mechanical, electrical, ventilation or air conditioning system;
- it provides access for persons with disabilities;
- it promotes energy or water conservation; or
- it maintains or improves the security of the residential complex or part of it.

These terms set out in subsection 126(7) of the RTA are not defined in the Act or the regulations, with the exception of "physical integrity". According to subsection 18(1) of O. Reg. 516/06, physical integrity means the integrity of all parts of a structure, including the foundation, that support loads or that provide a weather envelope and includes, without restricting the generality of the foregoing, the integrity of:

- the roof, exterior walls, exterior doors and exterior windows;
- elements adjacent to the structure that contribute to the weather envelope of the structure; and
- columns, walls and floors that support loads.

Subsection 126(8) provides that a capital expenditure to replace a system or thing is not an eligible capital expenditure for the purposes of this section if the system or thing that was replaced did not require major repair or replacement, unless the replacement of the system or thing promotes,

- access for persons with disabilities;
- energy or water conservation; or
- security of the residential complex or part of it.

Subsection 126(9) provides that a capital expenditure is not an eligible capital expenditure with respect to a rental unit for the purposes of this section if a new tenant entered into a new tenancy agreement in respect of the rental unit and the new tenancy agreement took effect after the capital expenditure was completed.

Work Undertaken by a Municipality, Local Board Or Public Utility:

According to paragraph (b) of subsection 18(1) of O. Reg. 516/06, if a landlord is obligated to pay for capital work undertaken by a municipality, local board or a public utility, the expenditure also qualifies as a capital expenditure (unless the work is undertaken because of the landlord's failure to do it).

For example, a municipality may upgrade the sewer system and require a landlord to pay for the service improvement by a special levy on the municipal tax bill. The landlord can claim the upgraded sewer system as a capital expenditure. The special levy charged by the municipality will be the costs incurred by the landlord.

If a municipality charges a landlord the costs for certain capital work because the landlord failed to do it, the work does not qualify as a capital expenditure. For example, a municipality issued a work order requiring a landlord to make repairs to the balconies of an apartment building because they were unsafe. The landlord failed to do the repairs. The municipality did them and charged the landlord the costs in the municipal tax bill. This work cannot be considered as a capital expenditure.

Had the landlord done the work as a result of a work order, the fact that a work order had been issued does not remove the work from the definition of a capital expenditure.

Leased Assets:

According to subsection 18(2) of O. Reg. 516/06, an expenditure on an item that is leased also qualifies as a capital expenditure if substantially all the risks and benefits associated with the leased asset are passed to the lessee and, at the commencement of the lease, any one or more of the following four conditions are met:

1. The lease provides that the ownership of the asset will pass to the lessee at or before the expiry of the lease;

2. The lease provides that the lessee has an option to purchase the asset when the term expires, at a price that is less than what the market value of the asset will be at that time;

3. The term of the lease is at least 75% of the useful life of the asset as determined in accordance with section 27 O. Reg. 516/06, but without regard to any part of section 27 that prevents the useful life from being determined to be less than 10 years; or

4. The net present value of the minimum lease payments is at least 90% of the asset's fair market value at the commencement of the lease.

According to paragraph 4 of subsection of section 18(2) of O. Reg.516/06, the net present value is determined using the interest rate fixed by section 20 of O. Reg. 516/06. The rate is the chartered bank administered conventional five-year mortgage interest rate on the last Wednesday of the month before the month in which the application is filed, as reported by the Bank of Canada.

Capital Expenditures that are "Incurred" and "Completed":

In addition to meeting the definition of capital expenditures, the items claimed must have been incurred by the landlord at the time the application is filed and they must have been completed during the specific time period required by the regulations.

Subsection 126(1), paragraph 2 of the RTA allows a landlord to apply for a capital expenditure that they (and/or the previous landlord) have incurred.

"Incurred" is defined in section 18 of O. Reg. 516/06. It means that payment in full of the amount of the capital expenditure, other than any hold back that is required under the Construction Lien Act, must have been made by the time the application is filed. If a capital expenditure relates to a lease, "incurred" means the assumption of the obligations under the lease. If an expenditure relates to work undertaken by a municipality, local board or public utility, "incurred" means that the work is completed.

In order for a capital expenditure item to be allowed, paragraph 2 of subsection 26 of O. Reg. 516/06 requires that the work must have been completed during the 18 month period that ends 90 days before the FED.

There are instances in which a project takes more than 18 months to complete. Since a landlord cannot apply before the project is completed and it would be unreasonable to conclude that the intention of the regulation was to exclude recovery for such projects, the Board will allow recovery, provided that the project was completed within the prescribed period. However, this approach does not allow a landlord who has undertaken several projects with regard to similar work, over an extended period, to recover for all of the projects in one application. For example, a landlord who repairs one part of a roof five years ago, does another repair three years ago and another within the last six months, will not be able to recover all that was spent in one application, on the theory that the work of repairing the roof was completed six months ago.

The Amount of a Capital Expenditure:

If an item qualifies as a capital expenditure, the Member must determine the amount to be allowed when calculating the allowance. Subsections 26(5) of O. Reg. 516/06 specify that the amount for a capital expenditure is calculated by totaling:

A. the purchase price, cost of leased assets, and the installation, renovation and construction costs, and

B. the value of the landlord's own labour,

less:

C. any grant or other assistance from a federal, provincial or municipal government or insurance, salvage, resale or trade-in proceeds.

Landlord's Own Labour:

The value of the landlord's own labour in carrying out the work related to a capital expenditure may be recognized when determining the amount of the capital expenditure item. Subsections 26(3) of O. Reg. 516/06 provides that the value of the landlord's own labour should be calculated by multiplying the amount of time the landlord spent by a reasonable rate of pay based on their experience and skill in the type of work done.

If the amount of time they spent is more than what is reasonable based on their experience and skill, the Board will allow the reasonable amount of time. The Board will only allow the value of the landlord's own labour that does not exceed what a skilled tradesperson would charge. The value of the landlord's own labour does not include any amount relating to the management and administration of the capital work.

This type of cost will normally only be recovered by landlords who are individuals and not by corporations whose employees or agents do work at the complex.

Government Loans and Grants:

If a landlord received financial assistance from the federal, provincial or municipal government, the appropriate amount of the grant or forgivable loan must be subtracted from the purchase price, installation, renovation and, construction costs of each affected capital expenditure item.

Revenue From Insurance, Salvage, Resale Or Trade-in:

In addition to government assistance, the landlord must also provide information regarding any revenue received from insurance, salvage, resale or trade-in proceeds. The amount of a capital expenditure must be reduced by the amount reported under these categories.

Useful Life:

According to subsection 27(1) of O. Reg. 516/06, the useful life of a capital expenditure item is determined from the prescribed Schedule subject to the following rules:

1. where the useful life set out in Column 2 of the Schedule is less than 10 years, the useful life of work done or a thing purchased shall be deemed to be 10 years;

2. where a thing is purchased and has previously been used, the useful life of the thing shall be determined taking in to account the length of time of that previous use;

3. if the work done or thing purchased does not appear in the Schedule, the useful life of the work or thing shall be determined with reference to items with similar characteristics that do appear in the Schedule; and

4. despite paragraphs 2 and 3 above, for the purposes of making a finding under this section, the useful life of work done or a thing purchased shall not be determined to be less than 10 years.

Subsection 27(2) further states that if the useful life of work done or a thing purchased cannot be determined under subsection 27(1) because the work or thing does not appear in the Schedule and no item with similar characteristics appears in the Schedule, the useful life of the work or thing shall be what is generally accepted as the useful life of such work or thing but in no case shall the useful life be determined to be less than 10 years.

Section 129 of the RTA provides that if the tenant continues to occupy the rental unit, the landlord will reduce the rent on the date and by the percentage increase that is attributed to the capital expenditure in the Board order. Section 38 of O. Reg. 516/06 provides the rules for calculating the date for the time the rent decrease can take place. The landlord will reduce the rent on the date and by the percentage increase that is attributed to the capital expenditure in the Board order.

ALLOCATION OF COSTS

If the amount of a capital expenditure or operating cost involves non-residential components or other residential complexes and/or the AGI application covers only some of the units in the complex, the Member will allocate the amount so that only the portion of the amount that is applicable to the units covered by the application is allowed.

Section 24 of O. Reg. 516/06 prescribes the rules for allocating operating costs and/or capital expenditures to the residential complex, if the costs also relate to non-residential components in the complex or other residential complexes. According to subsection 24(2) of O. Reg. 516/06, costs can be allocated based on one or more of these factors:

- the area (i.e. square footage) of the complex;
- the market value of the complex; or
- the revenue generated in the complex.

The usual approach is to allocate based on square footage. This is because, in the usual case, an expenditure will benefit all parts of a complex equally. If the allocation of costs would be unreasonable using any of these methods, the costs should be allocated in reasonable proportions according to how much of the costs and expenditures are attributable to the residential components in the complex or the residential complex. This is set out in subsection 24(3) of O. Reg. 516/06.

The decision on allocation is made with regard to each expenditure. It is therefore possible that different methods may be chosen when allocating different cost categories. Landlords are required to indicate in the application form which method(s) they have chosen to allocate the costs between residential and non-residential (or other residential) components. However, the Board may choose a different method found to be more reasonable.

A cost category may affect some or all of the units covered by the application. The Member will allocate the cost and allowance for a cost category if:

- the AGI application covers only some of the units in the complex; and

- the cost category affects units not covered by the application.

In this case, the Board must adjust the cost and allowance so that only the part of the cost and allowance that is applicable to the units covered by the application will be passed on to those units. Landlords are required to provide information in the application about which cost categories affect which units, and information about which units are covered by the application. However, the Board is not bound by this information and will allocate the cost based on a finding as to which units benefit from the expenditure.

The applicable costs and allowances are calculated by multiplying the total costs or allowances by an allocation factor. If an operating cost category affects units not covered by the application, the allocation factor is set out in subsection 21(1) of O. Reg. 516/06. The formula is:

$$\text{Allocation Factor} = \frac{\text{Total rents for rental units subject to the application \& affected by the operating cost category}}{\text{Total rents for rental units affected by the application}}$$

For the purpose of subsection 21(1) of O. Reg. 516/06, the rent for the rental unit that is vacant or not rented is deemed to be the average rent charged for the rental units in the residential complex.

The allowances for capital expenditure are calculated on a unit by unit basis. The method for calculating the allowance is determined under subsection 26(6) of O. Reg. 516/06 and the allowance for the unit for each capital expenditure takes into account the fact that the capital expenditure may not affect all rental units in the complex.

Release date: July 5, 2007

INTERPRETATION GUIDELINE 15 — AMENDING AN ORDER

Interpretation Guidelines are intended to assist the parties in understanding the Board's usual interpretation of the law, to provide guidance to Members and promote consistency in decision-making. However, a Member is not required to follow a Guideline and may make a different decision depending on the facts of the case.

The Board's authority to amend an order comes from section 21.1 of the *Statutory Powers Procedure Act*. It gives the Board authority to correct "a typographical error, error of calculation or similar error made in its order or decision." These are referred to as clerical errors.

The procedure for dealing with a request to amend an order can be found in Rule 28 of the Board's Rules of Practice.

WHAT IS A CLERICAL ERROR?

A clerical error may be a Board error, or an error made by a party in documentation submitted to the Board that ends up being transcribed into an order or decision. A clerical error may include any of the following:

- An incorrect name or address. For example, if the name or address is incorrect on the order but correct on the application, the error is likely clerical. If the name or address is incorrect on the application but the respondent received it and had an opportunity to participate in the proceeding, the error is likely clerical.
- An incorrect date. The order sets a date for doing something that is impossible to comply with or is not what the Member intended.
- An incorrect amount. The Member made an arithmetic error or misplaced a decimal point.
- An omission. The member inadvertently failed to include an essential term or condition in the order.

An error is not clerical if, for example:

- The name or address on the application is incorrect and the respondent may not have received the application.
- The error is brought to light by new evidence, or by evidence that was presented at the hearing but overlooked.
- The member has changed his or her mind on an issue.
- The error is a serious error.

DETERMINING CLERICAL ERROR

A party may request that an order be amended to correct a clerical error. The Member who issued the order will consider the request to amend unless the Member is on an extended absence: Rule 28.5. If the Member is on an extended absence, the Vice Chair will consider the request to amend: Rule 28.6.

Considering the Request to Amend

The Member should review the request to amend and dispose of it in accordance with Rule 28.7. In considering the request to amend:

- If the Member determines there is no clerical error, the Member will send a letter to the party who made the request informing the party that the request has been denied.

- If the Member determines there is an obvious clerical error that should be corrected, and the amendment will not cause prejudice to the other party, the Member may decide to amend the order without seeking submissions.

- The Member can also make any consequential amendments without seeking submissions.

- Where a party may be prejudiced by the amendment, the Member should invite submissions or hold a hearing in accordance with Rule 28.7.

Seeking Submissions

Submissions may be requested by way of a direction letter to the parties. The direction letter should:

- inform the other party that a request to amend the order has been received, and enclose the request;

- direct the parties to make submissions to the Board within a prescribed time. Generally a period of 10 to 15 days will be sufficient.

Where submissions are received, the Member may make a decision based solely on the submissions and the request to amend and without holding a hearing. If the request to amend is denied without holding a hearing, a denial letter should be sent to the parties.

Holding a Hearing

The Member may hold a hearing to determine if the order contains a clerical error. If the request to amend is denied after holding a hearing, an order will be issued explaining why the request to amend has been denied. If the request to amend is granted, an amended order will be issued.

AMENDING THE ORDER

If the Member determines that there is a clerical error in the order or decision and that it should be amended, an amended order will be issued that explains why the order is being changed and what the changes are, including any consequential amendments.

OTHER CONSIDERATIONS

Consequential Amendments

An amendment to one part of the order may require an amendment to another part. In some cases, it may also be necessary to "update" the order to reflect any amounts that have been paid or have become owing since the original order was issued.

Stays

A party may ask that the order be stayed until a decision is made. The request should explain the prejudice that a party will suffer if the order is not stayed until a decision is made.

A Member may decide to issue a stay of the original order, whether or not it was requested and without seeking submissions or holding a hearing.

A stay will not always be necessary. However, where the request to amend concerns an alleged error in an eviction order, and the Member determines that it may be necessary to seek submissions or hold a hearing, a stay will generally be issued. A stay may also be issued if the request to amend is received close to the effective date of the order, and the Member needs time to consider the request before making a decision.

The stay will be issued in the form of an interim order. If the request to amend is denied and the order is not amended, an order must be issued lifting the stay. If the request to amend is granted and order is amended, the stay must be lifted in the amended order.

Serious Errors

A member cannot amend an order to correct a serious error. A serious error can only be corrected by way of review under Rule 29 and Guideline 8.

If the Member determines that the order may contain a serious error, the Member may: a) deny the request to amend if the order does not contain a clerical error; or b) in exceptional cases, refer the matter to the Vice Chair who can initiate a review of the order.

Released Date: January 31, 2007

INTERPRETATION GUIDELINE 16 — ADMINISTRATIVE FINES

Interpretation Guidelines are intended to assist the parties in understanding the Board's usual interpretation of the law, to provide guidance to Members and promote consistency in decision-making. However, a Member is not required to follow a Guideline and may make a different decision depending on the facts of the case.

Purpose of a Fine

An administrative fine is a remedy to be used by the Board to encourage compliance with the *Residential Tenancies Act, 2006* (the "RTA"), and to deter landlords from engaging in similar activity in the future. This remedy is not normally imposed unless a landlord has shown a blatant disregard for the RTA and other remedies will not provide adequate deterrence and compliance. If an abatement of rent will provide an adequate remedy, an administrative fine may not be necessary.

An administrative fine should not be confused with costs. Administrative fines are payable to the Minister of Finance and not to a party. Costs may be ordered where a party's conduct in the proceeding before the Board was unreasonable and may be ordered payable to a party or to the Board. See Guideline 3, Costs, for details.

When can a Fine be Levied

A fine may be ordered in relation to the activities set out under:

- subsection 29(1), paragraphs 2 to 6 of the RTA relating to tenant applications alleging that the landlord, superintendent or agent of the landlord has:
    - withheld the reasonable supply of any vital service, care service or food that it is the landlord's obligation to supply under the tenancy agreement or deliberately interfered with the reasonable supply of any vital service, care service or food;
    - substantially interfered with the reasonable enjoyment of the rental unit or residential complex for all usual purposes by the tenant or a member of their household;
    - harassed, obstructed, coerced, threatened or interfered with the tenant during the tenant's occupancy of the rental unit;
    - altered the locking system on a door giving entry to the rental unit or the residential complex or caused the locking system to be altered during the tenant's occupancy of the rental unit without giving the tenant replacement keys; or
    - illegally entered the rental unit.
- subsection 41(2) and (3) where the landlord has breached an obligation:

- to not sell, retain or otherwise dispose of the tenant's property before 72 hours have elapsed after the enforcement of the eviction order; or,

- to make an evicted tenant's property available to be retrieved at a location close to the rental unit during the prescribed hours within the 72 hours after the enforcement of an eviction order.

• subsection 57(1), clause (a) to (c) relating to a former tenant's application alleging that:

- The landlord gave a notice of termination for personal use in bad faith, the former tenant moved out as a result of the notice or as a result of an application to or order made by the Board based on the notice and no person referred to in clause 48(1) (a), (b), (c), or (d) occupied the rental unit within a reasonable time after the former tenant vacated the rental unit;

- The landlord gave a notice of termination for personal use by the purchaser in bad faith, the former tenant moved out as a result of the notice or as a result of an application to or order made by the Board based on the notice and no person referred to in clause 49(1) (a), (b), (c), or (d) or 49(2) (a), (b), (c), or (d) occupied the rental unit within a reasonable time after the former tenant vacated the rental unit; or

- The landlord gave a notice of termination to demolish, convert, or to do extensive repairs or renovations in bad faith, the former tenant moved out as a result of the notice or as a result of an application to or order made by the Board based on the notice and the landlord did not demolish, convert, or repair or renovate the rental unit within a reasonable time after the former tenant vacated the rental unit.

• section 114 where the landlord has failed to give a new tenant written notice about the lawful rent for the rental unit where an order under paragraph 6, 7 or 8 of subsection 30(1) is in effect and the new tenant has made an application under subsection 115(1) to determine lawful rent or requiring the landlord to rebate rent paid in excess of any rent that may be lawfully charged.

The Board's authority to order an administrative fine in these circumstances is set out in the RTA under section 31(1)(d), 41(6), 57(3) paragraph 3, and 115(3) respectively.

Notice of Fine

Where a tenant requests a fine in an application, this will serve as notice to the landlord that a fine may be ordered. A Member may however, after hearing the evidence, consider ordering a fine even though it has not been requested. In either situation, the Member must give the parties an opportunity to make submissions on the issue.

Ordering a Fine

A Member may impose a conditional fine in an interim order to encourage compliance with the RTA. For example, a Member may order a fine for each day that the landlord fails to comply with a term or condition in the interim order, such as putting an illegally evicted tenant back into possession. The interim order should state precisely what the landlord is required to do and the consequences of failing to comply. The total amount of the fine, if any, should be set out in the final order based on the relevant circumstances as discussed at the hearing.

Where a landlord has committed several breaches, the Member need not order a separate fine for each breach. Rather, the Member may order one fine based on the overall pattern of activities alleged in the application.

In setting the amount of the fine, the Member may consider:

- the nature and severity of the breach
- the effect of the breach on the tenant
- any other relevant factors.

The amount of the fine should be commensurate with the breach.

Failure to Pay a Fine

Under section 196 of the RTA, where the Board receives information that an applicant owes money to the Board as a result of failing to pay any fine, fee or costs, the Board may, pursuant to its Rules:

- refuse to allow an application to be filed where such information is received on or before the day the application is submitted,
- stay or discontinue a proceeding where such information is received after the application has been filed but before a hearing is held,
- or delay issuing an order or discontinue the application where such information is received after a hearing of the application has begun.

See Rule 9, Refusing to Accept or Proceed with an Application, for details.

Amended December 08, 2008

INTERPRETATION GUIDELINE 17 — HUMAN RIGHTS GUIDELINE

Interpretation Guidelines are intended to assist the parties in understanding the Board's usual interpretation of the law, to provide guidance to Members and promote consistency in decision-making. However, a Member is not required to follow a Guideline and may make a different decision depending on the facts of the case.

Introduction

The Ontario *Human Rights Code*[55] (the "Code") is the primary source for human rights law at tribunals such as the Landlord and Tenant Board (the Board). By reason of subsection 47(1) of the Code, the Code applies to the Board as a provider of services and facilities. This means every person has the right to equal treatment, without discrimination, with respect to Board services and facilities, pursuant to section 1 of the Code. Although the Board's services and facilities are designed to be accessible, some persons may require additional accommodation from the Board in order to access its services and facilities.

The Board must interpret the *Residential Tenancies Act, 2006*[56] (the "RTA") in light of the Code. In *Walmer Developments v. Wolch*, the Divisional Court held that ". . .the Code is the law of Ontario and its provisions must inform any Ontario decision maker in its deliberations."[57] This means the Board must consider and apply the Code when, for instance, exercising its authority to delay or refuse an eviction, and determining, whether the landlord has accommodated the tenant to the point of undue hardship. The Code may also apply to certain applications filed by tenants against landlords.

According to subsection 47(2) of the Code, the Code is paramount over all other provincial laws, including the RTA. This is consistent with subsection 3(4) of the RTA which states that if a provision of the RTA conflicts with a provision of another law, other than the Code, the provision of the RTA applies. The Supreme Court of Canada has confirmed that an administrative tribunal such as the Board has authority to find that a provision of an Act does not apply if it conflicts with the Code.[58]

This Guideline addresses the following types of Code issues that may arise in Board proceedings:

1. A person requires accommodation from the Board in order to access the Board's services and participate in the Board's proceedings;

2. A tenant asserts that the Member should grant relief from eviction because they are covered by one or more of the categories in subsection 2(1)

---

[55] *Human Rights Code*, R.S.O. 1990, c.H-19, as amended

[56] *Residential Tenancies Act*, S.O. 2006, c. 17

[57] 2003 CanLII 42163 (ON S.C.D.C.), para. 18

[58] *Tranchemontagne v. Ontario (Director, Disability Support Program)* 2006 CanLII 14 (S.C.C.)

of the Code, such as disability, and the landlord has not accommodated them to the point of undue hardship;

3. A tenant asserts in a tenant's application that the landlord has contravened the Code; and

4. A party asserts that a provision of the RTA conflicts with the Code.

Code issues not considered by the Board

Some Code issues cannot be considered by the Board because the RTA does not apply to the situation. For instance, a person alleging that a landlord refused to provide them with a rental unit based on a Code ground of discrimination should contact the Human Rights Tribunal of Ontario. The Board has no jurisdiction to deal with such matters unless the person has paid a rent deposit and the landlord does not provide vacant possession of the rental unit, or return the rent deposit, in accordance with section 107 of the RTA.

1. Accommodation in a Board proceeding

According to section 1 of the Code, the Board is required to accommodate the needs of all persons who use the Board's services. Section 1 provides that every person has a right to equal treatment with respect to services without discrimination because of race, ancestry, place of origin, colour, ethnic origin, citizenship, creed (religion), sex (including pregnancy, gender identity), sexual orientation, age, marital status, family status or disability. Disability is defined by subsection 10(1) of the Code to include both physical conditions and mental disorders.

Section 183 of the RTA states that the Board shall adopt the most expeditious method of determining the questions arising in a proceeding that provides all persons directly affected an adequate opportunity to know the issues and be heard on the matter. Although the Board's services and hearings are designed to be accessible to as many people as possible, some persons covered under section 1 of the Code may require additional accommodation from the Board in order to have an adequate opportunity to know the issues and be heard on the matter.

a. Where a party requests accommodation

Parties seeking accommodation should make their needs known to Board staff as soon as possible, preferably in writing, so that the necessary arrangements can be made.

The party must participate in the accommodation process by working with the Board so that the appropriate accommodation can be implemented. Accommodation must be provided in a manner that respects dignity and allows the party to participate in the Board's process. More information about the Board's policy on accommodation, and how to request accommodation, can be found in the Board's *Human Rights Policy* **[policy currently under development]**.

In many cases, the needs of parties covered by section 1 of the Code can be accommodated with relatively minor changes to the Board's standard hearing procedures. For example, a party, witness or representative:

- with a physical disability may have difficulty bringing their evidence forward to the Member and require the assistance of security personnel;

- with a speech or hearing impairment may need all parties to speak slowly and loudly, or have the chairs in the hearing room positioned to enable lip reading;

- with a visual impairment may require the use of assistive devices;

- with diabetes may be permitted to consume juice or food in the hearing room as needed;

- with cognitive impairments may require multiple breaks during the hearing, a longer than usual scheduled hearing, a late or early start time for the hearing, additional time to present their evidence, or adjournments;

- with a disability relating to mental illness may need a support person (such as a social worker or family member) to sit with them during the hearing;

- may request that a hearing not be scheduled on a particular day because it is a religious holy day for that individual; or

- may be provided with an opportunity to consult with on-site Tenant Duty Counsel where available before proceeding with the hearing (applies to tenants only).

If, on the day of the hearing, a party believes that they do not have an adequate opportunity to participate in the proceeding and require accommodation, they should bring their concerns to the attention of the presiding Member as soon as possible during the hearing. Depending upon the circumstances, the Member may require the party to provide sufficient evidence to establish that they are covered under section 1 of the Code and need accommodation. The Member must be respectful of the party's privacy interests and should not require the party to disclose more information than is needed to make the necessary determination respecting the issue of accommodation.

If the party requesting accommodation is disclosing intimate personal information, the Member may consider excluding the public from the hearing room under Rule 24 of the Board's Rules of Practice, "Restricting Public Access to the Hearing" and section 9 of the *Statutory Powers Procedure Act*. However, the other parties to the application are entitled to remain in the hearing room, examine all of the evidence submitted to the Board, conduct cross-examination and make submissions solely with regard to the issue of accommodation as it relates to the Board's hearing procedures.

The nature and extent of any accommodation is determined by the Member on a case-by-case basis upon consideration of the evidence and submissions made by all of the parties. However, even if one party objects to the requested accommodation, the Member is still obliged to provide the accommodation necessary to permit the party to participate in the hearing.

If the party cannot be adequately accommodated at the hearing, the Member will generally grant an adjournment and liaise with Board staff to ensure that the necessary accommodation will be in place for the next hearing date.

b. Accommodation issues arising during a hearing

Members must be attentive to indications which suggest a party may require accommodation in order to participate in the hearing, even if the party does not request any accommodation from the Board. Pursuant to section 201 of the RTA, the Member may on their own initiative ask questions and request submissions from both sides to determine if the party requires accommodation. As discussed above, the Member may consider different methods of accommodation to ensure a fair hearing with an opportunity for participation by all parties.

c. Where the capacity of a party is at issue

Members must also be attentive to indications which suggest a party may be unable to participate in a hearing due to a lack of mental capacity, even if the party does not bring this issue to the attention of the Board. Pursuant to section 201 of the RTA, the Member may need to ask questions and request submissions from both sides to determine if the party understands the nature or purpose of the hearing, appreciates the possible consequences of the hearing and can communicate with their legal representative, if they have one.

Where a party may lack capacity and is not represented at the hearing, the Member may consider different methods of accommodation to ensure a fair hearing with an opportunity for participation by all parties, even if no request for accommodation has been made. Examples include standing down the hearing to allow a tenant to consult with on-site Tenant Duty Counsel, where available, or adjourning the hearing to allow the party to obtain assistance from a family member, social worker or another person of the party's choosing.

Under Ontario law, all adults are assumed to be capable unless they have been found to be incapable by an assessor appointed under the *Substitute Decisions Act, 1992*[59] (the 'SDA'). Such an assessment may result in someone else being appointed to look after that person's interests. The Board does not have the authority to find that a party to one of its proceedings is incapable within the meaning of the SDA or order that someone else represent that party in a Board hearing.

It should not be assumed that a person who is incapable of one thing is incapable of everything. A person who is incapable of making treatment decisions, or a person who is incapable of managing their money such that a guardian has been appointed, may still be capable of participating in a hearing and instructing their legal representative. Incapacity can be issue-specific.

d. Conduct during a Board hearing

Members have an obligation to ensure that all hearings are conducted in a manner that is respectful towards all of the participants. Members must also control the proceedings to ensure that the conduct of a party, witness, spectator or representative does not infringe upon another person's rights under the Code to equal treatment with

---

[59] *Substitute Decisions Act*, S.O. 1992, c.30, as amended.

respect to services. For example, a Member will not permit a hearing participant to make derogatory comments about a party's race, religion, or sexual orientation.

2. Landlord applications

Issues relating to any of the grounds set out in subsection 2(1) of the Code may be raised during Board hearings. Subsection 2(1) of the Code provides that everyone has the right to equal treatment with respect to housing, without discrimination because of race, ancestry, place of origin, colour, ethnic origin, citizenship, creed (religion), sex (including pregnancy, gender identity), sexual orientation, age, marital status, family status, disability, or the receipt of public assistance. "Disability" is defined by subsection 10(1) to include both physical conditions and mental disorders.

Code issues are most commonly raised when a landlord files an application to evict a tenant because of the tenant's conduct, and the tenant asserts that:

- the tenant has a disability;
- the landlord has discriminated against the tenant;
- the tenant's conduct is caused by the disability; and
- the landlord has not accommodated the tenant up to the point of undue hardship.

The Member must first determine, after hearing from all parties, whether the landlord has established that the tenant engaged in the alleged conduct. If the landlord does not meet this burden of proof, the application is dismissed. If the landlord meets the burden of proof, the Member will then consider the tenant's claim that the landlord has not met its obligations under the Code having regard to the following criteria:

a. Is the tenant protected under subsection 2(1) of the Code

The tenant must provide sufficient information to establish that they are covered by one or more of the categories set out in subsection 2(1) the Code, such as disability. Sometimes this will not be difficult for the tenant to establish because the disability is not in dispute. In other cases, the tenant may need to submit evidence, such as a letter from a doctor or other medical forms, to establish that they have a disability as defined in the Code.

The Member must be respectful of the tenant's privacy interests and should not require the tenant to disclose more information than is needed to make the necessary determination. For example, a party with a disability may not need to disclose their specific diagnosis if sufficient medical evidence about the impact or effect of the disability is submitted to the Member. If the tenant is disclosing intimate personal information, the Member may consider excluding the public from the hearing room under Rule 24 of the Board's Rules of Practice, "Restricting Public Access to the Hearing" and section 9 of the *Statutory Powers Procedure Act*. However, the other parties to the application are entitled to remain in the hearing room, examine all of the evidence submitted to the Board and make submissions.

b. Has the tenant been discriminated against contrary to the Code

If the Member determines that the tenant falls within one or more of the categories contained in subsection 2(1) of the Code, the tenant must next establish that the landlord has discriminated against the tenant. In some cases, the discrimination may be clear. For example, the landlord is seeking to evict the tenant simply because the tenant practices a particular religion. In other cases, the discrimination may be indirect, such as a rule or standard applied by the landlord that appears neutral but has the effect of discriminating against the tenant because the tenant belongs to one or more of the categories contained in subsection 2(1) of the Code. For example, a requirement that all tenants remove their belongings from cupboards and drawers to enable the landlord to fumigate all of the rental units may discriminate against tenants who are unable to perform such tasks because of a physical disability. If the landlord is seeking to evict a disabled tenant for failing to comply with this requirement, the Member would take such discrimination into account in applying the Code.

The Divisional Court in *Connelly v. Mary Lambert Swale Non-Profit Homes*[60] suggested that where the landlord's application for eviction is based on the tenant's conduct, the Member must also consider whether the conduct has been directly caused by the tenant's disability.

If the grounds for eviction contained in the landlord's application are unrelated to the tenant's membership within one or more of the categories contained in subsection 2(1) of the Code, the Member cannot find that the tenant has been discriminated against by the landlord. For example, if the landlord has filed an application for termination of the tenancy based on arrears of rent, the fact that the tenant has a hearing impairment is likely not relevant to the Member's determination of the merits of the landlord's application. However, even if the Member finds that the landlord's application is unrelated to the tenant's membership within one or more of the categories contained in subsection 2(1) of the Code, the Member may still take all of the tenant's circumstances into account when considering relief from eviction pursuant to section 83 of the RTA. Both scenarios are discussed below.

c. Has the landlord accommodated the tenant to the point of undue hardship

Once the Member determines that the tenant is covered by one or more of the categories contained in subsection 2(1) of the Code and has been discriminated against by the landlord, the legal burden shifts to the landlord to show that it has accommodated the tenant to the point of undue hardship.

Section 11 of the Code provides that a right under the Code is infringed where a person identified by a Code ground is excluded because of neutral rules or requirements that are not "reasonable and *bona fide* in the circumstances". According to subsection 11(2) of the Code, this determination requires a consideration of whether the needs of the group to which the tenant belongs can be accommodated without undue hardship to the landlord. In other words, section 11 allows the landlord to demonstrate that the requirement, qualification or factor applied by the landlord is

---

[60] 2007 CanLII 52787 (ON S.C.D.C.), para 8.

"reasonable and *bona fide*" by showing that the needs of the group to which the tenant belongs cannot be accommodated without undue hardship.

Subsection 17(1) of the Code contains a similar provision that specifically applies to disability. Subsection 17(1) states that a right is not infringed if the person with a disability is incapable of performing or fulfilling the essential duties or requirements attending the exercise of the right. In other words, there is no violation of the Code if the tenant is unable, because of a disability, to ". . . act as is reasonably required of a tenant"[61]. However, according to subsection 17(2) of the Code, this defence is not available to the landlord unless it can be shown that the needs of the tenant cannot be accommodated without undue hardship.

In *Walmer Developments v. Wolch*[62] the Divisional Court stated that the limitation on the rights of a disabled person in section 17 must be read narrowly, as befits the purpose of the RTA, and the requirement for accommodation of the needs of the person is a keystone of the Code.

In determining whether the landlord has satisfied its duty to accommodate the tenant pursuant to either subsection 11(2) or 17(2) of the Code, the Member should consider the following criteria:

- **Landlord's knowledge of the tenant's circumstances**

The Member must determine whether the landlord was aware, prior to filing the eviction application that the tenant is covered by one or more of the categories set out in subsection 2(1) the Code, such as disability. The duty to accommodate exists only for needs that are known to the landlord[63] However, this does not mean that a tenant with a disability is obliged to provide the landlord with full details of their medical condition and history. In *Eagleson Co-Operative Homes, Inc. v. Théberge*[64], the Court found that the landlord had received an uncontradicted medical opinion from the resident's doctor stating that she was unable to participate in any volunteer work due to medical reasons, and it was a violation of the Code to require a person with a mental disability to divulge private medical information as a condition of maintaining her accommodation.

Even if the tenant does not tell the landlord about the disability, the landlord cannot be willfully blind. If a disability is obvious, the landlord will be considered to have constructive knowledge of it and therefore should have attempted to address the issue with the tenant prior to taking steps to evict the tenant.

- **Tenant's role in the accommodation process**

If a tenant wants accommodation under the Code, the tenant has a duty to provide the landlord with sufficient information about their needs so that the landlord can determine possible accommodation. The tenant also has a duty to cooperate with the

---

[61] *Walmer Developments v. Wolch* 2003 CanLII 42163 (ON S.C.D.C.), para. 31.

[62] Ibid., para. 34.

[63] See *Bathurst-Vaughan Mall Limited v. Eini*, 2009 CanLII 3550 (ON S.C.D.C.)

[64] 2006 CanLII 29987 (ON S.C.D.C.).

landlord in the development and implementation of the accommodation. If the tenant refuses to cooperate, the landlord can argue it has fulfilled its duty to accommodate.

- **Has the landlord developed and implemented an appropriate accommodation plan**

The landlord will be expected to provide evidence about the steps the landlord has taken to address the problem, if any, prior to applying to the Board for eviction.

In developing accommodation for the tenant, the landlord should have regard to three guiding principles identified by the Ontario Human Rights Commission:

(1) accommodation must be provided in a manner that respects dignity;

(2) accommodation must be individualized to meet the needs of the specific person; and

(3) accommodation must provide for the inclusion of people protected under the Code.

Where the landlord is unable to immediately provide the ideal form of accommodation, other options such as phased-in, interim or alternative accommodation must be implemented by the landlord.

- **Will the accommodation cause undue hardship**

A landlord must accommodate the tenant up to the point that any further accommodation would cause undue hardship. The Courts have considered this issue in several decisions.

In *Walmer Developments v. Wolch*[65] the Ontario Rental Housing Tribunal (now the Board) found that the tenant had interfered with the reasonable enjoyment of the landlord and other tenants by engaging in conduct such as screaming loudly and causing food to catch on fire on her stove. The Divisional Court found that the Tribunal had erred in evicting the tenant because the Member had failed to consider the tenant's disability pursuant to the Code. At paragraph 35, the Court stated that the Tribunal ". . . must consider whether any disruption in the enjoyment of other tenants may be sufficiently alleviated by a reasonable accommodation of the disabled tenant without undue hardship to the landlord." The Court rejected the argument that the tenant could not, because of her disability, act as is reasonably required of a tenant, so as not to disturb her neighbours and found that accommodation would be appropriate in this case. The Court ordered the parties to enter into an arrangement whereby the landlord informs the tenant's relatives at the first sign of trouble, so that they can intervene.

In *Canadian Mental Health Association v. Warren*[66] the Tribunal found that the tenant had created disturbances within the residential complex by shouting, screaming, slamming doors, verbally abusing and threatening other tenants, activating the smoke detectors, continually threw garbage out of her second storey window and that her

[65] 2003 CanLII 42163 (ON S.C.D.C.).

[66] 2004 CanLII 16439 (ON S.C.D.C.).

unit was in such a state of hazardous disarray that it posed a real threat of fire. The Member determined that the tenant was disabled within the meaning of the Code. The Member accepted that the landlord's accommodation attempts included the negotiation and mediation of agreements which provided the tenant with relief from eviction, taking part in a "transition team" which had been formed to assist the tenant in resolving her problems, assigning caseworkers to deal with the tenant's needs, and installing less sensitive smoke detectors. The Member concluded that the landlord's accommodation met the requirements of section 17 of the Code and that the accommodation had now reached the point of undue hardship. The Divisional Court upheld the Tribunal's decision, finding that "there was overwhelming evidence of accommodation, to the point of undue hardship, on the facts before the Tribunal".

In *McKenzie v. Supportive Housing in Peel*[67] the Tribunal found that the tenant had seriously impaired the safety of the superintendent by stabbing the superintendent with a pen. The superintendent required medical attention and the tenant was convicted of assault. The tenant by her own testimony was disabled within the meaning of the Code. The member found that the landlord had done everything in its power to attempt to accommodate the tenant to the point of undue hardship, but that the tenant had refused to accept help. In upholding the Tribunal's decision, the Divisional Court quoted with approval the following passage from the ORHT decision:

> [3] . . .Therefore, I find that the Landlord has done everything in its power to attempt to accommodate the tenant to the point of undue hardship, and has thus satisfied its requirements under the Ontario Human Rights Code. Further, permitting the tenant to continue residing [in the] rental unit would constitute an undue hardship to the building Superintendent, in light of the safety concerns raised by the tenant's conduct.

In *Connelly v. Mary Lambert Swale Non-Profit Homes*[68], the Tribunal found that the tenant was addicted to drugs and was operating a crack house in the complex. The Divisional Court found that the tenant's drug addiction must be considered a disability, but upheld the Tribunal's order evicting the tenant. The Court held that:

> [10] On the finding of the Tribunal, no accommodation is possible. The appellant denied he was dealing drugs from his apartment. He denied that his conduct created difficulties both for the respondent and its tenants.
>
> [11] The Tribunal found that the appellant's operation of a crack house substantially interfered with the rights of the other tenants.
>
> [12] We reject any suggestion there is an obligation on the respondent to permit the tenant to operate a crack house in order to accommodate his disability. We conclude that such an attempt at accommodation would be an undue hardship to the respondent by substantially interfering with the rights of the other tenants.

Subsection 17(2) of the Code also prescribes three considerations when assessing whether an accommodation would cause undue hardship. These are:

---

[67] 2006 CanLII 7838 (ON S.C.D.C.).

[68] 2007 CanLII 52787 (ON S.C.D.C.).

(1) cost

(2) outside sources of funding, if any

(3) health and safety requirements, if any.

If issues relating to cost, outside sources of funding or health and safety requirements are relevant to the proceeding, it is the landlord's obligation to provide evidence respecting these three considerations if arguing that any or further accommodation would cause undue hardship.

Costs will amount to undue hardship if they are quantifiable, shown to be related to the accommodation, and are so substantial that they would alter the essential nature of the enterprise or so significant that they would substantially affect its viability.

For further guidance on undue hardship, see the Ontario Human Rights Commission's *Policy and Guidelines on Disability and the Duty to Accommodate* under "Policies" on the Commission's website at www.ohrc.on.ca.

- **Relief from eviction**

In *Walmer Developments v. Wolch*[69] the Divisional Court held that the Ontario Rental Housing Tribunal (now the Board) must consider and apply the Code when exercising its authority to grant relief from eviction. A Member considers such relief pursuant to section 83 of the RTA. Section 83 states that the Member must have regard to all the circumstances to determine whether it would be unfair to refuse the landlord's eviction application or postpone the enforcement of the eviction order.

If the Member determines that the landlord has failed to accommodate a tenant covered by one or more of the categories contained in subsection 2(1) of the Code up to the point of undue hardship, the Member must consider relief from eviction in accordance with clause (a) of subsection 83(1) of the RTA. However, even if relief is granted, the Member may still consider whether other types of conditions and requirements should be ordered to address the conduct or problem at issue. The authority to make such orders comes from subsection 204(1) of the RTA.

In some cases a Member may find that there are no Code-related grounds for relief for eviction. For example, the Member may find that the reason for the landlord's application is unrelated to the fact that the tenant belongs to one or more of the categories contained in subsection 2(1) of the Code, or that the landlord has met the obligation to accommodate the tenant to the point of undue hardship. However, in these circumstances the Member must still consider granting relief from eviction having regard to all of the circumstances of the parties pursuant to section 83 of the RTA. For example, there may be no connection between a landlord's application for arrears of rent and the fact that the tenant uses a wheelchair. However, the Member could take into account the difficulty the tenant may experience in finding alternative wheelchair accessible accommodation, and thus delay enforcement of the eviction order pursuant to section 83.

---

[69] 2003 CanLII 42163 (ON S.C.D.C.).

3. Tenant applications

A tenant may allege in a tenant's application that the landlord has contravened the Code. Such allegations may relate to a number of different sections of the RTA and the Code.

For example, a tenant may allege that the landlord has substantially interfered with the tenant's reasonable enjoyment of the rental unit in contravention of section 22 of the RTA by failing to make changes to the unit that are necessary to accommodate the tenant's physical disability. The Member's consideration of such a claim will be similar to that described above with respect to Code issues raised pursuant to section 83 of the RTA. The Member must first determine whether the tenant falls within one or more of the categories contained in subsection 2(1) of the Code and has been discriminated against by the landlord. The Member must then determine whether the landlord has accommodated the tenant to the point of undue hardship. If the tenant's claim is successful, the Member has the authority pursuant to clause (f) of subsection 31(1) of the RTA to order the landlord to make necessary changes to the rental unit or residential complex to accommodate the tenant's needs.

A tenant may also allege in a tenant's application that the landlord has harassed, obstructed, coerced, threatened or interfered with the tenant in contravention of section 25 of the RTA, and that the landlord acted in this way because the tenant is covered by one of the grounds set out in subsection 2(1) the Code. Such conduct may also contravene subsection 2(2) of the Code which provides that tenants have a right to freedom from harassment by the landlord or the landlord's agent. The Member will consider such claims in determining whether the landlord contravened the RTA, and if so, what the appropriate remedy should be.

4. Conflict between the RTA and the Code

Tribunals that can decide questions of law, such as the Board, have the jurisdiction to consider whether a legislative provision within its mandate is consistent with the Code. This does not mean that the Board has the authority to find that the legislative provision in question is invalid, as a Court may determine. However, if the Board finds that there is a conflict between a legislative provision and the Code, the Board has the authority to determine that the provision does not apply to the proceeding, pursuant to section 47 of the Code. Section 47 of the Code is applied when there is conflict between a legislative provision and the Code to ensure that the Code takes precedence.

Therefore, a party to a Board proceeding may argue that a particular section of the RTA should not be applied because it is in conflict with the Code's provisions.

Appendix 9

STATUTORY POWERS PROCEDURE ACT

R.S.O. 1990, c. S.22, as am. S.O. 1993, c. 27, Sched.; 1994, c. 27, s. 56; 1997, c. 23, s. 13; 1999, c. 12, Sched. B, s. 16; 2002, c. 17, Sched. F, s. 1; 2006, c. 19, Sched. B, s. 21, Sched. C, s. 1(1), (2), (4); 2006, c. 21, Sched. C, s. 134, Sched. F, s. 136(1), Table 1

1. (1) Definitions — In this Act,

"Committee" [Repealed 1994, c. 27, s. 56.]

"electronic hearing" means a hearing held by conference telephone or some other form of electronic technology allowing persons to hear one another;

"hearing" means a hearing in any proceeding;

"licence" includes any permit, certificate, approval, registration or similar form of permission required by law;

"municipality" has the same meaning as in the *Municipal Affairs Act*;

"oral hearing" means a hearing at which the parties or their representatives attend before the tribunal in person;

"proceeding" means a proceeding to which this Act applies;

"representative" means, in respect of a proceeding to which this Act applies, a person authorized under the *Law Society Act* to represent a person in that proceeding; ("représentant")

"statutory power of decision" means a power or right, conferred by or under a statute, to make a decision deciding or prescribing,

> (a) the legal rights, powers, privileges, immunities, duties or liabilities of any person or party, or
>
> (b) the eligibility of any person or party to receive, or to the continuation of, a benefit or licence, whether the person is legally entitled thereto or not;

"tribunal" means one or more persons, whether or not incorporated and however described, upon which a statutory power of decision is conferred by or under a statute;

"written hearing" means a hearing held by means of the exchange of documents, whether in written form or by electronic means.

(2) Meaning of "person" extended — A municipality, an unincorporated association of employers, a trade union or council of trade unions who may be a party to a proceeding in the exercise of a statutory power of decision under the statute conferring the powers, shall be deemed to be a person for the purpose of any provision of this Act or of any rule made under this Act that applies to parties.

1994, c. 27, s. 56; 2002, c. 17, Sched. F, s. 1; 2006, c. 21, Sched. C, s. 134(1), (2)

2. Interpretation — This Act, and any rule made by a tribunal under subsection 17.1(4) or section 25.1, shall be liberally construed to secure the just, most expeditious and cost-effective determination of every proceeding on its merits.

1999, c. 12, Sched. B, s. 16(1); 2006, c. 19, Sched. B, s. 21(1)

3. (1) Application of Act — Subject to subsection (2), this Act applies to a proceeding by a tribunal in the exercise of a statutory power of decision conferred by or under an Act of the Legislature, where the tribunal is required by or under such Act or otherwise by law to hold or to afford to the parties to the proceeding an opportunity for a hearing before making a decision.

(2) Where Act does not apply — This Act does not apply to a proceeding,

(a) before the Assembly or any committee of the Assembly;

(b) in or before,

(i) the Court of Appeal,

(ii) the Superior Court of Justice,

(iii) the Ontario Court of Justice,

(iv) the Family Court of the Superior Court of Justice,

(v) the Small Claims Court, or

(vi) a justice of the peace;

(c) to which the Rules of Civil Procedure apply;

(d) before an arbitrator to which the *Arbitrations Act* or the *Labour Relations Act* applies;

(e) at a coroner's inquest;

(f) of a commission appointed under the *Public Inquiries Act*;

(g) of one or more persons required to make an investigation and to make a report, with or without recommendations, where the report is for the information or advice of the person to whom it is made and does not in any way legally bind or limit that person in any decision he or she may have power to make; or

(h) of a tribunal empowered to make regulations, rules or by-laws in so far as its power to make regulations, rules or by-laws is concerned.

1994, c. 27, s. 56; 2006, c. 19, Sched. C, s. 1(1), (2), (4)

4. (1) Waiver of procedural requirement — Any procedural requirement of this Act, or of another Act or a regulation that applies to a proceeding, may be waived with the consent of the parties and the tribunal.

(2) Same, rules — Any provision of a tribunal's rules made under section 25.1 may be waived in accordance with the rules.

1994, c. 27, s. 56; 1997, c. 23, s. 13

4.1 Disposition without hearing — If the parties consent, a proceeding may be disposed of by a decision of the tribunal given without a hearing, unless another Act or a regulation that applies to the proceeding provides otherwise.

1994, c. 27, s. 56; 1997, c. 23, s. 13

4.2 (1) Panels, certain matters — A procedural or interlocutory matter in a proceeding may be heard and determined by a panel consisting of one or more members of the tribunal, as assigned by the chair of the tribunal.

(2) Assignments — In assigning members of the tribunal to a panel, the chair shall take into consideration any requirement imposed by another Act or a regulatoin that applies to the proceeding that the tribunal be representative of specific interests.

(3) Decision of panel — The decision of a majority of the members of a panel, or their unanimous decision in the case of a two-member panel, is the tribunal's decision.

1994, c. 27, s. 56; 1997, c. 23, s. 13

4.2.1 (1) Panel of one — The chair of a tribunal may decide that a proceeding be heard by a panel of one person and assign the person to hear the proceeding unless there is a statutory requirement in another Act that the proceeding be heard by a panel of more than one person.

(2) Reduction in number of panel members — Where there is a statutory requirement in another Act that a proceeding be heard by a panel of a specified number of persons, the chair of the tribunal may assign to the panel one person or any lesser number of persons than the number specified in the other Act if all parties to the proceeding consent.

1999, c. 12, Sched. B, s. 16(2)

4.3 Expiry of term — If the term of office of a member of a tribunal who has participated in a hearing expires before a decision is given, the term shall be deemed to continue, but only for the purpose of participating in the decision and for no other purpose.

1994, c. 27, s. 56; 1997, c. 23, s. 13

4.4 (1) Incapacity of member — If a member of a tribunal who has participated in a hearing becomes unable, for any reason, to complete the hearing or to participate in the decision, the remaining member or members may complete the hearing and give a decision.

(2) Other Acts and regulations — Subsection (1) does not apply if another Act or a regulation specifically deals with the issue of what takes place in the circumstances described in subsection (1).

1994, c. 27, s. 56; 1997, c. 23, s. 13

4.5 (1) Decision not to process commencement of proceeding — Subject to subsection (3), upon receiving documents relating to the commencement of a proceeding, a tribunal or its administrative staff may decide not to process the documents relating to the commencement of the proceeding if,

(a) the documents are incomplete;

(b) the documents are received after the time required for commencing the proceeding has elapsed;

(c) the fee required for commencing the proceeding is not paid; or

(d) there is some other technical defect in the commencement of the proceeding.

(2) Notice — A tribunal or its administrative staff shall give the party who commences a proceeding notice of its decision under subsection (1) and shall set out in the notice the reasons for the decision and the requirements for resuming the processing of the documents.

(3) Rules under s. 25.1 — A tribunal or its administrative staff shall not make a decision under subsection (1) unless the tribunal has made rules under section 25.1 respecting the making of such decisions and those rules shall set out,

(a) any of the grounds referred to in subsection (1) upon which the tribunal or its administrative staff may decide not to process the documents relating to the commencement of a proceeding; and

(b) the requirements for the processing of the documents to be resumed.

(4) Continuance of provisions in other statutes — Despite section 32, nothing in this section shall prevent a tribunal or its administrative staff from deciding not to process documents relating to the commencement of a proceeding on grounds that differ from those referred to in subsection (1) or without complying with subsection (2) or (3) if the tribunal or its staff does so in accordance with the provisions of an Act that are in force on the day this section comes into force.

1999, c. 12, Sched. B, s. 16(3)

4.6 (1) Dismissal of proceeding without hearing — Subject to subsections (5) and (6), a tribunal may dismiss a proceeding without a hearing if,

(a) the proceeding is frivolous, vexatious or is commenced in bad faith;

(b) the proceeding relates to matters that are outside the jurisdiction of the tribunal; or

(c) some aspect of the statutory requirements for bringing the proceeding has not been met.

(2) Notice — Before dismissing a proceeding under this section, a tribunal shall give notice of its intention to dismiss the proceeding to,

(a) all parties to the proceeding if the proceeding is being dismissed for reasons referred to in clause (1)(b); or

(b) the party who commences the proceeding if the proceeding is being dismissed for any other reason.

(3) Same — The notice of intention to dismiss a proceeding shall set out the reasons for the dismissal and inform the parties of their right to make written submissions to the tribunal with respect to the dismissal within the time specified in the notice.

(4) Right to make submissions — A party who receives a notice under subsection (2) may make written submissions to the tribunal with respect to the dismissal within the time specified in the notice.

(5) Dismissal — A tribunal shall not dismiss a proceeding under this section until it has given notice under subsection (2) and considered any submissions made under subsection (4).

(6) Rules — A tribunal shall not dismiss a proceeding under this section 25.1 respecting the early dismissal of proceedings and those rules shall include,

(a) any of the grounds referred to in subsection (1) upon which a proceeding may be dismissed;

(b) the right of the parties who are entitled to receive notice under subsection (2) to make submissions with respect to the dismissal; and

(c) the time within which the submissions must be made.

(7) Continuance of provisions in other statutes — Despite section 32, nothing in this section shall prevent a tribunal from dismissing a proceeding on grounds other than those referred to in subsection (1) or without complying with subsections (2) to (6) if the tribunal dismisses the proceeding in accordance with the provisions of an Act that are in force on the day this section comes into force.

1999, c. 12, Sched. B, s. 16(3)

4.7 Classifying proceedings — A tribunal may make rules under section 25.1 classifying the types of proceedings that come before it and setting guidelines as to the procedural steps or processes (such as preliminary motions, pre-hearing conferences, alternative dispute resolution mechanisms, expedited hearings) that apply to each type of proceeding and the circumstances in which other procedures may apply.

1999, c. 12, Sched. B, s. 16(3)

4.8 (1) Alternative dispute resolution — A tribunal may direct the parties to a proceeding to participate in an alternative dispute resolution mechanism for the purposes of resolving the proceeding or an issue arising in the proceeding if,

(a) it has made rules under section 25.1 respecting the use of alternative dispute resolution mechanisms; and

(b) all parties consent to participating in the alternative dispute resolution mechanism.

(2) Definition — In this section,

"alternative dispute resolution mechanism" includes mediation, conciliation, negotiation or any other means of facilitating the resolution of issues in dispute.

(3) Rules — A rule under section 25.1 respecting the use of alternative dispute resolution mechanisms shall include procedural guidelines to deal with the following:

1. The circumstances in which a settlement achieved by means of an alternative dispute resolution mechanism must be reviewed and approved by the tribunal.

2. Any requirement, statutory or otherwise, that there be an order by the tribunal.

(4) Mandatory alternative dispute resolution — A rule under subsection (3) may provide that participation in an alternative dispute resolution mechanism is mandatory or that it is mandatory in certain specified circumstances.

(5) Person appointed to mediate, etc. — A rule under subsection (3) may provide that a person appointed to mediate, conciliate, negotiate or help resolve a matter by means of an alternative dispute resolution mechanism be a member of the tribunal or a person independent of the tribunal. However, a member of the tribunal who is so appointed with respect to a matter in a proceeding shall not subsequently hear the matter if it comes before the tribunal unless the parties consent.

(6) Continuance of provisions in other statutes — Despite section 32, nothing in this section shall prevent a tribunal from directing parties to a proceeding to participate in an alternative dispute resolution mechanism even though the requirements of subsections (1) to (5) have not been met if the tribunal does so in accordance with the provisions of an Act that are in force on the day this section comes into force.

1999, c. 12, Sched. B, s. 16(3)

4.9 (1) Mediators, etc., not compellable — No person employed as a mediator, conciliator or negotiator or otherwise appointed to facilitate the resolution of a matter before a tribunal by means of an alternative dispute resolution mechanism shall be compelled to give testimony or produce documents in a proceeding before the tribunal or in a civil proceeding with respect to matters that come to his or her knowledge in the course of exercising his or her duties under this or any other Act.

(2) Evidence in civil proceedings — No notes or records kept by a mediator, conciliator or negotiator or by any other person appointed to facilitate the resolution of a matter before a tribunal by means of an alternative dispute resolution mechanism under this or any other Act are admissible in a civil proceeding.

1999, c. 12, Sched. B, s. 16(3)

5. Parties — The parties to a proceeding shall be the persons specified as parties by or under the statute under which the proceeding arises or, if not so specified, persons entitled by law to be parties to the proceeding.

5.1 (1) Written hearings — A tribunal whose rules made under section 25.1 deal with written hearing may hold a written hearing in a proceeding.

(2) Exception — The tribunal shall not hold a written hearing if a party satisfies the tribunal that there is good reason for not doing so.

(2.1) Same — Subsection (2) does not apply if the only purpose of the hearing is to deal with procedural matters.

(3) Documents — In a written hearing, all the parties are entitled to receive every document that the tribunal receives in the proceeding.

1994, c. 27, s. 56; 1997, c. 23, s. 13; 1999, c. 12, Sched. B, s. 16(4)

5.2 (1) Electronic hearings — A tribunal whose rules made under section 25.1 deal with electronic hearings may hold an electronic hearing in a proceeding.

(2) Exception — The tribunal shall not hold an electronic hearing if a party satisfies the tribunal that holding an electronic rather than an oral hearing is likely to cause the party significant prejudice.

(3) Same — Subsection (2) does not apply if the only purpose of the hearing is to deal with procedural matters.

(4) Participants to be able to hear one another — In an electronic hearing, all the parties and the members of the tribunal participating in the hearing must be able to hear one another and any witnesses throughout the hearing.

1994, c. 27, s. 56; 1997, c. 23, s. 13

5.2.1 Different kinds of hearings in one proceeding — A tribunal may, in a proceeding, hold any combination of written, electronic and oral hearings.

1997, c. 23, s. 13

5.3 (1) Pre-hearing conferences — If the tribunal's rules made under section 25.1 deal with pre-hearing conferences, the tribunal may direct the parties to participate in a pre-hearing conference to consider,

(a) the settlement of any or all of the issues;

(b) the simplification of the issues;

(c) facts or evidence that may be agreed upon;

(d) the dates by which any steps in the proceeding are to be taken or begun;

(e) the estimated duration of the hearing; and

(f) any other matter that may assist in the just and most expeditious disposition of the proceeding.

(1.1) Other Acts and regulations — The tribunal's power to direct the parties to participate in a pre-hearing conference is subject to any other Act or regulation that applies to the proceeding.

(2) Who presides — The chair of the tribunal may designate a member of the tribunal or any other person to preside at the pre-hearing conference.

(3) Orders — A member who presides at a pre-hearing conference may make such orders as he or she considers necessary or advisable with respect to the conduct of the proceeding, including adding parties.

(4) Disqualification — A member who presides at a pre-hearing conference at which the parties attempt to settle issues shall not preside at the hearing of the proceeding unless the parties consent.

(5) Application of s. 5.2 — Section 5.2 applies to a pre-hearing conference, with necessary modifications.

1994, c. 27, s. 56; 1997, c. 23, s. 13

5.4 (1) Disclosure — If the tribunal's rules made under section 25.1 deal with disclosure, the tribunal may, at any stage of the proceeding before all hearings are complete, make orders for,

(a) the exchange of documents;

(b) the oral or written examination of a party;

(c) the exchange of witness statements and reports of expert witnesses;

(d) the provision of particulars;

(e) any other form of disclosure.

(1.1) Other Acts and regulations — The tribunal's power to make orders for disclosure is subject to any other Act or regulation that applies to the proceeding.

(2) Exception, privileged information — Subsection (1) does not authorize the making of an order requiring disclosure of privileged information.

1994, c. 27, s. 56(12); 1997, c. 23, s. 13(11)

6. (1) Notice of hearing — The parties to a proceeding shall be given reasonable notice of the hearing by the tribunal.

(2) Statutory authority — A notice of a hearing shall include a reference to the statutory authority under which the hearing will be held.

(3) Oral hearing — A notice of an oral hearing shall include,

(a) a statement of the time, place and purpose of the hearing; and

(b) a statement that if the party notified does not attend at the hearing, the tribunal may proceed in the party's absence and the party will not be entitled to any further notice in the proceeding.

(4) Written hearing — A notice of a written hearing shall include,

(a) a statement of the time and purpose of the hearing, and details about the manner in which the hearing will be held;

(b) a statement that the hearing shall not be held as a written hearing if the party satisfies the tribunal that there is good reason for not holding a written hearing (in which case the tribunal is required to hold it as an electronic or oral hearing) and an indication of the procedure to be followed for that purpose.

(c) a statement that if the party notified neither acts under clause (b) nor participates in the hearing in accordance with the notice, the tribunal may proceed without the party's participation and the party will not be entitled to any further notice in the proceeding.

(5) **Electronic hearing** — A notice of an electronic hearing shall include,

(a) a statement of the time and purpose of the hearing, and details about the manner in which the hearing will be held;

(b) a statement that the only purpose of the hearing is to deal with procedural matters, if that is the case;

(c) if clause (b) does not apply, a statement that the party notified may, by satisfying the tribunal that holding the hearing as an electronic hearing is likely to cause the party significant prejudice, require the tribunal to hold the hearing as an oral hearing, and an indication of the procedure to be followed for that purpose; and

(d) a statement that if the party notified neither acts under clause (c), if applicable, nor participates in the hearing in accordance with the notice, the tribunal may proceed without the party's participation and the party will not be entitled to any further notice in the proceeding.

1994, c. 27, s. 56; 1997, c. 23, s. 13; 1999, c. 12, Sched. B, s. 16(5)

7. (1) **Effect of non-attendance at hearing after due notice** — Where notice of an oral hearing has been given to a party to a proceeding in accordance with this Act and the party does not attend at the hearing, the tribunal may proceed in the absence of the party and the party will not be entitled to any further notice in the proceeding.

(2) **Same, written hearings** — Where notice of a written hearing has been given to a party to a proceeding in accordance with this Act and the party neither acts under clause 6(4)(b) nor participates in the hearing in accordance with the notice, the tribunal may proceed without the party's participation and the party is not entitled to any further notice in the proceeding.

(3) **Same, electronic hearings** — Where notice of an electronic hearing has been given to a party to a proceeding in accordance with this Act and the party neither acts under clause 6(5)(c), if applicable, nor participates in the hearing in accordance with the notice, the tribunal may proceed without the party's participation and the party is not entitled to any further notice in the proceeding.

1994, c. 27, s. 56

8. **Where character, etc. of a party is in issue** — Where the good character, propriety of conduct or competence of a party is an issue in a proceeding, the party is entitled to be furnished prior to the hearing with reasonable information of any allegations with respect thereto.

9. (1) **Hearings to be public, exceptions** — An oral hearing shall be open to the public except where the tribunal is of the opinion that,

(a) matters involving public security may be disclosed; or

(b) intimate financial or personal matters or other matters may be disclosed at the hearing of such a nature, having regard to the circumstances, that the desirability of avoiding disclosure thereof in the interests of any person affected or in the public interest outweighs the desirability of adhering to the principle that hearings be open to the public, in which case the tribunal may hold the hearing in the absence of the public.

(1.1) Written hearings — In a written hearing, members of the public are entitled to reasonable access to the documents submitted, unless the tribunal is of the opinion that clause (1)(a) or (b) applies.

(1.2) Electronic hearings — An electronic hearing shall be open to the public unless the tribunal is of the opinion that,

(a) it is not practical to hold the hearing in a manner that is open to the public; or

(b) clause (1)(a) or (b) applies.

(2) Maintenance of order at hearings — A tribunal may make such orders or give such directions at an oral or electronic hearing as it considers necessary for the maintenance of order at the hearing, and, if any person disobeys or fails to comply with any such order or direction, the tribunal or a member thereof may call for the assistance of any peace officer to enforce the order or direction, and every peace officer so called upon shall take such action as is necessary to enforce the order or direction and may use such force as is reasonably required for that purpose.

1994, c. 27, s. 56; 1997, c. 23, s. 13

9.1 (1) Proceedings involving similar questions — If two or more proceedings before a tribunal involve the same or similar questions of fact, law or policy, the tribunal may,

(a) any other Act ore regulation that applies to the proceeding requires that it be heard in private.

(b) hear the proceedings at the same time, with the consent of the parties;

(c) hear the proceedings one immediately after the other; or

(d) stay one or more of the proceedings until after the determination of another one of them.

(2) Exception — Subsection (1) does not apply to proceedings to which the *Consolidated Hearings Act* applies.

(3) Same — Clauses (1)(a) and (b) do not apply to a proceeding if,

(a) the Act under which the proceeding arises requires that it be heard in private; or

(b) the tribunal is of the opinion that clause 9(1)(a) or (b) applies to the proceeding.

(4) Conflict, consent requirements — The consent requirements of clauses (1)(a) and (b) do not apply if another Act or a regulation that applies to the proceedings allows the tribunal to combine them or hear them at the same time without the consent of the parties.

(5) Use of same evidence — If the parties to the second-named proceeding consent, the tribunal may treat evidence that is admitted in a proceeding as if it were also admitted in another proceeding that is heard at the same time under clause (1)(b).

1994, c. 27, s. 56; 1997, c. 23, s. 13

10. Right to representation — A party to a proceeding may be represented by a representative.

1994, c. 27, s. 56; 2006, c. 21, Sched. C, s. 134(3)

10.1 Examination of witnesses — A party to a proceeding may, at an oral or electronic hearing,

(a) call and examine witnesses and present evidence and submissions; and

(b) conduct cross-examinations of witnesses at the hearing reasonably required for a full and fair disclosure of all matters relevant to the issues in the proceeding.

1994, c. 27, s. 56

11. (1) Rights of witnesses to representation — A witness at an oral or electronic hearing is entitled to be advised by a representative as to his or her rights, but such representative may take no other part in the hearing without leave of the tribunal.

(2) Idem — Where an oral hearing is closed to the public, the witness's representative is not entitled to be present except when that witness is giving evidence.

1994, c. 27, s. 56; 2006, c. 21, Sched. C, s. 134(4), (5)

12. (1) Summonses — A tribunal may require any person, including a party, by summons,

(a) to give evidence on oath or affirmation at an oral or electronic hearing; and

(b) to produce in evidence at an oral or electronic hearing documents and things specified by the tribunal,

relevant to the subject-matter of the proceeding and admissible at a hearing.

(2) Form and service of summons — A summons issued under subsection (1) shall be in the prescribed form (in English or French) and,

(a) where the tribunal consists of one person, shall be signed by him or her;

(b) where the tribunal consists of more than one person, shall be signed by the chair of the tribunal or in such other manner as documents on behalf of the tribunal may be signed under the statute constituting the tribunal.

(3) Same — The summons shall be served personally on the person summoned.

(3.1) Fees and allowances — The person summoned is entitled to receive the same fees or allowances for attending at or otherwise participating in the hearing as are paid to a person summoned to attend before the Superior Court of Justice.

(4) Bench warrant — A judge of the Superior Court of Justice may issue a warrant against a person if the judge is satisfied that,

(a) a summons was served on the person under this section;

(b) the person has failed to attend or to remain in attendance at the hearing (in the case of an oral hearing) or has failed otherwise to participate in the hearing (in the case of an electronic hearing) in accordance with the summons; and

(c) the person's attendance or participation is material to the ends of justice.

(4.1) Same — The warrant shall be in the prescribed form (in English or French), directed to any police officer, and shall require the person to be apprehended anywhere within Ontario, brought before the tribunal forthwith and,

(a) detained in custody as the judge may order until the person's presence as a witness is no longer required; or

(b) in the judge's discretion, released on a recognizance, with or without sureties, conditioned for attendance or participation to give evidence.

(5) Proof of service — Service of a summons may be proved by affidavit in an application to have a warrant issued under subsection (4).

(6) Certificate of facts — Where an application to have a warrant issued is made on behalf of a tribunal, the person constituting the tribunal or, if the tribunal consists of more than one person, the chair of the tribunal may certify to the judge the facts relied on to establish that the attendance or other participation of the person summoned is material to the ends of justice, and the judge may accept the certificate as proof of the facts.

(7) Same — Where the application is made by a party to the proceeding, the facts relied on to establish that the attendance or other participation of the person is material to the ends of justice may be proved by the party's affidavit.

1994, c. 27, s. 56; 2006, c. 19, Sched. C, s. 1(1)

13. (1) Contempt proceedings — Where any person without lawful excuse,

(a) on being duly summoned under section 12 as a witness at a hearing makes default in attending at the hearing; or

(b) being in attendance as a witness at an oral hearing or otherwise participating as a witness at an electronic hearing, refuses to take an oath or to make an affirmation legally required by the tribunal to be taken or made, or to produce any document or thing in his or her power or control legally required by the tribunal to be produced by him or her or to answer any question to which the tribunal may legally require an answer; or

(c) does any other thing that would, if the tribunal had been a court of law having power to commit for contempt, have been contempt of that court,

the tribunal may, of its own motion or on the motion of a party to the proceeding, state a case to the Divisional Court setting out the facts and that court may inquire into the matter and, after hearing any witnesses who may be produced against or on behalf of that person and after hearing any statement that may be offered in defence, punish or take steps for the punishment of that person in like manner as if he or she had been guilty of contempt of the court.

(2) Same — Subsection (1) also applies to a person who,

(a) having objected under clause 6(4)(b) to a hearing being held as a written hearing, fails without lawful excuse to participate in the oral or electronic hearing of the matter; or

(b) being a party, fails without lawful excuse to attend a pre-hearing conference when so directed by the tribunal.

1994, c. 27, s. 56; 1997, c. 23, s. 13

14. (1) Protection for witnesses — A witness at an oral or electronic hearing shall be deemed to have objected to answer any question asked him or her upon the ground that the answer may tend to criminate him or her or may tend to establish his or her liability to civil proceedings at the instance of the Crown, or of any person, and no answer given by a witness at a hearing shall be used or be receivable in evidence against the witness in any trial or other proceeding against him or her thereafter taking place, other than a prosecution for perjury in giving such evidence.

(2) [Repealed 1994, c. 27, s. 56(29).]

1994, c. 27, s. 56

15. (1) What is admissible in evidence at a hearing — Subject to subsections (2) and (3), a tribunal may admit as evidence at a hearing, whether or not given or proven under oath or affirmation or admissible as evidence in a court,

(a) any oral testimony; and

(b) any document or other thing,

relevant to the subject-matter of the proceeding and may act on such evidence, but the tribunal may exclude anything unduly repetitious.

(2) What is inadmissible in evidence at a hearing — Nothing is admissible in evidence at a hearing,

(a) that would be inadmissible in a court by reason of any privilege under the law of evidence; or

(b) that is inadmissible by the statute under which the proceeding arises or any other statute.

(3) Conflicts — Nothing in subsection (1) overrides the provisions of any Act expressly limiting the extent to or purposes for which any oral testimony, documents or things may be admitted or used in evidence in any proceeding.

(4) Copies — Where a tribunal is satisfied as to its authenticity, a copy of a document or other thing may be admitted as evidence at a hearing.

(5) Photocopies — Where a document has been filed in evidence at a hearing, the tribunal may, or the person producing it or entitled to it may with the leave of the tribunal, cause the document to be photocopied and the tribunal may authorize the photocopy to be filed in evidence in the place of the document filed and release the document filed, or may furnish to the person producing it or the person entitled to it a photocopy of the document filed certified by a member of the tribunal.

(6) Certified copy admissible in evidence — A document purporting to be a copy of a document filed in evidence at a hearing, certified to be a copy thereof by a member of the tribunal, is admissible in evidence in proceedings in which the document is admissible as evidence of the document.

15.1 (1) Use of previously admitted evidence — The tribunal may treat previously admitted evidence as if it had been admitted in a proceeding before the tribunal, if the parties to the proceeding consent.

(2) Definition — In subsection (1),

"previously admitted evidence" means evidence that was admitted, before the hearing of the proceeding referred to in that subsection, in any other proceeding before a court or tribunal, whether in or outside Ontario.

(3) Additional power — This power conferred by this section is in addition to the tribunal's power to admit evidence under section 15.

1994, c. 27, s. 56; 1997, c. 23, s. 13

15.2 Witness panels — A tribunal may receive evidence from panels of witnesses composed of two or more persons, if the parties have first had an opportunity to make submissions in that regard.

1994, c. 27, s. 56

16. Notice of facts and opinions — A tribunal may, in making its decision in any proceeding,

(a) take notice of facts that may be judicially noticed; and

(b) take notice of any generally recognized scientific or technical facts,

information or opinions within its scientific or specialized knowledge.

16.1 (1) Interim decisions and orders — A tribunal may make interim decisions and orders.

(2) Conditions — A tribunal may impose conditions on an interim decision or order.

(3) Reasons — An interim decision or order need not be accompanied by reasons.

1994, c. 27, s. 56

16.2 Time frames — A tribunal shall establish guidelines setting out the usual time frame for completing proceedings that come before the tribunal and for completing the procedural steps within those proceedings.

1999, c. 12, Sched. B, s. 16(6)

17. (1) Decision — A tribunal shall give its final decision and order, if any, in any proceeding in writing and shall give reasons in writing therefor if requested by a party.

(2) Interest — A tribunal that makes an order for the payment of money shall set out in the order the principal sum, and if interest is payable, the rate of interest and the date from which it is to be calculated.

1993, c. 27; Sched.; 1994, c. 27, s. 56

17.1 (1) Costs — Subject to subsection (2), a tribunal may, in the circumstances set out in rules made under subsection (4), order a party to pay all or part of another party's costs in a proceeding.

(2) Exception — A tribunal shall not make an order to pay costs under this section unless,

(a) the conduct or course of conduct of a party has been unreasonable, frivolous or vexatious or a party has acted in bad faith; and

(b) the tribunal has made rules under subsection (4).

(3) Amount of costs — The amount of the costs ordered under this section shall be determined in accordance with the rules made under subsection (4).

(4) Rules — A tribunal may make rules with respect to,

(a) the ordering of costs;

(b) the circumstances in which costs may be ordered; and

(c) the amount of costs or the manner in which the amount of costs is to be determined.

(5) Same — Subsections 25.1(3), (4), (5) and (6) apply with respect to rules made under subsection (4).

(6) Continuance of provisions in other statutes — Despite section 32, nothing in this section shall prevent a tribunal from ordering a party to pay all or part of another party's costs in a proceeding in circumstances other than those set out in, and without complying with, subsections (1) to (3) if the tribunal makes the order in accordance with the provisions of an Act that are in force on February 14, 2000.

(7) Transition — This section, as it read on the day before the effective date, continues to apply to proceedings commenced before the effective date.

(8) Same — Rules that are made under section 25.1 before the effective date and comply with subsection (4) are deemed to be rules made under subsection (4) until the earlier of the following days:

1. The first anniversary of the effective date.
2. The day on which the tribunal makes rules under subsection (4).

(9) **Definition** — In subsections (7) and (8),

"effective date" means the day on which section 21 of Schedule B to the *Good Government Act, 2006* comes into force.

1999, c. 12, Sched. B, s. 16(7); 2006, c. 19, Sched. B, s. 21(2)

18. (1) Notice of decision — The tribunal shall send each party who participated in the proceeding, or the party's representative, a copy of its final decision or order, including the reasons if any have been given,

(a) by regular lettermail;

(b) by electronic transmission;

(c) by telephone transmission of a facsimile; or

(d) by some other method that allows proof of receipt, if the tribunal's rules made under section 25.1 deal with the matter.

(2) Use of mail — If the copy is sent by regular lettermail, it shall be sent to the most recent addresses known to the tribunal and shall be deemed to be received by the party on the fifth day after the day it is mailed.

(3) Use of electronic or telephone transmission — If the copy is sent by electronic transmission or by telephone transmission of a facsimile, it shall be deemed to be received on the day after it was sent, unless that day is a holiday, in which case the copy shall be deemed to be received on the next day that is not a holiday.

(4) Use of other method — If the copy is sent by a method referred to in clause (1)(d), the tribunal's rules made under section 25.1 govern its deemed day of receipt.

(5) Failure to receive copy — If a party that acts in good faith does not, through absence, illness or other cause beyond the party's control, receive the copy until a later date than the deemed day of receipt, subsection (2), (3) or (4), as the case may be, does not apply.

1994, c. 27, s. 56; 1997, c. 23, s. 13; 2006, c. 21, Sched. C, s. 134(6)

19. (1) Enforcement of orders — A certified copy of a tribunal's decision or order in a proceeding may be filed in the Superior Court of Justice by the tribunal or by a party and on filing shall be deemed to be an order of that court and is enforceable as such.

(2) Notice of filing — A party who files an order under subsection (1) shall notify the tribunal within 10 days after the filing.

(3) Order for payment of money — On receiving a certified copy of a tribunal's order for the payment of money, the sheriff shall enforce the order as if it were an execution issued by the Superior Court of Justice.

1994, c. 27, s. 56; 2006, c. 19, Sched. C, s. 1(1)

20. Record of proceeding — A tribunal shall compile a record of any proceeding in which a hearing has been held which shall include,

(a) any application, complaint, reference or other document, if any, by which the proceeding was commenced;

(b) the notice of any hearing;

(c) any interlocutory orders made by the tribunal;

(d) all documentary evidence filed with the tribunal, subject to any limitation expressly imposed by any other Act on the extent to or the purposes for which any such documents may be used in evidence in any proceeding;

(e) the transcript, if any, of the oral evidence given at the hearing; and

(f) the decision of the tribunal and the reasons therefor, where reasons have been given.

21. Adjournments — A hearing may be adjourned from time to time by a tribunal of its own motion or where it is shown to the satisfaction of the tribunal that the adjournment is required to permit an adequate hearing to be held.

21.1 Corrections of errors — A tribunal may at any time correct a typographical error, error of calculation or similar error made in its decision or order.

1994, c. 27, s. 56

21.2 (1) Power to review — A tribunal may, if it considers it advisable and if its rules made under section 25.1 deal with the matter, review all or part of its own decision or order, and may confirm, vary, suspend or cancel the decision or order.

(2) Time for review — The review shall take place within a reasonable time after the decision or order is made.

(3) Conflict — In the event of a conflict between this section and any other Act, the other Act prevails.

1994, c. 27, s. 56; 1997, c. 23, s. 13

22. Administration of oaths — A member of a tribunal has power to administer oaths and affirmations for the purpose of any of its proceedings and the tribunal may require evidence before it to be given under oath or affirmation.

23. (1) Abuse of processes — A tribunal may make such orders or give such directions in proceedings before it as it considers proper to prevent abuse of its processes.

(2) Limitation on examination — A tribunal may reasonably limit further examination or cross-examination of a witness where it is satisfied that the examination or cross-examination has been sufficient to disclose fully and fairly all matters relevant to the issues in the proceeding.

(3) Exclusion of representatives — A tribunal may exclude from a hearing anyone, other than a person licensed under the *Law Society Act*, appearing on behalf of a party or as an adviser to a witness if it finds that such person is not competent properly to represent or to advise the party or witness, or does not understand and comply at the hearing with the duties and responsibilities of an advocate or adviser.

1994, c. 27, s. 56; 2006, c. 21, Sched. C, s. 134(7)

24. (1) Notice, etc. — Where a tribunal is of opinion that because the parties to any proceeding before it are so numerous or for any other reason, it is impracticable,

(a) to give notice of the hearing; or

(b) to send its decision and the material mentioned in section 18,

to all or any of the parties individually, the tribunal may, instead of doing so, cause reasonable notice of the hearing or of its decision to be given to such parties by public advertisement or otherwise as the tribunal may direct.

(2) Contents of notice — A notice of a decision given by a tribunal under clause (1)(b) shall inform the parties of the place where copies of the decision and the reasons therefor, if reasons were given, may be obtained.

25. (1) Appeal operates as stay, exception — An appeal from a decision of a tribunal to a court or other appellate body operates as a stay in the matter unless,

(a) another Act or regulation that applies to the proceeding expressly provides to the contrary; or

(b) the tribunal or the court or other appellate body orders otherwise.

(2) Idem — An application for judicial review under the *Judicial Review Procedure Act*, or the bringing of proceedings specified in subsection 2(1) of that Act is not an appeal within the meaning of subsection (1).

1997, c. 23, s. 13

25.0.1 Control of process — A tribunal has the power to determine its own procedures and practices and may for that purpose,

(a) make orders with respect to the procedures and practices that apply in any particular proceeding; and

(b) establish rules under section 25.1.

1999, c. 12, Sched. B, s. 16(8)

25.1 (1) Rules — A tribunal may make rules governing the practice and procedure before it.

(2) Application — The rules may be of general or particular application.

(3) Consistency with Acts — The rules shall be consistent with this Act and with the other Acts to which they relate.

(4) Public access — The tribunal shall make the rules available to the public in English and in French.

(5) Part III (Regulations) of the *Legislation Act, 2006* — Rules adopted under this section are not regulations as defined in Part III (Regulations) of the *Legislation Act, 2006*.

(6) Additional power — The power conferred by this section is in addition to any power to adopt rules that the tribunal may have under another Act.

1994, c. 27, s. 56; 2006, c. 21, Sched. F, s. 136(1), Table 1

26. Regulations — The Lieutenant Governor in Council may make regulations prescribing forms for the purpose of section 12.

1994, c. 27, s. 56

27. Rules, etc., available to public — A tribunal shall make any rules or guidelines established under this or any other Act available for examination by the public.

1999, c. 12, Sched. B, s. 16(9)

28. Substantial compliance — Substantial compliance with requirements respecting the content of forms, notices or documents under this Act or any rule made under this or any other Act is sufficient.

1999, c. 12, Sched. B, s. 16(9)

29. [Repealed 1994, c. 27, s. 56.]

30. [Repealed 1994, c. 27, s. 56.]

31. [Repealed 1994, c. 27, s. 56.]

32. Conflict — Unless it is expressly provided in any other Act that its provisions and regulations, rules or by-laws made under it apply despite anything in this Act, the provisions of this Act prevail over the provisions of such other Act and over regulations, rules or by-laws made under such other Act which conflict therewith.

1994, c. 27, s. 56

33. [Repealed 1994, c. 27, s. 56.]

34. [Repealed 1994, c. 27, s. 56.]

Forms 1 and 2 [Repealed 1994, c. 27, s. 56.]. *See now O. Reg. 116/95.*

Appendix 10

MORTGAGES ACT

R.S.O. 1990, c. M.40 as am. S.O. 1991, c. 6; 1993, c. 27, Sched.; 1997, c. 24, s. 215; 1998, c. 18, Sched. E, s. 183; 1999, c. 6, s. 38; 2000, c. 26, Sched. B, s. 14; 2005, c. 5, s. 42; 2006, c. 17, s. 252(1)–(13), (14) (Fr.), (15), (16)

. . .

27. Application of purchase money — The money arising from the sale shall be applied by the person receiving the same as follows:

Firstly, in payment of all the expenses incident to the sale or incurred in any attempted sale;

Secondly, in discharge of all interest and costs then due in respect of the mortgage under which the sale was made;

Thirdly, in discharge of all the principal money then due in respect of the mortgage;

Fourthly, in payment of the amounts due to the subsequent encumbrancers according to their priorities;

Fifthly, in payment to the tenants of the mortgagor of the rent deposits paid under section 106 of the *Residential Tenancies Act, 2006* where the rent deposit was not applied in payment for the last rent period,

and the residue shall be paid to the mortgagor.

1991, c. 6, s. 1; 1997, c. 24, s. 215(1); 2006, c. 17, s. 252(1)

. . .

PART V — MORTGAGEES IN POSSESSION OF RENTAL RESIDENTIAL PREMISES

44. Definitions — In this Part,

"landlord" has the same meaning as in subsection 2(1) of the *Residential Tenancies Act, 2006*; (*"locateur"*)

"mortgagee" includes a condominium corporation with a lien enforceable under subsection 32(6) of the *Condominium Act*; (*"créancier hypothécaire"*)

"rental unit" has the same meaning as in subsection 2(1) of the *Residential Tenancies Act, 2006*; (*"logement locatif"*)

"residential complex" has the same meaning as in subsection 2(1) of the *Residential Tenancies Act, 2006*; (*"ensemble d'habitation"*)

"same-sex partner" [Repealed 2005, c. 5, s. 42(1).]

"spouse" means a person,

(a) to whom the person is married, or

(b) with whom the person is living in a conjugal relationship outside marriage, if the two persons,

(i) have cohabited for at least one year,

(ii) are together the parents of a child, or

(iii) have together entered into a cohabitation agreement under section 53 of the *Family Law Act;*

(*"conjoint"*)

"tenancy agreement" has the same meaning as in subsection 2(1) of the *Residential Tenancies Act, 2006*; (*"convention de location"*)

"tenant" has the same meaning as in subsection 2(1) of the *Residential Tenancies Act, 2006*. (*"locataire"*)

1991, c. 6, s. 2; 1997, c. 24, s. 215(2); 1999, c. 6, s. 38(1);
2005, c. 5, s. 42(1), (2); 2006, c. 17, s. 252(2)–(6)

45. Single family home — (1) For purposes of this Part, a single family home is a residential complex that consists of a single dwelling unit or a primary dwelling unit and not more than two subsidiary dwelling units and that is not subject to a tenancy agreement when the mortgage is registered.

(2) Duplexes or triplexes — A residential complex that is a duplex or a triplex is not a single family home.

(3) When number of units determined — In deciding whether a residential complex qualifies as a single family home, the number of subsidiary units shall be the number that existed when the default under the mortgage occurred.

(4) Definition — For purposes of this section,

"subsidiary dwelling unit" means,

(a) an apartment or a subsidiary residential unit, including premises whose occupant or occupants are required to share a bathroom or kitchen facility with the owner, the owner's spouse, child or parent or the spouse's child or parent, where the owner, spouse, child or parent lives in the building in which the premises are located,

(b) a room or other subsidiary unit that is rented for residential purposes, including one that is rented to a member of the mortgagor's family or to an employee of the mortgagor.

1997, c. 24, s. 215(3); 1999, c. 6, s. 38(2); 2005, c. 5, s. 42(3)

46. Application — (1) In the event of a conflict between this Part and any other provision of this Act or any other Act, this Part prevails unless the provision or the Act states that it is to prevail over this Part.

(2) **Idem** — This Part applies despite any agreement to the contrary.

(3) **Idem** — This Part and section 27 apply to,

(a) tenancies of residential units and tenancy agreements whether entered into before or after the 13th day of June, 1991;

(b) mortgages, whether registered before or after the tenancy agreement was entered into, or the 13th day of June, 1991.

1991, c. 6, s. 2; 1997, c. 24, s. 215(4)

47. Person deemed to be landlord — (1) A person who becomes the mortgagee in possession of a mortgaged residential complex which is the subject of a tenancy agreement between the mortgagor and a tenant or who obtains title to the residential complex by foreclosure or power of sale shall be deemed to be the landlord under the tenancy agreement.

(2) **Person ceases to be landlord** — A person who is the landlord under the tenancy agreement ceases to be the landlord while another person is deemed to be a landlord under subsection (1).

(3) **Person deemed to be landlord** — A person who is deemed to be a landlord is subject to the tenancy agreement and to the provisions of the *Residential Tenancies Act, 2006* which apply to residential complex.

(4) **Person ceases to be landlord** — A person shall no longer be deemed to be the landlord under the tenancy agreement when the person ceases to be a mortgagee in possession.

(5) **Mortgagee's obligations continue** — Despite subsection (4), a person who is deemed to be a landlord under subsection (1) continues to be liable for the obligations of a landlord that were incurred while the person was deemed to be a landlord.

(6) **Notice to tenants** — A person who is deemed to be a landlord shall serve notice to all tenants of the change in landlord.

(7) **Idem** — The notice shall be in writing and shall provide the person's name and address.

(8) **Idem** — The notice may be in the form prescribed by the regulations made under this Act.

1991, c. 6, s. 3; 1997, c. 24, s. 215(5)–(8); 2006, c. 17, s. 252(7)

48. Possession — (1) No person exercising rights under a mortgage may obtain possession of a rental unit from the mortgagor's tenant except in accordance with the *Residential Tenancies Act, 2006*.

(2) **Person deemed to be landlord** — A person exercising rights under a mortgage who gives notice of termination of a tenancy shall be deemed to be a landlord under subsection 47(1).

1991, c. 6, s. 3; 1997, c. 24, s. 215(9); 2006, c. 17, s. 252(8)

49. Payment of rent by tenant — On or after default under the mortgage, a tenant who in good faith pays rent to a mortgagee who first serves notice on the tenant is released from the obligation to pay the rent to any other person unless the mortgagee instructs otherwise or a court orders otherwise.

1991, c. 6, s. 3

50. Mortgagee's rights after default — (1) Despite section 42, a mortgagee may at any time after the default under a mortgage on a residential complex make inquiries of the mortgagor regarding the existence of any tenancy agreement and require the mortgagor to provide a list of tenants, if any.

(2) Same — Despite section 42, a mortgagee at any time after default under a mortgage on a residential complex which is the subject of a tenancy agreement may,

(a) enter into the common areas of the residential complex for the purpose of inspection;

(b) demand production from the mortgagor or the mortgagor's tenant of a copy of the tenancy agreement if it is written; and

(c) demand from the mortgagor or the mortgagor's tenant any particulars of the tenancy agreement.

(3) Mortgagee not deemed mortgagee in possession — The mortgagee does not become a mortgagee in possession of the residential complex by any of the acts described in subsection (1) or (2).

(4) Obligations of mortgagor — In the circumstances described in subsection (1), the mortgagor shall provide the mortgagee with the information requested.

(5) Obligations of mortgagor and tenant — In the circumstances described in subsection (2), the mortgagor and the mortgagor's tenant shall provide the mortgagee with the information and documents requested and shall permit the mortgagee to enter the common areas of the complex.

(6) Application for compliance order — If a mortgagor or a mortgagor's tenant does not comply with subsection (4) or (5), the mortgagee may apply to the Superior Court of Justice for an order requiring compliance.

1991, c. 6, s. 3; 1997, c. 24, s. 215(10), (11); 2000, c. 26, Sched. B, s. 14(5)

51. Mortgagee not to interfere — (1) No mortgagee or person acting on behalf of the mortgagee shall,

(a) deliberately interfere with a reasonable supply of any service, such as heat, fuel, electricity, gas, food or water to a rental unit or to the residential complex in which it is located, whether or not it was the mortgagor's obligation to supply the service; or

(b) substantially interfere with the reasonable enjoyment of the rental unit or of the residential complex in which it is located for all the usual purposes by the mortgagor's tenant or household with the intent of causing the mortgagor's tenant to give up possession of the rental unit or to refrain from asserting any rights under this Act, the tenancy agreement or the *Residential Tenancies Act, 2006*.

(2) Offence — Any person who contravenes or fails to comply with this section is guilty of an offence and on conviction is liable to a fine of not more than $5,000 in the case of an individual and $25,000 in the case of a corporation.

1991, c. 6, s. 3; 1997, c. 24, s. 215(12); 2006, c. 17, s. 252(9)

52. Application to set aside tenancy — (1) The Superior Court of Justice may on application by the mortgagee vary or set aside a tenancy agreement, or any of its provisions, entered into by the mortgagor in contemplation of or after default under the mortgage with the object of,

(a) discouraging the mortgagee from taking possession of the residential complex on default; or

(b) adversely affecting the value of the mortgagee's interest in the residential complex.

(2) Idem — In considering the application, the judge shall have regard to the interests of the tenant and the mortgagee.

1991, c. 6, s. 3; 1997, c. 24, s. 215(13); 2000, c. 26, Sched. B, s. 14(5)

53. Termination of tenancy — (1) A person described in subsection 47(1) may obtain, under section 48 of the *Residential Tenancies Act, 2006*, possession of a single family home that is the subject of a tenancy agreement in the circumstances described in this section.

(2) Possession on behalf of purchaser — When a person described in subsection 47(1) has entered into a binding agreement for the purchase and sale of a single family home, the person may obtain possession of it on behalf of a purchaser who on closing would be entitled to give notice of termination under section 48 of the *Residential Tenancies Act, 2006*.

(3) Purchaser's undertaking in writing — The person described in subsection 47(1) shall obtain from the purchaser an undertaking in writing that states that the purchaser requires the single family home or any part of it occupied by a tenant for the purpose of occupation by himself or herself, his or her spouse or a child or parent of his or hers or of his or her spouse.

(4) Notice of termination — The notice of termination may be effective at least sixty days after it is given regardless of any fixed term of tenancy.

(5) Idem — In addition to the information required under section 43 of the *Residential Tenancies Act, 2006*, the notice of termination shall include a copy of the undertaking supplied by the purchaser.

(6) Form of notice — The form of notice of termination may be the same as the form used under section 48 of the *Residential Tenancies Act, 2006* except that it shall be modified to indicate that the mortgagee is obtaining possession on behalf of a purchaser who requires the single family home or any part of it occupied by a tenant for the purpose of occupation by himself or herself, his or her spouse or a child or parent of his or hers or of his or her spouse.

(7) Order for termination of tenancy — A person who has served notice may apply for an order terminating the tenancy and evicting the tenant under section 69 of the *Residential Tenancies Act, 2006*.

(8) Purchaser exercises rights of mortgagee — For the purpose of obtaining possession, a purchaser may exercise the rights of the person who served the notice of termination.

1991, c. 6, s. 4; 1997, c. 24, s. 215(14); 1999, c. 6, s. 38(3), (4); 2005, c. 5, s. 42(4), (5); 2006, c. 17, s. 252(10)–(13), (15)

54. Tenant's right to reoccupy — (1) If the purchaser does not within 180 days of the date of termination occupy the premises for his or her own use for a reasonable period, the tenant who was served notice under section 53 may bring an application to the Superior Court of Justice for an order directing that the tenant has the right to occupy the premises on the same terms that existed immediately before the date of termination.

(2) Limitation — An application by the tenant must be brought within 210 days after the date of termination set out in the notice of termination.

(3) Tenant's right to recovery — If the tenant makes an application or is entitled to make an application, and the premises are occupied by another tenant, the original tenant may bring an action against the purchaser to recover any costs and damages incurred as the result of the tenant having to vacate the premises.

1991, c. 6, s. 4; 2000, c. 26, Sched. B, s. 14(5)

55. Right to show single family home — A person described in subsection 47(1) may on reasonable notice show a single family home that is the subject of a tenancy agreement to a prospective purchaser at reasonable times.

1991, c. 6, s. 4; 1997, c. 24, s. 215(15)

56. Tenant's rights preserved — Nothing in this Part diminishes any rights which a tenant of a mortgagor has at common law or in equity where the mortgagee is bound by the tenancy agreement.

1991, c. 6, s. 5; 1997, c. 24, s. 215(16)

57. Service — All documents required to be served by this Part shall be served in accordance with section 191 of the *Residential Tenancies Act, 2006*.

1991, c. 6, s. 5; 1997, c. 24, s. 215(17); 2006, c. 17, s. 252(16)

58. Regulations — The Lieutenant Governor in Council may make regulations prescribing the form of notice described in subsection 47(8).

1991, c. 6, s. 5

SCHEDULE — NOTICE OF SALE UNDER MORTGAGE

(Sections 26(1) and 31(1))

Take notice that default has been made in payment of the money due under a certain mortgage dated the .... day of ...., 19.........., made between (*here state parties and describe mortgaged property*) which mortgage was registered on the .... day of ...., 19..........., in the registry division, etc. (*and, if the mortgage has been assigned, add*: and which mortgage was assigned to the undersigned on the .... day of ...., 19..........).

And I hereby give you notice that the amount now due on the mortgage for principal money, interest (*if so, add*: taxes, insurance premiums, *or other matters*) and costs, respectively, are as follows:

(*Set out items claimed to be due*)

And unless the said sums are paid on or before the .... day of ...., 19.......... (*a day not less than forty-five days from the service of the notice where the power of sale is exercised under Part II, or a day not less than thirty-five days from the service of the notice where Part III applies*), I shall sell the property covered by the said mortgage under the provisions contained in it (*or if so*: under Part II of the *Mortgages Act*).

This notice is given to you as you appear to have an interest in the mortgaged property and may be entitled to redeem the same.

Dated the .... day of ...., 19..........

(Signed) ....
Mortgagee

Appendix 11

ONT. REG. 282/98 — GENERAL REGULATION

made under the *Assessment Act*

O. Reg. 282/98 as am. O. Reg. 390/98; 721/98; 8/99; 46/99; 345/99; 351/99; 499/99; 605/99; 606/99; 105/00; 174/00; 356/00; 457/00; 679/00; 54/01; 62/01; 278/01; 45/02; 127/02; 418/02; 285/03; 347/03; 348/03; 349/03; 362/03; 363/03; 370/03; 397/03; 124/04; 198/04; 242/04; 243/04; 286/04; 388/04; 399/04; 419/04; 100/05; 211/05; 307/05; 365/05; 371/05; 536/05; 656/05; 406/06; 575/06; 126/07; 212/07; 528/07; 538/07; 90/08; 309/08; 389/08; 394/08; 437/08; 16/09; 101/09; 185/09

PART II — CLASSES OF REAL PROPERTY

Residential/Farm Property Class

3. (1) The residential property class consists of the following:

1. Land used for residential purposes that is,

i. land that does not have seven or more self-contained units,

ii. a unit or proposed unit, as defined in the *Condominium Act*,

iii. land owned by a co-operative, as defined in the *Co-operative Corporations Act*, the primary object of which is to provide housing to its members or land leased by such a co-operative if the term of the lease is at least 20 years,

iv. subject to subsection (2), land with seven or more self-contained units owned by a corporation with or without share capital each shareholder or member of which has a right, by virtue of being a shareholder or member of the corporation, to occupy one of the units,

v. subject to subsection (2), land with seven or more self-contained units owned by individuals only, each of whom has an undivided interest in the land and a right, arising from a contract with the other owners, to occupy one of the units, if at least half the units are occupied by the owners with a right to occupy them,

vi. land with self-contained units, organized as what is commonly known as a timeshare, that,

A. is owned by persons, each of whom has an undivided interest in the land and a right to occupy a unit on a periodic basis for at least one week at a time, or

B. is leased by persons, for terms of at least 20 years, each of whom has a right to occupy a unit on a periodic basis for at least one week at a time.

vii. a group home as defined in subsection 166(1) of the *Municipal Act, 2001*,

viii. a care home, as defined in the *Tenant Protection Act, 1997*, that does not have seven or more self-contained units and that is not included in the commercial property class under paragraph 2 of section 5,

ix. land used for residential purposes on a seasonal basis, including campgrounds.

x. land with self-contained units, organized as what is commonly known as a life lease project, in respect of which individuals (referred to in this subparagraph as "purchasers") have each entered into an agreement to purchase a right (referred to in this subparagraph as the "life lease interest") to occupy a unit for residential purposes within the project, if,

A. the term, not including renewals, of the life lease interest is equal to or greater than 20 years or is equal to the lifetime of the purchasers,

B. the purchasers have made one or more payments to the owner of the land on account of the purchase, and

C. the purchasers have a right to sell, transfer or otherwise dispose of the life lease interest in a manner determined under the terms of the agreement for the purchase.

xi. land that is a municipally-licensed rooming house.

xii. a recreational facility that is operated on a not-for-profit basis, if the use of the facility is restricted to residents of units in a residential subdivision, land-lease community or condominium or townhouse complex, as well as their guests, and if the facility is not open to the general public.

xiii. land on which a wind turbine tower as defined in subsection 45.4(5) is situated, but not the wind turbine tower, if,

A. the land immediately surrounding the land on which the wind turbine tower is situated is classified in the residential property class,

B. the electricity generated by the wind turbine tower is primarily for the operator's own use, and

C. the rated maximum output capacity of the wind turbine tower does not exceed 500 kilowatts.

2. Land not used for residential purposes that is,

i. farm land to which subsection 19(5) of the Act applies for the taxation year for which the land is being classified, other than land in the farm property class or land prescribed under section 44,

ii. land used by a non-profit organization for child care purposes that is either,

A. land owned by the organization, or

B. land leased by the organization, other than land that would otherwise be in the commercial property class or the industrial property class,

iii. land owned by a religious organization other than land occupied by a tenant and used for a commercial activity,

iv. land owned and occupied by a non-profit service organization, a non-profit private club, a non-profit cultural organization or a non-profit recreational sports club, other than land used as a golf course or ski resort,

v. land owned by a conservation authority, other than land occupied by a tenant and used for a commercial activity or land used as a golf course or ski resort,

vi. land used as a golf course, including buildings or structures used for the purpose of maintaining the golf course, but not including any other buildings and structures and the land used in connection with those other buildings or structures,

vii. land used as a driving range for at least four consecutive months a year but not including any buildings and structures and the land used in connection with those buildings or structures,

viii. land used as a ski resort, including ski-lifts and buildings or structures used for the purpose of maintaining ski hills or trails, but not including, any other buildings and structures and the land used in connection with those other buildings or structures,

ix. vacant land principally zoned for residential development but not principally zoned for multi-residential development.

x. buildings used exclusively for the purposes of storing private aircraft and land on which those buildings are located.

xi. land used to provide horse trail rides or horse riding lessons to the public.

3. For the 2000 and subsequent taxation years, the portion of land that is licensed or required to be licensed under Part II of the *Aggregate Resources Act* that is not in the farm property class or the industrial property class.

(2) Land described in subparagraph iv or v of paragraph 1 of subsection (1) is included in the residential/farm property class for 1999, 2000, 2001 or 2002 or in the residential property class for 2003 or a later taxation year only if the land was included in the residential/farm property class for the 1998 taxation year under subparagraph iv or v of paragraph 1 of subsection (1) as it read on December 31, 2002.

(2.1) In subparagraph 2 iv of subsection (1),

"cultural organization" means an organization that is established and maintained for cultural activities for Canadians of a specific ethnic origin, including First Nations peoples;

"service organization" means an organization whose primary function is to provide services to promote the welfare of the community and not only to benefit its members.

(3) In subparagraph vii of paragraph 2 of subsection (1),

"driving range" means an outdoor practice area for driving golf balls.

(4) In subparagraph 2 x of subsection (1),

"private aircraft" means an aircraft that is owned by one or more individuals and used exclusively for the recreational purposes of the owner or owners and not for any commercial purposes.

(5) If the assessment corporation requests the owner of land to verify that all aircraft stored in buildings are private aircraft, the owner shall do so before the land and buildings are classified in the residential property class under subparagraph 2 x of subsection (1).

(6) Subparagraph 2 xi of subsection (1) applies to the 2004 and subsequent taxation years.

O. Reg. 351/99, s. 1; 356/00, s. 1;
54/01, s. 1; 362/03, s. 1; 363/03, s. 2;
198/04, s. 2; 100/05, s. 1; 536/05, s. 1;
212/07, s. 1; 528/07, s. 1

Multi-Residential Property Class

4. (1) The multi-residential property class consists of the following:

1. Land used for residential purposes that has seven or more self-contained units other than land included in the residential property class under paragraph 1 of subsection 3(1).

2. Vacant land principally zoned for multi-residential development.

(2) Land in the new multi-residential property class is not included in the multi-residential property class.

O. Reg. 363/03, s. 3

Appendix 12

Human Rights Code

R.S.O. 1990, c. H.19 as am. S.O. 1993, c. 27, Sched.; 1993, c. 35, s. 56; 1994, c. 10, s. 22; 1994, c. 27, s. 65 [s. 65(7) not in force at date of publication.]; 1995, c. 4, s. 3; 1997, c. 16, s. 8; 1997, c. 24, s. 212; 1999, c. 6, s. 28; 2001, c. 13, s. 19; 2001, c. 32, s. 27; 2002, c. 18, Sched. C; 2005, c. 5, s. 32; 2005, c. 18, s. 17; 2005, c. 29, s. 1; 2006, c. 19, Sched. B, s. 10 (Fr.); 2006, c. 21, Sched. F, ss. 136(2), Table 2, 137; 2006, c. 30; 2006, c. 35, Sched. C, ss. 54(1), 132

Preamble

WHEREAS recognition of the inherent dignity and the equal and inalienable rights of all members of the human family is the foundation of freedom, justice and peace in the world and is in accord with the Universal Declaration of Human Rights as proclaimed by the United Nations;

AND WHEREAS it is public policy in Ontario to recognize the dignity and worth of every person and to provide for equal rights and opportunities without discrimination that is contrary to law, and having as its aim the creation of a climate of understanding and mutual respect for the dignity and worth of each person so that each person feels a part of the community and able to contribute fully to the development and well-being of the community and the Province;

AND WHEREAS these principles have been confirmed in Ontario by a number of enactments of the Legislature and it is desirable to revise and extend the protection of human rights in Ontario;

Therefore, Her Majesty, by and with the advice and consent of the Legislative Assembly of the Province of Ontario, enacts as follows:

Part I Freedom from Discrimination

1. Services

Every person has a right to equal treatment with respect to services, goods and facilities, without discrimination because of race, ancestry, place of origin, colour, ethnic origin, citizenship, creed, sex, sexual orientation, age, marital status, family status or disability.

1999, c. 6, s. 28(1); 2001, c. 32, s. 27(1), item 1; 2005, c. 5, s. 32(1)

2. (1) Accommodation

Every person has a right to equal treatment with respect to the occupancy of accommodation, without discrimination because of race, ancestry, place of origin, colour, ethnic origin, citizenship, creed, sex, sexual orientation, age, marital status, family status, disability or the receipt of public assistance.

(2) Harassment in accommodation

Every person who occupies accommodation has a right to freedom from harassment by the landlord or agent of the landlord or by an occupant of the same building because of race, ancestry, place of origin, colour, ethnic origin, citizenship, creed, age, marital status, family status, disability or the receipt of public assistance.

1999, c. 6, s. 28(2), (3); 2001, c. 32, s. 27(1), item 2; 2005, c. 5, s. 32(2), (3)

3. Contracts

Every person having legal capacity has a right to contract on equal terms without discrimination because of race, ancestry, place of origin, colour, ethnic origin, citizenship, creed, sex, sexual orientation, age, marital status, family status or disability.

1999, c. 6, s. 28(4); 2001, c. 32, s. 27(1), item 3; 2005, c. 5, s. 32(4)

4. (1) Accommodation of person under eighteen

Every sixteen or seventeen year old person who has withdrawn from parental control has a right to equal treatment with respect to occupancy of and contracting for accommodation without discrimination because the person is less than eighteen years old.

(2) Idem

A contract for accommodation entered into by a sixteen or seventeen year old person who has withdrawn from parental control is enforceable against that person as if the person were eighteen years old.

5. (1) Employment

Every person has a right to equal treatment with respect to employment without discrimination because of race, ancestry, place of origin, colour, ethnic origin, citizenship, creed, sex, sexual orientation, age, record of offences, marital status, family status or disability.

(2) Harassment in employment

Every person who is an employee has a right to freedom from harassment in the workplace by the employer or agent of the employer or by another employee because of race, ancestry, place of origin, colour, ethnic origin, citizenship, creed, age, record of offences, marital status, family status or disability.

1999, c. 6, s. 28(5), (6); 2001, c. 32, s. 27(1), item 4; 2005, c. 5, s. 32(5), (6)

6. Vocational associations

Every person has a right to equal treatment with respect to membership in any trade union, trade or occupational association or self-governing profession without discrimination because of race, ancestry, place of origin, colour, ethnic origin, citizenship, creed, sex, sexual orientation, age, marital status, family status or disability.

1999, c. 6, s. 28(7); 2001, c. 32, s. 27(1), item 5; 2005, c. 5, s. 32(7)

7. (1) Harassment because of sex in accommodation

Every person who occupies accommodation has a right to freedom from harassment because of sex by the landlord or agent of the landlord or by an occupant of the same building.

(2) Harassment because of sex in workplace

Every person who is an employee has a right to freedom from harassment in the workplace because of sex by his or her employer or agent of the employer or by another employee.

(3) Sexual solicitation by a person in position to confer benefit, etc.

Every person has a right to be free from,

(a) a sexual solicitation or advance made by a person in a position to confer, grant or deny a benefit or advancement to the person where the person making the solicitation or advance knows or ought reasonably to know that it is unwelcome; or

(b) a reprisal or a threat of reprisal for the rejection of a sexual solicitation or advance where the reprisal is made or threatened by a person in a position to confer, grant or deny a benefit or advancement to the person.

8. Reprisals

Every person has a right to claim and enforce his or her rights under this Act, to institute and participate in proceedings under this Act and to refuse to infringe a right of another person under this Act, without reprisal or threat of reprisal for so doing.

9. Infringement prohibited

No person shall infringe or do, directly or indirectly, anything that infringes a right under this Part.

Part II Interpretation and Application

10. (1) Definitions

In Part I and in this Part,

"age" means an age that is 18 years or more;

"because of handicap" [Repealed 2001, c. 32, s. 27(2).]

"disability" means,

(a) any degree of physical disability, infirmity, malformation or disfigurement that is caused by bodily injury, birth defect or illness and, without limiting the generality of the foregoing, includes diabetes mellitus, epilepsy, a brain injury, any degree of paralysis, amputation, lack of physical co-ordination, blindness or visual impediment, deafness or hearing impediment, muteness or speech impediment, or physical reliance on a guide dog or other animal or on a wheelchair or other remedial appliance or device,

(b) a condition of mental impairment or a developmental disability,

(c) a learning disability, or a dysfunction in one or more of the processes involved in understanding or using symbols or spoken language,

(d) a mental disorder, or

(e) an injury or disability for which benefits were claimed or received under the insurance plan established under the *Workplace Safety and Insurance Act, 1997*;

"equal" means subject to all requirements, qualifications and considerations that are not a prohibited ground of discrimination;

"family status" means the status of being in a parent and child relationship;

"group insurance" means insurance whereby the lives or well-being or the lives and well-being of a number of persons are insured severally under a single contract between an insurer and an association or an employer or other person;

"harassment" means engaging in a course of vexatious comment or conduct that is known or ought reasonably to be known to be unwelcome;

"marital status" means the status of being married, single, widowed, divorced or separated and includes the status of living with a person in a conjugal relationship outside marriage;

"record of offences" means a conviction for,

(a) an offence in respect of which a pardon has been granted under the *Criminal Records Act* (Canada) and has not been revoked, or

(b) an offence in respect of any provincial enactment;

"same-sex partner" [Repealed 2005, c. 5, s. 32(9).]

"same-sex partnership status" [Repealed 2005, c. 5, s. 32(9).]

"services" does not include a levy, fee, tax or periodic payment imposed by law;

"spouse" means the person to whom a person is married or with whom the person is living in a conjugal relationship outside marriage.

(2) Pregnancy

The right to equal treatment without discrimination because of sex includes the right to equal treatment without discrimination because a woman is or may become pregnant.

(3) Past and presumed disabilities

The right to equal treatment without discrimination because of disability includes the right to equal treatment without discrimination because a person has or has had a disability or is believed to have or to have had a disability.

1997, c. 16, s. 8; 1999, c. 6, s. 28(8); 2001, c. 13, s. 19; 2001, c. 32, s. 27(2)–(4); 2005, c. 5, s. 32(8)–(10); 2005, c. 29, s. 1(1)

11. (1) Constructive discrimination

A right of a person under Part I is infringed where a requirement, qualification or factor exists that is not discrimination on a prohibited ground but that results in the exclusion, restriction or preference of a group of persons who are identified by a prohibited ground of discrimination and of whom the person is a member, except where,

(a) the requirement, qualification or factor is reasonable and *bona fide* in the circumstances; or

(b) it is declared in this Act, other than in section 17, that to discriminate because of such ground is not an infringement of a right.

(2) Idem

The Commission, the Tribunal or a court shall not find that a requirement, qualification or factor is reasonable and *bona fide* in the circumstances unless it is satisfied that the needs of the group of which the person is a member cannot be accommodated without undue hardship on the person responsible for accommodating those needs, considering the cost, outside sources of funding, if any, and health and safety requirements, if any.

(3) Idem

The Commission, the Tribunal or a court shall consider any standards prescribed by the regulations for assessing what is undue hardship.

1994, c. 27, s. 65(1), (2); 2002, c. 18, Sched. C, s. 2

12. Discrimination because of association

A right under Part I is infringed where the discrimination is because of relationship, association or dealings with a person or persons identified by a prohibited ground of discrimination.

13. (1) Announced intention to discriminate

A right under Part I is infringed by a person who publishes or displays before the public or causes the publication or display before the public of any notice, sign, symbol, emblem, or other similar representation that indicates the intention of the person to infringe a right under Part I or that is intended by the person to incite the infringement of a right under Part I.

(2) Opinion

Subsection (1) shall not interfere with freedom of expression of opinion.

14. (1) Special programs

A right under Part I is not infringed by the implementation of a special program designed to relieve hardship or economic disadvantage or to assist disadvantaged persons or groups to achieve or attempt to achieve equal opportunity or that is likely to contribute to the elimination of the infringement of rights under Part I.

(2) Application to Commission

A person may apply to the Commission for a designation of a program as a special program for the purposes of subsection (1).

(3) Designation by Commission

Upon receipt of an application, the Commission may,

(a) designate the program as a special program if, in its opinion, the program meets the requirements of subsection (1); or

(b) designate the program as a special program on the condition that the program make such modifications as are specified in the designation in order to meet the requirements of subsection (1).

(4) Inquiries initiated by Commission

The Commission may, on its own initiative, inquire into one or more programs to determine whether the programs are special programs for the purposes of subsection (1).

(5) End of inquiry

At the conclusion of an inquiry under subsection (4), the Commission may designate as a special program any of the programs under inquiry if, in its opinion, the programs meet the requirements of subsection (1).

(6) Expiry of designation

A designation under subsection (3) or (5) expires five years after the day it is issued or at such earlier time as may be specified by the Commission.

(7) Renewal of designation

If an application for renewal of a designation of a program as a special program is made to the Commission before its expiry under subsection (6), the Commission may,

(a) renew the designation if, in its opinion, the program continues to meet the requirements of subsection (1); or

(b) renew the designation on the condition that the program make such modifications as are specified in the designation in order to meet the requirements of subsection (1).

(8) Effect of designation, etc.

In a proceeding,

(a) evidence that a program has been designated as a special program under this section is proof, in the absence of evidence to the contrary, that the program is a special program for the purposes of subsection (1); and

(b) evidence that the Commission has considered and refused to designate a program as a special program under this section is proof, in the absence of evidence to the contrary, that the program is not a special program for the purposes of subsection (1).

(9) Crown programs

Subsections (2) to (8) do not apply to a program implemented by the Crown or an agency of the Crown.

(10) Tribunal finding

For the purposes of a proceeding before the Tribunal, the Tribunal may make a finding that a program meets the requirements of a special program under subsection (1), even though the program has not been designated as a special program by the Commission under this section, subject to clause (8)(b).

2006, c. 30, s. 1

14.1 [Repealed 1995, c. 4, s. 3(1).]

15. Age sixty-five or over

A right under Part I to non-discrimination because of age is not infringed where an age of sixty-five years or over is a requirement, qualification or consideration for preferential treatment.

16. (1) Canadian Citizenship

A right under Part I to non-discrimination because of citizenship is not infringed where Canadian citizenship is a requirement, qualification or consideration imposed or authorized by law.

(2) Idem

A right under Part I to non-discrimination because of citizenship is not infringed where Canadian citizenship or lawful admission to Canada for permanent residence is a requirement, qualification or consideration adopted for the purpose of fostering and developing participation in cultural, educational, trade union or athletic activities by Canadian citizens or persons lawfully admitted to Canada for permanent residence.

(3) Idem

A right under Part I to non-discrimination because of citizenship is not infringed where Canadian citizenship or domicile in Canada with the intention to obtain Canadian citizenship is a requirement, qualification or consideration adopted by an organization or enterprise for the holder of chief or senior executive positions.

17. (1) Disability

A right of a person under this Act is not infringed for the reason only that the person is incapable of performing or fulfilling the essential duties or requirements attending the exercise of the right because of disability.

(2) Accommodation

No tribunal or court shall find a person incapable unless it is satisfied that the needs of the person cannot be accommodated without undue hardship on the person responsible for accommodating those needs, considering the cost, outside sources of funding, if any, and health and safety requirements, if any.

(3) Determining if undue hardship

In determining for the purposes of subsection (2) whether there would be undue hardship, a tribunal or court shall consider any standards prescribed by the regulations.

(4) [Repealed 2006, c. 30, s. 2(3).]

1994, c. 27, s. 65(2), (3); 2001, c. 32, s. 27(5), item 1; 2002, c. 18, Sched. C, ss. 1 (item 1), 3; 2006, c. 30, s. 2

18. Special interest organizations

The rights under Part I to equal treatment with respect to services and facilities, with or without accommodation, are not infringed where membership or participation in a religious, philanthropic, educational, fraternal or social institution or organization that is primarily engaged in serving the interests of persons identified by a prohibited ground of discrimination is restricted to persons who are similarly identified.

18.1 (1) Solemnization of marriage by religious officials

The rights under Part I to equal treatment with respect to services and facilities are not infringed where a person registered under section 20 of the *Marriage Act* refuses to solemnize a marriage, to allow a sacred place to be used for solemnizing a marriage or for an event related to the solemnization of a marriage, or to otherwise assist in the solemnization of a marriage, if to solemnize the marriage, allow the sacred place to be used or otherwise assist would be contrary to,

(a) the person's religious beliefs; or

(b) the doctrines, rites, usages or customs of the religious body to which the person belongs.

(2) Same

Nothing in subsection (1) limits the application of section 18.

(3) Definition

In this section,

"sacred place" includes a place of worship and any ancillary or accessory facilities.

2005, c. 5, s. 32(11)

19. (1) Separate school rights preserved

This Act shall not be construed to adversely affect any right or privilege respecting separate schools enjoyed by separate school boards or their supporters under the *Constitution Act, 1867* and the *Education Act*.

(2) Duties of teachers

This Act does not apply to affect the application of the *Education Act* with respect to the duties of teachers.

20. (1) Restriction of facilities by sex

The right under section 1 to equal treatment with respect to services and facilities without discrimination because of sex is not infringed where the use of the services or facilities is restricted to persons of the same sex on the ground of public decency.

(2) Minimum drinking age

The right under section 1 to equal treatment with respect to services, goods and facilities without discrimination because of age is not infringed by the provisions of the *Liquor Licence Act* and the regulations under it relating to providing for and enforcing a minimum drinking age of nineteen years.

(3) Recreational clubs

The right under section 1 to equal treatment with respect to services and facilities is not infringed where a recreational club restricts or qualifies access to its services or facilities or gives preferences with respect to membership dues and other fees because of age, sex, marital status, or family status.

(4) Tobacco and young persons

The right under section 1 to equal treatment with respect to goods without discrimination because of age is not infringed by the provisions of the *Smoke-Free Ontario Act* and the regulations under it relating to selling or supplying tobacco to persons who are, or who appear to be, under the age of 19 years or 25 years, as the case may be.

1994, c. 10, s. 22; 1999, c. 6, s. 28(9); 2005, c. 5, s. 32(12); 2005, c. 18, s. 17

21. (1) Shared accommodation

The right under section 2 to equal treatment with respect to the occupancy of residential accommodation without discrimination is not infringed by discrimination where the residential accommodation is in a dwelling in which the owner or his or her family reside if the occupant or occupants of the residential accommodation are required to share a bathroom or kitchen facility with the owner or family of the owner.

(2) Restrictions on accommodation, sex

The right under section 2 to equal treatment with respect to the occupancy of residential accommodation without discrimination because of sex is not infringed by discrimination on that ground where the occupancy of all the residential accommodation in the building, other than the accommodation, if any, of the owner or family of the owner, is restricted to persons who are of the same sex.

(3) Prescribing business practices

The right under section 2 to equal treatment with respect to the occupancy of residential accommodation without discrimination is not infringed if a landlord uses in the manner prescribed under this Act income information, credit checks, credit references, rental history, guarantees or other similar business practices which are prescribed in the regulations made under this Act in selecting prospective tenants.

1997, c. 24, s. 212

22. Restrictions for insurance contracts, etc.

The right under sections 1 and 3 to equal treatment with respect to services and to contract on equal terms, without discrimination because of age, sex, marital status, family status or disability, is not infringed where a contract of automobile, life, accident or sickness or disability insurance or a contract of group insurance between an insurer and an association or person other than an employer, or a life annuity, differentiates or makes a distinction, exclusion or preference on reasonable and *bona fide* grounds because of age, sex, marital status, family status or disability.

1999, c. 6, s. 28(10); 2001, c. 32, s. 27(5), item 2; 2005, c. 5, s. 32(13)

23. (1) Discriminatory employment advertising

The right under section 5 to equal treatment with respect to employment is infringed where an invitation to apply for employment or an advertisement in connection with employment is published or displayed that directly or indirectly classifies or indicates qualifications by a prohibited ground of discrimination.

(2) Application for employment

The right under section 5 to equal treatment with respect to employment is infringed where a form of application for employment is used or a written or oral inquiry is made of an applicant that directly or indirectly classifies or indicates qualifications by a prohibited ground of discrimination.

(3) Questions at interview

Nothing in subsection (2) precludes the asking of questions at a personal employment interview concerning a prohibited ground of discrimination where discrimination on such ground is permitted under this Act.

(4) Employment agencies

The right under section 5 to equal treatment with respect to employment is infringed where an employment agency discriminates against a person because of a prohibited ground of discrimination in receiving, classifying, disposing of or otherwise acting upon applications for its services or in referring an applicant or applicants to an employer or agent of an employer.

24. (1) Special employment

The right under section 5 to equal treatment with respect to employment is not infringed where,

(a) a religious, philanthropic, educational, fraternal or social institution or organization that is primarily engaged in serving the interests of persons identified by their race, ancestry, place of origin, colour, ethnic origin, creed, sex, age, marital status or disability employs only, or gives preference in employment to, persons similarly identified if the qualification is a reasonable and *bona fide* qualification because of the nature of the employment;

(b) the discrimination in employment is for reasons of age, sex, record of offences or marital status if the age, sex, record of offences or marital status of the applicant is a reasonable and *bona fide* qualification because of the nature of the employment;

(c) an individual person refuses to employ another for reasons of any prohibited ground of discrimination in section 5, where the primary duty of the employment is attending to the medical or personal needs of the person or of an ill child or an aged, infirm or ill spouse or other relative of the person;

(d) an employer grants or withholds employment or advancement in employment to a person who is the spouse, child or parent of the employer or an employee.

(e) a judge or master is required to retire or cease to continue in office on reaching a specified age under the *Courts of Justice Act*;

(f) a case management master is required to retire on reaching a specified age under the *Courts of Justice Act*;

(g) the term of reappointment of a case management master expires on the case management master reaching a specified age under the *Courts of Justice Act*; or

(h) a justice of the peace is required to retire on reaching a specified age under the *Justices of the Peace Act*.

(2) Reasonable accommodation

No tribunal or court shall find that a qualification under clause (1)(b) is reasonable and *bona fide* unless it is satisfied that the circumstances of the person cannot be accommodated without undue hardship on the person responsible for accommodating those circumstances considering the cost, outside sources of funding, if any, and health and safety requirements, if any.

(3) Determining if undue hardship

In determining for the purposes of subsection (2) whether there would be undue hardship, a tribunal or court shall consider any standards prescribed by the regulations.

(4) Same

Clauses 24(1)(e), (f), (g) and (h) shall not be interpreted to suggest that a judge, master, case management master or justice of the peace is an employee for the purposes of this Act or any other Act or law.

1994, c. 27, s. 65(4); 1999, c. 6, s. 28(11); 2001, c. 32, s. 27(5), item 3; 2002, c. 18, Sched. C, s. 4; 2005, c. 5, s. 32(14); 2005, c. 29, s. 1(2), (3); 2006, c. 30, s. 3

24.1 [Repealed 1995, c. 4, s. 3(2).]

25. (1) Employment conditional on membership in pension plan

The right under section 5 to equal treatment with respect to employment is infringed where employment is denied or made conditional because a term or condition of employment requires enrolment in an employee benefit, pension or superannuation plan or fund or a contract of group insurance between an insurer and an employer, that makes a distinction, preference or exclusion on a prohibited ground of discrimination.

(2) Pension or disability plan

The right under section 5 to equal treatment with respect to employment without discrimination because of sex, marital status or family status is not infringed by an employee superannuation or pension plan or fund or a contract of group insurance between an insurer and an employer that complies with the *Employment Standards Act, 2000* and the regulations thereunder.

(2.1) Same

The right under section 5 to equal treatment with respect to employment without discrimination because of age is not infringed by an employee benefit, pension, superannuation or group insurance plan or fund that complies with the *Employment Standards Act, 2000* and the regulations thereunder.

(2.2) Same

Subsection (2.1) applies whether or not a plan or fund is the subject of a contract of insurance between an insurer and an employer.

(2.3) Same

For greater certainty, subsections (2) and (2.1) apply whether or not "age", "sex" or "marital status" in the *Employment Standards Act, 2000* or the regulations under it have the same meaning as those terms have in this Act.

(3) Employee disability and pension plans: disability

The right under section 5 to equal treatment with respect to employment without discrimination because of disability is not infringed,

(a) where a reasonable and *bona fide* distinction, exclusion or preference is made in an employee disability or life insurance plan or benefit because of a pre-existing disability that substantially increases the risk;

(b) where a reasonable and *bona fide* distinction, exclusion or preference is made on the ground of a pre-existing disability in respect of an employee, pay-all or participant-pay-all benefit in an employee benefit, pension or superannuation plan or fund or a contract of group insurance between an insurer and an employer or in respect of a plan, fund or policy that is offered by an employer to employees if they are fewer than twenty-five in number.

(4) Compensation

An employer shall pay to an employee who is excluded because of a disability from an employee benefit, pension or superannuation plan or fund or a contract of group insurance between an insurer and the employer compensation equivalent to the contribution that the employer would make thereto on behalf of an employee who does not have a disability.

1999, c. 6, s. 28(12); 2001, c. 32, s. 27(5), item 4; 2005, c. 5, s. 32(15); 2005, c. 29, s. 1(4), (5)

26. (1) Discrimination in employment under government contracts

It shall be deemed to be a condition of every contract entered into by or on behalf of the Crown or any agency thereof and of every subcontract entered into in the performance thereof that no right under section 5 will be infringed in the course of performing the contract.

(2) Idem: government grants and loans

It shall be deemed to be a condition of every grant, contribution, loan or guarantee made by or on behalf of the Crown or any agency thereof that no right under section 5 will be infringed in the course of carrying out the purposes for which the grant, contribution, loan or guarantee was made.

(3) Sanction

Where an infringement of a right under section 5 is found by the Tribunal upon a complaint and constitutes a breach of a condition under this section, the breach of condition is sufficient grounds for cancellation of the contract, grant, contribution, loan or guarantee and refusal to enter into any further contract with or make any further grant, contribution, loan or guarantee to the same person.

2002, c. 18, Sched. C, s. 5

Part III The Ontario Human Rights Commission

27. (1) The Commission

The Ontario Human Rights Commission is continued under the name Ontario Human Rights Commission in English and Commission ontarienne des droits de la personne in French.

(2) Composition

The Commission shall be composed of such persons as are appointed by the Lieutenant Governor in Council.

(3) Appointment

Every person appointed to the Commission shall have knowledge, experience or training with respect to human rights law and issues.

(4) Criteria

In the appointment of persons to the Commission under subsection (2), the importance of reflecting, in the composition of the Commission as a whole, the diversity of Ontario's population shall be recognized.

(5) Chief Commissioner

The Lieutenant Governor in Council shall designate a member of the Commission as Chief Commissioner.

(6) Powers and duties of Chief Commissioner

The Chief Commissioner shall direct the Commission and exercise the powers and perform the duties assigned to the Chief Commissioner by or under this Act.

(7) Term of office

The Chief Commissioner and other members of the Commission shall hold office for such term as may be specified by the Lieutenant Governor in Council.

(8) Remuneration

The Chief Commissioner and other members of the Commission shall be paid such remuneration and allowance for expenses as are fixed by the Lieutenant Governor in Council.

(9) Employees

The Commission may appoint such employees as it considers necessary for the proper conduct of its affairs and the employees shall be appointed under Part III of the *Public Service of Ontario Act, 2006*.

(10) Evidence obtained in performance of duties

A member of the Commission shall not be required to give testimony in a civil suit or any proceeding as to information obtained in the performance of duties under this Act.

(11) Same, employees

An employee of the Commission shall not be required to give testimony in a civil suit or any proceeding other than a proceeding under this Act as to information obtained in the performance of duties under this Act.

(12) Delegation

The Chief Commissioner may in writing delegate any of his or her powers, duties or functions under this Act to any member of the Anti-Racism Secretariat, the Disability Rights Secretariat or an advisory group or to any other member of the Commission, subject to such conditions as the Chief Commissioner may set out in the delegation.

(13) Divisions

The Commission may authorize any function of the Commission to be performed by a division of the Commission composed of at least three members of the Commission.
2006, c. 30, s. 4; 2006, c. 35, Sched. C, ss. 54(1), 132(5)

28. (1) Acting Chief Commissioner

If the Chief Commissioner dies, resigns or is unable or neglects to perform his or her duties, the Lieutenant Governor in Council may appoint an Acting Chief Commissioner to hold office for such period as may be specified in the appointment.

(2) Same

An Acting Chief Commissioner shall perform the duties and have the powers of the Chief Commissioner and shall be paid such remuneration and allowance for expenses as are fixed by the Lieutenant Governor in Council.

2006, c. 30, s. 4

29. Functions of Commission

The functions of the Commission are to promote and advance respect for human rights in Ontario, to protect human rights in Ontario and, recognizing that it is in the public interest to do so and that it is the Commission's duty to protect the public interest, to identify and promote the elimination of discriminatory practices and, more specifically,

(a) to forward the policy that the dignity and worth of every person be recognized and that equal rights and opportunities be provided without discrimination that is contrary to law;

(b) to develop and conduct programs of public information and education to,

(i) promote awareness and understanding of, respect for and compliance with this Act, and

(ii) prevent and eliminate discriminatory practices that infringe rights under Part I;

(c) to undertake, direct and encourage research into discriminatory practices and to make recommendations designed to prevent and eliminate such discriminatory practices;

(d) to examine and review any statute or regulation, and any program or policy made by or under a statute, and make recommendations on any provision, program or policy that in his or her opinion is inconsistent with the intent of this Act;

(e) to initiate reviews and inquiries into incidents of tension or conflict, or conditions that lead or may lead to incidents of tension or conflict, in a community, institution, industry or sector of the economy, and to make recommendations, and encourage and co-ordinate plans, programs and activities, to reduce or prevent such incidents or sources of tension or conflict;

(f) to promote, assist and encourage public, municipal or private agencies, organizations, groups or persons to engage in programs to alleviate tensions and conflicts based upon identification by a prohibited ground of discrimination;

(g) to designate programs as special programs in accordance with section 14;

(h) to approve policies under section 30;

(i) to make applications to the Tribunal under section 35;

(j) to report to the people of Ontario on the state of human rights in Ontario and on its affairs;

(k) to perform the functions assigned to the Commission under this or any other Act.

1994, c. 27, s. 65(6); 2002, c. 18, Sched. C, s. 1, item 2; 2006, c. 30, s. 4

30. Commission policies

The Commission may approve policies prepared and published by the Commission to provide guidance in the application of Parts I and II.

2006, c. 30, s. 4

31. (1) Inquiries

The Commission may conduct an inquiry under this section for the purpose of carrying out its functions under this Act if the Commission believes it is in the public interest to do so.

(2) Conduct of inquiry

An inquiry may be conducted under this section by any person who is appointed by the Commission to carry out inquiries under this section.

(3) Production of certificate

A person conducting an inquiry under this section shall produce proof of their appointment upon request.

(4) Entry

A person conducting an inquiry under this section may, without warrant, enter any lands or any building, structure or premises where the person has reason to believe there may be documents, things or information relevant to the inquiry.

(5) Time of entry

The power to enter a place under subsection (4) may be exercised only during the place's regular business hours or, if it does not have regular business hours, during daylight hours.

(6) Dwellings

A person conducting an inquiry under this section shall not enter into a place or part of a place that is a dwelling without the consent of the occupant.

(7) Powers on inquiry

A person conducting an inquiry may,

(a) request the production for inspection and examination of documents or things that are or may be relevant to the inquiry;

(b) upon giving a receipt for it, remove from a place documents produced in response to a request under clause (a) for the purpose of making copies or extracts;

(c) question a person on matters that are or may be relevant to the inquiry, subject to the person's right to have counsel or a personal representative present during such questioning and exclude from the questioning any person who may be adverse in interest to the inquiry;

(d) use any data storage, processing or retrieval device or system used in carrying on business in the place in order to produce a document in readable form;

(e) take measurements or record by any means the physical dimensions of a place;

(f) take photographs, video recordings or other visual or audio recordings of the interior or exterior of a place; and

(g) require that a place or part thereof not be disturbed for a reasonable period of time for the purposes of carrying out an examination, inquiry or test.

(8) Written demand

A demand that a document or thing be produced must be in writing and must include a statement of the nature of the document or thing required.

(9) Assistance

A person conducting an inquiry may be accompanied by any person who has special, expert or professional knowledge and who may be of assistance in carrying out the inquiry.

(10) Use of force prohibited

A person conducting an inquiry shall not use force to enter and search premises under this section.

(11) Obligation to produce and assist

A person who is requested to produce a document or thing under clause (7)(a) shall produce it and shall, on request by the person conducting the inquiry, provide any assistance that is reasonably necessary, including assistance in using any data storage, processing or retrieval device or system, to produce a document in readable form.

(12) Return of removed things

A person conducting an inquiry who removes any document or thing from a place under clause (7)(b) shall,

(a) make it available to the person from whom it was removed, on request, at a time and place convenient for both that person and the person conducting the inquiry; and

(b) return it to the person from whom it was removed within a reasonable time.

(13) Admissibility of copies

A copy of a document certified by a person conducting an inquiry to be a true copy of the original is admissible in evidence to the same extent as the original and has the same evidentiary value.

(14) Obstruction

No person shall obstruct or interfere with a person conducting an inquiry under this section.

2006, c. 30, s. 4

31.1 (1) Search warrant

The Commission may authorize a person to apply to a justice of the peace for a warrant to enter a place and conduct a search of the place if,

(a) a person conducting an inquiry under section 31 has been denied entry to any place or asked to leave a place before concluding a search;

(b) a person conducting an inquiry under section 31 made a request for documents or things and the request was refused; or

(c) an inquiry under section 31 is otherwise obstructed or prevented.

(2) Same

Upon application by a person authorized under subsection (1) to do so, a justice of the peace may issue a warrant under this section if he or she is satisfied on information under oath or affirmation that the warrant is necessary for the purposes of carrying out the inquiry under section 31.

(3) Powers

A warrant obtained under subsection (2) may authorize a person named in the warrant, upon producing proof of his or her appointment,

(a) to enter any place specified in the warrant, including a dwelling; and

(b) to do any of the things specified in the warrant.

(4) Conditions on search warrant

A warrant obtained under subsection (2) shall contain such conditions as the justice of the peace considers advisable to ensure that any search authorized by the warrant is reasonable in the circumstances.

(5) Time of execution

An entry under a warrant issued under this section shall be made at such reasonable times as may be specified in the warrant.

(6) Expiry of warrant

A warrant issued under this section shall name a date of expiry, which shall be no later than 15 days after the warrant is issued, but a justice of the peace may extend the date of expiry for an additional period of no more than 15 days, upon application without notice by the person named in the warrant.

(7) Use of force

The person authorized to execute the warrant may call upon police officers for assistance in executing the warrant and the person may use whatever force is reasonably necessary to execute the warrant.

(8) Obstruction prohibited

No person shall obstruct or hinder a person in the execution of a warrant issued under this section.

(9) Application

Subsections 31(11), (12) and (13) apply with necessary modifications to an inquiry carried out pursuant to a warrant issued under this section.

2006, c. 30, s. 4

31.2 Evidence used in Tribunal proceedings

Despite any other Act, evidence obtained on an inquiry under section 31 or 31.1 may be received into evidence in a proceeding before the Tribunal.

2006, c. 30, s. 4

31.3 (1) Anti-Racism Secretariat

The Chief Commissioner directs the Anti-Racism Secretariat which shall be established in accordance with subsection (2).

(2) Composition

The Anti-Racism Secretariat shall be composed of not more than six persons appointed by the Lieutenant Governor in Council on the advice of the Chief Commissioner.

(3) Remuneration

The Lieutenant Governor in Council may fix the remuneration and allowance for expenses of the members of the Anti-Racism Secretariat.

(4) Functions of the Secretariat

At the direction of the Chief Commissioner, the Anti-Racism Secretariat shall,

(a) undertake, direct and encourage research into discriminatory practices that infringe rights under Part I on the basis of racism or a related ground and make recommendations to the Commission designed to prevent and eliminate such discriminatory practices;

(b) facilitate the development and provision of programs of public information and education relating to the elimination of racism; and

(c) undertake such tasks and responsibilities as may be assigned by the Chief Commissioner.

2006, c. 30, s. 4

31.4 (1) Disability Rights Secretariat

The Chief Commissioner directs the Disability Rights Secretariat which shall be established in accordance with subsection (2).

(2) Composition

The Disability Rights Secretariat shall be composed of not more than six persons appointed by the Lieutenant Governor in Council on the advice of the Chief Commissioner.

(3) Remuneration

The Lieutenant Governor in Council may fix the remuneration and allowance for expenses of the members of the Disability Rights Secretariat.

(4) Functions of the Secretariat

At the direction of the Chief Commissioner, the Disability Rights Secretariat shall,

(a) undertake, direct and encourage research into discriminatory practices that infringe rights under Part I on the basis of disability and make recommendations to the Commission designed to prevent and eliminate such discriminatory practices;

(b) facilitate the development and provision of programs of public information and education intended to promote the elimination of discriminatory practices that infringe rights under Part I on the basis of disability; and

(c) undertake such tasks and responsibilities as may be assigned by the Chief Commissioner.

2006, c. 30, s. 4

31.5 Advisory groups

The Chief Commissioner may establish such advisory groups as he or she considers appropriate to advise the Commission about the elimination of discriminatory practices that infringe rights under this Act.

2006, c. 30, s. 4

31.6 (1) Annual report

Every year, the Commission shall prepare an annual report on the affairs of the Commission that occurred during the 12-month period ending on March 31 of each year.

(2) Report to Speaker

The Commission shall submit the report to the Speaker of the Assembly no later than on June 30 in each year who shall cause the report to be laid before the Assembly if it is in session or, if not, at the next session.

(3) Copy to Minister

The Commission shall give a copy of the report to the Minister at least 30 days before it is submitted to the Speaker under subsection (2).

2006, c. 30, s. 4

31.7 Other reports

In addition to the annual report, the Commission may make any other reports respecting the state of human rights in Ontario and the affairs of the Commission as it considers appropriate, and may present such reports to the public or any other person it considers appropriate.

2006, c. 30, s. 4

Part IV Human Rights Tribunal of Ontario

[Heading amended 2006, c. 30, s. 5.]

32. (1) Tribunal

The Tribunal known as the Human Rights Tribunal of Ontario in English and Tribunal des droits de la personne de l'Ontario in French is continued.

(2) Composition

The Tribunal shall be composed of such members as are appointed by the Lieutenant Governor in Council in accordance with the selection process described in subsection (3).

(3) Selection process

The selection process for the appointment of members of the Tribunal shall be a competitive process and the criteria to be applied in assessing candidates shall include the following:

1. Experience, knowledge or training with respect to human rights law and issues.
2. Aptitude for impartial adjudication.
3. Aptitude for applying the alternative adjudicative practices and procedures that may be set out in the Tribunal rules.

(4) Remuneration

The members of the Tribunal shall be paid such remuneration and allowance for expenses as are fixed by the Lieutenant Governor in Council.

(5) Term of office

A member of the Tribunal shall be appointed for such term as may be specified by the Lieutenant Governor in Council.

(6) Chair, vice-chair

The Lieutenant Governor in Council shall appoint a chair and may appoint one or more vice-chairs of the Tribunal from among the members of the Tribunal.

(7) Alternate chair

The Lieutenant Governor in Council shall designate one of the vice-chairs to be the alternate chair.

(8) Same

If the chair is unable to act, the alternate chair shall perform the duties of the chair and, for this purpose, has all the powers of the chair.

(9) Employees

The Tribunal may appoint such employees as it considers necessary for the proper conduct of its affairs and the employees shall be appointed under Part III of the *Public Service of Ontario Act, 2006*.

(10) Evidence obtained in course of proceeding

A member or employee of the Tribunal shall not be required to give testimony in a civil suit or any proceeding as to information obtained in the course of a proceeding before the Tribunal.

(11) Same

Despite subsection (10), an employee of the Tribunal may be required to give testimony in a proceeding before the Tribunal in the circumstances prescribed by the Tribunal rules.

2006, c. 30, s. 5; 2006, c. 35, Sched. C, s. 132(6)

33. (1) Panels

The chair of the Tribunal may appoint panels composed of one or more members of the Tribunal to exercise and perform the powers and duties of the Tribunal.

(2) Person designated to preside over panel

If a panel of the Tribunal holds a hearing, the chair of the Tribunal shall designate one member of the panel to preside over the hearing.

(3) Reassignment of panel

If a panel of the Tribunal is unable for any reason to exercise or perform the powers or duties of the Tribunal, the chair of the Tribunal may assign another panel in its place.

(4) [Repealed 2006, c. 30, s. 5.]

(5) [Repealed 2006, c. 30, s. 5.]

(6) [Repealed 2006, c. 30, s. 5.]

(7) [Repealed 2006, c. 30, s. 5.]

(8) [Repealed 2006, c. 30, s. 5.]

(9) [Repealed 2006, c. 30, s. 5.]

(10) [Repealed 2006, c. 30, s. 5.]

(11) [Repealed 2006, c. 30, s. 5.]

(12) [Repealed 2006, c. 30, s. 5.]

(13) [Repealed 2006, c. 30, s. 5.]

1994, c. 27, s. 65(8), (9); 2002, c. 18, Sched. C, s. 1, item 3; 2006, c. 30, s. 5

34. (1) Application by person

If a person believes that any of his or her rights under Part I have been infringed, the person may apply to the Tribunal for an order under section 45.2,

(a) within one year after the incident to which the application relates; or

(b) if there was a series of incidents, within one year after the last incident in the series.

(2) Late applications

A person may apply under subsection (1) after the expiry of the time limit under that subsection if the Tribunal is satisfied that the delay was incurred in good faith and no substantial prejudice will result to any person affected by the delay.

(3) Form

An application under subsection (1) shall be in a form approved by the Tribunal.

(4) Two or more persons

Two or more persons who are each entitled to make an application under subsection (1) may file the applications jointly, subject to any provision in the Tribunal rules that authorizes the Tribunal to direct that one or more of the applications be considered in a separate proceeding.

(5) Application on behalf of another

A person or organization, other than the Commission, may apply on behalf of another person to the Tribunal for an order under section 45.2 if the other person,

(a) would have been entitled to bring an application under subsection (1); and

(b) consents to the application.

(6) Participation in proceedings

If a person or organization makes an application on behalf of another person, the person or organization may participate in the proceeding in accordance with the Tribunal rules.

(7) Consent form

A consent under clause (5)(b) shall be in a form specified in the Tribunal rules.

(8) Time of application

An application under subsection (5) shall be made within the time period required for making an application under subsection (1).

(9) Application

Subsections (2) and (3) apply to an application made under subsection (5).

(10) Withdrawal of application

An application under subsection (5) may be withdrawn by the person on behalf of whom the application is made in accordance with the Tribunal rules.

(11) Where application barred

A person who believes that one of his or her rights under Part I has been infringed may not make an application under subsection (1) with respect to that right if,

(a) a civil proceeding has been commenced in a court in which the person is seeking an order under section 46.1 with respect to the alleged infringement and the proceeding has not been finally determined or withdrawn; or

(b) a court has finally determined the issue of whether the right has been infringed or the matter has been settled.

(12) Final determination

For the purpose of subsection (11), a proceeding or issue has not been finally determined if a right of appeal exists and the time for appealing has not expired.

2006, c. 30, s. 5

35. (1) Application by Commission

The Commission may apply to the Tribunal for an order under section 45.3 if the Commission is of the opinion that,

(a) it is in the public interest to make an application; and

(b) an order under section 45.3 could provide an appropriate remedy.

(2) Form

An application under subsection (1) shall be in a form approved by the Tribunal.

(3) Effect of application

An application made by the Commission does not affect the right of a person to make an application under section 34 in respect of the same matter.

(4) Applications dealt with together

If a person or organization makes an application under section 34 and the Commission makes an application under this section in respect of the same matter, the two applications shall be dealt with together in the same proceeding unless the Tribunal determines otherwise.

(5) [Repealed 2006, c. 30, s. 5.]

(6) [Repealed 2006, c. 30, s. 5.]

(7) [Repealed 2006, c. 30, s. 5.]

(8) [Repealed 2006, c. 30, s. 5.]

1994, c. 27, s. 65(10); 2002, c. 18, Sched. C, ss. 1 (items 4, 5), 6; 2006, c. 30, s. 5

36. Parties

The parties to an application under section 34 or 35 are the following:

1. In the case of an application under subsection 34(1), the person who made the application.
2. In the case of an application under subsection 34(5), the person on behalf of whom the application is made.
3. In the case of an application under section 35, the Commission.
4. Any person against whom an order is sought in the application.
5. Any other person or the Commission, if they are added as a party by the Tribunal.

1994, c. 27, s. 65(12), (13); 2002, c. 18, Sched. C, s. 1, items 6, 7; 2006, c. 30, s. 5

37. (1) Intervention by Commission

The Commission may intervene in an application under section 34 on such terms as the Tribunal may determine having regard to the role and mandate of the Commission under this Act.

(2) Intervention as a party

The Commission may intervene as a party to an application under section 34 if the person or organization who made the application consents to the intervention as a party.

(3) [Repealed 2006, c. 30, s. 5.]

2006, c. 30, s. 5

38. Disclosure of information to Commission

Despite anything in the *Freedom of Information and Protection of Privacy Act*, at the request of the Commission, the Tribunal shall disclose to the Commission copies of applications and responses filed with the Tribunal and may disclose to the Commission other documents in its custody or in its control.

2006, c. 30, s. 5

39. Powers of Tribunal

The Tribunal has the jurisdiction to exercise the powers conferred on it by or under this Act and to determine all questions of fact or law that arise in any application before it.

1994, c. 27, s. 65(15)–(18); 2002, c. 18, Sched. C, s. 1, items 8–12; 2006, c. 30, s. 5

40. Disposition of applications

The Tribunal shall dispose of applications made under this Part by adopting the procedures and practices provided for in its rules or otherwise available to the Tribunal which, in its opinion, offer the best opportunity for a fair, just and expeditious resolution of the merits of the applications.

2006, c. 30, s. 5

41. Interpretation of Part and rules

This Part and the Tribunal rules shall be liberally construed to permit the Tribunal to adopt practices and procedures, including alternatives to traditional adjudicative or adversarial procedures that, in the opinion of the Tribunal, will facilitate fair, just and expeditious resolutions of the merits of the matters before it.

1994, c. 27, s. 65(20), (21); 2002, c. 18, Sched. C, s. 1, items 13–15; 2006, c. 30, s. 5

41.1 [Repealed 1995, c. 4, s. 3(3).]

42. (1) Statutory Powers Procedure Act

The provisions of the *Statutory Powers Procedure Act* apply to a proceeding before the Tribunal unless they conflict with a provision of this Act, the regulations or the Tribunal rules.

(2) Conflict

Despite section 32 of the *Statutory Powers Procedure Act*, this Act, the regulations and the Tribunal rules prevail over the provisions of that Act with which they conflict.

(3) [Repealed 2006, c. 30, s. 5.]

1994, c. 27, s. 65(23); 2002, c. 18, Sched. C, s. 1, items 16, 17; 2006, c. 30, s. 5

43. (1) Tribunal rules

The Tribunal may make rules governing the practice and procedure before it.

(2) Required practices and procedures

The rules shall ensure that the following requirements are met with respect to any proceeding before the Tribunal:

1. An application that is within the jurisdiction of the Tribunal shall not be finally disposed of without affording the parties an opportunity to make oral submissions in accordance with the rules.
2. An application may not be finally disposed of without written reasons.

(3) Same

Without limiting the generality of subsection (1), the Tribunal rules may,

- (a) provide for and require the use of hearings or of practices and procedures that are provided for under the *Statutory Powers Procedure Act* or that are alternatives to traditional adjudicative or adversarial procedures;
- (b) authorize the Tribunal to,
  - (i) define or narrow the issues required to dispose of an application and limit the evidence and submissions of the parties on such issues, and
  - (ii) determine the order in which the issues and evidence in a proceeding will be presented;

(c) authorize the Tribunal to conduct examinations in chief or cross-examinations of a witness;

(d) prescribe the stages of its processes at which preliminary, procedural or interlocutory matters will be determined;

(e) authorize the Tribunal to make or cause to be made such examinations of records and such other inquiries as it considers necessary in the circumstances;

(f) authorize the Tribunal to require a party to a proceeding or another person to,

(i) produce any document, information or thing and provide such assistance as is reasonably necessary, including using any data storage, processing or retrieval device or system, to produce the information in any form,

(ii) provide a statement or oral or affidavit evidence, or

(iii) in the case of a party to the proceeding, adduce evidence or produce witnesses who are reasonably within the party's control; and

(g) govern any matter prescribed by the regulations.

(4) General or particular

The rules may be of general or particular application.

(5) Consistency

The rules shall be consistent with this Part.

(6) Not a regulation

The rules made under this section are not regulations for the purposes of Part III of the *Legislation Act, 2006*.

(7) Public consultations

The Tribunal shall hold public consultations before making a rule under this section.

(8) Failure to comply with rules

Failure on the part of the Tribunal to comply with the practices and procedures required by the rules or the exercise of a discretion under the rules by the Tribunal in a particular manner is not a ground for setting aside a decision of the Tribunal on an application for judicial review or any other form of relief, unless the failure or the exercise of a discretion caused a substantial wrong which affected the final disposition of the matter.

(9) Adverse inference

The Tribunal may draw an adverse inference from the failure of a party to comply, in whole or in part, with an order of the Tribunal for the party to do anything under a rule made under clause (3)(f).

2006, c. 30, ss. 5, 11

44. (1) Tribunal inquiry

At the request of a party to an application under this Part, the Tribunal may appoint a person to conduct an inquiry under this section if the Tribunal is satisfied that,

(a) an inquiry is required in order to obtain evidence;

(b) the evidence obtained may assist in achieving a fair, just and expeditious resolution of the merits of the application; and

(c) it is appropriate to do so in the circumstances.

(2) Production of certificate

A person conducting an inquiry under this section shall produce proof of their appointment upon request.

(3) Entry

A person conducting an inquiry under this section may, without warrant, enter any lands or any building, structure or premises where the person has reason to believe there may be evidence relevant to the application.

(4) Time of entry

The power to enter a place under subsection (3) may be exercised only during the place's regular business hours or, if it does not have regular business hours, during daylight hours.

(5) Dwellings

A person conducting an inquiry shall not enter into a place or part of a place that is a dwelling without the consent of the occupant.

(6) Powers on inquiry

A person conducting an inquiry may,

(a) request the production for inspection and examination of documents or things that are or may be relevant to the inquiry;

(b) upon giving a receipt for it, remove from a place documents produced in response to a request under clause (a) for the purpose of making copies or extracts;

(c) question a person on matters that are or may be relevant to the inquiry, subject to the person's right to have counsel or a personal representative present during such questioning and exclude from the questioning any person who may be adverse in interest to the inquiry;

(d) use any data storage, processing or retrieval device or system used in carrying on business in the place in order to produce a document in readable form;

(e) take measurements or record by any means the physical dimensions of a place;

(f) take photographs, video recordings or other visual or audio recordings of the interior or exterior of a place; and

(g) require that a place or part thereof not be disturbed for a reasonable period of time for the purposes of carrying out an examination, inquiry or test.

(7) Written demand

A demand that a document or thing be produced must be in writing and must include a statement of the nature of the document or thing required.

(8) Assistance

A person conducting an inquiry may be accompanied by any person who has special, expert or professional knowledge and who may be of assistance in carrying out the inquiry.

(9) Use of force prohibited

A person conducting an inquiry shall not use force to enter and search premises under this section.

(10) Obligation to produce and assist

A person who is requested to produce a document or thing under clause (6)(a) shall produce it and shall, on request by the person conducting the inquiry, provide any assistance that is reasonably necessary, including assistance in using any data storage, processing or retrieval device or system, to produce a document in readable form.

(11) Return of removed things

A person conducting an inquiry who removes any document or thing from a place under clause (6)(b) shall,

(a) make it available to the person from whom it was removed, on request, at a time and place convenient for both that person and the person conducting the inquiry; and

(b) return it to the person from whom it was removed within a reasonable time.

(12) Admissibility of copies

A copy of a document certified by a person conducting an inquiry to be a true copy of the original is admissible in evidence to the same extent as the original and has the same evidentiary value.

(13) Obstruction

No person shall obstruct or interfere with a person conducting an inquiry under this section.

(14) Inquiry report

A person conducting an inquiry shall prepare a report and submit it to the Tribunal and the parties to the application that gave rise to the inquiry in accordance with the Tribunal rules.

(15) Transfer of inquiry to Commission

The Commission may, at the request of the Tribunal, appoint a person to conduct an inquiry under this section and the person so appointed has all of the powers of a person appointed by the Tribunal under this section and shall report to the Tribunal in accordance with subsection (14).

1994, c. 27, s. 65(23); 2002, c. 18, Sched. C, s. 1, item 18; 2006, c. 30, s. 5

45. Deferral of application

The Tribunal may defer an application in accordance with the Tribunal rules.

1994, c. 27, s. 65(23); 2002, c. 18, Sched. C, s. 1, item 19; 2006, c. 30, s. 5

45.1 Dismissal in accordance with rules

The Tribunal may dismiss an application, in whole or in part, in accordance with its rules if the Tribunal is of the opinion that another proceeding has appropriately dealt with the substance of the application.

2006, c. 30, s. 5

45.2 (1) Orders of Tribunal: applications under s. 34

On an application under section 34, the Tribunal may make one or more of the following orders if the Tribunal determines that a party to the application has infringed a right under Part I of another party to the application:

1. An order directing the party who infringed the right to pay monetary compensation to the party whose right was infringed for loss arising out of the infringement, including compensation for injury to dignity, feelings and self-respect.
2. An order directing the party who infringed the right to make restitution to the party whose right was infringed, other than through monetary compensation, for loss arising out of the infringement, including restitution for injury to dignity, feelings and self-respect.
3. An order directing any party to the application to do anything that, in the opinion of the Tribunal, the party ought to do to promote compliance with this Act.

(2) Orders under par. 3 of subs. (1)

For greater certainty, an order under paragraph 3 of subsection (1),

(a) may direct a person to do anything with respect to future practices; and

(b) may be made even if no order under that paragraph was requested.

2006, c. 30, s. 5

45.3 (1) Orders of Tribunal: applications under s. 35

If, on an application under section 35, the Tribunal determines that any one or more of the parties to the application have infringed a right under Part I, the Tribunal may make an order directing any party to the application to do anything that, in the opinion of the Tribunal, the party ought to do to promote compliance with this Act.

(2) Same

For greater certainty, an order under subsection (1) may direct a person to do anything with respect to future practices.

2006, c. 30, s. 5

45.4 (1) Matters referred to Commission

The Tribunal may refer any matters arising out of a proceeding before it to the Commission if, in the Tribunal's opinion, they are matters of public interest or are otherwise of interest to the Commission.

(2) Same

The Commission may, in its discretion, decide whether to deal with a matter referred to it by the Tribunal.

2006, c. 30, s. 5

45.5 (1) Documents published by Commission

In a proceeding under this Part, the Tribunal may consider policies approved by the Commission under section 30.

(2) Same

Despite subsection (1), the Tribunal shall consider a policy approved by the Commission under section 30 in a proceeding under this Part if a party to the proceeding or an intervenor requests that it do so.

2006, c. 30, s. 5

45.6 (1) Stated case to Divisional court

If the Tribunal makes a final decision or order in a proceeding in which the Commission was a party or an intervenor, and the Commission believes that the decision or order is not consistent with a policy that has been approved by the Commission under section 30, the Commission may apply to the Tribunal to have the Tribunal state a case to the Divisional Court.

(2) Same

If the Tribunal determines that the application of the Commission relates to a question of law and that it is appropriate to do so, it may state the case in writing for the opinion of the Divisional Court upon the question of law.

(3) Parties

The parties to a stated case under this section are the parties to the proceeding referred to in subsection (1) and, if the Commission was an intervenor in that proceeding, the Commission.

(4) Submissions by Tribunal

The Divisional Court may hear submissions from the Tribunal.

(5) Powers of Divisional Court

The Divisional Court shall hear and determine the stated case.

(6) No stay

Unless otherwise ordered by the Tribunal or the Divisional Court, an application by the Commission under subsection (1) or the stating of a case to the Divisional Court under subsection (2) does not operate as a stay of the final decision or order of the Tribunal.

(7) Reconsideration of Tribunal decision

Within 30 days of receipt of the decision of the Divisional Court, any party to the stated case proceeding may apply to the Tribunal for a reconsideration of its original decision or order in accordance with section 45.7.

2006, c. 30, s. 5

45.7 (1) Reconsideration of Tribunal decision

Any party to a proceeding before the Tribunal may request that the Tribunal reconsider its decision in accordance with the Tribunal rules.

(2) Same

Upon request under subsection (1) or on its own motion, the Tribunal may reconsider its decision in accordance with its rules.

2006, c. 30, s. 5

45.8 Decisions final

Subject to section 45.6 of this Act, section 21.1 of the *Statutory Powers Procedure Act* and the Tribunal rules, a decision of the Tribunal is final and not subject to appeal and shall not be altered or set aside in an application for judicial review or in any other proceeding unless the decision is patently unreasonable.

2006, c. 30, s. 5

45.9 (1) Settlements

If a settlement of an application made under section 34 or 35 is agreed to in writing and signed by the parties, the settlement is binding on the parties.

(2) Consent order

If a settlement of an application made under section 34 or 35 is agreed to in writing and signed by the parties, the Tribunal may, on the joint motion of the parties, make an order requiring compliance with the settlement or any part of the settlement.

(3) Application where contravention

If a settlement of an application made under section 34 or 35 is agreed to in writing and signed by the parties, a party who believes that another party has contravened the settlement may make an application to the Tribunal for an order under subsection (8),

(a) within six months after the contravention to which the application relates; or

(b) if there was a series of contraventions, within six months after the last contravention in the series.

(4) Late applications

A person may apply under subsection (3) after the expiry of the time limit under that subsection if the Tribunal is satisfied that the delay was incurred in good faith and no substantial prejudice will result to any person affected by the delay.

(5) Form of application

An application under subsection (3) shall be in a form approved by the Tribunal.

(6) Parties

Subject to the Tribunal rules, the parties to an application under subsection (3) are the following:

1. The parties to the settlement.
2. Any other person or the Commission, if they are added as a party by the Tribunal.

(7) Intervention by Commission

Section 37 applies with necessary modifications to an application under subsection (3).

(8) Order

If, on an application under subsection (3), the Tribunal determines that a party has contravened the settlement, the Tribunal may make any order that it considers appropriate to remedy the contravention.

2006, c. 30, s. 5

45.10 (1) Annual report

The Tribunal shall make a report to the Minister not later than June 30 in each year upon the affairs of the Tribunal during the year ending on March 31 of that year.

(2) Report laid in Assembly

The Minister shall submit the report to the Lieutenant Governor in Council who shall cause the report to be laid before the Assembly if it is in session or, if not, at the next session.

2006, c. 30, s. 5

Part IV.1 Human Rights Legal Support Centre

[Heading added 2006, c. 30, s. 6.]

45.11 (1) Centre established

A corporation without share capital is established under the name Human Rights Legal Support Centre in English and Centre d'assistance juridique en matière de droits de la personne in French.

(2) Membership

The members of the Centre shall consist of its board of directors.

(3) Not a Crown agency

The Centre is not an agent of Her Majesty nor a Crown agent for the purposes of the *Crown Agency Act.*

(4) Powers of natural person

The Centre has the capacity and the rights, powers and privileges of a natural person, subject to the limitations set out in this Act or the regulations.

(5) Independent from but accountable to Ontario

The Centre shall be independent from, but accountable to, the Government of Ontario as set out in this Act.

2006, c. 30, s. 6

45.12 Objects

The objects of the Centre are,

(a) to establish and administer a cost-effective and efficient system for providing support services, including legal services, respecting applications to the Tribunal under Part IV;

(b) to establish policies and priorities for the provision of support services based on its financial resources.

2006, c. 30, s. 6

45.13 (1) Provision of support services

The Centre shall provide the following support services:

1. Advice and assistance, legal and otherwise, respecting the infringement of rights under Part I.
2. Legal services in relation to,
   i. the making of applications to the Tribunal under Part IV,
   ii. proceedings before the Tribunal under Part IV,
   iii. applications for judicial review arising from Tribunal proceedings,

iv. stated case proceedings,

v. the enforcement of Tribunal orders.

3. Such other services as may be prescribed by regulation.

(2) Availability of services

The Centre shall ensure that the support services are available throughout the Province, using such methods of delivering the services as the Centre believes are appropriate.

2006, c. 30, s. 6

45.14 (1) Board of directors

The affairs of the Centre shall be governed and managed by its board of directors.

(2) Composition and appointment

The board of directors of the Centre shall consist of no fewer than five and no more than nine members appointed by the Lieutenant Governor in Council in accordance with the regulations.

(3) Appointment of Chair

A Chair designated by the Lieutenant Governor in Council will preside at meetings.

(4) Remuneration

The board of directors may be remunerated as determined by the Lieutenant Governor in Council.

(5) Duties

The board of directors of the Centre shall be responsible for furthering the objects of the Centre.

(6) Delegation

The board of directors may delegate any power or duty to any committee, to any member of a committee or to any officer or employee of the Centre.

(7) Same

A delegation shall be in writing and shall be on the terms and subject to the limitations, conditions or requirements specified in it.

(8) Board to act responsibly

The board of directors shall act in a financially responsible and accountable manner in exercising its powers and performing its duties.

(9) Standard of care

Members of the board of directors shall act in good faith with a view to the objects of the Centre and shall exercise the care, diligence and skill of a reasonably prudent person.

2006, c. 30, s. 6

45.15 (1) Government funding

The Centre shall submit its annual budget to the Minister for approval every year in a manner and form, and at a time, specified in the regulations.

(2) Approved budget included in estimates

If approved by the Minister, the annual budget shall be submitted to Cabinet to be reviewed for inclusion in the estimates of the Ministry.

(3) Appropriation by Legislature

The money required for the purposes of this Act shall be paid out of such money as is appropriated therefor by the Legislature.

2006, c. 30, s. 6

45.16 Centre's money not part of Consolidated Revenue Fund

The Centre's money and investments do not form part of the Consolidated Revenue Fund and shall be used by the Centre in carrying out its objects.

2006, c. 30, s. 6

45.17 (1) Annual report

The Centre shall submit an annual report to the Minister within four months after the end of its fiscal year.

(2) Fiscal year

The fiscal year of the Centre shall be from April 1 to March 31 of the following year.

2006, c. 30, s. 6

45.18 (1) Audit

The Centre must ensure that its books of financial account are audited annually in accordance with generally accepted accounting principles and a copy of the audit is given to the Minister.

(2) Audit by Minister

The Minister has the right to audit the Centre at any time that the Minister chooses.

2006, c. 30, s. 6

Part V General

46. Definitions

In this Act,

"board of inquiry" [Repealed 2002, c. 18, Sched. C, s. 7(1).]

"Commission" means the Ontario Human Rights Commission;

"Minister" means the member of the Executive Council to whom the powers and duties of the Minister under this Act are assigned by the Lieutenant Governor in Council;

"person" in addition to the extended meaning given it by Part VI (Interpretation) of the *Legislation Act, 2006*, includes an employment agency, an employers' organization, an unincorporated association, a trade or occupational association, a trade union, a partnership, a municipality, a board of police commissioners established under the *Police Act*, being chapter 381 of the Revised Statutes of Ontario, 1980, and a police services board established under the *Police Services Act*;

"regulations" means the regulations made under this Act;

"Tribunal" means the Human Rights Tribunal of Ontario continued under section 32;

"Tribunal rules" means the rules governing practice and procedure that are made by the Tribunal under section 43.

1994, c. 27, s. 65(24); 2002, c. 18, Sched. C, s. 7; 2006, c. 21, Sched. F, s. 136(2), Table 2; 2006, c. 30, s. 7

46.1 (1) Civil remedy

If, in a civil proceeding in a court, the court finds that a party to the proceeding has infringed a right under Part I of another party to the proceeding, the court may make either of the following orders, or both:

1. An order directing the party who infringed the right to pay monetary compensation to the party whose right was infringed for loss arising out of the infringement, including compensation for injury to dignity, feelings and self-respect.
2. An order directing the party who infringed the right to make restitution to the party whose right was infringed, other than through monetary compensation, for loss arising out of the infringement, including restitution for injury to dignity, feelings and self-respect.

(2) Same

Subsection (1) does not permit a person to commence an action based solely on an infringement of a right under Part I.

2006, c. 30, s. 8

46.2 (1) Penalty

Every person who contravenes section 9 or subsection 31(14), 31.1(8) or 44(13) or an order of the Tribunal is guilty of an offence and on conviction is liable to a fine of not more than $25,000.

(2) Consent to prosecution

No prosecution for an offence under this Act shall be instituted except with the consent in writing of the Attorney General.

2006, c. 30, s. 8

46.3 (1) Acts of officers, etc.

For the purposes of this Act, except subsection 2(2), subsection 5(2), section 7 and subsection 46.2(1), any act or thing done or omitted to be done in the course of his or her employment by an officer, official, employee or agent of a corporation, trade union, trade or occupational association, unincorporated association or employers' organization shall be deemed to be an act or thing done or omitted to be done by the corporation, trade union, trade or occupational association, unincorporated association or employers' organization.

(2) Opinion re authority or acquiescence

At the request of a corporation, trade union, trade or occupational association, unincorporated association or employers' organization, the Tribunal in its decision shall make known whether or not, in its opinion, an act or thing done or omitted to be done by an officer, official, employee or agent was done or omitted to be done with or without the authority or acquiescence of the corporation, trade union, trade or occupational association, unincorporated association or employers' organization, and the opinion does not affect the application of subsection (1).

2006, c. 30, s. 8

47. (1) Act binds Crown

This Act binds the Crown and every agency of the Crown.

(2) Act has primacy over other Acts

Where a provision in an Act or regulation purports to require or authorize conduct that is a contravention of Part I, this Act applies and prevails unless the Act or regulation specifically provides that it is to apply despite this Act.

48. Regulations

(1) Regulations

The Lieutenant Governor in Council may make regulations,

(a) prescribing standards for assessing what is undue hardship for the purposes of section 11, 17 or 24;

(a.1) prescribing the manner in which income information, credit checks, credit references, rental history, guarantees or other similar business practices may be used by a landlord in selecting prospective tenants without infringing section 2, and prescribing other similar business practices and the manner of their use, for the purposes of subsection 21(3);

(b) prescribing matters for the purposes of clause 43(3)(g);

(c) respecting the Human Rights Legal Support Centre;

(d) governing any matter that is necessary or advisable for the effective enforcement and administration of this Act;

(e) [Repealed 2006, c. 30, s. 9(1).]

(f) prescribing matters that the Commission shall consider in deciding whether or not to endeavour to effect a settlement under subsection 33(1).

(2) Human Rights Legal Support Centre

A regulation made under clause (1)(c) may,

(a) further define the Centre's constitution, management and structure as set out in Part IV.1;

(b) prescribe powers and duties of the Centre and its members;

(c) provide for limitations on the Centre's powers under subsection 45.11(4);

(d) prescribe services for the purposes of paragraph 3 of subsection 45.13(1);

(e) further define the nature and scope of support services referred to in subsection 45.13(1);

(f) provide for factors to be considered in appointing members and specify the circumstances and manner in which they are to be considered;

(g) provide for the term of appointment and reappointment of the Centre's members;

(h) provide for the nature and scope of the annual report required under section 45.17;

(i) provide for reporting requirements in addition to the annual report;

(j) provide for personal information to be collected by or on behalf of the Centre other than directly from the individual to whom the information relates, and for the manner in which the information is collected;

(k) provide for the transfer from specified persons or entities of information, including personal information, that is relevant to carrying out the functions of the Centre;

(l) provide for rules governing the confidentiality and security of information, including personal information, the collection, use and disclosure of such information, the retention and disposal of such information, and access to and correction of such information, including restrictions on any of these things, for the purposes of the carrying out of the functions of the Centre;

(m) specify requirements and conditions for the funding of the Centre and for the Centre's budget;

(n) provide for audits of the statements and records of the Centre;

(o) determine whether or not the *Business Corporations Act*, the *Corporations Information Act* or the *Corporations Act* or any provisions of those Acts apply to the Centre;

(p) provide for anything necessary or advisable for the purposes of Part IV.1.

1994, c. 27, s. 65(25); 1997, c. 24, s. 212; 2006, c. 30, s. 9

Part VI Transitional Provisions

[Heading added 2006, c. 30, s. 10.]

49. Definitions

In this Part,

"effective date" means the day sections 4 and 5 of the *Human Rights Code Amendment Act, 2006* come into force;

"new Part IV" means Part IV as it reads on and after the effective date;

"old Part IV" means Part IV as it reads before the effective date.

2006, c. 30, s. 10

50. Orders respecting special programs

On the fifth anniversary of the effective date, all orders that were made by the Commission under subsection 14(2) before the effective date shall be null and void.

2006, c. 30, s. 10

51. Application of s. 32(3)

Subsection 32(3) applies to the selection and appointment of persons to the Tribunal on or after the day section 10 of the *Human Rights Code Amendment Act, 2006* comes into force.

2006, c. 30, s. 10

52. (1) Tribunal powers before effective date

Despite anything to the contrary in the old Part IV, the Tribunal may, before the effective date,

(a) make rules in accordance with the new Part IV, including rules with respect to the reconsideration of Tribunal decisions; and

(b) when dealing with complaints that are referred to it under section 36 of the old Part IV,

(i) deal with the complaint in accordance with the practices and procedures set out in the rules made under clause (a),

(ii) exercise the powers described in section 39 of the new Part IV, and

(iii) dispose of the complaint in accordance with section 40 of the new Part IV.

(2) Application

Sections 41 and 42 of the new Part IV apply to rules made under clause (1)(a).

(3) Tribunal decisions made before effective date

Despite anything in the old Part IV, the following applies before the effective date with respect to a complaint that is referred to the Tribunal by the Commission under section 36 of the old Part IV on or after the day section 10 of the *Human Rights Code Amendment Act, 2006* comes into force:

1. Section 42 of the old Part IV does not apply to a decision of the Tribunal made with respect to the complaint.

2. Sections 45.7 and 45.8 of the new Part IV apply to a decision of the Tribunal made with respect to the complaint.

2006, c. 30, s. 10

53. (1) Complaints before Commission on effective date

This section applies to a complaint filed with the Commission under subsection 32(1) of the old Part IV or initiated by the Commission under subsection 32(2) of the old Part IV before the effective date.

(2) Commission powers continued for six months

Subject to subsection (3) and despite the repeal of the old Part IV, during the six-month period that begins on the effective date, the Commission shall continue to deal with complaints referred to in subsection (1) in accordance with subsection 32(3) and sections 33, 34, 36, 37 and 43 of the old Part IV and, for that purpose,

(a) the Commission has all the powers described in subsection 32(3) and sections 33, 34, 36, 37 and 43 of the old Part IV; and

(b) the provisions referred to in clause (a) continue to apply with respect to the complaints, with necessary modifications.

(3) Applications to Tribunal during six-month period

Subject to subsection (4), at any time during the six-month period referred to in subsection (2), the person who made a complaint that is continued under that subsection may, in accordance with the Tribunal rules, elect to abandon the complaint and make an application to the Tribunal with respect to the subject-matter of the complaint.

(4) Expedited process

The Tribunal shall make rules with respect to the practices and procedures that apply to an application under subsection (3) in order to ensure that the applications are dealt with in an expeditious manner.

(5) Applications to Tribunal after six-month period

If, after the end of the six-month period referred to in subsection (2), the Commission has failed to deal with the merits of a complaint continued under that subsection and the complaint has not been withdrawn or settled, the complainant may make an application to the Tribunal with respect to the subject-matter of the complaint within a further six-month period after the end of the earlier six-month period.

(6) New Part IV applies

The new Part IV applies to an application made under subsections (3) and (5).

(7) Disclosure of information

Despite anything in the *Freedom of Information and Protection of Privacy Act*, at the request of a party to an application under subsection (3) or (5), the Commission may disclose to the party any information obtained by the Commission in the course of an investigation.

(8) Application barred

No application, other than an application under subsection (3) or (5), may be made to the Tribunal if the subject-matter of the application is the same or substantially the same as the subject-matter of a complaint that was filed with the Commission under the old Part IV.

2006, c. 30, s. 10

54. Settlements effected by Commission

Section 45.9 of the new Part IV applies to the enforcement of a settlement that,

(a) was effected by the Commission under the old Part IV before the effective date or during the six-month period referred to in subsection 53(2); and

(b) was agreed to in writing, signed by the parties and approved by the Commission.

2006, c. 30, s. 10

55. (1) Where complaints referred to Tribunal

This section applies to complaints that are referred to the Tribunal by the Commission under section 36 of the old Part IV before the effective date or during the six-month period referred to in subsection 53(2).

(2) New Part IV applies

On and after the effective date, the new Part IV applies to a complaint described in subsection (1) as though it were an application made to the Tribunal under that Part and the Tribunal shall deal with the complaint in accordance with the new Part IV.

(3) Parties

The Commission,

(a) shall continue to be a party to a complaint that was referred to the Tribunal before the effective date; and

(b) subject to subsection (4), shall not be a party to a complaint referred to the Tribunal during the six-month period referred to in subsection 53(2).

(4) Same, exceptions

The Commission shall continue as a party to a complaint that was referred to the Tribunal during the six-month period referred to in subsection 53(2) if,

(a) the complaint was initiated by the Commission under subsection 32(2) of the old Part IV; or

(b) the Tribunal sets a date for the parties to appear before the Tribunal before the end of the six-month period.

(5) Same

Nothing in subsection (3) shall prevent,

(a) the Tribunal from adding the Commission as a party to a proceeding under section 36 of the new Part IV; or

(b) the Commission from intervening in a proceeding with respect to a complaint described in subsection (1).

2006, c. 30, s. 10

56. (1) Regulations, transitional matters

The Lieutenant Governor in Council may make regulations providing for transitional matters which, in the opinion of the Lieutenant Governor in Council, are necessary or desirable to facilitate the implementation of the *Human Rights Code Amendment Act, 2006*.

(2) Same

Without limiting the generality of subsection (1), the Lieutenant Governor in Council may make regulations,

(a) providing for transitional matters relating to the changes to the administration and functions of the Commission;

(b) dealing with any problems or issues arising as a result of the repeal or enactment of a provision of this Act by the *Human Rights Code Amendment Act, 2006*.

(3) Same

A regulation under this section may be general or specific in its application.

(4) Conflicts

If there is a conflict between a provision in a regulation under this section and any provision of this Act or of any other regulation made under this Act, the regulation under this section prevails.

2006, c. 30, s. 10

57. (1) Review

Three years after the effective date, the Minister shall appoint a person who shall undertake a review of the implementation and effectiveness of the changes resulting from the enactment of that Act.

(2) Public consultations

In conducting a review under this section, the person appointed under subsection (1) shall hold public consultations.

(3) Report to Minister

The person appointed under subsection (1) shall prepare a report on his or her findings and submit the report to the Minister within one year of his or her appointment.

2006, c. 30, s. 10

ONT. REG. 290/98 — BUSINESS PRACTICES PERMISSIBLE TO LANDLORDS IN SELECTING PROSPECTIVE TENANTS FOR RESIDENTIAL ACCOMMODATION

made under the *Human Rights Code*

O. Reg. 290/98 as am. O. Reg. 31/00; 646/00; 284/05

1. (1) A landlord may request credit references and rental history information, or either of them, from a prospective tenant and may request from a prospective tenant authorization to conduct credit checks on the prospective tenant.

(2) A landlord may consider credit references, rental history information and credit checks obtained pursuant to requests under subsection (1), alone or in any combination, in order to assess the prospective tenant and the landlord may select or refuse the prospective tenant accordingly.

(3) A landlord may request income information from a prospective tenant only if the landlord also requests information listed in subsection (1).

(4) A landlord may consider income information about a prospective tenant in order to assess the prospective tenant and the landlord may select or refuse the prospective tenant accordingly only if the landlord considers the income information together with all the other information that was obtained by the landlord pursuant to requests under subsection (1).

(5) If, after requesting the information listed in subsections (1) and (3), a landlord only obtains income information about a prospective tenant, the landlord may consider the income information alone in order to assess the prospective tenant and the landlord may select or refuse the prospective tenant accordingly.

2. (1) A landlord may require a prospective tenant to obtain a Guarantee for the rent.

(2) A landlord may require a prospective tenant to pay a security deposit in accordance with sections 117 and 118 of the *Tenant Protection Act, 1997.*

3. In selecting a prospective tenant, a landlord of a rental unit described in paragraph 1, 1.1, 2 or 3 of subsection 5(1) or subsection 6(1) of the *Tenant Protection Act, 1997* may request and use income information about a prospective tenant in order to determine a prospective tenant's eligibility for rent in an amount geared-to-income and, when requesting and using the income information for that purpose only, the landlord is not bound by subsection 1(3) and (4).

O. Reg. 646/00, s. 1

4. Nothing in this Regulation authorizes a landlord to refuse accommodation to any person because of race, ancestry, place of origin, colour, ethnic origin, citizenship, creed, sex, sexual orientation, age, marital status, family status, handicap or the receipt of public assistance.

O. Reg. 31/00, s. 1; 284/05, s. 1

5. This Regulation comes into force on the day clause 48(a.1) of the Act comes into force.

Appendix 13

ONT. REG. 373/06 — TABLE OF OPERATING COST CATEGORIES FOR 2007

made under the *Tenant Protection Act, 1997*

O. Reg. 373/06

1. Table for 2007 — The Table referred to in subsection 129(2) of the Act is the following for the year 2007:

TABLE FOR 2007

Column 1	Column 2	Column 3
Operating Cost Category	**Three-year Moving Average (%)**	**Weight (%)**
Insurance	7.52	6.06
Heating	9.83	24.38
Hydro	5.42	7.51
Water	6.11	3.89
Municipal Taxes and Charges	2.58	26.93
Administration	1.90	14.79
Maintenance	2.12	14.45
Miscellaneous	1.90	1.99

Appendix 14

ANNUAL RENT INCREASE GUIDELINES: 1975 to 2010

Year	Guideline Increase (%)
2010	2.1
2009	1.8
2008	1.4
2007	2.6
2006	2.1
2005	1.5
2004	2.9
2003	2.9
2002	3.9
2001	2.9
2000	2.6
1999	3.0
1998	3.0
1997	2.8
1996	2.8
1995	2.9
1994	3.2
1993	4.9
1992	6.0
1991	5.4
1990	4.6
1989	4.6
1988	4.7
1987	5.2
1986	4.0
1985	6.0

1984	**6.0**
1983	**6.0**
1982	**6.0**
1981	**6.0**
1980	**6.0**
1979	**6.0**
1978	**6.0**
1977	**8.0**
1976	**8.0**
1975	**8.0**

Appendix 15

Parental Responsibility Act, 2000

An Act to make parents responsible for wrongful acts intentionally committed by their children

S.O. 2000, c. 4 as am. S.O. 2006, c. 19, Sched. D, s. 16; 2006, c. 21, Sched. C, s. 126(1) (Fr.), (2), (3)

Her Majesty, by and with the advice and consent of the Legislative Assembly of the Province of Ontario, enacts as follows:

1. Definitions — In this Act, except as otherwise provided in section 10,

"child" means a person who is under the age of 18 years; (*"enfant"*)

"parent" means,

(a) a biological parent of a child, unless section 158 of the *Child and Family Services Act* applies to the child,

(b) an adoptive parent of a child,

(c) an individual declared to be a parent of a child under the *Children's Law Reform Act*,

(d) an individual who has lawful custody of a child, and

(e) an individual who has a lawful right of access to a child.

(*"père ou mère"*)

2. (1) Parents' liability — Where a child takes, damages or destroys property, an owner or a person entitled to possession of the property may bring an action in the Small Claims Court against a parent of the child to recover damages, not in excess of the monetary jurisdiction of the Small Claims Court,

(a) for loss of or damage to the property suffered as a result of the activity of the child; and

(b) for economic loss suffered as a consequence of that loss of or damage to property.

(2) Same — The parent is liable for the damages unless the parent satisfies the court that,

(a) he or she was exercising reasonable supervision over the child at the time the child engaged in the activity that caused the loss or damage and made reasonable efforts to prevent or discourage the child from engaging in the kind of activity that resulted in the loss or damage; or

(b) the activity that caused the loss or damage was not intentional.

(3) Factors — For the purposes of clause (2)(a), in determining whether a parent exercised reasonable supervision over a child or made reasonable efforts to prevent or discourage the child from engaging in the kind of activity that resulted in the loss or damage, the court may consider,

(a) the age of the child;

(b) the prior conduct of the child;

(c) the potential danger of the activity;

(d) the physical or mental capacity of the child;

(e) any psychological or other medical disorders of the child;

(f) whether the child was under the direct supervision of the parent at the time when the child was engaged in the activity;

(g) if the child was not under the direct supervision of the parent when the child engaged in the activity, whether the parent acted unreasonably in failing to make reasonable arrangements for the supervision of the child;

(h) whether the parent has sought to improve his or her parenting skills by attending parenting courses or otherwise;

(i) whether the parent has sought professional assistance for the child designed to discourage activity of the kind that resulted in the loss or damage; and

(j) any other matter that the court considers relevant.

3. (1) Definition — In this section,

"offence" has the same meaning as in the *Young Offenders Act* (Canada) and the *Youth Criminal Justice Act* (Canada).

"representative" means, in respect of a proceeding under this Act, a person authorized under the *Law Society Act* to represent the claimant, the child, or the child's parents in that proceeding. (*"représentant"*)

(2) Proof of conviction — In an action brought under this Act, proof that a child has been found guilty under the *Young Offenders Act* (Canada) or the *Youth Criminal Justice Act* (Canada) of an offence is proof, in the absence of evidence to the contrary, that the offence was committed by the child, if,

(a) no appeal of the finding of guilt was taken and the time for an appeal has expired; or

(b) an appeal of the finding of guilt was taken but was dismissed or abandoned and no further appeal is available.

(3) Same — For the purposes of subsection (2), a copy of a sentence order under the *Youth Criminal Justice Act* (Canada) showing that the original order appeared to be signed by the officer having custody of the records of the court that made the order is, on proof of the identity of the child named as guilty of the offence in the order, sufficient evidence that the child was found guilty of the offence, without proof of the signature or of the official character of the person appearing to have signed the order.

(4) Notice re evidence obtained under *Youth Criminal Justice Act* (Canada) — A person who presents evidence obtained under the *Youth Criminal Justice Act* (Canada) in an action brought under this Act shall first give the court notice, in the prescribed form.

(5) Record sealed — When evidence obtained under the *Youth Criminal Justice Act* (Canada) is presented in an action brought under this Act,

(a) the court file shall not be disclosed to any person except,

(i) the court and authorized court employees,

(ii) the claimant and the claimant's representative, and

(iii) the child, his or her parents and their representatives; and

(b) once the action has been finally disposed of, the court file shall be sealed up and shall not be disclosed to any person, except one mentioned in clause (a).

2006, c. 19, Sched. D, s. 16(1)–(5); 2006, c. 21, Sched. C, s. 126(2), (3)

4. *Youth Criminal Justice Act* (Canada) — For greater certainty, when information from records under the *Youth Criminal Justice Act* (Canada) is made available for the purposes of an action brought under this Act or presented as evidence in such an action, nothing in this Act affects any provision of the *Youth Criminal Justice Act* limiting disclosure or publication of the information.

2006, c. 19, Sched. D, s. 16(6)

5. Restitution — In determining the amount of damages in an action brought under this Act, the court may take into account any amount ordered by a court as restitution or paid voluntarily as restitution.

6. Joint and several liability — Where more than one parent is liable in an action brought under this Act for a child's activity, their liability is joint and several.

7. (1) Method of payment — In awarding damages in an action brought under this Act, the court may order payment of the damages,

(a) to be made in full on or before a fixed date; or

(b) to be made in instalments on or before fixed dates, if the court considers that a lump sum payment is beyond the financial resources of the parent or will otherwise impose an unreasonable financial burden on the parent.

(2) Security — The court may order security to be provided by the parent in any form that the court considers appropriate.

8. Insurers subrogated — An insurer who has paid an amount as compensation to a person in connection with the loss or damage is subrogated to the rights of the person under this Act to the extent of the amount.

9. Other remedies — Nothing in this Act shall be interpreted to limit remedies otherwise available under existing law or to preclude the development of remedies under the law.

10. (1) Parents' onus of proof in actions not under this Act — This section applies to any action brought otherwise than under this Act.

(2) Same — In an action against a parent for damage to property or for personal injury or death caused by the fault or neglect of a child who is a minor, the onus of establishing that the parent exercised reasonable supervision and control over the child rests with the parent.

(3) Same — In subsection (2),

"child" and **"parent"** have the same meaning as in the *Family Law Act*.

11. Regulations — The Lieutenant Governor in Council may, by regulation,

(a) prescribe forms to be used for requests under paragraph 119(1)(r) of the *Youth Criminal Justice Act* (Canada);

(b) prescribe a form for the purpose of subsection 3(4) (notice re evidence).
2006, c. 19, Sched. D, s. 16(7)

12. Repeal — Section 68 of the *Family Law Act* is repealed.

13. Commencement — This Act comes into force on a day to be named by proclamation of the Lieutenant Governor.

14. Short title — The short title of this Act is the *Parental Responsibility Act, 2000*.

Appendix 16

TABLE OF CONCORDANCE: *Tenant Protection Act, 1997* to *Residential Tenancies Act, 2006*

This table identifies the corresponding provisions of the *Tenant Protection Act, 1997* and the *Residential Tenancies Act, 2006*. Provisions without corresponding equivalents are denoted by a dash ("—") in the appropriate column. Provisions with significant amendments are highlighted in italics.

Tenant Protection Act, 1997	*Residential Tenancies Act, 2006*
—	1
1(1)	2(1)
—	2(1) "Board"
1 (1)"municipal taxes and charges" — before (a); see also O. Reg. 194/98, s. 1 item 1	*2 (1)"municipal taxes and charges" — before (a)*
1(1) "municipal taxes and charges" (a)-(c)	2 (1)"municipal taxes and charges" (a)-(c)
— see O. Reg. 194/98, s. 2	2(1)"municipal taxes and charges" (d)-(f)
1(1) "municipal taxes and charges" (d)	2(1) "municipal taxes and charges" (g)
1(1) "Tribunal"	—
1(1) "utilities"	*2(1) "utilities"*
1(1) "vital service"	*2(1) "vital service"*
1(1.1)	2(2)
—	2(3)
1(2)	2(4)
2	3
3(a)-(b)	5(a)-(b)
3(c)	*5(c)*
—	5(m)
3(d)-(l)	5(d)-(l)
3(m)	5(n)
4(1) before (a)	*6(1) before (a)*
4(1)	6(1)(a)
4(2)	6(2)
4(3); 3(e)	*6(1)(b)*
5(1) before 1	*7(1) before 1*

Tenant Protection Act, 1997	***Residential Tenancies Act, 2006***
5(1)1	7(1) 1
5(1) 1.1	7(1) 2
5(1) 2	7(1) 3
5(1) 3	*7(1) 4*
5(1) 4	7(1) 5
5(1) 5	7(1) 6
5(2)	7(2)
5(3)	7(3)
5(4)	7(4)
5(4.1)	7(5)
5(5)	7(6)
6(1)	*8(1)*
6(2)	8(2)
7	9
—	11
8	12
9	13
10	19
11	17
12	18
13	16
14	15
15	14
16	4
17	95
18	97
19	25
20	26
21(1) 1	27(1)1
21(1)2	27(1)2
21(1)3	*27(2)*
21(1)	3.1 27(1) 3
—	27(1) 4
21(1)4	27(1)5
21(2)	27(3)
22	28
23(1)	24
23(2)	35(1)

Tenant Protection Act, 1997	*Residential Tenancies Act, 2006*
24	20
25	21(1)
—	21(2)
26	22
27	23
28	36
29	33
30	*34*
31	40
32(1) 1	98(1)
32(1) 2	*29(1) 1*
32(1) 3	29(1)6
32(1)4	29(1)5
32(1)5	29(1)2
32(1)6	29(1)3
32(1)7	29(1)4
32(1) 8	*57(1)(a)*
32(1) 9	*57(1)(b)*
32(1)10	*57(1)(c)*
32(2)	*29(2); 57(2); 98(2)*
33(1)	98(3)
33(2)	98(4)
33(3)	98(5)
—	98(6)
34(1) 1	*30(1) 1 in part*
34(1) 2	*30(1) 2 in part*
34(1) 3	*30(1) 3 in part*
34(1) 4	*30(1) 4 in part*
34(1) 4.1	*30(1) 5 in part*
—	30(1) 6-8
34(1)5	30(1) 9
34(2)	30(2)
35(1)(a)	31(1)(a)
35(1)(a.1)(i)	*31(1)(b)(i)*
35(1)(a.1)(ii)	31(1)(b)(ii)
35(1)(b)	*31(1)(c), 57(3)2*
35(1)(c)	*31(1)(d), 57(3)3*
35(1)(d)	31(1)(e)

Tenant Protection Act, 1997	***Residential Tenancies Act, 2006***
35(1)(e)	*31(1)(f), 57(3)4*
—	57(4)
35(2)	*31(2), 57(3)1*
35(3)	31(3)
35(4)	31(4)
35(5)	31(5)
36	35(2)
37	35(3)
—	32
38	10
39(1)	37(1)
—	37(2)
39(2)	37(3)
39(3)	37(5)
39(4)	37(4)
—	37(6)-(11)
40(1)	38(1)
—	38(2)
40(2)	*38(3)*
41	39
42(1)	41(1)
42(2)	*41(2)*
42(3)	*41(3)*
42(4)	41(4)
42(5)	41(5)
—	41(6)
43(1)	43(1)
—	43(2)(a)
43(2)(a)-(b)	43(2)(b)-(c)
44	46
45(1)(a)	103(1)
45(1)(b)	86
45(2)	45; *103(2)*
46	47
47	44
48	96
49	91
50	92

Tenant Protection Act, 1997	*Residential Tenancies Act, 2006*
51(1)	48(1)(a)-(c)
—	48(1)(d)
51(2)	48(2)
51(3)	48(3)
51(4)	48(4)
52(1)	49(1)(a)-(c)
—	49(1)(d)
52(1.1)	49(2)(a)-(c)
—	49(2)(d)
52(2)	49(3)
52(3)	49(4)
52(4)	49(5)
53	50
54(1)	51(1)
54(2)	51(2)
54(3)(a)	51(3)
54(3)(b)	—
54(4)	51(4)
54(5)	51(5)
54(6)	51(6)
54(7)	51(7)
55	52
56	53
57(1)(a)	*54(1)(a)*
57(1)(b)	54(1)(b)
57(1)(c)	54(1)(c)
57(2)	54(2)(a)
—	54(2)(b)-(c)
58	55
59	56
60	58
61	59
62(1)	61(1)
62(2)	60(1)
62(3)(a)	61(2)
62(3)(b)	60(2)
62(4)	61(3)
63(1)	62(1)

Tenant Protection Act, 1997	***Residential Tenancies Act, 2006***
63(2)	62(2)(a)-(c)(i)
—	62(2)(c)(ii)
63(3)	*62(3) in part*
—	63
64	64
—	65
65	66
66	67
67	68
68	93
69	69
70(1)	*72(1)*
70(2)(a)-(b)	72(2)(a)-(b)(iii)
—	72(2)(b)(iv)
71(a)	*73(a)*
71(b)	73(b)(i)
—	73(b)(ii)
72(1)	74(1)
72(2)(a)	*74(2)(a)*
72(2)(b)	*74(2)(b)*
72(2)(c)	74(2)(c)
72(3)(a)	74(3)(a)
72(3)(b)	74(3)(b)
—	74(3)(c)
72(4)(a)	*74(4)(a)*
72(4)(b)	*74(4)(b)*
72(4)(c)-(e)	74(4)(c)-(e)
72(5)	74(5)
72(6)	74(6)
72(7)	74(7)
72(8)	74(8)
72(9)	74(9)
72(10)(a)-(b)	74(10)(a)-(b)
—	74(10)(c)
—	74(11)-(18); *see* 242(4)
73	75
74(1)	70
74(2)	76(1)

Tenant Protection Act, 1997	*Residential Tenancies Act, 2006*
74(3)	76(2)
74(4)	76(3)
75	71
76(1)-(6)	77(1)-(6)
76(7)	*77(7)*
76(8)	—
—	77(8)
77(1)(a)	78(1) 1
77(1)(b)-(c)	*78(1) 2 i.*
77(1)(d)	78(1) 2ii.
77(1)(e)	78(1) 3
77(1.1) 1, 2	78(3) 1
77(1.1) 3	78(3) 2
77(2)	78(2)
77(2.1) 1	*78(4) 4 ii*
77(2.1) 2	*78(4) 4 i*
77(2.1) 3	*78(4) 1*
77(2.1) 4	*78(4) 2, 3*
—	*78(4) 4 iii - v*
77(2.1) 5	*78(4) 5*
77(3)	*78(5)*
77(4)	78(6)
77 (4.1) 1	78(7) 2
77 (4.1) 2	*78(7) 5 i*
77 (4.1) 3	78(7) 1
77 (4.1) 4	*78(7) 3*
77 (4.1) 5	*78(7) 4*
—	*78(7) 5 ii - iv*
77(4.2)	78(8)
77(4.3)	*78(9), (10)*
77(5)	—
—	78(11)
78	79
79	42
80	94
81(1)	100(1)
81(2)	100(2)
82	101

Tenant Protection Act, 1997	***Residential Tenancies Act, 2006***
83(1)	80(1)
83(2)	—
—	80(2)
83.1	81
—	82; *see* 242(5)
84(1)	83(1); *see also* 242(3)
—	83(2); *see* 242(3)
84(2)	83(3); *see also* 242(3)
84(3)	83(4); *see also* 242(3)
84(4)	83(5); *see also* 242(3)
—	84
85	85
86(1)	87(1)
—	87(2)
86(2)	87(3)
86(2.1)	100(3)
86(3)	87(4)
86(4)	87(5), 100(4)
—	88
87(1)	*89(1)*
—	89(2)
88	90
89	102
90	*99*
91(1)-(2)	139(1)-(2)
—	139(3)
92	140
93	141
94	142
95	143
96(1)(a)	144(1)(a)
96(1)(b)	*144(1)(b)*
96(2)	144(2)
97	145(1)
—	145(2)-(4)
98	146
—	147
99(1)	148(1)

Tenant Protection Act, 1997	***Residential Tenancies Act, 2006***
99(2)	148(2)
99(3)	—
99(4)	148(3)
99(5)	148(4)
100	*149*
101(1)-(2)	150(1)-(2)
101(3)	*150(3)*
102	151
—	152(1)
103	152(2)
104	153
—	154
—	155
105	156
106	157
107	158
108	*159(1)*
—	159(2)-(4)
109	160
110(1)	*161*
110(2)	*29(1) 1; 29(2)*
110(3)(a)	*30(1)1*
110(3)(b)	*30(1)2*
110(3)(c)	*30(1)3s*
110(3)(d)	*30(1)4*
110(4)	30(2)
111	162
112	163
113	*164(1)*
—	164(2)
114(1)-(2)	*165*
114(3)	—
115	166
116	167
117	105
118(1)	106(1)
118(2)	106(2)
118(3)	106(3)

Tenant Protection Act, 1997	***Residential Tenancies Act, 2006***
118(4)	106(4)
118(5)	106(5)
118(6)	*106(6); 106(8)*
—	106(7)
118(7)	106(9)
118(8)	106(10)
118(9)	*106(8)*
118.1	107
119	108(a)
—	108(b)
120	*109(1) in part*
—	109(2)
121(1)	111(1)
—	111(2)
121(2)	*111(3)*
121(3)	111(4)
122	110
123	*112*
124	113
—	114
—	115
125(1)	104(1)
125(2)	104(2)
125(3)	*104(3) in part*
125(4)	104(4)
126	119
127(1)-(3)	116(1)-(3)
127(4)	*116(4)*
—	117
128	118
129(1)	*120(1)*
129(2)	*120(2)*
129(3)	*120(3)*
129(4)	*120(4), 120(5)*
130(1)	121(1)
130(2)	121(2)
130(3)	*121(3)*
130(4)	121(4)

Tenant Protection Act, 1997	*Residential Tenancies Act, 2006*
130(5)	121(5)
130(6)	121(6)
130(7)	121(7)
131	122
132(1)	123(1)
132(2)	*123(2)*
133	124
134	125
135	— *see* 258
136(1)-(4)	131(1)-(4)
136(5)	*131(5)*
137	132
138(1)1	126(1)1
138(1)2	*126(1)2*
138(1)3	*126(1)3*
138(2)	*126(2)*
138(3)	126(3)
—	126(4)
138(4)	126(5)
138(5)	126(6)
—	126(8)-(9)
138(6)	*126(10)*
138(7)	—
138(8)	*126(7)*
138(9)	—
138(10)	*126(11)*
—	126(12)-(13); *see* 242(7)
138(11)	*126(14) in part*
139	127
—	128
139.1(a)	129(a)
—	129(b)
139.1(b)(i)	*129(c)(i)*
139.1(b)(ii)	*129(c)(ii)*
140(1)	134(1)
140(2)	134(2)
140(3)(a)	134(3)(a)
140(3)(b)	—

Tenant Protection Act, 1997	***Residential Tenancies Act, 2006***
140(3)(c)-(d)	134(3)(b)-(c)
141(1)	136(1)
141(2)	136(2)
141(3)	—
141(4)	136(3)
—	137
—	138
142	130
143(1)	133(1)
143(2)	133(2)
—	133(3)
144(1)	*135(1) in part*
144(2)-(4)	135(2)-(4)
145	215
146	216
147	217
148	218
149	219
150	220
151	221
152	222
153(1)	223(1)
153(2)	*223(2)*
154	224
155	225
156	226
157(1)	*168(1)*
157(2)	168(2)
157(3)-(4)	—
158	169
159	170
160	171
161	172
—	173
162	174
163	175
164(1)-(5)	176(1)-(5)
164(6)	—

Tenant Protection Act, 1997	*Residential Tenancies Act, 2006*
165	177
166	178
167	179
168	180
169	181
170	182
171	183
172	185
173	186
174	187
175	188
—	189
176	190
177	— *see* 242(2)
178	191
179	192
180	193
181(1)	194(1)
181(2)	194(2)
181(3)(a)	—
181(3)(b)	*194(3)*
181(4)	194(4)
181(5)	194(5)
182(1)	195(1)(a); *see also* 242(6)
—	195(1)(b); *see* 242(6)
182(2)	195(2); *see also* 242(6)
—	195(3); *see* 242(6)
182(3)	*195(4); see also* 242(6)
—	195(5); *see* 242(6)
182.1	196
183	197
184	184
185	198
185.1	199
186(1)	*200(1)*
186(2)	200(2)
186(3)	200(3)
186(4)	200(4)

Tenant Protection Act, 1997	***Residential Tenancies Act, 2006***
187(1)(a)	201(1)(a)
187(1)(b)	*201(1)(b)*
187(1)(c)-(f)	201(1)(c)-(f)
187(2)	201(2)
187(3)	201(3)
187(4)	201(4)
188	202
—	203
189	—
190(1)-(4)	204(1)-(4)
—	204(5)
191	205
192	— *see* 242(2)
—	206
193(1)	*207(1)*
193(2)	207(2)
193(3)	207(3)
—	207(4)
193(4)	207(5)
193(5)	207(6)
193(6)	207(7)
194	208
195	*209(1)*
—	209(2)
196	210
197	211
198	212
198.1	213
199	214
200	227
201	228
202	229
203	*230*
204(1)	*231(1)*
204(2)-(6)	231(2)-(6)
205(1)	232(1)
205(2)	*232(2) in part*
206(1)1	233(c)

Tenant Protection Act, 1997	***Residential Tenancies Act, 2006***
206(1)2	*233(b)*
206(1)3	233(a)
206(1)4	233(h)
206(1)5	233(i)
206(1)6	233(j)
206(1)7	233(d)
206(1)8	233(k)
206(1)9	233(e)
206(1)10	233(f)
206(1)11	233(l)
206(1)12	233(g)
206(2)1	234(v)
206(2)2	234(a)
206(2)3	*234(y)*
206(2)4	234(w)
206(2)4.1	234(b)
206(2)5	234(c)
206(2)6	234(m)
—	234(n)
—	234(o)
206(2)7	234(p)
206(2)8	234(q)
206(2)9	234(r)
206(2)10	234(d)
206(2)11	234(e)
206(2)12	234(f)
206(2)12.1	234(g)
206(2)13	234(h)
—	234(i)
206(2)14	234(x)
206(2)15	234(j)
—	234(k)
206(2)16	234(l)
206(2)17	234(t)
206(2)18	234(s)
206(2)19	234(u)
206(3)	235(1)
206(3.1)	235(2)

Tenant Protection Act, 1997	***Residential Tenancies Act, 2006***
206(4)	236
206(5)	237
206(6)	*238(1)*
206(7)	*238(2)*
206(8)	239(1)
206(9)	239(2)
207(1)-(3)	240(1)-(3)
—	240(4)
208(1)1	241(1)2
208(1)2	241(1)3
208(1)3	241(1)1
208(1)4	*cf. 241(1)9*
—	241(1)4-5
208(1)5	241(1)6
—	241(1)7-8
208(1)6	241(1)10
208(1)7	241(1)11
208(1)7.1	241(1)12
—	241(1)13-15
208(1)8	241(1)56
208(1)9	*241(1)59*
208(1)10	241(1)60
208(1)11	*241(1)16*
208(1)12	*241(1)17*
208(1)13	*241(1)18*
—	*241(1)19-20*
208(1)14	—
208(1)15	*241(1)21*
208(1)16	*241(1)22*
—	*241(1)23-24*
208(1)17	*241(1)25 in part, 26 in part*
208(1)18	241(1)27
208(1)19	241(1)28
—	241(1)29-32
208(1)20	241(1)41
208(1)21	241(1)33
—	241(1)34-39
208(1)22	241(1)40

Tenant Protection Act, 1997	***Residential Tenancies Act, 2006***
—	241(1)42-55
—	241(1)57-58
208(1)23	241(1)72
208(1)24	*241(1)73*
208(1)25	241(1)74
208(1)26	*cf. 241(1)62*
208(1)27	241(1)61
—	241(1)63-65
208(1)28	241(1)66
208(1)29	241(1)67
—	241(1)68-69
208(1)30	241(1)71
208(1)30.1	241(1)70
208(1)31	—
—	241(1)75-76
208(1)32	241(1)78
208(1)33	241(1)77
208(2)	241(2)
—	244
—	245
—	247
210	—
—	*249*
211	*250*
—	251
212	—
213	*cf. 258, 259*
214	—
215	*252*
216	—
217	—
218	—
219	—
—	253
—	254
—	255
220	*256*
—	257

Tenant Protection Act, 1997	***Residential Tenancies Act, 2006***
221	—
222	*260*
—	261
223(1),(2),(8),(10)	*cf. 242(1); see also 243*
223(3); 223(9)	*cf. 246 ; see also 243*
223(4)-(7)	*— see 243*
223(11)	*— see 243*
224	—
225	—
226	—
227	—
228	*262*
229	*263*

Appendix 17

Table of Concordance: *Residential Tenancies Act, 2006 to Tenant Protection Act, 1997*

This table identifies the corresponding provisions of the *Residential Tenancies Act, 2006* and the *Tenant Protection Act, 1997*. Provisions without corresponding equivalents are denoted by a dash ("—") in the appropriate column. Provisions with significant amendments are highlighted in italics.

Residential Tenancies Act, 2006	*Tenant Protection Act, 1997*
1	—
2(1)	1(1)
2(1) "Board"	—
2 (1)"municipal taxes and charges" — before (a)	*1 (1)"municipal taxes and charges" before (a); see also O. Reg. 194/98, s. 1 item 1*
2 (1)"municipal taxes and charges" — (a)-(c)	1(1) "municipal taxes and charges" — (a)-(c)
2(1)"municipal taxes and charges" (d)-(f)	— *see O. Reg.* 194/98, s. 2
2(1) "municipal taxes and charges" (g)	1(1) "municipal taxes and charges" (d)
2(1) "utilities"	*1(1) "utilities"*
2(1) "vital service"	*1(1) "vital service"*
—	1(1) "Tribunal"
2(2)	1(1.1)
2(3)	—
2(4)	1(2)
3	2
4	16
5(a)-(b)	3(a)-(b)
5(c)	*3(c)*
5(d)-(l)	3(d)-(l)
5(m)	—
5(n)	3(m)
6(1) before (a)	*4(1) before (a)*
6(1)(a)	4(1)
6(2)	4(2)

Residential Tenancies Act, 2006	***Tenant Protection Act, 1997***
6(1)(b)	*4(3); 3(e)*
7(1) before 1	*5(1) before 1*
7(1) 1	5(1) 1
7(1) 2	5(1)1.1
7(1) 3	5(1) 2
7(1) 4	*5(1) 3*
7(1) 5	5(1) 4
7(1) 6	5(1) 5
7(2)	5(2)
7(3)	5(3)
7(4)	5(4)
7(5)	5(4.1)
7(6)	5(5)
8(1)	*6(1)*
8(2)	6(2)
9	7
10	38
11	—
12	8
13	9
14	15
15	14
16	13
17	11
18	12
19	10
20	24
21(1)	25
21(2)	—
22	26
23	27
24	23(1)
25	19
26	20
27(1) 1	21(1) 1
27(1) 2	21(1) 2
27(1) 3	21(1) 3.1
27(1) 4	—

Residential Tenancies Act, 2006	*Tenant Protection Act, 1997*
27(1) 5	21(1) 4
27(2)	*21(1) 3*
27(3)	21(2)
28	22
29(1) 1	*32(1) 2, 110(2)*
29(1) 2	32(1) 5
29(1) 3	32(1) 6
29(1) 4	32(1) 7
29(1) 5	32(1) 4
29(1) 6	32(1) 3
29(2)	*32(2)*
30(1) 1	*34(1) 1, 110(2)*
30(1) 2	*34(1) 2, 110(3)(a)*
30(1) 3	*34(1) 3, 110(3)(b)*
30(1) 4	*34(1) 4, 110(3)(c)*
30(1) 5	*34(1) 4.1, 110(3)(d)*
30(1) 6-8	—
30(1) 9	34(1) 5
30(2)	*34(2), 110(4)*
31(1)(a)	35(1)(a)
31(1)(b)(i)	*35(1)(a.1)(i)*
31(1)(b)(ii)	35(1)(a.1)(ii)
31(1)(c)	*35(1)(b)*
31(1)(d)	*35(1)(c)*
31(1)(e)	35(1)(d)
31(1)(f)	*35(1)(e)*
31(2)	*35(2)*
31(3)	35(3)
31(4)	35(4)
31(5)	35(5)
32	—
33	29
34	*30*
35(1)	23(2)
35(2)	36
35(3)	37
36	28
37(1)	39(1)

Residential Tenancies Act, 2006	***Tenant Protection Act, 1997***
37(2)	—
37(3)	39(2)
37(4)	39(4)
37(5)	39(3)
37(6)-(11)	—
38(1)	40(1)
38(2)	—
38(3)	*40(2)*
39	41
40	31
41(1)	42(1)
41(2)	*42(2)*
41(3)	*42(3)*
41(4)	42(4)
41(5)	42(5)
41(6)	—
42	79
43(1)	43(1)
43(2)(a)	—
43(2)(b)-(c)	43(2)(a)-(b)
44	47
45	45(2)
46	44
47	46
48(1)(a)-(c)	51(1)
48(1)(d)	—
48(2)	51(2)
48(3)	51(3)
48(4)	51(4)
49(1)(a)-(c)	52(1)
49(1)(d)	—
49(2)(a)-(c)	52(1.1)
49(2)(d)	—
49(3)	52(2)
49(4)	52(3)
49(5)	52(4)
50	53
51(1)	54(1)

Residential Tenancies Act, 2006	***Tenant Protection Act, 1997***
51(2)	54(2)
51(3)	54(3)(a)
—	54(3)(b)
51(4)	54(4)
51(5)	54(5)
51(6)	54(6)
51(7)	54(7)
52	55
53	56
54(1)(a)	— *57(1)(a)*
54(1)(b)	57(1)(b)
54(1)(c)	57(1)(c)
54(2)(a)	57(2)
54(2)(b)-(c)	—
55	58
56	59
57(1)(a)	*32(1) 8*
57(1)(b)	*32(1) 9*
57(1)(c)	*32(1)10*
57(2)	*32(2)*
57(3)1	*35(2)*
57(3)2	*35(1)(b)*
57(3)3	*35(1)(c)*
57(3)4	*35(1)(e)*
57(4)	—
58	*60*
59	*61*
60(1)	*62(2)*
60(2)	*62(3)(b)*
61(1)	*62(1)*
61(2)	*62(3)(a)*
61(3)	*62(4)*
62(1)	*63(1)*
62(2)(a)-(c)(i)	*63(2)*
62(2)(c)(ii)	—
62(3)	*63(3)*
63	—
64	64

Residential Tenancies Act, 2006	***Tenant Protection Act, 1997***
65	—
66	65
67	66
68	67
69	69
70	74(1)
71	75
72(1)	*70(1)*
72(2)(a)-(b)(iii)	70(2)(a)-(b)
72(2)(b)(iv)	—
73(a)	*71(a)*
73(b)(i)	71(b)
73(b)(ii)	—
74(1)	72(1)
74(2)(a)	*72(2)(a)*
74(2)(b)	*72(2)(b)*
74(2)(c)	72(2)(c)
74(3)(a)	72(3)(a)
74(3)(b)	72(3)(b)
74(3)(c)	—
74(4)(a)	*72(4)(a)*
74(4)(b)	*72(4)(b)*
74(4)(c)-(e)	72(4)(c)-(e)
74(5)	72(5)
74(6)	72(6)
74(7)	72(7)
74(8)	72(8)
74(9)	72(9)
74(10)(a)-(b)	72(10)(a)-(b)
74(10)(c)	—
74(11)-(18); *see also 242(4)*	—
75	*73*
76(1)	74(2)
76(2)	74(3)
76(3)	74(4)
77(1)-(6)	76(1)-(6)
77(7)	*76(7)*
—	76(8)

Residential Tenancies Act, 2006	***Tenant Protection Act, 1997***
77(8)	—
78(1) 1	77(1)(a)
78(1) 2 i.	*77(1)(b)-(c)*
78(1) 2 ii.	77(1)(d)
78(1) 3	77(1)(e)
78(3) 1	77(1.1) 1, 2
78(3) 2	77(1.1) 3
78(2)	77(2)
78(4) 4 i	*77(2.1)2*
78(4) 4 ii	*77(2.1) 1*
78(4) 1	*77(2.1) 3*
78(4) 2, 3	*77(2.1) 4*
78(4) 4 iii - v	—
78(4) 5	*77(2.1) 5*
78(5)	*77(3)*
78(6)	77(4)
78(7) 1	77 (4.1) 3
78(7) 2	77 (4.1) 1
78(7) 3	*77 (4.1) 4*
78(7) 4	*77 (4.1) 5*
78(7) 5 i	*77 (4.1) 2*
78(7) 5 ii - iv	—
78(8)	*77(4.2)*
78(9), (10)	*77(4.3)*
—	77(5)
78(11)	—
79	78
80(1)	83(1)
—	83(2)
80(2)	—
81	83.1
82; *see* 242(5)	—
83(1); *see also* 242(3)	84(1)
83(2); *see* 242(3)	—
83(3); *see also* 242(3)	84(2)
83(4); *see also* 242(3)	84(3)
83(5); *see also* 242(3)	84(4)
84	—

Residential Tenancies Act, 2006	***Tenant Protection Act, 1997***
85	85
86	45(1)(b)
87(1)	86(1)
87(2)	—
87(3)	86(2)
87(4)	86(3)
87(5)	86(4)
88	—
89(1)	*87(1)*
89(2)	—
90	88
91	49
92	50
93	68
94	80
95	17
96	48
97	18
98(1)	32(1) 1
98(2)	*32(2)*
98(3)	33(1)
98(4)	33(2)
98(5)	33(3)
98(6)	—
99	*90*
100(1)	81(1)
100(2)	81(2)
100(3)	86(2.1)
100(4)	*86(4)*
101	82
102	89
103(1)	45(1)(a)
103(2)	*45(2)(b) in part*
104(1)	125(1)
104(2)	125(2)
104(3)	*125(3)*
104(4)	125(4)
105	117

Residential Tenancies Act, 2006	***Tenant Protection Act, 1997***
106(1)	118(1)
106(2)	118(2)
106(3)	118(3)
106(4)	118(4)
106(5)	118(5)
106(6); 106(8)	*118(6)*
106(7)	—
106(9)	118(7)
106(10)	118(8)
106(8)	*118(9)*
107	118.1
108(a)	119
108(b)	—
109(1)	*120*
109(2)	—
110	122
111(1)	121(1)
111(2)	—
111(3)	*121(2)*
111(4)	121(3)
112	*123*
113	124
114	—
115	—
116(1)-(3)	127(1)-(3)
116(4)	*127(4)*
117	—
118	128
119	126
120(1)	*129(1)*
120(2)	*129(2)*
120(3)	*129(3)*
120(4), 120(5)	*129(4)*
121(1)	130(1)
121(2)	130(2)
121(3)	130(3)
121(4)	130(4)
121(5)	130(5)

Residential Tenancies Act, 2006	***Tenant Protection Act, 1997***
121(6)	130(6)
121(7)	130(7)
122	131
123(1)	132(1)
123(2)	*132(2)*
124	133
125	134
— *see 258*	*135*
126(1)1	138(1)1
126(1)2	*138(1)2*
126(1)3	*138(1)3*
126(2)	*138(2)*
126(3)	138(3)
126(4)	—
126(5)	138(4)
126(6)	138(5)
126(7)	*138(8)*
126(8)-(9)	—
126(10)	*138(6)*
—	138(7)
—	138(9)
126(11)	*138(10)*
126(12)-(13); *see also* 242(7)	—
126(14)	*138(11)*
127	*139*
128	—
129(a)	139.1(a)
129(b)	—
129(c)(i)	*139.1(b)(i)*
129(c)(ii)	*139.1(b)(ii)*
130	142
131(1)-(4)	136(1)-(4)
131(5)	*136(5)*
132	137
133(1)	143(1)
133(2)	143(2)
133(3)	—
134(1)	140(1)

Residential Tenancies Act, 2006	***Tenant Protection Act, 1997***
134(2)	140(2)
134(3)(a)	140(3)(a)
—	140(3)(b)
134(3)(b)-(c)	140(3)(c)-(d)
135(1)	*144(1)*
135(2)-(4)	144(2)-(4)
136(1)	141(1)
136(2)	141(2)
—	141(3)
136(3)	141(4)
137	—
138	—
139(1)-(2)	91(1)-(2)
139(3)	—
140	92
141	93
142	94
143	95
144(1)(a)	96(1)(a)
144(1)(b)	*96(1)(b)*
144(1)(c)	96(1)(c)
144(2)	96(2)
145(1)	97
145(2)-(4)	—
146	98
147	—
148(1)	99(1)
148(2)	99(2)
—	99(3)
148(3)	99(4)
148(4)	99(5)
149	*100*
150(1)-(2)	101(1)-(2)
150(3)	*101(3)*
151	102
152(1)	—
152(2)	103
153	104

Residential Tenancies Act, 2006	***Tenant Protection Act, 1997***
154	—
155	—
156	105
157	106
158	107
159(1)	*108*
159(2)-(4)	—
160	109
161	*110(1)*
162	111
163	112
164(1)	*113*
164(2)	—
165	*114(1)-(2)*
—	114(3)
166	115
167	116
168(1)	*157(1)*
168(2)	157(2)
—	157(3)-(4)
169	158
170	159
171	160
172	161
173	—
174	162
175	163
176(1)-(5)	164(1)-(5)
—	164(6)
177	165
178	166
179	167
180	168
181	169
182	170
183	171
184	184
185	172

Residential Tenancies Act, 2006	***Tenant Protection Act, 1997***
186	173
187	174
188	175
189	—
190	176
— *see* 242(2)	177
191	178
192	179
193	180
194(1)	181(1)
194(2)	181(2)
—	181(3)(a)
194(3)	*181(3)(b)*
194(4)	181(4)
194(5)	181(5)
195(1)(a); *see also* 242(6)	182(1)
195(1)(b); *see* 242(6)	—
195(2); *see also* 242(6)	182(2)
195(3); *see* 242(6)	—
195(4); see also 242(6)	182(3)
195(5); *see* 242(6)	—
196	182.1
197	183
198	185
199	185.1
200(1)	*186(1)*
200(2)	186(2)
200(3)	186(3)
200(4)	186(4)
201(1)(a)	187(1)(a)
201(1)(b)	*187(1)(b)*
201(1)(c)-(f)	187(1)(c)-(f)
201(2)	187(2)
201(3)	187(3)
201(4)	187(4)
202	188
203	—
—	189

Residential Tenancies Act, 2006	***Tenant Protection Act, 1997***
204(1)-(4)	190(1)-(4)
204(5)	—
205	191
— *see* 242(2)	192
206	—
207(1)	*193(1)*
207(2)	193(2)
207(3)	193(3)
207(4)	—
207(5)	193(4)
207(6)	193(5)
207(7)	193(6)
208	194
209(1)	*195*
209(2)	—
210	196
211	197
212	198
213	198.1
214	199
215	145
216	146
217	147
218	148
219	149
220	150
221	151
222	152
223(1)	153(1)
223(2)	*153(2)*
224	154
225	155
226	156
227	200
228	201
229	202
230	*203*
231(1)	*204(1)*

Residential Tenancies Act, 2006	***Tenant Protection Act, 1997***
231(2)-(6)	204(2)-(6)
232(1)	205(1)
232(2)	*205(2)*
233(a)	206(1)3
233(b)	*206(1)2*
233(c)	206(1)1
233(d)	206(1)7
233(e)	206(1)9
233(f)	206(1)10
233(g)	206(1)12
233(h)	206(1)4
233(i)	206(1)5
233(j)	206(1)6
233(k)	206(1)8
233(l)	206(1)11
234(a)	206(2)2
234(b)	206(2)4.1
234(c)	206(2)5
234(d)	206(2)10
234(e)	206(2)11
234(f)	206(2)12
234(g)	206(2)12.1
234(h)	206(2)13
234(i)	—
234(j)	206(2)15
234(k)	—
234(l)	206(2)16
234(m)	206(2)6
234(n)	—
234(o)	—
234(p)	206(2)7
234(q)	206(2)8
234(r)	206(2)9
234(s)	206(2)18
234(t)	206(2)17
234(u)	206(2)19
234(v)	206(2)1
234(w)	206(2)4

Residential Tenancies Act, 2006	***Tenant Protection Act, 1997***
234(x)	206(2)14
234(y)	*206(2)3*
235(1)	206(3)
235(2)	206(3.1)
236	206(4)
237	206(5)
238(1)	*206(6)*
238(2)	*206(7)*
239(1)	206(8)
239(2)	206(9)
240(1)-(3)	207(1)-(3)
240(4)	—
241(1)1	208(1)3
241(1)2	208(1)1
241(1)3	208(1)2
241(1)4-5	—
241(1)6	208(1)5
241(1)7-8	—
241(1)9	*cf. 208(1)4*
241(1)10	208(1)6
241(1)11	208(1)7
241(1)12	208(1)7.1
241(1)13-15	—
241(1)16	*208(1)11*
241(1)17	*208(1)12*
241(1)18	208(1)13
241(1)19-20	—
—	208(1)14
241(1)21	208(1)15
241(1)22	208(1)16
241(1)23-24	—
241(1)25-26	*208(1)17*
241(1)27	208(1)18
241(1)28	208(1)19
241(1)29-32	—
241(1)33	208(1)21
241(1)34-39	—
241(1)40	208(1)22

Residential Tenancies Act, 2006	***Tenant Protection Act, 1997***
241(1)41	208(1)20
241(1)42-55	—
241(1)56	208(1)8
241(1)57-58	—
241(1)59	*208(1)9*
241(1)60	208(1)10
241(1)61	208(1)27
241(1)62	*cf. 208(1)26*
241(1)63-65	—
241(1)66	*208(1)28*
241(1)67	*208(1)29*
241(1)68-69	—
241(1)70	*208(1)30.1*
241(1)71	*208(1)30*
—	*208(1)31*
241(1)72	*208(1)23*
241(1)73	*208(1)24*
241(1)74	208(1)25
241(1)75-76	—
241(1)77	208(1)32
241(1)78	208(1)33
241(2)	208(2)
242(1); see also 243	*243 cf. 223(1),(2),(8),(10)*
243	*223*
244	—
245	—
246; see also 243 *— see 243* *— see 243*	*cf. 223(3); 223(9)* *223(4)-(7)* *223(11)*
247	—
248	*209*
249	—
—	210
250	*211*
251	—
—	212
—	214
252	*215*
253	—

Residential Tenancies Act, 2006	***Tenant Protection Act, 1997***
254	—
255	—
—	216
—	217
—	218
—	219
256	*220*
—	221
257	—
258	135, 139.1; *cf. 213*
259	*213(4)*
260	*222*
—	224
—	225
—	226
—	227
261	—
262	*228*
263	*229*

Index

PENAL SANCTIONS

RES JUDICATA

SUBLETS AND ASSIGNMENTS

VITAL SERVICES